HANDBOOK OF EMERGENT METHODS

Handbook of Emergent Methods

EDITED BY
Sharlene Nagy Hesse-Biber
Patricia Leavy

THE GUILFORD PRESS
New York London

A Division of Guilford Publications, Inc.
72 Spring Street, New York, NY 10012
www.guilford.com

Printed in the United States of America

This book is printed on acid-free paper.

Last digit is print number: 9 8 7 6 5 4 3 2 1

Library of Congress Cataloging-in-Publication Data

Handbook of emergent methods / edited by Sharlene Nagy Hesse-Biber, Patricia Leavy.
p. cm.
Includes bibliographical references and index.
ISBN 978-1-59385-147-7 (hbk.)
1. Social sciences—Research. 2. Social sciences—Methodology. I. Hesse-Biber, Sharlene Nagy. II. Leavy, Patricia, 1975–
H62.H24536 2008
300.72—dc22

2007031575

Preface

Emergent methods arise as a means of accessing answers to complex research questions and revealing subjugated knowledge. These research techniques are particularly useful for discovering knowledge that lies hidden, that is, difficult to tap into because it has not been part of the dominant culture or discourse. Because they are techniques or tools, they can be applied to different methodologies and in different disciplines, making them highly pertinent to a range of researchers. The *Handbook of Emergent Methods* contains original review-length chapters that provide a comprehensive view of new and cutting-edge research methods in the social and behavioral sciences. The book includes both theoretical and empirical chapters from a range of disciplines so as to explore new methodologies in the service of innovative research questions. The purpose of the book is twofold: first, to present graduate students who are working on a thesis or dissertation with other options and approaches for thinking about their research questions; and, second, to provide researchers with a mode for exploring new research tools and lenses for uncovering information to enrich their research practice.

With 32 original chapters by leading scholars across the disciplines, the *Handbook* covers a broad range of innovative practices that are transforming traditional research methods approaches. These scholars are pioneers in the use of innovative research techniques and are willing to explore beyond the boundaries of their usual methods routines. They employ creativity, intellect, and their research imaginations to discover new tools or refashion old tools in the service of research questions that arise from emergent perspectives. Each author relates how the practice of a given method is not fixed over time but is subject to innovation. They discuss the reasons for the innovation—how it happens, and what makes this practice emergent while still remaining part of a traditional methods approach. Specific empirical examples are given to illustrate the emergent practice within a given method.

The *Handbook* also contains chapters on research methods that break out of traditional methods boundaries and may come about in a number of different ways. For example, some researchers may find that even when they stretch the traditional framework of a given method, they are unable to find a tool that works, given their particular research problem. Or a researcher may have access to new information or skills that are put to use in a given research endeavor that leads to the creation of a new method. In addition, innovations may evolve as a result of the creation of a technological innovation that, in turn, may provide the impetus for a new methods advance. Innovation may come about by combining tools across different disciplines or by mixing tools within a discipline. The source for the innovation may also come from funding agencies (private and public) that may promote or reward a particular form of innovation. We are particularly interested in those key innovations taking place within and across disciplines as a result of the development of new technologies.

The *Handbook* will appeal to graduate students and research practitioners who are interested in state-of-the-art methods practices. We envision that the *Handbook* will be used in upper-division undergraduate- and graduate-level advanced research methods courses, qualitative methods courses, and feminist research courses in various fields, including the social sciences, education, communications and media studies, health services, American studies, and the humanities. Both students and scholars will also benefit from in-depth section introductions that provide a context and overview of each section of the *Handbook*.

As the chapters in this handbook reflect, methodological diversity is becoming the new trend, as researchers from different disciplines—as well as those working in institutes or research centers—find themselves networking across the disciplines, creating multidimensional lenses through which to investigate the social world. These "hybrid" methodologies pose new questions that cannot necessarily be answered by traditional research techniques. In other words, it isn't about "more" methods for the sake of more, but rather, new methods designed to access aspects of social reality that would otherwise be rendered invisible. Paradigm interbreeding and evolution within the sciences and social sciences have ushered in the necessity of emergent research methods for the accurate assessment of new disciplinary and interdisciplinary questions. It is these "emergent research methods" that constitute the subject matter of this interdisciplinary handbook. We hope that this handbook will encourage readers to create accounts of their own emergent methods practices that will lead to further innovations within and across the disciplines.

We wish to acknowledge the support and assistance we have received toward the completion of our *Handbook*. First, we extend a heartfelt thanks to all the contributors who have worked so diligently to craft state-of-the-art methods chapters.

Sharlene Hesse-Biber: I want to thank my undergraduate research assistants at Boston College, Cooley Horner, Stacey Livingstone, and Colleen Madden. Thanks also to the undergraduate research grants office at Boston College and the Office of Research Administration for providing research assistant grants in support of the completion of the *Handbook*. My warm thanks to my husband, Michael Peter Biber, MD, and my daughters, Sarah Alexandra Biber and Julia Ariel Biber, for their love and encouragement during all phases of this project. I dedicate this work to my father, Zoltan Nagy, whose entrepreneurial spirit and boundless energy still influence a daughter who misses him dearly.

Patricia Leavy: I want to thank Stonehill College graduates Kathryn Maloney, Nathan Regan, and Paul Sacco for their tireless research assistance. I also want to thank Bonnie Troupe and Kathy Conroy for running the Summer Undergraduate Research Experience (SURE) program at Stonehill College through which I obtained such wonderful research assistance. Thank you as well to Academic Vice President Katie Conboy for providing research grants in support of the *Handbook*. My love to my family, and particularly my daughter, Madeline Claire, for all of the hugs and giggles during the long journey of putting this handbook together. Finally, I dedicate my work on this handbook to my students, who continue to shape my thinking about how best to serve the research muse.

Finally, we extend our thanks and gratitude to C. Deborah Laughton, Publisher, Methodology and Statistics, at The Guilford Press and her editorial staff for their expert advice, hard work, professionalism, and commitment to their craft. We also want to acknowledge Laughton's exemplary vision for the field of research methods and methodology that encourages her authors to pursue their research goals and creativity.

Contents

Interviewing

Ethnography

Arts-Based Practice

INTRODUCTION

Pushing on the Methodological Boundaries

The Growing Need for Emergent Methods within and across the Disciplines

Sharlene Nagy Hesse-Biber
Patricia Leavy

"Come to the edge," he said.
They said, "We are afraid."
"Come to the edge," he said.
They came.
He pushed them.
And they flew.
—APOLLINAIRE (as quoted in Eisner, 1997)

Within a rapidly changing and globalizing world, amidst social progress and change, as well as theoretical developments in multiple traditions both within and across disciplines, new research questions are being posed or reexamined. In order to answer these new questions and reexplore some old ones with our new insights and within our new and fluid context, new methods for gathering the data necessary for answering research questions have developed, as well as strategies for representing research findings. Emergent research methods have sprung forth as a result of where we have been, where we are, and where we envision ourselves going in the future. Research methods help illuminate something about social life. As noted feminist philosopher Sandra Harding (1987) explains, methods are techniques for gathering evidence. In other words, methods exist in order to service research questions that advance our understanding of the social world or some aspect of it. Therefore, as the social world and our understanding of it have progressed, so too has our repertoire of social research methods.

There is the illusion of a unity of knowledge within the disciplines, yet also an increasing acknowledgment of the "transgressive" quality of disciplinary knowledge:

> Nobody has anywhere succeeded for very long in containing knowledge. Knowledge seeps through institutions and structures like water through the pores of a membrane. Knowledge seeps in both directions, from science to society as well as from society to science. It seeps through institutions and from academia to and from the outside world. Transdisciplinarity is therefore about transgressing boundaries. Institutions still exist and have a function. Disciplines still exist and new ones arise continuously from interdisciplinary work. (Nowotny, 2007)

Interdisciplinary research provides an opportunity for researchers to think outside disciplinary boundaries (Hesse-Biber, Gilmartin, & Lydenberg, 1999; Kitch, 2007; Nowotny, Scott, & Gibbons, 2001). Emergent interdisciplinary models for conducting research that often reside both inside and outside traditional academic institutions such as research centers, institutes, and laboratories provide "contact methodological zones" for the raising of new research questions. These sites provide fertile ground for the development of new paradigmatic structures that will demand the necessity of emergent tools.

Philosopher Thomas Kuhn's concept of "paradigm" best describes the shifting nature of knowledge building. In his book *The Structure of Scientific Revolutions* (1970) he suggests that science, at any given historical moment, is framed by a particular paradigm or worldview. Turbulent paradigmatic shifts do occur within and across the disciplines. Paradigms are models of knowledge building that provide templates for studying social reality. They consist of the basic concepts and ideas by which a given discipline views the world. Kuhn notes that knowledge is shaped through the acknowledged dominant paradigm of every field of study. A paradigmatic shift in a given discipline, for example, can often create hybrid methodologies that begin to modify traditional disciplinary methods or even create innovative methods, all of which push not only the methodological borders of disciplines but also the paradigmatic borders. The practice of reevaluating traditional methods and generating new ones involves creativity, risk taking, and intuition. In this vein, consider the work of Chinese painter Lu Ch'ai, who in 1701 wrote in *The Tao of Painting* as follows:

> Some set great value on method, while others pride themselves on dispensing with method. To be without method is deplorable, but to depend on method [is] entirely worse. You must first learn to observe the rules faithfully; afterwards modify them according to your intelligence and capacity. The end of all method is to have no method. (as quoted in Janesick, 2001, p. 532)

Working with emergent methods is not about abandoning our disciplinary training but rather taking that training, adapting it, applying it, modifying it, and working beyond it as appropriate with respect to our research objectives.

Emergent methods are flexible; they can comprise qualitative methods or quantitative methods or a combination of these two types of methods. Emergent methods stress the interconnections between *epistemology*, who can know and what can be known; *methodology*, theoretical perspectives and research procedures that emanate from a given epistemology; and *method*, the specific techniques utilized to study a given research problem.

We can think of *methodology* as the bridge that brings epistemology and method together. In other words, methodology links epistemology and method, serving as the theoretical (defining the type of research problem) and procedural (defining how the research process should proceed, what methods to select, and how they are employed to get at the research problem) link between the two. A methodology can be modified during the research process to the extent to which a researcher's epistemological beliefs allow for revisions. As will be seen throughout many of the chapters in this *Handbook*, emergent methods typically require the researcher to remain flexible and open to modifications. In fact, emergent methods are often discovered as a result of modifying more conventional research projects when traditional methods fail to "get at" the aspect of social life the researcher is interested in. Consider Figure 1.

Figure 1 depicts what we perceive to be a cyclical process of methods innovation. Within a complex turbulent environment with multidirectional social, political, economic, technological, and academic forces in play, there is a general trend we can note. Social change, such as that brought about by such justice movements as the civil rights and women's movements, promotes theoretical and methodological innovation. We can also note, in Part III of this *Handbook*, that technological innovations also provide the impetus for asking new questions and revealing new realities. In other words, theory/methodology is often shaped by social, political, economic, and technological con-

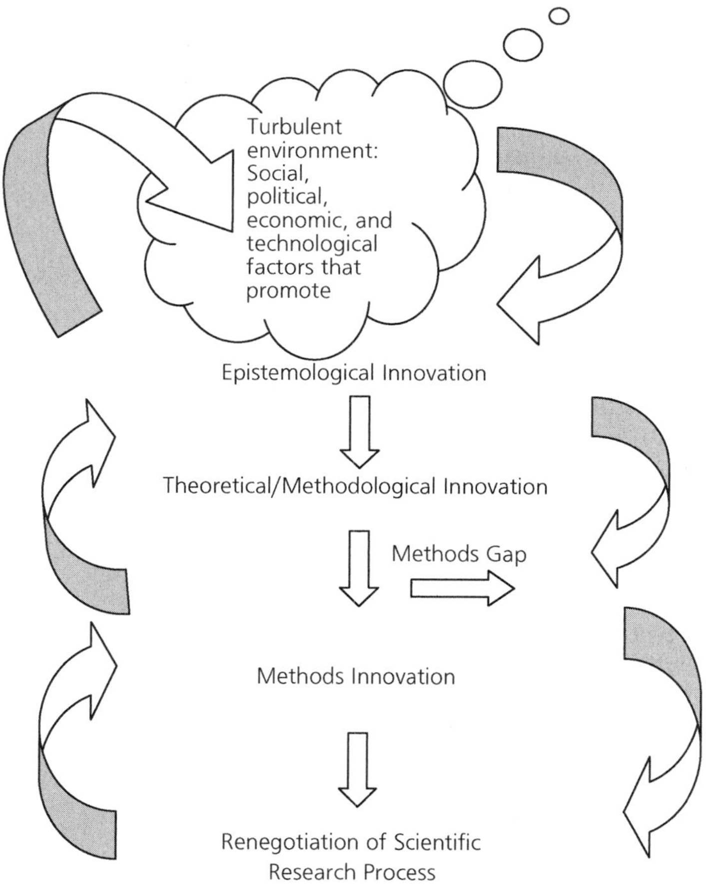

FIGURE 1. The emergent methods process.

texts that often drive methods innovation. As new theoretical and methodological perspectives emerge, a "methods gap" may occur. Therefore, methods innovations emerge in order to meet the insights and challenges posed by new theories. This is the point at which the "scientific landscape" changes—when paradigms experience ruptures, shifts, and revisions. Methods innovation drives a public renegotiation of "scientific standards" of assessment, validity, and other criteria by which knowledge is judged.

Researchers who utilize an emergent method may simultaneously find that they are negotiating both an "insider" and "outsider" researcher identity. As researchers, they are insiders, given their familiarity with the research process, yet the questions they now raise about what seemed familiar are now novel, and the methods tools they employ are not familiar. Their researcher positionality suddenly shifts, and they become explorers, outsiders who pose new research questions with unfamiliar research techniques. Trinh T. Minh-ha expresses this concept of multiple subjectivities as follows:

> Working right at the limits of several categories and approaches means that one is neither entirely inside or outside. One has to push one's work as far as one can go: to the borderlines, where one never stops, walking on the edges, incurring constantly the risk of falling off one side or the other side of the limit while undoing, redoing, modifying this limit. (1991, p. 218)

To successfully work with emergent questions and methods, a researcher often confronts a set of conundrums: How tied am I to the research techniques and ideas of my specific discipline? How committed am to I to my discipline's concepts and methods? If I were to experience conflict or tensions in my attempts to utilize a multidisciplinary or interdisciplinary position, how would I resolve them? How will I negotiate my research position—as an "insider," an "outsider," or both? If I conduct my research as an "outsider," will I be overly identifying with the other's perspective? If I conduct my research as an "insider," will I lose my ability to challenge my disciplinary perspective? These are a sample of the questions a researcher might confront when contemplating the use of emergent methods. It is not surprising, then, that the development of innovative methods has occurred congruent to increased scholarship on reflexivity. Reflexivity is the practice of actively locating oneself within the research process, including the representation stage. Reflexive practice seeks to minimize the unintentional effects of power in the research process through attention to the ways that biography, authorship, and textual representations mediate the knowledge-building process, to work with an emergent method and to successfully negotiate insider and outsider status require a highly reflexive process. Additionally, emergent methods often invite multiple meanings and contradictions due to the fact that different paradigms offer different and often opposing interpretations. Major theoretical developments, particularly those in the qualitative paradigm, have opened the way for researchers to create methodologies that actively seek multiple meanings, tensions, and alternate viewpoints (see Hesse-Biber & Leavy, 2006).

As with all research methods, emergent methods are about methodological innovation for the purpose of enhancing knowledge building and advancing scholarly conversations. Therefore, it is not surprising that there are major trends involving who and what acts as the impetus for methodological innovation. Here we review the primary catalysts for the development or renegotiation of research methods.

Those researchers who are innovating in both methodologies and methods share some common characteristics. Research on the personality characteristics of interdisciplinarians, for example, performed by Klein (1990) suggests that innovators are characterized by "reliability, flexibility, patience, resilience, sensitivity to others, risk-taking, a thick skin, and a preference for diversity and new social roles" (p. 182). These qualities appear to enhance the ability of those working in an interdisciplinary environment. Klein notes that interdisciplinarity requires excellent communication skills, as well as team-building abilities, in order to work with colleagues from diverse disciplines. Klein also states that "the wider the discrepancy between disciplines, and the greater the number of disciplines utilized, the wider the communication gap" (p. 183). To avoid this problem, an interdisciplinarian needs to be an exceptional communicator. Many of the methods reviewed in this volume take place at the edges of different disciplines, each with its own methodological perspectives. As interdisciplinarity spreads and garners a newfound legitimacy, new research questions heretofore unimagined are now being asked. In this way, the presence of emergent methods and its newfound visibility encourages the formulation of new questions about the social world—cyclically generating more methodological precision and innovation.

To reflect further on this issue, consider how research topics and questions develop. In addition to personal and professional interest in a topic and pragmatic concerns such as time and funding, the research questions posed are derived from collective literature on a particular topic and from our perception of our *ability* to illuminate a new dimension of it. As Eisner points out, "We tend to seek what we know how to find" (1997, p. 7). Moreover, sometimes we feel we're *on to something*, but traditional methods tools do not allow us to access it or represent it to an audience. Eisner elaborates: "Put another way . . . we report the temperature even when we are interested in the heat; we expect a reader to be able to transform numbers representing the former into the experience that constitutes the latter. New forms of data representation signify our growing interest in inventing ways to represent the heat" (1997, p. 7).

As evidenced throughout this handbook, many of the innovative methods now available to researchers have emerged as traditional methods have failed to get at "the heat." In this light it is not surprising that many qualitative emergent methods bring the intuitive process—always an implicit component of qualitative research—to the forefront. For example, the expanded use of metaphors during data collection and interpretation, now advocated by many qualitative researchers, offers a method for following and actively pursuing our "hunches" in order to see where they take us (see Dexter & LaMagdeleine, 2002; Moring, 2001; Todd & Harrison, Chapter 23, this volume). Likewise, performance methods such as ethnodrama and ethnotheater draw on the common practice of improvisation as a method for testing hypotheses. In other words, these methods allow researchers to explore the possibilities of "what if" (see Norris, 2000). These performance-driven methods use data collected via traditional qualitative methods (e.g., ethnography, interview, or public documents) that are interpreted through conventional or emergent inductive means and then presented dramatically through the writing of a script that is typically performed for an audience.

Paradigm Shifts

Let's take a specific look at how a shift in knowledge building can occur when paradigms for treating chronic pain bump up against one another. A Western "medical model" methodology embraces a "disease model" for understanding chronic pain. The "cure" of disease often involves intervention with drugs and neurotransmitters to block pain. Eastern models of medicine suggest the use of multimodal treatments that deal with the mind as well. This alternative approach to chronic illness believes in the synchronization of mind and body; treatment modalities suggested by this model often go against standard treatment practices of Western medicine. The following example takes us to the local hospitals of Portland,

Oregon, where patients are exposed to both Eastern and Western models for the treatment of chronic pain:

> Portland-area hospitals are using methods both ancient and modern—as varied as harp music and facet denervation—to treat patients suffering from chronic pain. Now that pain management has been mandated by the World Health Organization and the Joint Commission on Accreditation of Hospitals, physicians and hospital administrators are stepping up their efforts to make patients within the hospital, as well as outpatients, more comfortable. They are embracing a multidisciplinary approach and beginning to incorporate practices that until only recently were considered "fringe" or foreign.
>
> Hired in 2001 as Providence St. Vincent's first acupuncturist on staff, Dr. Loc Chandler works mostly with cancer patients. "Acupuncture can be very beneficial in decreasing pain," Chandler says. "It releases the body's natural painkillers, and changes the flow of blood to the brain." Chandler says that acupuncture can also help improve the patient's health in general, so that the patient can take fewer pain medications, perhaps resume driving a car, and participate more fully in his or her life.
>
> "We have to do a lot of listening to people about what they think will be most helpful to them," says Jocelyn Libby, a cancer counselor with Providence. "Pain is such a subjective thing." Libby, a registered nurse with a master's degree in counseling psychology, and a certification to teach mind–body skills, uses breathing, meditation and guided imagery to help outpatients cope with pain. (Laufe, 2004)

This excerpt is a good example of how cross-cultural paradigmatic encounters for treating chronic pain can result in a broader view of how to treat chronic pain with a set of emergent methods that incorporates both Western and Eastern treatment techniques. A Western model suggests intervention with drugs and neurotransmitters to block pain, whereas an Eastern model suggests the use of multimodality treatments that deal with the mind as well as the body.

Epistemological and theoretical advances in the social sciences have also led to other efforts at integrating the mind and body in our research endeavors. For example, feminism has long argued for an integration of the mind and body, and many emergent feminist practices result from this commitment. Interdisciplinary embodiment scholarship, influenced by psychoanalytic theory, feminism, and postmodern theory, has also seen major advances in recent decades. In essence, embodiment theory places the *body*, our corporeal reality, at the center of the knowledge-building process. The "inscribed body" refers to the ways in which the body serves as a site of social meanings marked by the sociohistorical context (Grosz, 1994; Hesse-Biber & Leavy, 2006). For example, this theoretical scholarship considers how bodies become raced and sexed. Furthermore, Merleau-Ponty (1962) rejects the Cartesian artificial separation of the mind and body and rather argues that all experiences occur through the lived body. Therefore, social scholars need to consider experience itself as embodied. New theoretical understandings of embodiment, which also seek to integrate the mind and body in our research, have propelled a host of methodological innovations. For example, performance studies are an outgrowth in part of this kind of theoretical work. Performance studies, which may involve drama, dance, or creative movement, all draw on embodied artistic practices in their representation of data. In health studies, the method of "health theater" can be used to show the physical, psychological, and emotional experience of living with a particular disease or disorder or of caring for someone with a particular ailment. This method is an adaptation of ethnodrama that occurs within the field of health studies as a way of accessing and dramatically representing the lived experiences of the ill, the disabled, and those who care for them. Health theater, like other performance-driven methods, explicitly unites the mind and body in the research process.

Neither the paradigm shifts nor the turn to interdisciplinarity within academia have occurred within a vacuum. Rather, social and political forces have shaped both the social world and our methods for learning about it. Entirely new paradigms have emerged as a result of the changing social world: examples include feminism, multiculturalism, queer studies, critical race theory, and third-world perspectives.

Within the social sciences new methodological perspectives make up the research landscape that challenge traditional standpoints on the nature of the individual and society. Such novel perspectives arose from the social justice movements, such as the civil rights movement and women's movement, in the 1960s and from the issues arising from the global economy. These innovative theoretical understandings of the social world challenge such traditional paradigms as positivism—a perspective that assumes a unified truth and whose goal is to "test" knowledge. They encourage, instead, the idea of multiple subjective perspectives on reality that seeks to question and thus expose the power dynamics of traditional paradigms by illuminating previously subjugated knowledge on the intersections of race, gender, sexuality, class, and nationality. Such novel paradigms often traverse disciplinary boundaries, opening up interdisciplinary space for dialogue on issues of social justice and oppression, and often embrace new perspectives emanating from a range of theoretical positions—feminist standpoint theory (Harding, 2004; Smith, 2004), postcolonial theory (Mohanty, 1988, 1992, 1999; Spivak, 1990), postmodernism (Nicholson & Seidman, 1995), ethnic studies (Perez, 1999), queer studies (Calvin, 2000), and critical theory and critical race theory (Wing, 2000).

All of these new perspectives push on traditional paradigmatic boundaries, bringing into visibility new research questions that emanate from the margins of the social world, especially from those whose knowledge has been subjugated: women, people of color, the poor, homosexuals, and so forth. These new questions, too, may require the use of new methods or the tweaking of more matured social methods such as ethnographies, surveys, or even the combining of macro and micro methods as in mixed methods designs to tackle these new questions. Another related general trend within all of these diverse perspectives is a critical and systematic reexamination of power *within the research process*. With greater attention to power in the research process, scholarship on reflexivity and authority has also flourished. In this regard, these perspectives offer alternative views of the researcher–researched relationship, subjectivity, authenticity, and many other issues. An outgrowth of these critical reexaminations of key ontological and epistemological issues is a reevaluation of traditional research practices from which innovative methods develop.

Technological Innovation

Sometimes the field of emergent methods is fueled not by new paradigmatic perspectives but through technological innovation that pushes on the boundaries of methodology. Key technological innovations are taking place within and across the disciplines. Consider the case of what happens when researchers discover a new technology—recombinant DNA—that allows researchers to find out whether an individual is in fact carrying genes for a range of diseases, from schizophrenia to breast cancer. With this new technology, doctors can test patients as an office procedure. The following is a conversation that took place among 50 primary care physicians from around the country who gathered at a conference to discuss the implications of this new technology, the new questions patients are certain to ask, and the issues and dilemmas they will face as a result of genetic testing. They have also come to gather new skills in order to prepare themselves for how they will practice medicine in the very near future.

The excerpt captures some of these dilemmas and was documented by one reporter covering the conference. We hear the voices of several doctors, as well as commentary from the reporter.

> "It is quite extraordinary to be in a lab doing southern blots [a method for sequencing DNA] one afternoon and to be listening to a rabbi talk about the genetic screening of a Jewish community in Brooklyn the next morning," said Nason Hamlin, an internist from rural Connecticut.
>
> While some doctors were drawn to the course to answer specific questions that had arisen in their practices, many came to satisfy their intellectual curiosity and to make up for a gap in their knowledge about genetics.
>
> For many, the most important aspect of the course was the attention to the ethical, legal and social issues raised by the efflorescence of genetic techniques. These issues ranged from the clinical–when do you tell patients that they carry a gene for a disease, and how do you tell them?–to the philosophical. "What is a good gene?" asked Susan Pauker, [Harvard Medical School] assistant clinical professor of pediatrics.
>
> The genetics revolution, the speakers noted, may be producing knowledge that is a double-edged sword. Although it may enable some patients to take preventive measures, it also may engender emotional problems for patients and larger social dilemmas as well.
>
> Patients may be told they are carriers for a gene that leads to a disease that has no cure. Or, in a family where a certain genetic ailment is common, those without the genetic defect may still suffer emotional problems, such as "survivor guilt." And genetic information, if made publicly known, might put a person's health insurance and job in jeopardy.
>
> Even good news–of a person learning he or she isn't a carrier for a lethal gene–may cause emotional turmoil. One 37-year-old woman at great risk for breast cancer–her sisters and mother suffered from the disease–was initially elated to learn that she didn't carry the defective gene, an elation which quickly turned to guilt, Collins said.
>
> "Everyone else has it but me," she told Collins. The woman required a year of intensive counseling to get over her guilt.
>
> . . . for the already born, the future has arrived when it comes to screening for genetic defects in the unborn. The obvious potential pitfall with such screening is that it will lead, more and more, to parental demand for the "perfect baby." Fetuses with even minor genetic problems might be aborted.
>
> . . . As the genetics revolution continues to explode there will be an ever greater number of "bad" genes that can be identified in screening tests. The challenge . . . for doctors will be to learn how to best communicate this information to their patients. (Landau, 1994)

We can see from this example that a new method, genetic testing fueled by technological innovation, has pushed on the boundaries of traditional medicine. Those physicians who deal directly with patients find that they are forced to confront a new set of issues and ethical dilemmas; they must also confront the need to acquire a new set of technical and socioemotional skills to better treat and communicate with their patients. New options of care are opened up to patients, and the idea of treating future illnesses is brought to the forefront, which has implications for a range of life decisions and choices. For example, should a child who is not medically perfect be aborted? One can also imagine a set of new scenarios based on genetic testing. Should genetic testing be part of a prenuptial agreement? What if your future partner comes with "bad genes"? To what extent can a patient's privacy be guarded from employers and insurers who may use this information in a way that is harmful to future job prospects and financial security? We can see that the emergence of a new technology and method creates a host of new questions and issues that reverberate within and across segments of disciplines and social groups.

Toward a History and Politics of Methods

The idea of a *Handbook of Emergent Methods* is embedded in a historical methods context. It is important to take notice of the changing character of methods throughout the history of the science and social science disciplines. Jennifer Platt's work on the history of American sociological research methods from the years 1920–1969 suggests the importance of studying the "evolution" of research methods in its own right, not just as an offshoot of sociological theory. Platt's study of the evolving nature of research methods suggests that we shift our attention from a focus on the "history of sociological theory" to an emphasized focus on the "history of research methods":

> The history of sociology has most commonly been written as the history of theoretical ideas. This has sometimes included methodological ideas, treated at an abstract and philosophical level, but has seldom given attention to practical research methods or, indeed, to empirical research. The history of theoretical ideas is an interesting and important area, but there has been proportionately too much of it for justice to be done to sociology as a whole. . . . The time has come to shift the balance of historical concern further in the direction of empirical research and ideas about its methods. (Platt, 1996, p. 1)

According to Platt, the history of sociological methods is one of a series of historical reinventions or reincarnations whereby methods tend to appear, disappear, and reappear, often given a new name depending on the discipline. Platt (1996) notes, for example:

> Beatrice Webb used participant observation before "participant observation" had been "invented" as a recognized technique. . . . Selvin . . . showed how Durkheim used analytic strategies which no one had formalized at the time. Lazarsfeld pointed out how Stouffer did novel things which he did not himself label as such, and for which Lazarsfeld received credit. (p. 32)

In fact, Platt suggests that some of the most popular research techniques of today, such as survey research, were methods historically linked to social reform movements striving to improve local communities rather than to the large-scale data collection instruments often used to collect data on national population trends. Contrary to survey research techniques today, Platt notes that the early surveys did not contain "fixed wording" choices, and they had little to do with seeking attitudinal information (1996, p. 45). Jennifer Platt notes that one of the ways to ensure that emergent methods do not disappear only to be rediscovered within and across the disciplines is to make sure that researchers *report* their use of innovative methods so that they do not remain invisible to mainstream researchers.

Qualitative researcher Janice Morse (2006) notes that although some methods can clearly be attributed to their developers, such as Barney Glaser and Anselm Strauss's (1967) book *The Discovery of Grounded Theory*, which emerged from the Chicago School of Sociology, many methods, especially those that are qualitative, such as ethnography, "have roots that are harder to identify" (p. 3) says Morse. There is a tendency for methods, even those whose method is well documented, to be used by another researcher. "The method is consciously or unconsciously tweaked, altered, adjusted, and improved" (p. 3). Sometimes, in fact, notes Morse, a method such as "grounded theory" is attached to Glaser and Strauss, but in fact the resulting use of the methods "does not resemble the method at all; and sometimes the method is modified and removed from the original developers, and another researchers' name is attached to the variation" (Morse, 2006, p. 3).

Janice Morse (2006, p. 4) provides a set of reflexive tips for the researcher as they go about their methods development:

1. "Be conscious of our methods, their origin, and our use of these strategies."
2. "If we develop a new method, or modify an old one, we must be . . . respectful and accurate in our representation of the original developer."
3. "Responsibility for this should be jointly

> on the shoulders of the reviewers, the editors, and the users of these methods."

What Morse notes, however, are that "methods take on a life" of their own. She states:

> What is the responsibility of the original developer if he or she does not agree with the new emerging form or even with the minor tweaks? Barney Glaser registers his complaints in print, in new volumes clarifying his methods and criticizing or supporting the work of others. Other researchers may ignore the new development, and over time, different schools may emerge, with distinct differences in their methods. At other times, we may find an "anything goes" approach that is messy, lackadaisical, and poor science. (2006, p. 4)

The *Handbook of Emergent Methods* therefore seeks to increase both the visibility and legitimacy of the range of new methods and scholarship within and across the disciplines and interdisciplines.

Problems and Resistance to Emergent Techniques

Despite the interlinking of theory and methods, particularly pronounced in emergent methodologies, there nevertheless remains a gap between new theoretical perspectives and new methods practices. We have observed, for example, how physicians need to educate themselves both about recombinant DNA and about how to implement this new information in the treatment context. They will need to acquire new knowledge and technological skills, as well as research techniques, in order to bridge the divide between theory and practice. An alarming gap between methods and theory—both within and across the disciplines—continues to be a concern within the social and behavioral sciences.

Some argue that there is an "experience gap" in a researcher's comprehension and utilization of emergent methods. Many researchers are trained in the use of a single primary method. Utilizing an innovative method may require that they leave their "methods comfort zone," forcing them to think outside their "methods box" (Hesse-Biber & Leavy, 2006). An intently advocated countermovement to emergent methods has been gaining force within the social sciences. "Specialization"—the specific intent to utilize one research method until achieving mastery—has had an increase in support. Denzin has commented on the deprivation of innovation that arises as a by-product of specialization:

> Other sociologists have tended to use methods with little thought for either their theoretical implications or their differing ability to shed light on theory. Many sociologists now use only one method in their studies—thereby eschewing the potential value of other methodologies. Small-group theorists rely nearly entirely upon the experiment, while family sociologists primarily use the survey technique, and students of organizations overemphasize field strategies such as participant observation. This tendency has given rise to a rather parochial, specialty-bound use of research methods. (Denzin, 1989, p. 3)

Yet, if a research question calls for the use of a hybrid method, such as the combining of qualitative and quantitative methods, how will these new methods tools be integrated in one research study? Is it reasonable to expect, for example, that a qualitatively trained researcher with an interpretative philosophy can successfully practice quantitative techniques such as survey research? How will numbers be integrated with words in pursuit of new research questions? When dealing with the visual arts and other art-driven methods, how can words be transformed into images and vice versa?

While new theoretical problems are being raised across the disciplines, the lack of training programs in emergent methods in the social science curriculum of academia and the ongoing divide between qualitative and quantitative methods (see Denzin & Lincoln, 1994) continues, despite a reduction of the "paradigm wars" (Teddlie & Tashakkori, 2003).

Only augmenting this dilemma is the new emphasis on learning methods techniques with a "cookbook" approach. The idea has been suggested that social research is like a recipe and that methods and methodologies are interchangeable ingredients, the links between theory and methods being completely ignored (see Seiler, 2004). Robert Merton notes the importance of theory–methods linkage: "Nor is it enough to say that research and theory must be married if sociology is to bear legitimate fruit. They must not only exchange solemn vows–they must know how to carry on from there. Their reciprocal roles must be clearly defined" (1967, p. 171).

Another concern raised by those who utilize emergent methods is the "funding gap" (Hesse-Biber & Leavy, 2006). Funding agencies, private and governmental, may prefer that researchers use traditional "tried and true" research methods. Funders may not want to give up the confines of their own "methods funding comfort zone." In *The Coming Crisis in Western Sociology* (1971), Alvin Gouldner suggests that funding institutions may unduly influence what is considered as an "acceptable method and research problem." What is "accepted," according to Gouldner, is applied research, what Gouldner coined as "theoryless theories" (p. 444). Despite this concern, a close inspection of the influence that funding of research has on research reveals that funding agencies' power to define what methods to use and what problems are worth studying is not definitive. Beyond the power that intellectual and economic interests of funding agencies may have to "tip the balance" somewhat, additional factors exist that must be considered in order to fully understand what types of projects receive funding (see Platt, 1996).

Academic context may also determine the specific research methods utilized in a research study. The research culture within a given university or department may affect what methods are utilized by faculty and taught to students. University and departmental environments may embrace certain methods practices. For example, in the 1920s, the University of Chicago came to be seen as solely advocating the practice of qualitative methods and newly emergent qualitative methods. Ignored were the significant number of faculty who employed quantitative methods within the Chicago School academic environment (Platt, 1996). Platt (1996) suggests that the invisibility of the quantitative work of the Chicago School was a result of quantitative methods' ability to cross disciplinary boundaries, thereby not seeming to be particularly identified with a specific department or school. When citing the work of Martin and Joan Blumer (1981), Platt notes that "Blumer and Blumer suggest that one reason is that those committed to quantitative work are much less interested in their history. They see the development of their field as cumulative advance, and so do not legitimate their activities by reference to ancestors" (1981, p. 265).

In this light, we also suggest that the resistance to emergent methodological practices is historical and must also be situated in the context of the privileging of quantitative data over qualitative data. Though qualitative research has gained legitimacy over the past several decades and renegotiations of the qualitative paradigm are a great source of emergent methodologies, there are many researchers and practitioners who still feel more comfortable with "hard science," associated with traditional quantitative techniques. Additionally, many qualitative researchers who have struggled for legitimacy (including publication opportunities and funding) may have a vested interest in "protecting" traditional qualitative techniques and not "watering them down" with new, cutting-edge methods. This parallels the fear many feminists have raised regarding postmodern theory; some feminists fear "giving up" identity categories such as "women" and "group voice" after struggling for these concepts to gain legitimacy for so many years (Hesse-Biber & Leavy, 2007). These feelings about protecting traditional qualitative methods are grounded in a fear that if we push on the methods border, "anything will go," and the legitimacy qualitative research has gained will be diminished. This is particularly salient given the critical theoretical perspectives from which many emergent methods have developed—perspectives that emphasize partial and situated knowledge over absolute truths.

Another potential resistance of researchers to using an emergent method is that it may require a researcher to rethink his or her epistemological and ontological perspective. Yet these notions of who can know and what can be known, held by researchers from different disciplinary backgrounds, may come together in what is termed "team projects." With team projects, researchers from a diverse array of disciplines may work together for a shared end result without having to sacrifice their particular epistemologies and ontologisms.

Innovation in the practice of social research is crucial. Researchers need to go beyond their own disciplinary boundaries to enhance their research vision of the social research landscape—what Laurel Richardson (2006) terms the "de-disciplining" of ourselves.

The intention of this introduction is not to generate an in-depth discussion of the social institutions that give rise to social research methods. However, it is a noteworthy observation, for it is often overlooked, yet serves as a reminder that there are a great number of factors both within and outside academia that must be analyzed in order to fully understand the phenomenon of why certain methods emerge and become standard and others linger on the periphery.

More than anything else, emergent methods are about advancing our understanding of the human condition. These new approaches—often initially criticized and even feared by those who feel more comfortable with conventional ways of knowing and traditional criteria for judging the usefulness of research (traditionally referred to as *validity* and *reliability*)—challenge our very conceptions of knowledge, including who creates it, what counts as knowledge, how it is to be disseminated and to whom, and how authenticity and trustworthiness can be achieved and evaluated. In other words, emergent methods force public scholarly conversations about knowledge and research, prompting a reevaluation of old standards and an exploration of the borders. In this way, these methods aid not only particular research projects but also the larger project of knowledge building and human discovery.

Goals of the *Handbook of Emergent Methods*

An important goal of this handbook is to provide a place for fresh insights on emergent methods. At this point in time, these methods are spread across a range of diverse disciplines, yet their practice is often hidden from the mainstream researcher's radar. The contributors to this volume address some of the following questions: How can alternative/emergent methods enhance our understanding of complex issues that emerge from interdisciplinary research? How can they enhance new paradigmatic approaches? The chapters represent state-of-the art work regarding emergent issues and methods. Authors provide in-depth examples of how a specific emergent method is applied in a research project, as well as examples of the types of questions that lend themselves to this type of innovation. Additionally, contributors who utilize a more traditional method in new ways address the impact of their innovations on conventional methods. These authors also address the factors that gave rise to this type of innovation within previously existing methods.

Furthermore, all authors were asked to address what they perceive to be the strengths and weaknesses of their innovations. For example: What are the problems and prospects of practicing this type of innovation? Why is it practiced by particular researchers? Why is it practiced within a particular disciplinary or interdisciplinary project?

Organization of the *Handbook*

Where are the new and powerful innovations taking place across the research process, from data gathering to interpretation and analysis? What are the new methods practices? In order to address these questions we have organized the *Handbook* into three parts.

Part I considers the historical context of emergent methods within and across disciplines and presents a host of emergent research methods as identified by known experts in the field. This section introduces a range of innovative practices that are transforming traditional research methods approaches. This part contains chapters that represent those methods that break out of traditional methods boundaries and may come about in a number of different ways. For example, some researchers may find it difficult to rework traditional methods of their discipline and seek new "hybrid" methods such as a mixed methods approach, in order to answer complex questions that often cross disciplinary boundaries. The development of new technologies, such as the Internet and global information systems (GIS), allow researchers to collect new data, ask novel questions, and provide the technology for answering these questions. Goodchild and Janelle (2004), for example, employ GIS tools to track spatial patterns of social behavior. The advent of GIS-based technological tools, once the province of geographers, now provide a means for social scientists to deepen and reconceptualize their understanding of social context through the integration of a special dimension into their research.

Funding agencies, both public and private, also push on the boundaries of methods practices with growing expectations that researchers should consider mixed methods and other innovative methods practices that hold the promise of synergizing research outcomes.

Part II of the handbook reviews innovation in research design and analysis. New research designs allow new research questions, making innovations in this area important when considering the future of interdisciplinary research. In this section mixed methods design innovations—which are necessarily hybrids—as well as other hybrid designs are considered. Moreover, by covering interpretation and analysis, this section of the handbook is about the meaning-making process with respect to emergent methods. For example, how do we make sense out of data that have been collected in nontraditional ways? How do we conceive of authenticity, trustworthiness, validity, and reliability with respect to emergent research methods and methodologies? New research methods may require a new internal and cross-paradigmatic system of checks and balances. How is this process being negotiated?

For example, poetry is now being used as a research method (particularly as a form of representation) in the social sciences. Among others, Laurel Richardson and Norman Denzin have written about the methodological capabilities of "poetic transcription" and related methods. One of the issues that have arisen from this representational form is the question of validity. Put simply, traditional measures of validity are not appropriate criteria for judging research poems. Accordingly, Sandra Faulkner (2005) provides the following lists of scientific and artistic criteria, as well as by her assessment of "poetic criteria":

Scientific criteria
Depth
Authenticity
Experience
Trustworthiness
Understanding of human experience
Reflexivity

Usefulness
Articulation of craft/method
Ethics

Artistic criteria
Compression of data
Understanding of craft
Social justice
Moral truth
Emotional verisimilitude
Evocation
Sublimity
Empathy

Poetic criteria
Artistic concentration embodied
Discovery/surprise
Conditional
Narrative truth
Transformation

As you can see, the measures of trustworthiness used to evaluate qualitative research and those used to judge the quality of artistic poetry merge in Faulkner's final list. In this way, "poetic criteria" do not privilege social scientific or artistic ways of creating and knowing "truth(s)." Rather, they propose the hybridization or merging of the two to create a third space for contemplating what counts as knowledge, paralleling the "third voice" produced out of poetic transcription. In this way, working through the challenges of creating criteria by which to judge and compare research poems as an emergent research practice is also a way that social scientists challenge and expand standard definitions of knowledge itself.

Finally, Part III of the handbook considers the impact of emergent technologies on emergent research methods. In this section we are looking for a review of the literature on key innovations taking place within and across disciplines as a result of the development of new technologies. The questions raised in this section include: What type(s) of new technologies are being utilized in the social sciences, humanities, and natural sciences? Do the questions drive the technology within existing disciplines or across disciplines? Who is carrying out these types of new technologically dependent emergent methods? Are there specific research questions that prompt the use of new methods that demand technological devices? Does technology drive the creation of new methods? How so? How has the Internet transformed traditional research methods? How does access to new software tools, such as network-based software and software for qualitative data analysis, transform the way methods are practiced?

References

Blumer, M., & Blumer, J. (1981). Philanthropy and social science in the 1920s: Beardsley Ruml and the Laura Spelman Rockefeller Memorial, 1922–29. *Minerva, 19*, 347–407.

Calvin, T. (Ed.). (2000). *Straight with a twist: Queer theory and the subject of homosexuality*. Urbana: University of Illinois Press.

Denzin, N. K. (1989). *The research act: A theoretical introduction to sociological methods* (3rd ed.). Englewood Cliffs, NJ: Prentice Hall.

Denzin, N. K., & Lincoln, Y. S. (Eds.). (1994). *Handbook of qualitative research*. Thousand Oaks, CA: Sage.

Dexter, S., & LaMagdeleine, D. R. (2002). Dominance theater, slam-a-thon, and cargo cults: Three illustrations of how using conceptual metaphors in qualitative research works. *Qualitative Inquiry, 8*(3), 362–380.

Eisner, E. W. (1997). The promise and perils of alternative forms of data representation. *Educational Researcher, 26*(6), 4–10.

Faulkner, S. L. (2005, May). *How do you know a good poem? Poetic representation and the case for criteria*. Symposium conducted at the 1st International Conference of Qualitative Inquiry, Urbana-Champaign, IL.

Glaser, B., & Strauss, A. (1967). *The discovery of grounded theory*. Chicago: Aldine.

Goodchild, M. F., & Janelle, D. G. (Eds.). (2004). *Spatially integrated social science*. New York: Oxford University Press.

Gouldner, A. W. (1971). *The coming crisis in Western sociology*. London: Heinemann.

Grosz, E. (1994). *Volatile bodies: Toward a corporeal feminism*. Bloomington: Indiana University Press.

Harding, S. (1987). Introduction. In S. Harding (Ed.), *Feminism and methodology* (pp. 1–14). Bloomington: Indiana University Press.

Harding, S. (Ed.). (2004). *The feminist standpoint theory*

reader: Intellectual and political controversies. New York: Routledge.

Hesse-Biber, S. N., Gilmartin, C., & Lydenberg, R. (Eds.). (1999). *Feminist approaches to theory and methodology: An interdisciplinary reader.* New York: Oxford University Press.

Hesse-Biber, S. N., & Leavy, P. (2007). *Feminist research practice: A primer.* Thousand Oaks, CA: Sage.

Hesse-Biber, S. N., & Leavy, P. (2006). *Emergent methods in social research.* Thousand Oaks, CA: Sage.

Janesick, V. J. (2001). Intuition and creativity: A pas de deux for qualitative researchers. *Qualitative Inquiry, 7*(5), 531–540.

Kitch, S. L. (2007). Feminist interdisciplinary approaches to knowledge building. In S. N. Hesse-Biber (Ed.), *Feminist research: Theory and praxis* (pp. 123–139). Thousand Oaks, CA: Sage.

Klein, J. T. (1990). *Interdisciplinarity: History, theory, and practice.* Detroit, MI: Wayne State University Press.

Kuhn, T. S. (1970). *The structure of scientific revolutions* (2nd ed.). Chicago: University of Chicago Press.

Landau, M. (1994). *Genetics: Conference tackles emerging questions.* Retrieved September 12, 2007, at *http://focus.med.harvard.edu/1994/Nov4_1994/Genetics.html*

Laufe, A. (2004). *New methods emerging to treat patients' chronic pain.* Retrieved September 12, 2007, at *http://www.bizjournals.com/portland/stories/2004/11/22/focus2.html*

Merleau-Ponty, M. (1962). *Phenomenology of perception* (C. Smith, Trans.). New York: Humanities Press.

Merton, R. K. (1967). *On theoretical sociology.* New York: Free Press.

Minh-ha, T. T. (1991). *Framer framed.* New York: Routledge.

Mohanty, C. (1988). Under Western eyes: Feminist scholarship and colonial discourses. *Feminist Review, 30,* 61–88.

Mohanty, C. (1992). Feminist encounters: Locating the politics of experience. In M. Barrett & A. Phillips (Eds.), *Destabilizing theory: Contemporary feminist debates* (pp. 74–92). Stanford, CA: Stanford University Press.

Mohanty, C. (1999). Women workers and capitalist scripts: Ideologies of domination, common interests, and the politics of solidarity. In S. N. Hesse-Biber, C. Gilmartin, & R. Lydenberg (Eds.), *Feminist approaches to theory and methodology: An interdisciplinary reader* (pp. 362–388). New York: Oxford University Press.

Moring, I. (2001). Detecting fictional problem solvers in time and space: Metaphors guiding qualitative analysis and interpretation. *Qualitative Inquiry, 7*(3), 346–369.

Morse, J. M. (2006). The politics of developing research methods. *Qualitative Health Research, 16*(3), 3–4.

Nicholson, L., & Seidman, S. (Eds.). (1995). *Social postmodernism: Beyond identity politics.* Cambridge, UK: Cambridge University Press.

Norris, J. (2000). Drama as research: Realizing the potential of drama in education as a research methodology. *Youth Theatre Journal, 14,* 40–51.

Nowotny, H., Scott, P., & Gibbons, M. (2001). *Rethinking science: Knowledge and the public in an age of uncertainty.* Cambridge, UK: Polity Press.

Perez, E. (1999). *The decolonial imaginary: Writing Chicanos into history.* Bloomington: Indiana University Press.

Platt, J. (1996). *A history of sociological research methods in America: 1920–1960.* Cambridge, UK: Cambridge University Press.

Richardson, L. (2006). Skirting a pleated text: De-disciplining an academic life. In S. N. Hesse-Biber & P. Leavy (Eds.), *Emergent methods in social research* (pp. 1–12). Thousand Oaks, CA: Sage.

Seiler, M. (2004). *Performing financial studies: A methodological cookbook.* New York: Prentice Hall.

Smith, D. E. (2004). Women's perspectives as a radical critique of sociology. In S. N. Hesse-Biber & M. Yaiser (Eds.), *Feminist perspectives on social research* (pp. 27–38). New York: Oxford University Press.

Spivak, G. C. (1990). *The postcolonial critic: Interviews, strategies, dialogue.* New York: Routledge.

Teddlie, C., & Tashakkori, A. (2003). Major issues and controversies in the use of mixed methods in the social and behavioral sciences. In A. Tashakkori & C. Teddlie (Eds.), *Handbook of mixed methods in social and behavioral research* (pp. 30–50). Thousand Oaks, CA: Sage.

Wing, A. K. (Ed.). (2000). *Global critical race feminism: An international reader.* New York: New York University Press.

PART I

Historical Context of Emergent Methods and Innovation in the Practice of Research Methods

Patricia Leavy
Sharlene Nagy Hesse-Biber

It is about exploring the edges and reexamining the meaning of research.

—EISNER (1997, p. 7)

This section of the *Handbook* reviews the historical context and range of emergent research methods. As made clear in the Introduction to this handbook, methods are not employed in a vacuum, nor do they develop in one. Rather, research methods are executed in the service of particular research objectives, and research projects are embedded in epistemological positions and theoretical frameworks. Moreover, as evidenced throughout this section of the *Handbook*, new methods emerge in response to large-scale historical, social, and political changes, as well as more specific paradigm shifts, theoretical developments, and epistemological innovations.

Research methods are the tools that researchers use in order to gather data and represent their research findings. These tools or techniques allow researchers to garner data about social reality from a host of sources, including individuals, groups, and texts in all mediums. Most research methods are employed from within either the qualitative or the quantitative paradigm, though some hybrid methods such as content analysis can be employed in both inductive and deductive ways. Qualitative researchers typically turn to inductive approaches grounded in a range of epistemological traditions that span feminism, postmodernism, and the interpretive school and often use ethnography, in-depth interviews, life histories, autoethnography, focus group interviews, case studies, discourse analysis, and content analysis. Quantitative researchers often rely on a different set of research methods that are grounded in the "scientific method," which espouses objectivity, neutrality, discovery, and verification, and that typically include experiments, surveys and questionnaires, evaluation, statistical analysis, and content analysis. Multimethod research, discussed in Part II of this handbook, may combine qualitative and quantitative methods within one research project.

Many methods innovations are hybrids. In other words, some of the emergent methods reviewed in this section of the *Handbook* merge qualitative and quantitative logic, transgress disciplinary boundaries, or combine the strategies of multiple methods. As we wrote in our book *Emergent Methods in Social Research* (Hesse-Biber & Leavy, 2006), emergent methods offer researchers "ways of coming at things differently" (p. 376). Traditional research practices may fail to access or illuminate the aspects of social reality we are interested in; when this occurs, methods innovation is necessary. The questions and consciousness raised by the social justice movements of the 1960s and 1970s, as well as the theoretical developments of the past several decades, have given rise to new questions and awareness, thus necessitating the development of new tools. In this way, methods innovations may be pursued with the intent of cultivating a congruency between epistemology, theory/methodology, and methods. Moreover, many emergent research practices aim to provide a tight fit between research purpose and research method, as well as form and content.

The first four chapters in this section provide a historical context for the development of emergent methods while also reviewing specific methods innovations. We begin with Karen M. Staller, Ellen Block, and Pilar S. Horner's chapter about the history of research methods. The authors offer a provocative discussion about the inherent challenges and tensions in writing a history of methodology in the social sciences. For the purpose of their chapter, they ultimately assert that "in the spirit of emergent methods, we sought to answer our research question—*What is the history of methods in the social sciences that helps explain the current context of emergent methods?*—using a creative approach to the problem" (p. 29). Through empirical research conducted with three evidentiary sources, Staller and colleagues outline a detailed account of the historical context in which research methods have developed and how our understanding of them has changed over time.

Chapter 2 traces emergent feminist research practices in greater detail. Sue V. Rosser provides a review of the history of gender inclusion within social research from a feminist perspective. She reviews how the social justice movements of the 1960s and 1970s created the environment from which feminists launched a challenge to positivist science so that many methodological innovations might emerge. Specifically, Rosser attends to how feminist theoretical perspectives have influenced corresponding methods practices. In this vein, Rosser provides an interdisciplinary historical review of the history of feminist research, the challenge to positivism and its conception of "objectivity," and the inclusion of difference more broadly. She then investigates the feminist use of "strong objectivity" as an emergent method and provides empirical examples of this concept.

Chapter 3 explores how postmodernism has influenced social research. Lisa Cosgrove and Maureen McHugh explore a post-Newtonian postmodern approach to social research. Cosgrove and McHugh trace how postmodern epistemological developments have prompted methodological innovations. They identify and review three methods that are congruent with postmodern perspectives on science, two qualitative and the third quantitative: phenomenology, discourse analysis, and satirical empiricism. Their chapter explores how these methods advance social action research, which they define as research that seeks to create "emancipatory knowledge." In this vein, Cosgrove and McHugh trace how postmodern perspectives on knowledge building have prompted methodological innovations that pay attention to the political nature of experience. In their conclusion they write:

> Taking the perspective that all research is "political"—at every stage in the research process we are endorsing certain values, worldviews, and beliefs and marginalizing others—we have outlined three empirical methods that embrace the sociopolitical grounding of experience. (p. 83)

Though Cosgrove and McHugh review emergent methods, they ultimately show how these methods contribute to larger conversations about the nature of the knowledge-building process. In this way, emergent methods move conversations forward. They write, "Our hope is that the three methods outlined . . . will encourage us to question the implicit assumptions that ground our work" (p. 83).

In Chapter 4, Melvin M. Mark contributes one of the few quantitative chapters in this part, within which he reviews how emergence can arise in the context of quasi-experimental designs. Mark reviews some common forms of emergence—or, at least, "quasi-emergence"—in quasi-experiments. However, before detailing alternative forms of emergence in quasi-experiments, Mark reviews the nature of and rationale for quasi-experiments, starting with an overview of randomized experiments that serves as a springboard to the topic of quasi-experiments. In this discussion Mark considers views of cause and effect, as well as the effect of the research process on the data. He further makes a case that many of the points made about emergence also apply to experiments.

The remainder of the chapters in this part of the *Handbook* review particular innovations in the practice of research methods. Most chapters center on the ways that conventional qualitative research methods have been adapted in order to ask and answer new research questions. In addition to providing context for the factors that have given rise to the emergent method, authors address questions such as:

- What is emergent about the method under review?
- What kinds of questions can be answered with this method?
- What is the impact of this new practice on the way the method is currently practiced?
- Where does the innovation in method take place in the research process—at the data-gathering stage, during data analysis, during interpretation, and/or at representation?
- What are the strengths and weaknesses of this innovation? What can it "get at" and what are its limitations? For example: What are the problems in and prospects for practicing this type of innovation?

The authors who discuss an innovation that remains within a traditional method also address the following question:

- In what ways is this method still part of a traditional methods approach?

The research methods chapters begin with two chapters about emergent methods in content analysis. In Chapter 5 Lindsay Prior reviews emergent-methods practices in the researching of documents. Prior provides a context for methodological innovation by asserting that documents enter into social affairs in two modes, both as receptacles of content and as agents in networks of action. Traditionally, social scientific research has focused on the collection and analysis of document content more than on documents as agents or actors. Prior reviews how approaching documents as topics rather than resources opens up a further dimension of analysis and that concerns the ways in which documents are used in social interaction and how they function. Once the focus shifts to the use and function of documents, the possibility of somewhat more dynamic (rather than static) styles of document analysis arise. It is in this vein that in recent decades new approaches to the study of documents have emerged. In Chapter 6 David Altheide, Michael Coyle, Katie DeVriese, and Christopher Schneider delineate and provide research examples of the practice of qualitative document analysis (QDA; also referred to as ethnographic content analysis, or ECA). Differing from other reviews of this subject, Altheide and colleagues consider QDA as an emergent methodology rather than a rigid set of procedures. Within this innovation, emergence primarily occurs in sampling and analysis. Altheide and colleagues also emphasize the importance of the research process, including the interaction between the researcher and the subject. Differing from other approaches to content analysis, "QDA is oriented to combining several steps in investigation with an explorer's eye to pursue concepts, data, and other information sources that emerge in the context of the thinking and discovering process of research" (p. 127).

Kathy Charmaz considers grounded theory as an emergent method of conducting qualitative research. Combining both inductive and abductive logic, Charmaz argues that grounded theory as a method is itself emergent because it is based on "emergent logic." Charmaz begins by defining emergent methods as "inductive, indeterminate, and open-ended." She posits that these methods are sensitive to the unanticipated directions that may emerge during the research process. In this vein, Charmaz suggests emergent methods are particularly useful for "studying uncharted, contingent, or dynamic phenomena."

The next four chapters cover a range of methods innovations in the area of interview studies, arranged from most quantitative to most qualitative. In Chapter 8 Frederick G. Conrad and Michael F. Schober explore new approaches to standardized interviewing, which they situate in the context of survey research in the social sciences. Conrad and Schober are particularly attentive to how new research practices in this area can contribute to "response accuracy" during data collection. They also consider how new technologies, including the Internet, provide new methodological possibilities. In Chapter 9 David Morgan reviews emergent approaches to focus group research. Morgan develops a "pragmatic approach" to understanding focus group research designs. He notes that researchers need to avoid thinking that there is "one right way to do focus groups." He notes that although researchers need to be aware of the variety of focus group research designs, it is imperative that researchers have "a clear understanding of the goals and outcomes for the project. . . . In other words, understanding why the research is being done is essential to answering questions about how to do the research" (p. 189). In Chapter 10, Monique M. Hennink discusses specific issues and strategies for conducting international focus group discussions. In particular, she notes how important it is to consider nuances in culture and language that can affect the validity of research findings. Rounding out the discussion of interview practices is Chapter 11, by Michael Frisch, which offers a rich description of innovations in oral history research, including how emergent technologies have influenced innovation in this area. Frisch begins by reviewing what he deems to have been "paradoxes" in the practice of oral history. For example, Frisch robustly describes the meanings and "textures rendered invisible" by traditional oral history practice, which relies on "orality." In this vein he writes:

> There are worlds of meaning that lie beyond words, and nobody pretends for a moment that the transcript is in any real sense a better

> representation of an interview than the voice itself. Meaning is carried and expressed in context and setting, in gesture, in tone, in body language, in pauses, in performed skills and movements. To the extent to which we are restricted to text and transcription, we will never locate such moments and meaning. (p. 223)

The chapter provides a strong case for how technology challenges the paradoxes on which traditional oral history practice rests. In this respect, Frisch's discussion of emergent practices in oral history illustrates the growing need for emergent methods as a way of accessing data that is otherwise unavailable.

The next four chapters consider emergent practices in ethnography and autoethnography. In Chapter 12 Jaber F. Gubrium and James A. Holstein offer a detailed account of innovations in narrative ethnography. The authors provide a retrospective and prospective review of this methodological practice, also arguing for the service provided by this method. Carol A. Bailey reviews emergent practices in ethnography and the rediscovery of "public ethnography." Unlike authors of chapters that focus on brand-new methods, Bailey makes a persuasive case for the ways in which public ethnography is reemerging as a strategy of inquiry. She details how sociology is centrally concerned with eradicating inequality and serving as an agent of social change. In this respect, the (re)turn to public ethnography is an attempt at dismantling false dualisms between activism and academia and finding methods that fit not only the research purpose but also the specific and more general intent that drives the research purpose. In Chapter 14 Christine S. Davis and Carolyn Ellis review the development of autoethnography as a research method in the social sciences. Davis and Ellis provide a discussion of single-voice narratives and then move into a review of emergent practices of coconstructed and relational narratives. Finally, they provide a discussion of "interactive focus groups," an emergent method they have created. This method brings new levels of collaboration and meaning making to the autoethnographic process. In this vein the authors write, "This is what I've learned about autoethnography: It is in the sharing that we heal, in vulnerability that we become strong, in laughter that we learn, and the more the merrier!" (p. 300). In addition to providing empirical examples from their own research, the authors demonstrate the strengths of the method throughout the chapter by writing in the very form of which they speak. In Chapter 15 Himika Bhattacharya reviews emergent methods in ethnographic research, focusing on new trends in critical collaborative ethnography. She presents several examples of critical ethnographic research studies across disciplines, including her own research on tribal women's experience of violence in the Northern Himalayan region of Lahaul, India. She raises some important issues regarding the practice of critical ethnographers and the role of the researcher within ethnographic practice: "How are we, as critical ethnographers, implicated in perpetuating and/or breaking hegemonic structures?" (p. 308). "What does it mean to be emancipated? How can we be transformed? And can we be transformed? What are 'acts of resistance'? . . . And when do we know that our 'acts of resistance' are ineffectual versus emancipatory and transforming?" (p. 316).

The last two chapters consider various emergent arts-based practices. In Chapter 16, Gunilla Holm provides a prospective view of the field of visual research methods situated in discussion of traditional practices in visual sociology and anthropology. Holm argues that visual methods are gaining prominence within the social sciences. She considers topics that include visual ethnography and action research, as well as many visual methods that have sprung forth as a result of technological developments, including photoblogs, photovoice, and video diaries. Chapter 17 rounds out the review of emergent arts-based research as Patricia Leavy reviews the development of methodological innovations in interdisciplinary performance studies. Performance modes such as drama and dance are often treated separately in the emergent literature on these methods practices, but the author reviews both ethnodrama and dance/creative movement research methods. Leavy also provides a discussion of the theoretical context in which performance-based methods have emerged as a means of gathering, analyzing, and representing data.

Part I of the *Handbook of Emergent Methods* provides historical context for methods innovations, considering the links between social and political change, theoretical and methodological development, and new perspectives in scientific standards. Researchers across the disciplines offer a range of perspectives on new methods practices—methods that have been rediscovered, methods that are being reworked to suit new research questions, hybrid methods, and entirely new methods tools. In their wisdom the contributors to Part I provide a range of ways that researchers can "explore the edges"—the cutting edge of methods practice—in service of long-standing and emergent research concerns.

References

Eisner, E. W. (1997). The promise and perils of alternative forms of data representation. *Educational Researcher, 26*(6), 4–10.

Hesse-Biber, S. N., & Leavy, P. (Eds.). (2006). *Emergent methods in social research*. Thousand Oaks, CA: Sage.

HISTORY

CHAPTER 1

History of Methods in Social Science Research

Karen M. Staller
Ellen Block
Pilar S. Horner

Science is a conversation between rigor and imagination.
—ABBOTT (2004, p. 3)

These fads come and go; ultimately, however, these tools are only as good as the scientific intuition and imagination of the researcher using them.
—BORGATTA (1969, p. xiv)

Our task was daunting: write a history of methods in the social sciences for a book on emergent methods in the new millennium. It seems worth pausing to tease out some of the inherent challenges in this undertaking and the choices that necessarily followed in order to carry it out.

One need only get as far as the words *write a history* to run into the first of these challenges. It turns out that historians have engaged in a lively methodological debate about the proper approach to producing histories. According to Jarausch and Coclanis (2001), during the 1960s a "new social history" emerged that shifted the object of study from affairs of state to such things as "societal changes, demographic transformations, or economic growth" (p. 12634). This shift in the *object* of study must be understood in the context of technological advances, including the introduction of mainframe computers in the 1950s, followed by the advent of personal computers and the introduction of widely available statistical software (such as SPSS in 1968 and SAS in 1972). These technological advances "made it possible to handle large amounts of data and to use complicated statistical procedures in customized form" (Jarausch & Coclanis, 2001, p. 12634). The net result was "a new hybrid, combining elements of historical research with social scientific analysis" (p. 12634). Mid-century technological advances permitted and promoted a shifting interest in the *object* of study and contributed to new methodological approaches in producing history.

So, in writing a history of social science methods, one approach available to us might be to quantify various uses of methods—perhaps by drawing evidence from prestigious journal articles or textbooks—to statistically analyze the data and then attempt to make sense of the findings. In other words, we could use frequencies or other numeric measures to investigate a social phenomenon and narrate a story on methods.

However, Jarausch and Coclanis (2001) go on to inform us that by the 1980s, "the seemingly unstoppable progress of the quantitative history project began to stall" and that during this time "many historians turned instead to cultural anthropology for methodological inspiration" (p. 12636). So it would seem that, as some limitations of quantitative approaches for investigating social history became apparent, historians began to reach across disciplinary lines in search of new methodological strategies to answer their questions.

Jarausch and Coclanis (2001) attribute the philosophical basis of this shift to the rise of postmodernism, which "deprecated the rationalism, universalism, and empiricism of historical social science" (p. 12636). In doing so, historians rejected "the rigorous, formal and remote, data-driven 'truths' sought by quantifiers" and instead substituted "in-depth microstudies" in order to "explore experience and meaning" (p. 12636). These methodological shifts (involving new theoretical approaches to history) resulted in new methods being employed and shifted the primary project from one involving quantitative to one involving qualitative data gathering. So it would seem that these postmodern historians rejected the idea that a sweeping, universal narrative could be told and instead focused on producing "microstudies" of smaller groups, making more contextualized and localized claims. Postmodern interpretivist researchers who have taken up the task of writing the history of *qualitative* methods also point to the early 1980s as a period of disruption and challenge. They conceptualize its history as a sequence of "turning points" or a "series of crises, ruptures, rifts, and even revolutions" (Lincoln & Denzin, 2003, p. 1).

For our project, an alternative and more postmodern approach to writing the history of methods might be to reflect on the messiness inherent in tracing ideas that commingle in time, space, and place. It would not assume a story easily reducible to a set of variables and resulting in a neatly unfolding grand narrative but might instead focus on the ruptures and contestations. These moments are particularly interesting and useful, for they point to movement from stagnation to growth. Feyerabend comments on the importance of such commotion when he notes that the "anarchic enterprise" of science "helps to achieve progress in any one of the senses one cares to choose" (Feyerabend, as cited in Crotty, 2003).

Of course, the question of history was not our only challenge in this assignment. Next came the matter of *social science*. Disciplines such as anthropology, sociology, psychology, political science, and economics are generally recognized as social sciences and are distinguishable from the natural sciences (geology, biology, astronomy) or the humanities (philosophy, literature, history). Nonetheless, the boundaries are not as clear as it might seem when considering a history of methods. Social scientists have routinely applied methods and methodologies borrowed from the natural sciences to social issues and social problems. Additionally, qualitative researchers have recently turned to the humanities for inspiration in their studies, utilizing poetry, fiction, drama, and performance as a way to design, disseminate, and make public their ideas (Denzin, 2003; Richardson & Lockridge, 2004). When it comes to a discussion of methods, such creative multidisciplinary weaving blurs the seemingly distinct boundary between "social sciences" and other areas of study.

Further complicating the task at hand—beyond worrying about what constitutes social science—is the relationship of any individual social science discipline to the methods it employs. Abbott (2004) argues that "with the possible exception of anthropology" no social science is primarily "organized around the use of one particular method" (p. 13). Anthropologists have made life comparatively simple by organizing the entire discipline around one method approach, known as ethnography. But what of other disciplines that have been more eclectic in their approaches? Abbott argues that these other disciplines have been organized around "various historical accidents"; for example, "economics is organized by a theoretical concept (the ideas of choice under constraint), political science by social organization (power), sociology by subject matter (city, family, etc.) and so on" (p. 5).

Historians of social science methods have taken different approaches to these disciplinary boundaries. Vidich and Lyman (2000), who examined the history of qualitative methods in sociology and anthropology, used comparative models. Others have studied the evolution of methods within a single discipline, such as Jennifer Platt (1996), who focused on the methods employed by sociologists between 1920 and 1960. It seemed that our assignment, however, was to think more broadly about methods across a wide variety of social sciences in order to set the context for a book on *emergent* methods. Given the lack of monogamy between most social science disciplines and their methods, it became evident that this history of methods was not best told as the history of a discipline (or two or three).

This led to yet another difficulty in our assignment. We also had to come to terms with the central object of investigation in this chapter, *methods*. The very term *methods* carries with it its own complications, particularly when distinguished from the idea of methodology and the relative role of theory. Not all social scientists agree on the distinctions separating these terms. In general, methods refer to the tools used in the research endeavor. For example, Harding (1987) defines methods as "a technique for (or way of proceeding in) gathering evidence" (pp. 2–3), whereas Crotty (1998) defines methods as "the techniques or procedures used to gather and analyze data related to some research question or hypothesis" (p. 3). Note here that Harding defines methods as tools for evidence gathering, and Crotty extends this definition to include linking evidence to the research question and to data analysis.

Harding (1987) goes on to define methodology as "a theory and analysis of how research does or should proceed" (pp. 2–3). For her, theory must be intrinsically related to methodology, therefore dictating how the entire research process is conducted. Similarly, Crotty (1998) defines methodology as "the strategy, plan of action, process or design lying behind the choice and use of some particular methods and linking the choice and use of methods to desired outcomes" (p. 3). Note, however, that he omits the word *theory* as organizing that strategy or plan of action. In fact, he relates theory to methodology slightly differently than Harding does when he addresses the relationship between theory and epistemology. Although both Harding and Crotty define epistemology as a "theory of knowledge," Crotty goes on to write that epistemology refers to the "theory of knowledge embedded in the theoretical perspective and thereby in the methodology" (p. 3). So for Crotty methodology would necessarily be infused with a theoretical perspective flowing from the researcher's epistemological position. Note that in both cases, a theoretical perspective is what gives shape to methodology, although in the former theory is an intrinsic element of methodology, and in the latter it is a necessary consequence of an epistemological position. The consequences of which approach is utilized will ripple through the research design.

For the purposes of this chapter, we refer to *methods* as tools of inquiry and *methodology* as a perspective or theory of social reality. For example, ethnography is a generally recognized technique for gathering data in a natural setting. So ethnography is a method or a tool for data collection. However, in deciding on how to approach an ethnographic project, one might shape it pursuant to a variety of possible theoretical positions, such as feminist ethnography, critical ethnography, or autoethnography. Therefore critical ethnography, autoethnography, or feminist ethnography are methodologies because they start from a certain perspective (or theoretical position) about social reality.

If our central task for this chapter is to consider the history of "methods," we are confronted with a distinct problem if we isolate these tools from the methodologies, or theoretical perspectives, by which researchers are organizing or utilizing them. Certainly there are a number of distinct methods (such as surveys, experimental designs, case studies, focus groups, etc.), but each requires putting together a coherent plan, or blueprint, that shares some common steps; in other words, the methodology. Mellenbergh and colleagues (2003) have conceptualized these as phases:

> The first phase consists of the *definition* of the research problem. The relevant literature is studied and the research problem is framed to a theoretical or practical context. The second phase is the *planning* of the study. The research problem is operationally defined in terms of a concrete design and measurement procedure. The third phase contains the *implementation* of the study. The study is actually carried out and the empirical data are collected. The fourth phase consists of the *analysis* of the data. The raw data are processed such that they yield information on the research problem. The final phase is the *reporting* of the study. The research problem and the study are described, and the results are interpreted. (p. 212)

These five phases reflect standardized approaches to research based in a natural science model. This particular sequential order carries with it some methodological assumptions about proper scientific construction. For example, the "relevant literature is studied" after a research problem is "defined" and the problem is "framed" through a "theoretical" lens. These researchers assert that variables must be operationally defined and "measured" (p. 212). So as the methods or tools in the process are identified, also apparent are some underlying methodological assumptions about proper science. Such a model may indeed offer a place to start, however, and we use the general component parts as a way to organize our subsequent discussion.

In studying the evolution of research discussions in a prominent handbook on research in teaching, Richardson (2001) noted "turbulence similar to that in other fields" involving postmodern questions that "jar the very foundations of our understanding of research. These questions concern the nature of knowledge, who owns it, who produces it, and how it should be used. . . . The conflicts go beyond the old qualitative–quantitative methodology controversy. . . . They now focus on the very nature of research and knowledge and the uses of research to improve practice" (p. 15483). In short, epistemological and methodological challenges necessitated changes in the methods employed by social scientists. Hesse-Biber and Leavy (2006) have explained emergent methods elsewhere as "the logical conclusion to paradigm shifts, major developments in theory, and new conceptions of knowledge and the knowledge-building process" (p. xi). Similarly, in 2003 Lincoln and Denzin wrote:

> The ferment in methods is not likely to come to an end soon. New methods, as well as new uses for older methods, are being invented almost daily. New venues for the application of old and revised methods—for example, the Internet (text and narrative analysis), photography, filmmaking, media representations (visual analyses), or community-centered cultures (focus groups)—arose with technological revolutions and increasing sophistication within the social science community. This is an incredibly fertile era for the revisiting of old methods and methodological strategies and the invention of new methods. (p. 11)

In our discussion of problematizing issues of (1) producing histories, (2) constituting strict boundaries of social science disciplines, and (3) standardizing methods and methodological processes, three things seem very clear. The first, as noted by Richardson (2001), is that postmodern questions "jar the very foundations of understanding of research" to its very core. Second, new technologies are both further complicating the process and creating new possibilities. These technologies are central to the creation of new and emerging methods. Third, researchers are now in a period in which "emergent methods," "turbulence," or the "ferment in methods" is creating an exciting context for methods and methodological experimentation and prompting contestation of once stable sets of procedures.

Our Model and Methods

For the purposes of this chapter, and in the spirit of emergent methods, we sought to answer our research question—*What is the history of methods in the social sciences that helps explain the current context of emergent methods?*—using a creative approach to the problem. We used three sources of empirical evidence: *Ulrich's Periodical Directory*, Sage Publishers' evaluation and methodology book list, and a comparative case study of leading journals in anthropology and sociology.

Ulrich's *Global Context and Scholarly Journals*

Ulrich's Periodical Directory is "a bibliographic database providing detailed, comprehensive, and authoritative information on serials published throughout the world." It calls itself "the global source for periodicals information since 1932" and "the most comprehensive online information source for the periodicals industry" (May 29, 2006). Indeed, this impressive resource for locating journals—both extinct and active—documents periodical life in all disciplines, over time, and in a global context. *Ulrich's* is marketed as a resource for librarians, publishers, and patrons; however, we have used it to consider the international growth of methodological conversations.

We created a database for our study that consisted of journals that were identified as academic/scholarly or refereed journals; that were cataloged under one of the following domains: social science, anthropology, education, sociology, or psychology; and that included in the title or key words the words *research*, *method*, *methods*, or *methodology*. The resulting titles were culled by eliminating those that were monographs, newsletters, proceedings, bulletins, or yearbooks. Due to our own limitations, we also eliminated any journals that were not in English, which included two in Chinese, two in Spanish (one from Mexico and the other from Spain), and one each in Japanese and German. The resulting list contained 313 journals representing 32 different countries. The earliest publication listing was from 1892.

Sage Publications Case Study

As a publisher, Sage has aggressively built a book list of methodology textbooks, handbooks, encyclopedias, and journals and currently leads the publication field in this area. These publications are important tools for educators, graduate students, undergraduate students, and researchers. Other publishers have produced significant contributions, but Sage Publications has dominated the methods market and for that reason offers important empirical evidence about the growth and evolution of methodology books over time. The Sage catalogue on *Research Methods and Evaluation* (2006) states:

> Since 1965, Sage has developed a reputation among scholars, researchers, instructors, and practitioners for publishing a superior list of methodology books across disciplines. We continue to expand our offerings and are passionately committed to bringing you
>
> - Cutting-edge research techniques
> - Best practices in and across social, behavioral, and health sciences, education and management
> - Pedagogically rich textbooks and course supplements
> - Accessible "how-to" guides for use in research and practice.

Sage is by no means the only publisher of methods books, nor do we mean to endorse the press by its selection for study. However, we do justify its selection for a case study based on the following four factors. First, Sage organizes its book list around research method and evaluation as a separate categorical topic independent of discipline (many publishers require you to identify a discipline first, before you can search for methods books). Second, because of Sage's dedication to developing a methods book list over a 40-year period, it provides a place to look at the longitudinal development of methods publication by topic, by genre, by discipline, and by product type and through quantitative measures. Third, because of Sage's determination to shape the methods market, the number (or volume) of publications makes historical trends more readily apparent than with publishers who publish fewer titles in this area. Fourth, its catalogue is easily available online and has search possibilities that aided in data analysis. For one thing, it is able to generate lists of titles with certain characteristics and then to sort them by author or by year of publication. This permitted an easy way to organize titles in historical sequence or by impact of specific authors in order to ask and answer questions about what was going on.

Therefore, Sage Publications serves as an excellent resource with which to examine the rise and development of research methods because of its mission to publish "cutting-edge research techniques," its marketing to both students and research practitioners, its 40-year history of building a research methods catalogue, the electronic organization of that catalogue, and its global reach.

Comparative Journal/Comparative Disciplinary Case Study

Finally, in order to examine the methodological trends more closely within the specific disciplines, we chose to look at the prefaces, prologues, and introductions written by the editors of three prominent method journals from the 1960s to the present. We examined two journals in sociology, *Sociological Methodology* (established in 1969) and *Qualitative Sociology* (established in 1978), and one in anthropology, *American Anthropologist* (established in 1888). We chose these disciplines specifically for their unique roles within the broader context of the social sciences. As noted earlier, sociology has been known for its organization around theory, whereas anthropology has been primarily organized around its favored method, ethnography.

These journals and their editorial essays were selected for several reasons. *Sociological Methodology* and *American Anthropologist* were chosen because (1) they are considered important journals by the American Sociological Association (ASA) and American Anthropological Association (AAA), respectively, and therefore enjoy a strong degree of respect and authority; (2) they both have a lengthy history and therefore reflect historical patterns; (3) all the data were easily and readily available through online resources; and (4) the editor's prefaces serve as a moment of reflection about the frontiers of the discipline. *Sociological Methodology* was chosen because it focuses specifically on methods, though it tends to privilege quantitative methodologies rather than those using qualitative data. Although *American Anthropologist* is not solely methodological, anthropology is uniquely linked to ethnography, so it serves as an excellent source for examining new trends and theories in anthropology, which are often accompanied by methodological accommodations. In addition, we included data from *Qualitative Sociology* because this journal emerged as a response to the quantitatively dominated journals and thus serves as a nice introduction to differing methodological viewpoints.

The dataset included a total of 107 pieces. In *Sociological Methodology*, 35 editor's notes were written by 12 different editors between the years 1969 and 2005; *Qualitative Sociology* contained 21 documents over a 9-year period, including 17 editorial notes or introductions and 4 special-issue introductions; and *American Anthropologist* contained 51 special editor notes, presidential addresses to the AAA, and prefaces to special issues published between 1959 and 2006.

Thus we combine the use of *Ulrich's Periodical Directory*, a Sage Publications case study, and a comparative interdisciplinary journal case study to examine changes, innovations, and trends in methods.

Model

Building on our earlier discussion involving Mellenbergh and colleagues (2003), it is our contention that we are in a period in which each *step* of the research process has been challenged and disrupted in profound and fundamental ways. Certainly research projects must include a research question (although that question may be articulated at the outset or evolve during the process); must embody some sort of methodological framework; must make implicit or explicit use of theory (although theory may frame the study, may be tested during it, or may be generated from it); must contain a stage in which the researcher identifies his or her relationship to the study and its participants (it can be arm's length, full participation, or anywhere in between); must contain a literature review or discussion that places the project in a broader context (but that might be conducted either before starting the project or after analyzing the data); must identify the study participants or location (a question of sampling, but this process can be highly systematic and rigid or not); must discuss a data collection stage in which material is gathered (but "data" can include a wide variety of things); must discuss a data analysis stage (but that analysis can range from subjecting it to statistical tests or conducting interpretive or negotiated processes); and finally must report findings, a stage in which the scientific story is produced and disseminated to others (this can be done in a classical scientific format or through more flexible and literary modes). In sum, there are many possibilities and choices available to a researcher as he or she goes about the research process.

The recent history of methods, at least from the 1960s onward, has been to challenge or trouble these steps and to untether them from their former places in the process—in part because of new epistemological and methodological conversations—thereby challenging the linear progressions assumed by Mellenbergh and colleagues (2003) and permitting them to be reconstituted in new and creative ways. We are in an age of dearrangement and rearrangement, an era ripe for fermenting methods in which researchers can borrow or adapt methods and capitalize on new technological advances. We attempt to construct this history of methods—leading up the era of "emergent methods"—by considering the historical challenges that have been raised at the various steps of the research process.

In Platt's work on the history of methods in sociology from 1920 to 1960, she notes that she "does not attempt to fill the gaps with a complete narrative history, but draws on narrative materials in relation to key thematic issues" (1996, p. 4). We have done the same. We sought to integrate our findings with existing literature on methods and methodology, disciplinary history, the philosophy of science, and other writings in the social sciences. First we contextualize our findings by examining the rapid growth of methodological conversation in the 1960s and the years that followed. We then turn to the increasingly global context of these discussions. These contextual discussions are then followed by six sections in which we consider the "troubling" of the steps in the research process as the natural extension of this explosion of methodological discourse that contributes to new methods.

History and Discussions

The 1960s and Beyond: Methodological Turbulence and Growth

In 2000, Denzin and Lincoln posited that today's "methodological revolution" would have been "beyond comprehension" in the mid-1970s. Indeed, in the decades leading up to the 1970s, conversations began to emerge on various fronts (particularly those with roots in the civil rights and feminist movements and from indigenous scholars) that challenged core assumptions about the scientific processes in the social sciences. Positivism, although not the only theoretical position posited in social science research, claimed a ubiquitous respectability prior to the 1960s. Social science was based in strategies that sought to verify knowledge, thereby revealing truths. These verification methods included "observation, mathematical calculation, experiment, and replication" (Brown, 2005, p. 202). Epistemologically rooted in objectivism's natural sciences, positivism was strenuously challenged by constructivism and subjectivism, as well as other postmodern views in the 1960s and following decades.[1] Brown and Strega (2005) argue that "the fundamental theoretical contestation and claim of postmodern theories is that social reality cannot be described or explained with certainty or in authoritarian terms," and for postmodern theorists, reality "is too complex, multiple, and fluid to be captured by singular, universal explanations found in enlightenment theories, with their attendant false/true dualisms" (pp. 56–57). From these different epistemological stances, new methodologies emerged and contributed to new orientations toward research design and the methods employed.

Thus one version of a history of methods could focus on the methodological tension between researchers who approached knowing the world through numbers, taking a more positivistic approach, and the backlash or challenges from the postpositivist and postmodern research communities, which argued for alternative philosophical assumptions to undergird scientific endeavors. In some circles this resulted in pitting the "quants" against the "quals." One source of empirical evidence that illustrates not only the jostling between these camps but also the exponential growth in conversations on methods in recent decades is the development of the Sage Publications book list.

Figure 1.1 depicts the number of Sage research methods publications plotted over time according to three publisher-identified categories: qualitative methods books, quantitative methods books, and total methods books (which includes evaluation and research methods in addition to qualitative and quantitative methods books). Three important points can be gleaned from this data. First, there has been a dramatic increase in methods books published since the initial debut, in 1976, of Ramon Henkel's *Tests of Significance* and Stuart Nagel's *Operations Research Methods*. By 2005 (the latest year of complete data) the book list included a total of 808 products. Second, the first qualitative book did not appear until 1983, with Garth Morgan's *Beyond Method: Strategies for Social Research*. Thus the entry of

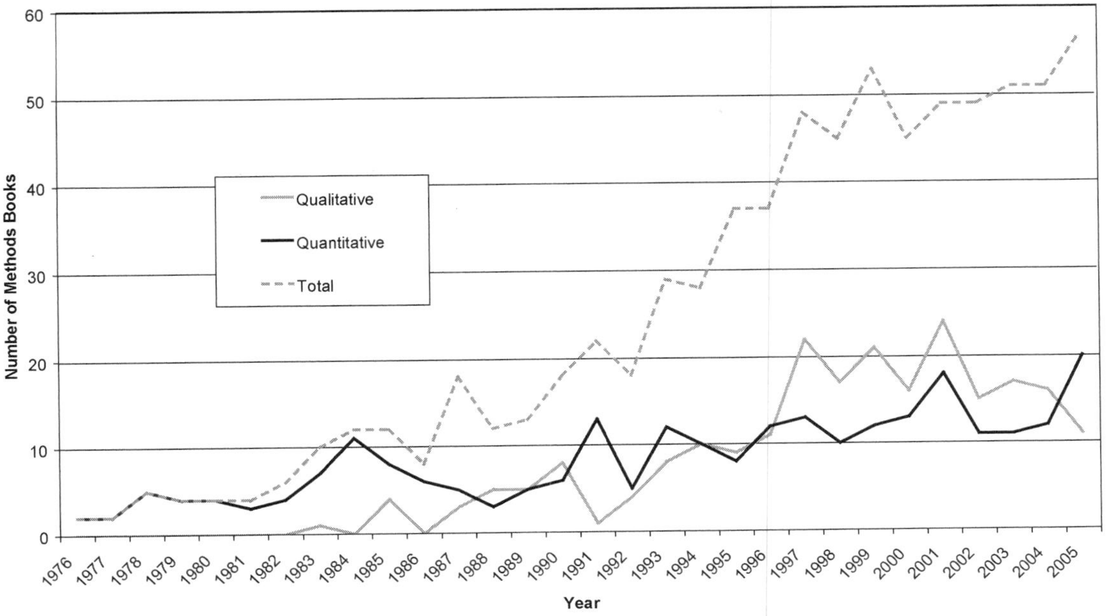

FIGURE 1.1. Sage Publications research methods books.

qualitative publications lagged 7 years behind the early quantitative books. Third, the relative numbers of quantitative- and qualitative-oriented books would seem to fall into four time periods. In the earliest period, from 1976 to 1987, quantitative books dominated the list; during a transitional period from 1987 to 1996, there was some jostling between the two; during a third period from 1996 to 2004, qualitative publications outnumbered quantitative ones. Finally, in the most recent years there again appears to be a balance between the two, suggesting, perhaps, that we might have settled on a middle ground that recognizes the important contributions of both approaches.

Some scholars have suggested that the increase in quantitative methods in the social sciences resulted from a desire to gain the respect generally afforded the hard sciences and professional schools–such as business, law, and medicine–within the academy. These professionalization initiatives coincided with, and may have even been fueled by, technological developments. Computer specialists who once communicated with mainframe computers and served as gatekeepers for social scientists during data analysis stages of the research process became obsolete as personal computers allowed any social scientist the luxury of storing enormous datasets and analyzing them using relatively easy-to-master statistical software such as SPSS or SAS. Thus individual social science researchers in any academic department could conduct sophisticated mathematical procedures. The popularity and dominance of quantitative methods would not have been possible without these advances, which made the tools to execute such methods widely available.

For example, in sociology, "major advances in quantitative research" took place in the 1960s, and "the decade saw the increased use of multivariate statistics—especially the introduction of path analysis, which built more complex causal models on the basis of multiple-regression analysis" (Calhoun & Duster, 2005, p. B7). Calhoun and Duster (2005) point to Otis Dudley

Duncan and Peter Blau's influential 1967 study of "The American Occupational Structure" as an exemplar. This pattern of quantification holds true in other disciplines as well. Psychology, which had first turned to "experimental quantification" in the 1930s and 1940s, intensified these efforts over time and resulted in the "new paradigm of a proper experiment," involving "a randomized design of control and experimental populations, yielding results that would, in most cases, be subjected to analysis of variance (ANOVA)"; the value of results was measured by tests of significance (Porter, 2001b, p. 12643). Economists also turned to quantification projects and introduced the term *quantitative economic history*, which referred to "a self-conscious movement dating from the 1950s and 1960s, also known as the 'new economic history' or 'cliometerics,' which set out to revolutionize the field by incorporating explicit economic analysis and quantitative methods into the study of past economic performance" (Wright, 2001, p. 4108). This pattern of turning toward numbers and utilizing positivistic methodological approaches to answer social science questions was repeated in virtually all disciplines.

It is not surprising that the earliest methods books published by Sage in the 1970s focused exclusively on statistical techniques (canonical analysis, factor analysis, analysis of covariance, etc.) or handling different types of quantitative data (ordinal data, panel data, multiple indicators). These books provided guidance to social scientists in integrating new forms of statistical analysis into their research designs and also furthered the trend toward increasingly quantitative work across the social sciences. Furthermore, the progression of these titles over time is also telling. For example, the earliest book devoted to computers was Philip Schrodt's *Microcomputer Methods for Social Scientists*, published in 1984. Others followed, but by 2001 there were entire books devoted to specific statistical software—SAS first, followed later by SPSS—and these texts now include specialized volumes for introductory and advanced material. Most recently, however, the market has been inundated with books targeted to reluctant students, such as Neil Salkind's *Statistics for People Who (Think They) Hate Statistics* (2008) and Dane Keller's *The Tao of Statistics* (2006). Even undergraduates in the social sciences are now expected as a matter of their basic education to be schooled in the fundamentals of statistical analysis. Note the dramatic evolution in expectation: These methods employing statistical techniques—which were once utilized only by specialists—are now routinely expected to be mastered (or at least tackled) by undergraduate students taking basic research methods courses.

In short, the contributions of quantitative work helped legitimize social science research by entering and adopting methodologies and methods that heretofore had been only the domain of the natural sciences. However, not all advances were seen as beneficial. One negative consequence of quantifying social phenomena in order to make sense of it was to silence or diminish the respectability of other, more qualitative approaches to social science research. For example, sociologists noted this phenomenon relative to one method—the personal narrative—and the resurgence or reclaiming of this qualitative method from more positivistic methodological perspectives during the 1960s:

> Although there is a history of personal narrative in early twentieth-century American sociology, this history was long obscured by the discipline's rush to quantification at mid century. The contemporary resurgence of interest in personal narratives dates from the 1960s and 1970s, originating in the Civil Rights movement and, even more powerfully, in second wave feminism. The strategy of consciousness raising—the effort to find both personal and political truth through the sharing of personal experiences—encouraged the flowering of autobiography, oral histories, and other narratives of the self. Feminist sociologists, especially those who had been active in the second

> wave of the women's movement, became interested in using personal narratives in their research as a way to give "voice" to women's experiences. Pioneering feminist scholarship of the later 1960s and 1970s privileged women's voices as part of the assault on androcentrism. In contrast to positivist traditions of thought, feminism emphasized reflexivity, sought out voices that spoke from alternative realities, and took those voices seriously without dismissing them as "mere" subjectivity. Here, the resurgence of interest in narrative must be understood as part of feminist scholarship's larger project of connecting scholarship and action and of understanding the workings of women's agency as part of a larger political agenda. (Pierce, 2003, p. 307)

As noted, the advent of the civil rights and feminist movements spurred serious critiques of virtually all aspects of the research process; this translated into focusing on new methods and methodological approaches, including, but not limited to, the narratives discussed by Pierce. In particular, the 1960s provided a new mix of ideas and renewed experimentation with a variety of methodologies. Critical theorists and Marxist discussions led to action-based research projects in which the goal was community change, such as participatory action research (PAR). In sociology, quantitative researchers were "often challenged by field researchers, specialists on social problems, those carrying on the reform traditions, and critical theorists" (Calhoun & Duster, 2005). Perhaps one of the most pivotal works to be published during this period was Barney G. Glaser and Anselm L. Strauss's *The Discovery of Grounded Theory* (1967), which sought to introduce rigorous techniques favored by quantitative researchers and unify it with data generated from field observations; in other words, staying true to a positivistic methodological tradition but employing new methods of data collection and analysis.

There were also calls during the 1960s to focus on naturalistic studies, everyday events and objects, and the ordinary and individualistic in many social science disciplines, including anthropology, sociology, history, and the newly emerging and expanding field of cultural studies. The focus was on the "commonplace and the seemingly trivial routines and activities of daily life" of ordinary people who were viewed as "creative actors rather than passive consumers or objects of domination" (Löfgren, 2001, p. 4969). There was a call among sociocultural anthropologists during the 1960s to "to study up, down and sideways" (Nader, 2002, p. 444). Furthermore, during the 1960s, "phenomenological sociology, inspired by Alfred Schutz, and ethnomethodology, promoted by Harold Garfinkle, emerged as alternative approaches that problematized objectivity, realism, and the social activities through which qualitative knowledge is created. Added to this mix during the same decade were the constructivism of Peter Berger and Thomas Luckmann, the dramaturgical approach of Erving Goffman" (Hall, 2001, p. 12614). These researchers frequently focused on everyday transactions, conversations, and events as the object of investigation.

Not surprisingly, the explosion of these conversations during the 1960s and thereafter and the dramatic diversity that ensued gave rise to the cacophony or methodological revolution we are seeing today. The most recent initiatives to "mix methods" seem like an attempt to create a bridge between these long-standing discussions. For example, at the time of this writing, Sage's newest methods journal is the *Journal of Mixed Methods Research*, edited by John Creswell and Abbas Tashakkori. Both of these editors have contributed other mixed methods books published by Sage: Tashakkori is coauthor of the *Handbook on Mixed Methods in Social and Behavioral Sciences*, and Creswell is author of several successful methods books, including one focusing on mixed method design.

Hesse-Biber and Leavy (2006) have noted that "some emergent methods quickly disappear, only to be rediscovered decades later emerging in a new discipline and even taking on a different conceptualization"

(p. 377). They point to "participant observation," which appeared in the 1920s but was unrecognized as a distinct mode of data collection until much later. Similarly, the current vibrant discussion of "mixed methods" has seen a renaissance. Nonetheless, one need only pick up the extraordinary work of Henry Mayhew from the 1860s, when he did an extensive study of London's poor and labor classes, to realize that in today's parlance he used and integrated an extraordinary array of "mixed" methods, including ethnographic observations, surveys, interviews, and meticulously collected quantitative and qualitative data. In short, the history of any of these methods is likely to have deep historical roots, and there are many rich traditions to draw from. But the current context of emergent methods is most immediately traceable to the explosion of conversations from the 1960s and thereafter.

Globalization and Challenges from the "Others"

Historically, anthropology distinguished itself from the other social sciences by initially turning its research eye toward the "exotic other," particularly nonliterate and primitive cultures throughout the world. As such, it offers an excellent starting point for considering the serious challenges to methodologies in which the researcher was in a position of power to speak authoritatively about "others."[2] Especially in an increasingly global context, this positionality is decidedly problematic. Leslie White asked in his presidential address to the AAA in 1965, "What will the ethnographer do when his preliterate tribes and cultures are gone?" (White, 1965, p. 630). As it turns out, the ethnographer has adapted his or her tools in order to examine culture within the context of contemporary issues. Many of the initial assumptions embedded in ethnography's methodological practices were contested, resulting in threats to authority, voice, representation of others, considerations of power and exploitation, and corresponding discussions of ethical practice. These discussions led to the upheaval and restructuring of research. As Lincoln and Denzin (2003) argue, "The peculiarly Western and masculine bent of the social sciences was effectively challenged by multiple discourses, including subaltern, indigenous, feminist, and border voices" (p. 3).

The challenges of globalization have led social scientists to include diverse paradigms in their research practices. In reaction to hegemonic discourse, there is pressure to hear and acknowledge the voices of these "others." This has influenced many aspects of social science methods, including challenges to research ownership, interpretation, and representation. For example, "ethical considerations about privacy, asymmetry of field research, and exploitation of subjects—raised especially by feminists and within anthropology—cast long shadows on the high modern quest for objectivity and validity in qualitative analysis" (Hall, 2001, p. 12614). Furthermore, "globalization fueled the internationalization of sociology. Soaring numbers of immigrants returned scholarly attention to classic sociological investigation of assimilation and ethnic identities, discrimination and access, and the continuing struggles of American minority groups for equal rights" (Calhoun & Duster, 2005, p. B7). Globalization has fundamentally altered research by problematizing what we know, how we know it, and even why we think we know it.

The effects of globalization are also reflected in the market for academic journals. For example, analysis of the entry of new journals in the *Ulrich's* database by decades illustrates the exponential growth in the latter half of the 20th century (see Table 1.1). The rapid growth of journals, internationally accessible, is attributable not only to the increasing numbers of journals published in the United States and United Kingdom but also to the introduction of methodology journals from around the world, including

TABLE 1.1. Number of New Journals by Decade of Entry

Decade	1920	1930	1940	1950	1960	1970	1980	1990	2000
Journal count	9	7	7	20	35	39	55	72	40

contributions from Africa (including Ethiopia, Ghana, Kenya, Zimbabwe, and South Africa); the Middle East (including Iraq and Israel); South Asia (including China, Thailand, Guam, the Philippines, Japan, and India), and South and Central America (including Mexico and Brazil), among others.

The *Ulrich's* database reflects this dramatic expansion and international inclusion of scholarly journals. Although these may, to some extent, signal within-country specializations, the fact that these journals and their articles are increasingly available on the Internet significantly alters the possibility of dissemination of ideas and enhances the possibility of scholarly cross-fertilization around the world.

As early as 1959, the journal *American Anthropologist* argued for an increase in collaboration and discussion with scholars from abroad. Goldschmidt (1959) called for more international submissions and more intellectual exchange between scholars from different countries while recognizing that this collaboration had become more difficult as scholars' methods and methodologies were departing from each other rather than converging. Goldschmidt saw this departure as being harmful to the discipline because "[it] runs counter to the precept that truth, and therefore presumably the scholarly and scientific pursuits, knows no national boundaries" (p. vii). Goldschmidt points to world events, such as the World Wars and the Depression, as possible causes for the decrease in international exchange. In 1965, the president of *American Anthropologist*, Leslie White, reminded anthropologists that international work is important because "all of the nations of the world today are intimately related to one another; what happens to one affects all the others" (p. 635). In 1990 and 1998, editors Dane Keller and Robert W. Sussman, respectively, put out a call for more contributions from international colleagues. Although these calls are not for methods advances specifically, international exchange certainly includes sharing methodological and methods innovations.

We are in a period of greater inclusion in which diversity of voices is embraced and in which cultural and contextual matters are of great interest and importance. We have turned a research eye both on the familiar and the unfamiliar, local and global. There is a growing international voice enhanced by the advent of new technology. The Internet, for example, shrink the world in time and space, allowing for broader dissemination of research products and conversations, thus creating new possibilities for a global forum to advance research.

Troubling the Research Process Step by Step

Although all research methodologies "rest on some ontological[3] and epistemological[4] foundation" (Strega, 2005, p. 201), disputes, disruptions, or debates often surface at the methods level. So the rapid expansion of ontological and epistemological challenges had a direct impact on methodological conversations and methods. The civil rights, feminism, gay liberation, and other civil rights-based movements that challenged patriarchy and other forms of oppression fueled both. Furthermore, rapid development of new technologies and increasing globalization have all contributed to the "troubling" of every phase of the research process. The following sections briefly examine the troubling of these various steps.

Troubling the Role of Researcher: The Researcher as "Variable"

One of the most important transformations in the research process began with questioning the role, authority, and responsibility of the researcher. Rather than finding ways to neutralize the influence of the researcher, as was attempted in more traditional survey designs, postmodern methodologies have embraced the notion that the researcher is a variable in the endeavor. As noted earlier, critical, queer, and standpoint theorists and feminist researchers have all given rise to critiques about the relationships between the researcher and the researched. Discourses emerged about "the self-as-researchers and the researcher-as-self. The idea of the 'voice from nowhere/voice from everywhere' was also criticized, as was the 'god's-eye view' of inquiry" (Lincoln & Denzin, 2003, p. 3). From these discourses emerged a new understanding of the role of the researcher, which acted as a catalyst for a series of other changes within the research process, and these discussions continue to challenge current researchers to approach their work with new cautions and considerations.

An evolution of titles on the Sage Publications method book list reflects the increasing presence of the researcher as part of the research project. The "researcher" was first introduced into the equation by Peter Adler in 1987. Since then, Sage has published several books on various aspects of the role of the researcher. These roles include, for example, participant observation (Jorgensen, 1989), investigating subjectivity (Ellis & Flaherty, 1992), insider/outsider team research (Bartunek & Louis, 1996), reflexivity and voice (Hertz, 1997), ethnographic self, fieldwork, and the representation of identity (Coffey, 1999), and reflexive methodology (Alvesson & Skoldberg, 2000).

We consider five implications that flow from introducing the researcher as a variable in the research process and that create new methodological possibilities as well as dilemmas. These are:

- By making the researcher present as part of the research process, his or her relationship to the research "subjects" must be explained.
- This new relationship between researcher and "subject" changes the nature of what constitutes data collection and analysis.
- The new focus on interpersonal relationships results in new concerns about authenticity, voice, and representation.
- The new relationships give rise to different ethical sensibilities and responsibilities.
- The introduction of the researcher as a variable in the process increases attention paid to reflexivity and allows the researcher to become a central focus of the process.

In the following section, each of these implications will be briefly considered.

First, when the researcher is present in the process, his or her relationship to the research "subjects" must be explained. Fontana (2001) noted this shift: "[traditionally], interactionists have attempted to remain as neutral and invisible as possible in order not to influence the study. Postmodern-informed interactionists make their presence felt in an attempt to establish a one-to-one partnership with respondents" (p. 15349). These interactions between researcher and researched have led to new language that recognizes the altered conceptualization. For example, the "people we used to call informants are becoming collaborators, and new priorities for field projects follow" (Nader, 2002, p. 447). Partnerships with respondents create an entirely new set of responsibilities toward participants and communities. For example, Maurer (2005) called us to account for "the enmeshment of the observer and the observed, together with their mutually reinforcing, yet oftentimes incongruent, knowledge formation" (p. 4).

Second, by reconceptualizing the role and influence of the researcher as something other than an objective arm's-length recorder or discoverer of the truth, such as a participant observer, researchers had to acknowledge how they entered and interacted with their research communities. In doing so, questions arose about how the researcher's presence does and should influence the subject matter under investigation. These issues extend beyond statistical problems associated with the Hawthorne effect and point to stronger ethical and foundational stances. For example, the use of critical theory methodologies such as PAR necessarily engages the researcher as part of community change efforts. Staggenborg (1998) discusses Verta Taylor's study on postpartum depression (PPD), she shared her own experiences with her research participants as part of the study and became an activist in the PPD support movement. In doing so, she "sought to break down the boundaries between the researcher and the researched. She shows how collaboration with activists can result in research that challenges previously held views, including both social scientific and feminist ideas" (Staggenborg, 1998, pp. 353–354).

New research relationships also influence the very notion of data and the findings that emerge from it and have given rise to related issues involving ethical responsibility to the participants, as well as the idea of interpretative control. Researchers must now consider the power dynamics between themselves and those researched (Herising, 2005). This consideration and reflexivity leads to a process in which the data collected may be the result of negotiation, but its interpretation is also a joint affair. "Researchers are no longer aloof observers collecting data"; rather, "data stems from a negotiated process between researcher and respondent" (Fontana, 2001, p. 15349). As Johannes Fabian argues, "The changed relationship between those who study and those being studied has forced anthropologists to consider the conditions under which their knowledge has been acquired. Evaluating the position of the observer and the observed includes consideration of the different views of those who study and those being studied" (as cited in Nader, 2002, p. 442).

Third, this new focus on interpersonal relationships and reliance on personal experiences and subjectivities has led to debates about authenticity and evidence. For example, the "narrative turn" in sociology, as well as many other disciplines, has challenged the notion that personal narratives can be read transparently as "authentic" experiences or voices. *Qualitative Sociologist* editor Jennifer L. Pierce (2003) pointed out that "feminist scholar Joan Scott's well-received caveat against the 'evidence of experience' points importantly to the ways that all narratives, even those claiming personal experience, are socially and historically constructed" (p. 308). In the wake of September 11, Mascia-Lees and Lees (2002) called for papers dealing with issues of terrorism and Islam, specifically considering ethical issues and implications for fieldwork. In particular, Mascia-Lees and Lees wanted to explore issues regarding the ethical presentation of images and media coverage of these sensitive topics.

Fourth, although ethical responsibility owed to research participants is not only the purview of qualitative researchers, new and arguably thornier dilemmas arise when the researcher acknowledges interpersonal relationships and responsibilities to individuals who participate in their studies, as many feminist researchers have done. One question that continues to trouble feminist scholars has been posited by Stacey (1988), who asks, "Can there be a feminist ethnography?" To which many researchers have replied "no." A central concern of this particular question has to do with the unequal power dynamics evident and inevitable in the research process.

Finally, the introduction of researcher as variable allows for inclusion of the personal in the research process, including discussions of reflexivity and a new emphasis on research strategies that employ the self as part of the project, such as autoethnography, autobiographical work, and narrative approaches. As Ellis and Bochner (1996) argue, autoethnography "took its place among genres for representing lived experience" (as cited in Lincoln & Denzin, 2003, p. 3) and has given rise to entirely new methodological approaches to ethnographic methods. Lived experiences are no longer limited to those "others" being studied but can now include the experiences of the researcher him- or herself.

Troubling the Role of Theory

The role of theory and its proper place in the research process have also been challenged. At least three basic questions have been raised. First is whether theory and method are distinct subfields or whether they belong wedded within a scientific process. To some extent this conversation relates to the idea that methodology always embodies some theoretical perspective relating to the researcher's epistemological positioning. However, questions about theory also relate to the scientific product. So a second debate exists over whether the goal of the research endeavor is to create comprehensive and sweeping explanations (as in grand theory) or whether theory should be local and contextualized. The third question is whether research projects should be theory driven or data driven. In the former the goal may be to test existing theory, whereas in the latter it may be to generate theory from empirical observations. In short, each of these ideas allocates different roles for theory relative to the research process.

During periods of quantification in the social sciences, while researchers engaged in a quest for better measures in order to enhance the rigor of their studies, philosophers and writers of science argued that theory provided the glue that held the research endeavor together. They argued that "only through theory had the measures attained scientific meaning" (Porter, 2001, p. 12638). Indeed, whereas some pursued abstract empiricism, others argued that grand theories were necessary to make sense of empirical findings generated through quantitative projects. In this context, theory took on an important role in guiding and interpreting the largely separate activity of conducting research.

These debates on the role of theory are not limited to quantitative researchers. For example, new technology has spawned the growing field of visual sociology that permits new methods for capturing, recording, and presenting data; however, this field of investigation also provides a clear example of the tensions between theory and abstract empiricism. Gold (1997) reflected that "despite the clear value of bringing [visual sociology and theory] together, visual sociology is troubled by a split between practitioners who are most interested in only one half of this equation: either making visual records of social life, on the one hand; or developing theoretical models for interpreting images, on the other . . ." (p. 4). Perhaps it is not surprising that visual sociology should be marked by a dichotomy so pivotal in the broader discipline and in the social sciences in general.

In their seminal and pioneering work on grounded theory, Glaser and Strauss bridged many of these tensions by creating a place for empirically based, naturally observed, rigorously measured "grounded theory." Charmaz (2001) reports:

> Glaser and Strauss developed grounded theory methods at a time when quantification had gained hegemony throughout the social sciences. Theory and research had become separate pursuits. The quest for quantified research findings resulted in the waning of qualitative studies. Except for an occasional classic study, most quantitative methodologists ignored qualitative research and related it to disciplinary sidelines, or treated it only as a precursor to rigorous quantitative research. Qualitative research was deemed impressionistic and anecdotal, unfitting the scientific quest for quantified facts. In contrast, Glaser and Strauss (1967) argued that qualitative research could stand as science in its

> own right, demonstrate rigor, and generate theory. (p. 6397)

As Charmaz noted, grounded theory was the unique progeny of the two intellectual traditions of its founders: "Strauss brought Chicago School pragmatism, symbolic interactionism, and field research to grounded theory" and "Glaser's training in survey research at Columbia University lent grounded theory its systematic approach, positivists' proclivities, and procedural language" (Charmaz, 2001, p. 6396). The net result was a new and rigorous approach to generating theory from empirically sound qualitative observations. As a consequence, theory occupied another location in the research process not as its starting point or as an interpretative framework but rather as the final product of the scientific endeavor.

By the 1980s the role of theory in sociology was undergoing a serious critique "as a modernist product" (Preda, 2001, p. 11866). Among other things, this critique resulted in "questions about the validity claims of scientific theories, the nature of scientific truth, and the status of the knowing subject" (Preda, 2001, p. 11866). Preda (2001) argued that this critique led to several conclusions about theory and knowledge:

> a) all knowledge is contextual and local; b) the validity claims of any scientific theory are not to be found in some abstract, universal criteria, but are rather the results of either negotiated consensus or power struggles; and c) as a consequence, the knowing subject does not dispose of universal criteria to ascertain the validity and truth of his or her knowledge. (p. 11866)

Under these conditions, theory and its role needed to be reevaluated, and the ensuing reformulation carried with it important implications. Preda (2001) concluded "[since] knowledge has a contextual and local character, it follows that scientific theories are reinterpreted according to local conditions; they are open-ended and cannot be controlled by their authors" (p. 11866).

Mellenbergh and colleagues (2003) noted that when facing conceptual issues involving research methodology, "one frequent choice confronted by researchers is that between *theory-driven* and *data-driven* approaches" (p. 213). Note how serious a conflict this is for the beginning researcher. Do you start with a theoretical framework in mind, which guides you through the process, or do you start by collecting information, such as through extensive observation (as in ethnography), and then begin to make sense of what you have observed? Do you use theory to explain and contextualize your findings? Some argue that a theory-free position is impossible because theory is embedded within, and wedded to, methodological choices. Others argue that even given an epistemologically inspired theoretical position, theory can also be used at different locations within the research process itself. When you free up the role of "theory," you create the opportunity to use theory for guidance, to trouble it, to test it, or to produce it (as in grounded theory). You can start with it (as in deductive projects or many of those beginning from positivistic orientations), or you can end with it (as in inductive projects or many of those beginning from constructionist orientations). Focusing on the contested history of methods untethers the role of theory within the research process and creates the opportunity for designers of emergent methods to consider how and where to utilize it in their own work.

The Object of Investigation and Evidence Supporting It

As times change, so does our understanding of what constitutes an appropriate object of study. In this section, we discuss three interrelated topics. First, we examine shifting ideas about what constitutes a proper object or subject matter for investigation. Second, as ideas about the object of investigation shift, we look at changes in ideas of what constitutes the empirical evidence (data) available to investigate that subject. Finally, as the notion of evidence changes, coupled with technological advances, we note evolutions in how evidence is captured or collected.

The researcher's object of study has changed over the years in a number of ways. As noted earlier, in anthropology and sociology, this shift was multifaceted and included concern with political and economic power; new fields or professional areas of investigation such as "science, medicine, law, media, and the environment" (Maurer, 2005, p. 2); new concern for everyday customs and practices, as well as lived experiences; and issues of gender and sexuality.

In the 1960s and 1970s, as anthropologists and sociologists turned to urban studies and studies of everyday life, there was a new emphasis on taking note of the "habits, rituals, routines, and traditions of daily life that 'culture' was embedded, as invisible to the actors as 'water to the fish,' to quote a popular metaphor from the 1970s" (Löfgren, 2001, pp. 4969–4970). Alternatively, Rosenau (2001) argued that "[postmodern] methodology focuses on the margins and postmodern social scientists highlight the unique and the unusual. They concentrate on the enigmatic and appreciate the unrepeatable. They seek to multiply paradox, to invent ever more elaborate repertoires of questions as much as to determine answers" (pp. 11868–11869). Whether the researcher focuses on everyday, commonplace practices or is concentrating on the unique and unusual, there is general consensus that studying a world that is in flux necessarily requires the researcher to remain flexible in the methods used for investigating their phenomena.

In reflecting upon her 4-year tenure as editor of *American Anthropologist*, Janet Keller (1994) took note of the opportunity to open a new dialogue among anthropologists:

> A dialogue in which the issues of gender and race; societal diversity; corporate practices; ethnicity, nation building, power, and authority; resource management and adaptation; human history and human evolution; reproduction and development; genetics; public and private symbol systems; and language-based interactions are centrally intertwined within both local and global frameworks. (p. 261)

In 2002 Laura Nader, guest editor for *American Anthropologist*, argued that the ethnography currently being written could not have been written during the first half of the previous century "because we had not yet developed sophisticated methodologies or theoretical perspectives that include studying political and economic power" (p. 445). Being free to study such things first required anthropologists to "liberate ourselves from limiting ideas about what constitutes ethnography in order to be freer to experiment with new subjects and representations" (Nader, 2002, p. 445). The net result was that anthropologists began to realize that "who we are, what we study, and with what consequence" had profoundly altered the discipline (Nader, 2002, p. 442).

Indeed, ethnography—in the hands of anthropologists, sociologists, and others—has taken on many new areas of investigation. Today, method textbooks offer guidance for ethnographers of different methodological, theoretical, and topical persuasions in diverse areas such as critical ethnography, feminist ethnography, applied ethnography, comparative ethnography, autoethnography, and urban ethnography.

Similarly, postmodern approaches in sociology and other disciplines, coupled with feminist and other critical theories, have led to a diversification of perspectives that emphasized areas of interest such as power and gender. For example, Preda (2001) noted, "postmodern diversification brings forth a fragmentation and multiplicity of gender and sexual identities. The distinction between genders becomes blurred; some forms of sexual identity formerly considered marginal gain a new significance and new sexual identities emerge" (p. 11867). In addition, and perhaps oddly, given the general mission of sociology to understand the world broadly, sociologists turned to personal narratives as a new method of investigation. In doing so they provided "unique insights into the connections between individual life trajectories and broader social structures" (Pierce, 2003, p. 308). More important, perhaps, personal narratives "offer a methodologically privileged location from which to comprehend human agency and subjectivity" and therefore better understand agency "simultaneously as inherent in individuals and as socially constructed" (Pierce, 2003, p. 308).

As the object of investigation changes, so too does the type of evidence (or data) necessary to support it. Narratives, for example, became a useful form of evidence in the study of human agency, as just noted. In addition, postmodern researchers, who value personal wisdom and lived experiences, were "counseled to look to music, art, poetry, and literature instead of census data and public opinion polls" (Rosenau, 2001, p. 11869). Historians turned to "previously untouched serial records, such as police files, employment registers, or draft books in order to infer from the behavior of ordinary people what they might have felt or thought" (Jarausch & Coclanis, 2001, p. 12635). Researchers focusing on "unobtrusive measures" have "showed how physical traces (erosion and accretion); the content of running records (sales records, credit card purchases), and contrived observations (e.g., hidden cameras) can be used as sources of data in research" (Cordray, 2001, p. 13778).

Quantitative researchers and those using statistical analysis for their studies necessarily concentrated on increased accuracy in measurement and new forms of evidence that would justify and support the increasingly sophisticated statistical tests and modeling being employed. As Fienberg and Kadane (2001) explain, "It is widely recognized that any statistical analysis can only be as good as the underlying data. Consequently, statisticians take great care in the design of methods for data collection and in their actual implementation. Some of the most important modes of statistical data collection include censuses, experiments, observational studies, and some surveys" (p. 15087). Furthermore, advances in technology made previously unavailable or difficult-to-obtain datasets more readily accessible. Jarausch and Coclanis (2001) claim, "the increasing availability of new and/or enhanced sources and datasets" presented "unprecedented research opportunities" (p. 12637).

Advances in technology resulted in a new emphasis being placed on certain kinds of empirical evidence. However, technological developments have also dramatically altered the way researchers can capture or record evidence. Commonplace technology such as audio and video recording, which we now take for granted, altered the possibilities in profound and fundamental ways when first introduced. Many of these technological advances were met initially with skepticism, suspicion, and amusement. However, adventurous and creative pioneering researchers saw the possibilities and sought to capitalize on them.

One example of this transition and the ensuing implications brought on by developing technology can be illustrated through the use of the camera. Consider, for example, anthropologist Margaret Mead, who lugged a tripod and camera with her to the field and began capturing "data" through photographs and film, much to the amusement of her anthropologist husband, Gregory Bateson. Most famously, Mead and Bateson made the 1952 documentary *Trance and Dance in Bali*, in which they carefully documented ritual dance activity of the Balinese. Long after Mead's initial analysis, her photographs and film footage are considered to be extremely important artifacts. But at the time, Mead and Bateson together engaged in methods debate over the usefulness (or not) of this practice (Mead & Bateson, 1977).

The initial struggle over this method of collecting data, coupled with technological advances, ultimately has given rise to an entire field of visual anthropology, which recognizes the usefulness of photographs and images as an *object* of study. So the photograph is no longer merely a method of data collection but rather serves as the central focus of study. In the 1970s Howard Becker published his "widely influential" "On Photography and Sociology," in which he inspired sociologists "to explore the visual dimensions of social life," giving rise to "the International Visual Sociological Association (IVSA), the inclusion of visual sociology sessions at ASA meetings, and the publication of a number of visually oriented books and articles in the sociological literature" (Gold, 1977, p. 3).

The advent of disposable cameras has led to emergent methods such as photovoice. This innovative methodology involves arming community members with cameras to document local social issues and problems in order to work toward community awareness and policy change (Wang & Pies, 2004; Wang, Morrel-Samuels, Hutchison, Bell, & Pestronk, 2004). Photographs serve not only as a method of gathering evidence but also as a way to engage community members, generate conversations, and provide a stimulus for change. Photovoice emerged because of technological advances in camera apparatus and also because of the willingness of critical theorists and methodologists to experiment with, and argue about, the usefulness of photographs and photography as part of the research process. These technological advances had far-reaching implications; they worked to change our conceptions of appropriate objects of study, they inspired new methods of data collection and preservation, and they also held important implications for data analysis and reporting.

Troubling Sampling and Its Purposes

Study sampling strategies are directly linked to the purpose and goals of the research project. Nonetheless, it is the rare postmodern researcher who has not been confronted with doubts about sample size and questions such as "are you sure you have enough?" At the heart of these questions are usually profoundly different understandings of the purpose of study. The "how many" and "how representative" are critical questions for population-based studies that use statistical analysis of large datasets in which the numbers are directly related to the mathematical assumptions undergirding the analysis.

The purpose of these studies is usually to uncover generalizable characteristics within a sample group in order to draw conclusions about a larger population. However, for postmodern researchers, particularly those focusing on subjectivities or on generating mini-narratives, the concern with how many may not be warranted. Such scholars would argue that the rich, local, and contextual nature of their work is not meant to be generalizable, though it can still contribute to knowledge about larger social institutions and processes. As noted by Rosenau (2001), "there are serious philosophical differences between postmodernism and the enlightenment norms of traditional science. Some postmodernists are uninterested in generalization, definitive explanations, replication, validity, reliability, etc. Neither prediction nor theory building are major concerns. They look to deconstruction as method" (p. 11868). Currently some researchers have addressed these methodological concerns by using mixed methods, which combine qualitative and quantitative methods in order to gain a more comprehensive understanding, both deep and broad, of the complex phenomenon under investigation. In short, the history of methodological debates over objects, purposes, and goals of studies have also ended up troubling procedures for selecting study sites and study samples.

For example, with the emergence of grounded theory in the late 1960s, researchers interested in theory building as part of an iterative process (moving back and forth between empirical evidence gathering and analysis) necessarily employed theoretical sampling strategies stemming from their unfolding findings. Similarly, analytic induction (AI) was "originally understood as an alternative to statistical sampling methodology," in the 1950s "took the form of tracing how negative cases led, step-by-step to the final state of the theory," and was largely touted as a useful method for revealing causal connections (Katz, 2001, p. 480). More recently, in the 1980s AI has become a standard method for "analyzing qualitative data in ethnographic research" (Katz, 2001, pp. 480–481).

Perhaps one of the best places to look for some of the tensions and debates over sampling strategies and study goals can be seen in the history and evolution of the case study. A case study, by definition, focuses on single units. Case studies, prior to the 1970s, "consisted primarily of historical studies of particular events, countries, or phenomena, with little effort to cumulate results or progressively develop theories" (Verba, 1967). However, during the 1970s, case study methodologists, "dissatisfied with the state of case study methods, and encouraged by the example of the formalization of statistical methods, began to formalize case study methods" (Bennett, 2001, p. 1514). Some scholars concentrated on case comparisons that utilized the logic of most and least similar cases in which "the researcher compares two cases that are similar in all but one independent variable and that differ in the outcome variable" (Bennett, 2001, p. 1514). Others distinguished "among various types of case study research designs and theory-building goals" and utilized ideas about similar types of cases and deviant cases to generate understandings of the phenomena under investigation (Bennett, 2001, p. 1514). In contrasting the work of Eckstein and Lijphart, Bennett (2001) notes:

> Their treatments differed, however, in that Lijphart relied greatly on statistical concepts and language. He was thus skeptical of the value of single case studies for building social science theories, and consistent with the widespread preference at the time for "large N" over "small n" methods, he urged researchers to consider several means of either decreasing the number of variables in their models or increasing the number of cases to be studied in order to make use of statistical rather than case study methods. (pp. 1514–1515)

In contrast, Eckstein "focused on the use of case studies for theory testing and argued that even single case studies could provide tests that might strongly support or impugn theories" (Bennett, 2001, p. 1515).

Later case study researchers focused on both within-case and cross-case comparisons. Bennett (2001) notes that within-case study researchers utilized methods "of 'congruence testing' and 'process tracing' as a means of checking on whether inferences arrived at through case comparisons were spurious" (p. 1515). More recently, he notes that case study methods have focused on "typological theory" that occupies "a middle ground between covering laws, or highly general abstract propositions, and causal mechanisms" (p. 1516). Bennett argues that we are currently in an era in which the "increasingly evident complementarity of case study and statistical methods is likely to lead toward more collaborative work by scholars using various methods" (p. 1518). In short, we are back to the point of mixing methods.

Note that these various uses and goals of case study methodology require the researcher to use different sampling strategies in order to control or develop an understanding of the phenomena under investigation. By clearly defining the researcher's goals, such as theory testing or revealing causal mechanisms, the sampling strategy necessarily follows. However, as there have been evolutions in the object of study and the goals of inquiry, there have necessarily been adjustments in how to approach the sampling stage of the research project.

Troubling Data Analysis: Discovering Truth or Constructing Answers?

Epistemological assumptions, embedded in the research process from the moment a research question is formulated, necessarily also dictate how data analysis will be approached. The researcher may be seeking to reveal or discover truths or may be making meaning of qualitative data. Findings may be described as "grounded" in the data or empirical evidence or they may be "mediated" or "negotiated" or "co-constructed" with study participants. Nonetheless, all of these endeavors fall under the general rubric of "data analysis."

For statisticians and quantifiers, the goals and processes of data analysis are undeniably linked to technological innovations in computers and statistical software. For example, in the 1920s and 1930s, during Pearson and Fisher's days:

> Pearson's laboratory employed dozens of women who used mechanical devices to carry out the careful and painstaking calculations required to tabulate values from various probability distributions. This effort ultimately led to the creation of the *Biometrika Tables for Statisticians* that were so widely used by others applying tools such as chi-square tests and the like. Similarly, Fisher also developed his own set of statistical tables with Frank Yates when he worked at Rothamsted Experiment Station in the 1920s and 1930s. (Fienberg & Kadane, 2001, p. 15086)

This cumbersome process changed dramatically in the 1960s, and these changes revolutionized the availability of computation to a broader community of social scientists. The first statistical packages appeared in the 1960s–for example, BMDP for work in biological and medical research and Datatext for the social sciences, with widely used statistical programs such as SAS and SPSS not long behind, as well as programs such as MINITAB for aid in teaching statistics.

However, it was not until some 30 years ago that sociologists began to make wide strides in disseminating technological information. Scientific journals such as *Sociological Methodology* began offering software packages "made available free of charge via the journal," with the editor stating his desire to "help readers to use the methods described in *Sociological Methodology 1996*"; he continues, "I have encouraged authors to make software available free of charge, preferably via StatLib, the electronic archive of statistical software at Carnegie-Mellon University" (Rafferty, 1996, p. xvi). Today, the inclusion of software with social science research methods textbooks for undergraduate and graduate students is common and helps to widely proliferate the use of specific software and statistical procedures.

Of course, the ease with which statistical data analysis can now be conducted is not without its worrying aspects. Some of these may sound dated, such as those expressed in 1969 by Borgatta, who warned:

> The main impact of the computer for social scientists has been in producing an instrument that can carry out data reduction and data analysis effectively. Enormous principal component factor analyses, for example, can be carried out in minutes, while two decades ago computation of such an analysis with twenty variables was virtually impossible. Beyond this, the computer has been a toy for a limited number of persons, and the achievements due to virtuosity of machine knowledge by social scientists have been meager. . . . It has become apparent that additional increments in computer capability have little demonstrable utility for social scientists. Indeed, it is doubtful that any of the machine advances that have occurred since 1960 have been of material relevance for social scientists, outside of data analysis.
>
> That large computers can be used has been demonstrated; the next question is, can they be used in a way that advances the science? The limitations here again are becoming apparent. In the absence of data drawn from well-conceived research, the giant computers are nothing more than playthings. (p. xiii)

A decade later a new editor, Karl F. Schuessler (1979), noted:

> While agreeing that an electronic revolution is taking place in their field (and of course in society generally), sociologists would probably disagree about its costs and benefits. Some fear

> that the computer has promoted the senseless application of complicated techniques to data of quite dubious worth. However, in these cases the fault lies not with the machine but with the user; the computer should not be blamed if it is misused.

These words of warning, although dated, reflect suspicion about new technologies and their impact on social science. Computer technology becomes a double-edged sword for analysts and researchers. New software offers power and ease of running statistical analysis, but the possibility on the other hand of doing sloppy analysis without a strong theoretical base has been seen as a dangerous path for social scientists.

Qualitative researchers have also explored new and innovative "data analysis" techniques, sometimes utilizing computer-assisted software and other times not. Much like the advent and advancement of statistical analysis software in quantitative research, so, too, have many new software packages been introduced in recent years to facilitate qualitative data analysis. The earliest of these were NUD*ist and Qualrus in 1981, followed by Ethnograph, HyperResearch, Atlas.ti and Nvivo, among others, in the 1980s and 1990s.

Developing and utilizing qualitative software can be particularly challenging, because postmodern views are often "introspective, intersubjective, and anti-objectivist, a form of individualized understanding" and therefore require an approach to analysis that honors these features (Rosenau, 2001, p. 11870). Researchers are more likely to describe their activities as making sense of the data through interpretive, constructive, or negotiated processes than as "discovering" things.

One vein of concern that runs through discussions on data analysis is that of rigor. How can researchers ensure that their work advances goals in scientifically strong work? The different approaches to data analysis shown previously note how inappropriate it would be to try to apply standards of rigor from one discourse to that of another. In 1976, for example, the editors of *Sociological Methodology* took particular note of the importance of understanding these distinctions while not permitting them to stand as barriers to cross-methodological discourse. Heise (1976) wrote:

> The traditional distinction between quantitative and qualitative research is, I hope, breaking down in the mid-1970s. Qualitative researchers have registered their argument that even structural-equation models rest implicitly on subjective decisions made by the scientist as a social actor and culturally bounded observer. On the other side, there is increasing recognition that qualitative does not necessarily mean nonquantifiable or without rigor. In a recent burst of methodological activity, logically and mathematically rigorous techniques of analysis have been extended to phenomena far beyond the usual domain of the general linear model. There is a new concern with describing and interpreting configurations and with analyzing data close to the content of ordinary social phenomena involving classifications and enumerations. In fact, every chapter in *Sociological Methodology 1976* reflects a concern with moving beyond the confines of the general linear model in order to handle more naturalistic and meaningful data and to address more directly the questions posed by complex sociocultural systems. (p. x)

Troubling Write-Ups of Scientific Reports

Given that the authority and role of the researcher has been challenged since the late 1970s, it has had major implications not only for the ways researchers relate to and interact with research participants but also for the way reports are "written up." Whereas researchers using more quantitative or positivistic methods tend to follow a fairly traditional structure in presenting their studies for publication—such as starting with a background and literature section, followed by theory, methodology, findings, discussion, and implications—postmodern and qualitative researchers have experimented with entirely different formats and grappled with different concerns. For example, although the Sage book list offers a variety of methods books on "writing up" qualitative research projects, there is no analogous genre of books to be found among the quantitative and statistical material.

To give a disciplinary example, Denzin and Lincoln (2000) have referred to dilemmas facing anthropologists in writing up ethnographic accounts as a "crisis in representation" (pp. 18–19). Some argue that an ethnographic account is little more than "stories (even 'fictions') and narratives rather than authoritative representations of reality" (Conrad, 2001, p. 6611). In part, this occurs because postmodernists value everyday experiences and "gravitate toward mininarratives" and partly because they tend to focus on "validity of multiple perspectives rather than privileging the authors' authority and singular truth" (Rosenau, 2001, p. 11869). Self-reflexivity has added a new dimension to writing up postmodern research reports. Reflecting on the process, the experience of the researcher, and the researcher's influence on the material adds new texture to written reports.

Lincoln and Denzin (2003) have argued that there is a "growing movement to reconnect art and science, literary forms" with "scientific information and social life" through the use of storied, performative, and narrative presentations (p. 4). So this crisis in representation has, in many ways, resulted in a return to the humanities and the arts in order to inform the social sciences. Lincoln and Denzin write:

> Even as the crisis of representation grows, the proposals for presentation expand accordingly. In part, the presentational revolution has emerged from critiques that bedevil the old dissociation of science from literature, of inquiry from spirituality, and of body from mind and many of the other bicameral dualisms that have plagued the Western mind, from St. Augustine to the present. The reemphasis on the human experience as an oral experience has led to experimentation in textual representation forms borrowed straight from literature and storied forms and from performance (p. 7).

Indeed, Norman Denzin has recently turned to "performance ethnography" as a new methodological approach that has implications not only for methods of conducting research but also for disseminating information (Denzin, 2003). In light of this new way of thinking, those once-brighter distinctions between art, literature, performance, humanities, and the social sciences are very blurred at the moment.

Conclusion

It is our hope that by going through this process of examining some recent debates in the history of methods and by organizing that discussion around the research process (rather than constructing history as a time line or a sequence of events) that we have led you to the precipice of the "emergent methods" further discussed in the following pages of this book. The scholars who write the subsequent chapters have found creative and pioneering ways to capitalize on the chaos currently confronting them. They are drawing from the old and lost methodological approaches, pulling together new threads, and embracing new technologies, thereby offering new and creative approaches to using methods and methodologies. In doing so, they introduce coherency to the process of inquiry in innovative and exciting ways.

As noted by Hesse-Biber and Leavy (2006), "[many] researchers were trained in the use of one primary method. Using an innovative method may require them to reach out across their own 'methods of comfort zone,' to think outside their normal everyday methods routine" (p. 378). Stepping outside of one's comfort zone is one aspect of the risk taking involved in pushing the envelope of methodological possibilities. Fontana (2001) has argued that "in trying to maintain the integrity of the phenomenon under investigation we should not fit the 'real world' to our method, as typical in survey research, but should adapt our methodology in the world and thus use flexible data collection strategies" and that our models of study "should be everchanging to fit the changes and events in the real world" (p. 15347). Emergent methods cry out for this kind of flexibility and environmental sensitivity. "There is," as Rosenau (2001) writes, "no easy methodological recipe for doing this type of [postmodern] research" (p. 11869).

For doctoral students or other beginning researchers, the choices may seem overwhelming. For example, our recent search of "social science method" books on Amazon.com resulted in 14,478 hits. Where does one start? The chapters that follow are meant as guidance, but we also hope that we have modeled some approaches for you. When faced with a question (in our case, to write a history of methods), ask yourself: How can I go about answering it? What should be the object of study? Where can I look for the sources of information, data, or evidence I need? How can I employ current technology? What do the various disciplines have to offer? How should the findings be presented and represented? Of course, you should look for guidance from those who have tackled similar projects in the past, but do not be afraid to ask how you can place yourself on the frontier, the cutting edge, of emergent methods as well. In our discussion, we explained that these steps are not in fact historically or currently determined. The research process has been "troubled"; it has been dearranged and rearranged by researchers and analysts throughout time. For example, new epistemological and methodological conversations and technological advances have led to new methods. However, this has not been unidirectional. Alternatively, new methods have given birth to new methodologies and fields of study. Take, for example, the introduction of the video recorder, which resulted in experimentation in methods of data collection but then gave rise to new critical theory methodological approaches such as photovoice and entirely new fields of study such as visual anthropology.

In this new digital age, with the World Wide Web, instant Internet access, and melding technologies, the choices available to us as researchers to capitalize on these new technologies are limited only by our own imaginative processes. For example, take the shift in the past several decades from the idea that a telephone is a stationary object used to place and receive calls to the current cell phone–a mobile unit that can serve as camera, video recorder and player, e-mail unit, text messager, radio, MP3 player, Web browser, calendar organizer, and global mapping device, as well as a phone. How can a cell phone be used as a tool to record, analyze, or transmit data or to serve as the object of investigation itself? A "phone" suddenly offers possibilities that would have been inconceivable 20 years ago.

The choices we make will give birth not only to innovative methods but also to entirely new ways of understanding our world. Although it may seem like an overwhelming number of options, the current fermenting of methods offers limitless possibilities for the creative researcher. This new frontier and the pioneers who explore it will profoundly and fundamentally change the shape and content of social science knowledge.

Notes

1. See Crotty (1998) for a fuller discussion of the link between epistemological and theoretical positions.

2. See, for example, Lacan (1977), in a speech originally delivered in Zurich in 1949, and Said (1978) for further discussion of the "Other."

3. Ontology refers to "a theory about what the world is like–what the world consists of and why" (Strega, 2005, p. 201).

4. Epistemology refers to "a philosophy of what counts as knowledge and 'truth' " (Strega, 2005, p. 201).

References

Abbott, A. D. (2004). *Methods of discovery: Heuristics for the social sciences*. New York: Norton.

Alvesson, M., & Skoldberg, K. (2000). *Reflexive methodology: New vistas for qualitative researchers*. Thousand Oaks, CA: Sage.

Bartunek, J., & Louis, M. R. (1996). *Insider/outsider team research*. Thousand Oaks, CA: Sage.

Bennett, A. (2001). Case study: Methods and analysis. In N. J. Smelser & P. B. Baltes (Eds.), *International encyclopedia of the social and behavioral sciences* (pp. 1513–1519). Amsterdam: Elsevier.

Borgatta, E. F. (Ed.). (1969). *Sociological methodology* (Vol. 1). San Francisco: Jossey-Bass.

Brown, L. (2005). The view from the poststructural margins: Epistemology and methodology reconsidered. In L. Brown & S. Strega (Eds.), *Research as resistance: Critical, indigenous, and anti-oppressive approaches* (pp. 199–235). Toronto, Ontario: Canadian Scholar's Press.

Brown, L., & Strega, S. (Eds.). (2005). *Research as resistance: Critical, indigenous, and anti-oppressive approaches*. Toronto, Ontario: Canadian Scholar's Press.

Calhoun, C., & Duster, T. (2005). The visions and divisions of sociology. *Chronicle Review, 51*(49), B7.

Charmaz, K. (2001). Grounded theory: Methodology and theory construction. In N. J. Smelser & P. B. Baltes (Eds.), *International encyclopedia of the social and behavioral sciences* (pp. 6396–6399). Amsterdam: Elsevier.

Coffey, A. (1999). *The ethnographic self: Fieldwork and the representation of identity*. Thousand Oaks, CA: Sage.

Conrad, P. (2001). Qualitative health research. In N. J. Smelser & P. B. Baltes (Eds.), *International encyclopedia of the social and behavioral sciences* (pp. 6608–6612). Amsterdam: Elsevier.

Cordray, D. S. (2001). Secondary analysis: Methodology. In N. J. Smelser & P. B. Baltes (Eds.), *International encyclopedia of the social and behavioral sciences* (pp. 13777–13780). Amsterdam: Elsevier.

Crotty, M. (1998). *Foundations of social research: Meaning and perspective in the research process*. Thousand Oaks, CA: Sage.

Denzin, N. K. (2003). *Performance ethnography: Critical pedagogy and the politics of culture*. Thousand Oaks, CA: Sage.

Denzin, N. K., & Lincoln, Y. S. (Eds.). (2000). *Handbook of qualitative research* (2nd ed.). Thousand Oaks, CA: Sage.

Ellis, C. S., & Flaherty, M. G. (1992). *Investigating subjectivity: Research on lived experience*. Thousand Oaks, CA: Sage.

Fienberg, S. E., & Kadane, J. B. (2001). Statistics: The field. In N. J. Smelser & P. B. Baltes (Eds.), *International encyclopedia of the social and behavioral sciences* (pp. 15085–15090). Amsterdam: Elsevier.

Fontana, A. (2001). Symbolic interaction: Methodology. In N. J. Smelser & P. B. Baltes (Eds.), *International encyclopedia of the social and behavioral sciences* (pp. 15347–15350). Amsterdam: Elsevier.

Gold, S. (1997). Introduction. *Qualitative Sociology, 20*(1), 3–6.

Goldschmidt, W. G. (1959). From the editor's desk. *American Anthropologist, 61*(1), vii–x.

Hall, J. R. (2001). History of qualitative methods. In N. J. Smelser & P. B. Baltes (Eds.), *International encyclopedia of the social and behavioral sciences* (pp. 12613–12617). Amsterdam: Elsevier.

Harding, S. (1987). *Feminism and methodology: Social science issues*. Milton Keynes, UK: Open University Press.

Heise, D. R. (1976). Prologue. *Sociological Methodology, 7*, ix–xii.

Herising, F. (2005). Interrupting positions: Critical thresholds and queer pro/positions. In L. Brown & S. Strega (Eds.), *Research as resistance: Critical, indigenous, and anti-oppressive approaches* (pp. 127–152). Toronto, Ontario: Canadian Scholar's Press.

Hertz, R. (1991). *Reflexivity and voice*. Thousand Oaks, CA: Sage.

Hesse-Biber, S. N., & Leavy, P. (2006). *Emergent methods in social research*. Thousand Oaks, CA: Sage.

Jarausch, K. H., & Coclanis, P. A. (2001). Quantification in history. In N. J. Smelser & P. B. Baltes (Eds.), *International encyclopedia of the social and behavioral sciences* (pp. 12634–12638). Amsterdam: Elsevier.

Jorgensen, D. L. (1989). *Participant observation: A methodology for human studies*. Thousand Oaks, CA: Sage.

Katz, J. (2001). Analytic induction. In N. J. Smelser & P. B. Baltes (Eds.), *International encyclopedia of the social and behavioral sciences* (pp. 480–484). Amsterdam: Elsevier.

Keller, J. (1994). Editorial. *American Anthropologist, 96*(2), 261–262.

Lacan, J. (1977). The mirror stage as formative of the function of the I. In *Ecrits: A selection* (pp. 1–7). New York: Norton.

Lincoln, Y. S., & Denzin, N. K. (2003). *Turning points in qualitative research: Tying knots in a handkerchief.* Walnut Creek: CA: AltaMira Press.

Löfgren, O. (2001). Anthropology of everyday life. In N. J. Smelser & P. B. Baltes (Eds.), *International encyclopedia of the social and behavioral sciences* (pp. 4969–4972). Amsterdam: Elsevier.

Mascia-Lees, F., & Lees, S. H. (2002). From the editors. *American Anthropologist, 104*(3), 713–714.

Maurer, B. (2005). Introduction to ethnographic emergences. *American Anthropologist, 107*(1), 1–4.

Mead, M., & Bateson, G. (1977). On the use of the camera in anthropology. *Studies in the Anthropology of Visual Communication, 4*(2), 78–80.

Mellenbergh, G. J., Ader, H. J., Baird, D., Berger, M. P. F., Cornell, J. E., Hagenaars, J. A. P., et al. (2003). Conceptual issues of research methodology for the behavioural, life and social sciences. *Statistician, 52*(2), 211–218.

Nader, L. (2002). Missing links: A commentary on Ward H. Goodenough's moving article "Anthropology in the 20th century and beyond." *American Anthropologist, 104*(2), 441–449.

Nagel, S. (1976). *Operations research methods: As applied to political science and the legal process.* Thousand Oaks, CA: Sage.

Pierce, J. (2003, Fall). Introduction. *Qualitative Sociology, 26*(3), 307–312.

Platt, J. (1996). *A history of sociological research methods in America: 1920–1960.* Cambridge, UK: Cambridge University Press.

Porter, T. M. (2001). Quantification in the history of the social sciences. In N. J. Smelser & P. B. Baltes (Eds.), *International encyclopedia of the social and behavioral sciences* (pp. 12638–12644). Amsterdam: Elsevier.

Preda, A. (2001). Postmodernism in sociology. In N. J. Smelser & P. B. Baltes (Eds.), *International encyclopedia of the social and behavioral sciences* (pp. 11865–11868). Amsterdam: Elsevier.

Rafferty, A. E. (1996). In this volume. *Sociological Methodology, 26,* xiii–xviii.

Research methods and evaluation [Catalogue]. Retrieved June 4, 2006, from *www.sagepub.com*

Richardson, L., & Lockridge, E. (2004). *Travels with Ernest: Crossing the literary/sociological divide.* Walnut Creek, CA: AltaMira Press.

Richardson, V. (2001). Teaching: Trends in research. In N. J. Smelser & P. B. Baltes (Eds.), *International encyclopedia of the social and behavioral sciences* (pp. 15483–15487). Amsterdam: Elsevier.

Rosenau, P. V. (2001). Postmodernism: Methodology. In N. J. Smelser & P. B. Baltes (Eds.), *International encyclopedia of the social and behavioral sciences* (pp. 11868–11871). Amsterdam: Elsevier.

Said, E. (1978). *Orientalism.* New York: Pantheon Books.

Schuessler, K. F. (1979). Prologue. *Sociological Methodology, 10,* ix–xviii.

Stacey, J. (1991). Can there be a feminist ethnography? In S. Gluck & D. Patai (Eds.), *Women's words: The feminist practice of oral history* (pp. 111–119). New York: Routledge.

Staggenborg, S. (1998). Introduction. *Qualitative Sociology, 21*(4), 353–355.

Strega, S. (2005). The view from the poststructural margins: Epistemology and methodology reconsidered. In L. Brown & S. Strega (Eds.), *Research as resistance: Critical, indigenous, and anti-oppressive approaches* (pp. 199–236). Toronto, Ontario: Canadian Scholar's Press.

Ulrich's Periodical Directory. (n.d.). Retrieved May 29, 2006, from *www.ulrichsweb.com*

Verba, S. (1967). Some dilemmas in comparative research. *World Politics, 20,* 111–127.

Vidich, A. J., & Lyman, S. M. (2000). Qualitative methods: Their history in sociology and anthropology. In N. K. Denzin & Y. S. Lincoln (Eds.), *Handbook on qualitative research* (2nd ed., pp. 37–84). Thousand Oaks, CA: Sage.

Wang, C. C., Morrel-Samuels, S., Hutchison, P., Bell, L., & Pestronk, R. M. (2004). Flint photovoice: Community building among youth, adults, and policy makers. *American Journal of Public Health, 94*(6), 911–913.

Wang, C. C., & Pies, C. A. (2004). Family, maternal, and child health through photovoice. *Maternal and Child Health Journal, 8*(2), 95–102.

White, L. A. (1965). Anthropology 1964: Retrospect and prospect. *American Anthropologist, 67*(3), 629–637.

Wright, G. (2001). Economic history, qualitative: United States. In N. J. Smelser & P. B. Baltes (Eds.), *International encyclopedia of the social and behavioral sciences* (pp. 4108–4114). Amsterdam: Elsevier.

CHAPTER 2

Gender Inclusion, Contextual Values, and Strong Objectivity

Emergent Feminist Methods for Research in the Sciences

Sue V. Rosser

The second wave of the women's movement and feminism that developed as a result of social and civil rights movements in the late 1960s and early 1970s in the United States spawned the academic arm of women's studies. Scholars working in the interdisciplinary field of women's studies and feminists working in traditional disciplines evolved feminist theories that created practices such as strong objectivity, contextual values, inclusion of women, and placing women in central focus in experimental research. In this chapter I explore how the emergent perspectives of feminist theories influence emergent feminist methods in the context of experimental research.

In the natural, physical, and technological sciences, questioning of positivist approaches and the inclusion of gender or other contextual values rank as emergent methods not yet accepted or even considered by most mainstream scientists. The humanities, in which context remains fundamental for scholarly analysis, originated much of the impetus for gender analysis; the inclusion of gender fits the long tradition in the humanities of examination of context and values. Although gender is often included as a variable in social sciences research that explores other issues, such as class, race, or politics, researchers in some social science subdisciplines, such as social psychology or sociology of the family, have tended more to explore the more subtle influences of gender on research methods and results than have those researchers in other social sciences that place a heavy emphasis on quantitative methods and on objectivity.

Most researchers in the behavioral, biomedical, and physical sciences are trained in the scientific method and believe in its power. Few, however, are aware of its historical and philosophical roots in logical positivism and objectivity. Positivism implies that "all knowledge is constructed by inference from immediate sensory experiences" (Jaggar, 1983, pp. 355–356). It is premised on the assumption that human beings are highly individualistic and obtain knowledge in a rational manner that may be separated from their social conditions. This leads to the belief in the possibilities of obtaining knowledge that is both objective and value-free, the cornerstone of the scientific method.

In the past two decades, feminist historians and philosophers of science (Fee, 1982, 1983; Haraway, 1978, 1989, 1997; Harding, 1986, 1993, 1998; Longino, 1990; Tuana, 1989, 1995), anthropologists (Martin, 1987, 1994, 1999; Rapp, 1999), and feminist scientists (Birke, 1986; Bleier, 1984, 1986; Fausto-Sterling, 1992; Keller, 1983, 1985, 1992; Rosser, 1988, 1994, 1998; Spanier, 1995) have pointed out the bias and absence of value neutrality in science, particularly biology. By excluding females as experimental subjects, by focusing on problems of primary interest to males, by utilizing faulty experimental designs, and by interpreting data based in language or ideas constricted by patriarchal parameters, scientists have introduced bias or flaws into their experimental results in several areas. These flaws and biases were permitted to become part of the mainstream of scientific thought and were perpetuated in the scientific literature for decades. Because most scientists were men, values held by them as males were not distinguished as biasing; rather, they were congruent with the values of all scientists and thus became synonymous with the "objective" view of the world (Chodorow, 1978; Keller, 1982, 1985) and the aspects of it that were studied.

A first step for feminist scientists was recognizing the possibility that androcentric bias would result from having virtually all theoretical and decision-making positions in science held by men (Keller, 1983). Not until a substantial number of women had entered the profession (Rosser, 1986) could this androcentrism be exposed. As long as only a few women were scientists, they had to demonstrate or conform to the male view of the world in order to be successful and have their research meet the criteria for "objectivity."

The demonstration that contextual values, including gender, bias not only the scientific research of individuals but also what is accepted as valid science by the entire scientific community represents one of the major contributions that feminism has made to science. In her 1999 book *Has Feminism Changed Science?*, Londa Schiebinger examined how the presence of women in traditionally male disciplines has altered scientific thinking and awareness, concluding that feminist perspectives have had little effect on mathematics and the physical sciences but more impact on biology, including medicine, archaeology, reproductive and evolutionary biology, and primatology. For example, Schiebinger describes influences on primatology as follows: "Feminist interventions have remade foundational paradigms in the field. Nonhuman females are no longer seen as docile creatures who trade sex and reproduction for protection and food, but are studied for their own unique contributions to primate society" (Schiebinger, 1999, p. 3).

Although the degree and the specifics of the impact of feminism on science, medicine, and technology vary from one subdiscipline to another, as Creager, Lunbeck, and Schiebinger, coeditors of *Feminism in Twentieth Century Science, Technology, and Medicine*, state: "Feminism connects gender to other systems that structure our lives and individual identities" (2001, p. viii). In linking with other systems, gender raises the issue of how context and values challenge traditional notions of objectivity.

Origins of This Emergent Method

During the late 1960s and 1970s, movements for equal rights for women, blacks, and working-class people that were re-emerging in the United States and Western Europe spawned academic, theoretical schools that questioned the possibility of objectivity and the influence of context on knowledge acquisition. Feminists asked whether androcentrism might permeate scientific and medical research. Departing from their Marxist origins, which held science to be separate from other human knowledge production, socialists wondered about the "social shaping" (MacKenzie & Wacjman, 1999) of science and technology. African American and other ethnic critiques asked about Eurocentric approaches to science and technology. Although each of these critiques had roots in a previous critique or tradition, the overlap among them and convergence around contextual values provided new demands on traditional objectivity.

Feminism

Beginning in the 18th century, political scientists, philosophers, and feminists (Friedan, 1963; Jaggar, 1983; Mill, 1970; Wollstonecraft, 1975) described the parameters of liberal feminism. The differences between 19th-century and 20th-century liberal feminists have varied from libertarian to egalitarian, and numerous complexities exist among definitions of liberal feminists today. A general definition of liberal feminism is the belief that women are suppressed in contemporary society because they suffer unjust discrimination (Jaggar, 1983). Liberal feminists seek no special privileges for women and simply demand that everyone receive equal consideration without discrimination on the basis of sex.

Most scientists would assume that the implications of liberal feminism for biology and other disciplines within the sciences are that scientists should work to remove the documented overt and covert barriers (National Science Foundation [NSF], 2002; Rosser, 2004; Rossiter, 1982: Vetter, 1988) that have prevented women from entering and succeeding in science. Although they might hold individual opinions as to whether or not women deserve equal pay for equal work, access to research resources, and equal opportunities for advancement, most scientists do not recognize that the implications of liberal feminism extend beyond employment, access, and discrimination to the acceptance of positivism as the theory of knowledge and belief in the ability to obtain knowledge that is both objective and value-free (Jaggar, 1983).

Given the high costs of sophisticated equipment, maintenance of laboratory animals and facilities, and salaries for qualified technicians and researchers, virtually no experimental research is undertaken today without governmental or foundation support. The choice of problems for study in research is substantially determined by a national agenda that defines what is worthy of study, that is, worth funding. As Marxist (Zimmerman et al., 1980), African American (Campbell, Denes, & Morrison, 2000), and feminist (Harding, 1998) critics of scientific research have pointed out, the scientific research undertaken in the United States reflects the societal bias toward the powerful, who are overwhelmingly white, middle or upper class, and male. Members of Congress and the individuals in the theoretical and decision-making positions within the medical and scientific establishments that set priorities and allocate funds for research exemplify these descriptors. The lack of diversity among Congressional and scientific leaders may allow unintentional, undetected flaws to bias the research in terms of what we study and how we study it. Examples from research studies demonstrate that unintentional bias may be reflected in at least three stages of application of the scientific method: (1) choice and definition of problems to be studied; (2) methods and approaches used in data gathering, including whom we choose as subjects; and (3) theories and conclusions drawn from the data.

Feminist critiques revealed the impact of distinct gender bias in choice and definition of health research problems. For example, many diseases that occur in both sexes have been studied in males only and/or by a male-as-norm approach. Cardiovascular diseases serve as a case in point. Research protocols for large-scale studies (Multiple Risk Factor Intervention Trial [MRFIT] Research Group, 1990; Grobbee et al., 1990; Steering Committee of the Physicians' Health Study Group, 1989) of cardiovascular diseases failed to assess gender differences. Women were excluded from clinical trials of drugs because of fear of litigation from possible teratogenic effects on fetuses. Exclusion of women from clinical drug trials was so pervasive that a meta-analysis surveying the literature from 1960 to 1991 on clinical trials of medications used to treat acute myocardial infarction found that women were included in less than 20% while the elderly were in less than 40% of those studies (Gurwitz, Nananda, & Avorn, 1992).

The choice of development of particular technologies from basic research may also reflect male priorities. Having large numbers of male engineers and creators of technologies also often results in technologies that are useful primarily from a male perspective (i.e., these technologies fail to address important issues for women users). In addition to the military origins of the development and funding of much technology (Barnaby, 1981; Norman, 1979), which makes its civilian application less useful for women's lives (Cockburn, 1983), men designing technology for the home frequently focus on issues less important to women users. For example, Berg's (1999) analysis of "smart houses" reveals that such houses do not include new technologies; instead they focus on "integration, centralised control and regulation of all functions in the home" (p. 306). "Housework is no part of what this house will 'do' for you" (Berg, 1999, p. 307). Knowledge of housework appears to be overlooked by the designers of smart houses. As Ruth Schwartz Cowan's (1976) work suggests, the improved household technologies developed in the first half of the 20th century actually increased the amount of time housewives spent on housework and reduced their role from general managers of servants, maiden aunts, grandmothers, children, and others to individuals who worked alone doing manual labor aided by household appliances (Cowan, 1976).

Using the white, middle-aged, heterosexual male as the "basic experimental subject" ignores the fact that females may respond differently to the variable tested; it also may lead to less accurate models, even for many men. For example, the standard dosage of certain medications is not only inappropriate for many women and the elderly, but also for most Asian men, because of their smaller body size and weight. Certain surgical procedures, such as angioplasty and cardiac bypass, initially resulted in higher death rates for women (Kelsey et al., 1993) and Asian men and required modification for the same reason (Lin-Fu, 1984).

Male dominance in engineering and the creative decision-making sectors of the information technology workforce may result in similar bias, particularly design and user bias. Shirley Malcom (personal communication, 1999) suggested that the air bag fiasco suffered by the U.S. auto industry serves as an excellent example of gender bias reflected in design; this fiasco would have been much less likely had a woman engineer been on the design team. Because, on the average, women tend to be smaller than men, women on the design team might have recognized that a bag that implicitly used the larger male body as a norm would be flawed when applied to smaller individuals, killing rather than protecting children and small women.

Theories may be presented in androcentric, ethnocentric, or class-biased language. An awareness of language should aid experimenters in avoiding the use of terms such as *tomboyism* (Money & Erhardt, 1972), *aggression*, and *hysteria*, which reflect assumptions about sex-appropriate behavior (Hamilton, 1985). Researchers should use evaluative terms such as *prostitute* with caution. Often the important fact for AIDS research is that a woman has multiple sex partners or is an IV drug user, not that she has received money for sex. The use of such terms as *prostitute* in analyzing data may induce bias by promoting the idea that women are vectors for transmission to men when, in fact, the men may have an equal or greater number of sex partners to whom they are transmitting the disease.

Many studies have explored the overt and covert links between the military, whose origins and current directions conjoin with masculinity in our culture, and the theories for applications drawn from the research funded for the military. For example, Janet Abbate (1999) studied the origins of the Internet in ARPANET, funded by the Department of Defense. The unique improvement of the Internet was that it was a network, overcoming the vulnerability to nuclear attack of the previous star configuration computer network.

Although liberal feminism suggests that true equity of women in the science and technology workforce would lead to inclusion of women in clinical trials and would correct bias in design to better serve women's interests, by definition, liberal feminism does not address the potential of gender to affect "fundamentals" (i.e., Do women scientists define, approach, or discover different fundamentals, such as string theory?). Liberal feminism accepts positivism as the theory of knowledge and assumes that human beings are highly individualistic and obtain knowledge in a rational manner that may be separated from their social conditions, including conditions of race, class, and gender. Because liberal feminism reaffirms, rather than challenges, positivism, it suggests that "fundamentals" would always remain the same. Now that they have become aware of potential bias, both male and female scientists and engineers can correct for such biases that previously resulted from failure to include women and their needs and interests.

Socialism

In contrast to liberal feminism, socialist feminism rejects individualism and positivism. Although socialist feminists argue that women's oppression predated the development of class societies, Marxist critiques form the historical precursors and foundations for socialist feminist critiques and define all knowledge, including science, as socially constructed and emerging from practical human involvement in production. Because knowledge is a productive activity of human beings, it cannot be objective and value-free because the basic categories of knowledge are shaped by human purposes and values. In the early 21st-century United States, capitalism, the prevailing mode of production, determines science and technology and favors the interests of the dominant class.

This Marxist/socialist theory undergirds the work of numerous scholars of science and technology who have used this framework for their studies, producing a large body of research commonly known as "the social shaping of science and technology" (MacKenzie & Wajcman, 1999). Different societies construct their material worlds, including the artifacts they create and use, in different ways. The culture of that society may use the artifacts or attach particular meanings to them differently at different times or historical periods. Thus a particular technology and science are situated in place, time, and culture (Lerman, Oldenziel, & Mohun, 2003).

Feminist scholars rightly point out that science and technology and the social shaping of technology (Wajcman, 1991; Webster, 1995) and science (Rose, 1994) have often been conceptualized in terms of men, excluding women at all levels. Socialist feminist critiques include women and place gender on equal footing with class in shaping science and technology. In this dual-systems approach (Eisenstein, 1984; Hartmann, 1981), capitalism and patriarchy function as mutually reinforcing parts of a system in which the sexual division of labor stands with wage labor as a central feature of capitalism and in which gender differences in wages—along with failing to count contributions of women to reproduction and child rearing as "productivity" in a capitalist economy—reinforce patriarchy and power differentials in the home. The social and technological shape each other. This so-called mutual shaping in times of technological change leads to contests over social categories such as gender being reflected in new interactions with the material world (Lerman et al., 2003). Some scholars (Fox, Johnson, & Rosser, 2006) have also called this mutual shaping of the social and technological the "co-creation of gender and technology" (p. 4).

Considerable research focus and dollars target diseases, such as cardiovascular disease, that are especially problematic for middle- and upper-class men in their prime earning years. Although women die from cardiovascular disease with the same frequency as men, on average women die at later ages. Hence, until recently, most cardiovascular disease research targeted white, middle-class men. Many of these studies, including the Physicians' Health Study (1989), were flawed due not only to factors of gender and age but also to factors of race and class (Marshall, 2005). Susceptibility to cardiovascular disease is known to be affected by lifestyle factors such as diet, exercise level, and stress, which are correlated with race and class. Because physicians in the United States are not representative of the overall male population with regard to lifestyle, the results may not be applicable even to most men.

Understandings of class relations emerging under capitalism and gender relations under patriarchy help to explain the intertwining of military and masculinity (Enloe, 1983, 1989; MacKenzie & Wajcman, 1999) that drives much technological innovation in this country and elsewhere. These understandings also explain how choices are made to develop technologies in a certain way, such as engineering decisions that favor expensive technologies for fewer rich people over relatively less expensive technologies, such as devices for the home, to aid many people, especially women. Caro's work (1974) revealed that Robert Moses, the master builder of New York's roads, parks, bridges, and other public works from the 1920s to the 1970s, had overpasses built to specifications to discourage buses on parkways. White upper- and middle-class car owners could use the parkways, such as Wantagh Parkway, to commute and to access recreation sites, including Jones Beach. Because the 12-foot height of public transit buses prohibited their fitting under the overpass, blacks and poor people dependent on public transit did not have access to Jones Beach (Winner, 1980). Socialist feminist approaches also suggest why men dominate the creation of new technologies, as access to venture capital, geographic mobility, and ability to work long hours may be as critical as technological expertise for the success of start-ups.

Designation of certain diseases as particular to one gender, race, or sexual orientation leads to overuse of that group in research protocols and the underuse of other groups. This not only cultivates ignorance in the general public about transmission or frequency of the disease, but also results in research that does not adequately explore the parameters of the disease. Most of the funding for heart disease has been appropriated for research on predisposing factors for the disease (such as cholesterol level, lack of exercise, stress, smoking, and weight) using white, middle-aged, middle-class males. Much less research has been directed toward elderly women, African American women who have had several children, and other high-risk groups of women. Virtually no research has explored predisposing factors for these groups, who fall outside the disease definition established from the dominant perspective.

Biases in populations sampled and choice and definition of problems raise ethical issues. Health care practitioners treat the majority of the population, which consists of females, minorities, and the elderly, based on information gathered from clinical research in which women and minorities are undersampled or not included. Bias in research thus leads to further injustice in health care diagnosis and treatment.

Current intellectual property rights agreements and laws provide opportunities for choices in technology development that further exacerbate class differences by transferring technologies developed using public moneys to the private realm through patents. The decisions regarding which products are developed falls under the influence of capitalist interests in profit margins. Such intellectual property rights function as a form of privatization (Mohanty, 1997). They permit decisions about which products will be developed to occur in the private, rather than the public, realm. This results in capitalist interests in the bottom line, rather than public needs and interests, dictating which products are developed. In the patenting of intellectual property, rights (and profits) get transferred from the public, who paid for the research with their tax dollars, to the private company, institution, or individual who controls the patent. Socialists might view this transfer from the pockets of the working class, who pay the taxes to underwrite federal research, to the patent holders in the private sector who will reap massive profits, as serving the interests of bourgeois capitalists. New technologies in genetic engineering, computer science, and engineering are often developed using federal grants (paid for by taxes).

African American/Racial Ethnic Critiques

Based on African American critiques of Eurocentric approaches to knowledge (Harding, 1998), African American, or black/womanist (Collins, 1990; hooks, 1992) feminism also rejects individualism and positivism for social construction as an approach to knowledge. In addition to rejecting objectivity and value neutrality associated with positivist approaches and accepted by liberal feminism, African American approaches critique dichotomization of knowledge, or at least the identification of "science" with the first half and "African American" with the second half of the following dichotomies: culture–nature; rational–feeling; objective–subjective; quantitative–qualitative; active–passive; focused–diffuse; independent–dependent; mind–body; self–others; knowing–being. Like socialism, African American critiques question methods that distance the observer from the object of study, thereby denying a facet of the social construction of knowledge.

Whereas socialism posits class as the organizing principle around which the struggle for power exists, African American critiques maintain that race is the primary oppression. African Americans critical of the scientific enterprise may view it as a function of white Eurocentric interests, with the methodology a reflection of those interests.

Just as socialist feminist theory provided insights into the gender and class distributions of science experiments and technological innovation, African American feminist critiques uncover the role of race in combination with gender. Racism intertwines and reinforces differing aspects of capitalism and patriarchy. African American feminists have examined the respective intersection of race and gender to provide a more complex, comprehensive view of reality. Many African American women are also uncomfortable with the word *feminism* because of its historical association with white women and ignoring of racial and ethnic diversity. Womanist (Steady, 1982), critical race theory (Williams, 1991, 1998), and black feminism (Collins, 1990), while all placing race in central focus, provide slightly differing critiques. Just as their African American sisters have done, Latina, Asian American, American Indian, and women from other racial and ethnic perspectives have developed critiques that place race/ethnicity and gender in central focus.

Data indicate that the initial designation of AIDS as a disease of male homosexuals, drug users, and Haitian immigrants not only has resulted in homophobic and racist stereotypes but also has particular implications for women of color. In 1981 the first official case of AIDS in a woman was reported to the Centers for Disease Control and Prevention (CDC). By 1991, $80 million had been spent since the inception of the Multicenter AIDS Cohort Study (MACS), designed to follow the natural history of HIV among gay and bisexual males (Faden, Kass, & McGraw, 1996). Although by 1988 the case reports for women were higher than the number for men had been in 1983, the year the MACS began (Chu, Buehler, & Berelman, 1990), it was not until the final quarter of 1994 that the first study on the natural history of HIV infection in women began. In 1998, the CDC reported that AIDS remains the leading cause of death among black females ages 25–44 and the second leading cause of death overall among those ages 25–44 (CDC, 1998). In the 21st century the majority of women diagnosed with AIDS are black or Hispanic.

When women of color are used as experimental participants, clinicians often hold stereotypical and racist views that limit accurate diagnosis. For example, numerous research studies have focused on sexually transmitted diseases in prostitutes in general (CDC, 1987; Cohen, Alexander, & Wofsy, 1988; Rosser, 1994) and African American women as prostitutes in particular. Several studies have also revealed that practitioners recognize and report at higher rates crack cocaine abuse in African American women and alcohol abuse in American Indian women compared with white women seeking prenatal care. In many cases, the women lost their children after they were born or had to serve jail time for detoxification. An American Civil Liberties Union study revealed that out of 53 cases brought against women for drug use during pregnancy in which the race of the woman was identifiable, 80% were brought against women of color (Pattrow, 1990, p. 2).

African American critiques also question methods that distance the observer from the object of study. Because technology, for the most part, involves practical application of more abstract, basic scientific research, the problem of the distance between engineer (researcher) and the technology (object of study) needs to be understood, discussed, and addressed to make technological research methodologies clearer to both developers and users. Unlike theoretical scientific projects, which do not necessarily have immediate practical outcomes, projects in computer science or engineering must accommodate the impact of the uses of technology with particular attention to the users of technology. When designing technologies, engineers, designers, and computer scientists would then not only ask how and under what conditions the technology would be used but would also have to allow the potential consumer to shape the design of the product. Potentially, gender, class, and race, along with other factors such as age and ability status, should be considered in defining who the user will be.

Challenges of Critiques and Strengths of Objectivity

Feminist, socialist, and racial/ethnic critiques provided powerful challenges to objectivity and positivism, with examples that revealed flaws and biases introduced through exclusion of gender, class, race, or other contextual values. In contrast, scientists held up the strengths of objectivity, including the reliability and verifiability of results. A debate erupted in the community, particularly among philosophers of science, about how methods employed by scientists can be objective and lead to repeatable, verifiable results.

Longino (1990) has explored the extent to which methods employed by scientists can be objective and lead to repeatable, verifiable results while contributing to hypotheses or theories that are congruent with nonobjective institutions and ideologies of the society: "Background assumptions are the means by which contextual values and ideology are incorporated into scientific inquiry" (Longino, 1990, p. 216). The institutions and beliefs of our society reflect the fact that the society is patriarchal. Even female scientists have only recently become aware of the influence of patriarchal bias in the paradigms of science (Rose & Rose, 1971; Rosser, 1992). For example, in the early primatology work, Yerkes (1943) chose the baboon and the chimpanzee as species for study primarily because their social organization was seen by the human observers to closely resemble that of human primates, with male dominance. It was not until a significant number of women entered primatology that the concepts of the universality and male leadership of dominance hierarchies among primates (Lancaster, 1975; Leavitt, 1975; Leibowitz, 1975; Rowell, 1974) were questioned and shown to be inaccurate for many primate species.

Recognition of the validity of these critiques of objectivity and the biases they might introduce into scientific research created a conundrum. How could the virtues of objectivity, such as reliability and verifiability, be retained while correcting for the bias resulting from the failure to include contextual values? Sandra Harding (1991, p. 148) suggested the solution of "strong objectivity."

Individuals holding identities or political "standpoints" outside the mainstream recognized biases in questions, methods, and theories permeating scientific investigation. Feminists identified androcentric biases, African Americans revealed Eurocentric biases, and socialists uncovered biases reflective of class. Harding (1998) suggests that starting from the "margins," or outside, provides a perspective on the contours of the paradigm or conceptual scheme not evident to the "insiders": "How might we accomplish our tasks of systematically identifying interests, cultural discourses, and ways of organizing the production of knowledge that (co-) constitute scientific projects–that coevolve with them and thus tend not to vary between legitimated observers–and of specifying the difference between those that enlarge and those that limit our knowledge?" (p. 140). Becoming aware of and including these outsider perspectives strengthens the objectivity of science while retaining its reliability and verifiability.

Types of Research Questions Appropriate for This Emergent Method

After Harding established the importance of "strong objectivity," as scientists began to accept and understand it, they wondered what types of research questions particularly lent themselves to this emergent method. The inclusion of gender becomes obvious in biological research dealing with species with males and females. For example, a laboratory exercise common in introductory biology courses uses the Siamese Fighting Fish, *Betta splendens*, and assumes a male norm and framework. The exercise implies that the only interaction occurring is between males, because only male responses to male, self, and female behavior are assessed. The female *Betta* is simply a passive object used to arouse the aggression of the males. Correcting the exercise to include an analysis of the female–female and female–male interaction would convey to the students a more significant role for females, while also constituting better science, as this is often the sole laboratory exercise devoted to animal behavior in the course. Including the gender in the context of this laboratory exercise experiment provides evidence of how strong objectivity/contextual values improve science. What researcher studying animal behavior of a species would not want to include the reaction of the female *Betta splendens*, as well as the male? Just as theories of dominance hierarchies as the only primate organizational behavioral patterns were overturned when female primatologists (Goodall, 1971; Hrdy, 1986; Lancaster, 1975) began to work in the field, some introductory laboratory exercises might demonstrate better science by a focus on issues of gender.

Similarly, in clinical research in humans, gender-based medicine now is understood as critical for providing practitioners with the necessary baseline to appropriately diagnose and treat all of their patients, both male and female, in the wake of the now demonstrated inadequacies of cardiovascular disease research conducted on male subjects only and extrapolated to women. Another example of how women appear to respond differently to drugs for treating or preventing cardiovascular disease comes from results of the Women's Health Study showing that women 45 years or older who took low-dose aspirin for 10 years had no fewer heart attacks but a 17% lower rate of stroke, just the opposite of the findings for men, who receive protection from hearth attacks but not stroke from aspirin (Ridker et al., 2005).

In clinical research, the impact of race, class, and sexual orientation and the context of other lifestyle factors becomes particularly relevant. The current debate over race-based medicine that surfaced surrounding both cardiovascular disease and certain types of cancer raises the issues of contextual values in an interesting way. Because "race" is not biologically determined, to what extent should it be used as a proxy to determine who might benefit from taking certain drugs demonstrated to be more effective in African Americans than Caucasians (Stein, 2006)?

In the physical sciences and technology, in which animals and people do not serve as the experimental subjects, gender, race, class, and other contextual values at first appear less relevant. Because people use technologies and products of basic physical science research, as the air bag example suggests, factors of gender and age do become significant. Policies that reflect contextual values, such as a desire to increase the number of women who use a particular technology, may uncover gender bias in designs that initially appeared gender neutral and may lead to new, innovative designs in engineering. The case of the cockpit design of the Joint Primary Aircraft Training System (JPATS) exemplifies such an innovation.

In direct ways, the use of the male norm excludes women as users of technology. Military regulations often apply Military Standard 1472 of anthropometric data so that systems dimensions use the 95th and 5th percentiles of male dimensions in designing weapons systems. This led to the cockpits of airplanes being designed to fit the dimensions of 90% of male military recruits (Weber, 1999). This worked relatively well as long as the military was entirely male. In the case of the JPATS, used by both the Navy and Air Force to train its pilots, the application of the standard accommodated the 5th–95th percentiles (90%) of males but only approximately the 65th–95th percentiles (30%) of females.

The policy decision by Secretary of Defense Les Aspin (1993, p. 1) to increase the percentage of women pilots uncovered the gender bias in the cockpit design. Designed to exclude only 10% of male recruits by dimensions, the cockpit excluded 70% of women recruits. Exclusion of such large numbers of women by dimensions alone made it extremely difficult to meet the military's policy goal of increasing the number of women pilots. The officers initially reacted by assuming that the technology reflected the best or only design possible and that either the goal for the percentage of women pilots would have to be lowered or the number of tall women recruits would have to be increased. This initial reaction, which represented the world viewpoint of men (de Beauvoir, 1947), changed. When political coalitions, the Tailhook scandal, and feminist groups reinforced the policy goal, a new cockpit design emerged that reduced the minimum sitting height from 34 to 32.8 inches, thereby increasing the percentage of eligible women (Weber, 1999, p. 379).

The JPATS example suggests that exploring or uncovering who is envisioned as the norm or default for whom the technology was engineered may uncover bias in design that superficially appears "neutral" with regard to gender, race, class, or other contextual values. For example, the Blacksburg Electronic Village, an online community network, "routes around" race and relies on the "digital default" of white, heterosexual, middle-aged, middle- to upper-class male (Silver, 2000, p. 143). This software "default" appears to parallel the use of white, middle-aged, middle- to upper-class men as the subjects or norm for cardiovascular disease. Does this normative "default" position help to explain the digital divide and African American's lower use of the Internet and computers?

Considerable research (Cockburn, 1983; Hacker, 1989) has documented the intertwining of masculinity with technology. Encouraged to be independent, autonomous, and distant, male engineers and computer scientists design technologies and information technology (IT) systems reflecting those characteristics and making them more comfortable for male users than female users.

As Bodker and Greenbaum (1993) suggest, the "hard systems" approach to computer systems development follows the positivist, linear, and technicist approach compatible with Western scientific thought. The technical capabilities, constraints of the machines, and rational data flow become the focus and driver of the technology design.

This "hard systems" design approach used by developers (mostly male) of computer systems assumes separation, distance, and independence on several levels: (1) Between the abstract systems development and the concrete real world of work: Separation ignores the often circular and interconnected forces of organization, assuming that they remain linear and unaffected by other hierarchical, power relations; (2) Between the developers and users: Because users do not contribute to the design of the system, their needs and suggestions that might make the system function more smoothly in the real world of work are ignored. The problems caused by this abstraction, objectivity, autonomy, and separation have spawned new methods, such as "soft systems" human factors approaches to solving the problems and mediating the gap.

The gender constellation predicted by psychoanalytic feminism also becomes transparent in technology: The men who design hardware systems design them in ways reflective of their perspective on the world, with which they feel comfortable. Such system designs tend to place priority on data and ignore relationships between people. Women, socialized to value connections and relationships, tend to feel uncomfortable with the hard-systems approach. As users, they find that the technology fails to aid much of the real-world work. The design inhibits or fails to foster good teamwork and other relationships among coworkers. Because the design does not reflect their view of priorities in the organization and work and actively ignores the reality of power and gender relations, women tend to be excluded, and to exclude themselves, from hard-systems design.

Critiques of IT from a psychoanalytic feminist perspective raise the very interesting question of how systems design might change if more feminine values and connection became priorities. Sorenson (1992) explored whether male and female computer scientists worked differently. He found that men tended to focus on mathematical models and computer programming, whereas women spent more time running experiments, reading scientific literature, and plotting data. After studying the technological and political values of men and women engineering students, graduate students, and junior research and development scientists at the Norwegian Institute of Technology, Sorenson found that women brought "caring values" to research in computer science. "Caring values" included empathy and a rationale of responsibility. "In computer science, this means that women have a caring, other-oriented relationship to nature and to people, an integrated, more holistic and less hierarchical world-view, a less competitive way of relating to colleagues and a greater affinity to users" (Sorenson, 1992, p. 10).

Understanding the importance of relationships and power, some women computer designers (Microsysters, 1988; Suchman, 1994) have attempted to link users with systems design as an explicit attempt to empower women. Some view this as an example of Harding's "strong objectivity."

Noting the differential use of particular technologies by individuals of different genders, races, and classes makes it easier to see some of the values, assumptions, and default positions that became embedded in the design of the technology. Although understanding how these contextual values become embedded in the design of these "objective" technologies is relatively difficult, technologies do represent applied research, developed for use by humans. Understanding how contextual values may be embedded and influence scientific theories becomes even more difficult than seeing it in scientific and technological applications.

In her book *Gender and Boyle's Law of Gases*, Elizabeth Potter (2001) provides an example from the history of science that documents how Boyle's contextual values surrounding his conservative political and religious beliefs led him to adopt the mechanistic model even though the experimental evidence supported either the mechanistic theory or that of animism, as proposed by Franciscus Linus, equally well. Despite his life as a bachelor, Boyle had a strong interest in gender, femininity, and women. Although Boyle wrote extensively about gender and the appropriate "modesty of body," as well as about the chastity and silence (Potter, 2001, p. 83) he expected of women, he separated his writing about gender from his writing about science.

Potter recreates the historical period in which Boyle conceived his law and undertook his experiments; during the civil war that raged in Britain in the 1640s, radicals threatened not only the absolute monarchy and decision-making authority and wealth of the king, church, and upper classes but also of men. The petitions presented by women claimed political equality with men and led to the establishment of civil marriage. Potter claims that because, as an upper-class male, Boyle was personally threatened by, and opposed to, the radicals, he rejected the animism that he saw as linked with radicalism. He chose the mechanistic model both because it comported well with the data (p. 108) and because it supported proper religion, monarchy, and the status quo with regard to class and gender. The same data could have been used to support an alternative law offered by Boyle's contemporary, Linus. Boyle did not clearly refute Linus's hypothesis on methodological or experimental grounds (p. 154).

Like that of Longino (1990), the work of other philosophers of science (Harding, 1986, 1998) and of feminist scientists (Birke, 1986; Rose, 1994) has demonstrated that androcentric bias infiltrates research because these values are shared by many in the scientific community. Potter suggests that Boyle's biases influenced his work, which was then accepted by the scientific community that also shared his values. His work also represented "good science," although the experimental evidence of the time did not permit distinction between Boyle's and Linus's hypotheses. In short, Boyle's conservative social, political, and gender values influenced his choice of the mechanistic model and his Law of Gases, thus demonstrating that Boyle's Law was not free of contextual values, but that it was still good science.

Perceiving the influence of values on modern scientific theories remains more difficult than perceiving such influences in a historical example. Keller's (1983) work on Barbara McClintock raises the question of why the model of the master molecule of DNA dominated in the face of increasing accumulated data demonstrating its inaccuracy for complex organisms.

The masculine worldview that surrounded Watson and Crick's "discovery" of the double helix as the control mechanism in the cell is well documented in Watson's (1969) own account of the discovery. Sayre (1975) and, to a certain extent, Maddox (2002) revealed Watson and Crick's exclusion and shameful treatment of Rosalind Franklin and their failure to acknowledge her substantial contribution to be one facet of their androcentrism. Feminist philosophers of science (Haraway, 1978) and feminist scientists (Hubbard, 1990; Keller, 1983) have demonstrated the androcentrism of reductionism and control inherent in the idea that life can be reduced to the DNA on the genes in the nucleus. (They also note that this gives the father equal status, as the father contributes DNA to the developing cell in amounts equal to that contributed by the mother.) They also point out that the hierarchical nature of the "central dogma" of DNA–RNA–protein parallels the hierarchical organizational charts of corporate structures (Keller, 1985), with unidirectional information flow from the top down.

The congruence of this hierarchical, reductionistic model, which centers unidirectional control for all life processes in the DNA found in the nucleus of the cell, with other social institutions, such as corporations, the Catholic Church, and the patriarchal family, led scientists to accept this model despite increasing contradictory evidence. Alternative models that emphasize interaction between the nucleus and cytoplasm and the importance of interrelationships and process (Nanney, 1957; Thomas, 1974) were proposed by scientists who represented a minority view during the "central dogma" era. Individuals who worked with more complex organisms (McClintock, 1950) warned that the Watson–Crick model did not explain the functioning of complex organisms. The views of these scientists were largely rejected, misunderstood, or ignored. Partially due to the biography of Barbara McClintock written by Evelyn Fox Keller (1983), and especially after McClintock's receipt of the Nobel Prize, reverse transcriptase and more interactive models contradicting DNA as the master molecule gained more acceptance.

Similarly, most of the traditional, theoretical models for the immune system focus on combat, competition, and boundaries. Both scholarly and popular accounts of the immune system depict it as maintaining the body's health, or self, through continuous warfare against the enemy, or foreign foe (Martin, 1999). This view of the importance of body surfaces and their boundaries, coupled with their ability to prevent entrance of foreign matter, fits with a mechanistic view of the body appropriate for the machine age of post–World War II America (Martin, 1999).

Emily Martin, in her 1994 book *Flexible Bodies: Tracking Immunity in America from the Days of Polio to the Age of AIDS*, skillfully analyzes language to reveal that we are in the process of a sea change regarding how the body is conceptualized. The older, steadier mechanical model has begun to give way to a new, fluid, complex systems model, exemplified in the new theories of the immune system. "Although they are not yet in the mainstream, a subset of immunologists favors what they call a network theory of the immune system. Imagery of the dance replaces traditional imagery of the immune system in battle against external foes" (Martin, 1999, p. 106). Flexibility characterizes the healthy immune system, just as it does the good dancer and the desired workforce. This shift from the mechanical model of the body to the flexible body model arose in the wake of the global economic system and the shift in the forces of production that began in the 1970s. In short, the acceptance of scientific models corresponds with the contextual values of the broader society.

How Does This Emergent Method Affect the Research Process?

How do the contextual values embedded in these theories affect the research process? Doesn't the theoretical model influence every stage of the research process, from formulation of the question through data gathering and approaches to data analysis to theories and conclusions drawn from the data and, finally, to applications?

Using the now historical example of cardiovascular disease, one can see how the contextual values that defined cardiovascular disease as a health problem primarily for white middle-class, middle-aged men influenced all stages of the research process. We know many of the historical reasons that determined this definition and research trajectory. Although cardiovascular diseases strike both men and women with approximately equal frequency, men experience cardiovascular disease approximately 10 years earlier on average than women because of the protective effects of estrogen in premenopausal women. In light of the Belmont Report (1978) and because of fears of teratogenic effects of drugs on the fetus, particularly after thalidomide and until the 1990s, very few premenopausal women participated in any clinical trials of drugs, including those for treating cardiovascular disease.

Not until a substantial number of women had entered medicine and science (Rosser, 1986) could this bias of androcentrism be exposed. Once the possibility of androcentric bias was discovered, the potential for distortion on a variety of levels of research and theory was recognized: the choice and definition of problems to be studied, the exclusion of females as experimental participants, bias in the methodology used to collect and interpret data, and bias in theories and conclusions drawn from the data. Researchers also began to realize that because the practice of modern medicine uses a biomedical approach based in positivist research in biology and chemistry and depends heavily on clinical research, any flaws and ethical problems in this research are likely to result in poorer health care and inequity in the medical treatment of disadvantaged groups.

This realization uncovered gender bias that had distorted some medical research. Women's health had become synonymous with reproductive health and obstetrics and gynecology. This meant that many diseases that occur in both sexes had been studied in males only or in studies that used a male-as-norm approach. Cardiovascular diseases served as a case in point. Research protocols for large-scale studies (Grobbee et al., 1990; MRFIT, 1990; Steering Committee of Physician's Health Study Group, 1989) of cardiovascular diseases failed to assess gender differences. A 1996 study including all prospective treatment and intervention studies published in the *New England Journal of Medicine*, the *Journal of the American Medical Association*, and the *Annals of Internal Medicine* between the months of January and June in the years 1990 and 1994 revealed that only 19% of the 1990 studies and 24% of the 1994 studies reported any data analysis by gender, despite the fact that 40% of the subjects were female (Charney & Morgan, 1996).

Excessive focus on male research participants and definition of cardiovascular diseases as "male" led to underdiagnosis and undertreatment of the disease in women. A 1991 study in Massachusetts and Maryland (Ayanian & Epstein, 1991) demonstrated that women were significantly less likely than men to undergo coronary angioplasty, angiography, or surgery when admitted to the hospital with a diagnosis of myocardial infarction, unstable or stable angina, chronic ischemic heart disease, or chest pain. This significant difference remained even when variables such as race, age, economic status, and other chronic disease, such as diabetes and heart failure, were controlled. A similar study (Steingart et al., 1991) revealed that women had angina before myocardial infarction as frequently as, and with more debilitating effects than, men, yet women were referred for cardiac catheterization only half as often. These and other similar studies led Bernadine Healy, a cardiologist and first woman director of the National Institutes of Health (NIH), to characterize the diagnosis of coronary heart disease in women as the Yentl syndrome: "Once a woman showed that she was just like a man, by having coronary artery disease or a myocardial infarction, then she was treated as a man should be" (Healy, 1991, p. 274). The male-as-norm approach in research and diagnosis, unsurprisingly, was translated into bias in treatments for women. Women exhibited higher death rates from coronary bypass surgery and angioplasty (Kelsey et al., 1993).

Women scientists, consumers, physicians, and politicians brought these revelations and other examples of bias and gaps in research and practice to the attention of the health community. After the 1985 U.S. Public Health Service survey recommended that the definition of women's health be expanded beyond reproductive health, the General Accounting Office (GAO) reported that the NIH expended only 13.5% of its budget on women's health issues. In 1990, the GAO criticized the NIH for inadequate representation of women and minorities in federally funded studies (Taylor, 1994), and the Congressional Caucus for Women's Issues introduced the Women's Health Equity Act. In 1991, Bernadine Healy established the Office of Research on Women's Health and announced plans for the Women's Health Initiative (Healy, 1991). The Women's Health Initiative, designed to collect baseline data and look at interventions to prevent cardiovascular disease, breast and colorectal cancer, and osteoporosis, seeks to fill the gaps in research and practice.

Impact of This Emergent Method

Inclusion of gender and other contextual values demonstrates how "strong objectivity" improves science through elimination of bias while still leading to verifiable and repeatable results of the scientific method. When cardiovascular disease (CVD) was defined as a problem for white middle-class men, the research results led to diagnoses and treatment applications effective for that population on which the research was done. Not surprisingly, the results led to less effective diagnoses and treatments in women, especially because it was known initially that this disease was affected by estrogen. The research also did not apply as well to other groups of men who differed from the research population because of their race, class, or other lifestyle factors. The problem was the embedding of certain assumptions, norms, or defaults—that CVD is a disease of white, middle-aged, middle-class men—in the theories and definitions of the research. The limitations of these assumptions were then overlooked when the research results were extrapolated beyond the research group to the entire population.

Inclusion of contextual values results in research on CVD in women, men of color, and individuals from varied socioeconomic strata, leading to a more accurate, inclusive model for CVD that has verifiable, repeatable results for all people, not just white, middle-class men. This demonstrates the power of this emergent method of inclusion. Women's symptoms are recognized as those of a heart attack when they arrive at the emergency room. They receive appropriate treatments because the diagnosis was accurate. If they require angioplasty or bypass, their chances of dying are less now than several years ago because the procedures have been normed and practiced on individuals, such as other women and Asian men, who have smaller vessels on average than does the white male population for whom the procedure was developed initially.

The inclusion of gender in the case of CVD clearly demonstrates more accurate diagnosis, treatment, and ultimate saving of lives. This elimination of gender bias in the research design contributes to better science. Designing and engineering products such as air bags, cockpits, and user-centered software that "work" for a larger percentage of the population, including most women, children, and smaller men, rather than just the average white male, also makes products accessible to more individuals and makes great economic sense. Designing software by beginning with the user also saves money and reduces frustration, particularly when the "default" user is defined as broader than the white, middle-class, heterosexual male.

Given the advantages of saving lives, making products accessible to more people, and, ultimately, cost savings, why weren't strong objectivity and inclusion of contextual values embraced immediately by all scientists and engineers? Difficulty of recognizing contextual values constitutes a primary obstacle to adoption of this emergent method. Most scientists try very hard to ask significant questions, design their experiments well to obtain data that answer those questions, analyze the data appropriately, and draw theories and conclusions from the data to provide people with accurate information on which to make decisions. They especially try to eliminate bias and not extrapolate beyond what the data warrant in issues of health and safety. In hindsight, the problems resulting from using only white, middle-aged, middle-class men to study CVD and then extrapolating the results to the entire population appear evident. Initially the problems appeared less evident, and, in fact, other factors, such as not using women in clinical trials because of fear of teratogenic effects in fetuses, predominated. Understanding the particular contextual values that might be relevant for a certain experiment or series of studies is difficult for scientists at the time when they design the experiment.

Although such understanding would be difficult for anyone, the education and training of scientists exacerbates this difficulty. As historians of science (Lloyd, 1996) have carefully documented, modern scientific training builds on Bacon's notions of science: "first, that he who would know Nature must turn away from mere ideas and abstractions and painstakingly attend to natural phenomena; and, second, that this painstaking attention cannot be regarded as mere contemplation" (Bacon, 1620/1901). Objectivity and positivism become defined as free from contextual values and as cornerstones of the scientific method. This definition led to the development of curricula for the education of scientists with requirements that focused on science and mathematics while excluding a focus on contextual values, even omitting courses in the history and philosophy of science. Divorced from the curriculum of the sciences, such courses and others that educate students in contextual values fell into the realm of the humanities and social sciences.

Recently, the medical and engineering curricula have begun to include more contextual values. The professional associations in these more applied areas of the sciences have demanded courses in ethics, social values, and human impacts. Some of these demands reflect the problems that became obvious when women were excluded from clinical trials and when products did not meet consumer safety or expectations.

The interdisciplinary exchanges between liberal arts faculty members and those in the applied areas of clinical medicine and engineering will help to further delineate the contours of this emergent method. Expanding beyond these applied areas to the more theoretical sciences will challenge both liberal arts and science and engineering faculty members to elaborate strong objectivity to improve research in basic science.

References

Abbate, J. (1999). Cold war and white heat: The origins and meanings of packet switching. In D. MacKenzie & J. Wacjman (Eds.), *The social shaping of technology* (2nd ed., pp. 351–379). Philadelphia: Open University Press.

Aspin, L. (1993). *Policy on the assignment of women in the armed forces.* Washington, DC: U.S. Department of Defense.

Ayanian, J. Z., & Epstein, A. M. (1991). Differences in the use of procedures between women and men hospitalized for coronary heart disease. *New England Journal of Medicine, 325*, 221–225.

Bacon, F. (1901). *Novum organum: I. Aphorism.* In J. Devey (Ed.), *The physical and metaphysical works of Lord Bacon* (p. 441). London: Bell. (Original work published 1620)

Barnaby, F. (1981). Social and economic reverberations of military research. *Impact of Science on Society, 31*, 73–83.

Belmont Report. (1978). Washington, DC: Department of Health, Education, and Welfare. (Publ. #0578-0012).

Berg, A.-J. (1999). A gendered socio-technical construction: the smart house. In D. MacKenzie & J. Wacjman (Eds.), *The social shaping of technology* (2nd ed.). Philadelphia: Open University Press.

Birke, L. (1986). *Women, feminism, and biology: The feminist challenge.* New York: Methuen.

Bleier, R. (1984). *Science and gender: A critique of biology and its theories on women.* New York: Pergamon Press.

Bleier, R. (1986). Sex differences research: Science or belief? In R. Bleier (Ed.), *Feminist approaches to science* (pp. 147–164). New York: Pergamon Press.

Bodker, S., & Greenbaum, J. (1993). Design of information systems: Things versus people. In E. Green, J. Owen, & D. Pain (Eds.), *Gendered by design: Information technology and office systems* (pp. 53–63). London: Taylor & Francis.

Campbell, G., Jr., Denes, R., & Morrison, C. (Eds.). (2000). *Access denied: Race, ethnicity and the scientific enterprise.* Oxford, UK: Oxford University Press.

Caro, R. (1974). *The power broker: Robert Moses and the fall of New York.* New York: Random House.

Centers for Disease Control. (1987). Antibody to human immunodeficiency virus in female prostitutes. *Morbidity and Mortality Weekly Report, 36*, 157–161.

Centers for Disease Control. (1998). Guidelines for evaluating surveillance systems. *Morbidity and Mortality Weekly Report, 37*, 1–18.

Charney, P., & Morgan, C. (1996). Do treatment recommendations reported in the research literature consider differences between women and men? *Journal of Women's Health, 5*(6), 579–584.

Chodorow, N. (1978). *The reproduction of mothering: Psychoanalysis and the sociology of gender.* Berkeley: University of California Press.

Chu, S. Y., Buehler, J. W., & Berelman, R. L. (1990). Impact of the human immunodeficiency virus epidemic on mortality in women of reproductive age: United States. *Journal of the American Medical Association, 264*, 225–229.

Cockburn, C. (1983). *Brothers: Male dominance and technological change.* London: Pluto Press.

Cohen, J., Alexander, P., & Wofsy, C. (1988). Prostitutes and AIDS: Public policy issues. *AIDS and Public Policy Journal, 3*, 16–22.

Collins, P. H. (1990). *Black feminist thought.* New York: Routledge.

Cowan, R. S. (1976). The industrial revolution in the home: Household technology and social change in the twentieth century. *Technology and Culture, 17*, 1–23.

Cowan, R. S. (1981). *More work for mother: The ironies of household technology from the open hearth to the microwave.* New York: Basic Books.

Creager, A. N. H., Lunbeck, E. A., & Schiebinger, L. (Eds.). (2001). *Feminism in twentieth century science, technology, and medicine.* Chicago: University of Chicago Press.

de Beavoir, S. (1947). *The second sex* (H. M. Parshley, Trans. & Ed.) New York: Vintage Books.

Eisenstein, H. (1984). *Contemporary feminist thought.* London: Allen & Unwin.

Enloe, C. (1983). *Does khaki become you?: The militarisation of women's lives.* London: Pluto Press.

Enloe, C. (1989). *Bananas, beaches and bases.* Berkeley: University of California Press.

Faden, R., Kass, N., & McGraw, D. (1996). Women as vessels and vectors: Lessons from the HIV epidemic. In S. M. Wolf (Ed.), *Feminism and bioethics: Beyond reproduction* (pp. 252–281). New York: Oxford University Press.

Fausto-Sterling, A. (1992). *Myths of gender.* New York: Basic Books.

Fee, E. (1982). A feminist critique of scientific objectivity. *Science for the People, 14*(4), 8.

Fee, E. (1983). Women's nature and scientific objectivity. In M. Lowe & R. Hubbard (Eds.), *Women's nature: Rationalizations of inequality* (pp. 9–27). New York: Pergamon Press.

Fox, M., Johnson, D., & Rosser, S. (Eds.). (2006). *Women, gender and technology.* Champaign: University of Illinois Press.

Friedan, B. (1963). *The feminine mystique.* New York: Norton.

Goodall, J. (1971). *In the shadow of man.* Boston: Houghton Mifflin.

Grobbee, D. E., Rimm, E. B., Giovannucci, E., Colditz, G., Stampfer, M., & Willett, W. (1990). Coffee, caffeine, and cardiovascular disease in men. *New England Journal of Medicine, 321*, 1026–1032.

Gurwitz, J. H., Nananda, F. C., & Avorn, J. (1992). The exclusion of the elderly and women from clinical trials in acute myocardial infarction. *Journal of the American Medical Association, 268*(2), 1417–1422.

Hacker, S. (1989). *Pleasure, power and technology*. Boston, MA: Unwin Hyman.

Hamilton, J. (1985). Avoiding methodological biases and policy-making biases in gender-related health research. In R. L. Kirschstein & D. H. Merritt (Eds.), *Women's health: Report of the Public Health Service task force on women's health issues* (pp. 54–64). Washington, DC: U.S. Department of Health and Human Services, Public Health Service.

Haraway, D. (1978). Animal sociology and a natural economy of the body politic. *Signs, 4*(l), 21–60.

Haraway, D. (1989). *Primate visions: Gender, race, and nature in the world of modern science*. New York: Routledge.

Haraway, D. (1997). Modest witness@second_millenium. FemaleMan© Meets Oncomouse™: *Feminism and technoscience*. New York: Routledge.

Harding, S. (1986). *The science question in feminism*. Ithaca, NY: Cornell University Press.

Harding, S. (1991). *Whose science? Whose knowledge?* Ithaca, NY: Cornell University Press.

Harding, S. (1993). Introduction. In S. Harding (Ed.), *The racial economy of science* (pp. 1–22). Bloomington: Indiana University Press.

Harding, S. (1998). *Is science multicultural? Postcolonialisms, feminisms, and epistemologies*. Bloomington: Indiana University Press.

Hartmann, H. (1981). The unhappy marriage of Marxism and feminism: Towards a more progressive union. In L. Sargent (Ed.), *Women and revolution* (pp. 1–41). Boston: South End Press.

Hawthorne, S., & Klein, R. (1999). *Cyberfeminism*. Melbourne, Australia: Spinifex.

Healy, B. (1991, July 24-31). Women's health, public welfare. *Journal of the American Medical Association, 266*, 566–568.

hooks, b. (1992). *Race and representation*. London: Turnaround Press.

Hrdy, S. (1986). Empathy, polyandry, and the myth of the coy female. In R. Bleier (Ed.), *Feminist approaches to science* (pp. 9–34). Elmsford, NY: Pergamon Press.

Hubbard, R. (1990). *The politics of women's biology*. New Brunswick, NJ: Rutgers University Press.

Jaggar, A. (1983). *Feminist politics and human nature*. Totowa, NJ: Rowman & Allanheld.

Keller, E. F. (1982). Feminism and science. *Signs, 7*(3), 589–602.

Keller, E. F. (1983). *A feeling for the organism*. San Francisco: Freeman.

Keller, E. F. (1985). *Reflections on gender and science*. New Haven, CT: Yale University Press.

Keller, E. Fox. (1992). *Secrets of life, secrets of death*. New York: Routledge.

Kelsey, S. F., James, M., Holubkov, A. L., Holubkov, R., Cowley, M. J., Detre, K. M., & Investigators from the National Heart, Lung, and Blood Institute Percutaneous Transluminal Coronary Angioplasty Registry. (1993). Results of percutaneous transluminal coronary angioplasty in women: 1985–1986. *Circulation, 87*(3), 720–727.

Lancaster, J. (1975). *Primate behavior and the emergence of human culture*. New York: Holt, Rinehart, & Winston.

Leavitt, R. (1975). *Peaceable primate and gentle people: Anthropological approaches to women's studies*. New York: Harper & Row.

Leibowitz, L. (1975). Perspectives in the evolution of sex differences. In R. R. Reiter (Ed.), *Toward an anthropology of women* (pp. 22–35). New York: Monthly Review Press.

Lerman, N., Oldenziel, R. & Mohun, A. (2003). *Gender and technology*. Baltimore: John Hopkins University Press.

Lin-Fu, J. S. (1984, July–August). The need for sensitivity to Asian and Pacific Americans' health problems and concerns. *Organization of Chinese American Women Speaks*, pp. 1–2.

Lloyd, G. (1996). Reason, science and the domination of nature. In E. F. Keller & H. Longino (Eds.), *Feminism and science* (pp. 91–102). Oxford, UK: Oxford University Press.

Longino, H. (1990). *Science as social knowledge: Values and objectivity in scientific inquiry*. Princeton, NJ: Princeton University Press.

Longino, H. (1996). Subjects, power and knowledge: Description and prescription in feminist philosophies of science. In L. H. Nelson, E. F. Keller, & H. Longino (Eds.), *Feminism and science* (pp. 264–279). Oxford, UK: Oxford University Press.

MacKenzie, D., & Wajcman, J. (1999). *The social shaping of technology* (2nd ed.). Milton Keynes, UK: Open University Press.

Maddox, B. (2002). *Rosalind Franklin: The dark lady of DNA*. New York: HarperCollins.

Marshall, E. (2005). Clinical trials: Keeping score on the sexes. *Science, 308*, 1571.

Martin, E. (1987). *The woman in the body*. Boston: Beacon Press.

Martin, E. (1994). *Flexible bodies: Tracking immunity in American culture from the days of polio to the age of AIDS*. Boston: Beacon Press.

Martin, E. (1999). The woman in the flexible body. In A. Clarke & V. Olesen (Eds.), *Revisioning women, health, and healing* (pp. 97–115). New York: Routledge.

McClintock, B. (1950). The origin and behavior of mutable loci in maize. *Proceedings of the National Academy of Sciences, 36*, 344–355.

Microsysters. (1988). *Not over our heads: Women and computers in the office*. London: Microsyster.

Mill, J. S. (1970). The subjection of women. In A. S. Rossi (Eds.), *Essays on sex equality* (pp. 123–242). University of Chicago Press. (Original work published 1869)

Mohanty, C. T. (1997). Women workers and capitalist scripts: Ideologies of domination, common interests, and the politics of solidarity. In M. J. Alexander & C. T. Mohanty (Eds.), *Feminist genealogies, colonial*

legacies, democratic futures (pp. 3–29). New York: Routledge.
Money, J., & Erhardt, A. (1972). *Man and woman, boy and girl.* Baltimore: John Hopkins University Press.
Multiple Risk Factor Intervention Trial Research Group. (1990). Mortality rates after 10.5 years for participants in the multiple risk factor intervention trial: Findings related to a prior hypothesis of the trial. *Journal of the American Medical Association, 263,* 1795.
Nanney, D. L. (1957). The role of cytoplasm is heredity. In W. E. McElroy & H. B. Glenn (Eds.), *The chemical basis of heredity* (pp. 134–166). Baltimore: Johns Hopkins University Press.
National Science Foundation. (2002). *Women, minorities, and persons with disabilities in science and engineering: 2002* (NSF No. 03-312). Arlington, VA: Author.
Norman, C. (1979, July 26). Global research: Who spends what? *New Scientist,* pp. 279–281.
Pattrow, L. M. (1990, Winter–Spring). When becoming pregnant is a crime. *Criminal Justice Ethics,* pp. 41–47.
Potter, E. (2001). *Gender and Boyle's law of gases.* Bloomington: Indiana University Press.
Public Health Service Task Force on Women's Health Issues. (1985). *Women's health* (Vol. II). Washington, DC: U.S. Department of Health and Human Services.
Rapp, R. (1999). One new reproductive technology, multiple sites: How feminist methodology bleeds into everyday life. In A. Clarke & V. Olesen (Eds.), *Revisioning women, health, and healing* (pp. 119–135). New York: Routledge.
Ridker, P. M., Cook, N., Lee, I-M., Gordon, D., Gazian, J. M., Manson, J. A., et al. (2005). A randomized trial of low-dose aspirin in the primary prevention of cardiovascular disease in women. *New England Journal of Medicine, 352*(13), 1293–1304.
Rose, H. (1994). *Love, power, and knowledge: Towards a feminist transformation of the sciences.* Bloomington: Indiana University Press.
Rose, H., & Rose, S. (1971). The myth of the neutrality of science. *Impact of Science on Society, 21,* 137–149.
Rosser, S. V. (1986). *Teaching science and health from a feminist perspective: A practical guide.* Elmsford, NY: Pergamon Press.
Rosser, S. V. (1988). Women in science and health care: A gender at risk. In S. V. Rosser (Ed.), *Feminism within the science and health care professions: Overcoming resistance* (pp. 3–15). New York: Pergamon Press.
Rosser, S. V. (1992). *Feminism and biology.* New York: Twayne/MacMillan.
Rosser, S. V. (1994). *Women's health: Missing from U.S. medicine.* Bloomington: Indiana University Press.
Rosser, S. V. (1998). The next millennium is here now: Women's studies perspectives on biotechnics and reproductive technologies. In B. Berner (Ed.), *New perspectives in gender studies: Research in the fields of economics, culture and life sciences* (pp. 7–35). Stockholm, Sweden: Almquist & Wilosell International.
Rosser, S. V. (2004). *The science glass ceiling: Academic women scientists and the struggle to succeed.* New York: Routledge.
Rossiter, M. (1982). *Women scientists in America: Struggles and strategies to 1940.* Baltimore: Johns Hopkins University Press.
Rowell, T. (1974). The concept of social dominance. *Behavioral Biology, 11,* 131–154.
Sayre, A. (1975). *Rosalind Franklin and DNA: A vivid view of what it is like to be a gifted woman in an especially male profession.* New York: Norton.
Schiebinger, L. (1999). *Has feminism changed science?* Cambridge, MA: Harvard University Press.
Silver, D. (2000). Margins in the wires: Looking for race, gender, and sexuality in the Blacksburg Electronic Village. In M. McCaughey & M. Ayers (Eds.), *Cyberactivism* (pp. 133–150). New York: Routledge.
Sorenson, K. (1992). Towards a feminized technology?: Gendered values in the construction of technology. *Social Studies of Science, 22*(1), 5–31.
Spanier, B. (1995). *Impartial science: Gender ideology in molecular biology.* Bloomington: Indiana University Press.
Steady, F. (1982). *The black woman culturally.* Cambridge, MA: Schenkman.
Steering Committee of the Physician's Health Study Group. (1989). Final report on the aspirin component of the ongoing Physician's Health Study. *New England Journal of Medicine, 321,* 129–135.
Stein, R. (2006, January 26). Race play key role in lung cancer risk. *Atlanta Journal Constitution,* A-16.
Steingart, R. M., Packer, M., Hamm, P., Coglianese, M. E., Gersh, B., Geltman, E. M., et al. (1991). Sex differences in the management of coronary artery disease. *New England Journal of Medicine, 325,* 226–230.
Suchman, L. (1994). Supporting articulation work: Aspects of a feminist practice of technology production. In A. Adam, J. Emms, E. Green, & J. Owen (Eds.), *Women, work and computerization: Breaking old boundaries–building new forms* (pp. 1–13). Amsterdam: North-Holland.
Taylor, C. (1994). Gender equity in research. *Journal of Women's Health, 3,* 143–153.
Thomas, L. (1974). *The lives of a cell.* New York: Viking.
Tuana, N. (1989). *Feminism and science.* Bloomington: Indiana University Press.
Tuana, N. (1995). The values of science: Empiricism from a feminist perspective. *Synthese, 104*(3), 441–461.
U.S. General Accounting Office. (1990). National Institutes of Health: Problems in implementing policy on women in study populations. Statement of Mark v. Nadel, Associate Director, National and Public Health Issues, Human Resources Division, before the Subcommittee on Health and the Environment, Committee on Energy and Commerce, U.S. House of Representatives, June 19, 1990.
Vetter, B. (1988). Where are the women in the physical sciences? In S. V. Rosser (Ed.), *Feminism within the sci-*

ence and health care professions: Overcoming resistance (pp. 19–32). New York: Pergamon Press.

Wajcman, J. (1991). *Feminism confronts technology*. University Park: Pennsylvania State University Press.

Watson, J. (1969). *The double helix*. New York: Atheneum.

Weber, R. (1999). Manufacturing gender in commercial and military cockpit design. *Science, Technology and Human Values, 22*, 235–253.

Webster, J. (1995). *Shaping women's work: Gender, employment and information technology*. New York: Longman.

Williams, P. (1991). *The alchemy of race and rights*. Cambridge, MA: Harvard University Press.

Williams, P. (1998). *Seeing a color-blind future*. New York: Noonday Press.

Winner, L. (1980). Do artifacts have politics? *Daedalus, 109*, 121–136.

Wollstonecraft, M. (1975). *A vindication of the rights of woman* (C. H. Poston, Ed.). New York: Norton. (Original work published 1792)

Yerkes, R. M. (1943). *Chimpanzees*. New Haven, CT: Yale University Press.

Zimmerman, B., et al. (1980). People's science. In R. Arditti, P. Brennan, & S. Cavrak (Eds.), *Science and liberation* (pp. 299–319). Boston: South End Press.

CHAPTER 3

A Post-Newtonian, Postmodern Approach to Science

New Methods in Social Action Research

Lisa Cosgrove
Maureen McHugh

Laboratories are excellent sites in which to understand the production of certainty.
—LATOUR (1999, p. 30)

In order to avoid the "production of certainty" of which Latour speaks, social scientists need to challenge the belief that an unmediated relationship between the world and our knowledge of it is possible. Rather than strive for (an impossible) objectivity, scientists should embrace the value-laden nature of our work by bringing issues of power to the forefront of our theories and methods. Appreciating the sociopolitical grounding of experience necessitates critical thinking about the epistemological and methodological choices that we make. Specifically, we need to explore the relationship between epistemology and methodology and recognize the impossibility of *any* method as a guarantor of truth. In this chapter we describe a post-Newtonian view of science, a view that is congruent with tenets from postmodernism, and we present several approaches to social science inquiry that are consistent with the goals of action research.

Modernism, Postmodernism, and Social Science Research

Traditional or mainstream social science research utilizes a modernist or Newtonian-based paradigm, one that is characterized by predictability, certainty, and causality. Our knowledge of the world, discovered via scientific methods, is understood to be valid and rational because knowledge, that is, scientific truths, exist independent of our values, beliefs, and ideologies. A Newtonian or modernist worldview requires strict adherence to a positivist–empiricist model, a model that privileges the scientific method of the natural sciences as the only valid route to knowledge. A positivist–empiricist model emphasizes the importance of scientific objectivity; the assumption is that reality is fixed and can be directly observed uninfluenced by the observer. There is an uncomplicated, unmediated relationship between sense experience and knowledge, between "reality" and our experience of it. Scientists study objects that they believe exist prior to and apart from their beliefs about those objects, and thus they believe that they are able to identify, study, and indeed discover the "truths" about their respective subject matter. A modernist paradigm does not focus on the connection between knowledge and power. Lowe (1991) explains why this is so: "[from a modernist perspective] knowledge is about something external to the knower and can be present objectively to the knower" (p. 43). Because true knowledge represents something real and unchanging about ourselves or about the world around us, there is no need to interrogate the relationship between power and truth; scientific facts exist a priori and are therefore presumed to exist independent of the scientific community who "discovers" them. For example, psychologists study and are able to discover ahistorical truths about agoraphobia, depression, self-esteem, and so forth. Insofar as social scientists utilize a modernist epistemology, they accept, at both the conceptual and methodological level, the belief in value-free facts and value-neutral science.

Although there is no one agreed-on definition, postmodernism may be described as a radical rethinking and questioning of some of our most taken-for-granted assumptions about the nature of reality, truth, and knowledge. It is an approach to knowledge generation and science that questions the belief in absolute or ahistorical truths by emphasizing the partial and impermanent nature of knowledge (Burr, 1995; Cosgrove, 2004; Gergen, 2001; Lowe, 1991). From a postmodern perspective, our knowledge or understanding of reality is always partial, resulting in a view of reality that is dynamic, incoherent, and fragmented. Also, researchers who utilize a postmodern framework underscore the power of language. In contrast to the modernist view that assumes that language reflects an a priori reality, a postmodern approach maintains that language mediates or even *constitutes* reality. The positivist–empiricist belief in direct (or unmediated) access to experience/reality is challenged. In this way, a postmodern critique upsets the fundamental dualities of modernist thought (e.g., subject–object, nature–culture, mind–body). The focus shifts from assuming that these dualisms are inherent and inevitable aspects of experience to examining how these dualisms structure our thought, ground our epistemology, and exert a profound influence over our methodological choices.

Thus, researchers whose work is influenced by postmodernism try to make explicit the epistemic commitments that warrant their concepts and theories. Reflecting on one's epistemic beliefs is the first step in challenging the science–politics dichotomy. The science–politics dichotomy assumes that "science" is uncontaminated by power, whereas the term *politics* implies competing interests and power dynamics (Cosgrove, 2004; Prilleltensky & Nelson, 2002). If this assumption goes unchallenged, the tendency is to celebrate accomplishments within the social sciences without attending to the ways in which many theories and interpretations of data reinforce stereotypes. For example, many social scientists tend to assume that race, gender, class, disability, and so on are discrete variables that can be inserted easily into empirical studies. This assumption leaves intact many heterosexist, racist, and classist beliefs, and it also leads to the commodification of diversity (Landrine, 1995). Challenging dichotomous and other forms of reductive thinking, especially the science–politics binary, helps researchers avoid the reification of social science categories (e.g., gender, race, class). Postmodernism provides an epistemological grounding for deconstructing, rather than reifying, difference because it helps us notice the complex processes through which these social categories are produced. Hence, it is a framework that allows researchers to grapple with epistemological issues and to think critically about what it means to be both culturally sensitive and politically engaged (Moghaddam & Studer, 1997). In addition, a postmodern framework redirects attention back to the larger sociopolitical context of individuals' experience. For these reasons a postmodern framework is of special relevance to social action research.

Phenomenology, Discourse Analysis, and Satirical Empiricism

In the following section we provide three examples of methods that have been influenced by epistemological developments in postmodernism. Two qualitative methods, phenomenology and discourse analysis, and one quantitative approach, satirical empiricism, are identified as three methods that are congruent with both social action research and a post-Newtonian view of science. In addition to describing the specifics of each method, we emphasize the complexity of determining what constitutes social action research or "emancipatory" knowledge. What sets social action research apart from mainstream approaches is its collaborative focus; social action researchers try to design studies and use the data gathered to empower the individuals and communities with whom they work (e.g., using collaboratively developed findings to inform public policy). Because all methods privilege certain views and marginalize others, pluralistic methods are needed in the struggle for social justice. That is, the use of qualitative methods does not in any way ensure that the lives of marginalized groups will be improved. In keeping with this perspective, we argue for a dialectical approach, and we attempt to transcend the qualitative–quantitative debate that remains entrenched in the social sciences by focusing on the conditions for postpositivist research.

Phenomenology

In recent years, as qualitative methods have gained greater legitimacy in the social sciences, more researchers have turned to phenomenology to inform their work. One of the main reasons for this is that a phenomenological approach is an *empirically based* descriptive method. Thus, although it is an approach that does not utilize statistical analyses to generate data, its epistemological grounding remains congruent with the empirical premise of social science research. At the same time, however, the philosophy on which a phenomenological approach is based provides an important challenge to the generalizability of laboratory-based research, and it exposes the limits of hypothesis testing. Various research methods are based on the philosophy of phenomenology, for the philosophy provides general guidelines for the social scientist (rather than outlining exact steps that must be taken). We describe the ways in which the philosophy of phenomenology is consistent with a post-Newtonian approach.

Edmund Husserl is credited as the founder of phenomenology. Responding to what he believed to be the crisis in science in the early 1900s, he maintained that the proper subject matter for psychology was consciousness (i.e., experience) and that psychologists should study lived experience. Husserl was critical of both idealist and materialist approaches evidenced in the social sciences, and he was prescient in his critique of psychology; in the early 1900s he saw clearly that psychology, like all modern sciences, was losing its philosophical grounding (Husserl, 1970). The implications of this loss were profound because, without a proper philosophical grounding, the focus was shifting quickly from description to causality. Husserl (1970) argued for a return "to the things themselves," meaning that psychologists should use descriptive methods to try to capture the meaning of individuals' experience. He emphasized the need for social scientists to investigate the personal, the life-world (*Lebensvelt*), in order to capture the radically experiential nature of human phenomena. Criticizing psychology (and other social sciences) for its adherence to positivist methods, he challenged the subjective–objective distinction. Specifically, he believed that psychology was rooted in what he termed the "natural attitude." Psychologists commit the dangerous error of naturalizing consciousness, "treating consciousness [experience] as if it were a part of the physical world and obeys the physical laws of nature" (Jennings, 1986, p. 1233). Here we see how Husserl's critique of positivism predates, and is congruent with, postmodern, post-Newtonian critiques of the social sciences. Both Husserlian phenomenology and postmodern, post-Newtonian epistemologies challenge many of the dichotomies of the modern sciences (e.g., subjective–objective), and both emphasize the importance of contextualizing the phenomena under investigation.

Hence phenomenology's project includes not only a critique of positivism but also suggestions for the conduct of human science research. That is, a phenomenological approach is not antiscientific; it is an empirical approach that challenges the belief that "being scientific" necessitates that the researcher start with hypothesis testing and that he or she is thereby confined to the laboratory. For example, a psychologist should not relinquish the goals of science (e.g., empirical rigor), but rather she or he appropriates those goals in a way that is consonant with her or his subject matter (human experience). This means that the researcher should privilege description (i.e., lived experience) over the measurement and quantification of behavior (Giorgi, 1985). Mainstream social science research, insofar as it is wedded to a Newtonian paradigm, decontextualizes the phenomenon under investigation and, hoping to control for extraneous variables, artificially imposes certain constraints on the phenomenon. Within a Newtonian paradigm the focus is on measuring behavior, rather than exploring the meaning of an individual's experience. As a growing number of feminist psychologists (e.g., Fine, 1992; Hollway, 1989; Lather, 1991) have noted, relying epistemologically and methodologically on quantification and measurement to the exclusion of the life-world makes for a rather hollow science and tends to produce alienated rather than emancipatory knowledge.

However, this is not to say that quantification has no place within psychology or the social sciences more generally; quantitative methods have and certainly can generate meaningful data. Fischer (1986) sums this point up well: "[a phenomenological approach] is not opposed to laboratory based research or to statistical analyses, so long as these methods are regarded as ways of describing human comportment, and so long as research into lived worlds is also acknowledged as a valid and related access to human events" (p. 349).

Although there is no "one" phenomenological method, all social scientists whose work is informed by phenomenological philosophy try to systematically and rigorously articulate the lived meaning and structure of experience. They do so by invoking two main tenets of a phenomenological methodology: intentionality and the phenomenological reduction. Husserl's notion of intentionality was a key component to his philosophy. Intentionality refers to the idea that what is fundamental to humans is that we are sense-making beings who are inextricably tied to the world. The intentional relation, that consciousness is always consciousness of something (Husserl, 1970), challenges the subject–object dichotomy that is at the heart of positivist social science research (see also Garko, 1999; Giorgi, 2005). Thus how we perceive the world must be understood vis-à-vis both our personal histories and the sociopolitical context in which we live.

The *phenomenological reduction* is somewhat of a misnomer in that the researcher is not "reducing" anything but instead is actively engaged in the dialogical research relationship. The reduction is more accurately described as a comportment, a way of listening to the participant, an effortful attempt to be faithfully present to the phenomenon under investigation. In this sense it is a methodological stance that requires the researcher to "bracket," or put out of play, his or her ideological, theoretical, or personal preconceptions. It should be noted, however, that Husserl never meant to imply that the reduction necessitated (or that one could even achieve) total presuppositionlessness. Rather, we can think of the phenomenological reduction as a "procedure designed to return us to experience as it is experienced; it is a [methodological] posture from which we can capture lived experience" (Keene, 1975, p. 39).

Giorgi, whose work has been influential in the field of psychology, outlined four essential steps in conducting phenomenologically based research. Insofar as the phenomenological character of this qualitative method is descriptive:

1. "The original data consist of naïve descriptions, prompted by open-ended questions, of experiences . . . it should be noted that this emphasis on description does not necessarily rule out quantification (a form of description) but simply that there is no pressure to quantify unless the demand arises intrinsically from the situation" (Giorgi, 1985, p. 69).

After asking participants for a narrative description of the phenomenon (e.g., the lived experience of agoraphobia) and after bracketing his or her presuppositions:

2. The researcher adopts a psychological attitude and breaks the description down into manageable units. That a psychological attitude toward the description must be adopted "means that we operate within the assumption that psychological reality is not ready-made in the world and simply seen and dealt with but rather that it has to be constituted by the psychologist" (Giorgi, 1985, p. 11). At the same time, however, the delineation of what Giorgi has termed "psychological meaning units" requires the researcher to remain faithful to the participant's description of the data.

3. Once meaning units have been identified, the researcher generates themes that express the psychological insight contained in the meaning units. This step is sometimes referred to as delineating the situated structure of the phenomenon under investigation.

4. The researcher then has the task of trying to synthesize and transform the meaning units into "a coherent but more general description that captures the complexity and richness of the psychological structure of all of the participants' lived experiences" (Giorgi, 1985, p. 10). The researcher thus tries to "transform a *phenomenal description* of the meaning units into a *phenomenological understanding* of the meaning of the phenomenon" (Garko, 1999, p. 173, emphasis added).

It is important to note that the phenomenological method is just that, a method, not a technique, and thus is different from content analysis, which is typically defined as an "objective" quantitative description of the "manifest content" of an experience. Because a phenomenological approach is not static or mechanical, the researcher does not impose artificial limits on the data, such as quantifying the data or limiting the data to the manifest content (Giorgi, 1985). Unlike other qualitative approaches, such as theme or content analysis, a phenomenological approach is not characterized by an attempt to try to uncover underlying truths about participants' experiences. The phenomenologically oriented researcher refuses the role of "omniscient narrator and summarizer" (Flyvjberg, 2001) of individuals' experiences. Making use of the Husserlian concepts of intentionality and the phenomenological reduction and bracketing, the phenomenologist appreciates the fact that it is impossible to "uncover" or gain access to an individual's "true" and unmediated experience. In other words, this qualitative methodology is characterized by *both* a commitment to the articulation of individuals' lived experiences *and* a commitment to analyzing the sociopolitical context in which experience is always embedded. By privileging reflexivity, challenging dichotomous thinking, and appreciating the richness and complexity of lived experience, a phenomenological approach is consistent with a postmodern, post-Newtonian epistemology.

Discourse Analysis

Like phenomenology, discourse analysis is a method, not a static technique. The main goal is to investigate how meanings are produced within narrative accounts (e.g., in conversations, newspapers, or interviews). The label *discourse analysis* does not describe a formulaic method; rather, it describes a set of approaches that can be used when researchers work with texts. Researchers who use a discourse-analytic approach emphasize the constitutive function of language, and they address the ways in which power relations are reproduced in narrative accounts. As Gill (1995) noted, the focus is on "what discourse is used to do in particular interpretive contexts" (p. 176). Discourse analysis is indebted to Derrida's (e.g., 1976, 1982) work on deconstruction and Foucault's (1979, 1980) work on the normalizing, regulatory, and prescriptive tendencies within contemporary biological and social science disciplines. "Deconstructing" a narrative account means that the researcher attempts to make implicit assumptions explicit by demonstrating how the reader is often persuaded by the use of various rhetorical strategies. That is, the reader is positioned by sometimes subtle, but nonetheless hegemonic, "regimes of truth" (Foucault, 1979). The analysis is deconstructive in the sense that the researcher tries to identify both what truths are being produced and what alternative perspectives or discourses are being negated or marginalized (Burman & Parker, 1993; Burr, 1995, 2003; Wilkinson & Kitzinger, 1995).

From a social action perspective, discourse analysis holds great appeal because it takes an explicitly political approach to the research process. The following question guides the work of discourse analysts: Whose interests are served, and whose interests are marginalized, by discourses that gain hegemony and authority? The goal is not to identify some underlying psychological truth. Instead of trying to develop a master narrative or an ahistorical explanation about a particular phenomenon, the purpose of the research is to use the analysis to empower participants. Burr (1995) sums this point up well: "[I]t is not a search for truth but for any usefulness that a researcher's 'reading' of a phenomenon may have in bringing about change for those who need it" (p. 162). By paying attention to the sociopolitical context of discourse and attempting to show how people are positioned by (or resist) dominant discourses, the researcher is better able to identify *structural* rather than *individual* change strategies. For example, if a researcher was interested in studying eating disorders in women and she or he chose discourse analysis as a method for examining interview data, the analysis might be informed by questions such as: What are the dominant discourses about femininity and appearance and how are women positioned by [i.e., how do they take up or understand] these discourses? How do women resist dominant discourses about femininity and appearance?

The specific steps or procedures that researchers use to identify discourses vary, because, as noted previously, there is no "one" discourse-analytic method. Indeed, researchers from a variety of disciplines (e.g., sociology, psychology, political science) do discourse-analytic work. However, an increasing number of researchers are trying to be more systematic and rigorous in delineating their procedures. For example, Potter and Wetherell (1996) have identified 10 stages in discourse analysis: developing the research question, sample selection, collection of records and documents, interviewing, transcription, coding, analysis, validation, report write-up, and application (pp. 158–176). Although all of the steps that they outline are important and worthy of consideration, it is beyond the scope of this chapter to address all of them. The following is a description of the analysis itself.

Whereas the traditional psychologist who uses qualitative methods does so with the hope that he or she can gain access to the real meaning of participants' experiences, a researcher who utilizes a discourse-analytic framework sees this as an impossible project. In much the same way that a researcher influenced by phenomenology would not assume that she or he can uncover an experience that exists "prediscursively," or "inside" the participant, a discourse analyst would not assume that she or he could obtain unmediated access to experience. That is, it is impossible for a researcher to discover the real meaning of a phenomenon or experience (e.g., depression in women) *because meaning does not exist prior to and apart from representational systems*. The discourse analyst starts from the belief that because meaning is produced in complex and intricate ways, any account of experience will inevitably be located within a complex network of power relations. Rather than trying to identify the real meaning of a narrative account, the discourse analyst tries to identify "the repertory of concepts and categories, and the system of ideas . . . that create a narrative . . . and further [the analyst asks] what does this repertory achieve?" (Marecek & Kartvez, 1998, p. 20).

Another important difference between discourse analysis and other traditional narrative methods is that the analysis focuses on both the consistencies and inconsistencies contained in any narrative account. The reason that the researcher does not gloss the inconsistencies in a participant's description or in other narrative accounts (e.g., a public policy statement) is that the discourse analyst recognizes that there are always multiple and competing discourses about any phenomenon. Although people are positioned by discourses that have gained dominance and authority, there are always less hegemonic discourses to which they can appeal. Thus, addressing inconsistencies and contradictions in a narrative account also helps the researcher to identify possibilities for resistance. The epistemological commitment to partial, historical, and contextual psychological "truths," together with an appreciation for the fact that there are always competing discourses about any phenomenon, shifts the focus away from intraindividual explanations of psychological phenomenon. Instead of asking causal questions about the etiology of an experience, the researcher turns his or her attention to how individuals construct and interpret their experience in relation to contemporary discourses and practices. Perhaps a specific example will clarify this point.

Far more women than men are diagnosed with depression each year. In fact, the *Diagnostic and Statistical Manual of Mental Disorders* conservatively reports that depression is twice as common in females as in males (American Psychiatric Association, 2000). Although researchers working in the field of women's health disagree about the reasons for the prevalence of depression in women, the vast majority of research focuses on etiological questions. Researchers appeal to intraindividual factors, such as a dysregulation of biogenic amines, to explain why so many women are depressed. Accepting the terms of our biopsychiatric discourse and assuming that depression is a neurobiologically based disease validates women's experiences of depression, but there is cost associated with embracing the medical model: We risk colluding with a biological essentialism that pathologizes women's bodies. Rather than assuming that depression is best conceptualized as an ahistorical disease and thus focusing on causal questions (i.e., questions about the etiology of this disease), the discourse analyst might examine how contemporary biopsychiatric discourses *about* depression converge on women's lived experiences *of* depression. The researcher can simultaneously accept biologically based explanations of behavior and mood and appeal to more contextual variables to understand depression in women. In this way, using discourse analysis not only challenges positivist notions about causality but also encourages researchers to study women's experiences of "having depression" without assuming that depression is best understood as an ahistorical, acontextual disease. Specifically, the discourse analyst would be interested in women's lived experience of depression, and he or she would also be interested in how contemporary cultural discourses (e.g., direct-to-consumer advertisements for medications to treat depression) affect women's interpretation of their experiences.

Finally, it should also be noted that movement away from "truth finding" and toward the function of discourse allows the researcher to address how useful the analysis may be for her or his constituents; it fosters a participatory research approach. In place of the positivist–empiricist investment in discovering the true meaning of the narrative under investigation, there is a greater appreciation for context and the politics of meaning. Taking this epistemological and methodological perspective encourages psychologists to contribute to social policy debates by working with and for marginalized groups. This is a much-needed contribution; a growing number of psychologists have discussed the crisis in our field's ability to respond effectively to social justice efforts (Fine & Barreras, 2001; Frost & Ouellette, 2004). For example, psychologists might analyze participants' narrative data about a particular phenomenon (e.g., the lived experience of homelessness), as well as analyze policy and/or media accounts of that phenomenon (e.g., the federal policy on homelessness) in an effort to make specific public policy suggestions (Cosgrove & Flynn, 2005).

Satirical Empiricism as Postmodern Perspective

Elsewhere, we have addressed the question, Can the current methods and paradigms of psychology, and science more generally, be used as tools for the study of women and gender? (McHugh & Cosgrove, 2002, 2004). In this section we focus on some of the ways in which a postmodern framework is congruent with a social action research agenda. Specifically we ask, Can a postmodern social scientist who does not subscribe to the positivist belief in value-neutral science continue to use the scientific method? Realizing the importance of the sociopolitical context of research, and recognizing that research often supports the status quo and reifies conceptions of difference, we offer satirical empiricism as a method that challenges essentializing and universalizing tendencies that are often present in traditional quantitative research approaches.

There is a long-standing tradition of using the scientific method to challenge status quo beliefs about marginalized groups. For example, in the field of feminist psychology, Hubbard (1981) encouraged scientists to "fight with science's own tools, refuting illogical and self serving explanations, exposing unsubstantiated claims, disclaiming poorly conceived and inadequately controlled experiments" (p. 216). McHugh and her colleagues (McHugh, Koeske, & Frieze, 1986) similarly subscribed to feminist empiricism as a corrective to gender bias in scientific accounts of women and gender. However, some scholars have seriously questioned the emancipatory potential of empiricist research traditions that rely on comparisons of group means. MacKinnon (1990) has been a vocal critic of sex-difference research as a means of women's liberation: "Difference is the velvet glove on the iron fist of dominance. If a concept like difference is a conceptual tool of gender and of inequality, it cannot deconstruct the master's house, because it has built it" (p. 213). Similar questions may be asked about research on other social groups insofar as that research also emphasizes differences and uses comparative analyses to identify differences between groups. For example, to understand the experiences and impact of race, is it really necessary or appropriate to compare Asian Americans, African Americans, and Latinos with European Americans? Research that compares dominant and marginalized groups often incorporates implicit assumptions concerning class, ethnicity, gender, and sexual orientation. Indeed, research is less likely to be published when it challenges, rather than supports, our cultural constructions of gender or other social groups. Hence, there is a tendency in mainstream psychological research to endorse stereotypes and blame subordinated groups for their own oppression (Fine, 1992).

In contrast to traditional empiricist methods that support and reify differences, we propose using what Hubbard (1981) referred to as the "master's tools" to *deconstruct* cultural constructions of difference. That is, we propose the use of satirical empiricism as a tool for exposing the implicit assumptions that justify oppression based on class, sexual orientation, ethnicity and race, and other social groupings. Following Irigaray's (1985) suggestion that we transcend androcentrism through mimicry and laughter, we argue for the expansion of satirical empiricism to illuminate the operation of other forms of biases in traditional social science research. In keeping with the definition of satire as the use of irony in order to expose or denounce abuses or errors, satirical empiricism can expose existing research that is ethically and epistemologically problematic.

Before moving on, it should be noted that other authors have applied satire to assist our understanding of problematic cultural biases embedded in our theory. For example, Kaplan (1983) pointed out that masculine-biased assumptions about what behaviors are healthy are codified in diagnostic criteria and may account for higher treatment rates in women. Her satiric suggestion that psychiatric taxonomy include a new diagnostic category of "excessive male independence" exposed the sexist biases in psychiatric diagnosis. Similarly, Tavris (1992) argued that if we lived in a world in which psychologists used women as the basis of comparison, we might be reading articles and books addressing "problems" such as male overconfidence, unrealistic self-assessment, aggression, and isolation rather than women's inadequacies. Satirical empiricism may be used to extend satire because it is an empirical method that can generate actual data concerning human behavior. In so doing, it can be used to provide stronger evidence that our epistemic commitments influence what is considered normative and what is deemed aberrant.

Satirical empiricism is a postmodern exercise in that it brings to the foreground implicit ideologies or worldviews in the design and interpretation of social science research. It makes use of the empirical method, particularly the use of comparative tests of group means, in a manner that exposes folly through exaggeration, irony, or reversal. The exaggeration involved in satire parallels the exaggeration of gender, race, and class differences inherent in traditional psychological research and exposes, through reversal or extension, the hidden assumptions in existing research. Employing satirical empiricism allows researchers to demonstrate how behavior is determined (or elicited) by context and helps them "deconstruct" (i.e., reveal) implicit beliefs that ground social science research. Also, it is a method that is congruent with postpositivist science in that it does not deny the value-laden nature of all research questions and methods; it recognizes the problems caused by traditional psychological approaches that decontextualize the individual from his or her environment; and it recognizes the need for social change. Satirical empiricists would agree with critics of the experimental methods of psychological science who contend that "the laboratory is itself an ecological context with demand characteristics and experimenter influence, not a setting in which to discover context-free basic processes" (Tricket, 1996, p. 212). That is, placing the individual in a novel or unfamiliar setting elicits behaviors different from those in "natural settings" and encourages decontextualized explanations of behavior. Controlled and artificial research situations may elicit more conventional behavior from participants, may inhibit self-disclosure, and may make the situation "unreal" to the participants (McHugh et al., 1986).

Part of the impetus for the development of alternative models such as the ones described here came from the criticism that the scientific method puts the experimenter in the position of influencing, deceiving, manipulating, and/or interpreting "subjects," a criticism discussed in the feminist literature as well. Yet satirical empiricists might create such a laboratory context in order to demonstrate the fact that context matters and that an experimental setting is itself a context. For example, a researcher might develop a laboratory analogue of a standardized aptitude test in order to investigate how stereotypic threat might be elicited in European American males. Similarly, one might conduct research in which the expectations of control that are usually held by middle-class and affluent individuals are not rewarded nor viewed as positive aspects of mental health but instead are interpreted as nonadaptive. The attitudes and responses of poor and working-class individuals would be interpreted as superior in terms of adaptability and interpersonal interactions. It might take effort to construct such a context, but scientists often try several versions of the task before they find a paradigm that produces the results they want.

It is not only in the construction (or the selection) of the context that researchers determine their results but also in the selection of the sample. An example explored by McHugh and Cosgrove (2004) involves the sample bias observed in research on gender differences in math. For example, Kimball (1995) points out that male math superiority is generally not found in more representative samples. In more racially and ethnically diverse samples and samples with more heterogeneity in terms of academic performance, there are far fewer gender differences than there are when the sample involves groups of white, middle-class, precocious adolescents tested on standardized tests (Caplan & Caplan, 1994). Favreau (1993) reported that only a few boys (outliers) account for gender differences in rough-and-tumble play; all girls and most boys engage in low to medium levels of aggressive play. A satirical empiricist approach might be to use the groups of white, middle-class, precocious teens from the math studies as a sample to examine gender differences in aggressive play and to study delinquent youths to examine gender differences in superior math ability. Another example of satirical empiricism would be to conduct research on work values or achievement orientation using a sample of immigrant, Latina, lesbian, and/or elderly individuals. Objecting to such samples as not being representative of the general population exposes the problems with samples used in traditional psychological research. Researchers frequently draw conclusions from samples of young European American college students (whose sexual orientations are not specified). Discomfort with drawing universal conclusions based on data collected from Latinas suggests there is something gendered or racial about the context or the constructs under study. Such research exposes the universalizing tendencies masked by cultural belief systems when the research "subjects" are predominantly white and male. In a similar vein, satirical empiricism could be used to uncover the powerful ways in which "ideologies of normative motherhood" (Connolly, 2000) function in psychological and sociological research on parenting. Specifically, this method could be used to explore the difficulties or pathologies experienced by children raised by stay-at-home middle-class mothers without any comparison groups or in comparison with children adopted by professional, affluent lesbians or gay men. This line of research would satirize our current approach, which pathologizes children of working and single mothers and legitimizes stay-at-home moms and heterosexual couples as parents. As these examples demonstrate, satirical empiricism could be used to deconstruct the androcentric, classist, and other assumptions that result in the privileging of certain comparison groups over others.

Satirical empiricism serves postmodern purposes in that irony not only produces laughter but also dissuades us from premature closure and helps us see the partialness of any "truth." Ferguson (1991) talks about irony as "a way to keep oneself within a situation that resists resolution in order to act politically without pretending that resolution has come" (p. 338). Taking her suggestion seriously increases the likelihood that we will resist the legitimization of a single perspective. Indeed, adopting an ironic approach can lead to a richer and more complex picture of the phenomenon under investigation and necessitates a re-visioning of the epistemological and methodological frameworks that underlie social action research and theory. Irony and satire have long been used as instruments of social change, serving political purposes by "problematizing through farce" (Ferguson, 1991, p. 338). Satirical empiricism is such a form of irony, problematizing standard empirical methods by exposing the assumptions and biases inherent in traditional psychology.

Conclusion

> Questioning makes one open, makes one sensitive, makes one humble. We don't suffer from our questions, we suffer from our answers. Most of the mischief in the world comes from people with answers, not from people with questions.
>
> —NEEDLEMAN (1990, p. 166)

The epistemological assumptions of traditional research paradigms may undermine our ability to develop a liberatory or social action research agenda. Although there have been numerous contributions made in the social sciences, for too long now scientists have been hampered by their investment in a Newtonian paradigm. In this chapter we have grappled with the question of what it means to try to address power dynamics and implicit biases at every stage in the research process. Taking the perspective that all research is "political"—at every stage in the research process we are endorsing certain values, worldviews, and beliefs and marginalizing others—we have outlined three empirical methods that embrace the sociopolitical grounding of experience. In much the same way that we do not believe that postmodernism is the answer, we do not believe that phenomenology, discourse analysis, and satirical empiricism are the only viable methods for scientists engaged in the struggle for social justice. Rather, our interest in a postmodern epistemology stems from the belief that it is time for a much-needed paradigm shift in the sciences. Our hope is that the three methods outlined in this chapter will encourage us to question the implicit assumptions that ground our work. Doing so will help us engage in the conduct of research with more humility.

References

American Psychiatric Association. (2000). *Diagnostic and statistical manual of mental disorders* (4th ed., text rev.). Washington, DC: Author.

Burman, E., & Parker, I. (Eds.). (1993). *Discourse analytic research: Repertoires and readings of texts in action*. New York: Routledge.

Burr, V. (1995). *An introduction to social constructionism*. New York: Routledge.

Burr, V. (2003). *Social constructionism* (2nd ed.). New York: Routledge.

Caplan, P., & Caplan, J. (1994). *Thinking critically about research on sex and gender*. New York: HarperCollins.

Connolly, D. (2000). *Homeless mothers: Face to face with women and poverty*. Minneapolis: University of Minnesota Press.

Cosgrove, L. (2004). What is postmodernism and how is it relevant to engaged pedagogy? *Teaching of Psychology, 31*, 171–177.

Cosgrove, L., & Flynn, C. (2005). Marginalized mothers: Parenting without a home. *Analysis of Social Issues and Public Policy, 5*, 127–143.

Derrida, J. (1976). *Of grammatology*. Baltimore: John Hopkins University Press.

Derrida, J. (1982). *Margins of philosophy* (A. Bass, Trans.). Chicago: University of Chicago Press.

Favreau, O. E. (1993). Do the *n*s justify the means? *Canadian Psychologist, 34*, 64–78.

Ferguson, K. E. (1991). Interpretation and genealogy in feminism. *Signs: Journal of Women in Culture and Society, 16*(21), 322–339.

Fine, F., & Barreras, R. (2001). To be of use. *Analysis of Social Issues and Public Policy, 1*.

Fine, M. (1992). *Disruptive voices: The possibilities of feminist research*. Ann Arbor: University of Michigan Press.

Fischer, W. (1986). On the phenomenological approach to psychopathology. *Journal of Phenomenological Psychology, 17*, 65–76.

Flyvbjerg, B. (2001). *Making social science matter: Why social inquiry fails and how it can count again*. New York: Cambridge University Press.

Foucault, M. (1979). *Discipline and punish: The birth of the prison* (A. Sheridan, Trans.). New York: Pantheon Books.

Foucault, M. (1980). *The history of sexuality* (Vol. 1, R. Hurley, Trans.). New York: Pantheon Books.

Frost, D. M., & Ouellette, S. C. (2004). Meaningful voices: How psychologists, as psychologists, can inform public policy. *Analysis of Social Issues and Public Policy, 4*, 219–226.

Garko, M. (1999). Existential phenomenology and feminist research. *Psychology of Women Quarterly, 23*, 167–175.

Gergen, K. J. (2001). Psychological science in a postmodern world. *American Psychologist, 56*, 803–813.

Gill, R. (1995). Relativism, reflexivity, and politics: Interrogating discourse analysis from a feminist perspective. In S. Wilkinson & C. Kitzinger (Eds.), *Feminism and discourse: Psychological perspectives* (pp. 165–186). Thousand Oaks, CA: Sage.

Giorgi, A. (1985). *Phenomenological and psychological research*. Pittsburgh, PA: Duquesne University Press.

Giorgi, A. (2005). Remaining challenges for humanistic psychology. *Journal of Humanistic Psychology, 45*, 204–216.

Hollway, W. (1989). *Subjectivity and method in psychology: Gender, meaning and science*. Thousand Oaks, CA: Sage.

Hubbard, R. (1981). The emperor doesn't wear any clothes: The impact of feminism on biology. In D. Spender (Ed.), *Men's studies modified: The impact of feminism on academic disciplines* (pp. 214–245). Oxford, UK: Pergamon Press.

Husserl, E. (1970). *The crisis of European sciences and transcendental phenomenology* (D. Carr, Trans.). Evanston, IL: Northwestern University Press.

Irigaray, L. (1985, Fall). Is the subject of science sexes? (E. Oberle, Trans). *Cultural Critique*, 73–88.

Jennings, J. (1986). Husserl revisited: The forgotten distinction between psychology and phenomenology. *American Psychologist, 41*, 1231–1240.

Kaplan, M. (1983). A woman's view of the DSM-III. *American Psychologist, 38*, 786–792.

Keene, E. (1975). *A primer in phenomenological psychology*. Washington, DC: University Press of America.

Kimball, M. M. (1995). *Feminist visions of gender similarities and differences*. New York: Harrington Press.

Landrine, H. (Ed.). (1995). *Bringing cultural diversity to feminist psychology: Theory, research, and practice*. Washington, DC: American Psychological Association.

Lather, P. (1991). *Getting smart: Feminist research and pedagogy within the postmodern*. New York: Routledge.

Latour, B. (1999). *Pandora's hope: Essays on the reality of science studies*. Cambridge, MA: Harvard University Press.

Lowe, R. (1991). Postmodern themes and therapeutic practices: Notes toward the definition of "family therapy": Part 2. *Dulwich Centre Newsletter, 3*, 41–52.

MacKinnon, C. A. (1990). Legal perspectives on sexual difference. In D. H. Rhodes (Ed.), *Theoretical perspectives on sexual difference* (pp. 213–225). New Haven, CT: Yale University Press.

Marecek, J., & Karvetz, D. (1998). Putting politics into practice: Feminist therapy as feminist praxis. *Women and Therapy, 21*, 17–36.

McHugh, M. C., & Cosgrove, L. (2002). Gendered subjects in psychology: Dialectic and satirical positions. In L. Collins, M. Dunlap, & J. Chrisler (Eds.), *Charting a new course: Directions in the psychology of women* (pp. 3–19). Westport, CT: Greenwood Press.

McHugh, M. C., & Cosgrove, L. (2004). Feminist research methods: Studying women and gender. In M. Paludi (Ed.), *The Praeger guide to the psychology of gender* (pp. 155–182). New York: Praeger.

McHugh, M. C., Koeske, R., & Frieze, I. (1986). Issues to consider in conducting nonsexist psychological research: A guide for researchers. *American Psychologist, 41*, 879–890.

Moghaddam, F. M., & Studer, C. (1997). Cross-cultural psychology: The frustrated gadfly's promises, potentialities, and failures. In D. Fox & I. Prilleltensky (Eds.), *Critical psychology: An introduction* (pp. 185–201). Thousand Oaks, CA: Sage.

Needleman, J. (1990). In B. Moyers (Ed.), *A world of ideas* (Vol. 2, pp. 158–166). New York: Doubleday.

Potter, J., & Wetherell, M. (1996). *Discourse and psychology: Beyond attitudes and behavior*. Thousand Oaks, CA: Sage.

Prilleltensky, I., & Nelson, G. (2002). *Doing psychology critically: Making a difference in diverse settings*. New York: Palgrave Macmillan.

Tavris, C. (1992). *The mismeasure of women*. New York: Simon & Schuster.

Tricket, E. J. (1996). A future for community psychology: The contexts of diversity and the diversity of contexts. *American Journal of Community Psychology, 24*, 209–229.

Wilkinson, S., & Kitzinger, C. (Eds.). (1995). *Feminism and discourse: Psychological perspectives*. Thousand Oaks, CA: Sage.

CHAPTER 4

Emergence in and from Quasi-Experimental Design and Analysis

Melvin M. Mark

Quasi-experiments are not the first thing that comes to mind when one thinks of emergent methods. The idea of emergence probably calls to mind more qualitative methods, especially those that allow ongoing modification of the research question, the focus of data collection, and interpretation as the inquiry progresses. In contrast, quasi-experiments, like other methods associated with a more quantitative, postpositivist tradition (Cook, 1985), are typically seen as fixed rather than emergent. With a quasi-experiment, or a randomized experiment for that matter, the research question and the data collection focus are typically thought to be (and, indeed, often are) determined in advance, with no modifications allowed midstream. Moreover, in quasi-experimental and experimental designs, interpretation is usually thought to be a final step that takes place after data collection is over, so that no opportunity would exist for ongoing interpretation to stimulate changes in data collection or hypothesis.

This chapter explores various ways in which emergence can and, at least sometimes, does arise in the context of quasi-experimental designs. Some relatively common forms of emergence—or, at least, "quasi-emergence"—in quasi-experiments are presented. Other forms of emergence, specifically an approach called principled discovery, are described here that are less common but that arguably deserve to be used more often. Before detailing alternative forms of emergence in quasi-experiments, however, I discuss the nature of and rationale for quasi-experiments, starting with a brief overview of randomized experiments. Randomized experiments provide a springboard to the topic of quasi-experiments. Moreover, many of the points made in this chapter about emergence also apply to experiments.

Experiments and Quasi-Experiments: Assessing the Effects of a Given Cause

Researchers, whether more basic or more applied in orientation, are often interested in assessing whether, and to what extent, one thing (which we can label a treatment, or intervention, or independent variable) makes a difference in another (which we can label an outcome, or effect, or a dependent variable). An evaluator specializing in early childhood education, for example, might do a study to see whether a new statewide, universal preschool program increases children's school readiness, their subsequent academic performance, and various other outcomes. Personnel specialists oftentimes estimate the effect of a training program on employees' performance to determine whether a program's benefits justify the investment. Medical researchers seek to identify the consequences of various drugs, surgical procedures, and other interventions. Legal and other scholars may study the effect of a change in a law or policy, such as seat belt or helmet laws, welfare reform, or over-the-counter sales of Plan B contraceptives, on one or more relevant outcomes (respectively, e.g., traffic fatalities, family income, or abortion rates). In many scholarly areas, much of theory testing involves assessing whether one variable causes a difference in another. For example, a social psychologist might test whether one form of a theoretically relevant persuasive message causes more attitude change than another. A neurochemist may administer an agent that blocks the uptake of a certain neurotransmitter to test its role in a biological process. To test a theory of movement, a kinesiologist might manipulate the starting and stopping positions that research participants are asked to adopt.

However, not all important questions involve assessing the effect of an intervention, broadly defined, on specified outcomes. Some questions are not causal in nature. One researcher may set out to describe the scope or intensity of a phenomenon, for instance, estimating the number of homeless mentally ill. Another researcher might be interested in understanding the lived experience of some group, say, individuals receiving a diagnosis of HIV. If the relevant research question is not causal in nature, then quasi-experiments are not a good choice. In addition, in some instances researchers are focused not on estimating the effects of a given cause but on identifying the cause of an observed effect. For instance, epidemiologists may strive to identify the cause of an outbreak of severe food poisoning (the effect). Even though the question involves causal inference, a quasi-experiment (at least as traditionally described) is not likely to be the method of choice. Again, quasi-experiments, like the randomized experiments they mimic, are best suited for estimating the effects of a given intervention. As the preceding questions and many other possible examples attest, however, this kind of question is very often precisely the research question of interest.

The Randomized Experiment

Randomized experiments are often referred to, though sometimes with controversy (e.g., Fletcher, 2004; Lederman & Flick, 2004), as the "gold standard" of causal methods (e.g., Institute for Education Sciences [IES], 2003). The real but implicit claim, I suggest, is that randomized experiments are the gold standard for estimating the effects of a given intervention (or treatment) on specified outcome variables. The implicit claim further seems to be that randomized experiments are the best method for estimating treatment effects in certain circumstances. Specifically, randomized experiments are most likely to be valuable, relative to other procedures for causal inference, when the outcome variable is influenced by several causal forces, when change over time is commonplace, and when there is interest in detecting effects that are modest in size relative to the changes in the outcome variable that are likely to occur given the causal background (Mark, in press). In the language of Donald Campbell and his associates (e.g., Cook & Campbell, 1979), randomized experiments are especially valuable when they control for alternative explanations that would otherwise be plausible. A randomized experiment may not be needed, or even sensible, in other circumstances. For example, even those who call the randomized experiment the gold standard show, in their everyday activities, the ability to make confident causal inferences without an experiment, as when they try replacing the batteries in their remote control to see if the remote now works. On the other hand, randomized experiments may be quite beneficial in other circumstances, such as in testing the effect of a new treatment for generalized anxiety disorder (GAD) relative to the existing therapy. Individual differences exist in the intensity of anxiety disorders, even among those who go to a therapist with the problem. Change can occur over time apart from any treatment effect: Some patients may show spontaneous recovery; others may worsen over time. Forces other than formal treatment can affect GAD, including changes in life circumstances. And we may not be satisfied with seeing only huge and dramatic treatment effects; it may be important to know about moderate and perhaps even small treatment effects. Unlike the remote control example, it will be harder in the case of a GAD therapy to be sure that any improvement in a patient's anxiety was the result of the treatment he or she received–as will be true for many, if not most, psychological, social, and educational interventions.

But what is a randomized experiment? In a randomized experiment, individuals (or other units) are randomly assigned to treatment conditions. That is, a flip of the coin, a table of random numbers, a computerized randomization program, or the like is used to decide, for example, whether each participant receives the new GAD treatment or the current best treatment. And why is the randomized experiment held by many as a gold standard, at least for the circumstances just described? Advocates of experiments point out that without random assignment, "selection differences" are likely to occur. This means that, even without the intervention making a difference, the individuals in the treatment group would probably differ initially from those in a comparison group on average. For example, the GAD sufferers who show up to try a new treatment would probably differ on average in several ways from those who elect (or are advised by their physicians) to receive the current standard treatment or from those who don't receive treatment at all. Random assignment facilitates causal inference primarily because it precludes any systematic bias due to initial selection differences.[1] Random assignment thus creates a fair comparison between the different conditions being examined, such as a new GAD treatment versus the standard GAD therapy (Boruch, 1997). Using the language of many methodologists and scholars of causal inference, because there is no systematic selection bias in a randomized experiment, the comparison group provides a strong estimate of the "counterfactual." For instance, the average outcome of the standard GAD treatment group will provide a strong estimate of how the patients in the novel-treatment group would have done on average *if* they had instead received the standard therapy. This contrasts with most cases in which participants self-select into treatment, are assigned by others (e.g., agency staff), or fall into a condition based on geography. In these and other circumstances without random assignment, systematic selection differences are likely.

Nevertheless, the randomized experiment has been soundly criticized on a variety of grounds (e.g., Fletcher, 2004; Lederman & Flick, 2003; Pawson & Tilley, 1997). Even respected advocates of randomized experiments note their limits and acknowledge the challenges in successfully implementing experiments outside of carefully controlled laboratory settings (for details on various problems and potential solutions, see Boruch, 1997; Cook & Campbell, 1979; Shadish, Cook, & Campbell, 2002). Of greatest interest here is that, even in circumstances in which a randomized experiment would in theory be an outstanding method for estimating the effects of an intervention, random assignment may not be feasible for practical or ethical reasons. Random assignment is not possible when a treatment is applied uniformly across some geographical area, for example (though a growing number of experiments randomly assign communities to condition; see Boruch, 2005). Random assignment will often be difficult to arrange when the researcher is not also the developer of the intervention being tested. Random assignment may be inconsistent with the rules or regulations that guide eligibility for some social or educational programs. In certain circumstances, random assignment may be (or may be perceived as being) ethically inappropriate. Such realities lead researchers to consider quasi-experiments.

Quasi-Experiments

When causal questions, specifically the desire to estimate the effects of an intervention, are central but random assignment is infeasible, researchers often resort to quasi-experiments. *Quasi* is the Latin term for "as if." Roughly, *quasi* means "like" or "an approximation." The term *quasi-experiment* thus refers to approximations of experiments, to "near experiments" that have several but not all of the characteristics of full-scale controlled experiments. Most important, quasi-experiments lack random assignment to conditions, but they include comparisons between different levels of a treatment variable. Contemporary knowledge about quasi-experiments derives primarily from the work of Campbell (1957, 1969) and his associates (Campbell & Stanley, 1966; Cook & Campbell, 1979; Shadish et al., 2002), which can be consulted for further information. As detailed in those works, there are several different quasi-experimental designs, which range in complexity and in how much confidence they generally provide about a treatment's effects.

One relatively simple quasi-experiment, which often can be implemented but almost as often will be inadequate, is the *one-group pretest–posttest design*. Imagine as an example that a new GAD treatment was evaluated by measuring clients' anxiety levels before therapy and then again after it. The problem with this simple design, of course, is that anxiety levels could change over time for a variety of reasons other than the treatment. These other sources of change could either masquerade as a treatment effect or mask a treatment effect that really exists. Several generic, alternative mechanisms exist that can lead to changes over time in anxiety and, more generally, in the kind of outcomes measured by researchers interested in human behavior. Following Campbell, these forces are called *internal validity threats*. For the moment, one example should suffice. Clients with certain psychological disorders typically appear for therapy when things are at their worst. Absent any treatment effect, clients often show some improvement. In the therapy literature, this possibility is called *spontaneous recovery*. In the methodological literature, it would be labeled as an instance of statistical regression (Campbell & Kenny, 1999). Regardless of what it is called, this pattern could make a treatment look beneficial when studied with the simple pretest–posttest design, even if the therapy really causes no improvement. This and other internal validity threats are discussed in more detail in a subsequent section.

A more complex design that can sometimes be implemented is the *interrupted time-series (ITS) design*. ITS designs use "time-series data," that is, repeated measurement of a quantitative outcome variable at (approximately) equally spaced intervals, such as days, months, quarters, or years, to estimate the effect of a treatment. In a *simple interrupted time-series design*, a series of pretest observations is collected, a treatment is introduced, and the series of (posttest) observations continues. For instance, GAD patients might report their anxiety on a monthly basis, so that the effect of a GAD treatment could be assessed using the ITS design. In essence, one uses the trend in the pretreatment observations, projecting it forward in time, to estimate what would have happened in the absence of a treatment effect. Is there, for example, an observable decline in reported anxiety relative to the pretreatment trend following implementation of the treatment? Unlike most other quasi-experimental designs, ITS designs allow an evaluator to observe the temporal pattern of the effect. This can be important. For example, the value of a GAD therapy might be judged differently if its effects die out after 3 or 6 months rather than persisting over a longer period. Even more important, the simple ITS design, with its series of pretest and posttest observations, can help strengthen causal inference. For instance, when viewed in a time series, statistical regression would typically show up as a visible worsening in the time periods before clients appear for treatment, followed by a return to precrisis levels. Such a pattern can be seen in an interrupted time-series design but would not be visible with only the two observations in the pretest–posttest design.

Both the simple one-group pretest–posttest and the simple interrupted time-series designs use comparisons of the same individuals (or aggregate units, such as communities) *across time* to gauge what the outcome would have been in the absence of the treatment. Alternatively, in other designs researchers compare *across groups* of different individuals (or aggregate units) at the same point(s) in time. When assignment to the different conditions is not random, designs of this sort are known as nonequivalent-groups designs. In nonequivalent-groups quasi-experiments, individuals self-select into different groups (e.g., individuals may choose to participate in a new GAD therapy or not); or they are assigned in some nonrandom fashion into the groups by others, such as program administrators (e.g., clinic intake staff may exercise their discretion in assigning some clients to a new therapy); or group assignment is determined by one's location (e.g., the new GAD therapy is implemented in one community's clinic but not another one); or some other nonrandom assignment process operates.

The simplest between-group design is the *posttest-only nonequivalent-groups design*. In this design, individuals (or other aggregate units such as schools or communities) fall into the treatment group, which receives the program, or into the control or comparison group, which does not receive the program (or receives some alternative program). Following the treatment, the members of both groups are measured on one or more outcome variables of interest. For instance, the posttreatment outcomes of those who sign up for a new GAD treatment might be compared with outcomes of others who do not sign up for the new therapy. The fundamental shortcoming of this design is the previously described validity threat of "selection." Put simply, the treatment group and the control (or comparison) group may differ initially on the outcome variable and/or on other relevant factors, and these initial differences may well obscure the actual effect of the program. Selection differences are typically quite plausible in circumstances in which the posttest-only nonequivalent-groups design would be implemented.

Accordingly, nonequivalent groups are often observed on a pretest (and, increasingly, on other preintervention measures), as well as a posttest. This results in what is called the *pretest–posttest nonequivalent-groups design*. The basic idea is to use the size of the pretest difference between groups to control for initial selection differences. One approach is to use "gain scores" to compare the two groups in the *amount of change*, on the average, between the pretest and posttest. Sometimes this will work reasonably well. At other times, the pretest does not do a good job capturing the relevant selection differences.

For example, if you were evaluating a program designed to prevent drug use, and if the pretest were given at an age before drug use usually begins, then a pretest measure of drug use will not capture very well the relevant selection differences between groups. Various measures of "risk" would do a better job. In practice, the challenge is in knowing whether the right pretreatment factors have been measured and included appropriately in the statistical analysis.[2]

The *regression-discontinuity design* is a special kind of nonequivalent-groups design. It requires a very different method of assignment to groups, quite unlike the self-selection or administrative discretion that creates groups in the typical nonequivalent-groups design. The regression–discontinuity design requires that, before the treatment is implemented, participants be measured on a special form of pretest sometimes called the *quantitative assignment variable*, or QAV (Reichardt & Mark, 1998). The design further requires that QAV scores, and QAV scores alone, be used to assign participants to conditions, according to a specified cutoff score on the QAV. That is, individuals whose QAV scores are above the cutoff value are assigned to one condition, whereas those whose QAV scores are below the cutoff are assigned to the other condition. Participants are subsequently measured on the outcome variable, and the treatment effect is estimated as a discontinuity in the QAV-outcome relationship at the cutoff. As an example, ethical concerns might lead us to measure anxiety in a group of patients and to provide the new (and, we hope, highly effective) GAD treatment to those patients who have the highest anxiety scores (and thus are thought to be in greatest need).

If the intervention had no effect on the subsequent posttest measure, the regression line for the treatment group and that for the comparison group should connect as one straight line, as shown in the solid lines (and ellipse) in Figure 4.1. In contrast, as implied by the design's name, a nonzero treatment effect will show up as a discontinuity between the two regression lines (assume that the effect is represented by the left-hand side and the dashed portion of the right-

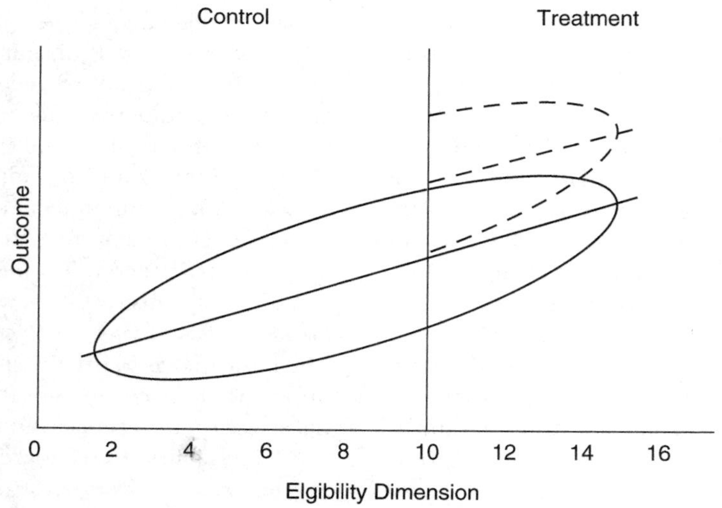

FIGURE 4.1. Hypothetical results from regression-discontinuity design, with (dotted line) and without (solid line) a treatment effect.

hand side in Figure 4.1). The graphical representation of regression-discontinuity findings, illustrated in Figure 4.1, highlights the source of the design's inferential strength. In general, it is implausible that any threat to validity, whether selection or statistical regression or another threat, would produce a discontinuity precisely at the cutoff between the treatment conditions.[3] Put informally, the question is: How likely is it that there would be a jump in scores on the outcome variable that coincides precisely with the cutoff on the eligibility criterion, unless there really is a treatment effect? Stated differently, unless the treatment really makes a difference, why would there be such a relatively big difference on the outcome variable between those individuals whose QAV scores are just below the eligibility criterion and those whose QAV scores are just above the cutoff?

The regression-discontinuity design is among the strongest quasi-experimental designs. At its best, the design comes close to the randomized experiment in terms of allowing confident causal inferences. Moreover, the design can be feasible in circumstances in which practical or ethical considerations rule out random assignment. In particular, random assignment may be unacceptable for treatments designed for those most in need (e.g., compensatory education programs) or most meritorious (e.g., promotions). In practice, however, until recently the regression-discontinuity design has rarely been used (Shadish et al., 2002; Trochim, 1984). Still, as noted in a following section, the opportunistic quasi-experimentalist may be on the lookout for those special circumstances that fit the requirements of the regression-discontinuity design.

There are a number of other quasi-experimental design options (see Shadish et al., 2002, for a comprehensive description). The preceding discussion should, however, suffice to lay the groundwork for a discussion of emergence in quasi-experimental research.

Emergence in Quasi-Experiments

Emergence can arise several ways in quasi-experiments. These are organized here into five categories: the application of the logic of validity threats and the selection of quasi-experimental design options; opportunism in quasi-experimental design; traditional emergent analysis options; sequential or iterative designs; and principled discovery as a data analysis strategy.

Validity Threats and the Selection of Design Options

Texts on quasi-experimental designs may seem to suggest that the researcher consults a menu of design options and then selects the strongest design that is possible to use in the upcoming study. In fact, in practice there can be an iterative and emergent characteristic to the creation of an experimental design. This iteration may take place early, as the researcher thinks through the plausibility of various internal validity threats and their implications for design.

For instance, imagine a researcher setting out to study the effects of a dorm-based training session intended to reduce college students' binge drinking. For the sake of economy, the researcher may consider using a simple one-group pretest–posttest design. Before the study begins, the researcher should think about how plausible a variety of validity threats are likely to be in the study. *History*, for instance, is a threat when some event other than the treatment also occurs between the pretest and posttest and could cause change in the outcome variable. In the case of the binge-drinking program, history would be a threat, for example, if the local police were to begin a well-publicized campaign against underage drinking. Alternatively, students' binge drinking might change simply because they are older at the posttest than they were at the pretest. This internal validity threat is called *maturation*. If history, maturation, statistical regression, or other internal validity threats seem likely to occur, the researcher is unlikely to be satisfied with a one-group pretest–posttest design (for further description of these and other threats, see Cook & Campbell, 1979; Shadish et al., 2002). Instead, the researcher might see the need for a nonequivalent-groups pretest–posstest design, comparing change in binge drinking in dorms that receive the program versus those that do not. Moreover, the researcher should consider which validity threats would be plausible for *this* design. In this sense, quasi-experimental design can be partly emergent, falling out of a process of assessing in advance the likelihood of various validity threats *in the specific context of the planned investigation.*

In this regard, it is important to realize that the fact that a validity threat can *generally* apply to a specific quasi-experimental design does not mean that it will operate in a *particular study* using that design. As an example, Eckert (2000) argued that the threats that, in principle, apply to the one-group pretest–posttest design often will not be plausible in evaluations of training programs (at least in terms of certain key outcome variables). For instance, he contends that maturation will not be a plausible explanation for sizable improvements in immediate posttests in most training evaluations because knowledge and skills generally would not rise markedly by maturation in such a short time. Thus, Eckert argues, training programs can often be studied with the easy-to-implement and relatively cheap one-group pretest–posttest design. As this example illustrates, the choice of a quasi-experimental design can emerge from conceptual analyses and thought experiments prior to the study (and perhaps from review of previous evidence, say, of relevant maturational patterns).

The iterative and emergent nature of selecting one's design is not always a priori, however. In some cases, potential validity threats are observed as a study proceeds, and additions to the quasi-experimental design are then made after the fact. Alternatively, a reviewer or critic of a study may suggest after the fact that a validity threat is plausible, and the researcher may then attempt to assess or rule out that threat. For example, the threat of history can be plausible in a one-group interrupted time-series design. If the initial design did not include features that help rule out history as a validity threat, the researcher may attempt to add such features post hoc, if events or critics raise the specter of history. For example, if a reviewer or other critic suggests a history threat, the researcher might seek time-series data for a control group that was not exposed to the treatment but that should have experienced similar historical forces. The researcher might instead stratify members of the treatment group into those who received more and those who received less exposure to the treatment. The assumption is that those who receive more of the treatment should (usually) show bigger effects if there is a real treatment effect but that history should (usually) not result in such a pattern of differential effects. A nonequivalent dependent variable might also be sought. This is another time-series variable that should be affected by the validity threat but not by the treatment. Alternatively, the researcher might use various techniques to see whether any historical event actually occurred that plausibly could have affected the outcome variable. Shadish and colleagues (2002) provide more detail on the threats that apply to the simple ITS design and on more complex ITS designs. Ross (1973) provides an early example of using a variety of efforts and additions after the initial time-series investigation.

In short, although quasi-experimental design is typically thought of as fixed, in practice there is at least sometimes a more iterative, emergent process of design and interpretation. The prototypical pattern seems to be that the researcher (1) tries to anticipate the plausibility of validity threats before the study and (2) then selects a quasi-experimental design in light of that exercise, considering various constraints and tradeoffs. However, (3) additional validity threats may emerge from observation or other evidence during the study, or subsequently from a critic, with either case entailing greater uncertainty about initially intended interpretation (i.e., that the study reasonably estimates the treatment effect). If an alternative interpretation emerges, (4) the researcher is likely to attempt to elaborate on the original design in response to the threat that has been raised. Then, (5) the process may reiterate, cycling back to an earlier step.

Opportunism in Quasi-Experimental Design

Traditional conventions for reporting quasi-experimental (and other quantitative) studies generally result in a relatively linear and rational narrative. In particular, the write-ups in most journals (or other reports) typically begin with an introduction that lays out the study's research area as completely preordained, independent of and conceptually preceding the methods. Later in the introduction, the specific research question or hypothesis usually is presented as an almost inevitable consequence of past theory and research, leavened by the skilled reasoning of the investigator. It is not a state secret, however, that the real, behind-the-scenes story of the development of the official narrative is rarely as linear and rational as the formal write-up suggests. This state of affairs is true for quasi-experimental investigations at least as much as for other types of studies, and perhaps more. The preordained top-down picture of the usual report may understate the emergence that led to the investigation. In part, this occurs because the appropriately opportunistic quasi-experimentalist is vigilant in looking for circumstances in which he or she can implement quasi-experimental designs that offer relatively strong causal inference for a substantive question of interest.

As an example, Mark and Mellor (1991) published the first study to show an important limitation on the hindsight bias. By way of background, the hindsight bias refers to the tendency of people, once the outcome of an event is known, to overestimate how predictable that outcome was in foresight. For example, after an election people claim they foresaw the outcome more accurately than they actually did before the election. Prior to the Mark and Mellor study, the hindsight bias had been demonstrated in a wide range of circumstances and identified by some scholars as among the most robust cognitive biases (Christensen-Szalanski & Willham, 1991; Hawkins & Hastie, 1990). In contrast, Mark and Mellor (1991) suggested that self-serving biases should reduce or eliminate the hindsight bias under certain conditions. In particular, when people directly experience a negative outcome for which they feel responsible (or feel responsible for not preparing for), they should not claim that the outcome was foreseeable. Indeed, if the negative outcome had been so foreseeable, presumably the person would have tried to avoid it, or at least prepare for it.

Mark and Mellor (1991) used the regression-discontinuity design to examine whether hindsight bias is reduced among people who experience a severely negative and self-relevant event. They measured union members from a company that had laid off a large number of workers. Whether a worker was laid off or not depended on the number of years he or she had been with the company. In other words, seniority served as the QAV. Employees below the seniority cutoff (19 years) were laid off, and those above the cutoff were not laid off, falling into what Mark and Mellor called the "survivor group." Six weeks after the layoff, both laid-off workers and survivors were surveyed and asked how predictable they thought the layoff was in advance. Results showed a dramatic discontinuity in hindsight bias exactly at the cutoff. The laid-off workers reported considerably less foreseeability than one would otherwise have expected. Perhaps the hindsight bias is not so robust after all (as subsequent experiments have confirmed; see Louie, 1999; Louie, Curren, & Harich,

2000; Mark, Boburka, Eyssell, Cohen, & Mellor, 2003).

Mark and Mellor's (1991) formal research report makes the entire investigation sound preordained and fixed. The behind-the-scenes story of this study reveals a more emergent picture. Mellor, an industrial/organizational psychologist interested in unions, had collected questionnaire responses from union members at plant sites where layoffs had occurred. Mellor approached Mark, a social psychologist, wondering whether they might collaborate, using the dataset to address social psychological questions. Mark had an existing interest in quasi-experimental design and was intrigued by the possibility of employing the rarely used but potent regression-discontinuity design. He also had an interest in the intersection of cognitive and affective or motivational processes. So he examined the variables in Mellor's dataset to identify ones that might reflect on substantively interesting social psychological questions. Mellor, as it happened, had surveyed participants about how foreseeable they thought the layoff was. The result was the initial paper (1991) demonstrating that self-serving biases can attenuate the supposedly robust hindsight bias.

Thus Mark and Mellor's (1991) research question emerged from an intersection of the available data (i.e., the survey question about the foreseeability of the layoff), the design options (i.e., the feasibility of employing the rare but potent regression-discontinuity design), and the hypothesis testing these allowed, as viewed from the perspective of Mark's background and interests as a social psychologist. Emergence of the research question is not a standard part of the traditional literature on quasi-experiments, nor in the conventional reporting of quasi-experimental investigations. But it does occur, as the Mark and Mellor study illustrates.

As another example, the existence of time-series data, in conjunction with an intervention of potential interest, has on occasion led to implementation of the interrupted time-series design. Consider the case of Steiner and Mark (1985), who presented a study of whether and to what extent community-based activist groups are effective. Past studies of community-based activist groups had focused more on process, duration, and image rather than on rigorous assessment of such groups' impact. Steiner and Mark reported an attempt to fill this gap in the past literature. Specifically, they examined the impact of a community action group that formed in protest of a bank's announced plan to increase the mortgage interest rates for a subset of its customers. Among its actions, the community action group organized a "mass withdrawal," encouraging people to stop doing business with the bank.

The Steiner and Mark (1985) journal article presents their investigation as an illustration of how the interrupted time-series quasi-experimental design can be used to investigate a question too often ignored in the literature on community organizations: How effective are such groups' actions? Once again, the behind-the-scenes story is more emergent. Steiner, then a graduate student in a research methods class taught by Mark, was looking for a suitable class paper. His mother worked at the bank that had been targeted by the community action group, and Steiner knew that this relationship would likely facilitate access to time-series data on the bank's holdings. The behind-the-scenes story again shows a kind of opportunism, with the investigators on the lookout for opportunities to employ a relatively strong quasi-experimental design, in this case the interrupted time-series design. It also shows the emergence of a research question from that opportunism. Notably, the research question was one of reasonable interest to Steiner and Mark, an I/O psychologist and a social psychologist, respectively.[4]

Take an additional, admittedly more speculative, example. Economists have in recent years demonstrated a growing interest in quasi-experiments, though typically under the label of "natural experiments." Seminal in this development was a pair of papers by David Card (Card, 1992; Card & Krueger, 1994) that tested the long-standing economic hypothesis that raising the minimum wage would reduce the employment rates of younger and less skilled workers. Card and Krueger (1994) tested this hypothesis by comparing employment in fast-food restaurants in New Jersey, which changed the state minimum wage in April 1992, with fast-food restaurant employment in nearby eastern Pennsylvania, where the minimum wage had not changed. Unlike in the typical researcher-controlled laboratory experiment, the field-based quasi-experimentalist must usually take advantage of the interventions that arise in the real world. This means that one must study whatever version of the treatment "nature" provides, whether or not the treatment is precisely as one would want for the research question at hand. The quasi-experimentalist often must also take advantage of existing data, as with Card's (1992) use of the *Current Population Survey* or Steiner and Mark's use of archival data on bank holdings (however, the quasi-experimental investigator can sometimes generate new data, as when Card and Krueger [1994] surveyed fast-food restaurants by phone and Mellor surveyed union members). In designing a quasi-experiment, the investigator must also usually take advantage of whatever design features the circumstances allow. For example, Card and Krueger were able to compare the pattern of change in New Jersey with that in nearby Pennsylvania, because Pennsylvania did not raise its minimum wage during the time period of the study. The same design would not have been possible if the increase in minimum wage had been the result of federal legislation.

In short, one's quasi-experimental design and research question are usually emergent, at least to some extent, in an interactive fashion. Sometimes the research question strongly guides the search for places at which a quasi-experimental test can be applied. For example, Card may have had a long-standing interest in the effects of the minimum wage on employment and vigilantly been looking for circumstances that would allow a test of the existing conventional wisdom. Even here, though, there is a kind of emergent dialectic between research question and the quasi-experimental design that can be implemented given conditions in the world. The precise research question to be tested would depend, for example, on the size of the increase in New Jersey's minimum wage (whether or not that size is ideal from a theoretical perspective) and on whether other adjacent states followed suit quickly (determining what can constitute the comparison group). In other cases, the design potentials more strongly guide the emergent research question. For instance, Mark and Mellor did not set out with a single-minded intent to test whether self-serving biases would attenuate hindsight bias. Instead, Mark saw that Mellor's union data would allow use of the regression-discontinuity design, and the self-serving bias and hindsight hypothesis emerged from the intersection of his social psychological background and the available data elements.

Admittedly, emergence in these cases may be different in kind from much of the emergence that arises in more qualitative investigations. In qualitative research, the interpretation that arises from early data collection may influence the revised research question that emerges for ultimate consideration. In the quasi-experimental cases discussed in this section, we see that the design options that are (or are not) available, rather than early data-driven interpretation, influence the research question that emerges.

This kind of emergence may appear to fly in the face of much traditional advice about research. Identify the research question first, we are told, preferably in the form of a quite specific hypothesis, and then select the methods that best test it (e.g., Sansone, Morf, & Panter, 2004). The conventional wisdom is: Do not let the tail of methods wag the dog of the research question. Sometimes the quasi-experimentalist follows this advice fairly closely, as in the speculative reconstruction of Card's work given earlier. Other times, there may be a far more emergent research question than traditional advice would allow, such as in the Mark and Mellor case. How is one to resolve this seeming tension? Strict adherence to the traditional advice would rule out work such as Mark and Mellor's—a consequence that does not seem uniformly desirable. An alternative is to recognize that: (1) there is no simple procedure for developing research questions and selecting methods that fits all cases; (2) unless you are primarily a methodologist, design opportunities should not lead you to invest in a research question you find substantively uninteresting; (3) alternatively, there may be value in selecting, from among the many research questions that interest you, one that is tractable (e.g., that can be tested well because of a natural experiment); and (4) the trade-offs that exist among different types of validity (e.g., internal vs. external) sometimes result in a preference for a more credible test of a less-than-optimal or modified hypothesis rather than a weaker test of the optimal or original hypothesis (e.g., even if Card and Krueger's quasi-experimental test was not ideal, perhaps because the magnitude of the wage increase was not theoretically optimal, that study may be preferable to an artificial study in a lab using a simulation). In this respect, emergence may be a property that should have some constraints. But in the development of hypotheses for quasi-experimental research, it may be an important property nonetheless.

Existing Emergent Analysis Options

Another source of some degree of emergence in quasi-experimentation stems from data analysis options that may be used. These methods provide an opportunity for the results of somewhat more exploratory data analyses to partially shape the specific hypotheses that are subsequently examined. These analysis options include classification methods to identify subgroups of individuals (or other subgroups), emergent methods for defining comparison groups, and relatively emergent methods for controlling for selection bias. The general topic of exploratory data analysis (Behrens, 1997; Tukey, 1977) could also be included in this section.

Classification Methods for Identifying Subgroups

In quasi-experimental or experimental studies, the possibility exists that the treatment effect is not constant across all kinds of treatment recipients (or contexts). Instead, the intervention may be more effective for one type of client than another (or for certain circumstances more so than others). In some studies, theory and past research may be sufficient to allow a priori predictions about the types of clients (or contexts) for which the intervention should be more effective. In other cases, the researcher may seek to identify empirically what subgroups of clients (or service delivery models or types of communities or contexts) exist. For example, cluster analyses might be conducted to see what subgroups of clients there are, as has been done to identify different categories of homeless individuals (cf. Humphries & Rosenheck, 1995; Kuhn & Culhane, 1998). The categories of clients that emerge can then be used to examine, in subsequent quasi-experimental analyses, whether the intervention is equally effective for the different types of clients.

Emergent Methods for Defining Comparison Groups

The treatment group in a quasi-experiment may be defined in advance. For example, in examining the hindsight of laid-off workers, Mark and Mellor (1991) used as a comparison the responses of layoff survivors at the same plants. In contrast, in some investigations the treatment group is defined but the cases that will constitute the comparison group must be selected. For instance,

Weitzman and her colleagues (2002) were asked to evaluate a foundation-funded community-based intervention intended to improve children's health outcomes. The foundation had gone through a process to select five cities as program sites at which the intervention would be implemented. How should the evaluators select a set of comparison-site cities for data collection? Weitzman and colleagues used cluster analysis and allowed an empirical answer to emerge. In essence, cluster analysis takes cases (usually individuals, but in this study, cities), examines them in a multidimensional space defined by the cases' scores on a variety of variables (e.g., population size, unemployment rates), and identifies clusters of cases that are "closer" to each other. Weitzman and colleagues used the cluster analysis results to select the comparison group. For each treatment site, a comparison-group site was selected that fell within the same cluster as the treatment-group city. Rather than being fully fixed in advance, the composition of the comparison group—an important feature of the quasi-experiment—emerged from this analysis.

Relatively Emergent Methods for Controlling for Selection Bias

Considerable effort and debate has taken place in recent years on the proper analysis of quasi-experimental designs, especially the nonequivalent-groups pretest–posttest design (Shadish et al., 2002). The focus of this debate is on the best way to control for selection bias. Earlier analysis procedures, such as the analysis of covariance (ANCOVA), tended to be more fixed in nature. ANCOVA controls statistically for initial differences, in essence matching individuals across treatment groups based usually on their pretest scores (or other initial scores), and essentially taking the average difference between the matched groups on the posttest as the estimate of the treatment effect. Some of the more recent alternatives are in a sense more emergent. For example, *propensity score analysis* involves two steps. In the first, a logistic regression is carried out, typically using a variety of available variables as predictors to estimate the predicted probability of being in the treatment (rather than the comparison) group. For instance, one might use a variety of variables to predict which GAD patients end up in a new treatment and which ones receive the existing therapy. Scores on each case's predictor variables are used to estimate the predicted probability, or propensity, of being in the treatment group. To control for selection bias, in the second step of the analysis the cases are usually stratified into subgroups (commonly five) based on their propensity scores, with the treatment effect computed as a weighted average based on the treatment- and comparison-group means within each subgroup. Alternatively, the propensity score can be treated as a covariate in ANCOVA (for descriptions of this and alternative analysis techniques, see Little & Rubin, 2000; Rosenbaum, 1995; Shadish et al., 2002; Winship & Morgan, 1999). In terms of emergence, the point is that the researcher does not begin with a fixed model of how to control for selection bias. Rather, the specifics of the statistical control model emerge from the empirical analysis.

Sequential or Iterative Designs

Quasi-experimental (and experimental) studies rarely, if ever, are designed in isolation from all other forms of inquiry. To the contrary, an experiment or quasi-experiment is typically preceded by a variety of activities. In some instances, these may be formally described by the researcher as prior studies in a multiple-study report. In other cases, the prior activities may be labeled as pilot tests or even construed as informal front-end work rather than as formal inquiry. Nevertheless, when viewed from the perspective of mixed method designs, this sequence of efforts allows a form of emergence in association with quasi-experiments (or experiments). In short, the longer stream of research activities often includes an initial period in which emergence is sought, to be followed by a relatively more fixed form of research during the quasi-experiment. (Indeed, some of the examples in the previous section, such as the use of classification methods, could be construed in this way.) The quasi-experiment can be preceded by another form of inquiry, the two can take place at the same time, or the quasi-experiment can be followed by another kind of study.

In the language of Caracelli and Greene (1997), quasi-experiments often take place in the context of an iterative mixed method or multiple method design. The term "mixed method" refers to combinations of qualitative and quantitative methods, whereas "multiple method" is more general and can include, for example, two quantitative methods. Iterative mixed method designs:

> are characterized by a dynamic and ongoing interplay over time between the different methodologies associated with different paradigms. Studies engaging in a single iteration can serve the mixed-method purpose of development in which the results from one method type are used to inform the development of the other method type. With multiple iterations, the study enables a progressive reconfiguration of substantive findings and interpretations in a pattern of increasing insight and sophistication. (p. 23)

Numerous examples exist of single-iteration mixed method (or multiple-method) sequences involving quasi-experimentation and other methods traditionally thought of as more fixed than emergent. For instance, quasi-experiments often employ self-report measures. Following the procedures endorsed by early theorists of self-report measurement, the development of such measures usually begins with more qualitative procedures, such as open-ended interviews or content analysis of related text. This procedure gives an emergent character to the development of the multiple-item scale's content, even though the scale will be fixed in form during the quasi-experiment. To take another example, even those known for advocating the use of quasi-experiments (and experiments) in program evaluation and applied social research (Shadish, Cook, & Campbell, 2002) suggest doing so in the context of a single-iteration design. For instance, Cook and Shadish (1994) endorse preceding a quasi-experiment with document analysis, interviews of stakeholders, and observation to better understand the program and the questions that should be addressed. It appears that quasi-experiments often are preceded by at least some degree of prior investigation. From Caracelli and Greene's (1997) view, the results of the initial work inform the development of the quasi-experiment in a single-iteration design.

Perhaps less frequently, quasi-experiments occur in the context of multiple iterations across method types. As Caracelli and Greene (1997) note, this kind of iterative design may allow enhanced and richer interpretation of findings. Mark, Feller, and Button (1997) describe and illustrate several specific benefits of having an experimental or quasi-experimental program evaluation preceded, accompanied, and followed by qualitative inquiry. Specifically, Mark and colleagues note the value of the more emergent methods for assessing the validity of the more quantitative findings, reframing some of the initial research questions, facilitating communication of the quasi-experimental results with vivid examples and quotes, enhancing explanation of the key quasi-experimental findings, examining implementation and adaptation, studying contextual factors, probing the limits of generalizability, and addressing emerging questions.

The point made here about quasi-experiments taking place in sequences of inquiry, parts of which are, by design, more emergent, is not new. For example, Carol Weiss, a major contributor to the theory and methods of program evaluation, was asked in an interview about her view of an earlier qualitative–quantitative debate. She responded:

> I had, from my very earliest research experience, used both qualitative and quantitative methods and I could see no contradiction; I could see various ways in which they could be combined. I saw that in developing a survey you always do some qualitative work first so that you know what the right questions are, and then you write the questions and try them out, rewrite them and try them out again. You can do quantitative work and follow it up with qualitative work to understand the pattern in the data. (Oral History Project Team, 2006)

In short, even to the extent that a quasi-experiment is fixed rather than emergent, it can and usually should take place in a longer series of inquiry that offers more emergence.

Principled Discovery

Principled discovery offers a form of emergence in quasi-experiments that perhaps most resembles the archetypical emergence in research, whereby an initial round of interpretation results in a reformulated research question. By way of background, it is important to recognize that virtually every quasi-experiment begins, if not with a specific hypothesis, then at least with a focal research question. For example, an evaluation of a new GAD therapy begins, if not with a hypothesis that the new therapy is more effective than the current standard therapy, then at least with a sharp focus on comparing the new and standard therapies. As another example, once Mark and Mellor's (1991) research question had emerged from their consideration of the available design options and data elements, they had a specific prediction that workers who were laid off would experience less hindsight than the survivors.

In quasi-experiments, the hypothesis (or focal question) commonly involves only the overall treatment–comparison group contrast (e.g., a new vs. a standard GAD therapy). On some occasions, the initial hypothesis may be more specific, indicating that the program will work better in some circumstances than others (e.g., it may be hypothesized that the new GAD therapy will be more beneficial for highly verbal clients than for less verbal ones). Nevertheless, in many (if not most) cases, the initial hypothesis will be quite coarse, involving only the average treatment–comparison group contrast. This is so even though generally it seems plausible that complexities and contingencies exist in the world such that the program is likely to have different effects for different types of clients or in different contexts. Given this expectation, how can researchers facilitate more emergence by using the data themselves to try to go beyond relatively simple initial hypotheses? And how can they do this without being misled by the well-known problem that chance will create pseudo-findings if one sifts through the data repeatedly (e.g., Diaconis, 1985)? Mark and colleagues (Mark, 2003; Mark, Henry, & Julnes, 2000) use the term "principled discovery" to describe methods that can allow for emergent revision and elaboration of the hypotheses but with procedures to reduce the likelihood of being misled by chance.

Like most quantitatively trained researchers, quasi-experimentalists have generally been trained in ways that emphasize the testing of a priori hypotheses while more or less ignoring emergent discoveries. The eminent statistician John Tukey decried this: "Exploration has been rather neglected; confirmation has been rather sanctified. Neither action is justifiable" (1986, p. 822). Rosenthal (1994), a psychologist and methodologist, concisely captured the situation: "Many of us have been taught that it is technically improper and perhaps even immoral to analyze and reanalyze our data in many ways (i.e., to snoop around in the data). We were taught to test the prediction with one particular preplanned test . . . and definitely not look further at our data. . . . [This] makes for bad science and for bad ethics" (p. 130).

Why does Rosenthal contend that there is bad ethics lurking in the emphasis on the confirmation of a priori hypotheses and the underemphasis on exploration? One answer is, first, that research has costs, including the time lost by participants, and, second, that failing to learn the more emergent possible lessons could undercut the benefits that research could generate. For example, ethical concerns would exist if a study of a new GAD therapy supported the conclusion that the new therapy is effective, whereas a more emergent approach would have shown that, though effective for most, the new therapy is actually less effective than the standard therapy for a certain type of client.

Principled discovery has been offered as a way to make for better science and better ethics, in Rosenthal's sense. In essence, principled discovery involves two primary steps. First, the researcher carries out some form of exploratory analyses. (In practice, this exploratory step is likely to follow analyses that test the a priori hypothesis, e.g., that a new therapy is more effective than the standard therapy.) The exploratory analyses may result in a finding that goes beyond the initial a priori hypothesis. Often, the discovery will show some contingency moderating the treatment effect. For example, a treatment may be more effective for men than for women. Or it might be helpful to most subgroups but harmful to a certain subgroup. In some instances, the discovery will point to an underlying mechanism (or mediator), that is, it might suggest how it is that the treatment leads to its effects.

The second general step of principled discovery requires the researcher to seek some form of independent (or quasi-independent) confirmation of the discovery. Replication is widely recommended as the ideal way to discipline discoveries (e.g., Behrens, 1997). Replication has much to be said for it, or course. And it can be quite feasible, especially in those areas of laboratory-based research in which studies can be mounted within a reasonable time frame. However, replication will not always be a feasible approach to disciplining a discovery in quasi-experiments. For example, quasi-experiments are often used to evaluate social or educational programs (Mark, Henry, & Julnes, 2000; Seltzer, 1994). These evaluations may take considerable time and sizable budgets to complete, making it unlikely that a replication could be undertaken easily. Moreover, decisions might have to be made about the program before a replication could be completed. Consequently, the second step of principled discovery will often require a test of some other implication of the new discovery, perhaps within the confines of the existing dataset. Examples are given subsequently.

The exploratory analyses that constitute the first step of principled discovery can be conducted using a wide variety of techniques (Mark, 2003; Mark, Henry, & Julnes, 1998). Almost any data analysis can be used in an exploratory fashion. For example, Tukey (1977) has pointed out that although researchers usually think of standard statistical techniques such as multiple regression as confirmatory, these analyses can be effectively used for exploration. In principled discovery, this would commonly involve testing for interactions (or, as these are also known, for moderated effects). That is, exploratory analyses would be conducted to see whether the treatment effect varies in relation to an existing measure of a client characteristic (or of a contextual attribute of different sites, or of some aspect of the treatment delivery). Although the exploratory use of multiple regression or another familiar technique may be the easiest way to undertake the first step of principled discovery, many other possibilities exist. As illustrated elsewhere (e.g., Mark, 2003), the options include multilevel modeling, exploratory data analyses, and classification methods.

Some tools of discovery are a bit arcane. For example, as Bryk and Raudenbush (1988) have pointed out, heterogeneity of variance (that is, more variability in the outcome variable scores in one group than another) can be a clue that there is an important discovery to be detailed. Bryk and Raudenbush examined an earlier study in which the treatment and control groups did not differ on the average but in which there was considerably more variability within the treatment group. One interpretation of this pattern is that the treatment helped some individuals but harmed others.

Other tools of discovery should seem familiar to researchers trained in the qualitative methods that are usually associated more with emergence. For example, discoveries will sometimes arise from inspecting the residuals from the analysis that tests the original a priori hypothesis (e.g., the treatment–control group comparison). Based on the residuals, one may be able to identify sites or cases that have larger or smaller outcomes than would be expected from standard predictors. These extreme cases can be compared and contrasted to see whether the variation in outcome appears to be associated with differences in types of participants or context or treatment implementation. Doing this will involve other data, such as background information on clients, which are used to see whether the extreme cases share any common characteristics. Additional data could be gathered after the extreme scores are identified, possibly including qualitative data. Overall, this approach to discovery in quasi-experimental (or experimental) research is analogous to the extreme-case technique discussed in the qualitative methods literature.

In the preceding and in several other ways (Mark, 2003; Mark et al., 1998), the quasi-experimental researcher can attempt to discover possible variations in treatment effectiveness. Of course, the researcher could stop there. The research report could present findings of the a priori tests of the original hypothesis and also summarize the discovery-oriented tests and findings. Caveats could be added about the exploratory findings, indicating that they should be treated as hypotheses awaiting replication. This approach may be quite appropriate for more basic research, in which an attempt at replication is likely to follow discoveries that are interesting enough to garner attention from other researchers. However, treating discovery as a means of generating hypotheses to be tested later may be inadequate for most quasi-experimental researchers. As noted earlier, for example, quasi-experiments are often used in evaluating social and educational programs, and decisions about a program may have to occur before replication could be conducted—if replication is even a feasible option. In addition, prospective consumers of evaluation findings may generate their own explanations for any discovery that is reported, and their self-generated accounts may lead them to rely on the finding, whether it is replicable or not. In short, the conventional call for "future research" may not suffice when reporting a discovery in an evaluation or other applied quasi-experiment.

At the same time, it is problematic for unanticipated discoveries in a quasi-experiment to be treated on an equal par with the findings of the a priori hypothesis. When a discovery occurs following exploratory analyses, chance exists as a plausible alternative explanation (perhaps along with other plausible alternative explanations). The more one slices and dices the data while exploring, the more likely it is that *something* will appear to be there, real or not. Consider this from the perspective of statistical significance, which is often used as a criterion for deciding whether a discovery is to be treated as real. In simplified terms, statistical significance means only that a given finding is unlikely to have arisen by chance if there really were no difference. The standard convention of "$p < .05$" means that a finding will be treated as real if it is large enough that it would have arisen by chance alone no more than 5 times out of 100. A corollary is that, if you conduct 100 exploratory tests and there really is nothing to be found, the expectation is that 5 of the tests nevertheless will be statistically significant. As Stigler (1987,

p. 148) stated with a clever turn of phrase, "Beware of testing too many hypotheses; the more you torture the data, the more likely they are to confess, but confession obtained under duress may not be admissible in the court of scientific opinion."

In short, then, the second step of principled discovery is important. In essence, this step calls for subjecting any discovery from the first step to replication or to some other kind of confirmatory tests. If replication is infeasible, the second step will usually involve other tests that can be carried out within the same dataset. In some cases, however, the researcher can go beyond the initial dataset. This might occur by integrating information from other datasets, as when information from school records is merged with data from an educational program evaluation. Or, in longitudinal investigations, a discovery from an early measurement wave might lead to the addition of new measures created to probe the initial discovery.

Regardless of the data sources, the second step of principled discovery will generally require an interpretation of the findings from the step 1 exploration. Indeed, emergence can be seen in the combination of the original discovery and its interpretation, which in turn facilitates further emergence in the form of a new, more specific test that can generate additional confidence in the emergent account. For example, a discovery, such as the discovery of differential effects across subgroups, may suggest an underlying mechanism that is responsible for the observed pattern of effects. This newly induced mechanism then helps generate a distinct prediction that should be true *if* the mechanism is operating. In the second step of principled discovery, this new prediction would be tested, perhaps using different variables in the same dataset (an example follows). In other cases, a discovery might suggest a more specific test, with the increased specificity of the second test providing greater confidence that the original discovery was not the result of chance. Imagine, for example, that initial exploratory tests reveal that an intervention was more effective when clients and therapists were matched on some background variable, such as parental socioeconomic status (SES), represented in the exploratory analyses simply as low versus high SES. This discovery could to some extent be disciplined by carrying out a more specific test of the matching hypothesis, with finer gradations of SES and the prediction that outcomes should be better *to the extent* that client and therapist match.

Principled discovery and its two primary steps are well illustrated by what Julnes (1995) calls the *context-confirmatory approach*. Julnes illustrated this approach in an evaluation of a "resource mother" program, in which staff provided support to new single mothers. In the a priori, planned test that compared program clients' outcomes with those of a comparison group, Julnes found that the program was effective on average. Even though many researchers would have been satisfied to stop at that point, Julnes chose to engage in some exploratory analyses. In the discovery phase, Julnes conducted additional regression analyses to see whether the overall positive treatment effect varied for different types of clients. These analyses revealed that the resource-mother program effects were larger for older than for younger mothers. Based on his knowledge and observation of the program, Julnes speculated that younger mothers' needs were more tangible and task oriented and that these needs were not necessarily met by the resource mothers, who often emphasized emotional support. In the disciplining step of principled discovery, Julnes conducted a new test of this emergent explanation. He classified support mothers based on the extent to which they provided tangible support versus emotional support. Subsequent tests confirmed that, as Julnes expected, the program was ineffective for younger mothers when the support mothers emphasized emotional support, but effective otherwise.

Principled discovery has considerable potential for enhancing emergent discovery in quasi-experimental (and experimental) research, while reducing the likelihood of being misled by chance findings. Despite its potential benefits, important practical limits will often apply to principled discovery. First, existing datasets may not include the additional variables needed to conduct a strong test of a new explanatory account. Second, statistical power may be inadequate for some discoveries, especially in smaller-sample quasi-experiments (Cohen, 1988; McClelland & Judd, 1993). Third, a single validity threat may be shared across both the test that provided the initial discovery and the test used to discipline it. Although these and other complexities do not render principled discovery invalid or useless, they may create challenges and make more it difficult to implement in some circumstances. Finally, principled discovery remains relatively new as a research strategy, and the kinks may not all have been worked out. To take but one example, it would be helpful to have user-friendly procedures that allow the researcher to calculate the extent to which a new principling test is truly independent of the test that generated the discovery. Despite these limitations, principled discovery can be a valuable, relatively emergent approach for going beyond the initial coarse research questions that motivate a quasi-experiment while minimizing false leads that otherwise would arise due to chance.

Summary and Conclusions

The question of whether, and to what extent, a treatment makes a difference on specified outcome variables is often critical. Estimating treatment effects is the primary method of theory testing in many areas of scholarship. Estimating treatment effects is also central in many areas of applied research. For example, in evaluating policies and programs, the question of the difference the policy or program makes on valued outcomes often predominates judgments of the policy or program's merit and worth. When estimating treatment effects is important and random assignment is infeasible, quasi-experimentation will often be the research design of choice.

Although quasi-experimentation, like the randomized experimental methods it approximates, is usually seen as fixed and preordained, different forms of emergence exist. The logic of validity threats and quasi-experimental design can create a kind of emergent design development process. By opportunistically seeking circumstances in which stronger designs can be implemented, quasi-experimental researchers may allow research questions, or at least variants on research questions, to emerge. Certain data analysis options, such as the use of clustering methods to select comparison group members, have an emergent character. Sequential or iterative designs, in which quasi-experiments are combined with other research designs, can create emergence beyond that of the quasi-experiment itself. Principled discovery can create an archetypical form of emergence whereby initial analyses suggest tentative interpretations that modify the focus of subsequent analyses.

Interesting forms of emergence are, of course, not guaranteed, even when the researcher seeks to facilitate it. For instance, the quasi-experimental researcher can conduct exploratory analyses; but interesting findings may not emerge, at least if there are no important contingencies limiting the overall treatment effect. Similarly, the opportunistic quasi-experimentalist may be vigilant in looking for circumstances that would allow for potent tests of hypotheses of interest; however, one could look for a long time without finding conditions that would support the use of a regression-discontinuity design to investigate a hypothesis in one's own research area. Emergence itself may be an emergent and somewhat unpredictable property.

Notes

1. Random assignment does not, however, guarantee that there will be absolutely no initial selection differences. Even when individuals are assigned at random to the new versus the current standard therapy groups, some (usually modest) difference is likely to occur initially. In a single experiment, random assignment guarantees that the initial selection differences between the groups are completely random, not that they are exactly zero. The gives rise to the second great benefit of random assignment: The classical statistical procedures of confidence intervals and hypothesis tests can take into account whatever random selection differences exist and can provide well-grounded statements about the warrant for confidence in one's results (Boruch, 1997; Reichardt & Mark, 1998).

2. Several alternatives to gain-score analysis exist for the pretest–posttest nonequivalent-groups design. One long-standing alternative analytical procedure is the analysis of covariance, or ANCOVA, using the pretest and other relevant preintervention factors as covariates. Other, more recent approaches include structural equation modeling, selection modeling, and, increasingly, the calculation and use of propensity scores (e.g., Little & Rubin, 2000; Rubin, 1974). Each of these involves a somewhat different approach toward controlling statistically for initial selection differences. Each approach should give unbiased estimates of the treatment effect if the assumptions underlying it hold. The problem in practice, however, is that it will generally not be possible to be fully confident that the assumptions underlying a specific analysis hold in a particular evaluation (Boruch, 1997), although advocates of each approach exist. Consequently, multiple analyses are often recommended for the pretest–posttest nonequivalent-groups design, in order to demonstrate that one's conclusions about the merit of a program are robust across different analytical assumptions (e.g., Reynolds & Temple, 1995).

3. However, the estimate of the treatment effect can be biased if the relationship between the QAV and the outcome variable is curvilinear but a linear relationship is fit to the data. To address this problem, curvilinearity in the data should be modeled in the analysis. In short, conventional statistical analysis of the regression-discontinuity design involves predicting the outcome variable in a series of regression analyses, where the predictors are the QAV (transformed by subtracting the cutoff value, so that the treatment effect is estimated at the cutoff point), a dummy code representing condition (e.g., treatment vs. comparison), and a term representing the interaction of condition and the QAV (note that the condition variable estimates the difference between conditions that exists over and above the relationship between the QAV and the outcome). In addition, polynomials of the transformed QAV and interaction are included and, if not significant, dropped out. Estimation of the polynomials serves to test for the possibility of a nonlinear relationship that could otherwise masquerade as a treatment effect. In addition, researchers who use the regression-discontinuity design should be aware that the design has substantially less power than a randomized experiment (Cappelleri, Darlington, & Trochim, 1994).

4. Consistent with the previous section on iterations between research design and validity threats, Steiner and Mark did additional, post hoc work to consider validity threats. Instrumentation is a threat that can occur, for example, if the introduction of a treatment is associated with a change in the way observations are defined or recorded. This is common, for example, in ITS studies of the impact of legal changes, where a law that changes the punishment for a crime also changes the definition of the crime. Steiner and Mark consulted bank officials to assess whether there had been changes in record keeping at the time of the community group's actions. Similarly, considering the threat of history, they looked for general changes in the local economy and asked bank officials and community members about historical events that might have caused a downturn in savings. They found no evidence of such changes.

References

Behrens, J. T. (1997). Principles and procedures of exploratory data analysis. *Psychological Methods, 2,* 131–160.

Boruch, R. F. (1997). *Randomized experiments for planning and evaluation: A practical guide.* Thousand Oaks, CA: Sage.

Boruch, R. F. (Ed.) (2005). Place randomized trials [Special issue]. *Annals of the American Academy of Political and Social Sciences, 598.*

Bryk, A. S., & Raudenbush, S. W. (1988). Heterogeneity of variance in experimental studies: A challenge to conventional interpretations. *Psychological Bulletin, 104*, 396–404.

Bryk, A. S., & Raudenbush, S. W. (1992). *Hierarchical linear models: Applications and data analysis methods.* Thousand Oaks, CA: Sage.

Campbell, D. T. (1957). Factors relevant to the validity of experiments in social settings. *Psychological Bulletin, 54*, 297–312.

Campbell, D. T. (1969). Reforms as experiments. *American Psychologist, 24*, 409–429.

Campbell, D. T., & Kenny, D. A. (1999). *A primer on regression artifacts.* New York: Guilford Press.

Campbell, D. T., & Stanley, J. C. (1966). *Experimental and quasi-experimental designs for research.* Skokie, IL: Rand McNally.

Cappelleri, J. C., Darlington, R. B., & Trochim, W. M. K. (1994). Power analysis of cutoff-based randomized clinical trials. *Evaluation Review, 18*, 141–152.

Caracelli, V. J., & Greene, J. C. (1997). Crafting mixed-method evaluation designs. In J. C. Greene & V. J. Caracelli (Eds.), *Advances in mixed-method evaluation* (pp. 19–32). San Francisco: Jossey-Bass.

Card, D. (1992). Do minimum wages reduce employment? A case study of California, 1987–89. *Industrial and Labor Relations Review, 46*, 38–54.

Card, D., & Krueger, A. B. (1994). Minimum wages and employment: A case study of the fast-food industry in New Jersey and Pennsylvania. *American Economic Review, 84*, 772–793.

Christensen-Szalanski, J. J., & Willham, C. F. (1991). The hindsight bias: A meta-analysis. *Organizational Behavior and Human Decision Processes, 48*, 147–168.

Cohen, J. (1988). *Statistical power analysis for the behavioral sciences.* Hillsdale, NJ: Erlbaum.

Cook, T. D. (1985). Post-positivist critical multiplism. In R. L Shotland & M. M. Mark (Eds.), *Social science and social policy* (pp. 21–62). Beverly Hills, CA: Sage.

Cook, T. D., & Campbell, D. T. (1979). *Quasi-experimentation: Design and analysis issues for field settings.* Skokie, IL: Rand McNally.

Cook, T. D., & Shadish, W. R. (1994). Social experiments: Some developments over the past 15 years. *Annual Review of Psychology, 45*, 545–580.

Diaconis, P. (1985). Theories of data analysis: From magical thinking through classical statistics. In D. C. Hoagland, F. Mosteller, & J. W. Tukey (Eds.), *Exploring data tables, trends, and shapes* (pp. 1–36). New York: Wiley.

Eckert, W. A. (2000). Situational enhancement of design validity: The case of training evaluation at the World Bank. *American Journal of Evaluation, 21*(2), 185–193.

Fletcher, G. H. (2004). Scientifically based research: Guidelines or mandates for product purchasing? *T.H.E. Journal, 31*, 22–24.

Hawkins, S. A., & Hastie, R. (1990). Hindsight: Biased judgments of past events after the outcomes are known. *Psychological Bulletin, 107*, 311–327.

Humphries, K., & Rosenheck, R. (1995). Sequential validation of cluster analytic subtypes of homeless veterans. *American Journal of Community Psychology, 23*, 75–98.

Institute for Education Sciences. (2003). *Identifying and implementing educational practices supported by rigorous evidence: A user friendly guide.* Retrieved February 17, 2007, from *ies.ed.gov/ncee/pubs/evidence_based/evidence_based.aspX*

Julnes, G. (1995, November). *Context-confirmatory methods for supporting disciplined induction in post-positivist inquiry.* Paper presented at the annual meeting of the American Evaluation Association, Vancouver, British Columbia, Canada.

Kuhn, R., & Culhane, D. P. (1998). Applying cluster analysis to test a typology of homelessness by pattern of shelter utilization: Results from the analysis of administrative data. *American Journal of Community Psychology, 26*(2), 207–232.

Lederman, N. G., & Flick, L. B. (2003). Never cry wolf. *School Science and Mathematics, 103*, 61–63.

Little, R. J., & Rubin, D. B. (2000). Causal effects in clinical and epidemiological studies via potential outcomes: Concepts and analytical approaches. In J. E. Fielding, L. B. Lave, & B. Starfield (Eds.), *Annual review of public health* (Vol. 21, pp. 121–145). Palo Alto, CA: Annual Reviews.

Louie, T. A. (1999). Decision makers' hindsight bias after receiving favorable and unfavorable feedback. *Journal of Applied Psychology, 84*, 29–41.

Louie, T. A., Curren, M. T., & Harich, K. R. (2000). "I knew we would win": Hindsight bias for favorable and unfavorable team decision outcomes. *Journal of Applied Psychology, 85*, 264–272.

Mark, M. M. (2003). Program evaluation. In S. A. Schinka & W. Velicer (Eds.), *Comprehensive handbook of psychology* (Vol. 2, pp. 323–347). New York: Wiley.

Mark, M. M. (in press). Credible evidence: Changing the terms of the debate. In S. I. Donaldson, C. A. Christie, & M. Mark (Eds.), *What counts as credible evidence in evaluation and evidence-based practice?* Thousand Oaks, CA: Sage.

Mark, M. M., Boburka, R. R., Eyssell, K. M., Cohen, L., & Mellor, S. (2003). "I couldn't have seen it coming": The impact of negative self-relevant outcomes on retrospections about foreseeability. *Memory, 11*(4/5), 443–454.

Mark, M. M., Feller, I., & Button, S. (1997). Integrating qualitative methods in a predominantly quantitative evaluation: A case study and some reflections. In J. Greene & V. Caracelli, (Eds.), *Advances in mixed-method evaluation* (pp. 47–59). San Francisco: Jossey-Bass.

Mark, M. M., Henry, G. T., & Julnes, G. (1998). A realist theory of evaluation practice. In G. Henry, G. W. Julnes, & M. M. Mark (Eds.), *Realist evaluation: An emerging theory in support of practice* (pp. 3–32). San Francisco: Jossey-Bass.

Mark, M. M., Henry, G. T., & Julnes, G. (2000). *Evalua-*

tion: An integrated framework for understanding, guiding, and improving policies and programs. San Francisco: Jossey-Bass.

Mark, M. M., & Mellor, S. (1991). The effect of the self-relevance of an event on hindsight bias: The foreseeability of a layoff. *Journal of Applied Psychology, 76,* 569–577.

McClelland, G. H., & Judd, C. M. (1993). Statistical difficulties of detecting interactions and moderator effects. *Psychological Bulletin, 114,* 376–390.

Oral History Project Team. (2006). The oral history of evaluation: Part 4. The professional evolution of Carol H. Weiss. *American Journal of Evaluation, 27,* 475–484.

Pawson, R., & Tilley, N. (1997). *Realistic evaluation.* Thousand Oaks, CA: Sage.

Reichardt, C. S., & Mark, M. M. (1998). Quasi-experimentation. In L. Bickman & D. J. Rog (Eds.), *Handbook of applied social research methods* (pp. 193–208). Thousand Oaks, CA: Sage.

Reynolds, A. J., & Temple, J. A. (1995). Quasi-experimental estimates of the effects of a preschool intervention: Psychometric and econometric comparisons. *Evaluation Review, 19,* 347–373.

Rosenbaum, P. R. (1995). *Observational studies.* New York: Springer-Verlag.

Rosenthal, R. (1994). Science and ethics in conducting, analyzing, and reporting psychological research. *Psychological Science, 5,* 127–134.

Ross, H. L. (1973). Law, science, and accidents: The British Road Safety Act of 1967. *Journal of Legal Studies, 2,* 1–75.

Rubin, D. B. (1974). Estimating causal effects of treatments in randomized and nonrandomized studies. *Journal of Educational Psychology, 66,* 688–701.

Sansone, C., Morf, C. C., & Panter, A. T. (2004). The research process: Of big pictures, little details, and the social psychological road in between. In C. Sansone, C. C. Morf, & A. T. Panter (Eds.), *The Sage handbook of methods in social psychology* (pp. 3–16). Thousand Oaks, CA: Sage.

Seltzer, M. H. (1994). Studying variation in program success: A multilevel modeling approach. *Evaluation Review, 18,* 342–361.

Shadish, W. R., Cook, T. D., & Campbell, D. T. (2002). *Experimental and quasi-experimental designs for generalized causal inference.* Boston: Houghton-Mifflin.

Steiner, D., & Mark, M. M. (1985). The impact of a community action group: An illustration of the potential of time series analysis for the study of community groups. *American Journal of Community Psychology, 13,* 13–30.

Stigler, S. M. (1987). Testing hypotheses or fitting models: Another look at mass extinction. In M. H. Nitecki & A. Hoffman (Eds.), *Neutral models in biology* (pp. 145–149). Oxford, UK: Oxford University Press.

Trochim, W. M. K. (1984). *Research design for program evaluation: The regression–discontinuity approach.* Newbury Park, CA: Sage.

Tukey, J. W. (1977). *Exploratory data analysis.* Reading, MA: Addison-Wesley.

Tukey, J. W. (1986). *The collected works of John W. Tukey: Vol. 4. Philosophy and principles of data analysis: 1965–1986.* Monterey, CA: Wadsworth.

Weitzman, B. C., Silver, D., & Dillman, K.-N. (2002). Integrating a comparison group design into a theory of change evaluation: The case of the Urban Health Initiative. *American Journal of Evaluation, 23,* 371–385.

Winship, C., & Morgan, S. L. (1999). The estimation of causal effects from observational data. *Annual Review of Sociology, 25,* 659–707.

DOCUMENT RESEARCH

CHAPTER 5

Researching Documents

Emergent Methods

Lindsay Prior

The moving finger writes and having writ, moves on. . . .
—*Rubáiyát of Omar Khayyám* (E. Fitzgerald, Trans.)

Writing and Action

The dynamic connection between writing and action that is highlighted in the opening quotation constitutes the central theme of this chapter. Oddly, it is a theme that is rarely taken up with issues relating to social research, despite the fact that writing plays such a large part in our own culture. Indeed, in our age and in our world, writing is more often than not seen as being divorced from action—as something that is static, immutable, and isolated from real human activity, contained as it is in books, World Wide Web pages, and other forms of documentation. Yet the plain fact is that writing has proved to be one of the most influential technologies ever invented, and the role of writing in underpinning forms of social organization and interaction is difficult to overestimate.

Writing is not, of course, coterminous with documentation; rather, it is contained within documentation (along with numerous other human creations such as maps, architectural plans, film, photographs, and other kinds of images). However, in this chapter I am not overly concerned with drawing distinctions between writing, text, and documentation but merely refer to documents in a generic sense—that is, as readable matter.

I have called on and extensively used documents in social research—mainly in the context of medical sociology—and it seems to me that they always enter into social affairs in two modes: (1) as receptacles of content and (2) as agents in networks of action. Traditionally, however, the main point of focus for sociologists and other social scientists has been on the collection and analysis of document content more than on documents as agents or actors. Indeed, a focus on documents as containers for content is well established in the social sciences. Documents in this frame can be approached as sources of information and the writing and images that they contain scoured for appropriate data. Thus letters, texts, photographs (and other images), biographies, and autobiographies, as well as documents containing statistical data, are typically regarded as a resource for the social science researcher—see, for example, Plummer (2001) and Scott (1990, 2006). Usually, various kinds of content analysis are adopted for such approaches; see Bryman (2004), Krippendorf (2004), and May (2001). Content analysis can also blend into discourse analysis, a form of analysis that examines how objects and relations between objects are represented and structured by means of text and talk (Wood, 2000).

On occasion, documents may also be studied as topic rather than resource, in which case the focus is, in part, on the ways in which any given document came to assume its actual content and structure. This latter approach is akin to what Foucault (1972) might have called the "archaeology of documentation"—looking, for example, at the first points at which certain objects in the world are mentioned and come into being or revealing the ways in which systems of classification of things in the world, such as birds, flowers, and viruses, change at specific points in time. (For examples of such strategies, see Prior, 2003.)

Approaching documents as topic rather than resource also opens up a further dimension of analysis, which concerns the ways in which documents are used in social interaction and how they function. And once we choose to focus on use and function, the possibility of somewhat more dynamic (rather than static) styles of document analysis arise. Indeed, in this vein it is evident that during recent decades new approaches to the study of documents have emerged. In the field of sociology these new visions may be seen to relate, in part, to developments in actor–network theory (Law & Hassard, 1999). In history and the history of science they relate to the newly emergent "geographies of knowledge" (Livingstone, 2005). In all cases the key theme involves a consideration of documents as objects and actors in a web of activity.

Examining the role of documents in a network generates questions about what documents "do," rather than what they "say"—though in the messy way of the world such distinctions hold only at a conceptual rather than an empirical level. In the following sections I expand on the issues that I have alluded to so far.

Content and Discourse

The use of documents as sources of evidence has a long and worthy tradition in the empirical social sciences. Even the nascent sociologists of the 19th century, such as Karl Marx, regularly called on documents as sources of data. In the case of Marx, of course, those documents were mainly British government official reports of agricultural, industrial, and commercial activity. These days the use of such "official" statistics and documentation is routine, and they can be approached either as a resource or as a topic, a distinction that I referred to earlier. Most documents that we encounter in everyday life, however, are not of the published and official variety but more likely come in unpublished and transitory forms. Thus, in everyday life, we are far more likely to encounter checkout receipts, newspapers, Web pages, advertising (junk mail) materials, and invoices from utility and credit card companies than official statistics about the economy, health, or labor markets.

The introduction of routine and everyday documents as data for social scientists can probably be attributed to researchers associated with the Chicago "school" of sociology during the 1920s and 1930s. Those early sociologists regularly used diaries; letters; and written descriptions of what it was like to be a gang member, a "jack-roller," or an ordinary resident in a "slum"; and they frequently supplemented such accounts with photographs (of people and places), as well as maps and the like. Thus Thrasher's (1927) study of gang membership and activities in Chicago (published as *The Gang*) is littered with extracts from such things as "gang boy's own story," "report of a private investigation," reports from the *Chicago Daily News*, and photographs of adolescent gang members, residential districts, and members of Chinese Tongs. A similar array of documents was used by Zorbaugh (1929) in his description of the Gold Coast and the slum; namely, personal life stories, school essays, the Illinois Lodging House register, the Chicago social register, maps, photographs, and diagrams, as well as a whole gamut of what were later to be called unobtrusive measures (Webb, 2000), such as "observations" of residents in the slum, in Little Sicily, and on Lake Shore Drive. However, in none of the studies could it be said that the analysis of the documentary materials was systematic and aimed at testing social theory; rather, it was selective and used to illustrate conjectures and claims that had already been decided on. Nevertheless, the tradition of using documents as a resource for research studies was established, and during subsequent decades a good number of sociological and anthropological studies used diaries, letters, biographies, and autobiographies as life histories and as important sources of social scientific data (Angrosino, 1989). Plummer (2001) provides an excellent overview of the field of "personal" documents and indicates how the use and study of such materials came to be associated with distinct methods of social scientific inquiry (as is the case with "biographical" methods, for example).

Scouring newspapers and other documents for supportive stories or evidence is one way of approaching document content, but a more systematic approach would require an analysis of the entire content of a document—looking at the segments that fail to fit hypotheses and theories, as well as at those that support hypotheses and theories. To undertake such tasks requires the adoption of some form of content analysis, and the analysis of content—whether it is from a newspaper story, a life history, a police report on a crime scene, or a social work report on a person with multiple problems—can take any one of a number of routes. In my own case, I usually like to begin any analysis by identifying the words used in a document, as well as the number of times that any given word is used. (This can be achieved through the use of simple concordance programs that are freely available on the Web.) Hence it is clear from the start that content analysis usually implies both enumeration and understanding of the various words within a text. For example, in Table 5.1, I have provided an indication of the number of times that particular words appeared in a patient-support-group leaflet for people who suffer from chronic fatigue syndrome (CFS; also known in the United Kingdom as

TABLE 5.1. Occurrence of Selected Words in a 2,315-Word Patient-Support-Group Leaflet on Chronic Fatigue Syndrome

Fatigue	55
Chronic	51
Illness	50
Syndrome	46
Research	29
Virus/viral/virology	23
Disease	19
Fibromyalgia	18
Depression	14
Immune/immune-related/immunology	9
Genetic	4
Psychology/psychological	4
Neurology/neurological	4
Psychoneuroimmunology	2
Psychiatric/psychiatrists	2
Mental	1
Mind	1

Note. Data from Prior (2003).

myalgic encephalomyelitis and in the United States as chronic fatigue and immune dysfunction syndrome). Given the name of the condition, the appearance in the document of *fatigue* and *chronic* more than 50 times apiece is not perhaps surprising. However, it is interesting to note that viruses seem to be associated with whatever is going on in the document (23 citations), as well as an entity referred to as *fibromyalgia* (18 citations), depression (14), genes (4), and something called *psychoneuroimmunology* (2).

The simple presence of these words is worthy of note and, for someone who knows the arguments and debates associated with the diagnosis and treatment of CFS, they are all highly significant. In general, however, rather than focusing on individual words, it is usually more important for the researcher to grasp (1) how the words relate to each other and (2) what is being implied by their use. Let us consider a brief example by moving up a level and looking at sentences and phrases rather than just words. Here is an extract from the aforementioned document:

> Is CFS genetic? The cause of the illness is not yet known. Current theories are looking at the possibilities of neuroendocrine dysfunction, viruses, environmental toxins, genetic predisposition, or a combination of these. For a time it was thought that Epstein–Barr virus (EBV), the cause of mononucleosis, might cause CFS but recent research has discounted this idea. The illness seems to prompt a chronic immune reaction in the body, however it is not clear that this is in response to any actual infection—this may only be a dysfunction of the immune system itself.

A number of things are evident from the passage, such as the cause of the illness being unknown; the possibility of the illness being caused by toxins, viruses, or endocrine disorder; the fact that the illness might be "genetic" or caused by immune dysfunction. Indeed, the suggestion is that whatever the cause might be, it is likely to be physiological (possibly neurological) rather than, say, psychological. Indeed, later on in the document, we get the following statement: "Emerging illnesses such as CFS typically go through a period of many years before they are accepted by the medical community, and during that interim time patients who have these new, unproven illnesses are all too often dismissed as being 'psychiatric cases.' This has been the experience with CFS as well."

So it is also clear that somebody somewhere has argued that CFS might be related in some way to psychological or psychiatric conditions, but the author of this document rejects such a claim because that would be to suggest that CFS is being "dismissed" or not "accepted" as a real illness simply because it is "unproven." In fact, were I to produce the document in full, it would be reasonably easy to see that throughout the text there is a tension between the claims of the writer—who asserts variously that CFS is a "real" and essentially "physical disease"—and some unknown others who have claimed that CFS is related to depression, anxiety, and other psychological problems. (Similar tensions are evident in debates concerning the nature of fibromyalgia; see Table 5.1). By examining such tensions in the chosen text, the analyst is drawn into a examination of a rhetoric of illness concerning the ways in which a disorder of unknown cause is represented and understood by different parties. It is at that point, however, that content analysis tends to drift into discourse analysis.

Unlike content analysis, discourse analysis is an awkward concept to capture. It has essentially concerned the ways in which things and our knowledge of things are structured and represented through text and talk. For instance, there is a considerable tradition within social studies of science and technology of examining the role of scientific rhetoric in structuring our notions of "nature" and the place of human beings within nature. The role and structure of scientific rhetoric in text has, for example, figured in the work of Bazerman (1988), Gross (1996), Latour and Woolgar (1979), Myers (1990), and Woolgar (1988), and it has even been extended beyond text and into the realm of visual representations (Lynch & Woolgar, 1990) and everyday talk (Gilbert & Mulkay, 1984). And in this vein there have been numerous studies examining how the objects of science, medicine, and technology have been, and are, structured through discourse. One particularly interesting set of studies has been that which has concentrated attention on the concept of the gene and the human genome and how genetics is both represented and recruited into scientific and other texts. (The recruitment of "genetic" into the foregoing text on CFS could itself form an interesting site for analysis.) For example, Lily Kay (2000) analyzed the role of metaphors of the gene and genetics in genetic science between the 1950s and the 21st century, indicating how the image of DNA as a code or text of instructions (recipe) or plan (blueprint) emerged only gradually during the second half of the 20th century. Thus she points out how, in the famous April 1953 *Nature* article by Crick and Watson on DNA, the authors referred only to the structure of DNA, and she then investigates how the idea of using concepts of grammar and semantics to describe genetic processes emerged during the 1960s, particularly relating to work on "messenger" RNA. Indeed, the first "word" of the genetic code (the UUU of RNA) was not identified until 1961. Kay argues that the Nobel Prize–winning work of Nirenberg and Mathei (who discovered the first word) would simply not have been possible without calling on and utilizing metaphors of communication and information science such as I referred to earlier.

Other writers have chosen to focus on genetic discourse in everyday culture (as reflected through news stories and the like), with equally interesting results. Thus Nelkin (2001), for instance, has noted how, in popular culture, DNA is not simply regarded as a "code," carrying and expressing information, but that it is also endowed with executive action. In short, DNA is represented through text as something that "makes things" (humans, cancers, and so forth) in a deterministic system.

In the following paragraph I present some of my own data (derived from a talk between a doctor and a client of a cancer genetics service in the United Kingdom) to illustrate some possibilities of this kind of approach. Although the data are derived from talk (rather than text per se), they serve to illustrate how analysis of a discourse can reveal detail about the ways in which, in any given culture, the world and the objects within it are represented and structured.

200 *Doctor*: And the genes are broken up into sections and so a gene that

201 controls a protein function in a body is not just one long coding

202 instruction it is in fact broken up into sections that then get joined

203 together. And those sections you can think of them as being volumes of

204 an encyclopedia. Basically between the two genes there are effectively

205 50 volumes. And it takes our laboratory a week to check each one,

206 which you can then work out quite quickly that that is effectively a year

207 to check every single one. That is just the practicality of the time scale.

208 The other problem though, if you are dealing with something as big as

209 something like an encyclopedia and you are looking for a mistake and

210 effectively what you are dealing with is just a code, a series of letters, then

211 you are looking for something like a missing paragraph or sometimes just

212 a missing word, or sometimes just a missing letter. And right down to

213 just a change on one letter can be all that is needed to have disastrous

214 effects.

215 *Patient*: Yeah.

A number of issues deserve attention here. The first is the extensive use of metaphor in this exchange. In particular, genes are referred to as "coding instructions" (lines 201–202, 210), "volumes of an encyclopedia" (203–204), a "series of letters" (210), words and/or paragraphs (211–212). And in accord with such rhetorical forms, mutations are referred to as "missing" words, letters, or paragraphs, as "mistakes" possibly brought about by a "change in just one letter" (213). The second issue of interest is in what may be called the actional components of the sentences that link genes to human physiology. Of particular significance is the way in which genes are said to "control" protein functions (line 201), and genetic rearrangements of DNA sequences (letters) are argued to be capable of having "disastrous effects" (line 213–214) on the human body. Such attention to the ways in which the use of tropes (such as metaphor) and syntax operate in text leads us to consider such text as "accounts" rather than as descriptions of the world—the research task being to dissect the ways in which the account structures the world. In the case of talk about genes and genetics, it is often the case that humans are represented as being at the mercy of their genes and determined by them.

As I have said, it could be argued that with both content and discourse analysis researchers are essentially seeking to use documentation as "resource"—that is, as a source of data for social scientific theorizing (of varying degrees of complexity). It is, however, possible to approach document content as topic. The very useful distinction between resource and topic was first introduced by Zimmerman and Pollner (1971), and picking up on this distinction can encourage us to ask a different set of questions about documentation. So instead of focusing merely on what documents contain, we can begin to ask how the documentation that we elect to examine came to assume the form that it did. This line of inquiry can be especially useful in the examination of the ways in which people "sort things out" (Bowker & Star, 1999). For instance, it is often instructive in matters of social research to ask how things come to be classified in a particular way (and not in other ways) and what rules are to be used to allocate objects to one realm rather than another. Thus we might, for example, ask questions concerning the "causes" of death, disease, and illness, such as, What can one die of? The answer to that question is invariably constrained by the content of a World Health Organization (WHO) manual, namely, the *International Classification of Diseases and Related Health Problems* (WHO, 1992). It is often referred to in an abbreviated form as the ICD. The current edition of the manual is the 10th, and so the abbreviation is, more accurately, ICD-10. ICD-10 provides a list of all currently accepted causes of death, and they are classified into chapters. Thus there are chapters relating to diseases and disorders of the respiratory system, the circulatory system, the nervous system, and so on. In different decades, different diseases and causes of death are added and deleted from the manual. HIV/AIDS is an obvious case of an addition, and it appears as a cause of death only in ICD-10, whereas "old age" as a cause of death was eliminated in ICD-6. Such taxonomies reflect aspects of human culture, and researching the "archaeology" of such documents can be instructive in itself.

A related publication—the *Diagnostic and Statistical Manual of Mental Disorders* (American Psychiatric Association, 2000), or DSM—is available for the classification of psychiatric conditions. One might say that the DSM provides the conceptual architecture in terms of which Western culture comprehends disorders of the mind. Posttraumatic stress disorder was, for instance, first recognized as a disorder only in DSM-III (first published in 1974), whereas multiple personality disorder (MPD) has undergone a few transformations and is no longer listed in the fourth revised edition of the DSM. The inclusion and deletion of such diagnostic categories can be used as key indicators of not merely how professional and technical discourse might have altered but also how political, legal, and socioeconomic processes impinge on the affairs of science and medicine (for a detailed example of the relationships between a form of scientific classification and styles of professional practice, see Keating & Cambrosio, 2000).

The standardization of taxonomies and the application of rules for allocating things and events to appropriate categories is important for various reasons, but not least for generating images of the world. For example, the ways in which events relating to crime, the economy, illness and disease, or education are classified and counted are fundamental to our understanding of long-term trends and our image of contemporary happenings. And as numerous analysts of official statistical accounts of the world have demonstrated (see, e.g., May, 2001; Prior, 2003), for any given society we can have as much or as little illness, crime, "success," and "failure" as we want–depending on how, exactly, we sort things out.

Unfortunately, once we are engaged with the ubiquitous messiness of the empirical world, many of these distinctions between content and discourse, topic and resource are difficult to hold to. For documents, like most phenomena, are fluid and somewhat slippery objects for analysis. Most important, documentation can have a dynamic as well as a static dimension, and in the following sections I aim to focus on the dynamic that affects the production and consumption of document content. I also aim to consider the ways in which documents can be considered as actors.

Studying Documents in Action

A focus on documents in action tends to encourage a focus on how documents are used (function) and how they are exchanged and circulated in various communities. Naturally, documents carry content–words, images, plans, ideas, patterns, and so forth–but the ways in which such content is actually called on and how it functions cannot be determined (though it may be constrained) by an analysis of its content. Indeed once a text or document is sent out into the world, there is simply no predicting how it is going to circulate and how it is going to function in specific social and cultural contexts. For this reason alone, a study of what the author(s) of a given document (text) "meant" or intended can only ever add up to limited examination of what a document "is." Thus the literary theorist de Certeau (1974/1984, p. 170) has stated that "Whether it is a question of newspapers or Proust, the text has a meaning only through its readers; it changes along with them; it is ordered in accordance with codes of perception that it does not control." In this regard an interest in the reception and reading of text has formed the focus for recent histories of knowledge that seek to examine how the "same" documents have been received and absorbed quite differently into different cultural and geographical contexts (see, e.g., Burke, 2000). A similar concern has arisen with regard to the newly emergent "geographies of knowledge" (see, e.g., Livingstone, 2005). In all cases the key theme involves a consideration of documents as objects and actors in a web of activity. In the following paragraph I consider two brief examples of the ways in which documents both enter into action and can function as actors in a network of processes.

My first example is (again) drawn from my own work and illustrates how documentation can form the occasion for talk and interaction, how it is drawn into interactions, and how it has effects on the performance of the interaction. The data are provided in Figure 5.1. The talk therein was gathered from a study of work in the same cancer genetics clinic that I mentioned earlier. In this instance a clinical geneticist (designated CG1) and a nurse-counselor (designated NC2) are discussing their understanding of the degree to which a given patient is at risk of inheriting a certain type of cancer-related mutation. The episode begins with NC2 asking to talk about a patient (line 1); following assent from the geneticist, NC2 very quickly

NC2: Do you want me to [talk] about this lady

[Looking at a pedigree or family tree]

[Consulting her notes]

CG1: Oh this isn't the one with 26 sibs, is it?

NC2: Yes it is. [Laughter] This is CW who herself has left breast cancer and having fairly active treatment. She has a huge number of siblings of whom a relatively appropriate number have malignancy. Her major reason to getting referred to us was actually the risk to her daughters. And if we actually look at her husband's side of the family they are actually at more risk because her husband's brother had breast cancer and her husband's sister had breast cancer at 37. I haven't been able to confirm but the history sounds very good from B.

[From records in hospital and cancer registry]

CG1: Right OK. I am just trying to remember does *Cyrillic* take account of males? I don't think it does, does it?

NC2: It didn't and it [calculated] a ridiculously inappropriate risk.

[A computerized device that draws pedigrees and calculates a risk of inheriting a cancer gene]

CG1: You just ignored it. You mean it came out as quite low?

NC2: Yes

[Pointing to pedigree]

CG1: But wouldn't that 37-year-old there?

NC2: Well because we were looking at her, and put the programs down to the . . . . I think the dilution effect of this ~~lot really~~.

[Pointing to males in the pedigree]

CG1: What we usually say is that a male equates to a bilateral female, same age.

NC2: He is 60 and he is well so we could DNA [she means give DNA]. I rang her and she was having treatment so she was quite poorly but quite anxious to come to clinic.

CG1: So is she aware that this side of the ~~family~~.

[Pointing to pedigree]

NC2: I have hinted that it is more an issue on this side of the family and that we would be able to explain the justification of that when she saw the family tree.

[Patient needs to see the printed pedigree in order to understand the problem]

CG1: But otherwise she is. . . . There are one, two

[Geneticist counts people on pedigree]

CG1 = Clinical Geneticist
NC2 = Nurse–Counselor

FIGURE 5.1. Documents as actors in episodes of interaction.

draws documentation into the discussion. She reads from her notes (the reason why the patient contacted the clinic; lines 5–6), she refers to a family history (or *pedigree*, as it is called in human genetics). She asks the participants to "look at" (line 6) the pedigree, and she refers to another set of documents (not present in the clinic) that it has not proved possible to check (cancer records or cancer registry; lines 8–9). In reply, the geneticist makes reference to a computerized decision aid that has drawn the pedigree (family history) and calculated the woman's risk of developing a cancer. In this case, the drawing has been composed by what Latour (1987) would refer to as an "inscription device" (known here as "Cyrillic," line 10). Cyrillic has also calculated the numerical risk (line 12) of inheritance—an estimate that NC2 has dismissed as "inappropriate." In lines 15–16 CG again brings the pedigree into discussion with NC2—the document (pedigree) forms the occasion for the talk; it is pointed at and used as evidence and counterevidence. Among other things, it serves as an actor that has assessed the risk of inheriting a mutation as "low," and that assessment has to be answered. It is answered in the following ways: it's "ridiculous," line 12; it doesn't "take account of males," lines 10–11; and it lets the males in the pedigree—referred to as "this lot"—"dilute" the estimate, lines 16–17. Yet in lines 23–25 it is suggested that the patient will not fully understand her problems unless she sees the pedigree that Cyrillic has drawn—at which point the pedigree will be used as "justification" for the concerns and analysis that the clinicians have arrived at (line 25). Finally, in line 26 we can witness how CG uses the pedigree as a counting device, adding up the people in the family tree of particular ages and disease states.

We can see, then, that the documents (notes, records, pedigrees) are central to the manner in which the interaction is sequenced and structured. Thus some documents (notes) are read; some documents (the pedigrees) are used as the occasion for the talk; some are pointed at and used to develop good arguments and justifications. What's more, the documents are linked to the speakers in distinct ways and in clear sequences and, among other things, serve to underline the ways in which the division of labor (between doctors and nurses) is underpinned in routine interaction (lines 1–2 and 16–19, specifically).

My second example illustrates a rather different way in which documents can enter into interaction and demonstrates how a document can influence action at a distance. The data are contained in Figure 5.2.

The figure contains extracts from a "special educational needs assessment" of a young boy. A psychologist executed the assessment. Once again, it is clear that we can choose to focus solely on the content of the document or to focus on the interactional dynamics that it is part of. For example, we might note the use of the categorization devices used in the assessment—such as "pleasant, likeable boy [with] a severely delayed/disordered phonological system"—and how the concerns of the psychologist structure the identity of the child. We might also take note of the grammar and syntax of the report, for example, "the boy has difficulty in accessing the curriculum." Yet we may also note that Part 3 of the assessment contains instructions for future action. How such action was to be implemented was the subject of a later section of the report that has not been reproduced here; nevertheless, it is clear that the report is designed not simply to categorize the child and his "problems" but also to instigate future action at a distance. It is instructing someone at a future date to do certain kinds of things. Indeed, this written assessment was also open to recruitment by parents, teachers, and others as an "ally," so as to demand more resources for the child even in the event of the "action" failing to take place. In that way the document (report) could also function (at a later point) as a warrant for further resources.

These two examples illustrate both how documents can be drawn into interaction

Part 2: Special Educational Needs.

(Here set out the child's special educational needs, in terms of the child's learning difficulties which call for special educational provision)

'Z' is a pleasant, likeable boy who has a severely delayed/disordered phonological system and a mild delay in his expressive language. His speech is largely unintelligible. Due to the severity of this delay he has difficulty in accessing the curriculum. He was slow to adapt to the social routines of the school day. His attention span is limited without adult support. He does show a high response in one to one situations with a known adult. Interaction with his peers is improving. Assessment of his non-verbal intellectual functioning is at the bottom end of the high average range, however, verbal intelligence falls into the low average range.

This pupil's special educational needs have been identified as follows:

1. *severe speech and language delay/disorder*
2. *poor social/interactive skills*

The attached reports contain more detail about 'Z's' specific attainments.

Part 3: Special Educational Provision.

Objectives. (Here specify the objectives which the special educational provision should aim to meet)

The objectives of the special educational provision to be made for this pupil should be:

1 To improve his receptive and expressive language skills
2 To develop early literacy and numeracy skills
3 To improve social/interactive skills

Educational provision to meet needs and objectives

FIGURE 5.2. Extracts from a "Statement of Special Educational Needs," Great Britain, 1999.

and how documents can function as actors in episodes of interaction. It is for this reason that in some previous publications I have referred to Goethe's "Sorcerer's Apprentice"—a poem that inspired a scene in the Walt Disney movie *Fantasia*. In the Disney movie we see how the apprentice, using his master's knowledge, enticed a household broom to carry buckets of water and free the apprentice from drudgery. Yet, when the time came for the apprentice to put the process to an end, the broom failed to stop—flooding the sorcerer's house. I would argue that documents have similarities to the active broom in that they are human creations, but they always retain the capacity to escape the intents of their designers so as to instigate new and sometimes radical processes of action.

Studying Documents in Networks

I have just suggested that documents can often be conceptualized as actors in networks of action. The idea of conceptualizing nonhuman agents as actors was first proposed by adherents of what came to be called actor–network theory, or ANT (see Callon, 1986; Law & Hassard, 1999). From the standpoint of this chapter, what was most important about ANT—over and above the suggestion that nonhuman agents might be considered as actors—was the notion that actors were linked in an actor network. Thus Michel Callon (1986), for example, linked the fisherman of Saint Brieuc Bay to the scallops that supported their livelihoods and spoke of the scallops very much as actors. (Other actors included a group of researchers, visitors to the bay, starfish, larvae, sea currents, etc.) The detail is not of importance here. What is important is that such a way of thinking fits into our notions of considering documents as members of networks—that is, as actors that can be recruited into webs of human activity and regarded by others as allies, enemies, or perhaps neutral agents or mere instigators of further actions. Once we adopt that point of view, then the key research questions revolve around the ways in which documents come to be integrated into networks and how they influence the development of the network. This kind of focus has, in some cases, led to important developments in research software to explore what we might call the relational aspects of humans and documentation. In what follows I outline a few examples. I concentrate first on World Wide Web pages as documents and sketch out how they can be approached in terms of the newly emergent social scientific frameworks.

In the first instance, of course, it is clear that Web pages can be scoured for their content alone. For example, in a study of antivaccination websites, Wolfe, Sharp, and Lipsky (2002) identified 22 such websites and noted that in all cases the documentation asserted that vaccines caused idiopathic illness; in 95% of cases, that vaccines erode immunity; and in 91% of cases, that vaccination policy was driven by profit motives rather than cares about health. These and other details concerning document content were acquired by the use of relatively simple coding techniques. The authors also noted that antivaccination sites used specific tactics for transmitting their messages. One favored strategy involved the use of personal stories, often from parents who served as witnesses to the fact that vaccination caused severe illness in their children. The use of personal stories in antivaccination texts is common, and such stories tend also to have a common structure. The structure normally recruits people into key roles and develops what might be called a heroic narrative of tragedy. Thus there is usually reference to a responsible parent, an irresponsible medical professional, an opposition between common sense and professional "knowledge," an atrocity or negative outcome of the lay–professional struggle (such as a child being disabled), and the expression of a determination to bring an end to such atrocities and the associated suffering. Such an analysis of story structure would, of course, inveigle us into a specific style of discourse analysis—in this case one that focused on narrative rather than on rhetoric. However, there remains a further strategy for the examination of antivaccination sites, and it involves looking at the networks that emerge out of the relations between such sites.

The possibility of examining relations between websites is, of course, built into websites ordinarily, for websites contain hyperlinks (to other Web pages), and by concentrating on the links between the Web pages it becomes possible to study how Internet documents relate to one another. In recent years the task of tracing the links between such sites has been facilitated by the use of Web crawlers. However, Richard Rogers, who has designed one such crawler (*www.govcom.org*), refers to issue networks and issue spaces rather than Web networks (see Marres & Rogers, 2005). An issue network is a network of pages that acknowledge each other by way of hyperlinks. I have provided a simple example of such a network in Figure 5.3.

This network consists of links relating to the field of pharmacogenetics. Put crudely, pharmacogenetics is aimed at tailoring specific types of medications (such as, say, antidepressants) to specific people or groups of people on the basis of what we

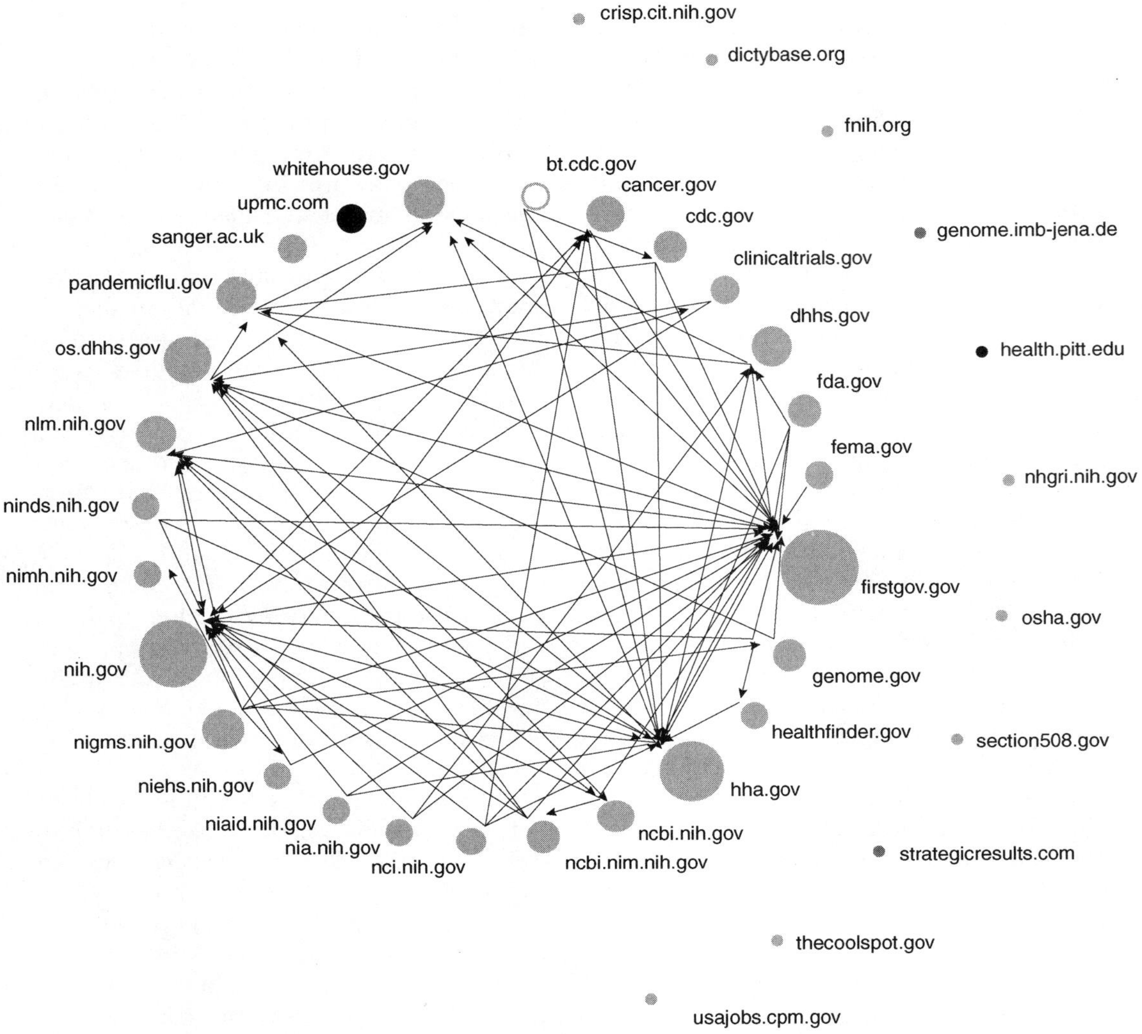

FIGURE 5.3. Relations between World Wide Web sites concerned with pharmacogenetics and antidepressants.

know about their genetic makeup or genotype. In the case of Figure 5.3, I was interested in discovering what kinds of connections might exist between the Web pages of institutions in which work on pharmacogenetics and antidepressants was being undertaken. One such site was the medical school at the University of Pittsburgh. I began by entering a few Web addresses into the Web crawler (such as the aforementioned university) and looked for links. Figure 5.3 represents some early results.

The links between Web documents may be considered as data in themselves, and they certainly point to factors such as the position of institutions (e.g., degrees of centrality), density of contact, and directions of contact. For example, even though the University of Pittsburgh (upmc.com) was entered as a starting point for the Web crawl, we can see that its relationship to most of the

Web pages in the diagram is peripheral. It appears only on the outer (upper left) edge of the main "globe." The sites that have the most contacts and connections and that are positioned inside the main globe are federal U.S. government sites. Indeed, the Web crawl is suggesting that the key actors in the world of pharmacogenetics are (1) in the United States (there is only one U.K. site and one German site, for example); and (2) concerned with the regulation of drugs rather than with their research or development. A more traditional representation of the same network is provided in Figure 5.4.

These two maps could, of course, be used as an initial research map for exploring the relationships between the various sites, though the exploration of such relationships would need to be supplemented by the use of other methods and techniques (such as in-

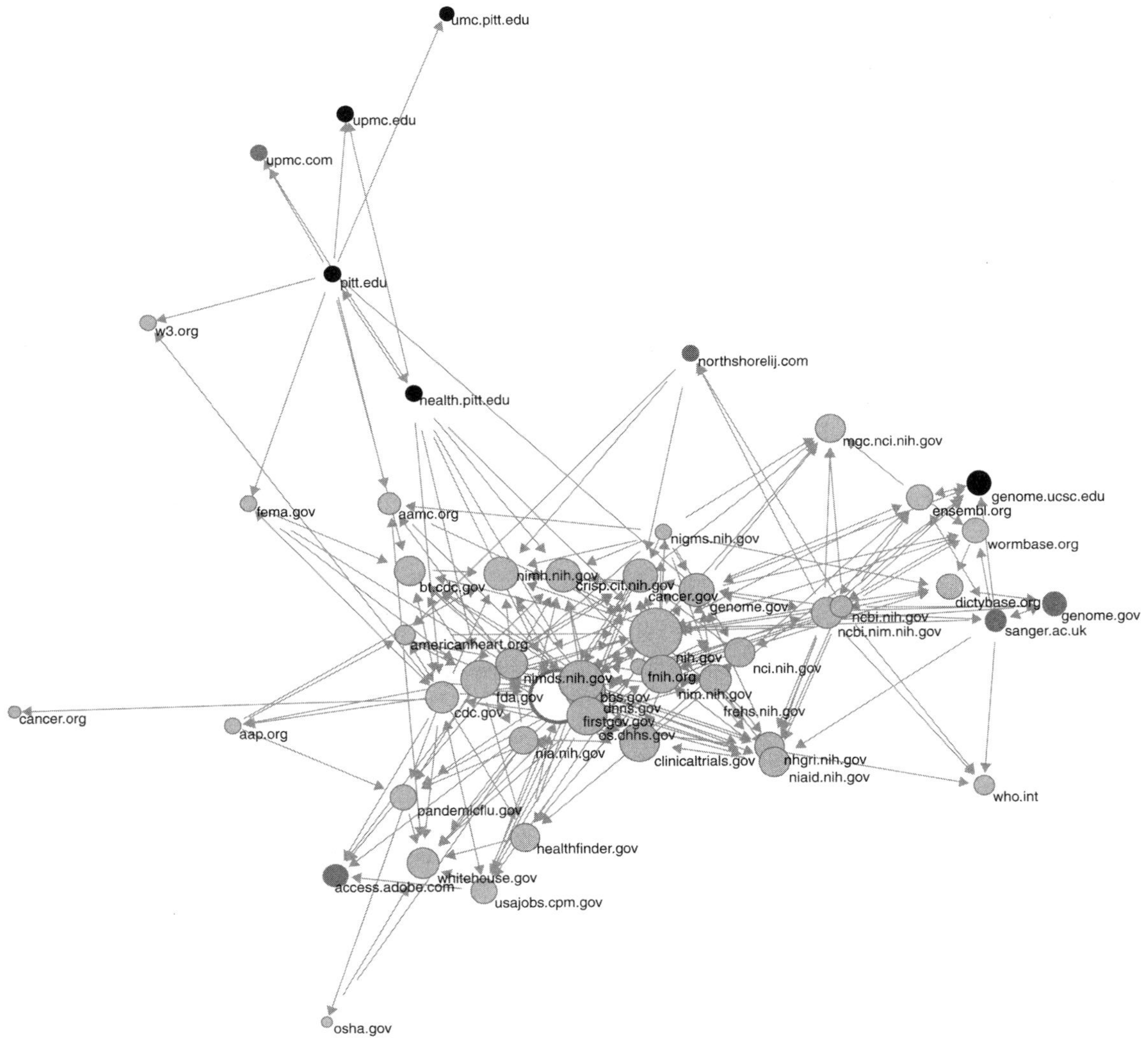

FIGURE 5.4. Networking documents: pharmacogenetics and antidepressants on the World Wide Web.

terview techniques or a range of ethnographic methods). Nevertheless, the provision of the Web map provides both a starting point and a ground on which hypotheses might be generated concerning notions of, say, "governance" in the field of pharmacogenetics. There is, however, a feature of social activity that is only touched on, rather than confronted, by the use of a Web crawler. It involves the fact that actor networks contain human as well as nonhuman actors.

By tradition, a focus on relationships between people in a network has been associated with social network analysis. Such analysis concentrates on the number of links between specific individuals, the degree to which an individual is central or peripheral to a given network, the density of interactional or contact nodes, and so forth (see Scott, 1999). However, as actor–network theorists emphasize, social networks cannot be reduced to relations between humans. Consequently, what is usually needed is an analysis of relationships between humans, organizations, and things (such as documents, machines, germs, etc.). For example, Cambrosio, Keating, and Mogoutov (2004) studied the nature of collaborative research networks and innovation in a specific field of biomedicine. The researchers were interested in how the people in the network collaborated, as well as the role of such things as antigen, antibody reagents (contained in bottles), and antibodies in a research network. One component of their investigation

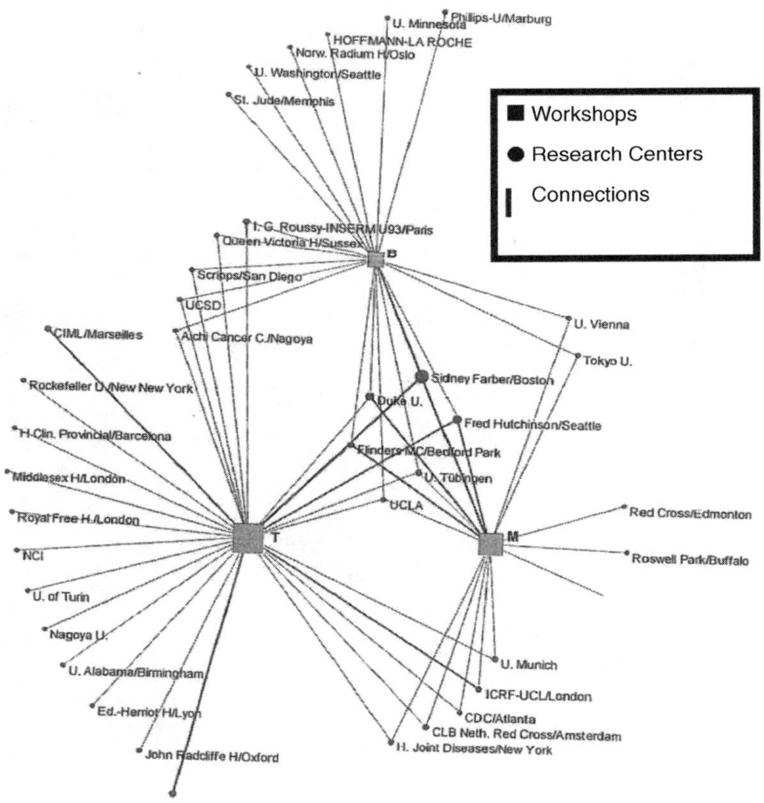

FIGURE 5.5. Human leukocyte differentiation antigens (HLDA): relations between workshops, research centers, and antigens. From Cambrosio, Keating, and Mogoutov (2004). Copyright 2004 by Sage Publications Ltd. Reprinted by permission.

concentrated on the relationships between research workshops and research laboratories in the development of particular (human leukocyte differentiation antigens, HLDA) antibodies, and Cambrosio and colleagues sought to develop a network map of the relations that linked the institutions and workshops to the antibodies. In doing that, they developed a network map, reproduced as Figure 5.5. In the context of this figure, the points T, M, and B represent different research workshops. The outer points represent the laboratories or research centers, and the size of the circles and squares are proportional to the number of antibodies submitted by each laboratory to each workshop. We can see immediately from the map how the relationships fan out, the relative importance of each of the three workshops, and which institutions are linked to which antibodies. Antibodies are not documents, of course, but the network map illustrates how documents could be mapped into a scheme of social relations and how it could be the documents that form the focus of attention rather than the human beings. However, such maps require dedicated software that can generate visual traces of an actor network, and in the case discussed the relevant technology was provided by Réseau-Lu (see Mogoutov, Cambrosio, & Keating, 2005).

Conclusion: A Lesson from Old World America

In the world of the Maya during the late classic period (600–850 A.D.), it seems evident (on the basis of archaeological data) that writing was an activity that was venerated and worshipped. Writing was regarded as an activity inspired by the gods and was something that linked humanity to the cosmos (Miller & Martin, 2004). On Mayan pottery, for example, one sees images of godly agents—the rabbit and the monkey in particular—recording the unfolding joys and tragedies of humanity in their jaguar-skin books. More important, stone carvings of the Mayan palaces suggest that writing was regarded as an animate force in its own right with its own power and being. Unfortunately, in our world, it is that sense of the power and influence of writing—and of documentation—that has been lost.

In the sections that have preceded this conclusion, I have attempted to outline the different ways in which the power of documentation can be captured by the empirical researcher. I have suggested that traditional approaches to documentation revolve around analysis of content, that content analysis can lead into various forms of discourse analysis, but that neither kind of analysis can capture the dynamic features of documentation. I have provided some illustrations of the ways in which documentation is often woven into the fine grain of interaction and how it influences episodes of interaction. I have further suggested that both theoretical and technical developments (in computer software) over recent decades have enabled us to focus far more on the relational properties of documentation and specifically on the role of documents as agents in networks of action. Having pointed toward such developments, I end this overview with an analogy that I believe to be useful when we consider how to approach the study of documents in human affairs. My analogy concerns an operatic libretto (the words and story-line of the opera). Taken on its own, a libretto rarely adds up to much. The text as narrative is often disjointed, repetitive, and lacking in depth. I cannot think of a single one that might hold a person's attention as a gripping tale. Yet a libretto is not intended to be analyzed in isolation. It demands to be analyzed in action. How it is integrated into the dramatic action on stage, how it relates to the melody and rhythm of the music, how it is called on (recruited or enrolled) and manipulated by the singers, how it is performed—all of these are of primary importance. Its substance as displayed on the inert page is of only secondary concern.

References

American Psychiatric Association. (2000). *Diagnostic and statistical manual of mental disorders* (4th ed., text rev.). Washington, DC: Author.

Angrosino, M. V. (1989). *Documents of interaction: Biography, autobiography, and life history in social science perspective*. Gainesville: University of Florida Press.

Bazerman, C. (1988). *Shaping written knowledge: The genre and activity of the experimental article in science*. Madison: University of Wisconsin Press.

Bowker, G. C., & Star, S. L. (1999). *Sorting things out: Classification and its consequences*. Cambridge, MA: MIT Press.

Bryman, A. (2004). *Social research methods* (2nd ed.). Oxford, UK: Oxford University Press.

Burke, P. (2000). *A social history of knowledge: From Gutenberg to Diderot*. Cambridge, UK: Polity Press.

Callon, M. (1986). Some elements of a sociology of translation: Domestication of the scallops and the fishermen of Saint Brieuc Bay. In J. Law (Ed.) *Power, action and belief: A new sociology of knowledge?* (Sociological Review Monograph No. 32, pp. 196–233). London: Routledge & Kegan Paul.

Cambrosio, A., Keating, P., & Mogoutov, A. (2004). Mapping collaborative work and innovation in biomedicine. *Social Studies of Science, 34*(3), 325-364.

de Certeau, M. (1984). *The practice of everyday life* (S. Rendall, Trans.). Berkeley: University of California Press. (Original work published 1974)

Foucault, M. (1972). *The archaeology of knowledge* (A. Sheridan, Trans.). New York: Pantheon.

Gilbert, G. N., & Mulkay, M. (1984). *Opening Pandora's box: A sociological analysis of scientists' discourse*. Cambridge, UK. Cambridge University Press.

Gross, A. G. (1990). *The rhetoric of science*. Cambridge, MA: Harvard University Press.

Kay, L. E. (2000). *Who wrote the book of life? A history of the genetic code*. Stanford, CA: Stanford University Press.

Keating, P., & Cambrosio, A. (2000). "Real compared to what?" Diagnosing leukemias and lymphomas. In M. Lock, A. Young, & A. Cambrosio (Eds.), *Living and working with the new medical technologies: Intersections of inquiry* (pp. 103–134). Cambridge, UK: Cambridge University Press.

Krippendorf, K. (2004). *Content analysis: An introduction to its methodology* (2nd ed.). London: Sage.

Latour, B. (1987). *Science in action: How to follow scientists and engineers through society*. Milton Keynes, UK: Open University Press.

Latour, B., & Woolgar, S. (1979). *Laboratory life: The social construction of scientific facts*. London: Sage.

Law, J., & Hassard, J. (Eds.). (1999). *Actor–network theory and after*. Oxford, UK: Blackwell.

Livingstone, D. N. (2005). Text, talk, and testimony: Geographical reflections on scientific habits: An afterword. *British Society for the History of Science, 38*(1), 93–100.

Lynch, M., & Woolgar, S. (Eds.). (1990). *Representation in scientific practice*. Cambridge, MA: MIT Press.

Marres, N., & Rogers, R. (2005). Recipe for tracing the fate of issues and their publics on the Web. In B. Latour & P. Wiebel (Eds.), *Making things public: Atmospheres of democracy* (pp. 922–935). Cambridge, MA: MIT Press.

May, T. (2001). *Social research: Issues, methods and process* (3rd ed.). Buckingham, UK: Open University Press.

Miller, M., & Martin, S. (2004). *Courtly art of the ancient Maya*. San Francisco: Fine Arts Museum of San Francisco with Thames & Hudson.

Mogoutov, A., Cambrosio, A., & Keating, P. (2005). Making collaborative networks visible. In B. Latour & P. Wiebel (Eds.), *Making things public: Atmospheres of democracy* (pp. 342–345). Cambridge, MA: MIT Press.

Myers, G. (1990). *Writing biology: Texts in the construction of scientific knowledge*. London: University of Wisconsin Press.

Nelkin, D. (2001). Molecular metaphors: The gene in popular discourse. *Nature Reviews, 2*, 555–559.

Plummer, K. (2001). *Documents of life. 2. An invitation to critical humanism*. London: Sage.

Prior, L. (2003). *Using documents in social research*. London: Sage.

Scott, J. (1990). *A matter of record: Documentary sources in social research*. Cambridge, UK: Polity Press.

Scott, J. (1999). *Social network analysis*. London: Sage.

Scott, J. P. (Ed.). (2006). *Documentary research* (Vols. 1–4). London: Sage.

Thrasher, F. M. (1927). *The gang*. Chicago: Chicago University Press.

Webb, E. J. (2000). *Unobtrusive measures*. Thousand Oaks, CA: Sage.

Wolfe, R. M., Sharp, L. K., & Lipsky, M. S. (2002). Content and design attributes of antivaccination websites. *Journal of the American Medical Association, 287*(24), 3245–3248.

Wood, L. A. (2000). *Doing discourse analysis: Methods for studying action in talk and text*. London: Sage.

Woolgar, S. (1988). *Science: The very idea*. London: Tavistock.

World Health Organization. (1992). *International statistical classification of diseases and related health problems* (10th rev. ed., Vols. 1–3). London: HMSO.

Zimmerman, D. H., & Pollner, M. (1971). The everyday world as a phenomenon. In J. D. Douglas (Ed.), *Understanding everyday life* (pp. 80–103). London: Routledge & Kegan Paul.

Zorbaugh, H. W. (1929). *The Gold Coast and slum: A sociological study of Chicago's near north side*. Chicago: University of Chicago Press.

CHAPTER 6

Emergent Qualitative Document Analysis

David Altheide
Michael Coyle
Katie DeVriese
Christopher Schneider

Our project is to delineate and provide research examples of the practice of qualitative document analysis (QDA; also referred to as ethnographic content analysis, or ECA) as an emergent methodology, rather than a rigid set of procedures with tight parameters. As the following pages illustrate, emergence primarily occurs in sampling and analysis. The research process and the interaction between the researcher and the subject matter is key. Although any content or document analysis can be narrowly cast, QDA is oriented to combining several steps in investigation with an explorer's eye to pursue concepts, data, and other information sources that emerge in the context of the thinking and discovering process of research. A document may be defined as any symbolic representation that can be recorded and retrieved for description and analysis. A qualitative approach focuses on describing and tracking discourse, including words, meanings, and themes over time. Utilizing protocols to tap documents in various information bases, QDA relies on immersion in the subject matter, conceptually informed conversation with numerous documents and examples, and theoretical sampling for systematic and constant comparison. However, getting to the point of focusing on specific terms as a feature of discourse requires constant exploration (Glaser & Strauss, 1967) and a willingness to check out other documents and sources. This process entails being flexible to nuances, surprises, and confusion. Ongoing research projects illustrate how some criminal justice discourse has "traveled" into other institutional realms, whereas in other instances, such as rap music, criminal justice terms are resisted and have been appropriated by "street culture." Our emphasis is on using the "findings" as a resource for illustrating the emergent process involved. An overview of QDA and its ethnographic and reflective nature is followed by a discussion of several projects.

Introduction to QDA

QDA is a method and research orientation that is informed by reflexive methodology in a mass-mediated age. The emphasis is on discovery and description, including searching for contexts, underlying meanings, patterns, and processes, rather than on mere quantity or numerical relationships between two or more variables, which is emphasized in traditional quantitative content analysis (Altheide, 1996; Berger, 1982). As a variant of quantitative content analysis, QDA is more interested in thematic emphasis and trends in communication patterns and discourse than in mere frequencies and statistically inferred relationships (Krippendorff, 2004). QDA, or ECA, refers to an integrated method, procedure, and technique for locating, identifying, retrieving, and analyzing documents for their relevance, significance, and meaning (Altheide, 1987, 1996). This approach is now widely recognized as a basic qualitative research method (Lewis-Beck, Bryman, & Liao, 2004). As Altheide (1996) stated:

> However, a major difference is the reflexive and highly interactive nature of the investigator, concepts, data collection and analysis. Unlike [quantitative content analysis] in which the protocol is the instrument, the investigator is continually central in ECA, although protocols may be used in later phases of the research. Like all ethnographic research, the meaning of a message is assumed to be reflected in various modes of information exchange, format, rhythm and style e.g., aural and visual, as well as the context of the report itself, and other nuances. (p. 16)

QDA follows a recursive and reflexive movement between concept development, sampling, data collection, data coding, data analysis, and interpretation. The aim is to be systematic and analytic but not rigid. Categories and "variables" initially guide the study, but others are allowed and expected to emerge throughout the study, including an orientation toward constant discovery and constant comparison of relevant situations, settings, styles, images, meanings, and nuances.

QDA emerged in a context of theoretical, epistemological, and methodological paradigm shifts and developments. Theoretical interests in the significance of social meanings, and particularly the role of the mass media in the social construction of reality and in contributing to how people define situations (e.g., new propaganda studies), led a host of researchers oriented to symbolic interaction, communication research, and cultural studies (as well as critical criminology) to understand how social reality was symbolically constructed, managed, packaged, and "sold" to audiences. Broader questions about social change and social control merged with a more active conception of the mass media as a significant social institution that fueled a rapidly expanding popular culture, particularly youth culture (Ferrarotti, 1988; Gronbeck, Farrell, & Soukop, 1991). The mass media came to be understood as key in the nexus of social order, a key to the ecology of communication, which refers to the structure, organization, and accessibility of information technology, various forums, media, and channels of information (Altheide, 1995). Emphasis shifts from "media effects" to media and modes of representation, including ideological and cultural forms. The significance of media formats and media–or the shape and structure of messages and images–is recognized.

The theoretical shifts were also accompanied by epistemological insights most aptly captured by the phrase "the reflexive turn," or the awareness that one's research methods could not be completely separated from research findings, that the process of knowledge was implicated in the product. These developments were informed by dissatisfaction with positivistic social science and the "welfare state" orientation identified by Gouldner (1970) and others, as well as the anti-Vietnam War, civil rights, and feminist social movements. Several social science departments (e.g., several campuses in the University of California system) acquired a "critical mass" of faculty and students interested in the social construction of reality and how this might apply to processes of social change, social control, and liberation. Researchers in anthropology (Geertz, 1973; Marcus, Clifford, & School of American Research, 1986; Marcus & Fischer, 1999), sociology (Denzin, 1989, 1997, 2003; Denzin & Lincoln, 1994, 2003), and communication (Gronbeck et al., 1991; Grossberg et al., 1998; Hall, 1988) celebrated and promoted this adjustment, which was also associated with "postmodernism." This newfound excitement was greeted by a publishing industry with open arms, offering more journal and book outlets for narrower niches, which could be sustained by less expensive, computerized operations and advertising. Qualitative research, especially work oriented toward symbolic interaction, flourished across all the human and social sciences, including education and, a bit later, the nursing and health professions. Many of these students would become professors who would publish qualitative research. Foreshadowed by the insights of numerous ethnomethodologists about the constitutive effect of language and action on social action (Cicourel, 1964, 1974; Douglas, 1967, 1970a, 1970b, 1971, 1976; Garfinkel, 1967; Lyman, 1989, 1997; Lyman & Scott, 1970), these critiques laid bare the subjective foundations of all research and freed researchers to innovatively explore texts for meaning and impact.

The theoretical shifts that informed the epistemological challenges contributed to methodological changes, which were also aided by developments in information technology, particularly the availability (and affordability) of massive information bases (e.g., LexisNexis). This had a major impact on all qualitative research, but most significantly for researchers studying documents. David Altheide's first use of an early version of LexisNexis in a graduate seminar on "news coverage" in the mid-1980s was supported by a small grant to cover the online cost of more than $100 per hour. An even larger information base that is more "user friendly" became available in the late 1990s as part of most major library services—and it was free to students and researchers. This shift was accompanied by the Internet explosion in information and information bases. For the first time, texts could be searched quickly and efficiently and narrative data collected, organized, and coded. The advent of various computer software programs no longer required that all text be reduced to numerical values and incorrectly treated (and calculated) as interval data (Cicourel, 1964). And there was a growing audience for such analyses. Documents abounded, but the research perspectives, questions, and orientations toward systematic "document analysis" were, essentially, lacking (Plummer, 1983).

The challenge, then, is to develop an approach to documents that can integrate what is now known about reflexivity and meaning. The key is to let one's research question(s) provoke, direct, and help engage the researcher in investigating relevant documents. Document analysis will expand as recording technologies improve and become more accessible, including print and electronic media, audiotapes, visuals (e.g., photos, home videos), clothing and fashion, Internet materials, information bases (e.g., LexisNexis), field notes, and so forth. Moreover, if a document is defined as any symbolic representation and meaning that can be recorded and/or retrieved for analysis, then virtually all of social science (if not all science, even those that rely on "measurements") involves documents, collecting data according to some logic or rubric and recording it in some form. Initial work with documents made it clear that the same logic being used in studying, say, newspaper articles could also be applied to an ethnographer's field notes or an interviewer's notes.

Toward an Emergent QDA

QDA analysis involves emergent and theoretical sampling (Glaser & Strauss, 1967) of documents from information bases (including those developed by a researcher, e.g., field notes), development of a protocol for more systematic analysis, and then constant comparisons to clarify themes, frames, and discourse. If one is interested in studying "TV violence," it is not an act of violence per se that is socially significant but rather how that act is linked to a *course of action* or a scenario as part of an *entertainment emphasis*—for example, "bad guys get shot by good guys in order to achieve justice." Or the use of violence may be somehow linked to bravery, cunning, skill, and sexual conquest. The latter are themes or general messages that are reiterated in specific scenarios. The aim, then, is to query how behavior and events are placed in context and what themes, frames, and discourse are being presented. The basic steps are not to be viewed as rigid, but rather, like Kant's famous "categories of the mind," the steps should be considered "regulative" but not "constitutive," or operationally defined as the precision and limit of the research act. Flexibility must be built into methodology in order to accommodate changing social circumstances and cultural context. The basic steps include:

- Pursue a specific problem to be investigated.
- Become familiar with the process and context of the information source, for example, ethnographic studies of newspapers, television stations, and so forth. Explore possible sources (perhaps documents) of information.
- Become familiar with several (6–10) examples of relevant documents, noting particularly the format. Select a unit of analysis, for example, each article (this may change).
- List several items or categories (variables) to guide data collection and draft a protocol (data collection sheet).
- Test the protocol by collecting data from several documents.
- Revise the protocol and select several additional cases to further refine the protocol.

A dynamic use of QDA is "tracking discourse," or following certain issues, words, themes, and frames over a period of time, across different issues, and across different news media. Initial manifest coding incorporates emergent coding and theoretical sampling in order to monitor changes in coverage and emphasis over time and across topics. For example, in a study of fear, a protocol was constructed to obtain data about date, location, author, format, topic, sources, theme, emphasis, and grammatical use of *fear* (as noun, verb, adverb). The contexts for using the word *fear* were clarified through theoretical sampling and constant comparison to delineate patterns and thematic emphases (Altheide, 2002). Materials were enumerated, charted, and analyzed qualitatively using a word processor and a qualitative data analysis program (NUD*IST) as well as quantitatively.

The constant comparison may extend across documents, information bases, discourse, frames, and even time. Indeed, a key aspect of tracking discourse is to follow certain issues, words, themes, and frames over a period of time, across different issues, and across different news media (Altheide, 1996; Berg, 1989; Grimshaw & Burke, 1994; van Dijk, 1988; Weiler & Pearce, 1992). Although there are many differences in some of the approaches, all share an assumption that symbolic representations are enmeshed in a context of other assumptions that are not stated as such. Our approach blends interpretive, ethnographic, and ethnomethodological approaches with media logic, particularly studies of news organizational culture, information technology, and communication formats. The capacity to examine numerous documents with specific conceptually informed search terms and logic provides a new way of "exploring" documents, applying "natural experimental" research designs to the materials, as well as retrieving and analyzing individual documents qualitatively. Moreover, because the technology permits immediate access to an enormous amount of material, comparative exploration, conceptual refinement, data collection, and analysis can cover a longer time period than other technologies afforded. This approach is aided by a process of creating a data collection protocol that is disciplined yet flexible. Involving 12 steps, tracking discourse entails initial familiarity with a sample of relevant documents before drafting a protocol, which is then checked for reliability and validity with additional documents. As noted, a protocol was constructed to obtain data about date, location, author, format, topic, sources, theme, emphasis, and grammatical use of *fear* (as noun, verb, adverb). However, materials may also be enumerated and charted.

Social research must accommodate emergent meanings and activities that often accompany technological changes, which help create new documents and social relationships. Adjustments in dealing with documents have already been made in nonacademic contexts. Documents are constantly emerging as our attention is directed through other social developments such as police work–evidence (e.g., DNA specimens), new technologies for capturing and transmitting images (e.g., digital cameras). (It is interesting that photographs have a special status as documents, which are more subject to copyright restrictions than is print.) People who analyze videotapes for evidence of participation in, for example, covert police activities are referred to as "forensic video analysts":

> Ms. Clancy, a founder of I-Witness Video, a project that collected hundreds of videotapes during the Republican National Convention that were used in the successful defense of people arrested that week, has assembled videotape of other public events made by legal observers, activists, bystanders and police officers. (Dwyer, 2005, p. 1)

Social science's use of documents must also become more sophisticated. Document analysts must also be reflexive of emergent sources, meanings, activities, and relationships. New documents may emerge. Indeed, studies of documents such as newspaper reports can lead one to query and explore other documents, such as television transcripts and government reports, or even interviews and observations of relevant individuals in certain settings. Price's creative work with information released under the Freedom of Information Act (FOIA) shows how anthropologists were censored and harassed during Senator Joseph McCarthy's rampage (Price, 2004) . More recently his work shows how outspoken foreign policy critic Edward Said has also been monitored by the FBI:

> The FBI's first record of Edward Said appears in a February 1971 domestic security investigation of another unidentified individual. The FBI collected photographs of Said from the State Department's passport division and various news agencies. Said's "International Security" FBI file was established when an informant gave the FBI a program from the October 1971 Boston Convention of the Arab-American University Graduates, where Said chaired a panel on "Culture and the Critical Spirit." Most of Said's FBI records were classified under the administrative heading of "Foreign Counterintelligence," category 105, and most records are designated as relating to "IS—Middle East," the Bureau's designation for Israel. (Price, 2005, p. 1)

A very basic aspect of social change, of course, is technology and accompanying changes in communication formats. We must adjust our research strategies accordingly. Focusing on recent information technologies provides documents for analysis. On the one hand, we do not study the use of the telegraph very much these days; nor do we study the use of the "land line" telephone very often. On the other hand, the advent of the cell phone has opened up many research questions, challenges, and opportunities. For example, the ubiquity of cell phones means that most people, especially youths, have one or two, and they are very familiar with various ways of using them—for example, voice, text, and "hands free." Using text messaging rather than "voice" blends print with aural communication, but in a shorthand sort of way, especially as photophones permit visual records of experience, emotions, and even intent, for example, sending sexual images to lovers and others. This technology can now be used as a substitute for the "old" approach of using diaries in which participants record certain behaviors, as users turn to "moblogs"—mobile-based weblogs—to chronicle impressions and experience (Glotz, Bertschi, & Locke, 2005).

Cell phones produce new documents—records of calls, as well as content. Moreover, the "content" of cell phones is recognized as a "real document"—that is, it can be subpoenaed for legal purposes. But another type of document is the record and location of the call itself. This capacity is becoming very important in expanded government and business surveillance efforts. Such documents can have numerous serious implications, such as the arrest warrants that were issued by the Italian government for 22 CIA agents who, under the policy of "rendition," kidnapped a religious leader from the streets of Milan and took him to Egypt, where he was reportedly tortured and eventually released (Wilkinson, 2005, p. 3). The conspiracy and plans directed by the CIA were easily confirmed when cell phone calls were traced to U.S. agency offices in Langley, Virginia, and elsewhere. The "cell" trail was so obvious that further analysis may suggest that the conspirators wanted to be tracked to the CIA:

> In the papers, [Italian] Judge Nobili wrote that she was persuaded of the Americans' involvement in part because of evidence that their cellphones were "all interacting with one another" at the time and scene of the abduction. . . . The American agents used their Italian cellphones at the precise moment Mr. Nasr was abducted; they kept the phones switched on for hours at a time, making it easier to track their movements; and they dialed many phone numbers in the United States, most of them in northern Virginia, including at least one number at agency headquarters.
>
> The police said they were able to retrace nearly every step the American operatives made during the nine days they were in Milan for the operation. They identified the suspects by examining all cellphones in use near the abduction, and then tracing the web of calls placed. Investigators said they were able to trace several calls by Americans on the road from Milan to Aviano, the joint American-Italian air base north of Venice. (Grey & Natta, 2005)

Documents emerge and change and in the process become more apparent and relevant to social science research as data. Documents are more stable, more reflective of social organization, activities, meanings, and social rules than most other forms of data used by social scientists. Documents are more reliable than observations, and, increasingly, social scientists are following the lead of anthropologists in becoming more adept at tracking the emergent interactive character of meaningful activity implicated in the relationship of documents (given symbolic meaning) and intentions.

Document analysis should not be limited to materials that can supplement other data collection methods. Although documents are often an "additional" source of information about a topic or problem that is being investigated with more traditional research design rubrics, technological and social changes render this distinction obsolete: Many relevant social activities, identities, meanings and relationships "exist" in documents and documentary interpretation. Such relevant sociological phenomena are appropriately studied *in situ*, where they occur, as they occur. In other words, they should be studied ethnographically, in the field, even if this field is cyberspace. Varieties of documents are increasingly a feature of basic social activities and, in some cases, the only place (e.g., computer games, virtual reality, and cyberspace symbolic realms) in which certain activities occur. Thus technological changes and communication format developments have transformed the nature and significance of documents for social research. The upshot is that documents play a different part in the research act than they once did.

Research with Internet documents is called for by the growing recognition that virtual reality has helped produce virtual identities. Documents on the Internet are integral to identity and self-conceptions, including how presentation of self is accomplished and organized. This development has been described as "net logic": "Consequently, the Internet is unique not because 'it conquers space and time,' but because it is the first strategy that operates according to a many-to-many (one-to-one) communications pattern or logic" (Surratt, 2001, p. 42).

Many people use documents as a "feature of identity," for example, Web pages; they are referred to in discussions, conversations, and even publications, meaning, "if you want to know more about me, who I am, what I stand for, the issues, and so forth, check out my Web page." The use of Internet documents goes beyond merely supplementing identity; in the realm of cyberspace (i.e., Internet/Web "spaces"), there are entire realms of interaction and life that are constituted by electronic documents–games, surveillance activities, and so forth. Indeed, game players sell portions of identities, strategies, skills, knowledge, prizes, honors, and costumes for "real money" on websites (e.g., eBay) where "real property" is exchanged.

QDA as a method and orientation to a mass-mediated world illuminates the nature and significance of power in the mass media and popular culture and the process of the social construction of reality, defining the situation and social control. Although social power is a complex topic, document analysis as an emergent methodology makes it much easier to demonstrate how power operates and the consequences of this operation. This is important in view of the often stated but incorrect claim that symbolic interaction in particular and ethnographic approaches in general are not capable of studying social power and "macro" issues.

Emergent document analysis enables researchers to meet the challenge of how to study social power. The first task is to become aware, often through dead ends and blind luck, about how certain organizations, such as the FBI and CIA, operate with regard to documents. These agencies clearly believe that documents are critical reflections of power, including illegal acts. Agencies jealously guard documents; they lie about their existence; and, when finally uncovered, they edit, that is, "redact," many pages. Price (2004) used Freedom of Information Act (FOIA) materials in a provocative analysis of how the FBI monitored anthropologists during the infamous McCarthy era:

> I filed over 500 FOIA requests and over 250 appeals in the course of searching this book. I aggressively filed numerous administrative appears to obtain the release of records that were initially withheld. I made it a practice to appeal many of the FBI's routine denials that they held any records on a particular anthropologist or organization. . . . Needless to say, not knowing what is being withheld creates difficulties in creating appellate arguments, and at times such appeals are shots in the dark. (p. 358)

And:

> The FBI's efforts to avoid full compliance with FOIA suggests that the organization resents requirements that it comply with FOIA, and FOIA censors frequently fail with impunity to comply with basic FOIA standards [several techniques are then listed]. . . . These practices are clear violations of both the spirit and the letter of the Freedom of Information Act, but

> the lack of congressional oversight allows these practices to continue. (p. 360)

Initially intending to study the role of anthropologists in World War II, Price shifted focus to the McCarthy era when a load of documents sought for one purpose arrived at his door. These materials were filled with references to McCarthy-era surveillance of anthropologists. One insight was that much of the information was incorrect but still had consequences:

> FBI files are frequently full of mistakes and misinformation, and it is generally impossible to evaluate the validity and reliability of the information. This is an important issue, and the "facts" in each FBI report cited and quoted in this book should be viewed with skepticism. These FBI documents are a record of the FBI and its violations of privacy and academic freedom. As such they help us study the FBI but they are not records to be trusted unto themselves. (p. 360)

Another example of how power shapes social life can be seen in documents tracking communications of government agents. One very simple way is to compare and contrast different documents in different "document bases" to show contradictory messages, as well as chart a path to culpability, which in some cases may openly challenge the veracity of politicians, who deny any wrongdoing. Consider the previous example of how cell phone calls by 22 CIA agents helped provide evidence that led to the Italian government issuing warrants for their arrest. This "covert" action could not have occurred without authorization of CIA officials, as well as the President of the United States. We read on the CIA's own Web page:

> Who decides when CIA should participate in covert actions, and why?
>
> Only the President can direct the CIA to undertake a covert action. Such actions usually are recommended by the *National Security Council* (NSC). Covert actions are considered when the NSC judges that US foreign policy objectives may not be fully realized by normal diplomatic means and when military action is deemed to be too extreme an option. Therefore, the Agency may be directed to conduct a special activity abroad in support of foreign policy where the role of the US Government is neither apparent nor publicly acknowledged. Once tasked, the intelligence oversight committees of the Congress must be notified. (Central Intelligence Agency, n.d.)

QDA Is Ethnographic

QDA involves immersion, exploration, contextual understanding, and emergent insights into social meanings, relationships, and activities. This process of understanding a subject matter is consistent with what is meant by ethnography (Altheide & Johnson, 1993; Becker, 1973; Brissett & Edgley, 1990; Cicourel, 1964; Denzin, 1978, 1997; Denzin & Lincoln, 1994; Douglas, 1970b, 1976; Douglas & Johnson, 1977; Emerson, 2001; Emerson, Fretz, & Shaw, 1995; Ferrell & Hamm, 1998; Goffman, 1959, 1968, 1974; Hammersley & Atkinson, 1983; Harper, 2003; Jorgensen, 1989; Lyman & Scott, 1970; Maines, 2000; Manning, 1987; Manning & Cullum-Swan, 1994; Nader, 1965; Van Maanen, 1988). We contend that qualitative document analysis forces us to reconsider what constitutes "ethnographic":

> It has been claimed that all research directly or indirectly involves participant observation in the selection of a topic, method of study, data collections, analysis and interpretation (Cicourel, 1964; Hammersley & Atkinson, 1983; Johnson, 1975). While it may seem evident that any sustained inquiry is constituted through a complex and reflexive interaction process, it is also apparent that some research methods, e. g., ethnography, embrace this process, while others, e.g., survey research and content analysis, disavow it. . . . I suggest that several aspects of an ethnographic research approach can be applied to content analysis to produce ethnographic content analysis (ECA),

which may be defined as the reflexive analysis of documents (Plummer, 1983). (Altheide, 1996, p. 14)

Usually associated with participant observation, ethnography requires firsthand experience with the natural setting in which social activity occurs. The guideline is for the researcher to understand the meanings and perspective of the members. But what exactly is meant by *ethnography* and *ethnographic*? A few important qualifications must be stated. Is there an ethnographic space or place one must be vis-à-vis other participants? Are there aural and visual requirements, such as that one must be able to hear and see (or even touch) the participants? First, simply being in a setting does not mean that the researcher is employing an ethnographic perspective; one can be unmindful and unaware of the members' perspectives and understanding. Great writers such as Ralph Ellison and James Baldwin (and numerous sociologists) have described how minority group members are often "invisible" and not taken into account by dominant group members, who seemingly ignore them as people. Clearly, immersion and involvement in the setting is essential, but that does not constitute an ethnography nor, for our purposes, provide an "ethnographic perspective." This perspective is derived from an awareness and a research orientation toward actively attending to the activities, language, meanings, and perspectives of members in the setting. Immersion, flexibility, and an openness to the relevant communication and symbolic representations that are congruent with the time, place, and manner of the subject matter is important. With these considerations in mind, we suggest that an ethnographic perspective can be brought to bear on symbolic communication in other than "physical spaces," including information bases and cyberspace. After all, ethnography is oriented toward description and clarification of perspective and meaning. If the key element involves human beings in a situation, then an ethnographic perspective entails being "there" with the people. However, if the research focus is not on human action per se but rather on symbolic meanings and perspectives within a different domain, then a research perspective and orientation can also be said to be "ethnographic" if it is oriented to emergence, discovery, and description. We claim, in this sense, that QDA is ethnographic in approach.

Document analysis becomes ethnographic when the researcher immerses him- or herself in the materials and asks key questions about the organization, production, relationships, and consequences of the content, including how it reflects communication formats grounded in media logic. The focus initially is on exploration, reading, looking, reflecting, and taking notes before more systematic and focused observations are undertaken. As is more apparent in the examples to follow, the focus is on process, meaning, and themes. Exploration is followed by identification of key terms, images, themes, and associated frames.

A key aspect of the process is to "design in" constant comparison with theoretical sampling in which the data, including the manifest and latent meanings of certain language and broader discourse, are examined and checked against other sources and associations. For example, if the sources used in certain documents do not include women, the researcher will query the documents to find out, first, whether this is an oversight and, second, whether examples of "women as sources" can be found in other, similar searches. The theoretical sampling promotes the quest for origins—the first time that a particular phrase was associated with a discursive frame—and the contexts in which this occurred.

In sum, this approach to documents is consistent with an ethnographic orientation toward immersing oneself in the subject matter. QDA is both a perspective and a method. Unlike conventional quantitative content analysis, which tends to be performed by "hired hand" researchers with little theoretical or methodological acumen, QDA is very interactive and requires extensive familiarity with a research topic, as well as a solid grounding in the character and organization of the documents under study. For example, anyone who studies newspaper reports should know something about how a newspaper and other news organizations actually function, either through a limited ethnography or through some literature.

Some of the emergent features of QDA are illustrated in the rest of the chapter. A number of comments have already been offered about QDA as "perspective," but as a method it is important to stress that there is a logic of discovery, comparative analysis, and critical synthesis, which are incorporated through a series of steps and procedures (e.g., developing, testing, refining a protocol), exploratory and then articulated theoretical sampling, critical comparison, and thematic analysis. However, the method is not rigid and does not preclude the "outlier" document or the "deviant case" from informing the project. The research commitment is to the research questions, which direct the researcher to domains of information rather than a specific ethnographic setting. More specific applications of this approach can be seen in ongoing research about how criminal justice terminology emerged and has moved or been incorporated into everyday life as part of the broader culture. Each of these cases is illustrated by the student's experiences and insights. A final overview follows these accounts.

The chapter continues with brief case studies illustrating QDA and emergence. We begin with Michael Coyle's project on the language of justice, followed by Chris Schneider's work on criminality in rap music, and then Katie DeVriese's account of how immersion in documents contributed to a discovery of the mediated path of *perp* and *junkie* into everyday discourse.

Case Studies of Emergent QDA through "Tracking Discourse" of Criminal Justice Terminology and Themes

Emergent Methods in Language of Justice Research (Michael Coyle)

As discussed in the beginning of this chapter, QDA is a research methodology centered on following the emergence of interpretations as they arise in the examination of document data. In this section, I demonstrate how in my own research I use documents and QDA to study words related to our understanding of "justice" and how the data interpretations I argue *emerge* within the research process itself.

Introduction

The phrase *the language of justice* refers to a research agenda that examines the language we use in everyday life to discuss justice. The emphasis is on the words we use to talk about our ideas and thoughts about justice, the words we use to describe our practices and traditions of justice, and finally the words we use to express our hopes and dreams about creating a just communal life.

Methodologically, my work rests on a foundation of qualitative methods and, more specifically, on analysis of media, dictionaries, and other documents. In essence, I study everyday discourse (language) as witnessed in such documents to uncover the processes of the construction of meaning in daily life. More specifically, I am interested in tracking the speech of moral entrepreneurs (i.e., people who develop and promote rule changes), to explore my hypothesis that *the language of justice reflects the social construction of human meanings around issues of justice and reflects the moral entrepreneuring of social control.*

Research Methods Foundations in Language of Justice Research

My methodology for document analysis and ECA relies on a model developed in the work of David Altheide and others (Altheide, 1987, 1996; Phillips & Hardy, 2002; Prus, 1996; Ragin, 1994). My research methods build toward my research goal: locating the process of social control as reflected and created in the social production of meaning and moral entrepreneurship and as evinced in daily discourse, that is, as observed in the documents of everyday life (newspaper articles, dictionaries, etc.). My research begins with the close reading of texts and moves to the creation and continuous development of emergent interpretations and to tracking themes, frames, and angles such interpretations suggest across documents in time and space—all of which is best described as a process of "tracking discourse" (Altheide, 2000).

This methodological process is best demonstrated with illustrations of such research. For example, in one project I began to track how moral entrepreneurs (media agents, political and civic leaders, criminal justice system managers, judges, etc.) use the word *evil* to describe "crimes" and "criminal actors." I began to closely read news documents (using the LexisNexis database) to track where and how *evil* and *crimes* were discussed together. As I examined document data, I developed interpretations of how these two concepts traveled together (themes/frames/angles). I began a *process* best described as a *construction of interpretations that emerged as I considered the data*. In other words, I tracked the discourse of "crime and evil" to locate interpretations. One important interpretation that emerged was that when "crime" or "criminal actors" are discussed as "evil," crime causation disfavors social construction, communal responsibility of deviancy definitions, or situational explanations. For example, one news headline reads, "Montreal Massacre Dead Killers Are Evil Not Insane" (*Toronto Star*, December 7, 1996). Another interpretation was that when "crime" or "criminal actors" are construed as "evil," crime causation favors other-than-human (metaphysical) explanations. For example, consider these headlines:

- "Defense Rips Witness as 'Diabolical Evil' " (*Chicago Sun Times*, September 30, 1992).
- "The Execution of Timothy McVeigh: As the Oklahoma City Bomber lives out his final days, still-struggling survivors take some solace in knowing evil did not triumph" (*Indianapolis Star*, April 15, 2001).

In this research project such interpretations were refined into a set of questions that were built into a protocol, which was then systematically applied to news stories. A finding based on this more thorough process gives my research a degree of reliability and validity.

The qualitative analysis of documents entails a process of interpretation that emerges in interactions with the material (data). In this sense, QDA treats documents as a community that is best understood ethnographically. Interpretation in QDA emerges as the researcher is *immersed* in a community of documents, as he or she *converses* with them by considering them together as a community that can speak, and as he or she *tracks* his or her emerging interpretations in this very community of documents. Thus a nonlinear hermeneutic develops focusing on returning again and again to the community of documents, much like an ethnographer would return to the village with his or her interpretations: immersion into the community, consideration of the community, interpretations of the community, and a return to the community to inquire of the value of the interpretations made.

This process of the *emergence of interpretation* is again best demonstrated with an illustration of such research. In another project I examined the phrase *innocent victim*. I encountered the phrase one morning while reading a newspaper. I was struck by how a reporter chose to describe the persons killed by the airplane that came through their tower office windows on September 11 as "innocent." In fact, it struck me as rather bizarre. I took this phrase and searched it in the LexisNexis major English-language newspapers database to see what I could discover about its contextual usages. I quickly became overwhelmed by the plethora of usages that had no intuitive sorting. But I noticed that for every 100 times the word *victim* is used, only once is the word *innocent* found anywhere near it. Comparative examinations still left me stumped and without interpretation. I decided to explore other avenues for ideas. Soon I found myself in the library tracing the long history and varied development of these two words in the history of English-language dictionaries from the 1600s to today. Along the way I discovered that integral to earlier definitions of both these words was the notion of agency.

With the notion of agency as possibly relevant, I returned to the LexisNexis database and began to look at the same community of "victim" and "innocent victim" documents. To my surprise I quickly discovered that the majority of uses of the phrase *innocent victim* relate to three categories of denial of agency: children, a circumstance of being overrun by the power of the state, and incidents involving actors attempting to refute responsibility that they have been called to accept. Similarly, a study of "victim" contexts demonstrates that agency is also relevant by its complete absence: Although the potential to declare that a presence or an absence of agency exists, it is simply not done; instead, for example, a person is declared a "victim" of disease or crime without any qualification as to innocence or guilt.

The examples of the "crime and evil" and "innocent victim" studies demonstrate the processes by which *interpretation emerges* and *emergent methodology operates*. This approach to research is defined by an ethnographic openness to themes that "surface" in the encounter and interpretation of data. This approach is less interested in *reading* to "uncover" or "displace" and more interested in *construing* to meaningfully encounter and *asking* about the social construction of meanings in everyday life.

Concerns and Opportunities

The strength of my research methodology is the diversity of sample. In media documents, such diversity allows the gathering of independent authors' (journalists, editors, etc.) decisions on how to use the words *evil* or *innocent victim*. In lexical documents, such diversity allows sampling of documents through several centuries. A weakness of this methodology is that media and lexicon documents project a particular expression of culture and language and have specific—and ever shifting—audiences in mind. Additionally, their creators belong to specific subcommunities. Finally, in my media studies, what I examine—newspapers—are only one form of media.

Various research and methodological problems arise during the lexicon studies and media document studies in my *language of justice* research. The methodological process of the lexicon studies is defined by its exploratory nature, for I have found no similar research precedent to draw methodology comparisons with. The media document studies are preceded by and follow closely much of the body of document analysis research methodology that precedes my own work and that I only point to here. However, the combining of these two methodologies toward my own research objectives has required inventiveness.

In the process of methodological invention, my guide has been what can best be described as the merging of Geertz and Altheide's methods (Altheide, 1996; Geertz, 1973). From the first I take "thick description," as, much like Geertz, I find the process of rich representation to be the best way to begin rich interpretation. I combine thick description with Altheide's QDA, which, with its use of *emergent meanings*, allows me to track discourse in line with categories I interpret to be of potential importance. Centrally, this methodology allows me both to construct falsifiable hypotheses and to avoid Geertz's "fictional ethnography."

The latter is important to contemplate in my research, for, although I readily abandon the modernist goal of "true" representation and interpretation, I do not find the label of "fiction" to be an honest description of quality ethnographic research in either document or interview analysis. Although it is not surprising that definitive interpretation is unlikely even when doing ethnographic analysis of dictionary entries, and although I do not consider that my use of *emergent meaning construction* produces "true" social meanings of media documents, it would be equally false to say that I expect my research product to be a fiction (other than in the postmodernist sense in which all interpretation is fiction). Instead, my methodology in lexicon studies and media document studies work produces emergent meanings that are verifiable on the basis of the fact that I began my research in order to discover how those meanings I discovered in the process of my research are, in fact, reflected in the data that I am considering. It is the *emergence* of their meaning that is most central to their own analysis. Importantly, the emergence of meanings itself is a process of discovery for ourselves. The difference between this and writing fiction is subtle but important.

It has been argued that *analytical categories* are inescapable, whether one uses qualitative or quantitative research methods (Atkinson, 1990). The modernist dream of representation is gone, and reflexivity seems permanently relevant and here to stay. Although in my preliminary work the lexicon studies initially seemed to be a site that would easily escape the label of interpretivist, ultimately choices had to be made to understand, to make themes, and so forth, of lexicon data. Such choices entail procedures that privilege certain analytical categories over others. In the media document studies, this is even more so the case, as it seems that such choices from the beginning are inevitable.

Both ECA and tracking-discourse methodologies are heavily ridden with such innate analytical category choices. None of these choices are an indication of bad methodology but rather are part and piecemeal of what Atkinson (1990) describes as the verisimilitude of texts. In creating narratives out of data, I have conformed to a canon of an appropriate mode of organization for the genre within which I operate. Using not only stylistic devices but also substantive analytical commitments in my lexicon studies and media document studies, I represent data in contextualized and meaningful chunks. As discussed earlier, this is exactly the outcome that the combining of Geertz's and Altheide's methodologies aims to produce.

Goffman (1989) has described the role of rationalizations in research, such as the analytical categories I have just discussed. He correctly argues that rationalizations in their broader sense are a constant companion to research methods, and he encourages making such rationalizations not only in interpretation but also even in deciding how to do the research itself. There is little difference between this argument and the process we discuss here, namely, *following emergent interpretations*. Although this may initially seem to be a subjectivism gone astray, eliminating all research value, the honesty of this approach is readily undeniable by anyone who has ever thought about and tried to solve a problem. In practice, all researchers invite, even crave, rationalizations to accomplish their work. Although some rationalizations will not help one to think about or to solve a particular problem, others will. It is, in fact, the ongoing process of rationalizations that makes research and its conclusions possible. The counterintuitiveness of rationalizations notwithstanding, I believe that in the lexicon studies and media document studies the intentional and conscious rationalizations work to accomplish and strengthen my research. I have found that this does not give license to betray all method, nor does it lead to Geertz's "fictional ethnography," as I had also feared. Instead, it provides the freedom to mix interpretations and meanings with imagination. Ultimately, the meaning-inserting and inherent chunking of data such methodology produces will contribute to my research, as the use of emergent meaning methodology will stave off both subjective alienation and fiction. Fiction and emotional appeals are examined in the next analysis of rap music.

Emergent Document Analysis in a Study of Rap Music (Christopher Schneider)

My project consists of an exploratory study of media depictions of rap music vernacular, specifically focusing on relevant terms thought to have derived from a preexisting institutionally specific discourse. Rap music can be loosely defined as a form of music that makes use of rhyme coupled with rhythmic speech that employs a particular vernacular spoken over a musical arrangement (Keyes, 2002). This study concerns an initial investigation of select words that emerge from a theoretical sampling of data. Although these words are thought to have specific or fixed meanings associated with criminal justice discourse, they are nonetheless frequently employed throughout rap music narratives. The aim is to identify and clarify some of the ways in which people might understand and negotiate social meaning conveyed through various media depictions of rap music, particularly the language and symbolism tied to criminal justice organizations and work. I became immersed in the qualitative analysis of documents in an effort to draw out subtle nuanced meanings in order to clarify the ways in which social meaning is created through rap music appropriations of criminal justice discourse and how resultant media depictions construct and create social understandings of rap music.

The crux of the process of emergence concerns not only the interaction between researcher and subject matter but also relies to some extent on the existent knowledge of the researcher. Music has always been an integral part of my life, even though I did not pursue my percussion training. My father was a professional musician for two decades, my mother was one of the first sound production managers in a larger urban market, and my younger brother (my only sibling) is currently an aspiring musician whose band has a sizable following in a large metropolitan area.

My avocation as a music collector contributed to my knowledge about and inclinations toward various ways to investigate the social significance of rap music, especially among youth. My involvement with music includes having collected music since my preteen years (initially with allowance money) and attending numerous concerts, as well as reading a host of trade publications that keep me informed on a variety of issues, including chart-topping albums and songs, forthcoming releases, and industry news and gossip. This background information proved to be very helpful in redirecting my attention to news media reports.

Research Method

My project begins with a musical recording—for instance, a compact disc—as a form of document, which can be retrieved and studied to better understand aspects of culture. My broad research questions about the social relevance of rap music, as well as how certain terms and symbols relevant to criminal justice discourse are portrayed, led me to reflect on music memories I have (i.e., thousands of songs heard and often collected), identifying certain terms, artists, and periods, and then to questions or, more correctly, research questions such as: When was this first used? Who (which group) used it first? What happened following this use? Was this controversial? What did it mean to the journalists (trade and general) who wrote about it? and so forth. I must, then, look for some other material, which in turn will raise some other questions, until I have exhausted the relevant queries for my project (until later, when other key matters will emerge!). This involves some reflection, quick analysis, and then a broad surveying of some other media material in an information base such as LexisNexis, which is a computerized database that houses (among other things) thousands of official media documents. I was particularly interested in sources such as newspaper reports and *Billboard* magazine.

I then look for some documents for comparative observation and description. Whereas the initial forays just discussed were informed by my experience and specific research queries, this next search is focused theoretically: Theoretical sampling utilizes conceptual comparisons that are drawn from reviewing existing data in an effort to qualify and test analytical categories. As noted before, this particular method is not guided by statistical representation but rather by theoretical relevance (Emerson, 2001). The crux, then, of theoretical sampling relies on sampling incidents and events that are indicative of categories, the resultant dimensions and properties, in an effort to foster a cogent conceptual relation to them (Strauss & Corbin, 1990).

Data Collection

Guided by my initial questions and some exploratory materials, more data were collected via theoretical sampling of (listening to) relevant rap music, including songs, albums, and particular artists that are either conducive to or reflective of some of the suggestions discussed in the broader research literature, for example, what has been identified or considered relevant and significant. The context of rap music is very important if one is to conduct informed research and not miss critical comparisons. For example, rap music derives from the remnants of the political turmoil of the 1960s civil rights movement in the United States. Nevertheless, rap music remained stagnant for nearly a decade until the Sugar Hill Gang released their hit single, "Rappers Delight," initiating this brand of music as a marketable commodity, although it was not until the mid-1980s that rap music established itself as an earmark of popular culture. In this regard, many consider Run-D.M.C. as rap music's first commercially successful mainstream act. Understandably, this became one of several "starting points."

After sampling the trajectory of rap music, from the Sugar Hill Gang and Run-D.M.C. to some of the more contemporary artists such as 50 Cent, I begin to recognize a consistency of particular terms emerging from the data (music). From these, three terms were carefully selected on the assumption that each was thought to have direct association to criminal justice discourse; these include *thug*, *pimp*, and *gangsta* (a derivation of *gangster*, a word almost always associated with criminal activity). Identifying these terms led to the next step in QDA, the drafting of a protocol to query each document and its context involving an instance of the term.

Before the development of a protocol, which is necessary to extract pertinent data from media documents, the terms *thug*, *pimp*, and *gangsta* were each entered independently into the LexisNexis search engine. Scanning a sample of "hits" helped inform the development of a protocol to guide a more refined focus on emergent frames and themes surrounding *thug*, *pimp*, and *gangsta*. Frames and themes are inextricably linked but not necessarily determinate of each other, although most documents usually refer to a particular point of view or frame and some documents will simply employ certain angles in reference to specific parts of a theme.

Findings

The preliminary systematic data collection was based on 15 articles selected from global news sources. A careful reading of the articles reveals a "morality" frame, which encompassed themes associated with violence, through such acts as murder, deception, misogyny, and so forth. The discourse used to convey these instances almost always involved criminal justice discourse, usually discussing these issues as violations of the law.

The discourse of *thug* is illustrative. As reported in *The Times (London)* (Saunders, 2005), the term *thug* is thought to have derived from the Urdu or Hindi word *t'hag*, which is literally translated as "deception." As a verb, to *thug* someone meant to trick, deceive, sometimes charm a person, and it was often synonymous with multiple murders. *Thugs* were bands of wandering criminals in India that would infiltrate unsuspecting groups of travelers, charm them (sometimes through musical performance and verse) so as to earn their trust, and then without warning murder their prey, steal their belongings, and move along to the next target group (Saunders, 2005).

In the United States, as reported in an article titled "Will the Real Thug Please Stand Up, and Lower That Gun," in the *New York Times* (Wilson, 2005), the symbolic imagery conveyed by the "thug" has since developed into an iconic law enforcement image, sometimes recognized in popular culture as a police shooting target. In this instance, then, the term *thug* is sometimes surreptitiously associated with a fictional character with the following attributes: white, male, husky, middle-aged, and clean-shaven, with thick dark hair. Nevertheless, the actual identity of *thug* remains mysterious, and although as a lexicon it is widely associated with negativity, the thug and its character attributes as reported are often rumored as either directly or indirectly related to character attributes of real former police officials, usually officers (Wilson, 2005).

The term *thug* was usually associated with a person who eludes capture, often through anonymity. Consider, for instance, the important association of the term *thug* with terrorism. For example, after the terrorist attacks in London in July, the *Agence France Presse* (July 22, 2005), reaffirmed the United States' support for Britain and the war on terror when it reported President Bush calling for the world to confront the "thugs and assassins" behind these attacks. Moreover, a thug was often described in the third-person tense unless the person in question could be positively identified (often through capture), when master status as a criminal superseded that of thug (anonymous), whereby the person's identity became associated with other terms more specific to issues of criminality.

The criminal justice notion of thug-as-a-bad-thing (person or act) was not apparent when it came to rap music. A theoretically drawn sample of songs reflects rap appropriations of the term *thug* as a form of endearment. For example, in rap vernacular, to be referred to as *thug*, either through self-proclamation (most often the case), by one's peers, by the criminal justice institution, by the media, or by others, is a social attribute associated with issues of autonomy and authenticity. In these instances, appropriation of the term *thug* seems to suggest a form of resistance whereby *thug* comes to represent a person who is not a member of the dominant social establishment, perhaps through possession of elusive paradoxical character attributes that construct meaningful status positions outside the boundaries of dominant cultural norms.

The data suggest that the morality frame, once central to criminal justice discourse, is less important, although the news media reports about rap music reflect dominant themes in popular culture concerning sex and drugs. Consider, for instance, the term *pimp*, which emerged from the data as a significant term and which until fairly recently (as an issue of morality) was widely and negatively associated with the illicit sex trade market; the term now appears in the television show *Pimp My Ride*, and has been used in a parody as an appeal to cubicle-tied office workers being offered a kit at $14.95, to "Pimp My Cubicle" (Stein, 2006).

The (re)appropriation and subsequent celebration of "pimp culture" has even permeated the university system. For example, Dooms (2005) reported that Howard University, in collaboration with Nelly (a widely known rap star), recently awarded a "P.I.M.P. Scholarship," a total award of $5,000 to the applicant who best described what made them "a pimp" or "Positive Intellectual Motivated Person." Although controversial, Nelly's organization has maintained that it is trying to change the meaning of *pimp*, which of course in criminal justice discourse has long been understood as man who solicits clients for prostitution.

In my search, the term *gangsta* by and large emerged from the data as either closely attached or directly attributed to a particular form or genre of rap music ("gangsta rap"), which was overwhelmingly reported as violent music that glorified drug use and misogyny, all consistent with themes associated with the morality frame briefly outlined previously. The data suggest that this genre of music, once understood largely as music exclusively associated with African American male urban disenfranchisement (sometimes infused with elements of cultural authenticity), has become somewhat of an anachronism. The personas of gangsta rappers Ice Cube, Ice-T, and others who are current mainstream actors seem to illustrate this point.

Our data suggest that the term *gangsta* in most instances has a direct negative association with our two previous terms, *thug* and *pimp*; but reciprocal searches did not reflect this association. This seems to indicate that the more closely one can associate terms (e.g., *thug*, *pimp*, etc.) with negative depictions of gangsta (rap), the more these terms are understood and, more important, constructed (reaffirmed) as negative. Within the perceived negativity of these terms when discussed in the context of rap music, *gangsta* then becomes more closely attached to negative images strongly associated with criminal justice discourse.

This is perhaps best exemplified in a report titled "[Spike] Lee Shoots Back at Gangsta Rap," reported in the *Hartford Courant* (Buck, 2005). This article was directed at criticizing the promotion of negative stereotypical images of African Americans as criminals, thieves, drug dealers, and so forth. The article reported Spike Lee (a famous movie director) as saying, "We're at a time now where young black males grow up and want to be pimps," and that, "something very dangerous is happening because this is not really the face of black Americans, but that's the image seen all over the world" (Buck, 2005).

When discussed in the context of gangsta (rap) then, *pimp* remains consistent with its traditional meaning and association with criminal justice discourse. Moreover, the preceding quote seems to adequately summarize the general premise of articles concerning gangsta (rap) that I reviewed for this project, each to varying degrees reporting negative images associated with perceptions of black criminality, including but not limited to glorification of violence, sex, and drugs, each as contextually specific to black Americans.

In regard to media depictions of the term *gangsta*, the resultant themes are strongly associated with the morality frame, substantiated through the use of discourse specific to the criminal justice institution. Moreover, through the examined media documents, media depictions of gangsta (rap) music then become attached almost exclusively to images that promote irresponsible behavior and that are sometimes further reinforced by reports prompting calls for censorship and for a boycott of media that promote these types of behaviors by endorsing this type of music.

In sum, this exploratory project is a brief attempt at understanding some of the ways in which people might understand meaning through media depictions of rap music. In these instances, meaning continues to be constructed through information that is disseminated and communicated through the media, through the organization, selection, and presentation of "objective" information.

The discourse of the criminal justice system and the (re)appropriation of its relevance in rap music seems to have solidified through our exploratory analysis of media depictions.

Moreover, this project reveals in part that rap music appropriations of criminal justice discourse as positive social attributes have at best been minimally successful. However, negative media depictions of the term *gangsta* seem to be especially significant when associated with rap. What is additionally necessary are future full-scale research endeavors to help inform and guide our general understanding of the overall importance the media has in the construction of rap music appropriations of institutionally specific discourses.

Tracking Perp *and* Junkie*: An Emergent Approach (Katie DeVriese)*

My work focuses on the way that words as symbols "travel" or move from criminal justice "discourse" into other realms. This project required a lot of flexibility and adjustment. This research analyzes how terms associated with an institutional discourse, in this case criminal justice, are propagated and normalized by the mass media. As key contributors to social power and the ways audiences define situations, the mass media play a significant role in maintaining social control by solidifying perspectives of self and other through their use of stigmatized language. I was particularly interested in the ways in which new words in public discourse reflect institutional orders of control and how the mass media can shape, intensify, or uphold social identities of individuals or groups of individuals by using particular and purposive language and symbols. The exploration of this relationship leads to the language of stigma and control in everyday life. However, this theoretical mapping entails a flexible conceptual scheme to follow the emerging data paths.

Research Methods

Conversations with David Altheide led to a list of possible terms to track across discourses. My initial overview of some news materials led to the focus on two terms of crime language; *perp*, as in perpetrator, and *junkie* were selected to explore in newspaper articles to clarify how the language of stigma is constructed in public discourse. (Some terms that I did explore—e.g., *OD* and *smack*—were not pursued because they did not flow into non–criminal justice and everyday language.) A few dozen newspaper articles were selected from LexisNexis and quickly read; I took notes, then reread the articles in search of certain themes and emphases that had been noted in previous research. Once initial patterns and themes had been documented, I expanded to other databases that included transcripts of prime-time television dramas and other television and radio news programs. I proceeded with the tracking-discourse approach, in which particular terms or topics are searched for and monitored over a period of time and across different types of media. This approach requires flexibility with search terms, sampling, and the creation of categories in order to achieve a more comprehensive analysis. In the initial stages of exploring documents, I allowed for comparison searches, which led me to develop other themes not originally expected, such as the appearance of *perp walk*. By expanding my search parameters and investigating other uses of the terms, I was able to distinguish between one-time uses and new and unexpected themes.

I searched for articles in LexisNexis under the General News category, among Major Papers, which included both domestic and international. I then created a protocol based on essential information extracted from each article. The protocol comprised title, date/year, newspaper, location of the terms *perp* or *junkie*, the context of the article (entertainment, crime-related, etc.), the identity of the perp(s) or junkie(s) (self-ascribed or ascribed by other), and the overall tone of the article (positive, negative, neutral, or light/humorous). The protocol was important in establishing stigmatized identity and was used to track different usages of the terms over time. Originally I searched for the terms *perp* and *junkie* in full text for the years 1980, 1990, and 2000. I realized that additional searches were needed, from as far back as the 1960s up until the present, to document the appearance of the terms and to elicit other connotations, leading me to new terms.

Data Collection and Analysis

The data collection and analysis stages were not completed in a linear but in a cyclical process. Analysis of initial documents would lead me to discover other themes and usages, which I would then go back to and conduct more searches using different search terms and different informational databases.

The term *junkie* first showed up in a few articles in 1972 and 1973 relating to drug addiction. *Junkie* did not appear again until 1977, when it was not only used in the article but exhibited in headlines as well. In the late 1970s *junkie* was used much more often and referred not only to drug addiction but also to an addiction to or obsession with such things as politics, sports, food, and entertainment (e.g., *political junkie, junk food junkie, basketball junkie, radio junkie*). There is an apparent difference between the identities of a junkie who is addicted to illegal drugs and a junkie who likes sports or TV maybe a little too much. A definite stigma is attached to someone who is addicted to drugs, and someone else usually ascribes the label of *junkie* to that person. On the other hand, those who are obsessed with politics, food, and so forth. usually label themselves as junkies, and the term is most likely used in a lighthearted or humorous way. Twenty-one articles containing the word *junkie* were collected, demonstrating the patterns that emerged.

Various themes emerged in relation to the use of *junkie* to refer to addiction, drug or otherwise. In one article about a celebrity caught with drugs, *junkie* is actually added to his name, suggesting that the celebrity and a junkie are synonymous. The label of *junkie* attaches a stigma that is inseparable from the individual. In some articles, particularly about movies and other forms of entertainment, it is even asserted that junkies have a particular look. An article about drugs in the movies emphasized beautiful people who become junkies, even taking on the junkie look that goes along with the stigma. It was noted that frequently, when the term *junkie* is used in any context, the article also uses other drug-related terms or phrases associated with it, for example, *getting a fix, getting a buzz,* or references to addiction. One article suggested that certain people are junkies, stereotyping the stigma of the label *junkie,* and it is a shock when an individual who does not fit within the stereotype is considered part of the stigmatized group.

Junkie also shows up in headlines, often possibly indicating that journalists use the word to grab the reader's attention. In some articles, *junkie* is used in the title, but in the text is replaced with *drug addict* or *drug abuser.* Again, the term *junkie* refers not only to drug users but also to individuals who are obsessed with some sort of activity or product. Examples of the use of *junkie* in headlines include "Report Debunks Junkie Criminal," "My Sister, the How-to Junkie," and "Passion for Politics: These Junkies Get Fix from Elections."

Once themes of addiction were determined, the term *junkie* was tracked in all transcripts of television and radio news programs available through LexisNexis. Most of the transcripts available contained only a short paragraph or two documenting main points, although some full transcripts of programs or segments were obtained. The first year in which the term *junkie* appeared in transcripts was 1983 (referring to drugs), but then it did not appear again until 1992 (with various meanings); each subsequent year contained more examples than the previous years. Eight transcripts were collected, and the protocol was filled out and attached to each transcript. The topics ranged from drug use to sports and political junkies and so forth, used in reference to crime or entertainment or as self-reference.

Additional patterns concerning identity were discovered from searching transcripts. The label *junkie* for someone accused of abusing drugs carries a stigma that is difficult to shake. This is exemplified when celebrities take legal action against tabloids that label them as such. In an episode of the *Geraldo* show about selling babies, Geraldo Rivera makes references to drug addicts as being the lowest of the low. He assumes that junkies and drug addicts are not held to the same standards as everyone else but still expects them to behave in a civilized manner. In an episode of *Turning Point with Diane Sawyer* from ABC News, special guest Barbara Walters interviews several people about their drug problems–a housewife, a doctor, a rock star, and an heiress. Several times throughout the program the guests make reference to how normal they look but that secretly they are "junkies." All previously had the assumption that "junkies" were certain kinds of people, that you could look at someone and know he or she was a drug addict. But from experience, they explain that anyone can be a junkie.

The term *perp* (short for "perpetrator") was searched in LexisNexis as well. It made its first appearance in the text of major newspapers in 1981. *Perp* was not used very often in the 1980s, and, interestingly, at least half of the time *perp* showed up as a short form for a financial term and was not related to criminal justice. From 1990 on, the instances of *perp* steadily increased each year. My first analysis of *perp* uncovered an inconsistent representation of the term, sometimes surrounded by quotation marks and other times not. Also inconsistent was the inclusion of what *perp* stood for. Several articles noted that *perp* was an abbreviation of *perpetrator*, although most articles did not explain the abbreviation. In some earlier appearances of *perp*, the term was used in a direct quote with someone in law enforcement and was not explained nor surrounded by quotation marks. The inclusion or exclusion of quotation marks was a pattern I followed over several decades to find that, over time, the quotation marks were being used less and less often. This suggested to me an assumption that readers knew the definition of *perp*.

After themes were determined in the initial selection of news articles, I decided to expand to other media documents. This came about one evening while I was watching a prime-time police drama and noticed how the term *perp* was used by the detectives and officers to assign a negative identity to an unknown or specific individual. The term *perp* was tracked in all transcripts of television and radio news programs available through LexisNexis. Most of the transcripts available contained only a short paragraph or two documenting main points, although some full transcripts of programs or segments were obtained. The first year in which the term *perp* appeared in transcripts was 1990, and each subsequent year contained more examples than the previous year. Seven transcripts were collected, and the protocol was filled out and attached to each transcript. Following the protocol developed from the initial analysis of news articles, I determined the identity of the perp, whether the term was self-ascribed or ascribed by another, and the tone in which the perp was identified. Examination of the documents revealed that the initial uses of *perp* in the mass media connoted a deviant person and that the term was assigned a stigma by someone else. As *perp* became part of the public discourse over time, the term was used in different respects, including in a nonstigmatized joking manner on the part of authors.

My subsequent search for *perp* in transcripts exposed more interpretations of perp identity. In a television review of a documentary on former President Nixon and the Watergate scandal, Nixon is degraded by the use of *perp*, signifying the attachment of a stigma to someone in a powerful position. In a story about an undercover African American police officer who was shot by other police officers, the term *perp* is used in relation to race. In this situation the person, because of his skin color, was assumed to be a perp, or criminal, suggesting that the race/ethnicity of a person can be used as an indicator of a type of person, creating a more complex stigma. In a story about violent muggers in New York City, a police officer interviewed compares perps to animals that are hunted. The indication is that there is a hierarchy of people and that perps are on the same level as animals.

In the beginning of the project, I searched only for the term *perp*. However, analysis of articles brought an unexpected new concept, the *perp walk*. Perp walk refers to the parading of someone in custody–often in handcuffs–in front of journalists and cameras. I looked through the articles and determined that *perp walk* occurred many times in the past decade. I went back and searched for *perp walk* in news articles and then in transcripts to find out when it first appeared and to track the term over time. *Perp walk* first appeared in newspapers in 1994 and in television and radio programs in 1991. The term was not used extensively until the early 2000s, particularly in 2002 with the corporate (Enron) and Martha Stewart scandals. *Perp walk* was displayed in quotation marks about half of the time. No consistent pattern was found. Twenty articles and 15 transcripts were collected, and the protocol was filled out and attached to each. The "perp walk" has been around for a very long time, but only recently has the term been used, especially with certain cases of celebrities or public officials. The term and use is so common now that it is even being parodied.

Some of the early articles were actually about the meaning and history of the perp walk. Several articles discussed the outlawing of perp walks in New York. The articles usually gave advantages and disadvantages of perp walks. One article discussed the societal value of the perp walk, in this case, restoring order. But it also mentioned the stigma associated with it, regardless of guilt. The perp walk as practice and meaning has been challenged in court as stigmatizing and unfair, implying that public shame often precedes a legal proceeding. After Manhattan federal judge Allen G. Schwartz ruled the perp walk unconstitutional, several articles came out either defending the ruling or criticizing it. One article presented arguments from expert anthropologists on the study of perp walks as a rite of passage. The perp's social status changes, the old status is stripped away, and a new status is assumed. However, the media are not dedicating much coverage to these legal questions about how they do their job. What reporting has appeared has been an oddly theoretical discussion, sidestepping basic questions and relying on frequent references to a "watchdog" press corps: intrepid, critical, responsible–and wholly unrecognizable to any regular consumer of corporate media.

Many of the articles and transcripts mentioned the perp walk in association with public figures, a way of shaming them for their alleged transgressions. The perp walk in this sense was used as a way of saying "the fact that you are famous doesn't mean you can get away with anything." The majority of articles focused on particular people, including Michael Jackson, Martha Stewart, and Kenneth Lay of Enron. The perp walk, being such a derogatory action, was also used for terrorists and priests suspected of child molestation. These perps were lumped into one category, regardless of crime or guilt.

Other articles made light of perp walks by suggesting what clothes should be worn or by analyzing the clothes that perps were wearing during their perp walks. An article about certain products that were getting noticed because of the perps who were wearing them said, in reference to the O.J. Simpson trial, "Do the perp walk–in Bruno Magli shoes" (Pogrebin, 1996). Another article made suggestions to Martha Stewart on the best outfit to wear for her public appearance.

In sum, this research tracked the terms *perp* and *junkie*, and subsequently *perp walk*, as examples of crime language that has been adopted by the mass media and incorporated into public discourse as stigmatized language. QDA was utilized, which allowed me the flexibility to investigate new and varied concepts that emerged during analysis. I used document analysis of articles, and later transcripts, found in the LexisNexis database to follow how the terms *perp*, *perp walk*, and *junkie* were introduced in the media and to document the change in usage over time and its eventual inclusion into common everyday language. As the analysis was conducted, patterns emerged to the introduction and contexts of the terms in the media. All terms saw a steady increase of inclusion in the news media over time, indicating the move of the language from a specific institution to commonplace knowledge.

Summary and Conclusion

QDA is an emergent methodology in several senses. In the most general sense, it views research as a process and not merely a series of fixed steps. Although there is a definite research design, it is kept open until the initial steps have been taken and familiarity with the materials achieved. More specifically, then, QDA is emergent for the following reasons. First, it emerged from conventional content analysis. Second, and more practically, the use of the method invites the researcher to interactively explore an initial body of documents to simultaneously "check out" any broad ideas or concepts, as well as to begin an immersion into both explicit and subtle symbolic representations, messages, and images that are relevant for the task at hand. This perspective empowers the researcher in using the method. Third, the research process will necessarily lead the researcher to explore additional documents that, in all likelihood, were not part of the original plan. Similarly, key words, symbols, concepts, and even "discourse" are likely to be partially discovered through the exploration. As in all ethnographic approaches, saturation and repetition begin to occur, and this marks the end of that particular phase of the research. Fourth, the use of theoretical sampling, or searching for documents, symbols, and so forth, entails structured emergence in that contradictions (or negations) of certain relationships are sought, particularly toward the end of conceptual closure, as a researcher investigates the parameters and dimensions of, say, a particular discourse (e.g., use of *gangsta* in nonrap music).

The strengths and weaknesses of this approach follow the classical lines of structured and unstructured research often used to describe quantitative and qualitative models, respectively. With exceptions, qualitative research is less replicable and therefore, according to the traditional positivist mantra, is less reliable. (Indeed, some positivists would even argue that validity depends on reliability.) It should be apparent to the reader by now that QDA is disciplined and systematic but that it is not highly structured throughout; it is a perspective as well as a method. There is a disciplined pursuit, a querying, comparative, and analytical phase to each project, but the parameters of each of these are not tightly constrained a priori; they are, rather, empirically informed by the materials and emergent questions. A key component of this approach is the development and guided pursuit of a protocol, a method of systematically querying the data. Thematic emphasis, how it is organized, when it emerged, and some of the social consequences can be demonstrated through this approach. For example, work on the "discourse of fear" established that fear "traveled" to other problems, issues, and sources, over time and across media. Moreover, this approach, along with that of other researchers, shows the connection between information sources and certain themes that appear in news and throughout public discourse. Establishing the entrepreneurial activity—and, ultimately, the "ownership"—of relevant terms, meanings, themes, and discourse is part of the overall project in which we are all involved. Nevertheless, although the research steps, including sampling, protocol construction, and coding categories, can be clearly stated, the emergent features of the research act make detailed replication very difficult.

A few more comments seem to be in order about theoretical sampling and generalizability. QDA is not primarily oriented toward making widespread generalizations; the research design is not set up for that. Theoretical sampling is employed instead of simple random sampling. Altheide's (1981, 1982) research on the Iranian hostage crisis demonstrated that the most significant and socially volatile, salient, and emotional aspects of propaganda and news coverage would be missed by virtually any sampling technique except for theoretical sampling. The reason is quite simple: The most important cultural and symbolic meanings for audiences and decision makers are not likely to be the most frequently occurring, although they might be. Any method that does not permit the discovery and inclusion of some of these "symbolically dense" narratives would miss important data.

One emphasis of QDA is to discover and demonstrate the nature and importance of thematic meanings in public discourse (i.e., in the case of news reports). As the brief case studies of Coyle, Schneider, Grimes, and DeVriese illustrate, this entails a broad vision to collect the optimum range of materials, which are then analyzed in some depth in order to answer the relevant research questions. That is the major goal. However, once the project is completed, a researcher could expand the question to include a broader sample of documents and/or to investigate other appropriate settings in order to explore similarities and differences in an emergent fashion. Finally, the researcher's reports become documents that others can explore, integrate, and systematically analyze for relevant substantive and methodological data. Thus the research act is also an emergent creative act, clarifying some questions while adding material for others to investigate.

References

Altheide, D. (1981). Iran vs. U.S. TV news!: The hostage story out of context. In W. C. Adams (Ed.), *TV coverage of the Middle East* (pp. 128–158). Norwood, NJ: Ablex.

Altheide, D. (1982, Fall). Three-in-one news: Network coverage of Iran. *Journalism Quarterly*, pp. 482–486.

Altheide, D. (1987). Ethnographic content analysis. *Qualitative Sociology, 10*, 65–77.

Altheide, D. (1995). *An ecology of communication: Cultural formats of control.* Hawthorne, NY: Aldine de Gruyter.

Altheide, D. (1996). *Qualitative media analysis.* Newbury Park, CA: Sage.

Altheide, D. (2000). Tracking discourse and qualitative document analysis. *Poetics, 27*, 287–299.

Altheide, D. (2002). *Creating fear: News and the construction of crisis.* Hawthorne, NY: Aldine de Gruyter.

Altheide, D. L. (2004). Ethnographic content analyses. In M. S. Lewis-Beck, A. Bryman, & T. F. Liao (Eds.), *The Sage encyclopedia of social science research methods* (pp. 325–326). Thousand Oaks, CA: Sage.

Altheide, D. L., & Johnson, J. M. (1993). Reflections on voice in ethnography. *Studies in Symbolic Interaction, 15*, 71–82.

Atkinson, P. (1990). *The ethnographic imagination: Textual constructs of reality.* London: Routledge.

Becker, H. S. (1973). *Outsiders: Studies in the sociology of deviance.* New York: Free Press.

Berg, B. L. (1989). *Qualitative research methods for the social sciences.* Boston: Allyn & Bacon.

Berger, A. A. (1982). *Media analysis techniques.* Newbury Park, CA: Sage.

Brissett, D., & Edgley, C. (1990). *Life as theater: A dramaturgical sourcebook.* New York: Aldine de Gruyter.

Buck, R. (2005, March 3). [Spike] Lee shouts back at gangsta rap. *Hartford Courant*, p. 6.

Central Intelligence Agency. (n.d.). Frequently asked questions. Retrieved from *https://www.cia.gov/about-cia/faqs/index.html#spyonamericans*

Cicourel, A. V. (1964). *Method and measurement in sociology.* New York: Free Press.

Cicourel, A. V. (1974). *Cognitive sociology: Language and meaning in social interaction.* New York: Free Press.

Denzin, N. K. (1978). *The research act: A theoretical introduction to sociological methods.* New York: McGraw-Hill.

Denzin, N. K. (1989). *Interpretive interactionism*. Newbury Park, CA: Sage.

Denzin, N. K. (1997). *Interpretive ethnography: Ethnographic practices for the 21st century*. Thousand Oaks, CA: Sage.

Denzin, N. K. (2003). Cultural studies. In L. T. Reynolds & N. J. Herman-Kinney (Eds.), *Handbook of symbolic interactionism* (pp. 997–1019). New York: AltaMira Press.

Denzin, N. K., & Lincoln, Y. S. (Eds.). (1994). *Handbook of qualitative research*. Newbury Park, CA: Sage.

Denzin, N. K., & Lincoln, Y. S. (2003). *Strategies of qualitative inquiry*. Thousand Oaks, CA: Sage.

Dooms, R. (2005, July 18). Howard student proud to win P.I.M.P. scholarship. *Black College Wire*. Retrieved from *http://www.blackcollegewire.org/culture/050718_pimp_scholar*

Douglas, J. D. (1967). *The social meanings of suicide*. Princeton, NJ: Princeton University Press.

Douglas, J. D. (1970a). *Deviance and respectability: The social construction of moral meanings*. New York: Basic Books.

Douglas, J. D. (1970b). *Understanding everyday life: Toward the reconstruction of sociological knowledge*. Chicago: Aldine.

Douglas, J. D. (1971). *American social order: Social rules in a pluralistic society*. New York: Free Press.

Douglas, J. D. (1976). *Investigative social research: Individual and team field research*. Beverly Hills, CA: Sage.

Douglas, J. D., & Johnson, J. M. (1977). *Existential sociology*. Cambridge, UK: Cambridge University Press.

Dwyer, J. (2005, December 22). New York police covertly join in at protest rallies. *New York Times*, p. 1.

Emerson, R. M. (2001). *Contemporary field research: Perspectives and formulations*. Prospect Heights, IL: Waveland Press.

Emerson, R. M., Fretz, R. I., & Shaw, L. L. (1995). *Writing ethnographic fieldnotes*. Chicago: University of Chicago Press.

Ferrarotti, F. (1988). *The end of conversation: The impact of mass media on modern society*. New York: Greenwood Press.

Ferrell, J., & Hamm, M. S. (1998). *Ethnography at the edge: Crime, deviance, and field research*. Boston: Northeastern University Press.

Garfinkel, H. (1967). *Studies in ethnomethodology*. Englewood Cliffs, NJ: Prentice-Hall.

Geertz, C. (1973). *The interpretation of cultures: Selected essays*. New York: Basic Books.

Glaser, B. G., & Strauss, A. L. (1967). *Discovery of grounded theory: Strategies for qualitative research*. Chicago: Aldine.

Glotz, P., Bertschi, S., & Locke, C. (Eds.) (2005). *Thumb culture: The meaning of mobile phones for society*. Bielefeld, Germany: Books on Demand.

Goffman, E. (1959). *The presentation of self in everyday life*. Garden City, NY: Doubleday.

Goffman, E. (1968). *Asylums: Essays on the social situation of mental patients and other inmates*. Chicago: Aldine.

Goffman, E. (1974). *Frame analysis*. New York: Harper & Row.

Goffman, E. (1989). On fieldwork. *Journal of Contemporary Ethnography, 18*, 123–132.

Gouldner, A. W. (1970). *The coming crisis of Western sociology*. New York: Basic Books.

Grey, S., & Van Natta, D. (2005, June 25). Thirteen with the C.I.A. sought by Italy in a kidnapping. *New York Times*. Retrieved from *http://www.nytimes.com/2005/06/25/international/europe/25milan.html?th&emc=th*

Grimshaw, A. D., & Burke, P. J. (1994). *What's going on here? Complementary studies of professional talk*. Norwood, NJ: Ablex.

Gronbeck, B. E., Farrell, T. J., & Soukup, P. A. (1991). *Media, consciousness, and culture: Explorations of Walter Ong's thought*. Newbury Park, CA: Sage.

Grossberg, L., Wartella, E., & Whitney, D. C. (1998). *Mediamaking: Mass media in a popular culture*. Thousand Oaks, CA: Sage.

Hall, P. (1988). Asymmetry, information control, and information technology. In D. Maines & C. J. Couch (Eds.), *Communication and social structure* (pp. 341–356). Springfield, IL: Thomas.

Hammersley, M., & Atkinson, P. (1983). *Ethnography, principles in practice*. London: Routledge.

Harper, D. (2003). Framing photographic ethnography: A case study. *Ethnography, 4*, 241–266.

Johnson, J. M. (1975). *Doing field research*. New York: Free Press.

Jorgensen, D. L. (1989). *Participant observation: A methodology for human studies*. Newbury Park, CA: Sage.

Keyes, C. L. (2002). *Rap music and street consciousness*. Urbana: University of Illinois Press.

Krippendorff, K. (2004). *Content analysis: An introduction to its methodology*. Thousand Oaks, CA: Sage.

Lyman, S. M. (1989). *The seven deadly sins: Society and evil*. Dix Hills, NY: General Hall.

Lyman, S. M. (1997). *Postmodernism and a sociology of the absurd and other essays on the "nouvelle vague" in American social science*. Fayetteville: University of Arkansas Press.

Lyman, S. M., & Scott, M. B. (1970). *A sociology of the absurd*. Pacific Palisades, CA: Goodyear.

Maines, D. R. (2000). The social construction of meaning. *Contemporary Sociology: A Journal of Reviews, 29*, 577–584.

Manning, P. K. (1987). *Semiotics and fieldwork*. Newbury Park, CA: Sage.

Manning, P. K., & Cullum-Swan, B. (1994). Narrative, content and semiotic analysis. In N. K. Denzin & Y. S. Lincoln (Eds.), *Handbook of qualitative research* (pp. 463–478). Newbury Park, CA: Sage.

Marcus, G. E., Clifford, J., & School of American Research. (1986). *Writing culture: The poetics and politics of ethnography: A School of American Research advanced seminar*. Berkeley: University of California Press.

Marcus, G. E., & Fischer, M. M. J. (1999). *Anthropology as cultural critique: An experimental moment in the human sciences*. Chicago: University of Chicago Press.

Nader, L. (1965). *The ethnography of law.* Menasha, WI: American Anthropological Association.

Phillips, N., & Hardy, C. (2002). *Discourse analysis: Investigating processes of social construction.* Thousand Oaks, CA: Sage.

Plummer, K. (1983). *Documents of life: An introduction to the problems and literature of a humanistic method.* London: Allen & Unwin.

Pogrebin, R. (1996, December 1). The product tie-ins from hell. *New York Times,* Sec. 4, p. 2.

Price, D. H. (2004). *Threatening anthropology: McCarthyism and the FBI's surveillance of activist anthropologists.* Durham, NC: Duke University Press.

Price, D. H. (2005). How the FBI spied on Edward Said. *CounterPunch, 12,* 1.

Prus, R. C. (1996). *Symbolic interaction and ethnographic research: Intersubjectivity and the study of human lived experience.* Albany: State University of New York Press.

Ragin, C. C. (1994). *Constructing social research: The unity and diversity of method.* Thousand Oaks, CA: Pine Forge Press.

Saunders, B. (2005, May 15). Beware the wild drovers; Indiana Jones got it all wrong: The thugs weren't bloody devotees of Kali. *The Independent,* p. 27.

Stein, R. (2005, March 6). Pimp my cubicle. *Newsweek,* p. 11.

Strauss, A. L., & Corbin, J. (1990). *Basics of qualitative research: Grounded theory procedures and techniques.* Newbury Park, CA: Sage.

Surratt, C. B. (2001). *The Internet and social change.* Jefferson, NC: McFarland.

van Dijk, T. A. (1988). *News as discourse.* Hillsdale, NJ: Erlbaum.

Van Maanen, J. (1988). *Tales of the field: On writing ethnography.* Chicago: University of Chicago Press.

Weiler, M., & Pearce, W. B. (1992). *Reagan and public discourse in America.* Tuscaloosa: University of Alabama Press.

Wilson, M. (2005, March 6). Will the real thug please stand up, and lower that gun. *New York Times,* Sec. 1, p. 39.

GROUNDED THEORY

CHAPTER 7

Grounded Theory as an Emergent Method

Kathy Charmaz

During its 40-year history, grounded theory has served as a major method for conducting emergent qualitative research.[1] What is an emergent method? I start with a working definition of an emergent method as inductive, indeterminate, and open-ended. An emergent method begins with the empirical world and builds an inductive understanding of it as events unfold and knowledge accrues. Social scientists who use emergent methods can study research problems that arise in the empirical world and can pursue unanticipated directions of inquiry in this world. Emergent methods are particularly well suited for studying uncharted, contingent, or dynamic phenomena. These methods also allow for new properties of the studied phenomenon to appear that, in turn, shape new conditions and consequences to be studied. By adopting emergent methods, researchers can account for processes discovered in the empirical world and direct their methodological strategies accordingly.

How does grounded theory fit the definition of an emergent method? In which ways does the grounded theory method advance the development of emergent methods? Grounded theory is predicated on an emergent logic. This method starts with a systematic, inductive approach to collecting and analyzing data to develop theoretical analyses. The method also includes checking emergent categories that emerge from successive levels of analysis through hypothetical and deductive reasoning. Grounded theory offers systematic analytic strategies that combine explicitness and flexibility.

Fundamental tenets of the grounded theory method include: (1) minimizing preconceived ideas about the research problem and the data, (2) using simultaneous data collection and analysis to inform each other, (3) remaining open to varied explanations and/or understandings of the data, and (4) focusing data analysis to construct middle-range theories. Rather than viewing only the product of inquiry—the completed grounded theory—as emergent, I argue that the *method* itself is emergent. Thus grounded theorists choose or create specific methodological strategies to handle puzzles and problems that arise as inquiry proceeds.

The publication of Barney G. Glaser and Anselm L. Strauss's *The Discovery of Grounded Theory* in 1967 marked the first systematic statement about how to construct emergent analyses. Prior to that time, students learned how to do qualitative research through an oral tradition of mentoring, as well as through immersion in fieldwork (Rock, 1979). The limited midcentury literature on qualitative methods attended to data collection (see, e.g., Adams & Priess, 1960; Junker, 1960) and attempted to answer quantitative concerns, such as achieving validity and reliability. Scholars had scarcely addressed how to handle the analytic phases of the research process.

Glaser and Strauss (1967) argued that qualitative research: (1) proceeded from a different logic than did quantitative inquiry and had its own rigor, (2) should be evaluated by different canons than those for quantitative research, (3) could integrate research and theory, and (4) democratized theory construction because any astute social scientist could engage in analytic practices that generated theory. Glaser and Strauss's arguments redirected the discussion of qualitative inquiry from methods of data collection to strategies for data analysis and challenged views about theory construction.

Prior to the work of Glaser and Strauss, midcentury theorizing had largely consisted of grand theories about societal structure, but these theories lacked empirical roots. Glaser and Strauss's arguments gained a receptive audience among established and aspiring qualitative researchers and provided them with ready justifications for doing inductive qualitative studies. Subsequently, grounded theory became the most cited qualitative research method across diverse disciplines and professions (Bryant & Charmaz, 2007b). Most researchers, however, adopted few, if any, of Glaser and Strauss's (1967) specific methodological strategies, and those who did often altered them beyond recognition as grounded theory.

Grounded theory is a method of explication and emergence. The method takes a systematic inductive, comparative, and interactive approach to inquiry and offers several open-ended strategies for conducting emergent inquiry (Charmaz, 2006; Charmaz & Henwood, in press). These strategies make grounded theory more than only inductive, because they encourage researchers to make conjectures and check them and therefore to engage in deductive reasoning as inquiry proceeds. Grounded theory strategies make the method explicit, and their open-ended qualities foster the development of emergent conceptual analyses. Grounded theory strategies prompt early analytic thinking and keep researchers interacting with their data and nascent analyses (Charmaz, 2006).

The logic of grounded theory provides a major contribution to emergent methods because grounded theory involves creative problem solving and imaginative interpretation.[2] Grounded theory strategies prompt the researcher to reach beyond pure induction. The method builds a series of checks and refinements into qualitative inquiry through an iterative process of successive analytic and data collection phases of research, each informed by the other and rendered more theoretical. In short, the grounded theory method emphasizes the process of analysis and the development of theoretical categories, rather than focusing solely on the results of inquiry.

The Place of Emergence in Grounded Theory

Any analysis of grounded theory as an emergent method must address the concept of emergence and its place in the method.

Emergence is a fundamental property of grounded theory—both in its products and, although perhaps unrecognized and sometimes contested, in its methodological strategies (see Bryant & Charmaz, 2007c; Charmaz, 2007b). The overriding stated objective of using grounded theory is to generate emergent theories from the data that account for the data.

Taking a step back and looking at emergence as a concept helps one to clarify its divergent understandings and uses in grounded theory. The concept of emergence assumes epistemological understandings and a theory of time. Disputes and misconceptions about what grounded theory is and should be occur at these foundational levels. Emergence is fundamentally a temporal concept; it presupposes a past, assumes the immediacy of the present, and implies a future. In keeping with George Herbert Mead (1932), the present arises from the past but has new properties. These novel elements of emergence distinguish the present from the past and make it distinctive. Emile Durkheim (1895/1982) takes the concept of emergence to its logical extension in his analysis of social structural change. His postulate of emergent reality holds that the whole is greater than and different from the sum of its parts. Emergence gives rise to a new phenomenon with qualitatively new properties.[3]

Whether or not researchers concur with Durkheim, they would agree that emergence means movement, process, and change. The concept of emergence takes into account that the unexpected may occur. The past shapes the present and future but does not make either wholly predictable. Emergent methods permit pursuing what researchers *could not* have anticipated. Grounded theory is particularly well suited to studying such areas because the method itself possesses emergent properties.

The language with which scholars construct the concept of emergence affects its use in the social sciences. Acts of distinguishing between past and present and differentiating the new from the old require language and shared meanings. Essentially, then, we understand the temporal dimensions of emergence through language. Individuals define and depict emergence through drawing on shared meanings. Nonetheless, innovations may occur as these individuals define and depict emergence and draw inferences from their studies. Thus emergence contains subjective elements, as well as collectively agreed-upon objective properties.

Grounded theory starts with an inductive logic but moves into abductive reasoning as the researcher seeks to understand emergent empirical findings. Abductive reasoning aims to account for surprises, anomalies, or puzzles in the collected data. This type of reasoning invokes imaginative interpretations because the researcher imagines all possible theoretical accounts for the observed data and then forms and checks hypotheses until arriving at the most plausible interpretation of the observed data (see also Charmaz, 2006; Reichertz, 2004, 2007; Rosenthal, 2004). For example, Patrick Biernacki's (1986) study not only employed abductive reasoning but also began because of puzzling findings that arose in an earlier small study of marijuana use. Biernacki had discovered that some individuals recovered from heroin addiction without formal treatment, something that health practitioners at that time believed to be impossible. What could account for this surprising discovery? Biernacki's study reveals his search for a theoretical explanation and the movement he made between detailed empirical data and an emergent interpretation of them.

Abduction allows for intuitive interpretations of empirical observations and creative ideas that might account for them (Dey, 2004; Reichertz, 2004, 2007; Rosenthal, 2004). Not only are the surprising data emergent, but the researcher's theoretical treatment of them is also emergent. Abductive reasoning can take the researcher into unanticipated theoretical realms.

Contested Meanings of Emergence in Grounded Theory

The original statement of grounded theory, as well as its current versions, emphasized emergence (see, e.g., Charmaz, 1983, 1990, 2006; Glaser, 1998, 2003, 2006; Strauss, 1987; Strauss & Corbin, 1990, 1998). Yet authors of different versions of grounded theory diverge in how they view and treat emergence in practice. Thus their divergent use of the concept of emergence in grounded theory has resulted in contested versions of the method (Charmaz, 2000, 2006; Clarke, 2005; Glaser, 1992, 1998; Strauss & Corbin, 1990, 1998).

As Kelle (2005) underscores, what emergence means in grounded theory has become a focal point in divisions and debates among its proponents. Glaser's (1992) subtitle, "Emergence vs. Forcing," exemplifies this division in his critique of Strauss and Corbin's (1990) grounded theory methods text. Other proponents' views on emergence are seldom as apparent or contentious as Glaser's but nonetheless shape their approaches to grounded theory. The method now has second-generation and, in some cases, third-generation spokespersons (see, e.g., Bryant & Charmaz, 2007a; Charmaz, 1983, 1990, 2003, 2006; Chenitz & Swanson, 1986; Clarke, 2005, 2006; Clarke & Friese, 2007; Stern, 1994a, 1994b; Wilson & Hutchinson, 1996). In addition, Glaser and Strauss and Corbin (1990, 1998; Strauss, 1987) have influenced numerous commentators, such as Boychuk-Duchscher and Morgan (2004), Dey (1999, 2004), Goulding (2002), Locke (1997, 2001), Lonkila (1995), May (1996), Melia (1996), and Uruquat (2007). The method has spread across diverse disciplines and professional fields, but its inextricable link to its originators continues. Thus I next clarify Glaser's and Strauss's early shared but later divergent views of emergence.

Glaser and Strauss's (1967) original statement portrays the analytic process as emergent in the sense that researchers develop increasingly more theoretical categories and connections as they engage in successive levels of data collection and analysis. Glaser and Strauss imply that these categories emerge automatically through invoking comparative methods. What facilitates the emergence of theoretical categories is less clear. In their book, Glaser and Strauss take a seemingly contradictory stance. They encourage researchers to conduct their research without preconceptions from earlier theory and research. Yet they assume that these researchers already possess sufficient theoretical sensitivity to discern and follow theoretical leads from examining their data. A fine line exists between asking theoretical questions and applying extant concepts. The subsequent tensions between asking and applying will substantially affect the extent to which grounded theory remains an emergent method or becomes a method of application.

The different strategies with which each originator attempted to resolve these tensions have influenced the development of the grounded theory method, as well as how later researchers have seen fit to use it. Numerous researchers have applied the method mechanically and prescriptively by treating grounded theory strategies as rigid, sequential rules rather than flexible, open-ended guidelines. Nonetheless, each of its originators has unwittingly fostered mechanical applications of the method. A renewed emphasis on using grounded theory as an emergent method can counter this trend.

The role of emergence remains central in Glaser's version of grounded theory. Glaser expands his view of emergence in his later works (1978, 1992, 1998, 2003) and sees it as a definitive property of grounded theory. In his version of grounded theory, emergent categories are objective, general, and abstract. Glaser asserts that the process of abstraction removes traces of subjectivity, raises the theoretical level of the analysis, and increases its generality and parsimony. In his view, using systematic comparative methods leads researchers to discover theoretical categories. Glaser admonishes his followers to "trust in emergence," as though the comparative process of working through levels of analysis will magically generate ideas. He treats emergence and the development of abstract categories as though they are devoid of interpretation and contends that abstraction is objective whereas description is interpretive (Glaser, 2002).[4] Similarly, Glaser (2003, p. 48) argues, "All knowledge is not perspectival. Description is perspectival; concepts that fit and work are variable." Nonetheless, variables are expressed in words and therefore import interpretation.

In his early works, Glaser (1978; Glaser & Strauss, 1967) aimed to use grounded theory to study emergent social or social psychological processes. In this case, emergence derived from the researcher's discovering a single overriding process in the field. The subsequent grounded theory would conceptualize that process by establishing the properties of its core categories or variables. Glaser has since abandoned the search for a single basic social process. He came to view this quest as misguided; it forced data into one framework at the expense of developing emergent categories and immobilized researchers who saw multiple processes in their research settings. Several former students from the 1970s and 1980s report having had similar reservations–and immobilizing setbacks–in their early studies (Charmaz, 2006; Clarke, 2005).

Glaser continues to view grounded theory as a variable analysis but has modified his view about which variables to seek. He now urges researchers to investigate how participants in a particular setting try to resolve their main concern. In 1992, Glaser asserted that research participants would tell the grounded theorist their main concern and their strategy for resolution, but by 2003 he viewed the main concern as latent and therefore assumed and largely unstated. Despite this change of view, Glaser continues to contend that researchers should focus on what emerges in the setting.

As analysis proceeds, potential tensions increase between invoking theoretical sensitivity and drawing on extant theoretical concepts. Glaser (1978, 1992, 1998) has relied on "theoretical codes" to guard against such tensions. "Theoretical codes" are an ad hoc, loosely integrated formulation of varied theoretical families of concepts, such as Glaser's well-known "Six Cs: Causes, Contexts, Contingencies, Consequences, Covariances, and Conditions" (Glaser, 1978, p. 74). Other coding families include those that invoke major sociological concepts such as "means-goals," "identity-self," and "consensus codes." What Glaser includes in a given coding family sometimes seems arbitrary and haphazard. The coding families are not necessarily mutually exclusive, and their boundaries are often indistinct. Substantive codes in a specific study may indicate a number of theoretical codes that cut across different coding families. Glaser asserts that theoretical codes provide the conceptual power to integrate substantive codes. His purpose in establishing theoretical codes is to give the substantive analysis new coherence at an abstract level. However, researchers might find these theoretical codes more helpful as possible directions rather than as definitive integrative links.

Strauss and Corbin's (1990, 1998) version of grounded theory relies less on emergence than does Glaser's version. Whereas Glaser enjoins researchers to initiate their studies by focusing on what is happening in the setting, that is, what the researcher defines as emerging there, Strauss and Corbin view starting points with a wider lens. They point out that, in addition to what emerges in the study, other influences, such as personal experiences, professional exigencies, and earlier ideas, may spark inquiry. Their introduction of techniques to apply to data, axial coding and the causal–conditional matrix, made grounded theory prescriptive and signaled critical departures from Glaser's version. Strauss and Corbin define axial coding as a way of specifying the dimensions of a category, relating categories to subcategories, delineating relationships between them, and bringing the data back together into a coherent whole after having fractured them during the initial coding (Charmaz, 2006, p. 186; Corbin & Strauss, 1988, p. 125). In this sense, Strauss and Corbin supply an alternative to Glaser's reliance on theoretical codes, but it requires application rather than relying on emergence. The conditional/consequential matrix is a coding device used to show the intersections of micro and macro conditions/consequences on actions and to clarify the connections between them. Strauss and Corbin present this matrix as an effective means of attending to structural context that links structures and situations.

The prescriptive character of Strauss and Corbin's books is something of a paradox, for Strauss had long emphasized Mead's analysis of temporality and the significance of agency, alternative actions, and indeterminacy in social life (Fisher & Strauss, 1979; Strauss, 1959/1969, 1993). Strauss's view of social life assumed emergence through dynamic processes of action (including interaction) and the construction and reconstruction of meaning. Perhaps sharp criticisms of Strauss and Corbin's 1990 book as technical and prescriptive led to their considerably more flexible view of grounded theory in the first edition of the *Handbook of Qualitative Research* (Strauss & Corbin, 1994). In addition, Margaret H. Kearney (2007) observes that Strauss received enormous pressure from graduate students to make grounded theory concrete and rule-bound.

The most recent version of grounded theory, constructivist grounded theory (Bryant, 2002; Charmaz, 2000, 2005, 2006; Clarke, 2005, 2006; Mills, Bonner, & Francis, 2006), retains the original focus on emergence but does so in relation to the conditions of the research and the standpoints and interactions of the researchers. Thus the research product includes more than what the researcher learns in the field. Whether or not researchers are conscious of what they bring to the study or of the conditions under which they conduct it, constructivists contend that all become part of the research process and product. The constructivist position views research as an emergent product of particular times, social conditions, and interactional situations. Constructivists argue that researchers' perspectives will direct their attention but not determine their research (see also Clarke, 2005, 2006). Unlike the view held by Glaser that researchers can and should remove themselves from the influences of their disciplines and the conditions of their research, constructivists aim to make these influences explicit.[5] Here researchers view themselves as embedded in the research process rather than as distanced observers of empirical phenomena. Thus constructivists attend to the conditions and relations of research, considering them part of the knowledge gained from the investigation.

Similarly, Clarke (2005, 2006) argues that classic grounded theory erases perspectives, positions, standpoints, and differences. Like the other constructivist approaches, Clarke's postmodern critique challenges the fundamental epistemological premises that support objectivist views and practices. Both Clarke (2005, 2006) and Charmaz (2006) observe that the generalizing thrust of Glaser's (1978, 1992, 1998, 2002) approach separates the conditions of research from the abstract concepts that the researcher generates. Glaser aims to gain objective concepts through observing many cases, which certainly helps to broaden the resulting scope of knowledge. Yet observing many cases does not necessarily answer the question of how the conditions of the research—the researcher's standpoints, interactions, and choices—affect the research process and product.

Constructivists reveal the significance of grounded theory as an emergent method: *The method does not stand outside the research process; it resides within it.*[6] Commentators often treat grounded theory as rule-bound, especially those influenced by Strauss and Corbin. At present Glaser also proffers rules, albeit a different set. Constructivists, however, view the emergent nature of the method itself as arising from researchers' questions, choices, and specific strategies and thus remain inseparable from their earlier and evolving perspectives. When constructivist grounded theorists enter research sites and engage their data, their perspectives may grow and/or change and thus permit the structure of inquiry, as well as its content, to be emergent. Researchers who treat grounded theory as consisting of a few flexible yet systematic guidelines create the conditions to define emergent categories.

A constructivist stance on emergence contrasts with both Glaser's (1978) theoretical codes and Strauss and Corbin's axial coding and conditional/consequential matrix at the level of grounded theory practice. Each of their respective approaches encourages researchers to force their data into extant categories. Adopting theoretical codes resounds of application, not emergence. If researchers use these theoretical codes to integrate their theories, where is the line between application and emergence? One solution is to pose theoretical questions about the nascent analysis rather than to apply theoretical concepts (see Charmaz, 2006, pp. 335–340) to it. Thus the theoretical questions that researchers pose arise from the particular issues grounded in the studied empirical world.

Emergence in Grounded Theory Practice

Grounded theory has evolved into a constellation of methods rather than an orthodox unitary approach.[7] My preceding discussion highlights major differences between Glaser and Strauss's classic statement, Glaser's development of it, Strauss and Corbin's version, and constructivist grounded theory. Nonetheless, these major versions of grounded theory also share certain similar guidelines and specific strategies in research practice. Hence I critique the strategies here and note crucial points at which researchers advance their emergent analyses or pursue directions that undermine emergence and their claims of having produced a grounded theory study.

Like those of many other qualitative researchers, grounded theorists' initial topics in new research arenas provide starting points of exploration—but not of specific research questions.[8] These questions depend on what arises in research sites and stories. Two defining properties of the grounded theory method create the conditions for emergent inquiry: (1) the systematic, active scrutiny of data and (2) the successive development and checking of categories. From the initial stages of research throughout the process, grounded theorists scrutinize their data by asking both action and analytic questions: "What is happening here?" and "What (theoretical category or theory) are these data a study of?" (Glaser, 1978, p. 57). The first question pushes the researcher to examine the empirical world—in close detail. The second question links this world to theoretical possibilities early on during data collection. Both questions encourage researchers to follow emergent leads systematically.

Emergent leads shape the search for emergent concepts. By interrogating their data repeatedly with these two questions, grounded theorists explicate, expedite, and enhance intuitive strategies that other qualitative researchers often invoke on a descriptive level. These strategies include probing beneath the surface: comparing data, checking hunches, refining emerging ideas, and constructing abstract categories from data analysis. Simultaneously, grounded theory makes these strategies more efficient and analytically effective by indicating how and when to use them. The iterative process of going back and forth between collecting and analyzing data raises the emergent levels of analysis.

Hence researchers' interactions and observations in the field affect both their developing analysis and their attempts to grapple with their constructed data. At each stage of the research process, new ideas, questions, and deeper refinements of earlier conceptions can emerge. A few crucial grounded theory strategies expedite the analytic process.

Because grounded theory relies on emergence, researchers should remain open to what happens in their research sites and settings. Narrow research problems and research questions seldom work until a grounded theorist has established intimate familiarity (Blumer, 1969; Lofland & Lofland, 1995) with the research topic or site.[9] This intimate familiarity with the topic gives grounded theorists a window to see emergent processes in their data, allowing them to pursue a specific research problem that addresses these processes.

In addition, the grounded theory goal of generating theoretical analyses that fit empirical reality requires researchers to gain an intimate familiarity (Blumer, 1969; Lofland & Lofland, 1995) with this empirical world. Researchers cannot assess how well their analyses fit their data unless they have gained intimate familiarity with the studied phenomenon. The openness of the grounded theory method allows researchers to develop an analysis of a major process, problem, or phenomenon in their data. Ironically, many researchers claim to adopt grounded theory to study narrowly defined preconceived problems in the field. Imposing either preconceived problems or narrow interests on a study stifles emergence and undermines effective use of grounded theory. Under these conditions, researchers treat grounded theory as a method of application rather than emergence.

Several grounded theory strategies have become part of the repertoire of the larger field of qualitative inquiry. Paradoxically, their translation into the lexicon of general qualitative methods has cost them emergent power and obfuscates the issue of whether and to what extent researchers' claims of using grounded theory can be supported (Charmaz, 2006; Hood, 2007). Simultaneous data collection and analysis has become common practice in qualitative research, although it marked a grand innovation when Glaser and Strauss first advocated it in 1967. They proposed that early data analysis would focus researchers' further data collection. In turn, this focused data would illuminate and inform construction of emergent categories.

At present, many qualitative researchers conduct simultaneous data gathering and analysis but do not necessarily use explicit comparative methods or adopt grounded theory forms of coding data. The grounded theory method integrates and streamlines data collection by constructing systematic comparisons throughout inquiry of data with data, data with code, code with code, code with category, and category with category.

Grounded theorists adopt an inductive approach yet move their nascent analyses beyond induction. In contrast, many qualitative studies remain solely inductive. These studies likely have a wider lens on the studied realities than do grounded theory studies, which progressively focus data collection and analysis. The grounded theory method not only calls for using comparisons to generate categories but also builds in checks that keep the researcher's ideas grounded in data. Grounded theorists go back to the setting to observe specific events or to ask key informants further, more specific questions to shed light on their developing theoretical categories.[10]

In my view, grounded theory strategies are few and flexible, so researchers may adapt them to the exigencies of their studies. Thus a researcher has latitude not simply to *choose* the methods but also to *create* them as inquiry proceeds. Grounded theory consists of transparent analytic guidelines; the transparency of the method enables researchers to make transparent analytic choices and constructions. The researcher can see and create a direct relationship between data and abstract categories.

Using Grounded Theory Guidelines

Effective use of the grounded theory method depends on adopting several of Glaser and Strauss's (1967; Glaser, 1978; Strauss, 1987) early grounded theory guidelines—with 21st-century caveats. Adopting comparative, interactive analytic strategies in coding, memo-writing, theoretical sampling, sorting, and integrating the analysis is only part of the grounded theorist's task. In keeping with constructivist premises, researchers must also (1) entertain a range of theoretical possibilities and (2) examine their own epistemological premises and research principles and practices. Grounded theory fosters openness to what is happening in the empirical world. That means studying data and developing an analysis from conceptualizing these data rather than imposing a theoretical framework on them.

Qualitative researchers often receive advice to choose research topics that affect their lives. Since the inception of the method, grounded theorists have pursued substantive topics in which they held a decided stake. Strauss and Glaser each had experienced the death of a parent before they began to study the social organization of dying. Elizabeth Cauhapé had experienced a midlife divorce before she undertook the dissertation research that led to her book, *Fresh Starts: Men and Women after Divorce* (1983). Adele E. Clarke had long-standing interests in women's reproductive health and in organizational analysis, which she combined in her 1998 historical study of the emergence of reproductive biology, *Disciplining Reproduction: Modernity, American Life Sciences and "the Problems of Sex."* Researchers who start where they are at may risk importing preconceived ideas into the study; however, engaging in reflexivity and invoking grounded theory strategies can challenge their previously taken-for-granted actions and assumptions.

What makes grounded theory distinctive? The comparative and interactive nature of grounded theory at every stage of analysis distinguishes grounded theory from other approaches and makes it an explicitly emergent method. First, crucial coding practices lay the foundation of grounded theory research. Second, writing progressively more analytic as opposed to descriptive, memos advances grounded theory practice. Third, a pivotal but often neglected grounded theory strategy, theoretical sampling, distinguishes grounded theory from other methods. Fourth, theoretical saturation is widely claimed but scarcely practiced. Following these four strategies enables researchers to make their theoretical analysis the basis for sorting and integrating their studies. I outline only how grounded theory strategies support emergent analyses here, as they are detailed elsewhere (Bryant & Charmaz, 2007b; Charmaz, 2003, 2006; Glaser, 1978; Strauss, 1987; Strauss & Corbin, 1990, 1994, 1998).

Coding Data

Coding begins the emergent process of analyzing data in grounded theory. Coding consists of at least two phases: initial coding and focused coding. Initial or open coding requires a close reading and interrogation of the data. This phase of coding moves grounded theorists' attention from the research field to the analysis of the data, as they engage in simultaneous data collection and analysis. Grounded theorists conduct coding as they gather data. Specific forms of grounded theory coding lead researchers to focus on possible meanings of the data and to stick closely to the data while actively interrogating them. By asking both of Glaser's questions, they can gain greater insight into their data and define what they might mean.

Most qualitative researchers code for themes and topics rather than actions and analytic possibilities. From the very beginning, coding for actions and theoretical potential distinguishes the grounded theory method and, likely, its product from other types of qualitative research. Researchers conduct initial grounded theory coding by comparing incidents or by coding word by word, line by line, or paragraph by paragraph. Coding in larger chunks works well with ethnographic data, whereas line-by-line coding is an excellent heuristic device for coding initial intensive interviews and certain types of narrative data. Coding with gerunds, that is, noun forms of verbs, such as *revealing*, *defining*, *feeling*, or *wanting*, helps to define what is happening in a fragment of data or a description of an incident. Gerunds enable grounded theorists to see implicit processes, to make connections between codes, and to keep their analyses active and emergent. Compare the excerpt of grounded theory coding with the one of general qualitative coding in Figure 7.1. The excerpt is taken from an interview with a woman I call Karen Liddell, who has a debilitating neck injury.

Note the difference between coding for topics as contrasted with grounded theory coding for actions. The general qualitative coding identifies topics about which the researcher can write; the researcher may use such topics as areas to sort and synthesize the material. The line-by-line grounded theory coding goes deeper into the phenomenon and attempts to explicate it. This type of coding gives researchers more directions to consider and already suggests emergent links between processes in the data. The codes indicate the simultaneous occurrence of a disintegrating marriage and family and the research participant's disintegrating self. The codes also indicate conditions under which each process occurs; readers gain a sense of what is happening in this statement and how it happens. The analytic level of the grounded theory codes ranges from describing a fragment of data, such as "disappearing husband," "being exhausted," and "explaining distress," to potential analytic categories such as "disintegrating self" and "disclosing a plausible identity." Karen Liddell imparts a sense of moving between past and present while describing her ex-husband's actions. I tried to portray this movement by coding him as an ex-husband in certain statements and a husband in others.

Grounded theory coding is interactive and comparative. Line-by-line coding forces the researcher to interact with the data. Even in so short an excerpt as I have provided in Figure 7.1, we can make some comparisons. Note how Karen tells the story of her husband's addiction and uses it to frame her story of her own struggle with addictive pain medications. In addition, the excerpt suggests conceptions of normal life compared with and juxtaposed against continual crises. My ideas and leads emerged while I grappled with the coding rather than from a reading of the entire interview. Grounded theorists may also gain emergent leads through identifying *in vivo* codes, which consist of research participants' direct statements. *In vivo* codes aid grounded theorists in discerning participants' meanings and in explaining their emergent actions.

After grounded theorists have established which initial codes are most frequent and/or significant, they engage in focused or selective coding. This coding allows them to sort and synthesize large amounts of data, thereby expediting their work. Grounded theorists scrutinize their focused codes to evaluate which ones best explain or interpret the empirical phenomenon. These codes then become tentative theoretical categories. Like their scrutiny of initial codes, which codes grounded theorists select to develop is an emergent process. They test their focused codes against the data by using them to examine large batches of data. When deciding which codes to raise to theoretical categories, they look for those codes that carry the weight of the analysis–what Clarke[11] calls "carrying capacity"–and that provide "analytic momentum" (Charmaz, 2006). Grounded theorists then treat these major focused codes as tentative categories subject to further analytic treatment.

Initial Grounded Theory Coding

Examples of Codes	*Initial Narrative Data to Be Coded*
Living with ex-husband's double life	My ex-husband had kind of a double life going on as it turns out; he
Disappearing husband Escalating disappearances Accounting for husband's disappearances	would disappear for two or three days at a time which became increasingly worse. He had colitis . . . part of it was
Defining hidden addiction Alluding to limits for self-explaining distress	his colitis but part of it, [as] it turned out was a hidden cocaine addiction so I couldn't continue to—in my chronic pain condition and his behavior, just kept
Being unable to function Disintegrating self Questioning survival of self/ of way of life Feeling hurt/betrayed Wanting husband's support for *her* pain	me so stressed out where I couldn't function emotionally and physically to a point. That's why I say my survival was at stake . . . it hurt me. And there was no support there for my pain
Carrying doubled responsibilities Expressing resentments (in tone of voice)	issue. . . . I always had to be the one who had to be strong because he'd be
Keeping life (family and business) together	gone on these disappearing things and then somebody had to hold down the fort and keep everything going when
Detailing ex-husband's lapses Timing then-husband's recovery/ explaining his complicating illness	this would happen. And then sometimes it would take him a week to recover because whatever he was
Feeling forced to be family emotional anchor	doing would cause his colitis to flare up, so I was always forced to be in the position of the emotional anchor in the
Being exhausted Feeling forced to escalate pain meds Seeing pain meds as allowing a normal life	family and it was so exhausting to me and again I had to keep escalating that pain medication then to continue on
Explaining extent of injury	and normally, then, at the time the disk was fully herniated so I was being
Externalizing questions about pain Revealing ambiguous cause of pain—physical and/or psychological	treated for chronic pain but there was still some questions to the validity of my pain factor whether it was
Questioning the possibility of addiction	emotionally induced or physically and some question as to whether it was a lot psychological, that I was perhaps,
Raising the specter of self-overmedicating Disclosing a plausible identity	you know, had a painful addiction and was just self-medicating.

General Qualitative Coding

Examples of Codes	*Initial Narrative Data to Be Coded*
Marital tensions	My ex-husband had kind of a double life going on as it turns out; he would disappear for two or three days at a time which became increasingly
Ex-husband's illness	worse. He had colitis . . . part of it was his colitis but part of it, [as] it turned out
Ex-husband's addiction	was a hidden cocaine addiction so I couldn't continue to—in my chronic pain
Stress	condition and his behavior, just kept me so stressed out where I couldn't function emotionally and physically to a point. That's why I say my survival was at stake . . . it hurt me. And there
Lack of support Pain issue	was no support there for my pain issue. . . . I always had to be the one
Pressures	who had to be strong because he'd be gone on these disappearing things and then somebody had to hold down the fort and keep everything going when this would happen. And then sometimes it would take him a week to
Family role	recover because whatever he was doing would cause his colitis to flare up, so I was always forced to be in the position of the emotional anchor in the family and it was so exhausting to me
Questions on source of pain	and again I had to keep escalating that pain medication then to continue on and normally, then, at the time the disk was fully herniated so I was being treated for chronic pain but there was still some questions to the validity of my pain factor whether it was emotionally induced or physically and
Possible addiction	some question as to whether it was a lot psychological, that I was perhaps, you know, had a painful addiction and was just self-medicating.

FIGURE 7.1. Comparison of grounded theory coding and general qualitative coding. Initial narrative data from Charmaz (2004).

Memo Writing

Grounded theorists typically define memo writing as the intermediate stage between data collection and writing a draft of a paper or chapter (Charmaz, 2003, 2006; Glaser, 1978, 1998). Yet memo writing is so much more. Memo writing is about capturing ideas in process and in progress. Successive memos on the same category trace its development as the researcher gathers more data to illuminate the category and probes deeper into its analysis. Memos can be partial, tentative, and exploratory. The acts of writing and storing memos provide a framework for exploring, checking, and developing ideas. Writing memos gives one the opportunity to learn about the data rather than just summarizing material. Through this writing, the grounded theorist's ideas emerge as discoveries unfold.

Memo writing is a distinct contribution of grounded theory, although most qualitative researchers now use some form of this method. Grounded theorists vary in the detail and analytic level of their memos. Essentially, however, memos first open the codes to scrutiny and then later examine the categories. Several guidelines are important for grounded theory memos: (1) title the memos for easy sorting and storage; (2) write memos throughout the entire research process; (3) define the code or category by its properties found in the data; (4) delineate the conditions under which the code or category emerges, is maintained, and changes; (5) compare the code or category with other codes and categories; (6) include the data from which the code or category is derived right in the memo; (7) outline the consequences of the code or category; (8) note gaps in the data and conjectures about it. Glaser (1998) urges researchers to write memos whenever and however they have an idea. Memos give grounded theorists something to work with, to ponder later, and to explore further.

Memo writing gives researchers the opportunity to stretch their thinking as they interrogate their data. Grounded theory approaches to memo writing shift qualitative inquiry into an explicit analytic endeavor. This type of memo writing prompts the researcher to move beyond description and storytelling. If, for example, I pursued the code "disintegrating self" in Figure 7.1, I would define each account of a "disintegrating self" according to properties I found in a range of interviews. Then I would try to outline the conditions in which each of these categories emerge and show how they might be related to other categories. I would see whether and to what extent the notion of a disintegrating self held when the social structure of a person's life was also disintegrating. I would then explore how other codes, such as "carrying doubled responsibilities" and "feeling hurt/betrayed," might fit into my emerging analysis. The analytic process of exploring meanings, weighing situations, and examining actions through memo writing raises questions that I could then try to answer through subsequent data collection.

Theoretical Sampling

Theoretical sampling keeps a study grounded. It is a method of sampling data for the development of a theoretical category. The term *sampling* here often leads to confusion and misunderstandings. Many researchers cannot separate the notion of sampling from studying populations and their characteristics. Hence they are able to envision sampling only as a procedure done before the collection of data. In contrast, researchers who subscribe to the grounded theory method conduct theoretical sampling only after they have tentative categories to develop or refine. For grounded theorists, emergent categories form the basis of theoretical sampling. Grounded theorists cannot anticipate where their theoretical inquiry will take them. Their tentative categories arise through the analytic process, and thus theoretical sampling may take them into new research sites and substantive areas.

Grounded theorists' major task in theoretical sampling is to fill out the properties of their categories. In keeping with grounded theory logic, they may seek comparative data to tease out hidden properties of a category. For example, if my data indicated that in each instance in which I found a disintegrating self, I also found a deteriorating social network, I might seek people who faced serious chronic conditions but had robust social networks. My subsequent comparisons could then illuminate to what extent and how the quality of a person's social network figures into his or her disintegrating self.

The logic of theoretical sampling distinguishes grounded theory from other types of qualitative inquiry. Through considering all possible theoretical understandings of their data, grounded theorists create tentative interpretations, then return to the field and gather more data to check and refine their categories. In this sense, grounded theory methods are abductive (Deely, 1990; Peirce, 1931/1958; Rosenthal, 2004). Abductive logic entails attempting to imagine all possible hypothetical accounts to explain surprising findings and then subjecting these hypothetical accounts to test. Abductive logic involves both imaginative interpretation and *reasoning* about experience, both of which grounded theorists invoke when they check and refine their categories. At this point, grounded theorists entertain all conceivable theoretical explanations for the data; they then proceed to check these explanations empirically through further experience–more data collection–to pursue the most plausible theoretical explanation (Charmaz, 2006). Thus a major strength of the grounded theory method is that these budding conceptualizations can lead researchers in the most useful, often emergent and unanticipated theoretical direction to understand their data.

Theoretical Saturation

Theoretical saturation means saturation of the properties of a theoretical category. Researchers define theoretical saturation as having occurred when gathering more data sheds no further light on the properties of their theoretical category. Much theoretical sampling is devoted to the quest of attaining theoretical saturation, and theoretical categories are mandatory for this achievement. Yet many qualitative researchers claim to have achieved saturation with no reference to theoretical concepts.

Theoretical saturation is another grounded theory strategy that found its way into the general lexicon of qualitative methods. Qualitative researchers who do not use grounded theory methods have stripped the term of its defining theoretical dimension. Instead, most of these other qualitative researchers talk of "saturation" of data, meaning that the same themes repeatedly arise in their data. Repetitive themes have very little to do with theoretical saturation and grounded theory when the repetitive data are not in service of a theoretical category.

Grounded theorists themselves have also diluted the strategy of theoretical saturation. Many researchers who claim grounded theory allegiance assert that they have achieved theoretical saturation without providing evidence for it (Morse, 1995). Very small initial samples in some grounded theory studies compound the problem of claims of theoretical saturation. How can researchers know that they have saturated a theoretical category if they have not gathered sufficient data to establish the parameters of the category or to explicate its properties?

Conclusion

The four grounded theory strategies of coding, memo writing, theoretical sampling, and theoretical saturation form the defining features of the method. How and when researchers employ these strategies emerges during the course of inquiry. Like applications of Elisabeth Kübler-Ross's (1969) stages of dying, followers of grounded theory have reified and rigidified its strategies. Efforts to make grounded theory mechanical and rule-bound erode the emergent qualities of the method and erase its potential for sparking new theoretical analyses. Despite efforts to make grounded theory prescriptive, its strategies have substantial flexibility, and researchers may adapt them to fit their emerging studies.

Grounded theory advances emergent methods because it is both inductive and abductive. The inductive, iterative process of going back and forth between data collection and analysis makes emergent grounded theory analyses focused and incisive. The abductive process of accounting for emergent findings raises the level of abstraction of the analysis and extends its "theoretical reach" (Charmaz, 2006, p. 128). Theoretical sampling and theoretical saturation provide solidity for the emergent analysis and keep it grounded.

Students and new PhDs may want the structure and seeming certainty that a procedural application of grounded theory may provide.[12] Although their wishes to follow rule-bound procedures are understandable, adopting and applying a procedural approach to grounded theory suppresses its emergent elements and likely stifles their own creativity. Learning to tolerate ambiguity permits the researcher to become receptive to creating emergent categories and strategies. Subsequently, the flexibility of constructivist grounded theory guidelines can frame inquiry and further imaginative engagement with data.

Acknowledgments

I thank Diana Grant, Sharlene Hesse-Biber, Matthew James, and Melinda Milligan for their comments on an earlier version of this chapter.

Notes

1. Consistent with conventional methodological parlance, I use the term *grounded theory* to represent the method as well as the completed grounded theory analysis of an empirical problem. A more precise distinction would call for distinguishing between the method of conducting research, the grounded theory method, and the product of that research, the substantive or formal grounded theory (Bryant & Charmaz, 2007c; Charmaz, 2003, 2006).

2. Here I allude to the pragmatist roots of grounded theory and the scientific but creative reasoning of C. S. Peirce. Strauss may not have engaged Peirce's concept of abduction explicitly in his writings, but he described grounded theory as an abductive method in his teaching—at least in the early years of the doctoral program at the University of California, San Francisco, when I was a graduate student.

3. The congruent views on emergence of Mead, an American pragmatist, and Durkheim, a French structuralist, reflect their realist assumptions of society preceding individuals and, likely, exposure to Henri Bergson's ideas. William James brought Bergson's ideas to the pragmatists, and Durkheim knew Bergson from their student days at the Ecole Normale. For more on Bergson's contributions, see his 1903/1961 and 1921/1965 works.

4. I am indebted to Matthew James, a paleontologist, for reminding me that natural scientists would disagree with Glaser's statement (personal communication, February 23, 2007). Glaser inverts conventional scientific reasoning here. Natural scientists treat description as straightforward, unproblematic, and replicable. They view the abstractions of description as interpretive.

5. Diana Grant (personal communication, February 23, 2007), who uses quantitative methods, points out that Glaser's position come close to the reified focus on researcher objectivity for which quantitative researchers are criticized.

6. My position here is analogous to Clarke's (2005) depiction of situations. In both cases, we aim to treat the whole phenomenon rather than focus on certain parts.

7. Glaser has recently modified his earlier insistence on representing the only version of grounded theory and now sees alternative versions as well (Bryant & Charmaz, 2007c).

8. Note that I specify new research arenas here. Grounded theorists may work in the same or related arenas on subsequent projects. If they do, having a rich reservoir of data and experience from prior studies may considerably expedite moving to a specific research question, as well as to conceptual analysis.

9. Grounded theory and naturalism (Lincoln & Guba, 1985; Lofland & Lofland, 1995) are congruent on this point.

10. Most grounded theory studies are interview studies. Grounded theorists who do not have access to interview participants more than once can form specific questions in the later interviews to check their theoretical categories.

11. Personal communication, February 28, 2005.

12. I am indebted to Melinda Milligan for suggesting the implications of the preceding analysis for students (personal communication, February 23, 2007).

References

Adams, R. N., & Preiss, J. J. (Eds.). (1960). *Human organization research: Field relations and techniques* (pp. 267–289). Homewood, IL: Dorsey Press.

Bergson, H. (1961). *An introduction to metaphysics* (M. L. Andison, Trans.). New York: Philosophical Library. (Original work published 1903)

Bergson, H. (1965). *Duration and simultaneity, with reference to Einstein's theory*. Indianapolis, IN: Bobbs-Merrill. (Original work published 1921)

Biernacki, P. (1986). *Pathways from heroin addiction: Recovery without treatment*. Philadelphia: Temple University Press.

Blumer, H. (1969). *Symbolic interactionism*. Englewood Cliffs, NJ: Prentice Hall.

Boychuk-Duchscher, J. E., & Morgan, D. (2004). Grounded theory: Reflections on the emerging vs. forcing debate. *Journal of Advanced Nursing, 48*(6), 605–612.

Bryant, A. (2002). Re-grounding grounded theory. *Journal of Information Technology Theory and Application, 4*(1), 25–42.

Bryant, A., & Charmaz, K. (2007a). Grounded theory in historical perspective: An epistemological account. In A. Bryant & K. Charmaz (Eds.), *The handbook of grounded theory* (pp. 31–57). London: Sage.

Bryant, A., & Charmaz, K. (Eds.). (2007b). *The handbook of grounded theory*. London: Sage.

Bryant, A., & Charmaz, K. (2007c). Introduction. In A. Bryant & K. Charmaz (Eds.), *The handbook of grounded theory* (pp. 1–28). London: Sage.

Cauhapé, E. (1983). *Fresh starts: Men and women after divorce*. New York: Basic Books.

Charmaz, K. (1983). The grounded theory method: An explication and interpretation. In R. M. Emerson (Ed.), *Contemporary field research* (pp. 109–126). Boston: Little, Brown.

Charmaz, K. (1990). Discovering chronic illness: Using grounded theory. *Social Science and Medicine, 30*, 1161–1172.

Charmaz, K. (2000). Constructivist and objectivist grounded theory. In N. K. Denzin & Y. S. Lincoln (Eds.), *Handbook of qualitative research* (2nd ed., pp. 509–535). Thousand Oaks, CA: Sage.

Charmaz, K. (2003). Grounded theory. In M. Lewis-Beck, A. E. Bryman, & T. F. Liao (Eds.), *The Sage encyclopedia of social science research methods* (pp. 440–444). London: Sage.

Charmaz, K. (2004). Premises, principles, and practices in qualitative research: Revisiting the foundations. *Qualitative Health Research, 14*, 976–993.

Charmaz, K. (2005). Grounded theory in the 21st century: A qualitative method for advancing social justice research. In N. K. Denzin & Y. S. Lincoln (Eds.), *Handbook of qualitative research* (3rd ed., pp. 507–535). Thousand Oaks, CA: Sage.

Charmaz, K. (2006). *Constructing grounded theory: A practical guide through qualitative analysis*. London: Sage.

Charmaz, K. (2007). Reconstructing grounded theory. In L. Bickman, P. Alasuutari, & J. Brannen (Eds.), *Handbook of social research* (pp. 461–478). London: Sage.

Charmaz, K. (in press). Grounded theory. In J. A. Smith (Ed.), *Qualitative psychology: A practical guide to research methods* (2nd ed.). London: Sage.

Charmaz, K., & Henwood, K. (in press). Grounded theory in psychology. In C. Willig & W. Stainton-Rogers (Eds.), *Handbook of qualitative research in psychology*. London: Sage.

Chenitz, W. C., & Swanson, J. M. (Eds.). (1986). *From practice to grounded theory: Qualitative research in nursing*. Reading, MA: Addison-Wesley.

Clarke, A. E. (1998). *Disciplining reproduction: Modernity, American life sciences, and "the problems of sex."* Berkeley: University of California Press.

Clarke, A. E. (2005). *Situational analysis: Grounded theory after the postmodern turn*. Thousand Oaks, CA: Sage.

Clarke, A. E. (2006). Feminism, grounded theory, and situational analysis. In S. Hess-Biber & D. Leckenby (Eds.), *Handbook of feminist research methods* (pp. 345–370). Thousand Oaks, CA: Sage.

Clarke, A. E., & Friese, C. (2007). Grounded theory using situational analysis. In A. Bryant & K. Charmaz (Eds.), *The handbook of grounded theory* (pp. 363–397). London: Sage.

Corbin, J., & Strauss, A. L. (1988). *Unending work and care: Managing chronic illness at home*. San Francisco: Jossey-Bass.

Deely, J. N. (1990). *Basics of semiotics*. Bloomington: Indiana University Press.

Dey, I. (1999). *Grounding grounded theory*. San Diego, CA: Academic Press.

Dey, I. (2004). Grounded theory. In C. Seale, G. Gobo, J. F. Gubrium, & D. Silverman (Eds.), *Qualitative research practice* (pp. 80–93). London: Sage.

Durkheim, E. (1895/1982). *The rules of sociological method*. New York: Free Press. (Original work published 1895)

Fisher, B. M., & Strauss, A. L. (1979). George Herbert

Mead and the Chicago tradition of sociology. *Symbolic Interaction, 2,* 9–26.
Glaser, B. G. (1978). *Theoretical sensitivity.* Mill Valley, CA: Sociology Press.
Glaser, B. G. (1992). *Basics of grounded theory analysis: Emergence vs. forcing.* Mill Valley, CA: Sociology Press.
Glaser, B. G. (1998). *Doing grounded theory: Issues and discussions.* Mill Valley, CA: Sociology Press.
Glaser, B. G. (2002). Constructivist grounded theory? *Forum: Qualitative Social Research, 3.* Retrieved October 20, 2002, from *http://www.qualitative-researh.net/fqs-texte/3-02/3-02glaser-e-htm*
Glaser, B. G. (2003). *Conceptualization contrasted with description.* Mill Valley, CA: Sociology Press.
Glaser, B. G. (2006). *Doing formal grounded theory: A proposal.* Mill Valley, CA: Sociology Press.
Glaser, B. G., & Strauss, A. L. (1967). *The discovery of grounded theory.* Chicago: Aldine.
Goulding, C. (2002). *Grounded theory: A practical guide for management, business, and market researchers.* London: Sage.
Hood, J. (2007). Orthodoxy vs. power: The defining traits of grounded theory. In A. Bryant & K. Charmaz (Eds.), *The handbook of grounded theory* (pp. 151–164). London: Sage.
Junker, B. H. (1960). *Field work: An introduction to the social sciences.* Chicago: University of Chicago Press
Kearney, M. H. (2007). From the sublime to the meticulous: The continuing evolution of grounded formal theory. In A. Bryant & K. Charmaz (Eds.), *The handbook of grounded theory* (pp. 127–150). London: Sage.
Kelle, U. (2005). "Emergence" vs. "forcing" of empirical data: A crucial problem of "grounded theory" reconsidered. *Forum: Qualitative Social Research, 6*(2). Retrieved May 30, 2005, from *www.qualitative-research.net/fqs.texte/2-05/05-2-27-e.htm*
Kübler-Ross, E. (1969). *On death and dying.* New York: Macmillan.
Layder, D. (1998). *Sociological practice: Linking theory and social research.* London: Sage.
Lincoln, Y. S., & Guba, E. G. (1985). *Naturalistic inquiry.* Beverly Hills, CA: Sage.
Locke, K. (1997). Rewriting the discovery of grounded theory after 25 years? *Journal of Management Inquiry, 5*(1), 239–245.
Locke, K. (2001). *Grounded theory in management research.* Thousand Oaks, CA: Sage.
Lofland, J., & Lofland, L. (1995). *Analyzing social settings: A guide to qualitative observation and analysis.* Belmont CA: Wadsworth.
Lonkila, M. (1995). Grounded theory as an emerging paradigm for computer-assisted qualitative data analysis. In U. Kelle (Ed.), *Computer-aided qualitative data analysis* (pp. 41–51). London: Sage.
May, K. (1996). Diffusion, dilution or distillation? The case of grounded theory method. *Qualitative Health Research, 6*(3), 309–311.
Mead, G. H. (1932). *The philosophy of the present.* La Salle, IL: Open Court.
Melia, K. M. (1996). Rediscovering Glaser. *Qualitative Health Research, 6*(3), 368–378.
Mills, J., Bonner, A., & Francis, K. (2006). The development of constructivist grounded theory. *International Journal of Qualitative Methods, 5*(1), 1–10.
Morse, J. M. (1995). The significance of saturation. *Qualitative Health Research, 5,* 147–149.
Peirce, C. S. (1958). *Collected papers.* Cambridge, MA: Harvard University Press. (Original work published 1931)
Reichertz, J. (2004). Abduction, deduction, and induction in qualitative research. In U. Flick, E. von Kardoff, & I. Steinke (Eds.), *A companion to qualitative research* (pp. 150–164). London: Sage.
Reichertz, J. (2007). Abduction: The logic of discovery of grounded theory. In A. Bryant & K. Charmaz (Eds.), *The handbook of grounded theory* (pp. 214–228). London: Sage.
Rock, P. (1979). *The making of symbolic interactionism.* London: Macmillan.
Rosenthal, G. (2004). Biographical research. In C. Seale, G. Gobo, J. F. Gubrium, & D. Silverman (Eds.), *Qualitative research practice* (pp. 48–64). London: Sage.
Stern, P. N. (1994a). Eroding grounded theory. In J. Morse (Ed.), *Critical issues in qualitative research methods* (pp. 212–223). Thousand Oaks, CA: Sage.
Stern, P. N. (1994b). The grounded theory method: Its uses and processes. In B. G. Glaser (Ed.), *More grounded theory: A reader* (pp. 116–126). Mill Valley, CA: Sociology Press.
Strauss, A. L. (1969). *Mirrors and masks.* Mill Valley, CA: Sociology Press. (Original work published 1959)
Strauss, A. (1987). *Qualitative analysis for social scientists.* New York: Cambridge University Press.
Strauss, A. (1993). *Continual permutations of action.* New York: Aldine de Gruyter.
Strauss, A., & Corbin, J. (1990). *Basics of qualitative research: Grounded theory procedures and techniques.* Newbury Park, CA: Sage.
Strauss, A., & Corbin, J. (1994). Grounded theory methodology: An overview. In N. K. Denzin & Y. S. Lincoln (Eds.), *Handbook of qualitative research* (pp. 273–285). Thousand Oaks, CA: Sage.
Strauss, A., & Corbin, J. (1998). *Basics of qualitative research: Grounded theory procedures and techniques* (2nd ed.). Thousand Oaks, CA: Sage.
Uruquat, C. (2007). The evolving nature of grounded theory methods: The case of the information systems discipline. In A. Bryant & K. Charmaz (Eds.), *The handbook of grounded theory* (pp. 339–359). London: Sage.
Wilson, H. S., & Hutchinson, S. A. (1996). Methodologic mistakes in grounded theory. *Nursing Research, 45*(2), 122–124.

INTERVIEWING

CHAPTER 8

New Frontiers in Standardized Survey Interviewing

Frederick G. Conrad
Michael F. Schober

Sample surveys are the empirical backbone of the social sciences, government policy, political campaigns, and corporate strategy. The method of collecting data that is generally assumed to provide the highest quality information is the standardized interview, either on the telephone or face-to-face. There are exceptions, of course, such as the collection of data about sensitive topics like drug use and sexual activities, for which self-administration (i.e., without an interviewer) is believed to increase the honesty of respondents' answers. However, by and large, if social researchers can afford to conduct interviews, they do so. Interviews generally lead to higher response rates than self-administration (particularly when conducted face-to-face) and allow respondents who cannot read (including those who are visually impaired) to participate.

Standardized interviewing is an approach to collecting survey data in which interviewers read questions exactly as worded to every respondent and are trained never to provide information beyond what is scripted in the questionnaire. The goal is to increase comparability across interviews so that different answers from different respondents cannot be attributed to different question stimuli. In principle, standardized interviewers are interchangeable; the answers should be the same no matter who asks the question.[1]

Uniform question presentation has not always been the industry standard (see Beatty, 1995, for a historical perspective on standardized interviewing). However, since the widespread deployment of telephone interviewing in the 1970s, standardization has been virtually synonymous with scientific social research (see Fowler & Mangione, 1990, for a clear statement of standardized interviewing practice and goals). Nonetheless, standardized interviewing has been criticized because the limits it places on what interviewers can say may prevent them from ensuring that questions are understood as intended. Thus standardized interviews might produce reliable results–that is, the same question produces the same answer, irrespective of who asks it–without producing valid results, because respondents may systematically misunderstand the question, effectively answering a question other than what the researchers intended to ask (Suchman & Jordan, 1990).

Our work (e.g., Conrad & Schober, 2000; Schober & Conrad, 1997; Schober, Conrad, & Fricker, 2004) has focused on the inaccuracies in survey responses that can arise from interviewers' inability to "ground" the meaning of questions (e.g., Clark & Schaeffer, 1989). The research is motivated by the fact that, in ordinary discourse, speaker and listener can achieve mutual understanding by discussing the meaning of what has been said; but in standardized survey interviews, the interviewer may not clarify what has been said if to do so requires more than a verbatim repetition of the question. It stands to reason that response accuracy should be inferior in just those cases in which respondents find questions to be ambiguous, for example, in which it is not clear which behaviors and events respondents should include and which they should exclude. The question for us is what the consequences are of licensing interviewers in such situations to say whatever they judge necessary to resolve the ambiguity and clarify the intended meaning of the question. We have called this approach "conversational interviewing" because interviewers are able to ground question meaning as in ordinary conversation. Conversational interviewing is similar in spirit to standardized interviewing–the goal being to produce comparable data–but emphasizes uniform *interpretation* rather than uniform *wording*.

In the first part of this chapter we review some of our research comparing strictly standardized interviewing with variants of conversational interviewing. We have observed substantial improvement in response accuracy when interviewers can help respondents determine which behaviors they should include and which they should exclude. Throughout, we focus on response accuracy rather than on more traditional survey measures of data quality such as response variance or missing data.

In the second part of the chapter we consider the implications of bringing ordinary conversational practices such as clarifying what has been said into automated self-administered survey "interviews." With new technologies, survey designers have the opportunity to explore a range of data collection methods in which computer interfaces incorporate more and more features of human interviewing. Text-based Web surveys can now add recorded human or synthesized voices, video (either live or recorded), or animated faces with varying degrees of verisimilitude and varying degrees of dialogue capability. We first examine the impact on data quality and user satisfaction of building clarification dialogue into textual questionnaires displayed in Web browsers and speech dialogue interviewing systems. We then consider some of the issues created when virtual interviewers–that is, avatars or animated agents–ask questions and clarify their meanings. In general, the issue concerns the degree to which respondents treat the interviewing agents as human-like or computer-like, but the issue is slightly different when the interviewing agents ask sensitive versus nonsensitive questions. Because designers can control so many features of the interviewing agent (e.g., facial appearance and vocal characteristics) and the way it interacts with respondents (e.g., its ability to engage in human-like dialogue), methodologists are forced to reconsider what standardization and comparability mean. For example, it is already possible to match features of the interviewing agent–gender, ethnicity, or age of voice or appearance–to those of each respondent. But when is this desirable and when is it undesirable?

Theories of Communication and Survey Interviews

Most large-scale surveys try to standardize what interviewers say. As described by Fowler and Mangione (1990), interviewers must read questions exactly as worded, they must probe neutrally, and they must never allow their own ideas to influence the respondents' answers. According to Fowler and Mangione, this practice reduces or eliminates what they call *interviewer-related error*—any systematic effect of particular interviewers on survey responses.

This view grows out of a long tradition in survey methodology of distinguishing between different sources of error and using different methods for reducing each type of error. For example, this view holds that respondent comprehension error is best handled by wording the question in ways that most respondents are likely to understand. By pretesting early versions of questions and revising those questions on the basis of the pretest results, misunderstanding can be largely reduced. Standardized interviewing presupposes that questions have been pretested and are universally interpretable. The argument is that if interviewers deliver pretested questions in a standardized way—exposing respondents to the same question stimulus (Fowler & Mangione, 1990, p. 14)—then researchers can be confident that differences in the answers stem only from the actual differences between respondents and not from any misunderstanding by some respondents or idiosyncrasies of interviewers' behavior (p. 15).

However, by separating interviewer behavior, respondent behavior, and question wording, this prevailing approach relies on a view of communication that has been discredited, at least for ordinary spontaneous conversations. This view, dating back to John Locke or perhaps even earlier, has been called, variously, the *message model* (Akmajian, Demers, Farmer, & Harnish, 1990), the *conduit metaphor* (Reddy, 1979/1993), and the *meaning-in-words assumption* (Schober, 1998). According to this view, speakers encode their thoughts into linguistic messages and send these messages to recipients by speaking, who decode them into their own thoughts. Thoughts and conceptual material are thus transferred from one head to the other via words.

Although the message model captures most people's intuitions about how communication works, it cannot account for all of what goes on in ordinary conversations (see also Clark, 1992, 1996; Gibbs, 1994; Maynard & Whalen, 1995). The problem is that the message model assumes that the meaning of speakers' words is in the words themselves. But it is not. Rather, speakers can use the same words to express vastly different meanings on different occasions (see Akmajian et al., 1990). Consider the word *red* (Clark, 1996). It denotes one color when referring to wine, another when referring to hair, another when describing a fire truck, and so on. Suessbrick, Schober, and Conrad (2000) observed that when respondents answered the question "Have you smoked at least 100 cigarettes in your entire life?" 54% of listeners interpreted this as including "cigarettes that you took a puff or two from," 23% interpreted this as referring to "cigarettes you partially smoked," and 23% interpreted it as meaning "only cigarettes that you finished." Given this sort of variability in the meaning of words, how do people ever manage to communicate?

One proposal is Clark and Wilkes-Gibbs's (1986) *collaborative* model (see also Clark, 1992, 1996; Clark & Brennan, 1991; Clark & Schaefer, 1987, 1989; Schober & Clark, 1989). This model generalizes observations by Paul Grice, Emanuel Schegloff, and others, bringing them into the psychological realm in ways that can be modeled and tested precisely (e.g., Cahn & Brennan, 1999). Under the assumptions of this approach, as people speak, they carefully monitor their addressees for evidence of understanding or misunderstanding, and they adjust their utterances, moment by moment, to ensure that their addressees understand them well enough for current purposes. Addressees, by providing such evidence, help mold the utterances speakers produce.

In this view, no utterance is complete until it has been *grounded*—until both participants have accepted that it has been understood. Understanding a reference in any particular utterance requires active participation by both speaker and addressee, and this can take several turns. Note that the point is not that words do not have conventional meanings; in fact, the conventional meanings of words provide important constraints on speakers' meanings. But speakers regularly use words in idiosyncratic ways that go far beyond dictionary definitions (see Clark, 1991; Clark & Gerrig, 1983). Speakers produce utterances based on their *common ground* with their conversational partners—that is, what they presume that they and their conversational partners mutually know, believe, and assume.

Experimenting with Alternatives to Standardized Interviewing

What might the collaborative view of language use imply for survey interviews? As we indicated earlier, standardized interviewers are prohibited from grounding the meaning of questions (although the rationale is not expressed in these collaborative terms). If a respondent asks a standardized interviewer to clarify a question (e.g., "What do you mean by 'household'?") the interviewer can reply only by administering one of a small set of "neutral" or nondirective probes, such as rereading the question or indicating that the interpretation of the question is the sole obligation of the respondent (e.g., "Whatever it means to you"). By withholding substantive clarification (as in rereading the question) and even encouraging respondents to interpret the question in their own way, the interviewer relinquishes control over what the question means to the respondent. The obvious cost of this practice is that respondents may not understand the questions the way the survey researchers intended and thus answer them inaccurately, jeopardizing the validity of the research.

We have conducted a series of experiments in which we have evaluated response accuracy and interaction patterns for strictly standardized and more collaborative "conversational" interviews, as well as for a range of interviewing techniques in between. In these studies, professional interviewers telephoned naive respondents either in the laboratory (Schober & Conrad, 1997; Schober et al., 2004) or at home (Conrad & Schober, 2000) and asked questions from large U.S. government surveys. In the laboratory studies, the "respondents" answered the questions on the basis of scenarios that described the work, housing, and purchases of fictional people. Because we created the scenarios, we knew the correct answers—according to official definitions—for each question–scenario combination, and so we could determine response accuracy. In the household study, the respondents answered questions about their own lives; we evaluated the response accuracy by less direct reinterview methods.

In each study, respondents participated in either strictly standardized interviews, following Fowler and Mangione's (1990) prescriptions, or less standardized, more collaborative interviews. In all interviews, questions were first posed exactly as worded, underscoring the shared commitment to standardization under the two approaches; the difference just concerns whether it is wording or underlying meaning that is standardized. In the more collaborative interviews, interviewers were then encouraged to ground understanding of question meaning, for example, by providing scripted definitions when respondents explicitly asked for them (Schober et al., 2004) or by using whatever words interviewers chose to make sure respondents understood the questions as intended (Schober & Conrad, 1997).

In all studies our basic question is which interviewing technique leads to more accurate responses. Of course, even in purely standardized surveys, interviewers can affect responses. What we have tested here is how the kinds of influences that occur in strictly standardized interviews affect response accuracy as compared with the kinds of influences that occur in more collaborative interviews.

Mapping Ambiguity

In all studies we used pretested questions from ongoing surveys whose words and grammar have been shown to be understandable but whose interpretation for some respondents on some occasions might be unclear. Consider a question such as "During the past year, have you purchased or had expenses for household furniture?" A respondent who has bought an end table should not have much trouble answering "yes," but a respondent who has bought a floor lamp may be less sure. Or consider a question such as "Last week, how many hours did you work?" This should be clear for a respondent who has a 9-to-5 job that includes overtime but less clear for a respondent who does business over lunch or solves work-related problems while jogging. We presume that the second respondent would be more likely than the first to request clarification, such as, "What do you mean by work?" or "Should I consider business lunches to be work?" We refer to this as a mapping ambiguity: the mapping between the question term and the respondent's circumstances is unclear. Interviewers following strictly standardized procedures cannot meaningfully resolve a mapping ambiguity; they would be obliged to use neutral probing techniques, including "whatever it means to you." More conversationally flexible interviewers could provide information to the respondent that would help clarify what the author of the question had in mind.

In our laboratory studies, we designed the fictional scenarios so that half corresponded to the questions in a straightforward way (straightforward mappings) and the other half corresponded to the questions in a more complicated way (complicated mappings). In the household study, we had no control over the frequency of complicated mappings. Our prediction was that response accuracy would be high for both standardized and more conversational interviewing when the mappings were straightforward; when the mappings were complicated, accuracy should suffer for strictly standardized interviewing but not as much—maybe not at all—for conversational interviewing. This pattern of results in the household study, in which mappings were not under our control, would indicate that complicated mappings are frequent enough in the real world to warrant further exploration of more collaborative interviewing techniques.

In order to ensure that conversational interviewers could answer respondents' substantive questions, we needed to teach them the official definitions of key concepts in the questions. Providing standardized interviewers with this knowledge might seem to violate the principles of standardization: The only role for definitions in the standardized interview is to be read in their entirety to all respondents on all occasions or not read at all. But the logic of our experiments required us to train all interviewers together on the concepts so that any accuracy differences could not somehow be attributed to different levels of knowledge between standardized and conversational interviewers. Standardized interviewers were told that the concept training was necessary so that interviewers would be able to judge when respondents had answered a question completely (see Beatty, 1995). In all studies the training lasted about 90 minutes; interviewers first studied the official definitions and then actively carried out exercises to ensure that they had grasped the concepts in detail.

After the concept training, interviewers were then trained in their respective interviewing techniques. The standardized instructions were based on guidelines that appeared in an interviewing manual for a survey on which many of these interviewers regularly worked and were consistent with Fowler and Mangione's (1990) approach. Using this material, we reviewed standardized question-asking and neutral probing techniques and supplemented this with role-playing exercises.

The interviewers who were trained to use more conversational techniques were instructed to initially read the question as worded. Then (depending on the study) they could substantively answer respondents' requests for clarification, either following a script or in their own words; they could also provide unsolicited clarification (scripted or in their own words) when respondents seemed to need it, even if respondents hadn't asked for help. In another study (Schober et al., 2004, Experiment 2), interviewers were not trained in a particular technique but were told to do whatever they ordinarily do.

Procedure

In the laboratory studies, respondents were given a packet of scenarios to study, and then they were questioned over the telephone about the scenarios. The respondents in conversational interviews were instructed to work with the interviewers to make sure they had interpreted the questions as the survey designers intended; they were encouraged to ask for clarification if they needed it. Response accuracy was measured as the percentage of questions for which responses matched what the official definitions indicated was correct.

Although the interviewers knew that respondents were answering on the basis of fictional situations, they were not familiar with the content of the individual scenarios, and so knowledge was allocated much as it is in real surveys: Interviewers knew the questions, and respondents knew about their own circumstances. We counterbalanced the items so that the respondents who were assigned to a particular interviewer always received different versions of the scenarios. This way the interviewers could not become familiar with the scenarios based on anything the earlier respondents might have said.

In the household study respondents were telephoned at home and asked about their own lives; no scenarios were involved. Because we could not directly determine the accuracy of the respondents' answers, we designed the experiment to provide two indirect measures. One measure was response change between interviews. All respondents participated in two interviews: The first was strictly standardized for all respondents, and the second was strictly standardized for half of the respondents and conversational for the other half. If respondents' circumstances mapped in a complicated way to the question concepts, they should be more likely to change their answers between an initial standardized interview and a subsequent conversational interview than between two standardized interviews. The reason is that in the conversational interviews the interviewers were instructed to clarify question meaning and correct respondent misconceptions, which could lead to different answers than provided in the initial interview. In contrast, in the second standardized interview, the interviewers were not permitted to clarify meaning or to correct initial respondent misconceptions; therefore, we hypothesized, responses would likely remain unchanged—reliable but incorrect.

The other measure in the household survey was the "legality" of respondents' explanations for their responses. If respondents answered "yes" when asked if they had made certain types of purchases, they were asked to briefly describe the purchase(s). These descriptions were then coded for their consistency with official definitions—their legality. For example, the definition of moving expenses explicitly excludes payments for do-it-yourself moving; a respondent who answered "yes" when asked if he or she incurred moving expenses and based this response on having rented a moving van would have provided an *illegal* explanation. When interviewers were licensed to clarify question meaning (in a conversational interview), we expected respondents to be more likely to base their responses on legal purchases than when interviewers were not able to clarify question meaning (in any of the standardized interviews).

Results

We first analyzed the transcripts of the interviews to verify that interviewers had followed our instructions and implemented the appropriate technique for each specific study. One way we demonstrated that interviewers followed instructions was by coding the various deviations from strict standardization and comparing their frequency between interviewing techniques. These deviations included rephrasing all or part of the question, providing all or part of a definition (either verbatim or paraphrased), converting the respondents' descriptions of their circumstances (the fictional scenario in the laboratory studies) into an answer, offering to provide clarification, confirming or disconfirming the respondent's interpretation of the question, and requesting particular information about the respondent's circumstances. For example, in the following exchange (from Schober & Conrad, 1997) the conversational interviewer paraphrased the long government definition of "household furniture" to answer the respondent's question:

I: Has Kelly purchased or had expenses for household furniture?
R: Um . . . is a lamp furniture?
I: No sir, we do not include lamps and lighting fixtures.
R: Okay, no.
(I: goes on to next question)

In strictly standardized interviewing, the interviewer should not have answered the respondent's request for clarification, because by doing so she helped interpret the survey question for this respondent buy may not have done so for another. Across the various studies, our coding gives us confidence that our interviewer training led to fundamentally different types of interaction. In the Schober and Conrad (1997) study, for example, 85% of the question–answer sequences in conversational interviews contained deviations from standardization, compared with only 2% in strictly standardized interviews.

We can now turn to response accuracy. Again, an accurate response in our experiments is one that is consistent with the official definition of the relevant concept. In our earlier lamp example, the correct answer is "no," because a lamp purchase does not qualify as a furniture purchase for the purposes of the survey from which this question was drawn; therefore, the respondent's answer was accurate.

Across all our lab studies (Schober & Conrad, 1997; Schober et al., 2004, Experiments 1 and 2), a general pattern emerges. When mappings between question concepts and people's circumstances (scenarios) are straightforward, all interviewing techniques lead to nearly perfect accuracy; virtually all respondents interpret question concepts in the ways that survey designers intended. But when mappings between question concepts and people's circumstances are complicated, strictly standardized interviewing leads to quite poor response accuracy (28%). Response accuracy improves when interviewers can provide clarification on request (57%), and it improves substantially more when interviewers can both offer clarification that they believe respondents need as well as provide it when respondents request it (77%). Response accuracy is highest when the interviewers who can both volunteer clarification and provide it on request can also use their own words to clarify question concepts, even if this departs from what is scripted (87%). This last group of interviewers can exercise much of the discretion and flexibility that is typical of everyday conversation.

These results are mirrored in the household study (Conrad & Schober, 2000), in which we used indirect measures of response accuracy. Respondents changed their answers more often when their second interview was conversational (22%) than when it was strictly standardized (11%). In addition, more responses were based on legal purchases when the second interview was conversational (95%) than when it was standardized (57%). For example, in conversational interviews respondents who answered "yes" to the question about moving expenses were more likely to do so because they had hired commercial movers or had had other expenses included in the definition than in standardized interviews, in which they were more likely to incorrectly respond "yes" because of excluded expenses such as do-it-yourself moving. This result was primarily due to interviewers' explaining what to count and what not to count, that is, grounding the meaning of the term. The improved response accuracy in conversational interviews suggests that respondents' actual circumstances (as opposed to the fictional scenarios presented in the lab studies) are complicated sufficiently often—at least for these questions—to justify exploring the technique further.

Fowler and Mangione (1990) have raised the concern that interviewers whose wording is not strictly standardized will damage the quality of the responses. They are particularly concerned that in questions about opinions, nonstandardized interviewers may bias respondents by presenting their own opinions or by reacting to the respondents' answers. Regarding interviewers' explaining the intent of questions, Fowler and Mangione are concerned that nonstandardized interviewers will mislead respondents by providing inaccurate information. In our experiments this has not been the case. For example, in the Schober and Conrad (1997) study, the information provided by conversational interviewers to clarify the question was accurate (conformed to the official definitions) in 93% of the cases in which it was given. This 93% consisted of 87% in which respondents received accurate information from interviewers and provided accurate answers, and only 6% in which respondents received accurate information but provided inaccurate answers. For the 7% of cases in which interviewers provided inaccurate information, respondents were still accurate about half the time. The 7% consisted of 4% in which respondents received inaccurate information from interviewers yet provided accurate answers, and only 3% in which they received inaccurate information and answered the question inaccurately. Overall, conversational interviewers provided highly accurate information. When they did provide inaccurate information, it did not necessarily lead respondents to produce incorrect answers; in fact, respondents produced incorrect answers resulting from inaccurate information only 3% of the time.

Closer analysis of the interviewer–respondent interaction (see Conrad & Schober, 2000; Schober & Conrad, 1997) shows that it really was interviewers' deviations from standardization that led to the increases in response accuracy. It would seem that interviewer intervention improved response accuracy whether respondents had requested clarification or not (that is, even when interviewers provided the information without the respondents' having asked for it). For example, in the Schober and Conrad (1997) study, for the 64 complicated-mapping cases in which interviewers provided unsolicited help, respondents produced 55 accurate answers, an accuracy rate of 86%. In contrast, for the 11 complicated-mapping cases in which interviewers did not provide any help, respondents produced only four accurate answers, an accuracy rate of 34%. This figure is close to the 28% accuracy rate for complicated mappings in standardized interviews and suggests that when conversational interviewers do not provide clarification but behave like their standardized counterparts, response accuracy will suffer.

Across our studies, this improvement in response accuracy came at a significant cost.

Conversational interviews took much longer than standardized interviews (from 80 to 300% longer, in the various studies); this was true for both straightforward and complicated mappings. Apparently, clarification just takes time. In Schober and colleagues (2004), experiment 1, the correlation between interview time and response accuracy across the five types of interviewing was .98. The more flexibility given to interviewers, the more accurately respondents answered, and the longer the interviews lasted. Practitioners will need to decide how certain they must be that respondents understand all questions as intended. If they are willing to live with some uncertainty, then it may be possible to shorten interviews while maintaining levels of response accuracy above what we observed for strictly standardized interviews.

The results of our studies should not be taken as the final word on the issue, nor should they be taken as showing definitively that conversational interviewing is always a good idea. Our studies have examined nonsensitive fact-based questions, and the results may not generalize to questions about sensitive topics or opinions in a straightforward way. Just like fact-based questions, opinion questions contain phrases with alternative possible interpretations—consider *abortion* or *approve*—and thus opinion surveys might benefit from more collaborative approaches to interviewing. But whether this can be done without influencing the opinions is unclear, especially because response accuracy for opinions cannot be validated as directly as it can for the fact-based questions in our studies. Nonetheless, O'Hara and Schober (2004) present evidence that differences in attitudes toward euthanasia are related to how respondents define the concept. One implication of this result is that presenting uniform wording does not guarantee uniform interpretation of the "attitude object," and so attitude researchers may well wish to standardize the attitude object by defining it as part of the question.

Our results also do not take into account the potential real-world costs of implementing more collaborative interviewing techniques. Beyond the potential expenses associated with increased interview length, interviewer training might have to be more intensive than it often is now. Interviewer behavior would have to be monitored even more closely to ensure that question meanings were being clarified appropriately and uniformly, without increasing interviewer variance. Far more effort would have to go into developing clear definitions for question concepts. To the extent that respondents find increased collaboration a burden, response rates could be affected.

Ultimately, the generalizability of our experimental findings on interviewing depends on the frequency of complicated mappings between questions and respondents' circumstances in real surveys; this frequency may vary from survey to survey. For the 10 questions we used in the Conrad and Schober (2000) national telephone sample, about 11% more answers changed when clarification was given (than when no clarification was given); we cannot say whether this is an accurate estimate of complicated mappings in other surveys, but it was based on actual questions from U.S. government surveys conducted with a national, representative sample. In the study by Suessbrick and colleagues (2000) mentioned earlier, respondents who answered questions about tobacco use such as "Have you smoked at least 100 cigarettes in your entire life?" exhibited a surprisingly large number of interpretations, with some respondents including only cigarettes they had finished, others including marijuana cigarettes and cigars, and others only cigarettes they had bought. This variability of interpretation was great enough that 10% of respondents changed their answers to this question when provided with a standardized definition. Because their answers determined what questions were presented in the remainder of the interview, a disturbingly large number of respondents were routed down what ultimately turned out to be the wrong questionnaire path. The Suessbrick and colleagues (2000) study was conducted in the laboratory with a convenience sample; nonetheless, the findings are consistent with other evidence (e.g., Belson, 1986) that suggests that ordinary words in survey questions are interpreted in numerous ways. Overall, our findings suggest that if complicated mappings are known to be rare, then strictly standardized techniques could lead to accurate responses at lower costs than collaborative techniques. If the complicated mappings are known to be frequent, or if (more realistically) their frequency is unknown, more collaborative techniques might be worth the increased costs their use would, no doubt, entail.

Dialogue Features in Automated Interviewing Systems

When respondents self-administer a paper-and-pencil survey or type and click answers on a Web survey, they are usually conceived of as doing something quite different than they are when they answer questions asked by a human interviewer. With self-administered questionnaires, respondents typically read rather than hear questions; they control the pacing of the interaction, and they write rather than speak their answers. Also, there is no interviewer present who might react to the respondent's answers (and potentially judge the respondent on the basis of those answers). The combination of such mode differences is no doubt what leads respondents to willingly report more socially undesirable behaviors (e.g., drug use and taboo sexual practices) in self-administered computer-based "interviews" than in actual interviews conducted by human interviewers (e.g., Tourangeau & Smith, 1996).

We propose, in contrast to the usual view, that new technologies used for presenting self-administered survey interviews fall on a continuum of anthropomorphism, with different kinds of self-administration incorporating different features of human interviewing (see Conrad & Schober, 2008). For example, textual administration steps closer to human administration when it is supplemented with audio files of computer-generated voices asking questions; computerized data collection becomes more like a human-administered interview when the text is replaced entirely with recorded human voices (see Couper, Singer, & Tourangeau, 2004). It becomes even more human-like when the interviewing system provides human-like prompts, feedback, and clarification. A self-administered questionnaire with a drawing of a human interviewer is less anthropomorphic than one with an animated, virtual interviewer whose lips move in synchrony with its speech and whose eyes blink; if the agent nods and smiles in response to answers, the system becomes yet more human-like.

If one conceives of interviewing as involving interaction between the respondent and an interviewing agent that is either a human or a computer program, ranging from fully conversational to robotically standardized, we can begin testing which features of interview interaction lead to high-quality data and respondent satisfaction (Conrad, Schober, & Coiner, 2007). We can also begin to better understand the nature of interviewing by decomposing interviewing behaviors into their separable parts and beginning to test what happens when we add features of human interviewing to self-administered interviews.

For example, interviewers, like most conversationalists, probably make certain assumptions about the respondent's abilities as a conversationalist: They probably judge whether a particular respondent is more or less likely to need help in understanding questions and may interpret a respondent's behavior for a particular question in light of such judgments. We refer to such judgments as "respondent models." Such models may not be useful to all interviewers, but to those who are empowered to provide clarification, that is, conversational interviewers, respondent models may help in calibrating the degree to which a respondent needs help at a particular moment in an interview.

We have implemented simple respondent models in text-based questionnaires displayed in a Web browser (Conrad, Schober, & Coiner, 2007, Experiment 2) and in a simulated speech-based system over a telephone (Ehlen, Schober, & Conrad, 2007). In the text-based system, respondents could click on a highlighted word in the question to request a definition; or, if respondents did not either click or type for more than a predetermined period of time, the system offered them a definition (see Figure 8.1). In the speech-based system, respondents could ask for clarification; or, if they exhibited spoken evidence of comprehension difficulty, such as *ums* and *uhs* or pauses (see Schober & Bloom, 2004, for evidence on which cues reliably predict misunderstanding of survey questions), the system offered them a definition. To the respondents, the speech system appeared to be automated—that is, it seemed to produce and recognize speech—but in actuality, a human experimenter played speech files in response to what respondents said in order to create the perception of automation. We developed versions of both systems that reacted differently depending on the respondent model.

When the interviewing system (whether text- or speech-based) could volunteer clarification, it interpreted respondent behavior (e.g., inactivity or silence) based either on a generic or a group-based (or "stereotype") respondent model. Under the generic model, the system treated the behavior of all respondents identically. Under the group-based model, a particular behavior (e.g., a pause of 2 seconds) was interpreted differently for respondents in different groups. The respondent attribute that we intended to model was mental quickness; a particular interval of no respondent activity or speech may signal difficulty for a quick respondent but ordinary thinking for a slower respondent. Thus help should be most useful after shorter lags for quick respondents and longer lags for slow respondents. Rather than assigning respondents to groups on the basis of their quickness, we used their age as a surrogate for quickness based on the well-known impact of cognitive aging on response time (e.g., Salthouse, 1976, 1982).

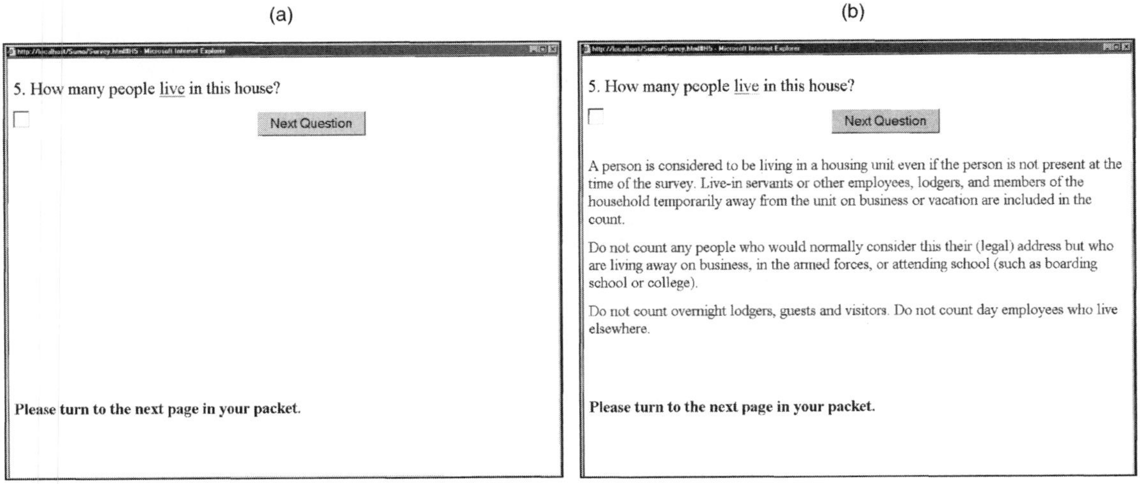

FIGURE 8.1. Survey question with linked definition (a) before and (b) after definition is displayed. From Conrad, Schober, and Coiner (2007). Copyright 2007 by John Wiley & Sons, Ltd. Reprinted by permission.

Therefore, under the group-based model, the system offered clarification sooner to younger respondents than to the older respondents.

With both the text-based and speech-based systems, respondents answered questions very similar to those used in the laboratory interview studies discussed earlier (Schober & Conrad, 1997; Schober et al., 2004), using either complicated or straightforward scenarios. As in the interview studies, our focus was on response accuracy for complicated scenarios. When group-based respondent models were used in either system, they improved response accuracy relative to generic response models, presumably because the clarification was better tailored to respondents' needs (see Figures 8.2 and 8.3). Irrespective of the model, enabling the system to both volunteer clarification and respond to explicit respondent requests increased response accuracy relative to cases in which respondents could obtain clarification only by explicitly requesting it. Any clarification the system provided led to greater accuracy than no clarification, which approximates what happens in standardized interviews, as well as in most current Web surveys.

Just as longer-than-normal response times may signal difficulty of some kind, quicker-than-normal response times may also reflect suboptimal performance. If a respondent answers immediately, it is unlikely that he or she has given as much thought to the task as the researchers would like. If this is the case, it may be possible to create more accurate respondent models by designing them so that the system offers help when response times are outside an optimal range, either too slow or too fast. We have dubbed this the "Goldilocks range" and used it to model respondent speech (Ehlen et al., 2007). As can be seen in Figure 8.3 (generic and stereotyped respondent models), response accuracy was better when the system could volunteer clarification based on either respondent silence or overly quick answers than when it could not provide clarification.

These findings suggest that some of what conversational interviews do can be implemented in self-administered surveys. But there are a number of caveats and questions that need to be addressed. For example, despite the apparent benefits of group-based models for response accuracy, some respondents found the system intervention unpleasant. For example, in postexperimental

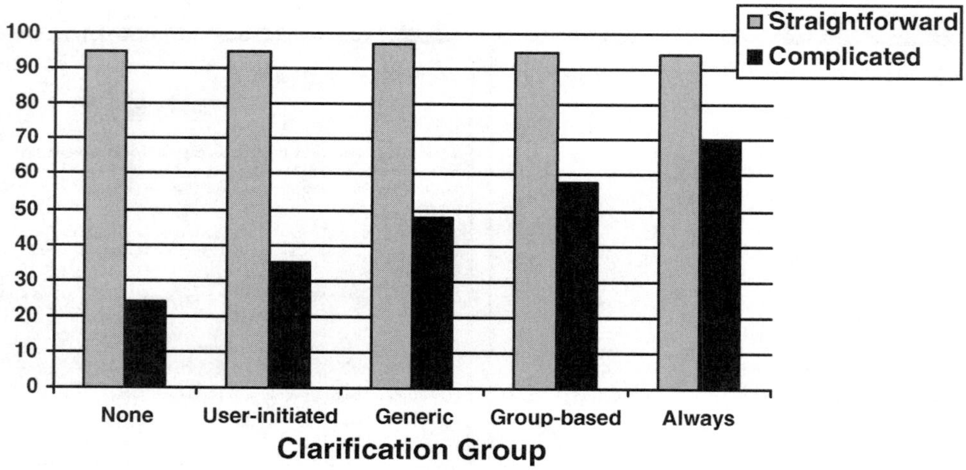

FIGURE 8.2. Response accuracy for textual question. From Conrad, Schober, and Coiner (2007, Experiment 2). Copyright 2007 by John Wiley & Sons, Ltd. Reprinted by permission.

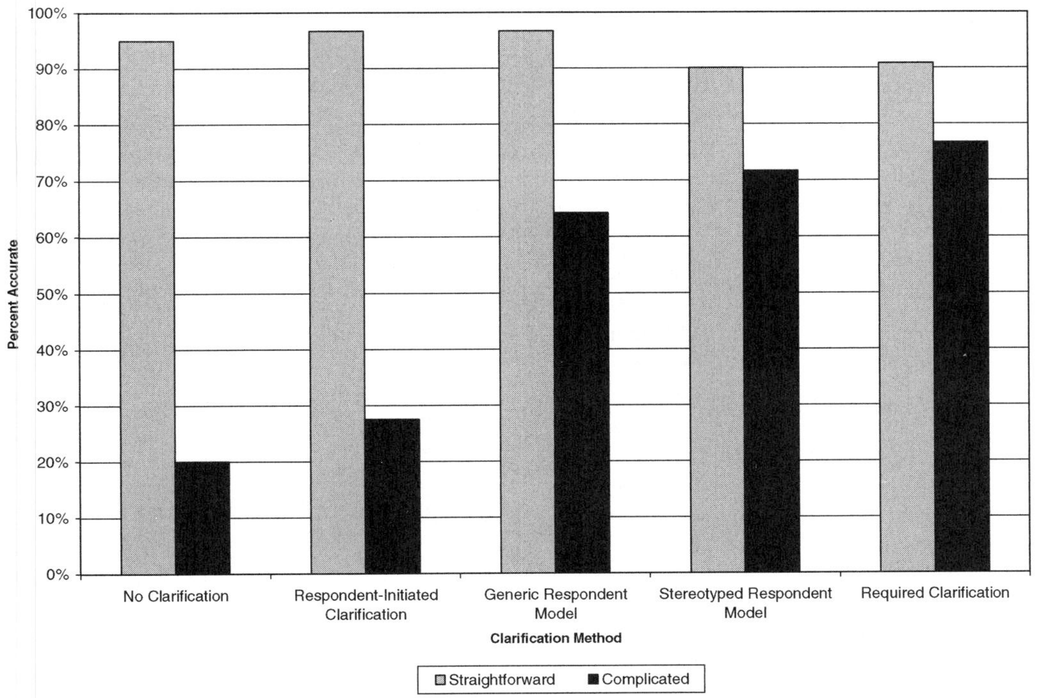

FIGURE 8.3. Response accuracy for spoken questions. From Ehlen, Schober, and Conrad (in press). Copyright by Elsevier. Reprinted by permission.

satisfaction questionnaires, a substantial portion of the older respondents indicated that they would prefer a human interviewer to the system that embodied a group-based respondent model, whereas they registered a preference for the computer-based system when it was built around a generic model or provided clarification only when respondents requested it by clicking. It could be that the modeling in this study is not as accurate as it might be and that better estimates of when respondents are having trouble might improve their satisfaction with the system. But the dissatisfaction of some respondents with this kind of system could also reflect a belief that respondents, not computers, should be in control of the interaction.

Despite the mixed impact on respondents' satisfaction, when interviewing systems offer clarification, they do so more effectively when they are based on respondent models. If interviewers and interviewing systems develop and use models of respondents, it seems likely that respondents similarly make certain assumptions about the abilities of the interviewer or interviewing system. Certainly an interface that provides clarification in conversationally savvy ways, such as adjusting its interpretation of respondent cues based on respondent characteristics, is likely to seem more human-like, or more animate. But what about embodying such animated characteristics in a virtual interviewing agent—that is, a computer-generated, graphical rendering of an interviewer—displayed in the user interface? This is sure to seem even more human. Due to the fact that animated agent technology is increasingly available, we believe it is a matter of time until survey researchers use it for collecting data. We have begun a series of experiments to explore situations in which animated agents as interviewers might help or hurt research. In order to study the impact of computerized interviewing agents that are more conversationally skilled than today's most advanced agents, we developed our agents by capturing the motions of human interviewers and using them to control the movement of graphical computer models.

This work is currently ongoing, but our experience to date suggests that the methodological concerns are quite different depending on the kinds of questions the interviewer asks. For example, when interviewing agents ask sensitive questions, do respondents assume that the agent can pass judgment on their answers as a human interviewer might? If so, they may well provide answers that are "adjusted" to be more socially desirable, as they do with human interviewers; if not, their answers will be as relatively free of social distortion as when they respond to questions that are unambiguously presented by a computer (e.g., Tourangeau & Smith, 1996). When interviewing agents ask nonsensitive, factual questions, the concerns are more focused on whether respondents believe that the interviewing agent can detect cues of response difficulty, for example, speech fluctuations and gaze aversion. If so, respondents may produce more of these cues, as we have observed in human interviews (Conrad, Schober, & Dijkstra, 2008; Schober & Bloom, 2004). Agents that are more facially realistic may encourage respondents to attribute to them the ability to detect cues of response difficulty. The agent's ability to respond to these cues, as well as to more explicit indications that help is needed, may be the most important factor, as we have observed in our studies of clarification.

An overriding issue that designers of interviewing agents will have to confront is what visual and vocal characteristics to give the agent. Human interviewers arrive on the job with certain characteristics–for example, in many organizations more interviewers are female than male. However, because the interviewer agents are animated, they can be imbued with any characteristics. It would surely be unwise to pair a female head with a male voice (see Louwerse, Graesser, Lu, & Mitchell, 2005), but other decisions are less obvious and may have a large impact on responses. For example, should a female agent wear a head scarf, or should a male agent wear a yarmulke? Should the agent match the respondent on characteristics such as age, gender, and race? If we knew the answers to such questions, we might be able to design interviewing systems that promise to make the results more credible and valid (see Conrad & Schober, 2008).

Discussion and Conclusions

We began this chapter by considering the limits of standardized interviewing as a path to comparable data across respondents, in view of the fact that different respondents can interpret the same words differently, particularly depending on how their circumstances correspond to the words. We provided evidence that allowing interviewers to choose their wording in order to make sure that respondents interpret the questions the same way and as intended can dramatically improve response accuracy, particularly when the correspondence between respondents' circumstances and question wording is ambiguous (complicated mappings). Our argument, in essence, is that standardizing meaning is more effective than standardizing wording in making data comparable. And introducing dialogue technology to self-administered surveys, as we discussed in the second part of this chapter, pushes us to rethink what counts as comparability in surveys.

To be more specific, if we think of wording versus meaning as one dimension on which comparability might be achieved, dialogue technology vastly increases the space of potential comparability. Although it is clear that the technology can help standardize respondents' interpretations by defining concepts much as human interviewers can do, it also makes it possible to tailor the interaction to respondents' abilities (e.g., mental speed), cultural conversational practices (e.g., some cultures are more tolerant of interruption than others), sensory abilities (e.g., font size or speech volume can be adjusted for the respondent), and so forth. Interviewing agents consist of many features (face, voice, clothing) that can be modified to match the respondent when desired (e.g., vocal similarity between speakers and listeners can lead to more positive ratings of speakers; Giles & Powesland, 1975) or to make them mismatch (e.g., a teenager may be less likely to inflate reports of drug use when the interviewing agent does not look like a peer). In this last case, dissimilarity could increase comparability by removing elements that lead some respondents to respond in a socially desirable way, but there may be no such effect for other respondents. Thus comparability may involve similarity to the interviewing agent for some respondents and dissimilarity for others.

The notion of comparability in standardized interviewing, we argue, deserves rethinking even in human interviews. Some characteristics of interviewers, such as vocal pitch range and race and gender, are immutable, but others are not: think of how differently warm an interviewer might be with different respondents, or how much more clarification or encouragement an interviewer might provide to different respondents. One could argue that this kind of variability is exactly what standardized interviewing intends to avoid–in the ideal, interviews would be so standardized that only one interviewer conducts them all. But is this really desirable? If we want to have truly comparable data, might it not be useful for interviewers to tailor their warmth or encouragement to the level that particular respondents need? Clearly, even having one interviewer does not necessarily standardize the stimulus to respondents. With interviewing agents, survey designers will need to make choices about what they mean by standardization and comparability and to decide which attributes to hold constant and which to allow to vary between respondents. We propose that the goal of collecting comparable data could end up requiring interviews that look rather different on the surface.

Note

1. It is widely acknowledged that interviewers' observable attributes can affect answers if interviewers differ on attributes that are relevant to the content of survey questions for which there may be more and less socially desirable answers. For example, in one study (Kane & Macaulay, 1993), female interviewers elicited more feminist responses from both men and women than did male interviewers. In another study (Hatchett & Schuman, 1975) black interviewers elicited more liberal responses to questions about racial topics than did white interviewers; for questions about nonracial topics, the answers were unrelated to the interviewer's race. We do not consider this kind of interviewer effect in the remainder of the chapter, that is, effects of the interviewer's observable characteristics; instead, we focus on the impact of interviewers' behavior on the accuracy of answers.

References

Akmajian, A., Demers, R. A., Farmer, A. K., & Harnish, R. M. (1990). *Linguistics: An introduction to language and communication* (3rd ed.). Cambridge, MA: MIT Press.

Beatty, P. (1995). Understanding the standardized/non-standardized interviewing controversy. *Journal of Official Statistics, 11*, 147–160.

Belson, W. A. (1986). *Validity in survey research.* Aldershot, UK: Gower.

Cahn, J. E., & Brennan, S. E. (1999). A psychological model of grounding and repair in dialog. In S. E. Brennan, A. Giboin, & D. Traum (Eds.), *Psychological models of communication in collaborative systems* (pp. 25–33). Menlo Park, CA: AAAI Press.

Clark, H. H. (1991). Words, the world, and their possibilities. In G. Lockhead & J. Pomerantz (Eds.), *The Perception of Structure* (pp. 263–277). Washington, DC: American Psychological Association.

Clark, H. H. (1992). *Arenas of language use.* Chicago: University of Chicago Press.

Clark, H. H. (1996). *Using language.* Cambridge, UK: Cambridge University Press.

Clark, H. H., & Brennan, S. E. (1991). Grounding in

communication. In L. B. Resnick, J. M. Levine, & S. D. Teasley (Eds.), *Perspectives on socially shared cognition* (pp. 127–149). Washington, DC: American Psychological Association.

Clark, H. H., & Gerrig, R. J. (1983). Understanding old words with new meanings. *Journal of Verbal Learning and Verbal Behavior, 22,* 591–608.

Clark, H. H., & Schaefer, E. F. (1987). Collaborating on contributions to conversations. *Language and Cognitive Processes, 2,* 19–41.

Clark, H. H., & Schaefer, E. F. (1989). Contributing to discourse. *Cognitive Science, 13,* 259–294.

Clark, H. H., & Wilkes-Gibbs, D. (1986). Referring as a collaborative process. *Cognition, 22,* 1–39.

Conrad, F. G., & Schober, M. F. (2000). Clarifying question meaning in a household telephone survey. *Public Opinion Quarterly, 64,* 1–28.

Conrad, F. G., & Schober, M. F. (Eds.). (2008). *Envisioning the survey interview of the future.* New York: Wiley.

Conrad, F. G., Schober, M. F., & Coiner, T. (2007). Bringing features of human dialogue to web surveys. *Applied Cognitive Psychology, 21*(2), 165–187.

Conrad, F. G., Schober, M. F., & Dijkstra, W. (2008). Cues of communication difficulty in telephone interviews. In J. M. Lepkowski, C. Tucker, M. Brick, E. de Leeuw, L. Japec, P. Lavrakas, M. Link, & R. Sangster (Eds.), *Advances in telephone survey methodology* (pp. 212–230). New York: Wiley.

Couper, M. P., Singer, E., & Tourangeau, R. (2004). Does voice matter? An interactive voice response (IVR) experiment. *Journal of Official Statistics, 20,* 551–570.

Ehlen, P., Schober, M. F., & Conrad, F. G. (2007). Modeling speech disfluency to predict conceptual misalignment in speech survey interfaces. *Discourse Processes, 44*(3), 245–266.

Fowler, F. J., & Mangione, T. W. (1990). *Standardized survey interviewing: Minimizing interviewer-related error.* Newbury Park, CA: Sage.

Gibbs, R. W. (1994). *The poetics of mind.* Cambridge, UK: Cambridge University Press.

Giles, H., & Powesland, P. E. (1975). *Speech style and social evaluation.* London: Academic Press.

Hatchett, S., & Schuman, H. (1975). White respondents and race of interviewer effects. *Public Opinion Quarterly, 39,* 523–528.

Kane, E. W., & Macaulay, L. J. (1993). Interviewer gender and gender attitudes. *Public Opinion Quarterly, 57,* 1–28.

Louwerse, M. M., Graesser, A. C., Lu, S., & Mitchell, H. H. (2005). Social cues in animated conversational agents. *Applied Cognitive Psychology, 19,* 693–704.

Maynard, D. W., & Whalen, M. R. (1995). Language, action, and social interaction. In K. Cook, G. Fine, & J. House (Eds.), *Sociological perspectives in social psychology* (pp. 149–175). Boston: Allyn & Bacon.

O'Hara, M., & Schober, M. (2004). Attitudes and comprehension of terms in opinion questions about euthanasia. *Proceedings of the American Statistical Association, Section on Survey Research Methods.* Alexandria, VA: American Statistical Association.

Reddy, M. J. (1993). The conduit metaphor: A case of frame conflict in our language about language. In A. Ortony (Ed.), *Metaphor and thought* (2nd ed., pp. 164–201). Cambridge, UK: Cambridge University Press. (Original work published 1979)

Salthouse, T. A. (1976). Speed and age: Multiple rates of age decline. *Experimental Aging Research, 2,* 349–359.

Salthouse, T. A. (1982). *Adult cognition: An experimental psychology of human aging.* New York: Springer-Verlag.

Schober, M. F. (1998). Conversational evidence for rethinking meaning. *Social Research, 65,* 511–534.

Schober, M. F., & Bloom, J. E. (2004). Discourse cues that respondents have misunderstood survey questions. *Discourse Processes, 38,* 287–308.

Schober, M. F., & Clark, H. H. (1989). Understanding by addressees and overhearers. *Cognitive Psychology, 21,* 211–232.

Schober, M. F., & Conrad, F. G. (1997). Does conversational interviewing reduce survey measurement error? *Public Opinion Quarterly, 61,* 576–602.

Schober, M. F., Conrad, F. G., & Fricker, S. S. (2004). Misunderstanding standardized language in research interviews. *Applied Cognitive Psychology, 18,* 169–188.

Suchman, L., & Jordan, B. (1990). Interactional troubles in face-to-face survey interviews. *Journal of the American Statistical Association, 85*(409), 232–253.

Suessbrick, A., Schober, M. F., & Conrad, F. G. (2000). Different respondents interpret ordinary questions quite differently. In *Proceedings of the American Statistical Association, Section on Survey Research Methods* (pp. 907–912). Alexandria, VA: American Statistical Association.

Tourangeau, R., & Smith, T. W. (1996). Asking sensitive questions: The impact of data collection mode, question format and question context. *Public Opinion Quarterly, 60,* 275–304.

Traum, D. R. (1994). A computational theory of grounding in natural language conversation. Unpublished doctoral dissertation, University of Rochester, Department of Computer Science.

CHAPTER 9

Emergent Approaches to Focus Group Research

David Morgan
Collin Fellows
Heather Guevara

At a recent international conference on qualitative research, one of the panelists began with an apology for the amount of time she needed to explain her methods, because "they aren't something traditional, like ethnography or focus groups." Yet only 20 years ago, the rare presentation that used focus groups started with a similar apology for and explanation of what was then a little-known method. Now, in the two decades since focus groups (re)emerged in the social sciences (Krueger, 1987; Morgan, 1987; Morgan & Spanish, 1984), their popularity has soared to the point that a Web of Science database search for articles from 2006 that used the term *focus groups* found more than 1,000 articles in that 1 year. Hence this chapter concentrates on newer or more innovative approaches to what is now a well-recognized method. It is also worth noting, however, that the history of focus groups illustrates how what was once a little-known, "emergent" method can become a widely used and even "traditional" research technique within a relatively short period of time.

Our overall approach in this chapter is to present these emergent alternatives to traditional ways of doing focus groups as a set of research designs. In particular, our goal is to make researchers aware not only of the range of options that are available for doing focus groups but also of how to evaluate those options for different purposes. This approach matches an overall position that there is no "one right way to do focus groups"—instead, there are many alternatives, and it is up to the researcher to select a set of options that are appropriate for any given project (Morgan, 1993). This amounts to a "pragmatic approach" to research design (Morgan, 2007, 2008), in which a clear understanding of the goals and outcomes for the project should determine decisions about the research design. In other words, understanding why the research is being done is essential to answering questions about how to do the research.

This chapter thus offers information about three emerging options for conducting focus groups, along with explicit advice about the kinds of goals that would be suited to each. The first section considers the broadest set of issues by describing ways to replace research designs that are determined before data collection begins with emergent designs for focus groups. The second section addresses the more specific option of conducting repeated focus groups rather than having the participants attend a single session. The third section is the most concrete, demonstrating one way to use stimulus materials and projective techniques via concept mapping. These three approaches all represent different options for doing focus groups, and each of them includes its own, more detailed, options about how to implement that particular approach. Consequently, we will do our best to give advice about both when and why to use these different options, as well as providing concrete examples for several of the different alternatives that we present.

Before doing so, however, we want to express a contrarian point of view about one area that we have explicitly excluded from consideration: online or "electronic" focus groups. We feel that, rather than offering a truly emerging approach, procedures for conducting online focus groups are still at "pretakeoff" stage. Although there are numerous articles about this topic, nearly all of them consist of descriptions of one possible way of doing online focus groups. Hence the current state of this area amounts to a number of competing alternatives with little or no consensus about how to move forward.

The one option that almost everyone agrees would work is to treat online focus groups as direct extensions of face-to-face focus groups by using a video conference to link the participants at their separate sites. This has the obvious advantage of eliminating the first half of the requirement that face-to-face focus groups must meet in the same place at the same time. In this format, a participant would be seated at a computer screen with a set of windows, with each window containing an ongoing video connection to one of the other participants. Although organizations with large budgets have been able to conduct similar video conferences for over a decade, this approach will be of limited value to most academic researchers until a great many more people have routine access to this technology. Hence, even though this video conference format has long been spoken of as the future of online focus groups, it seems to be a future that is very slow in arriving.

Rather than waiting for video conferencing that closely mimics the mechanics of face-to-face focus groups, researchers have made a number of attempts to adapt various forms of existing Internet technology as a way to conduct online focus groups. The basic strategy here is to create an analogy of the form: "A [specific technology] could be like focus groups if. . . ." For example, e-mail lists could be like focus groups if they could keep the same group of people routinely communicating back and forth about the same topics. Or Internet chat rooms could be like focus groups if there were a way to create relatively orderly exchanges among the participants. Or discussion boards could be like focus groups if it were possible to get most people to contribute to most of the discussion areas on a regular basis. For a general review of this literature, see Stewart and Williams (2005).

Note that each of these approaches begins with an Internet technology that was developed for some other purpose and then attempts to reshape it into something like a focus group. We are likely to see more efforts in this direction as new technologies emerge. For example, there is no reason that instant messaging or blogs could not be adapted to capture aspects of focus groups, and it is probably a safe bet that someone has already done so. Indeed, Williams (2006) describes conducting focus groups in which the participants appear as "avatars" in a simulated gaming environment. The major limitation of this general strategy is that each of these efforts concentrates almost entirely on the mechanics of creating manageable online interaction. Yet the value of focus groups is not merely due to the fact that they are interactive—if it were, then almost any kind of communication technology could reproduce what they have to offer. Instead, what is really important is that face-to-face focus groups routinely produce a kind of interaction that interests social science researchers (see Morgan, 2001, for a more detailed discussion of this basic point). This does not mean that online focus groups with existing Internet technologies should produce exactly the same kinds of interactions as face-to-face groups. What is missing, however, is a self-conscious movement beyond the minimal goal of managing interaction and toward the more important goal of producing the kind of interaction that has manifest value as data for social science research.

Overall, despite the number of articles offering "proof of concept" examples for various kinds of online focus groups, the research community has shown very little movement toward the adoption of any these innovations. Unless or until some consensus does emerge about the value of the interaction that can be generated through existing Internet technologies, we are left with the choice of continuing to wait for online video conferencing or developing the additional opportunities that face-to-face focus groups have to offer. This chapter clearly follows the latter path.

Emergent Designs for Focus Groups

Currently, many, if not most, focus group projects begin by determining a research design, then collecting data according to that design, and finally analyzing the resulting data. This amounts to a predetermined set of stages, with no allowance for emergence in either the basic aspects of the data collection or the larger research for the study. Yet the openness and flexibility of a more emergent approach is one of the central defining features of qualitative research. Hence this section argues for more uses of such emergence in focus groups.

Before laying out several pieces of practical advice for building more emergence into focus group research, we want to call attention to several more general points. First, this problem is not limited to research that uses focus groups, as individual research projects are just as susceptible to this predetermined sequence of design–collect–analyze. Thinking specifically about focus groups, however, the common tendency to plan the research in advance may well be due to the more complex logistics of putting together group interview sessions. This leads to our second general point: Allowing for emergence is not the same as a total lack of design or planning. Indeed, the key point of this section is that *it is possible to design for emergence*. Finally, even though we advocate more attention to doing focus group projects that take advantage of emergence, we do not deny the potential value of projects that choose to rely on predetermined designs. The key word here is *choose*, because the goal in any research design should be to use the approach that is best suited to the project's research goals. Unfortunately, at present the predetermined design–collect–analyze approach to focus groups often seems to be a mindless default rather than a conscious choice. Hence, we wish to promote a more emergent approach to focus groups as an explicit option for future research.

The majority of what follows (including the figures) is based on an article (Morgan, 2007) that describes two different approaches that emphasize emergence in focus groups. The difference between the two approaches depends on whether the design calls for a process of emergence *within* individual groups or *between* sets of groups. The presentation in this chapter concentrates on designing for emergence *between* sets of groups, both because these designs offer some of the most powerful options and because the alternative of designing for emergence with a single group is a relatively straightforward extension of existing practices. Still, we do want to say something about designs for emergence within groups before turning the bulk of our attention to designs that emphasize emergence between groups.

The simplest way to describe designs for emergence within groups is by comparison with the classic "funnel structure" for organizing the questions that guide focus groups (e.g., Krueger, 1998; Morgan, 1997). The funnel metaphor captures the idea of beginning the interview with broad, open questions that are oriented toward the participants' perspectives before shifting toward narrower questions that pursue the researchers' interests. Interestingly, one of the major goals in the "less structured" beginning for funnel interviews is to give participants the opportunity to raise topics that the research team may not have anticipated. Although this technique does recognize the value of learning about emergent topics during the course of the research, the predetermined content of the questions delays any use of this new information until the analysis stage. In contrast, a research design that was built on emergence would be flexible enough to modify the later data collection according to what was learned earlier.

Thus the use of broad opening questions in funnel designs recognizes the value of hearing about emergent topics, and designs that emphasize emergence within groups create opportunities to pursue this information. The easiest way to do this is to modify the funnel structure so that the initial open-ended portion of the interview is mirrored by a similar section near the end of the interview while the middle section contains the researchers' predetermined questions. This "hourglass" shape thus moves from broad questions to narrower topics and back to broad, open-ended questions. The advantage of this open section is that it allows the researcher to follow up on topics that were raised earlier and can now be pursued in more detail. Alternatively, if this particular group brought up rather little in the way of unanticipated material, then the moderator could ask about additional topics that were of interest to the research group or topics that emerged in earlier groups but were not raised in this group. This idea of using things that were learned in earlier groups begins to take us into the territory of emergence *between* groups, which is the central topic of this section.

The defining feature of research designs that emphasize emergence between groups is their ability to use insights from earlier groups to influence the nature of later groups. Figure 9.1 illustrates three different strategies for implementing this approach to emergent design. The first strategy, as shown in Figure 9.1a, is the most radical of the three because it allows not only the questions but also the kinds of participants to change on a group-by-group basis. In many respects, this design follows the classic approach from participant observation and ethnography, in which data collection and analysis are inseparably linked throughout the research process. Thus the project may begin with ideas about who to talk to in the later groups and the questions to ask them, but all of that is potentially open to change, depending on what the participants say in the first group. This strategy clearly offers the most opportunity for emergence by making the nature of each group contingent on the analysis of the earlier groups. At the same time, however, the possibility of changing direction on a group-by-group basis also presents the same problems that go along with any radical emphasis on emergence by making it almost impossible to plan in advance. This radical emphasis on emergence is thus a form of research design, but only a minimalist one.

The second strategy, as illustrated in Figure 9.1b, divides the full set of groups into distinctive subsets, which amounts to an intermediate option between a predetermined design for the whole project and a group-by-group emergence. This strategy is most pow-

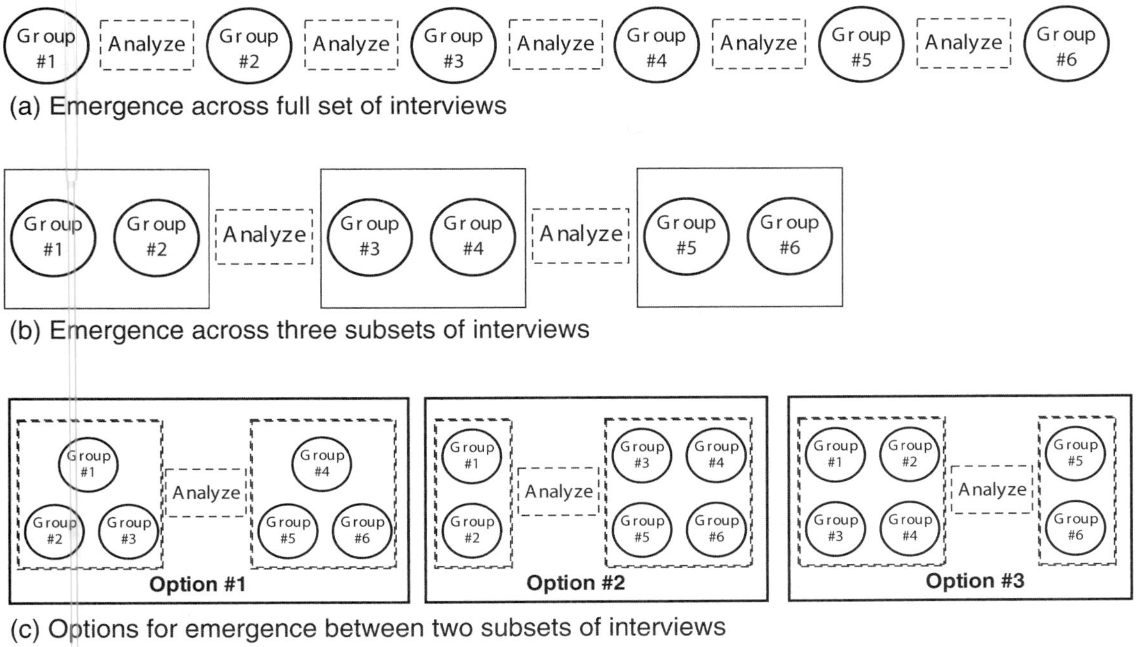

FIGURE 9.1. Designing for emergence between focus groups.

erful when there is a clear division of labor between the different stages, so that each stage serves a coherent function within the overall process of data collection and analysis. One particularly useful variant on this strategy shifts the basic funnel format from a within-group to a between-groups application. In that case, the first set of groups in Figure 9.1b would be relatively unstructured, with just a few broad questions that the moderator would use to facilitate the goal of hearing about as many different aspects of the overall topic as possible. The analysis of those initial groups would then determine both who should participate in the next set of groups and what the questions should be in those discussions. One likely format for this middle set of groups would be the classic within-group funnel questioning strategy, so that the research team could hear about the participants' perspectives in the early part of the interview and then shift to more directive, researcher-driven topics. The final set of interviews in this between-groups funnel would typically target issues that had not received sufficient coverage thus far. For example, the analysis of the previous groups might well show a high degree of "saturation" on some topics but less information in other areas, which would lead to a new interview guide that concentrated on filling those gaps. Alternatively, the analysis of the earlier groups might point to the desirability of hearing more from specific types of participants, which would lead to a shift in the group composition so that the final groups could capture the perspectives of those particular participants.

A concrete example of this approach comes from ongoing work with our colleague Peter Collier (2007). The goal in that project was to create a set of "peer mentor videos" that contained advice for students who were the first ones in their family to attend college (i.e., "first generation" students). The initial set of groups consisted of less structured interviews with successful first-generation students to hear about both the challenges they faced and the coping strategies they used. The second set of groups used more structured interviews with first-generation freshmen who were completing their freshman year. Here, the goals were to generate more depth and detail about the topics uncovered in the earlier discussions and to recruit a set of participants for the final set of groups. That third set of groups was dedicated to shooting the actual videos, concentrating on key topics from two earlier sets of groups. The participants for these sessions were students from the second round of groups who had experiences and thoughts that were especially relevant for the selected topics. Although this final set of groups was essentially "staged" to capture the desired material, this met the original goal of providing mentoring advice for future first-generation freshmen. In particular, the edited versions of these videos showed an equivalent set of students who described the challenges that first-generation students were likely to encounter, while also offering realistic strategies to meet those challenges.

In general, the three-part, funnel-like division between groups in Figure 9.1b has many attractive features; however, it is by no means the only way to separate the overall project into stages that allow for emergence between groups. Consequently, Figure 9.1c shows three different variations on between-groups designs that use two rather than three stages. The first of these two-part strategies divides the groups to allow for a "midpoint" analysis, in which insights that emerged in the first half of the project can influence the design of the second half. This design can be especially useful when the research team is working for an external sponsor or when the team itself contains multiple stakeholders; in these cases, the midpoint analysis often leads to an interim report or presentation that serves as the basis for making decisions about the remainder of the project. The second option illustrated in Figure 9.1c separates a smaller set of "start-up groups" from the bulk of the data collection. These earlier groups typically serve the same formative purpose as the first set of groups in a between-groups funnel design, such as Figure 9.1b, but in this case fewer initial data are necessary in order to "ground" the design for the remainder of the project. The third option uses a smaller set of "hold back" groups at the end of the data collection, which also typically borrows its function from the last set of groups in the between-group funnel. In this case, holding back a few groups until near the end of the project creates opportunities to cover new topics or hear from specific subgroups of participants, based on insights that emerged during the earlier groups. This final design strategy is particularly instructive because it demonstrates how designing for emergence makes it possible to pursue valuable data that could be lost if a project relied solely on a predetermined separation of research design, data collection, and analysis.

Overall, the basic goal of this section has been to expand the range of options that are available at the most basic level of connecting research design, data analysis, and data collection in focus groups. Even though allowing for emergence during the course of a research project is a classic element of qualitative research, it has been relatively rare in projects that rely on focus groups. Choosing this option is thus not a decision that should be taken without considerable thought. Even reviewers and colleagues who are familiar with more traditional approaches to focus groups may not be prepared for research designs that change and emerge during the course of the research. Furthermore, at the practical level, the flexibility that emergent designs offer for focus groups can also increase their complexity. Hence, even though emergent designs offer a powerful range of new options for doing focus groups, we have no intention of promoting them as inherently superior to more traditional forms of focus group research. Just like any other approach to research, these emergent designs make sense only when they match a set of goals that clearly justifies the choice of such a design.

Repeated Focus Groups

Repeated focus groups bring participants back from earlier sessions for a continuing discussion of related topics. This technique (which is also known as "reconvened" focus groups) is not strictly new, having received attention in the early marketing literature (Goldman, 1962) and at least some mention in social science treatments of focus groups (e.g., Bloor, Frankland, Thomas, & Robson, 2001; Krueger & Casey, 2000; Morgan, 1997). Recently, however, this approach has received increasing interest, which has led to clarifications in both the kinds of purposes it can serve and the kinds of procedures it requires.

There are currently two widely cited purposes for using repeated focus groups. The first reason is to gain insight into the ways that belief systems, social norms, and interaction styles are revealed in groups. This motivation for repeated groups is most common in social science applications, in which the goal is often, as we illustrate later, to learn about more complex "discourse processes" by hearing how the participants carry the things that were said and done in earlier groups into later groups. In particular, it creates the opportunity to hear how the beliefs and values that participants expressed in a first round of groups may have an impact on what is said or not said in a second round of groups (for an early example of such research, see Burgess, Limb, & Harrison, 1988a, 1988b).

The other common reason for using repeated groups, which we also illustrate, is to give the participants time to react to information before meeting again. This second motivation is most common in applied research, in which the purpose is to give the participants more time to consider the basic aspects of complex or unfamiliar topics before delving into a deeper discussion of those issues. In addition, the goal of increasing the participants' exposure to the topic may lead to assignments before the second session, such as diary keeping, television viewing, or Internet searching. Although it would easy to overstate the distinction between these two motivations for conducting repeated groups, it essentially amounts to a difference between giving the researcher more opportunity to observe relatively complex aspects of interaction versus giving the participants more opportunity to think about relatively complex topics.

These two different reasons for using repeated focus groups tend to match up with two different procedures for creating and recruiting such groups. The first approach requires that the participants in a second-round or later group must be the *identical* set of people who talked together in their first-round group. The obvious advantage of using identical sets of participants in each round of groups is the degree of continuity that it creates. The equally obvious disadvantage is the difficulty in maintaining this continuous participation. Another way to think about this disadvantage is that it translates into more complex recruitment procedures that require a search for people who are routinely available in the same time slot (e.g., Thursdays from 7:00–9:00). One common tactic for encouraging this kind of repeated attendance is to increase the monetary incentive for attending later groups (e.g., giving participants in a project with two rounds a substantial "bonus" for also attending the second group).

Relying on identical sets of participants from group to group is especially useful in projects in which the reason for repeated groups is to observe more complex types of interaction. This combination is more common in social science research, in which observing the same group members over time makes it possible to track how they express and use their belief systems. In essence, this strategy of bringing identical sets of participants back together assumes that ongoing interactions will influence what the individual members do and say in the later discussions. Of course, this goal can also increase the complexity of the analysis if it requires tracking the things that each individual member says in each group.

The second procedure for creating repeating groups draws the members of each later group from a larger pool of prior participants. Practically speaking, the first round of groups creates this pool of participants, who are all eligible to participate in any of the groups during the second round. Avoiding the requirement that the same set of people meet together as a group in every round of the repeated groups simplifies the recruitment process, although it does not eliminate all of the potential issues. In particular, if there is substantial attrition between the two rounds, then the later groups will need to be either smaller in size or fewer in number. In addition, there should be attention to the group composition so that none of the second-round groups contain too many participants who were all in the same first-round group. The practical tactics for addressing these issues are the same as those mentioned before—finding people who have a routine time slot available and offering additional incentives for completing the full set of groups.

Creating an initial pool of participants for follow-up groups is especially common in applied research projects that need to begin by exposing people to complex information. In that case, the goal is typically to get a more "deliberative" set of responses in the later discussions, based on the participants' exposure to the topic in the earlier groups. This procedure of using a pool of participants to create follow-up groups is well matched to the goal of providing individuals with more information that they can discuss in more depth during the second-round groups.

In general, there is a tendency to connect the two procedures for putting together repeated groups with the purposes that those repeated groups typically serve, but this tendency is just that, a tendency. Thus, even though the two examples we present here fit this pattern, it is also possible to imagine cases in which social science research on beliefs and interactions could benefit by drawing from a pool of participants or in which applied research on responses to new information could benefit from using an identical set of participants in each group.

Andrew McGregor (2004, 2005) provides an example of a social science-oriented project that used repeated groups with identical members in order to examine the discussions that emerged from those ongoing interactions. The project consisted of five groups of environmental activists who met three times over a 3-week period. The recruitment for each group drew from one of several similar residential area and environmental organizations, which undoubtedly made it easier to set up the repeated meetings, while also increasing the amount of experiences and beliefs in each group. As part of the goal of hearing how the groups developed their own ways of discussing the issues, McGregor used a relatively unstructured approach to moderating (Morgan, 1997), in which he provided few questions and did little to direct the conversations. As expected, the participants' overlapping backgrounds gave them a mutual vocabulary for expressing environmental issues, which rapidly developed into agreement about both the appropriate topics to pursue and the appropriate ways to pursue those topics. The ongoing interactions in the groups allowed this process to produce a "dominant discourse" that McGregor labeled "sustainable development" (i.e., human activities definitely do threaten natural resources, but this problem can be solved by proper management of the environment and the human threats to it).

McGregor was particularly interested in how this dominant discourse encouraged certain points of view while marginalizing others. Thus, even though most of the participants in each group agreed about most of the issues they considered, there were still a number of occasions on which people put forth ideas that did not coincide with this shared framework. For example, several of the groups discussed whaling, and this led some participants to declare that whales should not be considered in the same way as other animals, due to their unique intelligence. Even though that idea would be readily accepted in other settings (e.g., among animal rights supporters), other participants in these groups would challenge those views quite directly, with the result that those who initially suggested special considerations for whales eventually agreed with the dominant belief that whales should not be treated any differently from other endangered species. In part, this silencing of competing perspectives reflected the difficulty of finding acceptable ways to express nonconforming beliefs within the ongoing conversation, but it also highlighted the resources that the dominant discourse provided for participants who wished to challenge nonconforming ideas. Thus the key value of using repeated groups in this project was the opportunity to observe how a dominant discourse developed to the point at which it could marginalize and silence alternative points of view.

In contrast to using repeated groups with identical membership for social science research, the next example demonstrates the use of a pooled membership strategy for applied purposes. In this case, a commercial consulting firm examined voters' thoughts about various options for the public and private funding of political parties in Britain ("Public Perspectives," 2006). This relatively complex project began with a set of day-long "workshops" in each of four major cities, with 25–30 participants at each site. Small-group discussions at the start of the sessions showed that the participants' responses to this topic typically involved low levels of knowledge and high levels of cynicism. In the middle part of these first-round groups, the participants heard formal presentations about the most likely options for party funding, after which they debated different solutions and concluded by producing a sense of the five most popular options for party funding and a set of "guiding principles" for evaluating the options (e.g., transparency and accountability). In general, these initial sessions had the desired effect of taking the participants "from a situation of knowing little about party funding and having no opinion on the issue at the beginning of the day, to a situation where they were able to express a view on the subject" (2006, p. 2).

An analysis of the initial discussions pointed to three broad types of participants: a younger set of "disengaged citizens" who found it hard to decide about their preferences, an older set of "world-weary pragmatists" who were suspicious about public funding, and a set of "disillusioned idealists," who cut across age groups and were more in favor of public funding than the other groups were. The research team thus limited the participants in the second round to three subgroups who had at least some preferences with regard to funding options: the world-weary pragmatists and the disillusioned idealists, with the latter split according to younger or older age. By selecting participants who "were able to engage with the discussion in a relatively advanced way," the moderators were able "to explore issues in depth and detail that could only be given a cursory examination in the earlier sessions. Consequently the workshop had a real energy and was an example of a genuinely productive deliberative research" (2006, p. 79).

The participants met in their three subgroups throughout another day-long workshop, allowing them to work with others from the same age group who shared a similar outlook. These second-round groups started with discussions about the broad guiding principles from the previous groups and then moved on to consider the five widely popular options from the earlier sessions. Each of the three subgroups then brought their suggestions and conclusions to a "plenary meeting" of the group as a whole, which produced a final set of recommendations. Altogether, this project started with relatively uninformed and cynical participants, then applied a combination of information presentation, selective recruitment, and further deliberation, which ultimately resulted in thoughtful and well-articulated inputs to a policymaking process.

Overall, the options in this section demonstrate both the range of things that repeated focus groups can accomplish and the procedures that can be used to meet these goals. In this case, we have discussed the two most common pairings between the goals of either gaining greater access to group processes or helping participants work with more complex materials and recruitment procedures that use either identical group membership or pooled membership over time. In addition to these two widely practiced pairings, we have also argued for the value of exploring the other possible combinations of purposes and procedures for repeated groups. Once again, however, it needs to be emphasized that the overall goals for the research project should determine the value of these specific options, as well as whether it makes sense to use repeated focus groups at all. Like the other emergent approaches in this chapter, repeated groups create an additional option for conducting focus groups, but the value of this option must be weighed against the research purposes it is meant to serve.

Concept Mapping as an Example of Using Stimulus Materials and Projective Techniques

Compared with the way focus groups are used in fields such as market research (e.g., Mariampolski, 2001), social scientists tend to rely very heavily on pure discussion questions in their interviews. The alternative is to use more questions that involve stimulus materials, projective techniques, and so forth. More specifically, stimulus materials present the participants with pictures, stories, videos, or other forms of media as a basis for discussion, whereas projective techniques use a more creative, or Game-like, approach to spark an active conversation. In both cases, the approach is to use moderator-introduced items or activities as a way to generate less analytical and more imaginative responses. (See Krueger, 1998, for other examples of stimulus materials and projective techniques.)

In comparison, a great many social science interview guides tend to be much more analytically oriented. Even narrative approaches that emphasize storytelling usually concentrate on relatively coherent and well-organized accounts. This style of interviewing certainly makes sense when the participants are deeply engaged in the topics they are discussing. Groups of Alzheimer's disease caregivers or workers who have lost their jobs due to outsourcing can easily talk about their experiences, feelings, and opinions for 2 hours and more. For broader topics, however, with participants who are simply members of the general public, a continuing series of "left-brained" analytical questions can be quite tiring. Although social science researchers may be self-selected for their ability to participate in those kinds of conversations for hours on end, many community members are likely to appreciate the more free-form, "right-brained" opportunities that stimulus materials and projective techniques provide. In addition, the kind of discussion that these questions generate can make a valuable contribution to an otherwise highly scripted interview.

Our presentation concentrates on a single technique, concept mapping, which blends aspects of both stimulus materials and projective techniques. We believe that this combination can be particularly powerful in social science focus groups for two reasons. First, with regard to stimulus materials, these questions usually rely on media that are created outside the group and then introduced by the moderator; one such question might be "Take a look at these two different versions of a brochure about. . . ." That way of doing things has distinct advantages when the goal is to get reactions to preselected ideas that can be embodied in various media, but concept mapping also includes the option of letting each group generate its own stimulus materials. Second, with regard to projective techniques, those questions often rely on role playing or extended metaphors that originated in product marketing, such as: "Think of all the kinds of cars and trucks there are, and then imagine that this product was a car or truck—what kind would it be and why?" That approach can be difficult to adapt to social science topics, but concept mapping relies on activities in which the participants explore their own thinking on the issue at hand. (For more examples of projective techniques in product marketing, see Puchta & Potter, 2004.)

Concept mapping thus uses stimulus materials in the form of concepts and ideas that are either prepared beforehand or generated by the participants themselves. It also uses projective techniques by getting the group to work together in the process of arranging those concepts into a physical map. This combination of more open-ended, creative thinking and more active, group-based teamwork not only gives the participants a change of pace from analytical questioning but also has the potential to produce insightful data in its own right.

The goal in concept mapping is for the participants to produce a diagram or "map" that summarizes their thinking on a key topic or issue. The process involves making map-like patterns by arranging and connecting a set of ideas that are relevant to the discussion topic. Figure 9.2 shows a highly stylized set of examples of the final forms that concept maps may take. The remainder of this section presents a description of the mechanics of creating concept mapping in focus groups, followed by a discussion of broader research design options that match the different versions of this technique to more specific uses.

In some cases, the research team will already have chosen a list of concepts that are related to the topic, and those concepts will serve as stimulus material in the construction of the concept map. In other cases, in which the group itself generates the relevant concepts, a nominal group (Stewart, Shamdasani, & Rook, 2007) is a useful way to create that content. Here, the moderator would begin by providing a short, clear description of the core topic for the concept mapping exercise—in practice, this topic summary is often written on an easel pad for all to see or distributed as printed copies. The moderator then hands out cards or note paper and asks each participant to think about (or write down) two or three key things that are related to the core topic, things that can be summarized in just a few words.

Because of similarities in the concepts that participants generate individually, it is useful to go through a process of refining of these initial suggestions. One common way to do this is with a series of sheets of easel paper. The moderator first asks people just to read some of the ideas on their cards—not in any particular order, but just to get a sense of the different things that people mentioned. This will almost certainly yield examples in which people had very similar ideas, leading the moderator to say: "One topic that I heard at least a couple of people mention was. . . ." After writing down a set of related concepts, the moderator can ask: "What are some other things related to this category, not just things you had on your cards, but anything else we could use to fill out this list?" From there, the moderator moves onto a fresh sheet of paper and a new category ("What's another important set of things—something we haven't heard about yet?") and continues that process until the group agrees that the most important categories of concepts have been captured—usually ending with an "Other" category to hold any ideas that do not fit easily elsewhere.

A more participative technique for eliciting the initial content is to have group members work with large sticky notes or cards, about 5 by 7 inches. The participants begin by writing two or three ideas, one idea per card, using markers that allow other participants to read the cards from across the room. After each participant takes one idea card and posts it on the opposite wall, they direct the moderator to group together cards that have identical or very similar content. This should produce some areas that

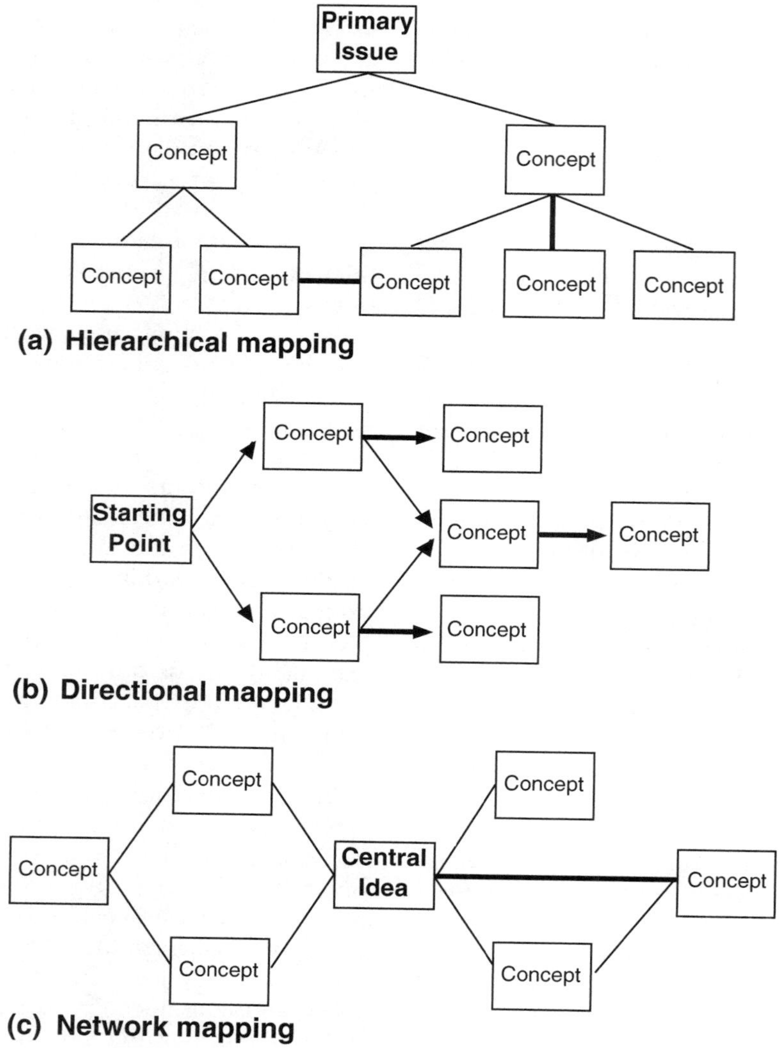

FIGURE 9.2. Three strategies for building concept maps.

are more full and others that are relatively empty, and the participants then take their remaining cards and place them either with similar cards or in blank spaces for cards that represent new ideas. Finally, the group advises the moderator, who considers each groups of cards, adding new ideas that can "fill out" an area, breaking up groups that are too heterogeneous, or grouping together smaller groups with similar content.

At the end of either of these "elicitation" sessions, the participants proceed to edit down this longer list by selecting the key concepts they want to include in their ultimate mapping. As a general guideline, 12–15 concepts is a good number for map-building activities in focus groups, because fewer items tend to make simplistic maps, whereas more items tend to be difficult to sort out in any consensual way. Of course, that suggested number should be adjusted to reflect both the complexity of the topic being mapped and the intellectual skills of the participants. For this selection process, it helps to emphasize that each item should have some relatively important connection to the overall topic and that the items in the set should all be relatively different from each other. In other words, the participants should drop items that are either peripheral to the core topic or very similar to other items in the set. One convenient way to accomplish this selection is by voting. A technique for speeding up that process is to give each participant a set of adhesive "dots" that each represent a vote for a particular concept. The participants then circulate and place their votes next to the items they want to retain for the actual mapping exercise.

Once the moderator has a set of concepts in hand, either through a predetermined process or the kind of elicitation just described, the next step is to have the participants arrange those items in a physical layout that captures the relationships between the concepts. The actual process of placing and linking concepts to create a concept map requires decisions about both a starting point for the map and a procedure for building on that starting point. Figure 9.2 shows simplified versions of three common ways of laying out and connecting the concepts that make up a concept map. Each of the three uses not only a different beginning point but also a different way of expanding from that beginning.

The process of hierarchical mapping, as shown in Figure 9.2a, starts with placing a "primary issue" at the top of the diagram and then proceeds by attaching additional concepts at lower levels in the hierarchy. This kind of concept map has been very popular in the education literature (e.g., Novak, 1998), and it is particularly useful for situations in which the concepts are likely to have a logical or relatively structured set of relationships to each other. In this case, the initial primary issue is often the same as the description that was used to elicit the list of concepts (or an equivalent statement, if the concepts were predetermined). The moderator begins by placing this statement at the top of the mapping space and spreading all of the concepts out at the bottom of the chart. The group then selects the two or three concepts that are most closely linked to that primary issue, which become the second level in the hierarchy. Along with drawing links from the primary issue to these second-level concepts, the moderator also asks about the nature of those connections or relationships and typically writes this information next to the connecting lines. That process continues as the moderator starts with one of the second-level concepts and asks the group to make and label connections from it to some of the remaining concepts, which become part of the third level, and so on. As the map emerges, it is also useful to ask whether there are other concepts that should be added; this is especially important at the end, as the group assesses its nearly complete map. That final step should also include a consideration of any other connections that should be drawn between concepts, including relationships that fall outside the orderly hierarchical structure, such as lines that cut across levels, and so forth.

An example of this process comes from a different part of our work with Peter Collier on first-generation college students. In this study of coping strategies, we wanted to get a systematic sense of the problems these students faced in their coursework and the range of options they used to address those problems. We investigated this issue through a series of group and individual interviews with graduate teaching assistants from the university's year-long "Freshman Inquiry" program. We used these instructors as "expert informants" and began each interview with a brainstorming session in which they generated a typical problem that many freshmen experienced, which served as the "primary issue" in their map. For example, more than one group chose problems related to students who did not realize until the last minute that they had two major assignments due at almost the same time. Next, the participants developed a list of issues related to their chosen problem and began the process of organizing these issues into a hierarchical map. Continuing the preceding example, the second level for the problem of overlapping due dates typically represented broad categories of coping strategies, and the third level contained specific versions of those coping strategies. One example of a second-level concept was "talking to professors," which included third-level items such as asking for an extension on one of the assignments, whereas another second-level strategy was "reorganizing own priorities," which included deciding to concentrate on one assignment while accepting a lower grade on the other. Overall, the collection of hierarchical maps from this project gave us both a strong list of different categories of problems and a clear sense of how various coping strategies fit into each of those problem areas.

Turning to other ways of constructing concept maps, Figure 9.2b illustrates directional mapping as an alternative strategy. In this case, the mapping process begins by placing one concept as a "starting point" along the left edge and then spreading to the right by attaching additional concepts. This kind of map is most commonly used to represent a process or something that happens over time, as indicated by the directional arrows in this diagram. In essence, each concept to the right of the starting point depends on the things that came "before" it, and the goal is to trace out that pattern of relationships. Adding an item on the right also creates the opportunity to expand the left side of the map by asking about other things that might be sources of the newly added concept; this strategy helps to prevent an overly linear style of thinking that is almost entirely driven by the initial starting point. Once again, the moderator asks for content to describe each link in the map and ends with a final consideration of any links that should be added, even if they cut across or "loop around" the overall flow of the main map.

The third option, network mapping, involves starting in the middle and then building a "network" of connections from there. This is the most flexible kind of mapping, and it is useful for issues and topics that involve a relatively free-form set of connections–as opposed to the "top-down" structure in hierarchical maps and the process or flow organization of directional mapping. In particular, network mapping does not even require the predetermined "central idea" shown in Figure 9.2c, which means that the procedures do not need to start with a single key concept, in the way that the other two options do. For this alternative, the moderator starts by having the group identify a pair of concepts that are closely connected and then asking whether that pair should be "near the center, off on one side, or maybe in a corner by themselves." If the initial pair is relatively central, then it probably makes sense to expand by asking about other concepts that are connected to one or the other or to both of them. Alternatively, if that initial pair is more isolated, the group can proceed by selecting another pair of closely connected concepts and then placing them in relation to the first pair. This flexible approach allows the pattern in the map to go beyond the web-like connections shown in Figure 9.2c. For example, the group may decide to break the concepts into two relatively distinct subsets with few or no connections between them, or they may create several loosely connected clusters with no real center. Once again, the mapping process usually ends by considering any further connections that might be added. With network mapping, however, there is also the option of stepping back near the end of the process to consider the whole question of using a central concept in the map. For example, if there was either a predetermined or group-selected central concept, they might consider whether there are any other concepts that could occupy that position. Or, if their emergent map did not contain a central concept, they might consider whether one of the items or groups of items might actually play that role. With any of these options for changing the central concept, the group can explore the consequences of organizing the map around that alternative before making their ultimate decision.

Considering Figure 9.2 as a whole, even though our presentation of these three options includes suggestions for deciding when each is more likely to be useful, we want to emphasize that all of these approaches can be used in a variety of ways that could fit a variety of circumstances. Unless one of these approaches is an obvious choice, we would urge research teams to spend some time debating the relative merits of each of these approaches to concept mapping. Another useful strategy would be to talk to key informants about what difference it might make to do things one way or another. Talking to key informants can also be useful for defining a primary issue, starting point, or central idea–which may be especially valuable information because the choice of a beginning point can have a strong influence on the development of the map as a whole. Ultimately, however, what matters most is not the specific format of the maps or the mapping process but rather the ability of the information in those maps to meet the research goals.

The theme of using research goals to drive actual decision making moves us up to the level of research designs, and there are several design options that have implications for the more mechanical procedures we have described so far. One key design decision is whether the mapping process will primarily serve as the basis for further discussions or whether the maps will be end products that function as sources of data in their own right. For example, when the concept maps serve as stimulus material for further discussions, a common strategy is to schedule a pair of questions within the overall session. In the first question, the moderator would use a relatively task-oriented approach to create the map, with less emphasis on talking about the content of the map. Instead, those discussions would be saved for the follow-up question that allows the group to take a more reflective look at both the overall structure of the map and the connections that created that pattern. Note that this second discussion could also include adding and subtracting concepts or rearranging the elements within the map. This approach is most useful when the goals behind the concept mapping are relatively exploratory and the research team wants to hear as much as possible about the participants' thinking on the issues being mapped.

In contrast, if the goal is to create a map that can serve as a basic source of data, then the initial process for creating it is usually more deliberative. In that case, the moderator would ask the group to discuss the nature of the separate links as they were being created, as well as stepping back from time to time to ask about the emerging structure of the overall map. Here, the process of adding and subtracting concepts and rearranging things would occur during the basic construction of the map rather than afterward. If this revision process creates a relatively messy map, then one solution is to redraw a clean version of the map immediately after the session. Also, if the mapping process makes it difficult to include important information about how and why the group created this particular map, then these data can be written up in a separate document or on the back of the map itself. Regardless of how the information is captured, the point is to leave each group with a relatively clean and well-documented map that serves as a source of data about that group's thinking. For example, if the goal is to compare how two different types of participants feel about a particular issue, then systematically working back and forth between the maps from each segment may play a central role in the ultimate analysis strategy.

Another possibility at the level of research design is to use a repeated groups approach, which typically uses the first round of groups to generate relatively clear-cut concept maps and the second round of groups to provide more in-depth reactions to those maps (for one specific and well-developed version of this technique, see Kane & Trochim, 2006). A comparison across segments would also be a useful application for this design, regardless of whether the repeated groups used identical or pooled membership. In this case, each group could discuss the same basic topic and produce a concept map during the first round. Then these maps could all be converted into a similar format for the second round, in which the groups would discuss and compare the full set of maps from the earlier groups. Consider the example of an agency that is considering a new program initiative or policy change. In the first round, several separate groups with agency staff and clients could each use the same set of predetermined concepts to create a map reflecting their thoughts. In the second round, groups composed of those same stakeholders could begin by discussing similarities and differences between the maps from the groups in their own category and then compare those maps with the ones produced by the other stakeholder group. The end result would thus be not only a sense of how each category of participants felt but also a picture of how they reacted to each others' thinking.

Overall, this section has presented a number of options for the basic process of concept mapping. Among those options are: using a hierarchical, directional, or network-based process for constructing the maps; creating the maps as a basis for further discussion or as a key piece of data; and conducting the mapping process in single or repeated sessions. What all of these variations have in common is an emphasis on an active group process that helps the participants visualize and work with their ideas, rather than continuing on the kind of analytical conversation that is currently at the core of most social science focus groups. Although we are certainly not opposed to that sort of analytical and deliberative process, we do believe that concept mapping provides a useful additional option, in terms of producing both an engaging discussion for the participants and a valuable form of data for the research team. Once again, this option makes sense only when it is carefully matched to a set of goals that are well matched to the kinds of data that concept mapping can provide.

Conclusions

Taken together, the three options we have described for conducting focus groups operate at very different levels within the research process as a whole. The use of emergent designs has the largest impact because it includes the potential for changing nearly every aspect of the overall research project. In contrast, using repeated groups provides a specific design alternative that can be considered along with such traditional focus group design issues as whether to segment the group composition, whether to use a more or less structured approach to conducting the group, and so on. Finally, concept mapping presents a specific technique for collecting data within focus groups, which can be used within any of a wide range of research designs for focus groups.

In all three cases, we have emphasized that our point in introducing these new techniques is not to replace more familiar ways of doing things but rather to increase the range of options that are available to focus group researchers. Furthermore, we have provided explicit advice about the most likely uses for these new approaches, because it does little good to broaden the range of options without providing guidance about when those options are most appropriate. At the same time, however, we do not want our "advice" and "guidelines" to be interpreted as rigid rules about what is or is not an appropriate use of these techniques. Instead, we hope that future researchers will develop creative new versions of the ideas we have presented here—with the obvious caveat that those new versions will require clear justifications of the reasons they are preferable to existing approaches for meeting the research goals of the project in question.

This need to rely on past traditions while also pursuing innovative new directions amounts to what the well-known historian of science Thomas Kuhn (1979) called *The Essential Tension* within any field of research. For focus groups, it appears that the glass is less than half full—with a heavy reliance on tradition and noticeably less pursuit of innovation. Although it is encouraging that we do have a solid set of lessons that we have learned from our prior practice with focus groups, we also need to promote more interest in developing emergent approaches that increase our capacities. Hence, one of the goals of this chapter is not just to add a specific set of new options to the existing way of doing focus groups but also to encourage more innovation from other researchers. It is thus fitting to conclude by recalling that only two decades ago focus groups as a whole were still "emerging" within the social sciences, and the success of that effort should be an encouragement to develop a variety of new versions of this method.

References

Bloor, M., Frankland, J., Thomas, M., & Robson, K. (2001). *Focus groups in social research*. Thousand Oaks, CA: Sage.

Burgess, J., Limb, M., & Harrison, C. M. (1988a). Exploring environmental values through the medium of small groups: 1. Theory and practice. *Environment and Planning A, 20*, 309–326.

Burgess, J., Limb, M., & Harrison, C. M. (1988b). Exploring environmental values through the medium of small groups: 2. Illustrations of a group at work. *Environment and Planning A, 20*, 457–476.

Collier, P. (2007, June). *Students first: Improving first generation students' performance and retention in higher education*. Address presented at the Peer Mentoring Initiative and Retention Summit, Minneapolis, MN.

Goldman, A. E. (1962). The group depth interview. *Journal of Marketing, 26*, 61–68.

Kane, M., & Trochim, W. M. (2006). *Concept mapping for planning and evaluation*. Thousand Oaks, CA: Sage.

Krueger, R. A. (1987). *Focus groups: A guide for applied research*. Thousand Oaks, CA: Sage.

Krueger, R. A. (1998). *Developing questions for focus groups*. In D. L. Morgan & R. A. Krueger (Eds.), *The focus group kit* (Vol. 3). Thousand Oaks, CA: Sage.

Krueger, R. A., & Casey, M. A. (2000). *Focus groups: A guide for applied research* (3rd ed.). Thousand Oaks, CA: Sage.

Kuhn, T. (1979). *The essential tension: Selected papers in scientific tradition and change*. Chicago: University of Chicago Press.

Mariampolski, H. (2001). *Qualitative market research: A comprehensive guide*. Thousand Oaks, CA: Sage.

McGregor, A. (2004). Sustainable development and "warm fuzzy feelings": Discourse and nature within Australian environmental imaginaries. *Geoforum, 35*, 593–606.

McGregor, A. (2005). Negotiating nature: Exploring discourse through small group research. *Area, 37*(4), 423–432.

Morgan, D. L. (1987). *Focus groups as qualitative research*. Thousand Oaks, CA: Sage.

Morgan, D. L. (1993). Future directions for focus groups. In D. L. Morgan (Ed.), *Successful focus groups: Advancing the state of the art* (pp. 225–244). Thousand Oaks, CA: Sage.

Morgan, D. L. (1997). *Focus groups as qualitative research* (2nd ed.). Thousand Oaks, CA: Sage.

Morgan, D. L. (2001). Focus group interviews. In J. Gubrium & J. Holstein (Eds.), *The handbook of interview research* (pp. 141–160). Thousand Oaks, CA: Sage.

Morgan, D. L. (2007). Paradigms lost and pragmatism regained: Methodological implication of combining qualitative and quantitative methods. *Journal of Mixed Methods Research, 1*(1) 48–76.

Morgan, D. L. (2008). *Designing for emergence in focus groups*. Manuscript forthcoming.

Morgan, D. L., & Spanish, M. T. (1984). Focus groups: A new tool for qualitative research. *Qualitative Sociology, (7)* 253–270.

Novak, J. D. (1998). *Learning, creating, and using knowledge: Concept maps as facilitative tools in schools and corporations*. Mahwah, NJ: Erlbaum.

Public perspectives: The future of party funding in the UK. (2006). Retrieved April 30, 2007, from *www.ipsos-mori.com/polls/2006/pdf/electoralcommission. pdf*

Puchta, C., & Potter, J. (2004). *Focus group practice*. Thousand Oaks, CA: Sage.

Stewart, D., Shamdasani, P., & Rook, D. (2007). *Focus groups: Theory and practice* (2nd ed.). Thousand Oaks, CA: Sage.

Stewart, K., & Williams, M. (2005). Researching online populations: The use of online focus groups for social research. *Qualitative Research, 5*(4), 395–416.

Williams, M. (2006). *Virtually criminal: Crime, deviance, and regulation online*. New York: Routledge.

CHAPTER 10

Emergent Issues in International Focus Group Discussions

Monique M. Hennink

Although social scientists have used focus group discussions for some time, changes are evident in the application of the method in the past decade. Not only has there been an increase in the use of focus group discussions, but the method is also employed within a wider range of disciplines and applied to more diverse research contexts than in the past. A noticeable change is the increasing application of focus group research in international and cross-cultural research. This broader application of focus group research has raised numerous challenges and issues that require fuller discussion to ensure that the methodological rigor is maintained despite changes in its application. Little has been written of these methodological issues arising in international focus group research in which researchers are unfamiliar with the language or culture of study participants. Much of the methodological literature is quiet about the influence of context and culture on the use of focus group discussions despite the fact that experienced international researchers face similar fieldwork challenges and decisions. Indeed, those experienced in international focus group research often use similar strategies to overcome fieldwork challenges, yet this knowledge remains within a select group. This chapter is based on a recently published book by Hennink (2007) that provides detailed coverage of the application of focus group research in international contexts. The book provides practical guidance on how to navigate the fieldwork decisions and practical challenges while maintaining the methodological rigor of international focus group research. This chapter highlights some of the methodological issues, challenges, and debates that arise when applying focus group research to international and cross-cultural settings.

International research, as discussed in this chapter, refers both to research conducted in another country *and* to cross-cultural research in one's own country. Both of these involve researchers working within an environment in which they are likely unfamiliar with the nuances of language, cultural milieu, and traditions of the study participants. This chapter focuses on four key areas of international focus group research that require additional consideration to the basic methodological requirements because of the international application of the method. The first issue is the need for researchers to recruit and train a field team fluent in the languages of the study population. The second is the management of language and translation issues in developing the discussion guide and in translation and transcription of the group discussions. The third area is adopting appropriate participant recruitment strategies relevant to communities with tightly knit social structures and social networks. The final challenge relates to managing practical aspects of the study context in the application of the method and ensuring that culture is adequately reflected in the outcomes of a focus group study. A brief overview of the focus group method is provided next for background purposes. It is not the intention of this chapter to describe the focus group discussion method in detail, as this is done adequately elsewhere (Bloor, Frankland, Thomas, & Robson, 2001; Fern, 2001; Greenbaum, 2000; Hennink & Diamond, 1999; Krueger & Casey, 2000; Morgan & Krueger, 1993; Ritchie & Lewis, 2003), but to highlight aspects in which the use of the method differs due to its international application.

Overview of Focus Group Discussions

A focus group discussion essentially involves a group of people discussing a specific range of topics. The discussion is facilitated by a trained moderator who encourages participants to share their views and respond to issues highlighted by a research team. Participants share homogeneous characteristics or experiences to facilitate productive interaction. In addition, the group discussion is typically tape-recorded and transcribed to produce research data. Focus group research is defined by Krueger and Casey (2000, p. 5) as follows:

> A focus group study is a carefully planned series of discussions designed to obtain perceptions on a defined area of interest in a permissive, non-threatening environment. Each group is conducted with six to eight people by a skilled interviewer. . . . Group members influence each other by responding to ideas and comments of others.

The discussion element and interaction between participants is a critical part of the method and sets it apart from other types of interview methods in qualitative inquiry. The group-based approach of nondirective interviewing allows the study participants to identify, define, and contextualize issues that are important to them. Furthermore, the group setting fosters an environment in which participants are able to describe, discuss, debate, disagree, and defend their views on the discussion topics. The discussion element is therefore critical not only in collecting diverse views and experiences but also in producing considered responses that are the outcome of group debate, justification, and acknowledgment. The group environment also produces a large quantity of rich data from each discussion.

Focus group discussions are conducted by a skilled moderator whose role is to facilitate the discussion and interaction between participants, to manage the group dynamics, to focus the discussion on the key issues while remaining flexible to new issues, to ensure that information collected is of sufficient depth and diversity to inform the research questions, and to foster a comfortable informal environment that is conducive to valid reliable information. The moderator thus has an important and challenging role. The moderator uses a discussion guide, which acts as a memory aid, to ensure that the key issues are raised during the discussion. Each group discussion should also have a note taker responsible for recording the key issues discussed and noting nonverbal communication that may assist in later interpretation of the data.

Focus group discussions are particularly suitable for exploratory research in which little is known about a research topic, for identifying new or unanticipated issues, and for collecting formative information to develop a survey or a new social program. Focus group discussions are suitable for seeking community-level views concerning social or cultural norms, for instance. However, focus groups are not appropriate for obtaining personal information due to the lack of confidentiality in a group environment. Focus group research is particularly suitable for inclusion in mixed method research designs that combine quantitative and qualitative methods (i.e., population survey and focus groups) or that combine several qualitative methods (i.e., in-depth interviews and focus group discussions) in a single study design. As a qualitative method of inquiry, focus group discussions are not designed to measure the prevalence of views or behavior within a larger population.

Emergent Changes in Focus Group Research

There have clearly been emergent changes in the use of focus group research, most notably over the past decade. Overall, there has been an increase in use of focus group discussions that stems from a broader range of disciplines and researchers who have adopted the method, as well as an increased application of the focus group method in diverse research settings, particularly in international and cross-cultural research. The context, influences, and implications of these changes are described briefly here.

First, the use of focus group discussions has broadened within the health and social sciences. Focus group discussions are now increasingly evident in public health, behavioral sciences, health promotion, evaluation research, health policy, and program planning. Second, focus group research is also being used in a greater variety of other disciplines, such as development studies, business studies, political sciences, and medical research, in addition to its traditional use in market research and social science disciplines.

Another emergent change in focus group research is seen in the increasingly diverse study contexts in which focus groups are used, particularly in international and cross-cultural research. The international application of focus group research is most evident in global health research that focuses on social and behavioral research issues—for example, research on cultural or behavioral aspects of HIV/AIDS in developing country settings, or on cultural norms surrounding breast-feeding within certain cultural settings, or in the development or refocusing of social programs. A further notable change within international focus group research is the broader range of organizations and professionals adopting the method in developing-country contexts. For example, it is now not uncommon for international and local nongovernment organizations, social marketing agencies, or government ministries to conduct focus group research. Finally, with increasing globalization, it appears that many pre- and postdoctoral students are also conducting research projects in international settings and including qualitative components in the study design.

These changed applications of focus group research result partly from developments in the evolution of research within the social sciences, in particular, the greater acceptability of qualitative research methods in recent years and the rise in mixed method research design. The increased use of focus group discussions is undoubtedly a product of the broader acceptability of qualitative research both within and outside academic research. There is now greater recognition of the benefits of qualitative methods in understanding complex social phenomena and an acceptance that some research issues remain unanswerable by quantitative or experimental research approaches. This recognition and acceptance of "alternative" nonquantitative approaches has led not only to an increased use of qualitative research within the health and social sciences but also to a broader application of qualitative methods in other disciplines. It could be argued that focus group discussions have become more appealing to professionals in a broader range of disciplines when compared with in-depth interviews, for example, due to their seemingly straightforward application and promise of large volumes of data. Indeed, the term *focus group discussions* has certainly become more recognized within the general community and in media reporting in recent years. However, the myth of focus group discussion as a "quick and cheap" approach to addressing a research problem still persists.

A second likely influence on the rise of focus group research across diverse disciplines is the more recent emphasis on mixed method research designs (Creswell, 2003; Creswell & Clark, 2007; Tashakkori & Teddlie, 2002). Mixed method study designs may use both qualitative and quantitative methods or combine several qualitative methods to investigate a research issue. This emphasis on mixed methods research has been embraced by researchers themselves and is also encouraged by research-funding bodies and editors of academic journals whose decisions to fund or to publish research studies are reflective of the preference for mixed method approaches. In addition, policymakers who adopt an evidence-based approach to decision making also value and request mixed method research studies. The focus on mixed method research has led to an inevitable increase in focus group discussions as a component of the study design. An additional effect of the rise in mixed method research is the use of focus group discussions among professionals from typically quantitative disciplines (i.e., demography, survey statistics, medicine) who use the method in addition to a survey, experimental design, or other quantitative methods. The net result of these changes in the evolution of social science research has been an increase in focus group research, a greater diversity of disciplines embracing focus group discussions, the exposure of focus group methods to traditionally quantitative disciplines, and the application of focus group research to an increasingly diverse range of study settings.

The application of focus group research to diverse study contexts is a testament to the flexibility of the method. When using focus groups in international and cross-cultural research, some adjustment of the method is often required in order to overcome challenges of the research context. Even though the basic principles of focus group research remain the same, some aspects of the method may be applied differently. Awareness of the different applications, the fieldwork decisions, and the challenges of conducting international focus group discussions is critical for novice researchers in order to retain methodological rigor and scientific validity. The challenge in conducting international focus group discussions is to maintain methodological rigor while remaining flexible in the face of the challenges of the research context: "Good quality focus group research, regardless of the context in which it is conducted, should reflect certain theoretical principles and be based on informed methodological decisions. Too often methodological rigor is overtaken by the management of fieldwork challenges" (Hennink, 2007, p. xvi).

Although the international application of focus group research is not in question, there exists little transparency in *how* the method is applied to international settings. As a result, novice researchers cannot become informed on the challenges, decisions, and strategies adopted by those experienced in international focus group research. Experienced researchers do use common strategies to manage fieldwork challenges; however, much of this experiential knowledge is not published, resulting in little transparency in the conduct of international focus group research. This transparency is fundamental to scientific rigor, as it fosters academic debate on methodological assumptions and consolidates agreement on aspects of the method that cannot be compromised and those that can be applied more flexibly in response to the study context. Currently, much methodological literature is written with an implicit assumption that focus group discussions will be conducted in settings in which the researcher shares the language and culture of the study participants. There is a strong need for researchers to share their experiences and challenges to guide the growing interest in international focus group research. Without clear guidance on the methodological pitfalls of and strategies in addressing these challenges, the quality of focus group research may be diminished despite its growing appeal.

Conducting international focus group discussion requires researchers to remain sensitive to cultural issues throughout the research process. Nevertheless, there are some parts of the research process in which differences in procedure are more notable, such as in the design of the discussion guide, in decisions during the data collection process (e.g., language issues, participant recruitment, group size management, seeking permissions, etc.), and in the acknowledgment of context and culture in data interpretation and reporting. These cultural and cross-cultural issues are discussed subsequently to highlight the specific challenges researchers confront as they embark on conducting international focus group research.

Field Team Training

With the increasing international application of focus group research, the need for training field moderators to conduct group discussions in local languages is paramount. The growing use of focus group discussions in international and cross-cultural settings has emphasized the critical importance of providing training for group moderators; however, strategies for effective in-country training are largely absent from the methodological literature. The need for guidance in training a field team will only increase with the continued growth of focus group research in diverse settings. In addition, researchers, too, often overlook the need for field training and fail to include time and resources for training in a research proposal, timetable, and budget.

Research investigators are typically trained or experienced in the use of qualitative methods but often have little understanding of the language and culture of the study population. As a result, research investigators are often unable to facilitate the group discussions themselves. This may be equally as true in cross-cultural research as in international research. For example, studies among Hispanic communities in the United States highlighted the fact that 70% preferred to speak to researchers in Spanish despite their level of acculturation and knowledge of the English language (Marin & Marin, 1991). Therefore, researchers need to seek appropriate moderators to conduct the group discussions in local languages. A suitable focus group moderator is one who has the language skills to communicate with study participants, has effective interpersonal skills to facilitate a group discussion, and is familiar with the methodological aspects of focus group research. Locating individuals at the study sites with this combination of skills is often a major challenge. Often those with appropriate language skills have limited experience in group facilitation or qualitative methods. In addition, those who do have experience in conducting research are more likely to be familiar with interviewing for a quantitative survey rather than with qualitative interview methods or group facilitation (Hennink, 2007). This mismatch of skills available at the field sites and those required to conduct effective focus group discussions means that providing training is a critical component of international focus group research.

Inexperienced researchers may attempt to use an interpreter through whom to communicate with study participants and conduct a group discussion rather than training a bilingual moderator. Trying to foster an effective group discussion through an interpreter has a negative effect on group dynamics, as the discussion becomes stifled while the interpreter relates each comment and question. The discussion will quickly be reduced to a question-and-answer session rather than a dynamic group discussion.

A focus group team comprises a moderator and a note taker. The goal of training a focus group team is to transfer the research skills of the study investigators to individuals with the linguistic proficiency to communicate with the study participants. Language proficiency is a critical requirement for conducting the group discussions; therefore, it is often the primary recruitment criteria when seeking group moderators. Researchers can then supplement these skills by providing training in focus group facilitation and methodological issues. Individuals with the required languages and interpersonal skills can often be trained to become effective focus group moderators.

In seeking individuals with the required language skills, international researchers often recruit potential moderators from a wide range of professional backgrounds, such as health or education professionals, university staff, students, civil servants, or in-country researchers. Some of these individuals may have previous experience as research consultants. In addition, some research projects may require several moderators, each fluent in different languages or simply with different demographic characteristics to match those of participants (e.g., male and female moderators, older and younger moderators, etc.). The variable research skills, experience, and expectations of these individuals underscores the need for comprehensive training to ensure that all members of the field team understand the focus group method, are trained to the same level of proficiency in group moderation, and have a clear vision of the purpose and expectations of the research project. Training these individuals is essential, as it: "provides the field team with the skills to conduct productive group discussions and to manage situations that may jeopardise the quality of the information collected. Without adequate training the group discussions may produce poor quality, biased or incomplete data" (Hennink, 2007, p. 77).

These training sessions can also be an effective exchange whereby the individuals receive training in group facilitation and at the same time provide valuable input to researchers on the social norms, cultural concepts, and use of colloquial expressions that may affect the conduct of the group discussions (Hennink, 2007).

All members of the focus group team should receive training. This includes the moderator(s), note taker(s), and those who will later translate and transcribe the group discussions. Members of the field team may contribute to several roles. For example, they may moderate one group discussion, become note takers for other group discussions, or translate or transcribe these or other group discussions. It is therefore beneficial to train the entire field team together on the roles and requirements of each task (i.e., moderation, note taking, and transcription) so that roles can be interchanged if necessary during fieldwork. The central figure in a group discussion is the moderator. Training for moderators needs to demonstrate how to effectively manage a group discussion that will elicit relevant, detailed, and sufficiently diverse information in order to adequately address the research issues. Training should also provide skill development in group facilitation strategies, developing rapport, managing group dynamics, and probing techniques. The moderators also need to have a clear understanding of the research objective so that they can focus the discussion on relevant topics and seek detailed information in these areas. In addition, moderators need to be trained in ethical issues, particularly on the protocols for seeking informed consent and maintaining confidentiality. Training for the role of note taker should include instruction on distilling key issues from a fast-paced group discussion, paraphrasing comments, nonjudgmental note taking, recognition of nonverbal signals, and how and when to note relevant colloquial terms and expressions from a discussion. The training should also stress that a note taker's record will become part of the research data. The note taker's role is critical if the recording device fails or if tape recording is refused by participants. In these situations the note taker's summary will be the only record of the discussion, and thus it needs to be clear and sufficiently detailed in order to provide an adequate reconstruction of the issues discussed.

Training should also be provided in the procedures for transcription and translation of the group discussions. Transcribers should be instructed in procedures for developing verbatim or abridged transcriptions of the discussion and whether simultaneous transcription and translation is expected. Clear instruction should be given to transcribers on the required format of transcripts, for example, whether transcriptions should include speaker identifiers, moderator questions, pauses, silences, laughter, interruptions, and so on. Transcribers also need instruction on when to retain colloquial terms or phrases in the original language. A common problem with the transcription of focus group discussion is that transcribers fail to produce a verbatim transcript or misunderstand the level of detail that is required in the transcription. Summary transcriptions, although requested in some research projects, often lose the detail and colloquial language that is evident in a verbatim transcript. Transcribers will also be responsible for translating the discussion into the language of the research investigators. Therefore, they need instruction on whether to simultaneously translate and transcribe the discussion or whether an intermediate transcript in the language of the discussion is needed.

Given the required skills outlined for each member of the focus group team, a training schedule should include the following components: orientation to the research topic, study participants, and study context; overview of key aspects of the focus group method; detailed instruction on the purpose, structure, and questions included in the discussion guide; and the operation of recording devices. Perhaps the most effective training strategy is to conduct mock focus group discussions to enable trainees to experience group facilitation, note taking, and transcription tasks. The first component of the training session should include an orientation on the study topic to highlight key issues and terminology that may be raised in the group discussions. The research objectives should be clearly outlined to enable moderators to focus the discussion on issues of central importance to the research objectives and away from those of marginal relevance. The second component of training should detail the principles of focus group research: "A common problem with trainee moderators is a lack of understanding of the focus group method and how to apply it effectively. Trainers need to clearly distinguish between the approaches for survey interviewing, in-depth interviews and focus group discussions" (Hennink, 2007, p. x).

The third and most lengthy part of the training session will focus on familiarizing trainees with the discussion guide, in particular the structure, question purpose, and phrasing of specific questions. If the discussion guide has been translated into another language, then the question meaning and wording should be reviewed. In some studies the training sessions are used to translate the discussion guide together with the trainees so that the questions reflect the colloquial style appropriate for the study participants. The fourth component of a training schedule, and perhaps the most valuable for skill development, is the inclusion of role-play sessions to enable trainees to experience their roles during a mock focus group discussion while receiving guidance from the research team. Initially, the role-play sessions should be conducted in the language of the research investigators to enable feedback on facilitation skills. Next, a mock group discussion in the actual language of the study participants will enable trainees to become familiar with the delivery of questions and probes. Such role-play sessions are often extremely valuable for building confidence among trainees in group facilitation and the method of interactive data collection through a group discussion. Finally, the training sessions should include a briefing on the study participants and study location and should highlight any issues that may influence the group discussion (e.g., problems of onlookers or noisy locations in outdoor groups). Instruction on the operation of recording devices should also be given. For a more detailed discussion on training field staff, see Hennink (2007), Ulin, Robinson, and Tolley (2005), or Maynard-Tucker (2000).

A comprehensive training schedule often takes between 3 and 5 days to complete. The length and components of the training schedule will be different for each research project, as there is inevitable variation in the basic skills of the field team, the complexity of the research instrument, and the resources available for field training.

Language and Translation

Two inevitable challenges when conducting international focus group research are language and translation. Not only do researchers need to consider the selection of languages to use in the group discussion, identify appropriate translators, and check the accuracy of translations, but they also need to consider how to translate the discussion in a way that preserves cultural nuances and subtle meanings. Although language and translation issues are fundamental to international and cross-cultural research, little common protocol exists concerning how to manage these issues and challenges despite the increase in international focus group research. Some of the decisions and strategies are highlighted here.

One of the first tasks in preparation for international focus group discussions is to identify the most appropriate language(s) in which to conduct the group discussions. If a study is conducted in several regions of the country with different linguistic traditions, it may be possible that several languages will be needed for the group discussions. The primary consideration in selecting appropriate languages for the group discussions should always be to identify the language in which the study participants feel most comfortable to converse. Selecting the most appropriate language(s) for the group discussion will be dependent on the context of the study, in particular whether there is a national language, regional languages, or a national *lingua franca.* For example, in some countries a national language is spoken and understood throughout the country, and the decision about a language for the group discussion is straightforward. However, in other countries, regional languages exist, so a study conducted in different regions of the country would require the discussion guide to be translated into several languages. For example, in Malawi the regional languages of the north and central areas are Timbuka and Chichewa, respectively. In Zambia, some of the regional languages include Bemba, Luvale, Lunda, and Kaonde. Furthermore, some countries have a national *lingua franca*, which is a common language of communication for people from different linguistic regions. This may be the language of a former colonial power (i.e., English, French, Spanish). When considering using the *lingua franca* for the focus group discussions, researchers must consider whether it will be understood by all the study participants, as participants who are uneducated or elderly may not be familiar with a national *lingua franca.*

There are two main tasks that require translation in international focus group research: first, the translations of the discussion guide (which is the list of questions to be used in the focus group discussion) into the language of the study participants; and, second, the translation of the group discussion itself into the language of the research investigators. The translation issues with each of these tasks are discussed here.

It is always recommended to translate the discussion guide into the language in which the group will be conducted (even if moderators are bilingual) rather than expecting a moderator to translate the questions spontaneously during the group discussion. A pretranslated discussion guide is enormously helpful for moderators, as they are able to use question wording that has been carefully prepared by the research team in appropriate colloquial language rather than having to quickly identify comparable local phrases while conducting the group discussion (Hennink, 2007). Use of a translated question guide also introduces some consistency between different moderators in a project.

Researchers need to decide who would be the most appropriate person to translate the discussion guide into the required local languages. It may seem appropriate to seek professional translators to conduct this task; however, the discussion guide should be translated into an informal, conversational style of language and use the level of colloquial language appropriate to the study participants. Professional translators may conduct a more formal translation, use technical language, or not use the colloquial style of language that is desired. Using an inappropriate style of language (e.g., too formal, too technical) can quickly alienate participants by creating an atmosphere that intimidates participant contribution. Professional translations of the discussion guide may also result in a literal translation of the words rather than translating the *meaning* or concept of the question. Instead of using professional translators, it is common practice to seek native speakers of the language(s) required to translate the discussion guide, such as teachers, health workers, university researchers, or other in-country professionals. Using these individuals to conduct the translations often leads to more ordinary, familiar phrasing of the discussion questions. In addition, the use of colloquial phrases can clearly establish the meaning of each question. Using local bilingual individuals to translate the research instrument can also result in valuable input on local nuances, colloquialisms, and common terminology that can enhance the discussion guide. Some terms in the discussion guide may not translate easily into local languages and may require discussion between the research team and those conducting the translation in order to clarify the intent of the question and identify equivalent phrases in the local language. It is critical to test the translated discussion guide to check that the translated questions are interpreted as intended by the study participants and that they elicit the type of information required for the study.

The second area in which translation is required in international focus group research is the translation of the group discussions from the local language into that of the research investigators for data analysis. Translation of the group discussions deserves careful attention because it results in the data for the study, and, if it is incorrect or incomplete, it will affect the data analysis and quality of study findings. As with the translation of the discussion guide, appropriate translators need to be identified. It is common practice to use the same strategy described previously of seeking local bilingual professionals to translate and transcribe the tape-recorded discussions rather than to seek professional translators. These bilingual individuals are not only familiar with local language(s) and able to translate the discussion into the appropriate informal style in which the discussion took place but also, more important, they are best placed to translate the subtleties of cultural expression, which often add enormous meaning to the transcriptions and may be lost in a more formal translation. The challenge in translating the group discussion is to balance the words of participants with the *meaning* of what is said in order to correctly convey the issues discussed in the group. It is also useful to retain, in the translated transcription, specific local terms, particularly those that represent cultural issues or concepts. For example, *purdah* (the segregation of the sexes in Islamic culture) is a recognizable cultural practice, and it is useful to retain this term in the transcription to maintain some of the cultural richness in the transcripts.

All translations should be checked for accuracy. The translated discussion guide should always be checked for cultural appropriateness and accuracy of the translations and to verify whether the translation has captured the meaning of each question or statement. The translated discussions should be checked for completeness and for accurate conveyance of the issues discussed. Often back-translation into the source language is used to check translation accuracy; however, a more appropriate approach to checking translation accuracy is to ensure that the translation has captured the *meaning* or essence of what is said, and this may involve using entirely different words from a literal translation. Checking the meaning of the translated text, as well as the cultural appropriateness, should be done with a local collaborator familiar with the language and context of the study.

Recruitment Challenges and Debates

When conducting international focus group research, the approach to participant recruitment will be influenced by the social structures of the study communities and therefore may require alternative approaches to those described in the methodological literature. In addition, some of the assumptions regarding group composition may be challenged, and researchers may also need to adopt strategies to manage the size of the group discussion. These issues are discussed next.

Participant recruitment for focus group discussions involves the selection of individuals with predefined characteristics. The type of recruitment strategy used will likely differ by the study context. Typically, research in developed countries will rely on technology-based strategies to recruit participants; for example, the use of electronic registers of residents, written invitations, telephone recruitment, or advertisements in print media. These strategies, however, assume the existence of electronic databases, a literate population, and universal telephone access (Hennink, 2007). Many methodological texts discuss only these types of recruitment strategies. However, such technology-based approaches may not be appropriate to international focus group research. Recruiting focus group participants in these contexts often involves utilizing existing social structures and acknowledging the local protocols of working in communities. Participant recruitment is therefore often conducted through an individual familiar with the characteristics of community members, rather than by approaching individuals directly. For example, participant recruitment is typically conducted through local gatekeepers, such as a community leader or chief, who would assist in identifying individuals with the required characteristics for the group discussion. A further distinction in international settings is that verbal recruitment of participants is most common due to low literacy levels in some communities. There is also a very short period of time between recruitment and the conduct of the group discussion. Often recruitment is conducted only 1 day prior to the group discussion, or sometimes even on the same day. This contrasts with more developed settings, in which recruitment is conducted more than a week in advance of the group discussion (Hennink, 2007). These differences in recruitment for international focus group research are not reflected in current texts on focus group discussions. There remains a need to broaden the published literature to include alternative approaches to participant recruitment for studies conducted outside of developed country settings.

A second area of participant recruitment that may differ in international focus group research is the degree of familiarity between focus group participants. One of the debates in the literature of focus group research is whether or not participants should be strangers and how acquaintance influences the dynamics of group discussion. The notion that focus group participants should be strangers to one another is thought to have its origins in market research approaches, which advocates that groups of strangers work most effectively (Morgan & Krueger, 1993). There are certainly numerous benefits in focus group discussions composed of individuals who are strangers. Among strangers, there is increased anonymity and confidentiality, which can lead to more honest contribution to the discussion and a greater level of detail in participants' contributions (Bloor et al., 2001; David & Sutton, 2004). Despite the clear benefits of recruiting a group of strangers, it is particularly challenging in communities with tightly integrated social structures (especially in rural areas) and dense residential environments in urban settings (particularly in urban slum areas). In addition, the methods of participant recruitment used in developed-country settings (e.g., telephone recruitment, electronic registers) may be more conducive to the recruitment of strangers, whereas recruitment strategies employed in developing countries are based on social networks and familiarity within a community (e.g., use of gatekeepers); therefore, the recruitment of strangers is less likely. Nonetheless, the integrated social structures of many communities in developing countries mean that recruiting participants who are truly strangers is extremely difficult. When conducting focus group research in these settings, researchers need to consider whether familiarity between group members will have an impact on the quality of their contributions and decide on the level of familiarity that would be acceptable to the study. For example, researchers may accept that some level of participant familiarity will be inevitable in the research context; however, they may actively minimize the presence of family members, relatives, or neighbors in the same group discussion (Hennink, 2007). One area requiring further investigation is whether familiarity between participants is beneficial for group dynamics. Participants in some cultural settings may feel more comfortable and willing to contribute to the group discussion if they are familiar with other members present (Ulin, Robinson, Tolley, & McNeill, 2002). The issue of familiarity in group composition needs to be given careful consideration and to be discussed with local collaborators who are knowledgeable about the social and cultural norms of the study community.

A further challenge for researchers is that recruitment strategies used in international settings often lead to the attainment of many more participants than is desirable in a group discussion. The recommended size for productive focus group discussion is between 6 and 10 participants; this allows sufficient time for each participant to contribute to the group discussion and enough participants to enable diverse issues and experiences to be identified (Krueger & Casey, 2000). It is advisable to remain within these recommended limits of group size despite the research context. However, in many international contexts, participants are recruited by a community leader who seeks community members with the required characteristics to meet at the study venue. This strategy often results in many more participants arriving at the group venue than are desired. For example, 20 or 30 participants will come when only 8 are needed. Recruited participants may bring friends or relatives; others may have heard that a community meeting is being held or simply join the group out of curiosity. Despite having carefully outlined the number of participants required, researchers may be faced with selecting participants from a large group of individuals. If researchers anticipate this situation occurring, they can prepare appropriate strategies for selecting group participants from the larger crowd without compromising the study quality. A range of strategies for this situation is described in Hennink (2007) and includes using a screening questionnaire to determine eligibility of those present; conducting simultaneous group discussions, if appropriate to the study design; prior selection of participants; and asking an assistant to turn away any participants who arrive after the required number of participants have been accepted.

Context and Culture

The culture of the study population and the context in which focus group discussions are conducted will undoubtedly influence the implementation of the method. The sociocultural context of the research will influence each stage of focus group research, including developing a culturally appropriate discussion guide, seeking appropriate translation of these questions, selecting a bilingual moderator, and obtaining a transcription of the group discussion that retains the cultural context in the expressions of participants. Cultural issues are ubiquitous in international and cross-cultural research; therefore, any outputs of international research need to reflect cultural issues. This is necessary in the description, interpretation, and reporting of international focus group research. In addition, the physical context (or location) in which a group discussion is conducted may need to be improvised once at the study site and may affect the quality of the data collected.

The location in which to hold a focus group discussion will vary by the context in which the research is conducted. Focus group discussions in international settings often improvise the venue once at the study site, for example, by conducting the group discussion in locations such as health facilities, church premises, and the homes of community leaders. At times these venues will not be available or suitable, so it is common practice to conduct focus group discussions in outdoor locations, such as in communal areas, under building verandas, in open areas, or in agricultural fields adjacent to the work sites of participants. In principle, there is no problem with conducting group discussion in outdoor locations provided that the location is quiet, private, and distraction free and that some arrangements are made for seating participants (e.g., chairs, benches, ground cover, etc.). However, there are inevitable compromises when conducting a group discussion outdoors that could affect the group discussion and quality of information collected. Outdoor groups will typically have problems with excessive noise, which will lower the quality of the tape recording. Distractions may affect participant's concentration, and a lack of privacy may affect the group dynamics and participants' willingness to contribute openly to the discussion. Microphones can be very sensitive and in outdoor locations may pick up surrounding sounds, such as people or traffic noise, and it may become difficult to distinguish the voices of community members from those of group participants. This can be particularly problematic during the transcription of the group discussions and will affect the data quality.

A common issue in conducting focus group discussions in outdoor locations is the presence of onlookers. Outdoor groups are particularly visible to community members and often attract the attention of curious onlookers (particularly if foreigners are present), who may observe the activity and listen to the group discussion. Although these onlookers have as much right to be in the communal space as the group participants, their presence reduces the group's privacy, and some participants may not contribute fully to the discussion with onlookers present. Therefore, discouraging onlookers is an important task for the research team. Simple strategies for discouraging onlookers are described in Hennink (2007) and include locating outdoor groups out of sight (e.g., behind a wall, hedge, or building) and away from central community areas; engaging with onlookers to take their attention from the group discussion; asking foreign researchers not to attend the discussion venue; or simply beginning the discussion to demonstrate to onlookers that the issues discussed will be of little interest so that they will leave of their own accord. Should these strategies fail, the presence of onlookers and any noticable effect on the group proceedings should be noted. Despite the difficulties, outdoor locations can be entirely suitable for a focus group discussion provided that researchers address issues of privacy, noise, and distractions. The challenge for the research team is to balance the ideal location with the options available at the study location.

Acknowledging the cultural context in which the research was conducted and providing an interpretation of the study findings through cultural understandings of the issues discussed increases the quality of international focus group research. Culture and context not only should influence the conduct of the research itself but also should be reflected in the report of study findings. Conveying the cultural context of the research provides an important background against which to understand the issues and implications of a study. The cultural context of the study can be reflected in the various parts of the study report. For example, the background section of the study report can provide description of the sociocultural context of the study population. The study results section can use verbatim extracts from study participants, photographs of the study setting, or reports from community stakeholders on the issues raised. Culture and context are most explicitly reflected in the interpretation of the study results and in shaping the policy implications of the study to reflect the economic, social, or cultural realities of the study environment.

Conclusion

This chapter has outlined some of the emergent issues in international focus group research. Table 10.1 highlights a range of key questions for consideration by researchers who plan to use focus group discussions in international and cross-cultural settings.

The broader application of focus group research to international and cross-cultural settings has highlighted a number of emergent issues, as well as challenges and debates. These emergent issues often lead researchers to adopt alternative strategies when conducting focus group research in international settings. Even though experienced researchers adopt common strategies

TABLE 10.1. Key Questions for International Application of Focus Group Discussions

1. Does the question guide reflect the cultural context of the group discussions?
2. Have appropriate local permissions been sought?
3. Who can best translate the question guide for meaning and colloquialisms?
4. Who can best moderate the group discussions in another language?
5. How (where and when) will the group moderators be trained?
6. Which language is most appropriate for group discussions?
7. How can social networks be used to facilitate participant recruitment?
8. Should participants be strangers or acquaintances?
9. How can confidentiality be maintained in group discussions within closely knit communities?
10. What strategies will be employed to manage too-large groups?
11. What types of locations will be available? Are outdoor locations likely to be used for the group discussions?
12. Who can best translate and transcribe the group discussions to maintain context and colloquialisms?
13. How can context and cultural nuances be retained in data analysis, interpretation, and reports?

to meet the challenges of international focus group research, there remains a need for greater transparency in reporting the procedures adopted. Understanding these common practices may prompt greater discussion in academic literature on the need for flexibility in focus group research that does not compromise scientific rigor. Awareness of the different applications of focus group research should also become part of classroom instruction on research methods. This will ensure that novice researchers are aware of appropriate applications of the method to maintain methodological rigor and scientific validity while meeting the challenges of international research contexts.

References

Bloor, M., Frankland, J., Thomas, M., & Robson, K. (2001). *Focus groups in social research.* London: Sage.

Creswell, J. (2003). *Research design: Qualitative, quantitative and mixed method approaches* (2nd ed.). Thousand Oaks, CA: Sage.

Creswell, J., & Clark, V. (2007). *Designing and conducting mixed methods research.* Thousand Oaks, CA: Sage.

David, M., & Sutton, C. (2004). *Social research: The basics.* London: Sage.

Fern, E. (2001). *Advanced focus group research.* Thousand Oaks, CA: Sage.

Greenbaum, T. (2000). *Moderating focus groups: A practical guide for group facilitation.* Thousand Oaks, CA: Sage.

Hennink, M. (2007). *International focus group discussions.* Cambridge, UK: Cambridge University Press.

Hennink, M., & Diamond, I. (1999). Using focus groups in social research. In A. Memnon & R. Bull (Eds.), *Handbook of the psychology of interviewing.* Chichester, UK: Wiley.

Krueger, R., & Casey, M. (2000). *Focus groups: A practical guide for applied research* (3rd ed.). Thousand Oaks, CA: Sage.

Marin, G., & Marin, B. (1991). *Research with Hispanic populations.* Newbury Park, CA: Sage.

Maynard-Tucker, G. (2000). Conducting focus groups in developing countries: Skill training for bi-lingual facilitators. *Qualitative Health Research, 10*(3), 396–410.

Morgan, D., & Krueger, R. (1993). When to use focus groups and why. In D. L. Morgan (Ed.), *Successful focus groups: Advancing the state of the art* (pp. 3–19). Newbury Park, CA: Sage.

Ritchie, J., & Lewis, J. (2003). *Qualitative research practice: A guide for social science students and researchers.* London: Sage.

Tashakkori, A., & Teddlie, C. (Eds.). (2002). *Handbook of mixed methods in social and behavioral research.* Thousand Oaks, CA: Sage.

Ulin, P., Robinson, E., & Tolley, E. (2005). *Qualitative methods in public health: A field guide for applied research.* San Francisco: Jossey-Bass.

Ulin, P., Robinson, E., Tolley, E., & McNeill, E. (2002). *Qualitative methods: A field guide for applied research in sexual and reproductive health.* Research Triangle Park, NC: Family Health International.

CHAPTER 11

Three Dimensions and More

Oral History Beyond the Paradoxes of Method

Michael Frisch

The Problem of Path-Defining Conventions

New ideas and new tools are producing striking departures in our understanding of work in the field of oral history—how it is done, how this process is understood, and to what ends methods are directed.

But before we can talk about emergent methods in oral history, we need to appreciate the structure and power of some conventional understandings of method since the emergence of oral history as a self-conscious "field" in the middle of the 20th century. These conventions continue to characterize oral history despite—and in some provocative ways because of—what seem to be dramatic departures both in intellectual approach and technological capacities, as we have turned the corner and taken off (or descended, as it can sometimes appear) into a rapidly changing 21st-century world.

These conventions and the generally unexamined assumptions on which they rest are best understood less as obstacles on some otherwise clear path, and more as seemingly natural elements defining a complex landscape of practice within which practitioners have learned to move comfortably and for most purposes quite effectively, along the pathways the patterns of convention have created. By understanding the path-defining power of these conventions more explicitly, we will be in a better position to appreciate how their recasting, or even removal, also removes the constraints on method, leaving open a new landscape in which, explored and mapped through practice, new pathways are beginning to emerge.

In this chapter I suggest three broad dimensions of limiting, path-defining convention, each of which embodies a highly consequential element of paradox. One is the paradox involved in how the ground of method is fundamentally conceived—what "doing" oral history has been assumed to involve. The second involves the paradox of orality—the difficulty that oral history has had in confronting, or put more directly its success in ignoring and avoiding, the oral dimension that defines and names the field itself. The third paradox, a more recent development, involves technology: how some new capacities centered on digitization and the Internet have tended to reinforce convention and turn methodological progress back on itself, as much as they have opened it up to new approaches and directions.

The Paradox of Method

The first paradox emerges from a simple observation. Most books, training programs, workshops, manuals, and methodological guides in oral history focus predominantly and in some cases exclusively on interviewing—organizing projects, planning and designing interviews, equipment and techniques for interviewing, interview skills and protocols, and all the related issues surrounding the generation and production of oral history documentation—and its preparation, usually through transcription, for whatever placement or use is to follow.

Because use and interpretation are necessarily context- and inquiry-specific, it has seemed sensible to focus more general training on the common elements of what any oral project must of necessity involve. If interviewing is what it is all about, then it is natural to see interviewing as the central focus of methodology. The attention conventionally accorded to interview transcription methodology is an extension of this focus—this is understood as part of what it means to generate interview documentation that can be readily used.

But relatively little attention is paid to the conditions that support the use of these documents. Though such matters are readily acknowledged as central concerns of the oral historian, methodology for the management, organization, description, and approach to working with the results of interviewing is conventionally seen as a more particular research- and context-driven concern. To the extent to which it involves more general considerations, it is conventionally imagined as something really "done," in terms of methodology, by librarians and archivists.

This interview-production profile may seem to have changed in recent years. It is certainly true that modern primers, guides, and handbooks have a very a different feel than do the narrower "how-to" manuals and workshops of earlier years. They now routinely include complex discussions of memory, narrativity, subjectivity, and dialogic complexity in the interview process itself—in its generalized processual dynamics and in the social and political relationships that construct these dynamics in particular ways. But in a sense such discussion is the exception that proves the rule: These matters are presented as foundational and theoretical, as orienting considerations to inform what we do, how we do it, and what we do with it. But they are not generally seen, or engaged, as fundamental elements of an operational methodology (Baum, 1991, 1995; Baum & Dunaway, 1996; Charlton, Myers, & Sharpless, 2006; Frisch, 1990; Ives, 1995; Hoopes, 1979; Perks & Thomson, 2006; Ritchie, 2003; Yow, 2005).

Now all this seems perfectly appropriate and straightforward—until it is realized how unusual these assumptions are in the context of historical methodology more generally. Methods courses and books in history, for instance, pay some attention to generating a documentary base—to searching, locating, and approaching source materials. But their center of gravity, the center of methodological concern, is in tools, concerns, protocols, caveats, and techniques for how historians work *with* documents. Notice the inversion of the assumptions noted before: in oral history, it is the generation of primary sources that is assumed to be central, with methods for engaging the documents seen as so particular and context- or inquiry-driven as to be hard to treat in anything other than a very broad, introductory way. But in broader historical training it is the reverse: working "with" primary sources is the common dimension shared across contexts and hence more usefully explored for diverse practitioners in greater methodological depth.

"Doing history" has thus seemed, in methodological terms, to revolve around doing something with the primary and secondary sources brought into view, whereas "doing oral history" has had a converse center of gravity in the generation of primary sources, a very different point in the process. I argue presently that the collapse of this distinction into a more unitary and inclusive definition is, for oral history, a central axis of emergent methods in the field. But understanding what has sustained this paradox of methodological centering for so long, and what may be propelling its evaporation now, requires an appreciation of additional paradoxes, of which the paradox of orality is the most expansive and compelling.

The Paradox of Orality

The Deep Dark Secret of oral history is that nobody spends much time listening to or watching recorded and collected interview documents. There has simply been little serious interest in the primary audio or video interviews that literally define the field and that the method is organized to produce. This is not really a secret, of course. On reflection, everyone recognizes that the core audio–video dimension of oral history is notoriously underutilized. The nicely catalogued but rarely consulted shelves of audio- and videocassettes in even the best media and oral history libraries are closer than most archivists want to admit to that shoebox of unviewed home-video cassettes in so many families—precious documentation that is inaccessible and generally unlistened to and unwatched. The content of these collections is rarely organized, much less indexed, in any depth, and the actual audio or video is generally not searchable or browsable in any useful way. As a result, the considerable potential of audio and video documents to support high-impact, vivid, thematic, and analytic engagement with meaningful issues, personalities, and contexts is largely untapped.

We all know, as well, that in most uses of oral history the shift from voice to text is extensive and controlling. Oral history source materials have generally been approached, used, and represented through expensive and cumbersome transcription into text. Even when the enormous flattening of meaning inherent in text reduction is recognized, transcription has seemed quite literally essential—not only inevitable but also something close to "natural." The assumption in this near-universal practice is that only in text can the material be efficiently and effectively engaged—text is easier to read, scan, browse, search and research, publish, display, and distribute. Audio or video documents, in contrast, inevitably have to be experienced in "real time." Even when there are guides, finding aids, indexes, or descriptions of the actual video or audio, these are likely to be in text that is disconnected from and not easily linked to the actual media, and particular points and passages are cumbersome to locate for auditing or viewing.

The basic point could not be simpler: There are worlds of meaning that lie beyond words, and nobody pretends for a moment that the transcript is in any real sense a better representation of an interview than the voice itself. Meaning is carried and expressed in context and setting, in gesture, in tone, in body language, in pauses, in performed skills and movements. To the extent to which we are restricted to text and transcription, we will never locate such moments and meaning, much less have the chance to study, reflect on, learn from, and share them.

But we have, for decades if not centuries, operated under the sometimes explicit, sometimes implicit, sometimes simply unexamined assumption that the gains from transformation into text—in everything from analytical access to ease of casual use and broader public sharing—are worth the price of lost meaning and texture rendered inaccessible. This assumption proceeds from the core assumption that oral and film or video documents are next to impossible to work with as a dimension of oral history practice, especially when they involve extensive collections and broader groups of imagined users interested in the material.

As a result, the paradox of orality takes two forms that both reinforce and are reinforced by the primacy of interview generation already discussed: Methodological treatments generally engage audio and video as such only at the level of collecting, including constantly updated discussions of digitization and new recording modalities, the choice between audio and video, and tools to assist transcription, whether involving mechanical aids or the lure of voice-recognition software. And there is usually discussion as well of the archival and preservation implications of choices in recording technology and storage media. But relatively little attention has been given to the implications of these developments for what happens next—to "doing" historical work with oral history documents. The orality of oral history, that is, and its broader, literal embodiment via video recording, remain generally unreachable in conventional approaches to oral history method.

The Paradox of Searching

Before turning to exploring how technologies for working with audio and video documentation erode the foundation on which this situation rests, we need to consider a final dimension of paradox in which technology has had in some ways the opposite effect—supporting and reinforcing the most conventional assumptions about the text-based interview transcript as the fundamental destination of oral history method. Here I refer to the immense and readily accessible power to search and navigate through text documents once they have been digitally rendered through word processing or scanning. Anyone can now explore easily the thousands of pages of transcripts in even a modest oral history collection. With increasingly common access to document files via the Internet, it is no harder to instantly search millions of pages across interviews and collections on a national and international level.

There is much to be said about the power of text-search tools for historical work, though like any tools these can be misused easily. Every teacher is familiar with the novice student who reports "I found the five references to such and such a topic" and the delicacy of helping such a student to understand that it is simply "five references" that have been found, it being in no way clear whether they represent the elephant's tail, its ear, or the whole animal. The stunning power of Google and other search engines only magnifies this problem, because the better the engines are and the more well trained we are at using them, the more likely it is that just about any quick search will yield *some* useful results—but this may be a far cry from a really adequate research exploration of what is available. And when the objects of searches are words or strings of words found across the transcripts housed in oral history collections, the dilemmas of search-engine reliance are in many ways compounded.

As a consequence, there is considerable concern among teachers and librarians that the contemporary search tools are producing a significant decline in research skills—the ability to work carefully, patiently, and skillfully with various levels of reference materials and all the tools they provide to explore a body of documentation at a level ensuring that needed information and ideas are not being overlooked. In the search-engine world it is simply too seductively easy to snag something on the run rather than to learn the skill of angling for it with just the right fly or lure suited to the setting, the conditions, and the object sought. In this sense, then, otherwise exciting and immensely useful technology still constitutes a formidable challenge that method must overcome.

Oral History and the Wobbly Stool

The focus on producing interviews rather than exploring them, the naturalized reliance on text over orality, and the deceptive power of digital searches of transcription—I suggest that these three limiting paradoxes in conventional oral history method are connected and mutually reinforcing to a very powerful extent. But by virtue of this very interdependency, the complex may be not nearly as solid as it has seemed: The loosening of any leg has the potential to render the whole stool unstable.

And in contemporary oral history practice, the wobble is indeed becoming very pronounced, owing especially to the loosening of the second and third legs of the stool I have described. New digital tools are offering powerful alternatives to the text-based linear search-engine approach to exploring information, and they are offering as well alternatives to text reliance itself based on new capacities to work directly with orality—with audio and video documentation as the primary source of oral history. And as these two legs of the stool take on new form, the third leg—the very locus and definition of oral history method—has to change as well if the three are to settle into a stable new form.

This is exactly what I think is starting to happen in oral history. And we can begin to appreciate it—to appreciate oral history's variation on the theme of emerging methods that this volume is surveying—by exploring some of the changes in audio and video documentation, new technologies for mapping and navigating it, and the intellectual implications of this combination for oral historical work.

Exploring Oral History Primary Sources as a Dimension of Method

Let me emphasize at the outset that I am not speaking here of presenting or displaying audio or video clips or excerpts from oral history interviews. Documentary has been doing this for quite a long time now, and it has come to seem as natural and inevitable as a destination for oral history in its audio or video primacy as the interview text transcript to which it is a kind of representational opposite. More recently, both the tools and the capacity to make, circulate, and instantly consume such media extracts—whether in elaborate documentary compositions, loops in exhibit kiosks, or fragmented clips posted to and downloaded from the Internet—have become so excitingly accessible as to transform this approach into a genuine media revolution whose implications are just beginning to be appreciated. Podcast Nation is a long way from the Cinémathèque Documentaire or Ken Burns and *The American Experience*.

I have more to say about this near the end of the chapter, but for now it will suffice simply to distinguish documentary presentation from oral history method as such. Documentary, old or new, involves what we can do "with" the selections from the primary sources that oral history creates. In contrast, the digital tools and approaches I discuss here, though obviously not irrelevant to documentary, center more on the prior process of defining, locating, and extracting such materials in the first place from the vast body of recorded oral history documentation. My argument is that these new capacities for working with primary sources imply and are beginning to propel a substantial reorientation in what it means to "do" oral history, which is to say, a considerably broadened conception of oral history method as such. Advancing this argument requires first some familiarity with the landscape in which all this is happening.

Navigating Audio–Video Communication

The digital revolution has two simple but profound ground-level implications. First, digitization means that in crucial respects all information can be considered the same. In digital form, there is simply no difference between text, photographs, drawings and models, music, speech, and visual information: All can be expressed as digital information that can be organized, searched, extracted, and integrated with equal facility. And, second, as every user of a CD or DVD knows, digitization means that any point in the data can be accessed instantly; one can move from point to point anywhere in the data without having to scroll or play forward or backward through the documentation in a linear way, as with tapes.

Both ideas are central to how digital technologies open new ways to work directly and easily with audio and video documents in their primary form. Oral history audio and video can now be placed in an environment in which specific passages of audio and video content can be linked to and reached via transcripts or, alternatively or in combination, various modes of annotation, cross-referencing tags, and other descriptive or analytical "meta-data." Interview passages are most often referenced through lexical content, but this is hardly a necessary condition; in many digital modes, it is as easy to tag and access passages for nonlexical content or qualities, whether these involve performance, context, or simply the palpable reality of affect through voice, tone, expression, body language, and the like.

By means of these reference tools, the audio–video materials themselves can be searched, sorted, browsed, accessed, studied, and selected for use at a high level of specificity. Indeed, with many of the emerging tools, users and researchers themselves can mark, assess, analyze, select, and export meaningful audio and video passages for a range of customized research, presentational, and pedagogical uses. On this software frontier, audio and video documentation becomes as richly and easily accessible as a well-organized text-based reference book and potentially far more easily usable.

Broadly speaking, the challenges in searching and exploring audio–video digital materials are less technical than they are intellectual and even philosophical. Technically, the objective is straightforward, though there are many evolving and competing ways of addressing it. Essentially, digital audio or video carries precise time stamps that mark the audio or video stream, like markers on a highway. Passages can be defined by identifying start and stop time codes for a particular passage or segment or even a word in a digital file, and a program can then go to and play such passages simply by locating the file and playing from start point to stop. When particular identifiers or combinations of identifiers have been associated with points in the data stream, the program can use these as filters for searching the audio–video content in order to instantly locate and play the audio or video passages associated with those reference terms, whether these be subject headings, cross-reference codes, or words in a transcript.

The real test of these tools is the ability to bring the user to relevant material and to permit this material to be explored efficiently and used easily. The analogy of a well-indexed reference book is helpful, but it is also somewhat deceptive, because whatever the mode of access, audio and video are inherently less skimmable than a page of text; content has to be experienced more or less in real time. And this raises the bar on meaningful access: A search leading to 35 passages, each between 2 and 4 minutes long, risks being impractical unless there are ways for the researcher to determine which ones are really worth the time it will take to review them. The underlying challenge of audio–video access is thus the organization and practicality of the cross-referencing and how this is connected to precise passages in the audio or video documentation—how the optimal qualities of access are defined and refined, and then how these can best be served by software tools.

Approaches to meeting this challenge are many and varied, with many choices driven initially by scale and volume. The most dramatic and comprehensive approaches to working with oral history audio–video deal with very large collections and seek to make them accessible at a meaningful level to the widest extent possible, increasingly through website access. Perhaps the most well known and most instructive example is the Survivors of the Shoah Visual History Foundation, the massive Holocaust-survivor oral history project initiated by film director Stephen Spielberg (*www.vhf.org*). Confronting a body of documentation amounting to hundreds of thousands of hours, the Foundation has invested very extensively in technologies for organizing and navigating a colossal, multilanguage archive. Its website offers rich insights into what it has done and how and the many ways in which this material is now open for exploration and use, much of it in video form.

Other illustrative award-winning large-scale projects include The Virtual Oral/Aural History Archive at California State University, Long Beach (*salticid.nmc.csulb.edu/cgi-bin/WebObjects/OralAural.woa*), led by Sherna Berger Gluck, in which extensive audio interviews have been put on line in a uniquely interactive, highly searchable format, and the Kentucky Historical Society's Kentucky Oral History Commission (*history.ky.gov/Programs/KOHC/index.htm*), recipient of a major Oral History Association award for its path-breaking approach to turning a broad archival collection into an explorable online resource.

A different kind of digital resource is the imposing Alexander Street Press project Oral History Online (*alexanderstreetpress.com/products/orhi.htm*), offering a huge cross-collection union catalogue of oral histories internationally, which even in its early form includes capacities to locate and access a considerable amount of audio documentation.

At the other end of this spectrum are tools for working closely with more discrete collections, by individual or team researchers, community projects, and the like. Here the interest is less likely to be in wholesale Web access for open-ended exploration and more likely to involve user-driven hands-on engagement with particular bodies of material, often for very particular purposes.

The work I have been doing via the Randforce Associates (*www.randforce.com*) stands closer to this pole. Using Interclipper (*www.interclipper.com*), software developed initially for focus group recording and analysis in the market research industry, one of our small-scale projects, for example, involves a collection of African American childhood stories being cross-referenced for use in community and classroom settings. Another is a law school alumni association's oral history project seeking to document educational and legal change, as well as to develop a "memory bank" useful in alumni relations and fund-raising. A third involves qualitative analysis of a discrete collection of intensive interviews conducted for a social science project assessing group dynamics. All of these examples involve discrete collections that require annotation and cross-referencing tailored to specific project content, needs, and intended uses.

Scale tends to drive choices in tools and approach, as well. The larger and more diverse the collection, the more overwhelming and complex the task of cross-referencing, annotation, and indexing becomes. Large archival projects, accordingly, have tended to rely on approaches that can be standardized—through controlled vocabulary thesauri and standardized subject headings—to the greatest extent possible. Their finding and navigation tools have tended to rely on full-text searches of preexisting transcripts, which then lead directly, via embedded time codes, to interview segments represented by audio or video files.

Many have been experimenting with various forms of automated markup and referencing by which artificial intelligence (AI) can process immense volumes of material, modeling the thought process of researchers so as to narrow dramatically the counter-productively large number of "hits" that cruder word or term searches tend to produce, even when refined through Boolean query combinations familiar to search-engine users. Such AI approaches are also increasingly significant in video work, in which vast bodies of material can be automatically organized by tagging schemes, some of which feature more sophisticated analysis of visual qualities such as shot changes, and are rendered searchable by global positioning system (GPS) location, face recognition, or other visual content tags.

There have been relatively fewer oral history applications of tools from what is known in the business, media, and governmental world as "digital asset management." But the implications and potential uses of techniques developing there are substantial. The large-volume video analysis offered by Streamsage software (*www.streamsage.com/index.htm*) is one good example; another is the Informedia Project at Carnegie Mellon University (*www.informedia.cs.cmu.edu*). In fact, the History Makers (*www.thehistorymakers.com*), an ambitious Chicago-based project documenting African American culture and history and our partner in the focused childhood story project noted earlier, is working with Carnegie Mellon's Informedia to build an accessible video archive of many thousands of hours of video life history interviews collected to date, with 1,200 hours already indexed in a recently completed prototype.

Tools for smaller scale work tend to share the characteristics of qualitative analysis approaches familiar in the social sciences. Well-known software such as N6 (formerly NUD*IST) (*www.qsr.com.au/products/productoverview/product_overview.htm*) and Ethnograph (*www.qualisresearch.com*) have for some time provided sophisticated software for mapping complex interview or other data by marking text with a range of researcher-driven observational, thematic, or categorical organizers, flexible and capacious database tools for helping meet age-old researcher needs to organize, sort, and rearrange information, whether reading notes or more structured research data. The Interclipper software I have been working with is one of the first tools to permit this kind of qualitative analysis of video and audio directly. It allows us to note and cross-reference—as easily as we cross-reference the place, names, or explicit content of a story—the emotional intensity, body language, thematic meaning, or pedagogical uses observable by watching the video of a narrator telling that story.

These descriptions of scale imply somewhat more general dimensions of approach that are worth clarifying as relatively independent variables, as they are found to varying degrees and combinations even in similarly scaled projects. Current and emerging approaches to mapping and accessing audio or video documentation can be helpfully organized—as on a literal map—as choices arrayed along four intersecting axes or dimensions, which singly and in combination have significant methodological implications.

The Cataloguing versus Indexing Axis

Drawing on a comfortably old-fashioned library frame of reference, a first dimension can be said to revolve around an axis with cataloguing at one end and indexing at the other. Traditionally, the purpose of a catalogue is to help you find a needed or relevant book, and the purpose of an index is to help locate content of interest within that book once you have found it. These are very different functions, but modern information tools are changing each and consequently narrowing the distance between them, opening up an intriguing middle ground.

No longer limited to the author plus one or two Library of Congress subject-heading cards that could lead to a book referenced in traditional card catalogues, digital catalogues can reach more deeply into the content of books, identifying sources through multiple search tags and varied combinations among tags, where there is material of interest even when this is not likely to be identified by the book's major subject-headings. Such catalogues offer greater power for describing materials precisely and in many diverse ways, and hence they vastly amplify meaningful access. In doing this, however, such descriptors still necessarily tend to be relatively general subject headings and do not necessarily identify or connect to specific passages.

Indexes have always been different in this respect. For hundreds of years, indexing has offered flexible tools for identifying very precise content, and dimensions of meaning or abstract theme as well, with no privileging or narrowing of opportunities in the process; when the index of a book directs readers to page 312, they have access to the full text surrounding the identified point or passage.

The traditional book index, in this sense, is less a restrictive filter or funnel than it is a kind of hypertextual alternative to linear reading, a way to explore the book in whole or part, driven by interest and inquiry rather than by the linear sequence of presentation. Indexes offer a way to follow themes or threads as they weave through the volume as a whole. In confronting demanding academic or scholarly books, I have told my students for years, it is always a good idea to study the index, which can be seen as offering a quickly apprehended schematic overview of the book's central concerns and approach. These concerns and approach are made particularly vivid in the way master idea headings jump out at the reader via the long indented lists of references and subreferences that only such headings (and not others less central to the argument or content) command.

Digitization is transforming the power of a traditional index as significantly as it is transforming subject-heading cataloguing in that various terms and dimensions of terms can be so easily combined in any order to filter and search the contents. Additionally, in digital realms there is no inherent barrier to extending the concept of indexing from one book to a shelf of related books or more, though this capacity to date has been deployed more commonly in the mode of full-text searches than in the richer, more complex mode of content indexing as such.

In electronic form, such approaches become more and more powerful, as if the entire book or group of books were being re-indexed on demand, with its content displayed and organized through the lens of any combination of index terms. The ease of manipulation and navigation and the analytical capacity these confer are reasons why contemporary information tools have so dramatically advanced the power of fluid, relational approaches to information, as this means that the same content can easily be explored from a variety of contrasting directions.

All of these considerations characterize emerging approaches to working with oral histories, most of which are located somewhere on the broad middle ground that blends indexing and cataloguing, a zone very much supported by new information tools and capacities. The contours of this ground and their implications for method become clearer when we consider this mapping in some other distinct dimensions of practice.

The Content- versus Meaning-Mapping Axis

The shift of emphasis from cataloguing to richer indexing suggests another dimensional axis for emerging practice: the distinction between content-driven mapping and exploration and what might be called meaning-driven, analysis-driven, or inquiry-driven mapping and exploration.

Many archivists and librarians have traditionally assumed this distinction to be central and controlling. It is the job of archivists to map content broadly, mainly by focusing on whole units, such as collections or perhaps specific interviews, rather than particular passages within documents. Archivists have generally been reluctant to privilege any particular approach to meaning or inquiry, much less to incorporate it in their taxonomies. In a recent discussion on the H-Oral electronic oral history discussion forum, for example, an American archivist termed anything other than collection- or interview-level indexing to be "ethically problematic":

> As an archivist it's not my job to create new meaning, it is just to try to stabilize the meaning of a recording or document in relation to the larger grouping from which it comes–to maintain it as best as possible within the intellectual context of its creation and use. Making new meaning is the job of a researcher using the materials. (Kolovos, 2004)

This is an understandable posture in traditional archiving, but its limitations in dealing with oral history audio and video are manifest because, as noted earlier, without being able to get closer to passages of interest, researchers simply will not be able to explore primary documentation given the time demanded by listening to or viewing recordings. This is exactly why most audio and video archives are so underutilized.

But the concept of referencing dimensions other than literal content is in no way a new or exotic one driven by media technology; indeed, it lies at the core of the most traditional indexing, as our previous discussion has suggested. When compared with the often unexamined assumptions that inform reliance on the search engines and key words at the center of contemporary approaches to information, traditional indexing offers some instructive insights.

Most obviously, indexes are not limited to nominal terms or to explicit words or locutions but can assign consistent terms that will group references to an event or place or person, whatever the explicit term of reference may have been. For instance, interviewees are unlikely always to refer to a particular strike by a consistent name, or by any name at all, when they are recalling anecdotes associated with it. But an indexer has no problem gathering these under one umbrella to which those looking for alternative terms can easily be directed, rendering the index a far more subtle and flexible tool than a word search alone.

Indexes also can and do include referencing of anything worth noting, from explicit nominal references to broader umbrella ideas to abstract themes. As such an index is maximally responsive to a user or researcher's approach to analysis, in which particular avenues of inquiry not reducible to content alone are often likely to be the basis of cross-sectional searching and navigation. People in interviews do not say "And now I will tell a story about gender relations in farm work." They just tell a story, which an indexer can reference under whatever headings seem appropriate–social relations, tools and technology, the business of farming, and so forth–so that a researcher interested in any of these will likely find their way to the story.

The distinction between content mapping and meaning mapping may have specific relevance to the promise of oral history in that personal narratives are the ground informing broader reflection and analysis of everything from specific historical contexts to the dynamics of life course and personality to the workings of memory and narrativity.

So this relationship between content and meanings–and how it is embodied both in the design of exploratory tools and in their use in oral history practice–is worth noticing as a second dimension around which various emerging approaches to audio and video access can be arrayed.

The Text versus Audio–Video Axis

A third dimension springs from the recognition that text transcriptions, even when not the "end," remain very important and useful as a practical means for accessing the audio or video stream efficiently. In many cases, of course, they are already available as resources once it is determined to bring the original audio or video into use more actively. In others, it has generally been felt that transcripts and powerful word searches, for all their limits, provide the most efficient tools for moving around in media if they can be linked to the audio or video.

In many of the leading oral history projects and archives managing digital audio–video collections, this has been the predominant approach: general reliance on text as the route to more specific passages of audio and video data through embedded time-coded links between transcription and particular portions of videos. Word-based searches speak to some of the archivists' concerns in that they remain content-based, rather than being driven by researcher-imposed themes, inquiries, or categories. And increasingly sophisticated word search tools move beyond the overly literal clumping of "hits" and search "false positives"; context and proximity controls, for example, can help distinguish a search interested in *bomb* and *airplane* from one focused on *bomb* and *Broadway*.

But the limits of this approach are clearly the inverse of its strengths, which is why many approaches, including a number of those referenced previously, have been seeking to transcend the limits of text for reaching dimensions of meaning or cross-referencing not explicit in the words of an interview, not to mention the potentially even broader range of content and meaning that is simply not lexical in any way.

In this regard, the degree and form of text reliance in searching and organizing represents a third axis useful for organizing emerging approaches. At one end is near-total reliance on text, with all searches based on the words in transcripts synchronized seamlessly to the audio or video stream. At the other end is a near-total dispensing with transcription as unnecessary and unhelpful, in contrast to searching or navigation based on descriptive and analytic cross-referencing not mediated through interview transcripts. Most approaches are coming to be located somewhere in between these poles, with various combinations of transcript-based and transcript-independent cross-referencing.

The Linear versus Multidimensional Axis

All of these considerations imply a final dimension by which emerging practices can be organized, though in a sense it offers a kind of summary axis consolidating the implications of the other spectra of variation I have surveyed.

Imagine a spectrum at one end of which is the essentially linear, funnel-like nature of search-engine queries, in which all possible references are treated similarly and the search is narrowed or particularized by restrictive or inclusive combinations that can zoom in on a more and more manageable group of "hits." At the other end of the spectrum is the multidimensional or multifield approach of a database, in which any piece of data can be identified in an unlimited number of discrete fields for each of which a taxonomy of choices can be offered.

A neighborhood, for instance, can be identified as having a particular ethnic composition, a particular socioeconomic status, an architectural character, a density level, or a value of whatever variable might be of interest; it is the same neighborhood, but it can be identified in terms of its particular value in any of these variable fields. What can seem new and intimidating when such terms as *relational database* are used has actually been quite familiar for a long time in commonsense usage. A cookbook might have a recipe for a Greek lamb stew indexed by ethnic origin; by type of dish, stew; and by both the general term *meat* and the specific, *lamb*–the variables are completely independent, and the book can be explored by initiating searches through any of them, in any order, which reveals how they are related and combined in the attributes of each recipe.

Such notions apply to meaning mapping as well: In our childhood story project, for instance, a single anecdote related in an interview might be located by searching choices in a content field (say, the journey north), in a typology of biographical stories (say, leaving home or conflict with parents), or by a searching a menu of broader historical or cultural topics (say, the Great Migration). And unlike random searches that might combine such explicit terms, in these modes a richer exploration is possible—for instance, we could select all stories about conflict with parents, subsorted by historical topic, or, alternatively, we could select all stories about the Great Migration subsorted by biographical theme. Either route would lead to our selected combination—leaving the South, conflict with parents, and the Great Migration—but in getting there we would also have a chance to discover and explore a wide range of combinations that we might never have thought to look for.

Mapping Current and Emerging Approaches

Taken together, our map of emergent approaches to working with audio–video materials involves four overlapping, interrelated, but conceptually and operationally distinct dimensions, or axes: (1) from cataloguing to indexing, (2) from content referencing to meaning or qualitative-analysis referencing, (3) from text-transcript-based audio or video access to direct or observational cross-referencing of audio or video as such, and (4) from one-dimensional descriptions of a unit of data to a multidimensional, multifield approach to data mapping.

I think it can safely be said that these distinctions are all very much in motion. Much of the "action" in current software development for oral history involves seeking various ways in which the capacities of every approach can be combined and more effectively mobilized for working with the audio–video documentation that is at the heart of all oral history.

And what all of these approaches have in common, what defines the current and prospective development of the field in this regard, is that one way or the other, from large-scale archive to small community projects to home and family collections, it is going to be more and more feasible to hear, see, browse, search, study, refine, select, export, and make use of audio and video extracts from oral histories directly through engaging the primary documentation itself. In the future rapidly unfolding, this mode, rather than piles or even digital files of text transcription, will become the primary, preferred way to explore and use oral history. And that returns us to the problem with which this chapter began: the implications for method, operationally and conceptually, that flow from "putting the oral back in oral history," from this profound reorientation to the core orality, voice, and embodiment found in oral history documents.

Toward Broadened Conceptions of Oral History Method

At the current moment, many leading approaches to digital oral history collections in general and to accessing their audio and video content in particular remain closer to the first-mentioned end of each of these dimensions: They are closer to cataloguing than to indexing, they are more oriented to content mapping than to meaning mapping, they are generally more reliant on transcript-driven searches than on nontranscript or observational referencing, and they seem more comfortable with and rely more on linear searches rather than relational database approaches to organization and navigation. These preferences are driven to a certain degree by scale, to an additional degree by the archival and library collection–management auspices of most of these projects, and to some extent as well by the state of current technology. But in oral history, they are driven perhaps more than anything else by cultural assumptions about research and practice that are not changing nearly as fast as are the tools that alter our relationship to audio and video data.

The challenge is much broader than oral history, of course. Changes in our relationship to audio and video in the broadest sense are manifest wherever one turns in a media–Internet culture recently drunk on the excitement of new capacities to access and manipulate audio and video. We engage a world of media at the click of a mouse. Cell phones, TVs, computers, and MP3 players are in the process of becoming more or less the same thing in terms of circulating and delivering media. And, as a consequence, it is coming to seem that we confront the danger of drowning in an ocean of data—or, which is also more or less the same thing, falling into the most glancing relationship to complex content through the superficial, instant-gratification consumption of brief clips in blogs or YouTube and the like.

Once the excitement of this unlimited capacity to immerse ourselves in media peaks, I believe that developing better ways of organizing and navigating content meaningfully will move to the center of attention, and not just in the mass-access world Google has created and will continue to dominate. Closer to home, the increasingly manifest need will be for customized approaches that more systematically and meaningfully combine mapping, exploration, and use in ways that respond to more particular needs and purposes.

For oral history, I believe that the most promising direction in this respect, the direction that emergent methods have both the need and capacity to develop, will be toward the opposite pole of each of the axes I have described: toward complex indexing, toward the mapping of meanings as well as content, toward alternatives to transcript word searches, and, especially, toward multidimensional or multifield cross-referencing in something closer to a relational database framework.

But oral historians are simply not yet comfortable thinking of their work in these terms, perhaps because of the field's grounding in traditional archiving at the one end and documentary production at the other, a point to which I return presently. And change will not be easy. Aside from the daunting technical, financial, and organizational demands of new approaches to collection management, and aside from the ways in which the appeal of inertia is actually increased rather than diminished by the intimidating scale of the challenge, I believe that moving in this direction requires a deeper cultural and intellectual reorientation in the way oral historians define the nature of their work—broadening the conception of method beyond its focus on interviewing, the point with which this chapter began.

Here again, the challenge is certainly more intellectual and cultural, in a disciplinary sense, than it is technological. And to a surprisingly encouraging degree, greater interdisciplinary experience and communication may do more than new tools alone to facilitate less inhibited movement in new directions for historians.

For the truth will be readily apparent to readers of this volume in a way less likely to be the case for an oral history audience; the notions I have advanced are close to commonplace and self-evident in other fields, particularly the social sciences and the qualitative-analysis methodologies developed there. The "other end" of the axes I have described, a direction in which I think oral historians will be moving, is the territory that has been most attractive in software development focused on researcher or user-driven qualitative analysis, or outside oral history in fields such as digital asset management or market research, as illustrated by some of the examples from my own practice previously discussed.

Social scientists are fully comfortable with the notion that the significance in data is not explicit or nominal, something to be navigated via the transcript, but rather something identified in response to an inquiry and then coded for sorting and analysis as such. A social psychologist documenting and studying conflict in a playground may not need or want to know whether the kids began fighting over a pail or a ball. The project is more likely to be concerned with developing and applying a typology of conflict-initiating behaviors, and its coders are trained to apply this typology consistently to categorize a body of video documentation so it can be studied meaningfully.

In my own interdisciplinary practice, it has been striking to me how unnatural such an approach feels to historians. Our work with oral history digital indexing frequently involves helping clients develop cross-referencing taxonomies for their projects. We know the syntax and capacities of the software we use and protocols for deploying it efficiently. But the clients know their material and its intended uses. Bringing these together—which the clients generally expect will be a matter of technological training and tool acquisition—more generally turns out to be something closer to a good graduate seminar.

The basic concept is easily conveyed and understood, often through the cookbook metaphor introduced earlier: A given recipe may be Chinese, made of tofu, and very spicy. These are not either–or choices of descriptor but rather dimensions of the same thing. And there could be many additional independent dimensions (cooking time, nutritional value, presence or absence of nuts or other allergens) with which any individual recipe could be described and within which choices for organizing a cookbook database of 10,000 recipes could be organized.

But what does this mean for the anecdotes in a story? For a given project, if every passage of interest could be mapped in at least three independent domains (our software offers three fields with codes assigned from drop-down controlled vocabulary menus), then what *are* those dimensions? What are the independent dimensions of historical meaning and reference for the project that are equivalent to our cookbook's ethnicity (item: Chinese), composition (item: vegetarian/tofu), and spiciness (item: very hot)? And for each dimension identified, what is the project-specific optimal granularity for mapping that dimension: Is Chinese–French–Italian sufficient, or should it be broken down, for example, to Mandarin, Hunan, Cantonese, and so forth?

In doing this work, we are discovering how exciting it is to think about interviews in this way—to experiment with different kinds of lenses, at different refractions, all of which reveal the material in distinctly different ways, and to then think about how these can be combined and manipulated to permit navigation and use in wonderfully expanded and fluid ways.

And so what began as an interest in particular tools for working with audio and video documentation directly, something previously unreachable, is evolving through practice into a fascination with the intellectual implications of this altered relationship to content—what it means to routinely approach historical testimony and narrative as inherently three-dimensional or more, an approach that, beyond offering new modes of exploration, permits new insights for questioning and interpreting what is being explored.

Toward a Postdocumentary Sensibility

Let me draw some of these ideas together by considering their implications not only for collection management, research, and scholarship but also for production, shifting focus at the end of this chapter to documentary, broadly considered, which is so often the "end" product of oral history in terms of public representation. Having noted at the outset that this also seemed outside the realm of a methodology focused on interviewing, I want to note here a powerful closing irony of sorts: that moving to a more multidimensional view of method permits the concept as a whole to become more unitary and encompassing, applicable to work in oral history from the initial interview to its final distillation and representation. The kind of general reorientation in method that I am advancing stands out in even sharper relief when considered against the backdrop of conventional assumptions about documentary.

Between Raw and Cooked

Documentary has been the mode in which oral history has most generally, and usefully, been mobilized for communicative, historical, and political purposes. And it has been in effect the long-standing solution of choice to the problem I have identified here. It has been the main resource for engaging and presenting those realms of meaning found in oral and embodied performance, the realms and dimensions that make our oral history collections valuable as such. Whatever the particular approach or format, documentary involves, virtually by definition, an exploration of a broader body of documentation in search of desired qualities or content, which leads in turn to some selection, arrangement, incorporation, and presentation of meaning grounded in that documentation, which takes the form of a presentation.

In documentary, of course, the "naturalness" or inevitability of text transcription is not the unexamined core assumption, though neither is its opposite, the subordination of text, as the documentary approach can be similar whether the object is a film or a book such as Theodore Rosengarten's (1974) *All God's Dangers: The Life of Nate Shaw* or my own *Portraits in Steel* (Frisch & Rogovin, 1993), in which oral histories were combined with Milton Rogovin's photographs so that images and text could represent parallel and resonant modes of documentary portraiture.

Rather, the central assumption in documentary is the inevitability and, indeed—as I have argued elsewhere—the indispensability of editorial intervention, selection, shaping, arrangement, and even manipulation. Documents may be found, even if this is perhaps less straightforward a matter than it can seem. But documentaries are not found; they are made, although it is also easy to avoid thinking carefully about what is involved in the process. Rather than mediating oral history through text, documentary requires the mediating of the oral history as a whole through some critical intelligence—the editor's, the artist's, the director's, the curator's, or the producer's.

Put differently, if audio-video oral history content itself has characteristically been seen as "raw" documentation that is almost impossible to search or navigate analytically, oral history documentation has become meaningful, sharable, and usable only when it is "cooked," in the form of a documentary selection or arrangement that is then served up to consumers. This "cooking" has seemed as necessary, natural, and inevitable in documentary as text transcription has seemed in working with oral history collections. Whatever the uses, political content, community purpose, or artistic and expressive intent, documentary has always presumed this kind of culinary role.

But what happens if that assumption, too, can be dramatically recast, or discarded altogether, when the potential of new technological tools is fully unfolded? Let me suggest two lines of approach that describe what is, in fact, happening already, each of which speaks to this question.

One—the more obvious and visible to date—involves the crucial issue of access and privilege, in which new modes are so dramatically democratizing access to the tools and processes of documentary production as to transform the approach profoundly. The most immediate and dramatic effect of new tools and techniques is to distribute widely the capacity for documentary production. The digital revolution has taken film from the darkroom and the movie studio into anyone's computer and elementary school classroom. It is redistributing to students, families, teachers, artists, social scientists, and activists the capacity to manage and exploit extensive bodies of documentation and to produce meaningful versions of it. All now have, easily at hand, exciting and increasingly affordable tools for consolidating and communicating the meanings they find in materials that matter to them and for purposes that matter to them.

The radical simplification and distribution of what had been highly restricted skills and equipment is, in this sense, surely transforming what up to now has been the privilege of the documentary producer—a transformation with political implications that are as unbounded as they are straightforward. A wide-open door changes not only access to the production room, but also the very nature of what takes place within, of what can be done, by whom and for what purposes.

However, another implication of new technology is far less obvious but potentially even more powerful and transformative. Here I refer to the implicit challenge posed to the assumption of pathed linearity, an assumption embedded in documentary production.

Most documentaries, even experimental ones that challenge the form, are necessarily a selection out of a broader body of material. They represent a linear product: a path through the material that embodies, supports, represents, or evokes a story being told, a point being made, a context or mood or texture being evoked and conveyed. This is the definitional difference between documentation and documentary. But it is precisely this distinction, as such, that new tools are subverting, in some potentially very exciting ways.

Almost all production in film and video now is taking place in such digital modes, and oral history editing is rapidly moving into this realm as well; it can safely be predicted that in 10 years tape will not be used at all in any form, whether magnetic or digital audio tape. There will be little use for and of CD-ROMs. All material will be in digital file formats for editing and for recording as well—witness the new generation of recorders that continue, quaintly, to look like tape recorders but that in actuality are small computers with enhanced audio and video recording capacity.

This digital transformation has only begun to be appreciated, even—perhaps especially—by those who work with these media routinely. Michael Haller, developer of the indexing software Interclipper, began as a documentary filmmaker, and he likes to observe that although everyone is now doing their editing and production in nonlinear digital editing modes, they still approach what they are producing in linear, analog terms—as a documentary that will begin here and end there, telling its story through a sequential arrangement of whatever materials are selected and refined through the digital editing process and leaving everything else behind, obscured in the archive or collection or left as outtakes from which the selection emerged. In this context, what would a contrasting method for documentary be like, one that proceeded from the fluid, flexible, multipathed, nonlinear access to core documentation?

The Expanding Domain of Method

The question is really the very same one that we have been considering at the other end of the oral historical process. The domain of method expands excitingly when the body of audio and video documentation can be explored in a searchable and easily navigated environment, a platform for the generation of paths and versions on a far more fluid, ongoing basis. In such modes, every search and inquiry can lead to a different focus or material for a different story, and each one is as instantly and continually accessible and easily constructed as any other.

The implications of this for documentary are as profound as for research with recorded interviews. To take a prosaic but instructive example, consider the family video collections that people are now being encouraged to transform into little documentary movies. Ask whether, instead of one, two, or even a file folder full of such precast movies or Web pages of photo files, it wouldn't be more interesting to imagine the material so organized and accessible that such a path could be instantly generated in response to any visiting relative, child's birthday, grandparent's funeral, sale of a house in the home town, or whatever might be occasioning interest in the relevant resources found in the video record. Such a located selection could easily be displayed, saved, and worked into a presentational form if it proved interesting. If not, it could be released to return to the database, awaiting some later inquiry or use.

Such notions apply to more complex settings and to more complex collections of documentation wherein accessibility for very different dimensions of question, evaluation, and application would make an easily navigable map far more useful and interesting than a preselected itinerary. This is precisely what new modes offer and, as this is realized, so too is the potential to imagine documentary itself as a natural extension of such nonlinear modes rather than as a linear path and destination. The documentary impulse and intelligence becomes more responsive, contingent, and sharable.

This is not a new idea by any means, and in fact its ancient provenance offers yet another dimension in which new tools ought best to be seen as permitting a return and rediscovery rather than an invocation to invention. Any reference work is a compilation of answers awaiting questions—as, indeed, is any book, the instantly and fluidly navigable book being in this sense the mother of all hypertext instruments in contrast to the scrolls it so easily superseded centuries ago. In this very same sense, new tools need only mean that audio and video documentation can become a similarly liberating, flexible resource for whatever questions and uses, situationally, are presented and by whatever diversity of users.

The Expanding Democracy of Method and Practice

The implications of such a reorientation of our relation to documentary source material are suggestive and potentially quite profound in practice. Beyond returning the power of "voice" to oral history, digital indexing of audio and video speaks to intellectual and political questions central to oral history discourse. The much-touted democratic promise of oral history has in fact usually been confronted by a variant of the raw–cooked choices noted earlier, restricted either to the "input" into collections or to the audience receipt of "output." In between has been the author, the mediator, the documentary filmmaker, the TV or radio producer, the shapers of whatever is selected from those oral histories for representation in public forms, whether through films, exhibits, books, radio and TV documentaries, and the like.

But as I have hoped to demonstrate here, new digital tools open the significant nonlinear, fluidly multipathed ground between these poles. Because audio–video indexing means that the entire content can be usefully, intelligently, and instrumentally searched and accessed at a rich level, it becomes a great deal more than a "raw" collection. And the same tools that provide that access permit anyone continually to "cook"—to explore a collection and select and order meaningful materials.

Implicit in this approach are whole new modes of publication and public access. Imagine, for example, the value of producing broadly distributed collections of richly mapped and thoroughly searchable interviews, music, and performance or other field documentation, in which users might find and make their own meanings. In producing such a documentary source, authorship would reside not in fixed path making but rather in the richness and openness of the mapping coordinates, codes, and finding tools offered to users.

Such modalities suggest something even more significant and potentially transformative in our relationship to audio and video documentation itself, a deeply and essentially nonlinear orientation that I term a *postdocumentary sensibility*. With accessible, meaningful, fluid, and nonprivileged access to the content of oral history, the authority of the mediating intelligence or documentary authorship is displaced by a sharable, dialogic capacity to explore, select, order, and interpret. In this mode, the privilege of a fixed documentary version that necessarily marginalizes other meanings or stories in the material—the very notion of document as starting point and documentary as product—is displaced by a notion of documentation and documentary as process, as an ongoing, contextually contingent, fluid construction of meaning.

As I have been emphasizing in a variety of ways, it really is not about tools or technologies—it is about practice. Change in tools and technologies is a constant, but changes in practice—in the most fundamental imagination of what we are doing and why—are not so inevitable or easily predictable. It may be that the money and power behind the mass digitization of everything will overwhelm us and that the kind of sensibilities I see as the greatest potential at this moment will end up as remote as all those subtle and fluid information skills collapsing before the incredible power of "quick-'n-dirty"search engines.

But I don't think so. A postdocumentary sensibility in film is really nothing more than the postinterview sensibility I have been arguing as the most exciting emergent potential for oral history method. The two come together in a unitary conception of that middle ground—a many-dimensioned field in which active interrogation and exploration is a constant possibility and in which this process stands at the very center of the notion of method itself. By making this possible with previously intractable audio and video documents, and by showing the power of method as a more general orientation and sensibility, whatever the nature of the documents and the uses made of them, new digital tools and the rich landscape of practice they support are proving powerful resources in restoring one of the foundational appeals of oral history and a worthy object of method: to open new dimensions of understanding and engagement through the broadly inclusive sharing and interrogation of memory.

References

Baum, W. (1991). *Transcribing and editing oral history*. Nashville, TN: American Association for State and Local History.

Baum, W. (1995). *Oral history for the local historical society* (3rd ed., rev.). Walnut Creek, CA: AltaMira Press.

Baum, W., & Dunaway, D. (Eds.). (1996). *Oral history: An interdisciplinary anthology* (2nd ed.). Walnut Creek, CA: AltaMira Press.

Charlton, T., Myers, E., & Sharpless, R. (Eds.). (2006). *Handbook of oral history*. Lanham, MD: AltaMira Press.

Frisch, M. (1990). *A shared authority: Essays on the craft and meaning of oral and public history*. Albany: State University of New York Press.

Frisch, M., & Rogovin, M. (1993). *Portraits in steel*. Ithaca, NY: Cornell University Press.

Hoopes, J. (1979). *Oral history: An introduction for students*. Chapel Hill: University of North Carolina Press.

Ives, E. (1995). *The tape recorded interview: A manual for fieldworkers in folklore and oral history* (2nd ed.). Knoxville: University of Tennessee Press.

Kolovos, A. (2004, November 17). *Re: Thesaurus building for oral history collections*. Archived message posted to H-Oral, http://h-net.msu.edu/cgi-bin/logbrowse.pl?trx=vx&list=H-Oralhist&month=0411&week=c&msg=%2b67UvPSp0W/vO6qOHgcEOw&user=&pw=

Perks, R., & Thomson, A. (2006). *The oral history reader* (2nd ed.). London: Routledge.

Ritchie, D. (2003). *Doing oral history: A practical guide* (2nd ed.). Oxford, UK: Oxford University Press.

Rosengarten, T. (1974). *All God's dangers: The life of Nate Shaw*. New York: Knopf.

Yow, V. (2005). *Recording oral history: A guide for the humanities and social sciences* (2nd ed.). Lanham, MD: AltaMira Press.

ETHNOGRAPHY

CHAPTER 12

Narrative Ethnography

Jaber F. Gubrium
James A. Holstein

Once upon a time, stories were told and written for what they were about. The ancients wrote love stories, recorded histories of military campaigns, produced treatises on flora and fauna, medical texts, and philosophical discourses, and recounted oral histories of countless domains of experience. Some told of the emotions, some of strategic actions, and others of the principles by which these operated. Some stories were written by literate members of their societies; others have been collected as simple yet enduring folk tales. Pictorial renderings, such as cave paintings and decorative displays, attest to narrative's longevity. Extended accounts are a signal feature of the way we have shared the world.

It is one thing, however, to share accounts of battles or lost love; it is quite another to contemplate narrativity or the storying process in its own right. This is a relatively recent development. Reflections on the process might foreground the general structure of battle reports as opposed to love stories, for instance. The difference between sharing stories, on the one hand, and noticing, cataloguing, and analyzing the corpus of narratives for similarities and differences on the other, is a leap in imagination, highlighting narrativity as something separate and distinct from the stories themselves.

As a matter of practice, we do not draw a sharp distinction between stories and the storying process. Nevertheless, something important happens when a distinction is made between them, offering grounds for thinking about narrativity as something interesting on its own. The distinction might best be viewed as a dialogue rather than a categorical difference. This allows us to explore the possibility that narratives have different or similar formats and, in turn, that different formats relate to what is told, to how and where narratives take place, and to how they are understood. This chapter outlines recent developments in the study of narrative practice that take these contextual features into account and present the need for narrative ethnography.

The Internal Organization of Narratives

The study of narrative has moved in two directions. The first of these "narrative turns" was launched by Vladimir Propp's (1928/1968) trailblazing book *Morphology of the Folk Tale*. Russian-born, Propp collected, but more important, called attention to the underlying features of Russian folk tales. He specified the internal shape of the folk tale, something that went beyond collection and appreciation. Like the myths and folk tales of other groups and nations, Russian folk tales dealt with diverse matters, from stories of family life, childhood, motherhood, birth, and death to villainy, loss, triumph, luck, desire, good, and evil. It was not the specific contents or moral twists that interested Propp, but rather how the actors and actions in a story functioned in the overall scheme of things.

Propp noticed similarities in otherwise diverse stories and argued that the fairy tale had a narrative form common to all storytelling. Actions and characters functioned in limited ways, despite the diverse subject matter. For example, a witch or a dragon provided the evil force in tales of struggle and victory. From a functional perspective, a dragon that kidnapped the king's daughter could serve the same function–as a force of evil–as the witch who snatched a baby from its mother's arms. Although dragons are not witches and king's daughters are not necessarily babies, it could be argued that they played identical roles in the accounts. As Terence Hawkes (1977, p. 69) explains, "The important thing to notice is that [Propp] is dealing with discernible and repeated structures [or functions]."

Since then, analysis of the internal organization of stories has flourished. Propp started a tradition of scholarship that now crosses linguistics, the humanities, and the social sciences, the aim of which is to theorize and catalogue the structures and functions of stories. For example, A. J. Greimas's (1983) interest in semantics led to a view of narrative structure modeled on Ferdinand de Saussure's (1915/1966) understanding of linguistic structure. In the following sections, we focus on the direction this view has taken in the social sciences. From psychologist Jerome Bruner's (1986) discussion of the narrative construction of mind, developmental theorist James Birren and his associates' (Birren, Kenyon, Ruth, Schroots, & Svensson, 1996) studies of life stories through time, and gerontologist Gary Kenyon and educator William Randall's (1997) work on autobiographical reflection to sociologist Catherine Kohler Riessman's (1990) analysis of the gender mediations of divorce talk, stories of inner lives and social worlds increasingly have been subjected to narrative analysis.

The Personal Self and Its Stories

Exemplary texts on the internal organization of narratives have distinct disciplinary flavors. Some deal with the personal self and its stories. Donald Polkinghorne's (1988) book *Narrative Knowing in the Human Sciences* is written from the perspective of a practicing psychotherapist. Polkinghorne's goal is to solve human and social problems. His disillusion with conventional social science research turned him to what he calls "narrative knowledge" as a way to understand how practitioners actually relate to their clients' troubles. Polkinghorne explains, "What I found was that practitioners work with narrative knowledge. They are concerned with people's stories: they work with case histories and use narrative explanations to understand why the people they work with behave the way they do" (p. x). Polkinghorne goes on to explicate the conceptual history of narrative knowledge as it developed in literature, psychology, and psychotherapy. One comes away from the book with a framework for orienting to personal accounts of experience in a new way.

Continuing in this vein, Dan McAdams's (1993) book *The Stories We Live By: Personal Myths and the Making of the Self* begins with a question: "What do we know when we know a person?" (p. 5). As simple as the question is, it is a key concern of personality psychologists such as McAdams (see also Crossley, 2000, 2003). His answer is that identity is a life story. Personal stories and selves have parallel narrative tones and imageries. The life course is a developing story, riddled with beginnings, false starts, sudden turns, reconceptualizations, recurrent themes, and "nuclear episodes." These are the "high points, low points, and turning points in our narrative accounts of the past" (p. 296). According to McAdams, as the *dramatis personae*, plots, and themes of our stories crystallize or change, our selves develop and transform in the process. McAdams explains that "the story is inside of us. It is made and remade in the secrecy of our own minds, both conscious and unconscious, and for our own psychological discovery and enjoyment" (p. 12). The answer to the question of what we know when we know a person or ourselves is found in the variety and vicissitudes of the stories within, which we live by.

The stories we live by in today's world are put into critical perspective in social psychologist Kenneth Gergen's (1991) book *The Saturated Self: Dilemmas of Identity in Contemporary Life*. Gergen is similarly concerned with the personal self, but in relation to the difficulties posed by the plethora of ways in which experience is currently storied. As the back cover of the book explains, "Today's ever-expanding communications technologies force us to relate to more people and institutions than ever before, challenging the way we view ourselves and our relationships." Gergen argues that contemporary life floods us with so many narratives of what we can be that the self is saturated, unable to center itself on any source of meaning and development. We are headed in all directions and thus in no direction at all. The self is "under siege," lost in a morass of possibilities that a teeming world of self stories presents to us. The self within is shuffled through the countless stories outside, turning the story inside of us into a communicative whirlwind. The self is besieged by a self-storying industry, whose cinematic and televisual images work against definitional closure, leaving the self anchorless in the process. The personal self echoes the narrative "collage of postmodern life" (p. 171), as one of Gergen's later chapters suggests.

The Relational Self and Its Stories

Not everything is this personal or this grim. Starting with George Herbert Mead's (1934) lectures at the University of Chicago on mind, self, and society, a tradition of thinking centered on the relational self has flourished alongside narrative research dealing with the personal self. Here the focus is on the self in relation to everyday life, in particular, the social interaction and situations through which self-understanding develops. Who and what we are in this context are not so much personal but relational stories; they are narratives that mirror the kinds of accounts we engage as we go about the business of living. Charles Horton Cooley (1903/1964) likened the relational self to a "looking glass," in which the narrative play of selfhood evolves through imagined accounts of who we might be (p. 184). This self is not so much located within as it is formed in communicative relation to others. The course of social interaction–both in real time and in our imaginations–inscribes the characters, plots, and themes of our identities.

The Chicago tradition came to early fruition in now classic research. W. I. Thomas and Florian Znaniecki's (1918–1920/1927) study of the immigration experience of Polish Americans in Chicago, titled *The Polish Peasant in Europe and America*, is a pioneering text of the genre. Indeed, except for a long introduction, Volume 1 of the two-volume compendium is composed solely of letters that the authors collected from Polish family members, written to each other between Europe and America. As the authors suggest, the letter writers' identities are located in the various accounts that depict who they were and what they have become as they describe a world left behind in relation to a world being currently lived in. The bits and pieces of life presented in the letters are records of attitudes within, the authors argue, whose predispositions to act tell of the relational selves that construct them.

Another key text of this genre is Clifford Shaw's (1930/1966) *The Jack Roller*, subtitled "A Delinquent Boy's Own Story." The subject matter is the career of a young male delinquent named Stanley. Stanley lives in a poor, crime-ridden neighborhood near the Chicago stockyards, not far from downtown. His life is a career of petty crime, including "rolling Jacks," or assaulting and stealing from working men, especially those drunk after nights out on payday. Stanley's story is presented as an extended account in his own words, featuring a social world whose relationships shape Stanley's view of who he is and was and his hopes for the future. Coining the "own story" technique, Shaw provides a glimpse of the delinquent life as Stanley spins his narrative. It is "one of a series of 200 similar studies of repeated male offenders under 17 years of age, all of whom were on parole from correctional institutions when the studies were made" (p. 1). Stanley's story is portrayed as a life record, whose themes and plotline offer a genuine glimpse of the social world under consideration. In contrast to those who orient to the personal self and its stories, Shaw's perspective suggests that the self's stories are less articulations of experience within than they are accounts that relate significant features of everyday life that are widely shared. Shaw explains:

> A second aspect of the problem of delinquency which may be studied by means of the "own story" is the social and cultural world in which the delinquent lives. It is undoubtedly true that the delinquent behavior of the child cannot be understood and explained apart from the cultural and social context in which it occurred. By means of personal documents it is possible to study not only the traditions, customs, and moral standards of neighborhoods, institutions, families, gangs, and play groups, but the manner in which these cultural factors become incorporated into the behavior trends of the child. (p. 7)

Thus begins a tradition of narrative analysis centered on how stories reveal the relational selves of storytellers. In this genre, stories are viewed as windows on distinctive social worlds. As Ken Plummer (2001) might put it, the stories are "documents of life." Stanley's story is about Stanley only to the extent that his experience has been shaped by the social life he has led. Although it is depicted as his "own story," he does not own it; rather, he conveys "in his own words" the subjective contours of a shared environment and experience, one centered on migration, poverty, disadvantage, crime, and incarceration. The content and shape of this account are idiosyncratic only insofar as Stanley brings biographical particulars and individual narrative habits to his report. What Stanley says is a story about a social world, not just about Stanley. It is important to emphasize that, although there are individual twists to such stories, their contents are viewed as patterned by social experience. The accounts tell us how inner life relates to distinctive social worlds.

This focus has been advanced in countless ethnographic case studies of social worlds depicted in participants' "own words" and "own stories." From William Foote Whyte's (1943) magnificent account of street corner life in an Italian American slum to Elliot Liebow's (1967) study of "Negro streetcorner men" in a poor African American neighborhood in Washington, D.C., to John Irwin's (1970) depiction of the social world of the felon and Elijah Anderson's (1976) portrayal of the "regulars," "wineheads," and "hoodlums" who narrate the social order and sociability of Jelly's bar and liquor store on the south side of Chicago, community members represent in their own words the lived features of particular social worlds and their related selves.

Catherine Kohler Riessman (1990) further develops the approach by analyzing stories not only for the ways plots depict social life but for the ways distinctive themes and the internal shape of accounts construct experience. Her book *Divorce Talk* shows how "women and men make sense of personal relationships," in this case divorce, through storytelling. The emphasis is on the way divorce is differentially plotted by men and women. The internal organization of the accounts Riessman discusses indicates *how* particular social experiences are put together by those under consideration, not just *what* those social experiences are like. Riessman offers us more active relational selves, selves that are not only shaped by their social worlds but that also, in turn, narratively inflect those worlds in their own right. Riessman is especially interested in illustrating how much difference the divorcing partners' gender makes in how divorced is storied. As the back cover of the book points out:

> To explain divorce, women and men construct gendered visions of what marriage should provide, and at the same time they mourn gender divisions and blame their divorces on them. Riessman examines the stories people tell about their marriages—the protagonists, inciting conditions, and culminating events—and how these narrative structures provide ways to persuade both teller and listener that divorce was justified.

The reference to "narrative structures" echoes Propp's pioneering functional analysis of Russian folk tales. The narrative turn in question is evident across the board. Stories are considered for their internal features, for their particular contents, and for the structural differences between individual accounts. Whether it is the function of a witch or a dragon, the true-to-life representation of a social world, or the construction of a form of experience by those differentially positioned in it, the internal features of stories have generalizable characteristics that move us beyond the idiosyncrasies of individual accounts. Fairy tales and reports of neighborhood experience have discernable narrative contours, in other words, suggesting that narrativity can be examined on its own terms for the manner in which it shapes what is known about its subject matter.

Analyzing Internal Structures

There now are several texts offering guidelines for conceptualizing and analyzing the internal organization of stories (see Clandinin & Connolly, 2000; Cortazzi, 1993; Daiute & Lightfoot, 2003; Herman & Vervaeck, 2005; Kenyon & Randall, 1997; Lieblich, Tuval-Mashiach, & Zilber, 1998; Riessman, 1993). Some are out of print and many are heavy on theory; two are exemplary because they are readily available and provide practical models for, and illustrations of, the analysis of life stories—Lieblich and colleagues' (1998) *Narrative Research* and Riessmann's *Narrative Analysis* (1993).

Lieblich and her associates distinguish three uses of narrative in social research. One is for exploratory purposes. When not much is known about a particular topic, narrative inquiry can be used to identify researchable questions. Small or strategic samples of narratives from focal populations might be collected as a prelude to the specification of variables that later can be operationalized for further study. Narratives also provide an in-depth view of the lifestyle of a particular group, such as a gang or a social movement. Developmental psychologists have used narratives to understand individual experience through time, especially in relation to significant life transitions. A second use is for research on stories themselves. This approach centers more on the formal aspects of stories than on their contents. Propp's contribution was pioneering in this regard. A third use of narratives is philosophical and methodological. Inquiry centers on what narrativity can contribute to our knowledge of individual and group experience and is often juxtaposed with the typically flat, thin contributions of positivistic methods.

The bulk of Lieblich and colleagues' (1998) text is devoted to the discussion of four strategies for analyzing the internal organization of life stories. The strategies stem from the intersection of two analytical dimensions: whether the whole story or a part, such as an utterance or theme, is under consideration and whether content or form is of primary interest. A holistic-content reading of narrative material deals with entire stories and their contents. For example, one might compare the content of stories of recent versus long-time immigrants for the extent to which they deal with adjustment or acculturated experiences. This is the kind of analysis that Thomas and Znaniecki (1918–1920/1927) undertook in examining the contents of letters written by Polish immigrants to America and their family members. A second strategy involves a holistic-form reading. The plotlines of stories might be compared as to whether they progress along a continuum, such as from scene-setting, characterization, and plot elaboration to climax and wrap-up. A third strategy involves a part-content reading. In this case, specific parts of stories are considered, such as particular categories of words, phrases, or self–other relationships. The fourth strategy involves a part-form reading. Here one might examine the relationship between narrative coherence as a facet of stories on the one hand and how coherence relates to the beginning, middle, and ending of stories on the other.

Riessman (1993) starts her text by noting that we do not have direct access to experience, arguing instead that because life comes to us in the form of stories, the analysis of narratives becomes a way of analyzing experience. Inasmuch as storytellers are active and shape their accounts, in addition to communicating information, stories represent our identities and our social worlds. However, although Riessman's constructionist spin on narrativity is clear, her presentation is limited to the analysis of stories' internal organization and does not extend to storytelling. The activeness she assigns to the storying process focuses on the textual results, not its practice. Still, it is valuable for the models she presents for doing narrative analysis.

One model is applied in Faye Ginsburg's (1989) study of the lives of 35 women activists in Fargo, North Dakota, who were divided in their views on the abortion issue. Riessman (1993) describes how Ginsburg explored the ways in which the women constructed their positions narratively, comparing the linguistic and substantive differences between pro-choice and right-to-life activists. The analysis showed that the women developed plotlines in very different ways. Using extensive excerpts from pro-choice activist Kay Ballard's story to illustrate Ginsburg's approach, Riessman notes in relation to several excerpts from the story:

> Kay illustrates the typical pro-choice plot line [absent in right-to-life stories]: being different in childhood (Excerpt 1); questioning the confines of motherhood through a particular reproductive experience (Excerpt 2); a conversion upon contact with feminism in the 1960s and 1970s (Excerpts 3 and 4); and a subsequent reframing of understandings of self, women's interests, and ideals of nurturance (Excerpts 4–7). (p. 30)

Another model is illustrated by Susan Bell's (1988) research on the stories of DES (diethylstilbestrol) daughters. Bell wished to explore how the women understood their risk for reproductive tract problems, including infertility and vaginal cancer. She was especially interested in what might have led to their becoming politically active in response to the adverse medical consequences for women. Bell used William Labov's (1972) structural categories and method of transcription in her analysis, coding stories into an initial *abstract* reference to the problem (e.g., "that sort of brought the whole issue of DES much more to the forefront of my mind"; Riessman, 1993, p. 36); followed by *orienting* information (e.g., "when I was around 19"; Riessman, 1993, p. 35); *complicating* action (e.g., a discussion of what happened to the storyteller as a result; Riessman, 1993, p. 35), and finally a *resolution* (e.g., "and that's when I um began to accept the fact, y'know, once it made sense"; Riessman, 1993, p. 36). Such stories might be analyzed for the point at which the voice of medicine is incorporated into the plot or when and in what way resistance to medical discourse develops. Alternatively, one might ask whether those who resist medical discourse and develop counterstories set this up narratively at the start so that a triumphant resolution follows. Regardless of the result, the point is not that the daughters engage in narrative machinations but rather that differences in experience have discernable narrative contours.

Turning to Narrative Practice

A second narrative turn takes us outside of stories themselves to the occasions and practical actions associated with story construction and storytelling (Bauman, 1986; Cicourel, 1974; Goffman, 1959; Gubrium & Holstein, 2001; Holstein & Gubrium, 2000b; Hymes, 1964). The focus is on *narrative practice*. Narrative practice is the broad term we use to encompass the content of accounts and their internal organization, as well as the communicative conditions and resources surrounding how narratives are assembled, conveyed, and received in everyday life. The complex and overlapping contexts of the storying process constitute *narrative environments*.

The transcript of a story provides limited information about the occasions on which the story was told. Certainly, chance utterances in a transcript might indeed refer to occasion, such as the question posed to the interviewer by the interviewee: "Is that the kind of thing you want to know?" But significant details about the setting are often missing. For example, the transcript may not reveal a setting's discursive conventions, such as what is usually talked about, avoided, or frowned on when it is mentioned. It does not disclose the consequences of telling stories in particular ways. Although there is no strict line of demarcation between, in this case, stories and storytelling, we need to know the details and working conditions of narrative occasions if we are to understand narrative practice. These details, in turn, can only be discerned from direct consideration of narrative environments.

Stories are assembled and told to someone, somewhere, at some time, with a variety of consequences for those concerned. All of this has a discernible impact on what is communicated and how that unfolds. A life story might be told to a spouse, to a lover, to a drinking buddy, to an employer, to a clergyperson, to a therapist, to a son or daughter, or to a fellow team member, among the huge variety of audiences to which narratives are conveyed. The occasion might be a job interview, part of a pickup line, a confession, or a recovery tale. The consequences might be amusing or life threatening. As we noted at the start, the environments of storytelling shape the content and internal organization of accounts, just as internal matters can have an impact on one's role as a storyteller.

Let us revisit Shaw's (1930/1966) presentation of Stanley's story in this regard. References to storytelling do appear in the text as Stanley describes his world, but Shaw's focus on the content of the story eclipses what is textually in view. Shaw is concerned with what accounts such as Stanley's can provide in the way of practical information about delinquents' social worlds and what that, in turn, can tell us about delinquency and how to deal with it. Shaw is not interested in narrative structure, plot development, or thematic organization; his focus is on sheer information for its worth in understanding the delinquent life. As he explains, case studies, especially in the form of subjects' own stories, are ideal for getting beyond the surface facts provided by official statistics to reveal social worlds on their own terms.

In considering what Shaw understandably overlooks, it is important to keep in mind that Stanley conveys some of his story in the context of his experiences in the Illinois State Reformatory, to which he was committed when he was 15 years old. Shaw points out that this "institution receives commitments of youthful male offenders between the ages of 16 and 26" (p. 103), so Stanley had many other delinquent youths to look up to. Status, apparently, was an important factor in their social ties, something that becomes glaringly obvious as Stanley tells his story. It raises questions about narrative ownership and the experiential fidelity of individualized accounts, even of those for which it is assumed that the self in question is not personal but relational. If Shaw argues that the delinquent boy's own story reveals his social world, he fails to notice that that social world is variegated and that Stanley actively shapes his story to fit its circumstances.

Describing the daily round of life in the institution, Stanley refers to his first days in a cell, which make him "heartsick," along with the part his cell mate plays in helping him "get used to things": "When the whistle blew for breakfast the next morning I was heartsick and weak, but after visiting with my cell mate, who took prison life with a smile and as a matter of course, I felt better. He said, 'You must as well get used to things here; you're a "convict" now, and tears won't melt those iron bars' " (pp. 103–104).

Stanley looks up to his cell mate Bill and, interestingly enough, virtually steps out of his story to inform the listener–reader that what he says about himself is narratively occasioned. Referring to his cell mate, Stanley explains:

> He was only seventeen, but older than me, and was in for one to ten years for burglaries. He delighted in telling about his exploits in crime, to impress me with this bravery and daring, and made me look up to him as a hero. Almost all young crooks like to tell about their accomplishments in crime. Older crooks are not so glib. They are hardened, and crime has lost its glamour and become a matter of business. Also, they have learned the dangers of talking too much and keep their mouths shut except to trusted friends. But Bill (my cell partner) talked all the time about himself and his crimes. I talked, too, and told wild stories of adventure, some true and some lies, for I couldn't let Bill outdo me just for lack of a few lies on my part. (p. 104)

Given the situated nature of this account—which narratively orients to Stanley's relationship with other inmates and what that means for his status in the setting—it is apparent that this is far from simply being Stanley's "own" story. Stanley actively shapes the account to enhance his standing with Bill and other inmates. The content and the theme of the story are as much a matter of his position under the circumstances as the story is a faithful rendition of his life. At this point in his narrative, Stanley virtually tells us that he occasionally does status work when he recounts his experience. His biographical work (Holstein & Gubrium, 2000a) cannot be separated from the circumstances of storytelling. We might figure in this regard that a particular narrative environment (the reformatory) and narrative occasion (a recollection within an interview) mediate the shape of the story being told. And there is reason to believe that other narrative environments and narrative occasions would do the same. The storytelling responds as much to the practical contingencies of storytelling as it reflects Stanley's ostensible experience. Stanley seems to know that the internal organization of his story and his role and circumstances as a storyteller are reflexively intertwined

There is other evidence of how Stanley's presence in the reformatory affects what he says about himself. In the following excerpt from the book, notice this time how Stanley laments his lack of narrative resources:

> So I listened with open ears to what was said in these groups of prisoners. Often I stood awestruck as tales of adventure in crime were related, and I took it in with interest. Somehow I wanted to go out and do the same thing myself.

> To myself I thought I was somebody to be doing a year at Pontiac, but in these groups of older prisoners I felt ashamed because I couldn't tell tales of daring exploits about my crimes. I hadn't done anything of consequence. I compared myself with the older crooks and saw how little and insignificant I was in the criminal line. But deep in my heart I knew that I was only a kid and couldn't be expected to have a reputation yet. I couldn't tell about my charge, for it savored of petty thievery, and everybody looked down on a petty thief in Pontiac. I felt humiliated in the extreme, so I only listened. (pp. 108–109)

The lament is doubly charged in that Stanley has not yet acquired the experience to fashion "tales of adventure" and "daring exploits," as he knew only petty thievery. He did not have these in his experiential repertoire to report. So he only listened, the idea being that experience and narrative go hand-in-hand in telling one's story. Neither is a simple by-product of the other.

Stanley broaches a different narrative environment a bit later. The occasion no longer involves storytelling between reformatory inmates, but rather among those who gather at an urban street corner, as Whyte's (1943), Liebow's (1967), and Anderson's (1976) protagonists do. Stanley now puts his story to work for a different purpose, one aligned with the representational needs of this occasion. What he does with words this time is a combination of status work and masculinity work:

> I went out to look for work, but it was scarce at the time. After a week of fruitless effort, I began to loaf around with the corner gang. These fellows were all working and doing well, but they had the habit of hanging around the corner and telling dirty stories about women. We took pride in telling about our exploits with such and such a girl, and tried to outdo each other in the number of women that we had conquered. (p. 118)

Storytelling and its occasions, then, are as important as the content of what is communicated. Both reflexively enter into the articulation of Stanley's inner life and social world, linking the fidelity of Stanley's story to the complex practices of narrativity.

The Need for Narrative Ethnography

We are fortunate that Shaw's (1930/1966) book reveals some of the narrative circumstances that shape Stanley's life story. But these come to us by way of Stanley, and Shaw, of course. What would we have learned had we been present in the reformatory or on the street corner in question? How might others' accounts have affected what Stanley talked about and how Stanley told his story? We do know from what Stanley says in Shaw's text that he was occasionally encouraged to enter conversations and even embellish his story; we also know that there were other occasions when he was reluctant to do so. His story apparently played a communicative role in some social worlds and was unheard in others. It is evident, too, that Stanley's feelings about himself and his identity as a young male delinquent and hanger-on were affected by these differences. All of this suggests that we might usefully turn directly to narrative environments—their occasions and practices—to understand the everyday contours of the storying process, as well as what is and is not put into words for communicating to others. Our analytical method needs to take account of not only what Stanley says and how he says it but also the narratively contingent conditions of assembling a story. In this particular case, it would include stories told by others about themselves, about Stanley, and about their common social worlds.

A word of caution is warranted at this point. We want to avoid judging Stanley's and others' accounts simply on the basis of individual memory, rationality, and communicative fidelity. Certainly, these characteristics affect what we know about people's lives. Some people remember very little, whereas others appear to communicate from photographic memories. Some seem eminently reasonable and straightforward in their accounts, detailing step-by-step what they have been through or what life has meant to them through time. Others' life stories meander. There are those whose stories hardly conform to what is otherwise known to be true, which might prompt us to figure that they are, perhaps, lying or "denying" experience, as some might put it. But evaluating stories on individual grounds fails to take account of the profoundly social configurations of narrativity, which, if known, might cast an altogether different light on ostensible shortcomings.

It is the social dimensions of narratives that we highlight in this chapter and that call for an emergent method that takes us outside of stories and their veridical relationship to storytellers and experience. Broadly, that method is *narrative ethnography*, that is, the ethnographic study of narrativity. The need for such an approach is clear. Even though *ethnography* has taken on so many meanings and usages in recent years that it is almost synonymous with qualitative inquiry (see Atkinson & Hammersley, 1994), we have something more specific in view. It is a method of procedure and analysis aimed at close scrutiny of social situations, their actors, and actions in relation to narratives. This involves direct, intensive observation of the field of study—in this case, the multifaceted field of narrative practice.

Being on the scenes of story construction and storytelling and considering how stories are shaped by the contingencies of communication is not simply window dressing for narrative analysis. Settings are integral parts of narrativity. Whoever heard of a story being told nowhere, at no time? Even stories told to researchers such as Shaw—or to therapists or in job interviews—are occasioned and conditioned by the narrative endeavor in place. Erving Goffman (1961) put this succinctly when he wrote of the need for ethnographic access to experience in his own work. Writing about the seemingly irrational, even the mad, he noted:

> My immediate objective in doing fieldwork at St. Elizabeth's [psychiatric hospital] was to try to learn about the world of the hospital inmate, as this world is subjectively experienced by him. . . . It was then and still is my belief that any group of persons—prisoners, primitives, pilots, or patients—develop a life [story] of their own that becomes meaningful, reasonable, and normal once you get close to it, and that a good way to learn about any of these worlds is to submit oneself in the company of the members to the daily round of petty contingencies to which they are subject. (pp. ix–x)

Concern with the production, distribution, and circulation of stories in society requires that we step outside of narrative material and consider questions such as who produces particular kinds of stories, where they are likely to be encountered, what their consequences are, under what circumstances particular narratives are more or less accountable, what interests publicize them, how they gain popularity, and how they are challenged. In this regard, we might ask how Stanley's story is told in relation to the inmate banter at Pontiac as opposed to the conviviality of the street corners he frequents. We might wonder how the "daily round of petty contingencies" of each setting and occasion for storytelling shapes Stanley's accounts. This would require us to examine the scenes of these occasions, to turn to stories as they are being put together or told (or not told, as the case might be on certain occasions), to listen to and take account of how they are received, to consider what might be preferred tellings in particular circumstances, and to explore the consequences of storying experience in conformity with or out of line with what is preferred. It requires that we give serious attention to the possibility that narrative environments and their occasions have preferred stories. In short, we need to examine narratives in full social context.

Narratives are not simply reflections of experience, nor are they descriptive free-for-alls. Not just anything goes when it comes to storying experience. Rather, narratives comprise the interplay between experience, storying practices, descriptive resources, purposes at hand, audiences, and the environments that condition storytelling. Narrative ethnography provides the analytical platform, tools, and sensibilities for capturing the rich and variegated contours of everyday narrative practice.

A growing collection of studies grounded in narrative ethnography has emerged in the past decade or so, although researchers have not necessarily adopted the rubric formally. Gale Miller's book, *Becoming Miracle Workers: Language and Meaning in Brief Therapy* (1997), is a rich, historical account of the shift in institutional discourse that led to altered ways of conceptualizing selves and doing therapy in an individual and family counseling clinic. Miller's approach to the ethnography of institutional discourse (Miller, 1994) has clear affinities with narrative ethnography as we portray it. His book is a powerful demonstration of how a comparative ethnographic approach provides insight into how lives, troubles, and their solutions are storied. Darin Weinberg's *Of Others Inside: Insanity, Addiction, and Belonging in America* (2005) pursues a similar theme. Whereas Miller discusses how therapeutic narratives changed over time in the same institution, Weinberg compares how two purportedly identical programs became dissimilar narrative environments to accommodate different residential treatment circumstances. Organizational differences are further highlighted in *Out of Control: Family Therapy and Domestic Disorder* (Gubrium, 1992), which describes narratives of family troubles in distinctly different therapeutic venues. Susan Chase's *Ambiguous Empowerment: The Work Narratives of Women School Superintendents* (1995) and Amir Marvasti's *Being Homeless: Textual and Narrative Constructions* (2003) offer nuanced examinations of the narratives of some of society's most and least successful members, accenting the contextually sensitive narrative work that is done to construct vastly different accounts of life and its challenges.

Before moving ahead, it is important to distinguish the version of narrative ethnography depicted in this chapter from another usage that focuses critically on the representational practices through which ethnographic reports emerge, a usage that especially works against the objectifying practices of ethnographic description. Some fieldworkers have used the term narrative ethnography to highlight *researchers'* narrative practices as they craft ethnographic accounts. This usage features the vibrant interplay between the ethnographer's own subjectivity and the subjectivities of those whose lives and worlds are in view. These ethnographic texts are typically derived from participant observation, but they are distinctive because they take special notice of the researcher's own participation, perspective, voice, and especially of his or her emotional experience in relation to the experiences of those being studied. Anthropologists Barbara Tedlock (1991, 1992, 2004), Ruth Behar (1993, 1996), and Kirin Narayan (1989) and sociologists Carolyn Ellis (1991), Laurel Richardson (1990a, 1990b), and others (Ellis & Bochner, 1996; Ellis & Flaherty, 1992) refer to "narrative ethnography" as their attempt to convey the reflexive, representational engagements of field encounters. H. L. Goodall's (2000) book *Writing the New Ethnography* is an exemplary rendition of this form of narrative ethnography.

In contrast, the narrative ethnography described in this chapter is less immediately self-conscious about researchers' representational practices. Accommodating naturalistic, constructionist, and ethnomethodological impulses and concerns, the approach focuses on the everyday narrative activity that unfolds within circumstantially situated social interaction, with an acute awareness of the myriad layers of social context that condition narrative production. The approach, although aware of the narrative practices of ethnographers, is more centrally concerned with the narrative practices of those whose experiences and lives are under consideration. We use the term narrative ethnography to signal the combination of epistemological, methodological, procedural, and analytical sensibilities that must be brought to bear to understand narrativity in social context.

Narrative Environments

Narrative ethnographers by trade, we have been in the habit of both listening to and taking systematic note of actual and possible stories in various settings. The methods of procedure have varied from in-depth life history interviews in nursing homes (see Gubrium, 1993) to courtroom observations that completely eschewed interviewing (see Holstein, 1993) to studies that combined observation, interviewing, and discourse analysis (see Gubrium, 1992). In systematically observing narratives-in-production, attending to the construction, use, and reception of accounts and textual material such as life records, we have found that the internal organization of narratives, although important to understand in its own right, does not tell us very much about the relation of stories to the worlds in which they circulate. Although the themes of stories such as accounts of sexual abuse or narratives of childhood sexuality might be identified and documented, discerning how these relate to particular social contexts requires an understanding of what people do with words in varied circumstances. As we noted in discussing Stanley's story, the same account might be appreciated in one setting or at one time and place but be disparaged, ignored, or unarticulated in others. The meanings of stories are poorly understood without careful consideration of the circumstances of their production and reception, which we broadly call their *narrative environments*.

Local Contingencies of Storytelling

Research reported in the book *Caretakers* (Buckholdt & Gubrium, 1979) is instructive. The ethnographic fieldwork centered on the social construction of children's emotional disturbance in a residential treatment facility called Cedarview. Through systematic participant observation, the study showed that narratives of children's inner lives, although available and occasionally communicated, were marginalized in a therapeutic environment that featured behaviorist interpretations and interventions. At Cedarview, an official token economy and behavior modification programming valorized narratives of visible behaviors and "consequences." This was the privileged, if not exclusive, discourse of problems and solutions—the master narrative in place, so to speak. The working rule was "stay out of children's heads," which served to caution all concerned to honor behavioristic principles.

Still, occasional consultations with a child psychiatrist rather than a behavioral psychologist provided communicative space for competing narratives, encouraging staff members and treatment teams to temporarily peek inside for understanding and explanation. On such occasions, encouraged by the consultant's deep psychiatric gaze, narratives that thematized early childhood disturbances, deep feelings, and hidden motives were taken to be more consequential for treatment decisions than were behaviorized accounts of children's activities. This complex narrative environment sometimes elicited accounts quite at odds with official therapeutic commitments. On such occasions, particular communicative niches gave voice to what otherwise were institutionally discredited narratives.

The value of these local contingencies was not lost on the staff, as they periodically found it helpful to account for children's conduct and progress in treatment, especially to one another, in deep psychological terms. These insights, however, were not conveyed to funding agencies; those stories reflected, instead, the facility's official treatment philosophy. Audiences, in other words, were important ingredients in the production, editing, distribution, and circulation of stories (also see Gubrium & Buckholdt, 1982). Questions of "how to put it" and what themes to highlight for particular purposes were noteworthy in the everyday formulation of stories about the children. Just as Stanley aligned the content and tone of his story with the local contingencies of narrativity in his social world, Cedarview staff members shaped their accounts in relation to the communicative contours of the circumstances they engaged in the process.

We should note that these actions were part of the local contingencies of storytelling and did not reflect a peculiar or cynical quality of Cedarview storytellers. Although the attitudes of individual staff members might indeed have been viewed as cynical by some, the systematic quality of narrative editing (Holstein & Gubrium, 2000b) throughout the facility—and, indeed, of any storytelling located in time and space—suggests that storytellers naturally attend to narrative circumstance in assembling their accounts. Except for biographical and institutional particulars, the stories of children's lives at Cedarview took shape in much the same way they would in similar narrative environments (see Goffman, 1961; Gubrium & Holstein, 2001). Such locally contingent features of storytelling are best captured ethnographically, a method that offers a view of the actual circumstances of narrativity. Without circumstantial knowledge, it would be too easy to turn, reductively, to the machinations or personal deficits of individuals or to a defective society for explanation. As the earlier quotation from Goffman (1961) reminds us, a significant share of the "meaningful, reasonable, and normal" is lost when we overlook "the daily round of petty contingencies" in everyday life.

Affirming Environments

Social settings vary as narrative environments. In our own work on narrativity within institutional settings, we have viewed them in terms of what Everett Hughes (1984) called *going concerns*. This was Hughes's way of emphasizing the work of maintaining particular ways of framing and doing matters of relevance to participants, including the work of formulating accounts. Such concerns vary in size, from families and friendship, support, and recovery groups to schools, courtrooms, correctional facilities, nursing homes, and therapeutic enterprises. A going concern such as a recovered-memory therapy group, for example, is an organized activity with the goal of recollecting the lost or otherwise hidden memories of adult survivors of sexual abuse. Joseph Davis (2005) found that, in the therapeutic settings he studied, memory enhancement and retrieval techniques were applied; survivors were encouraged to recall stories of childhood sexual contacts. They were urged to relive these experiences narratively and eventually to emplot them in relation to current psychological difficulties. In a much different context, sexuality education programs such as Teach Abstinence Until Marriage deploy other orienting stories, which are racialized when applied to European American, as opposed to African American, children. As Jessica Fields (2005) explains, the emplotment of sexual misbehavior among European Americans typically relates to the theme of childhood innocence, whereas parallel stories for African American youths rest on the theme of innate sexuality. The meanings of the substantive elaboration and themes of any particular account cannot be separated from socially situated narrative practice.

Each narrative environment affirms certain established stories and ways of narrating experience; they are going concerns that narratively construct, reproduce, and privilege particular accounts for institutional purposes. Conversely, one would expect counternarratives to be marginalized, "repaired," or otherwise challenged, if not kept in tolerable spaces. Across therapeutic concerns especially, the widely applied and well-recognized rhetoric of denial can be highly effective in both suppressing unacceptable stories and affirming the articulation of acceptable ones. Because the affirmed stories of such going concerns are often larded with globalized narratives such as therapeutic—as opposed to fatalistic or cosmic—discourses, the layered interplay between the local, the national, and the transnational can become a confluence of narrative affirmation. Narrative ethnography is necessary to capture this interplay in its full contextual richness.

Environments That Challenge Common Narratives

Narrative environments challenge, as well as affirm, various stories. Indeed, to theorize environments as either affirming or challenging particular narratives shortchanges the complex interplay between artful interpretation, institutional practices, and a constantly changing stock of narrative resources. It is unfortunate that so much theory building on these fronts is compartmentalized and specialized when many of the issues parallel one another. For example, the narration of selves and personal identity in institutional context is mediated by both official and unofficial structures and contingencies (see Gubrium & Holstein, 2001). But identity work (Holstein & Gubrium, 2000a) and biographical work (Gubrium & Holstein, 1995) are also abetted and sponsored by social movements that publicize rhetorics of preferred and disparaged frames of understanding (see Benford, 1993, 1997; Benford & Snow, 2000; Snow, 2003). If Hughes (1984) applies the term "going concerns" to institutions, then the application can be extended to the going concerns of movements toward change as well.

The empirical linkages between the narratively affirmed and the narratively challenging can be amazingly transformative. Research on the start of the Alzheimer's disease movement in the 1980s (Gubrium, 1986), for example, showed that marked differences in both local and global understandings of senile dementia formed in less than 5 years. The (re)discovery of Alzheimer's disease in 1979 quickly became a medical and experiential story affirming both a new subject with a diseased, as opposed to a naturally aging, brain and the research activities of a soon-to-be-hugely-successful medical and psychological enterprise. The Alzheimer's disease movement transformed, virtually overnight, the way professionals, families, the senile, and significant others narrated their relationship to the aging brain and its associated cognitive functions. As the senile became victims of a disease as opposed to aging, parties concerned with the aging enterprise—from the new National Institute of Aging to local caregivers—went into high gear to construct a social problem that became an issue of national and international importance (see Fox, 2000). It became evident that what was new and what was being affirmed were interwoven.

The application of these ideas to the construction of subjectivity is full of possibilities. Selves are not straightforwardly obvious in society. They must be identified as a matter of communicative practice. This is not constructive magic, in which new narratives for identity are conjured up out of thin air and absorbed into the social worlds and inner lives of those concerned. The process of identification and rhetorics of persuasion are practical and take place in lived circumstances—in narrative environments whose varied stock of accounts differentially serve to affirm or challenge both old and new stories about social worlds and their identities. Self stories come from somewhere, relate to larger stories, are shaped by other stories, and are affirmed and challenged through time by yet different and transformed narratives. Stories are relentlessly drawn through the gamut of contingent interests that bear on their particular content and shape. Narrative ethnography provides an encompassing sensitivity to the fluid contingencies, in this case the challenges, of narrative production.

Narrative Embeddedness

Narrative ethnography provides analytical access to the multilayered embeddedness of stories in relation to other stories. The analogy of nesting dolls is useful in considering a story's complex relation to its narrative environment. The smallest doll is embedded or nested in all the larger ones; each doll next in size both contains a smaller doll and is en-veloped by several bigger ones. Similarly, a life story such as Stanley's (Shaw, 1930/1966) is fully understood only when we take account of the other stories to which it relates and the occasions on which it is communicated. As Stanley almost glibly explains in passing, what he says or, in some settings, does not dare to say about himself is embedded in other stories that inform his own, as well as that inform him of the consequences of narrating his life in particular ways.

Stanley's story and the other narratives to which Stanley refers exist in complex relationship to similar accounts centered on "the" delinquent or "the" jack roller. This relationship has affirming and disconfirming facets. Stanley's own story is fueled by the bravado, status, and gender work of local storytelling. Shaw's (1930/1966) interest in understanding the lived experience of the delinquent and how this informs rehabilitation policy also tells us that Stanley's story is embedded in an environment of preferred narratives for wayward youths. Whereas Stanley's own story is deftly assembled, sharply thematized, and intriguingly developed through time, Shaw's, Stanley's, and our own reading of the account is nested in a variety of other stories, both local and more global. Indeed, a narrative of penal welfare and reform is the larger story in which Stanley's account and Shaw's narrative aims are nested. It is a story bound to a particular sense of criminal justice, told at a particular time and place (see Garland, 2001). Stanley's is hardly the singular narrative of a punk and small-time operator; its significance, although partially local, reverberates with the larger stories and circumstances in which it is embedded.

The idea of narrative embeddedness suggests that, in aiming to understand the broader meaning of accounts, it is useful to distinguish story from voice. As we reread Stanley's story, we can ask, Whose voice do we hear? The subtitle of Shaw's book—*A Delinquent Boy's Own Story*—implies that the text reflects Stanley's personal experience. As we read along, we ostensibly hear Stanley's voice. And, indeed, it is colorful, often natively elegant. It is both hopeful and depressing. But we do not hear cell mate Bill's voice, Shaw's voice, or the voices of countless other storytellers in Stanley's world, not to mention the voice that resonates with the scientific and policy undergirdings of the text. So then, we might ask, whose voice do we hear when Stanley gives voice to the jack roller? Featuring its narrative embeddedness, Stanley's story can be viewed as multivocal, voicing experience in the varied ways in which he has learned how to tell and not to tell his life, which are reflexively related to the unfolding life he describes. All the nesting narrative dolls, Stanley's included, vocalize together to construct his identity.

An ethnographic focus on narrative practice helps to avoid the reductionist and often romanticized aim of seeking to obtain the lived subject's "own" story, to hear it in his or her "own" voice, or to derive texts that convey accounts in individual subjects' "own" words. Although it is important in studying narrative practice to ground research in the vernacular and the everyday organization of accounts, it is equally important not to valorize what is individually conveyed as somehow unaffected by the environments in which is embedded. There are no narrative heroes or antiheroes who stand outside of, or rise above, their circumstances. Stanley adds flavor to his story, and his individual experiences provide the spice, but the resulting narrative stew is simmered in a more complex stock of ingredients.

There is another reductionist tendency that narrative ethnography helps us to avoid—societal reductionism. If an awareness of narrative embeddedness steers us clear of a romanticized concept of narrative ownership, it also helps us to contain the tendency to read stories as straightforward reflections of social structures or society at large. There are many phenomenal layers between the individual on the one hand and society on the other. These include what

Goffman (1983) once called the "interaction order" and what Hughes (1984), as we described, refers to as the worlds of going concerns, or the institutional order. Individual stories are embedded in both orders; they are not spun as whole cloth out of either personal or societal narratives. The lesson in this instance is that we do well not to figure that the sympathetic understanding and publication of Stanley's story, for example, simply reflects a discourse of reform. The story evidently has wended its way through diverse narrative environments, stretching from interpersonal claims to institutional imperatives, something far more complex than a totalized societal discourse would suggest.

Pursuing a narrative ethnographic approach to life stories in this regard leads us to consider the interactive and institutional mediations of accounts. It cautions against seeking to document "the" life story of a particular subject. It is a caveat against framing experience and its narrative contours in terms of master narratives, dominant discourses, or other totalized ways of framing narrativity. Rather, the leading concerns direct us to the multifaceted social contexts in which a story is embedded and how these contexts reflexively relate to stories and storytelling.

Narrative Control

Narrative ethnography opens to empirical inspection the social processes and circumstances through which narratives are constructed, promoted, and resisted. We can actually see and hear how those concerned actively call on or otherwise respond to the contexts, contingencies, and resources of narration to fashion their accounts. In other words, we can actually witness *narrative control* being exercised as ongoing social interaction and competing going concerns come into play. Such control is hardly straightforward and takes myriad forms. Here, we feature the ways in which interactional and institutional forms of control make their mark on narrative practice.

We use the concept narrative control as a way to foreground the ways in which the content and internal organization of stories are mediated by the complex environments in which they are embedded. But we need to be clear that we do not conceive of control in any deterministic or totally constraining way. Rather, we view it in terms of factors that work to shape and condition, rather than permit or prevent. A degree of narrative control was evident in many of our previous illustrations, in which locally preferred narrative themes and forms were either adopted or contested. We highlight related aspects of control in the following sections, which focus, respectively, on interactional and institutional forms of control. These forms of control reflexively enter into narrative accounts; neither form operates apart from the other.

Interactional Control

People seldom just "burst out" in stories. It takes work. For a narrative to emerge, the teller must be able to string together multiple sentences while retaining the attention of listeners without having them intrude into the conversation with anything more than signals that they are being attentive. A narrative space must be established in the give-and-take of social interaction. For the narrative to run its course, the speaker must sustain the line of talk—in cooperation with those listening to the narrative. In other words, in one way or another, narratives must be invited, incited, or initiated.

Perhaps the simplest way to introduce a narrative into a conversation is by way of a direct invitation or a question. This virtually solicits storytelling, inviting an extended response. We can see this most clearly in situations in which one party formally requests information from another. Interviews are a prime example. Whereas some interview formats (e.g., the survey interview) intentionally constrain and truncate responses, other formats (e.g., qualitative or life history interviews) intentionally activate or incite extended accounts (Gubrium & Holstein, 1995). The same is true of informal questioning in everyday conversation.

Stories, of course, are not always directly or explicitly invited. When they are not, they must be methodically introduced by the storyteller to be recognized as stories. Otherwise, they are likely to be viewed as gibberish or outbursts, so to speak. Harvey Sacks (1992a, 1992b) has noted that stories take more than a sentence to tell and that the initial challenge to storytelling is extending an account beyond that first sentence. Sacks and other conversation analysts have documented the range of conversational devices that may be used to secure the conversational "right" and "space" to extend a turn at talk, thus building it into a full-blown narrative production. Similarly, devices are available for continuing a story, staving off interruption, and sustaining a coherent line of talk across occasions at which the turn at talk might otherwise be brought to an end. Such continuations are artfully accomplished in concert between narrators and those attending to the narrative. Control, then, is not a property of one party to the conversation or the other but resides in the way that conversational partners cooperate in the emergence and development of a narrative.

Sometimes, complicity in actions that "keep the story going" also contributes to *where* the story is going. Listeners to stories can virtually induce the elaboration of particular dimensions of experience through their own story-facilitating actions. Consider the following instance taken from a nursing home interview. Grace Wheeler is a 70-year-old nursing home resident who shares a room with her 93-year-old mother, Lucy. Although Grace is the designated interviewee, in the following extract we can see how her story is guided, if not directed, by Lucy's contributions to the conversation, as Lucy vigilantly attends to Grace's telling of her life story.

INTERVIEWER: Why don't we start by your telling me about your life?

GRACE: Well that was quite a many years ago. I was born in Brinton Station, Ohio.

LUCY: She was a seven-month baby.

GRACE: I was a seven-month baby. That's what I was. [Elaborates story of growing up with her sisters and brother.] They've all been wonderful.

LUCY: They taught her. . . .

GRACE: And they taught me as well as my mom and dad. And then when radio and television came to the farm, why I learned from them. I love the quiz shows. (Gubrium, 1993, pp. 152–153)

It is clear that Lucy points the way for Grace's life story. But it is too simple to suggest that Lucy controlled Grace's story. Rather, Lucy offered resources and directions for Grace's narrative, but Grace herself picked up on Lucy's "suggestions" to elaborate and enrich her own account. They point here is not that the narrative is not really Grace's but that the narrative was jointly formulated out of this particular interactional environment.

Narrative ethnography allows us to see the sequence and circumstances from which Grace's ostensible life emerges. Such a view would not be available were we to simply track—by means of a transcript perhaps—the contours of Grace's story without noting the collaborative circumstances of its telling. Narrative ethnography gives us access to the myriad interactional practices that culminate in the production of narrative.

Institutional Control

Narrative control is not simply interactional. Indeed, many of its most profound manifestations are hardly visible because they derive from the most taken-for-granted aspects of a scene or setting. These features of control—preferred discursive regimes, for example—supply local accountability structures and conditions of possibility (Foucault, 1979) for how experience can be recounted. Inspection of narratives alone may not fully reveal the extent of control, but a comparative narrative ethnography can demonstrate how narrative environments figuratively speak the stories of their participants.

Consider, for instance, narratives of alcoholic lives that emerge under distinctly different organizational auspices. Alcoholics Anonymous (AA) is certainly the most widely recognized alcoholism treatment institution of our time. It is an especially ubiquitous and encapsulating narrative environment. In AA, alcoholism is construed as a spiritual and moral failure, not just a physical or mental disease. It is compounded by the victim's refusal to recognize that one's actions are not self-governed. Recovery comes about only when the victim accepts his or her weakness in the face of alcohol, turns over his or her fate to a "higher power," and takes the proper steps toward spiritual awakening and healing (see Denzin, 1987). This discourse of alcoholism provides an institutionally sanctioned way of understanding, and storying, drinking problems. Within the confines of AA, there is no other legitimate way of construing and talking about the problem of alcohol. The now-familiar "12 Steps" outline the institutionalized parameters of the problem and its solution. They provide a distinctive interpretive vocabulary for narrating alcoholism and recovery.

Within this narrative environment, alcoholism stories take distinctive shape. AA terminology offers familiar and available narrative resources that are available for accountable use in the countless contexts in which AA becomes salient. Although the language may not be formally imposed, its use is so pervasive that lives and experiences typically come to be storied in AA terms, as those terms are artfully applied by participants. This is evident, for example, in the following narrative conveyed by Jack, a member of an AA recovery group. Asked to share the meaning of his AA experiences with the entire group of recovering alcoholics, Jack stories his experience in this fashion:

> Step One. I know I'm powerless over alcohol. I take one drink and I can't stop. My life must be unmanageable. I have bills up to the ceiling and the family is about to leave and I've been put on notice at work. Step Two. I want to believe in God. I used to but I got away from the Church. But this isn't the God of my church. It's different. I want a God of love and caring. I know I was crazy when I drank. The last time I went out, I ended up in a motel room across town under a different name. Now that's not sane! Step Three. I want somebody else to run my life. AA and treatment seem to be doing a pretty good job right now, I hope I can stay with it. (Denzin, 1987, p. 70)

This narrative explicitly offers the AA steps as interpretive guides for understanding the alcoholism experience. AA principles shape the way the alcoholic's story is formulated; they are a veritable set of rules for narrating alcoholism. All testimonials are not this formulaic, but they pervade nearly all AA-related discussions. Regardless of venue, the narratives that emerge under AA's auspices draw on a shared stock of narrative resources from which stories may be crafted. Although narration is always artful, it invariably reflects AA's narrative environment.

Consider another alcoholic narrative that reconstructs the experience of being hospitalized for intoxication:

> I lay there on that hospital bed and went back over and reviewed my life. I thought of what liquor had done to me, the opportunities that I had discarded, the abilities that had been given me and how I had wasted them. . . . I was willing to admit to myself that I had hit bottom, that I had gotten hold of something that I didn't know how to handle by myself. So, after reviewing these things and realizing what liquor had cost me, I went to this Higher Power which to me, was God, without any reservation, and admitted that I was completely powerless over alcohol, and that I was willing to do anything in the world to get rid of the problem. In fact, I admitted that from now on I was willing to let God take over, instead of me. Each day I would try to find out what His will was, and try to fol-

> low that, rather than trying to get Him to always agree that the things I thought of myself were the things best for me. (Alcoholics Anonymous, 1976, pp. 186–187)

This classic AA narrative draws on AA themes, idioms, and vocabularies. Indeed, it is a virtual recitation—in AA language—of the prototype alcoholic's story. The language of the 12 Steps is apparent at every narrative turn, serving as the detailed building blocks of the story depicting the descending alcoholic, his self-realization, and his eventual recovery. Of course, in practice, available resources alone do not determine how experience is narrated, but it is equally clear that AA stories are adroitly crafted from a common stock of narrative building blocks.

Now consider how alcoholism narratives are distinctively constructed in a Secular Sobriety Group (SSG; see Christopher, 1988). The following extract recounts a conversation between an SSG member and some friends. Note how the narrator assembles aspects of self out of the particular set of resources and in relation to the specific institutional orientations that his SSG membership provides for him.

> "As you know," I said, "I've never kept my alcoholism a secret. I'm proud of my sobriety. Some other things in my life I'm not so pleased with, but sobriety is my most precious asset, my priority, my life-and-death necessity. . . . Now, from a factual perspective, I am just as alcoholic as I was prior to achieving sobriety; that is, I must reaffirm my priority of staying sober *no matter what!* I go to the market, work, see movies, make love, eat, sleep—all as a sober alcoholic. I'm a person with an arrested but lifelong disease. I place my sobriety and the necessity of staying sober before anything else in my life. . . . Alcoholism results in the inability to control one's drinking. Sobriety requires the acknowledgment of one's alcoholism on a daily basis, and it is never to be taken for granted. I must endure all my feelings and experiences, including injustices, failures, and whatever this uncertain life doles out. . . .
>
> "So," I continued, "in answer to your questions: I have my alcohol problem licked only on a daily basis and I continue to stay alive by protecting my conscious mind, by staying sober and avoiding the muddy waters of religion. I can't deal with reality by way of fantasy. . . . That's too scary for me. The more I stay in reality, in rationality, the better my chances. So, yes, my sobriety is a state of mind rather than mindlessness." (Christopher, 1988, pp. 87–88, original emphasis)

Clearly, the SSG has a different view of personal control than that offered by AA. Most prominently, of course, are differences with respect to spirituality. The SSG, however, also offers a distinct set of resources for conceptualizing and narrating the "alcoholic self." In practice, this translates into personal stories quite different from those assembled under the auspices of AA. As we can see in the SSG narrative, the alcoholic self is storied in terms of personal responsibility, unlike the AA self, which comes into its own only by surrendering to a higher power. The "conscious mind" is the center of self-control, in contrast with the AA self, which abandons personal control in favor of divine guidance. In SSG culture, the self is firmly grounded in secular reality, as opposed to the AA self, which centers itself in spirituality. The two recovery organizations provide sharply contrasting narrative resources and descriptive vocabularies, which, in turn, contribute to the production of distinctly different narratives of the alcoholism experience. Comparative ethnography allows us to view these differences in bold relief.

The Interplay of Interactional and Institutional Control

Institutional conventions constrain, promote, and otherwise shape narratives, but they alone do not determine how stories are formulated or what they are about. Nor does interactional control proceed in an institutional vacuum. Rather, it is the *interplay* between the artful exertions of interactional control and the organized narrative resources and restraints that ultimately shapes narrative practice.

For example, courtrooms and other "legalistic" settings would seem to be the quintessential constraining narrative environment. Rules and procedures virtually dictate who can speak, when one can speak, and what can be said. Yet, without the courtroom or hearing actors such as attorneys, judges, and hearings officers taking the initiative to implement the rules of the courts, proceedings would not take an institutionally "legal" cast. Rules must be invoked, but when they are, they constitute a controlling discursive environment for all practical purposes, one that can forcefully promote certain kinds of narratives or even altogether eliminate narrative production (see Miller & Holstein, 1996).

Similarly, less formal narrative environments provide narrative resources and parameters, but they do not dictate application. An element of interactional artfulness is always necessary. Consider, for example, how even a strictly defined set of narrative resources must be interactionally mobilized in the formulation of narratives in a treatment program for sufferers of posttraumatic stress disorder. As we shall see, the use of institutional discourse is subject to direct management with respect to prevailing narrative conventions. The means of control may be less formally asserted than in a courtroom, say, but they nevertheless condition narrative practice, suggesting if not imposing locally preferred narratives in the process.

Allan Young's (1995) study of a psychiatric unit of a Veterans Administration center providing inpatient treatment for victims of posttraumatic stress disorder (PTSD) is illustrative. In this facility, individual and group psychotherapy is aimed at addressing the etiology and symptoms of psychic distress. The psychotherapeutic philosophy guiding the PTSD program is fundamentally psychoanalytic, so the keys to recovery are said to be located in the victim's past. Problems must first be uncovered before they can be therapeutically addressed. The approach relies on two assumptions about PTSD: (1) the psychodynamic core of PTSD is a repetitive compulsion; the victim is psychologically compelled to reenact the behavior that precipitated the disorder in a futile attempt to gain mastery over the circumstances that originally overwhelmed him, and (2) to recover, the patient must recall his traumatic memory, disclose it to his therapist and fellow patients during group psychotherapy, and subject the memory and its narrative to therapeutic scrutiny. The facility thus has a well-articulated model of the disease, which provides staff and patients with a way of conceptualizing and characterizing PTSD (Young, 1995, p. 183).

The use of the center's model is obvious to participants and develops quite naturally as each displays his or her command of the language of the model and its application. But narrative control can sometimes become quite explicit in relation to the local priority of the model. When narratives emerge in ways that do not accord with the model, group participants may be reminded to "use the model," to rethink or "re-story" experience in line with the center's therapeutic discourse. In such instances, we literally hear the narrative environment being imposed in ongoing interaction. Consider the following exchange in a psychotherapy session involving Carol, the therapist, and a group of patients:

CAROL: Say to yourself, I've been punishing myself and people around me for twenty years. Say Jack, you *can* choose to stop.

JACK: Listen, Carol. On some nights, I feel anxiety going through my body like electricity. It started in Vietnam. It wasn't just a feeling. It was anxiety together with terrible chest pains and difficulty breathing. . . . And I'm still getting them.

CAROL: What would you call it?

JACK: Well, I know that it's called a "panic attack." But I didn't know it then.

CAROL: No, I mean what would you call it using the terms of the model—the model that you learned about during orientation phase?

JACK: I don't really know, Carol. My mind is confused right now.

CAROL: The model says that we're dominated by two drives, aggression and sex, and that—

JACK: Listen, Carol. When I got these attacks, I sure didn't want to get fucked, and I can't believe it was my aggression.

CAROL: We've got to think of these events, your difficulty breathing, we've got to think of them in terms of *guilt*, of your wanting to *punish* yourself. We need to get in touch with your conflict. . . . (Young, 1995, p. 245, emphasis in the original)

Jack's short initial story about his anxiety calls on a commonplace clinical vocabulary for describing the psychic distress that started in Vietnam. His use of "panic attack" to portray his experience is neither clinically incorrect nor commonsensically unfamiliar. Nonetheless, Carol moves to bring the articulation of the problem under the narrative purview of the model, asking Jack to think back to how he had originally been taught to conceptualize his problem "using the terms of the model." She continues to specify just what the model might say in relation to Jack's problems, only to be interrupted by Jack's assertion that the model did not seem to apply in this case. Insisting that he felt that neither his libidinal drives ("I sure didn't want to get fucked") nor his instinct toward aggression ("I can't believe it was my aggression") were behind his condition, Jack resists the application of the model. Carol, however, perseveres, insisting that "we've got to think of them" in terms specified by the model. Although resistance is always possible, the model as a narrative resource was a constant presence, a source of control available to be asserted in practice. Jack's story emerges in relation to the narrative controls in place, which are visible only through ethnographic examination of the therapy setting.

Conclusion

Herbert Blumer (1969) once argued that concepts are as much procedural as they are theoretical. They not only provide understanding but also sensitize us to ways of embracing the empirical world. Such is the case with narrative ethnography. The concept is theoretical in that it specifies a field and an object of inquiry—narrative practice. It is procedural in that it recommends methods that are necessary to capture the empirical material of narrative practice in its contextual complexity.

By framing our interest in stories in terms of narrative practice—the whats, hows, wheres, and whens of narrative production—our approach to narrative ethnography expands research concerns beyond the internal themes, structures, and structuring of stories to simultaneously and reflexively include narrative's external, contextual organization. It is no longer sufficient to seek the meaning of narratives by examining only their internal organization. Instead, we need to consider the social organization of the storying process as meaning-making activity in its own right. Following Goffman and others, narrative ethnography orients toward the situated character of accounts and turns to the interaction and institutional order to better understand the relation between narrative, experience, and meaning.

Narrative ethnography is an emergent method in that it requires the researcher to recombine and reconfigure tried-and-true technical approaches to data collection and management with new analytical sensibilities and emphases. Traditional narrative analysis has profitably focused on the internal organization of stories and has developed effective ways of discerning and describing narrative structures. Narrative ethnography encourages the combination of these methods with the tools of the ethnographic trade—close observation and interviewing, to name the most prominent. This expands the research purview beyond the narrative itself to the context of its production.

Narrative ethnography calls for new analytical sensitivities and emphases. The focus is on the contexts, conditions, and resources of the storying process. Narrative ethnography casts a wider net in an effort to describe and explicate the storying of experience in everyday life. The goal is to capture—through multifocal analysis—the contextual influences and dynamics that shape narrative. Narrative ethnography asks the researcher to be more inclusive in thinking about what constitutes appropriate data and how they should be analyzed. It prompts new questions about the storying process, directing attention textually outward as much as textually inward, so to speak. Existing analytical tools from conventional narrative analysis, conversation analysis, discourse analysis, textual analysis, ethnomethodology, deconstructionism, and other cutting-edge orientations to the dynamics of interaction provide a solid stock of analytic resources, but they need to be incorporated into the field of narrative analysis.

Narrative ethnography is informed and guided by an emergent stock of concepts and terms that describe narrative practice. This chapter has presented a number of these terms: narrative resources, narrative environments, narrative embeddedness, and narrative control. The challenge for the future is to expand the vocabulary to account for the widest possible range of analytical possibilities. Each new term or concept prompts new research questions. For example, the concept of narrative control leads us to ask what the mechanisms and sources of control might possibly be. This, in turn, points us to both interactional and institutional realms for possible answers. The terms narrative horizons, narrative composition, and narrative linkage (see Gubrium, 1993; Holstein & Gubrium, 2000b) point researchers to questions about possible realms of understanding and how they are combined into meaningful constellations by virtue of the procedural connections that are asserted in the process. Like all ethnography, the new questions for narrative ethnographers are open-ended. The research enterprise is exploratory and explanatory, aiming to shed light on the narrative process as much as on narrative products.

Of course, process and product are reflexively related. Perhaps the most innovative contribution narrative ethnography might make is to help researchers rethink taken-for-granted views of narrativity. Viewing narrative practice as situated social action allows the researcher to reconfigure traditional understandings. Structures that have conventionally been viewed as given and frequently treated as explanatory variables can now be seen as contextually conditioned social constructions—storied realities. Narrative ethnography provides us with the conceptual and methodological tool kit to empirically discern and describe narrative structures such as the family (Gubrium & Holstein, 1990), the self (Holstein & Gubrium, 2000b), and the life course (Holstein & Gubrium, 2000a). It provides a way of making visible the socially constructed and organized contours of these seemingly obdurate realities by featuring their storied presence in everyday life.

References

Alcoholics Anonymous. (1976). *Alcoholics Anonymous.* New York: Alcoholics Anonymous World Services.

Anderson, E. (1976). *A place on the corner.* Chicago: University of Chicago Press.

Atkinson, P., & Hammersley, M. (1994). Ethnography and participant observation. In N. K. Denzin & Y. S. Lincoln (Eds.), *Handbook of qualitative research* (pp. 248–261). Thousand Oaks, CA: Sage.

Bauman, R. (1986). *Story, performance, and event.* Cambridge, UK: Cambridge University Press.

Behar, R. (1993). *Translated women: Crossing the border with Esperanza's story.* Boston: Beacon Press.

Behar, R. (1996). *The vulnerable observer: Anthropology that breaks your heart.* Boston: Beacon Press.

Bell, S. (1988). Becoming a political woman: The reconstruction and interpretation of experience through stories. In A. D. Todd & S. Fisher (Eds.), *Gender and discourse: The power of talk* (pp. 97–123). Norwood, NJ: Ablex.

Benford, R. D. (1993). Frame disputes with the nuclear disarmament movement. *Social Forces, 71*, 677–701.

Benford, R. D. (1997). An insider's critique of the social movement framing perspective. *Sociological Inquiry, 67*, 409–430.

Benford, R. D., & Snow, D. A. (2000). Framing processes and social movements: An overview and assessment. *Annual Review of Sociology, 26*, 611–639.

Birren, J., Kenyon, G., Ruth, K.-E., Schroots, J., & Svensson, T. (Eds.). (1996). *Aging and biography: Explorations in adult development*. New York: Springer.

Blumer, H. (1969). *Symbolic interactionism*. Englewood Cliffs, NJ: Prentice Hall.

Bruner, J. (1986). *Actual minds, possible worlds*. Cambridge, MA: Harvard University Press.

Buckholdt, D. R., & Gubrium, J. F. (1979). *Caretakers: Treating emotionally disturbed children*. Thousand Oaks, CA: Sage.

Chase, S. (1995). *Ambiguous empowerment: The work narratives of women school superintendents*. Amherst: University of Massachusetts Press.

Christopher, J. (1988). *How to stay sober: Recovery without religion*. Buffalo, NY: Prometheus Books.

Cicourel, A. V. (1974). *Cognitive sociology*. New York: Free Press.

Clandinin, D. J., & Connolly, F. M. (2000). *Narrative inquiry: Experience and story in qualitative research*. San Francisco: Jossey-Bass.

Cooley, C. H. (1964). *Human nature and the social order*. New York: Schocken. (Original work published 1903)

Cortazzi, M. (1993). *Narrative analysis*. London: Falmer Press.

Crossley, M. (2000). *Introducing narrative psychology*. Buckingham, UK: Open University Press.

Crossley, M. (2003). Formulating narrative psychology: The limitations of contemporary social constructionism. *Narrative Inquiry, 13*, 287–300.

Daiute, C., & Lightfoot, C. (Eds.). (2003). *Narrative analysis: Studying the development of individuals in society*. Thousand Oaks, CA: Sage.

Davis, J. E. (2005). Victim narratives and victim selves: False memory syndrome and the power of accounts. *Social Problems, 52*, 529–548.

Denzin, N. K. (1987). *The alcoholic self*. Newbury Park, CA: Sage.

Ellis, C. (1991). Sociological introspection and emotional experience. *Symbolic Interaction, 14*, 23–50.

Ellis, C., & Bochner, A. P. (Eds.). (1996). *Composing ethnography: Alternative forms of qualitative writing*. Walnut Creek, CA: AltaMira Press.

Ellis, C., & Flaherty, M. (Eds.). (1992). *Investigating subjectivity*. Newbury Park, CA: Sage.

Fields, J. (2005). "Children having children": Race, innocence, and sexuality education. *Social Problems, 52*, 549–571.

Foucault, M. (1979). *Discipline and punish*. New York: Vintage Books.

Fox, P. J. (2000). The role of the concept of Alzheimer disease in the development of the Alzheimer's Association in the United States. In P. J. Whitehouse, K. Maurer, & J. F. Ballenger (Eds.), *Concepts of Alzheimer's disease* (pp. 209–233). Baltimore: Johns Hopkins University Press.

Garland, D. (2001). *The culture of control: Crime and social order in contemporary society*. Chicago: University of Chicago Press.

Gergen, K. J. (1991). *The saturated self*. New York: Basic Books.

Ginsburg, F. (1989). *Contested lives: The abortion debate in an American community*. Berkeley: University of California Press.

Goffman, E. (1959). *Presentation of self in everyday life*. New York: Doubleday.

Goffman, E. (1961). *Asylums*. Garden City, NY: Doubleday.

Goffman, E. (1983). The interaction order. *American Sociological Review, 48*, 1–17.

Goodall, H. L., Jr. (2000). *Writing the new ethnography*. Lanham, MD: AltaMira.

Greimas, A. J. (1983). *Structural semantics*. Lincoln: University of Nebraska Press.

Gubrium, J. F. (1986). *Oldtimers and Alzheimer's: The descriptive organization of senility*. Greenwich, CT: JAI Press.

Gubrium, J. F. (1992). *Out of control: Family therapy and domestic disorder*. Newbury Park, CA: Sage.

Gubrium, J. F. (1993). *Speaking of life: Horizons of meaning for nursing home residents*. Hawthorne, NY: Aldine de Gruyter.

Gubrium, J. F., & Buckholdt, D. R. (1982). *Describing care: Image and practice in rehabilitation*. Cambridge, MA: Oelgeschlager, Gunn & Hain.

Gubrium, J. F., & Holstein, J. A. (1990). *What is family?* Mountain View, CA: Mayfield.

Gubrium, J. F., & Holstein, J. A. (1995). Biographical work and new ethnography. In R. Josselson & A. Lieblich (Eds.), *Interpreting experience: The narrative study of lives* (pp. 45–58). Newbury Park, CA: Sage.

Gubrium, J. F., & Holstein, J. A. (Eds.). (2001). *Institutional selves: Troubled identities in a postmodern world*. New York: Oxford University Press.

Hawkes, T. (1977). *Structuralism and semiotics*. Berkeley: University of California Press.

Herman, L., & Vervaeck, B. (2005). *Handbook of narrative analysis*. Lincoln: University of Nebraska Press.

Holstein, J. A. (1993). *Court-ordered insanity: Interpretive practice and involuntary commitment*. Hawthorne, NY: Aldine de Gruyter.

Holstein, J. A., & Gubrium, J. F. (2000a). *Constructing the life course*. Lanham, MD: AltaMira Press.

Holstein, J. A., & Gubrium, J. F. (2000b). *The self we live by: Narrative identity in a postmodern world*. New York: Oxford University Press.

Hughes, E. C. (1984). *The sociological eye*. New Brunswick, NJ: Transaction Books.

Hymes, D. (1964). The ethnography of communication. *American Anthropologist, 66*, 6–56.

Irwin, J. (1970). *The felon*. Englewood Cliffs, NJ: Prentice Hall.

Kenyon, G. M., & Randall, W. L. (1997). *Restorying our lives: Personal growth through autobiographical reflection*. Westport, CT: Praeger.

Labov, W. (1972). The transformation of experience in narrative syntax. In W. Labov, *Language in the inner city: Studies in the Black English vernacular* (pp. 354–396). Philadelphia: University of Pennsylvania Press.

Lieblich, A., Tuval-Mashiach, R., & Zilber, T. (1998). *Narrative research: Reading, analysis, and interpretation*. Thousand Oaks, CA: Sage.

Liebow, E. (1967). *Tally's corner: A study of Negro streetcorner men*. Boston: Little, Brown.

Marvasti, A. (2003). *Being homeless: Textual and narrative constructions*. Lanham, MD: Lexington Books.

McAdams, D. P. (1993). *The stories we live by: Personal myths and the making of the self*. New York: Guilford Press.

Mead, G. H. (1934). *Mind, self, and society*. Chicago: University of Chicago Press.

Miller, G. (1994). Toward ethnographies of institutional discourse. *Journal of Contemporary Ethnography, 23*, 280–306.

Miller, G. (1997). *Becoming miracle workers: Language and meaning in brief therapy*. Hawthorne, NY: Aldine de Gruyter.

Miller, G., & Holstein, J. A. (1996). *Discupte domanis and welfare claims: Conflict and law in public bureaucracies*. Greenwich, CT: JAI Press.

Narayan, K. (1989). *Storytellers, saints, and scoundrels: Folk narrative in Hindu religious teaching*. Philadelphia: University of Pennsylvania Press.

Plummer, K. (2001). *Documents of life: 2*. London: Sage.

Polkinghorne, D. E. (1988). *Narrative knowing and the human sciences*. Albany: State University of New York Press.

Propp, V. (1968). *Morphology of the folk tale*. Austin: University of Texas Press. (Original work published 1928)

Richardson, L. (1990a). Narrative and sociology. *Journal of Contemporary Ethnography, 9*, 116–136.

Richardson, L. (1990b). *Writing strategies: Reaching diverse audiences*. Newbury Park, CA: Sage.

Riessman, C. K. (1990). *Divorce talk*. New Brunswick, NJ: Rutgers University Press.

Riessman, C. K. (1993). *Narrative analysis*. Thousand Oaks, CA: Sage.

Sacks, H. (1992a). *Lectures on conversation: Vol. I*. Oxford, UK: Blackwell.

Sacks, H. (1992b). *Lectures on conversation: Vol. II*. Oxford, UK: Blackwell.

Saussure, F. de. (1966). *Course in general linguistics*. New York: McGraw-Hill. (Original work published 1915)

Shaw, C. R. (1966). *The jack roller: A delinquent boy's own story*. Chicago: University of Chicago Press. (Original work published 1930)

Snow, D. A. (2003). Social movements. In L. T. Reynolds & N. J. Herman-Kinney (Eds.), *Handbook of symbolic interactionism* (pp. 811–833). Lanham, MD: AltaMira.

Tedlock, B. (1991). From participant observation to the observation of participation: The emergence of narrative ethnography. *Journal of Anthropological Research, 47*, 69–94.

Tedlock, B. (1992). *The beautiful and the dangerous: Encounters with the Zuni Indians*. New York: Viking.

Tedlock, B. (2004). Narrative ethnography as social science discourse. *Studies in Symbolic Interaction, 27*, 23–31.

Thomas, W. I., & Znaniecki, F. (1927). *The Polish peasant in Europe and America*. New York: Knopf. (Original work published 1918–1920)

Weinberg, D. (2005). *Of others inside: Insanity, addiction, and belonging in America*. Philadelphia: Temple University Press.

Whyte, W. F. (1943). *Street corner society*. Chicago: University of Chicago Press.

Young, A. (1995). *The harmony of illusions*. Princeton, NJ: Princeton University Press.

CHAPTER 13

Public Ethnography

Carol A. Bailey

After many years of flying under the radar, public ethnography is (re)emerging as a strategy of inquiry. Public ethnographers conduct research on and participate in the fight against repressive conditions. Public ethnographies are theoretically grounded and require rigorous data collection. Practitioners adopt compelling writing styles and utilize a variety of outlets and formats in an attempt to disseminate their findings to and engage in dialogue with other academics and the public at large (Brady, 2004; Sanday, 2003; Tedlock, 2005). They hope to motivate others to join in the struggle to create a better world. Lines between academics and activism are nonexistent for public ethnographers; research on social injustices and actively working to reduce them are epistemologically linked (Kleidman, 2004; Rodriguez, 2003; Sanday, 2003).

Interacting with graduate students over the years, I have found that many of them are attracted to sociology and anthropology because of their desire to "change the world." As only one of many examples, when he was a graduate student at the University of Wisconsin–Madison, Eric Haanstad wrote: "My goal, which I suspect I share with many students, is simply to help create positive social change in the world. I want to move towards economic and social equality whether through opening the minds of students, informing public policy or exposing social problems" (2001a).

Over the course of graduate students' academic careers, this drive to help others can become buried beneath the academic pressures of publications, grants, teaching, coursework, comprehensive exams, and the need to finish a dissertation before their funding ends. Warnings from faculty that "you'll never get published or hired with that topic" and chastisements that research should not be driven by ideology can direct students away from the very issues that drew them to the discipline in the first place. Even after students become faculty members, the requirements of academic life—numerous publications, grants, teaching, service—often continue to subsume what was once an ardent passion for reducing injustices.

I have long shared students' faith in sociology and other academic disciplines as positive agents of social change. At a tender age, I was inspired by Jane Addams's commitment to social reform and to an antiwar stance. As a graduate student in sociology, I was further influenced by the writings of Robert Lynd and C. Wright Mills, whose charge that sociologists develop ways to avoid or end international warfare is as important now as it was then (Horowitz, 1983, p. 89). In fact, this sentiment was echoed in 2003, when the membership of the American Sociological Association (ASA) passed a resolution calling for the "immediate end of the war against Iraq" (American Sociological Association, 2003). To me, eradicating inequality *is* the stuff of sociology. Thus I am energized by the hope that if public ethnography (re)gains legitimacy, this strategy of inquiry could be a vehicle by which graduate students to seasoned scholars can blend their efforts to reduce human misery with their research agendas.

Public Ethnography

Part of the difficulty with discussing public ethnography is that a well-codified definition of it does not yet exist. I proffer that a theoretically sound and methodologically rigorous form of scholarship can be considered a public ethnography if in general it meets the following conditions: (1) its primary means of collecting data is in-depth field research, (2) it is motivated by a desire to reduce social injustice, (3) it critiques the structures and social processes that promote inequality, (4) it includes active participation of the scholar in the fight against repressive conditions, and (5) its desired audience extends beyond academic circles to include some facet of the public at large.

Public ethnography is not just one but many things. It is, and yet is not, public interest anthropology, public anthropology, public sociology, participatory action research, activist anthropology, collaborative action research, critical medical anthropology, action anthropology, queer methods (Plummer, 2005), critical humanism (Plummer, 2005), scholar-activist approach (Kershaw, 2005), critical ethnography, advocacy anthropology, interpretive ethnography (Denzin, 1999), global ethnography, "militant" anthropology (Scheper-Hughes, 2005, *anthropology.berkeley.edu/nsh.html*), institutional ethnography, political anthropology, public-voice ethnography (Denzin, 2003), public interest sociology (Klein, 2005), engaged anthropology, and applied ethnography, among others.

Important subtle and not so subtle differences exist among these variants. For example, a critical ethnographer might engage in a critique of sociopolitical structures, whereas some applied ethnographers would not, such as those who are employed at such places as Xerox's Palo Alto Research Center, Intel, Microsoft, Wells Fargo, IDEO, Cheskin, and other high-tech firms (Fitzgerald, 2005; Kincheloe & McLaren, 2005). Those using a scholar–activist approach have a greater likelihood of framing their research within a theoretical position derived from Africana studies than does someone employing queer methods. Participatory action researchers tend to focus on local problems that might or might not include issues of health, the domain of critical medical anthropologists.

In addition to their differences, the aforementioned strategies of inquiry share many features. They can have similar methodological procedures, theoretical foundations, methods of data collection, and paradigmatic assumptions. The lines between different strategies are not always clear; they shift and are nonexistent at times, and the research questions and methodologies that underlie them seem to be converging (Lamphere, 2004). Consequently, it is not always certain how a particular study should be classified. For example, in this chapter I discuss several books as exemplars of public ethnography, but Douglas Foley and Angela Valenzuela (2005) identify them as critical ethnographies, and at the same time they are part of a series on public interest anthropology.

Even a less-than-engaged reader of this chapter will frequently notice that much of what is said herein applies to multiple methodologies and scholars of every ilk. I am making no claims otherwise. Rather, I am suggesting that the combination of motives, priorities, and a particular configuration of features distinguishes public ethnography from other strategies of inquiry. Given that sometimes we academics engage in methodological wrestling that drifts into much ado about nothing, I prefer to basically ignore the differences among closely related strategies. For the most part, I refer to similar research traditions under the umbrella term *public ethnography*; on occasion, I use the terminology used by the author I cite. Furthermore, I focus on and blend together discussions of sociology and anthropology and note that what is presented applies to some other disciplines, as well.

As the undergirding methodology of public ethnography, ethnography has a well-established canon and an array of excellent sources that offer guidance to practitioners. Thus I do not provide an overview of how to engage in ethnographic research other than to note that many of the features debated in the ethnographic literature—such as the "crisis of representation," reflexivity, evaluation standards, paradigmatic commensurability, and so on—also concern public ethnographers. Rather than covering issues discussed at length elsewhere, I focus on only a few features particularly relevant to public ethnographers.

Academic Context

Public ethnography has a long history in anthropology and sociology. Franz Boas, W.E.B. DuBois, and Jane Addams often are cited as quintessential examples of ethnographic researchers who during the first half of the 20th century engaged in social critique and activism. Less well known but equally important, St. Clair Drake, one of the few black anthropologists prior to World War II, engaged in applied, activist ethnography in the U.S. South, Chicago's Southside, the Tiger Bay community in Cardiff, Wales, and Ghana. Drake's combination of activism and ethnographic research contributed to the field of politically engaged ethnography and the development of African American studies (Weiss, 2006).

Although research on important social problems was being conducted in the 1920s, some sociologists began to move away from ethnographic research and concerns for social justice to quantitative techniques divorced from critiques of social systems. This trend gained momentum in 1929 when, during his presidential address to the American Sociological Society William Ogburn instructed sociologists not to become involved in social activism (Feagin, 2001, p. 8). With notable exceptions, ethnographic research on critical social problems was fairly quiet over the next several decades. In the 1960s, a smattering of renewed interest arose that continues to this day; however, this form of scholarship has yet to reclaim the high status it once held.

Although it never died, it was not until the end of the 20th century that public ethnography began to breathe fresh air. In these early days of the 21st century, it shows signs of reinvigorated health, aided by a series of events, only some of which are presented here. Public ethnography is being revitalized in part because of the renewed interest in public anthropology and public sociology, and thus my discussion of it is framed within the debates surrounding these.

The late 1990s were a fruitful time in sociology for research on important social problems, with the publication of several highly acclaimed urban ethnographies, such as those by Bourgois (1995), Anderson (1999), Duneier (1999), and Newman (1999). These authors used ethnographic methods to explore issues of racism and economic inequality and critiqued the social institutions that contributed to them. Around this same time, anthropologists expanded their commitment to public forms of anthropology, with college and university departments adding degree and certificate programs and training in public interest anthropology. The *American Anthropologist* mirrored this interest by publishing more politically engaged essays in a 5-year period than it had in the previous 100 years (Tedlock, 2005, p. 479). The decade ended with the presidential symposium at the 1999 American Anthropological Association annual meeting titled "A Public Anthropology!!!"

Agger (2000) ushered in the new decade with his book, *Public Sociology: From Social Facts to Literary Acts*. A year later, Feagin's (2001) presidential address at the American Sociological Association annual meeting reminded sociologists of the magnitude and horror of worldwide inequalities and strongly encouraged them to return to their roots by conducting research that could help eliminate forms of social oppression. Also in 2001, the University of California Press began its public anthropology book series, and *Public Anthropology: The Graduate Journal* was created as a forum for graduate students to share their research and argue for a more public form of anthropology.

A series of events in 2002 contributed to the growth of public ethnography and public sociology. The journal *Ethnography* and the Center for Urban Ethnography at the University of California, Berkeley, hosted an international conference, "Ethnografest," on the past, present, and future of ethnography (Wacquant, 2003). Pierre Bourdieu was to give the closing address on "Ethnography as Public Service." Unfortunately, he died before he was able to do so, but his commitment to social justice will no doubt continue to inspire social activists. That same year, the American Sociological Association and the University of California Press printed the first edition of *Contexts*, a magazine directed toward both academic and nonacademic audiences. *Context* markets itself as bringing sociological knowledge to bear on issues of public interest for purposes of generating policy and public debate. Also in 2002, Herbert Gans wrote in *Footnotes* that public sociology is needed and could lead to increased respect for the discipline.

In 2003, *Footnotes* introduced a new occasional column, "Public Sociology," designed to highlight the activities of sociologists who work with community members to improve the well-being of others. That same year, the Justice Action Network of Anthropologists was created at the American Anthropological Association meeting (Tedlock, 2005).

Interest in public sociology received a huge boost when "Public Sociologies" became the theme of the 2004 ASA annual meeting. Michael Burawoy's presidential address was titled "For Public Sociology." Burawoy (2004) defined public sociology as that which "engages publics beyond the academy in dialogue about matters of political and moral concern" (p. 1607). At this conference, ASA created the Task Force on Institutionalizing Public Sociologies.

The following year, Burawoy's address was published in *The British Journal of Sociology* and the *American Sociological Review*. His speech and additional articles by him led to a flurry of activity and responses in such publications as *Social Forces*, *The British Journal of Sociology*, *Critical Sociology*, and *Social Problems*.

In addition to public sociology, public ethnography itself began to receive specific attention. In 2005, a group of scholars held a 2-day seminar on public ethnography at the School of American Research. The cochairs and participants represented a variety of disciplines, such as anthropology, nursing, occupational science, occupational therapy, and political ecology. At this workshop, Barbara Tedlock and Nancy Lewis (2005) proposed a book series on public ethnography that would be "socially grounded and emotionally engaged, participatory, collaborative, and well-written" with the "hopes of educating and moving the public to action." The same year, public ethnography achieved an important milestone when the third edition of *The Sage Handbook of Qualitative Research* (Denzin & Lincoln, 2005) included a chapter titled "The Observation of Participation and the Emergence of Public Ethnography" (Tedlock, 2005). Although public ethnography, as I define it, is discussed elsewhere in the Denzin and Lincoln (2005) handbook and in earlier editions, other books, and journal articles, it finally reached the status of deserving its own chapter in this well-known series of handbooks.

Public sociology continued to garner attention in 2006 and 2007. At the 2006 annual meeting of the ASA, regular paper sessions, a thematic session, a refereed roundtable, and invited sessions on public sociology were held (American Sociological Association, 2006). Three edited books about public sociology were published during this time period (Blau & Smith, 2006; Clawson et al., 2007; Nicols, 2007). These events and others set the stage for the resurgence of interest in more activist forms of research. Nonetheless, despite its (re)emergence, public ethnography is not without its critics.

I think of public ethnography as just another in the list of adjectival ethnographies—critical, institutional, autoethnography, visual, corporate (Fitzgerald, 2005), analytic (Lofland, 1995), and so on (Hesse-Biber & Leavy, 2004). That is, public ethnographies are simply another legitimate choice in an array of options, an option that researchers can select or not. Consistent with my view, most public ethnographers would not argue that public ethnography is superior to other forms of inquiry, nor would they suggest that *all* scholars *should* engage in this type of scholarship. Still, public ethnographies generally are not considered as just one of many approaches. Opposition, quite emotional at times, exists to including public ethnography as a legitimate form of scholarship.

One concern expressed by opponents of public ethnography is that direct involvement in eradicating social injustices might decrease the legitimacy of sociology and anthropology in the eyes of other academics, elites, and the larger public (Feagin, 2001, p. 6). If sociological practice and professional organizations are viewed as not politically neutral, disciplinary expertise is too easily discounted, thereby reducing the persuasive power of sociology in debates about important social issues of concern to individual sociologists (Massey, 2007).

Additionally, some academics argue that politically motivated scholarship could lead to disciplinary requirements of a shared moral position. Given that more than a few public ethnographers are guided by theories that can be grouped under the label of critical theories, some fear that if the discipline became associated with a specific political position, it would be decidedly leftist, not a perspective that they share.

Another concern is that public ethnographies might negatively affect the position of sociology in the highly competitive battle for funding from the government, foundations, and other sources (Burawoy, 2005b, p. 75). After all, when they critique political and corporate structures that have ties to funding agencies, public ethnographers actively bite the hand that feeds them. This is not to imply that public ethnographies are never funded. Major funding agencies such as the National Science Foundation, National Institute on Drug Abuse, National Endowment for the Humanities, Ford Foundation, and Russell Sage Foundation have provided grant money for this type of scholarship. Whether the worries about the effect of public ethnographies on status and funding are realistic remains an unanswered empirical question.

Arguably, the assertion that has had the largest effect on preventing the legitimization of public ethnography is that it is not research. What Stephen Kemmis and Robin McTaggart (2003) write about participatory research also applies to public ethnography:

> Criticisms leveled against PR include that it lacks scientific rigor, confusing social activism

> and community development with research. Such practices may employ desirable means and serve desirable ends, but to confuse them with research—or, worse still, to disguise or dignify them as research—is a fundamental form of deception and manipulation, in this view. (p. 338)

Few academic incentives or professional rewards exist to encourage engagement in this type of research (Brady, 2004). Even when guided by academic theories and executed using established methodologies, activist research is rarely included in tenure and promotion guidelines. When it is evaluated within departmental reward structures, it is often classified as a service activity, typically considered less important than research and teaching (American Sociological Association Task Force on Institutionalizing Public Sociologies, 2005). The ASA task force proposes that if sociology is going to meet its promise of having relevance for addressing important social problems, then tenure and promotion guidelines need to include engaged research. The task force (2005) provides a series of recommendations that, if followed, would help guide departments in evaluating this kind of scholarship.

Increasingly, public ethnographers are making the case that the dichotomy between public sociology and anthropology and professional sociology and anthropology should be nonexistent. Yet the current conservative climate and the increased influence of legislators and powerful business interests within the academy might constrain, and may well prevent, a restructured reward system that would value publicly engaged scholarship (Ladson-Billings & Donnor, 2005, p.298). It is not likely that most of the next generation of graduate students will be supported if they want to conduct activist scholarship. Indeed, in an interview with Haanstad (2001b), Bourgois said that he thinks that, more than ever, prestigious anthropology departments are training students *not* to engage in research on important social problems.

Certainly, not all excellent schools shy away from public forms of scholarship. As a few of many examples, the departments of anthropology at the University of Oregon and the University of Pennsylvania and departments of sociology at the University of California, Berkeley, Florida Atlantic University, and Boston College support engaged scholarship. The University of North Carolina, Wilmington, will soon have a master's program in public sociology. The commitment to civil involvement at the University of Minnesota is so strong that budget requests from the colleges must identify their public engagement goals (Aminzade, 2004). Members of the department of sociology at the University of Minnesota sit on boards of nonprofit organizations, consult with community organizations, and testify at legislative hearings (Aminzade, 2004).

The University of Texas at Austin is an example of an excellent graduate department that emphasizes activist anthropology. Its students are required to engage in an activist research internship that lasts at least 6 months, from which they derive their master's report. Their program description states, in part, that:

> Activist anthropology is predicated on the idea that we need not choose between first-rate scholarship, on the one hand, and carefully considered political engagement, on the other. To the contrary, we contend that activist research can enhance the empirical breadth and the theoretical sophistication—as well as the practical usefulness of the knowledge that we produce as anthropologists. Finally, we intend to bring the activist anthropology track "home" in a dual sense: opening space for alternative forms of anthropological training within our department and university, and encouraging activist research on U.S. society, challenging the deeply seated dichotomy between "over there" (where political engagement happens) and "here" where more conservative premises often prevail. (*www.utexas.edu/cola/depts/anthropology/programs/activist/*)

In spite of the list of fine institutions that value engaged scholarship, the list is considerably longer of schools that offer few rewards for blending activism with research. Unless peers begin to value activist scholarship, Brady (2004) predicts that sociologists and anthropologists are not likely to veer from their present path. Foley and Valenzuela (2005) note that to prevent losing credibility within academic departments some critical ethnographers pull back into an academically safe space—being political but in an academically acceptable manner (p. 222). Others who desire to engage in scholarship that contributes to social change either leave research universities, teach at other types of institutions, are fired, or voluntarily leave academics altogether (Becker, Gans, Newman, & Vaughan, 2004). Thus public ethnographers and other politically motivated researchers struggle with the tensions among cultural critique, community and political activism, critiques of sociopolitical structures, and academic security (Foley & Valenzuela, 2005).

In Europe, the situation for public ethnographers is not as bleak as it is for those in the United States. Europeans tend to be more open to engaged scholarship, and the lines between public and professional sociology are more fluid and permeable (Barth, 2001). Burawoy points out that at times public sociology takes precedence over professional sociology in poor countries (2004, p. 1614).

In spite of barriers that often dissuade some scholars from conducting public ethnographies, a growing number of academics have the support, the training, or the secure position or are willing to define their own paths and create powerful scholarship that challenges the status quo.

Theory and Research Questions

Public ethnographers are sometimes labeled as atheoretical. On the contrary, public ethnographers come in all sorts of theoretical sizes and shapes. Some of the more common theories utilized by public ethnographers are critical race theory; a variety of types of cultural studies, critical, and feminist theories; Marxism and neo-Marxism; poststructuralist, womanism, postcolonial, postmodernism, standpoint, ethnic, queer, Aboriginal, and indigenous theories; critical pedagogy; and empowerment theories, to name just a few. One of the reasons that the label of nontheoretical is so easily attached is that even scholars whose ethnographies are theoretically well grounded often omit explicit and detailed discussions of their theoretical perspectives when they disseminate their work, just as they might exclude methodological details if not appropriate for their target audience. Thus public ethnographers are often falsely accused of conducting atheoretical research.

At times, the nontheoretical label is accurate. Norman Denzin, for example, calls for a type of interpretive ethnography that avoids the abstractions and high theory of traditional academic discourse (1999, p. 510). The argument is that these are less effective in scholarship rooted in a moral ethic that is repulsed by assaults on human dignity. In addition to speaking truth to power and a call to action, interpretive ethnographers aspire to a "higher, sacred goal" (Denzin, 1999, p. 518). If these can be better achieved without theory, then so be it.

Public ethnographers sometimes ask the *big* research questions, as called for in Feagin's ASA presidential address (2001). For example, four recent public ethnographies have focused on war. "What is war?" and "Why would humans engage in one of the most profoundly unpleasant activities imaginable—one capable of extinguishing humans themselves?" are the overarching research questions for Nordstrom's study of war and international profiteering (2004, p. 10). She also asks more specific research questions: "What happens to women, female guerrillas, children, and healers treating not only war wounds but also entire societies bleeding from assaults on their core institutions and values? How do civilians live their lives on the front lines? Who are the true brokers of war?" (p. 10).

Similarly, when examining the war in Chechnya that erupted in 1994, Tishkov's (2004) research question was, "Why do people who lived side by side start killing one another?" (p. xii). Alexander Hinton (2005) began his book with the question he first wanted to pose to the Khmer Rouge, who had enacted policies that resulted in the deaths of over one and a half million Cambodians, "Why did you kill?" (2005, p. 1). As a master's student at the University of Oregon, Hill (2001) worked with a team of researchers on the cultural politics of exhumation work in Guatemala. They exhumed some of the hundreds of thousands of people killed in Guatemala's civil war that ended in 1996. Part of her role as a public anthropologist was to examine how exhumations contribute to indigenous cultural survival in Guatemala. The research was intended, in part, to educate the public about the war in Guatemala with the hope that doing so would prevent further violence.

Research questions are not always as broad as those stated here, but public ethnographers invariably address a wide range of important social concerns. They study such issues as the AIDS crisis, environmental degradation, immigration, poverty, racism, human rights violations, health, corporate agriculture, pollution, pharmaceutical dumping, transnational labor migration, educational practices, the media, medical practices, the prison industry, class exploitation, hate crimes, slavery, homophobia, genocide, gender oppression, transnational corporations, sexual abuse, and addiction (Foley & Valenzuela, 2005).

Bourgois (1995) asserts that, historically, ethnographers have tended to shy away from these very topics. Whether anthropologists have ignored the social roots of human suffering–racism, imperialism, exploitation, and so on–has been a matter of considerable debate. Rather than engage in this controversy, I ask a more crucial question: Do we need more of this type of scholarship? I agree with those who argue that there is not enough attention paid by ethnographers to the sources of injustices, Furthermore, the full potential of this type of scholarship is truncated without public debate and social advocacy (Lamphere, 2004, p. 432).

Methodology

Prior to the discussion of methodological features of public ethnography, I once again provide two qualifiers: (1) public ethnographies are not methodologically monolithic, and (2) the methodology employed is not totally distinct from other ethnographies. Nonetheless, public ethnographers sometimes find themselves in territory for which how-to guides and other academic treatises on ethnographic research provide little guidance. Furthermore, they sometimes have to transgress some of the generally accepted canons of ethnographic research.

Public ethnographies are multifaceted. The list of "multiples" that are sometimes used when discussing public ethnographies includes *multimethod, multidimensional, multicultural, multiperspectival* (Kincheloe & McLaren, 2005), *multiethnic epistemologies, multimedia, multiple consciousness, multiple representations*, and *multivocal*. Four more, discussed here, are *multiple roles, multidisciplinary, multiple researchers*, and *multisited*.

Academics who engage in this strategy of inquiry invariably and simultaneously hold multiple roles within the context of the public ethnography. Sometimes a scholar operates from the familiar role of expert. At other times, he or she is the novice, the one who needs to learn from others. At any given moment, the public ethnographer might prioritize the role of committed activist over that of researcher, or vice versa. Nonetheless, if activism and research are two circles in a Venn diagram, public ethnographers inhabit the space where the circles overlap. This can be illustrated by way of two exemplary scholars, Paul Farmer and Nancy Scheper-Hughes.

Farmer is a medical anthropologist and physician at Harvard Medical School. He simultaneously conducts research on, frequently publishes about, and actively works toward the elimination of social ills. He is a founding director of Partners in Health, which is described as "an international charity organization that provides direct health care services and undertakes research and advocacy activities on behalf of those who are sick and living in poverty" (2005).

Another anthropologist who conducts public ethnographies is Scheper-Hughes, a professor of medical anthropology at the University of California, Berkeley, and director of the doctoral program in critical studies in medicine, science, and the body. She is a member of the Bellagio Task Force on Securing Bodily Integrity for the Socially Disadvantaged in Transplant Surgery and cofounder and director of Organs Watch, an organization that explores "the social and economic context of organ transplantation, focusing on the human rights implications of the desperate, world-wide, search for organs" (*anthropology.berkeley.edu/nsh.html*). Those involved in the organization conduct ethnographic research, engage in human rights investigations, and broadly disseminate their findings. She has a long list of publications on important social problems and an equally long list of service activities, such as being a consultant for women's reproductive health and AIDS in Brazil and a member of President Clinton's National Campaign against Youth Violence.

Although Farmer and Scheper-Hughes are exceptional, making contributions beyond what most public ethnographers can achieve, they exemplify the goals to which many public ethnographers aspire. I frequently utilize the original words of these two scholars and select others to illustrate public ethnography in practice. I do note that I could have chosen other, equally impressive, examples from a long list of scholars who conduct research and engage in humanitarian efforts.

Public ethnographies are described as multidisciplinary, interdisciplinary, transdisciplinary, and even counterdisciplinary (Kincheloe & McLaren, 2005). Usually the social issues that concern public ethnographers are so complex that, in an effort to provide an adequate analysis, they must draw on different disciplinary perspectives (Farmer, 2003; Kincheloe & McLaren, 2005). Rather than limiting themselves to the discipline within which they were trained, public ethnographers might blend archaeology, cultural anthropology, linguistics, biological anthropology, natural sciences, literary theory, cultural studies, sociology, geography, and so on (Sanday, 2003). Furthermore, academic disciplines, investigative journalism, scientific reporting, political engagement, and human rights work can get stirred together such that they are inseparable in the context of public ethnographies (Scheper-Hughes, 2004, p. 29).

Rather than conforming to the tradition of the lone ethnographer, public ethnographers tend to collaborate with others. As one example, Sanjek (1998) and a multiethnic team of 15 researchers conducted engaged scholarship in the Elmhurst–Corona neighborhood in Queens, New York, an extremely ethnically mixed community. Ethnographers from the social sciences might partner with other academics, graduate and undergraduate students, community organizations, nongovernmental organizations, farm workers, investigative reporters, documentary journalists, mental health professionals, civic associations, think tanks, economists, tenant associations, politicians, local activists, environmental experts, labor unions, immigrant groups, museum curators, trade associations, government officials, oversight committees, policymakers, grassroots activists, faith-based organizations, local residents, businesses, epidemiologists, biologists, physicians, and a host of other diverse groups and individuals (Burawoy et al., 2004; Fine, Weis, Weseen, & Wong, 2003; Tedlock, 2005).

Arguably, public ethnographies are more often multisited than traditional ethnographies that are rooted in specific settings. Although a public ethnography might begin in a particular location, the "field" for public ethnographies can be diffuse, fragmented, temporary, and on the move (Holmes & Marcus, 2005). In sharp contrast to other forms of ethnography, at times public ethnographers cannot even specify where the "field" of their fieldwork is located. For instance, during Nordstrom's (2004) research on violence, war, and profiteering, she was not always interested in "a place" (p. 15). Instead, as she notes, much of her work existed in the space of "place-less-ness," an invisible nonplace obscured by power and profit (p. 15). Using a writing style more consistent with literature than with academic discourse, she argues that no longer are single-sited studies sufficient given that locations swirl in a "fluid geographical space" where "humans feel the tug and pull of societal waves" that "move across vast global stretches" (p. 12). This amorphous nature of the "field" is particularly problematic for researchers who critique national or global structures that transcend, but have profound implications on, specific locations.

Hannerz (2003) suggests that term *translocal* might be a more appropriate description than either *multisited* or *multilocal* because it more accurately reflects the interest in the *relationships* among entities. Of major concern to some public ethnographers are the links, the interactions, the movements, the paths, and the intermingling of multiple locations, histories, cultures, individual acts, social actions and structures, ideals, objects, policies, and so on (Gille & Ó Riain, 2002; Nordstrom, 2004; Plummer, 1999). That is, public ethnographers explore the interconnectedness of larger social fields with discrete locations (Hannerz, 2003; Lyon-Callo & Hyatt, 2003; Rodriguez, 2003).

Nordstrom writes that to explore the connections between war and profiting, she had to go beyond a particular place because:

> The gun that fires the bullet in Mozambique was made in the USA, or Bulgaria, or Brazil, or China. It was traded through a vast network of agents, "advisors," and alliances—all of whom have a say in how the weapon should be used: who can legitimately be killed (and who cannot, starting with the arms vendors), and how this is all to be justified. (2004, p. 13)

Likewise, Scheper-Hughes's research on the organs-trafficking underworld was not confined to a particular setting. Instead she went to "police morgues, hospital mortuaries, medical–legal institutes, intensive care units, emergency rooms, dialysis units, surgical units, operating rooms, as well as to police stations, jails and prisons, mental institutions, orphanages and court rooms" (2004, p. 32).

In short, she followed the bodies of the dead, the not-quite-dead ("brain dead"), and those very much alive (Scheper-Hughes, 2004, p. 31). Her ethnography took her to Brazil, Argentina, Cuba, South Africa, Israel, the West Bank, Turkey, Moldova, Baltimore, New York City, and Philadelphia. Nonetheless, she never lost sight of people like Niculae Bardan, who was trafficked to Istanbul from his village of Mingir in rural Moldova so that his kidney could be removed and sold. Through her meticulous research, she connects the lives of the poor to transnational kidnapping by international brokers making multimillion-dollar deals.

Because of the fluid nature of public ethnographies beyond local contexts, the unit of analysis tends to change over time (Gille & Ó Riain, 2002, p. 286). Researchers might move from an analysis of individuals to groups, communities, organizations, institutions, nation states, and transnational corporations (Gille & Ó Riain, 2002; Plummer, 1999).

Another potentially problematic feature of public ethnographies involves relationships in the field. Tedlock indicates that public ethnography is rooted in "kindness, neighborliness, and a shared moral good" (2005, p. 474), but this description might provide only half of the story. Nurturing, close, and collaborative relationships, so highly touted in qualitative research, simply are not possible or desired with some individuals encountered by the public ethnographer. Public ethnographies sometimes require intermingling with, if not the "bad guys," then the "not-so-good guys" who make bad decisions and engage in bad practices that result in incredible hardship for others.

As is often the case with public ethnography, scholarship that examines power, authority, and structures that lead to human misery, inequalities, and exploitation invariably enters the territory of elites. Studying powerful individuals and institutions can result in the public ethnographer becoming trapped in methodological quagmires with little guidance on how to navigate them. Once one crosses into the world of the truly powerful, one might have to deviate from the standard advice on issues of sampling, access, gaining entry, gatekeepers, ethics, establishing rapport, relationships, interview styles and questions, observations, and so on (Ostrander, 1993; Undheim, 2006). As more and more scholars respond to the call to "stop studying the poor and start studying the people who make other people poor " (Becker et al., 2004, p. 274), the need for methodological guidelines for studying elites will increase (Undheim, 2006).

One major question that public ethnographers face involves whether they should extend the same confidentiality protection to all participants in their studies. If, after all, a goal is to engage in the type of activism that can stop abusive practices, then won't naming the repressors better serve this purpose than keeping their identities secret? Responses to this dilemma vary. Sometimes public ethnographers choose not to disclose identifying information. For example, one of the reasons Nordstrom (2004) gives for not breaking confidentiality was that: "exposing the name of the general who is profiteering from war will not illuminate the international networks of extra-legal economies and power—it will merely endanger my ability to return to this field site" (p. 15).

In contrast, some assert that confidentiality does not always have to be kept. Over 20 years ago, Bulmer (1982) wrote that scholars should be whistle blowers in some situations:

> Specifically social scientists are seen as having a responsibility to study those institutions or government agencies that are in a position to mistreat the disadvantaged, and if evidence of wrongdoing is discovered on the part of government officials or administrators, it should be publicly disclosed in an effort to discourage future wrongdoings—regardless of any promises made to the public officials to respect confidential information. (p. 21)

Protecting the confidentiality of the powerless is a given, but doing so can become extraordinary complex. Sometimes the risks of identifying those involved in a public ethnography are so high that scholars deviate from standard ethnographic practices. For example, Nordstrom (2004) states that she is willing to forgo detailed descriptions and verbatim quotes—on which valid and trustworthy ethnographies usually depend—in instances in which their inclusion could literally lead to death for local informants. Fortunately, most of the participants in public ethnographies do not have as much at stake as did Nordstrom's participants; yet many remain vulnerable to further abuses of power that could have serious negative consequences.

Value Commitments and Moral Imperatives

Public ethnographers usually locate themselves on the side of the debate that argues for the centrality of values in their scholarship. However, even though they assert that a moral–political stance is an appropriate part of engaged scholarship, uniformity does not exist regarding what constitutes a civil society, what the "authoritative definition of justice" is (Best, 2004, p. 158), or what the best mechanism is for achieving a more humane world. Setting aside the interesting, important, and complex question of whose values should be represented, public ethnographers tend to answer the question, Can valid and valued scholarship take an explicit moral position? with a resounding "yes."

For many public ethnographers, the pretense of value neutrality is not a feature of their work. Public ethnographers care about what they study; they want others to care and engage in public debate about repressive and unfair conditions; they want to work toward the amelioration of unjust practices. Although public ethnographers speak and write in tones appropriate for any given audience, in some of their work there is an undercurrent, if not a visible wave, of anger. Moral arguments are made; value statements are rampant. Farmer, for example, does not hide his ethical position:

> This book is a physician–anthropologist's effort to reveal the ways in which the most basic right—the right to survive—is trampled in an age of great affluence, and it argues that the matter should be considered the most pressing one of our times. The drama, the tragedy, of the destitute sick concerns not only physicians and scholars who work among the poor but all who profess even a passing interest in human rights. It's not much of a stretch to argue that anyone who wishes to be considered humane has ample cause to consider what it means to be sick and poor in the era of globalization. (2003, p. 6)

Farmer wants his book to achieve more than answer research questions:

> This book attempts to advance an agenda for research and action grounded in the struggle for social and economic rights, an agenda suited to public health and medicine and whose central contributions to future progress in human rights are linked to the equitable distribution of the fruits of scientific advancement. Such an approach is in keeping with the Universal Declaration but runs counter to several of the reigning ideologies of public health, including those favoring efficiency over equity. (2003, p. 18)

He continues: "Although the quandaries of the sick in industrialized countries are important and should never be dismissed, the failure of ethics to grapple with the tragedy of the modern era's *destitute* sick is nothing short of obscene" (p. 22).

Not surprisingly, public ethnographers are sometimes criticized, even discounted, because of their value stances and approach to scholarship. Granted, any scholar should expect to have his or her research evaluated by peers, and not all public ethnographies are well done. However, due to their explicit political nature and sometimes lack of adherence to standard methodology, they are particularly vulnerable to criticism. Powerful interest groups often lead the charge against public ethnographies, and they have done so for as long as this type of scholarship has been conducted. In the 1940s, for example, Goldschmidt (1978) conducted his fieldwork in three California towns on the consequences of industrialized food production and determined that class and ethnic conflicts were more common in communities with corporate farms than with family farms. His research was attacked by agribusiness interests, a member of Congress, a major newspaper, and a radio commentator, among others, who tried to prevent and did, in fact, delay its publication. More recently, Light's (2005) engaged scholarship highlighted how Blue Cross unfairly charged higher insurance rates for women and disadvantaged minorities. The governor's office spoke to Light's university president, who in turn contacted his dean, who finally informed him that he was not to continue his research and related advocacy on behalf of the clients of Blue Cross. As another example, Anderson and Berglund (2003, as cited in Tedlock, 2005) found themselves at risk of being sued if they did not modify their research findings to be less critical of a powerful conservation organization.

Similarly, Scheper-Hughes (2004) reports that once her research on organ trafficking began to be taken seriously in some realms, other academics devalued her research as too positioned, lacking in methodological rigor, and insufficiently theoretical. She was bluntly told that no place existed in anthropological research for political engagements or for taking a moral rather than a theoretical position. She recounts that she was not only criticized for adopting what was interpreted as an antiglobalization view of organ traffickers but also charged with being naive for buying "into the assumptive world of her informants, many of them poor, Third World, medically and technologically unsophisticated" (p. 31). Scheper-Hughes is not alone in being the recipient of such criticism. Kemmis and McTaggart (2003) state that other public ethnographers have been charged with aligning themselves with those they study in ways that are said to detract from the credibility of their work.

Editors who reviewed one of Scheper-Hughes's articles suggested that she should rewrite her paper "to explicate 'the novel intersections in geographical and social spaces, the formation of new and unexpected assemblages of institutions, biomedicines, actors, and ethics' " (2004, p. 36). Her critics considered that the "neocannibalism" that she so thoroughly documents in her work provided " 'an exciting new landscape where good and bad guys and goods are distributed in both expected and unexpected places' " (p. 36). This is curious advice when one reads the caption of a photo of Viorel that Scheper-Hughes included in a recent publication:

> Held like a hostage in the basement of a rundown hotel in Istanbul before he was trafficked into Georgia (Russia) where Viorel gave up his kidney under threats of physical violence. "If I hadn't gone through with it," he told me, "My body could be floating somewhere in the Bosperous Strait." (p. 54)

Public ethnographers, I believe rightfully so, do not couch events such as these as *novel intersections* and *exciting landscapes* in which good guys distribute goods. On the contrary, many public ethnographers do not feel compelled to hide moral outrage under the illusion of value neutrality and strict adherence to methodological orthodoxy.

Beyond the Academy

Public ethnographers who want to move beyond just understanding and explaining social inequalities to helping eradicate them elect to disseminate their results in new ways, beyond the confines of academics circles, and to engage the public in debate on important social problems (Lauder, Brown, & Halsey, 2004, p. 19). Arguably, more so than traditional modes of academic writing, public ethnographies are more accessible to nonacademic audiences because they are crafted to be clearly written, richly descriptive, powerful, and engaging (Becker et al., 2004). Public ethnographies generally eschew jargon-filled, pedantic, pretentious, obtuse, donnish, and elitist discourse. To use Diane Vaughan's phrase, public ethnographers attempt to be less "snobbish about their writing" (Becker et al., 2004, p. 275).

Sometimes public ethnographers reach a national, if not international, audience and are sought out by the media because of their expertise. Public ethnographers have appeared on *The Oprah Winfrey Show*, CNN, and the *Lehrer News Hour* and have been interviewed by Terry Gross on National Public Radio, Larry King, Ted Koppel, and journalists from *The New York Times* and the *Washington Post*. Farmer has won numerous awards, including the 2007 Austin College Leadership Award, the Conrad N. Hilton Humanitarian Prize, and the American Medical Association's International Physician

Award. I note the media attention and awards not to inspire young scholars to select a research agenda that might help them make money and garner fame (which is ultimately doubtful) but to reinforce the fact that public ethnographers are sometimes successful in making a large number of people aware of repressive conditions. Scheper-Hughes's audience included officials in multiple countries. For example, she shared some of her findings on illegal traffic in human organs with selected investigators from the U.S. Food and Drug Administration; the U.S. Attorney's Office in New York; FBI special agents with the State Department's Visa Fraud Division; the prime minister of Moldova; secretaries of health in the Philippines, Turkey, and South Africa; the Council of Europe; and the ethics committee of the United Network for Organ Sharing (UNOS), among others (Scheper-Hughes, 2004, p. 43). Additionally, she worked with the South African police to help round up organ traffickers and provided testimony to the United States Congress House Subcommittee on International Operations and Human Rights.

To facilitate reaching diverse audiences, public ethnographers move beyond the typical genres of social science research into a variety of forms and venues. Public ethnographers and their collaborators hold public symposia and create videos, museum exhibits, service learning opportunities, photography exhibits, CD-ROMs, websites, and hands-on collaborative projects (Lamphere, 2004). They write short stories, technological reports, executive summaries, magazine articles, press releases, op-ed pieces, and e-mails. They testify before Congress, make phone calls, speak on radio programs, and meet with numerous officials. They might write poetry, include poetry, or use a writing style that reads like poetry (Rhodes, 2004). They sometimes adopt such modes of presentation as performance pieces, such as ethnodramas and ethnographic theater. Performance pieces are written and performed in conjunction with the audience and are designed to be dialogical: The audience can become the actors, and vice versa. Through the process of repeatedly producing, performing, and critiquing the ethnodrama, stories get told in ways that are liberating and empowering (Denzin, 2003; Richardson, 2002; Tedlock, 2005).

Misuse of Public Ethnographies

Communicating with nonacademic audiences has its perils because of the risks of misrepresentation and misappropriation (Lamphere, 2003). During the radio or television interview, complex arguments can get reduced to one-sentence sound bites that misrepresent critical aspects of the findings and the intentions of the ethnographer (Lamphere, 2003; Stacey, 2004). Selective segments of publications can be pulled out of context and misappropriated for ends that are antithetical to views of the public ethnographer (Lauder, Brown, & Halsey, 2004). Bourgois (1995) worried about this. He feared that revealing details of the lives of the poor living in "El Barrio" would reinforce the already negative stereotypes of Puerto Ricans if the link he made between structural oppression and individual action was ignored.

Misappropriation is such a serious concern that public ethnographers would be wise to ask themselves a series of crucial questions: "*Have I considered how these data could be used for progressive, conservative, repressive social policies?* How might the data be heard? Misread? Misappropriated? Do you need to add a "warning" about potential misuse?" (Fine et al., 2003, p. 201). Etzioni (2005) echoes the view that those who want to speak to and with the public must carefully consider how to present their work so that it is not used in unintended ways. To help public ethnographers learn how to reach a larger public and navigate a conservative and often hostile media, the ASA Task Force on Institutionalizing Public

Sociologies (2005) recommends the creation of a "Tips and Tools" manual for interacting with such sources.

Why Public Ethnographies Matter

Why do scholars take the extended time and emotional energy to conduct this form of scholarship when often little academic credit exists for doing so? Public ethnographers answer this question with responses that are indicative of the moral impetus that drives them. *Because: children die from hunger; racism squashes the human potential; repressive immigration laws lead to laborers dying in the desert on their way to low-paying jobs; hatred of groups and individuals perceived as different, whether by sexual orientation, religion, or nationality, leads to violence; people sleep in the streets; people die of diseases that are treatable; homes and lives are destroyed because of self-serving decisions by policymakers; women and girls are raped; refugees flee war zones with nowhere to go; workers toil in horrible conditions while huge profits are reaped from their labor; soldiers and civilians die in war.*

Can public ethnographers have any impact on reducing human misery? Sometimes public ethnographies result in improved conditions for vulnerable populations; sometimes they are successful at inserting a new view into the public debate; sometimes there is no discernable outcome. It is impossible to know in advance whether one's research skills and advocacy will amount to anything. However, for the public ethnographer, trying and failing is not as great a sin as not trying at all. They are not willing to avert their gaze from human suffering and confine their careers to the academy. Despite the criticism and the lack of scholarly appreciation, public ethnographies still exist and might—as recent events have indicated—begin to thrive once more for the simple reason that they exemplify the very best that sociology and anthropology have to offer in the quest for a more just world.

References

Agger, B. (2000). *Public sociology: From social facts to literary acts.* Lanham, MD: Rowman & Littlefield.

American Sociological Association. (2003). *Statement against the war on Iraq.* Retrieved April 5, 2006, from *72.14.203.104/search?q=cache:BDbVRlGKOrYJ:www.sociologistswithoutborders.org/Manifestos/antiwarmanifesto.pdf+American+Sociological+Association+resolution+on+war&hl=en&gl=us&ct=clnk& cd=1*

American Sociological Association. (2006). *Preliminary program and agenda.* Retrieved July 16, 2006, from *convention2.allacademic.com/one/asa/asa06/index.php?click_key=1*

American Sociological Association Task Force on Institutionalizing Public Sociologies. (2005). *Public sociology and the roots of American sociology: Reestablishing our connections to the public.* Washington, DC: Author.

Aminzade, R. (2004). The engaged department: Public sociology in the Twin Cities. *Footnotes, 32.* Retrieved April 15, 2006, from *www2.asanet.org/footnotes*

Anderson, D., & Berglund, E. (Eds.). (2003). *Ethnographies of conservation: Environmentalism and the distribution of privilege.* New York: Berghahn Books.

Anderson, E. (1999). *Code of the street: Decency, violence, and the moral life of the inner city.* New York: Norton.

Barth, F. (2001, April 18). Envisioning a more public anthropology: An interview with Fredrik Barth. *Public Anthropology: Engaging Ideas.* Retrieved June 12, 2006, from *www.publicanthropology.org/Journals/Engaging-Ideas/barth.htm*

Becker, H., Gans, H., Newman, K., & Vaughan, D. (2004). On the value of ethnography: Sociology and public policy: A dialogue. *ANNALS of the American Academy of Political and Social Science, 594,* 264–276.

Best, J. (2004). Why don't they listen to us?: Fashion notes on the imperial wardrobe. *Social Programs, 51,* 154–160.

Blau, J., & Smith, K. (Eds.). (2006). *Public sociologies reader.* Lanham, MD: Rowman & Littlefield.

Bourgois, P. (1995). *In search of respect: Selling crack in El Barrio.* Cambridge, UK: Cambridge University Press.

Brady, D. (2004). Why public sociology may fail. *Social Forces, 82,* 1629–1638.

Bulmer, M. (1982). *Social research ethics.* London: Macmillan.

Burawoy, M. (2004). Public sociologies: Contradictions, dilemmas, and possibilities. *Social Forces, 82,* 1603–1618.

Burawoy, M. (2005a). 2004 American Sociological Association presidential address: For public sociology. *British Journal of Sociology, 56,* 259–294.

Burawoy, M. (2005b). The return of the repressed: Recovering the public face of U.S. sociology, one hundred years on. *ANNALS of the American Academy of Political and Social Science, 600,* 68–85.

Burawoy, M., Gamson, W., Ryan, C., Pfohl, S.,

Vaughan, D., Derber, C., et al. (2004). Public sociologies: A symposium from Boston College. *Social Problems, 51*, 103–130.

Clawson, D., Zussman, R., Misra, J., Gerstel, N., Stokes, R., Anderton, D., et al. (Eds.). (2007). *Public sociology: Fifteen eminent sociologists debate politics and the profession in the twenty-first century*. Berkeley: University of California Press.

Denzin, N. (1999). Interpretive ethnography for the next century. *Journal of Contemporary Ethnography, 28*, 510–519.

Denzin, N. (2003). *Performance ethnography: Critical pedagogy and the politics of culture*. Thousand Oaks, CA: Sage

Denzin, N., & Lincoln, Y. (Eds.). (2005). *The Sage handbook of qualitative research* (3rd ed.). Thousand Oaks, CA: Sage.

Duneier, M. (1999). *Sidewalk*. New York: Farrar, Straus, & Giroux.

Etzioni, A. (2005). Bookmarks for public sociologists. *British Journal of Sociology, 56*, 373–378.

Farmer, P. (2003). *Pathologies of power: Health, human, rights, and the new war on the poor*. Berkeley: University of California Press.

Farmer, P. (2005). *Partners in health*. Retrieved April 14, 2005, from *www.pih.org/whoweare/index.html*

Feagin, J. (2001). Social justice and sociology: Agendas for the twenty-first century. *American Sociological Review, 66*, 1–20.

Fine, M., Weis, L., Weseen, S., & Wong, L. (2003). For whom? Qualitative research, representations, and social responsibilities. In N. Denzin & Y. Lincoln (Eds.), *The landscape of qualitative research: Theories and issues* (2nd ed., pp. 167–207). Thousand Oaks, CA: Sage.

Fitzgerald, M. (2005). Corporate ethnography: High-tech companies are deploying ethnographers and anthropologists by the score to study how people actually use technology. *Technology Review: An MIT Enterprise*. Retrieved February 21, 2006, from *www.technologyreview.com/BizTech/wtr_15900,295,p1.html*

Foley, D., & Valenzuela, A. (2005). Critical ethnography: The politics of collaboration. In N. Denzin & Y. Lincoln (Eds.), *The Sage handbook of qualitative research* (3rd ed., pp. 217–234). Thousand Oaks, CA: Sage.

Gans, H. (2002). More of us should become public sociologists. *Footnotes, 30*(6). Retrieved April 15, 2006, from *www2.asanet.org/footnotes*

Gille, Z., & Ó Riain, S. (2002). Global ethnography. *Annual Review of Sociology, 28*, 271–295.

Goldschmidt, W. (1978). *As you sow: Three studies in the social consequences of agribusiness*. Montclair, NJ: Allanheld, Osmun.

Haanstad, E. (2001a). Anthropology revitalized: Public anthropology and student activism. *Public Anthropology: The Graduate Journal*. Retrieved March 3, 2006, from *www.publicanthropology.org/Journals/Grad-j/Wisconsin/haanstad.htm*

Haanstad, E. (2001b). *Being a public anthropologist: An interview with Phillippe Bourgois*. Retrieved March 15, 2005, from *www.publicanthropology.org/Journals/Gradj/Wisconsin/Bourgint.htm*

Hannerz, U. (2003). Being there . . . and there . . . and there! *Ethnography, 4*, 201–216.

Hess-Biber, S., & Leavy, P. (Eds.). (2004). *Approaches to qualitative research: A reader on theory and practice*. New York: Oxford University Press.

Hill, T. (2001). *Understanding the dead: The cultural politics of exhumation work in Guatemala*. Retrieved February 3, 2006, from *darkwing.uoregon.edu/~anthro/PublicAnth.html*

Hinton, A. (2005). *Why did they kill?: Cambodia in the shadow of genocide*. Berkeley: University of California Press.

Holmes, D., & Marcus, G. (2005). Refunctioning ethnography: The challenge of an anthropology of the contemporary. In N. Denzin & Y. Lincoln (Eds.), *The Sage handbook of qualitative research* (3rd ed., pp. 1099–1113). Thousand Oaks, CA: Sage.

Horowitz, I. (1983). *C. Wright Mills: An American utopian*. New York: Free Press.

Kemmis, S., & McTaggart, R. (2003). Participatory action research. In N. Denzin & Y. Lincoln (Eds.), *Strategies of qualitative inquiry* (2nd ed., pp. 336–396). Thousand Oaks, CA: Sage.

Kershaw, T. (2005). *The scholar activist approach*. Retrieved December 15, 2005, from *www.africanastudies.vt.edu/The%20Scholar%20Activist%20Approach.htm*

Kincheloe, J., & McLaren, P. (2005). Rethinking critical theory and qualitative research. In N. Denzin & Y. Lincoln (Eds.), *The Sage handbook of qualitative research* (3rd ed., pp. 303–342). Thousand Oaks, CA: Sage.

Kleidman, R. (2004). Community organizing as engaged scholarship. *Footnotes, 32*. Retrieved April 23, 2006, from *www2.asanet.org/footnotes/*

Klein, G. (2005). On the creation of "public interest sociology." *Footnotes, 33*. Retrieved April 15, 2006, from *www2.asanet.org/footnotes/*

Ladson-Billings, G., & Donnor, J. (2005). The moral activist role of critical race theory scholarship. In N. Denzin & Y. Lincoln (Eds.), *The Sage handbook of qualitative research* (3rd ed., pp. 279–301). Thousand Oaks, CA: Sage.

Lamphere, L. (2003). The perils and prospects for an engaged anthropology: A view from the Untied States. *Social Anthropology, 11*, 153–158.

Lamphere, L. (2004). The convergence of applied, practicing, and public anthropology in the 21st century. *Human Organizations, 63*, 431–441.

Lauder, H., Brown, P., & Halsey, A. (2004). Sociology and political arithmetic: Some principles of a new policy science. *British Journal of Sociology, 55*, 3–22.

Light, D. (2005). Contributing to scholarship and theory through public sociology. *Social Forces, 83*, 1647–1654.

Lofland, J. (1995). Analytic ethnography. *Journal of Contemporary Ethnography, 24*, 30–67.

Lyon-Callo, V., & Hyatt, S. (2003). The neoliberal state and the depoliticization of poverty: Activist anthropology and "ethnography from below." *Urban Anthropology and Studies of Cultural Systems and World Economic Development, 32*, 175–205.

Massey, D. (2007). The strength of weak politics. In D. Clawson, R. Zussman, J. Misra, N. Gerstel, R. Stokes, D. Anderton, et al. (Eds.), *Public sociology: Fifteen eminent sociologists debate politics and the profession in the twenty-first century* (pp. 145–157). Berkeley: University of California Press.

Newman, K. (1999). *No shame in my game: The working poor in the inner city.* New York: Knopf.

Nicols, L. (Ed.). (2007). *Public sociology: The contemporary debate.* Piscataway, NJ: Transaction Press.

Nordstrom, C. (2004). *Shadows of war: Violence, power, and international profiteering in the twenty-first century.* Berkeley: University of California Press.

Ostrander, S. (1993). Surely you're not in this just to be helpful: Access, rapport, and interviewing three studies of elites. *Journal of Contemporary Ethnography, 22*, 7–27.

Plummer, K. (1999). The "ethnographic society" at century's end: Clarifying the role of public ethnography. *Journal of Contemporary Ethnography, 29*, 641–649.

Plummer, K. (2005). Queer humanism and queer theory: Living with the tensions. In N. Denzin & Y. Lincoln (Eds.), *The Sage handbook of qualitative research* (3rd ed., pp. 357–373). Thousand Oaks, CA: Sage.

Richardson, L. (2002). Evaluating ethnography. *Qualitative Inquiry, 6* 253–255.

Rhodes, L. (2004). *Total confinement: Madness and reason in the maximum security prison.* Berkeley: University of California Press.

Rodriguez, C. (2003). Invoking Fannie Lou Hamer: Research, ethnography and activism in low-income communities. *Urban Anthropology and Studies of Cultural Systems and World Economic Development, 32*, 231–252.

Sanday, P. (2003, February). *Public interest anthropology: A model for engaged social science.* Paper presented at School of American Research Workshop on Public Interest Anthropology, Chicago. Retrieved February 25, 2006, from *www.sas.upenn.edu/~psanday/SARdiscussion%20paper.65.html*

Sanjek, R. (1998). *The future of us all: Race and neighborhood politics in New York City.* Ithaca, NY: Cornell University Press.

Sanjek, R. (2004). Going public: Responsibilities and strategies in the aftermath of ethnography. *Human Organization, 63*, 444–456.

Scheper-Hughes, N. (2004). Parts unknown: Undercover ethnography of the organs-trafficking underworld. *Ethnography, 5*, 29–73.

Stacey, J. (2004). Marital suitors court social science spin-sters: The unwittingly conservative effects of public sociology. *Social Problems, 51*, 131–145.

Tedlock, B. (2005). The observation of participation and the emergence of public ethnography. In N. Denzin & Y. Lincoln (Eds.), *The Sage handbook of qualitative research* (3rd ed., pp. 467–481). Thousand Oaks, CA: Sage.

Tedlock, B., & Lewis, N. (2005). *Public ethnography.* Retrieved February 25, 2006, from *www.sarweb.org/seminars/shortsempast/participants05-02ethnog. htm*

Tishkov, V. (2004). *Chechnya: Life in a war-torn society.* Berkeley: University of California Press.

Undheim, T. (2006). Getting connected: How sociologists can access the high tech élite. In S. Hess-Biber & P. Leavy (Eds.), *Emergent methods in social research* (pp. 13–42). Thousand Oaks, CA: Sage.

Wacquant, L. (2003). Ethnografest: A progress report on the practice and promise of ethnography. *Ethnography, 4*, 5–14.

Weiss, M. (2006). *Who was St. Clair Drake?* Retrieved April 14, 2006, from *sananet.org/drake.html*

CHAPTER 14

Emergent Methods in Autoethnographic Research

Autoethnographic Narrative and the Multiethnographic Turn

Christine S. Davis
Carolyn Ellis

I (Carolyn) began writing autoethnography in the early 1980s. My interest was in bringing the lived experience of emotions to social science research and doing research that was relevant to people's everyday lives. I wanted to resist the rationalist tendency to portray people exclusively as spiritless, empty husks with programmed, managed, predictable, and patterned emotions. Then my brother was killed in 1982 in an airplane crash on his way to visit me (Ellis, 1993). At the same time, my partner, Gene, entered the final stages of chronic emphysema. These events made the scientifically respectable survey of jealousy I was working on seem insignificant. Instead, I wanted to understand and cope with the intense emotions I felt about the sudden loss of my brother and the excruciating pain I experienced as Gene deteriorated. I turned then to my training as an ethnographer and began keeping field notes on the next few years of my relationship with Gene, how the relationship was affected by his illness, and how we coped with his deterioration. After 9 years of writing and rewriting, *Final Negotiations: A Story of Love, Loss, and Chronic Illness* (Ellis, 1995), was born. This text read more like a memoir or a novel, with conversations, thoughts, and feelings, than like a traditional social science text. Also violating usual social science practice, I was the main character, as well as the writer and researcher.

* * *

I (Cris) was first introduced to autoethnography as a method when I was an MA student in 1998 in communication studies. My professor at the University of North Carolina at Greensboro assigned me to give a book report on Carolyn Ellis's *Final Negotiations*. "I think you'll like it," he said.

"By the end of the first page, I do not like autoethnography, nor do I like Carolyn Ellis," I reported. "The writing is compelling, and the accounts so personal that I'm not sure I could look Carolyn Ellis in the eye after reading it," I continued. Somehow the honesty of Carolyn's writing evoked a sort of honesty in myself, and I found myself spewing criticisms I would not normally vocalize, especially to a professor and self-professed friend of the author.

The truth of the matter is, deep down, I admired Carolyn for her candor, her ability to reflect on her life and write about it. But, at the same time, I felt threatened by her openness. In my family of origin, feelings were hidden. "Life is not a soap opera," my father used to say. We children were punished for expressing our emotions, and my mother's own emotional problems produced scary things when she expressed her emotions. Problems at home were secrets, not to be revealed to anyone. Certainly not to be written about! Nor did we speak positively about ourselves, because that was bragging, and bragging set you up for criticism and ridicule. You have to have a strong ego to write autoethnography—to make yourself vulnerable to criticism about your most personal stories. I didn't have that strong an ego.

I ended my book report with the most telling response of all: "This book 'works' on many levels, for many reasons. First, whether or not I want to admit it, I relate to Ellis in many different ways.. ..Maybe I dislike Ellis because she talks about things I have kept hidden in myself. Maybe the book is compelling for the same reason."

Two years later, I sat in Carolyn's autoethnography class at the University of South Florida. Having been a PhD student of hers for two semesters, I was mesmerized by her charm, mentoring, and friendship. Under her tutelage, I wrote stories about my childhood and my parents' deaths. I wrote about secrets that I had never told anyone else, and I learned to become honest and open in my writing. I discovered the cathartic aspect of opening and writing and the scholarly aspect of telling and asking. Yet I still had much to learn.

* * *

In this chapter, we (Carolyn and Cris) review autoethnography and its definition and assumptions and follow its development as a methodological approach in social science research. We begin by discussing the genre of personal narratives, which focus on single-voiced narratives about the self. We move our discussion through the autoethnographic approaches of co-constructed narratives, reflexive interviewing, and interactive interviewing, which focus on relational multivoiced and multiauthored narratives. We end with a discussion of a newly developed method—interactive focus groups. In this development, autoethnographies become more dialogic, multivoiced, multiauthored, relational, and sensitive to context—where the interaction takes place—and respond to ethical issues of privacy and consent.

Autoethnography: Definition and Assumptions

Autoethnography is "research, writing, story, and method that connect the autobiographical and personal to the cultural, social, and political" (Ellis, 2004, p. xix). It is the study of a culture of which one is a part, integrated with one's relational and inward experiences. The author incorporates the "I" into research and writing, yet analyzes him- or herself as if studying an "other" (Ellis, 2004; Goodall, 2000).

As a method, autoethnography was developed partly to address the crises of legitimization (who can speak for this culture?) and representation (how can you speak for this culture?). Writing about one's own life or culture, it was thought, overcame the ethnical concerns associated with writing about the cultures of others. Autoethnography and the "new" reflexive ethnography lets us more fully understand the lived experiences and relationship practices of research participants and the multiple interpretations, experiences, and voices emergent in the culture we study (Bochner & Ellis, 1992; Mizco, 2003; Rappaport, 1993; Reed-Danahay, 2001). Whereas some autoethnographic writing traditionally has focused on the voice and point of view of the writer, other types have been more multivocal—including the voices of several authors or study participants (Ellis, 2004).

Typically written as evocative stories, autoethnographies move readers emotionally (Mykhalovskiy, 1997), using what Van Maanen (1988) called an "impressionist tale," one which includes striking stories with dramatic recall about remembered events in which the author was a participant. Autoethnography as a genre also frees us to move beyond traditional methods of writing (Gergen & Gergen, 2002), promoting narrative and poetic forms, displays of artifacts, photographs, drawings, and live performances (Ellis, 2004; Gergen & Gergen, 2002). Then evocative presentations of self "give pause for new possibilities and meanings and open new questions and avenues of inquiry" and representation (Ellis, 2004, p. 215).

Personal Narratives: One Voice/One Self

Autoethnographic narratives—personal accounts written as stories with characters, plot, and dialogue—traditionally have been written as first-person accounts of one's own experiences. Although autoethnography has historically linked the personal, other, and social (Ellis, 2002b), autoethnographic narratives still have tended to imply the ethnographer's "truth" and privilege the voice of the ethnographer as the main character in the story. In this type of autoethnography, other characters in the narrative often are not consulted in the writing of the narrative. When they are, the author's voice still dominates and determines how the experience is expressed. Although such autoethnographic narratives can be socially and interpersonally responsible, this practice of writing single-voiced accounts has raised many ethical issues and concerns of privacy, consent, and harm for autoethnographers. Although writing about one's own life or culture overcame some of the ethical concerns of speaking about and for cultures of unfamiliar others, personal narratives introduced equally problematic concerns about revealing the lives of intimate, often identifiable, others (see Ellis, 2007).

Many published autoethnographies fit the category of autoethnographic narratives. For example, Stacy Holman Jones's (2002) account, "The Way We Were, Are, and Might Be: Torch Singing as Autoethnography," ties together her story of seeing an ex-boyfriend with her viewing of the movie *The Way We Were* and with the genre of torch singing. In "Border Crossings: A Story of Sexual Identity Transformation," Beverly Dent (2002) tells her story of a sex-change operation within the context of family and friends. Lisa Tillmann-Healy (1996) tells the story of her struggle with bulimia within the context of her family and friends in "A Secret Life in a Culture of Thinness: Reflections on Body, Food, and Bulimia." Carol Rambo Ronai's (1996) "My Mother Is Mentally Retarded" is her account of growing up with a mentally retarded mother and abusive stepfather. Barbara Jago's (2002) story of depression, "Chronicling an Academic Depression," situates her mental illness within her academic department and university. In all of these evocative and creative examples of narrative autoethnography, the single writer's voice is paramount, points of view of supporting characters are filtered through the author's frames of reference, and the first-person experience of the supporting characters is not highlighted, nor does it seem to have been solicited.

Carolyn has written many of her stories as personal narratives. For example, "Maternal Connections" (Ellis, 1996) tells of caregiving for her ill mother. Though she later read this story to her mother, she first published it without consulting her mother or seeking her mother's interpretation. " 'I Hate My Voice': Coming to Terms with Minor Bodily Stigmas" (Ellis, 1998) is a narrative, autoethnographic story of Carolyn's mild physical speech imperfection. In this essay, she did consult the main characters in the story to make sure they did not object to her telling their stories of minor bodily stigmas, though she did not invite them to add their voices. "Shattered Lives: Making Sense of September 11th and Its Aftermath" (Ellis, 2002b) tells about Carolyn's experience at Dulles Airport during the September 11, 2001, terrorist attacks. She consulted the other main character in the story and incorporated his comments and let other characters read her story before it was published, but still Carolyn's voice, thoughts, and feelings provide the authorial voice for the study.

The following excerpt from "Shattered Lives" illustrates the primacy of Carolyn's authorial viewpoint:

> "Ladies and gentlemen, we're on schedule for our arrival at Dulles at 11:21," the captain says, immediately after our on-time take off at 9:10 A.M. "In fact, we'll have you at the gate early. The skies are clear and it should be a smooth flight."
>
> I am almost finished with the *USA Today* when suddenly the three flight attendants march decidedly and briskly in step to the front of the plane, enter the cockpit, and close the door. My body goes on alert. I look out the window; the sky is clear. I glance around the cabin; people continue reading and snoozing. I cock my left ear; the engine sounds smooth and steady. I look at my watch; it reads around ten A.M. Keeping a watchful eye on the cockpit, I return to my newspaper. When the flight attendants emerge in a matter of minutes and begin collecting trash, I relax and tell myself they must have responded to the captain turning off the fasten seatbelt sign. Not totally convinced, I submerge myself in the columns of numbers in the stock report.
>
> "May I have your attention please?" the captain says, interrupting my reading a few minutes later. "I have a very serious announcement to make." I am alerted by the grave tone of his voice as well as by the word "serious" he emphasizes. "It has nothing to do with the safety of the plane," he reassures quickly. I breathe a sigh of relief, yet my body tenses nervously and my breath catches as I am reminded of my brother's death in a commercial airplane crash in 1982 (Ellis, 1993).
>
> From my fifth row seat, I lean forward to hear what he is saying. Others do too. "Our plane is being diverted to Charlotte," he says into the quiet. Passengers groan in unison. Damn airlines, I think, my body relaxing into moral indignation. Seems like every time I fly now, there is a problem. "All planes in the air are being asked to land," the pilot continues. What? I return to alert. "There has been a terrorist attack. Ladies and gentlemen, I've been flying for twenty-five years, and I've never experienced anything like this. We'll let you know more as soon as we are informed. I really don't know what will happen once we land." (Ellis, 2002b, pp. 376–377)

Later in the narrative, Carolyn acknowledges the other and the other's story by speaking directly to readers and inviting them to tell their stories:

> I offer this story as my small contribution, meager as it may be, to helping others work their way through this tragedy and our shattered illusions. Along with stories of those killed, injured, lost, displaced, and left grieving for loved ones, and those heroes who risked their lives, the everyday stories of the rest of us—those not directly involved yet devastated by what happened and feeling deeply the country's collective grief—also merit telling. I provide my story as an incentive for you to put your own into words, compare your experience to mine, and find companionship in your sorrow (Mairs, 1993). I speak my story so that you feel liberated to speak yours without feeling guilty that others suffered more and there-

fore your story is not worth telling, your feelings unjustified. I believe we each need to find personal and collective meaning in the events that have transpired and in the disrupted and chaotic lives left behind. On the other side of our grief, we may then be inspired to live better lives—lives based on loving and caring relationships, community, and reaching out to those in need throughout the world. Finally, I tell and analyze this story to stimulate dialogue among social scientists and qualitative researchers about the meaning of the events of September 11th and the role they might play in understanding and helping others cope with this tragedy. (p. 378)

Cris, too, has written personal narratives in which she is the main character. For example, "Home" (Davis, 2005b) is Cris's account of her mother's final week in a hospice home and her subsequent death. Despite the topic—her mother's death—the story is clearly told from Cris's point of view. Her voice is paramount, whereas other characters (including her mother) are somewhat undeveloped and always supportive of the author's storyline. The following excerpt shows how Cris's mother's story has become Cris's story as she preempts the voice of the narrative:

> This morning, the day after Thanksgiving 1999, Karyn calls me early, waking me out of a deep sleep. "Something's wrong with Mom," she says. I rush over. When I get there, I find Mom sitting up in bed, supported by Karyn. Mom is moaning loudly and trying to say something, but what's coming out of her mouth are foreign-sounding nonwords, nonsense syllables that a child might make up before learning how to talk. Her right arm lies limp at her side. She's trying to communicate with us, and she's quite emotional about not being understood. Her face is contorted and her gestures expansive. When I walk into the room, she directs them at me.
>
> A stream of gibberish comes out of her mouth, and when I respond, "Mother, I'm sorry, I can't understand you," my upbringing to "never upset your mother" collides with reality. I can't understand or help her. As we play this charade, her moaning, crying, and spouting gibberish and me panicking, pleading, and failing, the Hospice nurse arrives. She walks into the bedroom just as Mom is trying to climb out of bed. (Davis, 2005b, pp. 393–394)

In these examples, the authors attempted to be open to multiple voices and truths but still wrote their story from a single and authorial point of view. The point of view of other characters, when given, was secondary to the voice of the author and typically filtered through the writer's voice. Although the authors drew attention to the "others" in the stories, the authorial voice still spoke for them.

Opening Up to Multivocality: Including Other Voices

Sometimes in autoethnographies authors occupy the role of researcher in the storyline rather than that of main character. For example, in reflexive dyadic interviews, the interview might take a conversational form in which the interviewer tries to tune in to the interactively produced meanings and emotional dynamics within the interview itself (Gubrium & Holstein, 1997). Though the focus is on the interviewee and the interviewee's story, the words, thoughts, and feelings of the researcher also are considered. Readers might be privy to the interviewer's reflections on his or her own story as he or she hears and/or tells the participant's story. The interviewer's account might involve telling what brought him or her to this research in the first place and how this knowledge of the self or topic is used to understand what the interviewee says. This account also might show the researcher's emotional responses in the course of the interview. In any case, the researcher's story isn't the focal point; instead, it enhances understanding of the topic. Including the subjective and emotional reflections of the researcher adds context and layers to the story being told about participants (see Berger, 2001; Ellis, 2004).

Much of Cris's work has featured reflexive dyadic interviews and resulting reflexive narratives. For example, "Sylvia's Story" (Davis, 2006) is a reflexive narrative about the experience of Sylvia, a caregiver of a child with mental illness. Cris presents herself as the ethnographer–researcher and highlights the role of Sylvia as caregiver and main character. This account is an attempt to reach multivocality and give another character a paramount voice, but Sylvia was not the coauthor, nor was she given an opportunity to comment on or reflect on the written narrative.

> The next time I see Sylvia is two weeks later when I conduct a personal interview with her. "My sister has cerebral palsy," I begin the interview. "When she was a child, she had the same surgery your daughter is going to have. It helped her a lot."
>
> I want to share a moment of connection, to show Sylvia that in some small measure, I understand her situation. Sylvia seems to appreciate the comment. She's full of hopes and dreams for her family, but she's still afraid of how those dreams are going to be realized. Some social security disability money she's been counting on has fallen through and she's concerned about paying her bills.
>
> "Call Nancy, and ask for her help," I advise repeatedly as I conduct the interview. I'm not sure if she will or not.
>
> I settle on the couch as Sylvia pours me a cup of coffee. It's my third cup this morning, and I should have declined her offer, but I just can't resist the smell of freshly brewed coffee. I breathe in the deep aroma as I sneak a look around the room. It is immaculate. I think of the clutter in my living room and wonder if my decorating style could be called "casual chic." I suppress a twinge of guilt over my deficient domestic skills as Sylvia joins me on the couch. . . .
>
> In response to my first interview question, she describes her foray into community mental health services. "My son, Rich, wouldn't go to school. He was actually Baker Acted a couple of times. He was hospitalized at Charter, the local mental health facility, and was pretty much out of control, and Charter referred me. . . .
>
> I nod in response, and Sylvia continues our interview with a story: "I knew that I was just basically overwhelmed and stressed out. I couldn't do this 24 hours a day. So, it was really difficult. I finally had to walk out of my own house. I was screaming, 'what do you want me to do, just try to kill myself and then you'll believe that I need help?' I kind of felt that way then. I was very, very depressed. You know, I used to sit around and go, 'what did I do wrong?' I would look at our old pictures of the family. I'd think about what I did that year, what I did the year before, what I did with the kids. What was it I did wrong? At first, obviously it's your fault, obviously it's your fault. You're the parent. Still, even now, in the back of my head, I think, what if I wasn't so impatient one day, and things like that?"
>
> This last comment makes me pause. I think of the times I've gotten angry at my stepdaughter for leaving dirty dishes in the sink or leaving a mess in the living room. I think of times I've been too busy or preoccupied to be the perfect mother that I wanted to be for her. I wonder how guilty I would feel if she had the problems that Sylvia's kids have. (Davis, 2006, pp. 1224–1225)

"With Mother/With Child: A True Story" (Ellis, 2001) represents a move in autoethnography toward not just focusing on other characters but actually attempting to get these characters to speak back to the text. In this emotional account of experiences of caregiving for her ill mother, Carolyn wrote the story from her own point of view but read the narrative to her mother and gave her an opportunity to voice her reactions. When Carolyn read this story to her mother before sending it for publication, the scene unfolded like this:

> I look up at my Mom still leaning toward me, both elbows propped on the left arm of her La-Z-Boy chair. Tears form in my eyes. I feel deep love for her as I read this story, as I recall the feelings I had for her the night the story took place. She looks directly at me as tears glisten in her eyes. I wait to see how she will respond. "That's really good," she says after a moment.
>
> "Really?" I ask.
>
> "Yes, I like it. Thank you so much for writing it."
>
> I am surprised she is thanking me. "You don't mind my writing stories about you?"

"No, I appreciate it. It's really nice that you do. I really want to thank you."

"Thank you for letting me write the story," I say. "So nothing in the story bothers you? About your getting dressed? Or your body? Anything you want me to take out?"

"No, I don't care. You can write anything you want. Anything," she says looking deep into my eyes.

I smile, wondering what this means, but not asking. Is she thinking of the secrets she told me after my father died? Does she notice that I skipped over some of the prose? Is she trying to reassure me that this was unnecessary? "Mom, maybe next time I come home I'll bring the story I wrote about Rex's [my brother's] death (1993). Would you be able to hear it? I know it's so hard for you."

"I think I could hear it now, though I might get tears in my eyes."

"We'd cry together," I assure her. "Oh, and I wrote another story about you that I've never shown you, about the time you were in the hospital for your gall bladder. I called it 'Maternal Connections'. Maybe I'll bring that home too."

"I'd like that. Is all that in that computer?" she suddenly asks, pointing toward my laptop.

"Yes, look." I turn the computer screen toward her and scroll through the pages. I want her to comment on specifics in the story and talk about what she was thinking and feeling. I want to analyze the story with her, banter the issues of control and independence back and forth, like I would with a colleague or in a class. I think of how multi-layered and multi-voiced that would make my story and my understanding, perhaps deepen our relationship even further. This kind of discussion also might help her know me better. But it's five o'clock and time for supper. As in the stories Mom watches on television, she's got the main plot line. She likes it. That's good enough for her. (pp. 613–614)

Interactive Autoethnography: Co-Constructed Narratives and Interactive Interviewing

Now, the narrative turn in ethnography has taken a spin. Ethnographic techniques that enable us to closely examine interactive events and at the same time deal with issues of reflexivity, subjectivity, emotional expression, modes of description, and narrativity (Bochner & Ellis, 1992) have evolved into creative techniques that also let us understand and give voice to the multiple participants we study. Autoethnography has evolved into multivoiced narratives in which we have begun to weave our stories with our relationships and co-construct both relationships and stories with our friends, lovers, and research participants (some of whom are the same persons). We use co-constructed narrative techniques in order to more fully understand the lived experiences and relationship practices of ourselves in interaction with others and the multiple interpretations, experiences, and voices emergent in our lives and in our stories.

Co-constructed narratives and interactive interviews are variations of this interactive multivocal approach (Ellis & Bochner, 2000). Some research under this genre consists of a type of collaborative interviewing process that includes multiple interviews that build trust and give the research participant time to read and respond to transcripts from previous interviews. Another variation is a co-constructive narrative process in which individually written stories are shared and then co-constructed and turned into a collaborative story by the participants. A third variation is to ask participants to individually write their stories, read each other's stories, and then get together to discuss understandings and findings. These variations often are combined in a single study. In all of these instances and types of multivocal autoethnography, the focus is on an intersubjective process of interpretation and understanding between the researcher and study participant, a state of vulnerability and sharing on the part of the researcher, and empathy and respect for the research participant (Ellis, Kiesinger, & Tillmann-Healy, 1997).

This interactive turn in ethnography offers an approach to research that is evocative, reflexive, multivocal, and dialogic. Cowriting our stories with others acknowledges our understanding that the memories in a system are jointly constructed through ongoing interaction and also can be remembered and shared jointly as "an ongoing joint enactment of the relationship parties" (Baxter, 1992, p. 334). Our relationships serve as the primary site for the construction of meaning, allowing us to take a dynamic, holistic view of the processes by which we create our reality (Daly, 1992; Mabry, 1999). Perhaps most important, interactive autoethnographic methods help equalize the hegemonic power relationship between research participants and researchers. They require that we pay attention to issues of voice, interpretation, interactions, dialogue, and reflexivity. They also give us a way to include the voice and feedback of all participants (Hawes, 1994; Owen, 2001; Reed-Danahay, 2001) and to understand how participants "assign meaning to their [own] realities," rather than simply reporting how we as researchers evaluate their realities through our own frames of reference (Daly, 1992, p. 8). This collaborative, dialogic process looks at the research relationship itself and "deal[s] with the personal experiences of the ethnographer" (Reed-Danahay, 2001, p. 412), as well as the relationship between our study participants and ourselves. When we understand our role as coparticipants in the research process, we recognize that in order to be dialogic researchers, we must be "engaged dialogically" through acknowledging both our own humanity and the humanity of our research participants (Czubaroff & Friedman, 2000; Mizco, 2003; Patton, 2002; Reed-Danahay, 2001). This stance on fieldwork was espoused by Conquergood (1991) "as the collaborative performance of an enabling fiction between observer and observed" (p. 190).

Co-Constructed Narratives

Co-constructed narratives offer the possibility of helping relational partners construct a story together to depict their experiences. In some cases, these narratives are mediated by a researcher. For example, the researcher might ask a couple to decide on a turning point in their relationship that they want to explore. Then the two participants independently construct a detailed chronology of events that took place, including emotional reactions to what happened, significant decisions that were made individually or collectively, conversations with each other and with third parties, and coping strategies. The couple write two separate stories or tell them into a tape recorder or directly to the researcher. Then they meet with the researcher, who observes them as they exchange and read each other's stories and collaborate in their attempt to create a co-constructed story about the experience. The researcher writes the story, inserting him- or herself in the character of researcher, and may even describe the interaction with participants.

In the following example, Cris conducted a mediated interview with two characters in her research, as they all attempted to make sense of the data. The resulting narrative is multivocal and collaborative (Davis, 2005a):

> Two weeks later, I have a chance to discuss my ideas about the dissertation with Nancy and Alan. We're at Jason's Deli again. I munch on salad as we talk.
>
> "One of the things that I'm trying to do with this research," I explain, "is to not be the expert, imposing my opinion on the rest of the team. I want this to be a partnership between me and the team. One of the things I'm discovering is how hard it is not to play the expert role. I wonder if it's hard for you and all the other professionals on the team, to have the family be a real true partner on the team." . . .
>
> Alan nods. "We've talked about this before. You have a situation of power, no matter what. If you're just talking about us being case managers, I don't even think about it anymore, being the professional versus the family, because we just do what we need to do to get things better."
>
> "But isn't the power differential still there, even if you don't think about it?" I protest.
>
> "To complicate matters," Nancy adds, "the financial assistance fund puts them in a subservient role since they have to ask for it, and it's

the state's money. We have to make decisions that are not just about adhering to the family's choice. A good example is the situation with the gas. I can't as an administrator just hand them the money because she wanted to go specifically to another, more expensive, company 'cause she was mad at the first company. By statutes, I had to say no, and that was a power decision. But I don't know that power necessarily needs to be looked at as something that is either inherently positive or negative. It's how you use it."

"How about the other professionals on the team?"

"That depends. As far as the regular team members, I don't know that I've been aware of any abuse of power or anything like that. The school psychologist definitely came over as the big expert, talking about a lot of negative things," Alan says.

"He didn't really understand our team," Nancy adds. "He was just invited that day as a guest."

"I don't think it was his fault," Alan responds, "but he came over powerfully and very negatively. I don't think it was his intention to do that, but at the same time I don't think he saw that family with the level of respect that the team members that know them do."

I nod. "I felt that he de-humanized them. Would you agree with that?"

Alan smiles. "I think that's what I just said."

"I've been noticing how the family, especially Kevin, seems to be doing better, and I wonder why you think that is," I ask.

Nancy sits forward. "I've thought a lot about this. We've given them more structure. The family financially isn't able to go a lot of places, and with the behavioral rewards, now they have something to look forward to every week. On Monday, they're already looking forward to what they're going to do on Saturday, and so they have a hope of things getting better."

Hope. Interesting. . . . "The main thesis of my dissertation is to look at what this team is constructing for themselves and the family, and I think one of the things that the team is constructing is hope."

They nod and I continue. "Alan, you and I have talked several times about this. One way you all are doing this is by changing your focus from the past and the present into the future. The past is problem-saturated. The present ain't so hot either, right? But when you focus them on the future, whether it's for the weekend, or next year when they'll have a bigger house, I think that's being hopeful. Could you comment on that?"

Nancy nods. "Yeah, I do agree. The other thing I think is that Mrs. Stewart doesn't see the team as impersonal. They may be straightforward with her about their opinion, but she doesn't doubt that they care about them and her children. That's created a different dynamic, 'cause she's not feeling like it's an 'us versus 'them' thing."

Alan interjects. "I think it's much more complicated than just hope. I agree that, in general, what we do and hope for is to improve and nurture. I also think that with this family, there's not an adversarial relationship within the team. We may have disagreements, but I don't see it being adversarial. Mrs. Stewart was very defensive at first, and everyone has done a nice job of getting to the point where it's a group of people that are in a non-adversarial relationship."

Hmmm. I'm not entirely sure that's true after my interview with the family. How interesting different points of view are. (Davis, 2005a, pp. 278–281)

Often in co-constructed narratives a researcher may write about his or her own experience with another participant, recruiting a person in his or her life to cowrite. For example, Cris's co-constructed narrative, "Sisters and Friends: Dialogue and Multivocality in a Relational Model of Sibling Disability" (Davis & Salkin, 2005), is jointly written by and about Cris's sister, who has a disability, and Cris, her able-bodied sibling. Written from dialogic personal interviews, personal reflections, e-mail exchanges, and instant-message conversations, the story consists of narrative vignettes, accounts of conversations between the authors, and reactions to each other's comments and writings. This first narrative opens with Cris's voice:

In February 1952, when my mother was 5½ months pregnant with my older sister Kathy, she met a fortune teller. The woman put her

> hand on mom's abdomen. "I see dancing legs," she predicted. "Your child will be a dancer."
>
> Two weeks later, my sister was born. She was baptized immediately. She was weighed for the first time when she was 5 days old; she weighed 2 pounds, 4 ounces. When she was 18 months old, her inability to walk, muscle spasticity, and lack of response to sounds was given a name: cerebral palsy. The cerebral palsy was thought to be caused by a lack of oxygen at birth. Her cognitive functioning was fine, but she was partially deaf and moved around only by vigorous crawling. It took four leg surgeries, huge leg braces and crutches, and years of physical therapy before she was able to walk.
>
> As the younger sister, I was born to exhausted, preoccupied parents with stored up expectations for their children. I learned independence as I used the physical therapy workroom as a playhouse, running up and down the stairs, along the parallel bars, and over the treadmills, as mom and the physical therapist worked with Kathy. I developed a fear of doctors as I sat alone in waiting rooms of doctor's offices, listening to Kathy's terrified screams down the hall as the doctor used an electric saw to remove yet one more cast. I acquired patience when I had to wait because it took Kathy longer to do things. I gained responsibility because it was my job to pick up both of our toys; after all, Kathy is "handicapped." (Davis & Salkin, 2005, pp. 207–208)

As the story progressed, both of our voices were heard:

> KATHY: The thing that took me most by surprise (and I confess hurt a bit) was that you were embarrassed by me. I've never been embarrassed by my disability. Yes, I hated being different but it was so much a part of me I was never embarrassed, and I've never thought anyone in the family was embarrassed because of it. . . .
>
> CRIS: I confess that my first reaction to your comment about your feelings being hurt was to take back saying I had been embarrassed. I'm ashamed to admit that I was embarrassed by your disability, and now I feel bad that I hurt your feelings. But then I think again. Why should I deny my feelings? If this paper is about being honest with each other, why shouldn't I admit what it was like from my point of view?. . . .
>
> KATHY: Hmm . . . what do I remember? I remember being worried about you at St. Paul's because of Nancy Spiker and her bullying you.
>
> CRIS: I can't believe you remember that! Nancy used to terrorize me, and I didn't know that anyone in the family even knew about it! It kind of feels nice to think that my "big sister" was in the background, keeping an eye on me. Wish I'd known it then. . . .
>
> KATHY: I'm not famous or make a lot of money but I think I've done pretty well—got two degrees and have a job I really like working with good people. It's not a bad life at all! Being disabled is just a part of me and I deal with it.
>
> CRIS: As Schulman (1999) points out, "sibling relationships are the only relationships that last a lifetime" (p. 1). You know, your disability will always be a part of me also, and, like you, I just deal with it.
>
> KATHY: When one has CP, one doesn't overcome it for it never goes away, one simply deals with it and does the best he/she can. (Davis & Salkin, 2005, pp. 227–229)

Ironically, although Cris conceived this story from the beginning as a multivoiced co-constructed narrative, bringing equal voice to both participants was incredibly challenging and probably never fully realized. As an academic researcher and writer cowriting with an educated yet "lay" coauthor, Cris found her voice to be primary and more prominent than Kathy's voice, which consisted primarily of memories and reactions to Cris's memories and analysis. But in the end, Cris and Kathy achieved some level of multivocality in the writing and a good dose of relational dialogue and understanding as a result of the effort.

Carolyn, along with her partner and coauthor, Art (Ellis & Bochner, 1992), also wrote a co-constructed narrative with equal voice about their reactions to a pregnancy and resulting abortion and its effect on their relationship. After independently constructing a detailed account of what had taken place and how they felt about it, they read each other's versions and then co-constructed a single story of what happened in both the male and female voices. In one scene, in which the authors take readers into what happened during the actual abortion procedure, their voices are presented side by side on the page. In other methods pieces, the authors discuss the advantages of doing co-constructed narratives over traditional interview stories and personal, one-voiced narratives (e.g., Bochner & Ellis, 1992). These two authors found that writing unmediated co-constructive narrative gave them the freedom to explore emotional trauma without worrying about doing emotional harm to other vulnerable participants or fearing loss of control of their words and personal experiences to another researcher. Additionally, they came to understand their relationship and feelings better and were able to unify the past with a hopeful future (see Ellis, 2004, p. 77).

Interactive Interviewing

Similar to, and in some cases used in conjunction with, co-constructed narrative, interactive interviewing is a conversation in which the researcher and the research participants engage in joint sensemaking and emergent understanding by mutual disclosure, sharing personal feelings and social experiences with each other (see also active interviewing; Holstein & Gubrium, 1995). Interactive interviewing requires engaging in multiple interview sessions, as well as potentially in shared activities other than formal interviews (Ellis et al., 1997; Holstein & Gubrium, 1995). In interactive interviews, usually two to four people act as researchers and participants. All participants share their stories as their relationships deepen. The understandings that emerge among all parties during interaction are as important as the stories each brings to the session.

In "Interactive Interviewing: Talking About Emotional Experience," Ellis and colleagues (1997) co-constructed a narrative about food, bodies, and eating disorders. They collected data through a series of interactive interviews and wrote the narrative collaboratively from interactions with each other and reflections on each other's writings.

Their last interview took place in a restaurant. Afterward, they independently wrote their stories of the event, including their thoughts and feelings. The following excerpt shows the importance of context in providing the opportunity to learn more about a research topic, as well as the importance of multiple voices in uncovering the complex feelings and thoughts that participants have about a topic:

> When Carolyn sits down across from her, Christine instantly is aware that they have never eaten together. Since she tends to synchronize her eating pattern with others, she panics. Will Carolyn eat quickly or slowly? Does she talk while eating? Is she a sharer? Will Carolyn, a seasoned ethnographer, be watching her every move?
>
> Lisa's stomach growls continuously as they sit talking without picking up their menus. Why don't they order? When finally the waitress stops to ask if they want an appetizer, Carolyn looks questioningly at Lisa and Christine. Lisa can almost taste the salty/greasy choices—oozing processed cheese nachos, fried mozzarella sticks, and hot chicken wings. But she's not feeling particularly "bad," and she knows Christine almost never eats appetizers. They shake their heads "no" simultaneously. Carolyn considered ordering some for the table, but after their response, she thinks that she really shouldn't have them either.
>
> Carolyn takes one of the menus tucked behind the salt and pepper shakers. Immediately Christine and Lisa reach for menus as well. It seems they have been waiting for Carolyn to make the first move. Right away Carolyn knows what she wants. But Christine and Lisa grasp their menus tightly, immersed, reading line by line. For what seems like minutes to Carolyn, they say nothing. Carolyn continues holding her menu in front of her face so they don't feel rushed. She'd like to know what they're thinking. Minutes go by.
>
> Craving a cheeseburger and fries, Lisa scans the menu for a low-fat selection. Christine feels she should be making table conversation, but, instead, pays attention only to the descriptions of each dish. Finally she asks Lisa, "What are you getting?"

> Carolyn offers, "I always get the lemon chicken. It's light."
>
> The word "light" catches Christine's attention. Light is something she feels after a urge. Now she feels the heaviness of her own body in contrast to Lisa's thinness. . . . Lisa orders the Italian chicken but instructs the waitress to leave off the dressing [She] waits impatiently for her meal to come, turning to look each time a server passes by with food. (Ellis et al., 1997, pp. 139–140)

Interactive forms of research also can be used in larger groups and communities, giving members the opportunity to reflect on their practices and processes. For example, Deb Walker's (2005) dissertation research on the construction of identity among community service volunteers at a domestic violence organization (Community Action Stops Abuse; CASA) used a collaborative research approach in which the research process gave participants the opportunity to reflect on their own volunteer experiences. As first-person narrator, Walker provided her account of being a volunteer at CASA and also represented the experiences of other volunteers, derived from formal interactive interviews and informal conversations and interactions over several years of fieldwork. Walker described community participants as coresearchers with equal voice:

> In the spirit of a collaborative action research project, I've obtained my participants' oral and written feedback about what I have written. I've allowed them to make revisions to early and subsequent drafts. They often disagreed about the sequencing of events, content of conversations, and methods of representation. They edited their own conversations and shared in their own descriptions. We negotiated disagreements about representation like we negotiated everything in this research project: dialogically, collaboratively, and respectfully. . . . All participants used as characters within this dissertation have read and verbally approved all versions and drafts of this work. At my participants' request, real names are used in this dissertation. (pp. 58–59)

Walker specifically discussed one challenge in giving participants equality, or perhaps even seniority, in voice, taking "member checks" to a new level:

> I, too, welcomed my participants' liberal editorializing. For example, Margaret, the legal advocate we meet in Chapter One, was distressed after reading early versions of the dissertation. She felt her character, especially as it was developed in Chapter Five, was unflattering. Margaret also expressed concerns about my representations of the domestic violence court clerks, who, in early drafts, were important, and rather unlikeable, characters. After listening to her concerns, reading her comments, and sharing our discussions with my advisors, I incorporated many of her suggestions. I inserted more sensory details from my field notes that we feel softens her portrayal. I agreed with Margaret that since I had not obtained consents from any of the domestic violence clerks, and recognizing that, like me, they were constrained structurally more than individually, I deleted all personal references to them, generalizing their representation significantly.
>
> However, Margaret and I disagreed as to the content of some of our early conversations. After re-reading my field notes and re-analyzing my purposes, I was dogged in my insistence that my representations of our mutual conversations were accurate and important. With much discussion and explanation, she has agreed to their inclusion. This process is representative of the multiple processes that occurred with all of my research participants as we co-constructed this dissertation. (pp. 61–62)

Elizabeth Curry's (2005) "research novel" also describes her interactions with CASA staff via a university–community initiative at the University of South Florida. Engaging in what Curry and Kenneth Gergen (2000) call "poetic activism," Curry used participant observation and interactive interviews to create a narrative that embraced the "ambiguities, contradictions, multiple identities and blurred boundaries" of their experiences (p. vi). As Curry states, "the heart of my dissertation is the relationship with the CASA workers and how scholarship and advocacy intersect with a philosophy of reciprocal and compassionate empowerment" (p. v).

Her dissertation included individual scenes of what could be termed *interactive participation*. For example, her first meeting with CASA staff is told in the context of reminiscing with the staff about that meeting in a "co-construction of their memories" (E. Curry, personal communication, April 4, 2006). A second chapter includes a conversation held between Curry and the executive director of CASA while they were swimming together, and a third describes staff feedback to a story Curry wrote about a focus group she had previously conducted with them. A fourth is a story about a staff member who was attacked by her estranged husband, told in the context of Curry's interview with the woman who was attacked and her interviews with other CASA workers. "At the end I find the staff comforting me," she says (E. Curry, personal communication, April 4, 2006).

Walker and Curry both show the potential of interactive research methods to engage the community in the research effort in a way that is empowering and enlightening, as well as multivocal and representative.

Interactive Focus Groups

Bringing the idea of interactive interviews to traditional focus groups, we have developed a methodological approach that we call *interactive focus groups*. This approach is especially well suited for understanding the dynamic interactions of a group or system. More than simply a large interactive interview, this method borrows characteristics from traditional focus groups, from interactive interviewing (Ellis et al., 1997; Holstein & Gubrium, 1995), from narrative recovery techniques (Delbecq, Van de Ven, & Gustafson, 1975), from the Delphi technique (de Meyrick, 2003; Fleming & Monda-Amaya, 2001; Neiger, Barnes, Thackeray, & Lindman, 2001), from interactive group interviews (Patton, 2002), from leaderless discussion groups (Stewart & Shamdasani, 1990), from interactive and constructivist therapy groups (Loos & Epstein, 1989), and from the therapy practice of reflecting teams (Andersen, 1987, 1995; Minuchin & Fishman, 1981; White, 1993).

In a traditional focus group, a moderator interviews a usually homogeneous group of 6 to 12 participants who are strangers to each other and uses the group process and interaction to stimulate a 1- to 2-hour discussion on the beliefs, attitudes, or motivations of participants on a specific, focused topic. The moderator typically follows a topical outline or interview guide consisting of open-ended questions. This definition implicates the importance of group interaction and social context to the collection of data, and this interaction leads to high-quality data through a process of participant questioning, challenging, elaborating, and disagreeing (Krueger & Casey, 2001; Merton, 1956, 1987; Morgan, 1988, 1996; Patton, 2002; Stewart & Shamdasani, 1990; Wilkinson, 1998). Ironically, despite the importance of the group interaction to the data collected, the interaction itself is rarely factored into the analysis.

Unlike traditional focus groups, which are highly constrained and organized (Myers, 1998), the group discussion in interactive focus groups tends to be unstructured, allowing "the widest range of meaning and interpretation" (Fontana & Frey, 2000, p. 652), and strives to create a type of polyphonic interviewing in which multiple perspectives are sought and discussed (Fontana & Frey, 2000). We are intentionally nondirective to let the natural interaction processes of the group come through with as little interference from us as possible. In addition, although the groups have a "ringleader," all participants are coresearchers, yielding a group process somewhere between that of a leaderless group and a group with all leaders. At different times, different participants may take the lead. At other times, the discussion seems more chaotic and unfocused.

Also unlike traditional focus groups, in which participants are strangers to each other and thus their interactions have few consequences past the group session (Myers, 1998), interactive focus groups consist of participants already in an existing "bona fide" group or relationship, and the purpose is to observe how their prior group culture plays itself out in the focus group environment.

Most important, these groups include an intentional process in which the researcher and the research participants engage in joint sensemaking and emergent understanding by mutual disclosure, sharing personal feelings and social experiences with each other. This entails multiple focus group sessions to build on previous sessions and encourage reflection, empathy, and trust between sessions. The focus of the group is threefold: to discuss the topic at hand, to reflect on the discussion in the group, and to analyze the discourse used in the discussion as a way of understanding how meaning is constructed in the group.

Interactive focus groups allow us to watch the system in action and interaction. In our analysis of these group sessions, we look at the conversation as a speech event or narrative, as suggested by Mishler (1986), to understand the joint construction of meaning taking place in the sessions. Through this process, we look at the conversational, narrative, and symbolic ways that the team as a system jointly constructs their reality.

Interactive focus groups are a moral and ethical methodological choice that let participants have a say in how the research is conducted, as they are able to exert control over the conversation. This approach provides an opportunity to tilt the balance of power in the research relationship from one single researcher to the group as coparticipants, providing what Andersen (1995) calls a "heterarchical" relationship, one in which power is infused through the other. Interactive focus groups have interpretive sufficiency (depth, detail, emotionality, nuance, and coherence) that represent multiple voices, enhance moral discernment and articulation, and promote social transformation (Christians, 2000; Madriz, 2000). As Christians (2000) stated, in this type of research, "because the research–subject relation is reciprocal, invasion of privacy, informed consent, and deception are nonissues. In communitarianism, conceptions of the good are shared by the research subjects, and researchers collaborate in bringing these definitions into their own" (p. 149).

There are, however, ethical concerns that must be taken into consideration when designing a study using any type of focus group methodology. A primary ethical consideration when conducting focus groups is the inability to guarantee confidentiality of the information discussed. Although group members can be asked to maintain both confidentiality and anonymity, participants cannot control for this nor guarantee it (Jones, 2003; Patton, 2002). Wilkinson (1998) notes a concern for potential bullying or intimidation between focus group members, and interactive focus groups are especially subject to group coercion or pressure to disclose information that participants may not have intended to disclose. Finally, creating a safe environment in which participants can share painful and emotional experiences is a challenge that must be met in any focus group, but especially in interactive focus groups because of the tendency for deeper disclosure in these sessions (Owen, 2001; Patton, 2002). In addition, because the end result of interactive focus groups is typically a group narrative, negotiating what to share with the outside world while being sensitive to individuals' needs for privacy is especially problematic.

Recently some significant examples of interactive focus groups have emerged. For example, Vangelis's doctoral dissertation (2006) used an interactive focus group approach to discuss issues of menopause with women who, like her, were undergoing that physical experience. Cris's dissertation research (Davis, 2005a) included a series of interactive focus groups in which she invited participants in the groups to metacommunicate about their shared group experience. In the final focus group, participants reacted to her tentative findings and suggested revisions and some findings of their own.

Cris is currently involved in a participant action research project sponsored by the Charlotte Institute for Rehabilitation at the Carolinas Medical Center. This research, which attempts to understand the communicative, interactive, social, cognitive, and biological components of irritability among people with traumatic brain injury (TBI), consists of a total of four ongoing groups meeting monthly for a year. Data from the group sessions are supplemented with entries from ongoing journals by all participants. Study participants—people with TBI, family members of people with TBI, health care providers, and university researchers—act as coresearchers, and all share the roles of planning, facilitation, responding, coding, and analyzing.

Cris and Carolyn together, along with colleagues Marilyn Myerson, Mary Poole, and Kendall Smith-Sullivan (2007), are in the process of an interactive focus group project we have tentatively titled "50-Something in 2006: It Ain't Your Mother's Middle Age." Through a series of interactive focus groups, we explore our experiences with being "plus or minus 50." We seek to understand how our experiences in this time of our lives contribute to our identities and how—through communication—we construct our identities as "new middle-aged" women. This project is characterized by an absence of a facilitator or leader, collaboration in forming of research questions, multiple voices, flexibility of conversation and direction, and collaborative writing.

In this coauthored "50-something" project, we five authors—all middle-aged (45–60 years old) and white professional women—discuss aging for women in 2006. These conversations take place in interactive focus groups, in which we all act as researchers and participants. The topic of the particular conversation in the following excerpt is women's bodies. Through our talk, we seek to view aging in a positive and healthy light, resisting society's negative stereotypes of aging women as "over the hill" and supporting each other in aging well. Yet we also show how we, too, are affected by the cultural contradictions of aging, as we discuss physical appearance, plastic surgery, weight gain, sexuality and desire, changing hormones, hot flashes, menopause, and physical and mental illness. The result is an open portrayal of how women communicate about their aging bodies, as illustrated in the following scene. Later in the conversation, we all move into researcher mode, sharing and analyzing at the same time.

> The tone is set, thinks Leslie, when Nancy suggests meeting in her hot tub. Her first reaction is "yikes," thinking ahead to her thickening thighs, bulging PMS belly and droopy boobs. However, she muses that she feels bonded enough with the rest of the group to feel comfortable in less garb. As soon as she recognizes her sense of ease, she begins to look forward to a gathering that combines scholarship and bubbling water jets. At home, as Leslie dons her low-cut, hot pink, one piece bathing suit and covers it with a short skirt and tank top in anticipation of the group session, she feels empowered and zippy. She waves goodbye to her husband and thinks that perhaps he wonders if her neon-colored swim outfit is just the beginning of some kind of liberal academic love-in. He says he will wait up for her. Maybe he also wonders if he will get lucky later, she thinks.
>
> We arrive at Nancy's on a gorgeous Florida spring evening. . . . Nancy's clothing choice—a dog-embossed t-shirt and shorts—mirrors Barbara's gray v-necked shirt and cropped pants in its carefree attitude, and contrasts with the suit Jan is still wearing straight from work. It rained this morning, and her layered haircut is frizzy, rendering her neither fully casual nor fully professional in her look. When Leslie arrives, she is dressed impeccably as always. Over her swimsuit, Leslie's short white skirt shows off her tanned, curved legs, and her tight-fitting bright red knit top showcases her sun-bleached blonde hair, which, like her makeup, is perfect. Catherine's bright red hair,

cut in a short shag style, matches her colorful, artistic knit pants suit and large, creative earrings and necklace.

Catherine and Jan retreat into back rooms to change into their swimsuits. They each grab their glasses of wine, Coke, and water and make their way to the back deck. Everyone watches as Nancy opens the lid to the hot tub. It is heavy, and Leslie and Jan set their drinks on the railing as they help her lift it off. Nancy shows us how to get into the tub safely.

"Put your feet in carefully, then sit your butt down," she instructs. "Be careful, hold on," she cautions as we gingerly step into the tub, one at a time, juggling our drinks as we lower our bodies into the steaming water.

"This is so much fun!" exclaims Barbara, as she follows Nancy into the tub.

"It's grown-up fun," Leslie clarifies, as we giggle and laugh.

Catherine follows Jan in. "The water is going over the edge when I sit down," she says cautiously.

"It's 'cause it's the five of us, Catherine!" Barbara retorts, refusing to let Catherine think her body weight alone has displaced the tubful of water.

"I don't think there's ever been this many people in here before," Nancy notes.

"I'm taking my shirt off now," Leslie announces, as she removes the top she is wearing over her swimsuit.

"Leslie, are you modest?" Nancy asks in a surprised tone.

"Yes, I know you wouldn't think that of me," Leslie admits as we giggle again.

"This is out of control," Barbara says.

"I love feeling out of control," Catherine responds.

"How do you all feel about being in bathing suits and in the hot tub?" Nancy asks.

"When I got up this morning," Catherine answers, "I thought, 'I'm going to be in a bathing suit tonight with everybody. Should I shave my legs?' I decided not to. So, here I am, hairy legs and all." We laugh again.

Nancy admits, "I haven't shaved my legs for about 35 years. I quit shaving when I was 20." Jan suppresses a twinge of surprise as she thinks of how hairy her legs are today, since she too decided not to shave for this event and wonders how hairy they would look if she quit shaving them entirely.

"But Nancy, you don't have any hair," Barbara protests.

"But I did. When you don't shave you don't get that really coarse hair."

"I have less pubic hair than I did," Barbara says.

"Me, too," Catherine chimes in.

Jan thinks of seeing her mother's sparse pubic hair when she was dying, and being surprised at how bare it was. But she was in her 70s and ill. She's surprised that women as young as Barbara and Catherine are saying they have less. She wonder if she has that to look forward to. She wonders if it matters.

Leslie joins in. "I'm not losing it, but I wanted to ask about graying pubic hair. I remember seeing my grandmother once walking around naked, and she had white pubic hair. It hasn't happened to me yet, but. . . ." Her voice trails off as we think for a minute.

Catherine responds first. "Yeah, do you ever get those catalogs in the mail for products for women going through menopause? Honest to God, they sell pubic hair wigs."

"No, they don't!" Leslie protests, as we all laugh.

"How do they attach them?" Barbara asks, as our laughter gets louder.

"Like pasties?" Leslie asks. Jan shudders at the entire thought.

Barbara says thoughtfully, "When you're 25, you do French wax to get rid of it, and when you're 45, you buy pubic wigs to make it more." We laugh.

For the moment, Jan can't think about aging pubic hair any longer, and, working against group resistance to a leader, she decides to attempt to assert some facilitator control over the conversation. She tries to frame the conversation theoretically. "Why are we all taking part in this research? My interest in this project is from a social construction point of view. I'm interested in the concept of middle age. I actually don't like the term, and I'm at an age that's probably considered middle age. Actually, someone said to me a month ago I was past middle age. I really didn't appreciate that." She nods her head for emphasis. "I think middle age is 45–60. I'm real curious, is middle age even an appropriate term for what we are? And if middle age is the only term we have right now, how do we as a society construct what being middle-aged means?"

"I think that women like us are socially constructing a different story," Catherine says. "We're not buying the canonical story about what it's like to be an older woman."

Nancy interjects, "What was one of the first conversations everyone had when we first walked in the door?"

Leslie laughs. "Oh my age, oh my this, oh my allergies. My innards are so, blah, blah blah."

"Right," Nancy says. She turns to Barbara. "Look what we talk about when we go walking every week."

Barbara and Nancy respond together. "How are your aches and pains today?"

"Yeah," Nancy says, "and it feels a lot like the conversations I used to hear my mother have."

Catherine responds thoughtfully. "I've written a little about my recent diagnosis with rheumatoid arthritis. I really made a point of not talking about illness most of my life, probably because of my mother's obsession with being ill. I've got to be in a lot of pain before I talk about being in pain."

"And then there's our bodies and how we look," Nancy says." I go to the mirror and look at my wrinkles probably the way my mother did and I pull my skin taut on my face, to see how it would look if it were tighter. I worry about gaining weight, and get on the scales every day." Nancy recalls how just this morning she stood looking in the mirror, pulling her facial skin first one way and then the other. When she heard her husband coming, she immediately pretended to be doing something else.

"We all talk about weight," Leslie admits. "We all talk about what maybe we shouldn't eat." Everyone nods.

"One of the articles I read said that middle-aged women are just depressed because they're no longer as beautiful and sexy and sexual as they were when they were younger," Jan says. "And that seems to be one common theme I saw in the way researchers described middle-aged women. They're a little saggier and not quite as sexual perhaps."

"Sexy or sexual or both?" asks Barbara.

"Both."

Barbara interjects. "We're a sex-oriented culture, and we're past the age of reproduction. And that's very much how middle age is defined."

Leslie says, "I'll tell you what, Demi Moore is marrying that toddler. She's pregnant at 42. He's 15 or 17 years younger. Now I have to say I think that's a victory for women." Nancy thinks that the pregnancy might be considered a victory of sorts, but she refuses to see marrying a younger man as in the same category.

"I think it's wonderful she's doing it, and I think it's sad she's doing it with all the plastic surgery," Jan adds, feeling the commonly conflicting feelings she has between her feminist self that thinks women should be allowed to age naturally and her narcissistic self that's influenced by our youth-oriented media and wants to continue to be as young and as beautiful as possible.

"I think we are redefining beauty, not because we don't care about it, but because we all care about looking good as middle-aged women. I'm not sure we're trying to look younger than we are," Nancy says.

Barbara agrees. "I feel better about my looks now than I did when I was in my 20s."

As the preceding excerpt shows, interactive focus groups let us analyze, reflect, and share in vivo, using our group discourse itself as a method of inquiry, as well as data to be further analyzed and discussed. Interactive focus groups provide a way to study interpersonal communication among women, studying ourselves as a "bona fide group" with an eye toward ecological validity (Poole, 1999; Sykes, 1990). The perspective we take through these groups helps us understand the role of social context in women's discourse of aging and the role of peer women in meaning making within this social context. As a group consisting solely of researchers, we reframe the role of the researcher in the process of reality construction. Interactive focus groups allow us to further equalize the hegemonic power relationship between traditional research participants and ourselves as researchers through a collaborative, dialogic process that makes us all coparticipants in the research process. In this process, we can view women's discourse on aging as it unfolds socially and continually in interaction between us as individual women and as women in a social system. We are able to investigate the impact of social processes on our construction of aging; look at how meaning is constructed through our communication; and understand how we are all part of the reflexive process of meaning construction. Through interactive focus groups, we get information on shared consciousness created in the group, how this consciousness creates a group identity, and the "communal process of collaborative emergence" (Poole, 1999, p. 61).

From autoethnographic narratives to interactive methods of interviewing and writing to interactive focus groups, we have taken the genre of autoethnography from a focus on "self" through a focus on "us" into a focus on "community." Interactive focus groups represent a dialogue of community, analyzed in process and about process.

Conclusion

Traditional ethnography has tended to emphasize research as a conduit of information that comes from informants to researchers and represents how things are. Autoethnography has moved this emphasis to a sea swell of meaning making in which researchers add their own stories and connect their experiences to those of others to provide stories that open up conversations about how we live and cope in relational, group, and institutional life. Autoethnography itself now includes groups and communities observing themselves rather than just the lone researcher reflecting on her or his emotional life. Hot tubs notwithstanding, autoethnography is not academic masturbation, and this is not an academic orgy, although it does represent a merging of selves that is certainly pleasurable to be a part of! Through narrative autoethnography, we connect with our readers as our experiences lead them to generalize to their own experiences and as analyzing our lives leads readers to analyze their own lives. In reflexive interviewing, interactive interviewing, co-constructed narratives, and interactive focus groups, we researchers have invited other participants to our party. We connect with them on the page through our joint experiences as they—and our readers— write their stories with us.

I (Cris) think of my mother's holiday dinners. Anyone and everyone was included; the more the merrier. The table was always formally set, yet around the table, raucous laughter, loud conversation, and warm comments could always be heard. This was a community built on sharing–food, understanding, and experiences. Interactive focus groups are much the same–a community based on shared experiences and shared understanding and, often, food! Interactive focus groups are a microcosm of the groups we study–a social construction of social construction, in a way. We do what groups do—talk, share, speculate, problem solve. We perform "group" under a microscope, analyze our performance, and even analyze our analysis. We perform, think, and write together, blending our thoughts, ideas, and voices into a coherent yet multivoiced analytical story.

This is what I've learned about autoethnography: It is in the sharing that we heal, in vulnerability that we become strong, in laughter that we learn, and the more the merrier! The secret is out. The party has begun.

Carolyn reads the last paragraph and smiles.

References

Andersen, T. (1987). The reflecting team: Dialogue and metadialogue in clinical work. *Family Process, 26*, 415–428.

Andersen, T. (1995). Reflecting processes: Acts of informing and forming. In S. Friedman (Ed.), *The reflecting team in action: Collaborative practice in family therapy* (pp. 11–37). New York: Guilford Press.

Baxter, L. A. (1992). Interpersonal communication as dialogue: A response to the "social approaches" forum. *Communication Theory*, *2*(4), 330–337.

Berger, L. (2001). Inside out: Narrative autoethnography as a path toward rapport. *Qualitative Inquiry*, *7*(4), 504–518.

Bochner, A. P., & Ellis, C. (1992). Personal narrative as

a social approach to interpersonal communication. *Communication Theory*, *2*(2), 165–172.

Christians, C. G. (2000). Ethics and politics in qualitative research. In N. K. Denzin & Y. S. Lincoln (Eds.), *The handbook of qualitative research* (pp. 133–155). Thousand Oaks, CA: Sage.

Conquergood, D. (1991). Rethinking ethnography: Towards a critical cultural politics. *Communication Monographs*, *58*(2), 179–194.

Curry, E. A. (2005). *Communication collaboration and empowerment: A research novel of relationships with domestic violence workers*. Unpublished dissertation, University of South Florida, Tampa.

Czubaroff, J., & Friedman, M. (2000). A conversation with Maurice Friedman. *Southern Communication Journal*, *65*(2/3), 243–255.

Daly, K. (1992). The fit between qualitative research and characteristics of families. In J. Gilgun, K. Daly, & G. Handel (Eds.), *Qualitative methods in family research* (pp. 3–11). Newbury Park, CA: Sage.

Davis, C. S. (2005a). *A future with hope: The social construction of hope, help, and dialogic reconciliation in a community children's mental health system of care*. Unpublished doctoral dissertation, University of South Florida, Tampa.

Davis, C. S. (2005b). Home. *Qualitative Inquiry*, *11*(3), 392–409.

Davis, C. S. (2006). Sylvia's story: Narrative, storytelling, and power in a children's community mental health system of care. *Qualitative Inquiry*, *13*(2), 1220–1243.

Davis, C. S., Ellis, C., Myerson, M., Poole, M., & Smith-Sullivan, K. (2007). *50-something in 2006: This ain't your mother's middle age*. Unpublished manuscript.

Davis, C. S., & Salkin, K. A. (2005). Sisters and friends: Dialogue and multivocality in a relational model of sibling disability. *Journal of Contemporary Ethnography*, *34*(2), 206–234.

de Meyrick, J. (2003). The Delphi method and health research. *Health Education*, *103*(1), 7–16.

Delbecq, A. L., Van de Ven, A. H., & Gustafson, D. H. (1975). *Group techniques for program planning*. Middleton, WI: Green Briar Press.

Dent, B. (2002). Border crossings: A story of sexual identity transformation. In A. P. Bochner & C. Ellis (Eds.), *Ethnographically speaking: Autoethnography, literature, and aesthetics* (pp. 191–200). Walnut Creek, CA: AltaMira Press.

Ellis, C. (1993). "There are survivors": Telling a story of sudden death. *Sociological Quarterly*, *34*(4), 711–730.

Ellis, C. (1995). *Final negotiations: A story of love, loss, and chronic illness*. Philadelphia: Temple University Press.

Ellis, C. (1996). Maternal connections. In C. Ellis & A. Bochner (Eds.), *Composing ethnography* (pp. 240–243). Walnut Creek, CA: AltaMira Press.

Ellis, C. (1998). "I hate my voice": Coming to terms with minor bodily stigmas. *Sociological Quarterly*, *39*(4), 517–537.

Ellis, C. (2001). With mother/with child: A true story. *Qualitative Inquiry*, *7*(5), 598–615.

Ellis, C. (2002a). Being real: Moving inward towards social change. *Qualitative Studies in Education*, *15*(4), 399–306.

Ellis, C. (2002b). Shattered lives: Making sense of September 11th and its aftermath. *Journal of Contemporary Ethnography*, *31*(4), 375–400.

Ellis, C. (2004). *The ethnographic I: A methodological novel about autoethnography*. Walnut Creek, CA: AltaMira Press.

Ellis, C. (2007). Telling secrets, revealing lives: Relational ethics in research with intimate others. *Qualitative Inquiry*.

Ellis, C., & Bochner, A. (1992). Telling and performing personal stories: The constraints of choice in abortion. In C. Ellis & M. Flaherty (Eds.), *Investigating subjectivity: Research on lived experience* (pp. 79–101). Thousand Oaks, CA: Sage.

Ellis, C., & Bochner, A. P. (2000). Autoethnography, personal narrative, reflexivity: Researcher as subject. In N. K. Denzin & Y. S. Lincoln (Eds.), *The handbook of qualitative research* (pp. 733–768). Thousand Oaks, CA: Sage.

Ellis, C., Kiesinger, C. E., & Tillman-Healy, L. M. (1997). Interactive interviewing: Talking about emotional experience. In R. Hertz (Ed.), *Reflexivity and voice* (pp. 119–149). Thousand Oaks, CA: Sage.

Fleming, J. L., & Monda-Amaya, L. E. (2001). Process variables critical for team effectiveness: A Delphi study of wraparound team members. *Remedial and Special Education*, *22*(3), 158–171.

Fontana, A., & Frey, J. H. (2000). The interview: From structured questions to negotiated text. In N. K. Denzin & Y. S. Lincoln (Eds.), *The handbook of qualitative research* (pp. 645–672). Thousand Oaks, CA: Sage.

Gergen, K. J. (2000). *An invitation to social construction*. Thousand Oaks, CA: Sage.

Gergen, M. M., & Gergen, K. J. (2002). Ethnographic representation as relationship. In A. P. Bochner & C. Ellis (Eds.), *Ethnographically speaking: Autoethnography, literature, and aesthetics* (pp. 11–33). Walnut Creek, CA: AltaMira Press.

Goodall, H. L. (2000). *Writing the new ethnography*. Walnut Creek, CA: AltaMira Press.

Gubrium, J. F., & Holstein, J. A. (1997). *The new language of qualitative method*. New York: Oxford University Press.

Hawes, L. C. (1994). Revisiting reflexivity. *Western Journal of Communication*, *58*, 5–10.

Holstein, J. A., & Gubrium, J. F. (1995). *The active interview*. Thousand Oaks, CA: Sage.

Jago, B. (2002). Chronicling an academic depression. *Journal of Contemporary Ethnography*, *31*, 729–757.

Jones, A. M. (2003). Changes in practice at the nurse–doctor interface. *Journal of Clinical Nursing*, *12*, 124–131.

Jones, S. H. (2002). The way we were, are, and might be: Torch singing as autoethnography. In A. P. Bochner & C. Ellis (Eds.), *Ethnographically speaking: Autoethnography, literature, and aesthetics* (pp. 44–56). Walnut Creek, CA: AltaMira Press.

Krueger, R., & Casey, M. A. (2001). *Designing and conducting focus group interviews.* Washington, DC: The Social Development Family in the World Bank.

Loos, V. E., & Epstein, E. S. (1989). Conversational construction of meaning in family therapy: Some evolving thoughts on Kelly's sociality corollary. *International Journal of Personal Construct Psychology, 2,* 149–167.

Mabry, E. A. (1999). The systems metaphor in group communication. In L. R. Frey (Ed.), *The handbook of group communication theory and research* (pp. 71–91). Thousand Oaks, CA: Sage.

Madriz, E. (2000). Focus groups in feminist research. In N. K. Denzin & Y. S. Lincoln (Eds.), *The handbook of qualitative research* (pp. 835–850). Thousand Oaks, CA: Sage.

Mairs, N. (1993, February 21). When bad things happen to good writers. *New York Times Book Review,* pp. 25–27.

Merton, R. K. (1956). *The focused interview: A manual of problems and procedures.* New York: Free Press.

Merton, R. K. (1987). The focussed interview and focus groups: Continuities and discontinuities. *Public Opinion Quarterly, 51,* 550–566.

Minuchin, S., & Fishman, H. C. (1981). *Family therapy techniques.* Cambridge, MA: Harvard University Press.

Mishler, E. G. (1986). *Research interviewing: Context and narrative.* Cambridge, MA: Harvard University Press.

Mizco, N. (2003). Beyond the "fetishism of words": Considerations on the use of the interview to gather chronic illness narratives. *Qualitative Health Research, 13*(4), 469–490.

Morgan, D. (1988). *Focus groups as qualitative research.* Newbury Park, CA: Sage.

Morgan, D. (1996). Focus groups. *Annual Review of Sociology, 22,* 129–152.

Myers, G. (1998). Displaying opinions: Topics and disagreement in focus groups. *Language in Society, 27,* 85–111.

Mykhalovskiy, E. (1997). Reconsidering "table talk": Critical thoughts on the relationship between sociology, autobiography, and self-indulgence. In R. Hertz (Ed.), *Reflexivity and voice* (pp. 229–251). Thousand Oaks, CA: Sage.

Neiger, B. L., Barnes, M. D., Thackeray, R., & Lindman, N. (2001). Use of the Delphi method and nominal group technique in front-end market segmentation. *American Journal of Health Studies, 17*(3), 111–119.

Owen, S. (2001). The practical, methodological, and ethical dilemmas of conducting focus groups with vulnerable clients. *Journal of Advanced Nursing, 36*(5), 652–658.

Patton, M. Q. (2002). *Qualitative research and evaluation methods.* Thousand Oaks, CA: Sage.

Poole, M. S. (1999). Group communication theory. In L. R. Frey (Ed.), *The handbook of group communication theory and research* (pp. 37–70). Thousand Oaks, CA: Sage.

Rambo Ronai, C. (1996). My mother is mentally retarded. In C. Ellis & A. P. Bochner (Eds.), *Composing ethnography: Alternative forms of qualitative writing* (pp. 109–131). Walnut Creek, CA: AltaMira Press.

Rappaport, J. (1993). Narrative studies, personal stories, and identity transformation in the mutual help context. *Journal of Applied Behavioral Science, 29*(2), 239–256.

Reed-Danahay, D. (2001). Autobiography, intimacy and ethnography. In P. Atkinson (Ed.), *Handbook of ethnography* (pp. 407–425). Thousand Oaks, CA: Sage.

Schulman, G. L. (1999). Siblings revisited: Old conflicts and new opportunities in later life. *Journal of Marital and Family Therapy, 25*(4), 517–524.

Stewart, D. W., & Shamdasani, P. N. (1990). *Focus groups: Theory and practice.* Newbury Park, CA: Sage.

Sykes, R. E. (1990). Imagining what we might study if we really studied small groups from a speech perspective. *Communication Studies, 41*(3), 200–211.

Tillmann-Healy, L. M. (1996). A secret life in a culture of thinness: Reflections on body, food, and bulimia. In C. Ellis & A. P. Bochner (Eds.), *Composing ethnography: Alternative forms of qualitative writing* (pp. 76–108). Walnut Creek, CA: AltaMira Press.

Vangelis, L. (2006). *Communicating change: An ethnography of women's sensemaking on hormone replacement therapies, menopause, and the Women's Health Initiative.* Unpublished dissertation, University of South Florida, Tampa.

Van Maanen, J. (1988). *Tales of the field.* Chicago: University of Chicago Press.

Walker, D. C. (2005). *Motive and identity in the narratives of community service volunteers.* Unpublished dissertation, University of South Florida, Tampa.

White, M. (1993). Deconstruction and therapy. In S. Gilligan & R. Price (Eds.), *Therapeutic conversations* (pp. 22–61). New York: Norton.

Wilkinson, S. (1998). Focus groups in feminist research: Power, interaction, and the co-construction of meaning. *Women's Studies International Forum, 21*(1), 111–125.

CHAPTER 15

New Critical Collaborative Ethnography

Himika Bhattacharya

> Critical ethnography must further its goals from simply politics to the politics of positionality. . . . Positionality is vital because it forces us to acknowledge our own power, privilege, and biases just as we are denouncing the power structures that surround our subjects.
>
> —MADISON (2005, pp. 6–7)

A Starting Definition

This chapter focuses on emergent methods in ethnography—more specifically, on new trends in critical collaborative ethnography. I discuss and draw on several examples of critical ethnographic research studies across disciplines, including my own experiences as a researcher completing a critical collaborative dissertation project embedded in feminist ideals in Lahaul, India. I discuss here the key issues that make this method emergent,[1] finally tying into a discussion of performance, researcher positionality, the development of new criteria for validity in this method, feminist and postmodern interventions, emancipatory potential of research, and the local–global connections that have reconfigured research practices across the world, especially those of the new critical collaborative ethnography.

From the outset, critical collaborative ethnography, which I define more fully subsequently, requires careful attention to questions about the research situation itself and the researcher's position within it—questions that would typically be omitted from a scholarly publication. As in my own case, these questions raise core issues that lie at the heart of any critical collaborative ethnography.

In her keynote address at the Third International Congress of Qualitative Inquiry held in May 2007, Soyini Madison discussed what she termed *dangerous ethnography*. She used the words *safe* and *dangerous* to illustrate the complex politics of researcher positionality, power, and privilege as intersections of race, gender, and class expand across continents. In part her discussion referred to questions about personal safety repeatedly asked of her and her mentor, Dwight Conquergood, by U.S. academics, as they conducted fieldwork in geographical places perceived as dangerous (he in immigrant neighborhoods of Chicago, she in Ghana). Her discussion brought to mind a set of questions asked about my own work.

I am repeatedly asked several types of questions concerning my work with women's experiences of violence in Lahaul, India, in general and sexual violence, rape, and marriage by abduction in particular. The first question concerns my own safety when working on such sensitive issues in such a community. Typically this question comes from people who meet me in the United States or from urban elite Indians in big cities such as Delhi, Bombay, and Calcutta: "Are you safe working in 'these places'?"[2] "Would they not abduct you, or force you? Are you not worried about a violent backlash?" As Madison (2007) noted of her work in Ghana, the focus is consistently on my safety rather than the safety of the women I work with. Each time I've been appalled by such concerns and made doubly aware of my own class and caste privilege in India. What is it that makes it easier to think of my safety and the "dangers" I expose myself to when doing this ethnography, rather than the dangers that the women I work with continue to face and handle on a daily basis?

The second kind of question usually tends to revolve around my own reasons for doing "this kind of work." A perfect example is this question I was asked rather suddenly in a recent appointment with a health professional at the University of Illinois at Urbana-Champaign: "Have you ever been raped? Hmmm. . . . I'm only wondering because of the work you do, you know." I was stunned into speechlessness.

Another question regarding my reasons for research came from an acquaintance employed by a fancy corporate firm in the United States: "People do this kind of research either if they've had a similar experience in their lives with violence or if they don't think they have the intellectual potential to get admission into business schools and make a lot of money. . . . Which of the two is true for you?" I said yes to the latter, to make him uncomfortable, and felt good at what I thought was him squirming.

Two years ago, at the U.S. embassy in Delhi, India, when I was being interviewed for renewal of my student visa, my interviewer—a white North American male—said, "India needs people like you, who study in the West, and return to work on these kinds of problems here. There's so much violence here. . . . I hope that's why you're getting this PhD—so you can help women in India . . . ?" I nodded in agreement, indicating that I intended to return as soon as possible armed with a doctoral degree validated by a U.S. university that would surely help me save India—hoping he would give me the visa if I did.

These are just a few examples of how I shift between multiple subject positions: a class- and caste-privileged member of the Indian urban elite, with access to worlds beyond the reach of those I work with; a survivor of sexual violence, my work viscerally inscribed on my body, freezing each time I hear questions about my reasons for this research; a woman wearing a *salwaar kameez*[3] (hoping that it displays the right amount of nationalistic fervor), made aware of my position in the world as a woman of color as I seek entry into the United States through approval from a white man sitting in New Delhi, who reminds me of the flag-waving, Support-Our-Troops bumper-sticker truckers I'm familiar with in Illinois and elsewhere in the United States (the bastions of civilization); the inherently contradictory position of a researcher conducting ethnographic fieldwork in the global south and now writing her work in the global north. I take these multiple positions I find myself in and work with those that I consider most politically problematic—those that place me within a particular racial, sexual, and kinship domain—and attempt to negotiate in my research these roles that I play in my life (Behar, 1993). The chapter that follows will make clear the centrality of these changing positions and identities to the theory and practice of the new critical collaborative ethnography.

What Is Critical Collaborative Ethnography?

The term *critical collaborative ethnography* has two main components: critical and collaborative. *Critical* refers to ethnographic practice that focuses on projects that challenge dominant hegemonic global structures at the intersection of race, gender, class, sexuality, and disability. Such ethnographic practice, as Madison (2005) notes in her important overview of the field, is said to have grown out of the "critical turn" in the social sciences—it refers to the "method" of critical "theory":

> Critical ethnography becomes the "doing" or the "performance" of critical theory. It is critical theory in action . . . in critical ethnography it is not my *exclusive* experience—that is autobiography, travel writing, or memoir (or what some people call *autoethnography*). I contend that *critical* ethnography is always a meeting of multiple sides in an encounter with and among Other(s), one in which there is negotiation and dialogue toward substantial and viable meanings that make a difference in the Other's world. (Madison, 2005, p. 15)

Hence, any ethnographic research project that lends itself to the "critical" turn in the social sciences is potentially a "critical ethnography." This turn is a major contribution of critical theory that brings together a hybrid body of theories across disciplines, ranging from postmodern to feminist to queer theory, and is invested in the significance of cultural representations, texts, practices, and subjectivities in understanding language, culture, and identity (Bhattacharya, 2008). These new ideas are exemplified in the works of Madison (2005), Lassiter (2005), Smith (2005), Mutua and Swadener (2004), Denzin (2003b), Goodall (2000), and Fine (1994), among others. A major emphasis on the Aristotlean notion of *praxis*,[4] then, marks this method. Simply put, critical ethnography is politically motivated ethnographic practice (Thomas, 1992).

Though "collaborative" research can be understood in a number of ways, in this context it refers to the notion of doing ethnography "with" people rather than "on" or "about" people. The idea of a traditional collaboration in ethnography is not new; it is something that has been part of ethnographic practice since before Malinowski's (1922) emphasis on the ethnographer's role as "participant observer" in the field. This early notion of collaboration was seen in research studies of American Indians, including the earliest ethnographic documentation of Native Americans (Lassiter, 2005). Native Americans within American anthropological tradition were the initial "collaborators" in the works of anthropologists (Mead & Bunzel, 1960). Subsequently, it was this notion of collaboration with the "native" that led anthropology into its modernist phase through the works of Malinowski (1922), especially in terms of grounding ethnographic tradition in fieldwork and participant observation, and then eventually through the Chicago School and into the interpretive turn (Geertz, 1973). However, in more recent times, the term *collaborative ethnography* has rejected the arrogance inherent in it earlier, whereby observation necessarily included collaboration but the overall research project did not. Recently it has come to include critical research practices that are conducted hand in hand with the research subjects—from fieldwork to writing—with a purpose of bringing about positive change in the lives of the researched. In

Luke Lassiter's (2005) words, critical ethnography is designed to:

> emphasize a more fully and critically conscious approach to the power relations inherent in all ethnography. Anthropologists and other social scientists called into question both the hegemony of Western-situated knowledge and the structures of power that engender ethnography. In an effort to resolve this "crisis of representation" feminists and postmodernists initiated a sustained critique of the ethnographic practice itself—from fieldwork to writing that lasts to this day. This critique and its implications for founding a reciprocal and collaborative ethnography on intersubjective grounds serve as the contemporary context for the building of a more deliberate and explicit collaborative ethnography—one that seeks to more honestly grapple with the divisions between Self and Other, between object and subject, and between academic and community-based knowledge, but also with the complexity of representing human experience in an ever-changing postcolonial and postindustrial world. (p. 48)

The term *critical collaborative ethnography* further refers to a practice of ethnography that is invested in questioning the boundaries and power relations between the researcher and the researched for the specific purpose of bringing about social action and social change. Such an ethnography has a political purpose and is conducted in collaboration with the researched community at different levels. Some of the key components of critical collaborative ethnography, then, are:

- It is politically motivated and emphasizes the need to affect social change processes.
- Often it involves more than a single researcher. The subjects of the study are also actively participating at different levels—in planning, conducting, and presenting the research.
- Even when it involves one researcher, he or she works with multiple nonacademic settings (such as nonacademic research institutions and community-based organizations).
- These projects that link academic scholarship to "real world" agencies and practical projects focus on researcher positionality and accountability.

Who Uses Critical Collaborative Ethnography?

This particular kind of ethnography is particularly useful for research projects that challenge hegemonic structures and call into question issues of power and privilege in the experiences of people across the world. Projects across disciplines that emphasize the collaborative, dialogic process between the researcher and the research community are often situated at the intersections of race, gender, class, caste, sexuality, disability, and globalization, are always challenging the false binary of the researcher–researched (Behar, 2003), and are central to the bulk of new critical collaborative ethnographic research.

In disciplines such as education research, critical collaborative research is also practiced as participatory action research. The field of health communication uses critical collaborative research practices extensively, as exemplified in the works of Parrott and Steiner (2003), Guttman (2000), Ford and Yep (2003), and Takahashi and Smutny (1998). In their collaborative project to promote sun protection to soccer-playing youths in order to reduce the risks of skin cancer, Parrott and Steiner talk about the importance of collaborative research practices, which, in their experience, go a long way in identifying healthcare solutions.

Different Levels of Collaboration

As Lassiter (2006) puts it, "At the core of collaborative ethnography is the magnification of ethical and moral commitments, established in the field and extended to the writing of ethnographic texts" (p. 20). The question of collaboration in critical ethnography, then, can exist both with regard to the researcher and the research participants, who must agree to conduct a collaborative project in the first place, and with regard to the representation in writing of the final research.

Though the term *critical ethnography* is sometimes used as a broad umbrella term to include what I refer to here as critical collaborative ethnography—for at present collaborative ethnographic practices are necessarily critical—it seems to me more useful to explicitly acknowledge the new sense in which the critical ethnographic becomes collaborative only when it uses the self–other interaction to bring about positive change through different stages of the project, from its initial conceptualization to the conduct of fieldwork, analyzing, and writing.

Case Examples of Levels of Collaboration

More recent critical ethnography is almost always collaborative, on the grounds that no performance[5] of the self is possible outside of the dialogue with the "Other"[6] (Madison, 2005). The levels of collaboration and participation can vary based on the kind of project undertaken. For example, in their collaborative projects, both Lassiter (2005) and Burawoy (2000) have used collaborative methods to different beginnings and ends. Burawoy and his students increased public awareness of academic theories by critiquing and dismantling canonized practices through community-based local ethnographies, which were collaborative mostly at the fieldwork level. Luke Lassiter and his team, on the other hand—for their project titled *The Other Side of Middletown*—conducted the project from start to finish with the inputs of Muncie, Indiana's, African American community, including the conceptualizing of the project, the fieldwork, and writing the final document. The collaborative writing and representation process led them to represent alternative points of view in the same project to reflect the positions of different participants in the project, such as younger and older community members, and their different interpretations (Lassiter, 2005).

Often critical ethnographers do not discuss details of their methodological and political collaborations; neither in their initial study nor afterward. However, Fine and Weis (1998), in their ethnographic study of the urban poor, extensively report on these issues in their formal report and also talk about their methodological reflections in later works (Fine & Weis, 2000). To clarify this variation a bit further, it may be useful for me to draw on my dissertation project, which grew out of an initial participatory action research study I conducted locally on broader community issues.

During my pilot study, the local women expressed the need to have their life stories documented and their voices heard. The subsequent fieldwork and initial analysis for this project was collaborative. However, my final thesis document is in English, a language other than the ones that the women I work with speak (Hindi and Tod), and is not at the same level of collaboration as other entirely collaborative projects. Although my writing is constantly in dialogue with the experiences performed to me and by me in Lahaul, the physical extent of collaboration at this stage is limited for several reasons, including requirements of graduate education in U.S. academia, translation issues, and distance from the field. So the overall point is that the specific context and purpose of the individual research project may shape or constrain its extent of collaboration and final form in a variety of ways.

What's "New" in New Critical Collaborative Ethnography?

The Performative Turn

This method within ethnographic practice has taken a turn toward performance, therefore redefining itself within the broader space of performance ethnography. "Doing fieldwork is a personal experience" (Madison, 2005, p. 8). Culture, then, is no longer something "out there" for the ethnographer to discover and write. It is, in fact, being coperformed everyday by the researcher and those *with* whom the research is being conducted. Conquergood (1991) challenged the idea of participant observation by discussing the arrogance inherent in it. According to him, the notion of observation positions the researcher as the expert on and about the research participants—the authoritative researcher who interprets and pronounces judgments on the cultures she or he is studying, as opposed to the self-reflexive practice of research being coperformed between the researcher and researched. Whether this is done through (auto)ethnography (Denzin, 2003a), critical performance ethnography (Madison, 2005), collaborative ethnography (Lassiter, 2005), or participatory action ethnography (Fine & Weis, 2000), these emergent practices have rearticulated the ways in which ethnography is performed and announced the call to move away from the Chicago School (Denzin, 2003a) to make way for multiple-voiced, indigenous, resistance-based performative research. The emergent scholarship in ethnography engages the ongoing conversation about how experience contains theory within it and why theory and experience can no longer be seen as binaries. By employing their situated experiences, ethnographers discuss the meaning, usefulness, and benefits of scholarship that underscores their lives and stories in the performance of culture and ethnography to discuss and challenge hegemonic cultural and social discourses.

Researcher Positionality in the New Critical Collaborative Ethnographic Project

New critical ethnographers (Fine & Weis, 2000; Lassiter, 2005; Madison, 2005, 2006) now refrain from drawing the boundaries that complicate further the objective–subjective debate, instead focusing on the details of situatedness and performance of experience. The move is in the direction of working with researcher positionality as a key component of new critical collaborative ethnography. I use Kenneth Burke's (1935; as cited in Wolcott, 1999) wonderful quote, part of the title of this section's subheading, to emphasize further this issue of ethnographic seeing and positionality. There are a myriad ways of seeing and not seeing the everyday performances of culture, and these ways are necessarily embedded in researcher positionality. For example, in my own work, I was positioned drastically differently in relation to what I could see, hear, and coperform when in dialogue with the women, as opposed to when I was in dialogue with members of the state's repressive machinery, such as the police. Simply put, I did not experience the same kind of dialogic coperformance with, say, the superintendent of police, who in conversations repeatedly undermined and erased the presence of violence in the lives of Lahauli women, as I did when I spoke to one of the study participants, who is a survivor of sexual and other forms of violence in her life.

Researcher positionality and self-reflexivity are constantly being reinstated in ethnographic research. What are the real dangers involved in doing ethnography? How are we, as critical ethnographers, implicated in perpetuating and/or breaking hegemonic structures? How do we position ourselves in relation to our research? How is my history, my body, my intellectual knowledge, inseparable from my work? We are all products of our histories, and ethnography has come a long way since researchers claimed to be "objective" detached observers, immersed in the culture of the Other. Now researchers are reflexively bending back to look at the self and self–other interactions more closely (Denzin, 2003b), collapsing the positivist boundaries that segregate the self from research and redefining the goals of ethnography in the direction of progressive, decolonizing, politically motivated research—what

Goodall (2000) calls "new ethnography" and what is often now referred to as critical collaborative ethnography. This "new" critical collaborative ethnography (Goodall, 2000; Lassiter, 2005) takes one step ahead by focusing on positionality (Madison, 2005) and the performance of culture. In new critical and collaborative ethnographic practices, the emphasis is on the significance of the issue that Madison (2007) raised so eloquently in her talk—the positionality of the researcher—which is at the core of the "emergent" in emergent ethnographies.

What warrants subjectively mediated meanings? This issue is discussed by critical collaborative ethnographers both in defending their underlying methodological underpinnings and in improving their research practices. Questions about objectivity, validity, and researcher reflexivity have been consistently debated and redefined over decades within qualitative research practices at large, and in ethnographic practice in particular. The development of the notion of objectivity (despite its multiple definitions) can be traced through its various foundationalist, positivist, postpositivist, and interpretive avatars and finally through new ethnographic lenses, as the various debates finally unify the current multitude of positions held by researchers across the board. From traditional Cartesian methodology of "seeing everywhere from nowhere" (Schwandt, 2001) to Thomas's (1992) reclaiming of ethnography as an objective science to Haraway's (1988) notion of "situated knowledge" to an emphasis on restructuring objectivity through standpoint theory to Madison's (2007) focus on grounding researcher positionality as the core of ethnographic performance in fieldwork and writing has been a long and fascinating path of ideas. Traditional notions of objectivity grounded in the possibility of making truth claims are at present largely discredited in the study of cultures and communities—the key sites of ethnographic research.

Some qualitative scholars (as discussed previously)—ethnographers and others—were grappling with the possibilities of drawing scientific criteria for validity of interpretive research. However, there were other scholars across disciplines, who were redefining the very boundaries of what is "scientific"[6] and what is not to begin with. Many new critical collaborative ethnographers (Lassiter, 2005; Madison, 2005) have critiqued this position as one that is embedded in inherently contradictory notions of the researcher at once making claims of creating truth-based knowledge and standing knee-deep in political judgment and positioning. Harding has claimed the space for a "robust objectivity" that privileges the situatedness of the researcher and the researched as scientific. Whereas earlier (as exemplified in Jim Thomas's 1992 book, *Doing Critical Ethnography*) it was within these redefined spaces of objectivity and science that critical collaborative ethnography was being grounded, it has now moved a step ahead in departing from trying to make scientific claims, focusing now on the coperformance of experience in the fieldwork and writing processes. The move has been to depart from empiricist positions and redefinitions of objectivity and scientific knowledge not only to acknowledge that research observations are theory-, value-, and perspective-laden and that knower and known are inextricably intertwined but also to state that no particular set of methods should be epistemically privileged. We do not have access to extralinguistic, external referents that would allow us to adjudicate from different knowledge claims.

Hence for new critical collaborative ethnographers the question is whether it is productive—epistemologically, ontologically, and politically—to debate what objectivity is and how to draw borders between the objective and subjective. Do we, as new critical collaborative ethnographers working hand in hand with our researched, embedded in and upholding our political positions, still need to define these boundaries? In Dwight Conquergood's words, "Borders bleed, as much as they contain. Instead of dividing lines to be patrolled or transgressed, boundaries are now understood as crisscrossing sites inside the post-modern subject. Difference is situated within, instead of beyond, the self" (Conquergood, 1991, p. 356).

Emerging Understandings of Validity for Critical Collaborative Ethnography

For critical collaborative ethnographers, research is inherently structured by the subjectivity of the researcher and the researched. They emphasize the importance of contexts in understanding or developing any criteria for validity in different ways. Some scholars have evolved new criteria for validity in interpretive research that is very relevant to critical collaborative ethnography. I first discuss three such criteria and then illustrate how the criteria can be used through an example of a study that is conducted from a critical collaborative approach.

The three criteria I mentioned are contextualized ("thick") description (Geertz, 1973), catalytic (validity) criteria (Lather, 2001), and triangulation. In contextualized, thick description, the attempt is to understand what goes into the phenomenon in question by searching out and analyzing symbolic forms, such as words, images, institutions, behaviors, and so forth, "in terms of which people actually represent themselves to themselves and to one another" (Geertz, 1973). The main focus here is in the description of the context. Thus descriptive validity will be possibly achieved by the quality of the fieldwork conducted.

Catalytic validity directs us to the possibility of the research moving to help those researched, to transform their world and experiences. Therefore, the criterion for this kind of validity will primarily focus on the reality-altering impact of the inquiry process (Lather, 2001). This would be determined largely by the nature of the research being conducted and the relationship of the researcher and participants: how much of the transformative potential guides the researcher's behavior, and the research at large, and how much of the research process leads the participants to gain self-understanding and self-direction. For critical collaborative ethnographers, catalytic validity is particularly useful to see how far the political and action-oriented goals of their research have been achieved.

Triangulation mainly refers to the multimethod focus of ethnographic research. The use of multiple methods helps in the attainment of a more rigorous, more in-depth understanding of the issue or phenomenon in question. It adds to the overall richness of the research and provides a much more varied set of fieldwork materials, as compared with the use of one single method.

Case Example for New Criteria

I discuss here an example of one critical collaborative project that uses the interpretive criteria just discussed. It is a framework for social work with groups of women who are being battered and raped by husbands and boyfriends that illustrates how the criteria discussed previously have been used in critical interpretive research. This study draws on feminist and social constructionist positions, anthropology, and narrative ideas and describes the framework, with examples from practice. The authors (Wood & Roche, 2001) and their students worked with multiple groups of such women, and the article is a composite of several women's experiences. They provide a thick and detailed description of the process of transformation-oriented intervention undertaken by a social worker with a group of five battered women in the United States. From 5:00 to 7:30 on Wednesday evenings, five women met with a social worker at a one-stop, community-based social services center. They were referred to the group by the local task force on domestic violence.

The group provided the women with a space in which they could talk and meet other women going through similar life experiences and immediately disrupted the isolation that batterers attempt to subject their partners to. The women also had a cover—a simultaneous 6-week children's play group that they brought their children to.

The main focus of the research was the act of protest. And through various kinds of leading questions, conversations, discussions, their acts of protest and resistance were brought out in the group situation and their transformative potential finally discussed. It illustrates a Freirian process of resistance, restructuring, and transformation (see Freire, 2001). The interrelated processes, which the researchers probe, describe, and discuss in great depth, are:

- Revealing and undermining oppressive social discourse.
- Seeking and detailing protest, the moving dynamic that both precipitates and constitutes change.
- Reconstructing identities and outlooks, a process based on and subsequent to the protest, which includes performing in definitional ceremonies.

For each part of the process, Wood and Roche (2001) provide detailed sections of the discussions and women's comments. The study is presented through the women's narratives, woven together with the narratives of the researchers. From the narratives, the themes emerge, and then finally the framework. By the end of the discussion, the women discovered their transformatory potential, and the fleshed out and detailed version of the framework emerges. Their work focuses on the emancipatory goal of their research and the freeing of the "unfreed mind" (Freire, 2001). In the last part of the study, the authors shift from the women and their lives to a larger discussion of future work, once the different processes in the framework fall into place.

The study focuses largely on the discussions and gives us details of each process, thereby fulfilling the descriptive criteria at that level. The entire focus of the project, including all the researcher's questions, processes, and discussions, for the group was directed toward a self-realization and recognition of change in the women, thereby meeting the catalytic criterion very well. By the end of the study, the women distinctly emerge as at least having recognized their potential and having encouraged each other's latent and manifest transformative potential. The researcher–social worker is a strong catalyst in this process.

To meet the triangulation criterion, the researchers use focus group discussions, sometimes starting off with open-ended questions to individual participants and sometimes leaving it open for the group. There is also a strong role as participant observers in which the researchers in their interactions with the group bring out various strong threads in the discussion. However, there is no individual interviewing or home visits (because of the delicate nature of the study, in this case, it could place the research participants at risk). Depending on the subject, other critical collaborative projects could use more in-depth, one-on-one interviews in meeting such criteria.

The Ethics of Doing New Critical Collaborative Ethnography

How are ethics defined for new ethnographies? How do we understand the operations of power in the standardization of ethics and institutional review boards (IRBs) in social science research? Do standards for the new critical collaborative project need to be context-driven? Who decides what is harmful and how? How relevant are the IRB requirements in collaborative projects being conducted in different contexts across the world? And, finally, how do ethics shape the collaborative practices between researcher and researched? These are a few of the complex challenges faced by new critical collaborative ethnographers today.

The ethics of research have come to mean different things to researchers in different contexts. Researchers now question who decides standards for academic research, such as those established through IRBs, in projects conducted in areas in which such standards may not match local contexts (Lincoln, 2005). How far does the researcher go in following standards set by units operating from Western universities in the global north?

Therefore, in critical collaborative ethnographic research, which is so context-specific, the ethics question has grown very complex. This is especially so with the move from the "detached observer" to the "engaged, critical collaborative ethnographer." The traditional approach to research required a researcher to focus on processes and methods, which were not participatory or self-engaging. From the value-neutral, we have moved to the value-inclusive (in which the researcher is aware of his or her subjectivities but still attempts to stay objective in order to present the interpretations of the researched people's lived experiences); value-committed (in which the commitment to a cause or the common good or an issue positions the researcher in a clearly subjective situation); value-skeptical (in which we accept the ambiguity and the ephemeral quality of interpretations and reality); and the value-engaged (in which the focus is on the researcher's willingness to risk his or her position with regard to all his or her values, commitments, perceptions, and realities).

The question of self-reflexivity, then, is deeply connected to the issue of ethics. How much of the experiences of the researched do we tell? How much of our own stories do we tell? How do we negotiate the power inherent in ethnographic writing? How do we tell the stories of those whom we work with? What, if any, is the right way to perform the stories performed to us? And what about our own values of our everyday lives; how do we locate ourselves as persons as we go through the processes of conducting research?

Case Example

To place this question within the perspective of my own practice, I need to keep in mind my own antecedents. From my position as a value-committed researcher, I have identified certain boundaries within which local practices of misogynistic violence occur, yet I discovered that these boundaries continued to change with the accumulation of new experiences and worldviews from the stories I coperformed with the women in my project. For example, their understanding of rape and/or sexual violence, which is entirely embedded within their context and often drastically different from definitions of rape provided through the legal, medical, media, and feminist discourses in India, leads me to question what I should do when representing their experiences. My decision is based on the kind of local and theoretical intervention I want my work to make. Eventually, my project is a collaborative, participatory one, with the women at the center, thereby leading me to focus on expanding the vocabulary of sexual violence as it exists in India (which currently excludes the meanings that these women ascribe to it).

Dangers of Critical Collaborative Ethnography: Issues of Researcher Accountability and Responsibility

Embedded in the discussions of validity and ethics in the new critical collaborative ethnography lie the multiple challenges raised by researcher accountability and responsibility when conducting politically charged ethnographies. I discuss here some key aspects to be kept in mind, illustrated through three practical examples:

1. This kind of ethnography aims to go a step beyond producing academic scholarship, and although researchers may have the

best of intentions, the circumstances in the field may require careful consideration, especially in relation to the limits of making political change through research. Moral political obligations of the researcher to individuals in the project need to be emphasized here in ways that distinguish between individual and institutional aims. For example, during my fieldwork, one of the participants, who was a low-caste woman, wanted to break the silence she had maintained regarding her experience of sexual violence. She wanted to tell the world her story and asked for my support in contacting a national TV show in Delhi or in publishing her story in a newspaper or magazine. Some members of the local women's collective felt it would be a good way to further their institutional struggle if they could present a woman's story with all its details. However, although I was inspired by this woman's courage and spirit and recognized that the women's group would greatly benefit from this, when asked for my opinion I gave my recommendations based on how such an event would affect the woman in question. I felt that the implications for her own safety and survival[7] in the community could be very negative, and I convinced her not to go public.

2. The researcher needs to be aware of the difference between the short-term impacts of a project and long-term sustained engagement and change at every step of the process and to be honest with the participants. Just as it is important to acknowledge privilege, it is also important to understand and discuss the powerlessness that researchers themselves may also face in relation to the operation of larger hegemonic structures in the community. Things can and will move in directions beyond the researcher's and the community's control. For example, during my initial work in Lahaul, a minor girl (age 12) was raped by a 25-year-old man. The girl's father wanted to fight the case legally, even though the rapist in question belonged to a very influential family of the neighboring village.[8] The local women's collective was at that point becoming more active in women's rights–related issues, and my own research project was to support their activities. We worked with the girl's family to campaign with the police department and the judiciary at the state level such that the case could be filed and fought legally. Finally, the rapist received only a 5-year sentence, and we were afraid that he would return to the same village on his release and harass the girl, who by then would be only 17. Although on the one hand this was a victory for the local group—as it was really the first conviction following rape in the valley—despite the length of the sentence, it was a terrible reality for the girl in question in relation to the aftermath that she might have to face after 5 years. The group finally decided to support her parents in moving the girl to another part of the valley after some years.

3. It is especially important for critical collaborative researchers to keep in mind the need to "return something" (Menon & Bhasin, 1998) to the field and to be clear with participants about the limitations of their work. Building trust and understanding the history that a community may have with previous research projects is key here. For example, when Parrott and Steiner (2003) in their collaborative health communication project began their formative research with farmers in rural southern Georgia with regard to pesticide container disposal, they were informed of an earlier research project in which the farmers were asked to save their pesticide containers for mass disposal. For years nobody came back or contacted them either to collect these containers or to ask them to stop collecting them. The new project had to address these issues first, and only then could they proceed.

The new critical collaborative ethnographic project needs to ask some important questions that challenge how we do our work. For example, when and how can critical collaborative ethnographic practice become dangerous, and for whom? How do we as researchers remain aware of the dangers that are contained in our projects and negotiate them?

Feminist and Postmodern Interventions

Critical collaborative ethnography, as I noted earlier, can be considered the methodology for critical theory (Giroux, 2001; Madison, 2005); its present form builds on several layers of participatory, action-based, indigenous, and collaborative ethnographic practices that focus on resistance, social change, and political action. If we go back to Luke Lassiter's[9] (2005) understanding of this new method, it becomes important to acknowledge the interventions made by feminist ethnographers across disciplines, who were among the first scholars to bring critical ethnography to the table, even as they were ignored by more established scholars (usually white Western male scholars; Lassiter, 2005). Some of the early feminist scholars—ethnographers and others—across disciplines questioned established power structures of race, gender, and nationality, as well as their own privilege in relation to those whom they researched, and also blurred the lines between critical and creative writing. Examples include Alice Cunningham Fletcher (1911), Margaret Mead (1928), and Ruth Landes (1947), to name a few. Later, Westkott (1979), hooks (1981), Klein (1983), Du Bois (1983), Spivak (1988), Stacey (1988), Haraway (1988), Moore (1988), Abu-Lughod (1993), Collins (1991), Visweswaran (1992), Ginsburg and Rapp (1995), Harding (1998), and Behar (2003) were among some of the leading feminist scholars in different disciplines who informed the field of ethnography by continuing to rework and renegotiate critical collaborative methods, amid the various developments occurring in anthropology and other disciplines, in sharpening this approach. The relationship between gender, power, and ethnography was repeatedly illustrated by many feminist ethnographers, and the new collaborative ethnography is a project embedded in ideals that problematize and politicize these relationships. But the division between objective and subjective is always problematic. Feminist ethnographers also problematize the binary of the objective–subjective debate, in emphasizing the significance of researcher positionality and context, both of which are key components for the new critical collaborative ethnography. Across disciplines they (Abu-Lughod, 1993; Madison, 2005) repeatedly illustrate the challenges of finding ways to bring multiple voices into any research study and break down hegemonic structures and practices. This is their priority, rather than struggling with the (im)possibility of making unbiased truth claims.

The postmodern moment, too, questions conventional methods of knowing, leading to the introduction of new methods. According to Richardson and St. Pierre (2005), "The core of postmodernism is the doubt that any method or theory, any discourse or genre, or any tradition or novelty has a universal and general claim as the 'right' or privileged form of authoritative knowledge. Postmodernism suspects all truth claims of masking and serving particular interests in local, cultural, and political struggles" (as cited in Denzin & Lincoln, 2005, p. 961).

The issues concerning the writing of ethnographic texts—the who, where, and how—challenge both postmodern*ism* (as aesthetic) *and* postmodern*ity* (as temporal frame) and force one to recognize the inherent contradiction in the postmodern condition—as it can be both liberating from and constitutive of hegemonies (Grewal & Kaplan, 1994). Transnational, indigenous feminist politics has raised these challenges to ethnography and critiqued it for homogenizing "third world experience" (Mohanty, 1991; Smith, 2005). Although these issues raise questions about the very nature of ethnographic research, that does not mean that the analytical and emancipatory goals of research need to be abandoned. They assist us, in fact, in further defining the aims of critical social science research.

Case Example

Have we in fact moved past the postmodern moment? For example, a woman from the Lahaula tribe I interviewed may not have crossed over into any modern space as understood in elite academic settings. Here, the postmodern assumption that "natives" have escaped modernity and are defining their world by themselves could appear highly dubious. In fact, these women, and others in similar positions across the world, may not even be aware of the complex verbal and conceptual ideas that scholars have been using to advance theories on their behalf. Instead, it might be more relevant to examine the complex contours of their social history: the kinship arrangements, customary laws, gender relations (violence included), and clan-based social arrangements. For example, in certain communities in India, such an examination would seek to identify practices that remain precolonial, that were drastically altered by colonialism, or that are still not entirely changed despite the growing impact of the global on the local. These continuing countercurrents refuse to conform to any concretely definable theoretical foundations. They refuse to be categorized even when wanting to take advantage of anything that notions of modernity and postmodernity might be able to supply. Richardson and St. Pierre (as cited in Denzin & Lincoln, 2005) argue that the move into the post-"post" period—"post-postmodernism"—has already occurred. "It is true, as the poet said, the center no longer holds. We can reflect on what should be at the new center" (Denzin & Lincoln, 2005, p. 26). These multiple and interconnected debates are the evolving challenges for the "new" critical collaborative ethnography.

Emancipatory Politics

Current and emerging understandings of the nature of the social world focus on shared meanings of action (whether viewed with interpretivist, constructivist, feminist, hermeneutic, or indigenous lenses) with a political purpose. If our final aim is toward the ultimate improvement of the human condition through our different struggles and positions, where is the space for objectivity, and why are we still trying to fit our experiences into the "cupcake model" provided for us, along the lines of the positivist natural sciences? Each context of social change will vary based on the fields of inquiry. And researchers will carry with themselves their own baggage, their history, positions, politics, and writing, into this context. Whether it is critical ethnography in education or anthropology or social work, the aim is to get there. The value-laden nature of inquiry becomes important here. How social meanings and individual meanings are constructed and used for political purposes is the major underpinning of such work.

Case Example

For example, in my research my aim stems from my commitment to a certain group of persons (the women I work with) and from the political stands that I take (with regard to the violence experienced by women). My work in that sense attempts to be emancipatory, both for me and for the women I work with. The premise of my research on violence against women positions me against certain ways of being in the world and in favor of certain others. The purpose of my research is inextricably interwoven with these facets of our roles in this semipedagogical order (in which, though there is no academe and no curriculum, there is teaching–learning occurring in a two-way, continuous manner between me as the "researcher" and the women who are my "researched"). My hope is that this relationship between us—on account of its give-and-take elements from both sides–becomes emancipatory for all of us, in the Frierian sense.

Emancipation, Resistance, and Social Action

According to Ngugi Wa Thongo (1986), the legality, as well as the life advancement power, of the Western, privileged written word established a postcolonial situation in which even "natives" worldwide tended to abide by the implications of the written text. From this understanding to the modernist phase was a significant leap. At the same time, certain colonial notions continued in the later postcolonial musings and struggles with research. The "underprivileged" and the "socially cheated" became the focus. New interpretive theories of the postmodern condition, critical theory, and feminism evolved. The recognition of the "native" as a colonial notion that needed to be decolonized and no longer deferred began to gain more and more prominence. The focus shifted to provide the space for voices that were earlier unheard. The need for emancipatory, facilitating research was recognized.

Here I would like to dwell on the notion of emancipation. What does it mean to be emancipated? How can we be transformed? And can we be transformed? What are "acts of resistance" (Freire, 2001) and when do they become ineffectual? And when do we know that our "acts of resistance" are ineffectual versus emancipatory and transforming? In order to move away from the binary of the "oppressed" and "oppressive system" as called for by Freire (2001), I look for acts of resistance. What are my acts of resistance? And are they futile? Or can this resistance bring about transformation? Several possibilities are contained in Freire's concept of the *conscientizacao*, a term that refers to "learning to perceive social, political, and economic contradictions and to take action against the oppressive elements of reality." Freire offers a model of emancipation that is rooted in a dialogic (which he understands as "revolutionary") way of looking at the world.

Much feminist scholarship also delves into ideas of emancipation, resistance, agency, and empowerment. Scholars caution feminist ethnographers to be mindful of the fine balance between appropriation (of women's life histories by the researchers for research) and empowerment (understood here as a way of including women's agency as they break the silence in allowing their experiences to be documented). In this sense what might be viewed by scholars in one particular context as particularly liberating could, in another context, have negative and unsettling consequences. Hence there is an important distinction between what the researcher accepts as historical truth (what is often considered "factual" truth) and narrative truth (a general perspective by a writer or a storyteller). This would be true specifically of societies that favor collective experience, tradition, and subjectivity over documented accuracy.

Case Example

Collective memory becomes important in the Lahaul context for the group's collective survival. For example, with regard to certain "traditional" forms of violence against women prevalent in their community, one segment of the society (primarily the men) provided nonfactual historical information that historically favors the society's collective memory (the men therefore are established as proprietors of this collective). In my case, the women are always at the center of my project. My analysis, as is seen in the works of many feminist scholars (Butalia, 2000; Menon & Bhasin, 1998), is made possible by juxtaposing their versions of specific experiences of marriage, violence, and medical practice with other versions, official or otherwise, and with available historical records (in the form of archival research). I look at these varied experiences of and about violence in Lahaul for themselves and through myself—even as they are changing, shifting, and often contradictory.

Global Reconfigurations

In more recent times, anthropology, through ethnographic research, has brought globalization into its discussion of specific contexts and concerns. Inda and Rosaldo (2003) propose that what ethnography brings to the larger discussion of globalization is the simultaneous focus on large-scale processes of increasing global interconnectedness and how individuals respond to these connections in culturally local ways. At the same time that the world is "experientially shrinking," the forces of interconnection are uneven (Allen & Hamnett, 1995), and this imbalance affects specific settings in distinct ways. Aspects of individual subjectivities are engaged through the power relationships constitutive of economic and political processes (Alexander & Mohanty, 1996; Ginsburg & Rapp, 1995).

For example, in my study on women's experiences of violence, what kinds of forces work on the men in performing these acts of violence, and what kinds of forces then engage the women in negotiating the new power relations? What are the global connections that create these local forces? Is it important or necessary to understand the discourses of these men and women in the local context to unravel the workings of global forces in specific ways? The questions we ask, the subject we study, and the ways in which we conduct our studies are all issues that are being reconfigured continually as the global is recognized as being *constitutive of* the local (Hart, 2002). Despite many challenges in terms of funding, credibility, and future prospects, new critical collaborative ethnographers, along with other qualitative scholars, are continuing to produce a healthy body of lively research. The point that they reiterate is that there is much in human experience that cannot be quantified and measured through the use of large survey questionnaires and that needs more in-depth, detailed understanding, interpretation, and writing in this globalized, shifting world.

Case Example

For example, in my initial quantitative research project in Lahaul, the statistical data based on surveys showed strong connections between a reduction in polyandry in the tribe and an increase in violence against women. The surveys, however, could not reveal other kinds of questions about how the transition from a traditional custom to a more modern system may have led to the greater abuse of women. In what ways does this more "acceptable" system exclude women from the central social and familial powers of the society? What forms of violence have increased? How and why? Is this new violence or a persistent but unperceived violence that has remained in the community for generations? How are we defining *violence*? Whose "violence" is the subject of our research? Chances are that *violence* is defined according to studies carried out within a Eurocentric, North American framework, legitimated by funded, published Western (Western-type) research grafted wholesale onto survey research designed for different parts of the world (such as, in my case, Lahaul, India). Chances are, too, that violence is defined in terms of a series of acts, practices, and criteria at this point well described in scholarly, legal, and popular publications in the West, such as whether physical force was involved; whether hospitalization was required; whether it was officially reported; whether any form of consent occurred; and so forth. However, as a counter, one of the key findings of my research on violence against women in Lahaul, India, is that the definition and evaluation of violence is not only dependent on the nature of specific acts but also on their aftermath, their consequences for the women's lives and their interpretation by the community.

But even these questions do not fully explore and embody the contextuality and the interactional complexity of this research. Each project's context must then lead the researcher(s) to make certain decisions about which methods to employ. The consistent reproduction of Eurocentric and Western facts, scales, and sources of knowledge claims through empirical research has had enormous impact on global social science research. Growing identification of their problems has led various groups of scholars and departments invested in feminist research (especially black and third world feminism), new critical collaborative ethnographic research, indigenous research, African American studies, Latina studies, Asian American studies, South Asian studies, queer studies, cultural studies, science and technology studies, disability studies, and critical theory to abandon them (Bhattacharya, in press). In their place these scholars are trying to redefine the politics of validity in knowledge, knowledge production, reproduction, representation, and of the question of who benefits.

Global Ethnographies

In the book *Global Ethnography* (Burawoy et al., 2000), the authors talk about the range of interpretations of what constitutes globalization. They span from James Clifford's (1997) work on the arrival of the Western anthropologist as the "exotic on the doorstep" (the migration of the once colonized to the country of the colonizers) to the discussion of disembedded time and space by Giddens (1990) to Appadurai's (1996) fragmented global "scapes" to Grewal and Kaplan's (1994) "scattered hegemonies." " 'Globalization', it seemed had become all things to all theorists, a black box of the nineties akin to 'structure' in the seventies" (Burawoy et al., 2000). Burawoy and colleagues (2000) talk about how he and his team of students split globalization into three "slices": transnational "forces"; flows, or "connections"; and discourse, or "imaginations."

In my work I first follow two of the three "slices" used by Burawoy and colleagues (2000)–that is, "transnational forces" and "connections"–to identify what constitutes the global aspects of everyday experiences. I connect the everyday individual experience of the women of Lahaul to the transnational forces and connections that are affecting them in the form of changing social, moral, and economic structures–through the state, the army, the media, and medical practice. I make an attempt at illuminating unseen connections (Treichler et al., 1998). Doing this then automatically leads me to discuss in greater depth the different discourses (the third "slice") that come together in this context. This issue of how the global is embedded in the local leads us to the current ongoing phase of critical ethnography–one that privileges everyday experiences of people across the world through transnational, global, feminist, and decolonized projects. In the introduction to *Global Ethnography* (Burawoy et al., 2000), Michael Burawoy says that different team members in his group raised the question of how their own migrations and the migrations of their friends, families, and fieldwork sites had brought home the focus on globalization as a way of understanding the everyday.

Conclusion

Critical collaborative ethnographers are constantly negotiating these spaces they inhabit, both in collusion and collaboration with the worlds (physical and discursive) that they migrate across. In the context of my practice, I have found myself running back and forth between my own ideological feminist position and my attempt to carefully distance myself from a cultural imperialism of sorts informed by an urban, elite, academic lens that imposes a specific definition of violence on the experiences of the women I work with.

Into each new situation I bring with me my baggage—of gender, race, caste, and class. I have had an urban upbringing in predominantly rural India and have been schooled at a convent run by missionary nuns. I have been a student of sociology and have also received training as a professional social worker. From then until I began my graduate education in the United States, I was working with rural communities in the farthest regions of India. These are my antecedents. They have necessarily conditioned me towards certain preferences and away from others. I would like to quote here a paragraph from the book *Writing Women's Worlds* (Abu-Lughod, 1993) that I find particularly relevant: "In an age when the boundaries of 'culture' have become difficult to keep in place, when books travel and when global politics appear increasingly uncertain, we have to anticipate the uncomfortable irony that our most enlightened endeavors might not be received as such by the subjects of our writings" (Abu-Lughod, 1993, p. 36).

Critical feminist scholars such as Abu-Lughod (1993), Visweswaran (1992, 1997), Haraway (1988), Moore (1988), Behar (2003), Madison (2005), and others have illustrated through their works the significance of positionality, power, and privilege in the ethnographic process from fieldwork to writing. They have highlighted several ways in which women studying women often struggle. This is especially true with regard to questions of the sameness of experience with (especially with patriarchal systems of domination), and the differences in experience from (often in terms of class, caste, and race) those women with whom they work.

These scholars have challenged the self–other binary for a project that includes the multiplicity of the self, as well as the multiple, overlapping, and interacting qualities of the other, which can no longer be ignored. Related to this, as I noted at the outset of this chapter, I navigate through, and negotiate with, the multiple subjective positions I inhabit—as researcher, caste- and class-privileged individual (especially in relation to those I work with), survivor of sexual violence, woman of color, and graduate student in the United States, to name a few. With this in mind, I foreground the questions about what kinds of lives I tell and what the real "dangers" are of my critical collaborative ethnographic project.

This takes me back to my opening quote from Madison (2005) at the beginning of this chapter and brings full circle the various issues that lie at the core of the new critical collaborative ethnography. Researcher positionality remains a constant thread all through the practice of this method. Finally, I would like to briefly reiterate that the new critical collaborative ethnography stands out as a particularly useful method for ethnographers who are invested in grounding their scholarship in processes of social change through collaboration with the people whom they work with. As mentioned earlier, this new ethnographic practice is gaining ground not only across subfields within the discipline of anthropology (such as development anthropology) but also across other disciplines, such as critical development studies, gender and women's studies, social work, queer studies, disability studies, science and technology studies, and critical cultural studies, to name a few.

The inextricable links between a critical political project committed to the performance and meaning of everyday experiences and a collaborative project embedded in the applied effects of the ethnographic experience, read through lenses that challenge existing race, class, gender, and several other dominant, oppressive structures, are where some of the key debates in this method are located and need to be further explored. Researcher positionality (Goodall, 2000; Madison, 2005); coperforming culture (Conquergood, 1991; Denzin, 2005); political purpose (Thomas, 1992; Madison, 2005); collaboration for political action (Fine & Weis, 2000; Lassiter, 2005, 2006); and indigenous, feminist, decolonizing collaborative research practices (Behar, 2003; Butalia,

2000; Mutua & Swadener, 2004; Smith, 2005) are some of the key ideas that are now being redefined.

Notes

1. When I use the terms *emergent*, *new*, and *recent* throughout the chapter, I try to stick with some of the most recent–year 2000 onward–conceptualizations of the method. However, I also refer to other theoretical interventions, such as feminist theory, that came from the mid-1980s onward and contributed hugely to this method and which continue to remain very relevant. I am not trying to present a linear order of how ideas developed across disciplines to influence this method; rather, it is my attempt to refer to chunks of intellectual thought that shaped critical collaborative ethnography.

2. In India, there is a long history of marginalization and "other-ing" of tribal communities in the mountain areas, such as the Lahaul tribe, on which my research is based. Such communities are termed uncivilized and lesser than the upper caste communities of the plains. This is similar to the kind of "other-ing" that is often visible in the United States in relation to domestic race politics, as well as with reference to parts of the world in the global south, such as India.

3. The *salwaar kameez* is a traditional two-piece outfit worn by women in many parts of North India.

4. Aristotle talked about forms of human activity as being twofold: productive activity and contemplative activity. In productive activity, he spoke of two distinct sets of activities again. First, *poiesis* and *techne*, which can be generally translated as "fabrication" or making/crafting and "technical know-how." Positivist (and some postpositivist) practice focuses on these two activities and defines knowledge as a product of something we use (*techne*/method). Second, he spoke of *praxis* and *phronesis*, translated as "action" (thus "being human" in terms of everyday life, and moral–political activity) and "practical wisdom" (i.e., wise judgment). Here, knowledge is *sui generis*–that is, understanding (knowledge) is a process in which we participate, and therefore it constitutes who we are (Gadamer, 1975).

5. The turn to performance in ethnography at large and in critical collaborative ethnography in particular is discussed in greater detail on page 308.

6. A lot has been written on this in the field of science studies.

7. Violent backlashes against low-caste women who dare to speak of the violence committed against them by members of the higher castes are still prevalent in different parts of India.

8. Often in such circumstances the girl's family is threatened by the influential network that the man in question may have and is forced to withdraw the case; hence the campaigning with the state departments was crucial for the case to even proceed.

9. See Lassiter's (2005) quote on page 306.

References

Abu-Lughod, L. (1986). *Veiled sentiment: Honor and poetry in a Bedouin society.* Berkeley: University of California Press.

Abu-Lughod, L. (1993). *Writing women's worlds: Bedouin stories.* Berkeley: University of California Press.

Alexander, J., & Mohanty, C. T. (1996). *Feminist geneaologies, colonial legacies, global movements.* New York: Routledge.

Allen, J., & Hamnett, C. (Eds.). (1995). *A shrinking world?: Global unevenness and inequality.* Oxford, UK: Oxford University Press.

Appadurai, A. (1996). *Modernity at large.* Minneapolis: University of Minnesota Press.

Behar, R. (1993). *Translated woman: Crossing the border with Esperanza's story.* Boston: Beacon Press.

Behar, R. (2003). Feminist ethnography as (experimental) genre. *Anthropology News, 44*(9), 40.

Bhattacharya, H. (in press). In L. M. Given (Ed.), *Encyclopedia of qualitative research.* Thousand Oaks, CA: Sage.

Burawoy, M., Blum, J. A., George, S., Gille, Z., Thayer, M., Gowan, T., et al. (2000). *Global ethnography: Forces, connections and imaginations in a postmodern world.* Berkeley: University of California Press.

Butalia, U. (2000). *The other side of silence.* Durham, NC: Duke University Press.

Clifford, J. (1997). Spatial practices: Fieldwork, travel, and the disciplining of anthropology. In A. Gupta & J. Ferguson (Eds.), *Anthropological locations* (pp. 185–222). Berkeley: University of California Press.

Collins, P. H. (1991). *Black feminist thought: Knowledge, consciousness and the politics of empowerment.* New York: Routledge.

Conquergood, D. (1991). Rethinking ethnography. *Communication Monographs, 58*(2), 179–194.

Denzin, N. K. (2003a). Methods of collecting and analyzing empirical materials. In N. K. Denzin & Y. S. Lincoln (Eds.), *Collecting and interpreting qualitative materials* (2nd ed., pp. 47–60). Thousand Oaks, CA: Sage.

Denzin, N. K. (2003b). The practices and politics of interpretation. In N. K. Denzin & Y. S. Lincoln (Eds.), *Collecting and interpreting qualitative materials* (2nd ed., pp. 458–498). Thousand Oaks, CA: Sage.

Denzin, N. K. (2005). Emancipatory discourses, and the ethics and politics of interpretation. In N. K. Denzin & Y. S. Lincoln (Eds.), *Handbook of qualitative research* (3rd ed., pp. 933–958). Thousand Oaks, CA: Sage.

Du Bois, B. (1983). Passionate scholarship: Notes on values, knowing and method in feminist social science. In G. Bowles & R. D. Klein (Eds.), *Theories of women's studies* (pp. 105–116). London: Routledge & Kegan Paul.

Fine, M. (1994). Dis-stance and other stances: Negotiations of power inside feminist research. In A. Gitlin (Ed.), *Power and methods* (pp. 13–55). New York: Routledge.

Fine, M., & Weis, L. (1998). *The unknown city: Lives of poor and working class young adults.* Boston: Beacon.

Fine, M., & Weis, L. (2000). *Speed bumps: A student-friendly guide to qualitative research.* New York: Teacher College Press.

Fletcher, A. C., & La Flesche, F. (1911). *The Omaha tribe: Twenty-seventh annual report of the Bureau of American Ethnology* Washington, DC: Government Printing Office.

Ford, L. A., & Yep, G. A. (2003). Working along the margins: Developing community-based strategies for communicating about health with marginalized groups. In T. L. Thompson, A. Dorsey, K. Miller, & R. Parrott (Eds.), *Handbook of health communication.* Mahwah, NJ: Erlbaum.

Freire, P. (2001). *Pedagogy of the oppressed.* New York: Continuum.

Gadamer, H. G. (1975). *Truth and method* (G. Barden & J. Cumming, Trans.). London: Sheed & Ward.

Geertz, C. (1973). *The interpretation of cultures: Selected essays.* New York: Basic Books.

Giddens, A. (1990). *The consequences of modernity.* Stanford, CA: Stanford University Press.

Ginsburg, F., & Rapp, R. (Eds.). (1995). *Conceiving the new world order: The global politics of reproduction.* Berkeley: University of California.

Giroux, H. (2001). Cultural studies as performative politics. *Cultural Studies–Critical Methodologies, 1,* 5–23.

Goodall, H. L. (2000). *Writing the new ethnography.* Walnut Creek, MD: AltaMira Press.

Grewal, I., & Kaplan, C. (1994). Introduction: Transnational feminist practices and questions of postmodernity. In I. Grewal & C. Kaplan (Eds.), *Scattered hegemonies* (pp. 1–33). Minneapolis: University of Minnesota Press.

Guttman, N. (2000). *Public health communication interventions: Values and ethical dilemmas.* Thousand Oaks, CA: Sage.

Haraway, D. (1988). Situated knowledges: The science question in feminism as a site of discourse on the privilege of parital perspective. *Feminist Studies, 14,* 575–599.

Harding, S. (1998). *Is science multicultural?: Postcolonialism, feminism, and epistemologies.* Bloomington: Indiana University Press.

Hart, G. (2002). *Disabling globalization: Places of power in Post-apartheid South Africa.* Berkeley: University of California Press.

hooks, b. (1981). *Ain't I a woman: Black women and feminism.* Boston: South End Press.

Inda, J., & Rosaldo, R. (2003). *Anthropology of globalization.* Oxford, UK: Blackwell.

Landes, R. (1947). *The city of women.* New York: Macmillan.

Lassiter, L. (2005). *The Chicago guide to collaborative ethnography.* Chicago: University of Chicago Press.

Lassiter, L. (2006, May). Collaborative ethnography matters. *Anthropology News,* p. 20.

Lather, P. (2001). Postmodernism, post-structuralism and post (critical) ethnography: Of ruins, aporias and angels. In P. Atkinson, S. Delamont, A. J. Coffey, J. Lofland, & L. H. Lofland (Eds.), *Handbook of ethnography* (pp. 477–492). London: Sage.

Lincoln, Y. (2005). Institutional review boards and methodological conservatism: The challenge to and from phenomenological paradigms. In N. K. Denzin & Y. S. Lincoln (Eds.), *Handbook of qualitative research* (3 rd ed., pp. 165–181). Thousand Oaks, CA: Sage.

Madison, D. S. (2005). *Critical ethnography.* Thousand Oaks, CA: Sage.

Madison, S. (2007, May). *Dangerous ethnography.* Keynote address at the Fourth Annual Congress of Qualitative Inquiry, Urbana-Champaign, IL.

Malinowski, B. (1922). *Argonauts of the Western Pacific.* London: Routledge.

Marcus, G. (1998). *Ethnography through thick and thin.* Princeton, NJ: Princeton University Press.

McLaren, P. (2001). Che Guevara, Paulo Freire, and the politics of hope: Reclaiming critical pedagogy. *Cultural Studies–Critical Methodologies, 1,* 108–131.

Mead, M. (1928). *Coming of age in Samoa.* New York: Morrow.

Mead, M., & Bunzel, R. L .(Eds.). (1960). *The golden age of American anthropology.* New York: Braziller.

Menon, R., & Bhasin, K. (1998). *Borders and boundaries: Women in India's partition.* Brunswick, NJ: Rutgers University Press.

Mohanty, C. T. (1991). Under Western eyes: Feminist scholarship and colonial discourses. In C. T. Mohanty, A. Russo, & L. Torres (Eds.), *Third world women and the politics of feminism* (pp. 51–80). Bloomington: Indiana University Press.

Moore, H. (1988). *Feminism and anthropology.* Minneapolis: University of Minnesota Press.

Mutua, K., & Swadener, B. B. (Eds.). (2004). *Decolonizing research in cross-cultural contexts: Critical personal narratives.* Albany: State University of New York Press.

National Center for the Dissemination of Disability Research. (2005). *What are the standards for quality research?* Washington, DC: Author.

Ngugi Wa Thongo. (1986). *Decolonising the mind.* Oxford, UK: James Currey.

Parrott, R., & Steiner, C. (2003). Lessons learned about academic and public health collaborations in the conduct of community-based research. In T. L. Thompson, A. Dorsey, K. Miller, & R. Parrott (Eds.), *Handbook of health communication* (pp. 637–650). Mahwah, NJ: Erlbaum.

Schwandt, T. (2001). A post script on thinking about dialogue. *Evaluation, 7*(2), 275–288.

Smith, L. T. (2005). On tricky ground: Researching the native in the age of uncertainty. In N. K. Denzin & Y. S. Lincoln (Eds.), *Handbook of qualitative research* (3rd ed., pp. 85–107). Thousand Oaks, CA: Sage.

Spivak, G. (1988). Can the subaltern speak? In C. Nelson & L. Grossberg (Eds.), *Marxism and the interpretation of culture* (pp. 271–313). Chicago: University of Illinois Press.

Stacey, J. (1988). Can there be a feminist ethnography? *Women's Studies International Forum, 11*(1), 21–27.

Takahashi, L., & Smutny, G. (1998). Community planning for HIV/AIDS prevention in Orange County, California. *Journal of the American Planning Association, 64*, 441–457.

Thomas, J. (1992). *Doing critical ethnography.* Newbury Park, CA: Sage.

Treichler, P. A., Cartwright, L., & Penley, C. (1998). *The visible woman: Imaging technologies, gender and science.* New York: New York University Press.

Visweswaran, K. (1992). *Fictions of feminist ethnography.* Minneapolis: University of Minnesota Press.

Visweswaran, K. (1997). Histories of feminist ethnography. *Annual Review of Anthropology, 26*, 591–621.

Westkott, M. (1979). Feminist criticism in the social sciences. *Harvard Educational Review, 49*(4), 422–430.

Wood, G. G., & Roche, S. E. (2001). Representing selves, reconstructing lives: Feminist group work with women survivors of male violence. *Social Work with Groups, 23*(4), 5–23.

ARTS-BASED PRACTICE

CHAPTER 16

Visual Research Methods

Where Are We and Where Are We Going?

Gunilla Holm

"Visual methods" are not purely visual. Rather, they pay particular attention to visual aspects of culture. Similarly, they cannot be used independently of other methods.
—PINK (2005, p. 17)

A sign that visual methods are gaining in popularity is the frequent inclusion of short sections on photography in recent introductory qualitative research methods books (Berg, 2007; Bogdan & Biklen, 2003; Flick, 2002; Warren & Karner, 2005; see also Prosser, 2000b, for a discussion about the exclusion of visual methods from earlier introductory research methods books). In these introductory books, photography and video are described as useful because they provide denser and permanent data. Videotapes, for example, are seen by Glesne (2006) as particularly useful for studying detailed everyday interactions.

Why would we use visual images instead of words? Ball and Smith (1992) argue that one reason would be that visual images are everywhere and that we are used to reading them. In fact, we are reading visual images all the time. Photographs were traditionally seen as capturing truth and reality. However, many researchers have recently asserted that images are not neutral and do not portray a truth but only the producers' and viewers' co-constructed understanding (Chaplin, 1994; Gibson, 2005). Images are produced with specific intentions in mind. Gibson (2005) argues that "how persons present themselves for the research camera is in itself data that provide a resource for analysis" (p. 3). She argues that this is the case even when the researcher is not physically present. The researcher's presence is felt already in that the participants would not be taking the photographs or shooting the videos without the researcher. The researcher always has a hand in setting up the parameters. Gibson describes how she eventually discovered that she had been looking for videos produced by the participants that focused on particular aspects of interest to her. Gibson uses a quote by Bourdieu to justify her stand:

> The crucial difference is not between a science which effects a construction and one which does not, but between a science that does this without knowing it and one which, being aware of this, attempts to discover and master as completely as possible, the nature of its inevitable acts of construction and the equally inevitable effects which they produce. (Bourdieu, 1996, as cited in Gibson, 2005, p. 4)

Hence, an image is a production of how the participants see or want to see themselves and their more factual position in a societal relationship (Bourdieu, 1998; Gibson, 2005). My research (Holm, 1997b) with teenage mothers clearly shows this tension between desired image and the more everyday position. The photographs the teen mothers took of each other reflect the image they want to give to others, and their more intimate writings together form an image of the girls. The photograph alone would allow the viewer to see the photograph only in relation to what they know about teen mothers and based on the girls' determination to be seen as happy girls with no problems. The girls' writing provides the more everyday position (see Figures 16.1.–16.4 on pp. 333–334). As Berger so aptly pointed out in his 1972 book *Ways of Seeing*, not only are the producer's intentions for a photograph important, but also the photograph invites many ways of seeing it because viewers see the photograph in relation to themselves.

Collier and Collier (1986) give a thorough introduction to the use of both photography and film- and videomaking in visual anthropology, but Collier (1967) argued against only taking pictures of what was found to be interesting in the eye of the researcher. Instead, he saw taking pictures of what was not understood as potentially illuminating as it could be used in interviews later in the research. In addition, he argued that taking photographs brings the researcher and the participants closer and that photographs are a way to learn about the nonverbal culture.

There are two main kinds of visual images, the still images consisting mainly of photographs, cartoons, or drawings and the moving images consisting of film and video (Prosser, 2000a). Traditionally, both ethnographic photographs and films have been used as illustrations, but not for analysis (Ball & Smith, 1992). Both kinds are discussed in this chapter. The grounding of visual methods in anthropology and sociology is explored briefly, and traditional approaches, as well as newer approaches, to visual research are reviewed.

The Roots: Visual Sociology and Visual Anthropology

According to Hockings (2003), the foundation for visual anthropology was laid between 1967 and 1974, when ethnographic films were produced at a rapid pace. By the time *Principles of Visual Anthropology* was published in 1975, the field was well established. However, visual anthropologists still had to defend their work, because it was considered too subjective, unsystematic, and unrepresentative. Collier had already tried to address these issues in 1967 by advocating a systematic approach with a research plan in which, for example, the order in which the photographs were taken was considered very important in order to represent the reality. Hockings emphasizes films within visual anthropology as the main tool for conveying research results and especially "films-as-a-constructed-text" (p. vii) as opposed to "films-as-record." "Films-as-a-constructed-text" is a product of the film producer, the subject, and the viewers. The current debate is substantially focused on visual anthropology's relationships to anthropology, as well as other fields working with images, such as art and documentary filmmaking (Banks & Morphy, 1997). As Ruby (2005; see also Banks, 2000) points out, ethnographic film is a much more common way than photography of communicating one's research, despite visual anthropology's roots in Bateson and Mead's (1942) photography. However, Banks (2000) also emphasizes that using photographs as illustrations in an anthropological study does not make it visual anthropology unless the photographs are analyzed in the written text.

The use of visual methods in sociology started in the 1960s (Warren & Karner, 2005). However, Flick (2002) argues that visual sociology was introduced by Becker in 1986 but states that Mead, already in 1963, had

> summarized the central purpose of using cameras in social research: they allowed detailed recordings of facts as well as providing a more comprehensive and holistic presentation of lifestyles and conditions. They allow the transportation of artifacts and the presentation of them as pictures and also the transgression of borders of time and space. They can catch facts and processes that are too fast or too complex for the human eye. Cameras also allow nonreactive recordings of observations, and finally are less selective than observations. Photographs are available for reanalysis by others. (Flick, 2002, pp. 149–150)

Grady (2001) summarizes visual research in sociology as follows:

> There are three major kinds of visual essay that a sociologist might be likely to produce: a photo-essay, a video documentary, or an analysis of visual data. . . . Many social science journals are interested in publishing analysis of visual data although they are only slowly beginning to publish actual images. . . . Currently . . . only *Visual Sociology* enthusiastically welcomes articles that contain visuals. (p. 112)

In sociology, visual methods are still considered too subjective by most. Harper (2000) has pushed the field forward, but his approach is also rooted in traditional sociological approaches with regard to theory and methods. However, Chaplin (1994) takes visual sociology a step further by arguing that visual images can be used to create new knowledge, and not only as data analyzed via traditional verbal approaches.

Kinds of Images

Three major kinds of visual images are used in visual research. First, applied sociologists, as well as critical and interpretative visual anthropologists, frequently use "subject-produced images" (Warren & Karner, 2005, p. 171). This means that the researcher asks the participants to either photograph or videotape aspects of their worlds, such as certain rituals or what their community is like, in order to allow researchers an inside view (see, e.g., Damico, 1985; Ziller, 1990). More recently, this kind of research has come to focus on producing a positive change in the participants' communities or life circumstances based on the participants' photographs of the community needs (White, 2003; see also later discussion about photovoice).

The second kinds of images are the researcher-produced images that are rooted in the use of documentary photography in anthropology. However, the images are not enough by themselves but need to be seen in a larger context. For example, Greenblat's (2004) use of photography with patients living with Alzheimer's disease shows how alive the patients can be despite their limited ability to express themselves with words (see also *www.alivewithalzheimers.com/homepage2/*). Greenblat provides a verbal context for understanding these photographs in relation to prevailing beliefs about people with Alzheimer's disease.

Bogdan and Biklen (2003) provide an extensive discussion about the researcher-produced images, how the photographer–researcher influences what is taken, and how this might make the photographs more subjective and provide an inaccurate record of artifacts or a situational map. Flick (2002) and Denzin (1989) also raise questions about the influence of the camera and how it will change the situation when participants pose for the camera or when the situation is arranged for the camera.

A third kind of image is the preexisting image. These may be, for example, old family pictures, newspaper photographs, or photographs of rituals and community events found in archives. These can be used as historical documents for tracing the development of a ritual or a family. However, they need to be treated with caution, because the context, as well as the intentions of the photographer, is often missing (Prosser & Schwartz, 1998). What are the factual circumstances of the photographs? Another untapped new source of preexisting images is photoblogs (*photoblogs.org*). A photoblog is similar to a regular blog, except photographs instead of words constitute the main form of communication. Individuals decide on how they want to document their worlds and lives by choosing the images they post on the Web. The possibility of using photoblogs for social science research is somewhat unclear (see Wakeford & Cohen, 2003). The accompanying text that provides the context and intentions for the photographs is usually minimal. The photographs are also often individual photos, not on a theme. However, if they are analyzed as textual diaries and logs usually are, the photoblogs might provide interesting and valuable insights into themes such as urban living and adults' views on children.

Photographs taken either by researchers (Heisley & Levy, 1991) or by the participants (Harrington & Lindy, 1998; van der Dos, Gooskens, Liefting, & van Mierlo, 1992) are commonly used as a strategy called *photo-elicitation* in interviewing. The photographs are selected for their potential in eliciting valuable information about the interviewee's views and beliefs. They are also used specifically for bringing back memories about particular events, people, or times. However, photographs taken by the participants can also be used as prompts in interviews. Felstead, Jewson, and Walters (2004, p. 111) refer to this approach as "auto-ethnography." Radley and Taylor (2003) asked postsurgery patients to photograph those aspects in the hospital that were important to them. The patients then explained the reason for taking the photographs and thereby brought to the researchers' attention aspects that they would not have thought to ask about as they were not seen as important. Overall, the researchers got a much more in-depth understanding of the impact the entire hospital setting has on the patients by encouraging passivity and compliance. The assumption in photoelicitation has been that the interviewees have a block of objective knowledge and information that needs to be unlocked. However, Harper (2003) argues that "the photograph loses its claim to objectivity in photo-elicitation. Indeed, the power of the photo lies in its ability to unlock the subjectivity of those who see the image differently from the researcher" (p. 195).

Content Analysis of Visual Images

A quantitative approach is often used in the content analysis of visual images. The images are classified according to criteria determined by the researcher, and then frequencies of occurrence are counted. It is often used in media research. However, as Bell (2001) points out, it is not a theory-based process but rather a technical and basic counting process that does not tell us much about meanings or effects of what is depicted. For example, gender of the depicted person or type of setting could be the basis for the counting. Content analysis is focused on comparisons. In other words, the hypothesis being tested might be that within the category of gender more men than women are depicted in a set of advertisements. Generalizations might not be possible or even desirable. With a large sample and the data put into a context, it is possible to see what the trends for the images are. However, for exploring the messages intended to be perceived from the pictures, a content analysis needs to be combined with a qualitative semiotic analysis. Bell argues that in order to obtain more informative data from the content analysis, it is better to establish variables with distinguishable values rather than just categories for classification.

Within popular culture studies, qualitative content analysis has been common for exploring films, magazines, and television. For example, there have been numerous studies of how schooling has been portrayed in popular films (Beyerbach, 2005; Bulman, 2005; Dalton, 1999; Farber & Holm, 1994a, 1994b; Lowe, 2001). These studies employ a very different kind of content analysis in which the visual images and the scenes are analyzed in relation to the verbal text holistically. Rarely is any kind of counting or straight categorization used. Similar kinds of analysis have been used in studies of gender issues in magazines, in which the images and the text are analyzed together but sometimes also separately (Holm, 1994, 1997a; Kehily, 1996).

Visual Ethnography, Action Research, and Photovoice

Pink (2005) criticizes earlier discussions of visual work (e.g., Collier & Collier, 1986; Prosser, 1996) both in sociology and anthropology as being too prescriptive and focused on issues related to objectivity and generalizations. She claims it is necessary to develop the visual ethnography approach while doing the fieldwork because each situation might require something different depending on the participants and the context. Pink advocates for an ethnographic approach in which reflexivity and "the relationship between the subjectivities of the researcher and informants" are key to the "negotiated version of reality" (2005, p. 20). Hence, there is no objective version of reality but a version based on the experiences of the researcher in collaboration with the participants.

Recent ethnographic work has taken on aspects of action research by being more participatory, as well as by being focused on change. Already in the 1980s, Dabbs (1982) gave cameras to participants and asked them to take photos of their lives. What was photographed was decided by the participants, and this method gave the researcher a way to better understand the views of the participants. Recently, photovoice has become a method used frequently, especially in public-health-related research. The research is combined with public advocacy. "Photovoice is a process by which people can identify, represent, and enhance their community through a specific photographic technique" (Wang, 2005). Photovoice basically means that the participants are given cameras to take pictures of aspects of their lives that they see as relevant and important for improving their community. Hence the difference between photovoice and the earlier method of distributing cameras to the participants is that the photovoice photos are used for advocacy for community improvement, as well as research. The photos taken by participants provide the researchers with an additional insight into the participants' lives that can be used together with more traditional data sources, such as interviews and observations.

According to Berg (2007), the main goals of photovoice as part of action research are:

1. Empowering and enabling people to reflect their personal and community concerns.
2. To encourage a dialogue and to transfer knowledge and information about personal and community issues through discussions about photographs among participants.
3. To access the perception of those not in control of various problem issues and share this information with those who are

in control (policymakers, politicians, health professionals, educators, etc.). (p. 234)

However, the method involves more than just giving cameras to participants. Wang (2005) describes the stages of photovoice as including "conceptualizing the problem; defining broader goals and objectives; recruiting policymakers as the audience for photovoice findings; training the trainers; conducting photovoice training; devising the initial theme/s for taking pictures; taking pictures; facilitating group discussion; critical reflection and dialogue; selecting photographs for discussion; contextualizing and storytelling; codifying issues, themes, and theories; documenting the stories; conducting the formative evaluation; reaching policymakers, donors, media, researchers, and others who may be mobilized to create change; conducting participatory evaluation of policy and program implementation." Wang also emphasizes that the way she uses the photovoice method is grounded in "the theoretical literature on education for critical consciousness, feminist theory, and documentary photography." Hence, photovoice is more than a technique. Photovoice projects are, so far, most common for community action (see, e.g., *www.photovoice.com/* and *www.photovoice.org*), often in combination with public health research. However, due to the documentary and action research nature of photovoice, it has not been widely used in education, anthropology, or sociology. However, before photovoice there were attempts, such as Holm's (1997b) study of the problematic education of teen mothers, to use photographs taken by the participants to indicate areas needing improvement. These kinds of studies have been mostly informative, and the strong advocacy component has been missing.

Video diaries are close to the photovoice approach but with a slightly different focus. A video diary is focused on the participant's own world. It is usually the participant who constructs the video of an aspect of his or her life, but the videotaping could be done by someone close to the person. For example, in Gibson's (2005) study of "the identities of young men with Duchenne muscular dystrophy . . . who rely on mechanical ventilation" (p. 2), the men created videos about who they were but also about how they wanted to be seen. In other words, even if the researcher was not present, she influenced the situation, because the video was produced for her as the audience. These videos were then discussed in interviews. Without the videos, the study would not have produced the kind of data it created. The videos were a form of communication very much located in the men's local situation but also in the larger ideology concerning people with theirs and other, similar medical conditions. An advantage of this research method was that the data could be watched and analyzed numerous times for additional details and understandings.

Design and Ethical Issues

Usually we think of sampling strategies during the initial design of a study, but in visual research the selection of images is an ongoing and complicated process. First, themes or areas to be photographed are decided, then the researcher decides on the photographs to be taken or on the participants who will be given cameras and who will decide on the photographs to be taken. Only certain images might be selected for analysis, and finally only a few images are selected for presentation. In addition, questions arise about whether the researcher should make decisions about images to analyze and include or whether the participants should be empowered to do so. This depends on the type of study and who is seen as owning the photographs (Prosser & Schwartz, 1998; Warren & Karner, 2005).

Glesne (2006) raises several questions about confidentiality and ownership with regard to videos and photographs. For example, do those photographed know what it really might mean to them if the photographs are made public? In other words, in what settings and to which audiences can the images be shown? These issues are not always made clear to the participants at the time of obtaining consent for photographing or videotaping. Participants might not be aware of all the possible ways a visual image can hurt them or provide advantages for them, even after giving their consent.

Whether cameras and video cameras help or hurt in the research process is argued differently by different researchers. Bogdan and Biklen (2003) argue that many researchers shy away from using cameras because cameras make them and their research more visible and make it harder to melt into the daily scene. The approach of drawing as little attention as possible with the camera is also supported by Flick (2002) and Denzin (1989). Others, such as Collier and Collier (1986), Pink (2005), and Margolis (1994), advocate a more collaborative approach and argue that taking photographs openly and immediately and sharing them opens up possibilities for interactions with the participants. The Bogdan and Biklen argument reflects a more traditional approach to doing ethnographic work in which the researcher uses what Prosser (2000a) calls the "softly, softly" approach–first, just walking around with a camera; then taking safe pictures of positive things; and only thereafter taking more sensitive pictures.

Gatekeepers are important in limiting access to photographing and filming, but researchers also need to scout out and avoid taking images of areas that the participants do not want to have photographed or filmed. In many places and situations, there is a very fine line between public and private space.

Denzin (1989) also raises the problem of manipulating the images, and this has become even more of a possibility with digital photography and video. The danger is the risk of data being lost in the manipulation. Harper (2003) argues that digital creation and manipulation of images have forever severed the perception that images are the same as the truth. Hence, he argues that data can be empirical without representing the true reality. Elaborating on this train of thought, according to Baudrillard (1988), we could argue that all visual images produced by researchers and study participants are simulacra and that a clear determination of what is real cannot be made.

Denzin (1989) further argues that the researcher's theoretical framework will influence the analysis. In addition, each researcher has his or her own style of taking photographs and videos that will influence what images are taken and how they are framed. However, these issues are not unique in working with visual images; they also emerge in work with verbal data. Researchers have their own styles of note taking; their theoretical frameworks will influence what they observe and what questions they focus on in interviews. Aesthetic manipulation of images is probably more tempting than manipulation of words. On the other hand, aesthetic choices will influence how an image is read. For example, Prosser (2000a), in his review of ethical issues in image-based research, points out that a photograph can easily be framed to draw on viewers' different emotions. Prosser also raises the question of why viewers consider the accuracy and truthfulness of film and photographs to be so important, as it is well known that photographers, directors, and editors make choices and cuts to portray their stories. Hence, he asks, "since we know that photography was never objective why do we hold on to the authenticity of the photograph?" (p. 124). Prosser quotes Kane (1994) in his explanation: "We believe the camera's eye can bring us truth, whether subjective (the snapshot of a loved one, the performance of a great actor) or objective (pictures of weather forecasts, police suspects, lab experiments). The photographic is the way we moderns test that reality is *out there*: we rely on its veracity more than we readily admit" (p. 124).

As Rose (2005) and Hall (1997) emphasize, the interpretation of "images is just that, interpretation, not the discovery of truth" (Rose, 2005, p. 2). The interpretations have to be based on a methodology and address cultural issues such as social differences and power. The more record-keeping type of photographs often used by sociologists (see also Collier & Collier, 1986) are problematic because they do not give us a sense of what meanings and experiences they hold for the participants (Pink, 2005).

The informed consent is one of the most difficult issues in visual research, as confidentiality cannot be promised if visual images of people are included in the final reporting. Visual research is also unpredictable, especially if the participants collect the images. If the participants photograph people and events in their lives, it is close to impossible to obtain institutional review board approval in advance for these kinds of images, as they will not be known in advance. Prosser (2000a) cites Graef's approach to informed consent as the best available approach in educational research: "My solution . . . is to provide as part of my rules for filming, a guaranteed viewing during the editing stage to all the key participants, with a firm promise to change anything that can be pointed out to be *factually inaccurate*. That extends to re-editing for *emphasis* as well (Graef, as cited in Prosser, 2000, p. 127, original emphasis).

However, this approach is not always possible. For example, in *Stolen Childhoods* (Morris, 2004), a documentary on global child labor, there were key participants from all over the world. Many of them would be impossible to locate or access, because the film took 7 years to make and because the children worked in illegal conditions. In addition, participants can approve of images they have made, but the people in the images might not approve of being part of a photo that is analyzed and published. As in other kinds of qualitative research, there is the risk that people who are not actual participants become drawn into the research inadvertently through photographs and video and therefore experience repercussions. Even self-analysis might include, directly or indirectly, other family members, friends, or colleagues who have not given their consent to being identified or having their actions recorded.

Analysis of Visual Text

Rose (2005) gives a detailed description of how to use different approaches to what she calls *visual methodologies*. She provides steps for doing a content analysis, a semiotic or psychoanalytic analysis, and two kinds of discourse analyses. It is a book from which to learn different analytical approaches to visual images based on her teaching of visual methodologies. On the other hand, Bogdan and Biklen (2003) raise numerous questions about the value of photographs and the camera and the analysis of visual images. They note, "Is it only an instrument, dependent on the skill and insightfulness of the one who is holding it? . . . [and] photos are not answers, but tools to pursue them" (p. 141). This is, of course, the situation with other data collection methods, as well, in qualitative research, and it should not dissuade anyone from using cameras and visual data. In-depth interviewing or participant observations also depend on the skill and insightfulness of the researcher. Interestingly, Felstead and colleagues (2004) found, in their study in which they shadowed participants by taking photographs of participants' work spaces in their homes, that "comparison of photographs with interview transcripts revealed that respondents were not always accurate or comprehensive in remembering, or even recognizing, where and how they work" (p. 110). Hence photographs and interviews complemented each other and raised questions about why the participants perceived their situations differently from the way they were portrayed in the photos.

Flick (2002) states that so far there has not been a visual data analysis method but that

> procedures of interpretation familiar from analyses of verbal data have been applied to them. In this respect such visual data are also regarded as texts: photos tell a story, visual data are sometimes transformed into text by transcription . . . , content summaries or descriptions are made before interpretation is carried out in order to be able to apply textual interpretation methods on visual material. (p. 153)

Flick, as well as Denzin (1989), argues that "films are understood as visual texts" (p. 156). However, it is important to remember that visual data are not always transcribed into a verbal form and that the end result may also be a visual narrative, such as a video or a series of photographs (Harper, 2003). Rose (2005) finds the discussion about the use of textual interpretation of visual images unproductive because visual images are rarely seen or presented isolated from other kinds of texts. Instead, Rose finds it important "to acknowledge that visual images can be powerful and seductive in their own right" (p. 10). The power of photographs can be seen in Holm's (1997b) study of teenage mothers who were asked to take photographs of their lives and write about their own thinking about their lives. In this case, the accompanying verbal text was not produced by the girl in the photo but by another girl in the same school, both to preserve confidentiality and also because it is not a particular girl's story that matters. It is important to create the entire group's stories. Together the series of photographs and the series of poems and writings give two very different stories, a visual one and a verbal one (see Figures 16.1.–16.4). The visual story is a happier story focused on how the girls want to be seen. The verbal one conveys the girls' struggles. The reader has to struggle with his or her own interpretations in order to develop a complex enough view of the girls that encompasses both the visual and

FIGURE 16.1. "I was mad. I still don't want no other baby, but it's here now so I can't stop it. I was crying and I was scared to tell my mother. 'Cause some people ain't ready to be a parent. I know I'm not. I wasn't thinking of having one now, not now. I could do without having kids."

FIGURE 16.2. "When I was born my father didn't claim me 'cause he didn't want to pay child support. I don't know why my mother let me know who he was—he didn't claim me."

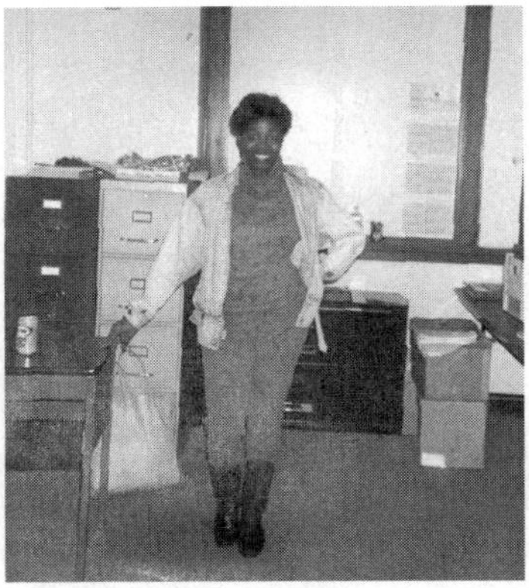

FIGURE 16.3. "Basically I just want to be successful. . . . Basically, I want to stay out of trouble. Just not getting more babies, that's for sure. I just take it one step at a time and stay away from all the bad stuff, try and do all the good stuff so I can set an example for my son."

FIGURE 16.4. "I've been in foster homes 'cause we had problems in our family, dealing with my father, he liked to do bad things to girls. You know what I'm talking about. I stay at home, ain't nowhere to go."

verbal narratives (Holm, 1997b, pp. 63, 67, 73, 77).

In the field, photo or video images are produced and given meanings that are seemingly important at that point. However, they are given academic meanings later in the analysis that may differ from the meanings invested in the images by the participants or the researcher in the field. Hence there are multiple meanings. For Pink:

> the purpose of analysis is not to translate "visual evidence" into verbal knowledge, but to explore the relationship between visual and other (including verbal) knowledge . . . this implies an analytical process of making meaningful links between different research experiences and materials such as photographs, videos, field diaries, more formal ethnographic writing, local written and visual texts, visual and other objects. These different media represent different types of knowledge that may be understood in relations to each other. (2005, p. 96)

Difficulties with Visual Data without Text

Most researchers see the need for written text to accompany visual images in order for the viewer to understand their meaning (Barthes, 1977). However, the accompanying words can be the words of the participants or the researchers. Pink (2005) argues that the visual image should be considered equal to the written word, even though images are rarely used as the main or only source of information. In daily life, text and images are interwoven.

Morse and Pooler (2002) had to focus only on what the participants' actions were as captured on tape when using videotaped data as a sole source for analysis. They found several advantages of working with such a dataset. For example, data can easily be replayed, viewing can be slowed down, and so forth. Researchers can discuss their disagreements and use particular scenes as examples of the emerging theory. Plus "showing, in addition to describing, is powerful and persuasive" (Morse & Pooler, 2002, p. 3). However, the difficulties emerge in how far one can go with such data. They saw it as possible to make inferences about what is taking place in a scene, but it was impossible to interpret what was going on based on only a conceptual framework. A scaffold is necessary in order "to work inductively: describing behaviors, questioning observations, verifying and confirming, and systematically creating or extending theory" (p. 6).

In teaching visual research methods, Holm, Huang, and Cui (2006) asked students to take pictures of what it meant to be a graduate student and discovered that the study participants would have benefited from instruction or practice in taking photographs. Even though all students had cameras and had taken pictures with a basic familiarity with photography, they did not have the visual vocabulary for taking photos of, for example, absences or certain moods or approaches to life. Several of the international students included photographs of their absent families and spouses who had stayed behind in their home countries, because they missed them. However, there was no clear distinction between these photographs and those that portrayed the families that were present. In other words, present and absent families were portrayed in a similar way. Hence, a brief text written by the participants as a complement to the photograph was necessary, or participants needed to be taught some basics about how situations can be portrayed in photography.

Figure 16.5 indicates that the student will not sacrifice the needs of her family for the sake of her studies, whereas Figures 16.6 and 16.7 indicate that the students have left their husbands (and children) behind in their home countries to pursue doctoral degrees in the United States. Figure 16.5 emphasizes the daily presence and priority of the family. Figures 16.6 and 16.7 signify the priority and daily absence of and their long-

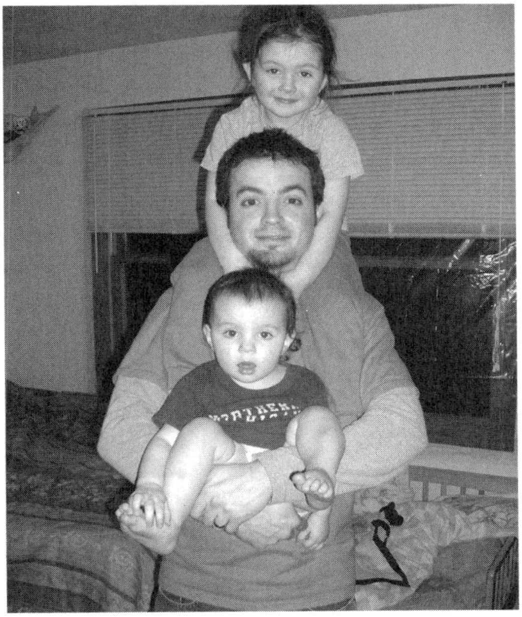

FIGURE 16.5. "The three things I will not sacrifice!"

FIGURE 16.6. "My husband and I."

FIGURE 16.7. "Staying far from family."

FIGURE 16.8. "Liquid energy."

ing for their families. This difference is difficult to detect, especially in Figure 16.6., despite the brief verbal titles of the photographs. Hence a contextualizing text is needed to complement the photographs. However, keeping the photograph as the main data source portrays the message of the importance of the family in a more powerful way by giving the reader a visual image of who the family members are.

It also became evident from the pictures that clear and specific instructions are needed for study participants. For example, the instructions were to take pictures of what it meant to be a graduate student, but some students interpreted this as having others take pictures of them as graduate students rather than taking the pictures themselves. Some also used pictures not specifically taken for this project. However, there are subtle differences between these three different kinds of pictures that made the analysis more complicated. Both Figures 16.8 and 16.9 portray the fact that doctoral students are always working. However, Figure 16.8, a photo that the student has taken of just his computer and a cup of coffee, also gives a sense of loneliness and isolation that the one with the student herself included in the photograph (Figure 16.9) does not.

In order to check on our interpretations of the photographs, we gave our verbal interpretations back to the students for review. Students agreed with our interpretations of their photographs. However, most students commented that once they saw the others' photographs they got additional ideas about how to express aspects of their lives they had not known how to express, such as the lack of time to participate in their children's extracurricular activities. This brings us back to photovoice, in which the study participants select and contextualize in groups the photographs they have taken (Berg, 2007). Working in groups allows the participants to think more broadly and deeply about what it is they want to say with their photographs.

FIGURE 16.9. "Killing two birds with one stone: Feeding the stomach and the brain."

The Future

The history of visual studies is rooted in anthropology (Banks, 2000; Collier & Collier, 1986; Ruby, 2005) and, to a lesser degree, in visual sociology (Becker, 1974, 2000; Harper, 1998, 2003). Most of the research within social sciences using visual methods is still conducted in those fields, whereas visual research methods are scarce in fields such as education. However, within many of the hard sciences, such as biology, health care, and medicine, photovoice and other visual research methods are becoming quite common. Institutional review boards (IRBs) are a major hurdle to conducting visual research in many fields, especially if children or other persons deemed vulnerable by IRBs are involved. More collaborative research would be beneficial for developing the methods and distribution of results despite these hurdles and disciplinary boundaries (Pink, 2003b). Interestingly, experience suggests that IRBs seem more willing to give permission for children to take photographs of their own milieus than they are to give permission to researchers to photograph children. For example, in a collaborative study with teachers in a bilingual immersion elementary school, we did a project based on how the students visually saw their community based on a unit on what community meant. Students were given cameras to photograph what they considered their community. Researchers would not easily have obtained permission from this particular IRB to enter children's homes or play areas to take photographs. Interestingly, most students selected the school or their bedrooms, pets, and possessions to photograph as representative of their communities (see Figures 16.10–16.12).

Visual researchers dwelt on issues of power and unequal relationships in their research, but only to a moderate extent. In traditional anthropological research, it was the researcher who took pictures of the colonized, not the colonized of the colonizers. Likewise, in more sociological research, it is those with power who take pictures of the powerless. Harper (2003) points out that academic researchers can take pictures of the homeless, but the homeless cannot enter academia to take pictures of life in the academic world. In addition to social class, there are other kinds of unequal relationships based, for example, on ethnicity, gender, and language.

FIGURE 16.10. My bedroom.

Technological advances keep changing the possibilities for using visual research methods. The digital revolution has changed how we collect data, using cameras that can take hundreds of photographs or videotaping with small and convenient cameras; how

FIGURE 16.11. Me and my pets.

FIGURE 16.12. Me and my stuffed animal collection.

we save, retrieve, analyze, and store data; and how we present our data and findings. This last aspect has not been discussed much in the research community, but we can now easily zoom in on certain aspects of a photograph and present our images with the help of computers. We can also print our photographs with more ease. Perhaps the most radical change is the hyperlogical way of data presentation as opposed to the traditional linear or narrative way. Harper (2003) points out that on the Web today:

> viewers can create their own paths through text, images, or even film and video clips. The most successful current example is Pieter Biella, Napoleon Chagnon, and Gary Seaman's (1997) interactive CD-ROM of the anthropological film *The Ax Fight*, by Timothy Asch, and additional hyperlinked materials. The interactive CD allows a viewer to view the actual film in any of several possible ways . . . the viewer can also link to scene-by-scene descriptions of the film, or can link to any individual shown in the film. . . . The CD contains complete footage and edited versions of the film, hundreds of photographs, and several full-length essays. The viewer can access any part of the film and digress to any of several analyses. The CD . . . represents the scientific expert whose claims are reinforced visually; on the other [hand], it deconstructs the authority of the scientist and makes the viewer the author of the viewing and learning experience. (pp. 180–181)

This is probably the most exciting development with regard to using video as a research tool. As the computer and the Web make videos more accessible and viewers more engaged, so do they open up more possibilities for viewers to examine photographs on their own. Alongside photovoice and photoblogs for collecting data, the CD-ROM provides new ways for sharing results and for viewers to be involved in the learning process. Ruby (2005) also points to digital interactive ethnographies as the most interesting development within visual anthropology. There is also a renewed interest in photography within anthropology, thanks in part to Pink's extensive work (1997, 2003a, 2004, 2005).

Most sociology and many anthropology departments do not offer courses in visual research methods, but some do. In very few other fields are courses in visual research offered. This is changing as Western culture is rapidly becoming more visual. Visual images such as advertisements are everywhere. Young people especially are becoming more tuned in to visual clues as youth culture is focused on consumption of digital images (computer, television, film/video, etc.). They are also more tuned in to producing images through creating Web pages, using cell phones with cameras, and so forth. More research is needed on how these images are produced, perceived, consumed, and interpreted.

In the field of evaluation, visual methods seem to be headed toward a brighter future. Walker (1993) suggested that in the evaluation of educational programs and educational research it would be useful to consider photographs in more ways than only as illustrations: "[We] neglect the power of the photograph to engage thought, extend the imagination and to undermine the implicit authority of the written word" (p. 73). Rosenstein (2002) sees it as an oversight that video is not even mentioned in program evaluation. She sees video as being particularly useful in the evaluation of teacher education programs. The overall use of photovoice in evaluation seems to be giving visual methods a boost.

In the field of sociology, visual sociologists are still working at the margins. Harper (2000) challenges visual sociologists to face the postmodern critique by building the visual research on sociological theory and by recognizing how ideology is built into photography. The so-called "new ethnographers" need to understand how their own work fits into the larger power relationships. At the more concrete level, Harper sees photoelicitation as the most promising visual research method within sociology.

Felstead and colleagues (2004) argue that photographs can challenge our taken-for-granted views and understandings of situations:

> Making and analysing images not only generated substantive findings but also created new leads in the research process and sensitised us to our own unquestioned assumptions. The *process* was valuable in itself, independently of its outcome. The photographs contained more information . . . than ever *could* have been captured by interview. Words could not have represented the wealth of detail contained in the photographs. (p. 109)

In summary, visual methods are becoming more commonly used and are breaking off and branching out from the traditional approaches used in anthropology and sociology. New fields such as evaluation, health care, and, to some extent, education are adopting visual research methods alongside other qualitative methods. In anthropology, visual research methods tend toward more participant involvement and collaborative work; in sociology, it is still more researcher-directed, even though photographs are sometimes taken by the participants. The approach is particularly collaborative in fields using photovoice. Despite these new developments, there are still some old but fundamental issues, such as confidentiality, consent, and power relations, that need to be further debated and researched.

References

Ball, M. S., & Smith, G. W. H. (1992). *Analyzing visual data*. London: Sage.

Banks, M. (2000). Visual anthropology: Image, object and interpretation. In J. Prosser (Ed.), *Image-based research. A sourcebook for qualitative researchers* (pp. 9–23). London: Routledge Falmer.

Banks, M., & Morphy, H. (Eds.). (1997). *Rethinking visual anthropology*. New Haven, CT: Yale University Press.

Barthes, R. (1977). *Image, music, text*. London: Fontana.

Bateson, G., & Mead, M. (1942). *Balinese character: A photographic essay*. New York: New York Academy of Sciences, v. 2.

Baudrillard, J. (1988). *Selected writings* (M. Poster, Ed.). Cambridge, UK: Polity Press.

Becker, H. S. (1974). Photography and sociology. *Studies in Anthropology of Visual Communication, 1*(1), 1–19.

Becker, H. S. (2000). Visual sociology, documentary photography, and photojournalism: It's (almost) all a matter of context. In J. Prosser (Ed.), *Image-based research: A sourcebook for qualitative researchers* (pp. 84–96). London: Routledge Falmer.

Bell, P. (2001). Content analysis of visual images. In T. van Leeuwen & C. Jewill (Eds.), *Handbook of visual analysis* (pp. 10–34). Thousand Oaks, CA: Sage.

Berg, B. (2007). *Qualitative research methods for the social sciences*. New York: Pearson.

Berger, J. (1972). *Ways of seeing*. London: British Broadcasting Association and Penguin.

Beyerbach, B. (2005). Themes in sixty years of teachers in film: Fast times, dangerous minds, stand on me. *Educational Studies, 37*(3), 267–285.

Bogdan, R. C., & Biklen, S. K. (2003). *Qualitative research for education: An introduction to theory and methods*. New York: Allyn & Bacon.

Bourdieu, P. (1998). *Practical reason*. Stanford, CA: Stanford University Press.

Bulman, R. C. (2005). *Hollywood goes to high school: Cinema, schools, and American culture*. New York: Worth.

Chaplin, E. (1994). *Sociology and visual representations*. London: Routledge.

Collier, J., Jr. (1967). *Visual anthropology: Photography as a research method*. New York: Holt, Rinehart & Winston.

Collier, J., Jr., & Collier, M. (1986). *Visual anthropology: Photography as a research method* (rev. & expanded ed.). Albuquerque: University of New Mexico Press.

Dabbs, J. M. (1982). Making things visible. In J. Van Maanen, J. M. Dabbs, & R. Faulkner (Eds.), *Varieties of qualitative research* (pp. 31–64). London: Sage.

Dalton, M. M. (1999). *The Hollywood curriculum: Teachers and teaching in the movies*. New York: Lang.

Damico, S. B. (1985). Two worlds of a school: Differences in photographs of black and white adolescents. *Urban Review, 17*, 210–222.

Denzin, N. K. (1989). *The research act* (3rd ed.). Englewood Cliffs, NJ: Prentice Hall.

Farber, P., & Holm, G. (1994a). Adolescent freedom and the cinematic high school. In P. Farber, E. Provenzo, Jr., & G. Holm (Eds.), *Schooling in the light of popular culture* (pp. 21–40). Albany: State University of New York Press.

Farber, P., & Holm, G. (1994b). A brotherhood of heroes: The charismatic educator in recent American movies. In P. Farber, E. Provenzo, Jr., & G. Holm (Eds.), *Schooling in the light of popular culture* (pp. 153–172). Albany: State University of New York Press.

Felstead, A., Jewson, N., & Walters, S. (2004). Images, interviews and interpretations: Making connections in visual research. In R. G. Burgess & C. J. Pooles (Series Eds.) & J. P. Poole (Vol. Ed.), *Seeing is believing?: Approaches to visual research* (pp. 105–121). London: Elsevier.

Flick, U. (2002). *An introduction to qualitative research.* Thousand Oaks, CA: Sage.

Gibson, B. E. (2005). Co-producing video diaries: The presence of the "absent" researcher. *International Journal of Qualitative Methods, 4*(3), Article 3. Retrieved March 8, 2006, from *www.ualberta.ca/~ijqm/backissues/4_4/pdf/gibson.pdf*

Glesne, C. (2006). *Becoming qualitative researchers: An introduction.* New York: Pearson.

Grady, J. (2001). Becoming a visual sociologist. *Sociological Imagination, 38*(1/2), 83–119.

Greenblat, C. S. (2004). *Alive with Alzheimer's.* Chicago: University of Chicago Press.

Hall, S. (Ed.). (1997). *Representation: Cultural representations and signifying practices.* London: Sage.

Harper, D. (1998). On the authority of the image: Visual methods at the crossroads. In N. Denzin & Y. Lincoln (Eds.), *Collecting and interpreting qualitative materials* (pp. 403–412). London: Sage.

Harper, D. (2000). An argument for visual sociology. In J. Prosser (Ed.), *Image-based research: A sourcebook for qualitative researchers* (pp. 24–41). London: Routledge Falmer.

Harper, D. (2003). Reimagining visual methods: Galileo to neuromancer. In N. K. Denzin & Y. S. Lincoln (Eds.), *Collecting and interpreting qualitative materials* (pp. 176–198). Thousand Oaks, CA: Sage.

Harrington, C., & Lindy, I. (1998, March). *The use of reflexive photography in the study of the freshman year experience.* Paper presented at the annual conference of the Indiana Association for Institutional Research Nashville, IN. (ERIC Document Reproduction Service No. ED 429473)

Heisley, D. D., & Levy, S. J. (1991). Autodriving: A photoelicitation technique. *Journal of Consumer Research, 18*, 257–272.

Hockings, P. (Ed.). (1975). *Principles of visual anthropology.* The Hague: Mouton.

Hockings, P. (Ed.). (2003). *Principles of visual anthropology.* New York: Mouton de Gruyter.

Holm, G. (1994). Learning in style: The portrayal of schooling in *Seventeen* magazine. In P. Farber, E. Provenzo, Jr., & G. Holm (Eds.), *Schooling in the light of popular culture* (pp. 59–80). Albany: State University of New York Press.

Holm, G. (1997a). Public texts/private conversations: Readings of a teen magazine from the girls' point of view. *Young, 5*(3), 20–29.

Holm, G. (1997b). Teenage motherhood: Public posing and private thoughts. In J. Jipson & N. Paley (Eds.), *Daredevil research: Re-creating analytic practice* (pp. 61–81). New York: Lang.

Holm, G., Huang, F., Cui, H. (with Ayyad, F., Bultsma, S., Gilling, M., et al.). (2006, June). *Being a doctoral student: A visual self-study.* Paper presented at the Ethnographic and Qualitative Research in Education Conference, Cedarville, OH.

Kehily, M. J. (1996, July). *More sugar?: Teenage magazines and sexual learning.* Paper presented at Crossroads in Cultural Studies conference, Tampere, Finland.

Lowe, R. (2001). Teachers as saviors, teachers who care. In P. B. Joseph & G. E. Burnaford (Eds.), *Images of schoolteachers in America* (pp. 201–209). Mahwah, NJ: Erlbaum.

Margolis, E. (1994). Video ethnography. *Jump Cut, 39*, 122–131.

Morris, L. (Director). (2004). *Stolen childhoods* [Film]. (Available from Galen Films, P.O. Box 4219, 18 State Road, Vineyard Haven, MA 02568)

Morse, J. M., & Pooler, S. (2002). Analysis of videotaped data: Methodological considerations. *International Journal of Qualitative Methods, 1*(4), Article 7. Retrieved April 8, 2006, from *www.ualberta.ca/~ijqm*

Pink, S. (1997). *Women and bullfighting: Gender, sex and the consumption of tradition.* Oxford, UK: Berg.

Pink, S. (2003a). *Doing visual ethnography.* London: Sage.

Pink, S. (2003b). Interdisciplinary agendas in visual research: Re-situating visual anthropology. *Visual Studies, 18*(2), 179–192.

Pink, S. (2004). Home truths: Changing gender in the sensory home. Oxford, UK: Berg.

Pink, S. (2005). *The future of visual anthropology.* London: Routledge.

Prosser, J. (1996). What constitutes an image-based methodology? *Visual Sociology, 11*(2), 25–34.

Prosser, J. (2000a). The moral maze of image ethics. In H. Simons & R. Usher (Eds.), *Situated ethics in educational research* (pp. 116–132). London: Routledge Falmer.

Prosser, J. (2000b). The status of image-based research. In J. Posser (Ed.), *Image-based research: A sourcebook for qualitative researchers* (pp. 97–112). London: Routledge Falmer.

Prosser, J., & Schwartz, D. (1998). Photographs within the sociological research process. In J. Prosser (Ed.), *Image-based research: A sourcebook for qualitative researchers* (pp. 115–129). London: Falmer Press.

Radley, A., & Taylor, D. (2003). Images of recovery: A photo-elicitation study on the hospital ward. *Qualitative Health Research, 13*(1), 77–99.

Rose, G. (2005). *Visual methodologies: An introduction to the interpretation of visual materials*. Thousand Oaks, CA: Sage.

Rosenstein, B. (2002). Video use in social science research and program evaluation. *International Journal of Qualitative Methods, 1*(3), Article 2. Retrieved February 8, 2006, from *www.ualberta.ca/~ijqm*

Ruby, J. (2005). The last 20 years of visual anthropology: A critical review. *Visual Studies, 20*(2), 159–170.

van der Dos, S. E., Gooskens, I., Liefting, M., & van Mierlo, M. (1992). Reading images: A study of a Dutch neighborhood. *Visual Sociology*, 7(1), 4–67.

Wakeford, N., & Cohen, K. (2003, July). *Photoblogging: Digital photography and sociology as strange chronicles*. Paper presented to the International Visual Sociological Association Meeting, Southampton, UK.

Walker, R. (1993). Finding a silent voice for the researcher: Using photographs in evaluation and research. In M. Scratz (Ed.), *Qualitative voices in educational research* (pp. 72–92). Washington, DC: Falmer Press.

Wang, C. (2005). *Photovoice: Social change through photography*. Retrieved July 19, 2006, from *www.photovoice.com/method/index.html*

Warren, C. A. B., & Karner, T. X. (2005). *Discovering qualitative methods: Field research, interviews, and analysis*. Los Angeles: Roxbury.

White, S. (2003). *Participatory video: Images that transform and empower*. Thousand Oaks, CA: Sage.

Ziller, R. C. (1990). *Photographing the self: Methods for personal orientation*. Newbury Park, CA: Sage.

CHAPTER 17

Performance-Based Emergent Methods

Patricia Leavy

All the world's a stage
And all the men and women merely players.
–SHAKESPEARE, *As You Like It* (Act II, Scene 7)

In recent decades performance has emerged as an interdisciplinary methodological genre in its own right, located within the expanded qualitative paradigm. Performance studies are diverse in both form and content and are used by researchers and practitioners in sociology, anthropology, health studies, education, dance studies, and theater arts in addition to other disciplinary, interdisciplinary, and multidisciplinary contexts. The performance genre has significantly influenced the shape of the qualitative paradigm, indicating that performance offers researchers a new way of thinking about and conducting social research. The move toward performance is not just about methodological innovation but is also a new epistemological grounding. In this regard Gray (2003) argues that performance challenges and disrupts conventional ways of knowing (p. 254). Oikarinen-Jabai (2003) suggests that a performance-based methodology allows researchers to transgress borders with their participants and offers a means for locating empowering spaces, exposing contradictions, and building empathy (p. 578).

Performance methods differ from other qualitative research methods as a result of the unique nature of performance. There is immediacy with the performance event that is not present, for example, in a conventional written report of research findings. Performances are also about "doing." Gray observes, "*Performance* is a verb" (2003, p. 254). Whereas interviews can be recorded and transcribed, performance exists only in the moment. Though some researchers videotape their performances as a part of their research methodology, a performance is a "live event" that may be taped but cannot be captured or experienced in the same way any other time than during that particular performance. As Saldana (1999) notes, performance events are temporal and ephemeral and so, although a recording may remain, the event itself does not. Moreover, no two performances are the same. Many factors, including environment, mood, intent, inflection, and so forth, help to give each performance its unique character. The exchange between the performer and the particular audience also varies depending on the context, broadly conceived (Langellier & Peterson, 2006).

Differing from traditional qualitative research findings, such as the writing up of interview data and the like, performances are accessible to much broader audiences. The highly specialized journals, academic jargon, and particulars of traditional academic writing often keep public audiences from benefiting directly from academic research. This is particularly true with respect to "meaning construction." When public audiences do consume academic writing, rare in itself, the intended meanings are typically laid out for the reader. In other words, the researcher has already determined the meanings and is privileged as the authority. Performances are not read; rather, they are *experienced*. Performances call forth multiplicity and are open to multiple meanings, which are derived from the *experience of consumption*, which may involve a host of emotional and psychological responses, not just "intellectual" ones. In this way and others, performance methods dismantle the rational–emotional dichotomy, with respect not just to the researcher's process but also to the consumptive process. Moreover, a performance constitutes an exchange between the actors–researchers and audience. A performance can be thought of as "a happening." In this vein, meaning is constructed and multiplied during the transfer. This process involves a negotiation of meanings of which the audience is a constituent part. Because performances are open to diverse audiences, performance studies have the potential to bring academic scholarship to much broader audiences, breaking down social class and other barriers, and doing so in a way in which the researcher ceases to be "the authority" and the performance text ceases to be the "authoritative voice" but, instead, the audience and researcher engage in a complex exchange through which multidimensional meanings emerge. In this way the turn toward performance as a research method and methodology is congruent with the larger move toward public sociology, as well as calls by qualitative researchers for the promises of induction to finally be more fully met. It is important to note, however, that the *potential* of performance-based research to extend social scientific knowledge outside of the academy has not yet been fully realized.

In social research, performance can serve many research purposes, including but not limited to consciousness raising, awareness, empowerment, emancipation, political agendas, discovery, exploration, and pedagogical goals. As Worthen (1998) suggests, performance is an investigation *and* a representation. As discussed later in the chapter, data collected through traditional qualitative research methods, such as ethnography, in-depth interviews, or focus group interviews, can be translated into performance texts in numerous ways, in some instances involving a traditional qualitative coding analytical process and, in some instances, relying on the tenets of drama explicitly during analysis and interpretation. Additionally, the emergence of performance methods has affected how traditional qualitative methods, particularly ethnography, are conceptualized and practiced. This demonstrates that emergent methods can also reshape the practice of conventional research methods.

As reviewed in this chapter, performance can be used as an entire research method or can serve any one part of the research process, though it is most often employed as a representational vehicle. As noted throughout the chapter, theories of performance are intertwined with the execution of performance methods. In this way, performance methods are an excellent vehicle for looking at the interconnectedness of theory and methods and how theoretical and methodological innovations emerge in relation to each other.

Given the wealth of performance-based methods in this chapter, I briefly review selected aspects of the academic context in which performance methods have developed, the similarities between performance arts and social research, and a selection of performance methods, including performance autoethnography, ethnodrama and ethnotheatre, reader's theater and health theater, and dance/creative movement as a representational form (though dance can also be used as a tool for gathering and interpreting data). Throughout the review I offer examples of empirical studies that have utilized these methods.

Academic Context

The move toward what Victor Turner (1974) deems a "performance paradigm" is linked to developments in embodiment research and the move toward bridging the mind–body connection, postmodern theoretical advancements, the larger academic move to interdisciplinary and multidisciplinary scholarship, and the impact of the social justice movements of the 1960s and 1970s, creating an awareness about ways to access "subjugated voices" and thus inspiring researchers to develop methods with this intent and capability.

Despite the new trend toward performance, sociologists have long incorporated aspects of performance into their disciplinary practices. For example, sociology was significantly influenced by the 1959 publication of Erving Goffman's groundbreaking book *The Presentation of Self in Everyday Life*, in which he employed the term *dramaturgy* to denote the presentation of self that people engage in during their daily life experiences. Building on Shakespeare's classic line, "All the world's a stage," Goffman wrote: "All the world is not, of course, a stage, but the critical ways in which it isn't are not easy to specify." This insight caused him to posit that social life mimics a stage, complete with "front" and "back" stages. The front stage is that which others see (in theater, this would be the actual performance, and in daily life, this is the public presentation of self), and the backstage is all of the behind-the-scenes stuff of life that others do not see (in theater, this would be the playwriting, the rehearsals, hair and makeup, etc.). Goffman's theoretical work posited that all aspects of social life involve performance, and his work continues to serve as an important text for sociology, a discipline centrally concerned with groups and with linking the macro and micro contexts in which individuals and groups operate. Qualitative researchers at the forefront of advancing performance methods continue to draw on the major tenets of Goffman's foundational work. For example, Denzin contends that our culture is dramaturgical and performance-based (2003, p. x).

Embodiment Research and Phenomenology

During the past few decades "the body" has become a central focus of an entire genre of academic scholarship. The body has garnered all of this attention due to the advances of feminist, postmodern, poststructural, and psychoanalytic theories of embodiment. These varied theoretical genres all share a critical perspective with respect to social power. These perspectives have also systematically exposed the artificiality of the Cartesian mind–body split and advocated for meaningful integration of these aspects of self. Additionally, these theoretical umbrellas perceive social actors as necessarily embodied actors and therefore assert that experience is embodied. Social reality is experienced from embodied vantage points. Embodiment theorists, as well as feminist and other critical scholars interested in "bodily experience," have advanced our collective understanding of how bodies become raced, gendered, sexed, and classed, among other topics.

Elizabeth Grosz (1994) has been at the forefront of merging feminist and psychoanalytic commitments in her work on embodiment. Grosz distinguishes between two major approaches to embodiment research. One approach is "inscriptive." By this Grosz means to suggest that the inscribed body is a site on which social meanings are created and resisted. Influenced by the work of poststructuralist Michel Foucault (1976) and feminist Susan Bordo (1989), Grosz explains, "The body is not outside of history, for it is produced through and in history" (1994, p. 148). The inscriptions exist on a continuum and may be "subtle" or "violent." For example, consider how this theoretical perspective could help us to understand how the mass-mediated images of female beauty that permeate American culture come into play in complex ways with respect to diverse women's embodied experiences. The inscriptions may result, cumulatively, in "subtle" ways, altering how women perceive and thus experience their bodies, and may also manifest in extreme body image disturbance, sexual dissatisfaction, alienation, depression, and so forth. More generally, the ways that bodies are gendered or raced are deeply implicated in existing relations of power (pp. 141–142).

The other major approach to embodiment research centers on "the lived body." It is within this theoretical category that a clear link between embodiment research and phenomenology emerges. In embodiment scholarship, "the lived body" refers to people's experiential knowledge, which necessarily occurs within a body. Grosz draws on the pioneering work of Merleau-Ponty (1962) who posits that we must look at the "necessary interconnectedness" of the mind and body (Grosz, 1994, p. 86). Merleau-Ponty argued that experience exists *between* the mind and body. Within this framework, the body is not viewed as an object, but rather as the "condition and context" through which social actors have relations to objects and through which they give and receive information (Grosz, 1994, p. 86). In other words, the body is a tool through which social life is experienced and meaning is created. In her research on pregnancy, in which she could not compartmentalize the bodily experience of pregnancy from other components of the experience, Tami Spry (2006) suggested that in order to truly access experiential knowledge, researchers must find ways to get at "enfleshed knowledge."

Embodiment theory seeks to offer a holistic or synergistic view of experience, noting that all experience is bodily and disrupting a long-standing paradigm that seeks to artificially separate the mind and body. As suggested throughout this *Handbook*, emergent methods develop within the context of theoretical advances. As noted in the introduction to this volume (p. 4), theoretical advances can cause a "methods gap" that prompt researchers to develop tools with which to explore the promises of theoretical advancements. The surge in highly complex embodiment theories has advanced our knowledge of embodiment and the physicality of experience, which in turn has facilitated methodological innovations, including recent explorations of dance and movement as methodological tools.

For example, Stinson (2004) explains that dance teaches a person to feel from the inside and, correspondingly, how to use the body as a source of knowledge and locus of meaning (p. 163). Drawing on theories of embodiment as she reflects on dance and movement as legitimate methods of social inquiry, Stinson posits the body as a microcosm for the world and a venue for understanding its meaning (p. 160). Moreover, influenced by phenomenological approaches to knowledge building, she further suggests that the entire body can be viewed as an experiential and memory repository for what we "know," which may emerge in improvisational dance in unexpected ways (p. 160). Furthermore, as noted throughout her body of work, dance is a site at which gender inscriptions on the body also come to the surface. Stinson suggests that dance itself has been gendered feminine, which is the reason that it occupies a lower status in the arts and social sciences than other forms of artistic expression.

Postmodern Theory

The emergence of postmodern theoretical perspectives over the past few decades has also prompted the exploration of performance-based methods. As postmodern theory rejects the totalizing or grand theories of modernism, scholars working from postmodern theoretical perspectives have sought to develop methodological strategies that mesh with theoretical insights. Denzin writes: "Under this postmodern performance aesthetic, the traditional audience disappears. The postmodern performance is both an interactive structure and an interpretive vehicle. Audience members are citizens from the local community, performers who bring their own interpretive frameworks to a performance event" (2003, p. 41).

Therefore, under this postmodern conception, the performance space gives way to what Madison (1998) terms a "performance of possibilities." In such a performance space, in which complex meanings are negotiated and dominant meanings are disrupted, the emancipatory potential of the performance event reveals itself. Moreover, as postmodern theorists have posed a serious challenge to conventional approaches to "truth" claims in relation to the texts we produce out of our research, so, too, have they offered insights about the importance of representation, including the interlocking nature of form and content. Finally, as feminism has propelled a meaningful exploration of reflexivity, postmodernists have also contributed to theoretical and methodological innovation in this area. In this regard, Denzin (2003) suggests that performance ethnography produces reflexive texts that are moral and politically self-aware.

Social Research and Drama: Craft in Qualitative Research

The merging of qualitative research practices and the dramatic arts, out of which performance-based research methods have emerged, has occurred within the context of larger linkages being identified between artistic practice and qualitative research. In order to discuss the relationship between social research and drama, I first briefly note convergences between social research and the arts more generally.

Artistic practice and the practice of qualitative research are both *crafts* that involve creativity, intuition, adaptability, and vision. I suggest that arts-based methods in general are "emergent" in that they are hybrids of artistic and scientific practices that, when merged, create a unique innovation beyond the sum of its parts. As Valerie J. Janesick (2001) notes, the researcher is the instrument in qualitative research, as in artistic practice. Moreover, both practices are holistic and dynamic, involving reflection, description, problem formulation and solving, and the ability to identify and explain intuition and creativity within the research process. It is with this awareness that Janesick calls qualitative researchers "artist–scientists." She also suggests that the function of qualitative research within the scientific paradigm can be better understood if we begin to more fully explore and disclose how we as researchers use creativity and intuition in our research projects.

Health care researchers Hunter, Lusardi, Zucker, Jacelon, and Chandler (2002) similarly argue that the creative arts can help qualitative researchers pay closer attention to how the complex process of meaning making and idea percolation shapes research. Hunter and colleagues posit that although meaning making is, of course, central to the research process, the "incubation phase" in qualitative research—the phase in which structured "intellectual chaos occurs" (p. 389) so that patterns may emerge and novel conclusions can be drawn—is not legitimized as a distinct phase of the research process and is, accordingly, hurried and often appears invisible in the final write-up. They suggest that the legitimized research process consists of the following four stages: (1) problem identification, (2) literature review, (3) methods, and (4) results (p. 389). Nevertheless, in qualitative research practice, the meaning-making process occurs as an iterative process (not a linear one), and meaning emerges through labeling, identifying, and classifying emerging concepts, interrelating concepts and testing hypotheses, finding patterns and generating theory (p. 389). Furthermore, there is an interface between interpretation and analysis. Hunter and colleagues argue that arts-based methods make this process explicit—allowing qualitative researchers to better accomplish what they already do. Art methods draw out the meaning-making process and push it to the forefront during practice and final representation.

The performance arts, primarily theater arts, are particularly useful for social researchers interested in accessing and revealing multifaceted dimensions of social life and communicating those dimensions to an audience with whom the meaning-making process then occurs. On a basic level, the performance arts and social research both seek to effectively tell people stories about the human condition. The process of conducting qualitative research and the process of creating a dramatic work bear striking similarities, and it this *convergence of process* that researchers are harnessing as they develop performance-based research methods. The affinity between the work of playwriting and performing and the craft of qualitative research is not surprising to scholars coming from the tradition of theater arts. Joe Norris (2000) suggests that the analytical work of qualitative researchers and theater practitioners bears similarities. In this vein he writes, "Much of what we do in process drama helps us to re-look at content to draw insights and make new meanings; this act can be considered a research tool (p. 44)." The improvisational techniques used in theater and dance may implicitly be a part of what qualitative researchers already do, and the development of performance-based methods may make this process more systematic and explicit. Norman K. Denzin suggests that improvisation is central to social research: "In the improvisation the researchers/actors articulated what they knew (data collection); framed it in the improvisation (analysis); and presented it to others (dissemination). Consequently, improvisation, even in its rudimentary form, is a research act" (2006, p. 44).

Langellier and Peterson (2006) note the main qualities of performance as *framed*, *reflexive*, and *emergent*. These qualities clearly correspond with many contemporary views of qualitative research. Johnny Saldana has been at the vanguard of discussing the relationship between the dramatic arts and social research. Saldana (1999) proposes that there is a fundamental similarity between the goals of qualitative researchers and playwrights in that they both attempt "to create a unique, engaging, and insightful text about the human condition" (p. 60). He further explains that theater practitioners have cultivated the following skills that are central to the practice of qualitative research:

1. enhanced sensory awareness and observation skills, enabling an attuned sensitivity to fieldwork environments;
2. the ability to analyze characters and dramatic texts, which transfers to analyzing interview transcripts and fieldnotes for participant actions and relationships;
3. the ability to infer objectives and subtext in participants' verbal and nonverbal actions, which enriches social insight;
4. sceneographic literacy, which heightens the visual analysis of fieldwork settings, space, artifacts, participant dress, etc.;
5. the ability to think conceptually, sym-

bolically, and metaphorically—essentials for qualitative data analysis; and

6. an aptitude for storytelling, in its broadest sense, which transfers to the writing of engaging narrative research reports. (p. 68)

The performance-based methods reviewed in this chapter draw on the strengths delineated by Saldana and aim to assist researchers in executing many different research objectives. Though performance studies can aid many research projects, in this chapter I consider how various performance-based methods can be used for accessing subjugated perspectives, consciousness raising, and adding new dimensions to our understanding of various aspects of social life. In the following sections I review several methodological practices and suggest specific strategies for using these methods.

Performance Autoethnography

The rise in performance-based methods is in part linked to the rise in incorporating autobiographical data in qualitative research in *explicit* ways. Although the researcher's perspective and personal writings have always (implicitly) been a part of ethnographic research—via standpoint, memo notes, and so forth—in recent decades this process has been brought to the foreground of professional conversations about ethnographic practice. It is within this context that Denzin (2003) argues that the turn to performance ethnography is linked to broader shifts in ethnographic practice. This comes to bear directly on the practice of ethnodrama and related methods discussed in the next section. However, the expansion of autobiographical data and other shifts within ethnography have also produced a move toward autoethnographic research and, more specifically, performance autoethnography.

Carolyn Ellis is at the forefront of autoethnographic research. She writes:

> What is autoethnography?" you might ask. My brief answer: research, writing, story, and method that connect the autobiographical and personal to the cultural, social, and political. Autoethnographic forms feature concrete action, emotion, embodiment, self-consciousness, and introspection portrayed in dialogue, scenes, characterization, and plot. Thus, autoethnography claims the conventions of literary writing. (2004, p. xix)

This method combines autobiographical writing with the conventions of narrative writing, at times incorporating fiction. Traditional ethnographic observations may also inform autoethnographic writing. Autoethnography may be communicated as a short story, essay, poem, novel, play, performance piece, or other experimental text. Aspects of the work may be fictionalized in order to create characterizations (which may be composites), or as a means of situating the piece within a particular cultural and historical context, or in order to evoke mood or emotionality, or for the purpose of following plot conventions. In autoethnographic writing, when fiction is employed it is as a means of revealing social meanings and linking autobiographic experiences of individuals to the larger cultural and historical context. Autoethnographic research can help qualitative researchers bridge the micro and macro levels of analysis and accentuate particular aspects of their work. As Ellis notes, this is a very distinct form of interrogation and writing.

A primary advantage of this method is the possibility it has to *raise self-consciousness* and thereby *promote reflexivity*. However, placing oneself at the center of the research process raises its own set of issues. Autoethnography requires the researcher to expose him- or herself and embark on an unpredictable emotional journey. Adding to the possible burden on the researcher, by opening up one's personal life and political beliefs to the public, a researcher lets go of some privacies and makes him- or herself vulnerable to possible criticism of a personal and professional nature. In this regard, Vickers claims that autoethnography is "writing on the edge–and without a safety net" (2002, p. 608). For this reason, as well as a measure toward validity, it is important to have a support team in place to offer feedback throughout the process (Tenni, Smyth, & Boucher, 2003).

Performance autoethnography combines the major tenets of autoethnography with the possibilities unleashed in a performance paradigm. Performance autoethnographies are highly reflexive texts that bring the personal into the public domain in ways that highlight links between biographical experience and social, institutional, material, historical context and then, via the performance aspect, seek to disrupt dominant ways of thinking by evoking emotional connections, inspiring social action, and inviting a complex, collaborative negotiation of meanings. In this regard Denzin suggests that performance autoethnography can be a "civic, participatory, collaborative project" (2003, p. 17).

Jonathan Wyatt (2005) wrote an (auto)ethnographic short story about his father's death. Through writing about his father's last days, death, and funeral, he also explored key issues of family, loss, and the father–son relationship. Communicated as a performance piece, Wyatt shared the narrative as a means of creating human connection with audience members and exploring, with others, central aspects of the human condition. The performance story format also allowed Wyatt to experiment with issues of time.

Laurie Thorp (2003) used the autoethnographic performance method to work through her agricultural education dissertation research, part of which is titled "Voices From the Garden: A Performance Ethnography." She found the method very effective for working through her own location within the shifting texts and for incorporating multiple voices, including that of her dissertation advisor, and the literature review into the research. Thorp's research comes from ethnographic research she conducted with approximately 150 children and 8 teachers, and, through autoethnography, the piece also chronicles her personal and professional experience during the research process, which was largely shaped by her father's death and her subsequent grieving process. In this performance piece, Thorp also documents her experiences working with an emergent research method and how others involved in the process, including her dissertation advisor, helped her navigate the process and modify her perceptions as necessary in order to reveal insights that would have remained dormant within a different methodological framework.

The cast and set are as follows: Six stools are on stage arranged in a semicircle. The characters, or "readers," are: Laurie Thorp, an elementary school teacher; an elementary school student; the dissertation advisor (renowned methodologist Yvonna Lincoln); a university student volunteer (Daniel Brooks); and the Poet Muse. Behind the six readers there are projected photographic images from the garden, and objects from the garden are placed at the foot of the stools. The houselights are dimmed, with soft lights on the six readers. Focusing on Thorp herself, the dissertation advisor, and the Poet Muse, as the three "characters" that allow for the greatest overt analysis and interpretation of the knowledge-building process itself, some excerpts from the script follow:

> DISSERTATION ADVISOR: Write your way through this darkness; you have a story to tell. (p. 314)
>
> POET MUSE: Voice is meaning that resides in the individual and enables that individual to participate in community. (p. 316)
>
> DISSERTATION ADVISOR: I might add that as Laurie relinquished control of the inquiry process, she came much closer to what is "really real" at this school than any research objectives or proposal could ever anticipate. (p. 318)
>
> LAURIE: Hold on to your hearts; I've saved the best for last. They don't get any better than

this. This is what makes research so damn rewarding. Just when you least expect it, the data jump out at you with a showstopper. And I can really toot the horn on this one 'cause I didn't figure it out, nope, not me. I puzzled and puzzled, cogitated and analyzed, and finally yelled uncle. So I met up for dinner one night with Gloria [*points to teacher*] and said, "Help, what does all of this mean?" She nearly took my breath away with her powers of insight and interpretation. (p. 322)

The use of these particular carefully constructed voices serve the script by making explicit the struggles—personal, epistemological, theoretical, and practical—that come to bear on the knowledge-building process. In this way, the script chronicles the meaning-making process itself from the perspective of the researcher who is struggling through it and in conversation with others. The conclusion of the script begins as follows:

> DISSERTATION ADVISOR: Laurie, I see our time is drawing to a close, but before we conclude, would you share some of the "lessons learned" from this, your journey of a lifetime?
>
> LAURIE: I must say that I'm a bit uneasy these days with recommending anything to anyone. Yet Clifford Geertz has said that as we traverse from "being there" to "being here," we somehow must find a place to stand. So, here is where I stand, for the time being: Open yourself to emergent design, emergent learning, emergent planning. Go ahead, let it unfold. I promise you won't be disappointed. It is liberating; you can't imagine what you will hear, what you will learn, and most important, what you will do.
>
> While you are there, stay awhile. Stay a long while. Prolonged engagement pays dividends, big dividends, in currency rarely traded these days: care, commitment, and human understanding.
>
> While you are waiting, be sure to reflect. And reflect out loud so we can all hear, I really mean it. Our closed system of discourse needs to reflexively come clean regarding our politics, our ethics, our ways of knowing, and all the other entanglements that occur in all research settings. Reflexivity acknowledges my vulnerability and I like that, for I am tired of the smooth, shiny certainty found in most academic journals.
>
> We hold the power of legitimized knowledge production in academia; make something happen. Don't become complacent with your privilege. Go ahead, you pick; there are hundreds of untold stories out there waiting to be told. . . .
>
> [*Laurie stands and moves to front and center*] There is a lump in my throat today that reminds me of the many difficult good-byes I've known in my life. . . . I am a daughter writing myself through grief. I am a woman writing myself into being. . . . (p. 323)

In Thorp's research it becomes clear that this methodology allows researchers to reflexively investigate the research process itself and how researchers move within it.

Ethnodrama, Ethnotheater, and Readers' Theater

Ethnodrama is a commonly used performance-based research method employed by researchers in many disciplines, including sociology, anthropology, education, and health studies, as well as interdisciplinary scholars. Many terms are used to denote ethnodramatic research, including *ethnodrama*, *ethnotheater*, *ethnographic performance texts*, and *performance ethnography*. Ethnodrama (and these related methods) combine qualitative data garnered from traditional qualitative methods, such as ethnography, interviews, or content analysis of public documents, with dramatic methods for interpreting and representing the data via the construction of a dramatic script that is typically performed. Though qualitative research can be represented as a script with the intent of being read and not performed, in this discussion I focus on ethnodramatic research that is performed.

The use of dramatic methods of interpretation and representation has been mistakenly construed by some as simply a flashy form for representing data, bells and whistles without substance; however, ethnodrama represents an expansion of the tenets of qualitative research. Moreover, the performance of ethnodramas is not merely a catchier way to represent data but rather a way to "get at," illuminate, and explore data that would not otherwise be accessible. This method reaches *dimensions* of social life that are often rendered invisible by traditional methods. Ethnodrama represents an epistemological departure from traditional qualitative research while allowing researchers to unearth the multiple meanings that new theoretical frameworks have exposed. The content cannot be separated from the form, and therefore the (re)presentation of data in dramatic fashion *implicitly changes the nature of the knowledge itself.*

Some qualitative researchers have explored ethnodrama for its ability to reach and effectively communicate the rich, textured, descriptive, tonal, situated, contextual experiences and multiple meanings that emerge in field research but that are incommunicable in a one-dimensional textual form of representation. Ethnodramatic performance is a strategy for getting closer to the general principles of ethnography (which guide many qualitative researchers, even those working with other methods). The performance medium allows researchers to explore the layers that constitute social life, the dimensionality of multisensory experiences that occur within natural settings in ways not enabled by traditional written representation. Ironically, given that ethnodrama is a stylized form of presentation, through attention to ambience, mood, color, sound, sight, plot, and story line consumers of ethnodramas gain deeper access to the "raw data" of ethnography. In this vein Denzin has famously claimed: "The performance text is the single, most powerful way for ethnography to recover yet interrogate the meanings of lived experience" (1997, pp. 94–95). This does not mean that ethnodrama is the right representation form for every ethnography; however, it is one valid method for getting closer to the principles of ethical ethnography, which itself has rightfully gained attention in recent years as discussions of voice, authorship, power, and authority have become central to renegotiations of the qualitative paradigm. When considering whether dramatic representation is appropriate for a particular project, Saldana writes that it is a matter of how the story the researcher seeks to communicate can be "validly, vividly, and persuasively told" (1999, p. 61).

Different strategies are available for writing a performance script. In some instances of ethnodrama, data are gathered using traditional qualitative methods and are analyzed and interpreted via qualitative methods such as grounded theory or other inductive coding procedures. In other cases, the data develop as a part of dramatically exploring a topic with the intent of writing and performing a play. In these instances the entire analytical and interpretive process may call on techniques adapted directly from the theater arts. I review these two avenues for approaching ethnodrama, though strategies offered for one can be implemented for the other, as these processes are themselves emergent.

Generally speaking, there are several standard components of a play that must be worked through in ethnodramatic script writing: characters, dialogue/monologues, plotting, structures, sceneography, and costuming.

Though the components of playwriting may be tackled in any number of ways, I begin with the issue of characterization. When using data garnered from traditional qualitative methods, such as interviews or ethnography, ethnodrama entails a process of transforming research participants into characters, and this can be accomplished in a variety of ways. During the interlinked processes of interpretation and script construction, it becomes evident that there are limitations to how many characters can appear in a script if they are to be properly "developed" and aid the overall narrative. Typically the number of participants in a study are reduced, resulting in the number of characters that appear in a script. This usually results in composite characters. Saldana (1999, 2003) notes that characters in the script can be constructed as composites so that the themes that emerged during data collection, which, for example, may have come forth in multiple interviews, can be used to formulate character "types." The compression of data into "types" can open the door to possible stereotyping, and so during this reductive process it is vital to make every effort at preserving the integrity of what the participants have shared. Attention to dimensionality assists this process. In this regard Saldana (1999, p. 62) provides guidelines for creating three-dimensional portrayals:

> 1. from interviews: what the participant reveals about his or her perceptions;
> 2. from fieldnotes, journal entries, or memoranda: what the researcher observes, infers, and interprets from the participant in action;
> 3. from observations or interviews with other participants connected to the primary case study: perspectives about the primary participant; and
> 4. from the research literature: what other scholars and theorists offer about the phenomena under study.

The process of characterization and dialogue writing are interlinked in this methodological practice. Though characters have a range of nonverbal forms of communication available, which in part is what differentiates ethnodrama from other representational forms, dialogue is central to the portrayal of characters and the execution of the storyline. Saldana (1999, pp. 63–66) posits that dialogue can reveal how characters react to one another (which may particularly appeal to researchers working from a symbolic interactionist framework), and monologues, when done well, can offer social insight (which may include the researcher's voice and voices from the literature review) and can also foster an emotional response from the audience (this connection being vital to performance-based methods). As dialogue and monologue are being written, researchers are also engaged in characterization. Again, these processes are interlinked. The writing of dialogue can assist with the compression of data and the creation of composite characters in ways that are nuanced, complex, and tonal. In other words, through the writing of dialogue, researchers can access multiple voices from their data, as well as the literature review, and thus offer a complex take on the data and open it up to multiplicity. In this regard, Saldana suggests applying the following strategies:

> Participant voices that come from two or more individual interviews can be interwoven to:
> 1. offer triangulation through their supporting statements;
> 2. highlight disconfirming evidence from their contrast and juxtaposition; and/or,
> 3. exhibit collective story creation through the multiplicity of perspectives. (p. 64)

In addition to writing characters and their dialogue, the researcher also has a role in the script. The place of the researcher within the text he or she collaborates to produce has become of paramount concern as a result of the advances of power-attentive epistemological and theoretical perspectives such as critical theory, postcolonial theory, postmodern theory, and poststructural feminism. The extent to which the researcher's analytical voice is present in the script is related to his or her view about how best to impart knowledge and facilitate the audience's understanding, which is determined in part by the goals of the study. For example, if an increased feminist consciousness is an intended outcome, then more overt interpretation—which may appear in the form a narrator's voice or character monologue—might be necessary. Saldana (1999, p. 66) proposes the following options for how a researcher may appear in the ethnodramatic text: "(1) a leading role, (2) an extra not commenting, just reacting, (3) a servant, (4) the lead's best friend, (5) an offstage voice heard on speakers, (6) a character cut from the play in an earlier draft." As with representations of research findings in more conventional forms, the role of the researcher's voice in the final text should not be diminished or glossed over. Ethical practice requires the researcher, particularly in the performance genre in which emotional connections are created between the performers and the audience, to disclose these choices.

Characters and their dialogue function to serve the story being communicated in a research play. In this regard, script construction also involves a process of plotting and creating a story line. Saldana (2003) clarifies these terms for a nontheater audience, defining plot as *the overall play structure* and story line as *the progression or sequence of events within the plot*. There are also structures that frame the play and communicate meaning. These structures are referred to as "units" in theater and traditionally include acts, scenes, and vignettes, which may be arranged in linear or episodic sequences (Saldana, 2003). The form and content cannot be separated within this method, and therefore structural choices about the "shape" of the play also inform the content or the narrative. Whether a more conventional interpretive process or one derived from the theater arts occurs, ultimately the researcher has to determine what narrative or narratives are being told. For the sake of producing an aesthetically pleasing play, Saldana suggests that the researcher attempt to retain and highlight "the juicy stuff" (1999, p. 61).

The ethnodrama format also allows researchers to present the visual components of social life, which are indistinguishable from human experience and our study of it. Though ethnographers have always sought to study people in their natural environment, the environmental components of the field site (visual, light and darkness, etc.) have only been able to be described, whereas performance methods allow these vital data to be shown. Therefore, in ethnodrama, the visual elements become inextricably bound to the data; they are presented richly as a constituent part of the data, not an addendum to it. Again, this is another way in which performance methods allow researchers to more robustly present their data and more deeply unleash the potential of ethnography. In this vein, sceneography relays information about the time, place, and social climate, and costumes help establish the "look" of the characters and show (Saldana, 2003, p. 228).

Some health care researchers have started using ethnodrama as a means of understanding various aspects of disease and illness. Mienczakowski, Smith, and Morgan (2002) employed ethnodrama to create a "health theater" project. Mienczakowski and colleagues assert that a performance-based methodology within health studies creates a space for the voices of marginalized health care recipients and caregivers (professional and personal). In this context, ethnotheater can be used to access and present subjugated voices, to educate, and to confront and work through stereotypes and misunderstandings pertaining to mental illness, stigmatized diseases, degenerative diseases, and gaps in the health care system. Health theater is a form of *public performance*, and thus ethical considerations abound. For example, when dealing with topics such as depression or suicide, stigmatized diseases, or degenerative illnesses, it is particularly important to be mindful of the potential impact that consuming the performance could have on audience members. In this regard, pilot performances are an effective safeguard, as are postperformance audience briefings (which also allow an opportunity for the emergence of multiple meanings).

Ethnodrama and ethnotheater are not the only methods available for researchers interested in performance strategies. Readers Theater and related collaborative drama-based methods can also utilize data collected from traditional qualitative methods. For example, Susan Finley (1998) presented a Readers' Theater piece based on interviews she had conducted with homeless people in New Orleans. Out of these interviews Finley created composite characters as "types" of youths identified in the data. The dramatic presentation of the data, in which each character spoke in the first person, allowed Finley to get at some of the authentic experience in a way that would not have been possible with traditional representational forms. When working with these kinds of dramatic methods, the data do not need to be collected in a conventional way. Data can also come from public sources.

Joe Norris (2000) is commissioned by agencies to create performance pieces and workshops on many subjects, and he typically uses public documents for data and inspiration. These public sources are used in a group analytical and writing process that follows an organized dramatic structure. He has collaborated in creating dramatic pieces exploring a diverse range of topics, including violence in schools, inclusion and exclusion, prejudice, sexuality, body image, addiction, equality and respect in the workplace, risk taking, and student teaching. He advocates a "spiral process" of play building in which all of the phases inform each other and the entire process has a dramatic structure (2000, pp. 46–48). As a part of this methodology, he has created a record-keeping system that he likens to "coding." Conceptualizing "record keeping" or "coding" as an "emergent process," he advocates using a series of files in which cast members place note cards with their thoughts, ideas, impressions, and so forth, throughout the process. Some of the file headings he uses are: "to be filed," "themes/issues," "metaphors," "scene ideas," "rehearsed scenes," "quickies" (short scenes and phrases), "keepers," "props/costumes/music needs," "external research data" and "potential titles" (p. 47). In this way, the analytical and writing process has reflexivity built into it (p. 46). Ultimately, as the performance approaches, Norris notes that a shift occurs from collection to compilation—a process guided by the question "what do we want this play to be about?" (p. 47)

Dance and Movement as a Performance-Based (Re)presentational Form

Dance is musical, visual, and performance-based. Similar to theater-based performance methods, dance and creative movement can serve all phases of the research endeavor. Dance is its own art form and discipline, and dance as a research method could constitute a chapter on emergent methods; however, for the purpose of this chapter, I very briefly consider the dance performance as a representational vehicle.

Carl Bagley and Mary Beth Cancienne's (2002) research provides an empirical example of using dance as a representational strategy in education research. Bagley is an education researcher, and Cancienne is a choreographer, dance expert, and scholar. While attending a conference, Cancienne was asked, virtually on the spot, to present a dance representing a dataset. Though she tried, she later concluded that the last-minute attempt failed; however, she wanted to try again under better circumstances, convinced that dance could be used to represent social research, like other performance vehicles.

For the collaborative project they developed, Bagley collected the data on the topic "impact of school choice on families whose children had special educational needs." Bagley conducted interviews and then selected 10 of the interviews as the final dataset for the project, at which point Cancienne was given the data so that she could create a dance that she thought represented them. Cancienne constructed an interpretative dance with words in order to preserve parents' voices and best convey the data. Cancienne portrayed the voices in abstract ways intended to communicate a particular set of meanings. For example, at one point in the dance a foot drew the name of a child on the floor as the parent spoke of the child's inability to write.

The researchers provide their viewpoints on the methodology they used, which is important given the relative newness of dance being employed in this capacity. Bagley reflected that the project was successful because people could connect with the data. The researchers viewed the data as unchanged from traditional textual form but felt that the dance performance infused it with new insight. Therefore, they concluded that the dance added *new dimensions* rather than new understandings (p. 15). Finally, in accord with the intent of all performance-based methods, the representation of the data in a dance format opened up a space for multiple meanings to emerge, though within the confines of a set of predetermined themes. Bagley and Cancienne write:

> In "dancing the data" we were able to facilitate a movement away from and disruption of the monovocal and monological nature of the voice in the print-based paper. Through a choreographed performance we were provided with an opportunity to encapture the multivocal and dialogical, as well as to cultivate multiple meanings, interpretations, and perspectives that might engage the audience in a recognition of textual diversity and complexity. (p. 16)

Dance as a representational form has the potential to add texture and tonality to the insights produced from traditional qualitative research. Congruent with the dance form itself, *the data retain movement* when presented to an audience, suggesting a dynamic and complex meaning-making process.

Conclusion

Performance-based research methods are a vast and interdisciplinary arena in which methodological innovation is occurring. As a result of many changes in the academic landscape, including the move toward interdisciplinarity, the expansion of the qualitative paradigm, the exploration of the arts in social research, advances in embodiment theory, postmodern theoretical advances, and feminism, researchers have developed a range of emergent performance methods. These methods are designed to get at and represent dimensions of social life that would otherwise remain invisible. Moreover, these methods are evocative and create emotional connections between audience members and performers–researchers–cocreators in the knowledge-building process. During this exchange a complex negotiation of meanings occurs. In this way and others, performance methods are a vehicle for accessing multiplicity *and* for promoting awareness and fostering social justice objectives.

References

Bagley, C., & Cancienne, M. B. (2002). Educational research and intertextual forms of (re)presentation. In C. Bagley & M. B. Cancienne (Ed.), *Dancing the data* (pp. 3–32). New York: Peter Lang.

Bordo, S. (1989). Feminism, postmodernism, and gender skepticism. In L. Nicholson (Ed.), *Feminism/postmodernism* (pp. 133–156). New York: Routledge.

Denzin, N. K. (1997). *Interpretive ethnography: Ethnographic practices for the 21st century*. Thousand Oaks, CA: Sage.

Denzin, N. K. (2003). *Performance ethnography*. Thousand Oaks, CA: Sage.

Denzin, N. K. (2006). The politics and ethics of performance pedagogy: Toward a pedagogy of hope. In D. S. Madison & J. Hamera (Eds.), *The Sage handbook of performance studies* (pp. 325–338). Thousand Oaks, CA: Sage.

Ellis, C. (2004). *The ethnographic I: The methodological novel about autoethnography*. New York: AltaMira Press.

Finley, S. (1998). *Traveling through the cracks: Homeless youth speak out*. Paper presented at the annual meeting of the American Education Association, San Diego, CA.

Foucault, M. (1976). Power as knowledge. In R. Hurley (Trans.), *The history of sexuality, Vol. 1: An introduction* (pp. 92–102). New York: Vintage Books.

Goffman, E. (1959). *The presentation of self in everyday life*. Garden City, NY: Anchor.

Gray, R. E. (2003). Performing on and off the stage: The place(s) of performance in arts-based approaches to qualitative inquiry. *Qualitative Inquiry, 9*(2), 254–267.

Grosz, E. (1994). *Volatile bodies: Toward a corporeal feminism*. Bloomington: Indiana University Press.

Hunter, H., Lusardi, P., Zucker, D., Jacelon, C., & Chandler, G. (2002). Making meaning: The creative component in qualitative research. *Qualitative Health Research Journal, 12*(3), 388–398.

Janesick, V. J. (2001). Intuition and creativity: A pas de deux for qualitative researchers. *Qualitative Inquiry, 7*(5), 531–540.

Langellier, K. M., & Peterson, E. E. (2006). Shifting contexts in personal narrative performance. In D. S. Madison & J. Hamera (Eds.), *Sage handbook of performance studies* (pp. 151–168). Thousand Oaks, CA: Sage.

Madison, D. S. (1998). Performances, personal narratives, and the politics of possibilities. In S. J. Dailey (Ed.), *The future of performance studies: Visions and revisions* (pp. 276–286). Annandale, VA: National Communication Association.

Merleau-Ponty, M. (1962). *Phenomenology of perception* (C. Smith, Trans.). London: Routledge.

Mienczakowski, J., Smith, L., & Morgan, S. (2002). Seeing words—Hearing feelings: Ethnodrama and the performance of data. In C. Bagley & M. B. Cancienne (Eds.), *Dancing the data* (pp. 90–104). New York: Peter Lang.

Norris, J. (2000). Drama as research: Realizing the potential of drama in education as a research methodology. *Youth Theatre Journal, 14*, 40–51.

Oikarinen-Jabai, H. (2003). Toward performative research: Embodied listening to the self/other. *Qualitative Inquiry, 9*(4), 569–579.

Saldana, J. (1999). Playwriting with data: Ethnographic performance texts. *Youth Theatre Journal, 14*, 60–71.

Saldana, J. (2003). Dramatizing data: A primer. *Qualitative Inquiry, 9*(2), 218–236.

Spry, T. (2006). Performing autoethnography: An embodied methodological praxis. In S. N. Hesse-Biber & P. Leavy (Eds.), *Emergent methods in social research* (pp. 183–211). Thousand Oaks, CA: Sage.

Stinson, S. W. (2004). My body/myself: Lessons from dance education. In L. Bressler (Ed.), *Knowing bodies, moving minds: Towards embodied teaching and learning* (pp. 153–168). London: Kluwer Academic.

Tenni, C., Smyth, A., & Boucher, C. (2003). The researcher as autobiographer: Analyzing data written about oneself. *Qualitative Report, 8*(1), 1–12.

Thorp, L. (2003). Voices from the garden: A performance ethnography. *Qualitative Inquiry, 9*(2), 312–324.

Turner, V. (1974). *Drama, fields, and metaphors: Symbolic action in human society*. Ithaca, NY: Routledge.

Vickers, M. H. (2002). Researchers as storytellers: Writing on the edge—and without a safety net. *Qualitative Inquiry, 8*(5), 608–621.

Worthen, W. B. (1998). Drama, performativity, and performance. *PMLA, 133*(5), 1093–1107.

Wyatt, J. (2005, May). *The telling of a tale: A reading of "A Gentle Going?"* Symposium conducted at the International Congress of Qualitative Inquiry.

PART II

Innovation in Research Methods Design and Analysis

Sharlene Nagy Hesse-Biber

There is a growing demand for new research methods designs and analysis procedures that will enable researchers to answer the range of research questions emanating from new theoretical contributions. The revolutionary works of feminists, postcolonialists, postmodernists, and critical theorists aim to expose the subjugated knowledge of oppressed groups that has often been left out of traditional research. Questions generated from these new theoretical models look at the intersections of race, class, gender, sexuality, nationality, and other hierarchical forms of social identity. Emergent questions often place subjugated groups at the center of inquiry. Feminist standpoint theory (Harding, 2004; Smith, 2004), for example, places women's concerns and knowledge at the forefront and is committed to issues of social justice and social change for women. Critical theory and critical race theory (Wing, 2000) upends conventional knowledge forms such as positivism by exposing the power dynamics underlying traditional knowledge practices and making visible the dynamic interconnections between gender, race, class, nationality, and so on. The emergent research designs and new forms of analysis presented in this section address these complex questions, which traditional research designs and analysis strategies are not able to adequately address (Hesse-Biber & Leavy, 2006).

Mixed methods research designs (those that combine both qualitative and quantitative research methods) are moving across the disciplines. The influence of these designs has accelerated considerably over the past decade (Bryman, 1988; Creswell, 1998, 2003, 2006; Greene & Caracelli, 1997; Morgan, 1998; Sandelowski, 2000; Sieber, 1973; Tashakkori & Teddlie, 1998, 2003). Researchers are witnessing an influx of mixed methods articles, books, and handbooks that tackle the thorny questions at the heart of basic assumptions about the nature of reality and a multilayered concept of "truth." Mixed methods designs are not simply about adding additional methods for the sake of "more" but rather, providing a synergistic approach to research design in which the different methods inform one another; in which the different methods are in conversation with one another, producing a more layered, multipronged approach to research. It is of critical importance that the research problem determine the feasibility and use of a mixed methods approach. Chapter 18, by Vicki L. Plano Clark, John W. Creswell, Denise O'Neil Green, and Ronald J. Shope, provides an excellent introduction to mixed methods research designs, starting with a discussion of the definition of mixed methods and the reasons for mixing methods. They present specific mixed methods design examples and compare and contrast these designs. They discuss the challenges researchers face in implementing a mixed methods approach and offer guidance in the application of mixed methods designs.

Currently, there are external pressures from funding agencies for researchers to inform social policy and those evaluations of policy that utilize qualitative, as well as quantitative, methods, and mixed methods appears to be a favored research design. In Chapter 19, Charles Teddlie, Abbas Tashakkori, and Burke Johnson point to the necessity of mixed methods research to more fully provide answers to complex social issues. They also point out the need for a research design that can satisfy a number of "stakeholders" whose perceptions and interests in studying a given problem differ. They note: "Different stakeholders sometimes will have different conceptions of what constitutes a quality conclusion. This complex process requires respect and understanding of different perspectives, and it requires that researchers carefully consider multiple perspectives during the conduct and writing up of research conclusions and recommendations" (p. 409). They provide detailed examples of how to implement a range of mixed methods designs.

The next two chapters in this section review innovative ways to analyze and link different forms of data. In Chapter 20, Sarah Irwin states that quantitative and qualitative data are both needed to address complex and multidimensional problems. In this regard, Irwin states:

> Different methods and sources of evidence will reveal specific slices through the phenomena and processes under study, and we need to understand better precisely how the evidence reveals a partial and particular picture. For example, in-depth interviews and survey responses may provide different lenses on people's perceptions of some particular event or state of affairs, and so different kinds of accounts are generated by the different media of data collection. (pp. 415–416)

Her chapter provides some excellent examples with respect to combining data from different levels of analysis (micro and macro) in order to enhance our understanding of social reality, and she explores how both types of data are "different *dimensions* of unitary problems" (p. 415). This touches on a prevalent theme reviewed throughout the *Handbook*, namely, an integration of macro and micro perspectives and the dynamic interplay between these dimensions of social experience. Irwin further notes that

> to understand an individual's values and subjective beliefs, we need knowledge of him or her as a person, knowledge of his or her proximate circumstances and experiences, and knowledge of the wider social structural contexts in which he or she is positioned. . . . Researching macro and micro is not just about "linking data"; it is an issue of how we conceptualize the phenomena we are investigating. (p. 415)

Moving from mixed methods research to other emergent analysis practices, Elisabetta Ruspini's chapter (Chapter 21) demonstrates how longitudinal data analysis can provide researchers with new ways to study gender and life course social changes. Chapter 21 provides an overview of what constitutes longitudinal research within the social sciences, as well as the strengths and weaknesses of longitudinal research designs. Ruspini provides some detailed examples of longitudinal research models for studying gender over the course of a lifetime.

Next, in Chapter 22, Joseph A. Maxwell and Barbara A. Miller aim to contribute to the "development of a theory of qualitative data analysis" (p. 461). The authors proceed to do this by focusing on the distinction between types of relationships, including those based on similarity (i.e., categorizing strategies such as coding that place similar or different data into separate categories independent of time or space) and those based on contiguity (a consideration of how data are related to each other in time and space; how data influence one another by focusing on connections between data segments). They describe each of these analysis strategies in detail and suggest that both are needed (they are complementary and mutually supportive of each other) to further advance our theoretical understanding of complex questions.

Offering another specific analysis procedure in Chapter 23, Zazie Todd and Simon J. Harrison see the use of metaphor as not just a "feature of language" but also a "feature of thought" (p. 480). They provide examples of specific analysis strategies using metaphors. They note:

> Some studies provide detailed analysis of many individual metaphors, commenting on how they link together. Other studies start with structural metaphors, providing little direct evidence of actual individual metaphors but using metaphor as a tool to interrogate wider theory or ideology. These might loosely be characterized as bottom-up and top-down approaches to metaphor analysis. (p. 480)

Finally, another important analytical tool is the "listening guide" described by Lynn Sorsoli and Deborah L. Tolman in Chapter 24. The listening guide's basic assumption is that contained within any person's narrative is not one story or one voice but rather a multiplicity of voices that can emerge from a single respondent's story. The listening guide provides a technique for getting at "multiple interpretive readings" of a singular narrative. This strategy picks up on issues raised in many of the methods chapters in Part I, in which multiplicity was many times revealed as a theoretical advance and methodological goal of contemporary qualitative research. Sorsoli and Tolman note that the listening guide provides a way for the researcher to capture "the ways different strands of narrative rise, fall, and intertwine, leading to a complex and nuanced understanding of participants' stories" (p. 495). Although they do not provide a full step-by-step guide to the entire listening process, the authors extract those factors that they found most essential and innovative within this process and present two detailed examples of how to analyze multivocality within their own research on the sexual experiences of adolescent girls, as well as trauma narratives of female survivors of sexual abuse.

The authors in this section remind us of how important innovation is throughout the research process. Innovation does not take place only at the data gathering stage but continues through analysis (what the data say) and interpretation (what the data mean) stages. The range of design and analytical strategies offered in this section are important ways to get at things differently so that all voices, especially those whose knowledge has been subjugated, can finally be heard. Through the use of emergent longitudinal designs, for example, we can capture micro and macro social change; through the use of a mixed methods design and analytical strategies we can draw on and combine a variety of data to enhance our understanding of complex social problems and thereby get at often hidden dimensions of our data.

References

Bryman, A. (1988). *Quantity and quality in social research.* New York: Routledge.

Creswell, J. (1998). *Quality inquiry and research design: Choosing among five traditions.* Thousand Oaks, CA: Sage.

Creswell, J. (2003). *Research design: Qualitative, quantitative, and mixed methods approaches* (2nd ed.). Thousand Oaks, CA: Sage.

Creswell, J. (2006). *Qualitative inquiry and research design: Choosing among five approaches* (2nd ed.). Thousand Oaks, CA: Sage.

Greene, J. C., & Caracelli, V. J. (Eds.). (1997). *Advances in mixed-method evaluation: The challenges and benefits of integrating diverse paradigms* (New Directions for Evaluation, No. 74). San Francisco: Jossey-Bass.

Harding, S. (2004). Rethinking standpoint epistemology: What is strong objectivity? In S. Hesse-Biber & M. Yaiser (Eds.), *Feminist perspectives on social research* (pp. 39–64). New York: Oxford University Press.

Hesse-Biber, S., & Leavy, P. (2006). *The practice of qualitative research*. Thousand Oaks, CA: Sage.

Morgan, D. (1998). Practical strategies for combining qualitative and quantitative methods: Applications to health research. *Qualitative Health Research, 8*(3), 362–376.

Sandelowski, M. (2000). Combining qualitative and quantitative sampling, data collection, and analysis techniques in mixed-method studies. *Research in Nursing and Health, 23*(3), 246–255.

Sieber, S. D. (1973). The integration of fieldwork and survey methods. *American Journal of Sociology, 78*(6), 1335–1359.

Smith, D. (2004). Women's perspective as a radical critique of sociology. In S. Hesse-Biber & M. Yaiser (Eds.), *Feminist perspectives on social research* (pp. 27–38). New York: Oxford University Press.

Tashakkori, A., & Teddlie, C. (1998). *Mixed methodology: Combining qualitative and quantitative approaches*. Thousand Oaks, CA: Sage.

Tashakkori, A., & Teddlie, C. (2003). *Handbook of mixed methods in social and behavior research*. Thousand Oaks, CA: Sage.

Wing, A. K. (Ed.). (2000). *Global critical race feminism: An international reader*. New York: New York University Press.

CHAPTER 18

Mixing Quantitative and Qualitative Approaches

An Introduction to Emergent Mixed Methods Research

Vicki L. Plano Clark
John W. Creswell
Denise O'Neil Green
Ronald J. Shope

For most of the past century, researchers relied on quantitative research to answer their research questions. However, in the 1980s and 1990s many researchers turned to an increased use of qualitative research. As researchers today have developed an understanding of and appreciation for both quantitative and qualitative approaches, they have begun to combine these two approaches in studies using mixed methods designs. In the past decade, mixed methods research has emerged as a major methodological movement across the social sciences, and many are starting to view it as a third approach to research, alongside quantitative and qualitative research (Johnson & Onwuegbuzie, 2004; Tashakkori & Teddlie, 2003). Researchers today need an introduction to mixed methods research so that they are familiar with its definition and can judge when it is the appropriate design to choose for a given research problem. They also need practical examples of how researchers are applying this approach in research studies.

In this chapter, we present an introductory overview of mixed methods research. We begin with its definition and discuss reasons that researchers choose this approach and the value that it can bring over other designs. Then we illustrate different examples of how mixed methods can be applied in practice for a range of research objectives. We introduce the major types of mixed methods designs, discuss the important features that distinguish these designs, and provide an exemplar study for each design. Finally, we consider the challenges that researchers face when choosing to implement a mixed methods approach and offer our advice for researchers considering mixed methods designs for their own studies.

What Is Mixed Methods Research and How Has It Emerged?

Like qualitative research and quantitative research, mixed methods research represents a collection of approaches, or designs, for collecting, analyzing, interpreting, and reporting data in empirical research studies. In particular, mixed methods approaches are those approaches to research in which the researcher decides to blend or combine both quantitative and qualitative methods. Although mixed methods can be discussed as a methodology with emphasis placed on the philosophical foundations of research (e.g., see Tashakkori & Teddlie, 1998), this chapter uses Creswell and Plano Clark's (2007) methods-based definition of mixed methods research. They define mixed methods research as a design for collecting, analyzing, and mixing both quantitative and qualitative data in a study[1] in order to understand a research problem.

Following from this definition, mixed methods research has three key features. First, a researcher collects both quantitative and qualitative data (e.g., the researcher may collect quantitative data using a questionnaire and qualitative data using focus group interviews). Second, the researcher analyzes these two datasets (e.g., the researcher could analyze the quantitative data for correlations and the qualitative data for themes). Third, the researcher mixes the two datasets in a meaningful way (e.g., by comparing and contrasting the results of the quantitative correlational analysis with the qualitative thematic findings) and develops an overall interpretation.

Combining quantitative and qualitative research into one study may not seem like an emerging approach to research. It is true that scholars have been discussing and applying multiple methods in studies for many years (e.g., Campbell & Fiske, 1959; Jick, 1979). However, only recently have researchers begun to view mixed methods research as a unique research approach that has philosophical foundations, its own terminology, systematic research designs, and specific procedures for designing, implementing, and reporting research using this approach (Creswell, 2003; Creswell, Plano Clark, Gutmann, & Hanson, 2003; Greene, Caracelli, & Graham, 1989; Tashakkori & Teddlie, 1998, 2003).

Evidence of the emerging interest in mixed methods research can be identified from many different sources. For example, there have been major publications that discuss mixed methods research as a design in its own right. These include *The Handbook of Mixed Methods in Social and Behavioral Research* (Tashakkori & Teddlie, 2003), *Research Design: Qualitative, Quantitative and Mixed Methods Approaches* (Creswell, 2003), and *Research and Evaluation in Education and Psychology: Integrating Diversity with Quantitative, Qualitative, and Mixed Methods* (Mertens, 2005). Many studies using mixed methods approaches have also been published across the disciplines (see, e.g., Plano Clark, 2005), and numerous disciplinary journals have published special issues on mixed methods research (e.g., Creswell, Fetters, & Ivankova, 2004, in family medicine; Hanson, Creswell, Plano Clark, Petska, & Creswell, 2005, in counseling psychology). In addition, major funding agencies, such as the National Institutes of Health (NIH) and the National Science Foundation (NSF), along with private foundations, such as the Robert Wood Johnson Foundation and the W. T. Grant Foundation, have advocated the use of mixed methods approaches and have published guidelines and/or offered workshops on their use. Finally, in the fall of 2005, the *Journal of Mixed Methods Research* was started by Sage Publications as a forum for publishing discussions and applications of mixed methods research. This growing acceptance of mixed methods research makes it a viable option for researchers as they consider what approaches to use for their studies.

Why Do Researchers Use Mixed Methods Approaches?

Researchers need to know more than a definition of mixed methods research; they also need to consider why they would want to use this approach. Many researchers have begun to turn to mixed methods approaches for their research due to the complexity of the research problems that are of interest today. These researchers choose this approach by considering its overall advantages and the added value this approach has over available single-method designs for addressing certain types of research goals.

Overall Advantage of Using Mixed Methods

In general, researchers decide to mix methods within their studies because the two methods together result in a better understanding of the problem being studied. This improved understanding arises when the complementary strengths of quantitative (numbers, trends, generalizability) and qualitative (words, context, meaning) approaches offset the different weaknesses of the two approaches (Brewer & Hunter, 1989). The following analogy, as told by a mixed methods researcher, illustrates the enhanced understanding that arises when multiple kinds of information are brought together to address a research problem:

> The story of the three blind men is that one blind man is holding the tail of an elephant, and [says] "OK, if this is an elephant, an elephant is long and skinny and it has wispy hairs on the end." And another one has the leg of the elephant, and he sticks his arms around it and holds it, and says, "Well, an elephant is something like a tree with a large solid trunk, very strong and sturdy." And then you have the third blind man who has a different part of the elephant, maybe the side of the elephant, and says, "Well an elephant is something that's long and broad like a wall and flat." And so if you had only any one of those views from the three blind men then you would say an elephant is either something long and wispy or something like the trunk on the tree or you might say that an elephant is something broad and long like a wall. But if you were able to have all three of those put in together and integrate them, then you might indeed come up with a better description of what an elephant is. (Plano Clark, 2005, p. 151)

As this story conveys, looking at a phenomenon from only one perspective can constrain our understanding of it. However, if we examine the same phenomenon using multiple perspectives that represent different but complementary views, then we are more likely to gain a better, more complete understanding. This is the overall argument for using mixed methods research by researchers who find value in combining quantitative and qualitative perspectives for addressing their research problems.

Value of Using Mixed Methods Approaches Over Single-Method Approaches

Although the logic of mixing methods, as told in the story of the blind men and the elephant, is often intuitively appealing to researchers, researchers also need to consider what this approach brings to a study over a single-method approach. That is, what is the value that a mixed methods approach has above and beyond using a single quantitative or qualitative method? This "added value" can arise in many different ways.

The value of a mixed methods approach arises partly from the multiple perspectives that can be included by combining quantitative and qualitative data in a study. For example, the researcher can examine statistical results and overall trends, along with in-depth individual perspectives and the context in which they occur. Researchers may also obtain stronger, more corroborated conclusions when the results are derived from two different types of data instead of only a single type. In addition, the researcher can use different types of data to examine different aspects of a phenomenon, such as both process and outcomes. This approach can also be used to achieve a more complete understanding by capturing multiple perspectives and/or different levels within a system when these different aspects require different methods.

The use of both quantitative and qualitative methods can also facilitate the incremental building of knowledge, particularly if the methods are used in a sequence. For example, a researcher can both develop a theory (e.g., by using a grounded theory approach) and test the theory (e.g., by following up with a survey). Mixed methods incorporates a level of flexibility that facilitates an emergent design, so that a researcher can build on initial findings without having to change the overall design (e.g., if qualitative interviews are conducted to explain specific quantitative results). In addition, the methodological rigor of a study can be increased by using multiple forms of validity/validation or by openly stating and addressing biases (as advocated in qualitative research) as part of the quantitative aspect of a mixed methods study.

Just as a mixed methods research approach offers numerous methodological advantages, it also brings value to a study in terms of its overall persuasiveness and emphasis on practical application. Mixed methods studies can produce more persuasive accounts of the phenomenon of interest because they combine statistical results with qualitative quotes and stories and therefore may appeal to a broader audience. Reports that combine both numbers and text may also help bridge the gaps between research and practice. Mixed methods research is also well received by practitioners because it aligns well with how practitioners address problems in practice (such as a physician who forms a diagnosis based on both lab results and a patient's description).

Finally, mixed methods approaches may bring added value to the researchers who engage in this type of research. When students and researchers apply mixed methods approaches, they further develop their own understanding of and expertise in both quantitative and qualitative methods, in addition to grappling with issues of how to mix the two. This broad experience with the different approaches may make them better prepared to face today's complex research questions.

Although a mixed methods approach may have value in addressing research problems, researchers must also carefully assess whether this approach fits the research problem of interest and is feasible for the researcher to carry out. Mixed methods studies are challenging designs that demand considerable time, resources, and skills to successfully implement both the quantitative and qualitative aspects. Researchers must also address important issues such as how the two datasets will be related to each other and how the study will result in an "added value" beyond the sum of the two aspects. We next consider types of research objectives that call for using a mixed methods approach, and later in this chapter we further discuss some of the challenges associated with using this design.

What Kinds of Research Objectives Call for Using Mixed Methods?

Once researchers decide that a mixed methods approach can bring value to their studies, they must also assess whether this approach fits the overall research problem and specific objectives of a particular study. There are many reasons that researchers choose to mix qualitative and quantitative methods in their research studies. We have identified objectives that are commonly found in published mixed methods studies, and eight of these objectives, along with corresponding sample studies, are discussed in the following sections.

Compare Quantitative and Qualitative Results

In many studies, researchers want to develop conclusions that are well substantiated. They may choose to collect both quantitative and qualitative information on the topic so that the findings from each data source can be compared. This may be accomplished by collecting two separate datasets (e.g., surveys and focus group interviews). When the two types of data provide corroborating evidence for a finding, then the researcher has additional evidence that this finding is valid. In some cases, the two datasets may result in contradictory evidence. When this occurs, the researcher may gain further insights by examining the divergence and may need to collect additional data to interpret the findings. Researchers may also choose to converge quantitative and qualitative data in order to produce a more complete picture of the topic of interest. When the two types of data provide complementary but different evidence on a topic, then the researcher develops a more complete understanding of the complexity of the topic.

Application of Comparing Quantitative and Qualitative Results

Yauch and Steudel (2003) compared quantitative and qualitative results in their examination of the organizational cultures of two small manufacturers. They chose to collect both qualitative data (observations, documents, interviews) and quantitative data (a survey measure of organizational culture) in order to develop a more complete and valid understanding of their research topic. For the quantitative data, they utilized a measure of organizational culture that had been previously documented in the literature. For the qualitative data, they collected documents, observations, and interviews. After they analyzed these two datasets separately using traditional quantitative and qualitative analytical procedures, they converged them by examining the quantitative and qualitative evidence for key findings to produce more valid conclusions. They included a table in their article that indicated which types of data (quantitative and qualitative) contributed to identifying each of the key dimensions of organizational culture for the two cases.

Validate Quantitative Data

Using surveys is a popular approach to studying trends in a population. Surveys need to have strong construct validity in order for meaningful conclusions to be drawn based on the data collected with the survey. If a survey has limited evidence supporting its construct validity or if the survey is being administered to a new population, then the researcher may want additional evidence to validate the survey data. In such a case, researchers can include a few qualitative open-ended questions as part of their survey questionnaire. These qualitative questions should address the same topics as the survey items and give participants a chance to provide additional information on these topics. Although the responses to a few open-ended items will not result in an extensive qualitative database, they can provide researchers with useful information that can be used to validate and illustrate the results obtained with the quantitative portion of the survey.

Application of Validating Quantitative Data

Morrell (2005) wanted to examine the role of shocks (single, jarring events) in nurses' decisions to leave their employment and to develop a typology of nurse turnover. He constructed a survey to measure variables that had been identified in the literature and through pilot work. He also included open-ended items on this structured survey. He analyzed the quantitative data using cluster-analysis analytical strategies that resulted in the identification of three clusters describing why nurses choose to quit. He used the qualitative responses as a means of validating these clusters as valid representations of nurse turnover.

Enhance an Experimental Study

Experimental designs are by definition quantitative procedures for testing a theory or measuring the effects of a treatment. However, even when conducting experimental research, some researchers find that a single dataset is not sufficient for addressing the objectives of their studies. Experimental researchers may include a qualitative component to enhance their study for a number of different reasons. For example, the qualitative data may be collected to enhance recruitment practices, to inform the development of a treatment, to examine the process of an intervention in addition to the outcomes, or to follow up on the results of an experiment. Therefore, researchers may choose to embed a qualitative approach within their experimental methodology either before, during, or after the intervention is administered.

Application of Enhancing Recruitment Practices for an Experimental Study

Donovan and colleagues (2002) developed an experimental trial to evaluate different courses of action for testing and treatment of prostate cancer in men. However, they found that they were having a difficult time with recruitment and obtaining participant consent, and therefore their experiment was in jeopardy due to inadequate participation. They proceeded to conduct qualitative, in-depth interviews before beginning the experiment to understand potential participants' interpretation of the study information and treatment descriptions. Using the themes that emerged from these interviews, they were able to redesign their recruitment procedures and increased their randomization rate from 40 to 70%. They were then able to conduct their experimental test using the different treatment conditions.

Application of Enhancing the Interpretation of Experimental Results

Bachay (1998) reported embedding a qualitative component within her experimental study of ethnic identity development of urban Haitian adolescents. She used a pretest–posttest control group design for the experimental approach, in which adolescent participants were randomly assigned to three treatment conditions (control, control with discussion, and experimental counselor-based intervention). Using standard measures, she compared the gains in ethnic development scores for the three groups and found no significant treatment effect, although she did find a significant difference based on gender. Within this intervention, she also collected qualitative information during open-ended interviews with all participants to explore the feelings and perspectives of the Haitian students with regard to their school experience. These interviews were conducted with all participants so as not to introduce a treatment bias across the groups, and they were thematically analyzed and used as evidence to further illuminate the experimental findings.

Explain How Mechanisms Worked within a Correlational Design

Qualitative data and findings can be embedded within correlational designs, in addition to experimental approaches. Correlational approaches are used to identify relationships among variables and to identify variables that predict a certain variable. Although quantitative data can be analyzed to identify significant relationships, these results do not always lead the researcher to understand why certain relationships occur. Researchers may choose to collect qualitative data as a means of explaining the mechanisms operating behind those relationships. This means that the researchers need to collect the qualitative data from the same participants (or a subset of the participants) who are providing the quantitative data.

Application of Explaining Mechanisms in a Correlational Design

Harrison (2005) embedded qualitative focus group interviews into her correlational study of the predictors of relationship building for participants in a mentoring program for undergraduate students majoring in education. Using a longitudinal design, she collected quantitative measures of the extent to which a positive relationship had formed, as well as predictors such as demographic characteristics, levels of program participation, and match of the personalities of the mentors and mentees. However, she wanted to explain why certain correlations occurred, in addition to predicting relationship outcomes. Therefore, she also explored the process of building positive relationships using focus groups with the same participants. The qualitative dataset augments her understanding of the significant relationships found among the quantitative variables.

Explain Quantitative Results

Researchers may collect qualitative data as a means of explaining certain quantitative results. That is, a researcher may begin studying a topic by collecting quantitative data using a quantitative instrument such as a survey or questionnaire. As these data are analyzed, the researcher may obtain results that cannot be readily explained. For example, the researcher may wonder why certain results were or were not significant. The researcher may also want to explain results that were unexpected or the reasons that extreme or outlier scores occurred. In such situations, the researcher can decide to collect and analyze qualitative data in a second phase of the study in order to explain specific aspects of the quantitative results. In this way, the qualitative data are used to follow up and explain initial quantitative results.

Application of Explaining Quantitative Results

Aldridge, Fraser, and Huang (1999) conducted a study of differences in classroom learning environments between Taiwan and Australia. They began their investigation with a survey study measuring student perceptions of different dimensions of classroom learning environments. When they analyzed these quantitative data, they were surprised to find that students in Taiwan had more positive attitudes toward science but that students in Australia held more positive perceptions of the learning environment. They then proceeded to collect extensive qualitative data (including classroom observations and interviews with students and teachers) in order to better understand these perceptions and to be able to explain this anomalous finding. The qualitative data were analyzed and were found to provide plausible explanations for the initial quantitative results.

Select Participants for In-Depth Study

Researchers may need quantitative information in order to purposefully select the best participants for an in-depth qualitative investigation. The use of quantitative results to guide participant selection can be particularly advantageous in studies using theoretical sampling, such as grounded theory studies. The quality of qualitative investigations depends largely on collecting data from the participants who can best inform the researcher about the phenomenon of interest. In some cases, finding the "best" participants can be facilitated by the use of quantitative results to identify participants with certain characteristics. The important characteristics are determined within the context of the study, but they could include demographic characteristics, quantitative indications of certain attitudes or experiences, or measures of performance.

Application of Selecting Participants for In-Depth Study

May and Etkina (2002) studied the differences in epistemological beliefs and self-reflection about learning physics concepts between students who demonstrated high conceptual gains and those with low conceptual gains in a college physics course. In the first phase of their study, they quantitatively analyzed the learning gains that were measured on a set of standard conceptual achievement tests. From their quantitative analysis, they identified students who consistently showed high levels of learning gains and students who consistently showed low levels of learning gains. They used these results to select participants from each of these groups as cases for an in-depth qualitative investigation of their use of reflection and applications of their epistemological beliefs in a series of documents completed as part of the course. In this way, they used their initial quantitative analyses to guide their purposeful sampling for their qualitative investigation.

Develop a Suitable Instrument

Researchers often want to measure relevant constructs using quantitative instruments (e.g., to measure the prevalence of a construct in a population). However, in some cases, the variables of interest are not known, or instruments that address these variables have not been reported in the literature. In such a circumstance, a researcher may turn to the literature for ideas, but often the literature provides an incomplete picture of the items and subscales that are appropriate for a new instrument or does not adequately represent individuals' perceptions and experiences. In other cases, instruments may exist, but they may not have been developed for the population that is of interest in the current study. For example, if the researcher is interested in underserved minority populations or populations with cultural differences, then preexisting instruments may be inadequate or inappropriate. When faced with these problems, researchers may decide to first collect qualitative data about the topic of interest. Once analyzed, the findings from the qualitative data can be used to identify important variables and provide the bases for developing or modifying an instrument so that its items and subscales are grounded in the perspectives of participants. After the instrument is developed and pilot tested, then the researcher can use this instrument to collect quantitative data in a second phase of the study.

Application of Developing a Suitable Instrument

Mak and Marshall (2004) collected qualitative data to guide the development of an instrument used in their study of perceived mattering in young adults' romantic relationships. Mak and Marshall wanted to test hypotheses about how perceived mattering related to other variables, but they first needed a description of the different dimensions of this concept, and then they needed a way of measuring it. Therefore, they began with a qualitative investigation of young adults' perceptions of mattering to romantic partners. They collected written responses from young adults and identified themes from these data. These findings guided the development of the questionnaire items and scales. Once the instrument was developed, these researchers followed the qualitative phase by using it to collect quantitative data to validate the questionnaire and to test their hypotheses.

Generalize Qualitative Findings

Researchers conducting in-depth qualitative investigations may be interested in generalizing their qualitative findings with quantitative data. Although this research objective has some similarities to developing an instrument, the focus is not on the instrument but on generalizing the results. For example, if the qualitative results were based on a small number of participants (as is typical in qualitative approaches), a researcher may want to see whether the findings also apply to a larger sample. Qualitative findings can take on different forms, including the identification of thematic categories, the development of a typology based on the qualitative data, or the generation of a conceptual model relating the qualitative findings. In some cases (but certainly not all), researchers may also want to quantitatively test these findings to help extend the research. This could involve returning to participants to collect quantitative data about variables identified in the qualitative phase (almost a form of member checking) or, more often, going to a new sample to quantitatively test the relationships found in the qualitative analyses. In this way, the quantitative data are used to extend the initial qualitative findings.

Application of Generalizing Qualitative Findings

Kretsedemas (2003) used a community-action research framework to guide his study of Haitian immigrants' experiences with service access following welfare reform. The study began with a series of interviews with 20 service professionals and Haitian community leaders. The analysis of this qualitative data resulted in the development of a typology of service barriers and hardships. The research team then conducted face-to-face structured survey interviews with 380 community residents. These quantitative data were collected and analyzed to extend and refine the theory generated from the qualitative phase and to assess the relationships among certain variables and relationships derived from the qualitative analysis and the literature.

This collection of objectives represents many of the reasons that researchers today choose to use a mixed methods approach in their research. Keep in mind that these objectives are illustrative and are not meant to be a comprehensive list. There certainly are additional objectives that call for a mixed methods approach, and some researchers combine multiple objectives within their studies. However, these objectives are among the most common in the literature, and, for researchers new to mixed methods, we recommend that they consider one primary objective to guide their mixed methods design choice. This will make the study's purpose clearer and make the study more straightforward to design and implement.

What Mixed Methods Designs Are Available?

At this stage, it is helpful to consider the basic types of mixed methods research designs and how they match the research objectives discussed previously. Although many design variants are possible for mixing quantitative and qualitative aspects within a study, Creswell and Plano Clark (2007) identified four major types of mixed methods designs that are currently being used by researchers. This classification system grew out of the foundational work of Greene, Caracelli, and Graham (1989), who identified six types of mixed methods approaches used in the evaluation literature and many other discussions appearing within the mixed methods literature (e.g., see Creswell et al., 2003; Morgan, 1998; Morse, 1991; Tashakkori & Teddlie, 2003). These design classifications represent distinct models and procedures that researchers can use to mix quantitative and qualitative data and analysis within their studies.

The four major mixed methods design types presented by Creswell and Plano Clark (2007) are the triangulation design, the embedded design, the explanatory design, and the exploratory design. These four designs are depicted in Figure 18.1 and discussed in the following sections.

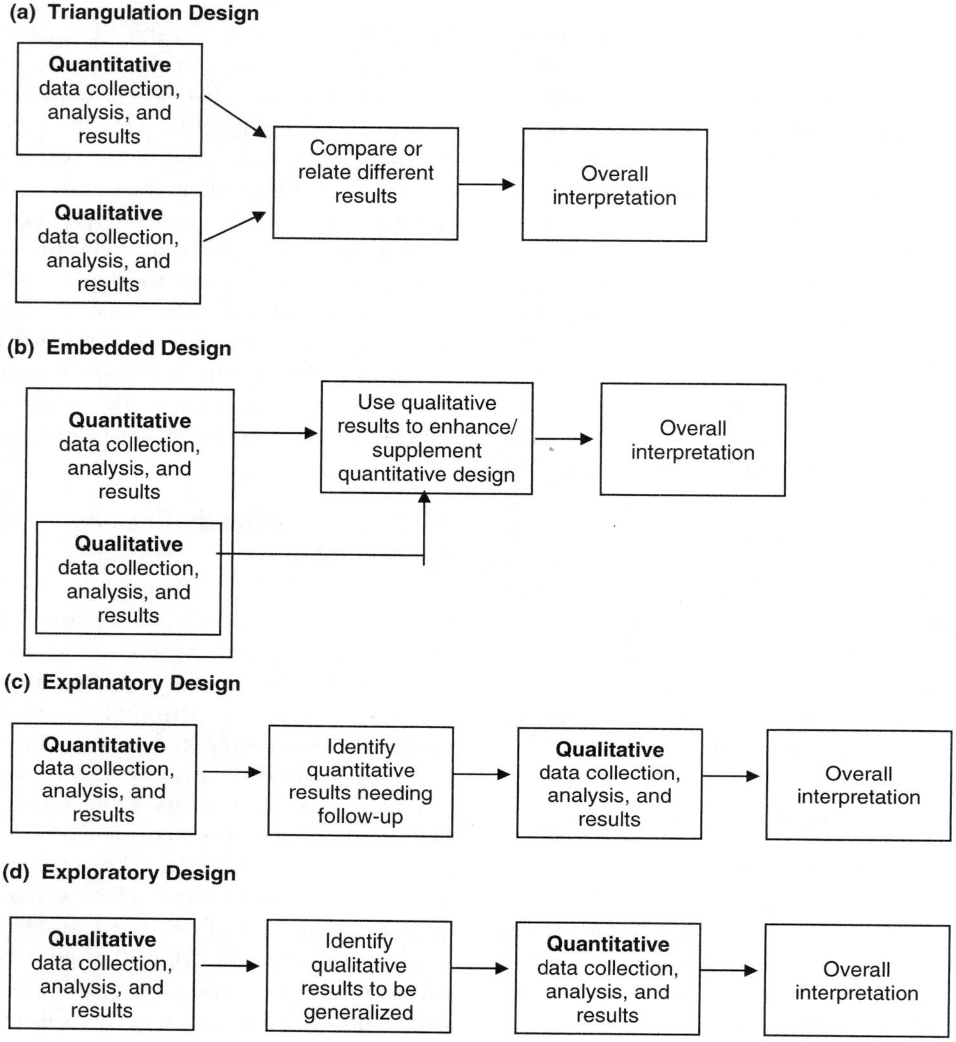

FIGURE 18.1. The four major mixed methods design types. Designs from Creswell and Plano Clark (2007).

The Triangulation Design

The triangulation design is a one-phase mixed methods design in which the quantitative and qualitative data are collected and analyzed during the same phase of the research process and are merged together into one interpretation (Creswell & Plano Clark, 2007). This concurrent (or parallel) implementation of the two types of methods is depicted in Figure 18.1a. Another characteristic of this design is that the quantitative and qualitative methods are usually given equal emphasis, so that each one contributes equally to addressing the study's research questions.

The triangulation design's overall intent is to develop a better understanding of a topic by obtaining two different but complementary types of data (Morse, 1991). This is accomplished by combining the strengths of quantitative research (large sample sizes, trends, generalizability) with the strengths of qualitative research (small sample sizes, contextual details, in-depth description) (Patton, 1990). This design is used when a researcher wants to compare quantitative and qualitative information in order to present well-corroborated conclusions (Creswell, 1999). It is also used when a researcher wants qualitative data to validate the results from a quantitative survey. Researchers using this design usually merge the results of the two datasets by comparing and contrasting them or by synthesizing what is learned from each (Plano Clark, 2005). In some examples, the researcher chooses to transform one type of data into the other type in order to directly relate findings from the two different datasets or to examine multiple levels of a system (Tashakkori & Teddlie, 1998).

The triangulation design may be the most popular mixed methods design, but it may also be the most challenging to implement well (Creswell et al., 2003). This design is popular because it has been discussed in the literature for a long time (see Greene et al., 1989; Jick, 1979), and it just makes intuitive sense to collect both types of data. It is also an efficient design because both types of data are collected and analyzed during the same phase of the study.

Despite its popularity, numerous challenges are associated with applying this design. Because both methods are emphasized and implemented at the same time, the researcher must have sufficient resources to manage the data collection and analysis and have expertise in both approaches or must work with a team that includes researchers with qualitative and quantitative skills. In addition, the researcher needs to design procedures for merging the two datasets, either through data transformation or during the interpretation. It can also be very difficult to converge or relate the two different datasets, particularly if the researcher did not design the quantitative and qualitative aspects to address the same concepts.

An Application of the Triangulation Design

Jenkins's (2001) article about rural adolescents' perceptions of what influences their ability to resist offers to use alcohol and drugs is an example of a study that used a triangulation design. Jenkins needed to collect both quantitative and qualitative data because she expected that adolescents' perceptions would differ based on the type of drug and based on individuals' levels of drug use. Therefore, she needed both qualitative data about adolescents' perceptions and quantitative data about adolescents' drug use to best understand this problem.

Jenkins collected quantitative data about drug use by administering a survey to all students enrolled in a rural high school in the Midwest. The survey asked participants about the frequency of their use of three types of drugs (beer, marijuana, and hard drugs). From the response data, the researcher classified each of the 361 participants as being nonusers, low-frequency users, or high-frequency users of each of the different substances. In this article, the quantitative analysis and results were limited, with only total counts being reported from the quantitative data. During the same phase of the research, Jenkins (2001) also collected qualitative data about why drug offers may be difficult to resist. The qualitative data included three open-ended items on the quantitative survey, which were completed by the same 361 participants who completed the survey. In order to enhance the credibility of this limited source of qualitative data, Jenkins conducted focus group interviews with 29 purposefully selected adolescents, in addition to collecting the written responses. Jenkins analyzed the qualitative written responses and found 15 categories that describe adolescent perceptions of what makes it difficult for an adolescent to resist an offer of beer, marijuana, and hard drugs. She used the focus group interview data to validate and elaborate on the qualitative written responses. The categories were described, and

Jenkins also transformed the qualitative data into quantitative counts by determining the percentage of participants whose responses included each of the categories. The qualitative categories were also related to the level-of-drug-use quantitative variable.

Jenkins (2001) used the one-phase triangulation design to describe adolescents' perceptions about resisting drug offers in relation to participants' own levels of drug use. The mixing of the quantitative and qualitative data occurred in the ways the data were analyzed, displayed, and interpreted in order to address the question of how the qualitative findings could be interpreted in relation to the quantitative results. The data were collected and analyzed during one phase of the study, and some of the data were even collected on the same instrument. Although not stated explicitly, this study appeared to place equal emphasis on the two methods, as both were necessary for addressing the study's purpose. The quantitative and qualitative data were merged at the end of the study by presenting tables that displayed both quantitative and qualitative information (drug type and level of use with the qualitative response categories) and by the overall interpretations that were made.

The Embedded Design

The embedded design is used when one type of data provides a supportive, secondary role in a study based primarily on the other type of data (Creswell et al., 2003). Unlike the triangulation design, which tends to mix at the level of data analysis and data interpretation, the embedded design tends to mix at the design level, with one type of data embedded within a methodology framed by the other data type (Caracelli & Greene, 1997). As shown in Figure 18.1b, most applications of embedded designs found in the literature use qualitative data in a supporting role within predominantly quantitative studies (such as experiments). However, it is also possible to embed quantitative data within a largely qualitative study (such as a case study).

Embedded designs are used when a researcher needs to answer two different research questions that require quantitative and qualitative data. In designs with a quantitative emphasis, the supplemental qualitative data are used to enhance the method or interpretation of an experiment or to explain relationships in a correlational design. The qualitative component may occur before, during, or after the quantitative intervention and/or data collection (Creswell, Fetters, & Plano Clark, 2005; Sandelowski, 1996). That means that, in embedded designs, the research methods may be implemented in a sequence or during the same phase of the study.

The embedded design offers a researcher a number of advantages as a mixed methods approach. For one, because the study is guided by a larger methodology, such as an experimental design, it can be appealing to those new to mixed methods because it can employ a familiar design. In addition, the emphasis on one data type makes this design more logistically manageable because the other data type receives lesser priority. Therefore, this design can be a good choice if time and resources are limited.

There are a number of challenges associated with the embedded design. For example, the researcher must clearly specify why the secondary dataset is needed and how these data will be used within the larger study. The researcher also must decide when and from which participants to collect the supplemental data. This is particularly important in experimental research, as researchers must ensure that their supplemental qualitative data collection does not introduce bias into the treatment. For example, a researcher may wait to collect the qualitative data until after the intervention is complete.

An Application of the Embedded Design

Rogers, Day, Randall, and Bentall (2003) embedded qualitative data within their randomized controlled trial of an intervention designed to enhance the management of antipsychotic medication by people diagnosed as suffering from schizophrenia. They collected qualitative data at two different times within their experimental design: before the intervention and after the intervention. Before the experimental trial began, they interviewed 26 patients in order to understand the meaning and use of medication from their perspectives. They then used their qualitative findings to inform the development of the intervention so that it would reflect the reality of the patients' lives.

The researchers randomly assigned participants to the three treatment conditions (treatment-as-usual control, compliance treatment, and patient-centered treatment designed from the qualitative results) tested in the randomized control trial. They collected quantitative data from all participants using a drug-attitude instrument before the intervention, at the end of the intervention, and at a 1-year follow-up. The focus of the quantitative data analysis was to determine which of the treatments led to the most positive attitudes.

In addition to collecting quantitative measures at the completion of the intervention, the researchers also conducted a second qualitative data collection. They interviewed 16 individuals who had participated in one of the intervention treatments (not in the treatment-as-usual control) and had scored positively or negatively on the outcome measure. The qualitative data were analyzed thematically to understand the meaning, contextual factors, and processes that occurred behind the outcome measures. They specifically wanted to be able to link patient narratives and quotes with the different outcomes, and they concluded by discussing the qualitative findings within the context of the interventions and the outcomes.

Rogers and colleagues (2003) used an embedded design to enhance their experimental study with qualitative data. They collected and analyzed a qualitative dataset before the experiment began to help design the treatment and then another after the experiment was complete to better understand the outcomes. Because this study was framed by experimental methodology, it clearly emphasized the quantitative approach, and the qualitative data served to enhance this experimental design. The researchers mixed the two data types in different ways. They embedded qualitative data before the intervention to inform how the experimental treatment was designed and again after the intervention was complete to explain the meaning and processes that had occurred. In addition, they used the quantitative results to help select the interview participants after the intervention, and they interpreted the qualitative findings within the context of the experiment in their final discussion.

The Explanatory Design

The explanatory design is a two-phase mixed methods design in which the quantitative and qualitative methods are implemented in a sequence. As depicted in Figure 18.1c, this design starts with the collection and analysis of quantitative data. This quantitative phase is then followed by the subsequent collection and analysis of qualitative data in a second phase. The qualitative phase of the study is designed so that it follows from, or is connected to, the results of the initial quantitative phase. Because this design begins quantitatively, investigators generally place greater emphasis on the quantitative methods in addressing the study's research questions.

The explanatory design's overall intent is to build from quantitative results about a topic to further qualitative examination. The qualitative data are used to explain, elaborate, or refine the initial quantitative results. Therefore, this design is well suited if a researcher needs additional qualitative information to explain interesting findings such as significant (or nonsignificant) results, outlier results, or surprising results (Morse, 1991). This design can also be used to select participants based on quantitative results for an in-depth qualitative investigation. In this case, the quantitative results can be used to form groups to guide a subsequent qualitative investigation (Morgan, 1998; Tashakkori & Teddlie, 1998) or to identify participant characteristics needed for purposeful sampling for a qualitative phase (Creswell et al., 2003).

Due to its two-phase implementation, the explanatory design has a number of distinct advantages. Two discrete phases mean that the project can be more manageable to implement, because the researcher only collects one type of data at a time. Having distinct phases also makes the study easier to report, because the different aspects of the study can be written in separate sections within one manuscript. These features make the explanatory design ideal for graduate projects and beginning mixed methods researchers. This design also appeals to many quantitative researchers because it begins with a strong quantitative orientation.

Although this design is straightforward, it is not without challenges. Its two-phase structure requires lengthy time for implementation because the quantitative and qualitative data are collected at separate times. Typically, the qualitative data will not be collected until the quantitative data have been analyzed so that the quantitative results influence the selection of participants and design of questions for the qualitative phase. In addition, it can be a challenge to secure institutional review board (IRB) approval for this design because the second phase cannot be fully planned until the first phase is complete. Researchers can describe tentative participants and data collection strategies for the qualitative phase at the planning stage but should recognize that a change in protocol may need to be filed before beginning the qualitative data collection.

An Application of the Explanatory Design

Ivankova (2004) used an explanatory design in her dissertation study of students' persistence in an online doctoral program. She began her study by conducting a cross-sectional Web-based survey of program participants. This survey contained items related to different internal and external factors (e.g., motivation, role of advisor) expected to relate to students' persistence. The quantitative data were statistically analyzed using univariate and multivariate techniques to determine the extent to which each factor predicted students' persistence in the program.

At the completion of the quantitative analyses, Ivankova had isolated the factors that predicted persistence, but she did not know why different factors were or were not significant predictors. Therefore, she conducted a second, qualitative phase to address this issue. Before starting the qualitative phase, she used the quantitative results to develop her interview questions and to purposefully select participants for the follow-up phase. She selected four individuals who were representative of the quantitative responses given by each of four groups based on program status (e.g., beginning, matriculated, graduated, or withdrawn/inactive). The qualitative data included one-on-one interviews, written documents, and artifacts. The data were analyzed within the four cases and across cases to explain how the different factors identified during the quantitative phase contribute to the students' persistence in the program.

Several features of the explanatory design are illustrated by Ivankova's (2004) study. Both quantitative and qualitative data were needed to identify predictor variables and to explain why these variables were significant. The mixing of the two types of data was guided by the question, How do the qualitative findings explain the statistical results obtained in the quantitative phase (Plano Clark, Creswell, Ivankova, & Green, 2005)? The data were collected and analyzed in a definite sequence, starting with a quantitative phase and then building to a qualitative phase. Ivankova reported that her study emphasized the qualitative phase more than the quantitative phase due to the extensive qualitative data collection and multiple levels of analysis. The two phases were connected in two ways. First, the quantitative results guided participant selection and interview question development for the qualitative phase. Second, the final discussion included an overall interpretation of what was learned across both phases of the study.

The Exploratory Design

Like the explanatory design, the exploratory design is also a two-phase mixed methods design. The exploratory design starts with the collection and analysis of qualitative data to explore a topic and then builds to a second phase in which quantitative data are collected and analyzed (see Figure 18.1d). The second, quantitative phase of the study is designed so that it builds on, or is connected to, the results of the initial qualitative phase. Because this design begins qualitatively, investigators generally place greater emphasis on the qualitative methods.

The exploratory design's overall intent is based on the need to initially explore a topic qualitatively before an adequate quantitative examination of the topic can be undertaken. Therefore, the second, quantitative phase builds on the initial exploratory qualitative results, and the quantitative data are used to measure, generalize, or test the qualitative results. This design is well suited if a researcher needs to develop or modify an instrument because one is not available (Creswell, 1999; Creswell et al., 2004) or to identify the important variables when the variables are unknown. It is also appropriate when a researcher wants to generalize results to different groups (Morse, 1991), to test aspects of an emergent theory (Morgan, 1998), or to explore a phenomenon in depth and measure its prevalence.

The exploratory design's two-phase approach makes it straightforward to implement and report. These features make the exploratory design a good choice for graduate projects and beginning mixed methods researchers. Although this design usually emphasizes the qualitative aspects of the study, the inclusion of a quantitative component can make the study more acceptable to quantitative-biased audiences (Creswell & Plano Clark, 2007).

This design also has a number of challenges. Just like the explanatory design, the exploratory design requires lengthy time for implementation, and researchers need to plan sufficient time to complete both phases. If an instrument is developed as part of this approach, then the researcher must also establish the reliability and validity of the instrument as part of the study. Finally, it can be a challenge to secure IRB approval for this design because the variables and instruments for the second phase will not be known until the first phase is complete. Researchers can describe tentative quantitative measures at the planning stage but should recognize that a change in protocol will need to be filed in the middle of the study.

An Application of the Exploratory Design

Myers and Oetzel (2003) used an exploratory design to study new employees' assimilation into organizational settings. They wanted to measure organizational assimilation within different types of organizational settings, but they reported that no such measure existed. Therefore, they began their study with a qualitative investigation of organizational assimilation. They conducted 13 one-on-one interviews asking participants to describe their assimilation experiences in order to address the research question, What are the dimensions of organizational assimilation? (p. 440). They analyzed the qualitative data using open coding to develop categories and then compared and refined the categories based on the data and what had been previously discussed in the literature. From this analysis, they reported six dimensions of organizational assimilation.

After describing the six dimensions that emerged from the qualitative analysis, Myers and Oetzel (2003) used these findings to develop an organizational assimilation instrument. They developed 61 items that represented the six dimensions and then administered this instrument to 342 employees across a wide range of different industries. They also collected data using two additional measures of constructs that were hypothesized to be related to organizational assimilation (such as job satisfaction). Using the quantitative data, they tested numerous hypotheses related to the different dimensions of organizational assimilation. They concluded that they had developed both a meaningful description of the dimensions of organizational assimilation and a valid means of measuring these dimensions across different types of organizations.

Myers and Oetzel (2003) applied the sequential exploratory design in their study. The data were collected and analyzed in a definite sequence. They needed qualitative data initially to explore participants' perceptions of organizational assimilation, and then they needed quantitative data to measure its dimensions. The mixing of the quantitative and qualitative data occurred in the development of the instrument. The researchers used the perceptions of the participants to design the instrument by identifying items and scales that represent the qualitative findings. Although not stated explicitly, this study appeared to place more emphasis on the initial qualitative phase that guided the direction of the entire study. The researchers connected the quantitative and qualitative phases by developing a quantitative instrument based on their qualitative findings, which was then implemented in the quantitative phase. Finally, the discussion section of the study included an overall interpretation of what was learned across both phases.

Important Features of the Major Mixed Methods Designs

By reflecting on the sample studies and examining the diagrams contained in Figure 18.1, we can identify important differences among the four major mixed methods designs. These differences relate to the mixed methods design features of weighting, timing, and mixing (Creswell & Plano Clark, 2007).

Equal or Unequal Weighting

Weighting refers to the relative emphasis or priority of the quantitative and qualitative methods within a mixed methods design (Morgan, 1998; Morse, 1991). Mixed methods designs can utilize an equal weighting when both methods are equally important for addressing the research questions. This is often the case in triangulation designs. Weighting can also be unequal. Unequal weighting occurs when one approach (quantitative or qualitative) is emphasized over the other approach (qualitative or quantitative) within the study. The embedded, explanatory, and exploratory designs usually have unequal weights. For researchers new to mixed methods research, we recommend using an unequal weighting. By emphasizing one method, the study may be more logistically manageable than if equal weight were given to both. Equal weighting implies that the researcher implements and reports both approaches with a relatively equal level of sophistication and thoroughness, but when unequal weighting is used, then the secondary method is often implemented at a less thorough and sophisticated level than the primary method.

Concurrent or Sequential Timing

Timing refers to the temporal relationship between the implementation of the quantitative and the qualitative methods (Greene et al., 1989). Timing usually relates to the times at which the different types of data are collected, but more important, it describes the times at which the different types of data are used (i.e., analyzed and interpreted) within the study (Morgan, 1998). As illustrated in the preceding example studies, there are two options for timing: concurrent and sequential. Concurrent timing implies that the quantitative and qualitative data are both collected and analyzed at roughly the same time and during the same phase of the research. Concurrent timing occurs in triangulation designs and some embedded designs. Sequential timing implies that there is a definite sequence to the two methods, with one type (quantitative or qualitative) being collected, analyzed, and interpreted before the other type (quantitative or qualitative). Sequential timing means that the study is implemented in two phases, and it is found in explanatory designs (quantitative first, then qualitative), exploratory designs (qualitative first, then quantitative), and some embedded designs (order depends on the study). Studies using concurrent timing are efficient because both types of data are collected and analyzed at the same time, but they require much effort and expertise. Therefore, we recommend that beginning mixed methods researchers consider using sequential timing. Although this approach may take more time to implement because of the two phases, the researcher will have to work with only one type of data at a time.

Mixing by Merging, Embedding, or Connecting the Data

Researchers implementing a mixed methods approach also must decide how they will mix the two types of data. Mixing is the explicit relating (or combining or integrating) of the two datasets, and it is an essential component of any mixed methods design. Mixed methods researchers can choose from three overall approaches to mixing: merging the data, embedding the data, or connecting the data (Creswell & Plano Clark, 2007).

Researchers attempt to merge their quantitative and qualitative data in triangulation designs by bringing the two data types together during analysis and/or interpretation. This is often done by simply comparing and contrasting the quantitative results with the qualitative findings to see whether the two datasets converge and agree with each other. The results can also be interpreted to see whether one set of findings corroborates the other set. Sometimes researchers take steps during the analysis to facilitate the merging of the two datasets. This can be accomplished by transforming one data set into data of the other type (Caracelli & Greene, 1993). Data transformation most often occurs when a researcher transforms qualitative results (such as themes) into quantitative counts (such as how frequently the theme occurred). The transformed data can then be related to the original quantitative data.

When using an embedded design, researchers mix the data by embedding data of one type within a design of the other type (Creswell & Plano Clark, 2007). Most often, qualitative data are embedded within a quantitative design, such as an experiment or correlational study, but researchers can also embed quantitative data within qualitative designs, for instance, incorporating descriptive statistics within a case study design. In either case, the embedded data serve to address a secondary purpose within the larger study. The researchers generally interpret these secondary findings within the context of the larger method and dataset.

The third type of mixing is used in explanatory and exploratory designs. In these designs, researchers connect an initial data collection and analysis (quantitative or qualitative) with a subsequent data collection and analysis (qualitative or quantitative). The mixing occurs in the connections made between the two datasets. For example, in an explanatory design, the researcher may identify specific quantitative results of interest and then collect qualitative data in an attempt to explain the quantitative results. The connection occurs in deciding which results need to be followed up on and/or in selecting participants to provide the needed information. In an exploratory design, the researcher builds from qualitative findings to collecting and analyzing quantitative data in order to quantitatively measure the initial findings. In this approach, the connection can occur by developing an instrument based on the qualitative findings and/or specifying variables or relationships to be measured. In addition, researchers using these sequential approaches bring the results together in their discussion and interpretations.

Researchers should utilize the approach to mixing that best matches their research problem and overall design choice. To ensure that the mixing is explicit and clear, we recommend that researchers state a mixed methods research question, in addition to quantitative and qualitative questions, within their mixed methods studies. These mixed methods questions foreshadow and direct the mixing that will occur within the selected design. For example, consider the following general questions that could be posed for a mixed methods study using each of the four designs:

Triangulation design

- Quantitative: What variables are significantly related?
- Qualitative: What themes emerge about the central phenomenon?
- Mixed methods: To what extent do the qualitative findings corroborate the quantitative results?

Embedded design

- Quantitative: Did the groups score significantly differently on the outcome measures?
- Qualitative: What were participants' experiences with the treatment?
- Mixed: How do the qualitative findings enhance the interpretation of the experimental outcomes?

Explanatory design

- Quantitative: Which variables are significant predictors?
- Qualitative: What are individuals' perceptions about the predicting variables?
- Mixed: How do the qualitative findings explain the quantitative results?

Exploratory design

- Qualitative: What dimensions describe the central phenomenon?
- Quantitative: What is the prevalence of the stated dimensions?
- Mixed: To what extent do the qualitative findings generalize to a specified population?

Examples of mixed methods research questions also appear in Table 18.1. This table summarizes the research objectives and sample studies provided earlier in this chapter. In addition, we have written a mixed methods question for each of these studies. These questions were not stated within the articles. However, we have written these questions to match the ways the authors reported mixing their quantitative and qualitative data. A number of considerations went into our development of the questions that appear in Table 18.1. We considered the intent for collecting both types of data, the way the data were used and mixed, and the overall design. In addition, we wanted the questions to be practical so they could help guide the mixing of two datasets within a study using a similar approach.

The need to write a mixed methods research question is only one of the challenges that researchers face when choosing to use a mixed methods design. Researchers need to be aware of the additional challenges associated with mixed methods designs so that they can assess whether this approach is feasible and, if it is, anticipate and overcome these issues. The following section provides an overview of key challenges, along with advice for addressing them.

TABLE 18.1. Examples of Suggested Mixed Methods Research Questions to Guide the Mixing of Quantitative and Qualitative Data to Meet Study Objectives

Design/objective	Example study	Suggested mixed methods research question
Triangulation design		
• Compare quantitative and qualitative results	Yauch & Steudel (2003)	To what extent do the quantitative results and qualitative findings agree?
• Validate quantitative data	Morrell (2005)	How do the qualitative responses validate the quantitative results?
Embedded design		
• Enhance an experimental design	Donovan et al. (2002)	How do the qualitative findings lead to improved recruitment practices?
	Bachay (1998)	How do the qualitative themes enhance the interpretation of the experimental results?
• Explain how mechanisms work within a correlational design	Harrison (2005)	How do the qualitative themes explain the relationships among the quantitative predictor and criterion variables?
Explanatory design		
• Explain quantitative results	Aldridge, Fraser, & Huang (1999)	How do the qualitative findings explain the anomalous quantitative results?
• Select participants for in-depth study	May & Etkina (2002)	How do high and low gainers differ among their perceptions of learning practices?
Exploratory design		
• Develop a suitable instrument	Mak & Marshall (2004)	Do the items based on the qualitative findings have construct validity?
• Generalize qualitative findings	Kretsedemas (2003)	How do the quantitative results refine the qualitatively generated theory?

What Are the Challenges Associated with Conducting Mixed Methods Research?

Although mixed methods research may be the best approach to many research questions, it is a challenging design because of the complexity inherent in collecting, analyzing, mixing, and interpreting quantitative and qualitative data. Mixed methods researchers must consider questions about the worldview(s) that provide the foundation for their research. In addition, they need to make sure they have sufficient skills, resources, and support to carry out these designs in a rigorous fashion.

Identifying a Worldview for Mixed Methods Research

The early years of mixed methods research were full of contention and debate about whether this approach to research was even possible (e.g., see Tashakkori & Teddlie, 1998). The essence of this debate was whether or not quantitative and qualitative methods could be combined when they each were based on different worldviews (sets of beliefs and assumptions that guide approaches to research). Scholars argued that quantitative methods arise from postpositivism and that qualitative methods arise from constructivism and therefore that these two methods are incompatible.

Today there are still some researchers who maintain that worldviews cannot be mixed and therefore that researchers cannot conduct mixed methods research (see, e.g., Denzin & Lincoln, 2005; Sale, Lohfeld, & Brazil, 2002). However, many researchers do not share this perspective and have adopted other stances on the question of worldviews and mixed methods research. At this time, the most commonly discussed stance on worldviews in the mixed methods literature says that mixed methods researchers can use the worldview of pragmatism as the foundation for their studies (see Tashakkori & Teddlie, 2003). Another perspective was stated by Greene and Caracelli (1997). They suggest that researchers can use multiple worldviews in a study and that those views should be honored and made explicit. Creswell (2003) agreed that researchers can use multiple worldviews, but he proposed that mixed methods researchers consider the question of worldview in relation to the specific design being applied. For example, an explanatory design may have a quantitative emphasis, and therefore researchers may implement this design using a postpositivist worldview. On the other hand, a triangulation design may use a pragmatic worldview to guide the concurrent collection, analysis, and mixing of quantitative and qualitative data. Therefore, a challenge of using mixed methods research is being familiar with ongoing questions about worldviews and being able to defend the design choice if questions emerge. Mixed methods researchers need to be familiar with these different perspectives so that they can anticipate questions and be able to articulate the stances that they bring to their studies.

The Minimum Skills

In addition to identifying one's worldview, mixed methods researchers also need to consider whether they have the minimum skills to successfully conduct this type of research. Ideally, researchers should have experience with quantitative and qualitative approaches separately before they consider using a design that combines the two. Basic quantitative skills include writing variable-oriented questions; knowing how to locate and administer quantitative instruments; being familiar with quantitative sampling procedures, common statistical tests, and analytical procedures (including statistical software programs such as SPSS or SAS); and understanding issues of validity and reliability. Qualitative skills and experience are also necessary. These skills include writing open-ended research questions that focus on a central phenomenon, being familiar with qualitative purposeful sampling procedures, having experience with coding and thematic development analytical procedures (including using qualitative data analysis software programs such as ATLAS.ti, MAXqda, or NVivo), and understanding issues of validation and reflexivity. There are many introductory research textbooks that discuss these important ideas (see, e.g., Creswell, 2005; Morse & Richards, 2002; Shadish, Cook, & Campbell, 2002).

Researchers who have skills only in either quantitative or qualitative approaches can still conduct mixed methods studies as part of a research team. A team approach can strengthen the study because it can help ensure that the necessary expertise is available for the study, to which team members can bring expertise in quantitative, qualitative, and mixed methods procedures. Being part of a team also facilitates a learning environment so that researchers can learn from those team members who are proficient in a particular area. However, mixed methods team research can also be a challenge when team members represent quantitative and qualitative specializations but have little understanding and appreciation of the other approach. In such cases, considerable effort may be needed to foster effective collaboration among team members.

Need for Sufficient Resources

Even when researchers have the minimum skills, they find that mixed methods studies take a great deal of effort to design and conduct. These designs require time to implement and to report. This is especially true of sequential designs that are implemented in two separate phases. In addition, researchers should keep in mind that qualitative data collection and analysis typically require more time than is needed for quantitative data, and they should plan accordingly within their studies. Although concurrent designs are more efficient due to their one-phase approach, they also require greater resources for data collection and analysis, because both types of data must be addressed at the same time. Therefore, concurrent designs are often more manageable when conducted by a research team instead of by an individual researcher.

Mixed methods research studies also require time to obtain necessary permissions, such as from research sites and from university IRBs. Although permissions are an essential piece of all research, they require careful consideration and planning in mixed methods studies. Because this approach to research is relatively new, it may need to be explained to stakeholders and reviewers. In addition, obtaining IRB approvals for sequential designs can be a particular challenge because the procedures for the second phase will not be set until the first phase is complete. In such cases, we recommend that researchers complete their applications for approvals by stating their tentative plans for both phases and then apply for a change in protocol or an addendum as the procedures become finalized.

Finally, mixed methods studies may also require more funding than studies using a single method. The increased costs may arise from collecting multiple types of data, using more resources (such as separate software for quantitative and qualitative analyses), and needing more highly trained assistants (who are familiar with both approaches).

Gaining Support for This Approach

Lastly, researchers implementing a mixed methods approach need to also secure support at various levels, including support from advisors and graduate committees, from funding agencies, and from reviewers and editors, when it comes time to publish. Openness to and acceptance of mixed methods approaches varies by discipline and even within areas in specific disciplines (Plano Clark, 2005). Overall, we have found that mixed methods research can be supported at all of these levels as long as it is rigorous and communicated in a clear and concise manner. Researchers can make a strong case for a mixed methods approach by using a rigorous design (such as one of the four discussed in this chapter), having detailed procedures for data collection and analysis, and offering a solid justification for both types of data being collected. Graduate students in particular may need to educate their committee members about mixed methods. We recommend that students locate good examples of mixed methods research from their fields of study (such as the studies cited in this chapter) and, with their advisor's support, bring these examples to their committee meetings and review the overall designs and procedures used in those studies with their committee members.

Mixed methods researchers also find it a challenge to describe clearly their procedures and reasons for using a mixed methods approach when writing proposals and journal articles. This is particularly an issue because these descriptions must fit within the traditional page limits (e.g., 30 pages). We recommend that researchers include a visual diagram (such as those pictured in Figure 18.1) in their proposals and manuscripts to give an overview of the design. These figures should include such details as the procedures used for collecting, analyzing, and mixing the data, the products produced at each step, and an overall timeline. Such a diagram is very helpful for graduate students and advisors proposing a mixed methods thesis or dissertation.

How to Start Planning a Mixed Methods Study

This chapter has presented a broad overview of mixed methods research, including how to define it, its overall value, research objectives that are a good match for it, the major designs, and the challenges associated with using this research approach. At this point, many readers may be convinced that they want to use mixed methods research to address their research problems, but they are unsure how to begin. Therefore, we offer the following series of steps as a way for researchers who are new to mixed methods to begin to plan a mixed methods study.

1. *Identify a research problem.* Studies begin by identifying a research problem that needs to be addressed. It is also helpful to write a title for the study at this initial stage. Although this title is tentative and will probably change, it helps to focus the study even at this early step.

2. *Evaluate initial considerations.* Initial considerations in planning a mixed methods study include one's worldview stance and whether the necessary skills, resources, and support are available. Most important, a researcher needs to evaluate whether the research problem is best suited to be addressed by a mixed methods design.

3. *State at least one quantitative and one qualitative research question.* Consider what questions you want answered in your study and state at least one quantitative research question and one qualitative research question.

4. *Identify the types of quantitative and qualitative data that will be collected.* We find that researchers new to mixed methods find it easier to consider the types of data that will be collected early in their planning process. List at least one form of each type of data that could help address your stated research questions.

5. *Identify the reason and/or objective for collecting both types of data.* Consider the reasons and objectives for collecting both quantitative and qualitative data presented in this chapter. Identify the reason and objective that best matches your overall research problem and questions. Although several reasons may seem appealing, select the one that is most relevant to your research goals.

6. *Determine how the data will be analyzed.* Specify procedures for analyzing both the quantitative and the qualitative data. Use rigorous procedures typically associated with each of the data types.

7. *Choose a mixed methods design type.* Reflect on the research problem, research questions, and reason for collecting both types of data that have been specified. Choose the mixed methods design type that best matches these considerations.

8. *Specify the timing, weighting, and mixing.* In addition to the selection of a major design type, attention should be paid to decisions about the timing, weighting, and mixing that will occur during the study. Decide whether the two data types will be used concurrently or sequentially, whether they will have equal or unequal weight in addressing the problem, and whether they will be merged together, connected, or embedded (one within the other).

9. *Write a mixed methods research question.* Now that you have thought through the design elements, consider the stated research goals, procedures for data collection and analysis, and mixed methods design. Write a mixed methods research question that will direct how the quantitative and qualitative data will be mixed. Examine the questions in Table 18.1 for examples.

10. *Draw a visual diagram of your procedures.* Draw a visual diagram that conveys the flow of activities as planned in your mixed methods study. This diagram should depict

when both types of data will be collected, analyzed, and interpreted. It can also indicate expected procedures and products. See Ivankova, Creswell, and Stick (2006) for additional advice for creating diagrams of mixed methods studies.

Although these steps are listed here in a logical order, like all research, the steps are interrelated and often iterative. Early decisions (such as the research questions) should continue to be refined as the design is further developed and implemented. Most important, the researcher must identify a research problem that calls for using a mixed methods design and pay close attention to designing rigorous quantitative and qualitative components, as well as considering how these components will be mixed and related. By completing these 10 steps, a researcher will have a clear plan for his or her mixed methods study that can be communicated, explained, and justified. From these initial steps, the researcher can continue to refine the questions, procedures, and design through the development of a proposal for the study.

Concluding Comments

Mixed methods designs are well suited to addressing a wide range of research objectives and should be matched to fit the specific questions and objects of the study. Triangulation designs are appropriate to use when a research problem requires the convergence of quantitative and qualitative results, the validation of quantitative survey data, the relating of qualitative findings to quantitative results, and/or the examination of multiple levels within a system. If a researcher needs to enhance an experiment or explain mechanisms at work within a correlational design, then an embedded design should be selected. Explanatory designs are used when a researcher needs to explain quantitative results with qualitative data or to use quantitative results to select participants for qualitative study. Finally, the exploratory design is the best choice if an instrument needs to be developed as part of the study or if there is a need to quantitatively generalize or test qualitative findings.

Whichever design is selected for a study, researchers need to carefully consider the relative priority of the quantitative and qualitative methods, the timing of the methods, and how the methods will be mixed. They also need to justify the reasons that a mixed methods approach is needed for their research problem. Consideration must also be given to ensure that researchers have sufficient skills, resources, and support to successfully plan, carry out, and report their mixed methods design.

Mixed methods research is a research approach that has emerged within the social, behavioral, and health sciences as a major methodological approach alongside quantitative and qualitative research (Tashakkori & Teddlie, 2003). Mixed methods designs are simply the best approach for addressing many of the research questions of interest today that seek to both understand and generalize findings. When well designed, this approach of mixing quantitative and qualitative methods brings value to a research effort above and beyond that accomplished by using a single method alone.

Note

1. Although mixed methods approaches can also be applied across multiple studies within a sustained research program, this discussion focuses on the use of mixed methods approaches within single studies.

References

Aldridge, J. M., Fraser, B. J., & Huang, T. I. (1999). Investigating classroom environments in Taiwan and Australia with multiple research methods. *Journal of Educational Research, 93*(1), 48–62.

Bachay, J. (1998). Ethnic identity development and urban Haitian adolescents. *Journal of Multicultural Counseling and Development, 26*(2), 96–109.

Brewer, J., & Hunter, A. (1989). *Multimethod research: A synthesis of styles.* Newbury Park, CA: Sage.

Campbell, D. T., & Fiske, D. W. (1959). Convergent and discriminant validation by the multitrait-multimethod matrix. *Psychological Bulletin, 56,* 81-105.

Caracelli, V. J., & Greene, J. C. (1993). Data analysis strategies for mixed-method evaluation designs. *Educational Evaluation and Policy Analysis, 15*(2), 195-207.

Caracelli, V. J., & Greene, J. C. (1997). Crafting mixed-method evaluation designs. In J. C. Greene & V. J. Caracelli (Eds.), *Advances in mixed-method evaluation: The challenges and benefits of integrating diverse paradigms* (pp. 19-32). San Francisco: Jossey-Bass.

Creswell, J. W. (1999). Mixed-method research: Introduction and application. In G. J. Cizek (Ed.), *Handbook of educational policy* (pp. 455-472). San Diego, CA: Academic Press.

Creswell, J. W. (2003). *Research design: Qualitative, quantitative, and mixed methods approaches* (2nd ed.). Thousand Oaks, CA: Sage.

Creswell, J. W. (2005). *Educational research: Planning, conducting, and evaluating quantitative and qualitative research* (2nd ed.). Upper Saddle River, NJ: Pearson Education.

Creswell, J. W., Fetters, M. D., & Ivankova, N. V. (2004). Designing a mixed methods study in primary care. *Annals of Family Medicine, 2*(1), 7-12.

Creswell, J. W., Fetters, M. D., & Plano Clark, V. L. (2005, April). *Nesting qualitative data in health sciences intervention trials: A mixed methods application.* Paper presented at the meeting of the American Educational Research Association, Montreal, Quebec, Canada.

Creswell, J. W., & Plano Clark, V. L. (2007). *Designing and conducting mixed methods research.* Thousand Oaks, CA: Sage.

Creswell, J. W., Plano Clark, V. L., Gutmann, M., & Hanson, W. (2003). Advanced mixed methods research designs. In A. Tashakkori & C. Teddlie (Eds.), *Handbook of mixed methods in social and behavioral research* (pp. 209-240). Thousand Oaks, CA: Sage.

Denzin, N. K., & Lincoln, Y. S. (Eds.). (2005). *Handbook of qualitative research* (3rd ed.). Thousand Oaks, CA: Sage.

Donovan, J., Mills, N., Smith, M., Brindle, L., Jacoby, A., Peters, T., et al. (2002). Improving design and conduct of randomised trials by embedding them in qualitative research: ProtecT (prostate testing for cancer and treatment) study. *British Medical Journal, 325,* 766-769.

Greene, J. C., & Caracelli, V. J. (Eds.). (1997). *Advances in mixed-method evaluation: The challenges and benefits of integrating diverse paradigms* (New Directions for Evaluation, 74). San Francisco: Jossey-Bass.

Greene, J. C., Caracelli, V. J., & Graham, W. F. (1989). Toward a conceptual framework for mixed-method evaluation designs. *Educational Evaluation and Policy Analysis, 11*(3), 255-274.

Hanson, W. E., Creswell, J. W., Plano Clark, V. L., Petska, K. P., & Creswell, J. D. (2005). Mixed methods research designs in counseling psychology. *Journal of Counseling Psychology, 52*(2) 224-235.

Harrison, A. (2005). *Correlates of positive relationship-building in a teacher education mentoring program.* Unpublished doctoral dissertation proposal, University of Nebraska, Lincoln.

Ivankova, N. V. (2004). Students' persistence in the University of Nebraska-Lincoln distributed doctoral program in educational leadership in higher education: A mixed methods study (Doctoral dissertation, University of Nebraska-Lincoln, 2004). *Dissertation Abstracts International, 65,* 04A.

Ivankova, N. V., Creswell, J. W., & Stick, S. (2006). Using mixed methods sequential explanatory design: From theory to practice. *Field Methods, 18*(1), 3-20.

Jenkins, J. E. (2001). Rural adolescent perceptions of alcohol and other drug resistance. *Child Study Journal, 31*(4), 211-224.

Jick, T. D. (1979). Mixing qualitative and quantitative methods: Triangulation in action. *Administrative Science Quarterly, 24,* 602-611.

Johnson, R. B., & Onwuegbuzie, A. J. (2004). Mixed methods research: A research paradigm whose time has come. *Educational Researcher, 33*(7), 14-26.

Kretsedemas, P. (2003). Immigrant households and hardships after welfare reform: A case study of the Miami-Dade Haitian community. *International Journal of Social Welfare, 12,* 314-325.

Mak, L., & Marshall, S. K. (2004). Perceived mattering in young adults' romantic relationships. *Journal of Social and Personal Relationships, 24*(4), 469-486.

May, D. B., & Etkina, E. (2002). College physics students' epistemological self-reflection and its relationship to conceptual learning. *American Journal of Physics, 70*(12), 1249-1258.

Mertens, D. M. (2005). *Research and evaluation in education and psychology: Integrating diversity with quantitative, qualitative, and mixed methods* (2nd ed.). Thousand Oaks, CA: Sage.

Morgan, D. L. (1998). Practical strategies for combining qualitative and quantitative methods: Applications to health research. *Qualitative Health Research, 8*(3), 362-376.

Morrell, K. (2005). Towards a typology of nursing turnover: The role of shocks in nurses' decisions to leave. *Journal of Advanced Nursing, 49*(3), 315-322.

Morse, J. M. (1991). Approaches to qualitative-quantitative methodological triangulation. *Nursing Research, 40,* 120-123.

Morse, J. M., & Richards, L. (2002). *Read me first: For a user's guide to qualitative methods.* Thousand Oaks, CA: Sage.

Myers, K. K., & Oetzel, J. G. (2003). Exploring the dimensions of organizational assimilation: Creating and validating a measure. *Communication Quarterly, 51*(4), 438–457.

Patton, M. Q. (1990). *Qualitative evaluation and research methods* (2nd ed.). Thousand Oaks, CA: Sage.

Plano Clark, V. L. (2005). Cross-disciplinary analysis of the use of mixed methods in physics education research, counseling psychology, and primary care (Doctoral dissertation, University of Nebraska, Lincoln, 2005). *Dissertation Abstracts International, 66,* 02A.

Plano Clark, V. L., Creswell, J. W., Ivankova, N. V., & Green, D. O. (2005, April). *Designing mixed methods studies: An interactive symposium.* Symposium presented at the meeting of the American Educational Research Association, Montreal, Quebec, Canada.

Rogers, A., Day, J., Randall, F., & Bentall, R. P. (2003). Patients' understanding and participation in a trial designed to improve the management of antipsychotic medication. *Social Psychiatry and Psychiatric Epidemiology, 38,* 720–727.

Sale, J. E., Lohfeld, L. H., & Brazil, K. (2002). Revisiting the quantitative-qualitative debate: Implications of mixed-methods research. *Quality and Quantity, 36,* 43–53.

Sandelowski, M. (1996). Using qualitative methods in intervention studies. *Research in Nursing and Health, 19*(4), 359–364.

Shadish, W., Cook, T., & Campbell, D. (2002). *Experimental and quasi-experimental designs for generalized causal inference.* Boston: Houghton Mifflin.

Tashakkori, A., & Teddlie, C. (1998). *Mixed methodology: Combining qualitative and quantitative approaches.* Thousand Oaks, CA: Sage.

Tashakkori, A., & Teddlie, C. (Eds.). (2003). *Handbook of mixed methods in social and behavioral research.* Thousand Oaks, CA: Sage.

Yauch, C. A., & Steudel, H. J. (2003). Complementary use of qualitative and quantitative cultural assessment methods. *Organizational Research Methods, 6*(4), 465–481.

CHAPTER 19

Emergent Techniques in the Gathering and Analysis of Mixed Methods Data

Charles Teddlie
Abbas Tashakkori
Burke Johnson

General Considerations Regarding Mixed Methods

There has been a great deal of interest in mixed methods (MM) research over the past decade, as evidenced by a rapidly growing body of literature (e.g., Creswell, 2003; Greene & Caracelli, 1997; Johnson & Onwuegbuzie, 2004; Tashakkori & Teddlie, 1998, 2003a). One result of the growing interest in this type of research is the emergence of a number of innovative techniques for answering complex research questions. The purpose of this chapter is to present three families of these new techniques and situate them within the MM research area on a number of salient dimensions. The three techniques are Internet-based iterative sequential MM designs, participatory MM designs, and group-case MM designs.

In order to do this, we first briefly discuss some differences in opinion between mixed methodologists and those individuals who have been called "purists," either from the qualitative (Qual) or quantitative (Quan) points of view. We then introduce the methods-strands matrix (Teddlie & Tashakkori, 2006), which presents a typology of research designs used in the behavioral and social sciences with an emphasis on those employing MM. This matrix helps structure the discussions of the emergent MM techniques discussed in this chapter and provides a framework for comparing them.

Paradigmatic Considerations Regarding MM

Before introducing the methods-strands matrix, we must first briefly discuss the three major "communities" of researchers operating in the social and behavioral sciences: quantitatively oriented researchers primarily working within the postpositivist paradigm and principally interested in numerical data and analyses; qualitatively oriented researchers primarily working within the constructivist paradigm[1] and principally interested in narrative (or text) data and analysis[2]; and mixed methodologists working primarily within the pragmatist paradigm and interested in both narrative and numerical data and their analyses. We subscribe to the definition of MM in the "Call for Papers of the *Journal of Mixed Methods Research*" (Sage Publications), which observes: "Mixed method research is defined as research in which the investigator collects and analyzes data, integrates the findings, and draws inferences using both qualitative and quantitative approaches or methods in a single study or program of inquiry."

There was a period (circa 1975–1995) of widespread disagreement between the Quans and Quals, which has been labeled the "paradigm wars" or "paradigms debate" (e.g., Gage, 1989). These disagreements were a product of the Quals' intense criticisms of problematic issues associated with what they called the "received tradition" of the positivist–postpositivist paradigm (e.g., the belief that there is a single, "fragmentable"[3] reality; the possibility of conducting "objective" research). In its place, many Quals posited constructivism (and its variants, such as interpretivism) as a better theoretical perspective for conducting research. Furthermore, authors (e.g., Guba & Lincoln, 1994; Lincoln & Guba, 1985) set up paradigm contrast tables including philosophical issues such as ontology, epistemology, axiology, the possibility of generalizations, the possibility of causal linkages, and so forth. These contrast tables presented fundamental dichotomous differences between paradigms on these basic philosophical issues, thereby indicating that the paradigms were not compatible with one another.

On the other hand, we believe that Qual and Quan approaches to research are not dichotomous and discrete. Every component or aspect of a study (e.g., research questions, data, data collection and analysis techniques, inferences, recommendations, etc.) is on a continuum of Qual–Quan approaches. As a result, studies differ in their degree of subjectivity, cultural relativity, value-ladedness, emic–etic perspective, and so forth. Figure 19.1 presents this continuum.

A major component of the paradigm wars was the incompatibility thesis, which stated that it was inappropriate to mix Qual and Quan methods due to fundamental differences in the paradigms underlying those methods. MM researchers countered this position with the compatibility thesis, which is exemplified by the following quote:

> However, the pragmatism of employing multiple research methods to study the same gen-

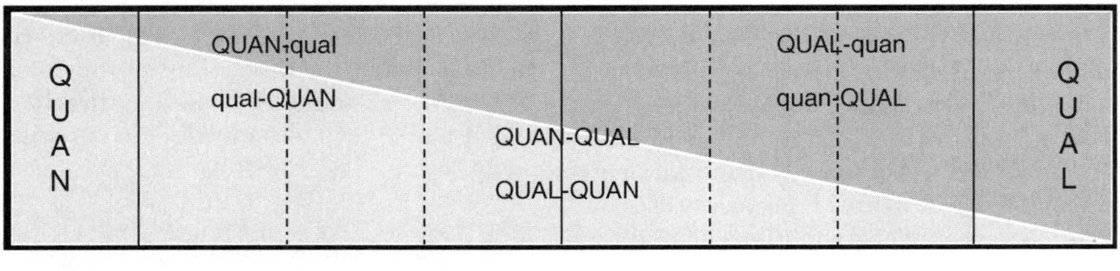

FIGURE 19.1. MM as a continuum of Qual and Quan integration. Used with permission of Tashakkori (2006).

> eral problem by posing different specific questions has some pragmatic implications for social theory. Rather than being wed to a particular theoretical style . . . and its most compatible method, one might instead combine methods that would encourage or even require integration of different theoretical perspectives to interpret the data. (Brewer & Hunter, 1989, p. 74)

The paradigms debate waned considerably in the mid-1990s and early 21st century (e.g., Patton, 2002), largely because "most researchers had become bored with philosophical discussions and were more interested in getting on with the task of doing their research" (Smith, 1996, pp. 162–163). Additionally, MM researchers were actively interested in reconciliation among the three communities, as the integration of different methods is a hallmark of the MM orientation. MM provided a justification and a place where Quan and Qual methods and approaches could be used together.

Despite this overall trend toward détente in the paradigms debate, the gap between the methodological "left" and "right" in educational research has widened recently in the United States. For instance, the installation of the Bush–Cheney administration in 2001 resulted in a small-scale reenactment of some aspects of the paradigms debate due to the establishment of a distinctly postpositivist Quan orientation in the United States Department of Education. Manifestations of that orientation include the passage of the No Child Left Behind Act (NCLB), which included a detailed definition of "scientifically based research" (SBR) and required federal grantees to expend their research funds on "evidence-based strategies" (e.g., Feuer, Towne, & Shavelson, 2002).

SBR emphasizes the utilization of randomized controlled trials or experiments (e.g., Eisenhart & Towne, 2003; Slavin, 2002, 2003). Experimentation is now considered by the Quan purists to be the "gold standard" for educational research in the United States, and there are "standard" texts that constitute the core logic for the movement (e.g., Boruch, 1997, 2002; Campbell & Stanley, 1966; Cook, 2002; Cook & Campbell, 1979; Shadish, Cook, & Campbell, 2002). SBR based on NCLB emphasizes experiments using random assignment to condition (or quasi-experiments where necessary), Quan methods, numerical data analysis, internal validity, summative evaluations of programs aimed at determining overall causal relations, and time- and context- free generalizations.

On the other side of the debate, Qual scholars continue to argue for the preeminence of their philosophical position and methods (e.g., Denzin & Lincoln, 2005a). The emergence of SBR and experimentation as the "gold standard" for educational research has led to predictable (and viable) charges of "scientism" from numerous critics who value Qual methods (e.g., Howe, 2004; Lather, 2004; Maxwell, 2004).

A new twist to these commentaries involves criticisms of the MM orientation from some scholars working within the Qual tradition (e.g., Denzin & Lincoln, 2005b; Howe, 2004). These assertions have been addressed elsewhere several times (e.g., Creswell, Shope, Plano Clark, & Green, 2006; Johnson & Onwuegbuzie, 2004; Tashakkori & Teddlie, 1998, 2003a). A synopsis of the assertions made by Denzin and Lincoln (2005b) and our responses is provided in the following list. We repeat these assertions in this chapter to alert readers to the positions that have been taken by some of the Qual purists; further discussion of these issues is beyond the scope of this chapter. In the following list, Denzin and Lincoln's (2005b, pp. 9–10) assertions regarding MM research are presented first, followed by the responses from the MM community:

- Denzin and Lincoln assertion: MM is a direct descendant of "classical experimentalism."
- MM community response: On the con-

trary, MM grew out of both the Qual and Quan traditions from applied research fields such as evaluation and education.

- Denzin and Lincoln assertion: MM presumes a "methodological hierarchy," with Quan methods at the top and Qual methods in a largely auxiliary role.
- MM community response: On the contrary, Qual and Quan methods have been given equal priority in MM since the earliest writing in the field (e.g., Brewer & Hunter, 1989; Greene, Caracelli, & Graham, 1989; Morse, 1991).
- Denzin and Lincoln assertion: MM divides inquiry into "dichotomous categories" (e.g., exploration vs. confirmation), with Qual work assigned to one category and Quan research to the other.
- MM community response: As indicated in Figure 19.1, many MM scholars refer to *continua* between different dimensions of Qual and Quan work, not dichotomies (e.g., Tashakkori & Teddlie, 2003a; Teddlie, 2005).
- Denzin and Lincoln assertion: MM "excludes stakeholders from dialogue and active participation in the research process."
- MM community response: On the contrary, MM researchers welcome the participation of stakeholders in the research process, as discussed in numerous MM studies (see, e.g., Bamberger, 1998; Mertens, 2005; Rao & Woolcock, 2004).
- Denzin and Lincoln assertion: The MM movement takes Qual methods out of their "natural home," which is within the critical, interpretive framework.
- MM community response: It is difficult for us to understand what a "natural home" for any research method is; instead, the MM perspective is that multiple frameworks or paradigms can be associated with any given method, so to claim that a method has a "natural home" is illogical from the MM point of view.

Types of MM Designs

Various scholars have created typologies of MM designs (e.g., Creswell, 2003; Creswell & Plano-Clark, 2006; Greene et al., 1989; Greene & Caracelli, 1997; Johnson & Onwuegbuzie, 2004; Morgan, 1998; Morse, 1991, 2003; Tashakkori & Teddlie, 1998, 2003a). Design types have been constructed on various dimensions such as priority, purpose, type of data, and type of analysis. Recently, Teddlie and Tashakkori (2006) presented a revised typology, which included a division of MM studies into MM and quasi-MM designs. In a *quasi-mixed design*, two types of data (Qual + Quan) are collected, but no integration of the findings or inferences occurs. In contrast, in true *mixed designs*, integration starts at the research questions and continues throughout until inferences are made based on data analysis and results.

Our typology is based on a 2 × 3 "methods–strands matrix"[4] that is generated by crossing two basic design dimensions:

1. *The type of methods employed in the study (monomethod or MM).* A monomethod design is one in which only the Qual approach (or only the Quan approach) is utilized with regard to type of questions, research methods, data collection and analysis procedures, and/or inferences. MM research was defined earlier in this chapter as involving both the Qual and Quan approaches.
2. *The number of strands of the study (monostrand or multistrands).* A strand of a research design is a complete phase of a study that includes three stages: the conceptualization stage, the experiential stage (methodological/analytical), and the inferential stage (see Tashakkori & Teddlie, 2003b). A monostrand design is a design that employs only a single phase, which encompasses all of the activities from conceptualization through inference. A multistrand design is one that employs more than one phase; there are multiple parts to the study, and each encompasses

all of the activities from conceptualization through inference.[5]

In this classification, MM multistrand designs are classified as concurrent/parallel, sequential, conversion, or fully integrated. In concurrent/parallel designs, the strands of a study occur in a parallel or synchronous manner (e.g., Qual + Quan),[6] whereas in sequential designs they occur in chronological order, with one strand emerging from or building on the other (e.g., Qual → Quan). In a conversion design, one form of data is transformed into another. The process of *quantitizing* involves converting Qual data into numbers that can be statistically analyzed (e.g., Boyatzis, 1998; Miles & Huberman, 1994), whereas the process of *qualitizing* involves transforming Quan data into narrative information that can be analyzed qualitatively (e.g., Tashakkori & Teddlie, 1998).

Although the three groups of methods discussed in the rest of this chapter utilize a combination of these design types, they are all *mixed studies. All three may utilize a form of the fully integrated MM design*. As we describe each in some detail, we also point to elements of their design in the overall typology presented here.

Internet-Based Iterative Sequential MM Designs

Description

Internet-based iterative sequential (IBIS) MM designs have a number of interesting characteristics, which describe the components of the definition of the term (MM, Internet-based, containing more than two strands that are combined iteratively). First, they are good examples of MM designs with *more* than two strands. These designs are seldom described in typologies of MM designs.

Second, the Internet-based nature of the IBIS-MM designs is important, because future research in the social and behavioral sciences will increasingly use that medium, especially in those studies employing questionnaires for data collection. The selection of IBIS-MM designs allows us to discuss the pros and cons of MM data collected over the Internet.

Third, IBIS-MM studies are intriguing from a design perspective in that they employ an iterative, sequential structure that allows for a repeated series of Qual → Quan (or Quan → Qual) data collection and analysis activities. There is a characteristic "ebb and flow" component of these studies in which inductive and deductive logic are used iteratively and in sequence, as described by the "cycle of research," the "chain of reasoning" (e.g., Krathwohl, 2004), the "cycle of scientific methodology" (Tashakkori & Teddlie, 1998), or the "research wheel" (Johnson & Christensen, 2008).

Finally, these studies sometimes employ the Delphi technique, an important technique that has been utilized in the social and behavioral science literature for the past 50 years. Although the original Delphi technique asked experts to forecast events in the future (e.g., Gordon & Helmer, 1964; Heylighen, 2003), it has also been utilized in a variety of studies in which group communication processes (with controlled feedback) are used to generate and refine expert information on a topic of interest (e.g., Wiersma & Jurs, 2005).

IBIS-MM designs cannot be characterized as totally new and different from previous research techniques used in the social and behavioral sciences, but they involve an innovative combination of design, method, and delivery mechanisms that result in a unique MM data collection and analysis technique.

Example

Teddlie, Creemers, Kyriakides, Muijs, and Yu (2006) used the Internet to conduct a multistage MM study, the purpose of which was to develop an internationally generated instrument (the International System for Teacher Observation and Feedback [ISTOF] teacher observation protocol) to measure teacher effectiveness in the classroom. ISTOF activities centered on the collection and analysis of a series of responses to queries delivered via e-mail to an international group of experts. Participants in the queries sequentially generated and rated: (1) *components* of effective teaching, (2) *indicators* of effective teaching, and (3) *items* that could be used to measure the components and indicators of effective teaching.

ISTOF employed the Delphi technique (e.g., Wiersma & Jurs, 2005), in which a group of experts is used to generate information on a topic of interest (i.e., teacher effectiveness) through a series of communications interspersed with controlled feedback. The Delphi technique has been used previously to identify behaviors related to effective teaching. In one such study conducted in Connecticut, experienced teachers responded to two rounds of questionnaires and generated 132 teacher behaviors that reflected effective teaching (Covino & Iwanicki, 1996) in that context.

A major difference between the Delphi technique employed by Covino and Iwanicki (1996) and the IBIS-MM design from ISTOF is that the former included two rounds of data collection, whereas the latter included six rounds. Descriptions of the Delphi technique normally involve two or three rounds of data collection and analysis (e.g., Wiersma & Jurs, 2005; Wilhelm, 2001), whereas IBIS-MM designs use three rounds or more.

There is one other point that should be discussed before we turn to a description of the activities involved in the multistage ISTOF study. Some researchers might argue that ISTOF is not an MM study because it involves a data collection strategy (questionnaires) often associated with Quan methods. We have argued elsewhere (e.g., Johnson & Turner, 2003; Teddlie & Tashakkori, 2008) that major data collection strategies (e.g., questionnaires, interviews, observations) do not "belong" to a particular methodological orientation (Quan, Qual, MM), as these strategies can be used to generate different types of data. For example, questionnaires have been used in numerous research studies to generate Quan (e.g., closed-ended, structured), Qual (e.g., open-ended, emic), or mixed (e.g., both) data.

Table 19.1 summarizes the overall design of the study as derived from recent articles (Teddlie & Reynolds, 2006a, 2006b). ISTOF stages 1–6 employed a sequential Qual → Quan → Qual → Quan → Quan → MM design in which one round of data collection led to a set of data analyses, which then led to another round of data collection, in an integrated, sequential manner. These six stages were conducted by a large group of international experts, whereas three other stages (also described in Table 19.1) involved a smaller group of "experts" with special conceptual and technical skills.

The ISTOF study was indeed mixed throughout, from the conceptualization to the experiential (methodological/analytical) to the inferential stages, as demonstrated by the following points:

- The research questions and data collection techniques were mixed. Qual questions included: What are the components of effective teaching? What are the indicators of effective teaching? These questions were answered using open-ended items. The Quan questions included: How do international experts rate the proposed components and indicators of effective teaching? Which are the most important or appropriate ones according to the international experts? These questions were answered using closed-ended items (rating scales, rank orders).
- Data analyses in ISTOF were mixed. Open-ended questions generated narrative data that were analyzed using the constant comparative method (e.g., Lincoln & Guba,

TABLE 19.1. Stages in the Development of ISTOF Using the IBIS-MM Approach: Sequential Six-Stage Qual–Quan–Qual–Quan–Quan–Mixed Design

Stage	Date	Activity	Methodological orientation
Preliminary stage	January–September 2004	Select country coordinators, country team members, chairs of committees	Not applicable
Stage 1: 17 countries	October–November 2004	1. Generation of potential *components* of effective teaching 2. Qualitative analysis of narrative data—content analysis	Qual
Stage 2: 17 countries, 257 individual responses	November 2004–February 2005	1. Ranking and 5-point scale rating of potential *components* of effective teaching 2. Quantitative analysis of numeric data—generalizability analysis	Quan
Stage 3: 16 countries	March–April 2005	1. Generation of potential *indicators* of effective teaching 2. Qualitative analysis of narrative data—content analysis	Qual
Stage 4: 19 countries, 213 responses	May–October 2005	1. 5-point scale ranking of potential *indicators* of effective teaching 2. Quantitative analysis of numeric data—generalizability analysis	Quan
Expert panels activity	November 2005–February 2006	Generation of potential *items* to assess effective teaching	Qual
Stage 5: 20 countries	March–April 2006	1. Ranking of potential *items* to assess effective teaching 2. Quantitative analysis of numeric data–generalizability analysis	Quan
Stage 6: 19 countries	May–June 2006	1. Overall 5-point scale rating of first version of teacher observation protocol 2. Rating of items on first version of teacher observation protocol (leave as is, change) 3. Final suggestions for altering items 4. Quantitative and qualitative analyses of numeric and narrative data	Mixed
Expert panels activity	June–July 2006	Generate the final version of the teacher observation protocol	Not applicable

1985). Closed-ended questions generated numerical data that were analyzed statistically through a series of generalizability studies (e.g., Shavelson, Webb, & Rowley, 1989).

- Integration of the Quan and Qual results occurred throughout the process, particularly in the "expert panels" activities that occurred first after stages 3 and 4 and then again after stages 5 and 6. These expert panels were composed of the most experienced and knowledgeable of the teacher effectiveness researchers participating in the study and involved their integrating the large amounts of Quan and Qual data that were generated from previous stages of the study.

During stages 1–6, the chair of the central committee sent out a series of questions (queries 1–6) to the country coordinators, who in turn relayed them to team members. Country coordinators collected all responses, typically via e-mail, and then transmitted those responses back to the central committee.

This IBIS-MM design resulted in the generation of a teacher observation protocol with seven *components* of effective teaching, 21 *indicators* of effective teaching, and 45 specific items to measure those components and indicators. Perhaps the most valuable aspect of this study was that "voices" from 20 different countries were heard and used in its development.

Strengths and Weaknesses

IBIS-MM designs, as exemplified by the ISTOF study, have a number of strengths and weaknesses, some of which are due to the characteristics of Internet research, the features of the Delphi technique, and the iterative nature of sequential designs. The IBIS-MM is a unique design in that it combines aspects of different existing techniques and integrates them in creative manners. It is to be expected that the strengths and weaknesses of the constituent techniques would be reflected in IBIS-MM design.

Strengths of IBIS-MM designs include:

1. IBIS-MM designs provide an excellent opportunity for participants to work with one another in situations in which they cannot meet as a group. This allows for more international research among scholars who would not normally be able to get together at one location for a wide variety of reasons.
2. IBIS-MM designs are created to capitalize on a characteristic "ebb and flow" component in which inductive and deductive logic are used iteratively and in sequence (i.e., the cycle of research). This design type allows research studies to evolve on the basis of the responses of the participants from the previous round. This characteristic of IBIS-MM designs provides a good counterargument to the qualitatively oriented purists (alluded to earlier in this chapter) who insist that MM research presumes a "methodological hierarchy," with Quan methods at the top and Qual methods in a largely auxiliary role.
3. The IBIS-MM design employed in the ISTOF study allows countries and individuals who typically cannot participate in an international study to do so, especially those from less developed or isolated locations. Therefore it allows the "voice" of these countries and individuals from Africa, Asia, and South America to be heard. This is particularly important in areas such as teacher effectiveness research (or educational effectiveness or school effectiveness) which has been dominated by the United States and other Western countries (e.g., the United Kingdom, Netherlands, Australia, Canada). ISTOF included participation from experts in countries such as Argentina, Belarus, Chile, India, Malaysia, and Nigeria, whose points of view were heard on the international stage in teacher effectiveness for the first time. This characteristic of IBIS-MM designs provides a good counterargument to the Qual purists, who insist that MM research "excludes stakeholders from dialogue and active participation in the re-

search process" (Denzin & Lincoln, 2005b, p. 9).

4. IBIS-MM designs can be a cost-efficient method of conducting international research with a moderately large number of participants. Research funds to conduct such international studies are difficult to find; therefore, the use of IBIS-MM designs is among the few ways that this type of international research can be carried out.

5. Turnaround on the Internet is obviously much quicker than through mailed pencil-and-paper surveys. The capacity of the Internet component of IBIS-MM designs is an area needing further exploration.

6. IBIS-MM designs can yield high participation rates, such as that which was recorded in the ISTOF project. The participation rate across all phases of the project was excellent, because the 20 research teams could respond at their convenience. Many teams also utilized the Internet within their own countries to generate responses, instead of physically meeting somewhere.

7. IBIS-MM designs, and other Delphi technique designs, prevent strong personalities from dominating the group with their opinions, as the group does not actually meet physically. Such domination can be a big problem in other research techniques, such as focus groups.

8. An unexpected side effect of the ISTOF study was the increased communication about teacher effectiveness research between team members within the same country. This serendipitously allowed for the further development of research traditions in areas in which they had not existed before.

Weaknesses of IBIS-MM designs include:

1. IBIS-MM designs may take considerable time to conduct due to the turnaround required and the effort required on the part of both the panel members and the researchers. ISTOF is a very good example of this, because the study took 10 months to assemble a team and another 21 months to carry out the six-stage process. Delays caused by one or two people can slow the entire process. For example, delays in the analysis of query #4 data in ISTOF, which were due partially to breakdowns in communication between the central and analysis committees, resulted in a delay of approximately 4 months.

2. Recruiting of participants can be difficult in IBIS-MM designs because of the challenging task of finding experts who meet the multiple necessary inclusion criteria. In the case of ISTOF, for instance, it was necessary that the country coordinators not only be experts but also be capable of assembling a viable team that would likely stay together throughout the project.

3. The success of subsequent rounds of studies using the IBIS-MM design requires that the research team properly analyze the data from the preceding round before setting up the next round of data collection. This is a fluid situation, especially in terms of generating and using the results from the content analyses of the Qual data. Researchers must be willing and able to recognize unexpected trends in the data and act accordingly in planning the next stage of a sequential IBIS-MM study.

4. Research teams using the IBIS-MM designs must be careful not to impose their points of view on the issue under study. This is always a problem, but it can be exacerbated in IBIS-MM designs, which require alternating between Qual and Quan analyses, the results of which lead to the next round of communication. Concerns about imposing one's point of view on the issue under study can be partially dealt with by having research teams composed of members with different points of view.

5. Research teams using IBIS-MM designs must be competent in analyzing both Qual and Quan data. This is the case in all MM studies, but it is exacerbated in cases in which errors in data analysis at one stage can lead to errors in the construction of queries for the next stage.

6. Participant attrition can be a problem in IBIS-MM designs, especially when studies

take almost 2 years and six rounds of data collection, as in the case of ISTOF. The ISTOF research team was fortunate in that the number of countries actively involved stayed at 16–20 throughout the six stages and that approximately 200 participants stayed with the project through to the end.

7. Communication in IBIS-MM designs does not allow face-to-face interactions; therefore, it is up to the researchers to ensure that there is adequate communication at the various stages of the study. Again, this was not a problem with the ISTOF project, which in fact spawned intercountry communication that was unexpected.

Participatory MM Designs

Description

Traditionally, large-scale development projects have been strictly Quan, usually involving survey designs in which data are collected via interviews with a variety of stakeholders. The instruments and protocols for data collection are often very structured, requiring the interviewer to read the questions without variation and to record the responses into prespecified and rigid response options. If prompting is needed, the prompts are predetermined, and the interviewer is required to read them. This strict level of structure is employed in order to ensure that the information about each participant (e.g., consumption patterns, household structure, family dynamics, attitudes and beliefs) is captured in the same way (i.e., based on the same stimuli). Despite their strengths and prevalence, these highly structured data collection procedures also have also been criticized for attempting to "replace [the] human surveyor with an idealized automaton" (Shaffer, 2002, p. 8).

Another issue in many research and evaluation projects that are funded or commissioned by international or transcultural agencies (e.g., projects on poverty analysis, economic development, and rural health) is that the research/evaluation questions, the design/procedures for answering them, and the final inferences that lead to policy decisions are made by individuals who are often outsiders to the context, culture, or social groups under investigation. What often seems to be an urgent need to outsiders is not seen as the most important problem by the participants, and what is perceived to be a solution by an outsider is not perceived to be a remedy by the individuals in need of social services (see, e.g., Bamberger, 1998; Gacitua-Mario & Wodon, 2006).

It is within the context of this insider–outsider distinction (Gacitua-Mario & Wodon, 2006; Johnson & Onwuegbuzie, 2004) that we find promising new methods of research and evaluation. Participatory econometrics (Rao & Woolcock, 2004) is an example of such a methodological innovation, attempting to remove the divide between the policy analysts, program participants, and policymakers. Participatory econometrics enables researchers to augment traditional Quan household, demographic, and needs assessment surveys with the strengths of the Qual methods of poverty assessment and program impact evaluation. Such augmentation occurs at all stages of research and evaluation, from the formulation of research questions to making inferences and providing policy guidelines for social programs.

The innovative aspect of the participatory MM design is in its flexibility in allowing participants (or recipients of the effects/interventions) to be actively involved in formulating questions, collecting and analyzing the data, and interpreting the results. This type of approach is in contrast to traditional large-scale social surveys or similar studies in which the participants are passive sources of information. Although participatory evaluation is not a new concept (see Patton, 2002, pp. 182–185), it has predominantly involved Qual methodology. We focus our coverage here on large-scale MM studies, with the hope of providing a model for many other MM studies.

Examples

To demonstrate this flexibility, we use an example from Rao and Woolcock (2004, p. 175). They summarize various iterations of a project in rural India that started with a question about marriage markets among potters in rural Karnataka but was later transformed to questions about domestic violence and other issues of importance to the lives of the participants:

> An initial interest in marriage markets thus evolved in several different but unanticipated directions, uncovering understudied phenomena that were of signal importance in the lives of the people being studied. Moreover, the subjects of the research, with their participation in PRAs [participatory rural appraisals] and PPAs [participatory poverty assessments], focus-group discussions, and in-depth interviews, played a significant role in shaping how research questions were defined, making an important contribution to the analysis and informing the subsequent econometric work, which tested the generalizability of the qualitative findings, measuring the magnitude of the effects and their causal determinants. (p. 175)

An implicit requirement of this type of approach is that researchers be open to both Qual and Quan questions, data collection and analysis techniques, and inferences. An even more important requirement is having the flexibility and the know-how to integrate insights gleaned from Qual approaches with those from Quan approaches. In short, these studies utilize MM, often involving teams of investigators with complementary research and evaluation skills, with a clear goal of trying to integrate the findings of the Qual and Quan components to generate a better understanding of the phenomena or problems. This type of methodology, and numerous variations of it, is found in many new projects conducted by large-scale organizations, such as the World Bank, the United Nations, and other nongovernmental organizations (NGOs).

Rao and Woolcock (2004, p. 173) have identified several premises that underlie this methodology and its variations (including what they call iterative participatory econometrics, or IPE). Among these premises is the necessity for the researchers to start a project with some general hypotheses and questions but to keep an open mind to the possibility that these hypotheses and questions might need to be changed as a project proceeds. It also necessitates the utilization of both Qual and Quan designs, data collection and analysis techniques, and integration of the results in order to "create an understanding of both measured impact and process" (p. 173). One of the most important requirements of the method is that the participants be actively involved in the formulation of the research questions, modifications of data collection procedures, interpretation of the results, and formulation of possible policy recommendations.

Data collection techniques in such participatory MM designs include "wealth rankings, oral histories, role playing, games, small-group discussions, and drawing village maps" (Rao & Woolcock, 2004, p. 170). Transformative (see Mertens, 2005) variations of the methodology are employed in order to initiate change by promoting dialogue and discourse, rather than simply obtaining information.

For example, a researcher might be able to facilitate socioeconomic and political change in the lives of the disadvantaged by helping "villagers or slum dwellers generate tangible visual diagrams of the processes that lead to deprivation and illness, of the strategies that are used in times of crisis, and of the fluctuation of resource availability and prices across different seasons, thereby helping them to conceive of potentially more effective ways to respond" (Rao & Woolcock, 2004, p. 170).

The grafting of such powerful Qual (participatory, transformative) methods with robust Quan surveys, field experiments, or ex post facto designs provides excellent tools for answering complex and vital research and evaluation questions. Such MM studies can be parallel (the Qual and Quan strands of the study are conducted almost independently), sequential (one strand follows the findings of a previous strand), or fully integrated (the Qual and Quan strands inform each other at multiple points or stages) (see Teddlie & Tashakkori, 2006). Rao and Woolcock (2004) have labeled a variant of what we call a fully integrated design as "iterative participatory econometrics," which is a sequential design in which the researcher regularly returns to the field "to clarify questions and resolve apparent anomalies" (p. 175).

Another example of this method involves an ongoing study reviewed by Rao and Woolcock (2004). The project, titled the Urban Poverty Project 2 (or UPP2), provides funds to poor communities so that they can establish infrastructure projects, with the goal of creating an accountable system of governance in poor urban communities. The following is a summary of various characteristics of the implementation and evaluation of the project:

- Two groups of poor communities were identified (matched) on the basis of "poverty scores." One group was identified as the UPP2 (intervention) group and the other as the comparison group. A survey was conducted in a random sample of these communities.
- Fieldwork was conducted by an interdisciplinary team of economists, urban planners, and social anthropologists for 2 or 3 days in each of the eight communities. The goal was to understand the program and plan the next steps of the methodology. The visits led to identification of questions, as well as previously unforeseen issues, such as the importance of key individuals and local religious organizations and the importance of customs and traditions in affecting the success or failure of a project.
- Following the fieldwork, a detailed structured questionnaire was developed as a part of the Quan survey of a sample of key participants.
- A household questionnaire also was constructed for implementation with a random sample of households and "microcredit groups" in the intervention communities.
- In each of the three regions, Qual baseline data were collected, consisting of case-based comparative analysis of the two intervention and two comparison communities with different levels of urbanicity (total of 12 cases).
- To gain insight into the role of custom and tradition in decision making, focus groups and in-depth interviews were planned for each community (1 week per community).
- It was predicted that the degree of generalizability of the Qual findings in the full group would be assessed via the Quan results.
- A 3-year follow-up, repeating all stages of the study, was planned as an attempt to increase certainty regarding the effects of the intervention.

On the surface, this type of methodology might seem unique to a specific field of research, such as poverty assessment or international development. Our purpose in focusing on these studies here is to initiate a crossover of the methodology to other areas of research and to other disciplines. For example, an educational or clinical field trial study might lend itself to such a participatory MM design in which the sampling design, data collection techniques, and even questions about types of attributes that are expected to be affected may be examined and refined in a participatory manner during the course of the investigation. Also, the fact that large-scale studies are conducted by teams of investigators with complementary skills and backgrounds does not negate the possibility of a single investigator using this methodology in smaller scale studies (e.g., in a doctoral dissertation). Many MM research studies are conducted by individual researchers with a sufficient mastery of both Qual and Quan methods to enable them to obtain useful information and gain understanding from listening to participants and other informants with local knowledge, as well as from peers who can act as professional reviewers and critical consultants.

Strengths and Weaknesses

Many of the strengths and weaknesses of participatory MM designs are also shared by the other two families of methods discussed in this chapter. A major strength of the participatory econometrics methodology and its variations is in empowering the stakeholders of development programs to actively engage in assessment of needs, to formulate questions, and to evaluate the effects. Adding this active voice of the participants would minimize the imposition of cultural and political agendas and investigators' values on the issues under investigation.

This type of methodology also allows the investigators to combine Qual and Quan approaches to answer research and evaluation questions that have traditionally been answered with one or the other (Qual or Quan) method. Participatory (and transformative) methods (e.g., rapid rural appraisal, participatory poverty assessments; see Rao & Woolcock, 2004, p. 170) enable researchers to collect data with predominantly illiterate populations in the developing world, using simple methods to "help outsiders learn about poverty and project impacts in cost-effective ways that reflect grounded experience" (p. 170).

Among the weaknesses of participatory MM designs, one might point to logistics and political controversies. Participatory MM designs need teams of investigators with distinct skills in Qual and Quan methods and techniques. Putting together such a team might be a difficult, costly, and time-consuming task for many smaller scale (or even large-scale) projects. Furthermore, members of such teams must have enough flexibility to keep an open dialogue between components of the investigation. Often, a skilled supervisor or moderator is needed to incorporate diverse and sometimes seemingly dissonant findings that emerge across the strands of the study. Absence of such an open and flexible opportunity for integration might lead to conflict and distrust and threaten the integrity of the project.

Group–Case MM Designs

Description

The third family of innovative methods examined in this chapter is called the *group-case method* (GCM).[7] The recent version of this innovative approach came about as a result of the continuing paradigm/science wars and the push by the G. W. Bush administration, through the Department of Education, to give priority to randomized field trials (often referred to as RCTs, which stands for randomized clinical/controlled trials) as the "gold standard" for determining the effectiveness and worth of educational programs (Office of Management and Budget, 2004). The push for RCTs and the medical research model has brought about numerous debates and suggestions by research methodologists (cf. Brass, Nunez-Neto, & Williams, 2006; Donaldson & Christie, 2005; Levine, 2003), with many calling for a wider array of methods to provide evidence of cause and effect in intervention programs.[8] GCM integrates ethnographic techniques, Brinkerhoff's (2003) success-case method (SCM), and experimental (or other Quan) designs into a broader and potentially stronger set of MM designs.

The SCM has been effectively used in business and applied settings to obtain a "quick read" on what innovations and programs appear to be working. It is based on Qual and Quan sampling and depth analysis of success cases. When expanded into the GCM, the approach often can be used to provide relatively strong evidence of cause and effect.

The idea of the success-case method is to find successes (even when most failed) and determine what was different for the success cases. Theoretically, several areas of literature are related to success-case evaluation, such as management theory in the 1980s and 1990s that focused on excellence and worker participation (e.g., Peters, 1987; Peters & Waterman, 1982/2004), total quality management (George & Weimerskirch, 1998), and the emerging field of positive psychology (Turner, Barling, & Zacharatos, 2005). A growing number of researchers also are learning of the usefulness of storytelling as a form of Qual data (Brown, Denning, Groh, & Prusak, 2005).

Van Haneghan and Johnson (2006) have shown how the SCM and traditional experimental research logic can be combined to form an MM approach that involves moving back and forth between (1) the *group* level (i.e., aggregate analysis, typically providing Quan data such as group means) and (2) the single *cases* level (individual case analysis, typically done through depth interviewing). This back-and-forth or iterative method is shown in Figure 19.2. We call this method the *group-case method* because its purpose is to use both group- and individual-level data to inform and strengthen the conclusions being drawn about a research question (e.g., Does a program work? How does it work?). Van Haneghan and Johnson argue that the group-case method can be used to strengthen causal conclusions by identifying multiple causes, showing process and time lines of events for each individual, and testing and ruling out some alternative or rival hypotheses that threaten traditional experimental research designs.

Epistemologically, the GCM relies on a "beyond reasonable doubt" standard for

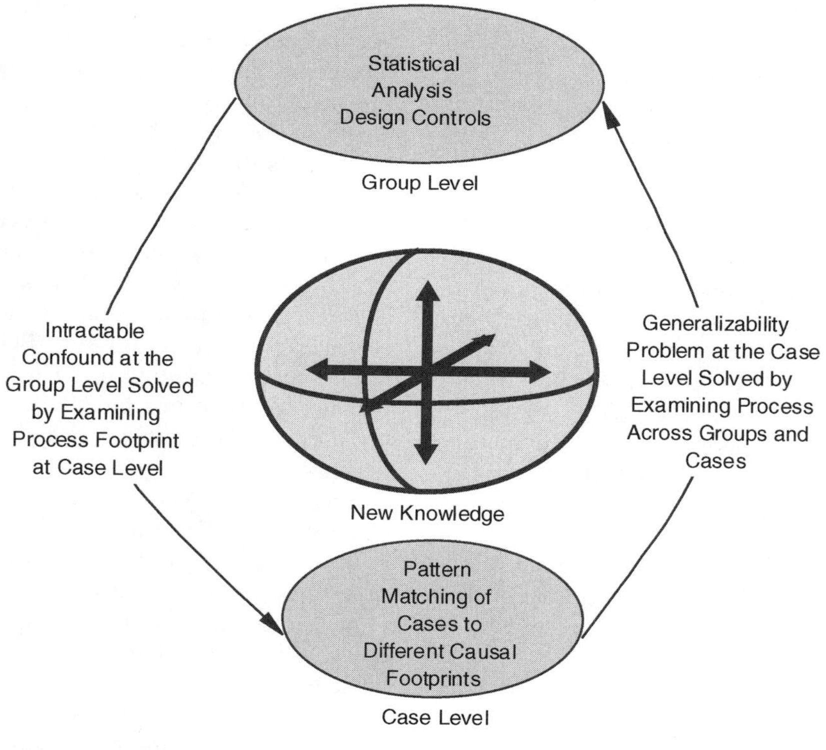

FIGURE 19.2. Cycling of analysis between group and case level. Used with permission of Van Haneghan and Johnson (2006).

judging evidence of causation, although different research communities can modify this criterion as they see fit. It utilizes comparison-group (counterfactual) logic, single-group pretest–posttest logic, and single-case research logic. The data are examined by comparing experimental and control groups, by examining those groups over time, and by collecting additional individual data to identify and rule out threats to validity. The integrative logic involves hypothesis/theory testing (i.e., a logic of justification), but it also provides a way to discover what works and why (i.e., a logic of discovery). Conclusions are strengthened through corroboration, explanation, and elaboration.

Sampling of individual cases for additional examination (i.e., beyond group-level study) in the GCM can take many forms, such as sampling only success cases, sampling success and nonsuccess cases from intervention and/or control groups, and selecting cases from study volunteers and nonvolunteers. Each type of resulting comparison will provide a different kind of information. In addition to considering the kinds of cases to be selected for additional study, decisions must be made about how many cases to select and how much time and effort to spend on each case (note the depth vs. breadth trade-off). Cases also can be selected and interview questions can be specifically geared toward checking for the presence of various threats to validity. Qual interviews can help identify or, on the other hand, help rule out various threats to internal (i.e., causal) validity (e.g., cross-group communication, history events), as well as threats to external (i.e., generalizing) validity (e.g., resentment, social reactivity, the influence of unique contextual characteristics, participant demographics, and other participant characteristics).

When operating at the individual or success–nonsuccess case level, the logic of inference to best explanation (or abductive reasoning) is useful for examining competing reasons for the success or nonsuccess and making sure that the intervention is a major part of the best explanation for the individual's success (rather than, e.g., spontaneous recovery or other positive influences on the case). When examining success and nonsuccess cases, an ideographic type of causal analysis is helpful in discerning the best causative explanation for each case. A useful strategy for understanding multiple cases is to examine the multiple individual paths from start to success, determining the presence of intervening mechanisms and documenting the routes to success. Is one route the most common? What factors help explain the different routes (e.g., contextual and other moderating factors)? During case analysis, consideration of rival explanations should always be operative for understanding each case, as well as for gaining a better understanding of the causal relationship suggested by the group-level analysis. The strategy of negative case sampling is helpful in locating exceptions to the general or average group-level finding. To better understand the group-level data, the case data should be used to unpack or disaggregate the data, shifting the focus from the "average person" to the actual people involved in the intervention. The case data (through ethnographic interviews) also can help in understanding the meanings of an intervention and changes in the viewpoints of program participants because of the program. In short, the case data are used to strategically add to what is found through the traditional RCT or other Quan component of a research study.

The steps in the GCM for studying program impact are as follows:

1. Plan the MM design, including, for example, a group-level Quan research design (e.g., a nonequivalent comparison-group design) to be used along with "depth" or ethnographic interviewing of sampled success and nonsuccess cases.
2. Identify the standard threats to internal and external validity of the group design.
3. Conduct the experiment and identify

what appear to be plausible threats to the quality of inferences (e.g., internal and external validity or legitimation; see Onwuegbuzie & Johnson, 2006; Tashakkori & Teddlie, 2003a).

4. During data analysis, identify success and nonsuccess cases, or identify any cases that are expected to potentially provide information about validity threats.
5. Collect intensive data from the cases (e.g., depth and process interviewing, asking questions about what occurred during the study internally and externally).
6. Integrate the data during analysis and use the case data to help explain the group/aggregate data; collect additional case data if needed.
7. Stop data collection and analysis when theoretical saturation has occurred (e.g., when a plausible story of what happened can be provided, along with sufficient justifying evidence).
8. Make meta-inferences based on the group and case data and write and communicate the research or evaluation report.

In short, the GCM is a general approach in which the researcher sees value in group-level or traditional aggregative and statistical approaches, as well as in case-level or disaggregative approaches, and the practitioner of this approach seeks to use group-level and case-level data collection, analysis, and interpretation to generate rigorous meta-inferences about phenomena of interest in social and evaluation research. An important part of the GCM is its iterative or dynamic process and its attention to generalizable conclusions, along with providing understanding and documenting the complexities of real-world phenomena. Researchers following this approach will see the usefulness of stories *and* numbers, cases *and* averages, and complexity *and* generality. More generally, the researcher using the GCM will focus on documenting complementarities found in multiple perspectives and will use multiple perspectives or theoretical lenses for seeing and understanding a phenomenon. The pure form of this "new" method will include group- and case-level data in a single, integrated research study.

Examples

The GCM has been, more or less, instantiated in what several psychologists and sociologists have independently labeled *experimental ethnography* (Cohen, Bowdle, Nisbett, & Schwarz, 1996; Sherman & Strang, 2004; Tweney, 2004). Experimental ethnography is an example of the GCM because, in this approach, group or aggregated data (e.g., means) are used along with multiple individual case data. In experimental ethnography, researchers blend concepts and approaches from mainstream scientific psychology with concepts and approaches from the disciplines of anthropology, sociology, and history (also see Caracelli, 2006; Caracelli & Greene, 1993; Maxwell, Bashook, & Sandlow, 1986). The exact meanings of the term *experimental ethnography* currently vary according to the researcher using the term.

One example of experimental ethnography is seen in a study by Sherman and Strang (2004). These researchers/methodologists first explain what they mean by the term *experimental ethnography*. They say that experimental ethnography is a social science approach that unites "the insights of stories and numbers" (p. 205) and that their version utilizes the insights of the ethnographer to improve traditional field experiments. They say that it is "a tool for answering questions about *why* programmatic attempts to solve human problems produce what effects, on average, in the context of the strong internal validity of large-sample, randomized, controlled field experiments" (p. 205). One goal is to "achieve experiments that create both a strong 'black box' test of cause and effect and a rich distillation of how those effects happened inside that black box, person by person, case by case, story by story" (p. 205).

They make a strong case for bringing down the wall between the standpoints of Quan and Qual research by using both. They want to do more than understand what they call "the average man" (p. 207), and they make the point that "as long as people are highly influenced by situational-specific emotions in their reactions to attempts to influence their behavior, the need will be great for adding knowledge about a social individuation in program effects," which involves addressing individuals' opinions "with individual-level stories as well as with numbers" (p. 207). Their description of experimental ethnography has much in common with what we are calling, more generally, the GCM in MM research, and their conceptualization influenced our own conceptualization of the broader GCM.

Sherman and Strang's (2004) application of the GCM, or experimental ethnography, focused on a *restorative justice* program. Restorative justice focuses on bringing together victims of crime with the perpetrators (as well as anyone affected by the crime) to help meet the needs of both (all) groups and offers a new strategy for dealing with crime. It involves "new values" such as "healing over punishment, reconciliation over anger, and reintegration over rejection" (p. 208). It includes interviews with victim and criminal and developing contracts for what the victim wants the perpetrator do and what the perpetrator agrees to do. Agreement about what activities the perpetrator is to carry out is reached through a conference between these individuals (which does not replace jail time but can be considered by judges). In addition to setting out activities to be carried out by perpetrators (e.g., getting off drugs, doing community service), the meeting can have therapeutic effects on both parties.

The field experiment done by Sherman and Strang included random assignment to experimental and control groups. The experimental group included perpetrator–victim pairs who participated in restorative justice activities; the control group pairs never met each other for conferences or any other activities associated with the program. The Quan results showed statistically significant differences between robbery victims in the intervention and control groups, with the intervention-group participants being, on average, less likely to experience posttraumatic stress disorder and more likely to experience normal employment patterns.

Qual case-level data were also collected, primarily through ethnographic interviews, prospectively (i.e., at more than one time point), that involved looking for changes; comparisons also were made with victims who were not part of the intervention. The Qual data enabled some development of grounded theory about the change process, and this suggested additional benefits for the victims (e.g., they adjusted better and returned to their normal lives quicker). The Qual data supported the Quan data and provided grounded theory about causal mechanisms and inductively derived hypotheses for future testing.

Another use of experimental ethnography is demonstrated in a study by Ryan Tweney (2004), who is interested in the history of scientific practices. Defining his version of experimental ethnography, Tweney says, "by *experimental ethnography*, I mean the attempt to understand scientific practices, both contemporary and historical, using procedures that replicate the practices under study, in an effort to more fully characterize their nature" (p. 732). Tweney thinks that textbook discussions of procedures of scientific practice have been oversimplified and too far removed from work by real scientists because of a bias toward only the nomothetic approach (searching for general psychological laws) and a lack of attention to disaggregative data and use of the ideographic approach (focusing on understanding individuals). His approach to the study of scientific practice (i.e., the thinking and behavior of scientists) is an integrative one. He relies on an experimental approach (in which the researcher creates and replicates a scientific practice and studies that practice) and an ethnographic approach (in which the researcher attempts to make the experiment authentic, and through this replication of historical conditions, the researcher gains a view into the rich cultural and historically situated meanings of scientific practice). In addition, Tweney and others in this area of research (e.g., Klahr, 2000; Simon, 1996) rely on diaries, historical case studies, and cognitive theory, along with laboratory simulations or replications of scientific practice. Much research in this area is focused on understanding the process and "logic" of scientific discovery.

Tweney (2004) has studied the scientific practices of the 19th-century scientist Michael Faraday (1791–1867), especially Faraday's work on the properties of thin films of metallic gold, which Faraday had hoped would lead to a better understanding of the interaction of light and matter. Tweney identified several heuristics used by Faraday and others. For example, researchers sometimes used analogy (both general and highly specific analogies, with the latter referring to disciplinary or research domain-specific analogies) to help generate new ideas about the operation of physical processes. Early on in scientific discovery, researchers often emphasized confirming evidence rather than disconfirming evidence. Researchers use the process of reconceptualization to create new theoretical lenses or windows to see and understand phenomena. They create models that are improved and changed over time. Finally, at times, researchers make *ceteris paribus* assumptions (trying to hold constant other factors), but at other times they relax these assumptions to gain understandings of phenomena in their natural, interactive, and complex environments. Tweney also pointed out the importance of "confusions" that face researchers and force them to reconceptualize their concepts, theories, and understandings of scientific objects. These reconceptualizations demonstrate the importance of the interaction of biography, situation, macro and micro contextual factors, heuristics, theory, and instrumentation in the process of scientific discovery.

An old but still highly innovative version of the GCM is what Gerald Fry and his colleagues (Fry, Chantavanich, & Chantavanich, 1981) called *ethnographic residual analysis*. These researchers called for the use of ethnographic methods along with Quan research methods more than 25 years ago, and, finally, the field appears poised to take this type of recommendation seriously. These researchers reported the results of adding ethnographic methods in three research studies. In the first study, the use of ethnographic interviewing helped the researchers to obtain measures that were appropriate in a different culture (Thailand). Here is their assessment of the first study:

> It is, however, doubtful that the model would have had such explanatory power if key concepts such as quality of school, ethnicity, and socioeconomic background had been measured in standard Western ways. The use of emic analysis to discover relevant Thai constructs certainly contributed to a more meaningful test of the Blau–Duncan model and a better, hopefully deeper understanding of the occupational attainment process in Thailand. (p. 149)

If these researchers had not conducted what they called *emic analysis*, the research would have been based on faulty measurement, and without good measurement even the "gold standard" RCT will fail completely.

In another of the studies reported by Fry and his colleagues (1981), econometric analysis was first carried out on survey and secondary Quan data to determine how well several variables predicted the rate of transition to the next grade level. They subtracted the predicted values from the observed values to identify residuals. They selected three cases for more extensive study. One province (the unit of Quan analysis) was selected because it had a large positive residual, one was selected because it had a large negative residual, and one was also included that was not an outlier (i.e., a typical province). Next, the researchers went to the three provinces and conducted in-depth interviews with multiple stakeholders (parents, children, teachers, administrators, villagers) and conducted field participant observations. The researchers were able to construct an additional predictor variable (called children's aspirations for children's future"), based on the Qual data, that significantly increased the variance explained in the model. Additional "variables" also aided in interpreting the results.

Strengths and Weaknesses

The particular strengths and weaknesses of the GCM will be contingent on the particular application. We can, however, outline several potential strengths and weaknesses of this innovative method. Here are the potential strengths:

- Case analysis and interviews help the researcher to rule out plausible alternative explanations of the program results (i.e., it strengthens internal validity) (Sackett & Mullen, 1993; Van Haneghan & Johnson, 2006).
- Interviews can serve as manipulation checks, as well as measurement checks (e.g., does the measure mean what the researcher assumes it means for the participants?).
- Interviews can help researchers better interpret results of significance testing, including nonsignificant results (e.g., Horodynski & Stommel, 2005; Wheatley, Brugha, & Shapiro, 2003).
- Ethnographic interviews document participants' meanings and tell their stories.
- Transferability (generalizability) can be increased through ethnographic interviews and observations when they document the characteristics of the people for whom a program works, show what motivates the participants, and show under what conditions a program works. Characteristics of program providers also need to be documented.
- When researchers study success cases "ethnographically," the group-level experiment gains a discovery dimension in addition to the traditional testing or justification dimension. Case analysis also can identify unintended outcomes, which helps provide a superior set of conclusions.
- The case data provide evidence of complexity, process, and situational factors (providing greater "process and contextual validity").
- Study of individual cases sheds light on ideographic and other microprocesses, in addition to providing information about traditional nomological relationships between variables.
- Use of Qual interviewing and observation, along with experiments, can help identify omitted variables and help researchers improve model specification, which is essential if statistical modeling is to be trusted.

Here are several weaknesses of the GCM:

- Application can be expensive because additional data collection with individuals typically is needed. This cost is added to the traditional group experimental method.
- Conducting a group-case study requires the use of both a Qual and a Quan researcher, or it requires a researcher trained in what Onwuegbuzie and Johnson (2006) call *commensurability legitimation*, which involves training in how to make gestalt switches between the "standpoints" of Qual research and Quan research.
- The GCM has not broadly penetrated the mainstream culture of Quan research (e.g., the RCT culture); hence, it is not always an option in some research situations.
- Currently, there might be a lack of funding for research based on this method because of the emphasis by the federal government on RCTs.

We believe that the strengths usually will outweigh the weaknesses, but this will depend on the situation or application. A strong argument in favor of the GCM is that it can add important information to what is considered to be the gold standard in federally funded educational evaluation and research. Because of the importance of the added information and the strengthened group design, one can conclude that the GCM is superior to RCTs. We look forward to seeing more applications of the method in the future.

A Comparison of the Three Methods

Each of the three innovative methods discussed in this chapter has a dominant strength that is linked to its primary purpose. The IBIS-MM is especially strong for collecting multiple rounds of questionnaire data quickly from people across the world to generate viewpoints and answers to the kinds of research questions that can be addressed using survey research (i.e., especially through open-ended questionnaires and interviews conducted over the Internet). Participatory MM is especially strong at increasing participant and stakeholder buy-in to evaluation/research findings because of the participation and joint construction of the evaluation product. Power differences (between coresearchers and participants) are especially reduced with this method. The GCM is especially strong at eliminating alternative explanations that can otherwise plague monomethod group (experimental) designs.

Generally speaking, no methodological hierarchy is required with any of these methods, nor should one be preferred. The style of the researchers (and the particular research questions needing answering) in each of these families of methods will determine whether the style-in-practice leans more toward traditional Qual, traditional Quan, or the more recent MM approach. The three methods were selected because they work especially well from an MM perspective, in which researchers must consider the phenomena and data from Qual and Quan "perspectives."

IBIS-MM, participatory MM, and group-case designs have several similarities because they all are MM designs.[9] All three of the innovative methods discussed here require that researchers take the idea of discourse seriously, allowing the voices of multiple participants and stakeholders to be heard. IBIS-MM designs create "groups" that interact on the Internet; participatory MM is specifically designed for participation and dialogue. GCM often requires a team of researchers (e.g., one at the group level and another to collect more in-depth interview data at the case level) that collects data on multiple perspectives and requires that researchers engage in discourse with each other and with participants.[10] The ideas of discourse and teams and multiple perspectives cut across the three innovative methods.

All three of the innovative methods also use multiple "logics." That is, all three methods use some form of iteration (allowing for change and improvement and integration of perspectives over time), and they all use a combination of logics of inquiry, such as abductive logic (generative, creative problem solving), inductive logic (generating grounded generalizations and theories), and deductive logic (deducing and testing observational consequences of theories and hypotheses). Although all three of the methods can be used by combinations of purists (e.g., Quan and Qual purists), an integration of the information obtained is necessary to gain the interactive benefits of using both Quan and Qual approaches; generally speaking, this will require someone skilled in the conduct of MM research. Understanding the concept of commensurability legitimation (or validity) is helpful as one attempts this difficult task (Onwuegbuzie & Johnson, 2006).

On the negative side, the innovative methods discussed here have a clear weakness of increased cost. They are more expensive than their monomethod counterparts. For example, participatory approaches take more skill, effort, and time because of the additional research practitioners (many of whom will have little or no formal training in the research process). GCM requires additional data collection, which also results in increased time and effort and, therefore, costs. In contrast, because the IBIS-MM utilizes the Internet for data collection, increased data-collection-related costs are less of a problem. At the same time, to the degree that the requirement of obtaining thick descriptions of participants' viewpoints is carried out, time and cost will increase; but, as in the other two cases, the improved product should be worth the increased cost. Whenever research teams are used, training costs will increase, and the process will take more time for discussion, integration, member checking, and reintegration/construction. In Table 19.2, we provide a brief summary of the three families of methods.

In conclusion, one of the main challenges in today's behavioral and social research settings is knowing how to obtain strong answers to complex research questions. The most important aspect of research is the quality of the conclusions that are made at the end of the studies (what we call *inference quality*). Politicians, policymakers, and stakeholders (e.g., parents, patients) are demanding strong accountability for the outcomes of research and evaluation projects. Different stakeholders sometimes will have different conceptions of what constitutes a quality conclusion. This complex process requires respect and understanding of different perspectives, and it requires that researchers carefully consider multiple perspectives during the conduct and writing up of research conclusions and recommendations. The importance of MM answers (which are based on multiple sources of evidence and perspectives) should motivate all of us to continue to educate policymakers and the public about the ways that MM research can integrate information and provide fuller, more widely usable solutions to social problems.

The three innovative families of methods discussed in this chapter only scratch the surface of the many innovations that currently are taking place in the fields of MM research and evaluation. We look forward to seeing more and more innovations as new combinations of Quan and Qual approaches are successfully used by researchers and evaluators and as these designs are formalized in the methodological literature. We also hope that an increasing number of researchers and evaluators will *explicitly* recognize that MM research might cost a little more but that it also can result in improved designs that in the past might have been overlooked. MM provides a place in which

TABLE 19.2. Comparisons among Three Emergent Families of MM Techniques

Dimension of comparison	IBIS MM designs	Participatory MM designs	Group-case MM designs
Field of origin	Education, economics	International development	Anthropology, psychology, sociology
Research design	Sequential with three or more strands	Sequential, iterative	Parallel/concurrent, sequential
Special techniques utilized	Delphi method	Rapid ethnography	Experimental ethnography, ethnographic residual analysis
Primary strength	Capitalizes on iterative Qual/Quan processes	Allows the involvement of the stakeholders in all stages	Strengthens experimental research and documents explanatory causation
Primary weakness	May take a long time to conduct	May require a team of investigators	May be expensive and require a team of investigators

innovations taking place in Quan and Qual research can be integrated and utilized.

Notes

1. There are many perspectives or traditions (e.g., critical theory) associated with Qual research in addition to constructivism and its variants, as noted by Creswell (1998), Denzin and Lincoln (2005b), and others. Glesne (2006, p. 7, italics in original) summarized the relative importance of constructivism as follows: "Most qualitative researchers adhere to social constructivism or a constructivist paradigm. . . ."

2. There are numerous references to Qual data as words, text, or narrative. For example, Schwandt (1997, p. 130) distinguished between Qual and Quan data as follows: "Perhaps the clearest use of the adjective [qualitative] is to distinguish between qualitative data–nonnumeric data in the form of words–and quantitative data–numeric data." In a general discussion of Qual data management and analysis methods, Ryan and Bernard (2000, p. 769) referred to qualitative data as both "text" and "narrative."

3. Lincoln and Guba (1985, p. 37) referred to a "fragmentable" reality that could be broken into "independent variables and processes, any of which can be studied independently of others."

4. The "methods–strands matrix" is presented in detail, together with descriptions and diagrams of various MM and quasi-MM designs, in a recent issue of *Research in the Schools* (Volume 13, no. 1) devoted entirely to current developments in MM research.

5. Dividing a strand into distinct stages allows for the transformation of one methodological approach to another within a strand; that is, a strand might start out as Qual, but then become Quan, or vice versa.

6. Morse (1991, 2003) developed the basic notational system used in MM research. One component of this system is whether projects are conducted simultaneously (concurrent or parallel designs, which are designated by a plus [+] sign) or sequentially (sequential designs, designated by an arrow [→]). In concurrent/parallel designs, Qual and Quan data may be collected simultaneously or at different times, independently or semi-independently. Unlike in sequential designs, analysis of one set is not required for the collection of the other.

7. Because of the newness of this approach, no single label for the GCM approach was available. The term group-case method was coined here as a useful descriptor. We prefer this label to the term success-case mixed method (Van Haneghan & Johnson, 2006) and to the term success-case method (because this is only a part of the group-case method). The group-case method is an update and expansion of extreme case analysis in mixed methods research and evaluation (Caracelli & Green, 1993; Tashakkori & Teddlie, 1998).

8. As Brinkerhoff (2003) points out, the success-case method appears to have been invented by him and another researcher, Barry Kibel (1999), each of whom worked independently without knowing of the other's work.

9. For a general list showing the strengths and weaknesses of MM research, see Johnson and Onwuegbuzie (2004).

10. For more information on the use of teams in MM research, see Shulha and Wilson (2003).

References

Bamberger, M. (1998). *Integrating qualitative and quantitative research in development projects*. Washington, DC: World Bank.

Boruch, R. F. (1997). *Randomized field experiments for planning and evaluation: A practical guide*. Thousand Oaks, CA: Sage.

Boruch, R. F. (2002). *The virtues of randomness*. Retrieved October 9, 2006, from *www.educationnext.org/20023/36.html*

Boyatzis, R. E. (1998). *Transforming qualitative information: Thematic analysis and code development*. Thousand Oaks, CA: Sage.

Brass, C. T., Nunez-Neto, B., & Williams, E. D. (2006). *Congress and program evaluation: An overview of randomized controlled trials (RCTs) and related issues* (Congressional Research Service Report Order No. RL33301). Washington, DC. Retrieved October 9, 2006, from *www.opencrs.com/rpts/RL33301_20060307.pdf*

Brewer, J., & Hunter, A. (1989). *Multimethod research: A synthesis of styles*. Thousand Oaks, CA: Sage.

Brinkerhoff, R. O. (2003). *The success case method: Find out quickly what's working and what's not*. San Francisco: Berrett-Koehler.

Brown, J. S., Denning, S., Groh, K., & Prusak, L. (2005). *Storytelling in organizations: Why storytelling is transforming 21st-century organizations and management*. Burlington, MA: Elsevier Butterworth-Heinemann.

Campbell, D. T., & Stanley, J. (1966). *Experimental and*

quasi-experimental designs for research. Chicago: Rand McNally.

Caracelli, V. J. (2006). Enhancing the policy process through the use of ethnography and other study frameworks: A mixed-method strategy. *Research in the Schools, 13*(1), 84–92.

Caracelli, V. J., & Greene, J. C. (1993). Data analysis strategies for mixed-method evaluation designs. *Educational Evaluation and Policy Analysis, 15*, 195–207.

Cohen, D., Bowdle, B. F., Nisbett, R. E., & Schwarz, N. (1996). Insult, aggression, and the Southern culture of honor: An "experimental ethnography." *Journal of Personality and Social Psychology, 70*(5), 945–960.

Cook, T. D. (2002). Randomized experiments in educational policy research: A critical examination of the reasons the educational evaluation community has offered for not doing them. *Educational Evaluation and Policy Analysis, 24*(3), 175–199.

Cook, T. D., & Campbell, D. T. (1979). *Quasiexperimentation: Design and analysis issues for field settings*. Boston: Houghton Mifflin.

Covino, E. A., & Iwanicki, E. F. (1996). Experienced teachers: Their constructs of effective teaching. *Journal of Personnel Evaluation in Education, 10*, 325–363.

Creswell, J., & Plano-Clark, V. (2006). *Designing and conducting mixed methods research*. Thousand Oaks, CA: Sage.

Creswell, J. W. (1998). *Qualitative inquiry and research design: Choosing among five traditions*. Thousand Oaks, CA: Sage.

Creswell, J. W. (2003). *Research design: Qualitative, quantitative, and mixed methods approaches*. Thousand Oaks, CA: Sage.

Creswell, J. W., Shope, R., Plano Clark, V. L., & Green, D. (2006, April). How interpretive qualitative research extends mixed methods research. *Research in the Schools, 13*(1), 1–11.

Denzin, N. K., & Lincoln, Y. S. (Eds.). (2005a). *Handbook of qualitative research* (3rd ed.). Thousand Oaks, CA: Sage.

Denzin, N. K., & Lincoln, Y. S. (2005b). Introduction: The discipline and practice of qualitative research. In N. K. Denzin & Y. S. Lincoln (Eds.), *Handbook of qualitative research* (3rd ed., pp. 1–42). Thousand Oaks, CA: Sage.

Donaldson, S. I., & Christie, C. A. (2005, October). The 2004 Claremont debate: Lipsey vs. Scriven. Determining causality in program evaluation and applied research: Should experimental evidence be the gold standard? *Journal of Multidisciplinary Evaluation*, p. 3. Retrieved August 5, 2006, from *evaluation.wmich.edu/jmde/JMDE_Num003.html*

Eisenhardt, M., & Towne, L. (2003). Contestation and change in national policy on "scientifically based" education research. *Educational Researcher, 32*(7), 31–38.

Feuer, M. J., Towne, L., & Shavelson, R. J. (2002). Scientific culture and educational research. *Educational Researcher, 31*(8), 4–14.

Fry, G., Chantavanich, S., & Chantavanich, A. (1981). Merging quantitative and qualitative research techniques: Toward a new research paradigm. *Anthropology and Education Quarterly, 12*(2), 145–158.

Gacitua-Mario, E., & Wodon, Q. (Eds.). (2006). *Measurement and meaning: Combining quantitative and qualitative methods for the analysis of poverty and social exclusion in Latin America*. Washington, DC: World Bank. Retrieved August 20, 2006, from *wbln0018.worldbank.org/LAC/lacinfoclient.nsf/d29684951174975c85256735007fef12/204feb702e946cf785256afc006baab4/$FILE/Measurement.doc*

Gage, N. (1989). The paradigm wars and their aftermath: A "historical" sketch of research and teaching since 1989. *Educational Researcher, 18*, 4–10.

George, S., & Weimerskirch, A. (1998). *Total quality management: Strategies and techniques proven at today's most successful companies*. New York: Wiley.

Glesne, C. (2006). *Becoming qualitative researchers: An introduction* (3rd ed.). Boston: Pearson, Allyn & Bacon.

Gordon, T. J., & Helmer, O. (1964). *Report on a long range forecasting study* (RAND Paper No. P-2982). Santa Monica, CA: RAND Corporation.

Greene, J., & Caracelli, V. (Eds.). (1997). *Advances in mixed-method evaluation: The challenges and benefits of integrating diverse paradigms* (New Directions for Evaluation, No. 74). San Francisco: Jossey-Bass.

Greene, J. C., Caracelli, V. J., & Graham, W. F. (1989). Toward a conceptual framework for mixed-method evaluation designs. *Educational Evaluation and Policy Analysis, 11*, 255–274.

Guba, E. G., & Lincoln, Y. S. (1994). Competing paradigms in qualitative research. In N. K. Denzin & Y. S. Lincoln (Eds.), *Handbook of qualitative research* (pp. 105–107). Thousand Oaks, CA: Sage.

Heylighen, F. (2003). *Web dictionary of cybernetics and systems*. Retrieved September 25, 2003, from *pespmc1.vub.ac.be/ASC*

Horodynski, M. A., & Stommel, M. (2005). Nutrition education aimed at toddlers: An intervention study. *Pediatric Nursing, 31*(5), 364–372.

Howe, K. R. (2004). A critique of experimentalism. *Qualitative Inquiry, 10*(1), 42–61.

Johnson, R. B., & Christensen, L. B. (2008). *Educational research: Quantitative, qualitative, and mixed approaches*. (3rd ed.). Thousand Oaks, CA: Sage.

Johnson, R. B., & Onwuegbuzie, A. (2004). Mixed methods research: A research paradigm whose time has come. *Educational Researcher, 33*(7), 14–26.

Johnson, R. B., & Turner, L. (2003). Data collection strategies in mixed methods research. In A. Tashakkori & C. Teddlie (Eds.), *Handbook of mixed methods in social and behavioral research* (pp. 297–320). Thousand Oaks, CA: Sage.

Kibel, B. M. (1999). *Success stories as hard data: An introduction to results mapping*. New York: Plenum Press.

Klahr, D. (2000). *Exploring science: The cognition and development of discovery processes*. Cambridge, MA: Bradford.

Krathwohl, D. R. (2004). *Methods of educational and social science research: An integrated approach* (2nd ed.). Long Grove, IL: Waveland Press.

Lather, P. (2004). This IS your father's paradigm: Government intrusion and the case of qualitative research in education. *Qualitative Inquiry, 10*(1), 15–34.

Levine, F. J. (2003). *American Educational Research Association's response to Rod Paige*. Retrieved May 6, 2004, from *www.eval.org/doeaera.htm*

Lincoln, Y. S., & Guba, E. G. (1985). *Naturalistic inquiry*. Beverly Hills, CA: Sage.

Maxwell, J. A. (2004). Reemergent scientism, postmodernism, and dialogue across differences. *Qualitative Inquiry, 10*(1), 35–41.

Maxwell, J. A., Bashook, P. G., & Sandlow, C. J. (1986). Combining ethnographic and experimental methods in educational evaluation. In D. M. Fetterman & M. A. Pitman (Eds.), *Educational evaluation: Ethnography in theory, practice, and politics* (pp. 121–143). Beverly Hills, CA: Sage.

Mertens, D. M. (2005). *Research and evaluation in education and psychology: Integrating diversity with quantitative, qualitative, and mixed methods* (2nd ed.). Thousand Oaks, CA: Sage.

Miles, M., & Huberman, M. (1994). *Qualitative data analysis: An expanded sourcebook* (2nd ed.). Thousand Oaks, CA: Sage.

Morgan, D. (1998). Practical strategies for combining qualitative and quantitative methods: Applications to health research. *Qualitative Health Research, 8*(3), 362–376.

Morse, J. (1991). Approaches to qualitative–quantitative methodological triangulation. *Nursing Research, 40*(2), 120–123.

Morse, J. (2003). Principles of mixed methods and multimethod research design. In A. Tashakkori & C. Teddlie (Eds.), *Handbook of mixed methods in social and behavioral research* (pp. 189–208). Thousand Oaks, CA: Sage.

Office of Management and Budget. (2004). What constitutes strong evidence of a program's effectiveness? Retrieved July 25, 2006, from *www.whitehouse.gov/omb/part/2004_program_eval.pdf*

Onwuegbuzie, A. J., & Johnson, R. B. (2006). The validity issue in mixed research. *Research in the Schools, 13*(1), 48–63.

Patton, M. Q. (2002). *Qualitative evaluation and research methods* (3rd ed.). Thousand Oaks, CA: Sage.

Peters, T. J. (1987). *Thriving on chaos: Handbook for a management revolution*. New York: Harper & Row.

Peters, T. J., & Waterman, R. H. (2004). *In search of excellence: Lessons from America's best-run companies*. New York: HarperCollins. (Original work published 1982)

Rao, V., & Woolcock, M. (2004). Integrating qualitative and quantitative approaches in program evaluation. In F. Bourguignon & L. A. Pereira da Silva (Eds.), *The impact of economic policies on poverty and income distribution: Evaluation techniques and tools* (pp. 8-1–8-23). Washington, DC: World Bank and Oxford University Press.

Ryan, G., & Bernard, H. (2000). Data management and analysis methods. In N. K. Denzin & Y. S. Lincoln (Eds.), *Handbook of qualitative research* (2nd ed., pp. 769–802). Thousand Oaks, CA: Sage.

Sackett, P. R., & Mullen, E. J. (1993). Beyond formal experimental design: Towards an expanded view of the training evaluation process. *Personnel Psychology, 46*, 613–627.

Schwandt, T. (1997). *Qualitative inquiry: A dictionary of terms*. Thousand Oaks, CA: Sage.

Shadish, W., Cook, T., & Campbell, D. (2002). *Experimental and quasi-experimental designs for general causal inference*. Boston: Houghton Mifflin.

Shaffer, P. (2002, July). *Assumptions matter: Reflections on the Kanbur typology*. Paper presented at the Conference on Combining Quantitative and Qualitative Methods in Development Research, University of Wales, Swansea. Retrieved October 25, 2006, from *www.swan.ac.uk/cds/pdffiles/SHAFFER.pdf*

Shavelson, R. J., Webb, N. M., & Rowley, G. L. (1989). Generalizability theory. *American Psychologist, 44*(6), 922–932.

Sherman, L. W., & Strang, H. (2004). Experimental ethnography: The marriage of qualitative and quantitative research. *Annals of the Academy of Social and Political Science, 595*, 204–222.

Shulha, L., & Wilson, R. (2003). Collaborative mixed methods research. In A. Tashakkori & C. Teddlie (Eds.), *Handbook of mixed methods in social and behavioral research* (pp. 639–670). Thousand Oaks, CA: Sage.

Simon, H. A. (1996). *The sciences of the artificial* (3rd ed.). Cambridge, MA: MIT Press.

Slavin, R. E. (2002). Evidence-based education policies: Transforming educational practice and research. *Educational Researcher, 31*(7), 15–21.

Slavin, R. E. (2003). A reader's guide to scientifically based research, *Educational Leadership, 60*, 12–16.

Smith, J. K. (1996). An opportunity lost? In L. Heshusius & K. Ballard (Eds.), *From positivism to interpretivism and beyond: Tales of transformation in educational and social research* (pp. 161–168). New York: Teachers College Press.

Tashakkori, A. (2006, July). *Growing pains? Agreements, disagreements, and new directions in conceptualizing mixed methods*. Keynote address presented at the second annual Mixed Methods Conference, Homerton School of Health Studies, Cambridge, UK.

Tashakkori, A., & Teddlie, C. (1998). *Mixed methodology: Combining the qualitative and quantitative approaches*. Thousand Oaks, CA: Sage.

Tashakkori, A., & Teddlie, C. (Eds.). (2003a). *Handbook of mixed methods in social and behavioral research*. Thousand Oaks, CA: Sage.

Tashakkori, A., & Teddlie, C. (2003b). The past and future of mixed methods research: From data triangulation to mixed model designs. In A. Tashakkori & C. Teddlie (Eds.), *Handbook of mixed methods in social and behavioral research* (pp. 671–702). Thousand Oaks, CA: Sage.

Teddlie, C. (2005). Methodological issues related to causal studies of leadership: A mixed methods perspective from the USA. *Educational Management and Administration, 33*(2), 211–217.

Teddlie, C., Creemers, B., Kyriakides, L., Muijs, D., & Yu, F. (2006). The International System for Teacher Observation and Feedback: Evolution of an international study of teacher effectiveness constructs. *Educational Research and Evaluation, 12*(6), 561–582.

Teddlie, C., & Reynolds, D. (2006a, April). *The International System for Teacher Observation and Feedback.* Paper presented at the annual meeting of the American Educational Research Association, San Francisco.

Teddlie, C., & Reynolds, D. (2006b, January). *Methodological issues associated with the development and validation of ISTOF.* Paper presented at the annual meeting of the International Congress for School Effectiveness and Improvement, Ft. Lauderdale, FL.

Teddlie, C., & Tashakkori, A. (2006). A general typology of research designs featuring mixed methods. *Research in the Schools, 13*(1), 12–28.

Teddlie, C., & Tashakkori, A. (2008). *Foundations of mixed methods research: Integrating quantitative and qualitative techniques in the social and behavioral sciences.* Thousand Oaks, CA: Sage.

Turner, N., Barling, J., & Zacharatos, A. (2005). Positive psychology at work. In C. R. Snyder & S. J. Lopez (Eds.), *Handbook of positive psychology* (pp. 715–728). Oxford, UK: Oxford University Press.

Tweney, R. D. (2004). Replication and the experimental ethnography of science. *Journal of Cognition and Culture, 4,* 731–758.

Van Haneghan, J. P., & Johnson, R. B. (2006). *Using mixed methods logic of inquiry to build a case for causation in educational programs.* Paper presented at the annual meeting of the American Educational Research Association, San Francisco.

Wheatley, S. L., Brugha, T. S., & Shapiro, D. A. (2003). Exploring and enhancing engagement to the psychosocial intervention "Preparing for Parenthood." *Archive of Women's Mental Health, 6,* 275–285.

Wiersma, W., & Jurs, S. G. (2005). *Research methods in education: An introduction* (8th ed.). Boston: Pearson, Allyn & Bacon.

Wilhelm, W. J. (2001). Alchemy of the oracle: Delphi technique. *Delta Pi Epsilon Journal, 43*(1), 6–26.

CHAPTER 20

Data Analysis and Interpretation

Emergent Issues in Linking Qualitative and Quantitative Evidence

Sarah Irwin

In this chapter I consider the value of using different kinds of evidence, from macro to micro, in exploring social processes. Quantitative and qualitative data provide particular lenses on these different "levels." However, we need to acknowledge that these levels are often not distinct research problems but rather different *dimensions* of unitary problems. For example, to understand an individual's values and subjective beliefs, we need knowledge of him or her as a person, knowledge of his or her proximate circumstances and experiences, and knowledge of the wider social structural contexts in which he or she is positioned. An inquiry into well-being may reveal a poor person to be more satisfied with his or her situation than a wealthy person. It is only by understanding the social distribution of wealth, the social organization of aspiration and constraint, and people's diverse circumstances that we can make sense of their perceptions and of the differences between them. Researching macro and micro is not just about "linking data"; it is an issue of how we conceptualize the phenomena we are investigating.

In this chapter I explore some examples in which using different sources of evidence can enhance our understanding and explanation of social processes. I argue that:

- Most of our research problems are complex and multifaceted. Different methods and sources of evidence will reveal specific slices through the phenomena and processes under study, and we need to understand better precisely how the evidence reveals a partial and particular picture. For example, in-depth interviews and survey responses may provide different lenses on people's perceptions of some particular event or state of affairs, and so different kinds of account are generated by the different media of data collection. Another illustrative example here is the way people provide accounts, in open-ended interviews, of their decisions about the best type of care for their children in terms of a moral choice, yet it is only by understanding (say, through survey evidence) that people in similar circumstances make the same kinds of "moral" choices that we can see that morality provides us with a partial account of the nature of their decision making.

• We need to keep under reflexive and critical scrutiny the categories we use to organize our thinking and order our data. This is consistent with seeking more expansive and systematically adequate explanations of the processes under study. For example, gender, age, and ethnicity are standard variables used to denote difference, yet these categories are not always adequately theorized in respect of the processes or patterns under investigation. They may be effective categories for revealing structures of inequality, for example, but qualitative research helps reveal that the salience of these categories of difference may vary across contexts, in respect of material inequalities, subjective orientations, and so on.

• Developing adequate conceptualizations of the phenomena and processes under investigation must remain at the heart of social analysis. We use theory-laden categories through which we interpret empirical evidence, itself shaped by our tools of data collection. Nevertheless, empirical data can supply us with tools for reinterrogating, expanding, or changing our conceptualization. In the examples in this chapter I consider how drawing together data from different sources and "levels" of the social can contribute to enhancing social explanation.

The chapter is organized as follows. In the next section I briefly explore some issues that emerge from recent debates on the value of mixing methods. I argue that we need to understand how methods and evidence entail concepts about the nature of what we are researching. Empirical evidence carries with it the assumptions that went into its making, but we need also attend to precisely how it bears on the research problem at hand. It may give a partial picture in that it shows only one "part" of the complex phenomenon under study. Importantly, we also need to be aware of the risk that a partial picture may be a distorting one. It may mislead us as to the salient processes shaping the phenomena we are researching. Additionally, it is inappropriate to treat macro patterns and knowledge of diversity as "background" context and qualitative evidence on meaning, interaction, value, and so on as holding a more direct line to "process." I introduce some issues and examples in considering how both macro- and micro-level lenses are important in building not just a broader picture but a more adequate understanding of social processes. The third section continues the theme of social explanation with reference to different models of adequacy in connecting theory and data. I look at the historical example of explanatory models used to understand the incidence of cholera in the 19th century. Critics have seen in the different models lessons about adequacy and progress in social science research. Some argue that now, still, standard ways of representing and modeling quantitative data are too abstracted from social phenomena and risk distorting the processes in which we are interested. We see how the form of data and modes of analysis shape our understandings in particular ways. Nevertheless, there is scope for empirical data analysis not merely to confirm prior assumptions but to contribute to theoretical expansion and transformation. The fourth section explores and develops some of the themes through a consideration of empirical data. The examples all share a concern with the link between people's attitudes and perceptions on the one hand and the social and economic structures in which they are embedded on the other. In recent research and theory there is a tendency to treat individual perceptions and values as a "layer" of subjective and normative understanding that is distinct from aggregate structures of distribution, for example. This has been a source of arguments that ideology prevents people from seeing the workings of an oppressive social system and of linked arguments that in late modern society, values and choices are more freed from social structural processes than they were in the past. However, people clearly hold diverse positions within such structures, and it is to these contexts and positions that we need to relate their subjective orientations. We can understand the links between micro and macro, and between subjective and objective, only if we have a sufficient understanding of social structural diversity. We need to move across levels of evidence in seeking to adequately understand subjective orientations. The examples I develop all reveal a connectedness of subjective orientations and social structure. Additionally, they show that bringing together evidence, which is a theoretical issue more than a technical one, can help us tackle puzzles of explanation and transform understanding.

Issues in Linking Methods

There has been a recent surge of interest in mixed methods research and its potential. The idea of mixing methods is not new. Many writers have long advocated using mixed methods, and many have done so in their research practices. But there has been a renewed interest among social scientists and funding agencies, in line with a perception that mixing methods provides a way forward and perhaps a renewal of our resources for tackling social complexity and contemporary social problems. Mixing methods is sometimes defined in different ways, but in general it can be taken to refer to bringing together qualitative and quantitative data collection and analysis (Teddlie & Tashakkori, 2003).

Many different rationales and schema have been devised for elucidating the different ways in which quantitative and qualitative strategies can be brought together. There are many ways to combine data and many examples of good practice in this area. Brannen (2005), Bryman (2001, 2005), Hammond (2005), Mason (2006), Moran-Ellis and colleagues (2006), Teddlie and Tashakkori (2003), and many others have explored and classified ways in which multimethod and mixed methods research proceeds. For example, there are sequential models, in which one strategy follows from the other in the design of the research. A preliminary qualitative (part of a) study might sensibly precede a quantitative (part of) one to generate insider knowledge and insights that would feed into the quantitative design. Alternatively, quantitative research might generate (among other things) a sampling frame from which key informant participants might be identified for a qualitative study. Another common reason for using mixed methods is that, in tackling complex issues with different component parts, different methods may be deemed most appropriate to different parts of a study. The pattern of enhancement, in which data from different methods are seen to be supplementary and adding value, or insight, was one of the most common uses of mixed methods that Bryman found in his content analysis of U.K. social science articles published between 1994 and 2003 (Bryman, 2005). Another common claim for mixed quantitative and qualitative research is that qualitative methods allow us to interpret the relationship between variables. Thus we might have evidence of associations at a macro level and infer a causal relationship, but we need qualitative research to develop and test out our understandings of individual action and interaction (cf. Goldthorpe, 2000). Another common usage of mixed methods is triangulation, in which data from different sources are used to enhance understanding or to explore validity by bringing different evidence to bear on the same problem (Bryman, 2001; Kelle, 2001). It may be, too, that different data sources allow for resolution of some puzzle and in this way help advance explanation (Erzberger & Kelle, 2003). In Bryman's content analysis, this was shown to be a relatively unusual rationale or outcome of research (Bryman, 2005).

I want to say more about the logic of bringing together different methods and/or data sources and how they may help access social process. Certainly it is widely recognized that evidence is theory laden, not theory neutral. Although there has long been debate about how particular methods shape what we see (e.g., Becker & Geer, 1957; Trow, 1957), this issue remains important. Linking different methods helps to crystallize some of the issues since we are more forced to confront the specificity of particular datasets.

One example of the specificity of data as a lens on social process comes from Deacon and his colleagues' (1998, as cited in Bryman, 2000) study of researchers' interactions with, and experience of, the mass media in Britain. Here, diverse kinds of evidence reveal a seemingly single object of analysis to be multifaceted. In their research, qualitative and quantitative data generated an apparent discrepancy, with the former suggesting a relationship of conflict between researchers and journalists that was absent from the quantitative evidence. What should we make of this discrepancy? It is here that arguments typically start up about how effectively different methods tap into the most important issues. But what is more interesting and productive is to consider how the different kinds of evidence reveal different facets of social experience. Both may be valid so long as we understand the nature of the method, the context in which the data are created, and the precise way such data accesses the issues under investigation. Deacon (1998, as cited in Bryman, 2001) showed that in their survey responses academics gave an "average" rating of their dealings with journalists, yet in semistructured interviews they were oriented to memorable encounters. We might suggest that atypical stories get played up in narrative accounts. They make a good story. They may also have an impact on people's lived experience far greater than the "average" rating reveals. Here we can see how different methods access (or "reconstruct") different facets of the same experience.

Research into values provides a second example of how data from a particular micro or macro perspective provide a specific and potentially distorting lens on our research questions. Mason (2002) argues, with reference to qualitative methods, that we should see "asking, listening, and interpretation" as theoretical projects: "how we ask and listen are theoretical enactments of our assumptions around where the phenomenon we are interested in are located, and how the interviewee and interview can illuminate the issues" (Mason, 2002, pp. 233–234).

In her substantive interest in researching values and morality in kinship relationships, Mason is concerned that people have sought an understanding of values and morals through abstract interview questions, arguing that these "direct attention to wrong or 'nonexistent' locations" and, further, that "they miss the point about morality in that they assume it is a thing rather than a process or practice" (Mason, 2002, pp. 233–234). Following a more in-depth line of inquiry to tackle this, we might invite people to provide "real-life" stories, yet we need to be aware that people may describe their decisions and behaviors in moral terms. For example, in deciding on the best type of care for their preschool child, or in making decisions about whether to work or care full time for preschool-age children, interviewees stress moral commitments and evaluative judgments (Duncan & Edwards, 1999). However, a wide picture reveals such moral accounts to be patterned in relation to social and economic constraints and opportunities, revealing "moral" judgements to be socially shaped (Duncan & Edwards, 1999; Duncan & Irwin, 2004). This is not to say that people are making up a moral account. They may choose to emphasize certain facets of their experience and choices, facets that may be important to them in their accounts to themselves, as well as to other people. Yet these may be partial accounts. In consequence, such accounts might lead us to overestimate moral reflexivity as a driver of behavior. It is not that accounts of belief, values, and choices are without value; far from it. However, we do need to have a clear understanding of how such data relate (or fail to relate) to our research question.

In this example we may see that a breadth of evidence that looks at responses across diverse contexts (whether through qualitative or survey means) allows us to see more clearly a patterning to the responses (Duncan & Edwards, 1999; Irwin, 2004). This patterning suggests that morality cannot be seen as an internal conversation in which individuals come to personal judgments about "doing the right thing," nor can it be understood only as an outcome of proximate context and interaction. The structured nature of such judgments reveals diverse contexts that shape moral and evaluative judgments (e.g., which is the best type of care for my preschool child?). "Up close" (in-depth) evidence reveals the importance to people of the moral content of their choices; "wide angle" (e.g., survey) evidence reveals the structured nature of their "choices." Evidence from only one of these sources provides only a part of a bigger picture, but it may also lead us to misapprehend the nature of "choice" as a singularly moral or social phenomenon. Evidence from both sources helps reveal the moral and social to be intertwined.

Methods, in part, create what we see. This must not lead us to relativism, in which we accept the validity of multiple, and possibly conflicting, accounts of the social world. Rather, it requires that we know more precisely how we are tapping into the processes in which we are interested and how our data offer a particular construction of and lens on such processes. We need conceive of data (from different sources and different methods) as offering specific kinds of evidence, as particular rather than all-revealing slices through our research problems.

The examples raise the question of how we may best access social process and how different data sources facilitate this. It is often said that quantitative research allows us access to pattern and qualitative method allows us access to process. Bryman (2005) supplemented his content analysis with semistructured interviews with 20 social scientists who have used mixed methods in their research. We can note that his interviewees referred to qualitative evidence accessing meaning and quantitative research supplying breadth (Bryman, 2005), and this is a common enough observation. At one level this is clear-cut and not problematic. However, just as it is inappropriate to accept too clear-cut a distinction between quantitative and qualitative strategies (e.g., Hammersley, 1992), so, too, we need to be cautious about dichotomizing pattern and process. They overlap and can usefully be seen as mutually made. Pattern and process are not distinct domains of social phenomena but, rather, different kinds of accounts of social phenomena.

Data on micro-level processes are often deemed to help illuminate pattern. Clearly, knowledge of micro-level beliefs, behaviors, interactions, and so on can help illuminate processes that may be hinted at by, but opaque to, quantitative research. However, social patterns are less often considered to illuminate process at a micro level. Certainly, a core stock in trade of qualitative analysis, which often proceeds from patterns found "within the data," is building understanding of patterns based on comparing cases. However, "external" quantitative data are often deemed background or context for micro-level research and not connected in a direct way. This is unfortunate. It may be essential to adequate knowledge of the positioning of individuals being researched and of the content of their beliefs. In the aforementioned example of values in respect to child care, people's values concerning "good mothering" (as a full-time care commitment or a combination of paid work and care) connect closely with their circumstances in respect to employment-based opportunities and constraints (Irwin, 2005). The constraints under which people act and perceive their experience may not be articulated by them (or not always reflected on). Nevertheless, we do not properly understand the nature of people's values and subjective orientations if we do not understand the contexts in which they hold meaning.

In short, it is important to acknowledge that qualitative research does not have some privileged direct line to process. As Kelle puts it, "structural nearsightedness clearly limits the explanatory power of research results derived exclusively from the qualitative investigation of actors' perspectives" (2001, p. 30). Often we cannot make proper explanatory sense of individual-level data if we do not have a handle on more aggregate structures. We may fail to understand crucial meanings, motivations, and understandings held by individuals, and accessible through qualitative research, if we are unable to locate them in the broader contexts and structures in which they are embedded and take on shape. Furthermore, social diversity means that we get not only a partial picture from people but also a view from a specific location within that diversity. The structured nature of social arrangements not only provides "context" for micro-level beliefs, behaviors, expectations, and so on but also shapes their content in important ways.

Qualitative research is often charged with a need to better locate the specific as part of the general and to locate contexts of action and belief as part of a wider social structure. Quantitative research is often charged with a need to better access such contexts. Recently, there is a growing interest in more sufficiently connecting micro and macro levels of evidence and analysis. However, clearly this is not just about supplying evidence pertaining to an "interconnecting" meso layer of context, although this would often help. It is a conceptual issue. How we best bring together methods and data is not at heart a methodological question but one that must be driven by tackling substantive research questions and guided by criteria of adequacy in how we connect theory and data. In this section I have argued that particular data sources offer a specific lens on multifaceted problems, and by itself this *may* be misleading. Additionally, I have argued that qualitative data may not necessarily access process, because we need an adequate understanding of structure and of diversity to adequately locate and interpret qualitative evidence. However, this is not simply a case of connecting qualitative to quantitative data sources. In the next section, I explore some issues in representing the "general picture" through quantitative data analysis.

Issues in Researching Social Causality

In addressing issues in linking theory and data, different writers have drawn on the fascinating historical example of the search for understanding the spread of cholera in the 19th century (Freedman, 1991; Turner, 1997). The example has been used to draw some lessons in the use of different kinds of evidence and modes of analysis for theoretical development. I summarize it again in order to consider some of the lessons drawn by previous writers and to add some observations about the nature of evidence we can bring to our research questions.

Through his work in mid-19th century England, John Snow developed an understanding of cholera as caused by a waterborne organism transmitted through human waste. It was only in 1884 that the bacterium was isolated and observable through newly powerful microscopes. Before that the nature of cholera and its incidence had to be deduced from an understanding of extant patterns. Snow's explanation went against the grain of accepted wisdom and understanding that the disease was caused by miasma, or poisonous particles carried in the air (Freedman, 1991; Turner, 1997). Scientific work that was in keeping with the contemporary understanding was being developed by William Farr, the superintendent of the Statistical Department of the Registrar General's Office. Turner describes the rival interpretations of Snow and Farr and how their different methods, assumptions, and questions shaped their very different understandings of the nature of cholera (Turner, 1997).

Farr, in line with miasma theory, had identified a pattern, within a major epidemic, of a strong inverse relation between the altitude of dwellings and the incidence of cholera. He took this as strong evidence in support of the prevailing theory. Turner emphasizes the limits to causal reasoning based on attempts to model cholera and its correlates without getting close enough to understanding its patterning "on the ground." In contrast, Snow developed his radically new theory through an approach that took him much closer to the transmission of cholera by an intensive, empirically based inquiry (hence the "shoe leather" in Freedman's [1991] title). Snow sought a situated understanding. He collected evidence surrounding the incidence and outbreaks of cholera, exploring the details of people's living arrangements and circumstances. He built evidence about the course of different outbreaks and found a strong clustering around water sources that evidence showed to be contaminated (Freedman, 1991). Through a series of naturally occurring experiments, Snow developed, elaborated, and tested out his theory. Although Farr came to accept the plausibility of Snow's conjectures, Turner argues that he simply added these into his statistical model and concluded that the key causal mechanism of transmission (contaminated water) simply held some additional effect (Turner, 1997).

In particular, Turner argues that the assumptions embedded in Farr's statistical models and the nature of the process of statistical modeling effectively blinded him to countervailing evidence that should have upended his theory. Additionally, Farr's method left him without effective means to falsify the theory. In short, the efficacy of statistical models is bounded by the correctness of assumptions that shape the model. Turner sees echoes in today's modeling and a tendency still to wrongly equate correlation and causality. He is concerned that we are too quick to assume causality in the absence of an understanding of underlying mechanisms or processes that reveal the internal workings of the causal process in which we are interested.

Turner argues that today, as in the 19th century, causal modelers risk being too distant from their data and that, although we have various tools for modeling associations, there remains the possibility that we are not correctly representing the mechanisms in which we are interested. Therefore "social scientists are a bit like Farr before his complete conversion to Snow's account of cholera" (Turner, 1997, p. 43). Causal models are no better than the assumptions on which they are founded. Sound knowledge is built, rather, on intensive empirical work, which holds qualitative insights and is available to testing and to falsification. Freedman, too, sees in Snow's work a more scientific approach to advancing explanation. He particularly stresses the value of Snow's development of questions and theory that could be tested against the empirical evidence and in a wide variety of settings and sees this as the model to emulate (Freedman, 1991). For Freedman:

> regression models are not a particularly good way of doing empirical work in the social sciences today, because the techniques depend on knowledge that we do not have. Investigators who use the technique are not paying adequate attention to the connection—if any—between the models and the phenomena they are studying. (1991, p. 304)

Turner and Freedman both favor methods and modes of data collection and analysis that lie much closer to "internal" processes than the relative abstraction of researching aggregate patterns and associations and causal modeling.

Other writers have made similar arguments. Advocates of a realist program of research see some conventional approaches to data and explanation as entailing a "black box" approach to causal analysis. For example, experimental method follows an input–output model, measuring differences before and after the introduction of some manipulation but often failing to engage adequately with the actual processes engendering change (e.g., Pawson & Tilley, 1997). In the experimental method cause is seen as external to that being measured, a force acting on an object (Goldthorpe, 2000; Pawson & Tilley, 1997). Similarly conventional approaches to statistical modeling, and variable-led analysis more widely, have been challenged for holding an inadequate representation of "internal mechanisms" and processes (Byrne, 2002; Pawson & Tilley, 1997). In their social realist perspectives, explanation needs to access internal processes, the "chemistry" of process, rather than simply deducing it from "external" evidence. Crucially, "generative theory sees causation as acting internally as well as externally" (Pawson & Tilley, 1997, p. 34). Nevertheless, adequately representing processes remains a challenge for social explanation.

For example, reflecting back on Turner's critique of Farr, we need to recognize that Farr believed that he had an appropriate and accurate representation of causal process. He thought he was approximating the "internal process." He was working with the prevailing theoretical understanding, and the evidence available to him appeared to confirm this theory (Turner, 1997). As Blalock (1991) says, it is only with the benefit of hindsight that we can distinguish so straightforwardly "between the tactics of the very few successful detectives and those of the presumably much greater number of failing detectives" (Blalock, 1991, p. 329). How can we know when a particular understanding is the best bet? Snow benefited from "natural experiments" in which he could develop and test out his developing theoretical propositions. An important principle, when we do not benefit from "natural experiments," is to create our own and make our assumptions available to testing (e.g., Blalock, 1991; Lieberson, 1992; Pawson & Tilley, 1997).

Turner (1997) and Freedman (1991) advocate strategies that seek to "get close" to "internal processes," with movement between proximate circumstances and broader patterns, and see this as important to developing theoretical inferences about causality. This movement across "levels" of evidence, between close up and wide angle, improves our understanding of process through deriving detailed empirical evidence, exploring general patterns, generating propositions, and testing them out across different contexts. It calls for working with all the available data to develop a more adequate theory. Blalock points out that the cholera example may be misleading as a metaphor for social science given that in the latter we are usually dealing with multiple causality and forms of contingency not evident in the cholera example (Blalock, 1991). Nevertheless, the case for moving between levels and subjecting theoretical propositions to test is every bit as key to enhancing social science understanding.

The cholera example, as others, shows how prior assumptions and expectations govern the ways in which we approach and analyze data. However, this is not to say that we are doomed to reproduce our prior conceptual frameworks. Empirical data can certainly challenge and even lead to a renewal of theory. Before exploring this in relation to some concrete examples of research, later in the chapter, I consider some recent criticisms of quantitative modeling. Again, we see concerns with the level of abstraction from the source data entailed in causal modeling, and an argument has been made that we need to build macro-level datasets, evidence, and analyses that can more closely represent social experiences, interactions, and patterns. Again, this is an argument about more adequately theorizing social process through interrogating the links between micro- and macro-level evidence.

The critics of variable-centered, or variable-led, quantitative modeling do not (generally) deny that the approach is necessary and valuable to representing patterns and regularities in social life (see Kemp & Holmwood, 2003, for a critique of those who do). After all, the knowledge of extant regularities is fundamental to exploring social life and its stable reproduction over time. However, in advocating a realist approach, various writers have been critical of variable-led analysis in which variables, at least at times, are seen to represent external forces acting *on* people or *on* social systems. Variable analysis in causal modeling necessarily looks at average effects (Byrne, 2005) and risks failing to get at where the social action is. For Lieberson and Lynn (2002), causal modeling is part of an inappropriate (classical-physics-derived) model of good science in the linking of evidence and theory. They argue that this model needs a radical reworking and that other models of scientific endeavor (such as the development of knowledge in evolutionary biology) provide better metaphors and guides for social science research (Lieberson & Lynn, 2002). Thus critics say that there is a tendency for variable-led analysis to insufficiently access context and to risk reifying variables as real forces. Byrne calls for death to the variable, a humorous yet serious challenge to those who place too much store by variable-led analysis in resolving conceptual problems. He insists that there is a risk that such analyses mislead as to generative mechanisms, in part through failing to engage with context and contingency. Byrne (2002) argues that:

> Variables describing complex systems are descriptions of properties of the system as a whole. We can consider them as the dimensions of a multi-dimensional state space with the actual character of the system at any point in time being represented by the set of values on measured variables considered as coordinates in that state space. However, the coordinates are more of an address than a description of causes: they tell us where–not why. (p. 7)

He desires an approach that is case based rather than variable based, in which it is possible to aggregate up from knowledge of individuals in contexts and that additionally recognizes that systems are more than the sum of their parts and have emergent properties; that is, they produce outcomes that could not be predicted on the basis of knowledge of the parts. He argues that there is an important potential site for convergence between qualitative research and method and quantitative method, should it take the route he advocates, seeing "[the] key link between the two [as] the focus on the case rather than some abstraction from the case reified and regarded as a variable" (Byrne, 2002, p. 160).

Byrne may be overstating the extent to which social scientists suppose that variable analysis somehow does the theoretical work for them. Many would see variables as providing us with probabilistic descriptions of social diversity. Social science researchers rarely insist that some cause *determines* some outcome. One can think of many examples in which researchers treat variable evidence in terms of "variate traces," which Byrne recommends: Variables provide a form of evidence, not a definitive account. Yet in practice reliance on variables does push toward a particular definition of the problem at hand. A variable-centered analysis offers a *particular* reconstruction and representation of the processes in which we are interested.

It is useful to reflect further on Byrne's concern that we reify variables. The methodological concern articulated by Byrne holds echoes within recent subject-based debates in sociologies of difference. Here some writers have argued that there is a risk that social differences are reified in research, as their salience is often assumed, where it needs to be explained or contextualized (e.g., Anthias, 1998, 2001; Epstein, 1988; Young, 1990, 1997). Some writers, including myself, have argued that categories of difference, such as ethnicity, gender, and class, are sometimes inappropriately treated as causes, rather than outcomes, of wider social processes (Anthias, 1998, 2001; Bottero & Irwin, 2003; Irwin, 2005). However, it may be crucial to research such divisions and not treat them as starting points for analysis. At a minimum we need to know when they count and why. What processes shape differences and give them salience (e.g., Bottero, 2004; Brubaker, 2002; Irwin, 2005; Siltanen, 1994)? In short, this requires an understanding of context and contingency and the shaping of diverse relevancies. There are parallels here with Byrne's advocacy of "mapping coordinates" of diversity and of taking a more taxonomic approach to ordering quantitative data through which we can remain more true to social context. For example, later in the chapter I show how gendered differences are being reshaped and how it is more useful to locate gender as an outcome of social relations (which are undergoing change) than to treat it as a static category or given social division.

In this section I have argued that we need to access underlying processes that shape the phenomena in which we are interested, a task that requires knowledge of contexts. Furthermore, we need to acknowledge that the way we categorize evidence entails theoretical assumptions. Neither qualitative nor quantitative research provides a privileged "direct line" to underlying processes. Qualitative evidence may speak more directly to process but will only do so where we can locate its specificity. Standard forms of quantitative data modeling and analysis have been challenged for being at too far a remove from specificity, for example, removed from perceptions, expectations, beliefs, behaviors, and modes of interaction as these relate to diverse contexts. Forms of evidence all carry theoretical assumptions and provide a particular, and theory-imbued, lens on our research questions. To improve our bearings on the processes in which we are interested, then, the use of different sources of evidence can help us. How we connect this evidence is a theoretical issue, and we need to reflect on how evidence relates to the social processes and phenomena in which we are interested. In the next section I focus on some empirical examples, drawing on evidence from different "levels" of the social in seeking to tackle problems of explanation and to enhance our understanding of social processes.

Subjectivity and Social Structure: Linking Data in Researching Social Diversity and Social Change

In all the examples in this section, I explore research areas in which some writers have identified what they see as a discrepancy or misalignment between people's social position on the one hand and their perceptions and attitudes on the other. Some writers argue that in the current era we have seen a loosening of the relationship between subjective orientations and social structural processes. I argue that such conclusions are misplaced. Rather than accounting for discrepancies by reference to categories external to the empirical data (such as ideologies), reinterrogating the data and exploring links between macro and micro evidence contributes to a renewed understanding of the mutuality of subjective orientations and social structural processes.

Youth and the Life Course: Exploring Attitudes and Social Diversity

First I take two examples from studies of youth and early adulthood. One is from qualitative and the other from quantitative research. Both show interesting insights into the link between position and disposition. We can draw out some general themes.

Various youth researchers have engaged in depth with the question of how values and choices on the one hand relate to structural processes on the other. One of the issues here has been addressing the gap between macro-level evidence that reveals clearly structured patterns of inequality and its reproduction and micro-level evidence of people's perceptions of choice and ownership of their destinies. In qualitatively based interviews, people will be likely to stress choice and agency in the stories they tell about themselves, in contrast to the quantitative evidence that reveals significant class-related inequalities in opportunity and constraint (e.g., Furlong & Cartmel, 1997). How do we understand the seeming discrepancy between the types of evidence? Some writers have posited ideological forces that obfuscate reality and encourage compliance with unequal and unjust social arrangements (for an extended discussion, see Irwin, 2005). However, it is more productive to consider how people's positions within the social structure will tend to engender and normalize particular views. Furthermore, as Nilsen and Brannen (2002) say, people are not routinely oriented to, nor typically particularly aware of, the external and structured forces that shape their lives so, "When structural forces and personal resources . . . support one another there is a tendency for the structural resources to take on an 'invisible' quality" (Nilsen & Brannen, 2002, p. 42.)

An example of the link between position and perception is revealed in a recent qualitative research project by Gillies and her colleagues (Gillies, Holland, & Ribbens McCarthy, 2003). Here a generational dimension is in evidence as young adults and their parents describe their perceptions of the formers' transitions to independence. Gillies and her colleagues stress the "embedded" nature of young adults' accounts, particularly the relational and interconnected nature of young people's understandings. The researchers argue that for young people describing their experiences, growing up was a process of taking control of their behavior and accepting responsibility for their decisions. Young people saw themselves as being at the center of their transition, as agents or authors of their progression to adult status. In contrast, interestingly, their parents emphasized their children's physical changes and the continuities they saw in their children's personalities as they progressed from childhood to adulthood. Young adults highlighted the ways in which they had changed since their childhoods, whereas parents reflected on consistencies.

We can see these differences as unsurprising outcomes of the interviews, but it is pertinent to remind ourselves that young people may emphasize agency and the "cult of the self" more than any other life-course group. Gillies and her colleagues stress that the individualism expressed by the youngsters "was clearly contained within a wider social context, characterised by interdependent family relationships" (Gillies et al., 2003, p. 47).

I would suggest that we can also usefully draw out something that remains implicit within their account–young adults and their parents are positioned differently and might be seen as offering different "vantage points" on the question of transition to independence. The young adults naturally enough experience themselves as being agents in a context in which boundaries are widening and the scope for their action expands as they seize greater autonomy and responsibilities. Parents may have a more "sociological" understanding of this transition, having some social distance from it (and possibly engaging in a fair degree of reflexive analysis about their children's position and how, as parents, to best relate to it). The vantage points of youth and parent are very different. Superficially they appear contradictory, but we can better see them as consistent–an example of how diverse values and perceptions are closely aligned with people's diverse social locations. We see more clearly the links between subjective orientations and objective structures if we delineate the diverse contexts that shape people's experiences and perceptions.

My second example draws on small-scale survey research that also points to a connectedness of social position and subjective dispositions. Within a survey exploring various aspects of work and family life of 92 young people, ages 16–34, all respondents were invited to rank claims to employment among people in different household and life-course circumstances (see Irwin, 1995, for details). They were asked to imagine that six people apply for a job and to assume that they are all equally qualified for the job. They were then asked "Who would you most like to see get the job? Who would you next most like to see get the job?" and so on. The six people in the vignette were described as: a young woman living at home; a young man living at home; a young woman living away from home; a married man with children, wife not working; a married woman, no child at home, husband not working; and a single mother with young children.

Of course the assumption about the perceived salience of household need is not buried very deeply, and one might see it as a self-corroborating exercise in which respondents rank in "need" order, merely reproducing the researchers' assumptions about the salience of need and obligations. In this we could see a clear example of the imposition of meaning. The researcher establishes, through structured questions, a conceptual framework to which respondents obligingly orient (regardless of its relevance to them). The researcher then mistakenly remains convinced of the value of the conceptual framework. We know from survey research how readily respondents engage in the task with which they are presented and rarely challenge the framework in which questions are asked, regardless of their perceived salience in the eyes of the respondent (e.g., Pawson, 1989). Yet in the responses to the question described previously is a patterning that suggests that something rather more interesting than "theory in, theory out" is going on.

It should be noted that the question was part of a small survey conducted in the context of an undermining of young adults' status in the United Kingdom in the late 1980s. A reading of the contemporary literature would suggest that ideological, individualizing processes prevented youths from seeing the extent of their exploitation and deteriorating relative position. Additionally, a reading of the literature would suggest that, at a minimum, a self-interested age preference would prevail. This implied that respondents would commend youth first. Few did. The overwhelming majority favored the claims of the single mother or the married man. This might at first seem to be a classic example of a self-corroborating exercise, in which respondents reflect back the assumptions embedded in the response categories. However, the patterning of responses suggests that we are accessing reflections on the structure of resource distribution from different vantage points within it. What is especially notable is that the young adults, who were themselves still dependent on parents and/or without dependents of their own, favored the claim of the single mother. A lack of financial obligations tallied with a likelihood of positive discrimination in favor of the single mother. Those who were themselves married or cohabiting or had dependent children of their own were far more likely to favor the claim of the married man whose wife was not working. This held for women as well as for men.

The example shows that we can usefully move away from age as the key variable in exploring age-related patterns and explore positions and attitudes as they relate to household/family need and commitments. To do so reveals the connectedness of micro-level perceptions and broader macro-level structures. The respondents' attitudes show a prioritizing of the claims of those with dependents, but within this structure their attitudes are patterned in relation to their own life-course position and circumstances in respect to household resourcing commitments. We can see a connection between individual orientations and the structures of distribution in which people are embedded, in which those with dependents are more likely to favor the male breadwinner's claim. Through considering diverse vantage points from within a variegated structure we can see more clearly the links between micro-level orientations and macro-level structures.

Clearly, then, this was not a self-corroborating exercise. Rather, it revealed a diverse pattern of attitudes shaped in relation to people's own household circumstances and a linked prioritizing of claims on work in relation to household needs. Respondents' attitudes reflected the structure of distribution and their position within it. The patterning of responses can be seen as an outcome of practical attitudes to distributional exigencies. In this sense evaluative judgments are shaped in relation to "what is" and reflect people's location within an asymmetrical pattern of distribution.

I have used both examples in the area of youth to argue that there is connectedness between people's outlooks, attitudes, and their social positioning. This theme of coherence between orientations and position within the social structure runs through the next two examples, which both relate to issues of gender and employment.

Work-Rich and Work-Poor Households: Using Data to Address Puzzles of Explanation

The details of my next example come from research conducted in the early 1990s, but the focus on puzzle solving and its value for social explanation retains its currency today. There is a parallel here with Erzberger and Kelle's (2003) advocacy of theoretical renewal as a response to divergent conclusions drawn from qualitative and quantitative evidence. The example is based on research into social relationships and economic change in the northeast of England, in the context of industrial restructuring through the 1980s (Morris, 1995). A concern was with the concentration of employment and unemployment at the level of the household. This showed a distinct patterning at a national level, a patterning paralleled in a survey of 790 couples in Hartlepool undertaken in 1989 (Irwin & Morris, 1993). The general patterning, which is well known, can be described as a division between work-rich and work-poor households. The period from the 1970s through the 1980s had manifested a growing concentration. In 1986, at a national level, 67% of men in paid employment had spouses also in paid work compared with 24% of unemployed men. Various studies revealed similar patterns, and researchers sought to understand the processes shaping this concentration of employment and unemployment at the household level among married couples. Much of the research was framed by the question: What do the wives of unemployed men do? A principal hypothesis of social policy researchers was that the social security structure provided a significant disincentive to work among women with unemployed husbands. At the time, social security and benefits for the unemployed carried very low earnings entitlements for dependents. Above a minimal earning allowance for the spouse, benefits were withdrawn, pound for pound. There was, therefore, a clear economic logic for a married woman not to work if her husband was drawing unemployment benefit or income support. This "social security" explanation remained a dominant understanding of causality in the patterning of work-rich and work-poor households.

Interestingly, some alternative, although complementary, explanations followed a similar theory of causality. For example, some argued the importance of a "bruised machismo" effect: that cultures of and beliefs about masculinity and breadwinning worked against a wife being employed if her husband was unemployed. However, in both explanations, there was a focus on the level of the household, with women's labor-force participation understood *in terms of their husbands'* labor-force status. We can note a gendered assumption here about his independence and her dependence and the assumption of some external causal process (social security disincentive structure, cultural mores) having an impact on couples and shaping unemployment outcomes.

A problem here lay with the failure to test out the assumptions embedded in the theory. Interestingly, though, this could be done. In the 1980 Women and Employment

Survey (WES), nonworking women married to unemployed men were asked to state their reasons for not themselves working. Eighty percent did not cite their husbands' employment status as a cause (Joshi, 1984). Of the 17% who said it was important, only 14 out of 58, or 4% of the total, said they did not work because their household benefits would be cut. This evidence was echoed in the Hartlepool survey. There was a concentration of employment and unemployment in households, with 67% of households having an employed male with an employed female partner, in contrast to 21% in which the male partner was unemployed. In open-ended questions within the survey, only 12% of nonworking women said they were unavailable to work because their spouses' benefits would be cut. This verbatim evidence, with its limited mention of benefits, appears to directly contradict the assumptions of the social security model of causality. It is a nice example of a research puzzle. To explain its resolution, we can, here, consider one particular finding (for more detail and discussion of further evidence, see Irwin & Morris, 1993).

Other studies sought to control for possible intervening factors to ensure that they had identified a "pure" causal effect. For example, they controlled by class, assuming that to do so was to control socioeconomic status. Thus if, for each class, employed husbands have employed wives and unemployed husbands have nonworking wives, we can be more confident that we have a pure causal effect: It is his labor-force status that affects her labor-force status. However, if we stop looking at women's status under the assumption that it is caused by their husbands' status, a different picture emerges. A range of indicators revealed a direct association between women's own positions and their husbands' labor-force status. For example, there was a strong association between women's own occupational standing (from their current or most recent jobs) and whether or not their husbands were unemployed, even controlling for the husband's social class. To illustrate, among unskilled husbands, 53% of those who were employed were married to women whose most recent jobs were in low-status occupations, in contrast to 90% of unemployed unskilled husbands. Broad class groupings are clearly very inadequate as a measure of social disadvantage and advantage. The example is drawn from wider evidence in the dataset that the concentration of employment and unemployment is more effectively explained by a similarity within couples of employment chances; the coincidence of spouses' unemployment is closely linked to their similar, independently held disadvantages in relation to employment opportunities. The new interpretation presents a direct challenge to the social security explanation. Importantly, the new analysis of the aggregate data provides an explanation that is in line with open-ended question data on women's self-reported experience. In consequence, it enables an improved understanding of the social structuring of advantage and disadvantage across households. Tackling contradictions arising from interpretations of available data and their reinterpretation can allow us to transform our understanding and develop a more inclusive explanatory framework.

The next example maintains the theme of gender relations and explores quantitative and qualitative data to reveal the close links between people's social position and their evaluations of the right thing to do in respect to work and care.

Reshaping Gender, Work, and Caregiving: Exploring the Connectedness of Attitudes and Social Position in a Context of Change

The example here is drawn from work in the area of gender, work, and caregiving. In it I draw together evidence in building a picture of diversity and change in women's commitments to child care and employment. The analysis offers an alternative account to the influential view that values are more autonomous of social circumstances than they were in the past (e.g., Beck, 1992; Beck & Beck-Gernsheim, 2002; and, from a different perspective, Hakim, 2000; see also Irwin, 2005, for the detailed account).

In the United Kingdom, full-time child care among women with preschool children is quite common. However, the incidence of full-time care has fallen dramatically over recent decades. The increase in labor-force participation rates has been most marked since the 1980s. Among women with children ages 0–4, in the years 1949, 1959, and 1969, overall employment participation rates stood at 14%, 15%, and 22%, respectively. The full- time employment participation rate across these years was constant at around 8%. In the years 1981, 1991, and 2001, the overall employment participation rate of women with children ages 0–4 rose from 24 to 42 to 54%, respectively. The full-time employment rates across these years rose from 6 to 13 to 18%, respectively.

There is a wealth of research in the area. Through the 1980s and 1990s, many writers emphasized continuity in women's position of relative disadvantage, given the extent to which the increase in participation was in part-time, flexible, and often low-paying work (e.g., Arber & Ginn, 1995; Hakim, 1996). More recently, there has been recognition that the growth of women's employment participation in late-20th-century Britain is bound up with important changes in the economic and social positioning of women and men (Bruegel & Perrons, 1998; Irwin, 1999, 2005; Walby, 1997). Several writers have presented evidence of an erosion of breadwinner patterns of household resourcing over the past three decades, with a rise in the incidence of dual-earner households and a growing importance of female earnings for household support. This does not betoken simply an improvement in the earnings of women, as it is also bound up with a decline in the relative adequacy of male earnings among some men, particularly those in manual-labor jobs (Bruegel & Perrons, 1998; Egerton & Savage, 2000; Irwin, 1995, 1999). I have argued elsewhere that these changes in women's and men's relations to employment, earning, and each other are linked to changes in occupational structures but are also not separable from changing norms about women's paid employment through family building, from women's claims for independence, nor from changing perceptions of adequate standards of living (Irwin, 2005).

A significant strand of recent research, in seeking to locate change, maintains that values are more important than they were in the past in shaping decisions about work and care. Some argue that attitudes and preferences play a significant role in shaping behaviors (e.g., Hakim, 2000; Hattery, 2001; Marks & Houston, 2002). However, although attitudes and preferences are clearly important motivators, we need to be cautious about seeing them as newly "loosened" from social structural arrangements. The data explored here are part of a wider argument that there is still a close alignment between subjective orientations and social and economic circumstances. There is evidence for this at different levels. We can see it in both general and more targeted social attitudinal data and their association with circumstance. We can see it in qualitative data that explore women's circumstances and their perceptions of the "right thing to do." What is notable about the latter is the link between many women's values and their current positions in a context of significant changes in women's relations to paid work and child care.

Attitudinal data provides a very particular lens, as do other kinds of data, on the processes in which we are interested (cf. Mason, 2002). Attitudinal data are sometimes treated like a thermometer, an instrument to measure the collective temperature, a kind of average of the national outlook on crucial issues. There are plenty of critics of attitudinal surveys; in particular, many find fault with the superficial nature of attitudinal statements. As discussed briefly earlier, responses are not mere artifacts of imposed meaning. In the examples here, they reveal a clear pattern of covariation with material and situational factors.

General attitudes toward women's roles and appropriate patterns of behavior among parents run broadly in parallel with actual changes in women's employment participation rates (e.g., Crompton, Brockmann, & Wiggins, 2003; Dex, 1988). So, for example, when asked whether a married woman with children under school age ought to work or stay at home, in 1965 78% of female survey respondents thought she should stay at home. In 1980, 60% of respondents thought she should do so (Hunt, 1968, and Martin & Roberts, 1984, as cited in Dex, 1988). In the 2002 British Social Attitudes Survey (BSAS), 46% of female respondents thought that women with a preschool-age child should stay at home. (In the 2002 BSAS women were asked: "Do you think that women should work outside the home full time, part time, or not at all under these circumstances?" for different categories, including when there is a child under school age.) Notably, the 1965 and 2002 figures compare particularly closely with actual participation rates at the time.

The preceding discussion of change is indicative only, but it gives a sense of a shift across the British population toward more pro-work attitudes on behalf of mothers of young children. Generalized attitudes may be of some interest in taking the national pulse, but they hold more limited use in understanding the actions of different parts of the social body. We can usefully consider in more depth the variable patterning of attitudes among those for whom the issues have a more direct salience. It is possible to see the close links between people's own circumstances and their attitudes when we do so. For example, working mothers are in favor of mothers working, and homemaker mothers are not. In the 2002 BSAS, 16% of homemaker mothers of preschool children felt that a woman in the same situation should work, and 64% felt that she should stay at home. In contrast, 66% of working mothers felt that such a woman should work, whereas 16% felt that she should stay at home (a ratio of 4:1 homemaker women favor staying at home; a ratio of more than 4:1 working women favor working). Clearly there is little evidence of a dissonance between experience and attitudes; rather, we see a noteworthy consistency.

We need to consider a risk that the link between attitudes and experience/situation is tautological. It is possible that, if people do not feel particularly strongly about something or have not much reflected on it, their response to an attitude statement may simply be based on their practical experience. What they are familiar with may simply translate for them, in giving a survey response, into the "right thing to do," even, perhaps especially, if they have not given it much thought. This is a risk and a potential problem for attitudinal survey research. However, we can plausibly expect that those for whom the question has most direct salience will have given it some thought—that is, they will see the statement as tapping into something relevant to them. Additionally, we can note that the patterning of attitudes is closely aligned to social circumstances more widely and not just to their behavior. At this point we can be more confident that the patterning of responses is not simply an artifact of the mode of asking questions.

Different datasets yield evidence of an association between people's circumstances and their attitudes. I consider an example of data gathered within a small survey, conducted as part of the research by the Economic and Social Research Council Research Group for the Study of Care, Values and the Future of Welfare (CAVA). In this "Life as a Parent" survey, the distributions of attitudes were explored. Women who were most in favor of full-time maternal child care (based on three attitudinal variables and described as "pro-maternal care") were identified, with a view to comparison with Hakim's (2000) argument that there is class-random diversity in their outlooks. It is notable that in this dataset the women were all in similar socioeconomic circumstances. The 14 out of

96 women interviewed who were "pro-care" were all relatively constrained in their employment options but were not among the most disadvantaged, and most of them were living with an employed partner. If these women worked, it was part time, and in only one case did the woman describe herself as working for "essentials," whereas half of the women who were not in the "pro-maternal care" group described themselves as working for this reason. A similar analysis of national-level BSAS data, using the two parallel attitudinal questions, also shows that those who are "pro-maternal care" fall within the lower half of household income groups but not among the lowest. This evidence runs counter to arguments that "values are becoming more important determinants of behaviour, relative to . . . social structural factors" (Hakim, 2000, pp. 80–81). It suggests ongoing links between values and circumstances.

We can also explore perceptions of the appropriate commitments of mothers through qualitative data. The Mothers, Care, and Employment (MCE) project was a qualitative study also conducted as part of the CAVA research project. It was conducted across different locales in Yorkshire and Lancashire, England. Parents (mostly mothers) of children age 14 and under were interviewed, with a particular focus on issues of value and people's sense of "doing the right thing" in respect to caring for their children (Duncan, Edwards, Reynolds, & Alldred, 2003; Duncan & Irwin, 2004; see also Duncan & Edwards, 1999). The data allow us to further reflect on general developments in the relative position of women in particular. It seems likely that the salience of work as a crucial component of women's identities has a greater spread across the population and that it is growing among groups for whom it has traditionally been a less definitive experience or expectation. The data show an alignment between circumstance and values, yet these values reveal a significant work ethic among women who are mothers of young children. This is a feature of middle-class respondents, many of whom see work as a core part of their identities. But it is also a theme for many white working-class respondents with more circumscribed opportunities and perhaps more circumscribed motivations for work. Women hold work as more central to their identities, and more white mothers, including working-class mothers, have a work-related identity, as well as a mother identity. This is consistent with the trends toward increased employment rates among women over the past quarter century. Although some groups of working-class mothers have always worked, employment participation among mothers of preschool children (0–4) is becoming more extensive. The MCE evidence reveals the very routine nature of work among women and suggests that it would disrupt their sense of themselves if they were to stop work fully through the family-building period.

Even among the relatively few, typically working-class, women defined by Duncan and colleagues (2003) as "primarily mother," who express clearly their high level of commitment to full-time parental care for their children, there is a clear sense of paid work as a core part of their identities. For example, Theresa encapsulates what Duncan terms a "primarily mother" orientation:

> "I believe if you have children you should fetch 'em up yourself rather than like you get your career mums who can go out to work and somebody else has fetched your child up and I don't believe in that really."

Nevertheless, this woman returned to work as a health care assistant when her child was 10 months old. She has a job-share arrangement with her husband, and both work 25 hours a week as care assistants. When asked "And you say that that is because you found it difficult to be just at home?", she replied:

> "Yeah. Yeah I found it hard work, I needed to see other people and do other things as well as be at home. I needed to be myself as well as being a mum."

That is, although her commitment to caregiving may be paramount, she still sees work and its sociability as core aspects of her identity.

Other interviewees expressed further dimensions of the importance of work to them. For example, Jessica said:

> "I work so that I can give my son everything that I've never had and so that I can provide for him and if he wants anything he can have it, not to spoil him but to make sure that . . . we can provide a decent standard of living."

In discussing her return to work when her son was young, she said:

> "I wanted to go back to work. I don't know why, but I did. I think it were, it were important for me to get back to being that person, not just being me little boy's mum."

Another respondent who encapsulates the "primarily mother" orientation was Christine, who said:

> "I couldn't see t'point of having a child and leaving him with somebody else."

Christine was from Barnsley, a traditional coal mining town and therefore a cultural context in which we might expect Duncan's "primarily mother" orientation (Duncan et al., 2003) to be common. Christine has five children and, despite her orientation, she has worked fairly extensively in unskilled (factory and cleaning) jobs while building her family. Her desire for work is financial, although such a motivation needs to be understood in the context of cultural expectations about adequacy. It is also linked to other aspects of her identity, especially the expectation of independence:

> "My husband always, always wanted me to stop working yeah. Ye know, this were always a bit of friction between me and [him] . . . 'cos he'd always say we'll cope and we'll manage ye know but I were always, I've always had money so I were always scared of just relying on his wage and then I'd say yeah, but what happens when I want summat and what happens if I want to do summat or I want to buy a new coat . . . do I ask you for money, I says: 'I don't think it'll work out like that' and he says 'yeah yeah of course you ask me' but ye know, its not, I can't. I've always had a job, from 19 I've always worked and I've always had me own money."

To work seems an important part of her identity and the kind of role model she wants to be for her children (traditionally associated with black women's orientations to work and care) (Duncan & Edwards, 1999):

> "I want my children to work, I want 'em to work, I want em to do good at school, as good as they can ye know, and try and try and get on."

So even among those who have few qualifications and who express Duncan's "primarily mother" orientation, it is notable that strongly expressed caregiving commitments are consistent with holding a significant work ethic. A sense of paid work appears to be a core component of the identity of a wide spectrum of women who have young children. It is common for this ethic to be bound up with women's desire for independence and autonomy.

As well as the importance of work to these women's sense of themselves and their self-esteem, it is notable that their views were not necessarily mirrored by their husbands, who, like Christine's, tended to "fall in" with their wives' plans following a position of doubt. The expressions here seem illustrative of the differential rate of change in women's and men's social positions. Another example of a husband falling in with his wife's desires is evident in the responses of Lisa, mother of five children. When asked if her husband was supportive when she returned to work, she said:

"When I first started for t'first few weeks he didn't like it—and we did have a few arguments and I says 'look, we either argue over t'fact that we don't see each other and you're tired and you're coming home and seeing to t'kids or we argue over money'. I says 'it's like Hobson's choice, which would you prefer? And he says 'I know you're right,' he says, 'carry on, we'll give it a bit longer,' and he's fine now, got used to it, the routine and there's no problem at all, he's quite all right with it."

The interview data is illustrative of individual-level experiences in a way that quantitative data cannot be, but it is consistent with the themes that are revealed through the general-level numerical data. From the 1970s there has been a marked rise in the employment rates of partnered mothers of young children. Work has become a more routinized experience within the family-building period. The quantitative evidence indicates that this is so for a larger section of the population. Qualitative data reveal the importance of work as a more core component of women's identities through the family-building period, and this includes working-class women who are relatively disadvantaged in their employment prospects. A pattern of mutuality between norms and women's (and men's) social positioning is evident in a period of significant changes in women's employment patterns. This is important. The different sources of evidence allow us to build a picture of diversity and change, and it is one that invites us to challenge and reinterrogate arguments that we are witnessing a historically new kind of division between norms and social structural processes. Different data sources give insights into social change, here notably change in the circumstances and social identities of women, and men, relating to employment and child care. Additionally, the evidence reminds us that gender, taken as a description of social division in those domains, is itself subject to change.

Across the examples I have given, I have drawn on different sources of evidence in reexamining the links between macro- and micro-level processes. In the examples of youth and of gender, work, and caregiving, I argued against accounts in which the subjective and objective are treated as distinct social "domains." Such accounts are associated with theoretical arguments of a new separation between social structural and subjective understandings. These arguments posit a new autonomy of values and choices, as in preference and individualization theories, and claims about ideology, in which external categories are imported to explain the seeming noncorrespondence of subjective and objective. However, a reinterrogation of data at different levels and an improved understanding of diversity and the locatedness of different vantage points allow us to see more clearly the connectedness of subjective and objective. It is by moving between levels of evidence that we can better access processes that shape diversity and change in gendered commitments to work and care. In the example of unemployment patterns, I addressed a puzzle arising from different data sources and their interpretation and sought a more expansive explanation through tackling and resolving the puzzle. All the examples reveal the connectedness of micro and macro, the subjective and the social structural. And in all, the use of evidence from different "levels" adds to our capacity to explain social pattern and process.

Conclusion

Linking methods is increasingly seen as a way forward in advancing social explanation. In this chapter I have argued that linking data from different levels of "the social" is important for many social science research questions and is crucial in cases in which we are seeking to understand social diversity and social change. Through a series of empirical examples, I have argued that bringing together macro- and micro-level data can contribute to better understanding of the connectedness of subjective orientations and social structural arrangements and improve our understanding of important social processes.

The linking of macro- and micro-level data is not first and foremost a technical issue but a conceptual one. Using a metaphor of our research problems as multifaceted, I have argued that different methods and different sources of data provide a *particular* lens on the social phenomena or processes being researched. Single sources of data can give us a partial picture, but it may also be one that is distorting. We cannot simply build up an adequate picture by piecing together the different components of evidence. Data themselves are not theory neutral but carry within them assumptions about how they relate to the phenomena under study. This does not mean that different data sources are incompatible. Nor does it mean that we will only reproduce the assumptions embedded within the data-collection tools. Seeking to bring together data can help clarify the nature of the phenomena under study by forcing us to confront the particularity and the theoretically imbued nature of different kinds of evidence. Linking data from different levels may make us aware not simply that what we see is part of a bigger story but that we may be in the wrong story altogether. Correspondingly, it has the potential to contribute to theoretical expansion or transformation.

References

Anthias, F. (1998). Rethinking social divisions: Some notes towards a theoretical framework. *Sociological Review, 46*(3), 505–535.

Anthias, F. (2001). The material and the symbolic in theorizing social stratification: Issues of gender, ethnicity and class. *British Journal of Sociology, 52*(3), 367–390.

Arber, S., & Ginn, J. (1995). The mirage of gender equality: Occupational success in the labour market and within marriage. *British Journal of Sociology, 46*(1), 21–43.

Beck, U. (1992). *Risk society: Towards a new modernity.* London: Sage.

Beck, U., & Beck-Gernsheim, E. (2002). *Individualization: Institutionalized individualism and its social and political consequences.* London: Sage.

Becker, H., & Geer, B. (1957). Participant observation and interviewing: A comparison. *Human Organization, 16*(3), 28–32.

Blalock, H. M. (1991). Are there really any *constructive* alternatives to causal modelling? In V. Marsden (Ed.), *Sociological methodology* (Vol. 21). Washington, DC: Blackwell.

Bottero, W. (2004). Class identities and the identity of class. *Sociology, 38*(5), 979–997.

Bottero, W., & Irwin, S. (2003). Locating difference: Class, "race" and gender and the shaping of social inequalities. *Sociological Review, 51*(4), 463–483.

Brannen, J. (2005). Mixing methods: The entry of qualitative and quantitative approaches into the research process. *International Journal of Social Research Methodology, 8*(3), 173–184.

Brubaker, R. (2002). Ethnicity without groups. *European Journal of Sociology, 43*(2), 163–189.

Bruegel, I., & Perrons, D. (1998). Deregulation and women's employment: The diverse experiences of women in Britain. *Feminist Economics, 4*(1), 103–125.

Bryman, A. (2001). *Social research methods.* Oxford, UK: Oxford University Press.

Bryman, A. (2005, October). *Why do we need mixed methods? Should we differentiate integration versus mixed methods?* Paper presented at the Economic and Social Research Council Research Methods Program Workshop on Mixed methods: Identifying the issues, University of Manchester, UK.

Byrne, D. (2002). *Interpreting quantitative data.* London: Sage.

Byrne, D. (2005). Complexity, configurations and cases. *Theory, Culture and Society, 22*(5), 95–111.

Crompton, R., Brockmann, M., & Wiggins, R. D. (2003). A woman's place . . . Employment and family life for men and women. In A. Park, J. Curtice, K. Thomson, L. Jarvis, & C. Bromley (Eds.), *British social attitudes: The 20th Report* (pp. 161–188). London: Sage.

Dex, S. (1988). *Women's attitudes towards work.* Basingstoke, UK: Macmillan.

Duncan, S., & Edwards, R. (1999). *Lone mothers, paid work and gendered moral rationalities.* Houndmills, UK: Macmillan.

Duncan, S., Edwards, R., Reynolds, T., & Alldred, P. (2003). Motherhood, paid work and partnering: Values and theories. *Work, Employment and Society, 17*(2), 309–330.

Duncan, S., & Irwin, S. (2004). The social patterning of values and rationalities: Mothers' choices in combining caring and employment. *Social Policy and Society, 3*(4), 391–399.

Egerton, M., & Savage, M. (2000). Age stratification and class formation: A longitudinal study of the social mobility of young men and women, 1971–1991. *Work, Employment and Society, 14*(1), 23–49.

Epstein, C. F. (1988). *Deceptive distinctions: Sex, gender and the social order.* New Haven, CT: Yale University Press.

Erzberger, C., & Kelle, U. (2003). Making inferences in

mixed methods: The rules of integration. In A. Tashakkori & C. B. Teddlie (Eds.), *Handbook of mixed methods in social and behavioral research* (pp. 457–488). Thousand Oaks, CA: Sage.

Freedman, D. A. (1991). Statistical models and shoe leather. In P. V. Marsden (Ed.), *Sociological methodology* (Vol. 21). Washington, DC: Blackwell.

Furlong, A., & Cartmel, F. (1997). *Young people and social change: Individualization and risk in late modernity.* Philadelphia: Open University Press.

Gillies, V., Holland, J., & Ribbens McCarthy, J. (2003). Past/present/future: Time and the meaning of change in the "family." In G. Allan & G. Jones (Eds.), *Social relations and the life course.* Houndmills, UK: Palgrave Macmillan.

Goldthorpe, J. (2000). *On sociology: Numbers, narratives and the integration of research and theory.* Oxford, UK: Oxford University Press.

Hakim, C. (1996). *Key issues in women's work: Female heterogeneity and the polarisation of women's employment.* London: Athlone Press.

Hakim, C. (2000). *Work–lifestyle choices in the 21st century: Preference theory.* New York: Oxford University Press.

Hammersley, M. (1992). *What's wrong with ethnography?* London: Routledge.

Hammond, C. (2005). The wider benefits of adult learning: An illustration of the advantages of multimethod research. *International Journal of Social Research Methodology, 8*(3), 239–255.

Hattery, A. (2001). *Women, work and family: Balancing and weaving.* Thousand Oaks, CA: Sage.

Irwin, S. (1995). *Rights of passage: Social change and the transition from youth to adulthood.* London: UCL Press.

Irwin, S. (1999). Resourcing the family: Gendered claims and obligations and issues of explanation. In E. B. Silva & C. C. Smart (Eds.), *The new family?* London: Sage.

Irwin, S. (2004). Attitudes, care and commitment: Pattern and process. *Sociological Research Online, 9*(3). Retrieved from *www.socresonline.org.uk/9/3/irwin.html*

Irwin, S. (2005). *Reshaping social life.* London: Routledge.

Irwin, S., & Morris, L. (1993). Social security or economic insecurity? The concentration of unemployment (and research) within households. *Journal of Social Policy, 22*(3), 349–372.

Joshi, H. (1984). *Women's participation in paid work: Further analysis of the Women and Employment Survey* (Department of Employment RP 45). London: Department of Employment.

Kelle, U. (2001). Sociological explanations between micro and macro and the integration of qualitative and quantitative methods. *Forum: Qualitative Social Research, 2*(1). Retrieved December 10, 2006, from *qualitative-research.net/fqs/fqs-eng.htm*

Kemp, S., & Holmwood, J. (2003). Realism, regularity and social explanation. *Journal for the Theory of Social Behaviour, 33*(2), 165–187.

Lieberson, S. (1992). Einstein, Renoir and Greeley: Some thoughts about evidence in sociology. *American Sociological Review, 57*(1), 1–15.

Lieberson, S., & Lynn, F. B. (2002). Barking up the wrong branch: Scientific alternatives to the current model of sociological science. *Annual Review of Sociology, 28*, 1–19.

Marks, G., & Houston, D. M. (2002). Attitudes towards work and motherhood held by working and non-working mothers. *Work, Employment and Society, 16*(3), 523–536.

Mason, J.(2002). Qualitative interviewing: Asking, listening and interpreting. In T. May (Ed.), *Qualitative research in action.* London: Sage.

Mason, J. (2006). Mixing methods in a qualitatively driven way. *Qualitative Research, 6*(1), 9–25.

Moran-Ellis, J., Alexander, V. D., Cronin, A., Dickinson, M., Fielding, J., Sleney, J., et al. (2006). Triangulation and integration: Processes, claims and implications. *Qualitative Research, 6*(1), 45–59.

Morris, L. (1995). *Social divisions: Economic decline and social structural change.* London: UCL Press.

Nilsen, A., & Brannen, J. (2002). Theorising the individual–structure dynamic. In J. Brannen, S. Lewis, A. Nilsen, & J. Smithson (Eds.), *Young Europeans, work and family: Futures in transition.* London: Routledge.

Pawson, R. (1989). *A measure for measures: A manifesto for empirical sociology.* London: Routledge.

Pawson, R., & Tilley, N. (1997). *Realistic evaluation.* London: Sage.

Siltanen, J. (1994). *Locating gender.* London: UCL Press.

Teddlie, C., & Tashakkori, A. (2003). Major issues and controversies in the use of mixed methods in the social and behavioral sciences. In A. Tashakkori & C. B. Teddlie (Eds.), *Handbook of mixed methods in social and behavioral research* (pp. 3–30). Thousand Oaks, CA: Sage.

Trow, M. (1957). Comment on "Participant observation and interviewing: A comparison." *Human Organization, 16*(3), 33–35.

Turner, S. (1997). Net effects: A short history. In V. R. McKim & S. P. Turner (Eds.), *Causality in crisis?: Statistical methods and the search for causal knowledge in the social sciences.* Notre Dame, IN: University of Notre Dame Press.

Walby, S. (1997). *Gender transformations.* London: Routledge.

Young, I. (1990). *Justice and the politics of difference.* Princeton, NJ: Princeton University Press.

Young, I. M. (1997). *Intersecting voices: Dilemmas of gender, political philosophy and policy.* Princeton, NJ: Princeton University Press.

CHAPTER 21

Longitudinal Research

An Emergent Method in the Social Sciences

Elisabetta Ruspini

Longitudinal Research, Social Change, and the Social Sciences

The problems of change have always occupied a central position in sociological thought. The modern social sciences have emerged as a response to an era of very rapid, all-embracing social changes—namely the development of capitalism that destroyed the older forms of social organization—and to the consequent need for greater understanding of social, economic, and political processes.

Social change indeed plays a central role in classical sociological thought. August Comte considered historical comparison to be the tool on which sociological research was based. Sociology is nothing if it is not guided by knowledge of historical evolution: "historical comparison of the diverse consecutive states of humanity is not only the main scientific insight of the new political philosophy . . . it also directly forms the basis of the science, of what it can offer as being most typical" (Comte, 1842, p. 268). The notion of differentiation (or specialization) was central in the work of Herbert Spencer, Emile Durkheim, and Talcott Parsons. Marx described the dynamics of the capitalist system. Max Weber established the dynamic power of culture, particularly religion, in social change (Haferkamp & Smelser, 1992; Smelser, 1981). Furthermore, Abrams (1982) argued that sociological explanations must always be of a historical nature, because social reality is historical reality, a reality in time. Accordingly, C. Wright Mills (1959) notes that "social science deals with the problems of biography, history and of the way they affect the body of social structures."

However, even though the analysis of social change represents the touchstone of sociology, and even though the subject studied in sociology is continuously undergoing transformations, the study of social change has, so far, not been developed to its fullest extent. This could depend on the combination of two elements, one theoretical and one methodological: first, the apparent difficulty of reconciling theories about social change—developed at the macrosociological level—with the changing life course patterns of individuals and with opportunities for analysis offered by empirical research (from the use of documents and empirical analysis of life histories to longitudinal surveys); second, the lack of longitudinal information about the social–demographic characteristics of both individuals and households and of techniques was designed to manipulate the longitudinal dimension.

The United States played a pioneering role in the development of longitudinal research. Indeed, the earliest attempts to gather and analyze dynamic data and, simultaneously, to use biographical data were all made in the United States, where, by the late 1920s to the early 1930s, many longitudinal studies on childhood were already well under way (for details, see Mednick & Mednick, 1984; Wall & Williams, 1970). Many, but not all, of these studies concentrated on the evolution of children's physical characteristics (Kessler & Greenberg, 1981; Sontag, 1971). In the 1920s and 1930s, social conditions in the United States also encouraged the development of life history and biography[1] research. In this period, particularly important research on biographies was carried out by the sociology department of the University of Chicago, which, primarily, launched these surveys in order to study urban margination.

The diachronic nature of phenomena such as deprivation or dependence on welfare began to be recognized thanks to the development of household panel surveys (HPS; see the section titled "Panel Design," for details). The results obtained from these studies encouraged a radical change in the way the phenomena were perceived. However, these results only really began to become available in the late 1960s in the United States and in the late 1980s in Europe. Thus, in this case, too, longitudinal research on prospective data[2] was first developed in the United States, where it was encouraged by the strongly pragmatic orientation of North American sociology and noted for its propensity to concentrate on analyzing and solving social problems. Indeed, the first household panel in history was the Panel Study of Income Dynamics (PSID) that was launched in the United States in 1968 and provided the inspiration for all subsequent HPS. One of the motivations for this project was the assumption that poverty was self-perpetuating. The panel design offered a way to determine whether such views corresponded with reality (Elder, 1985). Contrary to prevailing beliefs at the time, only a very small fraction of sample members who actually experienced poverty did so longer than a year or more. The same was true for welfare dependency: Welfare recipients remained on the welfare rolls for relatively short periods of time (Coe, Duncan, & Hill, 1982).

In Europe, many prospective longitudinal studies were set up in the early 1980s (particularly in the period 1984–1985). It was not by chance that prospective studies started in this period. Since the 1970s, all advanced industrial societies have been undergoing a period of profound socioeconomic changes: the differentiation and instability of family models and the consequent erosion of the protective role of the nuclear family; the growing importance of the service sector; the decline of secure employment, both in large manufacturing industry and in the tertiary sector, alongside which there had been increases both in the number of people experiencing either prolonged periods of unemployment or definitive ejection from employment—particularly among some social groups, such as women or youth—and in unstable, atypical, temporary, very-low-paid jobs. There are many approaches to describing the current changes in the world, such as the transformation to a knowledge-based society; globalization; postindustrialization;

post-Fordism; late, reflexive, or postmodernity (see, among others, Bauman, 1992; Beck, 1992; Bell, 1973; Giddens, 1990; Touraine, 1974). The main purpose of HPS is, in fact, to analyze income fluctuations and to describe and explain changes in the economic situation of the participants studied, with aspects linked to monitoring poverty providing the background.

Apart from noting that Anglo-Saxon cultures clearly dominate in the field, it should also be remembered that longitudinal studies in Europe have, in general, been developing at two different speeds, as the very high costs of such studies has made it difficult for less well-off countries to launch them. It is no coincidence that the countries of northern Europe (Germany, Sweden, Holland, Belgium, Great Britain) have been adopting a dynamic approach to the study of social phenomena for much longer than those in southern Europe, where there is still a severe lack of dynamic data available and no tradition of in-depth, longitudinal research.

Even if in the countries of southern Europe dynamic data are markedly slow to become available, it is now becoming easier to get access to both prospective and retrospective longitudinal data in Europe (see the later sections on panel design and event-oriented design). This will make it possible to develop an analytical prospective of life courses and constitutes one of the most important developments that has taken place in the area of official statistics in the past two decades (Ghellini & Trivellato, 1996). However, there is still a large gap between this increasing availability and everyday research practices, which, today, are still largely restricted to cross-sectional type analyses. A number of factors can explain the relative lack of available panel data and the small amount being produced; these factors include the high costs of gathering such data, the complexity of the data-gathering process, the complexity of the data gathered, and the fact that much of this information is reserved, which often inhibits the public distribution of such data.[3] Consequently, in many areas (e.g., those in southern Europe), longitudinal research is rarely used in social research, notwithstanding the fact that there is, clearly, a pressing need to produce such data and make it available. Longitudinal data are essential if a researcher wishes to measure social change and evolution through history. Moreover, as Rajulton and Ravanera (2000) argued, in spite of the general acceptance of the usefulness of longitudinal data, many researchers are still not ready to adopt suitable techniques for analyzing such data. This situation cannot be rectified unless we find a way to disseminate techniques of analysis to would-be users of longitudinal data. This is the reason that longitudinal research can be considered an emergent method in the social sciences.

Hence it is becoming more and more important to both construct and encourage wider use of longitudinal methodology—which places a high priority on longitudinal research and which could help in designing and setting up research activities—and, simultaneously, to exploit and make more available the few existing examples of longitudinal surveys. To do this there must be an exchange of information among those who have already worked and reasoned "longitudinally," those who would like to do so but are not sure how, and those who are wary of the consequences of approaching and dealing with dynamic data.

What Is Longitudinal Research?

The term *longitudinal* is used here to describe what can be defined as the minimum common denominator of a family of those methods that tell us about change at the individual or micro level (Menard, 1991; Rose, 2000; Zazzo, 1967). This family is the opposite of that described by the term *cross-sectional research*.

Longitudinal is a rather broad and imprecise term. Longitudinal data can be defined as data, gathered during the observation of participants, on a number of variables over time. This definition implies the notion of repeated measurements (Bijleveld et al., 1998, Chapter 1). Basically, longitudinal data present information about what happened to a set of units (people, households, firms, etc.) across time. The participants in a typical longitudinal study are asked to provide information about their behavior and attitudes regarding the issues of interest on a number of separate occasions in time (called the "waves" of the study) (Taris, 2000). In contrast, cross-sectional data refer to the circumstances of respondents at one particular point in time. Thus the term *longitudinal* refers to a particular type of relations between phenomena: the type that evolves over the course of time and that is termed *diachronic*, the opposite of *synchronic*.

There are many different methods that can be used to collect longitudinal data, which means that there are also many different types of research (Bijleveld et al., 1998; Buck, Gershuny, Rose, & Scott, 1994; Davies & Dale, 1994; Ruspini, 1999, 2002; Taris, 2000).

The most commonly used longitudinal designs are:

- Repeated cross-sectional studies (trend), carried out regularly, each time using a largely different sample or a completely new sample.
- Prospective longitudinal studies (panel), which repeatedly interview the same participants over a period of time.
- Retrospective longitudinal studies (duration data), in which interviewees are asked to remember and reconstruct events and aspects of their own life courses.

Of these three, prospective studies are considered the most "truly longitudinal" (and consequently preferable when analyzing micro social change), because they periodically gather information about the same individuals (Janson, 1990; Magnusson, Bergman, Rudinger, & Torestad, 1991) who are asked the same sequence of questions at regular intervals.

Repeated Cross-Sectional Surveys

A *cross-sectional survey* studies a cross-section of the population at a specific moment or point in time. Here, the term *cross-section* indicates a wide sample of people of different ages, education levels, religions, and so on. Thus details about an event or phenomenon are gathered once, and once only, for each participant or case studied. Consequently, cross-sectional studies offer an instant, but static, "photograph" of the process being studied. Their on–off nature makes such studies both easier to organize and cheaper by giving them the advantage of immediacy in offering instant results. This is the reason that they have always been the mainstay of both academic and market researchers.

However, cross-sectional studies are not the most suitable tools for the study of social change. Social scientists should be very careful when attempting to extrapolate longitudinal inferences on the basis of analyses of cross-sectional data, as they have to implicitly assume that the process being studied is in some sort of equilibrium.[4]

Because of this, cross-sectional surveys are usually repeated twice or more, at different points in time, each time using a completely new sample. In other words, the samples include entirely different cases, and any overlaps that may occur are so rare that they cannot be considered significant. The term *trend studies* is used for these repeated cross-sectional surveys (conducted at two or more occasions) on different samples. In order to ensure the comparability of the measurements across time, the same questionnaire should be used in all cross-sectional surveys.

Examples of repeated cross-sectional studies include the General Household Survey or the Family Expenditure Survey in Great Britain, the European Community Eurobarometer Surveys, the ISTAT (Italian National Institute of Statistics) Multipurpose Survey of Italian Families (*Indagine Multiscopo sulle famiglie italiane*), and the Bank of Italy Survey of Household Income and Wealth. Because these surveys are not based on the same sample, they offer only a means for analyzing *net changes* at the aggregate level—the *net effect* of all the changes (Firebaugh, 1997)—for example, comparisons between the incidence of poverty and the characteristics of the population below the poverty line at time t and at time $t - 1$ or between the pool of employed and unemployed in two different years.

Panel Design

Prospective longitudinal studies, especially HPS, follow individuals and families over time by periodically reinterviewing the same participants and providing multiple observations on each individual or household in the sample. Such studies involve not only a random sample of households but also all those members and subsequent coresidents, partners, and descendants who are repeatedly reinterviewed. These studies accumulate records of employment, income, family status, and attitudes over extended periods. This makes it possible to study change at the individual, that is, the *micro,* level (Gershuny, 1998, 2000; Hakim, 1987; Rose & Sullivan, 1996)—to analyze changes within the institutional, cultural, and social environments that surround the individual and shape the course of his or her life. Thus they offer a basis for further study of the dynamics of social phenomena—an advantage that Paul F. Lazarsfeld (Lazarsfeld, 1940, 1948; Lazarsfeld & Fiske, 1938) must have recognized when, in the late 1930s, he was the first to use longitudinal data when analyzing the relation between the mass media and changes in public opinion.

The term *panel data* covers a variety of data collection designs but generally refers to the repeated observation of a set of fixed entities (people, firms, nation states) at fixed intervals (usually, but not necessarily, annually). Thus there are various basic types of panels.

1. The first type are those that seek to ascertain the degree of stability or fluctuation of opinions and attitudes (usually surveys on political opinions or consumption); for example, *consumer panels,* which are used in market research in order to keep track, over time, of changes in purchasing and consumption patterns in relation to a particular product (Sudman & Ferber, 1979). The participants in such panels provide the researcher with information on a regular basis about their level of consumption of particular brands of products (van de Pol, 1989), and data collection is done at frequent intervals.

2. The most representative prospective surveys, HPS, are based on a probability sample of individuals or households and seek to discover what happens or has happened to the same participants over a certain period of time. The population from which the sample is drawn is made up of all the individuals resident or present in a given area or a subset of these. HPS are conducted using repeated interviews carried out at fixed intervals, which could be anything from every 2–3 months to once a year (with some important exceptions; see Ruspini, 2002, for details); the shorter the time interval, the easier it is for a relationship to develop with the household and the interviewees, which helps ensure a high and constant percentage of response over time. Usually, the composition of the population is dynamic in two ways: On the one hand, it changes over time both in terms of entrants—through, for example, births and immigration—and dropouts—through deaths and emigration. On the other hand, its basic aggregate units, households (which are also the sampling units of the HPS), also change continually, in the wake of events affecting family formation and dissolution (Trivellato, 1999). As I have already said, the clearest advantage these surveys offer is that they make it possible to study micro social change. When individuals are studied over time, it becomes possible to investigate the dynamics of both individual and family behaviors in the economic–social field and, also, the personal responses and adaptation strategies adopted in the face of previous circumstances and events. As already mentioned, important examples of HPS are, without doubt, the Panel Study of Income Dynamics

(PSID) in the United States, the German Socioeconomic Panel (GSOEP) in Germany, and the British Household Panel Study (BHPS) in the United Kingdom. But proof of the growing importance attributed to HPS can be found in the multiplicity of studies set up in recent years to examine and make comparisons, both *ex ante* and *ex post*, between longitudinal data. For example, in 1994, Eurostat launched a panel study, the European Community Household Panel (ECHP), which extends over all the member countries of the European Union. Four projects have been set up that seek to increase the *ex post* comparability of prospective panel studies: the Panel Comparability Project (PACO), which aims to build up an archive of longitudinal data that can be compared at the supranational level by drawing on various prospective longitudinal surveys currently under way in some European countries and in the United States; the PSID–GSOEP Equivalent Data File, an attempt to compare GSOEP and PSID data; the EPAG dataset (European Panel Analysis Group); and, last, the CHER (Consortium of Household Panels for European Socioeconomic Research) project, whose aim is to develop a comparative database for longitudinal household studies by harmonizing and integrating micro datasets from a large variety of panels.

3. It is important to distinguish between *rotating panels* and *split panels* (Kish, 1986, 1987). The former are surveys in which a new group of probabilistically chosen individuals is added to the sample at each successive wave in order to correct distortions that may have arisen within the sample between time t and time t_1 (e.g., one-sixth of the sample retire and are replaced by an equal number of employed persons). The idea is to keep samples of changing populations up-to-date. Sample size is controlled by stipulating the period of time that any participant will be included in the survey; that is, there is a limit on the length of time that each participant will participate in the panel (e.g., 2 years). Such rotation both serves as a good method of maintaining the original characteristics of the sample and reduces the distortion that would otherwise be created by natural loss of participants. This "refreshing" of the sample has the advantage that participants will develop "survey boredom" less easily, that there will be fewer testing and learning effects, and that there will be less panel mortality. Thus rotating panel surveys combine the features of both panel and repeated cross-section studies. Some important examples of studies that use rotation are: the Survey of Labour and Income Dynamics (SLID) in Canada; the Survey of Income and Program Participation (SIPP) in the United States; the Quarterly Labour Force Survey (QLFS) in the United Kingdom; and the Household Budget Continuous Survey (*Encuesta Continua de Presupuestos Familiares*, or ECPF) in Spain (Citro & Kalton, 1993; Kalton & Lepkowski, 1985).

Split panels are "classic" panels that include a rotating sample that is interviewed alongside another sample of the long-term panel members who are being followed over time. The rotating sample is interviewed once only and never again and serves as a control group in that they are not exposed to the potential effects of participating in the survey (attrition and conditioning). In other words, a panel study is combined with a repeated cross-sectional study (van de Pol, 1989) by flanking on–off independent samples with the long-term sample. The British Social Attitudes Survey (BSA) is an example of a split panel survey.

4. The fourth type are longitudinal cohort studies, or *cohort panels*. Cohort analyses are similar to panel studies, except that in cohort studies only a random sample of the individuals who experienced the same life event (birth, marriage, entering or leaving school, etc.) within the same time interval is followed over time. Usually a researcher will choose one or more cohorts and administer a questionnaire to a sample drawn from within that group; thus a number of generations are followed, over time, throughout their life courses.

One particularly important type of cohort is the "birth cohort," that is, the set of people who were born in the same year. Thus cohort studies may begin at birth but may also begin at a much later age (Davies & Dale, 1994; Taris, 2000); an example of this is panel studies on scholastic career (and/or on the transition from school to an active working life), in which the event origin used to identify the cohort is that of being present in (or entering or leaving) a given class in a given school year.

Unlike HPS, which contain dynamic populations that change over time because of births, deaths, immigration, and so forth, and in which family organization may change because of divorce, remarriage, a new marriage, or children leaving home, the main characteristic of this type of research is that a cohort is closed against new entries because such entries are, by definition, impossible (Ghellini & Trivellato, 1996). If, in every specific generation, the same people are followed over time, then the cohort study will be composed of a series of panel studies; however, if, for each observation, a sample is chosen from within each generation, the cohort study will consist of a series of trend studies. Cohort studies can be either prospective or retrospective. The former usually studies one or more cohorts at successive intervals over a period of time, whereas the latter gathers retrospective information about just one cohort at a time and may thus be made up of more than one study. Because of this, retrospective studies may simultaneously evince both cross-sectional features (samples are only interviewed once) and prospective panel features (they offer information about the life histories of the interviewees). Examples of the first group are the National Child Development Study (NCDS) and the 1970 British Cohort Study (BCS70), both British, and the series of National Longitudinal Surveys (NLS) carried out in the United States. The German Life History Study (GLHS) is a good example of the second group.

The underlying idea behind any cohort study is that long-term social change must be interpreted within the context of generational change. By following one generation throughout its entire life course, the consequences of growth, maturity, and aging are rendered visible. Furthermore, it also becomes possible to investigate the influence of a variety of events that take place over the course of time and, likewise, to understand whether a specific event has influenced an entire generation in the same way (Hagenaars, 1990). Consequently, cohort studies are particularly suitable when studying populations that are subject to radical changes (Olagnero & Saraceno, 1993).

5. *Linked or administrative panels* are derived, as a by-product, from data collected as part of public administration processes (census or administrative data). The value added may come from joining disparate data sources: for example, registration data linked to data from the census. In these cases, data items that are not collected primarily for panel purposes are linked together using unique personal identifiers (the combination of name, birth date, and place of birth is normally enough to identify individuals and enable linkage of administrative and/or other records). One good example of such panels is the ONS Longitudinal Study (LS) in the United Kingdom, organized by the Office of National Statistics (ONS); it is based on the census and vital events data (births, cancer, deaths) collected for a 1% sample of the population of England and Wales (approximately 500,000 individuals at any one point in time). The LS was established in the early 1970s. Whereas the original LS sample took all people who gave one of four dates of birth at the 1971 census, the study has been continuously updated to include new births and immigrants born on one of these dates; this distinguishes the LS from other longitudinal studies in which the sample is selected at one point in time (Centre for Longitudinal Studies, 1999). Another example is the *Enchantillon Démographique Permanent*, launched in 1968, in France; in this case, too, the study has involved more than 1% of the census population. A third example is the Turin Longitudinal Study (TLS) in Italy, which contains linked census data for all per-

sons who were resident in Turin at one or more of the last three decennial censuses (1971, 1981, and 1991). This archive uses record linkage to bring together information relating to events (such as mortality, migration, or ill health) that affect or that have affected Turin residents. The TLS has been widely used for investigating health inequalities, including infant and adolescent mortality and drug-related causes of death. Administrative panels are particularly widespread in the Scandinavian countries: the Finnish Longitudinal Study (launched in 1971), in which the whole resident population is being studied (Bynner, 1996); the IDA database (Integrated Database for Labour Market Research) in Denmark; the LINDA database (Longitudinal Individual Data for Sweden), and the Swedish Income Panel (SWIP).

Without doubt, administrative panels offer the least intrusive method of collecting longitudinal data. Moreover, the datasets obtained are large, thus sampling errors are small, even for small population subgroups; and they are also cheap. Another of the advantages of using register information as primary data in connection with surveys covering a longer period of time is that the effects of oblivion or memory can be reduced (Leth-Sørensen, 1997). However, they do have some clear disadvantages. Above all, they can offer only a very small variety of information, data that have often been collected with long intervals of time elapsing between one collection and the next (as in the case of census data); furthermore, such data often pose comparability problems. One common problem with register data is comparability between the years covered. For example, in SWIP, a fundamental problem for earnings and other variables obtained from tax records is changes in the tax code. During the period covered by the panel, there were two important changes in tax codes. In 1974, a number of transfers from the public sector (compensations for sickness, unemployment compensation, etc.) became subject to income tax. The tax reform at the beginning of the 1990s broadened the tax base, and therefore income recorded in 1991 and after is not strictly comparable with income recorded earlier (Gustafsson, 1997).

Furthermore, the analytical possibilities such panels offer are limited to those issues that correspond to the bureaucratic concerns of the administrators who collect the data (Gershuny & Buck, 2000). Last, these panel studies are frequently impeded by laws concerning data protection, which may make it difficult to obtain access to such data (Buck et al., 1994; Bynner, 1996).

Event-Oriented Design (Event History Data)

Repeated cross-sectional and longitudinal prospective data do have one important element in common that constitutes an important limitation for both: They are gathered at discrete points in time (e.g., every 6 months, or annually). Indeed, any analysis of the evolution of many types of social phenomena really requires continuous (in time) investigation of discrete events in order to permit the study of the sequence of both the events that have taken place and the precise intervals that may have elapsed between one event and another. Such information is crucial if one is to understand the development of a life course and the way in which events and processes are interrelated.

Because events are defined in terms of changes over time, it is usually accepted that the best way to study them together with their causes is to gather duration data or event history data and identify vectors that record what has happened to a sample of individuals or a collective, together with precise information about the point in time when these events took place.

Duration data are typically collected retrospectively through life history studies—which generally cover the whole life course of individuals—or through the use of event histories, gathered using either prospective panels or cohort studies. In the former case, samples of respondents are interviewed about aspects of their lives. For example, they may be asked about all jobs and spells of unemployment they have experienced since leaving school. In the latter case, members of a sample are tracked over time and questioned every so often about what has happened to them; for example, about all the important events that have affected household members since the last interview (Gilbert, 1993, p. 168).

Detailed information about each episode is collected: the duration of the event, the origin state, and the destination state. One example could be the event "first marriage": every individual who marries for the first time (*origin state* or *initial event*) starts off an episode that will finish only with the transition into the state of "no-longer married" (*destination state* or *terminal event*) (Blossfeld & Rohwer, 1995).[5]

Furthermore, such studies often collect information relating to repeated episodes or events (consecutive jobs, unions, separations, births, etc.) that take place both during and alongside parallel processes (work, matrimonial, family histories, etc.) and at different levels (micro, meso, and macro: e.g., individual work history, history of the firm in which the individual is employed, structural changes in the labor market). The underlying idea, or principle, is that an individual's life course can be understood only if and when it is placed into the context of the trajectories of his or her social life. Because the changes that take place at a macro level will potentially affect the life course of an individual, then this life course should not be isolated from the situation in which it is set (Mayer, 1990). In other words, these data make it possible to analyze developments within the institutional, cultural, and social contexts in which an individual's life course is unfolding. By focusing on these events and transitions in individual lives, the interaction between action and structures can be closely observed.

Thus, in an event-oriented matrix, each line vector corresponds to the duration of one state or episode; for example, it could express a work/job episode (first job, second job, and third job). If only one episode is considered for each case (e.g., the birth of the first child or the first marriage), then the number of vectors will correspond to the number of cases examined. If, however, these are repeated and/or parallel episodes, the number of which may vary greatly from one individual to another, the sum of the episodes that characterize *each* individual life course represents the total of line vectors in the data matrix.[6]

One good example of a study oriented toward events is the already cited German Life History Study (GLHS), which is made up of a set of retrospective cohort studies that seek to gather detailed information about both events in the lives of the participants involved and their most important activities. The study is made up of diverse studies of cohort samples drawn from the population of Germany. These cohorts were not followed over time but were contacted *just once* during the data-gathering activities. The groups were chosen in such a way that the transition phase between school and work coincided with periods that were particularly important from the historical point of view: the immediate postwar (World War II) period; a period of fast economic growth (boom); a period of expansion within the welfare state, and a period of contraction in the economy (slump). The fundamental hypothesis underlying this study was that specific historical conditions would have had an equally specific impact on the working lives of those interviewed. As well as information about education and work, the GLHS also offers information about other important aspects of individual life: cultural background, family and residential history, and so forth (Blossfeld, Hamerle, & Mayer, 1989, pp. 17–25).

One further example is the United Kingdom 1980 Women and Employment Survey (WES), which collected very detailed work histories from a nationwide sample of more than 5,000 working women between 16 and 59 years of age living in Great Britain (Martin

& Roberts, 1984). I should also mention the ILFI, *l'Indagine Longitudinale sulle Famiglie Italiane* (Longitudinal Survey on Italian Families), a prospective panel study with a retrospective first wave (Schizzerotto, 2002).

It is important to remember that longitudinal research is rarely based on one investigative method alone but commonly on a mix of methods. Some examples of longitudinal mixed designs are:

1. Repeated cross-sectional studies, one part of which is done in the form of panel studies. For example, the British Social Attitudes Survey (BSAs) or the Bank of Italy Survey of Household Income and Wealth (SHIW) are repeated regularly on a largely different sample but with a small part done as a panel study (Jowell, Brooks, Prior, & Taylor, 1992);
2. Prospective studies gather information systematically through the use of calendars and/or suitable batteries of questions that aim to retrospectively investigate the life of the interviewee but not necessarily to inquire about the same subject each time. One typical example is HPS (Household Panel Studies), the most important of these being the PSID in the United States, the GSOEP in Germany, and the BHPS in Great Britain.
3. Cohort studies are also prospective and/or retrospective (two British examples of this being the National Child Development Study and the Birth Cohort Study). As I have already said, a cohort has been defined as "the aggregate of individuals who experienced the same life event within the same time interval" (Ryder, 1965, p. 845): birth, marriage, moment of entry in the labor market, moment of diagnosis of a particular disease, and so forth.

The Heuristic Potential of Longitudinal Research

There is no doubt about the heuristic potential of either prospective or retrospective longitudinal data. Indeed, such data make it possible to:

- analyze the duration of social phenomena
- highlight differences or changes, between one period and another, in the values of one or more variables
- identify *sleeper effects,* that is, connections between events and transitions that are widely separated in time because they took place in very different periods, as in the relation between childhood, adulthood, and old age (Elder, 1985; Hakim, 1987). For example, the experience of old age has much to do with hardship in the adult years and one's responses to it; the same event or transition followed by different adaptations can lead to very different trajectories (Elder & Liker, 1982; Negri, 1990). Also, caregiving at a young age has a significant effect on earnings and risk of poverty in later life, as young caregivers are often absent from school and fail to gain even the basic qualifications (Olsen, 1996; Payne, 2001)
- describe subjects' intraindividual and interindividual changes over time and monitor the magnitude and patterns of these changes
- explain the changes in terms of certain other characteristics (these characteristics can be stable, such as gender, or unstable, i.e., time-varying, such as income; Bijleveld et al., 1998, p. 3).

Longitudinal data also contribute to identifying the causes of social phenomena, or at least they help to do this by allowing antecedents to be specified and consequences identified. The temporal ordering of events is often the closest we can get to causality; the structure of causality inherent in social processes may be reconstructed as a specific sequence of events leading to a certain state (Leisering & Walker, 1998b). More specifically, longitudinal studies not only allow the researcher to study the segment of the population that at different points in time finds itself caught within a specific situation, such as poverty or unemployment, but also, because of their very nature, can be used to examine the flows into and out of such a situation, thus opening up many paths for both causal analysis and inference (Duncan & Kalton, 1987; Rose, 1993, 2000).

With longitudinal data, it is also possible to develop causal theories that link individual dynamics with the dynamics of institutions and social structures (Gershuny, 1998, 2000), which makes it possible to fit the events studied both into individuals' biographies and into the family and social contexts they are part of, permitting in-depth analysis of social and demographic processes in terms of both the choices and the determining factors that underlie different behaviors.[7]

Longitudinal data also allow us to construct more complicated behavioral models than purely cross-sectional or time-series data do (Davies & Dale, 1994, p. 4; Hsiao, 1986, p. 3). More precisely, longitudinal data allow models to be constructed that are better able to take into account some of the complexities of the ways in which people conduct their lives, that is, models that allow improved control over the myriad of variables that are, inevitably, omitted from any analysis. Because of the complexity of human behavior and because of our limited ability to model it, there is always considerable heterogeneity in the response variable, even among people with the same characteristics. For example, women with the same age, level of education, and number of children will show considerable differences in their level of labor market participation. There are also other influences that may differ between these women that have not been measured and cannot be taken into account in the model. Omitting these variables may produce misleading results, particularly if the variables omitted are correlated with one of the explanatory variables. Indeed, the effect of unobserved individual characteristics, which generally do not vary over time, can drastically undermine the results of analyses carried out on cross-sectional samples, because parameter estimates will be inconsistent. By using longitudinal information, one is better able to check for the effects of missing or unobserved variables, thus attenuating the effect of "unobserved heterogeneity"—a key econometric problem that often arises in empirical studies—namely, the assertion that the real reason one finds (or does not find) certain effects is because of omitted (mismeasured or not observed) variables that are correlated with explanatory variables. This problem can easily be overcome by exploiting the time invariance of the unobserved individual characteristics—a plausible assumption in many instances—and by the fact that repeated observations on the same individuals are available[8] (Hsiao, 1985, 1986; Mátyás & Sevestre, 1996; Trivellato, 1999).

Furthermore, the development of research projects that use longitudinal data serves to build a "bridge" between "quantitative" and "qualitative" research traditions and encourages a reassessment of the concepts of qualitative and quantitative research themselves. The tendency to view the two research traditions as reflecting different epistemological positions and divergent paradigms has exaggerated the differences between them; consequently, quantitative and qualitative research are often depicted as mutually exclusive models of the social process.

Bryman (1988, pp. 65–66) stated that there is an implicit longitudinal element built into much qualitative research; the general image that the qualitative researcher conveys about the social order is one of interconnection and change. Great emphasis is placed on social life as an interlocking series of events; this emphasis can be seen as a response to the qualitative researcher's concern with reflecting the reality of everyday life, which takes the form of a stream of interconnecting events. Longitudinal surveys usually combine both extensive (quantitative) and intensive (qualitative) approaches. For example, if panel data trace individuals and households over time by gathering information about them at regular intervals, they also include relevant retrospective information, so that the respondents have continuous records in key fields from the beginning of their lives. This makes it possible to develop an analytical prospective of individual life courses.

Longitudinal Research and (Some of) Its Drawbacks

Even though dynamic data offer a highly innovative and precious tool for the analysis of social phenomena, they do, nonetheless, have certain inherent disadvantages.

Dynamic analysis is, in itself, highly complex; longitudinal studies are usually very expensive both in terms of the money and of the time and energy they require. Not only do we have to ensure that the same participants can be measured repeatedly over the course of many years, but we also run great risks if the research team cannot be preserved over the duration of the study. Last but not least, the world of longitudinal research is extremely heterogeneous.

The higher costs of longitudinal studies are due not only to the fact that we measure a sample of N participants at least twice and thus have to collect repeated measurements but also, mainly, to the fact that we have to *follow* the participants over time: We have to track people who change homes, who form new families, who move to another municipality. We also have to ensure cooperation in all subsequent waves, as we cannot replace participants who refuse or are lost with others who did not participate in the previous measurement occasion. Apart from the actual research costs themselves (tracking and tracing techniques), the organizational costs of longitudinal research are tremendous: Not only do we have to ensure that the same participants can be traced repeatedly over their life course, but we also need to preserve the research team over the duration of the study (Bijleveld et al., 1998).

Consequently, longitudinal studies are usually carried out only by large research organizations, and they need national and often governmental support.

The Limitations of Repeated Cross-Sectional Design

The obvious advantages of cross-sectional designs over longitudinal ones (e.g., saved time and expense and absence of attrition) are compelling when the research question does not involve a focus on continuity and change (Copeland & White, 1991, p. 20).

However, because they do not use the same sample, trend studies enable change to be analyzed only at the macro level (e.g., comparisons of the proportion of the population that is below the poverty line at time t and at time $t - 1$). Given that the same individuals are not followed over a period of time, that is, participants are not reinterviewed, such studies are not suitable if one is seeking to identify the causal mechanisms that govern social change (Menard, 1991).

Problems Connected with Panel Design

Prospective studies have unmistakable methodological strengths, but they are expensive and time-consuming (Bijleveld et al., 1998). Both Duncan (1989) and Blossfeld and Rohwer (1995) have summed up the problems posed by panel studies:[9]

- Above all, physiological changes in the size of the sample (attrition) at each successive period of data gathering represent a process of selective reduction in the number of participants involved. Attrition occurs when respondents leave the panel—because of refusal to answer, physical incapacity of the respondent to provide information, and/or failure to follow up sample cases—after having participated in one or more consecutive waves, including the first wave of the study. This thinning process is not random: If those who leave the study are not typical of those who started it, any longitudinal data will become biased to the same extent, and this will produce a nonrepresentative sample (a "biased" sample). Attrition happens because of a refusal to continue or through death or emigration;

thus it can distort conclusions drawn on the basis of information supplied by that section of the sample that has survived and remained.[10]

• Dealing with missing answers is a problem from a longitudinal point of view. Getting rid of the information from missing cases in cross-sectional studies is not a major problem, but, if it is done at each wave of panel studies, it may lead to severe distortion within the panel, which will, at the end of this process, exhibit very different features from those it started out with.

• There is a higher risk of error than in cross-sectional data because errors accumulate over time (Fuller, 1987). For example, if data about income gathered at time t has errors, this could lead to false transitions appearing concerning phenomena such as poverty or unemployment (Duncan, 1992).

• The nature of the answers given can be influenced by repeated participation in the panel (*panel conditioning* or *problem of sensitization* or *time-in-sample bias*).[11] The problem of panel conditioning is "the situation when repeated questioning of panel members affects their survey responses, either by altering the behaviour reported or by changing the quality of the responses given" (Kalton, Kasprzyk, & McMillen, 1989, pp. 249–250). Precisely because they are repeated, panel studies tend to influence the phenomena that they are hoping to observe. During subsequent waves, interviewees often answer differently from how they answered at the first wave. The reason may be that they have lost some of their inhibitions, that they have acquired new information in the meantime, or that they have had new, different experiences during the time that has elapsed between one wave and the next. Participants may also react differently during a second survey simply because they have had the experience of the first one. Thus, conversely, participation in a panel survey may also improve the quality of the data (Duncan, 2000).[12]

• Panel data offer information that is related only to predetermined points in time (data are usually gathered annually, i.e., at discrete time points). Thus the researcher cannot know about the course and evolution of events in the period that has elapsed between one collection time and the next. Furthermore, prospective studies are often limited to a few waves only and, consequently, cover only a short period of time. Indeed, a particular situation under way at the moment in time at which information is being gathered may distort individuals' answers (*fallacy of historical period*).

There are also problems that are inherent in the structure of the panels themselves.

First of all, panel data files are usually extremely large; the majority of existing household panels have initial samples of around 5,000 households and more than 10,000 individuals.

The high level of complexity of the structure of HPS is also a problem. Such studies have two temporal dimensions (cross-sectional and longitudinal), and, furthermore, the data are usually gathered and stored at three levels: the household, the individual, and the period or length of time (*spell-files*), in which the unit analyzed is neither the family nor the individual but the event. Thus the structure of such data makes it possible to combine two separate units of analysis (family and individual) and, consequently, to create longitudinal files (by linking one wave to another through the use of original and unique individual and household identifiers or key variables) on the basis of either prospective or retrospective longitudinal information that has been gathered at either the aggregate or the individual level.

Thus HPS are "complex" in the sense that they consist of a number of different data structures or files with differing focuses (some referring to the particular households studied at particular waves, some referring to individuals, some referring to particular events that the individuals surveyed have experienced) and often of repeated files that have the same structures but relate to different points in historical time (i.e., files describing respondents' circumstances in successive years or waves). This implies that analysts must apply some additional concepts to those involved in the analysis of more straightforward survey datasets. The real value of this sort of dataset comes from the investigator's ability to link the various files together so as to connect information in a number of straightforward ways: for example, attaching household-level information to the individual respondents or connecting individual respondents' information over time. The crucial concept is that of a "key variable," which serves to identify particular records within files as belonging to particular households or individuals. It is these key variables that may be used for linking records between them.

Successful navigation through individual wave and cross-wave files is therefore a complex task and requires careful documentation. The user documentation is crucial to making longitudinal analysis both easier and more straightforward. It should contain essential information required for the analysis of data and information, as well as information that will assist users when linking and aggregating data across waves (Freed Taylor, 2000). Bailar (1984) and David (1991) have identified a number of topics as being essential for the documentation of a panel dataset: design of the survey (sample, questionnaire, field procedures; coding, editing, linkage, treatment of missing data; etc.); design of the panel dataset (following rules,[13] verification of linkage, periodicity); facts of the survey (what is known about the data, including inconsistencies and anomalies); facts about the panel (information that is needed to understand how to condition data collected in later waves on data collected in prior waves); and, last, analyses (which record the completed work already carried out on the data).

Last, the complexity and the diversity of the structure of longitudinal data, both from the point of view of files and of variables, pose considerable problems to those who try to compare household panel survey data. In a work on the impact of gender on the dynamics of poverty, which was conducted using both GSOEP and BHPS data (Ruspini, 2000), both the complexity of the files and the diversity of the structure of the data created marked problems for comparative analysis. More specifically, it was difficult to use the GSOEP data, as it necessitated a complex task of recoding the data. The reason was that major changes had taken place regarding the structure of the variables, which had often changed both values and name from year to year. Indeed, while in BHPS data, file variables are named independently of the position they hold in the questionnaire and remain the same over the years, except for the first letter of the name of the file (a for 1991; b for 1992; etc.). In the GSOEP file, the variable depends on the number given to that question in the questionnaire (i.e., on its position within the questionnaire), and because the structure of the questionnaire changes from year to year, the name of the variable changes, too.

Retrospective Design and Its Drawbacks

Retrospective data are less expensive than prospective longitudinal data, as they are usually gathered during one single wave. However, they do have certain disadvantages connected, in particular, to the distortion due to the inevitable, often unconscious, selectivity of individuals' memories when elaborating their biographies, when remembering. Long-term retrospective data tend to be more unreliable than prospective data: the longer the recall period is, the more unreliable retrospective data tend to be.

1. One disadvantage is linked to the quantity of information that an individual is able to remember on one occasion (i.e., when the retrospective interview is carried out). Many participants simply forget things about events, feelings, or considerations, and even when an event has not been wholly forgotten, they may have trouble recalling it (memory loss and retrieval problems).

2. In general, the quality of the data diminishes the further back in time the interviewee is asked to go. There are two main problems with memory: the *omission* effect—some events that could be important for the study are not revealed—and the *telescope* effect—the time at which the event took place is not remembered accurately. One particular type of memory error occurs when respondents omit relevant pieces of information. Respondents may be unable to recall a particular item, or they may be unable to distinguish one item from another in their memories (Linton, 1982). Even if all relevant events have been correctly remembered, if asked *when* they happened, respondents tend to report events as having taken place more recently than they actually did (forward telescoping). The inverse may also occur: Some participants place events further away in the past than they actually happened (backward telescoping). Generally, people tend to assume that distant events happened more recently than they actually did, whereas the reverse applies to recent events (Schwarz, 1996; Schwarz & Sudman, 1994; Taris, 2000). One particular case of the telescope effect occurs when interviewees link the event being studied to certain particular periods (Billari, 1998). Thus only a period that has a well-defined limit, usually the preceding wave, should be used; this helps to reduce the effects of telescoping and, to some extent at least, to keep a check on them (Janson, 1990; Sudman & Bradburn, 1982).

3. Furthermore, the ways in which individuals interpret their own past behavior will be influenced by subsequent events in their lives. Participants tend to interpret and reinterpret events, opinions, and feelings so that they fit in with their (the participants') own current perceptions of their lives and past lives and constitute a sequence of events that "bears some logic." This tendency has been called "modification to fit a coherent scheme" (Bijleveld et al., 1998).

4. Retrospective questions concerning cognitive and affective states and attitudes are particularly problematic because it is very difficult for interviewees to remember accurately the changes related to particular states of mind, how long these states lasted, and the precise order in which they took place.

5. In some other areas of interest—such as income or state of health—it is quite difficult to collect information retrospectively (e.g., information about monthly earnings, blood pressure, weight loss or gain, etc.).

6. Like panel studies, retrospective studies are also subject to distortions, which are caused by changes within the sample, changes brought about by death, emigration, or a refusal to continue.

7. Last, the length of time required for each interview may also be a major problem. Interviews usually last from 1 to 2 hours: the longer the interview, the "richer" will be the information obtained about the life of the interviewee (Billari, 1998).

Gender, Social Change, and Longitudinal Research

Among the areas of longitudinal research that have been identified as being of particular concern to policymakers are the following:

- Dynamic analyses of labor income (Joshi & Davies, 2002)
- Analysis of career trajectories (Gallie & Paugam, 2000; Scherer, 2000)
- Poverty and income dynamics (Ashworth, Hill, & Walker, 2000; Jarvis & Jenkins, 2000; Muffels, 2000; Walker & Ashworth, 1994)
- The gender dimension of poverty (Ruspini, 2000)
- Child poverty, child achievement, and parenting (Ashworth, Hill, & Walker, 1992, 1994; Hill & Jenkins, 1999)
- Well-being of the elderly (Bound, Duncan, Laren, & Oleinick, 1991; Burkhauser & Duncan, 1988, 1991; Coe, 1988; Lillard & Waite, 1995)

- Social exclusion (Schizzerotto, 2002; Walker, 1995)
- Analysis of welfare use (Saraceno, 2002; Walker & Ashworth, 1994)
- Analysis of the achievements and failures of welfare states (Goodin, Headey, Muffels, & Dirven, 1999)
- Household change; household formation and dissolution (Blossfeld, 1995; Ermisch, 2000; Jarvis & Jenkins, 1998)
- Dynamic issues of disability (Adler, 1992; Eustis, Clark, & Adler, 1995)
- Transitions, for example, into/out of the labor force; from youth to adulthood (Billari, 2000; Lucchini & Schizzerotto, 2001; Schizzerotto & Lucchini, 2004).

Within these, gender is one of the most interesting dimensions of social change, but it is also more controversial and less investigated in many European contexts. A blanket of silence continues to shroud thinking on the transformations of gender identities and on the effects caused by these changes on the relationships between men and women, their forms of cohabitation, and experiences of fatherhood and motherhood.

However, empirical results sustain the view that women and men have been affected differently by social change and that women are probably the most important actors in social change, as they have seen their patterns of life and expectations change more fundamentally than those of men. Indeed, life course changes are more pronounced for women than for men, both in the family and in the labor market. For example, the latest generations of women, in particular, are well aware of the need for cultural training to achieve a satisfactory life. They achieve higher performances, their school careers proceed more smoothly, and they consider study more important; at the same time, they have high expectations regarding their entry into the labor market. Various research studies (see, e.g., Bianco, 1997; Schizzerotto, Bison, & Zoppé, 1995) show that, for girls, the lengthening of the training process brings much greater advantages than for boys: it facilitates finding work and enables them to qualify for good jobs.

Moreover, women's risk of poverty has diversified since the patterns of social exclusion have multiplied. Both employment and the family structure are becoming less stable in protecting individuals from falling into poverty. Family life course changes include a decline in marriage, an increase in separation and divorce and in cohabiting unions, and an increase in births out of wedlock. Current employment transformations also influence women's risk of poverty: unemployment and marginal forms of employment, a decline in lifetime occupations, and shrinkage in permanent contract career ladders. These phenomena are interlinked in a complex manner. Changes in the labor market have created a complex scenario marked by a reduction in the number of opportunities for obtaining permanent jobs and by a parallel increase in flexibility. Obviously, the transformations currently under way do not have the same impact either on the diverse groups that make up society or on the individuals within each family, for some individuals are more vulnerable than others. Families in which the head of the household is a woman, often separated or divorced and with dependent children, are far more vulnerable than families in which the head of household is a male or in which an adult male is present (Duncan & Edwards, 1997; Lewis, 1997; Millar, 1989). As an example, Jarvis and Jenkins (1998) have shown that among separated British couples, women usually experience a substantial drop in household income and living standards, whereas for men they either rise or stay much the same. Last, those changes are creating a crisis for the institutional framework that was originally conceived for a different kind of organization of family life: welfare systems are still largely structured according to the idea of a "male breadwinner" and of a "secondary" female wage earner, an idea that is built into welfare provisions. Thus women's poverty is gradually becoming more visible.

On the one hand, whereas women are beginning to make their presence in society increasingly more substantial and visible (though not without contradictions), on the other hand, there is a feeling that the process of reformulating male identity, although already taking place, is still in an initial phase and has not yet taken a precise direction. Some men have accepted the challenges and invitations emerging in the process of the change in female identities, but often along with regrets, doubts, and perplexity; others have instead rejected them, reacting with fear and aggressiveness, tending toward an "attachment to models of stereotyped virility," reinforcing the model of masculinity that repudiates feminine characteristics and falls back on physical or verbal aggression, sexual harassment, and homophobic attitudes. The different reactions vary according to the different characteristics of the men involved in terms of age and generation, level of education, ethnic culture, and social class. They do not constitute a uniform group, nor is it possible to speak of a single male role. Masculinity is not always equivalent to power. Men lead many different types of lives and have many different interests. Although men, masculinity, and men's powers and practices were for a long time generally taken for granted (gender was largely seen as a matter of and for women; men were generally seen as ungendered), the nature of men and masculinities is now changing. Men have become the subject of growing academic, policy, and media debates. Not only are men now increasingly recognized as gendered, but they, or rather some of them, are increasingly recognized as a gendered social problem to which welfare systems may or, for a variety of reasons, may not respond. This can apply in terms of violence, crime, drug and alcohol abuse, buying of sex, accidents, driving, and indeed the denial of such problems as sexual violence. Social and health statistics show that life in Western society demands a high price from men. Males are overrepresented among drug abusers and prison inmates. The life expectancy of men is shorter than that of women. Boys display more problematic behavior patterns in school than girls and constitute a larger proportion of the pupils who require remedial measures at primary school level. The dropout rate for boys is considerably higher than for girls. All these issues are relevant to the development of new ways of being a man and will play a decisive part in the development of a culture of gender equality.

One of the areas in which male gender roles have changed the most involves men's fatherly roles. Fathers neither have nor operate a single model of fatherhood; research indicates that fatherhood leads men to make the most explicit break with traditional forms of masculinity. Today, men and fathers are expected to be accessible and nurturing, as well as financially supportive, for their families and children. Indeed, studies on the impact of father involvement in child care on later child outcomes confirm the importance of early paternal investment both in caregiving and in improving opportunities for women. However, the father's involvement in caregiving tasks and housework seems twofold. On the one hand, according to some evidence, men in general are spending more and more time with their children (changing diapers, playing), albeit still less than mothers do. On the other hand, the father's involvement in housework remains low, contributing to women's feelings of overload, particularly for full-time working mothers. Fathers are also unlikely to take parental leave, even when it is offered. And it is true that most noncustodial fathers spend very little time with their children.

The dynamic perspective can help us to improve our understanding of how women's and men's lives are evolving and in what direction and how the gender dimensions of the system of social inequality are changing. As already said, longitudinal data provide the essential empirical basis for understanding the relationship between individuals' (women's and men's) behavior and social change.

The importance of longitudinal data cannot be overemphasized as both a national resource and a resource for comparative analysis. However, many aspects of the existing longitudinal surveys and of longitudinal research itself could be improved, in order to increase their value in making a truly gender-sensitive research approach possible. The research challenge now is to analyze and understand the gender dimension of change, that is, *both* the consequence of social change on women's and men's life courses *and* the role of women and men as actors of change. This also means there is an urgent need for social research to make more use of longitudinal data and to bring a gender-sensitive perspective into diachronic analysis (Ruspini & Dale, 2002, pp. 262–266).

• First of all, research on the gender dimension of social change needs to be contextualized with information on actors in the private domestic sphere and also outside households. Previous research has shown that there is likely to be extreme inequality between husband and wife and deprivation on the part of the wife and children. Much work has also shown the extent to which women adapt their lives to combine employment with family care. First, women "go without" more often than men; some women are denied access to resources, and some voluntarily go without to increase the amount available for their partners and children (see, among others, Brannen & Wilson, 1987; Graham, 1987; Ruspini, 2001). Moreover, as Payne (1991) suggested, some resources, such as the family car, heating for the home, and hot water, are apparently bought jointly, but consumption is not shared equally. Most wives use their income to buy things for the family or add their earnings to the housekeeping money (day-to-day living expenses, food, cleaning materials). Women's pay is typically spent on household necessities and only rarely and in smaller amounts on women's own needs (Pahl, 1989, 1995). Thus women and men often hold different views over necessary expenditures and the ways in which money can be saved (Charles & Kerr, 1987; Graham, 1987; Wilson, 1987), and this pattern of consumption in low-income households makes women's task of making ends meet more difficult. This means that surveys need to ensure that information is collected about all relevant actors, which may require questions about the flows of time and economic resources that lie outside the walls of the household. Furthermore, detailed information on family composition and change, on the division of tasks and duties inside the households, and on the shape and variations of networks of informal exchange are needed.

• In addition, another relevant issue concerns the need to analyze the process of gender role developments, the intergenerational transmission of gender-role stereotypes and biases, and the transformations of these stereotypes (Helwig, 1998). These biases, for example, relate to the acceptance of domestic responsibilities and "moral obligations" toward family needs or the limitation of occupational aspirations. This could successfully be done by collecting longitudinal information on men, women, and children, both prospectively and retrospectively, and also by analyzing the socioeconomic situation of the parents and grandparents of the respondents–the latter in order to see whether and to what extent the gender division of duties and the processes of dependence are transmitted intergenerationally. Through differential reinforcements learned first in the home and then reinforced by other adults such as teachers, by school experiences, by the child's peers, and by television viewing, boys and girls are taught to do "boy and girl things," to pursue "gender appropriate" school and academic subjects, and to aspire to occupations that fit their own gender. For example, children's toy preferences have been found to be significantly related to parental sex typing (Etaugh & Liss, 1992; Henshaw, Kelly, & Gratton, 1992) with parents providing gender-differentiated toys and rewarding play behavior that is gender stereotyped.

Boys are more likely than girls to have maintenance chores around the house, whereas girls are likely to have domestic chores, such as cooking and doing the laundry (see, e.g., Basow, 1992). This assignment of household tasks by gender leads children to link certain types of occupational aspirations. Another interesting issue is the development of the "economic world" of children and the exploration of gender differences from childhood to adolescence in economic socialization. Empirical evidence suggests that there are strong differences between boys and girls in money socialization processes. Different familial experiences promote in children feelings of independence or of fear, autonomy or dependency, and feelings of expertise or shame concerning financial matters. For example, recent research carried out in Italy showed that young girls tend to be less interested in economic issues and slightly more concerned about "not wasting money on useless things" compared with their male peers. Differences between men and women increase with age (Rinaldi & Giromini, 2002). If both mothers and fathers contribute to the gender stereotyping of their children, fathers have been found to reinforce gender stereotypes more often than mothers (Witt, 1997). It also seems that children whose mothers work outside the home are not as traditional in sex-role orientation as children whose mothers are not economically active (Weinraub, Jaeger, & Hoffman, 1988). Thus social change and the roles played by women within these changes are contributing to the modification of gender-role stereotypes.

• It is also important that topics and questions be compiled in a way that is gender-sensitive. A first, crucial methodological challenge for gender-sensitive research is how to open the family "black box" in order to understand the extent to which social exclusion processes and poverty are masked and to analyze the factors that underlie a system of inequality that hinges on gender differences. This can be done through increased availability of variables that specifically aim to depict the three processes involved in the acquisition and expenditure of resources within the family: the entry of resources into the household; the allocation and control of resources; the expenditure of resources. Another methodological challenge is to dig into the connection between the concepts of dependence and unpaid work and, at the same time, to measure progress toward gender equality in economic autonomy. Important suggestions come from Millar (2000) and Joshi, Dale, Ward, and Davies (1995). They argue that the issue of how to place individuals within the household and capture not only their contributions to the resources of that household but also their dependence on those resources lies in the examination of sources (not just levels) of income. Another topic relates to the conceptualization of employment and unemployment, in which differences in cultural expectations require questions that are gender-sensitive. For example, occupational class analyses should use classifications that more adequately reflect meaningful distinctions between women's occupations and the need to consider both a woman's domestic roles and her structural position (Arber, 1990).

• The inclusion of topics relevant to the analysis of gender differences will not only encourage the greater use of these important resources but will also open them up to a much broader range of researchers. This also raises the need to ensure that analysis tools are accessible and that longitudinal data do not become seen as too difficult to use by the average social scientist, especially if he or she does not possess a strong statistical background. With comparative longitudinal analysis, in particular, simple, accessible techniques of data analyses are an essential first step in the research process. This issue is of growing importance, because longitudinal comparative datasets, both *exante* and *ex post*—such as the already mentioned ECHP, PACO, or CHER datasets—are now available for analysis by academics.

Thus new methods of inquiry and new tools are required to help understand not only this fast and radical social change but also the dynamic nature of women's and men's lives and the shifts taking place in the role of social institutions. This should encourage a move toward richer and more sensitive methods of (longitudinal) data gathering and the development of techniques that permit dynamic interpretation of the gender dimension of social change.

Notes

1. There are various types of biographical approaches: (1) life history analysis; (2) study of the life course; and (3) study of life events (Olagnero & Saraceno, 1993).

2. Prospective longitudinal studies are usually based on a probability sample of individuals/families and carried out by means of repeated interviews at fixed intervals.

3. These problems could be resolved, while still respecting privacy, through the work of collecting and distributing files of data held in the diverse archives to be found in many European countries: Austria (WISDOM), Belgium (BASS), Denmark (DDA), France (BDSP), Germany (ZA), Hungary (TARKI), Italy (ADPSS), Holland (STAR), Norway (NSD), Sweden (SSD), Switzerland (SIDOS), and the United Kingdom (UK-DA). These archives have been organized into a consortium; Council of European Social Science Data Archives, which aims to act as an international network for promoting and facilitating the exchange of data required for research. Website: *www.nsd.uib.no/cessda/europe.html.*

4. For a discussion on the advantages and disadvantages of cross-sectional versus longitudinal studies data, see, among others, Blossfeld and Rohwer (1995), Coleman (1981), Davies (1994), Davies and Dale (1994), and Rajulton and Ravanera (2000).

5. The period between two changes of state (e.g., from "being employed" to "being unemployed") is called an *episode*, *waiting time*, or *spell*. The change from one spell to another is commonly termed a *transition* or (terminal) *event* (Taris, 2000, p. 95).

6. Within the history of life events, the unit analyzed may be not only the individual him- or herself but also the event itself. In this case the line vectors concern individual histories relating to that event (the birth of children, hospitalization, retirement, etc.). Transitions may be considered instead (the transition from a part-time to a full-time job, from maternity to work), thus considering more than one data collection episode about events that are continuous over a period of time.

7. For further details, see Courgeau and Lelièvre (1988), Davies and Dale (1994), and Kasprzyk, Duncan, Kalton, and Singh (1989).

8. The consequence of this advantage is that the dependence structure between the repeated observations must be identified, and this has become a delicate matter in the treatment of these data (Capursi, 1993).

9. See also Magnusson and Bergman (1990).

10. For a comparative analysis of attrition in HPS, see Singh (1995).

11. Cf. Bailar (1989); Corder and Horvitz (1989); Waterton and Lievesley (1989).

12. For most phenomena reported in surveys, panel participation mainly affects the way in which behavior is reported—that is to say, responses—whereas it does not affect behavior itself (Trivellato, 1999).

13. Those rules that are designed to follow up and to update the initial sample, so as to ensure that on every wave the sample remains cross-sectionally representative of the population (Trivellato, 1999).

References

Abrams, P. (1982). *Historical sociology*. Ithaca, NY: Cornell University Press.

Adler, M. C. (1992). The future of SIPP for analyzing disability and health. *Journal of Economic and Social Measurement, 18*, 91–124.

Arber, S. (1990). Opening the black box: Understanding inequalities in women's health. In P. Abbott & G. Payne (Eds.), *New directions in the sociology of health* (pp. 37–56). Brighton, UK: Falmer Press.

Ashworth, K., Hill, M. S., & Walker, R. (1992). *Economic disadvantages during childhood* (Working Paper No. 17). Centre for Research in Social Policy, Loughborough University of Technology.

Ashworth, K., Hill, M. S., & Walker, R. (1994). Patterns of childhood poverty: New challenges for policy. *Journal of Policy Analysis and Management, 13*(4), 658–680.

Ashworth, K., Hill, M. S., & Walker, R. (2000). A new approach to poverty dynamics. In D. Rose (Ed.), *Re-*

searching social and economic change: The uses of household panel studies (pp. 210–229). London: Routledge.

Bailar, B. (1984). The quality of survey data. In *Proceedings of the Survey Research Section* (pp. 43–59). Alexandria, VA: American Statistical Association. Retrieved from *www.amstat.org/sections/sems/proceedings/papers/1984_009.pdf*

Bailar, B. (1989). Information needs, surveys and measurement errors. In D. Kasprzyk, G. J. Duncan, G. Kalton, & M. P. Singh (Eds.), *Panel surveys* (pp. 1–24). New York: Wiley.

Basow, S. A. (1992). *Gender stereotypes and roles* (3rd ed.). Pacific Grove, CA: Brooks/Cole.

Bauman, Z. (1992). *Intimations of postmodernity*. London: Routledge.

Beck, U. (1992). *Risk society: Towards a new modernity*. London: Sage.

Bell, D. (1973). *The coming of post-industrial society: A venture in social forecasting*. London: Heinemann.

Bianco, M. L. (1997). *Donne al lavoro: Cinque itinerari fra le diseguaglianze di genere*. Torino, Italy: Scriptorium.

Billari, F. (1998). *Appunti di demografia sociale*. Padua, Italy: University of Padova.

Billari, F. (2000). *L'analisi delle biografie e la transizione allo stato adulto: Aspetti metodologici e applicazioni ai dati della seconda Indagine sulla Fecondità in Italia*. Padova, Italy: Cleup.

Bijleveld, C. C. J. H., & van der Kamp, L. J. Th. (with Mooijaart, A., van der Kloot, W. A., van der Leeden, R., & van der Burg, E.). (1998). *Longitudinal data analysis: Designs, models, and methods*. London: Sage.

Blossfeld, H. P. (Ed.). (1995). *The new role Of women: Family formation in modern societies*. Boulder, CO: Westview Press.

Blossfeld, H. P., Hamerle, A., & Mayer, K. U. (1989). *Event history analysis: Statistical theory and application in the social sciences*. Hillsdale, NJ: Erlbaum.

Blossfeld, H. P., & Rohwer, G. (1995). *Techniques of event history modeling: New approaches to causal analysis*. Hillsdale, NJ: Erlbaum.

Bound, J., Duncan, G. J., Laren, D., & Oleinick, L. (1991). Poverty dynamics in widowhood. *Journal of Gerontology, 46*(3), 115–124.

Brannen, J., & Wilson, C. (1987). Introduction. In J. Brannen & C. Wilson (Eds.), *Give and take in families: Studies in resource distribution* (pp. 1–17). London: Allen & Unwin.

Bryman, A. (1988). *Quantity and quality in social research*. London: Routledge.

Buck, N., Gershuny, J., Rose, D., & Scott, J. (Eds.). (1994). *Changing households: The BHPS 1990 to 1992*. Colchester, UK: University of Essex.

Burkhauser, R. V., & Duncan, G. J. (1988). Life events, public policy, and the economic vulnerability of children and the elderly. In J. L. Palmer, T. M. Smeeding, & B. B. Torrey (Eds.), *The vulnerable* (pp. 55–88). Washington, DC: The Urban Institute Press.

Burkhauser, R. V., & Duncan, G. J. (1991). United States public policy and the elderly: The disproportionate risk to the well-being of women. *Journal of Population Economics, 4*(3), 217–231.

Bynner, J. (1996). *Use of longitudinal data in the study of social exclusion: A report for the Organisation for Economic Co-operation and Development, Social Statistics Research Unit*. London: City University.

Capursi, V. (1993). *Some issues in longitudinal data analysis with categorical variables*. Palermo, Italy: University of Palermo Istituto di Statistica Sociale e Scienze Demografiche e Biometriche.

Centre for Longitudinal Studies. (1999). *Research review 1999*. London: University of London Institute of Education.

Charles, N., & Kerr, M. (1987). Just the way it is: Gender and age differences in family food consumption. In J. Brannen & G. Wilson (Eds.), *Give and take in families* (pp. 155–174). London: Allen & Unwin.

Citro, C., & Kalton, G. (Eds.). (1993). *The future of the Survey of Income and Program Participation*. Washington, DC: National Academy Press.

Coe, R. D. (1988). A longitudinal examination of poverty in the elderly years. *Gerontologist, 28*(4), 540–544.

Coe, R. D., Duncan, G. J., & Hill, M. S. (1982, August). *Dynamic aspects of poverty and welfare use in the United States*. Paper presented at the Conference on Problems on Poverty, Clark University.

Coleman, J. S. (1981). *Longitudinal data analysis*. New York: Basic Books.

Comte, A. (1842). *Cours de philosophie positive* (Vol. 1). Paris: Costes.

Copeland, A. P., & White, K. M. (1991). *Studying families* (Applied Social Research Methods Series, vol. 27). London: Sage.

Corder, L. S., & Horvitz, D. G. (1989). Panel effects in the National Medical Care Utilization and Expenditure Survey. In D. Kasprzyk, G. J. Duncan, G. Kalton, & M. P. Singh (Eds.), *Panel surveys* (pp. 304–318). New York: Wiley.

Courgeau, D., & Lelièvre, E. (1988). *Analyse démographique des biographies*. Paris: Institut National Etudes Démographiques.

David, M. (1991). The science of data sharing: Documentation. In J. E. Sieber (Ed.), *Sharing social science data: Advantages and challenges* (pp. 91–115). London: Sage.

Davies, R. B. (1994). From cross-sectional to longitudinal analysis. In A. Dale & R. B. Davies (Eds.), *Analysing social and political change: A casebook of methods* (pp. 20–40). London: Sage.

Davies, R. B., & Dale, A. (1994). Introduction. In A. Dale & R. B. Davies (Eds.), *Analysing social and political change: A casebook of methods* (pp. 1–19). London: Sage.

Duncan, G. J. (1989). *Panel studies of poverty: Prospects and problems*. Ann Arbor: University of Michigan, Survey Research Center.

Duncan, G. J. (1992). *Household panel studies: Prospects and problems* (Working Papers of the European Scientific Network on Household Panel Studies, no. 54). Colchester, UK: University of Essex.

Duncan, G. J. (2000). Using panel studies to understand household behaviour and well-being. In D. Rose (Ed.), *Researching social and economic change: The uses of household panel studies* (pp. 54–75). London: Routledge.

Duncan, G. J., & Kalton, G. (1987). Issues of design and analysis of surveys across time. *International Statistical Review, 55*, 97–117.

Duncan, S., & Edwards, R. (Eds.). (1997). *Single mothers in an international context: Mothers or workers?* London: UCL Press.

Elder, G. H., Jr. (1985). Perspectives on the life course. In G. H. Elder, Jr. (Ed.), *Life course dynamics: Trajectories and transitions, 1968–1980* (pp. 23–49). Ithaca, NY: Cornell University Press.

Elder, G. H., Jr., & Liker, J. K. (1982). Hard times in women's lives: Historical influences across 40 years. *American Journal of Sociology, 88*, 241–269.

Ermisch, J. (2000). Using panel data to analyse household and family dynamics. In D. Rose (Ed.), *Researching social and economic change: The uses of household panel studies* (pp. 230–249). London: Routledge.

Etaugh, C., & Liss, M. B. (1992). Home, school, and playroom: Training grounds for adult gender roles. *Sex Roles, 26*, 129–147.

Eustis, N. N., Clark, R. F., & Adler, M. C. (1995). *Disability data for disability policy: Availability, access and analysis*. Retrieved September 11, 2007, from aspe.hhs.gov/daltcp/home.htm

Firebaugh, G. (1997). *Analyzing repeated surveys* (Sage University Paper Series on Quantitative Applications in the Social Sciences [QASS], no. 115). London: Sage.

Freed Taylor, M. (2000). Dissemination issues for panel studies: Metadata and documentation. In D. Rose (Ed.), *Researching social and economic change: The uses of household panel studies* (pp. 146–162). London: Routledge.

Fuller, W. A. (1987). *Measurement error models*. New York: Wiley.

Gallie, D., & Paugam, S. (Eds.). (2000). *Welfare regimes and the experience of unemployment in Europe*. Oxford, UK: Oxford University Press.

Gershuny, J. (1998). Thinking dynamically: Sociology and narrative data. In L. Leisering & R. Walker (Eds.), *The dynamics of modern society* (pp. 34–48). Bristol, UK: Policy Press.

Gershuny, J. (2000, August). Time budgets, life histories and social position. In E. Ruspini (Ed.), Longitudinal analysis: A bridge between quantitative and qualitative social research. *Quality and Quantity* [Special issue], pp. 277–289.

Gershuny, J., & Buck, N. (2000). *ESRC national strategy for longitudinal studies: Enquiry into social scientists' requirements for longitudinal data*. Colchester, UK: University of Essex, UK Longitudinal Studies Centre. Retrieved September 11, 2007, from *www.iser.essex.ac.uk/activities/NSLS-Enquiry.php*

Ghellini, G., & Trivellato, U. (1996). Indagini panel sul comportamento socio-economico di individui e famiglie: Una selezionata rassegna di problemi ed esperienze. In C. Quintano (Ed.), *Scritti di statistica economica 2*. Naples, Italy: Rocco Curto Editore.

Giddens, A. (1990). *The consequences of modernity*. Cambridge, UK: Polity Press.

Gilbert, N. (1993). *Analyzing tabular data: Loglinear and logistic models for social researchers*. London: University College London Press.

Goodin, R. E., Headey, B., Muffels, R., & Dirven, H.-J. (1999). *The real worlds of welfare capitalism*. Cambridge, UK: Cambridge University Press.

Graham, H. (1987). Women's poverty and caring. In C. Glendinning & J. Millar (Eds.), *Women and poverty in Britain* (pp. 221–240). Hemel Hempstead, UK: Harvester Wheatsheaf.

Gustafsson, B. (1997, March). *The Swedish Income Panel (SWIP)* [Application to the Swedish Council for Planning and Co-ordination of Research], University of Gothenburg, Göteborg, Sweden.

Haferkamp, H., & Smelser, N. J. (Eds.). (1992). *Social change and modernity*. Berkeley: University of California Press.

Hagenaars, J. A. (1990). *Categorical longitudinal data: Log-linear panel, trend and cohort analysis*. London: Sage.

Hakim, C. (1987). *Research design: Strategies and choices in the design of social research*. London: Allen & Unwin.

Helwig, A. A. (1998, March). Gender-role stereotyping: Testing theory with a longitudinal sample. *Sex Roles: A Journal of Research, 38*(5), 5–6. Retrieved September 11, 2007, from *www.findarticles.com/p/articles/mi_m2294/is_n5-6_v38/ai_20749197*

Henshaw, A., Kelly, J., & Gratton, C. (1992). Skipping's for girls: Children's perceptions of gender roles and gender preferences. *Educational Research, 34*, 229–235.

Hill, M., & Jenkins, M. S. (1999). *Poverty among British children: Chronic or transitory?* (Working Paper no. 99-23). Colchester, UK: University of Essex, Institute for Social and Economic Research.

Hsiao, C. (1985). Benefits and limitations of panel data. *Econometric Reviews, 4*, 121–188.

Hsiao, C. (1986). *Analysis of panel data*. Cambridge, MA: Cambridge University Press.

Janson, C.-G. (1990). Retrospective data, undesirable behavior, and the longitudinal perspective. In D. Magnusson & L. R. Bergman (Eds.), *Data quality in longitudinal research* (pp. 100–121). Cambridge, UK: Cambridge University Press.

Jarvis, S., & Jenkins, S. (1998). Marital dissolution and income change: Evidence for Britain. In R. Ford & J. Millar (Eds.), *Private lives and public responses: Lone parenthood and future policy* (pp. 104–117). London: Policy Studies Institute.

Jarvis, S., & Jenkins, S. (2000). Low-income dynamics in 1990s Britain. In D. Rose (Ed.), *Researching social and economic change: The uses of household panel studies* (pp. 188–209). London: Routledge.

Joshi, H., Dale, A., Ward, C., & Davies, H. (1995). *Dependence and independence in the finances of women aged 33*. London: Family Policy Study Centre.

Joshi, H., & Davies, H. (2002). Women's incomes over a synthetic lifetime. In E. Ruspini & A. Dale (Eds.), *The gender dimension of social change: The contribution of dynamic research to the study of women's life courses* (pp. 111–131). Bristol, UK: Policy Press.

Jowell, R., Brooks, L., Prior, G., & Taylor, B. (1992). *British social attitudes: The 9th report*. Aldershot, UK: Avebury.

Kalton, G., Kasprzyk, D., & McMillen, D. B. (1989). Nonsampling errors in panel survey. In D. Kasprzyk, G. J. Duncan, G. Kalton, & M. P. Singh (Eds.), *Panel surveys* (pp. 249–270). New York: Wiley.

Kalton, G., & Lepkowski, J. (1985). Following rules in SIPP. *Journal of Social and Economic Measurement, 13*, 319–329.

Kasprzyk, D., Duncan, G. J., Kalton, G., & Singh, M. P. (Eds.). (1989). *Panel surveys*. New York: Wiley.

Kessler, R. C., & Greenberg, D. F. (1981). *Linear panel analysis*. London: Academic Press.

Kish, L. (1986). Timing of surveys for public policy. *Australian Journal of Statistics, 7*, 1–12.

Kish, L. (1987). *Statistical design for research*. New York: Wiley.

Lazarsfeld, P. F. (1940). Panel studies. *Public Opinion Quarterly, 4*, 122–128.

Lazarsfeld, P. F. (1948). The use of panels in social research. In *Proceedings of the American Philosophical Society, 42*, 405–410.

Lazarsfeld, P. F., & Fiske, M. (1938). The "panel" as a new tool for measuring public opinion. *Public Opinion Quarterly, 2*, 596–612.

Leisering, K., & Walker, R. (1998). Making the future: From dynamics to policy agendas. In L. Leisering & R. Walker (Eds.), *The dynamics of modern society* (pp. 265–285). Bristol, UK: Policy Press.

Leth-Sørensen, S. (1997). *The IDA database: A longitudinal database of establishments and their employees*. Copenhagen, Denmark: Danmarks Statistik.

Lewis, J. (Ed.). (1997). *Lone mothers in European welfare regimes: Shifting policy logics*. London: Kingsley.

Lillard, L., & Waite, L. J. (1995). Till death do us part: Marital disruption and mortality. *American Journal of Sociology, 100*(5), 1131–1156.

Linton, M. (1982). Transformations of memory in everyday life. In U. Neisser (Ed.), *Memory observed: Remembering in natural contexts* (pp. 107–118). San Francisco: Freeman.

Lucchini, M., & Schizzerotto, A. (2001). Mutamenti nel tempo delle transizioni alla condizione adulta: un'analisi comparative. *Polis/Polis: Ricerche e Studi Società e Politica in Italia*, pp. 18–33.

Magnusson, D., & Bergman, L. R. (Eds.). (1990). *Data quality in longitudinal research*. Cambridge, UK: Cambridge University Press.

Magnusson, D., Bergman, L. R., Rudinger, G., & Torestad, B. (Eds.). (1991). *Problems and methods in longitudinal research: Stability and change*. Cambridge, UK: Cambridge University Press.

Martin, J., & Roberts, C. (1984). *Women and employment: A lifetime perspective*. London: Her Majesty's Stationery Office.

Mátyás, L., & Sevestre, P. (Eds.). (1996). *The econometrics of panel data: Handbook of theory and applications* (2nd rev. ed.). Dordrecht, the Netherlands: Kluwer Academic.

Mayer, K. U. (1990). Lebensverlaufe und sozialer Wandel: Anmerkungen zu einem Forschungsprogramm. In K. U. Mayer (Ed.), *Lebensverläufe und sozialer Wandel* (pp. 7–21). Opladen: Westdeutscher Verlag.

Mednick, S. A., & Mednick, B. (1984). A brief history of North American longitudinal research. In A. M. Sarnoff, M. Harway, & K. M. Finello (Eds.), *Handbook of longitudinal research: Vol. 1. Birth and childhood cohorts* (pp. 19–21). New York: Praeger.

Menard, S. (1991). *Longitudinal research*. London: Sage.

Millar, J. (1989). *Poverty and the lone-parent family: The challenge to social policy*. Aldershot, UK: Avebury.

Millar, J. (2000). Genere, povertà e esclusione sociale. *Inchiesta, 128*, 9–13.

Muffels, R. J. A. (2000). Dynamics of poverty and determinants of poverty transitions: Results from the Dutch Socioeconomic Panel. In D. Rose (Ed.), *Researching social and economic change: The uses of household panel studies* (pp. 165–187). London: Routledge.

Negri, N. (1990). Introduzione. In N. Negri (Ed.), *Povertà in Europa e trasformazione dello Stato sociale* (pp. 11–72). Milan, Italy: Franco Angeli.

Olagnero, M., & Saraceno, C. (1993). *Che vita è: L'uso dei materiali biografici nell'analisi sociologica*. Rome: La Nuova Italia Scientifica.

Olsen, R. (1996). Young carers: Challenging the facts and politics of research into children and caring. *Disability and Society, 11*(1), 41–54.

Pahl, J. (1989). *Money and marriage*. London: Macmillan.

Pahl, J. (1995). His money, her money: Recent research on financial organisation in marriage. *Journal of Economic Psychology, 16*(3), 361–376.

Payne, S. (2001). Malattia e ruoli femminili: La relazione tra dipendenza economica, responsabilità di cura e povertà. In C. Facchini & E. Ruspini (Eds.), *Salute e disuguaglianze: Genere, condizioni sociali e corso di vita* (pp. 177–207). Milan, Italy: Franco Angeli.

Rajulton, F., & Ravanera, Z. R. (2000, May). *Theoretical and analytical aspects of longitudinal research*. Paper presented at the annual meeting of the Canadian Population Association, Edmonton, Alberta.

Rinaldi, E., & Giromini, E. (2002). The importance of money to Italian children. *International Journal of Advertising and Marketing to Children, 3*(4), 53–59.

Rose, D. (1993). *European household panel studies*

(Working Papers of the ESF Network on Household Panel Studies, no. 45). Colchester, UK: University of Essex.

Rose, D. (2000). Household panel studies: An overview. In D. Rose (Ed.), *Researching social and economic change: The uses of household panel studies* (pp. 3–35). London: Routledge.

Rose, D., & Sullivan, O. (1996). *Introducing data analysis for social scientists.* Milton Keynes, UK: Open University Press.

Ruspini, E. (1999, July–August). Longitudinal research and the analysis of social change. In E. Ruspini (Ed.), Longitudinal analysis: A bridge between quantitative and qualitative social research. *Quality and Quantity* [Special issue], *33*(3), 219–227.

Ruspini, E. (2000). *L'altra metà della povertà. Uno studio sulla povertà femminile in Germania e Gran Bretagna.* Rome: Carocci Editore.

Ruspini, E. (2001). The study of women's deprivation: How to reveal the gender dimension of poverty. *International Journal of Social Research Methodology: Theory and Practice*, *4*(2), 101–118.

Ruspini, E. (2002). *Introduction to longitudinal research.* London: Routledge.

Ruspini, E., & Dale A. (Eds.). (2002). *The gender dimension of social change: The contribution of dynamic research to the study of women's life courses.* Bristol, UK: Policy Press.

Ryder, N. B. (1965). The cohort as a concept in the study of social change. *American Sociological Review*, *30*, 843–861.

Saraceno, C. (Ed.). (2002). *Social assistance dynamics in Europe.* Bristol, UK: Policy Press.

Scherer, S. (2000). Assetti istituzionali e differenze di genere nell'accesso al mercato del lavoro. *Inchiesta*, *128*, 75–84.

Schizzerotto, A. (Ed.). (2002). *Vite ineguali: Disuguaglianze e corsi di vita nell'Italia contemporanea.* Bologna, Italy: il Mulino.

Schizzerotto, A., Bison, I., & Zoppé, A. (1995). Disparità di genere nella partecipazione al mondo del lavoro e nella durata delle carriere. *Polis*, *9*(1), 91–112.

Schizzerotto, A., & Lucchini, M. (2004). Transitions to adulthood. In R. Berthoud & M. Iacovou (Eds.), *Social Europe: Living standards and welfare states* (pp. 46–68). Cheltenham, UK: Edward Elgar.

Schwarz, N. (1996). *Survey research: Collecting data by asking questions.* In G. R. Semin & K. Fiedler (Eds.), *Applied social psychology* (pp. 65–90). London: Sage.

Schwarz, N., & Sudman, S. (Eds.). (1994). *Autobiographical memory and the validity of retrospective reports.* New York: Springer Verlag.

Singh, C. (1995). *A comparative analysis of attrition in household panel studies* (Comparative Research on Household Panel Studies [PACO project], Document No. 10). Luxembourg: CEPS/INSTEAD. Retrieved September 11, 2007, from *www.ceps.lu/pdf/11/art930.pdf?CFID=319120&CFTOKEN=43759969&jsessionid=2030792fd7cb44485921*

Smelser, N. J. (1981). *Sociology.* Englewood Cliffs, NJ: Prentice Hall.

Sontag, L. W. (1971). The history of longitudinal research: Implications for the future. *Child Development*, *42*, 987–1002.

Sudman, S., & Bradburn, N. A. (1982). *Asking questions.* San Francisco: Jossey-Bass.

Sudman, S., & Ferber, R. (1979). *Consumer panels.* Chicago: American Marketing Association.

Taris, T. W. (2000). *A primer in longitudinal data analysis.* London: Sage.

Touraine, A. (1974). *The post-industrial society.* London: Wildwood.

Trivellato, U. (1999, July–August). Issues in the design and analysis of panel studies: A cursory review. In E. Ruspini (Ed.), Longitudinal analysis: A bridge between quantitative and qualitative social research *Quality and Quantity* [Special issue], *33*(3), 339–352.

van de Pol, F. J. R. (1989). *Issues of design and analysis of panels.* Amsterdam: Sociometric Research Foundation.

Walker, R. (1995). The dynamics of poverty and social exclusion. In G. Room (Ed.), *Beyond the threshold: The measurement and analysis of social exclusion.* London: Polity Press.

Walker, R., & Ashworth, K. (1994). *Poverty dynamics: Issues and examples.* Aldershot, UK: Avebury.

Wall, W. D., & Williams, H. L. (1970). *Longitudinal studies and the social sciences.* London: Heinemann.

Waterton, J., & Lievesley, D. (1989). Evidence of conditioning effects in the British Attitudes Panel Survey. In D. Kasprzyk, G. J. Duncan, G. Kalton, & M. P. Singh (Eds.), *Panel surveys* (pp. 319–339). New York: Wiley.

Weinraub, M., Jaeger, E., & Hoffman, L. W. (1988). Predicting infant outcomes in families of employed and nonemployed mothers. *Early Childhood Research Quarterly*, *3*, 361–378.

Wilson, G. (1987). Money: Pattern of responsibility and irresponsibility. In J. Brannen & C. Wilson (Eds.), *Give and take in families: Studies in resource distribution* (pp. 136–154). London: Allen & Unwin.

Witt, S. D. (1997, Summer). Parental influence on children's socialization to gender roles adolescence. *Adolescence*, *32*, 253–259.

Wright Mills, C. (1959). *The sociological imagination.* New York: Oxford University Press.

Zazzo, R. (1967). Diversité, realité, et mirages de la méthode longitudinale: Rapport introducif au symposium des études longitudinales. *Enfance*, *2*(20), 131–136.

CHAPTER 22

Categorizing and Connecting Strategies in Qualitative Data Analysis

Joseph A. Maxwell
Barbara A. Miller

Quantitative research has a detailed and systematic general theory, known as statistics, that informs and guides how data analysis should be done. As defined by Kerlinger, statistics is "the theory and method of analyzing quantitative data obtained from samples of observations in order to study and compare sources of variance of phenomena, to help make decisions to accept or reject hypothesized relations between the phenomena, and to aid in making reliable inferences from empirical observations" (1979, p. 185). Tesch (1990) argued that "statistics books . . . are remarkable in the sense that they all say pretty much the same thing" (p. 3). Although this applies more to introductory texts than to advanced work, and although there are numerous controversial topics within statistics, there is nevertheless considerable agreement on those theoretical principles that guide quantitative data analysis. Even disagreements, such as the recent controversy over null hypothesis significance testing, are usually based on widely, if not universally, shared theoretical principles.

Qualitative research has no comparable theory to statistics. Although there are now a substantial number of descriptions and justifications of how qualitative analysis can or should be done, there is little generally accepted theory that provides an underlying rationale for what qualitative researchers do when they analyze data. Anselm Strauss's statement, "we have a very long way to go yet in understanding how we do qualitative analysis and how to improve our analysis" (1988, p. 99), still seems accurate.

In this chapter, we hope to contribute to the development of a theory of qualitative data analysis. We approach this goal by applying to qualitative analysis a distinction, widely used in linguistics, between two types of relationships: those based on similarity and those based on contiguity (Jakobson, 1956; Lyons, 1968, pp. 70–81; Saussure,

1916/1986). These relationships are often respectively termed *paradigmatic* and *syntagmatic*.

Similarity and contiguity refer to two fundamentally different kinds of relationships between things, neither of which can be assimilated to the other. Similarity-based relations involve resemblances or common features; their identification is based on comparison, which can be independent of time and place. In qualitative data analysis, similarities and differences are generally used to define categories and to group and compare data by category. We refer to analytical strategies that focus on relationships of similarity as *categorizing* strategies.[1] Coding is a typical categorizing strategy in qualitative research.

Contiguity-based relations, in contrast, involve juxtaposition in time and space, the influence of one thing on another, or relations among parts of a text; their identification involves seeing actual *connections* between things, rather than similarities and differences. In qualitative data analysis, contiguity relationships are identified among data in an actual context (such as an interview transcript or observational field notes). Contiguity relationships may also be identified among abstract concepts and categories as a subsequent step to a categorizing analysis of the data. We refer to strategies that focus on relationships of contiguity as *connecting* strategies; in earlier work (e.g., Maxwell, 1996), we had called these "contextualizing strategies." Some narrative approaches to interview analysis are examples of primarily connecting strategies, as are microethnographic approaches (Erickson, 1992) to observational data.

Our purpose in this chapter is to give the distinction between these two approaches to analysis a more systematic theoretical grounding and to apply this distinction more widely and explicitly to methods for analyzing qualitative data. We see the distinction between similarity-based categorizing and contiguity-based connecting as fundamental to the conceptual processes and strategies on which qualitative data analysis is based. We would also argue that the similarity–contiguity distinction is involved in such broader distinctions as those between variance theory and process theory (Mohr, 1982), variable-oriented and case-oriented approaches (Ragin, 1987), structural and functional analyses of discourse (Linde, 1993), and sociological and historical analysis (Wieviorka, 1992), but these wider issues are beyond the scope of this chapter.

We begin by explicating the similarity–contiguity distinction, the basis for our distinction between categorizing and connecting strategies. We then describe each of these two strategies in more detail, presenting the strengths and limitations of each approach, and discuss ways of integrating the two approaches. We conclude with some observations on the use of computers in qualitative data analysis.

Similarity and Contiguity

The distinction between similarity and contiguity, generally credited to Saussure, was first explicitly stated by David Hume in his *A Treatise of Human Nature* (1739/1978). Hume defined three ways in which ideas may be associated: by resemblance (similarity), by contiguity in time or place, and by cause and effect. He then argued that causation is a complex relation based on the other two, leaving resemblance and contiguity as the two primary modes of association. Hume used this distinction widely, but not systematically, in the *Treatise*, discussing, for example, how sympathy was the result of the operation of both resemblance and contiguity: "Nor is resemblance the only relation, which has this effect. . . . The sentiments of others have little influence, when far remov'd from us, and require the relation of contiguity, to make them communicate themselves entirely" (p. 318).

The similarity–contiguity distinction has been most widely employed in linguistics, into which it was explicitly introduced by Saussure (1916/1986).[2] Saussure distinguished between associative (similarity-based) and syntagmatic (contiguity-based) relations, and grounded his theory of language in this distinction. This distinction was given its most explicit presentation in an article by Jakobson titled "Two Aspects of Language and Two Types of Aphasic Disturbances" (1956). In this paper, Jakobson developed the distinction with reference to language, establishing the currently prevalent terms *paradigmatic* and *syntagmatic* and explicitly basing these on similarity and contiguity, respectively. He then applied this distinction to aphasia, identifying two types of aphasia, which he labeled *similarity disorder* and *contiguity disorder*, each reflecting a loss of one of these two essential components of language. A key point in Jakobson's argument is the *complementarity* of the two dimensions; he argued that the loss of either dimension resulted in an inability to use language effectively.

Jakobson's ideas were picked up and further developed by numerous other writers. Barthes, in his *Elements of Semiology* (1968), used a similar contrast, that between "system" and "syntagm." Levi-Strauss (e.g., 1958/1963, 1966) employed a number of related distinctions, including paradigmatic–syntagmatic, metaphor–metonym, and harmonic–melodic, to analyze kinship, myth, and primitive thought. Such distinctions were fundamental to the approach that became known as "structuralism." Holdcroft (1991) stated that "the principle that linguistic units have no significance apart from their syntagmatic and associative relations, and so necessarily belong to a system, is the central thesis of Saussurean structuralism" (p. 104).

Structuralism as a movement tended to assume that languages, cultures, or literary works could be analyzed in terms of a small number of invariant distinctions that were presumably grounded in basic structures of thought. This approach tended to ignore human agency and to present "totalizing" analyses that left no room for alternatives. These views were criticized by authors labeled (by themselves or others) as poststructuralist, postmodernist, or deconstructionist, and structuralism has largely been abandoned (see *en.wikipedia.org/wiki/Structuralism*). Partly as a result, the similarity–contiguity distinction has mostly fallen out of use in social science.

More recently, however, Bruner (1986) used Saussure's and Jakobson's distinction to define two different approaches to understanding, which he called "two modes of thought": the paradigmatic, or logico-scientific mode, and the narrative mode. However, he did not elaborate on the distinction itself, focusing instead on the narrative mode as an alternative to traditional "scientific" thinking.

Jakobson's application of the similarity–contiguity distinction to aphasia suggests that there may be a neurological basis for this distinction. Research on memory by the psychologist Tulving (1983; Tulving & Craik, 2000) and others provides some support for this view. Tulving distinguished two distinct, though interacting, systems of memory, which he called *semantic memory* and *episodic memory*. Semantic memory is memory of facts, concepts, principles, and other sorts of information, organized conceptually rather than in terms of the context in which they were learned. Episodic memory, in contrast, is memory of events and episodes, organized temporally in terms of the context of their occurrence. Extensive experimental research (Tulving & Craik, 2000) has supported this distinction, as have studies demonstrating that memory loss may selectively affect one or the other of these systems (Mayes, 2000), and brain imaging has shown that encoding or retrieving information from the two memory systems engages different areas of the brain (Nyberg & Cabeza, 2000; Wheeler, 2000).

In applying the similarity–contiguity distinction to qualitative data analysis, we are not claiming that this is an obligatory distinction, or that it takes precedence over other ways of conceptualizing analysis. We do believe that it is a *useful* distinction, one that clarifies some important aspects of qualitative data analysis and can lead to improvements in how we do analyses.

Similarity and Contiguity Relations in Qualitative Data Analysis

To our knowledge, the extensively developed theoretical analysis of these two types of relationships has never been explicitly applied to qualitative data analysis. Although the role of similarity in categorizing is often recognized, the importance of contiguity relations in other types of analysis is rarely stated, and the similarity–contiguity distinction itself, though often implicitly recognized and described, is not linked to existing theoretical work on this distinction.

A particularly clear presentation of how this distinction is involved in the actual processes of data analysis is that of Smith (1979):

> I usually start . . . at the beginning of the notes. I read along and seem to engage in two kinds of processes–comparing and contrasting, and looking for antecedents and consequences. . . .
>
> The essence of concept formation [the first process] is . . . "How are they alike, and how are they different?" The similar things are grouped and given a label that highlights their similarity. . . . In time, these similarities and differences come to represent clusters of concepts, which then organize themselves into more abstract categories and eventually into hierarchical taxonomies.
>
> Concurrently, a related but different process is occurring. . . . The conscious search for the consequences of social items . . . seemed to flesh out a complex systemic view and a concern for process, the flow of events over time. In addition it seemed to argue for a more holistic, systemic, interdependent network of events at the concrete level and concepts and propositions at an abstract level. . . . At a practical level, while in the field, the thinking, searching, and note recording reflected not only a consciousness of similarities and differences but also an attempt to look for unexpected relationships, antecedents, and consequences within the flow of items. (p. 338)

A similar distinction is found in many accounts of qualitative data analysis. For example, Seidman (1998, p. 101 ff.) described two main strategies in the analysis of interviews: the categorization of interview material through coding and thematic analysis, and the creation of several different types of narratives, which he calls "profiles" and "vignettes." Other versions of this distinction are Patton's (1990), between content analysis and case studies; Weiss's (1994), between "issue-focused" and "case-focused" analysis; and Coffey and Atkinson's (1996), between "concepts and coding" and "narratives and stories." However, none of these authors examined the principles on which these distinctions are based, and the similarity–contiguity distinction is frequently confounded with others. For example, Ezzy (2002, p. 95) distinguished narrative analysis from coding primarily in terms of its being more holistic, interpretive, and "in process" and as employing a constructivist approach and "situated relativity."

A few authors provide a more explicit recognition of this distinction. Sayer, in discussing theoretical abstraction and structural analysis, distinguished between " 'substantial' relations of connection and interaction and 'formal' relations of similarity or dissimilarity" (1992, p. 88), but made no further use of this distinction. And Dey (1993, pp. 94, 153 ff.), specifically addressing qualitative data analysis, used Sayer's distinction to discriminate between creating categories and making comparisons, on the one hand, and "linking data," on the other. Despite this, Dey focused mainly on using specific links between data segments to create links between categories, rather than on developing a more extensive connecting analysis of actual data.

Before we discuss the use of categorizing and connecting strategies in qualitative data analysis, we provide a brief overview of the qualitative analysis process. Although we describe this in terms of "steps," we want to emphasize that these do not usually occur in a strict linear sequence and that there can be frequent movement between the different components, with each influencing the subsequent application of the others (Maxwell, 2005).

Qualitative Data Analysis: An Overview

The initial step in the analysis of qualitative data is *reading* the interview transcripts, observational notes, or documents that are to be analyzed (Dey, 1993; Erickson, 1986; Smith, 1979). This initial reading will result in notes and memos on the material read and in tentative ideas about categories and relationships in the data.

The next step is the identification of units of data that will be addressed by subsequent analytic procedures. This step has been called "unitizing" by Labov and Fanshel (1977, pp. 38–40) and Lincoln and Guba (1985, p. 344) and "segmenting" by Coffey and Atkinson (1996, p. 26) and Tesch (1990, p. 91); Seidman (1998, p. 100) described it as "marking what is of interest in the text." It has been discussed extensively in linguistics but has often not been recognized as a distinct step in qualitative research, instead being subsumed in subsequent categorizing steps.

Segmenting the data is obviously involved in categorizing analyses, but it is often an implicit process in narrative and other connecting approaches, as well, although it rarely is explicitly discussed. For example, Gee (2005, pp. 118–128), in his approach to discourse analysis, segments speech into units that he calls "lines" and "stanzas," based on both linguistic cues and the content of the utterance. This step is as necessary to narrative and other connecting strategies as it is to categorizing ones (Linde, 1993, pp. 61–67; Riessman, 1993, p. 58), although the particular way it is done will depend on the type of analysis selected, as well as on the length of the segments.

At this point, there are a number of analytic options available to the researcher. We see these as falling into three main groups: memos, categorizing strategies (such as coding and thematic analysis), and connecting strategies (typically involved in narratives, case studies, and ethnographic microanalysis). Memos are an important technique for analyzing qualitative data (Miles & Huberman, 1994; Strauss & Corbin, 1990), but they can be used for either categorizing or connecting purposes, or to perform other functions not related to data analysis, such as reflection on methods.

Categorizing Strategies

The most widely used categorizing strategy in qualitative data analysis is coding. In coding, the data segments are labeled and grouped by category; they are then examined and compared, both within and between categories. Coding categories "are a means of sorting the descriptive data you have collected . . . so that the material bearing on a given topic can be physically separated from other data" (Bogdan & Biklen, 2003, p. 161). Coding and sorting by code creates a similarity-based ordering of data that replaces the original contiguity-based ordering.

Many qualitative researchers have treated coding as the fundamental activity in analysis and the only one that involves manipulation of actual data (e.g., Ryan & Bernard, 2000). For example, LeCompte and Preissle stated that "the next step [after writing an initial summary] is to begin the time-consuming and laborious process of pulling apart field notes, matching, comparing, and contrasting, which constitutes the heart of analysis" (1993, p. 237).

Tesch (1990, pp. 115–123) referred to this replacement of an original contextual structure by a different, categorical structure as "decontextualizing and recontextualizing." She described recontextualizing as follows: "The [data] segment is settled in the context of its topic, in the neighborhood of all other segments of the data corpus that deal with the same topic" (p. 122). However, this new set of relationships is based on similarity rather than contiguity and is thus not a "recontextualization" in the usual sense of "context," that is, a set of phenomena that are connected in time and space. This new set of relationships is quite different from a contiguity-based context, and confusing the two can lead to the neglect of actual contextual relationships. In addition, reordering the data in terms of particular categories can create analytic blinders, preventing the analyst from seeing alternative relationships (particularly connecting relationships) in the data.

Both of these problems are illustrated by Atkinson's description (1992) of how his initial categorizing analysis of the teaching of general medicine affected his subsequent analysis of his surgery notes:

> [O]n rereading the surgery notes, I initially found it difficult to *escape* those categories I had initially established [for medicine]. Understandably, they furnished a powerful conceptual grid. Moreover, they exercised a more powerful physical constraint. The notes as I confronted them had been fragmented into the constituent themes. (pp. 458–459)

On returning to his original notebooks, Atkinson found:

> I am now much less inclined to fragment the notes into relatively small segments. Instead, I am just as interested in reading episodes and passages at greater length, with a correspondingly different attitude toward the act of reading and hence of analysis. Rather than constructing my account like a patchwork quilt, I feel more like working with the whole cloth. . . . To be more precise, what now concerns me is the nature of these products as *texts*. (p. 460)

Other researchers (e.g., Mishler, 1984, 1986) have also seen the neglect of context as a major defect of coding and other categorizing strategies. Mishler argued that "the meanings of questions and answers are not fixed by nor adequately represented by the interview schedule or by code-category systems" (1986, p. 138) and claimed that systematic methods of narrative analysis are required to understand research interviews.

The categories generated through coding are typically linked into larger patterns; this subsequent step can be seen as contiguity-based, but the connections are made between the categories themselves, rather than between segments of actual data. In addition, using connecting techniques only on the categories, rather than the data, results in an *aggregate* account of contiguity relationships and can never reconstitute the specific contextual connections that were lost during the original categorizing analysis.

Most qualitative researchers are aware of the dangers of decontextualization in using categorizing techniques. Works on qualitative methods often warn about context-stripping and the need to retain the connection of coded data to their original context. However, attention to context is often seen only as a *check* or *control* on the use of categorizing analytic strategies, and most works say little about how one might *analyze* contextual relationships. For example, Lofland and Lofland (1984) argued:

> Splitting the materials into mundane, analytic, and fieldwork files will facilitate staying "on top" of what is happening and evolving an analysis. But it also tends to obscure that nebulous quality called "context." . . . You should therefore keep a full set of your materials in the order in which you originally collected them. . . . [I]t is useful simply for reading and reviewing from beginning to end, as a stimulus to thinking about larger patterns and larger units of analysis. (pp. 134–135)

Thematic analysis is also a categorizing strategy, although the units categorized as similar or different are usually larger than those typically involved in coding data. The theme *itself* often has an internal connected structure: a relationship between two concepts or actions, a proposition or belief, a narrative or argument, or other, more complex sets of relations. However, its identification and establishment *as* a theme—showing that it is more than an idiosyncratic occurrence—is inherently a categorizing process. Also, as is the case for linking categories, the relationships among the components of a theme are *generic* relationships, not ones between actual data.

The most common alternative to coding and thematic classification in qualitative research is the "case study" (Patton, 1990, pp. 384 ff.). In this approach, the unique context of each case is retained, and the data are interpreted within that context, to provide an account of a particular instance, setting, person, or event. However, case studies often employ primarily categorizing analysis strategies (e.g., Merriam, 1988; Yin, 2003, pp. 101–111), and their main advantage is that the categorizing (coding, thematic analysis, etc.) occurs within a particular case rather than between cases, so that the contextual relationships are harder to lose sight of. Qualitative case studies *can* be highly contextual or connected in their analysis (e.g., clinical case description), but they are not inherently so.

Connecting Strategies

Narratives, portraits, and case studies are often included in qualitative research reports as an accompaniment to categorizing analysis, and Barone (1990, p. 358) argued that most qualitative texts are a mixture of narrative and paradigmatic (categorizing) design features. However, such uses of narrative are often largely presentational rather than analytical; even Patton, who clearly used case studies as an analytic strategy, confounded this claim by describing case studies as "presenting a holistic portrayal" (1990, p. 388). Such presentational techniques partially compensate for the loss of contextual ties that results from a primarily categorizing approach, but they rarely are integrated with what is seen as the "real" analysis or go beyond what is apparent in the raw data. Here, we are concerned with narrative or contextual approaches that involve data *analysis*, rather than being limited to the presentation of raw or edited data.

Connecting analytic strategies do not simply preserve data in their original form. Instead, they are ways to analyze and reduce data. This is generally done by identifying key relationships that tie the data together into a narrative or sequence and eliminating information that is not germane to these relationships. For example, Patton (1990, pp. 386–390) and Seidman (1998, pp. 102–107) discussed the steps involved in selecting data to create case studies and "profiles," respectively.

The process of doing connecting analysis has received less attention than categorizing analysis. Narrative analysis is the most prevalent approach that has emphasized alternatives to categorizing analysis, but much of narrative research, broadly defined, involves categorizing as well as connecting analysis, and the distinction has not been clearly defined.

For example, Lieblich, Tuval-Mashiach, and Zilber (1998) defined two dimensions of narrative analysis: (1) holistic versus categorical approaches and (2) a focus on content versus form. The first dimension was described as "very similar to the distinction between 'categorization' and 'contextualization' as proposed by Maxwell (1996)." However, Lieblich and colleagues' characterization of holistic analysis focused mainly on the holism rather than the connecting nature of the analysis: "in the holistic approach, the life story of the person is taken as a whole, and sections of the text are interpreted in the context of other parts of the narrative" (p. 12). Their examples of the holistic approach emphasized a thematic analysis of the material and the use of these themes "to create a rich picture of a unique individual" (p. 15) and, in multiple case studies, a focus on similarities and differences among the cases. It is only in the discussion of the actual process of reading holistically that specifically connecting strategies, such as following each theme throughout the story and noting the context of each transition between themes, appeared (p. 63). (For this strategy, the authors cited Brown et al., 1988, an early version of the "listening guide" approach described below.)

Many connecting strategies focus on the structure or significance of the narrative conveyed by the data (the latter usually being an interview transcript). These narrative strategies are informed by different disciplines. Discourse analysis and other approaches that draw primarily from linguistics (e.g., Gee, 2005; Mishler, 1986 usually operate on a close, textual level, on which the semantic connections between different parts of the text are examined. One such strategy is the functional analysis carried out by Labov and his colleagues (1972, 1982; Labov & Fanshel, 1977; Labov & Waletzky, 1967). In their early work they focused on the temporal sequence of action within a narrative; in subsequent work, they attended to the larger social meanings conveyed by the narrative structure. Such works usually fall into the "holistic-form" category described by Lieblich and colleagues (1998).

A second kind of narrative strategy is informed more by sociology, anthropology, and clinical psychology. This approach is less concerned with the structure of the text and more with the meaning of that text for the participant; these works usually fit the "holistic-content" category of Lieblich and colleagues (1998). Seidman's "profiles" are one example of such an approach. In creating a profile from an interview transcript, Seidman (1998) first identifies and synthesizes the basic story line by reducing the text to those elements that are seen as important parts of the person's story. These segments are then crafted into a first-person account, normally (but not invariably) keeping the same order in which they appeared in the transcript (pp. 100–107).

Contiguity-based analytic strategies are not limited to narrative approaches. What Erickson (1992) called "ethnographic microanalysis of interaction" involves the detailed description of local interaction processes and analysis of how these processes are organized (p. 204). The analytic process "begins by considering whole events, continues by analytically decomposing them into smaller fragments, and then concludes by *recomposing* them into wholes. . . . [This process] returns them to a level of sequentially connected social action" (p. 217). Thus, instead of segmenting events and then *categorizing* these segments to create a structure of similarities and differences among these, this approach segments the data and then *connects* these segments into a relational order within an actual context.

Narrative strategies, as well as most other connecting strategies, do not rely exclusively on contiguity. As described previously, they also tend to utilize categorization, to a greater or lesser extent, to discern the narrative structure of the data (Linde, 1993, pp. 65–66). For example, identifying elements of plot, scene, conflict, or resolution in a narrative, as in approaches that focus on form rather than content (Lieblich et al., 1998), inherently involves classification. However, such classification is used to identify the elements of a narrative in terms of how they relate to other elements rather than to create a similarity-based ordering of the data in terms of its *content*. Thus Mishler (1986) describes some forms of narrative analysis that employ coding and categorization, but the categories he presents are *functional* rather than substantive categories. Such categories "provide a set of codes for classifying the 'narrative functions' of different parts of the account" (p. 82), rather than constituting the basis for a reorganization of the data. Such categorization can be a necessary complement to a connecting analysis, rather than as a separate analytic process.

Narrative and contextual analyses, as strategies based primarily on contiguity rather than similarity, have disadvantages of their own. In particular, they can lead to an inability to make comparisons and to gain insights from the similarity or difference of two things in separate contexts. Some of our students have avoided coding their interviews or field notes, convinced that coding would destroy the contextual relations that they considered most important. However, if we persuaded them to try coding, they often said that it vastly increased their understanding of the data, because it broke them out of the fixed contextual frameworks within which they were working and allowed them to see other relationships that they had been blind to. As one student wrote:

> At first, I resisted coding. The process seemed mechanical and reductive to me. I didn't want to violate the organic unity of my interviews, many of which had deeply moved me. To fracture these conversations into discrete pieces of information seemed like taking a pair of scissors and cutting up family photographs. However, as I started coding I soon realized what a powerful tool it was. To my amazement, I found connections between the interviews that I hadn't previously suspected. Not only did my informants share similar experiences, they sometimes used the same language to discuss those experiences. This was exciting, for I began to see that what had at first seemed like a mass of incoherent, intractable material did, indeed, have pattern and shape—and that in spite of the unique personalities and circumstances of my informants' lives, there were commonalities in both their experiences and the way they looked at things. (Huang, 1991)

An exclusive emphasis on connecting strategies can create what another student called an "imprisonment in the story" of a particular narrative—a failure to see alternative ways of framing and interpreting the text or situation in question. Wieviorka argued that comparison "may help deconstruct what common sense takes to be unique or unified" (1992, p. 170) and generate alternative perspectives.

Displays as Categorizing and Connecting Strategies

Displays (Miles & Huberman, 1994), as techniques for data analysis, can also be divided into similarity-based and contiguity-based forms. Miles and Huberman described a wide variety of displays, but most of these fall into two basic types: matrices and networks. Matrices are essentially tables formed by the intersection of two or more lists of items; the cells in the table are filled with data, either raw or summarized, allowing comparison of the similarities and differences among the cells. The lists forming the matrix can be of individuals, roles, sites, topics, or properties of these, and can be organized in numerous ways, creating a large number of different types of matrices. Networks, in contrast, are visual maps of the relationships (for Miles and Huberman [1994], usually temporal or causal relationships) among individuals, events, social units, or properties of these.

We see matrices and networks as, respectively, similarity-based and contiguity-based displays. Matrices are a logical extension of coding; they are created by constructing lists of mutually exclusive categories and then crossing these to create cells. Such displays may then be used to make connections across items in a row or column, but these connections link the results of the original categorization that was used to create the matrix. Networks, on the other hand, are a logical extension of narrative or causal analysis, organizing events or concepts by time and by spatial or causal connection; they capture the contiguity-based relationships that are lost in creating matrices. Miles and Huberman (1994) provided examples of networks that link specific events, as well as those that link more abstract categories, although none were included that link actual data segments. They also presented a substantial number of hybrid forms that involve both categorizing and connecting analysis, such as time-ordered matrices and segmented causal networks.[3]

Integrating Categorizing and Connecting Strategies

We have alluded to some of the advantages of combining categorizing and connecting strategies for analyzing qualitative data. However, even authors who explicitly discuss both types of strategies, such as Seidman (1998) and Atkinson (1992; Coffey & Atkinson, 1996), rarely address how to produce a successful combination. Implicitly, they seem to see the two as alternative, or parallel but separate, analytic approaches.

Although the separate use of the two approaches is legitimate and often productive, there are other possibilities as well. The most common is the sequential use of the two types of strategies, beginning with one and then moving to the other. For example, most qualitative researchers who employ coding strategies eventually develop a model of the causal connections or relational patterns among the categories, as discussed earlier. However, this final step rarely involves direct analysis of data and usually receives little explicit discussion (prominent exceptions are the work of Strauss, discussed shortly, and of Miles and Huberman).

Researchers who employ initial connecting or narrative strategies, on the other hand, often conclude by discussing similarities and differences among the cases or individuals analyzed (this is the reverse of the previous strategy of connecting categories into a relational sequence or network). For example, Erickson (1992) describes the final step in ethnographic microanalysis as the "comparative analysis of instances across the research corpus," to determine how typical these analyzed units of interaction are (p. 220).

We suggest that it may be useful to think of this process in terms of categorizing and connecting "moves" in an analysis, rather than in terms of alternative or sequential overall strategies. At each point in the analysis, one can take either a categorizing step, looking for similarities and differences, or a connecting step, looking for actual (contiguity based) connections between things. In fact, it is often productive to alternate between categorizing and connecting moves, as each move can respond to limitations in the results of the previous move.[4]

A widely used approach to qualitative analysis that seems to us to employ this strategy is the "grounded theory" method (Strauss, 1987; Strauss & Corbin, 1990). The initial step in analysis, which Strauss called "open coding," involves segmenting the data, attaching conceptual labels to these segments, and making comparisons among the segments. However, many of the subsequent steps in analysis are predominantly connecting, despite being described as forms of coding; Strauss and Corbin used "coding" to mean "the process of analyzing data" (1990, p. 61). Thus Strauss's next step, "axial coding," consists of:

> specifying a category (*phenomenon*) in terms of the *conditions* that give rise to it; the *context* . . . in which it is embedded; the action/interactional *strategies* by which it is handled, managed, carried out; and the *consequences* of these strategies. (Strauss & Corbin, 1990, p. 97, original emphasis)

This is almost a definition of what we mean by connecting analysis; the main difference is that Strauss and Corbin (1990) describe these connections as being to *categories*, rather than to data segments. The analytical steps subsequent to open coding involve making connections among categories, developing a "story line" about the central phenomena of the study, and identifying "conditional paths" that link actions with conditions and consequences. Confusingly, Strauss and Corbin referred to these contextual connections as "subcategories," stating that "they too are categories, but because we relate them to a category in some form of relationship, we add the prefix 'sub'" (p. 97).

Strauss continually integrated categorizing steps into these later stages: "Having identified the differences in context, the researcher can begin systematically to group the categories. . . . This grouping again is done by asking questions and making comparisons" (Strauss & Corbin, 1990, p. 132). However, Strauss said very little about the grouping of *data* by category. Categorization, in the grounded theory approach, is manifested primarily in the development and comparison of concepts and categories. Nor does he deal with the analysis of specific contextual relations in the data, operating mostly in terms of relations among concepts.[5]

A similar alternation of strategies, but one that stayed much closer to the actual data, was employed by Miller (1991) in her study of adolescent friendships. We therefore present an extended account of this study in order to illustrate one way in which these two strategies can be integrated.

We also have a second goal in presenting this example. The preceding account of the two different approaches to data analysis has been essentially categorizing rather than contextualizing; it classifies and compares the two types of strategies, rather than presenting them in any real context or clarifying the proper situations in which to use either strategy. To complement this analysis, then, the following account is a narrative or case study by Miller of her analysis. We hope that it will illustrate by example both the difference between a contiguity-based account and a similarity-based one, as well as how to identify when to use categorical strategies and when to use connecting strategies. The account is written in the first person because it is a narrative of Miller's own struggle to make sense of her data.

A Narrative Example

"Once upon a time. . . . " While this account of data analysis is no fairy tale, it is nonetheless a story set in time and shaped by particular questions. Working with interviews with adolescents about their friendships, it seemed important to look closely at the features of the friendships, to understand in specific terms what they mean for the adolescents involved. In short, this seemed to call for a categorizing analysis, a close investigation of the components that seem to make up a relationship, for the purpose of investigating similarities across the friendships of different adolescents.

I therefore began my analysis by formulating coding categories, coding the data, and constructing matrices. I coded the data for such elements as closeness, talk among friends, and dependence. These codes, for each interview, were then collected in matrices so that I could look across interviews for each concept. This helped me to focus on specific features of the data, informed by my research agenda as well as by the comments made by the adolescents themselves. With the completion of the matrices, though, two pressing issues emerged.

The first was that there was extensive overlap of data between the cells of the matrices. For example, many adolescents explained that part of being close to their friends involved talking with them. The matrix for closeness did not, however, capture the complexity of that talk, which involved information from other cells. These matrices seemed too simplistic for the complex, interconnected data I felt I had.

The second issue was that an essential aspect of the data was missing; namely, the narrative nature of the adolescents' accounts of their friendships. In their interviews, the adolescents did not offer isolated bits of information about their friends. Instead, what I heard were the stories of their relationships with their friends. As adolescents talked about their friends and explained why their friendships were important, they described their shared past and created a context from which to understand their relationship. This narrative quality of the data, and its implications for understanding their relationships, were lost in the process of coding and of creating the matrices.

To deal with the limitations of the matrices, and to capture the narrative quality of the data, I moved to what became the second phase of the analysis: the construction of narrative summaries. These summaries are narrative in that they seek to preserve the context and story of the relationship, yet they are summaries since they are my analytic abridgements of the narratives heard. These narrative summaries made use of extensive quotes from the data, but often involved a reorganization of the data to achieve what I, as the reader, perceived to be a concise account of the friendship narrative.

These narrative summaries were effective in holding on to the context as well as the story of the friendship. They did not, however, directly help me understand more clearly the meaning of that friendship experience for these adolescents. For that, I needed to look more closely at their relationships in light of my understanding of the larger context of that friendship. The next phase of my analysis, therefore, was to integrate the results of my categorizing and contextualizing strategies. This led to more depth within the concepts represented in the matrices; the category of closeness between friends, for example, was contextualized. By holding the narrative summaries against the matrices, I could track the meaning of closeness across different friendships for a particular adolescent or between adolescents, or trace its significance throughout a particular friendship.

Data analysis had become, for me, an iterative process of moving from categorizing to contextualizing strategies and back again. My understanding of the narrative context of the friendships informed my interpretation of the particular concepts and categories I had identified as important in these adolescents' friendships. At the same time, the particular concepts I focused on in the categorizing analysis allowed me to look at the narratives in new ways, and to see contextual relationships that were more complex than the temporal ordering of events within the narratives. My understanding of the meaning and experience of friendship for these adolescents was not stripped of the context, which the adolescents provided, nor was it locked into and limited to individual friendship stories. Coding and matrices were combined with narrative summaries to achieve an understanding of the interviews that neither could have provided alone.

A final example of a strategy that we see as combining categorizing and connecting "moves" in analysis is the "listening guide" strategy (Gilligan, Spencer, Weinberg, & Bertsch, 2003) for analyzing interviews. This strategy, which the authors describe as a "voice-centered relational method," involves a sequence of readings (the authors use the term *listenings*) of the interview transcript, each focused on a different aspect of the speaker's expression of her experience within the context of the research relationship. This approach is premised on the idea that a person's voice is polyphonic rather than monotone, that different "voices" can be identified within an interview.

The first listening is typically for the "plot" of the interview—what stories are being told and in what contexts—and the researcher's response to these. The second listening is for the voice of the "I" who is speaking—how does this person speak about him- or herself? This involves underlining all passages containing an "I," along with the associated verb and any other important words, and creating a separate text with only these segments, keeping them in their original order. Subsequent listenings depend on the specific purposes and questions of the research, but they are typically contrapuntal, focusing on contrasting issues and "voices." In Gilligan's original use of this method, the focus was on differences between men's and women's moral judgment, and the listenings were for the voices of justice and of care, and of a separate and a connected self. These later listenings are not necessarily specified in advance; they may be inductively developed. The final step is to pull together an interpretation of this person's perspective on these issues.

The listening for different "voices" is clearly a categorizing move in that it identifies segments that are similar in some way—they are first-person statements, or they deal with a particular issue. However, in contrast to traditional coding, these segments are not fragmented and reorganized by topic; they are kept in sequential order. In the case of "I" statements, these segments are used to create an "I poem" that captures the "associative stream of consciousness" (Gilligan et al., 2003, p. 260) running through the interview; this is a connecting step in analysis. As in Miller's example, the analysis is composed of a mix of categorizing and connecting moves, with each strategy compensating for the deficiencies of the other. For example, the "I poem" 's initial categorizing step allows the listener to focus specifically on the voice of "self" without the interference of extraneous material, foregrounding this aspect of the narrative, and the connecting step of preserving the chronological order of the statements allows the listener to follow the sequential links between these statements.

Like Atkinson (1992; Coffey & Atkinson, 1996), we see categorizing and connecting approaches as inherently complementary strategies for data analysis. The complementarity of similarity and contiguity relations in language is generally recognized and is a central theme in the article by Jakobson (1956/1987) cited earlier. However, what seems distinctive about the approach that we advocate is that it involves an explicit, finer grained integration of the two strategies, rather than seeing these as separate, independent analyses.[6]

It seems to us that the defects in qualitative analysis that result from ignoring one or the other of these relationships among qualitative data are analogous to the communicative disturbances found in the two types of aphasic patients described by Jakobson. The use of computers in qualitative research is a case in point.

Computers and Qualitative Data Analysis

Computer programs for analyzing qualitative data have had a major influence on how analysis is done (Weitzman & Miles, 1995) and will undoubtedly have even greater impact in the future. However, so far, computers have been used primarily for categorizing rather than connecting types of initial data analysis, due to the ease and power with which computers can perform similarity-based functions such as sorting and comparison.

There is thus a danger that, following what Kaplan (1964, p. 28) called *the law of the instrument*, the ease of using computers for categorizing analysis will reinforce this approach and lead to the neglect of connecting strategies. Pfaffenberger argued:

> A technology is like a colonial power—it tells you that it is working in your best interests and, all the while it is functioning insidiously to dim your critical perception of the world around you. You will remain its victim so long as you fail to conceptualize adequately what it's up to. (1988, p. 20)

In contrast, Tesch claimed that "computers, like scissors, are tools. In themselves, they have no influence on the research process" (1993, p. 279). This view neglects the ways in which the *decision to use* particular tools, such as the decision to use scissors rather than some other technique, involves assumptions, often unconscious ones, about the nature of analysis (e.g., that it begins with "cutting up" the data). Such tools privilege certain analytic strategies and inhibit others.

For example, Agar (1991, p. 181) was once asked by a foundation to review a report on an interview study that it had commissioned investigating how historians worked. The researchers had used the computer program The Ethnograph to segment and code the interviews by topic and collect together all the segments on the same topic; the report discussed each of these topics and provided examples of how the historians talked about these. However, the foundation felt that the report had not really answered its questions, which had to do with how individual historians thought about their work—their theories about how the different topics were connected and the relationships they saw between their thinking, actions, and results.

Answering the latter question would have required an analysis that elucidated these connections in each historian's interview.

However, the categorizing analysis on which the report was based fragmented these connections, destroying the contextual unity of each historian's views and allowing only a collective presentation of shared concerns. Agar (1991) argued that the fault was not with The Ethnograph, which is extremely useful for answering questions that require categorization, but with its misapplication. As he commented:

> I don't mean to pick on The Ethnograph. On the contrary, later I describe a study where, if The Ethnograph had been available, I would have been the first in line. I do mean to say that a program like The Ethnograph represents a *part of* an ethnographic research process. When the part is taken for the whole, you get a pathological metonym that can lead you straight to the right answer to the wrong question. (p. 181)

Connecting uses of computer software do exist. For example, "theory-building" programs (Weitzman & Miles, 1995) can assist in searching for correlations, testing hypotheses about relationships, and establishing sequences. Padilla (1991) describes the use of the program HyperQual to develop "concept models," networks of concepts that are "assembled inductively from individual and small groups of concepts developed during the analysis" (p. 267). However, these uses are based on a prior categorizing analysis, and the connecting functions focus on conceptual linkages rather than on linking actual data, as discussed earlier in the section on categorizing strategies.

More recently, Richards (2005) described a number of ways of using computers to establish links among data and data files. However, she focused mainly on links between different *types* of data, such as between fieldnotes and memos, and on links between *different* interviews or observations, as well as links between data *categories*. Richards's emphasis was almost entirely on categorizing analysis, and she did not discuss linking data *within* a specific context, or of identifying relationships of contiguity rather than similarity/difference.

Despite this, there are ways that computers can be used to assist in the direct connecting analysis of qualitative data. One way is to mark, extract, and compile selected data from a longer text, simplifying the task of data reduction in producing case studies, profiles, and narratives. This is a function that any word processor can perform, but one that could be improved by software specifically designed for this purpose. Another is to use graphics programs (such as Inspiration) to develop network displays of events and processes (Miles & Huberman, 1994). This process resembles what Padilla (1991) has done with HyperQual, but it deals with specific events and connections rather than with relations among abstract or generalized concepts. So-called hypertext programs (Coffey & Atkinson, 1996, pp. 181–186; Dey, 1993, pp. 180–191) allow the user to create electronic links among any segments, within or between contexts; a few of the more structured "theory building" programs, such as ATLAS/ti and HyperRESEARCH, not only will do this but also will display the resulting networks (Weitzman & Miles, 1995). Software that is designed to facilitate such strategies could move case-oriented, connecting analysis beyond what Miles and Huberman (1994) call "handicraft production" and could help to prevent the "pathological metonym" that Agar warns against.

In summary, we have argued that the distinction between similarity-based (categorizing) and contiguity-based (connecting) analytic strategies is a useful theoretical tool, both for understanding how qualitative researchers analyze data and for seeing how to improve our analyses. The two strategies are best seen as complementary and mutually supporting, rather than being antagonistic and mutually exclusive alternatives, for each has its own strengths and limitations. We think that Wieviorka's (1992) statement about sociological and historical analyses (which we see as analogous to categorizing and connecting strategies) also applies to qualitative data analysis: that "research will advance not by confusing but by combining these approaches" (p. 163).

Notes

1. Categorization in qualitative analysis is almost always based on similarity, despite the existence of theories of categorization (e.g., Lakoff, 1987) that include contiguity-based relationships (e.g., metonymy), as well as similarity-based ones.

2. This distinction was used by several authors during the 19th and early 20th centuries, including the anthropologist Sir James Frazer and the philosopher Charles Peirce, but without crediting Hume. Saussure also makes no mention of Hume.

3. The reference to causality may seem inconsistent with connecting analysis, as the investigation of causality is often taken to be the exclusive property of quantitative methods. We disagree with this claim and see causal explanation as relying primarily on the analysis of contiguity, rather than similarity, relationships. Our view is grounded in a realist, rather than a positivist, understanding of causality and causal explanation, one that sees causality as involving the actual processes by which one entity or event influences another, rather than the regular association of variables (Manicas, 2006; Maxwell, 2004). This is quite consistent with Saussure's claim (Jakobson, 1956, p. 61) that relationships of similarity and difference are *virtual* relationships, while relationships of contiguity are *actual* relationships. The use of narratives to understand and explain causal relationships has been an important strategy in history and the social sciences for many years (Abbott, 1992; Allison & Zelikow, 1999; Bates, Greif, Levi, Rosenthal, & Weingast, 1998).

4. This strategy is somewhat analogous to Abbott's description (2004, pp. 162 ff.), in his discussion of the "fractal" nature of many debates in the social sciences, of the significance of "moves" based on one or the other of the two opposed positions (e.g., positivist and interpretivist or realist and constructivist).

5. Gerson (1991) addressed these issues in grounded theory research, using a distinction between heterogeneity heuristics and compositional heuristics that is similar to that between categorizing and connecting relations. Heterogeneity heuristics analyze similarities and difference among phenomena within a category, while compositional heuristics address the relationships among categories and between phenomena and categories. However, Gerson's compositional heuristics include relations that involve similarity as well as contiguity, such as taxonomic relations; the ones that most closely resemble what we call connecting relations are his part–whole and sequential relations.

6. We are here drawing on Caracelli and Greene's (1997) distinction between "component" and "integrated" designs for combining qualitative and quantitative methods.

References

Abbott, A. (2004). *Methods of discovery: Heuristics for the social sciences*. New York: Norton.

Agar, M. (1991). The right brain strikes back. In N. G. Fielding & R. M. Lee (Eds.), *Using computers in qualitative research* (pp. 181–194). Thousand Oaks, CA: Sage.

Allison, G., & Zelikow, P. (1999). *Essence of decision: Explaining the Cuban missile crisis* (2nd ed.). New York: Longman.

Atkinson, P. (1992). The ethnography of a medical setting: Reading, writing, and rhetoric. *Qualitative Health Research, 2*, 451–474.

Barone, T. (1990). Using the narrative text as an occasion for conspiracy. In E. Eisner & A. Peshkin, *Qualitative inquiry in education: The continuing debate* (pp. 305–326). New York: Teachers College Press.

Barthes, R. (1968). *Elements of semiology* (A. Lavers & C. Smith, Trans.). New York: Hill & Wang.

Bates, R. H., Greif, A., Levi, M., Rosenthal, J.-L., & Weingast, B. R. (1998). *Analytic narratives*. Princeton, NJ: Princeton University Press.

Bogdan, R., & Biklen, S. K. (2003). *Qualitative research for education: An introduction to theory and methods* (4th ed.). Boston: Allyn & Bacon.

Brown, L. M., Argyris, D., Attanucci, J., Bardige, B., Gilligan, C., Johnston, K., et al. (1988). *A guide to reading narratives of conflict and choice for self and voice*. Cambridge, MA: Harvard University Press.

Bruner, J. (1986). Two modes of thought. In J. Bruner, *Actual minds, possible worlds* (pp. 11–43). Cambridge, MA: Harvard University Press.

Caracelli, V. J., & Greene, J. C. (1997, Summer). Crafting mixed-method evaluation designs. In *Advances in mixed-method evaluation: The challenges and benefits of integrating diverse paradigms* (New Directions for Evaluation, no. 74, pp. 19–32). San Francisco: Jossey-Bass.

Coffey, A., & Atkinson, P. (1996). *Making sense of quali-*

tative data: Complementary research strategies. Thousand Oaks, CA: Sage.

Dey, I. (1993). *Qualitative data analysis: A user-friendly guide for social scientists*. London: Routledge.

Erickson, F. (1986). Qualitative methods. In M. Wittrock (Ed.), *Handbook of research on teaching* (3rd ed., pp. 119–161). New York: Macmillan.

Erickson, F. (1992). Ethnographic microanalysis of interaction. In M. D. LeCompte, W. L. Millroy, & J. Preissle (Eds.), *Handbook of qualitative research in education* (pp. 201–225). San Diego, CA: Academic Press.

Ezzy, D. (2002). *Qualitative analysis: Practice and innovation*. London: Routledge.

Gee, J. P. (2005). *An introduction to discourse analysis: Theory and method*. New York: Routledge.

Gerson, E. M. (1991). Supplementing grounded theory. In D. R. Maines (Ed.), *Social organization and social process: Essays in honor of Anselm Strauss* (pp. 285–302). Chicago: Aldine.

Gilligan, C. Spencer, R., Weinberg, M. C., & Bertsch, T. (2003). On the listening guide: A voice-centered relational method. In P. M. Camic, J. E. Rhodes, & L. Yardley (Eds.), *Qualitative research in psychology: Expanding perspectives in methodology and design* (pp. 157–172). Washington, DC: American Psychological Association.

Holdcroft, D. (1991). *Saussure: Signs, system, and arbitrariness*. Cambridge, UK: Cambridge University Press.

Huang, B. (1991). Unpublished manuscript, Harvard Graduate School of Education.

Hume, D. (1978). *A treatise of human nature* (L. A. Selby-Bigge, Ed.) (2nd ed.). Oxford, UK: Oxford University Press. (Original work published 1739)

Jakobson, R. (1987). Two aspects of language and two types of aphasic disturbances. In R. Jakobson & M. Halle, *Fundamentals of language* (pp. 55–82). 's-Gravenhage: Mouton.

Kaplan, A. (1964). *The conduct of inquiry: Methodology for behavioral science*. San Francisco: Chandler.

Kerlinger, F. N. (1979). *Behavioral research: A conceptual approach*. New York: Holt, Rinehart & Winston.

Labov, W. (1972). The transformation of experience in narrative syntax. In W. Labov (Ed.), *Language in the inner city: Studies in the Black English vernacular* (pp. 354–396). Philadelphia: University of Pennsylvania Press.

Labov, W. (1982). Speech actions and reactions in personal narrative. In D. Tannen (Ed.), *Analyzing discourse: Text and talk* (pp. 219–247). Washington, DC: Georgetown University Press.

Labov, W., & Fanshel, D. (1977). *Therapeutic discourse: Psychotherapy as conversation*. New York: Academic Press.

Labov, W., & Waletzky, J. (1967). Narrative analysis: oral versions of personal experience. In J. Helm (Ed.), *Essays on the verbal and visual arts* (pp. 12–44). Seattle: University of Washington Press.

Lakoff, G. (1987). *Women, fire, and dangerous things: What categories reveal about the mind*. Chicago: University of Chicago Press.

LeCompte, M., & Preissle, J. (1993). *Ethnography and qualitative design in educational research* (2nd ed.). San Diego, CA: Academic Press.

Levi-Strauss, C. (1963). *Structural anthropology* (C. Jacobson & B. G. Schoepf, Trans.). New York: Basic Books. (Original work published 1958)

Levi-Strauss, C. (1966). *The savage mind*. Chicago: University of Chicago Press.

Lieblich, A., Tuval-Mashiach, R., & Zilber, T. (1998). *Narrative research: Reading, analysis, and interpretation*. Thousand Oaks, CA: Sage.

Lincoln, Y. S., & Guba, E. G. (1985). *Naturalistic inquiry*. Thousand Oaks, CA: Sage.

Linde, C. (1993). *Life stories: The creation of coherence*. Oxford, UK: Oxford University Press.

Lofland, J., & Lofland, L. (1984). *Analyzing social settings: A guide to qualitative observation and analysis*. Belmont, CA: Wadsworth.

Lyons, J. (1968). *Introduction to theoretical linguistics*. Cambridge, UK: Cambridge University Press.

Manicas, P. (2006). *A realist philosophy of social science: Explanation and understanding*. Cambridge, UK: Cambridge University Press.

Maxwell, J. A. (1996). *Qualitative research design: An interactive approach*. Thousand Oaks, CA: Sage.

Maxwell, J. A. (2004, August). Using qualitative methods for causal explanation. *Field Methods, 16*(3), 243–264.

Maxwell, J. A. (2005). *Qualitative research design: An interactive approach*. Thousand Oaks, CA: Sage.

Mayes, A. H. (2000). Selective memory disorders. In E. Tulving & F. I. M. Craik (Eds.), *The Oxford handbook of memory* (pp. 427–440). Oxford, UK: Oxford University Press.

Merriam, S. (1988). *Case study research in education: A qualitative approach*. San Francisco: Jossey-Bass.

Miles, M. B., & Huberman, A. M. (1994). *Qualitative data analysis: An expanded sourcebook* (2nd ed.). Thousand Oaks, CA: Sage.

Miller, B. A. (1991). *Adolescents' relationships with their friends*. Unpublished doctoral dissertation, Harvard Graduate School of Education.

Mishler, E. (1984). *The discourse of medicine: Dialectics of medical interviews*. Norwood, NJ: Ablex.

Mishler, E. (1986). *Research interviewing: Context and narrative*. Cambridge, MA: Harvard University Press.

Mohr, L. (1982). *Explaining organizational behavior*. San Francisco: Jossey-Bass.

Nyberg, L., & Cabeza, R. (2000). Brain imaging of memory. In E. Tulving & F. I. M. Craik (Eds.), *The Oxford handbook of memory*. Oxford, UK: Oxford University Press.

Padilla, R. B. (1991). Using computers to develop concept models of social situations. *Qualitative Sociology, 14*, 263–274.

Patton, M. Q. (1990). *Qualitative evaluation and research methods* (2nd ed.). Thousand Oaks, CA: Sage.

Pfaffenberger, B. (1988). *Microcomputer applications in qualitative research*. Thousand Oaks, CA: Sage.

Ragin, C. C. (1987). *The comparative method: Moving beyond qualitative and quantitative strategies*. Berkeley: University of California Press.

Richards, L. (2005). *Handling qualitative data: A practical guide*. London: Sage.

Riessman, C. K. (1993). *Narrative analysis*. Thousand Oaks, CA: Sage.

Ryan, G. W., & Bernard, H. W. (2000). Data management and analysis methods. In N. K. Denzin & Y. S. Lincoln (Eds.), *Handbook of qualitative research* (2nd ed., pp. 769–802). Thousand Oaks, CA: Sage.

Saussure, F. de (1986). *Course in general linguistics*. La Salle, IL: Open Court. (Original work published 1916)

Sayer, A. (1992). *Method in social science: A realist approach* (2nd ed.). London: Routledge.

Seidman, I. E. (1998). *Interviewing as qualitative research: A guide for researchers in education and the social sciences* (2nd ed.). New York: Teachers College Press.

Smith, L. (1979). An evolving logic of participant observation, educational ethnography, and other case studies. *Review of Research in Education, 6*, 316–377.

Strauss, A. (1987). *Qualitative analysis for social scientists*. Cambridge, UK: Cambridge University Press.

Strauss, A. (1988). Teaching qualitative research methods courses: A conversation with Anselm Strauss. *International Journal of Qualitative Studies in Education, 1*, 91–99.

Strauss, A., & Corbin, J. (1990). *Basics of qualitative research: Grounded theory procedures and techniques*. Thousand Oaks, CA: Sage.

Tesch, R. (1990). *Qualitative research: Analysis types and software tools*. New York: Falmer Press.

Tesch, R. (1993). Personal computers in qualitative research. In M. D. LeCompte & J. Preissle (Eds.), *Ethnography and qualitative design in educational research* (2nd ed., pp. 279–314). San Diego, CA: Academic Press.

Tulving, E. (1983). *Elements of episodic memory*. Oxford, UK: Oxford University Press.

Tulving, E., & Craik, F. I. M. (Eds.). (2000). *The Oxford handbook of memory*. Oxford, UK: Oxford University Press.

Weiss, R. S. (1994). *Learning from strangers: The art and method of qualitative interview studies*. New York: Free Press.

Weitzman, E. A., & Miles, M. B. (1995). *Computer programs for qualitative data analysis*. Thousand Oaks, CA: Sage.

Wheeler, M. A. (2000). Episodic memory and autonoetic awareness. In E. Tulving & F. I. M. Craik (Eds.), *The Oxford handbook of memory* (pp. 597–608). Oxford, UK: Oxford University Press.

Wieviorka, M. (1992). Case studies: History or sociology? In C. Ragin & H. Becker (Eds.), *What is a case?* (pp. 159–172). Cambridge, UK: Cambridge University Press.

Yin, R. K. (2003). *Case study research: Design and methods* (3rd ed.). Thousand Oaks, CA: Sage.

CHAPTER 23

Metaphor Analysis

Zazie Todd
Simon J. Harrison

We use metaphor every time we call something by another name. Far from being merely a poetic device, metaphor is ubiquitous in everyday language. Moreover, by categorizing the world for us, metaphor creates cognitive frames that may have real-world consequences. For example, in the days following the Hurricane Katrina disaster in New Orleans, the media and military increasingly used metaphors of a war zone to describe the situation (Tierney, Bevc, & Kuligowski, 2006). One consequence was that the military, called in to help, began to apply restrictions on reporting that were similar to those they would apply in a war zone, and reporters found it difficult to gain access to New Orleans. Another consequence was that residents who had stayed in New Orleans found it difficult to move around the city because the military were under orders to arrest them; thus it was hard for them to check on neighbors, and the community was unable to help itself:

> Officials increasingly responded to the debacle in New Orleans–a debacle that was in large measure of their own making–as if the United States were facing an armed urban insurgency rather than a catastrophic disaster. As the situation in New Orleans was increasingly equated with conditions of a "war zone," strict military and law enforcement controls, including controls on media access to response activities such as body recovery, were seen as necessary to replace social breakdown with the rule of law and order. (Tierney et al., 2006, p. 74)

Thus the "war zone" metaphor corresponded not only to aspects of the disaster itself that made the area like a war zone but also to the responses of the military in dealing with the situation. Hence, as Tierney and colleagues (2006) put it in the title of their article, "metaphors matter."

Many social scientists will already be familiar with the idea of metaphor as a tool for description or for the construction of theory; for example, Foucault's (1977/1991) metaphor of the panopticon served to critically illustrate aspects of modern society and is still a point of reference for many researchers (e.g., Walby, 2005). In this instance, however, metaphor is being used as an analytical tool to frame the social scientist's thoughts; the focus of this chapter is instead on the analysis of metaphors in texts, such as semistructured interviews, focus groups, newspaper reports, and policy documents.

Metaphor analysis has its roots in cognitive linguistics, and it is increasingly becoming of interest to the social scientist. Although metaphor has been studied at least since Aristotle, it was Lakoff and Johnson's (1980) *Metaphors We Live By* that changed the landscape of metaphor research. In this and subsequent books, they argued that metaphor, rather than being a feature of language, is a feature of thought. Patterns of conceptual metaphor, they argued, underlie much of our everyday cognition. Today, social scientists have become interested in using methods derived from cognitive linguistics, whether or not they subscribe to the belief that metaphor is cognitive rather than linguistic. However, there are some problems for social scientists wishing to use this method. First, much of the published work on conceptual metaphor relies on brief examples, taken out of context or presented with little additional information. Although this method might be appropriate in linguistics, which often relies on native-speaker judgments, it is a little disconcerting for the social scientist versed in the idea that qualitative researchers need to present plenty of examples of contextualized evidence. Second, many researchers who use metaphor analysis, even in a social science context, do not specify the details of how they have conducted their analyses. This chapter aims to explain why metaphor analysis is useful to the social scientist and how to do it. Of course, many methodological issues are mentioned in this chapter that cannot be described in detail due to space limitations. The interested reader is referred to additional reading where appropriate.

One of the interesting things about metaphor analysis as an emergent method is that, so far, there are no fixed and established ways of conducting a metaphor analysis. Different studies take their own approaches, sometimes working at the level of individual metaphors and sometimes working at the macro level of overarching metaphors that provide a frame to a text and may or may not have individual instantiations. Thus the level of evidence provided in reports also varies tremendously. Some studies provide detailed analysis of many individual metaphors, commenting on how they link together. Other studies start with structural metaphors, providing little direct evidence of actual individual metaphors but using metaphor as a tool to interrogate wider theory or ideology. These might loosely be characterized as bottom-up and top-down approaches to metaphor analysis. It is also an interdisciplinary approach that has its roots in cognitive linguistics and that is beginning to be used across the social science disciplines.

Metaphor analysis could be particularly useful as a technique to bring studies of cognition into studies of discourse. This point is made by Wodak (2006, p. 184) when she says that there is "a cognitive link between language/discourse and society." She notes that when summarizing news stories, people do not just use stereotypes but also draw on their own personal experience; thus there is something personal and idiosyncratic about their response. She says "stereotypes and prejudicial beliefs are thus enforced and manifested inter alia by metaphors, analogies, insinuations as well as stories" (Wodak, 2006, p. 185). An understanding of metaphor can help to bridge the personal and the cultural and link wider societal discourses to individual cognition. The potential of theories of embodiment (arising from metaphor research) have also been discussed by Rennie and Fergus (2006), who draw on these theories in order to develop the process of categorization in grounded theory. During the process of interpretation, they suggest that analysts draw on their own experience and memories to assist them in making sense of the data. They argue that this process will lead to the development of better categories. Again, this deals with the personal and idiosyncratic nature of meaning and drawing these together to create links with wider issues.

Another interesting feature of the ongoing development of metaphor analysis as a method is that it draws on both quantitative and qualitative traditions. Metaphor is a device that is used in the construction of meaning, and thus we can immediately see a link with qualitative methods that are interpretive or constructivist in their approaches. At the same time, metaphor is something that can be identified and hence measured or counted, lending itself to a numerical analysis. Thus metaphor analysis can be undertaken in either a slightly more qualitative or a slightly more quantitative approach. For examples of the use of statistics in metaphor analysis, see Corts and Pollio (1999) and Cameron and Stelma (2004).

Metaphor in Cognitive Linguistics

The idea of a metaphor analysis comes from developments in cognitive linguistics, in which metaphor has long been recognized as a ubiquitous form of speech. In 1980, Lakoff and Johnson discovered that many conventional phrases could be grouped according to the metaphors that explained and motivated them. For example, many phrases are motivated by the metaphor LIFE IS A JOURNEY: "She was at a crossroads in her life," "he didn't know which career path to follow," "I feel like I'm stuck in a rut," "we're on the right track," and other such examples. The abstract notion of life (the target domain) is explained through the more concrete physical experience of a journey (the source domain). In this case, the metaphor is seen as conceptual because it motivates the way that people think. In order to distinguish conceptual metaphors from conventional metaphors, conceptual metaphors are conventionally written in capital letters. This theory suggests that metaphor is not just a linguistic phenomenon but something that is crucial for cognition: "Far from being merely a matter of words, metaphor is a matter of thought—all kinds of thought. . . . It is indispensable not only to our imagination but also to our reason. Great poets can speak to us because they use the modes of thought we all possess" (Lakoff & Turner, 1989, p. xi). It is not suggested that people are consciously using metaphor in this way; rather, the "conceptual metaphors serve as part of the unconscious conceptual foundation for everyday thought" (Gibbs & Franks, 2002, p. 161).

Lakoff's experientialist approach is presented as a third way between realism and social constructionism. A key feature of the experientialist approach is that thought is seen as both embodied and imaginative. There is some empirical evidence that people do use metaphor to think about abstract concepts. For example, Gibbs, Costa Lima, and Francozo (2004) have shown that in both American English and Brazilian Portuguese, desire is talked about using metaphors of hunger. This is illustrated by the following quote from one of their participants:

> All I used to do since about the time I was 11 or 12 was play with computers. Computers, especially playing computer games, was all I could ever think about. Any time I heard that some new game had come out, I would get this craving in the pit of my stomach where I just had to have the game and learn all I could about it and become a master at it. It was like I could never get enough of these games—they sort of were my main source of mental fuel for many years. I was like this throughout high school, but I am now pretty much burned out on them (but I still play occasionally). I've had my fill so to speak. (p. 1198)

Here we can see some concrete instances of hunger metaphors: "a craving in the pit of my stomach," "I could never get enough," "mental fuel," "burned out," and "had my fill." Gibbs and colleagues found similar expressions in both of the languages they studied, although there were also some cultural differences. This led them to argue that the abstract notion of desire is thought of through the embodied experience of hunger. For a fuller consideration of the notion that metaphor is embodied, consult the work of Gibbs (1994, 2006).

These ideas of embodiment are not infallible. Some critics raise the questions of whether the theory is falsifiable (Vervaeke & Kennedy, 1996), whether the approach could still be subsumed under an objectivist theory (Green & Vervaeke, 1997), and whether it might be unable to cope with certain types of abstract thought (Vervaeke & Kennedy, 2004). Whereas some social constructionists reject the notions of embodiment, other critical discourse analysts find points of contact between the two approaches. Koller (2005) addresses points of overlap between critical discourse analysis and cognitive linguistics. It is beyond the scope of this chapter to consider these epistemological issues in any detail. We note, however, that social scientists who have started to use metaphor analysis have done so while adopting a range of epistemological positions and that one can recognize the discursive power of metaphor while still debating theories of metaphor.

What Kinds of Data?

Metaphor analysis can be conducted on any kinds of textual data. Although originally used on naturally occurring written texts in linguistics, it can also be used to analyze interview transcripts from semistructured interviews or focus groups and transcripts of conversations. A level of transcription suitable for grounded theory will also be suitable for metaphor analysis. Metaphors can also occur visually; see, for example, Forceville (1996).

Steen (1999) has described a step-by-step procedure for metaphor identification by cognitive linguists. This is very helpful because many linguistic studies of metaphors do not clearly state how the metaphors were identified. Steen's procedure is designed to produce a set of conceptual metaphors by working closely through a text. This method, and some potential difficulties with it, is discussed in detail by Semino, Heywood, and Short (2004). Steen begins with metaphor identification and goes on to consider the ideas behind the metaphors. In turn, the ideas are examined to ascertain the relevant comparisons, and then analogies are identified between properties. The fifth stage involves the identification of the underlying mappings and the naming of the conceptual metaphors thus uncovered. This procedure is devised for cognitive linguists and may not be easily accessible to social scientists without a linguistic or philosophical background. Semino and colleagues illustrate the problem of deciding whether something is metaphorical or literal, and they describe various analytical decisions that might or might not be used and the consequences of that approach. However, it is the later stages of the process that they find particularly problematic. They demonstrate, with their data, two different ways of applying Steen's process that lead to different results. For any qualitative method, although it might be accepted that different analysts might sometimes have different interpretations, one would prefer them not to differ too wildly.

Metaphor Identification

The first step in the analysis is the identification of metaphors within a text. This can be taken to mean both metaphors and similes and to include conventional metaphors, as well as novel metaphors. The identification process is not always clear. For one thing, the boundary between a literal and a metaphorical phrase can be fuzzy. In these cases, the researcher must make his or her own judgments as to whether a phrase is literal or metaphorical, perhaps in discussion with other members of the research team. It may well be necessary to check a dictionary before making a decision as to whether or not something is metaphorical. And just to complicate matters further, sometimes an utterance can stand as both literal and metaphorical, that is, both meanings can make sense and seem to be conveyed by the speaker. It is important to remember that decisions about metaphor identification should be taken in the context of the text being analyzed, as well as in terms of patterns in the English language as a whole.

The cognitive–linguistic tradition of a metaphor preexisting as a "thought" (e.g., Lakoff & Johnson, 1980) or quasi object, which is then taken up and used in a context by a speaker or writer, suggests that it must be possible to make a correct, accurate identification. As already stated, one of the assumptions of some linguistic and psychological researchers is that "metaphor is primarily a matter of conceptual structure, and derivatively a matter of language" (Steen, 2002, p. 389). We would like to suspend judgment on this assumption here because it imposes a distinction and assumption on language use that steers analysis toward examining this distinction (in psychology, at any rate) and because by implication it insists on the assumption of metaphor as a device that bounds "it" (or "them"). Bounding a metaphor as a device imposes its own metaphorical mapping (METAPHORS ARE OBJECTS) on the identification process; that is, the assumption primes the process. We may wish to adopt this assumption, however, if we want to identify "ontological metaphors" (e.g., Kovecses, 2002; Lakoff & Johnson, 1980), but it must be acknowledged that there is no one "correct" identification of the metaphor objects in interpretation. Crisp, Heywood, and Steen (2002) put the identification problem definitely: "there can be no single absolute answer to the question of what to count as the unit of metaphor" (p. 67), suggesting that it is not just the word that is a problem here, and, as Cameron states, having "necessary and sufficient conditions for metaphoricity produces insuperable problems" (1999, p. 105). What "counts" as a metaphor is perhaps less important than the "work" done in communication by the metaphorical "sense" of the word or phrase; rather, as Ricoeur puts it, "the power of metaphor to project and reveal a world" (2003, p. 108)—not a world of disconnected thought objects or syntactical rules, though, but of transactional experience expressed. Davidson (2005), too, emphasizes the interactive function of language, noting: "What matters, the point of language or speech . . . , is communication" (p. 120), though perhaps the literal function of metaphor, Davidson asserts, swings too far in the other direction. We do not agree that metaphor "belongs exclusively to the domain of use" (1978, p. 31); this would invalidate the use of "conceptual metaphor" even with a suspension of the empirical realist grounding of concepts.

The linguistic "insuperable problem" that Cameron (1999) identifies reflects a difficulty for qualitative social scientists wishing to explore metaphor in deciding what portion of the text—word, phrase, and so forth—is metaphorical and what is literal and whether it is as, if not more, important to detail what the speaker is implicitly referring to by the use of metaphorical language than to endow words with a metaphor tag in order to examine their relationship with concepts of thought. Cameron asserts that "it is important for the researcher to be clear about whether research is focusing on metaphor in language or in thought when setting up analytic frameworks" (p. 12). However, this assertion cannot always be grounded with certainty, especially if a constructionist epistemology is adopted; could it be a matter of both thought and language? The context of the phrase or passage needs to be taken into account when identifying metaphors.

Taking the "whole phrase" metaphor identification as a "unit" of identification (a *discourse unit*, in Steen's [2002] term) may help bridge the gap between the cognitive–linguistic approach, which presumes preexisting metaphorical structuring, and the discourse analysis approach, which emphasizes construction and context. Therefore, in deciding on identification, the researcher must pay attention to the *aims* of the analysis. The aim is to go beyond "revealing" a structural "systematicity" (borrowed from cognitive linguistics) of concepts and to examine the intentions (conscious or not) driving the use made by speakers of metaphorical language in the action of speaking (within a particular rhetorical frame) and in the context of the questions asked. In other words, how the speaker uses metaphorical language to express ideas about a subject within the frame of the interview situation can become a tool for effective communication within the context of the situation. This is also pivotal in how speakers use this "coherence" to construct their position in relation to wider societal issues. This is similar to the linguistic notion of "information management" (Tomlin, Forrest, Pu, & Kim, 1997) and shares an aim with discursive psychology: the need to contextualize. The act of communicating in such a fashion evokes an interaction for which we agree on conceptual definitions as part of this communicative act and whether they "exist" as mental concepts or not. Though many applied linguists embrace the need for contextualization (e.g., Cameron, 1999), linguists such as Steen and members of the "Pragglejaz" group he set up attempt to unify identification of metaphors as part of an analysis procedure that aims to "minimize measurer bias" (2002, p. 388) and to produce "demonstrably reliable results" (p. 389). The methods of analysis employed suited their aim, which was to come to agreement on which words or "discourse units" in a selected text may be metaphorical and why. However, taking an interpretive hermeneutic approach may make such questions unanswerable.

How to Conduct a Metaphor Analysis

We illustrate the method of metaphorical analysis with a short extract from a semi-structured interview with a schoolteacher. In this passage from the interview, the teacher is talking about some of the problems with her job as a teacher:

> "There are so many things that can make it go wrong, and so many things you're up against, that I don't think . . . in every area there is something. You can't say 'this section of teaching has no problems.' In everything whether it be resources that you haven't got enough of, or they're the wrong ones, or they're broken, or space, time, money, children, colleagues, management. Every area you look there is some type of problem, so I don't think you can feel contented because of the nature of the job. But I think you can get those rewards, if you have those 'magic moments' which are getting few and far between, because it's one of those jobs which you never actually finish, (yes), there is always something else to be done, so you can't say 'yes, we've got it done' 'cos there's a load of other things round the corner waiting to be done."

The first stage of metaphor analysis is to identify the metaphors in the text. This can be done by simply underlining words or phrases that the researcher understands to be metaphorical. It is worth remembering that this will include conventional, as well as novel, metaphors, since both can contribute to a metaphorical understanding. In this case, underlining the metaphors gives us the following:

> "There are so many <u>things that can make it go wrong</u>, and so many <u>things you're up against</u>, that I don't think . . . in <u>every area</u>

> there is something. You can't say 'this section of teaching has no problems.' In everything whether it be resources that you haven't got enough of, or they're the wrong ones, or they're broken, or space, time, money, children, colleagues, management. Every area you look there is some type of problem, so I don't think you can feel contented because of the nature of the job. But I think you can get those rewards, if you have those 'magic moments' which are getting few and far between, because it's one of those jobs which you never actually finish, (yes), there is always something else to be done, so you can't say 'yes, we've got it done' 'cos there's a load of other things round the corner waiting to be done."

A closer examination of individual metaphors shows that some phrases are quite complex. In line 656 of Figure 23.1, the phrase "there's a load of other things around the corner" contains several metaphors. The "things" referred to are problems, and although "a load of" them means a lot, it also references the idea of weight, thus suggesting that problems are heavy and burdensome. They are also "round the corner," which is also metaphorical, because they are not literally around the corner; instead, it refers to the idea that they are currently out of sight and not yet known.

Figure 23.1 illustrates the next stage of the metaphor analysis. Here we can see that the identified metaphors are listed in the standard notation of conceptual metaphor propositions, along with the line numbers they relate to. It is still possible to identify more metaphors. For example, line 653, "but I think you can get those rewards," uses REWARDS ARE OBJECTS TO BE POSSESSED, and some notation is missing, too, such as in line 651: "Every area you look there is some type of problem" should include: CONTEMPLATION IS A VISUAL ACT and WORK IS PHYSICAL SPACES also. This illustrates the importance of revisiting the identification process as you compare the metaphors with other passages in the text and with other transcripts; it is often the case that a second (or even third) pass will "reveal" more metaphors, or different ones. We are keeping in mind Low's (1999) sensitivity and familiarity "dangers." Crisp (2002) makes the point that the "standard notation" of conceptual metaphor (which this resembles) may mislead us into thinking that these conceptual categories of ontological relationships are "much simpler things than they really are" (p. 10). Setting aside the point that we will not ever know "what they really are," this reminds us that this is still an interpretation, subject to change and revision with revisits, and that the metaphors identified are only working hypotheses in the loosest sense of the term; both oversensitivity and overgeneralization are possible and may obscure the sense of the text. It may be that if an analysis of "systems" is being attempted, much of this detail will be necessarily simplified into higher level interpretative categories that appeal directly to the text for their validity, rather than the complete listings of "ontological" metaphors, as these "systems" more succinctly explain the relationships in system structure.

The possibility of "incorrect" analysis is not, of course, due to an objective standard of "correct" identification (this is an interpretation) but to the usefulness of such identification in the emerging coherence. We can see in Figure 23.1 that some phrases are constructed with particular metaphorical relationships that are sometimes complex, such as that in line 656ii: "there's a load of other things round the corner waiting to be done." Other phrases seem to be constructed with a more straightforward metaphor, such as in line 652: "so I don't think you can feel contented because of the nature of the job." Yet this is not as simple as it first appears; we have identified WORK IS AN ORGANIC BODY to deal with "the nature of the job," but this job is represented as a force that is a barrier to the contentment of the represented person-object (you), so WORK IS A BARRIER could also be added

	"Gemma" Stress in teaching.		
647	There are so many things that can make it go wrong, and so many things	647	WORK IS A FAULTY MACHINE/ACTIONS ARE FORCES/EVENTS ARE FORCES
648	you're up against, that I don't think . . . in every area there is something. You can't say	647ii	PROBLEMS ARE OBSTACLES/PROGRESSION IS MOVEMENT
649	"this section of teaching has no problems." In everything whether it be resources that	648	PROBLEMS ARE OBJECTS/WORK IS A CONTAINER
650	you haven't got enough of, or they're the wrong ones, or they're broken, or space,	649	TEACHING IS AN OBJECT/TEACHING IS A STRUCTURE/ PROBLEMS ARE ATTACHED OBJECTS
651	time, money, children, colleagues, management. Every area you look there is some	650	RESOURCES ARE TOOLS
652	type of problem, so I don't think you can feel contented because of the nature of the	651	PROBLEMS ARE RELATED OBJECTS
653	job. But I think you can get those rewards, if you have those "magic moments" which	652	(idiom) WORK IS AN ORGANIC BODY
654	are getting few and far between, because its one of those jobs which you never	653	REWARDS ARE OBJECTS
655	actually finish, (yes), there is always something else to be done, so you can't say "yes,	654	REWARDS ARE SCARCE OBJECTS/TIME IS A CONTAINER (idiom)
656	we've got it done" 'cos there's a load of other things round the corner waiting to be	654ii	WORK IS A MOVING OBJECT (?)/TIME IS A CONTAINER
657	done.	655	WORK IS A TRANSFORMATION/WORK IS A FORCE(?)
		655ii	WORK IS A TRANSFORMED OBJECT
		656	WORK IS HIDDEN OBJECTS (personification)/TIME IS A ROAD/ WORK IS A FUTURE TRANSFORMATION/TIME IS A PERSON MOVING TOWARD OBJECTS/WORK IS A JOURNEY

FIGURE 23.1. Identification of "conceptual" metaphors ("ontological metaphors") in a passage of transcribed interview.

here. It should be noted, too, that the physical layout of the analysis here preserves the whole passage (though not the whole text), as well as listing the metaphorical propositions. For the sake of management, it should be accepted that this process is not a complete one, and the decision of where to stop categorizing should be made with the aim of the analysis in mind. The detail of the identification and coding will be subject to time and text amount constraints, but, if possible, at least two complete "runs" through the text should result in a satisfactory working list.

Building the Metaphorical Relationships

So far, we have been working with just one passage. At this stage, it can be useful to record instances across passages that use common concepts, such as TIME IS A RESOURCE, or WORK IS A CONTAINER. The task here is to examine where similar concepts have a relationship and where similar "mappings" of metaphors apply. So, for example, when this participant talks about work, is it in relation to time or to problems with children, parents, relationships with colleagues? When she talks about these elements, are there recurrent examples in the same or different passages; are the contexts the same or not? This sounds very messy and complicated, but the process involves interpreting from your identifications which relationships are dominant, so the amount of cross-referencing is dependent on the detail of analysis required. The participant in Figure 23.1, for example, expresses, among other things, problems such as objects in a work "container." Can this be found elsewhere, and in what context? In another passage she talks of "the worst sort of behavior problems that are just downright rude children," and later "those with the social problems." This expression of "problem objects" does not explicitly mention work, and here is the implied part of the interpretation. As she *is* talking about her work in this example, these problems are "contained" within it by implication. Therefore, WORK IS A CONTAINER will contain, in this context, PROBLEMS ARE OBJECTS. An inferred relationship has been interpreted that can be compared with the sense of the passage in which the phrase produced the identification. If she were talking about problems as objects in another context, for example, with her children at home, the inferred relationship would not stand.

It may be useful to graphically illustrate the emerging metaphorical sense of the passage, or text. This helps to categorize the implication visually and to test new propositions that must be accounted for. A concept such as TIME is expressed through many metaphorical conventions–as a resource, a container, an object, a moving self-object within a container, and so forth–but often is not explicitly referred to; or, if it is referred to, common idioms are used that do not necessarily imply a time consideration, such as "at the end of the day. . . . " These should be noted as idioms but not listed as metaphors. Time as a container, or a series of containers, is very commonly implied, such as when our participant says, "We don't have them [the children] all morning, every morning. . . . " Work is also subject to time (work takes place "in" time); TIME IS A CONTAINER is an implied superordinate concept within which the other metaphorical relationships (work, self, problems, children, learning, etc.) must be expressed. These conceptual implications are your interpretation of the offered metaphorical coherence that you presume was the intention of your participant, and of course we should be cautious with these inferred relationships and not mistake them for models of behavior. A graphical representation of the participant's metaphorical expression of her work might look like that in Figure 23.2 (simplified).

As can be seen in Figure 23.2, when talking about her work, the participant talks of how her efforts "moving" children "put loads and loads of effort into him [the child]." For example, in a "container" la-

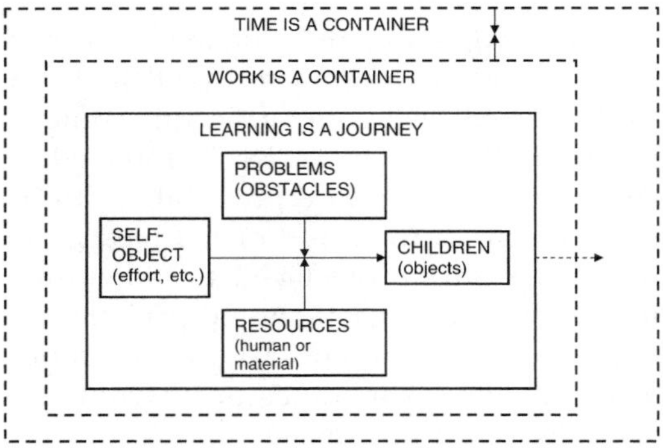

FIGURE 23.2. A (simplified) graphical illustration of the relationship of metaphorical propositions in the expressions of a primary school teacher and her work.

beled LEARNING IS A JOURNEY, the metaphor is illustrated when the participant notes, "They're [the children] really just nowhere, we're going to get nowhere at all . . . and its annoying because it's set back so many years." Not all talk about learning here will imply a journey that the children or the teacher (or both) are taking (hence metaphors are *partial* in context; Lakoff and Johnson, 1980), which is the caveat with this simplified illustration, but talk of a teacher–child relationship with the objective of learning is part of her work ("in" the container), which is restricted by the time allocated to it; the implication that work takes place in a particular amount of time is expressed by such phrases as "trying to fit it all in, all the different areas into a week." The dashed boxes of work and time represent the changing "size" of these in relation to each other, which she expresses both explicitly (as in the last example) and implicitly. The arrows represent the (simplified) relationships of objects of forces that express this understanding in answer to my questions. Therefore, an area of anxiety or stress for this teacher is the expansion of work to the limits (or beyond) of time available (represented as the arrows opposing each other) and supported by implied relationships.

Such an illustration anchors the analysis so that a reconstruction of the participant's metaphorical story can be developed. Of course, this is an interpretation that must be considered in the light of instances of expression that do not fit its suggested relationships; the illustration represents a preferred interpretation based on a subjective identification that is influenced by the prior assumptions of the researcher and the experience of the interview context. It is not a model for hypothesis testing (it does not permit predictions to be made, except as a loose conjecture). One can, with the help of the illustration, appreciate the systematic nature of the metaphorical relationships expressed and visually observe a hierarchy of relationships developing by explicit reference and implication. It should not be the last word of analysis, though, as its one-dimensional aspect misses important metaphorical overlaps and multiplicities. For example, the self can be represented as a moving object in a static landscape but also as a stationary object observing multiple containers (perhaps comparing different events) within the same passage, so coherence does not mean consistency (for a detailed discussion of consistency, coherence, and the partial nature of metaphor, see Kovecses, 2002; Lakoff & Johnson, 1980). This developing analysis can help direct subsequent analyses of text on the same subject, so in this case, other primary school teachers asked the same (or similar) questions. One can then suggest a system of metaphor relationships that, though simplified, can aid in understanding those participants and the researcher. A more comprehensive analysis should be done in the form of the "retelling" of the metaphorical relationships as prose, which can include the multidimensional nature of overlapping metaphor domains.

"Structural" Metaphors as the Second Level

The identification of "structural" metaphors (Lakoff & Johnson, 1980) allows an interpretation of the specific use of metaphors to shape expression; they will usually be more explicit and deliberate. These resemble the metaphors that people would most commonly associate with the word. Such metaphors provide more precise entailments as to the intended mapping of ideas, so the metaphor TIME IS A RESOURCE (discussed in Lakoff & Johnson, 1980, pp. 61–68) is found with the common idea of "*using* one's time," for example, which allows certain other related ideas (entailments) on the theme to be used "legitimately" as they make sense in the context of the metaphor: time is spent, recovered, lost, and so forth. The identification of such metaphors can account for many of the instances in which the phrase does not fit the "emerging" system and is more likely to center on words rather than propositions. Our interpretation finds no hard boundary between the structural and the ontological; TIME IS A RESOURCE, for example, is part of an overall system of relationships (in that we, as objects, use, lose or recover it), but it allows a more detailed and specific understanding of the subject, such as might be too multidimensional to illustrate in the form of Figure 23.2. Our teacher participant, for example, described the effect on her children of the lack of time in the week for physical education as leaving them "sat and stagnant," a deliberate use of a natural–biological structural metaphor not only to allow related entailments of decay but also to implicitly emphasize that the children should be the opposite—"flowing" and "healthy." The effort here is to decide whether such metaphors are in the service of the proposition, and if so, do they help structure the meaning of the passage? With "sat and stagnant," this is the case, because the subject of the passage is "trying to fit it [work] all in, all the different areas into a week," and, by implication, *the consequences of the failure to do so*. In this case, "sat and stagnant" describes the implied consequence of the subject of the passage by giving the consequence of the "failure to fit the work in" a structure, that of CHILDREN ARE BIOLOGICAL FORMS, which, if not allowed to move and grow, will stagnate, or fail.

Some Potential Problems

In many metaphor studies, only one person identifies and analyzes the metaphors. Although this is often the most convenient way to analyze the data, it may be preferable to have a second coder for at least some of the data. The second coder could check the identification of metaphors and/or the grouping of metaphors together. Low (1999) has pointed out several problems with only having one coder, including "unilateral identification," in that the researcher creates his or her own identification criteria from "informed intuition" (p. 49). This is appealing due to the hermeneutic freedom it allows (always taking into account reflexivity, of course). Low's "serious dangers" are worth noting when identifying and coding metaphors, especially the notions of sensitivity and familiarity. Briefly, Low points to the danger of a "heightened sensitivity" to recently studied metaphors and the danger of "overinterpreting" particular expressions (p. 49). This should not, however, dissuade a researcher from examining systems of metaphor use or inducing certain metaphorical themes that emerge in analysis. Heightened sensitivity can also mean interpretative insight. The possibility of a thematic structuring of metaphor (as schemas, scripts, etc.) is explored by some researchers (see Cameron, 1999, p. 18), and thematic induction that is not purely linguistically bound could be a useful avenue of research, if the aim is not purely linguistic. Familiarity, too, is worth bearing in mind, especially due to the detail that an "ontological" identification demands. Low makes an important point that "the more the researcher reads (and reflects on) a text, the more metaphors tend to be identified" (p. 50).

Of course, it may not be feasible to have two coders work with an entire set of text, and it might be enough for the second coder to work with a suitable sample. How researchers treat the second set of codings will depend on whether they are working more within a quantitative or qualitative tradition. If the intention is to count the metaphors, a traditional reliability check would be appropriate; this is not just to see whether both coders identify the same metaphors but also whether they group them in the same way. However, if the work is more within a qualitative tradition, one might have little interest in the reliability statistic; instead, the researchers might be more interested in using the cases in which the coders differed as ways of questioning their analysis and further testing their ideas about the data.

What to Do with an Interesting Metaphor

Metaphor is ubiquitous. It is not surprising, then, that qualitative researchers conducting other kinds of analyses will sometimes find particularly interesting metaphors in their data. What should one do if this is the case?

Perhaps the first thing to do is to check the text immediately surrounding the metaphor to see whether the metaphor is part of a cluster. Because metaphors are often used conversationally to sum up an idea or to introduce a new one, it is quite likely that there are other metaphors nearby in the text that connect to this metaphor. If so, it will be helpful to think about these as a group, rather than simply to consider the metaphor in question. This may give added insight into what the metaphor means, demonstrate shared meaning between participants (e.g., in focus group data), or even illustrate contradictions within accounts.

Several studies have shown that novel metaphors are clustered in lectures (Corts, 2006; Corts & Pollio, 1999) and in sermons (Corts & Meyers, 2002). Common to both of these situations is that the speaker is explaining something and speaking uninterrupted for some time. The metaphors produced in these bursts are generally coherent. For example, Corts and Pollio (1999) found a cluster of several phrases that could be grouped as AGING IS AN ATTACK: Aging was described as "an attack on one's ego" and something that people tried to "fight back." Furthermore, Corts (2006) found that gestures were often related to the metaphorical clusters, so if your data include video footage, this is worth bearing in mind.

Metaphors that occur in figurative bursts appear to be different from those that appear in other parts of the monologue:

> Figures in a topical burst are generally novel and more likely to be coherent than those not in a burst. In addition, they employ analogies and metaphors more often than other categories of figurative language. Finally, figures contained within a topical burst are derived from a root metaphor that is essential both to the presentation and understanding of the topic being presented; in other words, it is a representation rather than a description. (Corts, 2006, p. 229)

Thus, if the metaphor is part of a figurative burst of speech, it is likely that it is an important one for the structure of the text at that point.

Another question to ask is, Is the metaphor part of a systematic group? As well as checking in the immediate vicinity of the metaphor itself, it is worth looking more widely in the text to see whether there are other metaphors that reference the interesting metaphor in question. If so, perhaps it is a systematic metaphor that underlies the text as a whole.

Is it part of a commonly occurring conceptual metaphor? It is also worth checking to see whether the metaphor in question fits into a commonly occurring conceptual metaphor, as identified by cognitive linguists. Could it be related to LIFE IS A JOURNEY, for example, or GOOD IS UP? If so, does this help you to make sense of other aspects of the data? George Lakoff keeps an online list of conceptual metaphors that can be used to check against (*http://cogsci.berkeley.edu/lakoff*).

If the metaphor in question was found using a nonmetaphor analysis method, then it is quite possible that some aspects of that method will be at odds with some aspect of conceptual metaphor theory, given the experientialist approach of cognitive linguistics. But even if one does not want to buy into the idea of conceptual metaphors, it is still useful to know that there are particular metaphors that are very common in talk and that tend to occur in groups. Read Gibbs (1994) for examples of how novel, poetic metaphors are understood in terms of underlying conceptual metaphor groupings.

It is always possible that the metaphor in question is an isolated example of a particularly novel utterance. In this case, if it does not seem to help structure the organization of the text, perhaps it is just a throwaway example that is of relatively little other importance.

There will always be a temptation to use a striking metaphor as the title or subsection of an article in which it might relate quite strongly to central ideas contained within that article. In this case, we can quietly be grateful to our participants for providing us with such a lovely example.

Finally, of course, in the case of data collected from interviews, it is important to check whether the metaphor was actually produced first by the researcher. Social scientists are quite used to thinking about designing interview schedules that will not bias the responses and ensuring that questions are not leading, but "metaphor" is not normally on the list of things to check for. If you intend to conduct an analysis of the metaphors produced, it is important to check that the researcher has not prompted them.

Examples of Studies That Have Used Metaphor Analysis

Charteris-Black (2006) examines the metaphors used to talk about immigration by right-wing politicians in the 2005 election campaign in the United Kingdom. He analyzed speeches from the Conservative Party and the manifestoes of the Conservative Party and the British National Party. Disaster metaphors (such as floods) were used to describe both immigration and the immigration system. Container metaphors (the NATION IS A CONTAINER) were also used, but "while the container metaphor is a general rhetorical legitimization strategy of the right, the emotion schema metaphor is used according to political positioning with the more extreme disaster reflecting the more extreme political position" (Charteris-Black, 2006, p. 578). Thus it is not simply a case of identifying the metaphors that are used but also of paying attention to the way in which they are used by different groups of people. Oberlechner, Slunecko, and Kronberger (2004) is an interesting study for its examination of the metaphors produced in semistructured interviews. In fact, they have analyzed answers to just the first two questions of a large set of interviews with finance experts (traders and journalists), and the second of those questions was a direct request for a metaphor or analogy. Thus they were able to compare the metaphors produced in response to an implicit question with those given in response to an explicit question. The fact that there were differences is a warning to metaphor analysts working with interview data that they need to word their questions very carefully indeed. El-Sawad (2005) takes a critical interpretive approach to analyzing interviews about people's careers. He finds that although some of the "textbook" metaphors are used, such as journey and competition metaphors, there are also a number of metaphors that do not appear in the academic career literature, such as imprisonment and surveillance metaphors. One of the interesting things about this article is the way El-Sawad considers the positive and negative implications of the metaphors used. And finally, because metaphors can also be visual, it is interesting to read an analysis of both visual and textual metaphors in Velasco-Sacristán and Fuertes-Oliver's (2006) study of gendered metaphors in advertising. Their study of advertisements in *Cosmopolitan* magazine shows how metaphor is used to hide as well as to reveal.

The diversity of these studies shows the diversity of research questions for which metaphor analysis can be useful. One of the strengths of the approach is its ability to identify common patterns underlying apparently different texts or parts of texts, which can make it a powerful tool for understanding the ideological implications of text. Another main strength of the approach is its attention both to the topic of what is being said (in terms of the content of the metaphors) and the conversational manner in which it is said (through consideration of the metaphor usage). Perhaps one of the main problems is the difficulty of agreeing on exactly what is and is not a metaphor, which ultimately remains up to the native speaker or researcher's judgment.

Conclusions

Metaphor analysis has developed from cognitive linguistics and is of interest to the social scientist because of its recognition of the discursive power of metaphor. Cognitive linguists see metaphor as both conceptual and embodied, but although this may make the approach unsuitable for analysts who are uneasy considering cognition, critical discourse analysts are also showing an interest in the approach. This chapter has outlined one way of conducting a metaphor analysis; for an alternative detailed approach, see Steen (1999) and revisions suggested by Semino and colleagues (2004). Metaphor analysis can be conducted on any kind of text, whether naturally occurring or collected from interviews or focus groups. The approach can also handle visual data, particularly as it would posit relationships between visual and verbal metaphors. Finally, the ubiquity of metaphor means that scholars using other kinds of analysis are also likely to come across metaphors, and some knowledge of metaphor theory may be helpful in making decisions about whether to privilege those metaphors in their analysis.

References

Cameron, L. (1999). Operationalising metaphor for applied linguistic research. In L. Cameron & G. Low (Eds.), *Researching and applying metaphor* (pp. 3–28). Cambridge, UK: Cambridge University Press.

Cameron, L. J., & Stelma, J. H. (2004). Metaphor clusters in discourse. *Journal of Applied Linguistics, 1*(2), 107–136.

Charteris-Black, J. (2006). Britain as a container: Immigration metaphors in the 2005 election campaign. *Discourse and Society, 17*(5) 563–581.

Corts, D. P. (2006). Factors characterizing bursts of figurative language and gesture in college lectures. *Discourse Studies, 8*(2), 211–233.

Corts, D. P., & Meyers, K. (2002). Conceptual clusters in figurative language production. *Journal of Psycholinguistic Research, 31*, 391–408.

Corts, D. P., & Pollio, H. R. (1999). Spontaneous production of figurative language and gesture in college lectures. *Metaphor and Symbol, 14*, 81–100.

Crisp, P. (2002). Metaphorical propositions: A rationale. *Language and Literature, 11*(1), 7–16.

Crisp, P., Heywood, J., & Steen, G. (2002). Metaphor identification and analysis: Classification and quantification. *Language and Literature, 11*(1), 55–69.

Davidson, D. (1978). What metaphors mean. In S. Sacks (Ed.), *On metaphor*. Chicago: University of Chicago Press.

Davidson, D. (2005). The social aspect of language. In D. Davidson, *Truth, language and history* (pp. 109–127). Oxford, UK: Oxford University Press.

El-Sawad, A. (2005). Becoming a "lifer"?: Unlocking career through metaphor. *Journal of Occupational and Organizational Psychology, 78*(1), 23–41.

Forceville, C. (1996). *Pictorial metaphor in advertising.* Routledge: London.

Foucault, M. (1991). *Discipline and punish: The birth of the prison.* (A. Sheridan, Trans.). London: Penguin. (Original work published 1977)

Gibbs, R. W., Jr. (1994). *The poetics of mind: Figurative thought, language and understanding*. Cambridge, UK: Cambridge University Press.

Gibbs, R. W., Jr. (2006). Metaphor interpretation as embodied simulation. *Mind and Language, 21*(3), 434–458.

Gibbs, R. W., Jr., Costa Lima, P. L., & Francozo, E. (2004). Metaphor is grounded in embodied experience. *Journal of Pragmatics, 36*(7), 1189–1210.

Gibbs, R. W., Jr., & Franks, H. (2002). Embodied metaphor in women's narratives about their experiences with cancer. *Health Communication, 14*(2), 139–165.

Green, C. D., & Vervaeke, J. (1997). The experience of

objects and the objects of experience. *Metaphor and Symbol, 12*, 3–17.

Koller, V. (2005). Critical discourse analysis and social cognition: Evidence from business media discourse. *Discourse and Society, 16*(2), 199–224.

Kovecses, Z. (2002). *Metaphor: A practical introduction.* Oxford, UK: Oxford University Press.

Lakoff, G., & Johnson, M. (1980). *Metaphors we live by.* Chicago: University of Chicago Press.

Lakoff, G., & Turner, M. (1989). *More than cool reason.* Chicago: University of Chicago Press.

Low, G. (1999). Validating metaphor research projects. In L. Cameron & G. Low (Eds.), *Researching and applying metaphor* (pp. 48–65). Cambridge, UK: Cambridge University Press.

Oberlechner, T., Slunecko, T., & Kronberger, N. (2004). Surfing the money tides: Understanding the foreign exchange market through metaphors. *British Journal of Social Psychology, 43*, 133–156.

Rennie, D. L., & Fergus, K. D. (2006). Embodied categorizing in the grounded theory method. *Theory and Psychology, 16*(4), 483–503.

Ricoeur, P. (2003). Metaphor and the semantics of discourse. In P. Ricoeur (Ed.), *The rule of metaphor: The creation of meaning in language* (pp. 74–116). London: Routledge Classics.

Semino, E., Heywood, J., & Short, M. (2004). Methodological problems in the analysis of metaphors in a corpus of conversations about cancer. *Journal of Pragmatics, 36*, 1271–1294.

Steen, G. J. (1999). From linguistic to conceptual metaphor in 5 steps. In R. W. Gibbs, Jr. & G. J. Steen (Eds.), *Metaphor in cognitive linguistics* (pp. 57–77). Amsterdam: Benjamins.

Steen, G. J. (2002). Identifying metaphor in language: A cognitive approach. *Style, 36*(3), 386–407.

Tierney, K., Bevc, C., & Kuligowski, E. (2006). Metaphors matter: Disaster myths, media frames, and their consequences in Hurricane Katrina. *Annals of the American Academy of Political and Social Science, 604*, 57–81.

Tomlin, R. S., Forrest, L., Pu, M. M., & Kim, M. H. (1997). Discourse semantics. In T. A. van Dijk (Ed.), *Discourse as structure and process: Discourse studies: A multidisciplinary introduction* (Vol. 1, pp. 63–111). London: Sage.

Velasco-Sacristán, M., & Fuertes-Oliver, P. A. (2006). Towards a critical cognitive-pragmatic approach to gender metaphors in advertising English. *Journal of Pragmatics, 38*, 1982–2002.

Vervaeke, J., & Kennedy, J. M. (1996). Metaphors in language and thought: Falsification and multiple meanings. *Metaphor and Symbolic Activity, 11*(4), 273–284.

Vervaeke, J., & Kennedy, J. M. (2004). Conceptual metaphor and abstract thought. *Metaphor and Symbol, 19*(3), 213–231.

Walby, K. (2005). How closed-circuit television surveillance organizes the social: An institutional ethnography. *Canadian Journal of Sociology [Cahiers Canadiens de Sociologie], 30*(2), 189–214.

Wodak, R. (2006). Mediation between discourse and society: Assessing cognitive approaches in CDA. *Discourse Studies, 8*(1), 179–190.

CHAPTER 24

Hearing Voices

Listening for Multiplicity and Movement in Interview Data

Lynn Sorsoli
Deborah L. Tolman

It has become increasingly common for researchers to use narrative methods to identify and analyze stories that emerge from interviews. Although it is understood that the form and content of narratives may vary, it is often implicitly assumed that a person's "story" is singular and transparent; typically, qualitative researchers emphasize presenting this story in a participant's "voice," also singular. In this chapter, we discuss the Listening Guide—a technique that demands that researchers listen for two or more different "voices" threaded through narratives in interview data. This technique involves multiple interpretive readings and careful explorations of the ways different strands of narrative rise, fall, and intertwine, leading to a complex and nuanced understanding of participants' stories. Although a variety of stories can be explored with this method, research questions involving marginalized experiences, including those involving social stigma, shame, or secrecy, are particularly well suited for a Listening Guide analysis.

In this chapter, we offer a brief background to the Listening Guide, but we do not detail each of the steps involved in implementing this method, as the full sequence of steps has been amply discussed elsewhere (see Brown, Debold, Tappan, & Gilligan, 1991; Gilligan, Spencer, Weinberg, & Bertsch, 2003). We choose instead to focus our efforts on the elements we have found to be the most essentially innovative and useful about this technique in our own work: the identification and analysis of "contrapuntal" voices in narrative data (Gilligan, Brown, & Rogers, 1990; Gilligan et al., 2003). In order to illustrate the value of this method to qualitative research, we offer two detailed examples of analyses of the voices we have identified in our data. The first example arises from studies of the sexual experiences of adolescent girls and examines the ways in which their own desire is and is not present in their narratives. In this example, we identify different voices that can be present in girls' narratives of sexual desire, introduce the concept of alignment, and present an examination of the ways the first person narrator is and is not aligned with one of these voices. In the second example, we discuss the struggles female survivors narrate over decisions to disclose experiences of sexual abuse in their relationships. This second example illustrates an analysis of the movement between voices in narratives (i.e., when different voices enter and exit) and presents a theoretical understanding of the presence of these voices in trauma narratives. Later, we discuss some ways that learning and using this method can affect approaches and strategies for collecting interview data, including the underlying epistemology.

The Listening Guide: History and Theoretical Framework

The Listening Guide is a qualitative method with psychodynamic, literary, clinical, and feminist foundations (Brown et al., 1991; Brown & Gilligan, 1992; Brown, Tappan, Gilligan, Miller, & Argyris, 1989). The short history of this method begins with several developments in psychology, including Kohlberg's method of eliciting decision-making narratives to identify stages of moral development (Kohlberg & Elfenbein, 1975; Kohlberg & Puka, 1994) and an increasing interest in life history as a psychological method (Erikson, 1993). In the 1980s, feminist and clinical psychologists began to discern the possibilities of narratives as an entrée to the psyche and to less linear dimensions of human experience, especially more marginalized dimensions. Traditional reductive methods of coding narratives demanded that data be coded into predetermined and/or mutually exclusive categories and relied on the quantification of qualitative data. This coding process "disappeared" much of what was most compelling in narratives, the unanticipated, undertheorized aspects of lives, and tended to simplify complex social and emotional experiences. Interest in studying and interpreting narrative had spurred dissatisfaction with the costs of quantification, and there was an urgent need to begin to develop and refine systematic methods for analyzing qualitative data (Bruner, 1987; Mishler, 1986).

In the late 1980s, Carol Gilligan and the students who constituted the Harvard Project on Women's Psychology and Girls' Development[1] focused on bringing both feminist and literary perspectives to the analysis of narratives. The initial innovation drew on Gilligan and Belenky's (Belenky, Clinchy, Goldberger, & Tarule, 1986; Gilligan, 1982) queries of women's stories about their actual experiences with moral dilemmas; that is, going back to a truly empirical (i.e., observational) approach with a feminist lens and a clinical bent toward listening, and subsequently hearing threads of love and care intertwined with concerns about fairness and equity in narratives ostensibly illustrating morality. These inquiries led to a new question about girls' moral development. Rejecting the compression of girls' narratives about their own experiences into categories that could be analyzed statistically, the group began to develop an innovative method of systematic analysis: the Reading Guide (Brown et al., 1988, 1989). As this method was developed with a broader range of narratives and populations (e.g., Reindl, 2001; Steiner-Adair, 1991; Tolman, 2001), the emphasis shifted from reading transcripts toward the context in which the narratives originated—the actual physical and embodied telling of stories in a relational process with an interviewer whose central task was to listen (Brown & Gilligan, 1992; Gilligan et al., 1990)—and the name was changed to the Listening Guide. As the Listening Guide has continued to mature, its malleability has allowed it to create ways of listening to and understanding narratives about many kinds of human experiences and development. As a result, a body of literature illuminating how this method can be used rigorously and systematically has begun to emerge.

The Listening Guide centers on "voice"—not as a metaphor but as a physical, embodied entity—as one of the primary ways inner thoughts and feelings can be communicated to an outside audience. Like narrative analysis and phenomenology, it relies on the epistemic principle that eliciting and analyzing narratives is one appropriate mechanism for understanding the ways research participants make meaning of their experiences. It is in narratives that we move closer to a participant's perspective; the stories people tell reveal who they are in a unique light, offering essential information about the reality they have constructed from their experiences. In addition, the telling of such stories is inherently contextualized by relationships, including the relationships the teller has engaged in across his or her lifespan and the relational dimensions of the self that have evolved over time. In the case of research, the relationships developed during interviews are important, as well, and a researcher's relationship with the data can also come into play during an in-depth interpretive analysis. Because of the Listening Guide's acknowledgment of and attention to both relationship and voice, as well as the ways they are intertwined, the method has been characterized as voice-centered and relational (Brown et al., 1991; Brown & Gilligan, 1992; Gilligan et al., 1990, 2003).

In addition, in accord with psychodynamic theorists of the self (e.g., Fairbairn, 1954; Jung, 1954; Winnicott, 1965), the Listening Guide acknowledges that multiplicity is an expected aspect of the psyche and that shifting from one "state of mind" to another is a frequent psychological process. People pass regularly from one state of mind to another many times in a day, often without realizing it, and particularly in response to difficult relational experiences. Multiple, even contradictory, perspectives on any given experience (which can be "voiced" in concert in narratives) are not only acceptable but are to be anticipated. Shifts in language can expose the presence of these subtle psychological processes, and qualitative methods of analysis are ideal for exploring the complex orchestration of these multiple voices. The Listening Guide offers a systematic and rigorous way to identify and analyze the theoretically relevant shifts that occur during interviews, opening a novel window for understanding both the existence of these multiple layers of psychic life and what they can reveal about lived experiences.

While maintaining an allegiance to narrative as a fruitful manner of exploring lived experience, the Listening Guide also duly acknowledges that people may have difficulty putting certain experiences into words and may resist talking about other experiences, especially experiences that reveal violations of acceptable or conventional thoughts, feelings, or behaviors, given the teller's positionalities and those of the subjects of the narrative. Some trauma survivors, for example, have lived through experiences they are not able to narrate easily. Physiological and cognitive factors limit their abilities to construct cohesive narratives about their experiences, and thus understanding the inner worlds of survivors and the meanings they have made from their experiences often involves a careful consideration of disjointed fragments (Harvey, Mishler, Koenen, & Harney, 2000; Sorsoli, 2004; Waites, 1997). Other experiences can be difficult to put into words because revealing these experiences can have social or material implications and consequences. In the dominant, patriarchal society of the United States, adolescent girls are not supposed to have sexual desires; for girls, a yearning to share stories about planning and carrying out sexual encounters can be overridden by the sense of indecency that permeates girls' sexuality in our cultural context (Tolman, 2001, 2002; Tolman & Brown, 2001). Complicated ways of speaking have also been evident in connection with experiences of depression and anger for both girls and women (Brown, 1999, 2003; Gilligan & Machoian, 2002; Jack, 1991, 1999a; Machoian, 2005), young women's experiences of eating disorders (Reindl, 2001; Steiner-Adair, 1991), and boys' desires for relationships (Way, 2001). Given the existence of such roadblocks, the Listening Guide does not assume that research participants are always able to deliver straightforward accounts of their experiences. Rather, one operating assumption of this psychodynamic, feminist method is that when talking about "forbidden" experiences, participants may offer accounts that are nuanced, multifaceted, and densely packed with diverse meanings and cryptic messages.

As a method, the Listening Guide grows out of and contributes to feminist standpoint theory (Nielsen, 1990), which emerged in response to the recognition that women were rarely if ever included in research purported to be about "people." Feminist standpoint theory involves the explicit goal of bringing women's perspectives, experiences, and, in the case of qualitative research, actual voices into the research process, including research questions, measurement development, sampling procedures, and validation, as well as the identification of what constitutes meaningful and significant behaviors or phenomena. It also demands acknowledgment that women are not a monolithic group, that their diversity yields diverse experiences, and that other groups have experienced oppression and are also not represented in research. The Listening Guide was developed specifically to approach and understand these kinds of marginalized and understudied experiences. In fact, the Listening Guide method is predicated on the need to be "resisting listeners" (Brown & Gilligan, 1992); that is, to listen under parts of a narrative with an ear tuned to how marginalized and oppressed people negotiate their lives on the flip side of power (Miller, 1976). The method actively encourages researchers to begin to unravel some of this complexity.[2] Although every person's voice contains multiple melodic lines that can be explored qualitatively, it is often in regard to experiences that are the most complicated, taboo, or awkward to share with others that this method's goal of tuning into the rhythms, harmonies, and disjunctures present in research interviews can be the most illuminating.

Learning to Listen for Multiple Layers

Understanding the nuances of complex personal narratives requires examining them from many different angles and slowly building an interpretation from the perspective each angle or part offers (Brown et al., 1989; Sorsoli, 2007), which is the reason that the Listening Guide lends itself so well to these types of data. The Listening Guide involves multiple interpretive readings of the same text: Initial readings for "plot" and "self" are followed by separate readings for two or more distinct "voices." The method was originally premised on a distinction between two specific voices that could be heard in narratives describing moral conflicts (see Brown et al., 1989, 1991). One of these voices, the voice of "care," articulated a concern with loving and being loved and being responsive in relationships; the other voice, the "justice" voice, reflected a dedication to fairness and equality. Gilligan and colleagues (1990) described these voices as "contrapuntal," likening narrative to a piece of music. The two voices—or parts—work with and against each other in time and tone to infuse meaning. Linguistically, the word *contrapuntal* signifies that although they are not necessarily opposites, the two voices are strongly differentiated and embody different perspectives, in the original case reflecting a shifting consciousness about a moral dilemma.

Although originally the method was designed for the analysis of discrete narratives—a single personal narrative arising in response to an interviewer's specific prompt—the concept has since been expanded to thinking about narratives and talk across full interview transcripts, and researchers quickly found that the key concepts of the method could be applied to a wide array of human experiences. The justice and care voices had emerged in Gilligan's research as different approaches to morality, as well as the inner conflicts that can arise in situations requiring moral decision making, and these original two contrapuntal voices became examples of how to study morality. Other research projects demanded the identification of distinct voices relevant to that work, in response to the particular theoretical frameworks and analytical questions guiding them. In fact, the importance of theory in the identification of salient voices is a characteristic that sets the Listening Guide method apart from other qualitative methods, such as grounded theory approaches, which set theory (i.e., preconceived concepts) aside in favor of letting emic constructs emerge from the data and which begin with open coding (Strauss & Corbin, 1998). With the Listening Guide, researchers' implicit and explicit theories guide research design, including interviewing protocols and practices, and thus are present in many ways throughout a research project. The interplay between theory and data is critical to both the identification of these voices and their subsequent interpretation—that is, we use theory to identify relevant voices and voices to shed light on theory. In fact, theory itself can be influenced by listening to voices of human experience, as Gilligan's work illustrates.

At first glance, it may be difficult to distinguish the Listening Guide from other narrative methods. In fact, researchers using other methods of narrative analysis might conceivably code a narrative's content similarly, particularly if coded categories are not required to be mutually exclusive. Such researchers might subsequently look for themes in these content categories or simply analyze the presence or predominance of one type of content across interview transcripts. For example, an analysis could potentially explore recovery from traumatic events in terms of the presence of themes of empowerment across a series of interviews at sequential time points during the course of a therapeutic intervention. The significance of the Listening Guide technique is that it begins with but is designed to go *beyond* questions of predominance and theme, questions primarily devoted to understanding the content of narratives, to an analysis of the alignment and dynamics of the separate voices that can be present in narratives, which is primarily an analysis of form and flow. That is, this analysis is not simply an analysis of content, but also about the ways certain types of content are communicated.

Another characteristic that sets the Listening Guide apart from other methods of narrative analysis involves the way it utilizes context. Lieblich, Tuval-Mashiach, and Zilber (1998) suggest that narrative analyses can be differentiated on two dimensions that classify whether the analysis prioritizes a story's form or its content and whether it examines narratives holistically or seeks patterns in coded portions of the material. The Listening Guide works in the very center of this coordinate system, embracing the idea that narrative is not static and offering the essential innovation of tracking the dynamic relationship that exists between the various voices that can be present in interview texts. Put more simply, rather than coding and then sorting the data into various categories for analysis—which requires researchers to seek patterns in decontextualized data—this method examines the presence of these voices in the context of the full interview and in the context of the other voices that may be present. As a layered method of interpreting narratives, it emphasizes both content (i.e., what participants say) *and* form (i.e., the way the content is expressed) equally; it codes specific portions of narratives but still examines them holistically (i.e., in context). Although it can be used in many different ways, the traditional Listening Guide analysis involves examining the relationship between contrapuntal voices, as well as the relationship between a participant's first-person voice and one or more of the contrapuntal voices, noting where and when these voices appear and disappear and the ways in which they are woven together in the context of a participant's narrative. The techniques devoted to examining narration and voice as dynamic processes differentiate this method from other analytical techniques designed to explore personal narratives solely for their content.

Finally, the Listening Guide can be utilized at both the case and cross-case levels. Patterns in voices across cases can be identified, most often using conceptually clustered matrices (Miles & Huberman, 1994), in order to develop an understanding of a given phenomenon across a group of people, both in terms of similarities and differences. This kind of cross-case analysis has been demonstrated in multiple groups of women and girls across a variety of phenomena (e.g., Brown, 1999, 2001, 2003; Jack, 1991, 1999a; Tolman, 2002), perhaps because female voices can easily become muffled or distorted in a Western culture that disavows or denigrates their experiences. In this historical and cultural context, research on the lived experiences of girls and women (and often boys and men) (see, e.g., Way, 2001) demands a conscientious qualitative interviewer and data analyst who thinks about the kinds of experiences that are silenced in this culture and about the importance of being a responsive listener—a listener who is resistant to disconnection and encourages participants to say what they know instead of hiding behind a curtain of niceness and propriety (Brown & Gilligan, 1992). The following example illustrates the use of the Listening Guide in research with adolescent girls' sexual desires.

Adolescent Girls and Sexuality: Speaking of (No) Desire

Because the sexual desires of adolescent girls are relentlessly silenced in this patriarchal society whereas boys' desires are normalized and exaggerated, to address the missing discourse of girls' desire (Fine, 1988) in research literature (Tolman, 1991), it has been necessary to create a safe, relational space in which girls feel they can speak about the "unspeakable" topic of their own embodied sexual feelings and experiences in and with such feelings. A key to this "interruption" is identifying the taboo nature of the topic, the rarity of adults' wanting to know this information from and about young women, and the authentic desire to know that the researcher brings to the interview. Aside from or in addition to stating this stance, the researcher needs to be comfortable talking about sexuality and asking questions in a very straightforward and nonjudgmental way (Tolman, 2002). Although the reality of women's sexual desires has now begun to enter the public discourse, media messages still send out intense pressure for adolescent girls to be the passive sexual objects of men (Kim, Sorsoli, Schooler, & Tolman, 2006; Sorsoli, Porche, & Tolman, 2005), and Fine's nearly two-decade-old analysis that young women are "educated away from positions of sexual self-interest" (1988, p. 42) continues to ring true.

Given the pressure on girls to disconnect from and denigrate their experiences of sexual desire, the fact that they may narrate such experiences in a fragmented, discontinuous, incoherent, or incomplete manner is not surprising. Theory suggests that girls' narratives of sexual desire would likely involve a multiplicity of voice. Understanding the accounts rising from in-depth interviews with girls demands a form of analysis—like the Listening Guide—that can hold the variety of ways in which a single narrative could have multiple layers and exploit the fact that each narrative can be seen or heard from multiple perspectives. Asking girls directly to give voice to sexual desire gives them permission to transgress, and so the stories they tell reveal complexity. It is not simply that a veil is lifted and a once-muted voice can be heard clearly. When anyone speaks, her or his words are always being filtered through systems of power and socially constructed ideas about what it is possible to say or even to know (Foucault, 1980), which is why looking beyond the content of narratives to the ways they unfold and the types of voices they incorporate is such a necessary innovation for psychological studies. This method clears space for such transgressive experience to move from margin to center (Fine, 1994; hooks, 1984), shifting our focus. In what ways can and do girls experience and/or communicate a sexual self (Jordan, 1997; Tolman, 1991, 2002), and in what ways is this sexual self aligned with the first-person narrator?

In order to understand the ways a first-person narrator can be more or less aligned with a distinct voice, we start by reading for the self and identifying places where the self is present across a particular text. The task of placing the self in the center of a narrative about desire can feel as treacherous as it might feel liberating, which is one reason that the technique of listening for the self in girls' narratives of sexual desire can lead to such rich findings. Originally, what we are calling a self reading identified the narrator's representation of herself as a protagonist in a specifically prompted story told about moral conflict–what she thought, felt, believed, said, and did during the context of the events narrated (i.e., her psychological experience of the moral dilemma). In a Listening Guide analysis, a self reading involves identifying and underlining the portions of an account narrated in the first person. Most often these are places where *I* is the subject or the object of a verb ("I went . . . ," "I saw . . . ," "I said . . . ," "she was counting on me," "he did it to me"), although occasionally interview participants also use other pronouns to represent personal experiences. For example, participants may use the second person, "you just kind of know," to refer indirectly to themselves. All of these types of references are considered in a reading for self.

We will illustrate reading for self with the following excerpt, which was taken from a 2-hour interview conducted with a 16-year-old girl who has the pseudonym Isabel. The interview was designed to explore her experiences of sexual pleasure, sexual desire, including feeling "sexy," and sexual fantasies. Isabel declares that she is a feminist and is articulate and intelligent. During the interview, she struggles to talk about her experiences with desire, a question that turns out to be one of her own. She says that she thinks and writes a lot about desire, especially her distress and confusion about not feeling it. The underlined portions of the following excerpt illustrate what we would emphasize if reading this transcript for self (for simplicity, we will not underline every "I" statement):

> "Maybe I'd go to a college campus just to hunt out the guys, and and they're just not there. And maybe it's because I don't know them, but nothing's like striking a chord. Um, and then, I <u>I guess in the past like month</u>, or I mean it's been going on for a while, but <u>I just started to get really scared</u>, like, '<u>Oh my God, I'm asexual</u>,' (laughs) you know, I'm like nothing's happening. <u>I'm not finding anybody</u> and <u>when I fantasize, I don't fantasize about having sex</u>. And, and <u>I don't think that I'm a lesbian</u>, which would be fine with me if I were, but <u>I just don't think I am</u>. And I don't think, um, I mean <u>I'm pretty sure that I'm like heterosexual</u>, but there's no sexual urge there. And <u>I keep like checking</u>, like, you know, like, um, tracing my birthday back, and like, <u>I'm only 16</u>. So maybe it's coming next year. Like, it better hurry, cause you know, there's just like no impetus there for like, losing virginity."

When we listen for the self in her narrative, we hear her concern and confusion regarding her own sexual desires. She says: "In the past month, I just started to get really scared . . . Oh my God, I'm asexual. . . . I'm not finding anybody . . . when I fantasize, I don't fantasize about having sex. . . . I don't think I'm a lesbian . . . I just don't think I am. . . . I'm pretty sure that I'm heterosexual. . . . I keep checking . . . I'm only 16." In this segment of her interview, she conducts her own analysis of her lack of desire, invoking culturally available sexuality theories as potential explanations, including asexuality, sexual identity, and the content of her fantasy life.

One way to analyze a transcript for the presence of self is to create an "I-poem" (see Debold, 1990; Gilligan et al., 2003). The poem is created by taking these underlined references to self (*I*, with the occasional verb and associated object) out of the context of the full narrative in order to hear variability in how the narrator represents him- or herself. With each phrase on a separate line without punctuation, the I-poem takes on the appearance and sound of free verse; holding the separate representation of self against the fuller narrative can illuminate how a participant experiences the phenomenon under study in unique ways. For example, in the context of an exploration of narratives focusing exclusively on the early memories of trauma survivors, it is interesting to see "I don't remember . . . I don't remember . . . I don't remember" emerge in the formation of an I-poem. Some researchers do not distill a reading for self into a discrete I-poem but retain a "self voice" as one of several salient voices. Tolman (2002), for example, braided developmental theory, which suggests that girls' experiences with their desire are highly contextualized by individual circumstances, with Adrienne Rich's (1983) feminist theory that female sexuality is organized by the institution of heterosexuality. The coupling of these two perspectives led Tolman to listen specifically for several voices in her exploration of girls' sexual desire: She included one voice that spoke about and contextualized experiences of the self (i.e., a self voice) with others that reflected the institution of heterosexuality. Instead of constructing an I-poem in her analyses, Tolman contrasts the self voice with the other voices present in girls' narratives.

Because we are illustrating an analysis of alignment, we will move away from the I-poem as well and now that we have read for the self, we will turn toward the contrapuntal voices. The involvement of theory in the choice of contrapuntal voices can be crucial to an analysis; theory offers a way of seeing/constructing reality and, thus, asking questions about it. By attending to theory, we seek to ensure that we do not pose our questions so narrowly that we miss salient aspects of experience or so broadly that we fail to frame the phenomenon under question. Multiple realities are available to researchers, and it is theory that enables us to zero in on and front one of them for a specific reason. Theory enables the identification of multiple voices as it helps "turn up the volume" so that we can more easily hear the voices that are in tune with theoretical expectations, and those that are somehow either "at odds" with mainstream constructions of the phenomenon or covered up by such constructions. As mentioned earlier, it was the braiding of two distinct theories that led Tolman to listen in a particular way to girls' narratives. Listening to the ways the institution of heterosexuality might be reflected in girls' stories of desire in interviews with adolescent girls about sexuality, she focused on voices that were theoretically relevant and identified a duet: an erotic voice and a response voice (that is, she noted that an expression of desire is often complemented by a response to the existence of this desire).[3] The erotic voice illuminates the experience of wanting and desire, whether the speaker labels it sexual or not. This voice speaks the existence of bodily sensations, or knowledge, or sexualized romantic fantasies, and how these dimensions of desire operate in her or as she has observed them in others. Using the same segment of interview as before, the erotic voice is italicized below. In this particular narrative, rather than hearing about desire, we will actually hear a denial of sexual feelings:

> "Maybe I'd go to a college campus just to hunt out the guys, and and they're just not there. And maybe it's because I don't know them, but *nothing's like striking a*

chord. Um, and then, I I guess in the past like month, or I mean it's been going on for a while, but I just started to get really scared, like, 'Oh my God, I'm asexual,' (laughs) you know, I'm like *nothing's happening.* I'm not finding anybody and *when I fantasize, I don't fantasize about having sex.* And, and I don't think that I'm a lesbian, which would be fine with me if I were, but I just don't think I am. And I don't think, um, I mean I'm pretty sure that I'm like heterosexual, but *there's no sexual urge there.* And I keep like checking, like, you know, like, um, tracing my birthday back, and like, I'm only 16. So *maybe it's coming next year.* Like, *it better hurry,* cause you know, *there's just like no impetus there* for like, losing virginity."

In this excerpt, the erotic voice says "nothing's striking a chord . . . nothing's happening . . . when I fantasize, I don't fantasize about having sex . . . there's no sexual urge there . . . maybe it's coming next year . . . it better hurry . . . there's just no impetus there." She talks about desire as though it is completely out of the realm of her experience even though the indication is that it is expected and normal, a feeling that she wants to have and for which she is waiting impatiently. The way she speaks about desire differs from the erotic voices of other girls who incorporate it as part of their experience and say things like "I really really wanted him really bad" ("Amber," in Tolman, 2002, p. 159) or "I wanted it to be that way. I wanted to be able to feel pleasure. . . . And I wanted to be able to enjoy it" ("Barbara," in Tolman, 2002, p. 142).

Once the self and contrapuntal voices have been identified in the transcripts, the researcher can examine the alignment of the self with respect to each of the contrapuntal voices—in this particular example we examine the alignment of the self with only one voice, the erotic voice. When we talk about alignment between voices, we are talking about harmony or agreement. In a sense, this is like reliability: Is one voice contradicting the other or do the voices present a cohesive whole? Are both voices telling the same story? (In the past, we would underline each voice with a different-colored pencil. This technique makes alignment visual: Multiple lines of different colors underlining the same portion of narrative illustrate the degree of alignment.) In short, alignment is the relationship between the first-person presentation of self and one or more of the contrapuntal voices identified.

Understanding whether the self voice is aligned with a contrapuntal voice offers powerful information and insight. Whereas a person may acknowledge the orientation of a contrapuntal voice or know its logic, that same person may not represent ownership of those thoughts and beliefs (i.e., speak these thoughts or beliefs in the first-person voice). For example, the one girl might first say "Girls don't need a boyfriend to feel complete," only later to say, "I don't know what I'd do without my boyfriend. I only feel good when I'm with him." The first sentence in this example is a depersonalized or general statement about the "reality" that girls do not need to be dependent on boys, whereas the second sentence in this example is spoken in a first-person voice, presumably revealing her lived experience. The two statements express contrasting ideas about whether a girl can be complete without a romantic partner; however, the self, the protagonist *I*, is present only in the second statement. If this happened only one time in a transcript, it would be ambiguous to interpret. However, if this is a pattern across a particular girl's interviews, a researcher might interpret it as evidence suggesting that although she champions the feminist narrative that girls do not need boys, her personal narrative reveals the enactment of a more traditional feminine ideology. What we seek to understand is whether the presentation of voices constitutes a pattern of alignment for a particular case (i.e., whether the self is equally represented across voices or more aligned with a particular voice) and, ultimately, whether the pattern holds across cases. In the excerpt we are using as an example, the self reading is underlined and the erotic voice is in italics; the bold letters indicate the one place where the two voices overlap:

> "Maybe I'd go to a college campus just to hunt out the guys, and and they're just not there. And maybe it's because I don't know them, but *nothing's like striking a chord*. Um, and then, I I guess in the past like month, or I mean it's been going on for a while, but I just started to get really scared, like, 'Oh my God, I'm asexual,' (laughs) you know, I'm like *nothing's happening. I'm not finding anybody* and ***when I fantasize, I don't fantasize about having sex***. And, and I don't think that I'm a lesbian, which would be fine with me if I were, but I just don't think I am. And I don't think, um, I mean I'm pretty sure that I'm like heterosexual, but *there's no sexual urge there*. And I keep like checking, like, you know, like, um, tracing my birthday back, and like, I'm only 16. So *maybe it's coming next year*. Like, *it better hurry*, cause you know, *there's just like no impetus there* for like, losing virginity."

When we assess the alignment of self with the erotic voice in this example, we see that the two rarely overlap—the fonts offer a visual representation of the independence of the two voices.[4] One statement ("when I fantasize, I don't fantasize about having sex") identifies the self as devoid of sexual fantasy, whereas the other statements in the erotic voice refer to desire as a thing distinct from the self, an "it" that is not there, may come next year, and needs to hurry. The way Isabel describes her experience is not simply that she does not experience desire but that "it" has not come, and she is waiting for "it" to make its way to her. The absence or presence of the first-person pronoun may indicate a psychodynamic interplay and can be a marker of psychological shifts—narrators often shift away from the use of first person when experience or knowledge is difficult to claim (see Cohn, Mehl, & Pennebaker, 2004; Muhlhausler & Harre, 1990). The *I* goes missing in girls' narratives of desire in many ways. For example, a girl could talk about other people's desires without ever broaching her own (i.e., she could talk all around desire but never claim it), or a girl can speak about being desired or desirable from the third person (i.e., she might describe boys looking at her and imagine them wanting to ask her out, but never say "I feel sexy"), reflecting that a girl knows that she is desirable because of the way a boy responds to her and not because of what she herself is feeling. In these cases, and the preceding case, the protagonist of desire is someone beyond the self, offering a specific way to understand these participants' experiences.

Female Survivors of Sexual Abuse: Unlearning Not to Speak

The second example we discuss approaches the very difficult topic of sexual abuse. Adults who were sexually abused as children often find it challenging to disclose their experiences; these difficulties tend to linger long after the original events and have the potential to severely disrupt the recovery process. As Herman (1992) describes, recovery from trauma unfolds in three stages, each stage encompassing its own central task, including the "establishment of safety," "remembrance and mourning," and "reconnection." Although these stages suggest an orderly progression, the actual process of recovery is gradual and dynamic: Each stage may be revisited many times, although perhaps in different ways, over a long course of time. Notably, at each stage of recovery, both relationships and disclosure are fundamentally important, as recovery cannot occur in isolation (Herman, 1992). Another key aspect of the process involves the empowerment of the survivor, who must become the author of his or her own recovery. We draw the following example from a study that was designed to enter an ongoing exploration of how trauma survivors, both treated and untreated, make meaning of their experiences at different points in their lives and at different stages of recovery, while also examining where and how disclosure might fit into this process.

During the interviews conducted for this study, it seemed that there were shifts in the ways participants spoke about relationships and disclosure; early readings of transcripts confirmed these impressions. Because the research literature suggests that both relationships and disclosure can be fraught with complexity for trauma survivors (Chu, 1992; Herman, 1992), the presence of ambivalence in these narratives was not surprising. At certain times the participants spoke about a deep desire to be in authentic relationships with others and about an urgent need to share their thoughts, emotions, and experiences in these relationships; at other times, the same participants described a fundamental distrust of relationships and questioned the value of sharing these experiences, as well as the ability of language to accurately convey them. We can understand these two stances as different voices, each of them reflecting concerns about disclosure but representing different philosophical orientations and logic. The first voice draws attention to a desire or need to "tell" and the importance of openness or honesty; it holds the possibility of connection or relationship. The second voice, however, reflects disconnection and distress and involves a desire or need to "hide," "forget," or "silence" experiences, even experiences not explicitly related to abuse; it either rejects relationships or emphasizes the dangers that disclosure and relationships may hold. An important distinction between these two voices involves the degree to which the participants assume that it is safe and valuable to articulate and share their thoughts, feelings, and experiences.

Because the first voice operates from the perspective that neither speaking nor relationships are safe, and because theory suggests that chronically silencing the self and constant feelings of danger in relationships can have disastrous psychological effects (Chu, 1992; Jack, 1991, 1999b), we call the first voice a "voice of distress." For many different reasons ("it wasn't very important," "it wasn't very interesting," "I don't think there was anyone I would ever have tried to speak to," "I felt bad," "I was embarrassed," "I was the one to blame"), the perception embodied by this voice is that the self must be pulled out of relationships. In other words, "not saying" is understood as the only reasonable, safe option. Examples of this voice (in italics in the following excerpts) illustrate the ways in which these specific portions of the interviews are characterized by shame, doubt about self-worth, and, in relationships, a desperate need to hide. The woman speaking, whose pseudonym is Lauren, was 33. She had been raised in Europe, spoke three languages fluently, and held a PhD. Her parents were well educated and married. She had a twin brother and five older siblings. She was unsure of her age at the time of the onset of the abuse; however, she knew that one of her older brothers had repeatedly sexually abused her. She had never seen a therapist at the time of these interviews and had spoken to only two people, neither one a family member, about her history of abuse:

> "I don't think I even confided in my sister . . . at that age. *I didn't have much to say. I remember things that happened at school I wasn't happy about, but I didn't tell anyone. I didn't tell my sister. I always thought that it wasn't very interesting and it wasn't very important and, or I felt, you know, bad about certain things.*"
>
> "If things bothered me with the school teacher or something, I thought that was, *I was probably at fault* anyway, *so* I would—*there was no point in me trying to find comfort when . . . I was the one to blame.*"
>
> "*I don't think there was anyone I would ever have tried to speak to. I mean, my parents were fairly distant.* Um. Even, like, you know, they would ask you about whether there was a, there was someone in the class you

liked, you know, a first first sort of um . . . attraction to a classmate and so on and even if there was anything, *I would be very embarrassed to tell them anyway, even if they tried to talk to get me to, to um, to say anything.*"

The second recurring voice in the interviews with these survivors reflected endurance and empowerment and thus was called a "voice of resilience." The presence of this second voice illustrates the fact that, in spite of their difficulties with words and in relationships, these women felt a great pressure (and a great desire) to tell their stories. In direct contrast to the first voice, this second voice holds the perspective that relationships and connections do exist, can be safe, and can provide comfort and assistance ("I would have benefited," "this person supports me") and that speaking is a viable, desirable option ("I will need to discuss it"; "I want people to know this"). Declaring this voice to be about resilience reflects the theory that reconnection and disclosure are associated with recovery and psychological health (Miller & Stiver, 1997; Pennebaker, 1999, 2003). This voice (in bold in the following excerpts) is characterized by a desire to be seen and heard and to be more fully and authentically present in relationships:

"**And now I think that, yeah, I would have benefited from . . . talking to people. I mean, particularly to close friends, that they would maybe understand me better or they would have been able to help me.**"

"I never thought about it because until now, it never was an issue. It just didn't exist. It was so far back. **So, now, now I started thinking about it and now I want to tell everyone. People on the street. Listen to me!**"

"**I feel like, I think it's more important for me to speak out than for them to know maybe**. And uh . . . in the long run, you know, my close friends . . . I don't know. **I think it's important [for them] to know that it, that this is part of me and that it has shaped me in a way** . . . and um . . . I mean, in the same way that I would hope that . . . you know, some of these friends would would tell me about their more . . . you know, with similar experiences, um . . . recent or past. **I just, it's just, you know, a way of having a more complete picture . . . of me.**"

"But now I, you know, at this very moment, in these coming months it's more for me . . . just to to uh . . . take the . . . to uh . . . take the step of of opening up and and also **I think . . . for me it will be the case of . . . I know they are out there and I know they support me. I know they are with me in that fight. You know, if I tell them, then I think it's all these connections that I have. And when I feel, you know, if I feel stress about it or depression, I can think, 'Well, I know that this person is thinking about me, and I know that this person supports me.'** "

Once we have identified these two voices in the data, we can begin to analyze the relationship between them. As mentioned earlier, the analysis of the relationships between the various voices we identify (including, potentially, the self voice) is what distinguishes this method from a more traditional type of narrative analysis (e.g., a thematic analysis) that may simply examine the kinds of themes that are present and/or whether one theme dominated a set of narratives. For example, another researcher could have coded the same content that is called here a voice of distress and called it instead "hiding" or "secrecy"; and we can imagine a similar parallel process concerning the resilient voice and/or the erotic voice described earlier, as well. That is, users of other narrative methods could have potentially coded the same material for analysis. However, beyond the coding process, what happens in a Listening Guide analysis (which includes examining the coded content in the context of full narratives, as well as in relation to other coded portions of text) sets apart findings arising from this method from those that would result from more traditional forms of analysis. The clear focus on *ways* of speaking and the underlying or latent meanings words hold, in addition to *what* is being said concretely, distinguishes a voice-centered analysis from a content or thematic analysis.

It is also important to reiterate that these voices are in some ways distinct from content: When we identify a "voice," it is not simply that the speaker is talking about a certain topic—we are considering the philosophical and psychological underpinnings of what is being said and using these to differentiate one voice from another. For example, both voices identified in this particular analysis involve content related to disclosure, but each represents a different orientation with regard to the prospect of safe disclosures. For the purposes of a Listening Guide analysis, it would not be useful to identify a single "voice of disclosure" that simply designates that the participant is talking about disclosure experiences in the way we might code for disclosure if we were doing grounded theory; rather, the voices in this type of analysis are designed to capture differences in underlying beliefs about disclosure that may shift in time or relationship. The voices thus are connected to and illustrate the complex multiplicity of the psyche. As mentioned earlier, the distinct presence of theory that includes the recognition of polyphonic narrators with multilayered psyches and guides both the identification of the contrapuntal voices and their interpretation also distinguishes studies that utilize the Listening Guide from other approaches.

As illustrated in the earlier examples about sexual desire, the Listening Guide can be used to explore the relationships between voices by examining how the self aligns with one or more of the contrapuntal voices identified in the interview data. For example, we could have explored Lauren's tendency to say such things as "I should talk about this," "I want to talk about this," or "I need to talk about this" in comparison to such things as "people need to share difficult experiences" or "one wants others to know." As discussed earlier, the difference between these types of statements is the position taken up by the narrator. In the first set of examples, the narrator is speaking in the first person about her own experiences, whereas in the second set, the narrator is speaking more generally, as if about the experiences of others. As outlined earlier, the question underlying this type of analysis would be about the orientation with which the narrator tends to align—that is, whether or not the first-person narrator speaks more frequently in a "voice of resilience" or a "voice of distress."

However, a second way to undertake a Listening Guide analysis is to explicitly examine the relationship between the two contrapuntal voices themselves. For survivors, speaking can be very complicated. Listening to or conducting interviews, we see clearly that the desire to speak coexists with a desire to be known beyond words—and both are accompanied by a deeply ingrained belief that speaking will cause the disruption of relationships (Sorsoli, 2004). Speaking also has the tendency to bring floods of emotions, sometimes quite unexpectedly, that can be very difficult for survivors to manage. Given the relational difficulties that tend to accompany early traumatic experiences such as sexual abuse, it makes sense that these narrators would often seem to vacillate frantically between wanting to be seen and heard (i.e., voicing resilience) and not wanting to be seen and heard (i.e., voicing distress). In other words, they understably waver between believing that it is possible and believing that it is impossible to be safe sharing what is real for them, such as their thoughts, their emotions, and their experiences, which results in the audible struggle between these two voices. The palpable presence of this struggle (and the clinical importance of its outcome) is the reason that an analysis of the relationship between the two contrapuntal voices is such an appropriate application of the Listening Guide.

Because our interest was in what the shifting of these voices could contribute to an understanding of the dynamics of resilience as conveyed in trauma narratives, we looked specifically to portions of the interviews where both voices were present to explore the pattern in the relationship between the two voices. When attempting to establish the existence of a pattern in the dynamic relationship between voices, it is critical to consider the unit of analysis, such as discrete narratives or speaking turns, so that the dynamic can be analyzed systematically and findings can be interpreted. Each of the following examples represents one speaking turn, that is, each example was in response to a single comment or question of the interviewer. As in earlier examples, the voice of distress is presented in *italics* and the voice of resilience is in **bold**:

"**It's it it is . . . hard, but then . . . you know, call a cat a cat. This is what happened**. *And you can use,* unless you know exactly what you, which word describes what, *you can be misled by . . . you know, using other words. You know, intercourse or fooling around or you know, intimacy, sexual relationship, what do they really mean*?"

"**I always talk about it in English.** Maybe [French] describes the things . . . too clearly. So *I'm afraid of the word.* Whereas *in English they, there's sort of a cover.*"

"*I can't say anything. I can't say anything. I just close up and then I say, 'Oh forget it. Forget it.'* **And then I get so frustrated because I want to say it, but it it doesn't come out.**"

"**I told my father that we could have done with a little bit more attention.** He said, 'Yeah, I know. We let you grow like weeds.' **I said, 'Yeah, you did.'** And uh, he said, 'Well yeah, but you know, who do you think should would have needed more attention?' You know, and he said like, 'Certainly not this and this' like mentioning my oldest brothers and so on. *And at that stage I was I was too scared to say, 'Well, I would have.' So I didn't say anything. Not a thing.*"

"**I have to, you know, be open. This is a part of me. This is just as important as anything else.** You know the thing is . . . okay so, the story with my brother is one thing, but one thing **I've always wanted to . . . tell people, tell my friends,** but . . . **I I wanted to tell someone or I wanted to discuss or . . . or exchange views about was . . . was what happened what happened to me in terms of intimate relationships, you know, for ten years, when nothing, or fifteen years, nothing happened.** And and all these all these horrible experiences and why did it happen, why did it happen to me? Why did it happen again? And why was it that no one was interested in me? Why? You know, all these things. And all these things have always bothered me. *And I thought, I always wondered why . . . do [I] have this need . . . to tell someone about my private life . . . and my intimate relationships when no one wants to hear about that*?"

Again, it is not simply the presence or predominance of one or the other of these two different voices across an interview transcript but the movement between the voices (i.e., where one voice rises and the other falls) that captures our interest here. Because we can see these voices in the context of the full narrative, rather than extracting the voices into categories for separate analysis, we can see them as dynamic entities. In the preceding examples, looking at the presence and movement between these two voices tells a compelling story about Lauren's inner experiences. Although both voices are present in each excerpt, her narratives exhibit a pattern: She often begins a speaking turn with a voice of resilience ("I have to be open. This is a part of me"; "I told my father we could have done with a bit more attention"), but ends with the voice of distress ("I was too scared to say, 'Well I would have.' So I didn't say anything"; "Why do I have this need to tell someone about my private life? No one wants to hear that"). The movement between these voices suggests that Lauren, despite an initial resilient stance, quickly falls back into the distress of silence, which is certainly understandable; at the time of this interview, Lauren had seen a therapist only once in her entire life, even though she had been repeatedly molested and raped by an older brother.

As mentioned earlier, theory can be important at several points in a Listening Guide analysis, including the process of interpreting the findings. For clinicians, a natural way to understand the existence of these shifts between voices is to consider a theoretical system of "parts." Internal family systems (IFS) therapy (Goulding & Schwartz, 1995; Mann & Schwartz, 2002; Schwartz, 1999), for example, works explicitly with systems of parts and, like the Listening Guide, suggests that each of them has "a distinct voice or character, complete with idiosyncratic desires, style of communication, and temperament" (Mann & Schwartz, 2002, p. 135). In accord with the Listening Guide, the internal family systems model takes the position that multiplicity is a normal aspect of the psyche, which differs from other views that suggest that these parts are internalized representations of significant others or are the result of traumatic experiences that shatter a once unitary mind. In IFS, each of the separate parts serves a different function in the psychological system. Lauren's case, while exhibiting the ways a resilient narrative about wanting to be heard can be overcome by an old and very difficult story that "no one wants to hear that," thus can also be interpreted as a system of parts in which one of the parts wants to speak out, whereas another feels safer in silence. The goal of an internal family systems therapist is to understand the network that exists among and between the parts, improving relationships between the parts and thus reducing psychological distress. As a research method, the Listening Guide highlights the existence of these parts as they appear in narratives and attempts to understand the relationships between these distinct ways of conveying experiences, taking into consideration how they reflect inner experiences, as well as responses to the outer environment.

Highlighting the ways the voices in this analysis reflect differing orientations toward relationships and examining the ways they shift in time offers a very intriguing way to understand the inner experiences of these survivors. Overall, listening to these different voices as different stories being told about experience suggests that understanding their presence and shifts between them may be helpful in the recovery process. A child in an abusive environment may learn that silence offers a certain degree of emotional safety and, over the years, may lose consciousness of her or his power to choose to speak, automatically slipping back into silence whenever she or he senses risk or conflict. Although not speaking may have served them well in the past, survivors struggle to relearn how to voice their thoughts and feelings. That is, their developmental edge involves "unlearning" not to speak. As a result, recovery may involve empowering a survivor to be not only the author of her or his own recovery but also the author of her or his narrative, engaging a consciousness about the choice to speak instead of being subject to seemingly uncontrollable shifts back into silence. Although certainly not generalizable in the statistical sense, qualitative research such as this can offer important insight into survivors' experiences with disclosure and girls' experiences of sexual desire, even though designing and conducting this type of research comes with a certain set of challenges.

The Challenges of Using a Voice-Centered Relational Method

Research with adolescent girls revealed that "holding firmly" to standard practices of psychological research—such as an experimental design, structured interviews, and a neutral, detached interviewing style—could prevent the formation of positive connections with study participants and limited a researcher's ability to follow participants where they wanted to go (Brown & Gilligan, 1992). Shifts in procedures that allowed the discovery of new information and the emergence of the Listening Guide centered around the practice of relationship and "listening to the complexities of voice" (Brown & Gilligan, 1992, p. 20), both during interviews and later during analysis. We have found that these shifts in research practices are critical because the successful use of the Listening Guide method depends greatly on the quality of the data collected for analysis. Our experience suggests that semistructured clinical interviews (conducted in a relational interviewing style) yield complex narratives and thoughtful internal reflection of a quality that can be impossible to gather with traditional structured approaches to interviewing.

By describing the interviews as clinical, we do not mean to suggest that the researcher take on the role of a therapist. However, like clinicians, a clinical interviewer does not assume that language is transparent and understands that both language and the psyche are layered. In addition, like clinicians, we ask questions that enable the participant to share life experiences and, while listening to their answers, we follow the cadence, rhythm, and tone of narratives for information about the threads that warrant following and where to go next. Like Freud (1963), we set before ourselves "the task of bringing to light what human beings keep hidden within them" (p. 69) and seek to follow participants' associative logic. During interviews, we listen closely and on many levels, conscious that there may be hints of insight or information lingering behind the words that are actually said.

As with other narrative research, interview protocols designed to be used in conjunction with the Listening Guide focus on eliciting specific, concrete experiences (Chase, 2003), and on this level we listen during interviews for a degree of coherence and detail that will allow us to visualize (Weiss, 1994) the setting in which the plot takes place and the characters involved. On a second level, we are listening for the ways these narrated experiences do and do not fit into the theoretical frameworks that guide our research and for how well our protocol is capturing lived experiences of the phenomenon, conscious that we may need to ask different questions, in a different order, or with different wording in order to connect with our participants. On a third level, looking ahead to our analysis, we listen for the ways the self is portrayed in the narratives and potentially the ways different aspects of the phenomenology we are studying are voiced. On all of these levels, we are conscious about the importance of "going deep" in terms of the phenomenon we are studying. Sometimes this means momentarily abandoning our interview protocol to follow a participant where she or he wants to lead us.

Because of the way it tunes researchers' ears toward the potential existence and recognition of multiple voices, learning the Listening Guide can change how narration sounds even during the interviewing process. However, the beginning of a research project, and particularly during the first few interviews, the different voices that can be present in interviews can be difficult if not impossible to hear. It is often necessary to read interview texts multiple times before one is able to go beneath the surface narrative and hear the separate voices it contains. And yet, if distinct voices exist, they become increasingly clear over time. As we become more familiar with the data our protocols elicit, we also become increasingly aware of patterns in actual, real-time speech, and, as mentioned earlier, the practice of untangling these threads can lend itself to listening for their presence during interviews. Similar to listening for the presence of metastatements, moral language, and inner dialogues (Jack, 1999c), tuning our ears for these voices can both help us to understand our participants' experiences and to ask appropriate, sensitive follow-up questions.

Although listening for shifts in voice and/or orientation characteristics is relatively common among psychotherapists (see, e.g., Dierks, 1996; Krueger, 2002), researchers are often less aware of the multiplicity of voice that can be heard during interviews. Texts on interviewing skills sometimes base adequacy of accounts on factors such as story development, detail, and visualizability (e.g., Weiss, 1994), and narrative analysts tend to seek coherence (e.g., Bluck & Habermas, 2000). Unlike these other ways of judging data, listening for voices is not simply about the content that is present but the ways in which it is being expressed. Sometimes certain vocal markers suggest a hidden "understory"—for example, long pauses, drops or raises in pitch, a quickening of pace, or laughter that seems out of place can suggest to an interviewer that perhaps the whole story is yet to be told; other times the body becomes involved in the telling of the story, and wrenching hands, unacknowledged tears, or a dazed look signal that something important may be going unsaid. Seeking stories that lie just underneath the surface, or seeking a voice or perspective that offers an alternative to the dominant discourse, either within a particular interview or in society in general, can be a particularly fruitful way to generate deep understandings of complex phenomena.

As feminist researchers, in our interviews we focus on encouraging participants to tell their own stories on their own terms and to reflect on the meanings those stories hold for them—and we listen with an awareness of the social forces that may affect the ability to articulate one's experiences (Anderson, Armitage, Jack, & Wittner, 1990). We are also aware that the processes that influence the relationships of others may also influence our research. This means acknowledging that at certain points during our interviews, participants' desires to speak and to be in the research relationship with us may shift. For example, when asked about her first interview during her second interview, Lauren, the survivor discussed earlier, said, "I had a very very positive impression about the first interview. . . . I could sense not only interest, but . . . compassion and um . . . so it, I mean it created a very very comfortable environment, uh, where I felt very safe to talk." Later, however, at the end of the second interview, she admitted, "I came back here and I thought, you know, I'm going back into this house and talking to this person who I told my entire life and suddenly . . . you know, it made me feel like . . . do I really want to see you again?" When asked how she felt about the fact that she had stayed and revealed even more about herself, she said that even though she had been afraid before coming into the interview, once she started talking she remembered how safe it felt and was glad she stayed. During an interview sometimes these shifts are difficult to perceive; however, they are often much more noticeable during the process of analysis. A rich story may wither when pursued with follow-up questions; a tiny suggestion of a story may continue to grow and develop over time. Because of the potential impact on research, considering such shifts in relational dynamics can be extremely important and can help us to become even more responsive to participants' needs. The key to being responsive, as it is with much of successful research, is listening well.

Researchers attempting to use the Listening Guide will undoubtedly find that that this technique, although adaptable, works better for particular types of research questions (psychological or phenomenological) and for particular types of data (clinically oriented in-depth interviews). As with all research, credible results rely on good study design, which demands that careful consideration be given to purpose, conceptual context, research questions, and methods of data collection and analysis (see Maxwell, 1996). Furthermore, for a Listening Guide analysis to be persuasive, researchers must be extremely rigorous and systematic in the application of the method and the documentation of the analysis process, including how narratives or transcript portions are chosen for analysis (if full transcripts are not the unit of analysis) and how voices are defined and later identified in text. Findings reached at each individual level of analysis must be carefully documented for each case, and significant attention must be given to a thoughtful integration of these separate findings to produce a compelling research product. Because of the rigor involved, using this method can be quite time-consuming. Occasionally, in spite of extensive front-end efforts, findings can be difficult to interpret—for example, when a clear, compelling pattern does not emerge.

On the other hand, the existence of multiple potential interpretations of the findings is one reason the Listening Guide works well as an exploratory method. It encourages complex understandings of the data and can be quite adept at generating new questions that should be explored, either in the present or the future, and either qualitatively or quantitatively. The method also works extremely well when it is used in concert with other narrative methods or as a part of a well-designed mixed method study, as Tolman and Szalacha (1999) have illustrated. As a final note, as Gilligan and colleagues (2003) also suggest, it is not our intention to pronounce our approach *the* definitive way to understand and conduct a Listening Guide analysis. Instead, we offer this chapter as a guide to the particular way in which *we* have implemented this method, focusing on the procedures and elements we have found to be the most productive and innovative in our work. For us, analyzing contrapuntal voices has been a rich and fascinating process. We have found that extraordinary and often unanticipated findings arise from this unique way of listening to narrative data. Indeed, perhaps one of the most valuable things this method does is draw attention to a lost art: listening. By encouraging us to listen, gently but tenaciously, and on many levels, it reintroduces the complexity and humanity of listening and being heard back into the research landscape.

Notes

1. The members of the Harvard Project on the Psychology of Women and the Development of Girls were Lyn Brown, Elizabeth Debold, Judy Dorney, Barbara Miller, Annie Rogers, Mark Tappan, Jill Taylor, Deborah Tolman, and Janie Ward. Other students contributing to conversations about the Listening Guide method include Dianne Argyris, Jane Attanucci, Betty Bardige, Kay Johnston, Dick Osborne, Grant Wiggins, and David Wilcox.

2. The method also incorporates procedures for the analyst to acknowledge his or her own salient experiences explicitly, not to "remove bias," but to identify potential ways of hearing that could "drown out" the experiences that participants describe, so that such "voicing over" can be avoided or ameliorated (see Gilligan et al., 2003).

3. In her main body of work, Tolman practices this method listening for a third, theoretically-driven voice of embodied sexuality (see Tolman, 2002). Most often requiring a direct question about bodily sexual feelings (which are not part of acceptable discourse for girls about their sexuality), this voice is often difficult to discern and strongly aligned with the erotic voice.

4. Early users of the Listening Guide underlined the voices with various colored pencils, each color representing a different voice/reading. At every level of analysis, the transcripts became increasingly colored, and the colors themselves illustrated visually the presence, absence, ebb, and flow of the various voices present. Although we still believe that marked transcripts help researchers to stay in contact with the data, advances in technology allow us new entrées into qualitative data analysis. For example, we can now enter and code our transcripts using the program Atlas.ti. Doing so, we can actually quickly analyze whether two voices often overlap or occur in close proximity. Furthermore, if we record interviews digitally, we can now create hyperlinks to actual participants' voices—this can be particularly useful when analyzing a complicated narrative, as it allows coders and analysts to easily review the exact vocal qualities of the statements on which codes need to be based.

References

Anderson, K., Armitage, S., Jack, D. C., & Wittner, J. (1990). Beginning where we are: Feminist methodology in oral history. In J. M. Nielsen (Ed.), *Feminist research methods: Exemplary readings in the social sciences* (pp. 94–112). Boulder, CO: Westview Press.

Belenky, M. F., Clinchy, B. M., Goldberger, N. R., & Tarule, J. M. (1986). *Women's ways of knowing: The development of self, voice, and mind.* New York: Basic Books.

Bluck, S., & Habermas, T. (2000). The life story schema. *Motivation and Emotion, 24*(2), 121–147.

Brown, L., Argyris, D., Attanucci, J., Bardige, B., Gilligan, C., Johnston, K., et al. (1988). *A guide to reading narratives of conflict and choice for self and moral voice.* Cambridge, MA: Harvard Graduate School of Education, Center for the Study of Gender, Education, and Human Development.

Brown, L. M. (1999). *Raising their voices: The politics of girls' anger.* Cambridge, MA: Harvard University Press.

Brown, L. M. (2001). White working-class girls, femininities, and the paradox of resistance. In D. L. Tolman & M. Brydon-Miller (Eds.), *From subjects to subjectivities: A handbook of interpretive and participatory methods* (pp. 95–110). New York: New York University Press.

Brown, L. M. (2003). *Girlfighting: Betrayal and rejection among girls.* New York: New York University Press.

Brown, L. M., Debold, E., Tappan, M. B., & Gilligan, C. (1991). Reading narratives of conflict and choice for self and moral voices: A relational method. In W. M. Kurtines & J. L. Gewirtz (Eds.), *Handbook of moral behavior and development: Vol. 2. Research* (pp. 25–61). Hillsdale, NJ: Erlbaum.

Brown, L. M., & Gilligan, C. (1992). *Meeting at the crossroads: Women's psychology and girls' development.* Cambridge, MA: Harvard University Press.

Brown, L. M., Tappan, M. B., Gilligan, C., Miller, B. A., & Argyris, D. E. (1989). Reading for self and moral voice: A method for interpreting narratives of real-life moral conflict and choice. In M. J. Packer & R. B. Addison (Eds.), *Entering the circle: Hermeneutic investigation in psychology* (pp. 141–164). Albany: State University of New York Press.

Bruner, J. (1987). Life as narrative. *Social Research, 54*(1), 11–32.

Chase, S. E. (2003). Learning to listen: Narrative principles on a qualitative research methods course. In R. Josselson, A. Lieblich, & D. P. McAdams (Eds.), *Up close and personal: The teaching and learning of narrative research* (pp. 79–99). Washington, DC: American Psychological Association Press.

Chu, J. A. (1992). The therapeutic roller coaster: Dilemmas in the treatment of childhood abuse survivors. *Journal of Psychotherapy Practice and Research, 1*(4), 351–370.

Cohn, M. A., Mehl, M. R., & Pennebaker, J. W. (2004). Linguistic markers of psychological change surrounding September 11, 2001. *Psychological Science, 15*(10), 687–693.

Debold, E. (1990, April). *Learning in the first person: A passion to know.* Paper presented at the Laurel–Harvard Conference on the Psychology of Women and the Development of Girls, Cleveland, OH.

Dierks, J. M. (1996). Listening within: A brief therapy model for use with Gestalt theory. *Gestalt Journal, 19*(2), 51–99.

Erikson, E. H. (1993). *Gandhi's truth: On the origins of militant nonviolence.* New York: Norton.

Fairbairn, W. R. D. (1954). *An object-relations theory of the personality.* Oxford, UK: Basic Books.

Fine, M. (1988). Sexuality, schooling, and adolescent females: The missing discourse of desire. *Harvard Educational Review, 58*(1), 29–53.

Fine, M. (1994). Working the hyphens: Reinventing the self and other in qualitative research. In N. K. Denzin & Y. S. Lincoln (Eds.), *Handbook of qualitative research* (pp. 70–82). Thousand Oaks, CA: Sage.

Foucault, M. (1980). *The history of sexuality: Vol. 1. An introduction.* New York: Vintage Books.

Freud, S. (1963). *Dora: An analysis of a case of hysteria.* New York: Simon & Schuster.

Gilligan, C. (1982). *In a different voice: Psychological theory and women's development.* Cambridge, MA: Harvard University Press.

Gilligan, C., Brown, L. M., & Rogers, A. G. (1990). Psyche embedded: A place for body, relationships, and culture in personality theory. In A. I. Rabin, R. A. Zucker, R. A. Emmons, & S. Frank (Eds.), *Studying persons and lives* (pp. 86–147). New York: Springer.

Gilligan, C., & Machoian, L. (2002). Learning to speak the language: A relational interpretation of an adolescent girl's suicidality. *Studies in Gender and Sexuality, 3*(3), 321–340.

Gilligan, C., Spencer, R., Weinberg, M. K., & Bertsch, T. (2003). On the Listening Guide: A voice-centered relational model. In P. M. Camic, J. E. Rhodes, & L. Yardley (Eds.), *Qualitative research in psychology: Expanding perspectives in methodology and design* (pp. 157–172). Washington, DC: American Psychological Association.

Goulding, R. A., & Schwartz, R. C. (1995). *The Mosaic mind: Empowering tormented selves of child abuse survivors.* New York: Norton.

Harvey, M. R., Mishler, E. G., Koenen, K., & Harney, P. A. (2000). In the aftermath of sexual abuse: Making and remaking meaning in narratives of trauma and recovery. *Narrative Inquiry, 10*(2), 291–311.

Herman, J. L. (1992). *Trauma and recovery.* New York: Basic Books.

hooks, b. (1984). *Feminist theory from margin to center.* Boston: South End Press.

Jack, D. C. (1991). *Silencing the self: Women and depression.* Cambridge, MA: Harvard University Press.

Jack, D. C. (1999a). *Behind the mask: Destruction and creativity in women's aggression.* Cambridge, MA: Harvard University Press.

Jack, D. C. (1999b). Silencing the self: Inner dialogues and outer realities. In T. Joiner & J. C. Coyne (Eds.), *The interactional nature of depression: Advances in interpersonal approaches* (pp. 221–246). Washington, DC: American Psychological Association.

Jack, D. C. (1999c). Ways of listening to depressed women in qualitative research: Interview techniques and analyses. *Canadian Psychology, 40*(2), 91–101.

Jordan, J. V. (1997). Clarity in connection: Empathic knowing, desire, and sexuality. In J. V. Jordan (Ed.), *Women's growth in diversity: More writings from the Stone Center* (pp. 50–73). New York: Guilford Press.

Jung, C. G. (1954). *The development of personality.* New York: Pantheon Books.

Kim, J. L., Sorsoli, C. L., Schooler, D., & Tolman, D. L. (2007). From sex to sexuality: Exposing the heterosexual script on primetime network television. *Journal of Adolescent Health, 40*(1), e9–e16.

Kohlberg, L., & Elfenbein, D. (1975). The development of moral judgments concerning capital punishment. *American Journal of Orthopsychiatry, 45*(4), 614–640.

Kohlberg, L., & Puka, B. (1994). *Kohlberg's original study of moral development.* New York: Garland.

Krueger, D. W. (2002). *Integrating body self and psychological self: Creating a new story in psychoanalysis and psychotherapy.* New York: Brunner-Routledge.

Lieblich, A., Tuval-Mashiach, R., & Zilber, T. (1998). *Narrative research: Reading, analysis, and interpretation.* Thousand Oaks, CA: Sage.

Machoian, L. (2005). *The disappearing girl: Learning the language of teenage depression.* New York: Dutton/Penguin Books.

Mann, B. J., & Schwartz, R. C. (2002). Internal systems therapy. In F. W. Kaslow (Ed.), *Comprehensive handbook of psychotherapy: Vol. 4. Integrative/eclectic* (pp. 455–474). Hoboken, NJ: Wiley.

Maxwell, J. A. (1996). *Qualitative research design: An interactive approach.* Thousand Oaks, CA: Sage.

Miles, M. B., & Huberman, A. M. (1994). *Qualitative data analysis: An expanded sourcebook* (2nd ed.). Thousand Oaks, CA: Sage.

Miller, J. B. (1976). *Toward a new psychology of women.* Oxford, UK: Beacon.

Miller, J. B., & Stiver, I. P. (1997). *The healing connection: How women form relationships in therapy and in life.* Boston: Beacon Press.

Mishler, E. (1986). *Research interviewing.* Cambridge, MA: Harvard University Press.

Muhlhausler, P., & Harre, R. (1990). *Pronouns and people: The linguistic construction of social and personal identity.* Oxford, UK: Blackwell.

Nielsen, J. M. (1990). Introduction. In J. M. Nielsen (Ed.), *Feminist research methods: Exemplary readings in the social sciences* (pp. 1–37). Boulder, CO: Westview Press.

Pennebaker, J. W. (1999). The effects of traumatic disclosure on physical and mental health: The values of writing and talking about upsetting events. *International Journal of Emergency Mental Health, 1*(1), 9–18.

Pennebaker, J. W. (2003). The social, linguistic and health consequences of emotional disclosure. In J. Suls & K. A. Wallston (Eds.), *Social psychological foundations of health and illness* (pp. 288–313). Malden, MA: Blackwell.

Reindl, S. M. (2001). *Sensing the self: Women's recovery from bulimia.* Cambridge, MA: Harvard University Press.

Rich, A. (1983). Compulsory heterosexuality and the lesbian existence. In A. Snitow, C. Stansell, & S. Thompson (Eds.), *Powers of desire: The politics of sexuality* (pp. 177–205). New York: Monthly Review Press.

Schwartz, R. C. (1999). The Internal Family Systems model. In J. Rowan & M. Cooper (Eds.), *The plural self: Multiplicity in everyday life* (pp. 238–253). Thousand Oaks, CA: Sage.

Sorsoli, C. L., Porche, M. V., & Tolman, D. L. (2005). "He left her for the alien": Girls, television, and sex. In E. Cole & J. H. Daniel (Eds.), *Featuring females: Feminist analyses of media* (pp. 25–39). Washington, DC: American Psychological Association.

Sorsoli, L. (2004). Echoes of silence: Remembering and repeating childhood trauma. In A. Lieblich, D. P. McAdams, & R. Josselson (Eds.), *Healing plots: The narrative basis of psychotherapy* (pp. 89–109). Washington, DC: American Psychological Association.

Sorsoli, L. (2007). Where the whole thing fell apart: Race, resilience, and the complexity of trauma. *Journal of Aggression, Maltreatment and Trauma, 14*(1–2), 99–121.

Steiner-Adair, C. (1991). New maps of development, new models of therapy: The psychology of women and the treatment of eating disorders. In C. L. Johnson (Ed.), *Psychodynamic treatment of anorexia nervosa and bulimia* (pp. 225–244). New York: Guilford Press.

Strauss, A., & Corbin, J. (1998). *Basics of qualitative research: Techniques and procedures for developing grounded theory* (2nd ed.). Thousand Oaks, CA: Sage.

Tolman, D. L. (1991). Adolescent girls, women and sexuality: Discerning dilemmas of desire. *Women and Therapy, 11*(3–4), 55–69.

Tolman, D. L. (2001). Echoes of sexual objectification: Listening for one girl's erotic voice. In D. Tolman & M. Brydon-Miller (Eds.), *From subjects to subjectivities: A handbook of interpretive and participatory methods* (pp. 130–144). New York: New York University Press.

Tolman, D. L. (2002). *Dilemmas of desire: Teenage girls talk about sexuality.* Cambridge, MA: Harvard University Press.

Tolman, D. L., & Brown, L. M. (2001). Adolescent girls'

voices: Resonating resistance in body and soul. In R. K. Unger (Ed.), *Handbook of the psychology of women and gender* (pp. 133–155). New York: Wiley.

Tolman, D. L., & Szalacha, L. (1999). Dimensions of desire: Bridging qualitative and quantitative methods in a study of female adolescent sexuality. *Psychology of Women Quarterly, 23*(1), 7–39.

Waites, E. A. (1997). *Memory quest: Trauma and the search for personal history*. New York: Norton.

Way, N. (2001). Using feminist research methods to explore boys' relationships. In D. L. Tolman & M. Brydon-Miller (Eds.), *From subjects to subjectivities: A handbook of interpretive and participatory methods* (pp. 111–129). New York: New York University Press.

Weiss, R. S. (1994). *Learning from strangers: The art and method of qualitative interview studies.* New York: Free Press.

Winnicott, D. W. (1965). *Maturational processes and the facilitating environment: Studies in the theory of emotional development*. New York: International Universities Press.

PART III

The Impact of Emergent Technologies on Research Methods

Sharlene Nagy Hesse-Biber

The number one benefit of information technology is that it empowers people to do what they want to do. It lets people be creative. It lets people be productive. It lets people learn things they didn't think they could learn before, and so in a sense it is all about potential.

—BALLMER (personal communication, February 17, 2005)

Emergent technologies have pushed against the boundaries of how both qualitative and quantitative researchers now practice their research craft. In this section of the *Handbook*, authors raise issues regarding how to effectively apply new technological innovations, including the use of the Internet, mobile technologies, geospatial technologies, self-organizing maps, and the incorporation of computer-assisted software programs to collect and analyze both qualitative and quantitative data.

In Part III, we explore the promises and perils that emergent technology usage holds for research methods practice. The contributors look at how emergent technologies are practiced within the research process and what issues these technologies raise, as well as the questions new technologies allow researchers to address in a range of disciplines. We discuss the costs and benefits of new computer software technologies for the research process, as well as the potential misuse of these techniques for methods practice. We begin this part with Christine Hine's discussion of the role of Internet technology in facilitating mixed methods research. Steven Jones (1999) described the Internet as an "engine of social change" (p. 2) in that it has "modified work habits, education, social relations generally, and . . . our hopes and dreams" (p. 2). The Internet originated in the early 1960s and has now mushroomed into a venue to which individuals turn for a variety of information. According to comScore Networks' World Metrex Service, the Internet is reaching over 747 million individuals worldwide as of 2007, having grown by 10% since 2006 (*http://www.comscore.com/*, retrieved September 12, 2007). Individuals from around the world spend, on the average, 27 hours each month on the Internet (*http://www.clickz.com/showPage.html?page=3625168*, retrieved September 12, 2007). Sudweeks and Simoff (1999) note:

> The Internet has given birth to new research fields or has diversified existing research fields, or has diversified existing research fields connected with human activities, including computer-mediated communication (CMC), computer-supported cooperative work (CSCW), electronic commerce, virtual communities, virtual architecture, various virtual environments and information design. (p. 29)

What Sudweeks and Simoff (1999) found is that with the advent of Internet technologies, traditional researchers need to adapt to the Internet environment in which "communication technologies and socio-cultural norms challenge existing research assumptions and premises" (p. 30). The Internet challenges some basic philosophical assumptions that researchers have about the nature of the social reality. To what extent is the Internet an extension of social reality, or in fact a new environment, with a different set of laws and social conventions (p. 31)? To what extent do positivist assumptions about the nature of the social reality hold up within an Internet environment? To what extent do interpretative models of subjective experience that focus on individuals in their relation to others hold up within an Internet context (p. 31)?

Compounding these issues is the changing technological nature of the Internet environment that incorporates a variety of modes of accessing information in a multimedia format. The use of iPods and other devices that link into a virtual environment provide a multitude of ways to view and access information. There is, in fact, a data-overload of information. The ability to hyperlink information also now allows the access to information in a nonlinear fashion (p. 32).

In Chapter 25, Christine Hine takes up the new research designs and techniques in social research that have emerged as a result of the growth and development of the Internet. She looks at a variety of research methods, both quantitative and qualitative, that have been undertaken but focuses her lens on ethnographic practice and how it has evolved and transformed since the advent of the Internet. She provides both theoretical issues and in-depth examples of how ethnographers invent new research practices and tweak existing practices. Early researchers working with the Internet were from the field of psychology and social psychology. They wanted to conduct experiments on the impact of "reduced social cues"—that is, What happens to interaction over the Internet when individuals cannot rely on face-to-face interaction? How does this interaction vary when individuals know each other?

Other researchers were interested in understanding Internet culture as a social formation in its own right, which ultimately came to be known as "cyberculture." Researchers employed ethnographic methods in order to understand online and offline interactions between users. One of Christine Hine's major points is that although there have been some very creative twists on established research methods, there still remains a strong application of traditional research methods to Internet research. She notes, "Internet researchers come from diverse disciplines and bring their methods with them. There is thus no single accepted means of addressing the Internet. Internet research itself is not a discipline but an interdiscipline, a field or a research network populated by heterogeneous perspectives . . ." (p. 537).

In Chapter 26, Claire Hewson narrows the discussion to how the Internet as a technology can interface with a specific research design or, in this case, mixed methods. Hewson begins her chapter by outlining the pros and cons of Internet-mediated research, including some thorny ethical issues faced by researchers. She presents in-depth examples of Internet-mediated research (IMR). She covers some key quantitative approaches to Internet research—surveys, experiments, and structured observations, as well as unobtrusive research using content analytic techniques applied to archival online data and online documents.

Qualitative approaches to studying IMR consist of getting at the experiences of those who use the Internet via open-ended interviews, instant messaging, or e-mail discussions. Qualitative methods such as interviewing run into a set of new challenges for the researcher who employs them to conduct Internet research. Sometimes researchers find that their interaction with respondents entails a time lag, whereby the interview is not conducted in "real time" but the interviewer waits for the respondent to comment later in time. There is also the concern that meaning may be lost in the interview situation because nonverbal cues are missing from the interaction. Ways of establishing rapport with the respondent must take place differently, especially with the lack of face-to-face interviewing and verbal communication (except for some emotions that can be expressed linguistically—such as a smile notation, for example). The use of in-depth observational techniques such as participant observation in chat rooms and discussion groups, along with webcam technology, can now allow the analysis of multimedia data. However, these new technologies can affect a respondent's anonymity. Hewson notes "what is private and public online needs to be carefully considered" (p. 556). Some researchers chose to be nonparticipants and to access only archived material or observe only real-time interactions without participating in order to offset some of these issues.

A novel approach that has been gaining popularity is that of mixed methods designs that combine both qualitative and quantitative methods in either single or multiple studies within a single mode (online or offline) or different modes (both online and offline). Hewson discusses both sequential and concurrent mixed methods Internet research. She notes:

> IMR mixed-mode studies may also be useful in research that aims to explore the nature of potential differences in online and offline behaviors. For example, some studies have compared the characteristics of online and offline interviews in order to examine whether the idiosyncratic features of each mode of administration (some of which were discussed earlier, e.g., presence or absence of extralinguistic cues) may have an impact on the way the interview proceeds. Such studies are of interest in their own right, as explorations of behavior in an online medium. (p. 562)

Bella Dicks and Bruce Mason, in Chapter 27, take up hypermedia technology, another technological innovation that promises to provide researchers with a rich medium for getting at meaning in the research process. New approaches have arisen for analyzing multimedia data beyond text with the advent of digital technology, welcoming the use of still images, sound, and moving images into the analytical process. Computer programs have the ability to hyperlink data, allowing researchers to move from one type of meaning to another in a nonlinear process, linking, for example, text with images and sound. Chapter 27 takes the reader through the methodological implications of using multimedia data and illustrates the paucity of discussion on the methodological implications of using such mixed-media data. Although the use of visual methods is addressed in the literature, other media forms, such as sound, have not received such widespread discussion. In addition, the discussion of alternative media forms tends to be done in isolation with little attention focused on the mixing of different media forms. The intention of their chapter is to focus on multimedia methods that can capture what the authors see as the "multisensory nature of the social worlds we study" (p. 571). They also address how to represent research findings in a multimediated format.

Dicks and Mason focus on ethnographic hypermedia environments (EHE). These are experimental environments that demonstrate how the researcher can link together various forms of media data, such as textual and video data. Hypermediated data allow the possibility of multiple representations of the data. They note: "hyper/multimedia approaches seem to provide the means of addressing some of the critiques mounted against standard realist genres of representation in qualitative social research" (p. 576). Hypermedia allows a range of subjective meanings and interpretations. They argue, "Hyperlinks, by contrast, allow numerous directions to be followed with a simple click of the mouse. At the same time, the computer screen itself offers what Bolter calls a 'topographical writing space' that brings together the written word, images, and sound and opens up new opportunities for multimedia representation" (p. 578). Linking various forms of multimedia data also increases an individual's ability to network across different forms of knowledge building and "different knowledge domains" (p. 580). Dicks and Mason offer in-depth examples of hypermedia/multimedia research projects. They reframe the research process from data generation and recording to analysis, interpretation, representation, and dissemination of findings from a multimediated perspective. The advent of hypermedia allows the researcher to create, if you will, audit trails—to take the reader through the set of connections the researcher makes with these varied data. One is able to convey to the reader the complexity of one's analysis and interpretation.

The next five chapters introduce a variety of new technologies and software programs that hold great promise of assisting with the gathering of new types of research quantitative and qualitative data, as well as enhancing the researcher's ability to analyze large volumes of data in order to get at multiple layers of meaning. In Chapter 28, Ingrid Mulder and Joke Kort discuss the role of emerging mobile technologies (context-aware applications). They note that applications such as the mobile phones that are already part of everyday life may be used to capture subjective experiences in real time. Most current measures of subjective experience rely on traditional tools and methods, such as laboratory experiments and interviews, that provide a one-shot measure of experience that does not fully capture the micro and macro (contextual) factors that frame an individual's ongoing subjective experiences. Mei-Po Kwan, in Chapter 29, discusses the use of geospatial technologies as a research method. As a feminist geographer, Kwan employs geographic information systems (GIS) to qualitatively explore the gendered, classed, raced, and sexualized aspects of how space is perceived and utilized. In her chapter, she explores the recent trends in the use of geospatial technologies by feminist researchers within and outside the discipline of geography. She is concerned about the traditional uses of this technology by researchers that often excludes issues of difference. She stresses the need for practitioners of geospatial technologies to

> contest the dominant meanings and uses of GT [geospatial technologies] and to participate in struggles against the oppressive or violent effects of these technologies . . . geospatial practices need to be recorporealized and embodied. This involves not only reintroducing long-lost subjectivities (of the researcher/user, as well as of the researched and those affected by these technologies) back into geospatial practices but also making emotions, feelings, values, and ethics an integral aspect of geospatial practices. (p. 614)

In Chapter 30, Natalia Sarkisian provides the reader with a detailed description and in-depth examples of a new software tool for analyzing large quantitative data sets. The tool, SOM, or self-organizing mapping, self-organizes networks by finding patterning in large-scale datasets. The software "learns" from the data in that it adapts its patterns of relationships based on what it learns from the data. As Sarkisian notes:

> The neurons of self-organizing networks learn to recognize groups of similar data points and move toward them in such a way that those neurons that are physically located near each other move toward similar sets of data points. In the case of self-organizing maps, the map units adjust to the probability density of the input data. The result is a topological "map" of the input data, dense where many data points are located and more dispersed where the data density is low. (p. 629)

In fact, Sarkisian notes that emergent technologies such as neural networks mimic brain functioning as it relates to sensory perceptions.

Computer-assisted qualitative data analysis (CAQDAS) and its impact on emergent methods in qualitative research is the subject of Chapter 31. Sharlene Nagy Hesse-Biber and Christine Crofts introduce the historical development of computerized software for the analysis of qualitative data, as well as discuss the range of functions of software products, including prequalitative programs and those specific to qualitative analysis, as well as coding and retrieving software and theory generation software products. Hesse-Biber and Crofts suggest taking a "reflexive approach" to the selection of computer-assisted software programs for qualitative analysis that places the standpoint of the user at the center of software decision making. They provide a number of sensitizing questions to assist users in the selection process and note that these questions "remind users that they are in control of the analysis process and that no technological tool, regardless of its features, can independently 'perform' analysis" (p. 666). Hesse-Biber and Crofts discuss the strengths and weakness of CAQDAS software for qualitative analysis and address future directions for software development, including the analysis of multimedia data—digitized video and audio.

In Chapter 32, Nigel Fielding provides an excellent description of the role of qualitative software in the field of qualitative methods. He looks at how computer-assisted software can assist in the integration, as well as interrelation, of qualitative and quantitative data and provides specific examples of software packages to demonstrate the variety of analysis functions of specific software packages. He outlines some emergent techniques that rely on grid computing and high-performance computing (HPC) to enable researchers to handle a range of archived qualitative data, as well as allowing researchers to access multimodal data (images, sounds, text, and statistics).

Emergent technologies will continue to move toward the development of artificial intelligence—that is, technologies that rely on expert systems, such as the advent of neural network mapping software described by Natalia Sarkisian or the "fourth generation" of computer-assisted software to analyze qualitative data described in Chapters 31 and 32—that also incorporates "expert system" theory. Such technological innovation may increasingly enable the researcher with many of the "human" work involved in coding and analyzing data. As Evans (2002) notes:

> Ultimately, we can expect a system that will monitor, process, and code texts and images with little human intervention. This system may be able to retrieve and manage great quantities of material and may actively identify opportunities for content analysis, devise and test content analytic hypotheses, and even learn as it does so. In other words, it is not feasible to begin working toward a kind of magic in content analysis. Furthermore, this magic is appropriate and even necessary if content analysts are to take full advantage of opportunities

> afforded by the emerging era of electronic databases and interactive media. (Evans, 2002, as cited in Chapter 31, this volume, p. 671)

There are, however, concerns expressed about the downside of technological innovation, especially when there is the real possibility that technology will overshadow human agency. Hesse-Biber (1995) summarizes these apprehensions with the metaphor of "Frankenstein's monster" and notes that "while computers have the potential to revolutionize the field, there is also a possibility for things to run out of control" (p. 26). Her concerns about the use of computer-assisted software for analyzing qualitative data are applicable to many of the new technological innovations discussed in this *Handbook*.

One concern is that using computerized analysis techniques may take out the "craft" or the creative aspects of conducting research, especially as this relates to the analysis of qualitative data—by distancing the researcher from his or her data. As creativity and instinct are increasingly becoming legitimized aspects of research, as noted elsewhere in this volume, the increase in the use of computerized analysis strategies may bump up against other trends in unexpected ways.

The ability of software programs to analyze audio or video data brings up new concerns of data protection and confidentiality. Another concern lies in the ability to adequately train users in the new software programs and the potential for these new software programs to be misapplied as a result of the lack of adequate training or understanding of their use with regard to the particulars of social research.

Natalia Sarkisian's comments on these issues are most applicable here when she discusses the limitations of neural network models. She notes:

> Neural networks are often presented as an assumption-free method of data analysis, in that it is expected that neural networks will be able to provide good output results free of error and bias no matter what. . . . Thus, the good old rule of "garbage in, garbage out" is often neglected when using neural network methodologies. But, although neural network models are more robust, they are not assumption-free . . . their assumptions are just milder and less explicit and, unfortunately, more frequently ignored. (p. 651)

Sarkisian also points out the vast amount of creativity and analytical skills that are required in interpreting neural network analysis: "The researcher must be able to figure out how to interpret the map, to identify the important conceptual domains, to explain what they mean, and to examine how they are related to each other" (p. 651).

Whatever innovations in technology occur in the coming years, it is likely that researcher feedback will step up to provide software developers with valuable "research user experience" in future software development and revisions to existing software programs. It is crucial that researchers using emergent technologies and emergent methods be in communication with each other and that this communication continue to be strengthened. As evidenced throughout this volume, these collaborations and research networks are vital to moving scientific conversations forward—conversations about the best research practices. There are a plethora of new lines of communication, from a number of online user groups and developer groups to electronic mailing lists for users of specific computer software programs. Cross-disciplinary training is also important, and relevant institutions need to create an environment in which employees can learn these technologies, which may include explicit incentives, that do not raise barriers.

This *Handbook* is also an important venue for relaying the theory and practice of emergent methods. Emergent methods are likely to have a very strong impact on the field of social research, as researchers strive to answer difficult and complex social issues within and across their disciplines and within the global society as whole.

References

Hesse-Biber, S. (1995). Unleashing Frankenstein's monster: The use of computers in qualitative research. *Studies in Qualitative Methodology*, 5, 25–41.

Jones, S. (1999). Studying the Net: Intricacies and issues. In S. Jones (Ed.), *Doing Internet research: Critical issues and methods for examining the net* (pp. 1–28). Thousand Oaks, CA: Sage.

Sudweeks, F., & Simoff, S. J. (1999). Complementary explorative data analysis: The reconciliation of quantitative and qualitative principles. In S. Jones (Ed.), *Doing Internet research: Critical issues and methods for examining the net* (pp. 29–56). Thousand Oaks, CA: Sage.

CHAPTER 25

Internet Research as Emergent Practice

Christine Hine

This chapter explores the emergence of research designs and techniques in the face of the recent development and growth in social significance of the Internet. While covering a number of different research traditions, the chapter focuses particularly on the applications of ethnography to the Internet. I first describe the establishment of Internet research as a distinctive field of inquiry before exploring some ways in which the perceived novelty of the Internet has provided the occasion for new research practices to emerge. Various ways in which researchers have adapted their methods to accommodate the social phenomena that they experience on the Internet are described; ultimately, however, most methodological solutions are strongly in dialogue with conventional approaches. The chapter thus concludes with an assessment of the extent to which Internet research methods can appropriately be characterized as innovative.

Internet research was founded in large part on the recognition that the Internet could act as a novel site for social formations. Early Internet research produced considerable interest in research methods, as researchers sought to explore how established methods such as interviews, ethnography, and survey research might be applicable in the new environment. There was a widely held belief that the Internet was novel in socially significant ways, and this perception fueled anxiety about the applicability of approaches transferred from face-to-face settings. In this sense, the methods now available have emerged in the face of the technology, or at least in response to the forms of social interaction that have become visible on the Internet and to the expectations we have about those forms of social interaction. This emergence has happened in dialogue with existing methodological practice, and it has proved problematic to overemphasize breaks with tradition, particularly where questions of research ethics are concerned.

Internet research techniques have thrived on the social sites produced by ordinary Internet users through their everyday use. E-mail has become mainstream, and research practices such as online interviews have built on the increasing transparency of e-mail as a medium for social interaction and become widely accepted by social researchers. Online forums such as bulletin boards, newsgroups,[1] MUDs,[2] and, recently, MMORPGs[3] offer up the possibility of new forms of social formation, such as online community, and have been conceived of as field sites for ethnographic work. Hyperlink analysis and new forms of social network analysis have been built on the availability of Internet data and offer ways of exploring emerging geographies of connection. Websites have offered ways for researchers to present their research and engage with research users, and recently blogs[4] offer intriguing possibilities for opening up research-in-progress for consumption and comment. New sites, therefore, provide new phenomena to study and opportunities for development of new techniques and new forms of engagement with research participants and users. The willingness of Internet researchers to innovate in the face of what appear to be socially innovative practices by users has led Internet research to build up an exciting and fast-maturing array of research techniques. If we think of Internet research practice as restricted to tinkering with techniques, however, we may be neglecting some significant emergent innovations in research design and conceptualization.

Recent Internet research focuses on the embedding of computer-mediated interactions in everyday life and stresses the complex patterning and connections enacted within increasingly media-saturated lives. Viewed in this way, the Internet may also provide the opportunity for alternative conceptualizations of research objects to develop, focusing more on exploring connections than on techniques adapted for discrete sites. Emergent practices of Internet research thus recently focus on exploring the varied textures of contemporary social life as lived through a variety of media, within which the Internet is only one option. Using this approach, the ethnographer allows the research project itself to be emergent through practices of tracing and exploring connections and experiencing boundaries in action, rather than the project and site being defined in advance. A focus on Internet research, therefore, can bring to the fore both the emergence of new techniques and the emergent qualities of the whole research project as an object crafted in dialogue with the goals and experiences of the researcher.

From Experiments to Cyberculture

For almost as long as we have been using computers to communicate, there have been social researchers trying to understand how that communication happens and what its implications might be. Inevitably, different disciplines have been involved along the way, and each has brought its own research methods to bear on the problem. Much of the early work on the effects of particular media on communication processes and outcomes was conducted from the perspectives of social psychology. The effects on group processes were therefore a particular focus of attention, and these effects were often explored through experimental research designs. A particularly well-known perspective on this issue is the "reduced social cues" model, established largely through experimental studies of the effects of medium on group decision making (Kiesler, Siegel, & McGuire, 1984; Sproull & Kiesler, 1986). This form of experiment involves distribution of a task to groups allocated to either face-to-face interaction or a computer conferencing system and the analysis of the resulting interaction according to variables based on levels of participation, content of contributions (such as emotional content or aggression), and task performance. This kind of analysis suggested that consistent differences between media were to be expected, based on the extent to which they allowed social context cues to be transmitted. These cues (e.g., gender, facial expression, intonation) were thought to be absent in textual communications, leading to disinhibiting effects on users. People using textual media were, therefore, expected to participate on a more equal basis but also to display higher levels of aggression.

These experimental approaches suggested that regular effects on interaction might be produced by particular media and also promoted a view of textual computer-mediated communication as inherently limited. Some critics of this perspective within social psychology suggested that, rather than simply comparing computer-mediated interactions with their face-to-face counterparts, it was also important to study computer-mediated interactions under different social conditions. This approach suggested that different outcomes could be observed depending on the extent to which participants were anonymous to one another and the way in which the task was presented to them as either a group endeavor or an individual challenge (Lea & Spears, 1991; Spears, Lea, & Lee, 1990). In addition to experimentally based critiques, observational studies on computer-mediated communication also suggested that consistent effects in equalizing hierarchies were not experienced (Mantovani, 1994). In both cases, the importance of context in shaping the meaning of computer-mediated communication was asserted. Systematic experimental studies of the psychology of Internet behavior continue to have a significant place in the field (Joinson, 2003) and have been particularly interesting on a methodological level in exploring how far application of surveys via the Internet can be designed to enhance rather than inhibit disclosure (Joinson, 2005). Nonetheless, the experimental approach to the Internet has lately been complemented by a rapidly maturing set of methods that seek to explore Internet culture in its own right and downplay the importance of comparing Internet with face-to-face communication. These approaches have also begun to seek to understand Internet use as a situated phenomenon, both as deployed by particular social groups and as integrated into diverse lives. This approach to Internet research has its roots in a set of studies that questioned the "reduced social cues" model of computer-mediated communication and suggested that online social formations could be studied through naturalistic approaches.

In the following sections I explain in more depth the methods deployed by researchers working in this field, beginning with studies that first established the value of applying ethnographic methods to online settings, and then moving on to the diverse ways of mapping online phenomena and exploring their links to offline social life that have developed. First, however, I briefly situate the emergence of this field, drawing heavily on an account by Silver (2000). According to Silver, the field, which he terms *cyberculture studies*, had its origins in the popular cyberculture that developed in the early 1990s. At this time stories began to appear in the popular media about the Internet, and dedicated media outlets, such as *Wired* magazine, appeared, along with newspaper supplements and television shows. *Information superhighway* became a popular term with politicians, and the Internet became a site for the expression of extreme hopes and fears about society. Commercially, Internet companies became a favorite place to invest money, and the dot-com bubble grew. Culturally, the Internet was represented as a new frontier and a site for the reinvention of society. At around the same time as this popular cyberculture was booming, the academic field that Silver describes as cyberculture studies began to emerge, building on this air of expectation and novelty. Cyberculture scholars began studying the social formations that were appearing online. Strong links with postmodern theory shaped a particular focus on identity play and the discursive construction of culture and community.

Silver (2000) suggests that the early phase of cyberculture studies has been succeeded by critical cyberculture studies, which is less celebratory in style and focuses on the integration of the Internet into a widely construed social life rather than narrowly focusing on the online world and treating it as a separate social sphere. The critical cyberculture style of research focuses on social and political factors that shape use of the Internet and explores the processes of interpretation through which it is made meaningful. The Internet, in this approach, becomes more thoroughly contextualized with other spheres of social life, and Internet research becomes more continuous with other approaches to social research (Hine, 2004). Nonetheless, some very specific research techniques have developed in order to allow social researchers to make sense of Internet use *as* social interaction. Internet research is far from being an established discipline in its own right (Baym, 2005; Jones, 2005), but as a field of research that has provided a focal point for researchers from diverse disciplines, it has inevitably had much to say about the applicability of existing methodological approaches to the Internet (Hine, 2005a). Although there is much continuity with existing methods, there have also been creative adaptations of traditional approaches and the opportunity for dialogue about the adequacy of various approaches (Hine, 2005b). In the following sections I explore in more detail some areas in which methodological issues have arisen for Internet researchers, focusing first on the establishment of the Internet as an appropriate field site for ethnography.

Claiming the Internet as a Field Site

A significant part of the popular cyberculture, which crossed over into cyberculture studies within an academic context, was its interest in the possibilities of new kinds of social formation happening online. Howard Rheingold, a journalist, was particularly influential in promoting the idea that online formations could be a new kind of community (Rheingold, 1993). He described experiences of participation in the WELL, an online conferencing system in which he claimed that people formed close bonds and sustained relationships, albeit largely through textual communication. Developers of MUDs began to write about the emergence of social structures in these online settings (Bruckman, 1992; Curtis, 1996). This kind of phenomenon seemed very different from the restricted and impersonal interactions that some psychological models had predicted. Preconceptions about the limits of computer-mediated communication provided a foil for empirical, often naturalistic, studies that aimed to find out just what people were doing with the technologies newly at their disposal. Academic studies of online social phenomena began to emerge, and the term *cybersociety* (Jones, 1995) was coined to capture the growing sense that rich and complex social phenomena were possible in text-based environments after all.

Both popular cyberculture and cyberculture studies were thus intrigued by the emergence of social phenomena on the Internet. Within academic contexts, a range of disciplinary approaches began to colonize the Internet as a field site, deploying their existing methods and adapting them to suit the conditions encountered online. The study of online communities, in particular, was built on the application of ethnographic approaches. The participant-observation approach to in-depth understanding of cultural complexity appeared to be particularly appropriate for capturing the kinds of emergent structures that were being encountered. Ethnography aspires to be a holistic approach to understanding culture, a discipline that studies lived experience in its own right and expects diverse aspects of experience to be interconnected. The ethnographer's participation is a means to engagement with those who inhabit the chosen domain and a means to reflection on the various forms of experience that the domain encompasses. Claiming to do ethnography in an online setting is therefore a quite strong claim about the nature of the social interactions that go on there, both between participants and between the ethnographer and the research participants. This need not be considered a straightforward instance of the recognition of affinity between a method (ethnography) and an application domain (online forums). Rather, the emergence of online ethnography can usefully be thought of as the product of a particular set of claims about the nature of social interactions in online settings. Early Internet ethnographers were pioneering a view of the Internet as a cultural domain in its own right, to which the notion of holistic inquiry could legitimately apply.

The early Internet ethnographies established a version of participant observation for online settings that relied on varying combinations of reading messages, posting contributions or surveys, e-mailing participants, and arranging face-to-face meetings. Correll (1995) carried out an ethnography of a lesbian bar hosted on a bulletin board system and conducted ethnography primarily by observing the interactions that went on in the (purely textual) bar environment, although she also carried out e-mail and telephone interviews and met some participants in person. Baym (2000) carried out an ethnographic study of a newsgroup focused on a popular soap opera (*rec.arts.tv.soaps*, or r.a.t.s). Her ethnography comprised 3 years of observation and participation, aiming toward a naturalistic understanding of what went on in the online group, supplemented by more direct engagement with participants through qualitative online surveys. Baym studied the emergence of a culture rich in humor and interpersonal relationships.

Baym argued that the online context provides a particularly useful place to study the practices of being an audience. She suggested that we have a chance to see the richness and breadth of social practices that engaging with a soap opera entails within this online environment. She compares this approach favorably with the artificial settings created in focus groups and with narrower understandings of the audience as interpreters of text. Baym positioned her study thus: "When I tell the story of r.a.t.s as an audience community, then, I am seeking to show how a collection of previously disconnected individuals took their shared interest in a pop culture text and transformed it into a rich and meaningful interpersonal social world" (2000, p. 21). As well as being a means to reflect on the richness of online social formations, the ethnography of this particular kind of formation is thus also a strategic contribution to a wider field of audience studies.

Some versions of online ethnography focus more on documenting the online experience itself rather than using the Internet as a means to observe a non-Internet specific social phenomenon, as Baym did. Markham (1998) found a reflexive style of ethnography useful for exploring the multiple experiences of the Internet. Rather than finding a single way to conceptualize the Internet experience, she argued that it operated under different circumstances as a tool, a place, and a way of being. She arrived at this position as much through her own use of the Internet to carry out the research as through the interviews she conducted with people she met online. She focused particularly on her own experiences as a means to question aspects of the online environment that might otherwise be taken for granted if we looked at the goings-on within a particular field site. She also found herself drawn into some unconventional writing practices in order to portray the experiences she had:

> writing of moments, presenting narrative fragments, speaking with the voices of others, speaking for myself, and speaking as a scholar all seem well-suited to an ethnography of this place I created with many other people, where few boundaries are heeded and most tradi-

> tions and norms arise and are woven out of fragmented exchanges of texts. (Markham, 1998, p. 19)

This version of ethnography stresses the importance of going online as a means to an in-depth understanding of the online experience but focuses less on strategic contributions to the understanding of other social phenomena. It also largely dispenses with the notion of a discrete field site, other than the online world itself, as a field of experience.

Internet ethnography has addressed a wide range of different forms of social interaction. One of the most common early sites was the newsgroup, as studied by Baym (2000). These subject-based discussion forums were asynchronous and often archived, meaning that researchers could follow messages as posted in real time but could also trawl back through archives and carry out systematic historical investigations. Researchers could also lurk without participants being aware of their presence if they wished, although this, of course, limits the possibilities for engagement. Ethnographers have also been particularly interested in text-based social realities (such as MUDs [multi-user domains]) in which users can interact in real time, describing both their characters and the environments that they inhabit (Kendall, 2002; Schaap, 2002). Here real-time interaction can be challenging for the researcher to keep track of and participate in meaningfully, but log files can be saved for later review. Recently, graphical environments, such as massive multiplayer online games, have provided stimulating sites to study and new challenges for ethnographers in finding appropriate ways to participate, record data, and engage with users (Taylor, 1999) and in developing an appropriately skilled player to be present in the first place. Various forms of Internet interaction, therefore, offer up possibilities as ethnographic field sites, but each offers its own challenges in terms of the techniques the researcher needs in order to be effectively present and to record significant events. Ethnographers in more conventional settings have often had to develop specific linguistic and practical skills in order to engage with their informants, and Internet ethnography is possibly little different in this regard, although the particular skills are new.

Although Internet ethnography is a diverse field, a large part of the rhetorical establishment of the complexity and social richness of Internet social formations depended on the claim that ethnography in some form was indeed an appropriate method. If the phenomena encountered online were rich enough to count as culture, then it seemed apparent that ethnographic methods would apply and vice versa. This is not to suggest, however, that it was straightforward to work out how to be an ethnographer online. Ethnographers of online field sites have had to struggle with concerns about how to develop appropriate presence and how to present themselves in their interactions with participants, how far to trust the revelations that online informants made to them, whether to carry out wholly overt research or to exploit the enhanced possibilities of covert research that the Internet offers, and how to cope with the resulting deluges of data (Fox & Roberts, 1999; Guimarães, 2005; Kanayama, 2003; Lindlof & Shatzer, 1998; Paccagnella, 1997; Rutter & Smith, 2005). None of these issues are confined to Internet ethnography. Nonetheless, perceptions of the Internet as providing for novel forms of social interaction cast a particular spotlight on questions about the applicability and reliability of methods. In particular, the perception of the Internet as a domain in which identity play was rife highlighted concerns about the authenticity of interpretations made on the basis of online observations alone (Paccagnella, 1997).

This air of anxiety about the application of conventional methods to online interaction and the possibility that fundamental assumptions might be threatened have fueled considerable methodological reflection in relation to other established methods, such as interviews (e.g., Illingworth, 2001; Kivits, 2005; Madge & O'Connor, 2002) and discourse analysis (Herring, 1996a, 2001), as well as ethnography. A further area of particularly intense examination has been the ethics of using Internet data in social science research. Here the concern is whether researchers may have been overenthused by the accessibility of the Internet as a field site and been "swarming over the virtual landscape, peering around at virtual natives and writing busily in their virtual field notes" (Stone, 1995, p. 243) without due respect for the people involved. Some feared that Internet researchers, in their excitement about this new field and led by the aura of innovation that surrounds it to assume that usual conventions of informed consent did not apply, were inappropriately neglecting ethical frameworks for respectful research.

The extent to which existing ethical standards should apply to online settings was much debated, with particular concerns about the necessity and practicality of negotiating informed consent (e.g., Fox & Roberts, 1999; Frankel & Siang, 1999; King, 1996; Sharf, 1999; Waskul & Douglass, 1996). The Association of Internet Researchers prepared a set of guidelines to assist researchers in coming to appropriate decisions about the use of Internet data (Ess & AoIR Ethics Working Committee, 2002). It became clear that a single model was unlikely to suit all situations. There was variation between disciplines, and some disputed the automatic application of a human-subjects model to Internet research ethics (Bassett & O'Riordan, 2002; Herring, 1996b; White, 2002). Bruckman (2002) strongly advocated the deployment of informed consent wherever possible, but, with Hudson, later argued that some circumstances merited application for a waiver of informed consent, notably chat rooms in which participants could be left unaware that they were being studied and in which the research was not considered to be harmful in any way (Hudson & Bruckman, 2004, 2005). The ethical dimension of online research has proved to be a particularly rich source of debate, enlivening an area of concern often otherwise considered settled.

Thus far I have described research that concentrates on the online sphere as a relatively discrete cultural domain. This way of thinking has been productive of considerable efforts to develop appropriate methods for the exploration of the new domain: The possibility that new social phenomena might be arising on the Internet raises the possibility that methodological adjustments may be required. The image of the Internet as apart from everyday life provided impetus for this air of innovation. However, this portrayal clearly does not exhaust the useful ways in which to think about the Internet, and it became apparent to many researchers that the Internet was often not a discrete sphere but was embedded in everyday life in diverse ways. This realization brought its own methodological challenges, particularly in carving out manageable objects of study. Many researchers have risen to these challenges and tried to develop methods that allow them to move between online and offline and to examine the ways in which the Internet becomes a part of everyday life. In the next section I turn to this body of research to explore the methodological solutions that have emerged through attempts to address the Internet as an embedded phenomenon.

Interweaving the Internet with Everyday Life

Although the treatment of online domains as field sites for ethnographic research in their own right was a persuasive step in taking online social experiences seriously, it was apparent early on that this approach did not encompass all of the significant things to say about the Internet. Miller and Slater (2000) in particular made a strong pitch that the Internet was rarely, if ever, experienced as a separate domain of virtual experience and instead should be studied as it was made meaningful in particular contexts. Their ethnography of the Internet began in Trinidad, and while they explored online contexts that Trinidadians used, they focused in particular on the ways in which Trinidadians made sense of the Internet and made it their own. Miller and Slater made a very distinctive contribution to the establishment of methods for studying the Internet with their proposal for a focus on comparative ethnographies of the Internet in context. Their approach to understanding the Internet as interwoven with everyday life and made meaningful in specific contexts is, however, shared across different methodological traditions. Mackay (2005) argues that we can usefully draw on existing approaches to the study of media audiences and media consumption in domestic settings for our explorations of new media, such as the Internet. Mackay shares with Miller and Slater the concern that we should not reject established research designs through too great a focus on the Internet as a new form of social space. Bakardjieva and Smith (2001) similarly draw on face-to-face interviews and tours of the home to understand the embedding of new media in domestic contexts. These researchers remind us that the Internet coexists with and is consumed within more conventional social spaces and thus continues to be amenable to established methods.

Approaches that explore the embedding of the Internet within everyday life have become more prominent in recent years, in the phase that Silver (2000) describes as critical cyberculture studies. Wellman and Haythornthwaite's (2002) collection brings together chapters from a diverse set of qualitative and quantitative methodological approaches, including surveys, home visits, and time-use diaries, all seeking to explore the Internet as an integral feature of daily life. Woolgar (2002) also assembles a diverse set of disciplinary perspectives to explore the implications of the Internet and new media for contemporary social life. This collection arrives at the conclusion that we need methodologies that give us detailed insight into the origins and usage of these new technologies and that do not assume in advance what will count as real or virtual or what the connections between them will be. Howard and Jones (2004) also assemble a diverse array of methodological approaches in their exploration of new media as "embedded media" (Howard, 2004). Implicit within these collections is the strong suggestion that the integration of the Internet with everyday life is a complex topic that is amenable to and benefits from a combination of approaches. The methods used in these collections are recognizable from pre-Internet days and encompass surveys, interviews, diaries, focus groups, observation, documentary and historical analysis, and experimental or comparative studies.

At the same time as this return to traditional methods and research designs as a way of viewing the Internet within its everyday contexts was occurring, other researchers were trying to develop approaches that would enable them to explore the diverse connections that suffused the Internet. While rejecting the notion that cyberculture was a discrete sphere always to be studied apart from offline life, these approaches acknowledged the rich social complexity of the Internet and aimed to develop research designs that still did it justice. Rejecting both the online and the offline as self-evident field sites within which an investigation could be contained, these approaches sought to traverse the online–offline boundary and explore the ways in which this boundary was (or was not) relevant in organizing social experience. A variety of forms of study thus emerged to combine studies of online and offline sites. Howard (2002) proposed a network ethnography that used network analysis of online data as a means to orient offline investigations. He described this novel combination of methods as a particularly suitable way to go about studying the kind of distributed organizations increasingly enabled by new technologies.

Howard (2002) proposed a particular methodological combination aimed at addressing a specific organizational form.

Other approaches have proposed pursuing the connections that arise through the course of the study in a more adaptive fashion and have been less prescriptive about the appropriate way to combine online and offline. In *Virtual Ethnography*, Hine (2000) proposed a connective approach to the study of the Internet that would be open to its qualities as both a cultural site and a cultural artifact and would explore diverse ways in which the Internet was made meaningful. The case study through which this approach was developed was a media event. Through a connective ethnographic approach it proved possible to explore the ways in which use of the Internet was interpreted in the media and the ways in which people expressed their responses to the media event and their understandings of the Internet in their Web pages and message board posts. Subsequently, in work on scientists' uses of the Internet, a similar approach has been used to explore the ways in which emerging uses of the Internet make sense within a particular material culture, political and institutional context, and communication ecology (Hine, 2007, 2008).

Constable's (2003) work on long-distance relationships also combines online participation and observation with explorations of the contexts within which online activities take place and make sense, using each to inform the other. She studied mailing lists and websites on which American men were meeting women from China and the Philippines to find marriage partners. Constable also traveled to visit people that she met online, and thus she was able to contextualize her online observations in the settings from which they originated. Orgad (2005a, 2005b) also combines online and offline methods in her study of the uses of the Internet by women living with breast cancer. She argues that online and offline experiences contextualize one another and that neither should automatically be taken as preceding or explaining the other. By moving between contexts, the researcher is encouraged to question her own assumptions and use the two contexts to interrogate one another.

Connective approaches can seem very attractive when trying to understand the experience of heavy users of new media. In this kind of study it can be important to follow people as they inhabit various media spaces and to reflect both on how they came to be there and how their potential as social actors is shaped by various forms of engagement. This approach is exemplified by Leander and McKim (2003) in their proposals for studying the online practices of adolescents. They propose a diverse set of strategies for going online with adolescents, following bodies and flows of information and studying the construction of boundaries. They also suggest that the notion of "context" is far too static to capture the diverse ways in which experiences inform and interact with one another. In the process of taking on the complexity of these situations, Leander and McKim found themselves drawn "to imaginatively expand current methodologies" (p. 237). Once again, the Internet provides a challenge to established methodologies, not necessarily because it is not amenable to existing approaches but because it stimulates the imagination of the researcher in new directions.

As well as enabling the study of the experience of individuals, connective approaches have also been deployed to understand the origins and uses of some online objects. In their work on scientific databases on the Web, Beaulieu and Simakova (Beaulieu, 2005; Beaulieu & Simakova, 2006) draw on various strategies to work out how the databases have become embedded in the Internet and in scientific practices. Specifically, they advocate an ethnographic approach to hyperlinks that enables the ethnographer to use them as a means to move around the field of the World Wide Web exploring the connections of the database. An ethnographic treatment of hyperlinks also involves reflection on the circumstances through which they arise and their diverse meanings. This approach connects with work on the ethnography of infrastructure (Star, 1999), using the hyperlink as a means to both pursue the reach of an infrastructure for knowledge production and to reflect on its contingency.

The connective and mobile studies that I have described aim to combine online and offline research in contingent ways that reflect everyday experiences and the experienced reality of the Internet. In moving away from the security of a predefined field site, whether online or offline, these ethnographers threaten their links to the ethnographic tradition. Researchers increasingly find themselves drawn away from self-contained field sites and into the exploration of heterogeneous connections when they set out to explore lived experiences that traverse the online–offline boundary. It then becomes problematic to sustain the claims about in-depth and holistic analysis on which ethnography founds itself as a distinctive method, because engagement becomes more fleeting. Field sites increasingly appear as a construct of the researcher rather than as preexisting entities. These mobile and partial approaches have therefore often had to justify themselves on grounds both of their strategic importance as ways of addressing a particular lived social reality and in terms of their methodological foundations. In this latter respect, ethnographies that cross between online and offline settings have usefully been able to draw on some currents of contemporary anthropological thinking. The media-saturated world is spatially and socially complex, and this fact has translated into a new focus for ethnographers on the ways that the field is constituted (Amit, 1999; Gupta & Ferguson, 1997) and the strategies that can be deployed for seeing the global in the local (Burawoy, 2000). An acceptance of multi-sited approaches (Marcus, 1995, 1998) to the study of contemporary culture has been particularly useful in positioning connective studies of the Internet as a part of wider ongoing trends in ethnographic methodology

Although connective ethnographies have emerged as a particular means of coming to grips with the embedding of the Internet into everyday life, it would not be fair to represent this emergent practice as wholly novel. Ethnographies of the Internet take diverse forms, but their justification is rooted in conventional versions of ethnography. The early versions of Internet ethnography tended to stress the cultural richness and complexity of the Internet in itself and consequently relied on very conventional notions of ethnographic engagement and field site translated to the new medium. Various forms of connective and mobile ethnography have recently engaged with the Internet experience and moved further away from the traditional notion of field work, but they have still maintained a connection with ethnographic principles through ongoing debates about the constitution of the field. This version of ethnographic principles maintains the notion of the lived experience of the ethnographer as a means to engagement with those who form the subjects of the research and as a reflexive tool for exploration of difference. It is sometimes controversial to characterize the end product as ethnography, but there are many researchers aiming to draw on the ethnographic spirit to orient their studies of the embedded Internet and to find ways of capturing its richness and complexity.

Tracing Patterns and Tracking Networks

Ethnographers of the Internet tend to rely on the reflexive engagement of the ethnographer with the field as their primary methodological focus. Internet data, however, can be overwhelming in its diversity and sheer volume. Mobile and connective approaches intensify this concern, as they involve casting off the idea of any kind of exhaustive or intensive engagement with a bounded field. In this circumstance, various forms of systematic data storage and exploration become appealing. However, Internet data also have some major methodological attractions that researchers from other traditions have been able to capitalize on. The quantity and availability of Internet data have thus, in themselves, provided the conditions for some innovative methodological approaches to emerge. In particular, the ease of capturing Internet data and exploring patterns within them has inspired some innovations. In this section I explore some of the new research designs that the accessibility of Internet data on a large scale has inspired and once again consider the research traditions with which these approaches connect.

From the early days of Internet research, there have been some large-scale projects that attempt to characterize the Internet experience. ProjectH (Sudweeks, McLaughlin, & Rafaeli, 1998) was a content analysis of a large sample of messages posted on the Usenet newsgroups, organized as an international collaborative project. The organization of the project itself was a matter for some reflection, as the collaborative work was largely carried out using the same media that the group set out to study (Sudweeks & Rafaeli, 1996). Content analysis is a familiar approach for such a large-scale endeavor, and it translated relatively easily to the Internet situation, in which the focus was on the content of individual messages. The threaded structure of Internet discussions does, however, pose some challenges for analysis of content, and where social structure is significant, a straightforward content analysis seems less appealing. To address this issue, Smith (1999) developed a means of analyzing Usenet data to explore important features of participation and social structure. His NetScan facility (*netscan.research.microsoft.com*) allows researchers to explore temporal aspects of newsgroups that interest them, together with the posting profiles of participants and links with other newsgroups. NetScan plays on the availability of Internet data to provide a means for researchers, and, of course, participants themselves, to visualize qualities of the ongoing interactions.

Visualization of Internet patterns and connections has been both a popular phenomenon and a useful tool for researchers. In their book on the mapping of the Internet, Dodge and Kitchin (2000) assemble an impressive collection of visualizations that capture the geography of the Internet itself, depict specific spaces on the Internet, and explore connections between online and offline geographies. The accompanying *Atlas of Cyberspace* (*www.cybergeography.org/atlas/*) offers further stimulus for imagining the Internet as social space and, argues Dodge (2005), could provide a useful methodological tool in its ability to highlight potentially sociologically interesting patterns and thus provoke the design of innovative research projects.

Beyond the role of visualizations as stimuli to the imagination of researchers, there have also been research traditions that focus on production of visualizations as an analytical tool. Social network analysis in particular thrives on the Internet, both because the Internet provides interesting new phenomena to explore and because the ready availability of Internet data provides new ways to capture information on social networks (Garton, Haythornthwaite, & Wellman, 1997). Social network analysis has also been applied to the connections between blogs (Herring et al., 2005). The most obvious site for carrying out network analysis on the Web is, of course, the analysis of hyperlinks themselves. Link analysis has become a well-established method for visualizing the differentiated space of the World Wide Web (Thelwall, 2004), although what a hyperlink means is always open for interpretation in sociological terms (Thelwall, 2006). A form of link analysis has also been used effectively in exploring the extent to which offline connections and affinities are reflected in links between websites (Rogers & Marres, 2000) and between blogs (Rogers, 2005).

On another scale, researchers have conceived of the Web as reflecting offline developments through the emergence of Web spheres that contain diverse websites connected with an event, such as an election or the 2004 Indian Ocean tsunami (Foot & Schneider, 2006; Schneider & Foot, 2005). Web sphere analysis has been conceived as a method that begins with the research team collecting an archive of websites connected with the issue of interest through successive searches and the pursuit of connections. Developments in time can be explored through capture of snapshots. Subsequent analysis of the Web sphere is carried out through annotation and extended forms of content analysis focusing on text, visuals, and interactive features, allowing for characterization of the Web sphere and exploration of regular features and patterns. Successive Web spheres relating to recurring events such as elections can be captured and compared to explore how Internet use varies over time.

In this form of research there has often been a suspicion about reliance on ready-to-hand Internet tools such as popular search engines. If one seeks a controlled sample of hyperlinks, or a representative Web sphere, reliance on search engines would mean abdicating control over the timing of sampling and the criteria for selection. In link analysis, a crawler under the control of the researcher would often be preferred (Thelwall, 2004). In Web sphere analysis the researcher might combine several different ways of identifying websites of interest, including use of multiple search engines and following of links (Schneider & Foot, 2005). Beaulieu (2005) found that some very important ways in which the databases she was interested in were embedded in other sites were not visible using search engines. Use of search engines needs to be treated with caution in social research in order not to take on board an unwanted influence on shaping the object of study. Nonetheless, it is possible to use ready-to-hand tools in an ethnographic spirit, drawing on the reflexive tradition to think about the ways in which these tools effectively shape the Internet experience for all users (Hine, 2007).

There are diverse ways of conceptualizing the World Wide Web as an object of study (Schneider & Foot, 2004), and in large part we, as social scientists, do this through the methodologies at our disposal to imagine our projects (Mitra & Cohen, 1999; Wakeford, 2000), but we also do this through our own experiences as members of an Internet-saturated culture. As Silver (2000) argues, the origins of cyberculture studies have close connections with the emergence of a popular cyberculture. It seems likely that our current research uses of the Internet are still shaped by perceptions from the broader culture of Internet use in which we participate. This shapes, also, the tools that seem reasonable to deploy within our own research process. Thus far in this chapter I have described Internet research as a somewhat disengaged phenomenon, in which Internet researchers treat Internet users as the "other" to be described and explained. The reflexive element to Internet research has also become apparent, however, in the adoption of new media technologies by Internet researchers in the research process itself, challenging this disengaged stance. New media have sometimes offered ways of reconceiving the outputs of the research and rethinking the relationship between researchers and those about whom they write. Sometimes this is a relatively mild adaptation, such as the use of online journal publishing, whereas in other cases the intervention in the research process is more radical.

The emergence of various forms of online publishing has helped to make the products of research more widely accessible, and Internet researchers have been very active in developing online journals. Online journals tend, however, to mimic the style of printed journal articles, and hence are not particularly innovative in form, largely reproducing the prevailing tendency toward an impersonal authorial voice and the presentation of research results as a nonnegotiable finished artifact. Other uses of the Internet by researchers, notably personal websites and blogs, have been recognized by some as having potential for a more radical rethinking of research practice. Posting of interim research results on personal websites provides interesting ways to engage with research participants and allows participants to research the researcher before a meeting. This has the potential to provide some interesting shifts in relations between researcher and researched, although of course some communities will be more attuned to these possibilities than others. Having researched for some time among fellow academics, I am aware that my personal website and the writings that it offers have been particularly helpful in building trusting research relationships with this community.

A number of Internet-related books have developed websites to accompany the text, allowing the presentation of enhanced visual materials and provision for more interaction with data (see, e.g., Foot & Schneider, 2006; Miller & Slater, 2000). Blogging (the maintenance of regularly updated diaries and the accompanying practices of mutual linking and commenting by communities of bloggers) has also been adopted by Internet researchers as a means to engage with the research process and has offered some intriguing ways to think about the role of the medium of presentation in shaping the project itself (Paquet, 2002). Mortensen and Walker (2002) described the use of blogs in their research on online gaming communities, finding that the continually updated and networked form provided a means of reflection that led them to see writing the blog as a way of doing the research, thus tying the act of writing into the process. Blog researcher Lilia Efimova (*blog.mathemagenic.com*) has reflected extensively in her own blog about the impacts that the form has had on her work. In particular, she explores the adoption of blogging as a means to develop a reflexive autoethnographic style. New media, therefore, have provided stimulus to the rethinking of research practice, not just in the new social phenomena they offer up to be studied but also in the opportunities they offer to rethink the research process. A number of Internet researchers have thus made the move from tracking connections and tracing patterns to participating in the networks themselves.

Conclusion: How New Is Internet Research?

I have described here a series of ways in which the emergence of the Internet has stimulated discussion of research methods and research ethics and has provided the occasion for new techniques to be developed. Even when the techniques are recognizable from existing traditions, the advent of the Internet has stimulated debate about their resilience in the face of this new medium. As well as developing techniques to address the particular qualities of the Internet as a social phenomenon, researchers have also concentrated on diverse ways of conceptualizing research projects. There prove to be many ways of conceiving of the Internet and the World Wide Web as objects of research, each oriented toward a particular set of research questions and building on a particular research tradition. Internet researchers come from diverse disciplines and bring their methods with them. There is thus no single accepted means of addressing the Internet. Internet research itself is not a discipline but an interdiscipline, a field or a research network populated by heterogeneous perspectives (Baym, 2005; Hine, 2005a). Researchers who orient their work toward the Internet are thus also often still rooted in more conventional disciplines. This possibly accounts for some of the insistence on linking the methods for studying the Internet back to established traditions. Internet research approaches are rarely claimed as radically new, being presented more often as extensions in the spirit of existing traditions. It is in their uses of new media for presenting the processes and products of research that some Internet researchers seem to come closest to radical innovations. More often, however, innovations in Internet research are presented as minor adjustments (Jankowski & van Selm, 2005) or as ultimately not troubling fundamental epistemological principles (Beaulieu, 2004).

There is, then, ambivalence about the innovative status of the Internet itself and the associated methodologies of social research. Although the perceived novelty of the Internet has encouraged many, including social researchers, to get involved and to take seriously the prospect of new phenomena, the experience has often been a more rooted one, mingling a sense of continuity with tradition with its air of novelty. In order to be a sustainable resource, Internet use and Internet research methods have to be meaningful in the context of everyday life and recognizable academic disciplines. The emergent practice of Internet research tries to take seriously our feeling that something new might be going on but without casting off the disciplinary traditions that ground our reflections and provide the field on which debates about methodological adequacy are played out.

Notes

1. An asynchronous text-based form of communication on the Internet. Newsgroups are usually dedicated to discussion of a subject area specified in the name of the group.

2. A MUD is a multiuser dungeon (or domain); a synchronous form of textual communication. Players are represented by characters who interact with one another and with an environment that is also wholly textual.

3. An MMORPG is a massive, multiplayer online role-playing game. These online environments allow players to participate in real-time interactions within graphical environments. Actions are carried out by graphical avatars representing the players, supplemented by textual chat and sometimes speech.

4. Online diaries.

References

Amit, V. (Ed.). (1999). *Constructing the field*. London: Routledge.

Bakardjieva, M., & Smith, R. (2001). The Internet in everyday life: Computer networking from the standpoint of the domestic user. *New Media and Society*, *3*(1), 67–83.

Bassett, E. H., & O'Riordan, K. (2002). Ethics of Internet research: Contesting the human subjects research model. *Ethics and Information Technology*, *4*(3), 233–247.

Baym, N. (2000). *Tune in, log on: Soaps, fandom and online community*. Thousand Oaks, CA: Sage.

Baym, N. (2005). Introduction: Internet research as it isn't, is, could be and should be. *Information Society*, *21*(4), 229–232.

Beaulieu, A. (2004). Mediating ethnography: Objectivity and the making of ethnographies of the Internet. *Social Epistemology*, *18*(2–3), 139–163.

Beaulieu, A. (2005). Sociable hyperlinks: An ethnographic approach to connectivity. In C. Hine (Ed.), *Virtual methods: Issues in social research on the Internet* (pp. 183–198). Oxford, UK: Berg.

Beaulieu, A., & Simakova, E. (2006). Textured connectivity: An ethnographic approach to understanding the timescape of hyperlinks. *Cybermetrics*, *10*(1). Retrieved October 10, 2006, from *www.cindoc.csic.es/cybermetrics/articles/v10i1p6.html*

Bruckman, A. (1992). *Identity workshop: Emergent social and psychological phenomena in text-based virtual reality*. Retrieved October 10, 2006, from *www-static.cc.gatech.edu/~asb/papers/identity-workshop.rtf*

Bruckman, A. (2002). *Ethical guidelines for research online*. Retrieved October 10, 2006, from *www.cc.gatech.edu/~asb/ethics*

Burawoy, M. (Ed.). (2000). *Global ethnography: Forces, connections and imaginations in a postmodern world*. Berkeley: University of California Press.

Constable, N. (2003). *Romance on a global stage: Pen pals, virtual ethnography and "mail order" marriages*. Berkeley: University of California Press.

Correll, S. (1995). An ethnography of an electronic bar: The lesbian cafe. *Journal of Contemporary Ethnography*, *24*(3), 270–298.

Curtis, P. (1996). Mudding: Social phenomena in text-based virtual realities. In P. Ludlow (Ed.), *High noon on the electronic frontier: Conceptual issues in cyberspace* (pp. 347–373). Cambridge, MA: MIT Press.

Dodge, M. (2005). The role of maps in virtual research

methods. In C. Hine (Ed.), *Virtual methods: Issues in social research on the Internet* (pp. 113–128). Oxford, UK: Berg.

Dodge, M., & Kitchin, R. (2000). *Mapping cyberspace.* London: Routledge.

Ess, C., & Association of Internet Researchers Ethics Working Committee. (2002). *Ethical decision-making and Internet research: Recommendations from the AoIR ethics working committee.* Retrieved October 10, 2006, from *www.aoir.org/reports/ethics.pdf*

Foot, K. A., & Schneider, S. M. (2006). *Web campaigning.* Cambridge, MA: MIT Press.

Fox, N., & Roberts, C. (1999). GPs in cyberspace: The ethnography of a "virtual community." *Sociological Review, 47*(4), 643–671.

Frankel, M. S., & Siang, S. (1999). *Ethical and legal aspects of human subjects research on the Internet.* Retrieved October 10, 2006, from *www.aaas.org/spp/sfrl/projects/intres/report.pdf*

Garton, L., Haythornthwaite, C., & Wellman, B. (1997). Studying online social networks. *Journal of Computer Mediated Communication, 3*(1). Retrieved October 10, 2006, from *jcmc.indiana.edu/vol3/issue1/garton.html*

Guimarães, M. J. L., Jr. (2005). Doing anthropology in cyberspace: Fieldwork boundaries and social environments. In C. Hine (Ed.), *Virtual methods: Issues in social research on the Internet* (pp. 141–156). Oxford, UK: Berg.

Gupta, A., & Ferguson, J. (Eds.). (1997). *Anthropological locations: Boundaries and grounds of a field science.* Berkeley: University of California Press.

Herring, S. (Ed.). (1996a). *Computer-mediated communication: Linguistic, social and cross-cultural perspectives.* Amsterdam: Benjamins.

Herring, S. (1996b). Linguistic and critical analysis of computer-mediated communication: Some ethical and scholarly considerations. *Information Society, 12*(2), 153–168.

Herring, S. C. (2001). Computer mediated discourse. In D. Schiffrin, D. Tannen, & H. E. Hamilton (Eds.), *Handbook of discourse analysis* (pp. 612–634). Malden, MA: Blackwell.

Herring, S. C., Kouper, I., Paolillo, J. C., Scheidt, L. A., Tyworth, M., Welsch, P., et al. (2005). Conversations in the blogosphere: An analysis "from the bottom up." In *Proceedings of the Thirty-Eighth Hawai'i International Conference on System Sciences (HICSS-38)* (p. 107b). Los Alamitos: IEEE Press.

Hine, C. (2000). *Virtual ethnography.* London: Sage.

Hine, C. (2004). Social research methods and the Internet: A thematic review. *Sociological Research Online, 9*(2). Retrieved October 10, 2006, from *www.socresonline.org.uk/9/2/hine.html*

Hine, C. (2005a). Internet research and the sociology of cyber-social-scientific knowledge. *Information Society, 21*(4), 239–248.

Hine, C. (2005b). Virtual methods and the sociology of cyber-social scientific knowledge. In C. Hine (Ed.), *Virtual methods: Issues in social research on the Internet* (pp. 1–13). Oxford, UK: Berg.

Hine, C. (2007). Connective ethnography for the exploration of e-science. *Journal of Computer Mediated Communication, 12*(2). Retrieved October 10, 2006, from *jcmc.indiana.edu/vol12/issue2/hine.html*

Hine, C. (2008). *Systematics as cyberscience: Computers, change and continuity in science.* Cambridge, MA: MIT Press.

Howard, P. (2002). Network ethnography and the hypermedia organization: New organizations, new media, new methods. *New Media and Society, 4*(4), 551–575.

Howard, P. N. (2004). Embedded media: Who we know, what we know, and society online. In P. N. Howard & S. Jones (Eds.), *Society online: The Internet in context* (pp. 1–27). Thousand Oaks, CA: Sage.

Howard, P. N., & Jones, S. (Eds.). (2004). *Society online: The Internet in context.* Thousand Oaks, CA: Sage.

Hudson, J. M., & Bruckman, A. (2004). "Go away": Participant objections to being studied and the ethics of chatroom research. *Information Society, 20*(2), 127–139.

Hudson, J. M., & Bruckman, A. (2005). Using empirical data to reason about Internet research ethics. In H. Gellersen, K. Schmidt, M. Beaudovin-Lafon, & W. Mackay (Eds.), *Proceedings of the European Conference on Computer-Supported Cooperative Work (ECSCW)* (pp. 287–306). Paris: Kluwer Academic. Retrieved October 10, 2006, from *www.static.cc.gatech.edu/~jhudson/publications/ecscw05.pdf*

Illingworth, N. (2001). The Internet matters: Exploring the use of the Internet as a research tool. *Sociological Research Online, 6*(2). Retrieved October 10, 2006, from *www.socresonline.org.uk/6/2/illingworth.html*

Jankowski, N. W., & van Selm, M. (2005). Epilogue: Methodological concerns and innovations in Internet research. In C. Hine (Ed.), *Virtual methods: Issues in social research on the Internet* (pp. 199–207). Oxford, UK: Berg.

Joinson, A. (2003). *Understanding the psychology of Internet behaviour: Virtual worlds, real lives.* Basingstoke, UK: Palgrave Macmillan.

Joinson, A. (2005). Internet behaviour and the design of virtual methods. In C. Hine (Ed.), *Virtual methods: Issues in social research on the Internet* (pp. 21–34). Oxford, UK: Berg.

Jones, S. (2005). Fizz in the field: Toward a basis for an emergent Internet studies. *Information Society, 21*(4), 233–237.

Jones, S. G. (Ed.). (1995). *Cybersociety: Computer-mediated communication and community.* Thousand Oaks, CA: Sage.

Kanayama, T. (2003). Ethnographic research on the experience of Japanese elderly people online. *New Media and Society, 5*(2), 267–288.

Kendall, L. (2002). *Hanging out in the virtual pub: Mascu-*

linities and relationships online. Berkeley: University of California Press.
Kiesler, S., Siegel, J., & McGuire, T. W. (1984). Social psychological-aspects of computer-mediated communication. *American Psychologist, 39*(10), 1123–1134.
King, S. A. (1996). Researching Internet communities: Proposed ethical guidelines for the reporting of results. *Information Society, 12*(2), 119–127.
Kivits, J. (2005). Online interviewing and the research relationship. In C. Hine (Ed.), *Virtual methods: Issues in social research on the Internet* (pp. 35–49). Oxford, UK: Berg.
Lea, M., & Spears, R. (1991). Computer-mediated communication, deindividuation and group decision-making. *International Journal of Man-Machine Studies, 34*(2), 283–301.
Leander, K. M., & McKim, K. K. (2003). Tracing the everyday "sitings" of adolescents on the Internet: A strategic adaptation of ethnography across online and offline spaces. *Education, Communication and Information, 3*(2), 211–240.
Lindlof, T. R., & Shatzer, M. J. (1998). Media ethnography in virtual space: Strategies, limits, and possibilities. *Journal of Broadcasting and Electronic Media, 42*(2), 170–189.
Mackay, H. (2005). New connections, familiar settings: Issues in the ethnographic study of new media use at home. In C. Hine (Ed.), *Virtual methods: Issues in social research on the Internet* (pp. 129–140). Oxford, UK: Berg.
Madge, C., & O'Connor, H. (2002). Online with the e-mums: Exploring the internet as a medium for research. *Area, 34*(1), 92–102.
Mantovani, G. (1994). Is computer-mediated communication intrinsically apt to enhance democracy in organizations? *Human Relations, 47*(1), 45–62.
Marcus, G. (1995). Ethnography in/of the world system: The emergence of multi-sited ethnography. *Annual Review of Anthropology, 24*, 95–117.
Marcus, G. (1998). *Ethnography through thick and thin*. Princeton, NJ: Princeton University Press.
Markham, A. (1998). *Life online: Researching real experience in virtual space*. Walnut Creek, CA: AltaMira Press.
Miller, D., & Slater, D. (2000). *The Internet: An ethnographic approach*. Oxford, UK: Berg.
Mitra, A., & Cohen, E. (1999). Analyzing the web: Directions and challenges. In S. Jones (Ed.), *Doing Internet research: Critical issues and methods for examining the Net* (pp. 179–202). Thousand Oaks, CA: Sage.
Mortensen, T., & Walker, J. (2002). Blogging thoughts: Personal publication as an online research tool. In A. Morrison (Ed.), *Researching ICTs in context* (pp. 249–279). Oslo, Norway: InterMedia Report.
Orgad, S. S. (2005a). From online to offline and back: Moving from online to offline research relationships with informants. In C. Hine (Ed.), *Virtual methods: Issues in social research on the Internet* (pp. 51–66). Oxford, UK: Berg.
Orgad, S. S. (2005b). *Storytelling online: Talking breast cancer on the Internet*. New York: Lang.
Paccagnella, L. (1997). Getting the seats of your pants dirty: Strategies for ethnographic research on virtual communities. *Journal of Computer Mediated Communication, 3*(1). Retrieved October 10, 2006, from *jcmc.indiana.edu/vol3/issue1/paccagnella.html*
Paquet, S. (2002). *Personal knowledge publishing and its uses in research*. Retrieved October 10, 2006, from *radio.weblogs.com/0110772/stories/2002/10/03/personalKnowledgePublishingAndItsUsesInResearch.html*
Rheingold, H. (1993). *The virtual community: Homesteading on the electronic frontier*. Reading, MA: Addison-Wesley.
Rogers, R. (2005). Poignancy in the US political blogsphere. *Aslib Proceedings, 57*(4), 356–368.
Rogers, R., & Marres, N. (2000). Landscaping climate change: A mapping technique for understanding science and technology debates on the World Wide Web. *Public Understanding of Science, 9*(2), 141–163.
Rutter, J., & Smith, G. W. H. (2005). Ethnographic presence in a nebulous setting. In C. Hine (Ed.), *Virtual methods: Issues in social research on the Internet* (pp. 81–92). Oxford, UK: Berg.
Schaap, F. (2002). *The words that took us there: Ethnography in a virtual reality*. Amsterdam: Aksant Academic.
Schneider, S. M., & Foot, K. A. (2004). The web as an object of study. *New Media and Society, 6*(1), 114–122.
Schneider, S. M., & Foot, K. A. (2005). Web sphere analysis: An approach to studying online action. In C. Hine (Ed.), *Virtual methods: Issues in social research on the Internet* (pp. 157–170). Oxford, UK: Berg.
Sharf, B. (1999). Beyond netiquette: The ethics of doing naturalistic research on the internet. In S. Jones (Ed.), *Doing Internet research: Critical issues and methods for examining the Net* (pp. 243–256). Thousand Oaks, CA: Sage.
Silver, D. (2000). Looking backwards, looking forwards: Cyberculture studies, 1990–2000. In D. Gauntlett (Ed.), *Web.Studies: Rewiring media studies for the digital age* (pp. 19–30). London: Arnold.
Smith, M. A. (1999). Invisible crowds in cyberspace: Measuring and mapping the social structure of Usenet. In M. A. Smith & P. Kollock (Eds.), *Communities in cyberspace: Perspectives on new forms of social organization* (pp. 195–219). London: Routledge.
Spears, R., Lea, M., & Lee, S. (1990). Deindividuation and group polarization in computer-mediated communication. *British Journal of Social Psychology, 29*(2), 121–134.
Sproull, L., & Kiesler, S. (1986). Reducing social-context cues: Electronic mail in organizational communication. *Management Science, 32*(11), 1492–1512.
Star, S. L. (1999). The ethnography of infrastructure. *American Behavioral Scientist, 43*(3), 377–391.
Stone, A. R. (1995). *The war of desire and technology at the close of the mechanical age*. Cambridge, MA: MIT Press.

Sudweeks, F., McLaughlin, M., & Rafaeli, S. (Eds.). (1998). *Network and netplay: Virtual groups on the Internet*. Cambridge, MA: MIT Press.

Sudweeks, F., & Rafaeli, S. (1996). How do you get a hundred strangers to agree: Computer mediated communication and collaboration. In T. M. Harrison & T. D. Stephen (Eds.), *Computer networking and scholarship in the 21st century university* (pp. 115–136). New York: State University of New York Press.

Taylor, T. L. (1999). Life in virtual worlds: Plural existence, multimodalities, and other online research challenges. *American Behavioral Scientist, 43*(3), 436–449.

Thelwall, M. (2004). *Link analysis: An information science approach*. Amsterdam: Elsevier.

Thelwall, M. (2006). Interpreting social science link analysis research: A theoretical framework. *Journal of the American Society for Information Science and Technology, 57*(1), 60–68.

Wakeford, N. (2000). New media, new methodologies: Studying the web. In D. Gauntlett (Ed.), *Web.Studies: Rewiring media studies for the digital age* (pp. 31–42). London: Arnold.

Waskul, D., & Douglass, M. (1996). Considering the electronic participant: Some polemical observations on the ethics of on-line research. *Information Society, 12*(2), 129–139.

Wellman, B., & Haythornthwaite, C. (Eds.). (2002). *The Internet in everyday life*. Oxford, UK: Blackwell.

White, M. (2002). Representations or people? *Ethics and Information Technology, 4*(3), 249–266.

Woolgar, S. (Ed.). (2002). *Virtual society?: Technology, cyberbole, reality*. Oxford, UK: Oxford University Press.

CHAPTER 26

Internet-Mediated Research as an Emergent Method and Its Potential Role in Facilitating Mixed Methods Research

Claire Hewson

This chapter considers the possibilities afforded by the Internet for facilitating and enhancing primary research in the social and behavioral sciences. Possibilities for facilitating mixed methods approaches, in particular, are also explored. Primary Internet research has been referred to as *Internet-mediated research* (IMR) and characterized as the gathering of novel, original data (via the Internet) with the aim of subjecting them to analysis to provide new evidence in relation to a specific research question (Hewson, Yule, Laurent, & Vogel, 2003). This can be contrasted with *secondary* Internet research, which uses the Internet to locate secondary information sources, such as online journals, newspapers, library databases, and so on. In secondary Internet research the goal is not to generate new evidence in relation to a specific research question but to locate, assimilate, and summarize preexisting evidence and arguments and reports of primary research, as, for example, in conducting a literature review. Useful sources on conducting secondary Internet research include Hewson and colleagues (2003, Ch. 2) and O'Dochartaigh (2001). The focus of this chapter is on primary Internet research. Since the publication of some early explorations of IMR methods, appearing around the mid- to late 1990s (e.g., Hewson, Laurent, & Vogel, 1996; Pettitt, 1999; Szabo & Frenkl, 1996), recognition of the validity of the approach and the implementation of these methods by both experienced researchers and students alike have increased rapidly. Many researchers now consider the Internet a valuable and important data-gathering tool that may facilitate and enhance research possibilities within the social and behavioral sciences. *Mixed methods* research has been broadly defined as referring to the combined use of both qualitative and quantitative methodologies within the same study to address a single research question (Hewson, 2006). In the past decade or so, mixed methods approaches also have become increasingly widely used and recognized as a valid alternative to either purely quantitative or purely qualitative designs. This recognition is reflected in the emerging availability of entire books devoted to the topic (e.g., Creswell & Plano-Clark, 2006; Greene & Caracelli, 1997; Tashakkori & Teddlie, 1998, 2003), including a recent four-volume set (Bryman, 2006), and the appearance of the new *Journal of Mixed Methods Research* (see *www.mmr.sagepub.com*). As Creswell (2003) notes, such texts were not available a decade ago. As it became increasingly apparent, however, that more and more researchers were utilizing mixed methods designs across a broad range of disciplines, scholars came to recognize that some kind of formal categorization of the various design choices available and guidelines for implementation were in demand (e.g., Tashakkori & Teddlie, 1998).

Thus both Internet-mediated research and mixed methods approaches can be described as emergent research methods. Also, both have cut broadly across disciplinary boundaries within the social, behavioral, and human sciences, having been used, for example, in research in psychology, sociology, geography, education, political science, cognitive science, marketing, health, and nursing. Although a handful of researchers to date have combined these two emergent methods and implemented mixed methods designs within an Internet-mediated research context, there has so far been limited explicit discussion of the advantages, disadvantages, scope, and novel possibilities the Internet offers for supporting mixed methods research (see Hewson, 2007, and Mann & Stewart, 2000, for some initial reflections, however). Summaries within the IMR literature have, to date, tended to focus on issues relevant to either quantitative (e.g., Reips, 2002) or qualitative (e.g., Mann & Stewart, 2000) research strategies. Many of these issues will, of course, also be relevant to mixed methods approaches, which combine both quantitative and qualitative elements in research. Given the limited discussion of the topic so far, a goal of this chapter is to review some IMR mixed methods designs that have been implemented to date and offer some reflections on the potential benefits of combining IMR and mixed methods approaches, especially in comparison with traditional offline mixed methods procedures. The chapter first provides an overview and evaluation of quantitative and qualitative approaches in IMR. This is then followed by a brief account of the growth and influence of mixed methods approaches within the social and behavioral sciences before going on to examine examples of IMR mixed methods designs. The key features of each approach discussed are summarized and the benefits, drawbacks, caveats, and issues that emerge highlighted. Examples from the literature are used throughout to illustrate the techniques described. Although it is beyond the scope of this chapter to provide detailed implementation guidelines for the techniques discussed, reference to useful existing guides and resources are provided. Because it is essentially at the *data-gathering* stage of the research process that Internet-mediated approaches differ from traditional offline approaches, focus will be primarily on this stage.

Internet-Mediated Research

The increasing popularity and extensive growth of Internet-mediated research methods over the past decade or so is reflected both in the growing body of literature in this area and in the range of Internet study-hosting websites that now exist online. See, for example, the WebExperimental Psychology Lab (*www.psych.unizh.ch/genpsy/Ulf/Lab/*

WebExpPsyLab.html), Online Social Psychology Studies (*www.socialpsychology.org/expts.htm*), Online Psychology Research UK (*www.onlinepsychresearch.co.uk*) and the Hanover College Psychology Department Psychological Research on the Net page (*psych.hanover.edu/research/exponnet.html*). Articles reporting the results of IMR studies are now becoming abundant in influential journals such as *Behavior Research Methods, Instruments, and Computers*, *Social Science Computer Review*, *Computers in Human Behavior*, *Journal of Computer-Mediated Communication*, and *Public Opinion Quarterly*. Furthermore, chapters on IMR are now starting to appear in research methods textbooks (e.g., Bryman, 2004; Fraley, 2007; O'Brien, 1999), and research methods courses, especially at postgraduate level, are beginning to incorporate discussion of the approach. Disciplines that appear to have been at the forefront in engaging with this recently emerging method for conducting social and behavioral research, based on the sheer volume of published articles they have produced on the topic, include psychology, sociology, and marketing research. Within these disciplines a range of IMR approaches have been adopted, though some disciplines have heavily favored particular techniques; for example, marketing researchers have drawn mainly on survey-based approaches, which reflects the techniques most commonly used in this area in traditional offline research. Psychologists, too, have made extensive use of IMR surveys and questionnaires but also have implemented experimental designs and observational approaches.

In considering the range of approaches possible in IMR, it is useful to consider the distinction between what have been termed *reactive* and *nonreactive* methods. A particular feature of IMR is the scope it offers for gathering *nonreactive* data via nonreactive methods. Essentially, reactive methods are those in which the researcher sets up a research situation with the explicit intent of gathering primary research data and in which participants are recruited and take part in the full knowledge that they are participating in a research study. An issue that thus emerges with such methods is the extent to which behaviors may be influenced by the research context and therefore potentially lack ecological validity. Nonreactive methods, in contrast, derive data from sources of information that were not originally created within an explicit research context. Here, "reactivity" of participants' behavior should not be an issue, because the behavior is occurring naturally without awareness of any specific research context or goals that may otherwise serve to bias or influence the behavior. Examples of reactive methods are questionnaires, interviews, experiments, and disclosed observation. Nonreactive methods have been taken to include undisclosed observation and analysis of documents and archives. However, rather than seeing reactive and nonreactive methods as distinct categories, it may be more useful to view any particular method as lying somewhere on a continuum between reactive and nonreactive extremes. Elaboration of this perspective and a more detailed consideration of reactivity in social and behavioral research are provided by Fritsche and Linneweber (2006). These authors describe a range of data-gathering approaches, classifying these as ranging from the most nonreactive forms–for example, analysis of "traces" of behavior, as in "garbology" (the study of the contents of peoples' garbage cans; see Jupp, 2006, for a description of this technique)–to the most reactive forms, for example, interviews. Somewhere in between lie approaches such as undisclosed participant observation, in which, although participants may be unaware of any research goals, the researcher will be aware of them and thus can potentially influence the behaviors that occur. In IMR, the automatic logging of many forms of online interaction and behaviors creates a wealth of data sources that may prove useful for nonreactive methods of research. Archives of online discussions may be analyzed, for example; or "log file analysis" may be used, which involves tracing information about features such as which Web page links people have visited, how many times, and how long they have spent there (see Fritsche & Linneweber, 2006, for further discussion of nonreactive data-gathering methods using the Internet). Having introduced the nature and scope of IMR methods, I now outline some salient general advantages and disadvantages of the approach before going on to look at specific methods and tools in more detail.

General Advantages, Disadvantages, and Ethical Issues in IMR

By now, the general advantages, disadvantages, pitfalls, and caveats in IMR have been well documented (see, e.g., Birnbaum, 2004; Hewson, 2003). Nevertheless, they are worth summarizing here. Further discussion of the issues most pertinent to either quantitative or qualitative approaches, in particular, is provided in the relevant subsections following.

Advantages of IMR

One of the key general advantages of IMR that has been widely recognized within the literature to date is the ready access to a vast and diverse population of potential research participants, namely the *Internet-user population* (IUP), which the Internet affords. This feature may incur various possible benefits, including facilitating cross-cultural research due to the collapsing of geographical boundaries (e.g., Pohl, Bender, & Lachmann, 2002); facilitating access to small and/or specialist populations, which can be traditionally difficult to obtain (e.g., as in Coomber's [1997] Internet survey of drug dealers); and enhancing statistical power due to the ability to quickly obtain large samples. Indeed, Musch and Reips (2000) have reported that, in their survey of researchers who had used Internet-mediated research, the potential for obtaining a large number of participants and high statistical power were the two most important reasons cited for using the approach.[1] A second key appeal of IMR is its ability to enhance both the time and cost efficiency of a piece of research, compared with traditional offline approaches. This advantage is due to features such as the ability to automate presentation of materials and storing of data, which can reduce both photocopying and data input costs, as well as researcher time. Particularly noteworthy is the ability of the Internet to allow automated simultaneous presentation of materials to a very large and geographically diverse number of participants, which could potentially dramatically reduce the cost and time scale of a piece of research. The ready availability of IMR data in text-based or digitized format (typically) can serve to eliminate the need for transcribing and can provide data that are already in a format that can be readily imported into data analysis software packages such as SPSS (Statistical Package for the Social Sciences) or the qualitative analysis package NVivo. This, again, may help in greatly reducing costs associated with data manipulation and storage, which are often necessary in traditional offline research methods.

Other benefits of IMR may emerge from the nature of the online communication medium itself. One of the idiosyncratic features of the Internet is the way in which it can give rise to fairly high levels of interactivity while also maintaining relatively high degrees of anonymity, for example, as in online text-based chat interactions in which the conversants have no information about each other's physical characteristics. Hewson and colleagues (1996) have commented on this feature, suggesting that such heightened levels of anonymity may serve to reduce biases due to perceptions of biosocial attributes, such as gender, socioeconomic status, ethnicity, and so on. The potential confounding effects of such biases in research with human participants has long been recognized (Murray & Sixsmith, 1998). There is also some evidence that the enhanced levels of anonymity in online contexts may encourage people to be more candid and willing to discuss personal and sensitive topics and less prone to responding in a socially desirable manner (e.g., Joinson, 1999, 2001). The Internet may also open up possibilities for implementing research designs that traditionally have been impracticable, or even impossible, using offline methods. Thus, for example, the logs of electronic text-based interactions that are automatically created in many online communication settings (e.g., discussion groups, bulletin boards, mailing lists, e-mail exchanges, etc.) can create opportunities for conducting unobtrusive observational research in a way not previously possible in many offline contexts. Bordia (1996) reports successfully implementing an unobtrusive naturalistic study of rumor transmission using the Internet by locating and searching discussion archives on Usenet, Internet, and Bitnet to obtain instances of rumors generated within these online discussion forums. Bordia comments on the benefits of such an IMR approach compared with traditional offline approaches in being able both to observe unobtrusively and to locate instances of rumor transmission more quickly and easily than has previously been possible using traditional methods. Thus the ready data trail left by the vast number of electronic communications online creates a wealth of easily accessible material that can provide a valuable resource for use in such unobtrusive observation studies. Another example of new possibilities afforded by IMR methods is the enhanced potential for conducting cross-cultural research studies (as noted earlier), which may not be feasible using traditional methods due to practical and financial constraints.

Disadvantages of IMR

Given the advantages of IMR just noted, both in enhancing and facilitating a range of types of research, as well as opening up new possibilities that have been previously difficult to implement offline, many researchers are excited about the opportunities that IMR approaches may offer to support social and behavioral research. However, it is also important to recognize the potential drawbacks associated with this new data-gathering medium and the possible implications of these drawbacks for both the validity and reliability of IMR studies and for the proper implementation of relevant ethical guidelines for research. One issue that was prominent in early discussions of IMR concerned the extent to which the Internet-user population constitutes a dramatically skewed and unrepresentative sample of the "population at large." A common claim at the time was that the IUP was, in fact, dominated by white, high-earning, high-socioeconomic status, highly computer-literate males working in professional fields (e.g., Schmidt, 1997; Stanton, 1998; Szabo & Frenkl, 1996). Considering the history of the development of the Internet, these concerns were probably once very legitimate. The Internet as we know it today grew out of ARPANET (Advanced Research Projects Agency Network), commissioned in 1969 by the U.S. Department of Defense for research into computer networking. It was not until 1982, with the introduction of Transmission Control Protocol (TCP) and Internet Protocol (IP) that the Internet effectively began. It was toward the end of the 1980s that the Internet began to expand rapidly. In 1987 the number of available Internet hosts ("hosts" are computers that act as a point of access to the Internet and are typically configured to allow a number of individual computers to connect via a network) was around 10,000. In 1988 this had increased to 60,000 and in 1989 to over 100,000. Recent estimates put the number of Internet-accessible hosts at around 490 million (Internet Systems Consortium, 2007), with estimates of the entire IUP having now exceeded the 1 billion mark (Computer Industry Almanac, 2006). The massive expanse of the Internet over the past few decades is thus undeniable. Furthermore, taking into account the diverse range of functions and services the Internet now provides, such as allowing people to order groceries, manage bank accounts, book travel tickets, pay bills, buy insurance, search for a partner, and so on, alongside the ever-decreasing costs of Internet access, it would be difficult to offer convincing counterarguments to the claim that the IUP not only has expanded massively in size but also has become massively diversified in terms of representing a broader section of the worldwide population than ever before. This is not, of course, to deny that there are still some major restrictions on who has Internet access. Access is still essentially limited to moderately affluent individuals within industrially developed nations. Still, this nevertheless constitutes a population of potential research participants of quite astounding proportions when considered in light of the populations typically practically accessible via traditional methods. For further arguments that sample bias should not be considered a major barrier to implementing IMR studies across many research domains, see Hewson (2003, especially Ch. 3). This view is now becoming increasingly widely accepted, as is apparent from the increasing number of researchers implementing IMR studies across a range of disciplines and research domains. Ultimately, it is up to the individual researcher to assess the extent to which sampling via the Internet is likely to be able to generate samples of the type required for any particular research study. As has already been noted, the Internet may be particularly useful for accessing small, specialist populations. It may, however, be less appropriate (currently, at least) for obtaining large, representative probability samples due to the lack of a central register of all Internet users and associated difficulties in measuring the sampling frame in IMR methods. At present, the relationship between sampling approaches in IMR and the types of samples these may generate is an ongoing research topic that has so far been explored to a limited degree only. One thing that does seem apparent is that the landscape of this issue is ever changing, as the Internet continues to rapidly expand and diversify.

Another key issue in IMR, which constitutes a potential disadvantage and a possible threat to data validity and integrity, is the reduced levels of researcher control over and knowledge of participant behavior, participation context, and presentation of stimulus materials (e.g., Hewson, 2003; Krantz, 2001). Not only may system variations (hardware configurations, network performance, etc.) lead to differences in the way participants experience study materials, but participants may also undertake a study under a range of contrasting conditions, such as in a crowded busy computer laboratory, among a group of friends who are offering advice, in a state of intoxication, and so on. Some participants may even consider it a challenge to deliberately try to sabotage a study, for example, by backtracking to view prior materials in a memory experiment or by hacking into the system to obtain information about alternative experimental conditions (though procedures can be implemented that help minimize the probability of success of such attempts; see, e.g., Hewson et al., 2003, Ch. 6). IMR studies are particularly vulnerable to such unwanted (and often unanticipated) sources of variation, as these are far more difficult to detect than in many traditional settings, that is, in which the researcher is present. Issues of control are, of course, particularly relevant to experimental IMR designs, in which tight control over extraneous variables is crucial (see further discussion of experimental approaches later in the chapter). A potential drawback in IMR that is more relevant to *qualitative* approaches, such as online interviewing or observational studies of online conversational interactions, concerns the possible disadvantages that may emerge due to the idiosyncratic nature of the online communication medium. In particular, online interactions typically embody a lack of extralinguistic cues that are normally available in face-to-face settings, such as facial expressions, tone of voice, body language, and so on. Although this feature was noted earlier as having potential advantages–in terms of its role in enhancing levels of anonymity and thus possibly encouraging more candid and honest responses—a number of potential disadvantages also emerge. These include difficulty in establishing good levels of rapport with participants (e.g., Strickland et al., 2003) and possible ambiguities (e.g., Bowker & Tuffin, 2004) and a lack of depth (e.g., Davis, Bolding, Hart, Sherr, & Elford, 2004) in the communication process (see further discussion of these issues later in the chapter).

In summary, the aforementioned possible advantages and disadvantages associated with using the Internet as a data-gathering tool in primary social and behavioral research must be carefully considered when assessing the validity and potential value of any IMR study. Although the advantages an IMR approach affords are appealing, of primary concern is whether IMR procedures are likely to be able to generate valid, reliable,[2] useful data that are informative in relation to the research question at hand. The extent to which the potential barriers discussed may be problematic for IMR requires further exploration. However, encouragingly, there is a growing body of research (discussed further later) that indicates that IMR studies can often produce valid, reliable results at least comparable to those obtained in similar studies implemented offline. This suggests that factors such as lack of control and sample bias may have a minimal impact in posing threats to the validity of IMR results, in many areas at least.

Ethical Issues in IMR

Due to certain key features of the data-gathering process in IMR, in particular the lack of direct interpersonal proximity between researcher(s) and participant(s), which tends to give rise to enhanced levels of anonymity and privacy, and the way in which information is transmitted and stored in an electronic medium across networked computers, certain ethical concerns emerge. These concerns relate to both whether and how it may be possible to properly implement existing ethical guidelines for conducting research with human participants and how to resolve novel ethical dilemmas that emerge due to the nature of the Internet as a new medium for primary research. The main issues to date concern how to obtain informed consent from participants, how to make sure they have been properly debriefed, how to ensure anonymity (where relevant) and confidentiality of data, and how to resolve the issue of the blurred boundary between the public and private domains online. In relation to the first point, obtaining consent from participants is possible using a range of techniques, such as asking them to tick a consent box on a Web page, to click on a link to participate in a study, or to sign and return a consent form either electronically (e.g., by e-mail) or via postal mail. However, certain issues, such as being sure that a participant has actually read and understood the prior consent form and being able to verify that he or she meets the necessary requirements to be able to properly give informed consent (e.g., being over 16 years of age), emerge as problematic due to the lack of interpersonal proximity in an IMR context. Debriefing participants is also problematic for the same reason. Without being in direct proximal contact with participants, it is difficult to verify that they have properly digested and understood any debriefing information presented. Debriefing procedures in IMR need to be carefully thought out so as to maximize the chance that participants are properly debriefed, for example, by making sure that debriefing information is presented not only after completion of a study but also if a participant exits prematurely (e.g., by closing down his or her Web browser). Implementing effective procedures for obtaining informed consent and debriefing participants is perhaps most relevant in relation to IMR contexts in which researchers have the least direct contact with research participants, such as in Web-based surveys and experiments. When using IMR procedures with greater levels of interpersonal interaction between researcher(s) and participant(s), such as in-depth interviews, the researcher will be in a better position to monitor and assess the reactions of participants throughout the study.

Although ensuring anonymity and confidentiality can be important in all types of research, especially when assurances of these conditions have been given during the informed-consent stage, these features should be given particular consideration when using research procedures that aim to elicit detailed, elaborate information from participants, particularly when this information is of a sensitive nature and analyzed on an individual basis (as opposed to aggregating group data), such as occurs in an in-depth, one-to-one interview on a personal topic. A number of obstacles may emerge in relation to ensuring anonymity and confidentiality in IMR. The use of personal e-mail accounts–for example, in conducting an online interview–will invariably lead to both reduced levels of anonymity and increased threats to the security and confidentiality of responses compared with other approaches (e.g., using online chat facilities). Anonymity may be compromised because an e-mail address may often allow the owner of the e-mail account to be traced, for example, by a Web search of all the employees at a particular organization. Furthermore, because e-mail messages are relayed across a number of computers between leaving the sender and arriving with the recipient, they may potentially be intercepted at any point in this process, thus posing a threat to confidentiality. The confidentiality of participants' responses may also be threatened if secure systems for the storing of data are not carefully implemented (see Hewson et al., 2003, for guidance on securely storing data). Anonymity may also be unwittingly compromised by quoting participants' comments, such as from an online discussion forum, along with their online pseudonyms or user names. Although this approach may at first glance be considered sufficient to guarantee anonymity, as it does not reveal a participant's "true" offline identity, a number of authors have pointed out the degree of investment that may often go into a person's online identity and the repercussions of treating such pseudonyms, or "identities," as truly anonymous (see, e.g., Frankel & Siang, 1999). Also, even when quotes are rendered fully anonymous, a search on the World Wide Web may easily allow an individual quote to be traced back to a particular member of a discussion forum in a way that simply cannot occur in offline approaches, as the original data source (e.g., a transcribed interview) will not be publicly accessible in the same way.

The issue of the blurred distinction between the private and public domains online is especially relevant to observational approaches in IMR, in which a researcher may face dilemmas over whether it is necessary to obtain informed consent from participants in certain settings (such as in studying verbal exchanges on a public discussion board). Currently, there is no established set of standards on the correct ethical procedures relating to the use of nonreactive observational data derived from online communications (both in real time and archived), though a number of authors have reflected on the issue (e.g., Flicker, Haans, & Skinner, 2004). At present, as with many of the ethical issues raised in IMR, it will be up to the individual researcher to make appropriate judgments and decisions based on the current research context. Although it is beyond the scope of this chapter to consider ethical issues in IMR in any greater depth than the brief summary just provided, a number of useful articles that discuss these issues in more detail exist. For example, see Birnbaum and Reips (2005); Elgesem (2002); Ess (2007); Kraut and colleagues (2004); and Pittenger (2003). At the time of this writing, the British Psychological Society (2007) had just published a set of guidelines for ethical practice in psychological research online.

The previous sections have outlined some general issues relating to Internet-mediated research as a new, emergent, and evolving method. As more and more researchers come to adopt the approach, these issues will gain clarity, and additional solutions, recommendations, and guidelines will emerge (for existing guidelines, see, e.g., Dillman & Bowker, 2001; Hewson, 2003; Reips, 2002). However, the current state of play seems to be that IMR provides a potentially valuable approach, as indicated by its emerging popularity and the reported success of many studies implemented to date. The following sections review the main tools, methods, and techniques available in IMR, providing illustrations of studies that have been carried out to date across a range of research domains and disciplines.

Quantitative Approaches in IMR

For useful summaries of the issues involved in quantitative Internet-mediated research, see Birnbaum (2004) and Reips (2002). The key quantitative research strategies that have been implemented online to date include surveys and questionnaires, experiments, and (primarily linguistic) observation studies and document analysis. The first two of these strategies have by far dominated discussions of quantitative methods in IMR.

Surveys and Questionnaires

Internet surveys and questionnaires have most commonly been administered by placing them on the World Wide Web (WWW) as a Web form, constructed using HTML (hypertext markup language) and associated technologies such as JavaScript (a client-side scripting language[3]) to allow more sophisticated functionalities. JavaScript, for example, can support features such as checking response completeness, timing participants, and randomizing stimuli. There are numerous general introductory guides to HTML, including both books (e.g., Castro, 2002) and online guides (see, e.g., "Basic HTML Programming," n.d.), that may be useful for the researcher wishing to construct a Web-based survey. For a more thorough account of the range of technologies available for supporting Web-based survey and questionnaire research and how to use them, see Hewson and colleagues (2003). For a useful introductory guide that explains in detail how to develop HTML-based Web pages and how to implement a simple Web-based questionnaire or survey, see Birnbaum (2001). More sophisticated implementations, along with supporting code, are presented in Göritz and Birnbaum (2005). Web-based resources for supporting implementation of online surveys and questionnaires are also available, and these may be especially useful for researchers who do not have high levels of computer literacy or programming experience or access to external technical support. These resources include (at the time of writing) the freely available SurveyWiz (*psych.fullerton.edu/mbirnbaum/programs/surveyWiz.htm*) and the formerly free but now commercial WWW Survey Assistant (*www.mohsho.com/ s_ware/home.html*). A Web-based questionnaire or survey provides a user-friendly interface that allows respondents to view questions, input their answers, and easily submit the form after completion by simply hitting a "send" button.

Surveys and questionnaires can also be administered by e-mail, which has the advantage of requiring only minimal levels of researcher technical expertise (or available technical support) and technological equipment but that offers less control over factors such as presentation and response format. This means that variations between participants on these factors will be more likely to occur, which may detrimentally affect levels of reliability and validity. Web-based survey methods, as just discussed, not only have an advantage in being better able to constrain such possible sources of variation but also provide scope for gathering additional information, such as response patterns and completion times. Ultimately, it is up to the individual researcher to decide on the relative importance of each of these factors and make choices based on the particular research context and goals and the resources available. Further discussion of issues in IMR survey and questionnaire approaches can be found in Dillman and Bowker (2001),

Couper (2000), and Fox, Murray, and Warm (2003). Design guidelines can be found in Dillman (2006) and in Schonlau, Fricker, and Elliott (2002). Despite concerns raised earlier about potential threats to validity in online questionnaire and survey research—for example, due to a lack of control over and knowledge of a range of possible sources of variation—some researchers have reported support for the validity of online questionnaire administrations by successfully replicating effects that had been previously established in offline contexts. Voracek, Steiger, and Gindl (2001), for example, report administering a sexual jealousy questionnaire online in which they replicated established sex differences commonly found in offline administrations. Such findings would appear to indicate that, at least in some contexts, online participants can be trusted to be honest and reliable in the information they provide about characteristics such as their gender, attitudes, and beliefs. Similarly encouraging results have been obtained in studies that have set out to test the validity of psychometric test instruments administered online. The question of whether such online tests are able to provide valid and reliable measures of psychometric constructs (e.g., personality) comparable with those achieved in offline administrations has been an ongoing research topic in this area (see Buchanan, 2001, for a review). A number of studies comparing online and offline administrations of the same psychometric test instrument have shown each approach to yield comparable results in terms of psychometric properties such as factor structures and internal reliabilities (e.g., Anderson, Kaldo-Sandstrom, Strom, & Stromgren, 2003; Buchanan & Smith, 1999; Hewson & Charlton, 2005). Some such studies, however, have failed to find equivalence of online and offline versions of a test instrument (e.g., Johnson, 2000). As noted by Buchanan (2001), before adapting any test instrument for administration via IMR methods, it should first be tested and validated within this medium. Also, it should not be assumed that test norms will be equivalent for online and offline administrations of the same test instrument, given the idiosyncratic features of the online medium (as noted earlier) and the potential differences in the typical characteristics of Internet-accessed and traditional offline samples.

Experiments

Experimental designs have been fairly widely implemented in IMR. Informative discussion of the approach can be found in Birnbaum (2000) and Reips (2007). Implementational details are provided in Birnbaum (2001) and Reips (2001), and for more advanced techniques see Schmidt (2002). Descriptions of resources available to help in constructing Internet experiments are provided in Wolfe and Reyna (2002) and Yule and Cooper (2003). In general, implementing an experiment online places the greatest demands on the researcher in terms of the levels of technical expertise and sophistication of equipment required compared with the other IMR strategies discussed here. Issues relating to levels of researcher control are of particular importance in experimental IMR designs, in which tight control over extraneous variables is key to ensuring the validity of the data obtained. Although it is generally difficult to gauge the extent of variability that may occur in an IMR experiment—technical procedures being able to constrain both presentation of stimuli and participant behavior to some extent but not entirely (e.g., the conditions under which participation occurs can never be properly controlled or known in IMR, due to the lack of researcher presence)—studies that have set out to validate experimental procedures in Internet-mediated research have produced promising results. For example, McGraw, Tew, and Williams (2000) report the results of a series of IMR experiments, noting that these were successful in replicating established psychological phenomena, such as the Stroop effect. Similarly, in a psycholinguistic experiment delivered online, Corley and Scheepers (2002) replicated syntactic priming effects typically found in offline contexts. This would suggest not only that the types of variations that may potentially occur in IMR experiments are not overly problematic (at least in contexts such as those just mentioned) but also that IMR experiments that rely on fairly precise, accurate timings are possible. In more complex implementations, however, there may be greater scope for problems to emerge. Givaty, van Vaan, Christou, and Bulthoff (1998) implemented a series of multimedia spatial cognition experiments online, in which participants were required to navigate around a 3-D virtual environment. Virtual-reality modeling language (VRML) was used to present 3-D graphics over the Internet in an attempt to simulate the types of conditions typically presented in laboratory experiments in this area while benefiting from the ability of an IMR approach to facilitate data gathering from much larger samples than is possible in laboratory studies of this type (due to practicable constraints, such as time, cost, etc.). Givaty and colleagues (1998) highlight some of the technical issues that emerged in their Internet experiments, especially relating to difficulties in constraining participants' behaviors to within the range required by the experimental design. Although some such behaviors could not be fully constrained as desired due to the ability of participants to vary parameters via their Web browser settings, for example, the authors offer solutions and guidelines that aim to maximize the validity of data obtained in these types of virtual-reality applications in IMR. As with online questionnaire- and survey-based approaches, the scope and range of experimental procedures that may be successfully implemented in IMR is an ongoing research topic.

Observation and Document Analysis

Traditionally, quantitative researchers have tended to make use of *structured* observation approaches, in which a coding scheme using predetermined categories is applied in recording what is being observed in *real time* (though behavior may also be recorded using audio and video, to allow for subsequent analysis in a more relaxed time scale). In an Internet-mediated research context, this approach may be applicable, for example, when recording observations of real-time online interactions, such as online discussions in Internet chat rooms, or the behavior of participants within a virtual online environment such as a role-playing game. However, the beauty of the Internet for supporting observational research lies largely in the opportunities it creates for conducting observational analysis using traces of online behaviors that have already been logged and stored electronically. The most obvious application for this approach is linguistic observation, given the wealth of easily accessible and searchable logs of online discussions available on the Internet. Bordia's (1996) study of rumor transmission using online discussion threads is an example of quantitative observational IMR. When using such archives in observational IMR, the researcher will thus not need to make choices about the appropriate coding schemes to be used in recording behaviors. Rather, it will be at the data *analysis* stage that it becomes apparent whether a more quantitative or qualitative research orientation is being adopted. However, it is still useful to refer to quantitative IMR observation approaches as "structured observation" to distinguish these from more qualitative unstructured approaches, given that a structured coding scheme will typically be applied at the data analysis stage. Using linguistic archives of online interactions thus provides a promising avenue for structured observation approaches in IMR. Real-time observations using multimedia and virtual-reality environments may also be plausible (though these techniques require further exploration), and here automatic logging of many aspects of behavior is also feasible and may confer an advantage for IMR over more traditional approaches. The tools and techniques available for observational research online are explored further in the next section on qualitative approaches. These tools and techniques can be useful for both qualitative and quantitative observational research approaches, however. Although there are few examples of either purely quantitative or purely qualitative observational IMR studies, a number of researchers have adopted a mixed methods approach in IMR observational research (e.g., Herring, Johnson, & DiBenedetto, 1998; Sotillo & Wang-Gempp, 2004), as described later in the chapter.

Closely related to observational approaches in an IMR context is document analysis, as this approach also makes use of online archives, or "documents." The distinction between these two approaches, as outlined by Hewson (2007), is useful for the purposes of the present discussion. Hewson classifies observational research in IMR as that which makes use of archives of (or real-time) *interactions* between two or more individuals, whereas document analysis makes use of static documents available online, which do not involve interactions between individuals; e.g., artwork, government documents, newspaper articles, personal Web pages, and so on. This distinction is approximate, however, and certain online sources may straddle the boundary between these two categories. For example, weblogs, or "blogs," are online personal diaries that initially emerged as written documents posted on the Web by a single author. However, blogs have now also developed to take on a more interactive nature, acting sometimes more like open bulletin boards to which various people may post comments and responses to each other[4] (Hewson, 2007). In traditional research, document analysis has been characterized as "The detailed examination of documents across a wide range of social practices, taking a variety of forms from the written word to the visual image" (Wharton, 2006). Document analysts traditionally may make use of public documents, such as contracts of employment, records of educational achievement, mass media documents, and private documents, such as letters, diaries, and photographs (Wharton, 2006). Resources readily available for document analysis in IMR include personal and corporate Web pages, newspaper articles, academic papers, weblogs, images and photographs, official public documents, and so on. Document analysts may make use of either quantitative or qualitative analysis techniques (as noted previously), and the documents available online may be equally useful for either approach. Quantitative document analysis has been closely associated with quantitative *content analysis* (indeed, some authors seem almost to treat document analysis and content analysis as synonymous; see, e.g., Robson, 1993). Content analysis involves quantitative measures of the frequency of appearance of particular elements in the text (Scott, 2006).

Several examples of quantitative document analysis in IMR exist. Nastri, Pena, and Hancock (2006), for example, report the results of a quantitative content and speech act analysis of "instant messaging" (IM) away messages. Rains and Young (2006) have carried out a content analysis of e-mail signatures. Examples of qualitative approaches to document analysis in IMR are provided in the next section. Document analysis can be considered an example of a nonreactive method in that the documents used have been produced without any intention or knowledge that they will be used as data in primary research (though documents *could* be solicited with explicit research goals in mind; e.g., see the description of the study by Hessler et al., 2003, later in the chapter).

To summarize, surveys and questionnaires, experiments, and quantitative approaches to (i.e., structured) observation and document analysis all seem viable in an IMR context, and successful examples of all these approaches have been reported within the literature. However, issues such as how to maximize levels of researcher control emerge in many contexts. Also, especially with more complex experimental designs, demands on levels of researcher expertise and for availability of equipment can be high. Nevertheless, the results to date are promising in terms of the range of quantitative research techniques that can be adapted to an IMR environment and the evidence for the validity of such approaches across a range of domains. Quantitative techniques in IMR have been implemented across a broad range of disciplines, though those disciplines that have tended to draw most on quantitative research strategies traditionally—for example, experimental and questionnaire-based approaches in psychology and survey-based approaches in sociology and marketing research—appear to also have made greater use of these techniques within an IMR context.

Qualitative Approaches in IMR

Mann and Stewart (2000) have identified interviews, observation, and document analysis as the main tools used by qualitative researchers, and these approaches have been most extensively discussed in relation to qualitative-oriented IMR approaches. Qualitative research is characterized by an emphasis on generating rich, in-depth, elaborate data that are amenable to a "thick" interpretative description in which participants' meanings can be explored. To this end, qualitative researchers tend to use less structured, more open-ended approaches than those characteristic of quantitative research strategies. Thus unstructured and in-depth interviews and observational and document analysis techniques are commonly employed (for further discussion of qualitative approaches to research, see Berg, 2006; Creswell, 2003). For useful overviews of the tools, techniques, and issues involved in qualitative IMR, see Hewson (2007) and Mann and Stewart (2000).

Interviews

Online interviews are possible using either e-mail or online "chat" (e.g., Internet Relay Chat [IRC][5]) and IM[6] tools. Within the IMR literature a distinction has been drawn between *synchronous* and *asynchronous* forms of online interaction. Thus whereas e-mail tends to be used more asynchronously, online chat and instant messaging technologies are typically used for more synchronous forms of communication. The implications for online qualitative interviews of using either a synchronous or an asynchronous approach have been discussed widely. In general, there is evidence that asynchronous approaches can allow more elaborate, deeper, considered responses (as well as, perhaps, more accurate ones due to the potential to check documents and other relevant sources), but they may suffer from reduced conversational "flow"[7] (e.g., Bowker & Tuffin, 2004; Murray & Sixsmith, 1998). Synchronous online interviews, on the other hand, have been identified as potentially being able to improve the flow of a conversation due to the close temporal relation of exchanges between conversants, but they also can tend to be more superficial and playful and lead to less considered, elaborate responses due to the social and conversational norms that have come to characterize such online chat interactions (e.g., Davis et al., 2004). One particularly salient issue in relation to both synchronous and asynchronous online interviewing approaches is the lack of extralinguistic cues and enhanced levels of anonymity that typically prevail. As noted earlier, it has been suggested that heightened levels of anonymity may be beneficial in encouraging participants to be more candid and open, which may lead them to feel more comfortable and willing to discuss sensitive topics and disclose personal information. This could be particularly useful in an online qualitative interview context, and, indeed, evidence for such effects has been reported (e.g., Madge & O'Connor, 2002; Murray & Sixsmith, 1998). On the other hand, enhanced levels of anonymity may also lead to difficulties in establishing levels of rapport (e.g., Bowker & Tuffin, 2004; Strickland et al., 2003), as participants may feel discomfort and tend toward being more reticent as a result of the lack of personal cues (such as appearance, gender, age, etc.)

available from the researcher. However, several researchers have reported effective techniques for overcoming this problem, including implementing explicit procedures for disclosing personal information to participants at the start of a study (e.g., Madge & O'Connor, 2002).

As well as issues related to the *enhanced levels of anonymity* that the reduced availability of extralinguistic cues in an online interview situation creates, further advantages and disadvantages may emerge from this feature. On the one hand, a lack of extralinguistic information could lead to ambiguities in the communication process; for example, it may be more difficult to discern whether a comment is intended to be serious, sarcastic, or simply friendly and humorous without reference to cues derived from features such as facial expression and tone of voice. On the other hand, a lack of extralinguistic cues could perhaps serve to further encourage more frank and honest responses and greater levels of self-disclosure due to a reduced sense among participants of "being judged." Another feature of online interviews is their potential for creating more balanced power relationships between participants and between researcher(s) and participants due to the lack of readily available information about biosocial attributes and other relevant cues (e.g., sex, age, ethnic origin, socioeconomic status, educational level, etc.), which may often play a role in defining social hierarchies in group interactions (e.g., Murray & Sixsmith, 1998). Some authors have pointed out, however, that many cues to an individual's personal attributes remain even online, such as the use of gendered language styles (e.g., Herring, 1993; Postmes & Spears, 2002). For a more thorough discussion of the extent to which the Internet may or may not confer a "democratizing" effect in interpersonal interaction, see Mann and Stewart (2000). The Internet has the potential to support both one-to-one qualitative interviews (see, e.g., Davis et al., 2004; Murray & Sixsmith, 1998) and focus group interviews (see, e.g., Madge & O'Connor, 2002), both synchronously and asynchronously. One-to-one interviews can be conducted synchronously using chat software and asynchronously using e-mail, for example, as noted previously. Focus groups can be implemented synchronously, also using chat facilities, and asynchronously, using mailing lists or discussion forums (see Hewson, 2007, and Mann & Stewart, 2000, for more detailed discussion of the use of these tools for conducting one-to-one and focus group interviews in IMR).

Observation and Document Analysis

Whereas quantitative strategies in observational research have made use of structured approaches, qualitative observational research has drawn extensively on unstructured techniques, such as forms of participant observation whereby the researcher aims to immerse him- or herself in a group in order to engage in a close, rich, detailed understanding of the behaviors, social norms, and shared meanings within the group. In IMR qualitative participant observation is made possible due to the numerous online communities that exist, largely within language-based environments such as Internet chat rooms, discussion boards, and newsgroups. A researcher wishing to undertake such research with online communities will need to obtain consent from group members unless an undisclosed approach is utilized, in which case the ethical issues concerning what is private and public online need to be carefully considered. *Nonparticipant* qualitative observation is equally feasible, and probably easier to carry out, due to the wealth of archives of interactions available online. As with quantitative approaches, the qualitative researcher may choose to make use of such archived logs of interactions or to observe in real time. In real-time observations it is often possible to create automatic logs of the interaction, which then may serve the purpose of archives, though logs may fail to capture some features, such as the timings of exchanges, for example. In nonparticipant observation approaches, issues relating to public and private spaces online and whether it is necessary to gain informed consent from participants are also important. Observations of both synchronous and asynchronous online exchanges are possible (supported by the range of technologies discussed earlier in relation to IMR interview approaches). As with quantitative approaches, the primary scope for conducting qualitative observational research in IMR involves linguistic observation. Here, the ready availability of the resulting data in electronic text-based format is especially useful and can eliminate the need for transcribing, which is typically a necessary and time-consuming stage in traditional offline linguistic observation studies. There is scope for going beyond linguistic observation studies, however. One possibility is the observation of interactions within online multiuser virtual environments, such as MUDs (multiuser dungeons, the name reflecting the origin of these environments as places where participants played the role-playing game Dungeons and Dragons), MUSEs (multiuser simulation environments), and MOOs (MUDs-object-oriented). These are places online where people meet up to interact, often within a role-playing fantasy game setting. The online 3-D virtual-reality environment "second life" is a more recent example of this type of online community, which, since opening to the public in 2003, has expanded rapidly, at the time of this writing having a reported 7 million users from around the world (*secondlife.com/whatis*). Other possibilities for online observational research that goes beyond text-based interactions are conceivable due to the availability of webcams, which allow the transmission of video data. However, at the time of this writing, such approaches are still hampered by technical issues, which at present limit their usefulness in supporting IMR (see, e.g., Hewson, 2007). Nevertheless, although extralinguistic cues, such as facial expressions and tone of voice, have been considered essentially absent in online communications (as noted earlier), the existence of devices such as emoticons (e.g., smile: :-), wink and smile: ;-), kiss: :-*), acronyms (e.g., LOL: "laughing out loud," ROTFL: "rolling on the floor laughing"), and use of capital letters to indicate shouting, for example, provides more scope for analysis of extralinguistic features than may at first be obvious. Studies that have engaged with qualitative observational research techniques in IMR tend also to have made use of quantitative approaches and are therefore discussed in the next section on mixed methods approaches in IMR.

Document analysis has been considered earlier, largely within a quantitative framework. There appear to be fewer examples available of purely qualitative approaches to document analysis using IMR methods. As with observational techniques, qualitative document analysis engages with the data in a less structured way than in quantitative approaches. Emphasis is less on quantification and categorization and more on uncovering the richness of meanings and interpretations embedded within the text. *Textual analysis* is a document analysis technique that uses qualitative procedures in order to assess the significance of particular ideas or meanings within the document (see Scott, 2006, for further discussion of this technique). Examples of qualitative document analysis in IMR include Thoreau's (2006) analysis of representations of disability by disabled people, using articles (text and images) from *Ouch!*, a magazine website produced largely by and for disabled people. Heinz, Gu, Inuzuka, and Zender (2002) also report a qualitative document analysis study in which they carried out a rhetorical–critical examination of texts and images on gay, lesbian, bisexual, and transgender websites.[8] Hessler and colleagues (2003) report what may be considered a "solicited document analysis" study within a qualitative framework. These authors carried out a qualitative study on adolescent risk behavior and report successfully eliciting daily diary entries from consenting volunteer participants by e-mail, leading to the generation of "rich and extensive narratives of everyday life as seen through adolescent eyes" (Hessler et al., 2003, p. 111).

To summarize, interviews and (unstructured) observation and document analysis are all feasible in qualitative IMR approaches. The next sections discuss the possibilities for combining both qualitative and quantitative research within a mixed methods framework. Examples of such approaches within IMR and the advantages that the combination of these two emergent research methods may afford are explored, after a brief explanation of mixed methods approaches more generally.

Mixed Methods Approaches

For an accessible introduction to mixed methods approaches, see Creswell (2003). For a more in-depth account, including discussion of the philosophical underpinnings of qualitative, quantitative, and mixed methods approaches to research and historical developments in the acceptance and use of these methods, see Tashakkori and Teddlie (1998). Pioneering work in this area has been presented by Greene, Caracelli, and Graham (1989), who reviewed and described the design features of 57 mixed methods studies. Since then, within the past decade or so, the approach has become increasingly widely accepted as a valid alternative research strategy to either purely qualitative or purely quantitative approaches across a range of disciplines. Mixed methods studies have been carried out in sociology, psychology, administration, and educational research, for example (Tashakkori & Teddlie, 1998). Discussion of mixed methods approaches has also recently filtered into key introductory research methods textbooks (e.g., Creswell, 2003). Tashakkori and Teddlie have described mixed methods studies as those "that combine the qualitative and quantitative approaches into the research methodology of a single study or multiphased study" (p. 17). They also draw a distinction between "mixed methods" and "mixed model" approaches, describing the latter as those that "combine the qualitative and quantitative approaches within different phases of the research process" (p. 19). Essentially, Tashakkori and Teddlie seem to be characterizing mixed methods approaches as those that mix qualitative and quantitative strategies specifically at the "methodology" stage, whereas mixed-model approaches mix these strategies at stages other than those that form part of the methodology of a study. What is perhaps not entirely clear from their account is which phases constitute the *methodology* of a study. The illustrations presented help to clarify this, however. For present purposes, the "methodology" stage(s) will be taken to include those elements relating to the *methods* employed in a study; that is, design, data gathering, and data analysis. Stages that lie outside of the methods of a study include, for example, problem formulation and inference processes (i.e., drawing conclusions from study results). One example that Tashakkori and Teddlie present as an illustration of a mixed methods design is Dressler's (1991) study of social conditions and health. Here, open-ended ethnographic interviews were used initially, and the results of these were used to inform the construction of structured survey instruments. An illustration of a mixed model approach is the *parallel mixed model* study reported by Taylor and Tashakkori (1997). These authors investigated school restructuring effects and combined both qualitative and quantitative techniques at the data collection, data analysis, and inference stages. Data were collected by asking teachers to respond to a quantitative survey instrument with closed-ended questions and also to answer qualitative open-ended questions. Additionally, classroom observations were carried out, and focus groups were conducted with teachers, students, administrators, board members, and parents. Qualitative and quantitative approaches were also used both in analyzing the data and in drawing conclusions from the results. Tashakkori and Teddlie describe the inference process as drifting "simultaneously between inductive and deductive." Thus it would appear to be the interplay of qualitative and quantitative processes at the *inference* stage (which is not part of the *methodology*) that characterizes this study as mixed model rather than mixed method.

The distinction between mixed methods and mixed model approaches seems useful. Because the focus of interest in this chapter is on the role of the *Internet* in supporting research methodologies, however, and because it is at the data-gathering stage that an IMR approach becomes relevant and distinct from traditional offline approaches, it is mixed methods and not mixed model approaches that are of primary interest here. Of course, the different stages of a research study will interact such that decisions made at the problem-formulation stage, for example, will affect the way data are collected.

Several authors have attempted to provide a categorization scheme for classifying different types of mixed methods designs. Although there has been considerable overlap in the types of dimensions on which different mixed methods designs have been perceived to vary, different authors have adopted slightly different terminology. Creswell (2003) provides an accessible and clear characterization of what he refers to as different *mixed methods models* (not to be confused with *mixed model* approaches, as just mentioned; Creswell uses the term *models* here to mean essentially "categories" or "types" of mixed methods designs). Creswell identifies six key types of mixed methods designs. These are distinguished by the way they differ in terms of the choices made concerning *implementation* (whether data are collected sequentially or concurrently), *priority* (whether either the qualitative or quantitative approach is given priority), *integration* (the stage in the research process at which qualitative and quantitative data are integrated), and whether or not an "overall theoretical perspective (e.g., gender, race/ethnicity, lifestyle, class)" (Creswell, 2003, p. 211) is adopted to guide the entire design process. Creswell notes that sequential designs are generally easier to implement but embody the drawback of requiring a longer data collection period. Concurrent approaches (which Tashakkkori & Teddlie, 1998, refer to as "parallel") are less easy to implement but quicker to execute. Creswell identifies the *concurrent triangulation strategy* as the most familiar mixed methods model, whereby "a researcher uses two different methods in an attempt to confirm, cross-validate, or corroborate findings within a single study" (Creswell, 2003, p. 217). Here quantitative and qualitative techniques may often be combined so as to offset the weaknesses inherent in one method with the strengths of the other method (Creswell, 2003). The concept of "triangulation" is itself strongly associated with mixed methods approaches and refers essentially to the process of attacking a problem or question from several angles, or perspectives, in order to gain a more comprehensive and better informed account (though many varieties of triangulation have been identified; e.g., see Tashakkori & Teddlie, 1998). Although such categorization schemes for mixed methods approaches have emerged relatively recently, certain mixed methods designs have been around for rather longer. For example, a classic illustration of a sequential approach is survey instrument development, in which themes and statements are obtained initially from participants via qualitative interviews and then are used to create specific statements to develop a quantitative survey instrument that is subsequently validated with a large sample representative of a population (Creswell, 2003).

It is worth pointing out that some authors have objected to a mixed methods approach on theoretical grounds, arguing that qualitative and quantitative research strategies are based on such fundamentally different ontological and epistemological claims that they cannot be coherently combined (see Smith, 1983, for a discussion of the compatability or otherwise of qualitative and quantitative research strategies). Nevertheless, an increasing number of authors are advocating the approach, arguing that the traditional divide between, and perceived incompatability of, qualitative and quantitative research strategies is not useful, because both have their own relative strengths and weaknesses (e.g., Eid & Diener, 2005; Johnson & Onwuegbuzie, 2004). The philosophical position (or "paradigm") underlying this view is *pragmatism*. According to Tashakkori and Teddlie, writing in 1998, the long-standing *paradigm wars*, in which researchers debated the relative merits of quantitative and qualitative approaches, were over and had become superseded by a paradigm-relativist pragmatist orientation. Pragmatists argue that a research strategy should be chosen based on what is most appropriate in addressing the research question at hand and that either qualitative or quantitative approaches, or a combination of both, may be most suited to meeting a particular research goal. Pragmatists thus urge for recognition of the value of both qualitative and quantitative approaches and accept the usefulness of combining elements of each of these strategies within a single study to address a particular research question. They therefore aim to break down the traditional divide between qualitative and quantitative approaches to research design, data gathering, and data analysis (Tashakkori & Teddlie, 1998).

Advantages and Disadvantages of Mixed Methods Approaches

All mixed methods approaches place fairly intensive demands on researcher levels of expertise, requiring familiarity with both qualitative and quantitative research designs, methods, and analysis techniques, which may be seen as a potential drawback of, or at least a barrier to, the approach. Also, the mixing of both quantitative and qualitative strategies tends to increase the complexity of a piece of research, which may also place additional demands on the types of resources, tools, and equipment required (e.g., relevant software packages). Mixed methods approaches will also typically impose an extended time scale on a piece of research compared with monomethod approaches, particularly when using sequential designs. However, the value of mixed methods approaches lies in their ability to provide converging strands of evidence in relation to a single research question and thus provide a richer and more comprehensive picture (cf. the concept of triangulation). Also, mixed methods strategies have been described as useful for approaching questions at different levels. For example, in some situations, quantitative techniques may perhaps be more appropriate at one level of analysis, whereas qualitative techniques may be most suitable at another level, for example, as in Tashakkori and Teddlie's (1998) description of a study in which a survey was administered to a large number of high school students across different schools, school principals were interviewed in depth, and schools were extensively observed for social-psychological dynamics. Here the qualitative school-level data may help make the quantitative survey data more meaningful, and vice versa (Tashakkori & Teddlie, 1998). Despite the practical considerations that may present barriers in undertaking mixed methods studies, the present discussion adopts a perspective in agreement with the general sentiments of Tashakkori and Teddlie, who state,

> We stress the importance of the predominance of the research question over the paradigm, and we encourage researchers to use appropriate methods from both [qualitative and quantitative] approaches to answer their research question. For most applications in the social and behavioral sciences, these research questions are best answered with mixed method or mixed model research designs rather than with a sole reliance on either the quantitative or

qualitative approach. (Tasakkori & Teddlie, 1998, p. x)

Mixed Methods Approaches in IMR

In this section, the role of the Internet in supporting mixed methods research is considered, with emphasis on the way in which combination of these two emergent research methods may lead to particular benefits over and above those that accrue when they are used individually. To start with, it is useful to draw up a typology of the main types of IMR studies under consideration in this chapter, categorized according to two key relevant dimensions: first, whether they adopt a qualitative or quantitative orientation or both and, second, whether they use a single or mixed mode approach. In the current context, "mixed mode" specifically refers to the use of both online and offline methods of data collection within a single study, whereas "single mode" uses only one or the other of these media. Thus a study in which questionnaires are administered both in pen-and-paper format *and* electronically via the Internet would be a mixed mode IMR study, as would be a research design that involved first administering questionnaires to participants online and then following this up with offline face-to-face interviews. It should be noted that terms such as *mixed mode*, *multimode*, *mixed methods*, *multimethod*, *mixed methodology*, and so on have been used in a variety of ways, and their domains of reference have been varied and not always clear. For the purposes of the present discussion, the definition of mixed methods, as outlined earlier, is used throughout (unless otherwise specified)—that is, the use of both qualitative and quantitative research strategies within the methodology of a single research study or series of studies. Mixed mode is used here in a restricted way to refer to mixed mode *IMR* designs, that is, those that combine both offline and online data-gathering procedures, as just outlined.

Consideration of the various possible combinations of mode (online or offline) and research strategy (quantitative or qualitative) in IMR studies gives rise to the four main classifications of research design shown in Figure 26.1.

Thus the simplest design in the preceding classification scheme is *c*, which uses either a qualitative or quantitative approach and a single mode of administration only. Because we are here considering IMR approaches, that is, those that make use of the Internet in one way or another to gather data, then the single mode of administration must be online. However, either a quantitative or a qualitative strategy could be adopted (see the examples provided in earlier sections for such designs). An online in-depth qualitative interview, using an Internet-based communication tool such as e-mail or online chat, would be an example of this type of design. Study type *d* in Figure 26.1 has also been discussed in relation to studies that set out to validate Internet-mediated research procedures by comparing administrations of the same instrument or procedure in both offline and online contexts, such as delivery of a personality scale in both pen-and-paper and Web-based format. Because this approach has been fairly commonly implemented in IMR, the next section considers the value and scope of this type of design. The subsequent section then considers mixed methods designs in IMR, that is, those that combine both qualitative and quantitative approaches—designs *a* and *b*. These may use either a single online mode of administration (design *a*) or a combination of online and offline modes (design *b*).

	Same mode (online)	Different modes (online and offline)
Qual and Quan	Mixed methods[a]	Mixed methods, mixed mode[b]
Qual or Quan	Qual or Quan[c]	Mixed mode[d]

FIGURE 26.1. Classification scheme for different types of IMR design.

Because the issues that emerge in relation to each of these two varieties are very similar, they will be discussed together under the generic term *mixed methods IMR studies*.

Mixed Mode IMR Studies

Mixed mode IMR studies have, as described earlier, often been adopted in order to validate IMR procedures and techniques. One variant of such *IMR validation studies* sets out to replicate online effects that have previously been shown to be robust in offline contexts, the idea being that this would then serve to support the validity of the online implementation medium. The second type administers (simultaneously or sequentially) a procedure in both online and offline contexts in order to compare results. Although the tendency has been to assume that convergence with offline results serves to validate online data, the reverse may also be the case (Hewson, 2007). For example, an Internet sample may be more diverse and representative than a traditional sample (e.g., consisting of psychology undergraduates), in which case the Internet data may be considered more trustworthy and valid in terms of being more representative and generalizable to a broader population. The use of IMR procedures may thus be valuable in further validation of test instruments initially developed using smaller, more restricted samples (see, e.g., Hewson & Charlton, 2005). As well as being used to validate online (or offline) procedures, IMR mixed mode studies may also be useful in research that aims to explore the nature of potential differences in online and offline behaviors. For example, some studies have compared the characteristics of online and offline interviews in order to examine whether the idiosyncratic features of each mode of administration (some of which were discussed earlier, e.g., presence or absence of extralinguistic cues) may have an impact on the way the interview proceeds. Such studies are of interest in their own right, as explorations of behavior in an online medium. Other mixed mode studies have had the primary goal neither of looking for comparability of online and offline procedures nor looking for contrasts but have simply used the approach because it has been seen as beneficial in enhancing the data-gathering process. For example, Workman (1992) reports using electronic media to support offline participant observation fieldwork, noting that although the electronic medium did not replace traditional methods, it was useful for scheduling meetings and gaining additional information from, for example, bulletin board systems (BBS) and mailing lists. Similarly, Davis and colleagues (2004) commend the possibilities for and potential benefits of mixed mode IMR studies, noting that the use of both online and offline methods together can generate datasets that may complement each other by providing a type of information that the other may lack.[9] Thus, while recognizing certain limitations of the data they obtained from online synchronous chat interviews (due mainly to problems with ambiguity and a lack of depth and detail in participants' responses), Davis and colleagues suggested that such approaches could nevertheless be useful when combined with other offline methods, such as face-to-face interviews, which they also used in their study. Thus, conceivably, online methods may prove useful in making initial contact with participants and perhaps eliciting information that might be difficult to otherwise obtain in a face-to-face setting (e.g., due to social desirability effects or the inconvenience of having to attend an interview site), which can then be followed up, after contact has been established, using offline methods, which may offer different types of benefits such as being more efficient and effective in eliciting richer, more elaborate, and less ambiguous data.

Advantages and Disadvantages of Mixed Mode IMR Studies

Some advantages of mixed mode studies have already been noted, including their role in validating online and offline procedures, comparing online and offline behaviors, and providing additional support when used alongside offline data-gathering procedures. Also, mixed mode IMR studies may help obtain more representative samples. Hewson (2003), for example, has suggested that the bias toward overrepresentation of females in much psychological research (due to the heavy use of psychology undergraduate students) may be addressed by concurrently using both offline and online methods to recruit participants and administer a study. Hewson thus assumes the overrepresentation of males in at least some accessible online contexts. Although this is probably still true, the changing demographics of the Internet user population has no doubt closed the gender gap somewhat, and in some forums women may well be overrepresented. However, the key point here is that the diversity and range of online contexts available, for example, the enormous number of general and specialist interest online discussion forums, provides great scope for targeting and accessing samples with certain desired qualities, whether these be gender-specific, age-specific, or more broadly representative. This may indeed provide scope for researchers to supplement traditional offline samples in ways that are of benefit to the research question at hand and in cases in which practicable constraints might make accessing such samples offline difficult. Of course, certain populations are still underrepresented on the Internet (e.g., the homeless), and this is the reason that using offline and online sampling procedures concurrently may prove valuable. Another role for mixed mode IMR studies is in allowing broader generalizations to be drawn about the robustness of experimental and other research and assessment procedures (e.g., psychometric testing). This point relates to the variability inherent in IMR procedures due to the lack of control over contextual variables, as noted earlier. For example, as Hewson and Charlton (2005) point out, administering a psychometric scale or questionnaire online and obtaining the same results (e.g., psychometric test properties) as have been obtained in offline administrations (e.g., pen and paper) lends support to the robustness of the testing procedures and constructs being measured. Thus, in the development of a new scale, this approach may be useful right at the outset, especially as gathering supplementary data online can be quick and efficient. This will allow a test of the robustness of a procedure not only across the kinds of (to some extent unknown) variations that no doubt occur in IMR implementations but also across diverse samples.

Mixed mode IMR studies can thus be useful for a range of purposes. The main disadvantage is probably the extended time scale involved in conducting a mixed mode study. However, in concurrent approaches, given the ease of data collection on the Internet due to ease of automation, this may be of minimal impact. Sequential approaches could prove to be more time-consuming, but again the scope for automation in IMR means that this may not be a major drawback. Another disadvantage may be the need for levels of technical expertise, as outlined earlier, in implementing an IMR phase of a study. As with all types of research, the potential advantages and disadvantages of any particular approach need to be assessed in relation to the research goals and the resources available.

Mixed Methods and Mixed Methods, Mixed Mode Approaches in IMR

Studies working solely within either quantitative or qualitative research traditions have dominated the IMR literature to date. However, some authors have implemented mixed methods designs, especially more recently, as these have become increasingly popular within traditional offline research contexts. Examples of these studies follow.

Sequential Mixed Methods Designs

Several authors have reported implementing sequential mixed methods IMR studies. Madge and O'Connor (2002) found the approach useful in their study of the experiences of new parents. They initially recruited participants via the Internet by posting an invitation for participation in a quantitative survey to the website *babyworld.co.uk.* The survey was also placed on the Babyworld website, with permission of the site managers. On submission of survey responses, participants were then invited to continue in a follow-up phase, which involved taking part in qualitative online focus groups. Fifteen out of the 155 participants who completed the survey agreed to take part in this second phase of the study. Madge and O'Connor's approach thus provides a good example of how IMR can be useful to quickly and effectively gather a large volume of quantitative data initially in order to gain a broader, more generalizable impression and then to follow this up with more in-depth qualitative data-gathering procedures that allow greater, more detailed insights into individual participants' perspectives. Madge and O'Connor note the success of their online focus group procedures in generating such rich, elaborate data, with some of the advantages of online qualitative interview approaches outlined earlier coming into play, such as high levels of elaboration and self-disclosure. Susan Herring and colleagues have also made use of sequential mixed methods approaches in a series of IMR studies looking at online communication. Herring and colleagues (1998), for example, conducted a study in which the first phase involved observing mailing list discussion postings and subjecting these to quantitative analysis, considering, for example, the frequency and length of postings from different group members. Herring and colleagues were particularly interested in gender differences in participation in the discussion. After the quantitative analysis phase, Herring then went on to follow up on these results by posting an open-ended survey to the mailing list group asking for participants' perceptions of a particular discussion thread that had occurred and been subjected to quantitative analysis. The results of utilizing these two types of data—linguistic observation and participants' self-reports—proved interesting in this study. Overall, whereas men were found to dominate the discussion thread when objective quantitative measures such as the frequency and length of postings were considered, the perceptions of male contributors about the relative contributions of men and women conflicted with the information derived from these objective measures. Men perceived women to have been dominating the discussion, even when the reverse was true. This ability to compare lay perceptions and objective observational measures is especially useful, as the two may often conflict, and this is itself an interesting research topic. Kendall (1999) also notes the value of being able to compare self-report and observational data in IMR, having made use of this approach in a concurrent mixed methods design (see the next subsection). In IMR the range of accessible text-based data amenable to observational analysis and the ease in many cases of contacting the contributors of this data via newsgroups, mailing lists, and so on make this approach quite practicable. An example of a sequential[10] mixed methods, mixed mode IMR study has been presented by Strickland and colleagues (2003). In a study of migraines in perimenopausal women, these authors recruited participants to first complete several online quantitative questionnaires and then take part in asynchronous online focus groups. Finally, participants were asked to take part in a telephone interview. These authors report the approach as moderately successful, though some issues emerged relating to difficulties in establishing good levels of rapport with participants.

For both Herring and colleagues (1998) and Madge and O'Connor (2002), the choice to implement sequential mixed methods approaches seemed appropriate in meeting the research goals. Herring and colleagues were interested in tapping people's subjective perceptions of an online discussion thread *after* having taken part in that discussion. Had they used a concurrent approach, in which participants were asked to answer survey-type questions while the discussion was going on, this may have influenced the way the discussion proceeded. Of course, nonreactive observational data and reactive self-report data can also be collected concurrently in IMR. Madge and O'Connor were interested in following up on a quantitative survey using qualitative in-depth interviews, and having survey results available prior to conducting the interviews can be potentially useful in guiding the focus and content of these interviews and the range and relevance to participants of the topics explored. Thus in such sequential designs the first phase of a study can feed into the design and procedure of the second phase. In Strickland and colleagues' (2003) study, it was not clear whether such a strategy was adopted or not, though the data-collection stages were delivered sequentially to individual participants. Some examples of concurrent mixed methods IMR studies that have been implemented to date are now provided.

Concurrent Mixed Methods Designs

Kendall (1999) has implemented a concurrent mixed methods, mixed mode IMR design, which made use of face-to-face interviews, group participation sessions, and information gathered via newsgroups and mailing lists. Kendall points out the benefits of being able to easily acquire both self-report and observational data using IMR methods. Ward (1999) has implemented a concurrent mixed methods IMR design, using online methods only (i.e., single mode), by combining observational data and semistructured interviews to study online communities, making use of e-mail and BBS.[11] The communities Ward studied were located via two websites: @Cybergrrl and Women Halting Online Abuse (WHOA). Ward reports the approach as being successful in generating a rich understanding of these online communities' perceptions and experiences. Sotillo and Wang-Gempp (2004) report what may be described as a concurrent mixed methods study, in which they downloaded archives of political discussions from a public bulletin board in order to produce a corpus of texts, which were then subjected to both quantitative and qualitative analyses. Thus this study implemented a mixed methods strategy at the analysis stage, essentially, rather than at the data-gathering stage (the data gathered were clearly amenable to both forms of analysis). As already noted, many of the potential data sources online, such as discussion archives, Web pages, online documents, and so forth, are amenable to analysis using either qualitative or quantitative techniques.

The preceding examples indicate that researchers are starting to use mixed methods designs in IMR, though to date the approach is far from having been extensively explored. Much more common are mixed mode studies that do not aim specifically to mix qualitative and quantitative strategies but mix online and offline data-gathering methods or research designs working within a solely qualitative or quantitative tradition. This is not especially surprising, given that IMR and mixed methods approaches are both still relatively recently emerging methods. Also, it does not seem obvious that any one discipline has been especially prominent in leading the way in IMR mixed methods approaches. It would seem that IMR mixed methods designs may be potentially useful across a broad range of disciplines and research domains. Identifying the types of research questions that lend themselves to the various approaches within IMR, and mixed methods IMR approaches in particular, is an ongoing topic of investigation.

Advantages of Mixed Methods Approaches in IMR

A number of advantages of using online methods to facilitate mixed methods research seem immediately apparent. Obviously, mixed methods approaches in IMR will inherit the advantages and disadvantages (as outlined earlier) of the respective quantitative and qualitative methods on which they draw. However, some features of

IMR seem particularly relevant in relation to facilitating mixed methods designs, compared with implementation of such designs in traditional offline research. One salient feature relates to the barriers to implementing traditional mixed methods approaches outlined earlier, most notably, the additional time and costs involved in conducting what in mixed methods approaches is typically a larger scale study than using either quantitative or qualitative strategies alone. Here the enhanced efficiency often characteristic of the IMR data-gathering process may be especially beneficial. Thus, as noted, traditional mixed methods approaches–especially sequential designs–tend to involve lengthy and costly data collection and analysis procedures. The cost- and time-saving benefits to the researcher, which are general features of IMR approaches, due to factors such as the ease of access to participants, automation of various stages of the research process, and so on, may clearly benefit traditionally time-consuming mixed methods studies. Furthermore, the digitizing of data that occurs in IMR may aid mixed methods approaches by automatically rendering data available in a format that can be readily transported between different data management software packages, including those designed for both qualitative and quantitative forms of analysis (Mann & Stewart, 2000). One of the points noted about mixed methods approaches, which could act as a potential barrier, was the need for researchers to be well versed in both qualitative and quantitative forms of analysis. Although the implementation of IMR mixed methods approaches obviously does not eliminate this demand on researchers' levels of expertise, the easy import of data into supporting analysis software packages may serve to facilitate the data analysis process, freeing up more time for the researcher to engage with the relevant data analysis techniques because he or she will not have to spend vast time and costs on data input and formatting. IMR mixed methods approaches may also reduce the demands placed on participants (which may often also be high) because of the greater control offered over time and place of response. Using IMR to implement mixed methods research could also offer the benefit of enhancing triangulation techniques in which methods are combined in order to offset each other's inherent weaknesses with their respective strengths. Thus some IMR data-gathering techniques may offer novel advantages compared with existing offline procedures because of their particular characteristics (such as heightened levels of anonymity and privacy in online interactions, potentially leading to reduced social desirability effects), and these may be especially useful in a mixed methods design. Of course, methods may also be mixed *within* one research orientation (i.e., qualitative or quantitative), such as in the use of both synchronous and asynchronous interviews online to provide data for a qualitative research study. On the other hand, a researcher might decide that the data generated by asynchronous interviews may be better suited to analysis using qualitative techniques, whereas those generated by synchronous approaches may be more suited to quantitative analysis techniques. All these issues and questions demand further exploration. Nevertheless, at a time at which the relative advantages and disadvantages of the various possible IMR procedures are still being uncovered (e.g., Reips, 2002) and in which trade-offs are clearly apparent in making choices about which approach to use, it would seem sensible to suggest making use of more than one method or strategy. This suggestion may naturally lead to mixed methods designs in which a key goal is to take advantage of the potential benefits of both qualitative and quantitative approaches by combining these to address an individual research question.

To summarize, the preceding discussion has provided some preliminary reflections on the use of IMR to conduct mixed methods studies, considering the experiences of researchers who have adopted the approach to date. Internet-mediated research is still young, and mixed methods approaches are just coming to fruition and widespread recognition. As more researchers join those pioneers of IMR mixed methods research mentioned here, the benefits and drawbacks of marrying these two approaches will become increasingly clear.

Conclusions

Both Internet-mediated research and mixed methods approaches are emergent research methods. This chapter has explored the former, in particular, and shown it to be a promising approach that has generated a diverse range of successful studies to date, both within qualitative and quantitative research traditions and across a broad range of disciplines and research domains. The ability of IMR to facilitate and benefit mixed methods approaches in particular was also considered, after describing some examples of such studies. Although this particular combination of emergent methods remains to be further utilized and explored, in terms of the benefits it can offer and the range of questions to which various designs may be usefully applied, some initial suggestions have been offered here about the value of IMR in supporting mixed methods approaches. Future studies are required to clarify the extent of the value of this approach. However, at present the combination looks promising.

Notes

1. However, it is not clear the extent to which this finding may reflect a bias among survey respondents toward those working primarily within quantitative rather than qualitative research traditions.

2. Note that the concepts of validity and reliability are relevant primarily to quantitative approaches to research. Qualitative parallels to these concepts are "trustworthiness," "dependability," and "confirmability" (Denzin & Lincoln, 2000).

3. "Client-side" scripts are those that run on the client computer, that is, the remote computer that is connected to a host Web server. Javascript commands embedded within an HTML form are executed by the Web browser on the client computer. In contrast, "server-side" scripts run on the Web server itself. CGI (Common Gateway Interface) scripts are an example of the latter type (see Hewson et al., 2003, for a more detailed discussion of these Internet technologies).

4. Examples of blogs can be accessed via the Yahoo! list, available at *buzz.yahoo.com/buzz_log/entry/2005/03/08/1300/*.

5. Such as mIRC, for Windows operating systems, available at *www.mirc.com* for a one-time fee of $20.

6. Such as Microsoft's MSN Messenger for Windows, freely available at *messenger.msn.com*.

7. As Hewson (2007) notes, the term *conversational flow* can take on a variety of specific meanings. However, in the current context, it can be taken as referring to the topics covered, links drawn between subthemes, and the time scale of the interview dialogue.

8. In fact, although Heinz, Gu, and Zender (2002) describe their study as qualitative, they do also make extensive use of quantitative analysis approaches, thus producing a mixed methods design.

9. This idea is somewhat related to the notion of triangulation mentioned earlier, whereby different methods (e.g., quantitative and qualitative or online and offline) may be combined in order to offset each other's weaknesses.

10. The study was sequential from the participants' point of view, at least. However, because participants were allowed to complete the questionnaires in their own time at their leisure, and because the researchers determined when to set up the online focus groups by waiting until a group of four or five participants had completed the questionnaires, this meant that individual participants could be at different stages of the study at any time. This required the researchers to be engaged in managing data collection from different phases of the study (i.e., questionnaires, focus groups, interviews) simultaneously.

11. Strictly speaking, based on the definition of mixed methods provided earlier, it is questionable whether this study should in fact be described as "mixed methods," the discussion hav-

ing been presented largely within a qualitative analysis framework. Nevertheless, it is a useful example of the combined use of different data-gathering methods in IMR.

References

Anderson, G., Kaldo-Sandstrom, V., Strom, L., & Stromgren, T. (2003). Internet administration of the Hospital Anxiety and Depression Scale in a sample of tinnitus patients. *Journal of Psychosomatic Research, 55*(3), 259–262.

Basic HTML programming. (n.d.). Retrieved September 8, 2007, from *www.cs.cf.ac.uk/Dave/PERL/node1.html*

Berg, B. L. (2006). *Qualitative research methods for the social sciences* (6th ed.). Boston: Allyn & Bacon.

Birnbaum, M. H. (Ed.). (2000). *Psychological experiments on the Internet*. San Diego, CA: Academic Press.

Birnbaum, M. H. (2001). *Introduction to behavioral research on the Internet*. Upper Saddle River, NJ: Prentice Hall.

Birnbaum, M. H. (2004). Human research and data collection via the Internet. *Annual Review of Psychology, 55*, 803–832.

Birnbaum, M. H., & Reips, U.-D. (2005). Behavioral research and data collection via the Internet. In R. W. Proctor & K.-P. L. Vu (Eds.), *The handbook of human factors in Web design* (pp. 471–492). Mahwah, NJ: Erlbaum.

Bordia, P. (1996). Studying verbal interaction on the Internet: The case of rumour transmission research. *Behavior Research Methods, Instruments, and Computers, 28*, 149–151.

Bowker, N., & Tuffin, K. (2004). Using the online medium for discursive research about people with disabilities. *Social Science Computer Review, 22*(2), 228–241.

British Psychological Society. (2007). *Report of the working party on conducting research on the Internet: Guidelines for ethical practice in psychological research online* (Report No. 62/06.2007). Leicester, UK: Author.

Bryman, A. (2004). *Social research methods* (2nd ed.). Oxford, UK: Oxford University Press.

Bryman, A. (2006). *Mixed methods*. Thousand Oaks, CA: Sage.

Buchanan, T. (2001). Online personality assessment. In U.-D. Reips & M. Bosnjak (Eds.), *Dimensions of Internet science* (pp. 57–74). Lengerich, Germany: Pabst Science.

Buchanan, T., & Smith, J. L. (1999). Using the Internet for psychological research: Personality testing on the World Wide Web. *British Journal of Psychology, 90*, 125–144.

Castro, E. (2002). *HTML for the World Wide Web with XHTML and CSS: Visual QuickStart guide* (5th ed.). Berkeley, CA: Peachpit Press.

Computer Industry Almanac. (2006). *Press release: Worldwide Internet users top 1 billion in 2005*. Retrieved September 8, 2007, from *www.c-i-a.com/pr0106.htm*

Coomber, R. (1997). Dangerous drug adulteration: An international survey of drug dealers using the Internet and World Wide Web (WWW). *International Journal of Drug Policy, 8*(2), 71–81.

Corley, M., & Scheepers, C. (2002). Syntactic priming in English sentence production: Categorical and latency evidence from an Internet-based study. *Psychonomic Bulletin Review, 9*(1), 126–131.

Couper, P. (2000). Web surveys: A review of issues and approaches. *Public Opinion Quarterly, 64*(4), 464–494.

Creswell, J. W. (2003). *Research design: Qualitative, quantitative and mixed methods approaches* (2nd ed.). Thousand Oaks, CA: Sage.

Creswell, J. W., & Plano-Clark, V. L. (2006). *Designing and conducting mixed methods research*. Thousand Oaks, CA: Sage.

Davis, M., Bolding, G., Hart, G., Sherr, L., & Elford, J. (2004). Reflecting on the experience of interviewing online: Perspectives from the Internet and HIV study in London. *AIDS Care, 16*(8), 944–952.

Denzin, N. K., & Lincoln, Y. S. (2000). *The handbook of qualitative research*. Thousand Oaks, CA: Sage.

Dillman, D. A. (2006). *Mail and Internet surveys: The tailored design method* (2nd ed.). Hoboken, NJ: Wiley.

Dillman, D. A., & Bowker, D. K. (2001). The Web questionnaire challenge to survey methodologists. In U.-D. Reips & M. Bosnjak (Eds.), *Dimensions of Internet science* (pp. 159–178). Lengerich, Germany: Pabst Science.

Dressler, W. W. (1991). *Stress and adaption in the context of culture: Depression in a Southern black community*. Albany: State University of New York Press.

Eid, M., & Diener, E. (Eds.). (2005). *Handbook of multimethod measurement in psychology*. Washington, DC: American Psychological Association.

Elgesem, D. (2002). What is special about the ethical issues in online research? *Ethics and Information Technology, 4*, 195–203.

Ess, C. (2007). Internet research ethics. In A. Joinson, K. McKenna, U. Reips, & T. Postmes (Ed.), *Oxford handbook of Internet psychology* (pp. 487–502). Oxford, UK: Oxford University Press.

Flicker, S., Haans, D., & Skinner, H. (2004). Ethical dilemmas in research on Internet communities. *Qualitative Health Research, 14*, 124–134.

Fox, J., Murray, C., & Warm, A. (2003). Conducting research using Web-based questionnaires: Practical, methodological, and ethical considerations. *Social Research Methodology, 6*(2), 167–180.

Fraley, R. C. (2007). Using the Internet for personality research: What can be done, how to do it, and some concerns. In R. W. Robins, R. C. Fraley, & R. F. Krueger (Eds.), *Handbook of research methods in personality psychology* (pp. 130–148). New York: Guilford Press.

Frankel, M., & Siang, S. (1999). *Ethical and legal issues of human subjects research on the Internet: Report of a workshop*.Washington, DC: American Association for the Advancement of Science. Retrieved October 2, 2006, from *www.aaas.org/spp/sfrl/projects/intres/report.pdf*

Fritsche, I., & Linneweber, V. (2006). Nonreactive methods in psychological research. In M. Eid & E. Diener (Eds.), *Handbook of multimethod measurement in psychology* (pp. 189–203). Washington, DC: American Psychological Association.

Givaty, G., van Vaan, H. A. H. C., Christou, C., & Bulthoff, H. H. (1998). *Tele-experiments: Experiments on spatial cognition using VRML-based multimedia*. Retrieved September 10, 2007, from *www.ece.uwaterloo.ca/vrml98/cdrom/papers/givaty/givaty.pdf*

Göritz, A. S., & Birnbaum, M. H. (2005). Generic HTML form processor: A versatile PHP script to save Web-collected data into a MySQL database. *Behavior Research Methods, Instruments and Computers*, *37*(4), 703–710.

Green, J. C., & Caracelli, V. J. (Eds.). (1997). *Advances in mixed method evaluation: The challenges and benefits of integrating diverse paradigms* (New Directions for Program Evaluation, Vol. 74). San Francisco: Jossey-Bass.

Greene, J. C., Caracelli, V. J., & Graham, W. F. (1989). Toward a conceptual framework for mixed method evaluation designs. *Educational Evaluation and Policy Analysis*, *11*(3), 255–274.

Heinz, B., Gu, L., Inuzuka, A., & Zender, R. (2002). Under the rainbow flag: Webbing global gay identities. *International Journal of Sexuality and Gender Studies*, 7(2/3), 107–124.

Herring, S. C. (1993). Gender and democracy in computer-mediated communication. *Electronic Journal of Communication*, *3*(2). Retrieved September 8, 2007, from *http://ella.slis.indiana.edu/~herring/ejc.txt*

Herring, S. C., Johnson, D. A., & DiBenedetto, T. (1998). Participation in electronic discourse in a "feminist" field. In J. Coates (Ed.), *Language and gender: A reader* (pp. 197–210). Oxford, UK: Blackwell.

Hessler, R. M., Downing, J., Beltz, C., Pelliccio, A., Powell, M., & Vale, W. (2003). Qualitative research on adolescent risk using e-mail: A methodological assessment. *Qualitative Sociology*, *26*(1), 111–124.

Hewson, C. (2003). Conducting psychological research on the Internet. *The Psychologist*, *16*(6), 290–292.

Hewson, C. (2006). Mixed methods research. In V. Jupp (Ed.), *The Sage dictionary of social research methods*. London: Sage.

Hewson, C. (2007). Gathering data on the Internet: Qualitative approaches and possibilities for mixed methods research. In A. Joinson, K. McKenna, U. Reips, & T. Postmes (Ed.), *Oxford handbook of Internet psychology* (pp. 405–428). Oxford, UK: Oxford University Press.

Hewson, C., & Charlton, J. P. (2005). Measuring health beliefs on the Internet: A comparison of paper and Internet administrations of the Multidimensional Health Locus of Control Scale. *Behavior Research Methods, Instruments and Computers*, *37*(4), 691–702.

Hewson, C., Laurent, D., & Vogel, C. M. (1996). Proper methodologies for psychological and sociological studies conducted via the Internet. *Behavior Research Methods, Instruments, and Computers*, *32*, 186–191.

Internet Systems Consortium. (2007). *Internet domain survey, July 2007*. Retrieved September 8, 2007, from *www.isc.org/index.pl*

Johnson, J. A. (2000, March). *Web-based personality assessment*. Poster session presented at the annual meeting of the Eastern Psychological Association, Baltimore.

Johnson, R. B., & Onwuegbuzie, A. J. (2004). Mixed methods research: A research paradigm whose time has come. *Educational Researcher*, *33*(7), 14–26.

Joinson, A. N. (1999). Social desirability, anonymity and Internet-based questionnaires. *Behavior Research Methods, Instruments and Computers*, *31*, 433–438.

Joinson, A. N. (2001). Knowing me, knowing you: Reciprocal self-disclosure in Internet-based surveys. *Cyberpsychology and Behavior*, *4*(5), 587–591.

Jupp, V. (2006). Garbology. In V. Jupp (Ed.), *The Sage dictionary of social research methods* (p. 125). London: Sage.

Kendall, L. (1999). Recontextualizing "cyberspace": Methodological considerations for on-line research. In S. Jones (Ed.), *Doing Internet research: Critical issues and methods for examining the Net* (pp. 57–74). London: Sage.

Krantz, J. H. (2001). Stimulus delivery on the Web: What can be presented when calibration isn't possible. In U.-D. Reips & M. Bosnjak (Eds.), *Dimensions of Internet science* (pp. 113–130). Lengerich, Germany: Pabst Science.

Kraut, R., Olson, J., Banaji, M., Bruckman, A., Cohen, J., & Couper, M. (2004). Psychological research online: Report of Board of Scientific Affairs' advisory group on the conduct of research on the Internet. *American Psychologist*, *59*(2), 105–117.

Madge, C., & O'Connor, H. (2002). On-line with e-mums: Exploring the Internet as a medium for research. *Area*, *34*(1), 92–102.

Mann, C., & Stewart, F. (2000). *Internet communication and qualitative research: A handbook for researching online*. Thousand Oaks, CA: Sage.

McGraw, K. O., Tew, M. D., & Williams, J. E. (2000). The integrity of web-delivered experiments: Can you trust the data? *Psychological Science*, *11*(6), 502–506.

Murray, C. D., & Sixsmith, J. (1998). E-mail: A qualitative research medium for interviewing? *International Journal of Social Research Methodology: Theory and Practice*, *1*(2), 103–121.

Musch, J., & Reips, U.-D. (2000). A brief history of Web experimenting. In M. H. Birnbaum (Ed.), *Psychological experiments on the Internet* (pp. 61–87). San Diego, CA: Academic Press.

Nastri, J., Pena, J., & Hancock, J. T. (2006). The construction of away messages: A speech act analysis.

Journal of Computer-Mediated Communication, 11(4), article 7. Retrieved October 1, 2006, from *jcmc.indiana.edu/vol11/issue4/nastri.html*

O'Brien, L. P. (1999). The Internet and qualitative research: Opportunities and constraints on analysis of cyberspace discourse. In M. Kopala & L. A. Suzuki (Eds.), *Using qualitative methods in psychology* (pp. 77–88). London: Sage.

O'Dochartaigh, N. (2001). *The Internet research handbook: A practical guide for students and researchers in the social sciences.* London: Sage.

Pettitt, F. A. (1999). Exploring the use of the World Wide Web as a psychology data collection tool. *Computers in Human Behavior, 15*(1), 67–71.

Pittenger, D. J. (2003). Internet research: An opportunity to revisit classical ethical problems in behavioural research. *Ethics and Behaviour, 13*(1), 45–60.

Pohl, F., Bender, M., & Lachmann, G. (2002). Hindsight bias around the world. *Experimental Psychology, 49*(4), 270–282.

Postmes, T., & Spears, R. (2002). Behaviour online: Does anonymous computer communication reduce gender inequality? *Personality and Social Psychology Bulletin, 28*(8), 1073–1083.

Rains, S. A., & Young, A. M. (2006). A sign of the times: An analysis of organizational members' email signatures. *Journal of Computer-Mediated Communication, 11*(4), article 8. Retrieved October 1, 2006, from *jcmc.indiana.edu/vol11/issue4/rains.html*

Reips, U.-D. (2001). The Web experimental psychology lab: Five years of data collection on the Internet. *Behavior Research Methods, Instruments, and Computers, 33*(2), 201–211.

Reips, U.-D. (2002). Standards for Internet-based experimenting. *Experimental Psychology, 49*(4), 243–256.

Reips, U.-D. (2007). The methodology of Internet-based experiments. In A. Joinson, K. McKenna, U. Reips, & T. Postmes (Ed.), *Oxford handbook of Internet psychology* (pp. 373–390). Oxford, UK: Oxford University Press.

Robson, C. (1993). *Real world research: A resource for social scientists and practitioner-researchers.* Oxford, UK: Blackwell.

Schmidt, W. C. (1997) World Wide Web survey research: Benefits, potential, problems, and solutions. *Behavior Research Methods, Instruments, and Computers, 29*, 274–279.

Schmidt, W. C. (2002). A server-side program for delivering experiments with animations. *Behavior Research Methods, Instruments, and Computers, 34*(2), 208–217.

Schonlau, M., Fricker, R. D., & Elliott, M. N., Jr. (2002). *Conducting research surveys via e-mail and the Web.* Santa Monica, CA: RAND Corporation.

Scott, J. (2006). Content analysis. In V. Jupp (Ed.), *The Sage dictionary of social research methods* (pp. 40–41). London: Sage.

Smith, J. K. (1983). Quantitative versus qualitative research: An attempt to clarify the issues. *Educational Research, 12*, 6–13.

Sotillo, S. M., & Wang-Gempp, J. (2004). Using corpus linguistics to investigate class, ideology and discursive practices in online political discussions. In V. Connor & T. A. Upton (Eds.), *Applied corpus linguistics: A multidimensional perspective* (pp. 91–122). Amsterdam: Rodopi.

Stanton, J. M. (1998). An empirical assessment of data collection using the Internet. *Personnel Psychology, 51*(3), 709–725.

Strickland, O. L., Moloney, M. F., Dietrich, A. S., Myerburg, J. D., Cotsonis, G. A., & Johnson, R. (2003). Measurement issues related to data collection on the World Wide Web. *Advances in Nursing Science, 26*(4), 246–256.

Szabo, A., & Frenkl, M. D. (1996). Consideration of research on Internet: Guidelines and implications for human movement studies. *Clinical Kinesiology, 50*(3), 58–65.

Tashakkori, A., & Teddlie, C. (1998). *Mixed methodology: Combining qualitative and quantitative approaches.* Thousand Oaks, CA: Sage.

Tashakkori, A., & Teddlie, C. (2003). *Handbook of mixed methods in the social and behavioral sciences.* Thousand Oaks, CA: Sage.

Taylor, D. L., & Tashakkori, A. (1997). Towards an understanding of teachers' desire for participation in decision making. *Journal of School Leadership, 7*, 1–20.

Thoreau, E. (2006). Ouch! An examination of the self-representation of disabled people on the Internet. *Journal of Computer-Mediated Communication, 11*(2), 442–468.

Voracek, M., Steiger, S., & Gindl, A. (2001). Online replication of evolutionary psychology evidence: Sex differences in sexual jealousy in imagined scenarios of mate's sexual vs. emotional infidelity. In U.-D. Reips & M. Bosnjak (Eds.), *Dimensions of Internet science* (pp. 91–112). Lengerich, Germany: Pabst Science.

Ward, K. J. (1999). The cyber-ethnographic (re)construction of two feminist online communities. *Sociological Research Online, 4*(1). Retrieved September 8, 2007, from *www.socresearchconline.org.uk/socresearchonline/4/1/ward.html*

Wharton, C. (2006). Document analysis. In V. Jupp (Ed.), *The Sage dictionary of social research methods* (pp. 79–81). London: Sage.

Wolfe, C. R., & Reyna, V. F. (2002). Using NetClock to develop server-side Web-based experiments without writing CGI programs. *Behavior Research Methods, Instruments, and Computers, 34*(2), 204–207.

Workman, J. P. (1992). Use of electronic media in a participant observation study. *Qualitative Sociology, 15*(4), 419–425.

Yule, P., & Cooper, R. P. (2003). Express: A Web-based technology to support human and computational experimentation. *Behavior Research Methods, Instruments, and Computers, 35*(4), 605–613.

CHAPTER 27

Hypermedia Methods for Qualitative Research

Bella Dicks
Bruce Mason

What Are Multimedia?

Technological innovations are increasingly allowing researchers to utilize diverse types of media in their data, but discussion of the implications of mixing media in data records is still undeveloped. Visual methodology has been extensively addressed in recent literature (Banks, 2001; Emmison & Smith, 2000; Harper, 1998; Pink, 2001; Rose, 2001), but other media—such as sound—are only just beginning to receive attention in methodological discussion (e.g., Bauer, 2000; Lashua, Hall, & Coffey, 2006). And—the main point—each medium tends to be discussed in isolation. Little attention has been paid to the methodological implications of combining or mixing media or to the distinctive or similar modes of meaning that different media convey. For example, when a researcher uses both audiotapes and photographic images to record a situation or event in the field, can we say that these represent the "same" data, or even the same event? What is the relationship between that sound recording and those images? How should they be analyzed in relation to each other? Too much attention paid only to the visual realm tends to occlude the importance of the other perceptual senses we bring to bear in apprehending any physical social setting. Increasingly, it seems necessary to replace the idea of visual methods with that of *multimedia methods*, as we increasingly come to recognize the multisensory nature of the social worlds we study (see Dicks, 2006; Dicks, Soyinka, & Coffey, 2006; Pink, 2006).

It is also necessary to think about multimedia at different stages of the research process. One quite obvious gap is the lack of discussion of the implications of screen-based *representation* of research findings in social research. Multimedia is usually considered only in relation to the generation of data (e.g., how to handle a camera in the field) and the making and interpretation of data records (e.g., how to analyze images). Few academic authors take advantage of multimedia in presenting their research findings. Instead, writing usually takes over, at least outside the domain of visual anthropology and film. This means that multimedia data records are generally represented in monomedia forms through written reports and analyses produced by researchers. Conversations from the field appear as snatches of quoted material; interactions are described through written narrative. A series of reductions throughout the research process are implied in this classic process of "writing up." The first reduction occurs when the researcher represents his or her multisensory understanding of the research setting by means of the more limited media available for data recording (fieldnotes, audio recordings, photographs, video recordings). The second is when those records are once more transformed through writing up, when he or she adopts the conventions of the printed page to produce the finished representation. We argue that in the process, despite the considerable powers of description undisputedly available via the written word, diverse modes of meaning are inevitably closed down. Yet the world of print is currently being challenged: Electronic journals are multiplying, and it is clear that images and sound can easily be represented within them. The conventions and parameters for incorporating multimedia into scholarly articles remain, however, unclear and largely untested. This chapter discusses the dilemmas of bringing multimedia and hypermedia approaches into the "writing up," or representational, phase of qualitative research, as well as in the other phases of a study. This, after all, is the moment in which the researcher strives to represent his or her findings publicly in a form that is readable, expressive, convincing, persuasive, and—above all—interesting. The introduction of electronic media into this task of creation is an exciting, yet also potentially troubling, prospect.

What Are Hypermedia?

The other strand of methodological innovation implicit in the possibilities of the computer screen is *hypermedia*. A simple definition of hypermedia is that it brings together *hypertext* (which is simply "clickable writing," as institutionalized on the World Wide Web via HTML and its characteristic highlighted links) and *multimedia* (the use of a variety of media to communicate, typically including sound, still images, moving images, graphical images, and so forth—but also, as in emergent virtual-reality domains, tastes and smells, too). Hence, *hypermedia is clickable multimedia*. This means that the resultant electronic text may be made up of a diversity of sounds and images alongside writing (the written word will continue to play a large part in any scholarly work, for obvious reasons). Hypermedia scholarly texts can mirror simple Web pages (perhaps with only basic "next" and "back" links), or they can have complex structures that encourage more multilinear kinds of exploration—hence the word *environment* rather than *text* captures the kind of reading experience they provide. They can be hosted on the Web, possibly with password-protected access, or they can be distributed via portable media such as CDs, DVDs, and flash drives. So far, few academic hypermedia environments exist, though there are some notable examples that are discussed later on, including our own work.

Ethnographic Hypermedia Environments

Together with colleagues, we have spent a number of years examining the potential of hypermedia for the conduct and authoring of ethnographic research (Dicks, Mason, Coffey, & Atkinson, 2005). This has involved the construction of an experimental "ethnographic hypermedia environment" (EHE), which is being developed at Cardiff University School of Social Sciences. Figures 27.1–27.4 show some screen shots from our EHE. They show how it is organized into two

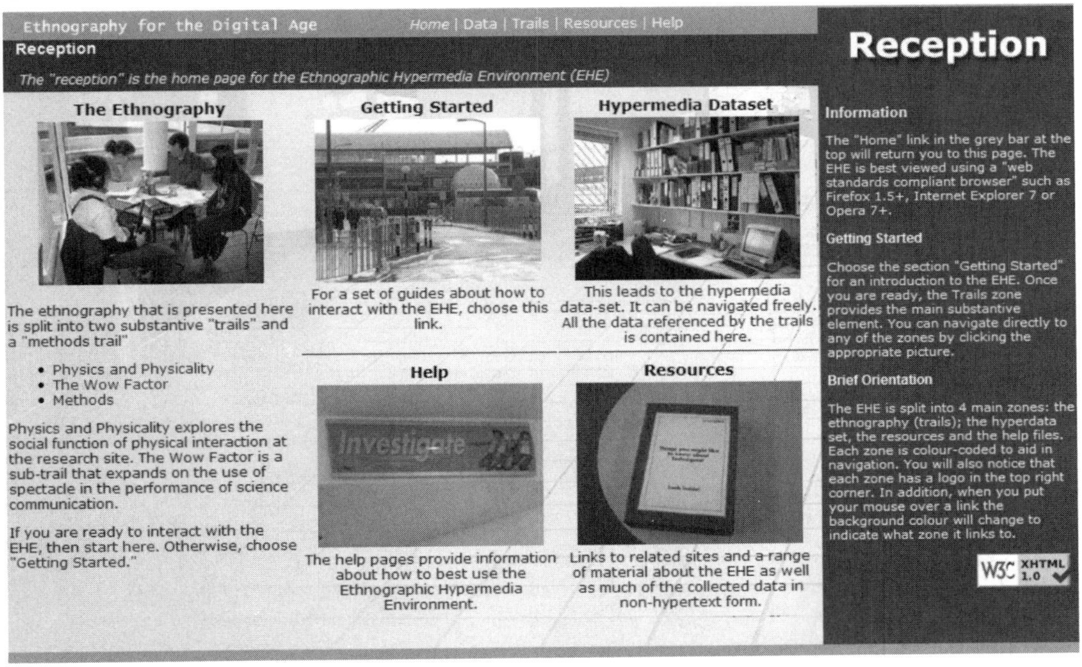

FIGURE 27.1. The start page of the EHE.

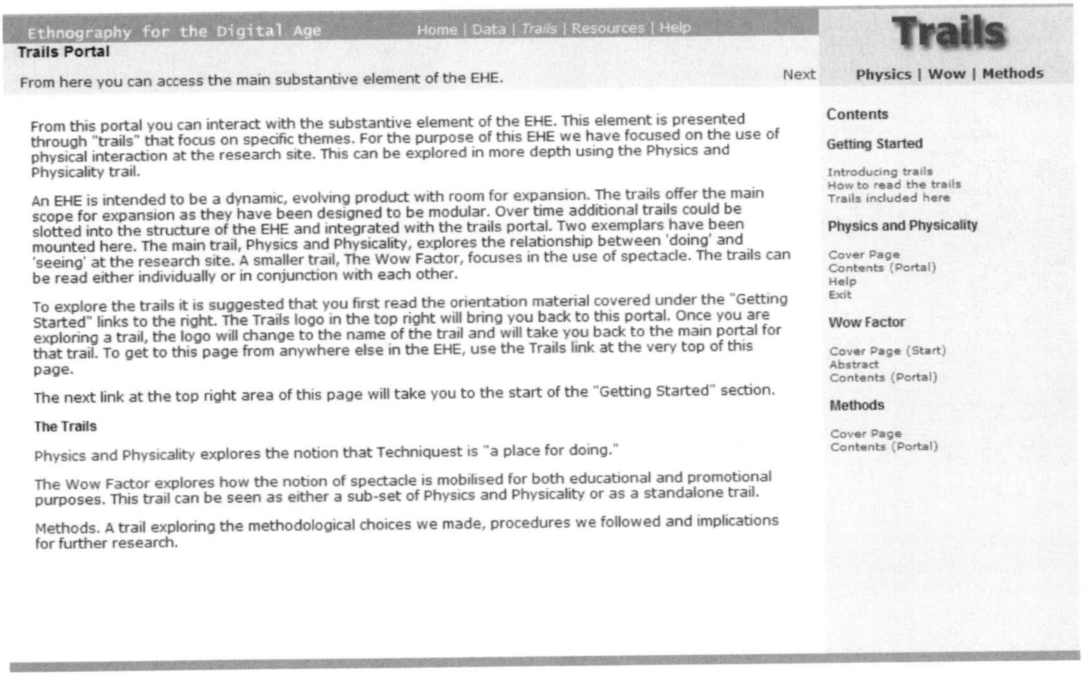

FIGURE 27.2. The "trails" portal of the EHE.

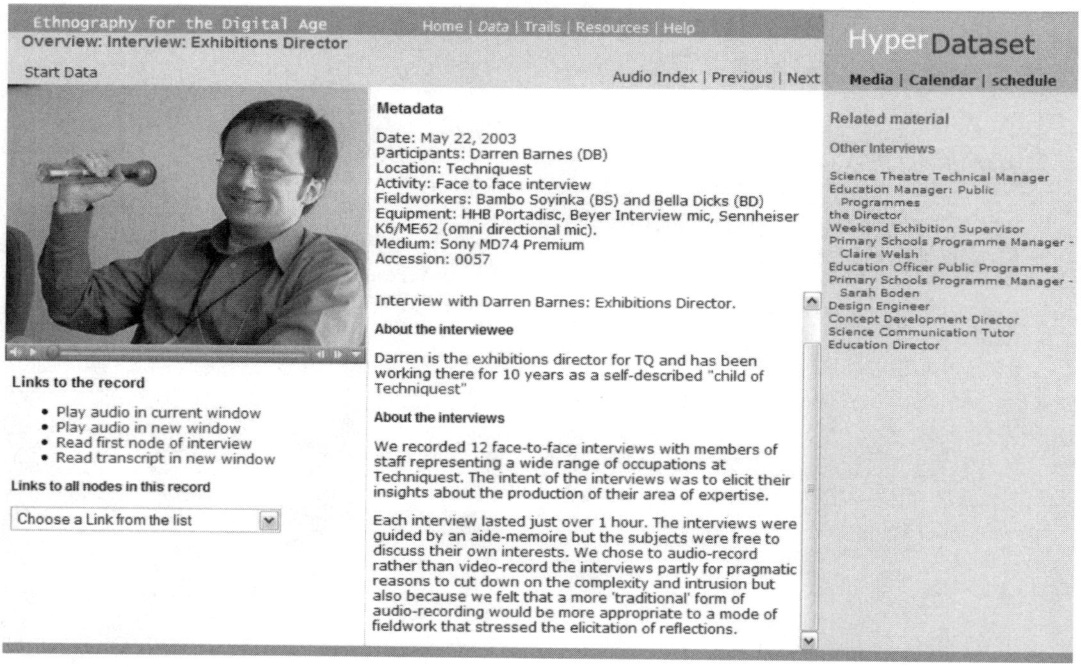

FIGURE 27.3. Example "data record" overview.

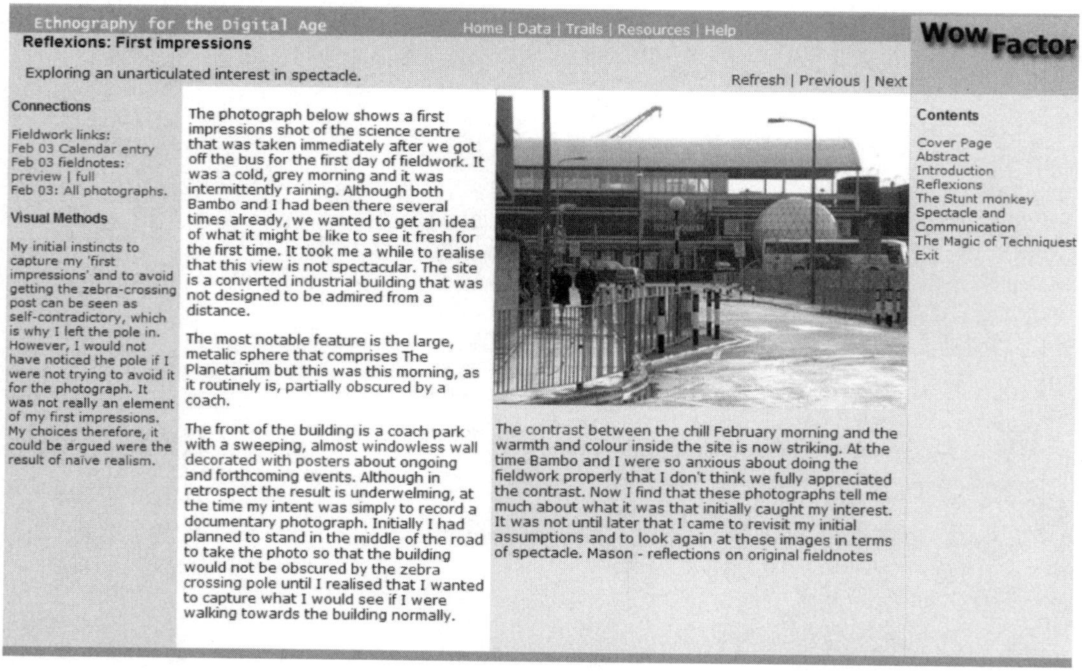

FIGURE 27.4. Example of a screen shot from a "trail."

"interpretative trails" that together present aspects of the *ethnography*, another trail that presents the project *methodology*, a hyperlinked *dataset* that allows the reader to browse all the data records, and various "help" pages. The idea of a "trail" captures that need within academic exposition, already alluded to, for an ordered sequence of "steps" enabling an argument or narrative to be built up. The major innovation that an EHE affords, in our view, is the capacity to link data and analysis together and to allow the reader to inspect these linkages. It accordingly allows a potentially transparent and interactive form of engagement with qualitative data. If fully implemented, we envisage a hypermedia environment for qualitative research that would link every data record with other data records and also with pages from interpretative trails in a way that could illuminate the complex (and necessarily always unfinished) insights of sociological and cultural interpretation. A data record could be linked to another in a way that creates a juxtaposition capable of showing unexpected contradictions, concordances, and relationships. In our own work, we have implemented many, but far from all, of the links we would like to see. Still, as Geertz (1973) put it, "Cultural analysis is intrinsically incomplete. And, worse than that, the more deeply it goes the less complete it is" (p. 29).

Although a reader can enter the "hyperdataset" and simply browse the data records without having to encounter the authors' voices, the EHE is designed to offer ethnographic interpretation, too. When the reader embarks on one of the two interpretative trails, he or she is being introduced to the ethnographers' analysis of an interactive science discovery center that tries to combine fun and education in the communication of science; an analysis that explores, in particular, the interactions between "seeing" and "doing" (Trail 1) and "magic" and "science" (Trail 2). While on a trail, the reader encounters graphically designed screens that contain quite small amounts of verbiage as compared with classic print but with highlighted links embedded within that take him or her onto new screens, bring new text into other areas of the same screen, or, frequently, activate video or audio pop-up windows. The experience is similar to reading a complex Web page, but the linking is much more conceptually driven.

The reader can check which part of the trail he or she is in via the "contents" pages on the left-hand side. Clicking through the screens unfolds a number of narrative strands covering several topics, illuminated where appropriate by links to the data and to other parts of the EHE. As with any ethnographic writing, quotations and other excerpts from the data are deployed within the "text" of the trail. However, it is always possible to link the quote directly to the data. When exploring a trail, the data is always immanent in a way that is not feasible within conventional print. Thus, in the EHE, it is possible to follow links that move between trails and between trails and data. Because it is possible to lose the thread of an argument very easily in hypertext, there are various navigational aids (such as ever-present "next" and "back" buttons, color coding to indicate whereabouts, and contents pages). Creating the EHE is like building a house that keeps on getting larger and fuller as those living inside increase, and it is likely that we will never be able to say it is finished. Nevertheless, we hope it gives an idea at least of the potential of hypermedia for the representation of qualitative research.

It is important to point out that hypermedia is neither a method nor a technology. It utilizes computer technology but is not coterminous with it. For example, a simple indexing system in a printed book utilizes hypertext in that it instigates links between items of text situated at different locations; if we added pictures to these indexes, we would have a print-based example of hypermedia. Nevertheless, the amount and complexity of linking that can be achieved through print is necessarily very limited compared with the ease and scope of computer-based linking (or *hyperlinking*). For this reason, hypermedia is best thought of as something that has properly emerged only in the computer era. It is not, however, an emergent *method* as such. One could think of utilizing hypermedia in a range of established qualitative methods, including ethnography, interview-based research, focus groups, systematic review, narrative research, discourse-analytical research, and so forth. Hypermedia, then, is a link-based representation enabled by new digital technology. It can be utilized both in the analysis and interpretation and in the presentation and dissemination stages of research projects. In pointing this out, we do not mean to imply that the business of interpretation does not go hand-in-hand with that of representation, or indeed that the two activities do not merge into one another. We are simply alluding to that moment in the research project when the researcher—although still interpreting and reinterpreting the data as long as he or she continues to engage with them—is now embarked on the process of writing up, thinking about how to present a set of findings to the intended audience.

In impinging on these different activities, hypermedia does, therefore, have a number of implications for methodology, or at least for the ways in which research is conventionally conducted and approached. These implications will become clearer as the discussion progresses—parts of which will be concerned with multimedia issues alone, whereas others address the impact of the hyperlink itself.

The Emergence of Hypermedia and Multimedia Approaches

As already noted, neither multimedia nor hypermedia are primarily methodological innovations. Their trajectories of development have occurred elsewhere. In hypermedia two fields of development have predominated: one technological, concerning the refinement of linking technology in computer science (such as the development of HTML and XML), and one literary, through experimentation with narrative linking in hypertext fiction and "electronic literature" (see Joyce, 1995; Landow, 1997; Moulthrop, 1993). In multimedia, conversely, the major impulse has been Web design and graphical design, in which the emphasis is on audience impact and experience. It is only in very recent times that these terms have started to appear in the research methodology literature in social science. Their potential use here is distinct from these more established literary or commercial applications. Technological innovation is one factor behind their appearance on the qualitative methods scene; advances in digital technology (enabling digital convergence, loss-free data transfer, and high-volume data storage) have made them newly affordable, usable, and accessible. Researchers, it is clear, now have new choices of data recording and representational technologies that were not available before. The question is: To what end can these opportunities be best used?

It is worth noting that although the methodological potential of hyper/multimedia approaches has been opened up by new technological capabilities, it is not driven by them; rather, it has emerged within the context of long-standing methodological debates in the field of qualitative research. In particular, hyper/multimedia approaches seem to provide the means of addressing some of the critiques mounted against standard realist genres of representation in qualitative social research. These question how the researcher is able to *know* aspects of the social world in all its necessary complexity and produce truth-claims about it. This set of challenges has not just involved the so-called textual turn in ethnography, in which the status and authority of ethnographic writing has been interrogated (see the classic 1986 text by Clifford and Marcus that defined this turn); some commentators consider that qualitative research as a whole has experienced a triple crisis—of representation, legitimation, and praxis (see Denzin & Lincoln, 2000). The entire project of scientific research has historically assumed the possibility of an objective observer, separated from the messiness of the social world and armed with a neutral language of observation. Recognizing the crumbling of such certainties under the influence of new perspectives (including feminism, postmodernism, postcolonialism, and the politics of representation in general), qualitative researchers and ethnographers have turned to a range of representational methods for acknowledging the subjectivity and contingency of interpretation. These have included dialogic approaches (Dwyer, 1977, 1979; see also Holquist, 1990), the use of theatrical devices (Mienczakowski, 2001), poetry (Richardson, 1992, 2000), and fiction. These approaches are also related to the more general promotion of biographical and autobiographical work in anthropology and sociology (Hastrup, 1992; Plummer, 2001; Reed-Danahay, 1997; Stanley, 1992). They strive to convey the extent to which knowledge about a research setting is coconstructed through the subjective interpretations of both the researcher and his or her informants and involve a more overt recognition of the role played by the researcherself in the context of situated research relationships (see Coffey, 1999; Ellis & Bochner, 2000).

In such experimental approaches, authors' self-conscious attempts to communicate complexity have not always been successful or well received. The danger is that the sense-making capacities of qualitative knowledge can be lost in the effort to present multiple perspectives while avoiding truth-claims that discriminate between one possible interpretation and another. This leads some highly reflexive research to lose what Kincheloe (2005) terms the "rigor of complexity," which is "displaced not by scientific reductionism but by an excessive fascination with unsituated personal experience" (p. 343). Kitzinger (2004), in this regard, warns of the dangers in some feminist analyses of equating women's voices with their actual experiences and seeing these voices as embodying an "authentic" female/feminist discourse. She argues against presenting voices as though they were self-validating; authors should instead acknowledge and account for their own methodological and political stances in making sense of what these voices say. Among other things, this means having the confidence to show where data do and do not validate one set of interpretations over others. Brewer (2004) is one of many scholars who argues that ethnography should not abandon confidence in its authority (derived from the depth of the data and the particular skills of the ethnographer) to make carefully substantiated empirical generalizations. These debates about the status of "postparadigm" qualitative knowledge are complex and varied, and it is not our intention to try and do justice to them here. The essential problems involve questions of ontology, ethics, politics, rhetoric, and epistemology that underpin the entire edifice of interpretive research. Coming to terms with them requires adopting a style of representation that fits one's underlying assumptions about knowledge and truth.

Hypertext, we suggest, is sufficiently malleable to allow for the display and exploration of multivocality yet also to accommodate an overarching authorial voice conveying a credible analysis. We do not accept the argument that print resists complexity whereas hypertext embraces it (as advocated by, e.g., Landow, 1997); nevertheless, it is clear that print has established a framework of conventions that circumscribe what can be said and how. Bolter (2001) has advanced a historically informed analysis of print that illustrates, for example, the ways in which, over the ages, the inclusion of images on the printed page was gradually reserved for children's writing and how in the process images became denigrated. At the same time, print adopted the "outline" structure of hierarchically ordered chapters, sections, and paragraphs, in block print surrounded by white space with nothing in the margins. Print-based media, in these ways, have become limited in the extent to which they can convey multiple lines of inquiry simultaneously. Instead, ideas have to be marshaled into a linear exposition that proceeds by well-recognized and familiar steps. Hyperlinks, by contrast, allow numerous directions to be followed with a simple click of the mouse. At the same time, the computer screen itself offers what Bolter calls a "topographical writing space" that brings together the written word, images, and sound and opens up new opportunities for multimedia representation.

Although Bolter's analysis is not concerned with social science per se, the arrival of hyper/multimedia approaches seems to mesh with the concerns of postparadigm methodology. These approaches invite an engagement with tensions between authority and contingency, hierarchical argumentation and polyvocality. With its "rhizomatic" qualities (like the underground stem in botany, sending out shoots and roots from multiplying nodes in unpredictable directions; see Deleuze & Guattari, 1980/1987; Landow, 1997), hypertext offers a means of highlighting the multiple paths that interpretation can take. Wesch (2001), writing as an ethnographer, identifies five primary qualities of hypermedia: it is (1) multilinear, (2) multisided, (3) multilayered, (4) multimedia, and (5) multivocal. By creating a multidimensional structure, hypermedia enables a multiplicity of voices to be brought into dialogue and juxtaposition with each other, while at the same time allowing various degrees of order to be imposed on content. Most of all, it provides a way for authors to make clear the linkages between their own interpretations and the data (see examples later in the chapter). Accordingly it can potentially address some recurrent questions about scientific authority in qualitative research: How can I show how my data records substantiate my analysis? How can I present a persuasive account that still communicates the contingency and reflexivity of my analysis? How can I convey the complexity of my data and research relationships without sacrificing coherence and readability? What kind of representational media are best suited to the description of *x*? What kind of representation does the video camera afford as opposed to the fieldnote or stills camera? What are the diverse voices and interlinkages in my data, and how can I make sense of and best represent these? Let's now take a brief look at two of the underlying issues behind the emergence of such questions and consider how they might be addressed through hypermedia and multimedia approaches.

Complexity and Bricolage

Recent writings on qualitative methods stress the importance of exploring multiple dimensions of the object of study; Richardson (2000) likens this to noting the many different kinds of light that a crystal refracts. The problem, however, with amassing diverse kinds of data is bringing it all together into a unilinear printed research report. Most writers will recognize this problem. In selecting the successive building blocks of a linear argument, one is inevitably placing elements in relations of importance to each other: first this has to be established, then that, and so forth. Things have to be left out; certain aspects have to be prioritized and others marginalized. This is part of the skills and crafts of writing up, and indeed we have already noted the importance of sequentiality to academic writing. But it does not easily accommodate the multistranded networks of relationships that make up this "crystal." Denzin and Lincoln (2000) introduce the concept of *bricolage* (originally coined by Levi-Strauss) to designate the multiple techniques for data generation and analysis required in order to approach the phenomena under investigation in a nonreductive way. However, methods cannot simply be added together; making sense of the different insights they permit entails synthesizing different horizons of meaning. In Kincheloe's (2005) discussion, it is not only about combining methods but also disciplines (including "ethnography, textual analysis, semiotics, hermeneutics, psychoanalysis, phenomenology, historiography, discourse analysis" and others); this involves integrating diverse forms of knowledge in relations of "simultaneity" (p. 323).

Kincheloe's discussion does not address how such complexity and simultaneity might be conveyed in writing or, indeed, in other kinds of representation; yet such questions are vital. If a monolinear print narrative is to do justice to them, the different insights and conclusions produced by the multiple approaches adopted need to be brought together without giving the impression that one is more authoritative or correct than another. Producing a single-stranded narrative exposition may not be the best way of achieving this. Electronic representation that makes use of hyperlinks and multimedia is one way of allowing these more complex and multifaceted aspects of a study to come to the fore outside the demands of print. As we discuss further later, however, hypermedia representation does not mean sacrificing linearity in argument and exposition; on the contrary, sequencing can easily be, and, in our view, needs to be, retained. However, hypermedia allows a *multi*linear exposition to be presented, in which one thread of interpretation can be presented as simultaneous with another. (For example, the three "trails" in our own EHE offer the reader parallel and interlinked lines of inquiry; in a book, though achievable, this would be somewhat unwieldy.)

There are losses and dangers, of course, associated with this. In spite of its powerful linking capacities, hypermedia can end up simply presenting different interpretations in an unconnected way and failing to produce the synthesis at which multiple methods, arguably, should aim. It can also result in confusing, unstructured, and frustrating experiences for readers. Furthermore, the researcher can strive to present multiple interpretations using hypermedia, but these interpretations remain the products of his or her own analytical approach, rather than emerging from those of others (later we mention multiauthored Web 2.0 technologies that subvert the idea of the single omnipotent author). At one end of the continuum, hypermedia can simply offer a database of empirical materials that readers have to find their own way through. At the other, it can have a tightly controlled instructional format with a strong authorial voice. Indeed, hypermedia writers are faced with a recurrent dilemma in organizing content: the closing down or opening up of threads and pathways for the reader to follow. What level of authorial control, or, conversely, reader choice, to adopt is a key decision, as are choices about structure and the density of argumentation. Our preference is to use hypermedia for the classic purposes of scholarly exposition and to explore its potential for communicating authored interpretations based on rigorous empirical analysis. Every scholar, we would assume, wishes to convince the reader of a set of truths that his or her study has produced—even if these are multiple truths. Hypermedia does not mean sacrificing persuasiveness or authoritativeness. Our own experimentation suggests that it can be used to produce ordered narratives through providing the reader with the means of tracing connections between interpretation and data. In this sense, it both imposes structure (through navigational controls) and introduces freedoms (through reader interactivity). It has the capacity to offer the reader a way to engage on his or her own terms with a project's evidential base—directly, rigorously, and critically. Certainly, it should not be thought that hypermedia can be a panacea for the "crisis of representation" in qualitative research. Nevertheless, when analysis is directed at coming to terms with complexity, it follows that representation needs to do justice to it; in such projects, electronic screen-based media can be of considerable value.

Relationships and Networks

There is another, broader set of resonances that helps explain the emergence of hypermedia approaches in qualitative methodology. The kernel of these approaches taps into the idea of establishing *networks of links* between differently located domains and items of knowledge, something that is central to the way knowledge is thought of, organized, and communicated in contemporary society. As computer networks allow the communicational world to expand and diversify and wider access to diverse information to open up, so the potential for people to make links and perceive relationships between different knowledge domains also expands (Castells, 2004). The barriers between relatively specialized knowledge domains (academic, professional, technical) become more leaky, and multiskilling takes over from specialization. For example, Kress and Van Leeuwen (2001) point to the ways in which the previously demarcated professional domains of magazine and newspaper production (in which written content was produced separately from its layout and representation) have merged together, so that a journalist has to be competent in images, layout, and design, as well as the production of written copy. If they embrace screen-based technologies, qualitative researchers, too, will be taking on skills of design and presentation that were previously left to the publisher.

Digital technologies, it seems, have brought an end to established divisions among domains of knowledge. There is, of course, a chicken-and-egg situation here, for it is clear that current computer technology both facilitates the representation of complex networks and relationships and also encourages their proliferation. So it is with hypermedia and qualitative research. An increasing tendency to question the authority claims of realist qualitative research, for example, and to demand fuller and more honest accounts of the research process seem to call out for digital hypermedia; at the same time, digital hypermedia and multimedia themselves encourage demand for more user-friendly, interactive, and transparent forms of engagement with data. Accordingly, hypermedia can be used by researchers to direct the reader's attention to the network of linkages and connections that exist within a dataset. For example, hypermedia environments allow all the data records to be made available for the reader to explore and interpret. Direct hyperlinks can be put in place between aspects of the author's exposition and the dataset, allowing readers to assess the nature of the link, and hence the knowledge claim, with which they are being presented. We return to the powerful capacities of the hyperlink later.

A further point is that the sheer range of media that people use in their normal everyday lives has increased exponentially. We can now communicate with each other through a whole range of portable devices. For example, young people's identities can hardly be studied without taking into account their use of new technologies, such as mobile phones, camera phones, Internet phones, iPods, e-mail, online chat rooms and social networking websites (e.g., MySpace), Wi-Fi devices, and the like. In order to understand how they are used in social networks, it is clear that researchers will need to come to terms with them and find ways of recording and analyzing their content. Digital platforms are the obvious way to bring these diverse media together. In addition, the ubiquity of *design* in everyday spatial environments draws our attention to the multiple dimensions of different media. Kress and Van Leeuwen (2001) point out that, as more and more of the manufactured material world becomes subjected to the practices of design, more media are coopted into the processes of making meaning (they give the example of the sound a car door makes when it closes, sound designers having been employed to simulate the requisite satisfying click). Hence new technology changes more and more media into modes—that is, into codified systems of meanings. Accordingly, the researcher confronts an ever-expanding and increasingly codified universe of meaning in studying the settings of everyday life. Multimedia and hypermedia enable at least an approximation of this complexity to be represented on the computer screen for analysis and interpretation. None of this is to denigrate writing or to suggest that writing cannot adequately describe key aspects of contemporary life. Rather, it is to point to the proliferation of multimedia and network-based knowledge and to suggest that we should at least be exploring the possibilities of multi/hypermedia in engaging with and describing them in our studies.

Examples of Hypermedia/Multimedia Qualitative Research

What exactly is a hypermedia environment for qualitative research? Most of the extant examples, and there are few, have been produced by ethnographers, many working within the discipline of visual anthropology. Our own work belongs to sociology, but all of our experimentation in hypermedia so far has been dedicated to the conduct and representation of ethnography. Ethnography is a fieldwork-based method that generates a large amount of complex, diverse, and multilayered data. We wanted to experiment with ethnographic materials for these very reasons, as hypermedia offers a way of accommodating and exploiting large amounts of complex data. Indeed, we have introduced the term *ethnographic hypermedia environment*, or EHE, to refer to the "product" generated. We present illustrations of our own work shortly, but first we wish to draw attention to other examples of hypermedia ethnography we have encountered. These include Peter Biella and colleagues' *Yanomamo Interactive: The Ax Fight* (Biella, Chagnon, & Seaman, 1997), Peter Biella's *Maasai Interactive* (in press), Robert Gardner's interactive DVD release of his film *Dead Birds* (2004), Sarah Pink's *The Bullfighter's Braid* (1997) and *Interweaving Lives* (1999), Jay Ruby's *Oak Park Stories* (2005–2006) and Roderick Coover's *Cultures in Webs* (2003). Some of these are discussed further later. They illustrate the variety of work that is possible in hypermedia: some of it using quite complex linking; others retaining tightly organized structures and using the hyperlink mainly for navigation; and it is fair to say that there is quite a diversity of style and outcome to be found. Works using hypermedia as a combined visual, aural, and written medium are only just starting to appear (e.g., Coover, 2003; this is what our own work is trying to develop). By contrast, visual ethnographers have seen the potential of hypermedia largely through the lens of the camera. Their CDs and DVD-ROMs are either heavily characterized by film and image, with relatively little in the way of integrated text–image–sound experimentation, or predominantly biased toward written exposition, with photographs and video as illustrative materials. This has meant that complex multimedia hyperlinking capabilities still remain relatively unexplored.

The visual anthropologist Sarah Pink has produced two CD-ROMs, *The Bullfighter's Braid* (1997) and *Interweaving Lives* (1999) that present her ethnographic fieldwork and analysis with female Spanish bullfighters. These are primarily designed as learning tools that introduce students to the uses of photography and video in ethnographic research. There is a tight "outline" structure (with primary sections of 10–14 pages or so, containing opportunities to click into expansions of the argument). In all relevant ways, *The Bullfighter's Braid* is as linear as a printed book. Pink's other ethnographic CD, *Interweaving Lives* (1999), works in a similar manner. Here the contents screen for each section is an animated loom, suggesting a weaving metaphor, and each section is a "strand," yet the work still consists of sections and pages within each section. Pink's primary focus explores the effects of new media on still and moving images rather than on hypermedia per se. In this respect her work can be seen as a progression from earlier works, such as Kersenboom-Story's *Word, Sound, Image* (1995), which features an illustrative interactive CD (CD-i) along with a printed book. Kersenboom's empirical work is focused on Tamil oral performance, and although the book comprises a conventional, linear monograph and the CD-i element is merely illustrative, she urges further exploitation of multiple modes of representation (written, visual, musical, spoken) in order to communicate the full complexity of such cultural forms. Another early pioneer of this model was Ricki Goldman-Segall, whose monograph *Points of Viewing* (1998) contains links to an associated website with extensive video clips. The book describes her ethnographic study of schoolchildren's computer culture, and her primary fieldwork involved extensive videotaping of the children. A reader can open the website, type in the page number of the reference, watch the relevant video clip, and also leave comments about the clip directly on the Web pages. Since these first few scattered examples, this model of printed book plus accompanying CD, DVD, or website is becoming more common. Web-hosted video, in particular, is now easier to develop and access, as today's digital video streaming allows much larger and better quality video files to be played directly from the Web. Kirsten Foot and Steven Schneider's book, *Web Campaigning* (2006), also has an accompanying digital installation available on the Web. These Web pages grant access to a vast archive of websites created by the authors and hyperlinked to fieldnotes and memos made during the process of their research into the historical evolution of political online campaigns in the United States.

In terms of works native to the Web, that is, which do not exist in conventional print form, Wesch's *Nekalimin.net* (2006) is a notable example. This (as yet unfinished) hypermedia ethnography utilizes Web-based multimedia to present a wide range of material relating to the author's fieldwork in the Nekalimin Valley of Papua New Guinea. It includes fieldnotes, historical documents, images, video, and academic papers. Wesch adopts a layered structure for the Web pages, in which the top layer contains scholarly exposition (or theses) and the lower layers contain voices from the field: ethnographic vignettes; stories told by informants; the author's own fieldnotes and multimedia data records, including videos, photographs, audio files, and maps. Such a structure at first sight suggests a hierarchical organization that privileges the authorial voice of the ethnographer, and Wesch (2001) is well aware of this tendency in ethnographic writing. He sees hypermedia's greatest potential as "the possibility of allowing our subjects' voices to be heard" but recognizes that this "also poses its greatest dilemma—that these voices might be shaped, manipulated, and actually swallowed by the media environment." His work proceeds by the principle of "making multiple and purposive layers and links that can show the blooming, buzzing complexity of life behind those voices—ultimately presenting author and subject as co-creators of the representation."

Of hypermedia works distributed on CD-ROM or DVD, Peter Biella's hypermedia ethnography of his anthropological fieldwork with the Maasai, *Maasai Interactive* (in press) gives a glimpse of the potential of the medium. Although Biella traces his intellectual heritage to the work of hypertext experimenters Landow and Delaney and the original hypertext program Intermedia, he explicitly designed *Maasai Interactive* very differently. Intermedia was designed to encourage "textual randomness" (Landow & Delaney, 1991, p. 9), whereas Biella's hypermedia is "committed to non-random, non-broken readings and analyses" (Biella, 1993b, p. 319). The screen of *Maasai Interactive* is divided into quadrants, with each quadrant showing specific types of data, including voice recordings, photographs, and video. The top left area of any screen is always the primary focus, with the rest of the screen providing supplementary information. As readers progress, they "travel" from screen to screen, and each new screen provides a new primary focus with its supporting information. Biella's intent, then, is not to puzzle or challenge the reader; rather, he claims that "contrary to Landow and Delaney, the consequence of exposure to hypermedia is not *necessarily* a growing conviction of textual 'randomness' or incorrigible 'fragmentation' " (1993b, pp. 320–321; original emphasis). *Yanomamö Interactive: The Ax Fight* (Biella, Chagnon, & Seaman, 1997), another of his works, is designed to be viewed alongside a textbook and video documentary of Asch and Chagnon's classic ethnographic film, *The Ax Fight* (1975). As with *Maasai Interactive*, the screen is divided into quadrants and designed to be simple to use.[1] In both cases, Biella's travel metaphor facilitates ease of use while providing an element of homology between the fieldworker's journey to the "field" and the viewers' journeys through the CD-ROM.

The most innovative example we have seen so far of hypermedia ethnography on CD-ROM is Rod Coover's *Culture in Webs*. In the CD-ROM, Coover (2003) writes of the navigational powers offered by a network structure of hyperlinks: "these movements can be both revealing and concealing in how they shift thought and focus, transgress conventional domains and disciplines, and juxtapose through collage and montage contrasting ideas and images." Coover's work comprises three hypermedia "essays," "Theory, Practice and Performance," in which he explores the potential of digital media for communicating a particular view of culture. The first essay discusses the work of contemporary documentary filmmakers such as Robert Gardner and Trinh T. Minh-ha, discussing how they succeed in using the medium to show the complexity and contingency of the life-worlds they depict. Coover reflects in this essay on the use of film to "construct associative webs of referents" through fragmentary images that mean, he argues, that "the objects pictured can no longer serve a single narrative." Nevertheless, when Coover presents his own ethnographic work in the other two essays, we do not gain much of a sense of life as a web of referents, mainly because Coover has chosen to present a strongly authored written analysis that does not make use of association but rather writes about the subjects in quite a distanced way. Images play merely an illustrative role. There is little sense here of the author using hypermedia as a means of allowing multiple and contradictory perspectives and voices to come through. Instead, the aim is a more modest one that shows the different effects obtainable by three different uses of hypermedia: (1) a long, scrollable text with video insets; (2) a photographic essay on a local wine harvest in France, and (3) text, video, and photographs made of different Ghanaian musical performances in the context of national political change. Like Biella's CD-ROM, it does not make much use of hyperlinking, perhaps because it, too, adheres to a unilinear structure. The reader has a clear sense of direction and progress provided by each screen's "next" arrows or buttons. Nevertheless, the interactive nature of these CD-ROMs—the reader's ability to click around them at will and their use of digital media such as photographs, video pop-ups, and audio recordings—produce a striking collage effect, highlighting juxtapositions between images, text, and sound.

All of the aforementioned hypermedia writers—from Pink to Coover—are situated within visual ethnography and use hypermedia to explore the interconnections between images and written text. They do not, however, fully exploit the narrative multidirectionality provided by hypertext. Our EHE work at Cardiff, by contrast, emerged from early reflections in the 1990s on the use of data coding programs in qualitative research; perhaps as a result we were focused on methodological issues from the outset, rather than on visual communication. These issues, for us, center on hypertext's ability to allow the reader to engage directly with data records and to allow writers to explore in the process the tension between authorial control and "voices from the field." We thus make more use of hyperlinking than any other of the hypermedia ethnographies we have encountered. Our work, therefore, is not primarily multimedia ethnography but rather an experiment in qualitative hyperlinking. This means that it constructs a reasonably dense network of hyperlinks that grant access both to examples of linear scholarly exposition and to a complete set of data records in multimedia form, both of which can be explored freely by readers.

Our experimentation has been funded (by the Economic and Social Research Council in the U.K.) over several periods, and we have had the benefit of more than one researcher. We have not brought in technical computing skills, as we set out to explore what could be done by social scientists lacking computer programming backgrounds. On the whole, the experience has taught us that this kind of work is extremely labor-intensive. After analysis is complete,[2] a vast amount of work remains to be done in order for a navigable and meaningful EHE to be constructed by hyperlinking data records to authored interpretation. Every data record has to be broken into nodes, carefully archived and tagged with metadata so that each data node can be identified when a reader stumbles across it. Then, meaningful hyperlinks have to be made between these data nodes and the authored interpretative texts (organized in our case into "trails"), so that every pertinent piece of data can be located and read, and then the trail can be rejoined at the same point. All this has to work while the reader forges his or her own path through the whole. The structure of the trails must be carefully planned, and consistent navigational tools put in place. Screen design has to be thought through so that the semiotic modalities of color, font, image, screen position, and layout work to help orient the reader and minimize opportunities for losing one's way.

All this takes an immense amount of time and is something that is likely to be beyond the resources of a single author. Nevertheless, once a hypermedia framework has been constructed, other projects can be conducted using the same blueprint, hence cutting down on the amount of new linking work that needs to be done. It is arguable that so-called Web 2.0 technologies offer a solution by turning the hypermedia project into an open, interactive site that can become a collective endeavor, with contributions from informants and participants as well as "experts." Rather than personally labeling and linking every possible piece of related data in order to create a fully immersive hypermedia environment, authors could choose to adopt a "wiki" format (as in the popular online encyclopedia, *Wikipedia,* and indeed in Web 2.0 social networking sites [e.g., YouTube, MySpace]), which allows informants and participants, other academics, and indeed the general public to make contributions, allowing the work to grow and develop organically over time. Although interesting and promising in itself, such an endeavor would represent quite a radical departure from standard academic output. In this sense, we do not envisage that it could offer a substitute for authored scholarly work within the dominant institutional context of today. Hence, we now continue by discussing, as our ideal case, a hypermedia environment that could be used for communicating scholarly exposition via multimedia resources and hyperlinks.

Definitions of Multimedia: Modes and Media

At this point, it is useful to define our terms. To start with *multimedia,* what does this imply in the context of qualitative social research? The term *medium* is in itself ambiguous, as it commonly refers both to products and tools. A medium can be the means by which something is represented, as well as being the representation itself. In this chapter we use the term *medium* in the way that Kress and Van Leeuwen (2001, p. 22) advocate, that is, media "are the material resources used in the production of semiotic products and events." This can mean both tools and products. The key point in Kress and Van Leeuwen's framework is that the distinctions between media are not as clearcut as one might suppose. That is, one cannot specify the "meaning" of an image as opposed to sound, or taste as opposed to touch. Instead, every medium deploys one or more semiotic resources, or "modes," that are both abstract and rule-governed; hence, one can talk of the "grammar" of the image in that it implies a multiplicity of modes—including perspective, size, shape, color, and so forth—that operate according to communicative (cultural) conventions.

A mode is a resource for meaning in the sense that it sets off particular cultural associations in our minds, such as the color blue connoting calm and restfulness; red, danger; or green, nature. Those aspects of physical settings amenable to vision deploy numerous modes, including size, shape, position, perspective, and color; combined with sound, taste, touch, and smell, this means that the social settings we study need to be thought of as highly complex semiotic environments. Hence, in thinking about *multimedia*, Kress and Van Leeuwen (2001) propose that we need a *multimodal* approach that is fully sensitized to the various meaning effects of the different modes that are pulled into relationship with each other in a communicative environment. This is the reason that, as Kress (1998) argues, the term *multimedia*, as used in computer-mediated communication, does not simply mean adding the visual and the lettered modes together but the production of a distinctive, multisemiotic space of representation—what Bolter (1990) calls the distinctive and novel "writing space" of the computer screen. But multimodality is not restricted to computer-based media. Instead, it is all around us in the everyday physical settings we inhabit and study. Simply put, multimodality means that different modes interact with each other to produce a universe of meanings that is more than the sum of its parts (Kress, 1998). Below we discuss multimodality in relation to (1) the actual fieldwork settings we study, (2) the data records we construct via observation and elicitation, and (3) the resultant texts we produce to disseminate our findings. First, however, it is useful to revisit the distinction—important for understanding multimodality—between data and data records.

Multimedia in Data and Data Records

The preceding discussion has suggested that multimedia should not be thought of as an issue only for data analysis (as it commonly is). Indeed, it is just as important an issue for the data-generation stage of a research project, during the activities of observation, listening, participation, and/or interviewing. In other words, we need to distinguish between multimedia data in the field and multimedia data in the materials through which we attempt to record our observations or elicitations of the field. Data are multisensory; they are what we are able to *perceive* in the field through all of our senses, including sight, hearing, touch, smell, and even taste. They are by their very nature composed of diverse media (they are likely to include sounds, objects, visual designs, people's actions and bodies, etc.). So multimedia within the field are not the same thing as multimedia within data records. The latter are our attempts to transform our observations and elicitations of the phenomenal world into a separate set of permanent recordings (through media technologies such as fieldnotes, camera images, etc.). The tools available to do this—from pen to video camera—restrict the modes that can be represented. Yet often this modal reduction goes unnoticed or uncommented on in methods texts. As Emmison and Smith (2000) point out in relation to visual methods, social science has traditionally seen visual "data" predominantly as camera images (still or moving). They argue:

> Stated in its bluntest form our reservations about an image-based social science rest on the view that photographs have been misunderstood as constituting forms of data in their own right when in fact they should be considered in the first instance as *means of preserving, storing or representing information*. (p. 2, emphasis added)

Hence they argue that visual data are not "what the camera can record but . . . what the eye can see" (p. 4).

One merit of this insight is that it directs our attention to the inevitable problems that occur in making data records. For example, it is clear that "what the eye can see" cannot be equated with what the camera reproduces. The human eye and brain are processing a number of modes implicit in the visual realm: not only obvious ones such as the size, shape, color, and relative and perspectival positions of phenomena but also the visible aspects of their nonvisual modes, such as texture. Other modes–such as taste, smell, weight, and density–require different senses to perceive them: touch, taste, smell. And then of course there is the whole universe of sounds that are amenable to the human ear: background sounds and what they say about the relative positions of things; human voices; the sounds of nature; music; mechanical noises; and so forth. Many of these will be lost when a record is made. Audio recordings of speech, for example, appear simply to copy it, yet they lose many of the modes accompanying speech, such as facial expression, gesture, and gaze, that contribute to its meaning-making power. Furthermore, when we ask our participants to sit down in soundproof environments for interviews, we close off all the surrounding soundscapes that are part of the original context of interaction (Lashua et al., 2006). Accordingly, it is clear that the human brain does not erect barriers between different sensory data, but brings all of the senses to bear on interpreting given phenomena; yet recording media artificially separate them. All of these multiple and complex modes of meaning cannot be simply "captured" by the audio recorder or video camera, as a very long tradition of critique in the fields of visual anthropology and sociology has demonstrated (Crawford & Turton, 1992; Harper, 1998; Loizos, 1993; Nichols, 1994). There are the obvious reductions associated with the switch from multimodal field data to the limited modalities of the two-dimensional image and one- or two-track sound tape. Then there are all the long-recognized and much-debated problems of the inherent subjectivity of camera work and the impossibility of a positivist science of the image. All these point to the inappropriateness of the terms *recording* or *capturing* and bring us up against long-running debates in representation theory and the poetics and politics of film (see Barbash & Taylor, 1997; Clifford & Marcus, 1986; Taylor, 1994; Weiner, 1994).

For all of these reasons, it is useful to approach the question of multimedia through the conceptual framework of multimodality, as discussed earlier. This shifts our focus away from just the qualities of something called "the image" to thinking about all the sensory properties of the field settings we study. How can we best keep these in focus as we make records of our interactions with them, knowing that the records are necessarily reductions and transformations? Let's think, then, about multimedia at four stages of the research process:

1. Fieldwork and data generation
2. Data recording
3. Data analysis/interpretation
4. Representation and dissemination of analytical findings

We take each of these in turn and consider the potential impact that multimedia and hypermedia might have on each.

Fieldwork and Data Generation

We have already pointed out that it is the social world that is characterized by truly multiple media, and not our data records. Because our data records reduce everyday-world media to recording media, absenting some modes altogether and prioritizing others in the process, the only time we can "tune in" to the full range of media and modes perceivable is during the data-generation phase (i.e., the time we spend looking, observing, participating in, and eliciting information about the research setting). There is merit in spending a preliminary phase tuning in to the semiotics, rhythms, and regularities of the research setting before adopting recording media. This may encourage us to be more conscious about applying our full range of senses in perceiving it. How do different aspects of the environment and its everyday situations communicate? What is visual about these? What is aural? What are the various material resources deployed in the interactions under investigation? What are the recurrent types and rhythms of movement and sound and how significant are they? Are there particular temporal qualities, spatial relations, regularities of action that require interpretation? (And then, once these questions have been answered, one has to decide which techniques of elicitation, observation, and/or participation will best bring these qualities out.) Only then should we decide which recording media to use. Take the field setting of an infant classroom as an example. How does the layout of furniture, the colors of its wall displays, and the shapes of the desks and toys within it work together to anchor particular meanings of childhood and pedagogy? Or—perhaps more likely—to suggest contradictory meanings? How, then, do the children's and teacher's interactions within it become shaped and constrained by these conventions? Or, conversely, how do they appear to subvert or rework them? How does the segmentation of time, regulated by the timetable, constrain the interactions that take place? Given these complex social and semiotic interplays, how best to elicit the desired information and how to record this?

In our own multimedia fieldwork at Cardiff, we studied a science discovery center that was marketed to children as a "fun place to learn." It deliberately sets out to distinguish itself from classroom-placed learning. The main visitor area (see Figure 27.1) is dotted with brightly colored exhibits that respond in some way to the visitor's touch (hence supposedly communicating a principle of science, such as forces or gravity). These exhibits put into play action–reaction sequences that then constitute a mode of communication. But exhibits also communicate meanings through their sheer physical materiality, working through the modes of color, texture, shape, position, opaqueness/light, and weight. Each exhibit is encased in a single wooden module that is hard and solid (texture and shape). Furthermore, each exhibit is positioned at a certain child-accessible height and at a certain distance from other exhibits (physical position). And each casing is machine spray-painted to give a highly glossy finish (light) in bright, primary colors of yellow, blue, green, and red (color). All of these different modes work together to produce a space that deliberately evokes children's play areas. In the process, they help to shape the ways in which it is "read" and experienced by visitors (i.e., as a fun, safe, playful space). In addition, science is reproduced here as mechanical, practical, and applied (rather than theoretical or abstract), with the emphasis always on a human-initiated functionality. The environment promotes an individualist, skills-centered, and competitive approach to learning, in that each exhibit involves the rewarding or frustrating of individual performance. The exhibits' modalities thereby combine to position children as the active performers of tasks designated as "fun" rather than the passive recipients of expert knowledge, as in older models of classroom and textbook learning (Kress, 1998). We had to select methods to represent the science center's modalities quite consciously, using a range of media that included written fieldnotes to convey modes not amenable to audio–visual recording media.

Multimodality in research settings such as a science center or classroom thus involves all kinds of modes that may not show up in data records unless they have been consciously represented. Hence thinking about multimodality in the data-generation phase is clearly valuable. This approach draws attention to the different resources or grammars that allow people and environments to communicate and produce meaning—whether consciously (as the product of design) or unconsciously (simply through convention or habit). It also underlines the situated nature of interaction in that it occurs within environments themselves redolent with meaning, not as static contexts of action but as active agents in the contingencies of action. Furthermore, it can help to show how the structuring qualities of cultural reproduction (the regularities of classroom design, the enduring social conventions of a lesson, the habitual ways for a teacher to speak, etc.) can be brought into dialogue with the spontaneous and contingent nature of actual everyday interactions. The challenge is to find a means of representing these dialogues that allows all the modes involved to be kept in mind.

Expanding one's repertoire of recording media does at least help in approximating multimodal realities. Yet there are related risks. First, as Hastrup (1992) points out, many aspects of social life and interaction are not amenable to visual (or indeed audio) recording. A photograph excels in recording spatial relations; it fails dismally at representing the sociality of interactions–as anyone's attempts at taking party photos demonstrate. Writing should not be downgraded in multimedia fieldwork, as it plays a crucial role, not the least of which is that field notes describe those social and cultural aspects of the research setting that are crucial but neither visible nor audible. Second, once visual and audio records have been made, it is easy to treat these *as* data and to forget that, although neatly catalogued and archived, they still remain the partial and subjective "traces" that we assembled under less-than-ideal conditions while immersed as actors in the unfolding drama of action in the field. This is particularly the case with video footage, which we frequently take to be the perfect record of "what really happened." Instead, we need to recognize it as our active temporal and spatial intervention in the field of action itself. There is no easy answer to such problems. Thinking back to the field and, where feasible, successively revisiting it may at least help bring back into dialogue with the "finished" records we take to our desks the multisensory and physical experience of being there–unencumbered by notepad or camera.

Production of Data Records

Let's now think in more detail about the data records we might make of our hypothetical classroom situation. Semiotically, a photograph of a class in action communicates in quite specific ways, some of which are peculiar to the medium of the still image (freezing an instant in time and showing up momentarily suspended gestures, movements, and expressions and the *spatial* interrelationships between teacher, pupils, their work, the furniture, walls, displays, and so on). If we make a sound recording of it, we will be attuned to quite different modalities: to the *temporal* unfolding of sound-in-action; the cadences of speech; the didactic techniques of instruction or the turn-taking of conversation; the sound of emotions, as in laughter or anger; the interaction between speech and other noises; the multilayered soundscapes of the classroom as a whole. Sound, which disappears as it is produced, leaving no trace, seems to "flow" and thence to mark the passage of time. Our own audio recordings of the science center show otherwise unnoticed aspects of the messages circulating in the space (such as its high-tech credentials yet everyday functionality, its accessible scienticity, its vaguely futuristic feel), communicated in part via the sounds emitted by the exhibits (e.g., a repeated computerized note emitted by the "hot-air balloon" exhibit imparts a regular rhythm to the space over and above the chaotic sounds of children shouting and running).

A video recording of the exhibits area, by contrast, will distract our attention away from the specificities of both background space and sound, as the eye will be trained on action and movement, and the mind will be striving to make sense of the space in terms of the familiar scripts and narrative blueprints that make up our cultural knowledge of science center or classroom behavior. The moving images and soundtrack of videotape focus attention on the physical action and speech of bodies, although they also allow the spatial semiotics of the environment to be inspected. Then again, a field-note description of the same space will produce a more overtly narrative account, in which the visual modes of color, size, shape, and the aural modes of speech and sound are unlikely to be described except as they impinge on the particular narrative being constructed. In any case, where present, they will be represented through writing–a kind of translation. In our own fieldwork, written field notes played an important role, as key aspects of the communicative affordances of the science center exhibits were produced through their weight, texture, and solidity–modes that cannot adequately be represented via cameras.

Each of the different records produced, it should be remembered, is the outcome of a particular subjective position taken up, consciously or not, by the person who has made them. This person is an active agent situated within the dynamics of the social interactions happening all around; at the same time he or she inhabits a nexus of cultural discourses that help shape his or her responses. In this sense, the picture is not "taken" by the camera; rather, each photograph, video sequence, or field note is generated from the perspective of a social actor occupying a particular social and spatial location in relation to the "object" under study at a particular instant or series of instants in time. Where and when we stand in the room, what we are looking for, how we see ourselves in relation to others, and how they see us–all these go to make up the particular representational artefact we produce when using pen, camera, and recorder. In this sense, recordings are made, not taken. In our own work, we experimented with simultaneous use of two video cameras, both trained on the same situation but from different positions. But even then we cannot say that these double-takes, as it were, produced greater objectivity. What they did was introduce yet another subjective perspective. Thinking through these subjectivities alongside the particular semiotic modalities of each medium makes clear what a complex job the researcher then has in making sense of these records. Images cannot simply be approached as though they were data in their own right. Being recordings, they are of quite a different order from field data themselves.

When different recording media are utilized together in data generation and the resultant records subjected to analysis, interpretations are produced from the researcher's subjective engagement with each of them in *combination*. Hence, data records become *multi*media at the moment they are assembled together. How to bring photographs into dialogue with video and sounds? How to decide what it all adds up to? The temptation is to assign each medium a slot in an objective hierarchy, or pecking order, in which video (being the medium that employs the greatest number of modes) is seen as offering "the true record of what happened." However, as visual theorists have long pointed out, film is always partial: even when a video camera is left running unmanned, it is still highly selective, for real life does not coalesce neatly in front of a lens. It is therefore necessary to be reflexive about these different media and the particular conditions under which each record was made. Rather than focusing solely on observable media, it is important to appreciate what each medium can and cannot convey and to be aware of the different (or, indeed, similar) kinds of meanings that different media afford. This means thinking carefully about which recording medium to adopt to capture different aspects of the fieldwork setting. This is not easy, for, as Pink (1997) observes, "it is confusing to hold an image of something which we know was real, but at the same time be convinced by theory that it is not."

Analysis of Data Records

Once the choices of recording media have been made, data records need to be catalogued and sorted for analysis. Here, we are confronted by a problem. There is no such thing as multimedia data records; instead, there are records in different media. What we will be faced with are different collections of media: audio recordings, transcripts, photographs, video footage, field notes, and other written memoranda, perhaps scanned documents and graphical images. These cannot all be lumped together and analyzed as if they were "multimedia." For one thing, the analysis of written records (such as field notes and transcripts) has evolved quite separately from that of image records such as photographs (although it is true that recent computer software programs such as HyperResearch and Atlas-ti for qualitative data analysis have multimedia capabilities for analysis of audio and video text, as well as still images with mapping capabilities). Second, the specific modalities of writing as opposed to images means that different skills are required to analyze them. Audio–visual footage is even more complex to analyze. We do not propose here to provide an overview of issues in the field of visual analysis, which are dealt with well elsewhere (e.g., Banks, 2001; Dicks et al., 2005; Pink, 2001; Rose, 2001). However, our own experience suggests that data records in different media are best analyzed separately before being interlinked together. We touch on some of the problems involved in this bringing together of data analysis conducted on different types of media.

First, we take the analysis of written media records. This has long been dominated by techniques for the thematic coding of audio transcriptions or fieldnotes, followed by the bringing together of coded segments (code and retrieve). This process has been facilitated in recent years by various software packages for the computer-assisted qualitative data analysis (CAQDAS), on which there is an extensive literature (e.g., Coffey, Atkinson, & Holbrook, 1996; Dohan & Sanchez-Jankowski, 1998; Fielding & Lee, 1998; Kelle, 1997; Lee & Fielding, 1991). Coding is a method of data reduction via indexing. Segments of the data records are marked with one or more codes that correspond to the researcher's emergent interpretation. This reformulation of the data into an index or set of codes enables the researcher to operate on a more abstract level and focus on the relationships among different aspects of the corpus. CAQDAS programs facilitate the coding process by providing a wide range of tools that can partially automate the process, make it easier to manage lists of codes, set up relationships between codes, and easily search and retrieve codes or fragments of data that have been indexed with codes. If the dataset has been adequately coded, then the relationships among codes should provide insights into the actual data.

CAQDAS development has been dominated by indexical "code and retrieve" approaches (though see Kelle, 2000).[3] These, as Coffey and colleagues (1996) argue, are not necessarily the most appropriate technique for every project. Conversely, the hypertext approach to data analysis works on a cross-referencing system in which text segments are linked together on the basis of a specified relationship between them. Kelle's (1997) riposte to Coffey and colleagues claims that there is in effect little difference between indexing/coding and cross-referencing/hyperlinking. Whether one indexes text segments or directly links them together, the same sort of insight is produced. However, our own experiments suggest otherwise. As with coding, hypertext requires repeated readings of the data, but the analysis of the data progresses in a somewhat different manner. Using the StorySpace hypertext program developed by Eastgate Systems, it is possible to create a complex network of nodes, each of which contains either data records or interpretative texts (authorial commentary). Whereas CAQDAS links segments of data record to researcher-generated codes in a data-to-code model, the hypertext strategy links segments of data record to other segments of data record in a data-to-data model (although data records can also, of course, be linked to interpretative texts in a data-to-memo model, or even to thematic nodes, mimicking a data-to-code model). The data-to-data model institutes a somewhat different conceptual approach to the data record, because the major task for the researcher is not deciding which code to assign to a segment of data but which other segments of data to link with the segment of data currently being considered. This is distinctive from coding, as the whole point of an index is to create links between data and index, not data and data.[4]

Hyperlinking also involves labeling the nature of the link among segments (something that Kelle's [1997] discussion neglects). This focuses attention on identifying the varied kinds of relations among different segments rather than purely on relations of similarity, as in indexing. The researcher does not have to identify an overarching code that adequately sums up multiple pieces of text content (which can often be frustrating, as meanings are rarely precisely replicated across a whole corpus). Instead, the researcher examines the nature of the relationship between two or more segments. Over time, these relationships can be grouped together into link families. A number of distinguishable themes will indeed be amassed, but each will consist of a field of interrelationships rather than a series of nested and interwoven codes that try to label each piece of content. The major difficulty of the hypertextual approach, presently, is the lack of off-the-shelf software. The burden of interpretation in hypertext lies in the linking, but no currently available software allows the analysis of hypertext links. In comparison, CAQDAS programs specialize in running logical inquiries about the coding structure of the marked-up data. No such software can interrogate link structures in a comparable way. If the hypertext strategy is to be developed, procedures for doing this and programs that can perform those procedures need to be created. This requires both theoretical analyses of hypertext links and practical implementations of those analyses. If such software is created, it can be put to a wide range of uses. Although we have focused on the handling of ethnographic data here, it could also be used to aid in, for example, the creation of "mind maps" for semiological approaches to image analysis (Penn, 2000), or television shows (Rose, 2000).

Now we turn to analysis of records in other media. Earlier we introduced hypertext as a method of analysis that represents an alternative to traditional coding. It should be noted that a hypertextual analysis of video footage is not (yet) technically feasible (there is no software to our knowledge that allows one to break digital footage into thematic segments and then connect related ones together with named links). Instead, video can be analyzed via coding and annotation. In order to effect a finely tuned level of analysis of captured video, some means of labeling and categorizing video segments is needed. This can be done manually or through software that enables segments of footage to be transcribed, labeled, annotated, and then grouped together and later searched for those that are thematically interlinked. One such program is the freeware package Transana. In ATLAS/ti and HyperRESEARCH, similarly, files in AVI format can be imported, cut into shorter sequences within the program, labeled, and then linked to texts of any kind (e.g., annotations, other video sequences, sound clips, graphics, etc.). This means that video footage and sound tracks can be as intensively coded as written text (always providing that the requisite computer disc storage space is available).

However, the question of whether conventional coding is at all appropriate for video analysis remains. Videotaped interviews can be treated in a similar way to conventional interview transcripts, with the added extra levels of meaning that nonverbal communication conveys. But video of social actors engaged in "natural" action cannot easily be reduced to a finite number of manifest categories due to the critical *narrative* dimensions of the footage. In our view, it is not really appropriate to treat video data as analogous to interview transcripts. Coding may not be the best way of dealing with video footage. Instead, the researcher might well adopt a more flexible and interpretative approach to the data that does not try to break it down into categories based on the same procedures as for textual analysis. In the case of extended footage of naturally occurring action, the reduction of footage to codes and indexes is not always appropriate—though it can be useful for familiarization purposes, in that attaching thematic labels to sections of footage helps the researcher map and negotiate it efficiently (in any case, logging the footage remains essential). At Cardiff, we have experimented with adopting a narrative rather than a thematic approach, creating edited "descriptive sequences" of significant ethnographic events.[5] These condense footage down into viewable sequences pertaining to the ethnographically significant events in which we are interested. Selected segments of these have then been hyperlinked into the rest of the EHE.

For the still image, some CAQDAS programs (such as Atlas-ti and HyperResearch) allow photographs to be annotated and/or thematically linked in a way that allows them to be assembled into a network of associated themes. Sound, too, can be analyzed in depth on its own terms, though this is something in which we have not yet developed much expertise or experience. The challenge is to bring all these differently derived insights together. Video footage can be left "raw," divided into sequences "as shot," or edited into montages. If a digital environment is being used, then editing can be done on the computer, using one of the video editing programs such as Adobe Premiere. Photographs can be edited with a similar package, such as Adobe PhotoShop. Sound, too, can be separately edited, using software such as Sound Forge. Again, there is not enough space to include a proper discussion of these programs here (see Dicks et al., 2005, for further comment).

Representation Using Hyper/Multimedia

Qualitative researchers have been slow to experiment with new electronic kinds of writing up or representation. It is true that hypertext principles have, to a limited extent, been incorporated into one or two computer-aided qualitative data analysis software packages. This suggests that the value of hypertext for qualitative analysis is beginning to be recognized. It remains the case, however, that once analysis is complete and writing up commences, the traditional "unilinear"[6] printed text usually takes over, in which images and other media play only a supporting role, if any. It is, nevertheless, obvious that the ready availability of simple digital reproduction will tempt many to bring images and sound into their work in the near future and to present them via the Web. However, considerable problems are involved in producing scholarly work via multimedia and hypermedia approaches. Writing conventions in academic research have been honed and refined over many decades and depend on a complex rhetoric of persuasion—even though submerged beneath the apparently neutral conventions of scientific reporting (as Atkinson, 1990, observes in the case of ethnographic writing). The risk is that the addition of multimedia develops haphazardly without an in-depth understanding of how it can best work for academic argumentation, if it can work at all.

To elaborate on this further, we should remember that the computer screen is very different from the printed page. Bolter (1999, p. 300), for example, has characterized it as a new topographical "writing space" in which writing becomes "writing *with* places, with spatially realised topics." This emphasis on space and the arrangement of elements within it points to the importance of careful planning and screen design when laying out hypermedia "pages." As readers of Web pages know, it is easy to overload the screen with animated flashy multimedia that fail to do anything other than momentarily distract our attention. If they embrace hypermedia for academic representation, authors will have to become multimedia designers, too—and there are many skills involved in this that are not native to social scientists. Lemke (2002a), for example, shows how coherence in Web pages is achieved by the complex interweaving of visual and verbal semantics. Color and typeface become important aspects of the screen's cohesion. A developing body of work on discourse analysis, linguistics, and semiotics is trying to codify and make sense of these new image–writing–sound combinations (see Iedema, 2003; Macken-Horarik, 2004). Developing a map of the kinds of multimodal implications of particular screen design choices is an important task awaiting qualitative researchers in the digital age. There is also a question about whether computer screens are a suitable medium for the kinds of dense argumentation that most academic work requires. In our own work, we have discussed the many barriers preventing an easy transfer of scholarly argumentation from the printed page to hyperlink-based media (Dicks & Mason, 2003; Dicks et al., 2005). These problems center on the issue of sequentiality in hypermedia representations: how to ensure that the reader can follow a linear argument or exposition while still benefiting from the freedom to explore the work at will. For some, there is no contradiction between hypermedia and scholarly exposition. Peter Biella, an anthropologist, declares that "hypermedia will allow film and scholarship to join forces" (1993a, p. 165). In a pioneering and much-quoted essay, he discusses the potential of hypermedia for scholarly argumentation and identifies eight formal attributes that make up what he calls the "scholarly apparatus" in print-based social science writing. Biella sees film as inherently unscholarly because its linearity and necessary brevity cannot accommodate these formal requirements. Hypermedia, by contrast, allows the filmmaker to utilize these eight formal attributes of the full scholarly apparatus. Hypermedia does not, for Biella, represent a challenge to the terms on which scholarly exposition rests. Instead, it is the means by which film can assume the necessary scholarly attributes that allow it to be taken seriously in the discipline. The result combines these with the insights that, in Biella's view, only film can convey: "the ability to communicate a compelling sense of intimacy with the subject, an oceanic insight into something new and startlingly important . . . an unprecedented, privileged sense about people who would otherwise remain unknown" (p. 164). The implications of his argument point in the direction of highly structured hypermedia productions that cogently and clearly communicate the results of authored scholarship.

However, Biella's is only one view of what hypermedia can mean. Those whose experience of hypermedia has been influenced by discussions of "electronic literature" and by educational applications of hypertext offer an evaluation that is more focused on the "rhizomatic" qualities of hypertext itself. This perspective emphasizes the affinities between multilinear writing and the associative qualities of human cognition (as in the arguments of hypertext's original proponent, Vannevar Bush). Here, too, efforts have been made to open up a dialogue between multilinear hypertext and the demands of scholarly work. David Kolb, a philosopher and social theorist, has experimented with hypertext in his philosophical work and has discussed in a number of essays both the benefits and drawbacks of scholarly hypermedia. He underlines how the demands of scholarly exposition require quite different kinds of reading engagement than the conventional Web page or piece of digital fiction. When writing scholarly, argumentative essays, Kolb (1998) points out:

> I'm not just setting out structure to be strolled through and admired—not: "ooh, how complex and interesting!" Nor am I building a structure to be explored and discovered as in a mystery narrative—not: "now I see the whole structure that was presented only in glimpses!"

> . . . Nor am I just creating a world that readers try on—not: "so this is what it feels like to have this point of view." . . . There are specific assertions and propositions to be judged and assented to. The reader should exit from the text changed, but in a self-critically evaluative way.

Hence, in scholarly writing, we are doing something quite different from a standard Web page; in social research, furthermore, we are presenting the reader with an argument that draws its authority from (usually) its basis in empirical evidence. The problem is structuring electronic texts so that the legitimacy and credibility of research findings are preserved. As Kolb observes, "hypertexts have no edge of the page." In order to ensure that readers encounter, follow, and are persuaded by the argumentation proffered, devices such as outlines, tables of contents, summaries, navigational aides, and such need to be used. This returns us to Biella's point that scholarly exposition has to meet the requirements of intellectual work (for clarity, debate, evidence, argumentation, cross-referencing, bibliographic attributions, etc.) that are reflected in the expectations of, for example, peer review.

In many cases, perhaps even most, writers will find it easiest to meet these requirements by retaining a tight structure that controls the labyrinthine qualities of hypertext. This can be done by restricting hyperlinks to illustrative roles (e.g., through video popups) and navigation to forward–back movement. By tightly controlling the sequencing of pages, the author can establish a clear hierarchy of voices—those of the author, of fieldwork informants, of other writers, commentators, and academics—which makes it easier for him or her to engage in established academic debates through authoritative and substantiated unilinear argumentation. Yet authors may also want the reader to see how other interpretations could be reached or how the same data can be analyzed to produce different insights. They might want to show the reader how to trace different paths through the data records and how to encounter the full complexity of voices that characterize the field. They also might want to challenge the reader to see through the rhetoric of persuasion that underpins classic unilinear academic writing. In some ethnographic writing, for example, representation becomes the complex activity of weaving together stories that are self-consciously partial and multiple. This kind of narrative interweaving can certainly be done on the printed page, but the results are arguably rather messy. Such attempts are struggling to convey the consciousness of radical interconnectivity and contingency that, arguably, lies at the heart of contemporary cultural analysis. It is a consciousness that hypertext effortlessly embodies, even imposes. Perhaps sticking to the print form to convey it is more a function of the persistence of powerful publishing conventions and status markers in academia than of representational considerations alone. Our suggestion, on the whole, is that qualitative researchers will want to continue producing their own interpretations and presenting these as authoritative readings. In so doing, they may well wish to underscore the contingency of their interpretation but also to ensure that the reader can identify, make sense of, and follow it. A well-structured hyperlinked trail can do this.

There are also potential dangers in hyperlink-based writing. In postparadigm ethnography (see earlier in the chapter) many writings attempt to *expose* the rhetoric of ethnographic representation—to make it visible and hence to denaturalize the arguments and claims that ethnographers have traditionally made. Yet rather than offering enhanced visibility, hypertext can end up making connections more opaque. As Barbules (1998) warns of the Web, the invisibility of links can serve to naturalize relations between items, making it difficult for the reader to perceive precisely what connection is being made. Readers of hypermedia environments may well expect that a link expresses particular logical relationships. Hence, one node linked to another (sequencing) may be read as cause and effect, particularly where this is suggested by beliefs about the world "outside." One way of addressing this problem is to make the functions of links more explicit. We also concur with Lemke (2002) in arguing for using links in a motivated manner. Just because we *can* make a link, we should not necessarily do so; we must avoid the temptation of linking everything to everything else, which will produce only incoherence.

The Potential of the Hyperlink

In our view, it is the hyperlink that provides the key to understanding the potential of hypermedia and multimedia for qualitative research. When an author links two items (or nodes) together, he or she is not simply providing a bridge between them. Instead, he or she is introducing a third entity—the specification of a relationship between the two nodes. This third entity not only brings two items together but also alters the meaning of each in the process. Writing for the multimedia computer screen brings the possibility of exploring both *collage* (the juxtaposition of different media on a Web page) and *montage* (the provision of links to let the reader navigate from one screen or screen element to another). These two sets of relationships do not simply act as navigational tools; they allow new dimensions of meaning to emerge. For example, juxtaposing an informant's account and authorial commentary does not simply add together two voices; rather, each forces us to read the other in its own light. Similarly, the complex rhetoric of hyperlinking has begun to be charted outside the field of qualitative social research methods. Barbules (1998), for example, has noted the restricted meanings that typical Web links evoke. These usually follow the conventions of metaphorical, metonymical, or synecdochal semantic relationships. However, these types of links will not necessarily be the most appropriate ones for hypermedia scholarly authors. The links they make must generate ordered knowledge rather than work largely through associations.

On the Web, the most significant thing can be connected together with the most trivial. Once links are followed, it is up to readers to consider what, if anything, it all means. This would not generate an effective form of communication for most scholarly researchers. But it raises interesting questions about the kinds of links that qualitative researchers are likely to find most valuable. There is the question of how far links should be generated from within the data, and therefore be project-specific, or whether a common set of links could be established that would serve all projects. The rhizomatic qualities of hypertext also suggest their own rhetoric, which has the potential to take ethnographic representation in new directions. Bricolage and juxtaposition, for instance, can be used to suggest alternative or contrasting interpretations of the same situation or event. Ethnographers will undoubtedly wish to take advantage of hypertext's labyrinthine qualities in ways that we have not attempted to address here.

We end by outlining four distinguishing features of hypermedia that enable us to ponder some of the losses and gains involved in working with it at different stages of the research process.

1. The division of labor between the analysis and representational stages of research is blurred in hypermedia—meaning that the activity of "writing up" becomes increasingly interwoven with that of analysis. Data records can be hyperlinked to and with authored interpretative texts in an evolving network of interconnections between analysis, representation, and data.

2. The electronic computer screen does not naturally lend itself to the construction of a long sequential narrative. Instead, it is better to construct short, hyperlinked pieces of content, either written text or multimedia, and lay out alternative pathways for the reader to follow, some (but not all) of which will be marked out by the author.

3. Digital-age researchers are not confined to "lettered" representation or even to verbal language. The capacity to incorporate

still and moving images, as well as sound, means that the burden of meaning is no longer carried by written words alone. As a result, new ways of integrating these different modalities need to be found that have much to do with practices of *design*.

4. An ethnographic hypermedia environment is not finished when the author has finished preparing it. Because the medium is electronic and evolving, readers can annotate and comment, contributing directly to the "text." In addition, the ethnographic hypermedia environment can be linked to and with other electronic texts, foregrounding its connections outward and undermining the idea of fixed-content boundaries.

Although this chapter has outlined some of the potential that these features bring, we have alluded to the losses and dangers, too. For example, academic authors will not want their electronic hypermedia to be approached as though it were simply another website offering what is often superficial information. In the ages of multichannel and mobile electronic communication, readers have become more expectant of having multiple choices in informational environments and are more able to "parallel process" different materials simultaneously. Web pages tend to acknowledge and reinforce the expectation of a short attention span. Through its superficial analogies with computer gaming, hypertext may encourage a trial-and-error, experimental approach to reading: "just click and see." Although beneficial in some cases, it can also engender a distracted, uncritical approach in which links are merely activated rather than reflected on and pages consumed in a restless and ever-mobile manner—perhaps with a view to getting to the "juicy" bits lurking in the labyrinth. Video content may be sought and activated as "entertainment" in preference to written sections. Hypertext certainly encourages actively mobile transits, as opposed to the more reflective approach that many would argue is encouraged by the book. Yet the fact that readers are required actively to click and explore an EHE may also provoke greater engagement levels, critical distance, and sense of ownership over the content. More research needs to be done into how readers do relate to academic hypertext and multimedia.

Furthermore, there is the undisputedly tricky nexus of issues raised by ethical principles (which we discuss at length elsewhere; see Coffey et al., 2006). In audio and video editing programs, traditional televisual techniques of blurring faces or distorting voices are unlikely to be enthusiastically embraced by qualitative researchers, as they lose the semiotic qualities of facial and vocal expression and involve quite an intrusive technological add-in, as well as possibly insinuating an equivalence between research participants and the familiarly anonymous images of television "victims" and "criminals." The question of identifying informants is likely to be an increasing problem as wider access to data becomes possible. Electronically stored and retrieved digital datasets, for example, allow fairly easy access to the original data (password-protected websites, our own preferred option, provide one kind of solution to this). One has to be careful to find out about and apply the relevant ethical codes and laws (including laws of copyright, data protection, and freedom of information). Video, in particular, raises a host of ethical dilemmas in that anonymization becomes virtually impossible. In general, of course, the principles of active, informed consent should be applied to all research practice, so the means of distribution should be made clear to all participants and their consent and understanding ensured as to where, when, and under what conditions their data (including their own images) might be made public. More work is urgently needed on the ethical challenges of hypermedia and electronic representation in the age of an increasing proliferation of images but also of increasing concern for the privacy, safety, and integrity of personal identities.

Conclusion

This chapter has discussed some of the key issues to consider in applying hypermedia and multimedia to qualitative research. We have discussed things to bear in mind when using hypermedia at four phases of a research project: fieldwork and data generation, data recording, data analysis and interpretation, and representation and dissemination of findings. Perhaps it is in this last—the presentation of our research to an audience—that hypermedia has the greatest potential to influence the way we think of our data. Hypermedia representation encourages us to recognize that analysis and interpretation are always contingent due to its ability to keep two dimensions simultaneously in view. On the one hand, hypermedia highlights the *openness* of meaning by allowing readers access to the entire dataset and thus encouraging the reader to trace and test out the connections between data and interpretation that have been made by the researcher, as well as to make new ones of his or her own. On the other hand, it provides a means of communicating fully realized scholarly arguments by the careful construction of ordered trails (through sequential linking), allowing the author to guide the reader along his or her preferred interpretative routes through the corpus. This novel kind of double articulation allows the reader to grasp the relationship between meaning potential (what sense *could* be made of the universe of meanings suggested by the corpus of data) and meaning production (what sense *has* been made by the particular researcher). Whereas the traditional model of print representation grants the reader access only to the latter (except where data records, and this is very rare, are included in appendices or accompanying resources), hypermedia keeps both in view. In allowing a representation of the relationship between the two, it shows the basis on which a particular interpretation has been reached.

In conclusion, we recognize that the printed book or article (and, differently, the film) remains a well-established, institutionally legitimate, and powerful rival to any new form of scholarly authorship that may emerge in the computer age. Rather than replacing either of these, hypermedia will find its own place. Indeed, it is likely that there will be a continuum of use. Academics may adopt many hypertextual techniques to complement their word-processed presentations and, indeed, may increasingly construct those presentations on the basis of hypertextually aided analysis. They may, however, stop short of the kind of fully hyperlinked authoring discussed here. Time and other resource constraints are likely to be a big factor in mitigating against fully realized, scholarly multimedia environments on the computer screen. Nevertheless, the era of print *monopoly* is surely fading away as the benefits of Web-hosted dissemination become clearer to many, including the academic publishing industry. This fact, in combination with the reverberations of postparadigm qualitative research that encourages calls for more transparent and proactive forms of reader engagement with scholarly texts, may well mean that hypermedia does begin to catch on. Certainly, in relation to multimedia, it is hard not to envisage a future in which researchers write up their research electronically, so that they can display the video, sound, and other representational media that they will undoubtedly be using to ever greater degrees. And once text transmutes from page to screen, it would be unlikely for authors not to take up the potential of the hyperlink—albeit, one would hope, with the benefits of further study into the potentiality of link semiotics and rhetoric for scholarly exposition. The relations between analysis and representation, reading and writing, images and writing, written and spoken word, and movement and stasis are all potentially reconfigured in hypermedia. As the page blurs into the screen, these relations will continue to require further reflection from qualitative researchers.

Notes

1. Excerpts from the CD-ROM and book can be found on Biella's website at *www.anth.ucsb.edu/projects/axfight/updates/biellaintroduction. html.*

2. In actual fact, analysis itself can proceed through utilizing the hyperlink; we expand on this later.

3. There is an exception to this generalization in textual biblical studies. As Kelle notes (1997, 2000), cross-referencing is form of textual analysis that has long been used in the study of religious texts and has been implemented in programs marketed specifically as "text analysis" (e.g., Code-A-Text) rather than "data analysis."

4. This is quite a complex assertion that could be further explored. Depending on the definition of hypertext being utilized–for example, Aarseth's (1997) very general depiction of hypertext as a form of electronic text–an electronically coded dataset could be seen as a type of hypertext. Even if this stance is taken, however, a coding structure is only very minimally hypertextual. Interestingly, some CAQDAS programs, such as Atlas-ti, *do* now possess some hypertext functionality, but it tends not to be integrated with the coding mechanisms.

5. One member of the Cardiff team, Bambo Soyinka, has been largely responsible for developing this approach.

6. The terms *unilinear* and *multilinear* are somewhat awkward but are, we believe, more accurate than the traditional linear versus nonlinear dichotomy that has previously been posited for text and hypertext.

References

Aarseth, E. (1997). *Cybertext.* Baltimore: John Hopkins University Press.

Asch, T., & Chagnon, N. (1975). *The ax fight* [Videotape]. Watertown, MA: Documentary Educational Resources.

Atkinson, P. A. (1990). *The ethnographic imagination: Textual constructions of reality.* London: Routledge.

Banks, M. (2001). *Visual methods in social research.* London: Sage.

Barbash, I., & Taylor, L. (1997). *Cross-cultural filmmaking.* Berkeley: University of California Press.

Barbules, N. C. (1998). Rhetorics of the Web: Hyperreading and critical literacy. In I. Snyder (Ed.), *Page to screen: Taking literacy into the electronic era* (pp. 102–122). London: Routledge.

Bauer, M. W. (2000). Analyzing noise and music as social data. In M. W. Bauer & G. Gaskell (Eds.), *Qualitative researching with text, image and sound: A practical handbook* (pp. 263–281). London: Sage.

Biella, P. (1993a). Beyond ethnographic film: Hypermedia and scholarship. In J. R. Rollwagen (Ed.), *Anthropological film and video in the 1990s* (pp. 131–176). Brockport, NY: The Institute.

Biella, P. (1993b). The design of ethnographic hypermedia. In J. R. Rollwagen (Ed.), *Anthropological film and video in the 1990s* (pp. 293–341). Brockport, NY: The Institute.

Biella, P. (in press). *Maasai interactive* [CD-ROM]. Belmont, CA: Wadsworth.

Biella, P., Chagnon, N. A., & Seaman, G. (1997). *Yanomamö interactive: The ax fight* [CD-ROM]. Belmont, CA: Thomson-Wadsworth. (Available from *www.anth.ucsb.edu/projects/axfight/index2.html*).

Bolter, J. D. (1990). *Writing space: The computer, hypertext, and the history of writing.* Hillsdale, NJ: Erlbaum.

Bolter, J. D. (1999). Topographic writing. In P. A. Mayer (Ed.), *Computer media and communication: A reader.* Oxford, UK: Oxford University Press.

Bolter, J. D. (2001). *Writing space: Computers, hypertext and the remediation of print* (2nd ed.). Hillsdale, NJ: Erlbaum.

Brewer, J. D. (2004). The ethnographic critique of ethnography. In C. Seale (Ed.), *Social research methods: A reader* (pp. 405–408). London: Routledge.

Castells, M. (2004). *The power of identity* (2nd ed.). Oxford, UK: Blackwell.

Clifford, J., & Marcus, G. E. (Eds.). (1986). *Writing culture: The poetics and politics of ethnography.* Berkeley: University of California Press.

Coffey, A. (1999). *The ethnographic self.* London: Sage.

Coffey, A., Atkinson, P., & Holbrook, B. (1996). Qualitative data analysis: Technologies and representations, *Sociological Research Online, 1*(1). Retrieved November 7, 2007, from *http://www.socresonline.org.uk/socresonline/1/1/4.html*

Coover, R. (2003). *Culture in webs: Working in hypermedia and the documentary image.* Watertown, MA: Eastgate Systems.

Crawford, P. I., & Turton, D. (Eds.). (1992). *Film as ethnography.* Manchester, UK: Manchester University Press.

Deleuze, G., & Guattari, F. (1987). *A thousand plateaus: Capitalism and schizophrenia* (B. Massumi, Trans.). Minneapolis: University of Minnesota Press. (Original work published 1980)

Denzin, N., & Lincoln, Y. (Eds.). (2000). *Handbook of qualitative research* (2nd ed.). Thousand Oaks, CA: Sage.

Dicks, B. (2006, July). *Visual methods in the context of multimodality.* Paper presented at ESRC Research Methods Festival, Oxford, UK.

Dicks, B., & Mason, B. (2003). Ethnography: Academia and hyperauthoring. In O. Ovieda, J. Barber, & J. R. Walker (Eds.), *Texts and technology*. Cresskill, NJ: Hampton Press.

Dicks, B., Mason, B., Coffey, A., & Atkinson, P. (2005). *Qualitative research and hypermedia: Ethnography for the digital age*. London: Sage.

Dicks, B., Soyinka, B., & Coffey, A. (2006). Multimodal ethnography. *Qualitative Research, 6*(1), 77–96.

Dohan, D., & Sanchez-Jankowski, M. (1998). Using computers to analyze ethnographic field data: Theoretical and practical considerations. *Annual Review of Sociology, 24*, 477–498

Dwyer, K. (1977). On the dialogic of ethnology. *Dialectical Anthropology, 2*, 143–151.

Dwyer, K. (1979). The dialogic of ethnology. *Dialectical Anthropology, 4*, 205–241.

Ellis, C., & Bochner, A. P. (2000). Autoethnography, personal narrative, reflexivity: Researcher as subject. In N. K. Denzin & Y. S. Lincoln (Eds.), *Handbook of qualitative research* (2nd ed., pp. 733–768). Thousand Oaks, CA: Sage.

Emmison, M., & Smith, P. (2000). *Researching the visual: Images, objects, contexts and interactions in social and cultural inquiry*. London: Sage.

Fielding, N., & Lee, R. (1998). *Computer analysis and qualitative research*. London: Sage.

Foot, K. A., & Schneider, S. M. (2006). *Web Campaigning*. Cambridge, MA: MIT Press.

Gardner, R. (2004). *Dead birds* [Videotape]. New Haven, CT: Yale Peabody Museum.

Geertz, C. (1973). *The interpretation of cultures*. New York: Basic Books.

Goldman-Segall, R. (1998). *Points of viewing: Children's thinking*. London: Erlbaum.

Harper, D. (1998). On the authority of the image: Visual methods at the crossroads. In N. Denzin & Y. Lincoln (Eds.), *Collecting and interpreting qualitative materials* (pp. 403–412). London: Sage.

Hastrup, K. (1992). Anthropological visions: Some notes on visual and textual authority. In P. I. Crawford & D. Turton (Eds.), *Films as ethnography* (pp. 8–25). Manchester, UK: Manchester University Press.

Holquist, M. (1990). *Dialogism*. London: Routledge.

Iedema, R. (2003). Multimodality, resemiotization: Extending the analysis of discourse as multisemiotic practice. *Visual Communication, 2*(1), 29–57.

Joyce, M. (1995). *Of two minds: Hypertext pedagogy and poetics*. Ann Arbor: University of Michigan Press.

Kelle, U. (1997). Theory building in qualitative research and computer programs for the management of textual data. *Sociological Research Online, 2*(2). Retrieved November 6, 2007, *www.socresonline.org.uk/socresonline/2/2/1.html*

Kelle, U. (2000). Computer-assisted analysis: Coding and indexing. In M. W. Bauer & G. Gaskell (Eds.), *Qualitative researching with text, image and sound* (pp. 282–298). London: Sage.

Kersenboom-Story, S. C. (1995). *Word, sound, image: The life of the Tamil text*. Oxford, UK: Berg.

Kincheloe, J. L. (2005). On to the next level: Continuing the conceptualization of the bricolage. *Qualitative Inquiry, 11*(3), 323–350.

Kitzinger, C. (2004). Reflections on three decades of lesbian and gay psychology. *Feminism and Psychology, 14*(4), 523–530.

Kolb, D. (1998, July). *Ruminations in mixed company: Literacy in print and hypertext together*. Presentation notes for KMI, Milton Keynes, UK. Retrieved November 6, 2007, at *http://www.dkolb.org/ht/ou-dk.html*

Kress, G. (1998). Visual and verbal modes of representation in electronically mediated communication: The potentials of new forms of text. In I. Snyder (Ed.), *Page to screen: Taking literacy into the electronic era* (pp. 53–79). London: Routledge.

Kress, G., & Van Leeuwen, T. (2001). *Multimodal discourse*. London: Arnold.

Landow, G. P. (1997). *Hypertext 2.0: The convergence of contemporary critical theory and technology* (rev. ed.). Baltimore: John Hopkins University Press.

Landow, G. P., & Delaney, P. (1991). Hypertext, hypermedia and literary studies: The state of the art. In P. Delaney & G. P. Landow (Eds.), *Hypermedia and literary studies* (pp. 3–50). Cambridge, MA: MIT Press.

Lashua, B., Hall, T., & Coffey, A. (2006, April). *Bring the noise: "Soundscape" in the context of recorded interviews*. Paper presented at the British Sociological Association annual conference, Harrogate, UK.

Lee, R. M., & Fielding, N. G. (Eds.). (1991). *Using computers in qualitative research*. London: Sage

Lemke, J. L. (2002). Travels in hypermodality. *Visual Communication, 1*(3), 299–325.

Loizos, P. (1993). *Innovation in ethnographic film*. Manchester, UK: Manchester University Press.

Macken-Horarik, M. (2004). Interacting with the multimodal text: Reflections on image and verbiage in *ArtExpress*. *Visual Communication, 3*(1), 5–26.

Mienczakowski, J. (2001). Ethnodrama: Performed research—limitations and potential. In P. Atkinson, A. Coffey, S. Delamont, J. Lofland, & L. Lofland (Eds.), *Handbook of ethnography* (pp. 468–476). London: Sage.

Moulthrop, S. (1993). You say you want a revolution?: Hypertext and the laws of media. In E. Amiran & J. Unsworth (Eds.), *Essays in postmodern culture*. Oxford, UK: Oxford University Press.

Nichols, B. (1994). The ethnographer's tale. In L. Taylor (Ed.), *Visualising theory* (pp. 60–83). New York: Routledge.

Penn, G. (2000). Semiotic analysis of still images. In M. W. Bauer & G. Gaskell (Eds.), *Qualitative researching with text, image and sound* (pp. 227–245). London: Sage.

Pink, S. (1997). *The bullfighter's braid: Unravelling photographic research* [CD-ROM]. Visual Images and Ethnographic Research I, Centre for Social Research, University of Derby, UK.

Pink, S. (1999). *Interweaving lives, producing images, creating knowledge: Video in ethnographic research* [CD-ROM]. Visual Images and Ethnographic Research II, Centre for Social Research, University of Derby, UK.

Pink, S. (2001). *Doing visual ethnography*. London: Sage.

Pink, S. (2006, July). *Using visual methods to understand other people's experience*. Paper presented at ESRC Research Methods Festival, Oxford, UK.

Plummer, K. (2001). *Documents of life: 2. An invitation to critical humanism*. London: Sage.

Reed-Danahay, D. (Ed.). (1997). *Auto/ethnography: Rewriting the self and the social*. Oxford, UK: Berg.

Richardson, L. (1992). The consequences of poetic representation: Writing the other, rewriting the self. In C. Ellis & M. G. Flaherty (Eds.), *Investigating subjectivity: Research on lived experience* (pp. 125–138). Newbury Park, CA: Sage.

Richardson, L. (1994). Writing: A method of inquiry. In N. K. Denzin & Y. S. Lincoln (Eds.), *Handbook of qualitative research* (pp. 516–529). Thousand Oaks, CA: Sage.

Richardson, L. (2000). Evaluating ethnography. *Qualitative Inquiry, 6*(2), 253–255.

Rose, D. (2000). Analysis of moving images. In M. W. Bauer & G. Gaskell (Eds.), *Qualitative researching with text, image and sound* (pp. 246–262). London: Sage.

Rose, G. (2001). *Visual methodologies*. London: Sage.

Ruby, J. (2005–2006). *Oak Park stories* [4 CD-ROMs]. Watertown, MA: Documentary Educational Resources.

Stanley, L. (Ed.). (1992). *The auto/biographical I*. Manchester, UK: Manchester University Press.

Taylor, L. (Ed.). (1994). *Visualising theory*. London: Routledge.

Weiner, A. (1994). Trobrianders on camera and off: The film that did not get made. In L. Taylor (Ed.), *Visualising theory: Essays from V. A. R. 1990–1994* (pp. 54–59). New York: Routledge.

Wesch, M. (2001, November). *Hypermedia's greatest potential (dilemma): Preserving and presenting creativity*. Paper presented at Futures Conference, Washington, DC. Retrieved October 10, 2006, from *www.mediatedcultures.net/phantom/png/nekalimin/home6.html*

CHAPTER 28

Mixed Emotions, Mixed Methods

The Role of Emergent Technologies in Studying User Experience in Context

Ingrid Mulder
Joke Kort

In the past years, we have seen a rapid proliferation of (mobile) emerging technologies, also referred to as ubiquitous, pervasive, or context-aware applications. Many of these applications are inherently personal in nature; they stay or travel with one person most of the time and are therefore used in various contexts. Evaluating such technologies is challenging. Whereas some aspects of the user experience can be captured and evaluated properly with traditional methods and tools, such as lab experiments and interviews, various other aspects, such as subjective experiences, are harder to reproduce in a lab or to collect with traditional methods. These subjective experiences are best obtained in real life: the different contexts in which a user uses the product or service.

In the ongoing debate on user experience and usability, many seem to interpret user experience as a wider concept than usability. Consequently, user-experience methods have to tackle more or other dimensions than traditional usability methods. Moreover, as mobile devices and services tend to become more and more personalized and adaptable to the user, user experiences generally tend to evolve over time, and the user's experiences in prolonged use of applications are often crucial to their success. Thus long-term studies, ranging from weeks to months, are needed in order to capture the issue of evolving user experiences (Vermeeren & Kort, 2006). Still, however, long-term, *in situ* evaluation is often considered to be too complex or too expensive in relation to the benefits it provides over other methods.

One possible approach in resolving this issue could be to use emerging information and communication technologies themselves to (remotely) collect user experience-related data. Such technologies may enable researchers to capture different aspects of a user's context, activities, and experiences. Furthermore, they provide a means to study a user in his or her context in a prolonged, less resource-intensive, and less obtrusive way than most current evaluation methods and tools, as they are often personal in nature and stay with the user all the time (ter Hofte, Otte, Peddemors, & Mulder, 2006). Differently stated, these emerging technologies have the potential to study the broad concept of user experience in context.

Experience in Context

Dealing with experiences of people using emergent technologies to communicate and cooperate is quite different from dealing with the experience of one person using one machine. Therefore, we speak of a mediated "human-to-human" experience–in line with the shift from *user*-centered to *human*-centered design; also in keeping with Koskinen and Battarbee (2003), who state that "we co-experience things with others in situ, and in elaborating experiences in stories afterwards" (p. 44).

Thus experience is not only the here-and-now experience of a certain interaction or event; it is also how people remember this interaction or event. In this, the context (e.g., the place where interaction happens) plays an intriguing role. Here, we assume that experiences that people have when they use emergent technology to communicate and cooperate are social experiences, happening in a social context, and that such experiences are social constructions, because these experiences are constructed while people are interacting with each other.

> Experience is a very dynamic, complex and subjective phenomenon. . . . The experience of even simple artefacts does not exist in a vacuum but, rather, in dynamic relationship with other people, places and objects. Additionally, the quality of people's experience changes over time as it is influenced by variations in these multiple contextual factors. (Buchenau & Fulton Suri, 2000, p. 424)

As defined by Mulder and Steen (2005), user experiences can be seen at three levels. The macro level of experience refers to experiences as an (economic) offering (Pine & Gilmore, 1999) or the impact on society. The micro level refers to the experience of using emergent technology; it focuses on the interaction of a person with the product or service (e.g., Marcus, 2004). The intermediate level, the meso level represents the social interaction and sharing of experiences aimed for by "we-centric services," that is, services that are coexperienced (see the next section for an example of a "we-centric" service). We-centric services seem be of particular added value for dynamic groups of people that sometimes collaborate on event-driven tasks, such as police officers who need to cooperate with other police officers or with ambulance personnel (ter Hofte & Mulder, 2003). By articulating what we-centric, context-aware adaptive services are from the perspective of end users, it becomes clear that such services can have benefits. The nature of such services poses a range of delicate questions about:

1. Dynamics within a group and social appropriateness (we-centric)
2. Dynamic contexts, tasks and ubiquitous computing (context-aware)
3. Sensitivity of user-data, control and self-management (adaptive)

In keeping with this view (as illustrated in Figures 28.1 and 28.2), experience defined from a traditional product development perspective can be referred to as micro level, whereas the service provided concentrates on a macro level. The experiences people have when they communicate and collaborate using we-centric services can be distinguished as the meso level. Figure 28.1 illustrates these three levels of experiences. Having experiences introduced as socially

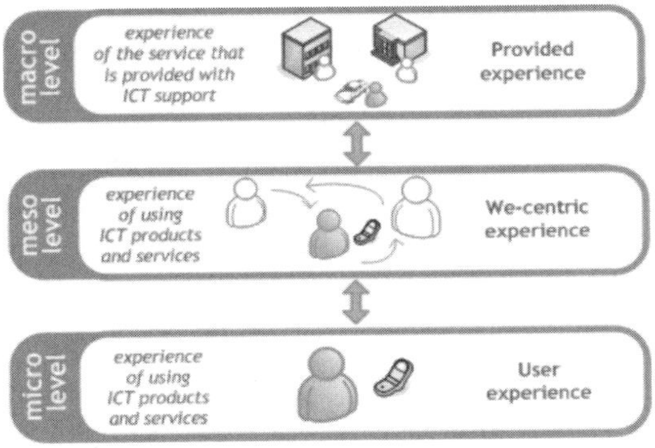

FIGURE 28.1. Three levels of experience (from bottom to top): a micro level that refers to people's experiences of using innovative technology; the meso level of we-centric experience of communication and cooperation supported by these technologies; and a macro-level experience of the service provided by people (meso) with these emergent supports.

constructed and socially contextualized, Figure 28.2 shows a more in-depth view on this meso level of experience, including feelings and thoughts, intentions and motivation, and (motivated) action and behavior.

Figure 28.2 shows that we-centric experience or coexperience consists of feelings and thoughts, intentions and motivation, and (motivated) action and behavior and that it is influenced by the context. In the next section we illustrate how emergent

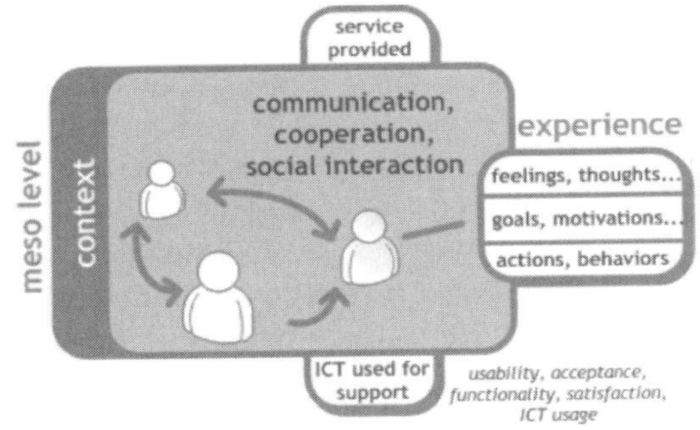

FIGURE 28.2. Experience on the meso level happens when people communicate and cooperate with one another supported by emergent technology.

technology can play a role in understanding the user behavior and experience in context.

Example: "We-Centric" Service and Emerging Technology

WeCare, a service currently under development, perfectly illustrates how emerging technology can be used to study and evaluate experiences, contextual influences, and user behavior.

WeCare is a service developed to alleviate the burden of informal caretakers of a person with dementia. Informal caretakers who provide care to dementia patients who live at home often provide this care full time, given that the condition of the person with dementia only gets worse. Related to this full-time care, informal caretakers, especially the main caretakers, often experience stress that might result in burnout. The goal of WeCare is to improve the quality of life for both the person with dementia and the informal caretakers. WeCare supports informal caretakers with different organization and communication means through a personal desktop computer and mobile phone. WeCare enables better management and care provision for the person with dementia by better and more flexibly dividing the caregiving tasks among the group of informal caretakers. An informal caretaker can keep his or her calendar up-to-date via WeCare, indicating times at which care can be provided. The main caretaker also keeps the calendar of the person with dementia up-to-date and can formulate caregiving tasks for this person. Bulletin boards created for the group of caretakers of the person with dementia provide means to communicate within informal care groups. WeCare matches the calendar information of informal caretakers and the help requests formulated by the main caretaker. Help request notifications are sent to informal caretakers via e-mail or text message. An informal caretaker can respond to a help request by accepting or rejecting the request, which is accordingly placed in his or her calendar as a caregiving task. In addition, the WeCare service is also available on a mobile phone for contexts in which no personal computer is available; this mobile service enables, for instance, viewing one's own or a care receiver's calendar for the current and following day. In this way, the main informal caretaker can formulate help requests for the person with dementia via his or her mobile device.

WeCare and Emerging Technology in Concept Development

In the early stages of the development of WeCare, the main research questions were focused on how informal care is currently provided and managed within informal caregiving groups and how the informal care for a person with dementia could be improved, resulting in less stress for the (main) informal caretaker and a higher quality of life for the dementia patient. For this, detailed insight is needed about the daily structure and organization of the informal care and the experiences of caregiving (e.g., whether the caregiver has stress or peace of mind). Once this insight is obtained, concepts that can alleviate negative experiences and enhance the quality of life can be formulated. The insight needed in the current situation is about when experiences and specific behaviors, such as stress and coping behavior, occur and which specific aspects within a person's context cause the experience and behavior. Common methods used to obtain this insight are observations, diary studies, interviews, and questionnaires. However, to study experiences such as stress and coping behavior during daily caregiving, how stress develops over time, and what causes the stress to occur is sometimes difficult with these methods: first, because they are performed over a specific and often short period of time in a limited number of contexts (e.g., observations) and, second, because they are often based on recall (e.g., interviews and questionnaires), which makes it difficult to obtain insight about the variance in the exact causes and context in which stress, for example, occurs.

To gain the desired insight, we need tools that enable us to frequently monitor experiences, behaviors, and contextual variables over a longer period of time, preferably during daily caregiving. To prevent research becoming too time- and resource-consuming, these tools should be largely automated and require minimal effort of the researcher and the informal caretaker.

WeCare and Emerging Technology during Evaluation

After WeCare has been implemented, it will be tested in a field trial with two or three informal caregiving groups over a period of several weeks. Examples of questions that need to be answered during the evaluation are whether it was easier to find someone who could perform specific care at a specific moment, whether one experienced the same or other problems as before, and what caused the positive or negative effect. Could it be possible that people do not check their mail frequently enough to respond properly to help requests in time? Are the calendars flexible enough and therefore the right means to assign help requests in ad hoc "emergency" situations?

Many of these types of questions are difficult to answer in detail when applying common methods such as questionnaires, interviews, and observations. Here, too, we would like to be able to monitor service usage and the experience that goes with it at the moment something important happens. We could, for example, register the time at which a help request is posted and monitor the response times and responses of caregivers. Furthermore, we could ask a caregiver what he or she thought of the help request and whether the match with this caregiver was suitable or not and for what reasons. Monitoring service usage and being able to send, for example, a short questionnaire to a caregiver based on this service usage (e.g., the acceptance or rejection of a caregiving task) could provide the right means to gain detailed insight into the user's experiences during evaluation.

Experience Takes Time

In order to study the concept of experience, another discriminating aspect of experience needs to be taken into account: Experience takes time (van Vliet & Mulder, 2006). This fact can be looked on in two ways. One way is to look at experience as having a certain development "curve" in time: It builds up, peaks, and then "fades" (see Figure 28.3). An interesting example in this case is the peak–end phenomenon (Kahneman, Diener, & Schwarz, 1999); this is the phenomenon by which, for instance, the pain experienced during a surgical intervention is best relieved not by quickly ending it but by slowly decreasing the inconvenient painful actions. Objectively, the pain is being extended unnecessarily, but overall it is experienced by the patient as less stressful.

A second way to look at the time aspect is to extend it even beyond a certain situation or "curve" and to stress the importance of the expectations being brought into the situation and the memories being taken out of the situation. Previous experiences and expectations influence the present experience. This present experience leads to more experiences and modified expectations. The user's experience is a result of a motivated action in a certain context. This is in keeping with how process-centered models define user experience; see, for example, Kankainen (2003). In both cases experiences can be analyzed as the state at a certain moment in time, or as a movement, a flow with a certain duration and course. This can be regarded as a "snapshot" versus a "movie" perspective on experiences (Mulder & van Vliet, 2005).

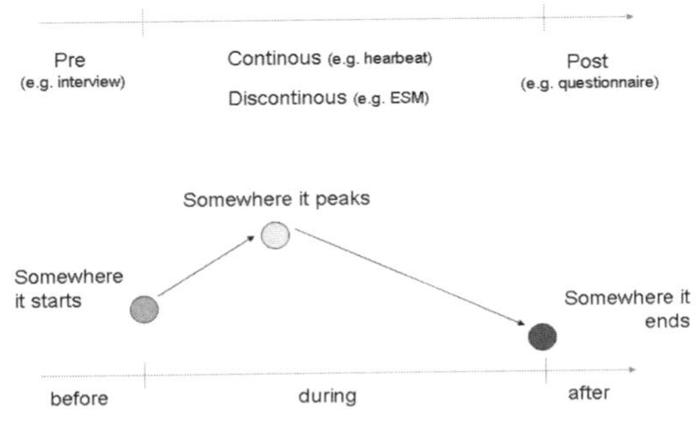

FIGURE 28.3. Measuring experience.

Methods of storytelling and experience diaries seem to be appropriate for capturing the memories and interpretations of experiences (afterward) and might come close to measuring experience; however, they also might not be suitable for measuring experiences when they occur. Experience sampling methods, on the other hand, seem to be more appropriate for capturing here-and-now or momentary user experiences (e.g., "I feel safe here and now") and in this way staying close (in time) to the actual experience.

Measuring Experience in Context

User-experience research not only poses the need for new user-research methods and tools, but services and applications are also growing in complexity, which makes them harder to study and evaluate. This complexity emerges, for example, in extensive applications (Brinck & Hofer, 2002); in integrated services with multiple stakeholders (Faber et al., 2003); in interacting devices (fixed and mobile); and in switches between contexts and target groups (de Poot, Kort, & Langley, 2004). High-quality usage research across the entire service or application design cycle has grown increasingly difficult (Ivory & Hearst, 2001). Event and other types of logging might provide a possible solution to the research problems encountered when evaluating complex services. Event logging, which originated in website and browser logging analysis, has made its way into logging and analyzing window, icon, menu, pointing (WIMP) events (Brinck & Hofer, 2002; Ivory & Hearst, 2001). Different typologies and frameworks have been introduced since. Most typologies, frameworks, and methods focus on usability evaluation through rules-based (e.g., by guidelines) or models-based (e.g., goals, operators, methods, and selection rules [GOMS] models) analyses and have already been proven to work (Ivory & Hearst, 2001). However, these methods are mainly aiming for recognizing usability or interface problems, often neglecting the fact that information and communication technology (ICT) and related products and services encompass more than just the performance of specific tasks and usage. As is central in this chapter, it is just this subjective experience that plays a very important role in product acceptance, appreciation, adoption, and success. When studying the user experience, not only the quantitative information obtained via logging but also the qualitative subjective experience needs to be captured to gain a fully detailed insight into the user's experience. In user-experience research the context in which experiences take place is an important element to monitor.

From a different perspective, mobility and mobile devices can also be used as a means to get closer to the user's experience. In other words, mobile devices can be used to assess experiences in the field (ter Hofte & Mulder, 2003). Emergent technologies, especially those with context-sensitive services, can measure certain aspects of experience to better adapt to people's needs—for example, when one is in a hurry, the service filters out nonurgent messages. By doing field studies, experiences can be measured in context—*in situ*, in real time—and can consequently be translated into meaningful system parameters. In this way emergent technologies offer a platform of new challenges for studying experience in a nonobtrusive way.

A few research tools have emerged recently that support *in situ* evaluation using the hardware (sensors) and software functionalities of contemporary mobile devices, such as personal digital assistants (PDAs) and "smart phones." Examples include context-aware experience sampling (CAES; Intille, Rondoni, Kukla, Ancona, & Bao, 2003), ContextPhone (Raento, Oulasvirta, Petit, & Toivonen, 2005), MyExperience (Froehlich, Chen, Consolvo, Harrison, & Landay, 2007), and SocioXensor (Mulder, ter Hofte, & Kort, 2005). Generally, these tools can automatically log objective data about human behavior and the context in which it takes place, such as where, when, and with whom and how communication takes place. Often, they can also automatically log usage of mobile applications. Using experience sampling or diary techniques, some of these tools can also record self-reports of subjective data, reflecting, for example, the mood of the user (e.g., stressed, happy, sad). The data collected in the field can typically be uploaded at convenient moments to a central server, where researchers can access and analyze the data to obtain more insight into the relationships and interactions between users, their experiences, human behavior, social context, and application usage.

These types of tools or platforms often meet one or more of the following requirements, consistent with requirements put forward from measuring experiences:

- Support *in situ* measurements
- Over longer periods of time
- As unobtrusively as possible
- Largely automated
- Over multiple users
- Capture qualitative data as well as quantitative, subjective data

In the remainder of this chapter we elaborate on the opportunities these tools and platforms can offer to social science research.

Logging Relationships between Users

Dynamic patterns of physical proximity in a population can be logged with wearable devices explicitly designed for this purpose, such as the infrared-based sociometer device (Choudhury & Pentland, 2002). Moreover, it becomes increasingly feasible to use short-range radio-based techniques present in contemporary mobile devices for this purpose. Examples include the Bluetooth-based BlueAware system that runs on a contemporary "smart phone" (Eagle & Pentland, 2005) and the wireless local area network–based systems for presence, location, instant messaging (PLIM) (Peddemors, Lankhorst, & de Heer, 2003) and Reality Mining (Eagle & Pentland, 2003) that run on PDAs.

Logging physical location and correlating the logs can be another indirect means to log proximity. In recent years, various location-sensing techniques have become available based on infrared receivers, radio frequency identification tags, small global positioning system (GPS) receivers, and, very recently, location services provided by mobile phone networks (Hightower & Borriello, 2001). Logging physical location itself can provide insight into the relation between location and personal social network dynamics. Note that not every research question requires logging physical locations with GPS precision; in some situations it may be sufficient to log the cell phone identification of a mobile phone network that a mobile phone is connected to.

When people access shared resources, for example, browsing the Web, editing files from a shared network drive, or reading or posting in newsgroups, in a sense, they are present at a location in cyberspace. By correlating these logs, we can capture dynamic patterns of proximity of users in cyberspace (e.g., when people are on the same Web page, on the same website working in the same project workspace; see, e.g., work on CoCoBrowse [ter Hofte, Mulder, & Verwijs, 2004] and/or browsing on Web pages with similar content; see, e.g., research on I2I [Budzik, Bradshaw, Fu, & Hammond, 2001]).

Logging Communication

Perhaps even more important than logging physical proximity is the ability to log people in communication; when, with whom, and how long? Communication patterns through electronic means, such as telephone, e-mail, and instant messaging, are relatively easy to log (see, e.g., de Vos, ter Hofte, & de Poot, 2004; Fisher & Dourish, 2004; Garton, Haythornthwaite, & Wellman, 1997), and tools such as MetaSight (*www.metasight.co.uk*) are commercially available. In systems such as instant messaging, it is even technically feasible to log which groups of contacts are currently opened and closed, thus giving an impression of which parts of a social network are currently relevant. Nevertheless, despite the increasing use of these electronic means, there are strong indications that face-to-face communication still plays a crucial role in many organizational settings (Allen, 1997). The sociometer and Reality Mining systems can also log face-to-face communication patterns based on capturing and processing audio.

Dynamic Social Network Sampling

Sometimes it is hard to log the dynamics of personal social networks unobtrusively, for example, when no adequate sensing technology is available or when a momentary subjective judgment of a human is needed. In these cases techniques from the experience sampling method can be used. The experience sampling method (ESM; Csikszentmihalyhi & Larson, 1987) is a research method in which respondents typically carry a mobile electronic device with them (e.g., a PDA, smart phone, mobile phone, or pager) for 1 or 2 weeks. At random moments during the day (8–12 times per day), a respondent gets a signal to answer a very short questionnaire (2–20 seconds) consisting of closed-ended questions. One or more questions may inquire about factual information; at least one inquires about the respondent's momentary experience, for instance, a feeling, emotion, and/or opinion. ESM seeks to maximize the validity of data collected by avoiding or minimizing the retrospective recall that is present in other self-report techniques, such as surveys and interviews. It is more obtrusive than logging but typically less obtrusive than direct observation methods such as ethnography or videotaping.

Using experience sampling, dynamics of social networks can be sampled, for example, by asking questions such as "Who are you with"? Also, experiences can be captured that relate to the momentary personal social network situation. Moreover, dynamic social network logging techniques can be used to detect relevant moments to take an experience sample, for example, directly after a meeting or a telephone conversation.

Social network (modeling and) analysis focuses on structural patterns of relations among actors, typically people, but also organizations. Basic units of analysis are relations and transitive relations (ties) between actors. A social network structure can be expressed with various measures, including range, density, centrality, groups, and positions. Most social network models view the network structure as a static property of a social network. More recently, efforts have been undertaken to create models and techniques that can deal with the dynamic emergence and evolution of social networks (see, e.g., Breiger, Carley, & Pattison, 2003).

Example: SocioXensor, Emergent Technology as Research Instrument

SocioXensor (Mulder, ter Hofte, & Kort, 2005) is an extensible tool kit that exploits the hardware sensors and software capabilities of contemporary mobile devices, such as PDAs and smart phones, to capture objective data about human behavior and social context (e.g., proximity, communication, application usage), together with sampling of subjective user experiences (e.g., needs, frustrations, and other feelings). The aim is to provide the social sciences with a research instrument to gain a much deeper, detailed, and dynamic insight into these phenomena and their relations. In turn, these outcomes can inform the design of successful emergent technology and context-sensitive applications.

SocioXensor focuses on the collection of data *in situ*, avoiding retrospective recall, which is encountered in other self-report techniques, such as surveys and interviews. More specifically, SocioXensor typically can collect data at times and locations that would be impractical or very costly with ethnography and lab studies, while maximizing the chance that participants will exhibit their natural behavior in their natural context. SocioXensor can be more obtrusive than logging, but it is typically less obtrusive than direct observation methods such as ethnography (which allow for very rich data capturing) or lab experiments.

SocioXensor fits into an evolutionary prototyping research and design strategy and can be used in field trials to get answers to formative and summative evaluation questions, such as:

- In which contexts do information and communication needs arise, and how often?
- What (combination) of contextual information is relevant for an application?
- In which contexts are application features actually used?
- What (combination of) contextual information predicts a user experience of an application?
- Did the user experience of an application improve? In which contexts?

The SocioXensor method guides researchers in their choices of which questions to ask, which schedule to follow to obtain user experience data, which human behavior and context data sensors to use, and which application usage data to log. In order to answer these questions, the SocioXensor instrument allows the capture of three types of data.

User-Experience Data

Subjective information, such as opinions and feelings, can be obtained using an experience sampling procedure. At random moments during 1 or 2 weeks, respondents get a signal to answer a very short questionnaire (3–30 seconds) consisting of closed-ended questions. One or more questions may inquire about factual information, but at least one inquires about the respondent's momentary experience, such as feelings and/or opinion. An example of such a question is, "Did you experience information overload in the last 2 hours?"

Human Behavior and Context Data

Raw, objective data about human behavior and context (e.g., location, proximity, activity, and communication) can be captured unobtrusively through device technologies on mobile devices and wearables (e.g., Global System for Mobile Communications [GSM] cell IDs, GPS location data, Bluetooth device detection, audio microphone, call logs, contact data, and calendar data). This raw context data can be used in later analyses to find relations and predictiveness of user experiences: for example, which raw context data predicts low tolerance for interruptions? Which raw context data predicts which colleague might be able to help you given your current context?

Application Usage Data

Raw, objective data about the usage of the application that is being studied is collected. The raw data may range from low-level keystrokes and screens to high-level application events. Note that in formative evaluation usage of SocioXensor, these types of data are typically not collected.

Challenges for Future Research

Exploiting emergent technologies to enable longer term, *in situ* evaluation studies brings up several issues to be resolved (see also Mulder, ter Hofte, Kort, & Vermeeren, 2007). One such issue may be that of confidentiality. Mobile devices have a large impact on how we organize our daily life, how we work, make friends, and seek entertainment. The amount of communication increases, and because communication is less bounded to certain locations (you no longer talk about work only at the office and about private things only at home), the mixture of public and private "space" is inevitable: Public places now get invaded with private conversations (lovers calling each other on the train), and text messages may disturb intimate moments. This mobility of communication raises several new discussions about issues such as the private space entering the public space and monitoring people's activity with location-based services (Brown, Green, & Harper, 2003). Another issue to be resolved relates to the researcher's problem of how to set up an evaluation for unknown contexts and contextual effects. What variables should be measured? Can one know in advance what variables need to be measured? Additionally, how should a researcher deal with the massive amount of data from an in-context user-experience evaluation with a large variety of data from a prolonged use of an application by a potentially large number of users?

In conclusion, emergent technologies might be useful as unobtrusive research methods to enable us to study interacting people in their daily context. However, there are some challenges for future research to work on in order to exploit emergent technologies as research instruments for social scientists.

One such issue is that of "missing data." Although GPS is commonly used, sometimes not all GPS coordinates can be captured. Also, the issue of power consumption needs some attention. The use of emergent technology requires power, which might not be a problem in Western countries. However, charging mobile devices more often than usual might influence the behavior of the participants. Even though contextual research has been preferred, as it captures the whole, real-life situation and therefore provides researchers with a rich input, not all context variables are always taken into account. Finally, privacy is a very important issue that requires more attention, as context information often has a personal character. How can the user be allowed to control the release of his or her personal context information? Moreover, how can the user be enabled to control his or her provided context information?

Without a doubt, emergent technologies provide a wealth of possibilities for monitoring. However, there are as yet no agreed-on generic methods for logging, only system events, but these are detailed and not always complete. Often logging is incorporated into the ICT product or service during implementation. This implementation is not always straightforward, or even possible, without access to the source code. Many of the automated tools alone do not deliver the desired insight; they need to be combined with common methods, such as interviews and focus groups, which provide either input for the automated measurements (which things should be captured and asked for during experience sampling) or additional information after the automated measurements (clarifications of specific experience sampling data, behaviors, or contexts in which it appeared).

In this chapter we promoted the idea of using emergent technology for *in situ* data collection and investigated the challenges to studying behavior by using current and emergent technology in a more objective and less obtrusive way. Current methods largely rely on observed data, more often than not gathered afterward. Nowadays, hardly any attention is paid to addressing methodologies and analysis techniques for capturing experience during user–system interactions. Therefore, the applicability of methods that try to capture experiences during (real time) user–system–context interactions need to be taken into account. The main issue here is to study the (nonlinear) dependencies between context variables and subjective experiences (cause and effect) in interaction, which require new methods for capturing experience. However, interpreting the data and translating the data into meaningful predictors for designing emergent technology needs to be addressed in future research. For understanding—more or less predicting—behavior in context, and in particular for its reliable and comprehensive assessment, subjective as well as objective methods, qualitative as well as quantitative methods, *in situ* as well as laboratory methods need to be combined. Additionally, more research into methodological guidelines and tool requirements for data analysis is necessary—in particular, analysis techniques for correlating objective behavior and subjective user-experience data into relevant design context parameters. As said before, opportunities for data collection are obvious; however, how to analyze these enormous data files is less straightforward. Which techniques are appropriate for this kind of research? How can we relate all the different data sources and obtain results? The problem is not only the sheer volume but also which information is usable, at which abstraction level, and what is not necessary to capture. You still need to know what you are interested in!

Acknowledgments

The research for this chapter has been done in the Freeband User Experience project. Special thanks for the collaboration on SocioXensor and our mixed methods research go to Henri ter Hofte and Marc Steen. The Freeband Communication program (*www.freeband.nl*) aims at the generation of public knowledge in advanced telecommunication technology and applications in the Netherlands. Freeband FRUX is a joint effort of Delft University of Technology, Dutch Police/ICS, Ericsson, Free University, Telematica Instituut, TNO Information & Communication Technology, Waag Society, and Web Integration.

References

Allen, T. J. (1997). *Architecture and communication among product development engineers*. Cambridge, MA: MIT Press.

Breiger, R., Carley, K., & Pattison, P. (Eds.). (2003). *Dynamic social network modeling and analysis: Workshop summary and papers*. Washington, DC: National Academic Press.

Brinck, T., & Hofer, E. (2002). Automatically evaluating the usability of web sites. In *Proceedings of the Conference on Human Factors in Computing Systems: Extended Abstracts* (pp. 906–907). New York: Association for Computing Machinery.

Brown, B., Green, N., & Harper, R. (Eds.) (2002). *Wireless world: Social and interactional aspects of the mobile age*. London: Springer.

Buchenau, M., & Fulton Suri, J. (2000). Experience prototyping. In *Proceedings of the Symposium on Designing Interactive Systems*. New York: ACM Press.

Budzik, J., Bradshaw, S., Fu, X., & Hammond, K. J. (2002). Clustering for opportunistic communication. In *Proceedings of the 11th International World Wide Web Conference*. New York: ACM Press.

Choudhury, T., & Pentland, A. (2002). *The sociometer: A wearable device for understanding human networks*. In *Computer-Supported Cooperative Work '02 Workshop: Ad hoc Communications and Collaboration in Ubiquitous Computing Environments*. Retrieved May 1, 2007, from *http://www.media.mit.edu/~tanzeem/TR-554.pdf*

Csikszentmihalyi, M., & Larson, R. (1987). Validity and reliability of the experience-sampling method. *Journal of Nervous and Mental Disease, 175*, 526–536.

de Poot, H., Kort, J., & Langley, D. J. (2004). Enhancing presence and context awareness in collaborative settings. In P. Cunningham & M. Cunningham (Eds.), *eAdoption and the knowledge economy: Issues, applications, case studies* (pp. 1325–1332). Amsterdam: Ios Press.

de Vos, H., ter Hofte, G. H., & De Poot, H. (2004). IM [@Work]: Adoption of instant messaging in a knowledge worker organisation. In *Proceedings of the 37th annual Hawaii International Conference on System Sciences* (HICSS-37), IEEE.

Eagle, N., & Pentland, A. (2003). Social network computing. In *UbiComp 2003: Ubiquitous Computing, 5th International Conference, Lecture Notes in Computer Science, 2864*, 289–296.

Eagle, N., & Pentland, A. (2005). Mobile matchmaking: Proximity sensing and cueing. *IEEE Pervasic Computing, 4*(2), 28–34.

Faber, E., Ballon, P., Bouwman, H., Haaker, T., Rietkerk, O., & Steen, M. (2003, June). *Designing business models for mobile ICT services*. Paper presented at the 16th Bled Ecommerce conference, Bled, Slovenia.

Fisher, D., & Dourish, P. (2004). Social and temporal structures in everyday collaboration. In *Proceedings of the Conference on Human Factors in Computing Systems* (pp. 551–558). New York: ACM Press.

Froehlich, J., Chen, M., Consolvo, S., Harrison, B., & Landay, J. (2007). MyExperience: A system for in situ tracing and capturing of user feedback on mobile phones. *Proceedings of MobiSys 2007*, San Juan, Puerto Rico.

Garton, L., Haythornthwaite, C., & Wellman, B. (1997). Studying online social networks. *Journal of Computer Mediated Communication, 3*(1). Available at http://jcmc.indiana.edu/vol3/issue1/index.html

Hightower, J., & Borriello, G. (2001). Location systems for ubiquitous computing. *Computer, 34*(8), 57–66.

Intille, S. S., Rondoni, J., Kukla, C., Ancona, I., & Bao, L. (2003). A context-aware experience sampling tool. In *Proceedings of the Conference on Human Factors in Computing Systems* (pp. 972–973). New York: Association for Computing Machinery.

Ivory, M. Y., & Hearst, M. A. (2001). The state of the art in automating usability evaluation of user interfaces. *ACM Computing Surveys, 33*(4), 470–516.

Kahneman, D., Diener, E., & Schwarz, N. (Eds.). (1999). *Well-being: The foundations of hedonic quality*. New York: Sage.

Kankainen, A. (2003). UCPCD: User-centered product concept design. In *Proceedings of the 2003 conference on Designing for User Experiences*. New York: ACM Press.

Koskinen, I., & Battarbee, K. (2003). Introduction in user experience and empathic design. In I. Koskinen, K. Battarbee, & T. Mattelmäki (Eds.), *Empathic design: User experience in product design* (pp. 37–50). Edita, Finland: Edita.

Marcus, A. (2004). Six degrees of user spaces. *User Experience, 2*(6).

Mulder, I., & Steen, M. (2005, May). *Mixed emotions, mixed methods: Conceptualising experiences of we-centric context-aware adaptive mobile services*. Paper presented at the Third International Conference on Pervasive Computing, Munich, Germany. Available at *http://www.fluidum.org/events/experience05/*

Mulder, I., ter Hofte, G. H., & Kort, J. (2005, August 30–September 2). SocioXensor: Measuring user behavior and user eXperience in ConteXt with mobile devices. In L. P. J. J. Noldus, F. Grieco, L. W. S. Loijens, & P. H. Zimmerman (Eds.), *Proceedings of Measuring Behavior 2005: The 5th International Conference on Methods and Techniques in Behavioral Research* (pp. 355–358). Wageningen, the Netherlands: Noldus Information Technology.

Mulder, I., ter Hofte, G. H., Kort, J., & Vermeeren, A. P. O. S. (2007, September). MobileHCI 2007 Workshop on the role of mobile devices and emergent technology in in-situ evaluation, MobileHCI2007, Singapore. Available at *http://insitu2007.freeband.nl*

Mulder, I., & van Vliet, H. (2005). *The experience sketchbook: Exploring experience research*. Enschede, the Netherlands: Freeband.

Peddemors, A., Lankhorst, M., & de Heer, J. (2003). Presence, location and instant messaging in a context-aware application framework. In *Proceedings of the 4th International Conference on Mobile Data Management (MDM2003), 2574*, 325–330.

Pine, B. J., & Gilmore, J. H. (1999). *The experience economy*. Boston: Harvard Business School Press.

Raento, M., Oulasvirta, A., Petit, R., & Toivonen, H. (2005). ContextPhone: A prototyping platform for context-aware mobile applications. *IEEE Pervasive Computing, 4*, 51–59.

ter Hofte, G. H., & Mulder, I. (2003, December). Dynamic personal social networks: A new perspective for CSCW research and design. *SIGGROUP Bulletin, 24*(3), 139–142.

ter Hofte, G. H., Mulder, I., & Verwijs, C. (2004). Close encounters of the virtual kind: Exploring place-based presence. *AI and Society, 20*, 151–168. Available at *http://dx.doi.org/10.1007/s00146-005-0013-6*

ter Hofte, G. H., Otte, R. A. A., Peddemors, A., & Mulder, I. (2006, November). What's your lab doing in my pocket? Supporting mobile field studies with SocioXensor. In *Computer-Supported Cooperative Work 2006 Conference Supplement* (pp. 109–110). Banff, AB, Canada.

van Vliet, H., & Mulder, I. (2006). Experience and design: Trojan Horse or Holy Grail? In E. L. C. Law, E. T. Hvannberg, & M. Hassenzahl (Eds.), *User eXperience: Towards a unified view. Proceedings of the Second COST294-MAUSE International Open Workshop: User Experience–Towards a Unified View* (pp. 58–62). Retrieved May 1, 2007, from *http://www.cost294.org/ux-workshop-nordichi2006/*

Vermeeren, A. P. O. S., & Kort, J. (2006). Developing a testbed for automated user experience measurement of context aware mobile applications. In E. L. C. Law, E. T. Hvannberg, & M. Hassenzahl (Eds.), *User eXperience: Towards a unified view* (pp. 33–38). *Proceedings of the Second COST294-MAUSE International Open Workshop: User Experience–Towards a Unified View*. Retrieved May 1, 2007, from *www.cost294.org/ux-workshop-nordichi2006/*

CHAPTER 29

Emergent Methods in Feminist Geography

Mei-Po Kwan

Feminist geography has experienced tremendous growth in the past three decades. It is a highly diverse subfield of geography with practitioners from a variety of epistemological and methodological perspectives (e.g., Moss, 2002; Nelson & Seager, 2005). Although several strands of feminist geography can be identified in the literature (Pratt, 2000), the most active of these in recent years is feminist geographies of difference—a strand that is attentive to the construction of gendered identities across multiple axes of difference (e.g., race, ethnicity, age, sexuality, religion, and nationality) and the geographies of the body. Research in this strand mainly draws on cultural, poststructural, postcolonial, and psychoanalytic theories, while turning away from objectivist epistemologies.

Although working with different substantive foci and methods, the central constructs in the work of feminist geographers are space and place. They explore the complex relationships between bodies, identities, places, and power and examine the processes through which oppressions and inequalities are embedded in, and produced through, material and symbolic space (Nelson & Seager, 2005). In addition, feminist geographers share some common concerns. First, they hold that the material and discursive construction of gendered identities is crucial for understanding difference in the lived experiences of individuals. Second, any claim to transcendent objectivity or truth is considered untenable, as all knowledge must be acquired through knowers situated in particular subject positions and social contexts (Haraway, 1991; Harding, 1991). Instead, feminist geographers recognize the partiality and situatedness of all knowledge and the importance of critical reflections on one's subject position relative to research participants, the research process, and the knowledge produced (reflexivity) (England, 1994; Gibson-Graham, 1994; Rose, 1997). Third, feminist geographers share a commitment to progressive social change that reduces social inequality and oppression of marginalized groups in general, and gender inequality in particular. An important element of this commitment is an integration of feminist theories and practice in various forms of activism.

Feminist geographers have actively engaged in debates about methods and methodologies in the past decade or so (Sharp, 2005). Special issues on feminist methods have been published in many journals, including *The Professional Geographer*, *Gender, Place and Culture*, and *ACME*. They have dealt with a variety of themes, including fieldwork, quantitative methods, and geographic information systems (GIS). From these methodological reflections, it is apparent that feminist geographers tend not to hold particular research methods as distinctively feminist. Instead, they emphasize the need to choose research methods that are appropriate for the research questions and data (Cope, 2002; Kwan, 2004; Lawson, 1995). Increasingly many feminist geographers advocate the use of multiple methods in a single study, so that the weaknesses of each single method may be compensated by the strengths of another (McLafferty, 1995; Moss, 1995; Rocheleau, 1995; D. Rose, 1993).

Feminist geographers have recently begun to explore geospatial technologies (GT) as methods in geographical research (Kwan, 2002a, 2002b; McLafferty, 2005; Pavlovskaya, 2002, 2004). GTs include a broad range of technologies for collecting, storing, displaying, or analyzing geographical information (e.g., GIS, global positioning systems [GPS], and remote sensing). Although much has been written about the limitations and social implications of geospatial technologies since the early 1990s (e.g., Curry, 1994; Pickles, 1995; Sheppard, 1993), the potential of GT as a research method in feminist geography has been explored only in recent years. In feminist urban geography and political ecology, for instance, GIS and remote sensing are involved in qualitative research that explores women's gendered and sexualized experiences and land-cover change in various cultural contexts (e.g., Cieri, 2003; Nightingale, 2003). There is also research by feminist geographers that seeks to renegotiate the meanings of GT at the intersection of science, art, and subjectivities (e.g., Kwan, 2002a, 2007). Outside geography, feminist scholars in cultural and media studies have explored the role of GT as new representational media (e.g., Parks, 2001). These recent studies by feminist scholars within and outside geography suggest that GT may be creatively used to enhance our understanding of the gendered, classed, raced, and/or sexualized experiences of places.

In this chapter I highlight these recent developments in GT as emergent methods in feminist geography. I explore the ways in which they hint at alternative geospatial practices that are more relevant to the contemporary world, especially in light of the recent waves of wars and violent conflicts (Chomsky, 1988, 2003; Enloe, 1989; Gregory, 2004; Hannah, 2005; Hyndman, 2005). I emphasize the need for researchers, developers, and users (hereafter, "practitioners") to contest the dominant meanings and uses of GT and to participate in struggles against the oppressive or violent effects of these technologies. Drawing on insights from feminist science and technology studies, I suggest that geospatial practices need to be recorporealized and embodied. This involves not only reintroducing long-lost subjectivities (of the researcher/user, as well as of the researched and those affected by these technologies) back into geospatial practices but also making emotions, feelings, values, and ethics an integral aspect of geospatial practices (Kwan, 2007). Only then will moral geospatial practices become possible, and only then can we hope that the use and application of these technologies will lead to a less violent and more just world.

Bodies Matter

GT are designed, created, and used by humans, and a large proportion of their application is for understanding or solving problems of individuals and social groups. Bodies, however, are often absent or rendered irrelevant in contemporary practices of GT. This "omission of the body" happened in two different but related senses (Johnson, 1990, p. 18). First, although bodies are involved in the development and use of GT, there is little room in these technologies to allow for any role of the practitioner's subjectivities, emotions, feelings, passion, values, and ethics. Second, despite the fact that a large number of bodies are affected by the application of GT (e.g., people profiled by geodemographic application; civilians who were annihilated by GPS-guided "smart bombs" that missed their targets), bodies are often treated merely as things, as dots on maps, or even as if they do not exist (Gregory, 2004; Hyndman, 2005).

The dominant disembodied practices of GT, however, are contestable, as they are largely the result of a particular understanding of science and scientific objectivity. This historically specific and socially constructed notion of science, as Donna Haraway (1991) argues, is predicated on the positionality of a disembodied master subject with transcendent vision. With such disembodied and infinite vision, the knower is capable of achieving a detached view into a separate, completely knowable world. The kind of knowledge produced with such disembodied positionality denies the partiality of the knower, erases subjectivities, and ignores the power relations involved in all forms of knowledge production (Foucault, 1977). Haraway (1991, p. 189) calls this decorporealized vision "the god-trick of seeing everything from nowhere."

To bring bodies back in and make them relevant to geospatial practices, the vision enabled by GT should be reclaimed from the abstract, disembodied practices through recorporealizing all visualizations as embodied and situated practices. I have called this appropriation of vision "feminist visualization" (Kwan, 2002a, p. 645), which is grounded in "the view from a body . . . versus the view from above, from nowhere, from simplicity" (Haraway, 1991, p. 195). As I argued, feminist geographers can appropriate the power of modern GT and contest the dominant meanings and uses of these technologies. In order to do this, feminists should develop alternative geospatial practices for representing the world in ways that question or destabilize dominant representations, which are often imbued with various silences (especially on subaltern groups) and insensitive to the effects of oppression and violence (Nash, 1994; Sparke, 1998).

The critical project that aims to recorporealize geospatial technologies entails several important elements. First, we should reconfigure the dominant visual practices in conventional geospatial practices with the explicit intent to counter their omniscient vision and objectifying gaze. Second, we should create and experiment with new geospatial practices that can better represent the complex realities of gendered, classed, raced, and sexualized spaces and experiences of individuals. These new practices should take into account the existence of different kinds of bodies (e.g., pregnant, disabled, old, mutilated, dead) and their socially encoded meanings in relation to specific spatial, temporal, and cultural contexts (Domosh & Seager, 2001; Laws, 1997; Longhurst, 2001; G. Rose, 1993). They should also allow practitioners of GT to become more sensitive to how identities are socially constructed and negotiated and to the effects and outcomes of the power relations involved in the use and application of GT. Third, we should develop more reflexive modes of collecting, using, analyzing, and visualizing geographic data. This "implies a sensitivity to power relations within the field, an awareness of the ethical role of the researcher and a commitment to the progressive deployment of research as well as an understanding of how the researcher and the researched have been gendered, sexualized, raced and classed" (Jenkins, Jones, & Dixon, 2003, p. 58). Perhaps one of the most important elements of the project is bringing the role of emotions, desires, passion, values, and ethics to bear on geospatial practices (Sharp, Browne, & Thien, 2004). If the world is imbued with complex emotional geographies, GT can become more relevant only if they allow us to take the geographical effects of feelings (e.g., love, hate, hope, and fear) into account.

Drawing on recent works by feminist geographers and scholars, I explore in what follows several issues pertinent to any attempt to recorporealize GT. For example, what notions may provide useful guidelines for practitioners of GT in their everyday politics and practice? What kind of strategy may be used to contest the dominant meanings and uses of GT, especially those that have violent outcomes? What kind of critical engagement with GT would facilitate the emergence of a less violent and more just world? How to bring about material change to the politics and practice of GT?

Lived Experiences and Personal Knowledge

Two areas in which feminist theory has been applied effectively with GT are in urban geography and political ecology. Feminist urban geographers have explored how GIS and remote sensing may enhance our understanding of the multiple meanings and realities of women's gendered/sexualized experiences in various cultural contexts. An example is Marianna Pavlovskaya's (2002, 2004) study of the interaction between urban restructuring and the livelihood of urban residents in post-Soviet Moscow. In the study she examines the survival strategies of urban households in a period of rapid economic change. She explores the complex links between urban restructuring, the micro geographies of neighborhoods, and economic activities inside individual households. Pavlovskaya shows that the most rapidly growing segments of the tertiary sector in the urban economy of Moscow are not responding to the daily needs of urban households in Moscow. She also uses GIS maps effectively to illuminate the multiple economies at the household level using a variety of data—including ethnographic data collected through in-depth interviews with families and street-level details (e.g., individual buildings).

Marie Cieri's (2003) study of queer tourism in Philadelphia also highlights how GT can be used to explore the gendered and sexualized geographies of urban space. Her project explores lesbian social space in the context of mainstream promotion of queer tourist space in greater Philadelphia. Cieri compares official information and representations of queer tourist spaces with what exists on the ground and in the spatial perception of a group of lesbian and bisexual women in the study area. With data collected through participant observation and in-depth interviews and using a variety of geospatial techniques (GIS and remote-sensing analysis, map overlays, as well as other types of visual collages), she found that queer tourism promoters tend to conflate lesbian tourism with gay male tourism, though there are considerable differences in the spaces of consumption between lesbians and gay males. To tell the geographic stories of her participants, she develops a new visual method (in the form of a PowerPoint slide show). Through expanding the representational capacity of GT, the method she developed can be considered as "a way of transferring some of the power inherent in the generation and communication of geographic information to those who generally lack it" (Cieri, 2003, p. 148).

Important progress has also been made in cultural and political ecology. An important focus of this work is to improve the ability of GIS to represent human knowledge, meanings, and emotions through a detailed comparison of the knowledge provided by GIS and remote-sensing data with the personal knowledge and perceptions of research participants collected through qualitative methods (e.g., in-depth interviews or oral histories). As recent studies have shown (e.g., Jiang, 2003), there are significant discrepancies between the "objective" knowledge represented by visual images generated with GIS or remote-sensing technologies and people's partial and situated knowledge. These studies used mixed methods to show that a careful comparison of these two types of knowledge may yield significant insights into people's personal knowledge of the environment and the underlying social, cultural, and political processes.

One of these studies used ecological oral histories. In her study on community forestry in Nepal, Andrea Nightingale (2003) interrogates nature–society relations by examining how cultural understandings of forestry and the social–political contestations embedded within forest use affect the implementation of a resource-based development program. Her study challenges dominant representations of forest change (i.e., aerial photo and other remote-sensing data) through demonstrating how they provide only a partial story of forest change in the study area. She accomplished this through an analysis of the discrepancies between the story told by aerial photos and the stories told by local villagers (ecological oral histories). The discrepancies between local knowledge of the villagers and the photos indicate that the villagers know the more accessible areas of the forest better. These areas are of great value and importance to them, and the improvement they see in these areas represents a dramatic change to them. Furthermore, the dramatic improvements the villagers talk about actually referred to small areas of significant improvement in key places, whereas the images captured by the aerial photos were devoid of local meaning. Her study highlights the partiality and limitations of GIS or remote-sensing data as representations of local knowledge. It also demonstrates that the use of qualitative methods and GIS data can yield rich insights by analyzing the discrepancies between the stories told by different sources of materials, including oral histories, participant observation, in-depth interviews, aerial photos, and quantitative vegetation inventory.

Recorporealizing Geospatial Technologies

Another area in which the dominant uses of GT are being contested is in feminist art, cultural, and media studies. These works use GT to express meanings, memories, feelings, and emotions about places. Their primary goal is to recorporealize geospatial practices through incorporating the practitioner's subjectivity as an integral element of the project. These projects are more expressive than representational or analytical, and they often take the form of creative visual or artistic work (e.g., GPS-assisted travelogues and 3-D GIS video). I describe three of these attempts to disrupt conventional GT practice.

Subjective Mapping

Lisa Parks (2001, p. 209), a cultural critic and video artist, contests the meanings of GPS through using it as an interactive technology for "plotting the personal." She explores whether GPS can be used to document human movement and everyday experiences in a way similar to that of photography, home video, and travelogues. She highlights the paradoxical nature of GPS and argues the need for critical strategies for struggling with the meanings and uses of satellite technologies. She states, "the satellite occupies a remote orbital position beyond users' reach and outside of the field of vision; satellites have historically been controlled by states and used in myriad ways without citizens' knowledge, involvement or consent; and satellites are high-tech, high-capital and high-maintenance devices that are seemingly beyond the purview of the popular and the personal" (Parks, 2001, p. 210). Parks contends that what state-sponsored and commercial digital mapping projects share is their quest for total vision and total knowledge of the planet. She argues that the personal plot she explored works against this centralization of vision and knowledge by insisting that GPS need not be used to articulate the agendas of the state or business. Instead, it can be used as a means of storytelling and a technology for self-expression.

Parks explored GPS as a means of articulating the politics of location through linking and interpreting an individual's global position (location data produced through satellites) with his or her subject position (historically and socially constituted identities). She illustrates how GPS maps might produce such politics through discussing two GPS tracks of her movements that she recorded in two recent trips, one in California and the other in Alice Springs, Australia. As Parks (2001, p. 216) puts it, "At each juncture I entered a waypoint, ensuring that each moving trace would be remembered. I was reminded here of my own mobility relative to theirs—and that my GPS map of California would look quite different from that of a migrant worker, a Chinese pharmacist, a high-tech executive or a groaning seal for that matter." She suggests that GPS maps (or personal plots) offer "new ways of visualizing social difference that are based on human movement rather than physiognomy or pigmentation" (Parks, 2001, p. 211). These visualizations, she argues, enable us to conceptualize more precisely how identities are constituted through material rather than figurative movements.

Like travel photography, Parks (2001, p. 213) suggests, "the GPS receiver, rather than capturing an objective record, instead generates a visual display that may activate memories of subjective perspective, of a particularly situated point of view." GPS not only registers location coordinates but also records the highlights, landmarks, and special events of one's journey—those personal experiences that are not coded within conventional maps. In this sense, Parks argues, the GPS map combines the objective and omniscient discourse of cartography with the subjective, grounded experience of the user. Visual representation of the moving body by GPS introduces the possibility of subjective mapping. Although represented as a series of lines and dots, the body's movement transforms the map from an omniscient view of territory into an individualized expression. By plotting the personal, GPS inscribes embodied practices into the discourse of mapping and allows the user to call into question the objective status of the map by inflecting it with personal movement. The producer of the GPS map is none other than the body that traveled, walked, or moved along a certain trajectory carrying a GPS receiver. The practice of plotting the personal, then, figures the user as a subject produced through a series of movements and encounters. Drawing on Paul Virilio (1997) and Gilles Deleuze (1986), Parks calls this subject "the trajective self," referring to a space in between the subjective and objective that accounts for the ongoing condition of bodily movement.

Furthermore, as Parks (2001, p. 214) suggests, "GPS mapping involves the act of self-positioning by recording and displaying movements from here to there. The goal of the personal plot is not to reproduce panoramic vistas, but rather to display one's changing position and archive one's routes." The GPS maps therefore represent the possibility of a mediated experience, as they often necessitate storytelling and narration, because what they reveal is seen and experienced from very specific and personal points of view. When used as a technology of self-reflection, GPS invites the user to see him- or herself as a subject-in-motion, as a reader and a writer, reflexively inscribing personal trajectories onto the text of the social world of his or her everyday life. In this light, as Parks argues, GPS receivers can be used as technologies of self-expression, creating spatial interpretation and social understanding as much as they can be used as tracking and monitoring devices.

Refigured Visuality

In a similar vein, I contest the omniscient and objectifying vision of GIS-based 3-D geovisualization by exploring new ways to portray human movement and everyday experiences. Drawing on the methods in visual ethnography, visual sociology, and the critical study of visual culture (e.g., Banks, 2001; Rose, 2001), I created a 3-D GIS "movie" that is more an artistic and expressive visual narrative than an objective recording generated with the aid of scientific visualization. As Sarah Pink (2001, p. 88) suggests, video can be used for "ethnographic diary-keeping, note-taking (including surveys of the physical environment, housing, etc.)" or for "recording certain processes and activities." However, such video materials should not be treated merely as visual facts. Rather, they are representations, in which the collaborations and strategies of self-representation of those involved were part of their making. For visual ethnographers, video is not simply a data-collecting tool but a technology that participates in the negotiation of social relationships and a medium through which ethnographic knowledge is produced.

Based on these notions of video as a visual method, I developed a method that may be called "collaborative 3-D GIS videography," which refers to the creation of videos using scenes rendered by a 3-D GIS to represent the person-specific experience and story of a particular research participant. The video that I produced is based on the oral history of a Muslim woman (who was a key informant of the study) about her feelings when traveling and undertaking activities outside her home shortly after September 11, 2001 (hereafter "9/11"). The purpose of the study is to understand the impact of anti-Muslim hate crimes on the everyday lives of Muslim women in Columbus, Ohio, after 9/11. One day several months after 9/11, I traveled with her while she was driving her minivan to undertake her normal out-of-home activities. As we passed through various routes, she recalled her feelings and fear when she saw particular buildings or stores (and her oral narrative was recorded). Using the textual transcripts of such audio recordings, the field notes that I took on that day, and the activity diary and the map sketches she completed during an in-depth interview, I portray her body's space–time trajectory in a 3-D GIS with the intent to reflect her feelings and emotions.

Contrary to the high-angle perspective commonly used in 3-D geovisualization, the video that I produced adopts her point of view (in the literal sense) as the vantage point. The moving scenes of the video show what she saw (captured and rendered by 3-D GIS) as she drove through various routes in the study area on a particular day after 9/11. Her movement is portrayed as a person-specific space–time trajectory, which is color-coded to reflect the level of fear and perceived danger she experienced. The buildings along the road are also color-coded to indicate the level of perceived danger she experienced. As audio clips from her oral narrative were also incorporated into the video, the video shows the routes and the spaces her body had moved through. It also tells her story through the scenes and her oral narrative as she recalled what happened to her life and how she negotiated the hostile urban spaces after 9/11. It shows what she saw and experienced from her personal point of view (i.e., from the position of a driver who was traveling along various roads in the study area). It is a powerful form of individualized storytelling based on her personal movements, memories, feelings, and emotions.

The 3-D GIS video I produced is, therefore, not an "objective" or "impartial" video recording of anything that can be captured by a conventional video camera. Its scenes have many physical elements that are considered to be parts of the objective reality and scientifically visible "facts" of the study area (e.g., buildings and roads). But they are rendered from the GIS database with symbolic and artistic techniques, which helped create an expressive visual narrative that was produced collaboratively with the informant. For instance, a green line was used to represent the tiny comfort zone that she experienced as she was driving her minivan through a major road in the study area, whereas the oppressive effect of the hostile urban environment was symbolically represented by coloring the surrounding buildings as red blocks. Furthermore, instead of being filmed, represented as a protagonist, and being watched, this informant does not appear in the video. She is the person who saw and acted, and only her feelings, memories, and experiences find expression in the video. The video produced is therefore not only about her but also for her, the person who is situated at the center of its production. The video contests the objectifying gaze of conventional 3-D geovisualization practices through this spatial and visual organization of its elements.

Geospatial Aesthetics

As Parks's and my own work have shown, GT can be appropriated and used as a means of self-expression, and their meanings and uses can be contested in surprising ways. For instance, there are attempts to use GT in artwork. The earliest one was perhaps Marilyn Taylor's (n.d.) *Time Pieces*, which explores how the space–time rhythm of our daily activities defines us and constitutes our sense of place. The work is an assemblage of seven three-dimensional towers constructed of clear acrylic plates, as well as brass tubing and armback connectors. Each of the transparent towers has a map on the inside of its top and bottom panels, and the passage of time is represented by its vertical axis. Each of the maps (created by GIS) shows when and where Taylor went over the course on each day of a week (as recorded by a GPS). Running between these maps is a copper wire that marks location and time simultaneously. Each 1-inch increment of wire is equal to 5 minutes, except where there are brass coils (each of which denotes an hour).

Contrary to Marilyn Taylor's creation of tangible art objects with GT, I have explored GIS as an artistic medium for generating digital artwork with GIS software and data. I have explored the aesthetic potential of GIS through experimenting with various artistic styles and techniques (Figures 29.1 and 29.2). (A color version of these figures is available at *http://geog-www.sbs.ohio-state.edu/faculty/mkwan/AffectGT.html.*) As GIS is not developed and designed for artistic work, my GIS art project primarily intends to challenge the dominant understanding of GT as scientific apparatus for producing objective knowledge and controlling the world. I intend to destabilize the fixed meanings of GT that have precluded their use in novel and creative ways. Through my GIS art I also articulate my discontent with the massive scale of militarism, violence, and misery of the contemporary world, often assisted by the noncivilian use of GT (Gregory, 2004; Hyndman, 2005). I also protest against the use of these technologies in any applications that violate personal rights and privacy (e.g., geodemographic and surveillance applications).

The digital spaces of my GIS have been my "spaces of resistance" (Pile, 1997, p. 1). Cultural politics, as Don Mitchell (2000, p. 159) suggests, "are contestations over meanings, over borders and boundaries, over the ways we make sense of our worlds, and the ways we live our lives." My GIS art project was initiated as I reflected on the wars and violent conflicts in the Middle East subsequent to the attacks at the World Trade Center and the Pentagon on 9/11. In the project, GIS was used to create digital images that are aesthetically pleasing, but none of the visual elements in these images corresponds to any particular object in the world. Through this nondiscursive and nonrepresentational GIS art practice (Rose, 1997), GIS is momentarily dissociated from any precepts of science, objectivity, transcendent vision, exploitation, surveillance, or control. I thus participated in the cultural politics of contending the meanings of GT (albeit at a personal level). Through this geospatial aesthetics grounded on my concern about the role of GT in global violence, I insist that GT should be used primarily for

FIGURE 29.1. Digital image created with three layers of geographic data (contours, rivers, and soils). Artistic effects were added to the original image with image processing software.

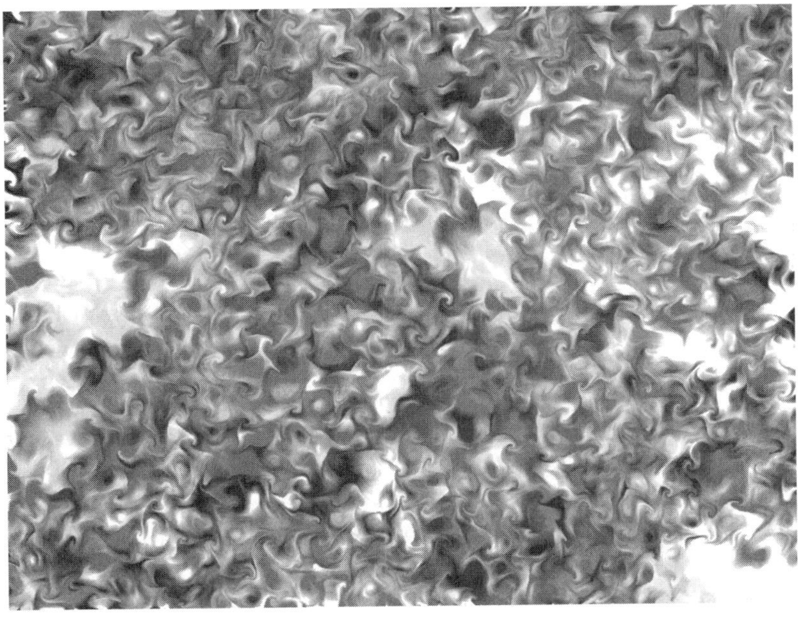

FIGURE 29.2. Digital image created with triangulated irregular network (TIN) data. Artistic effects were added to the original image with image processing software.

creating a more just and peaceful world—as when they are used in research on environmental justice or for empowering marginalized social groups (e.g., McLafferty, 2005). GIS was appropriated as a medium of passionate politics (hooks, 2000) for countering the dominant practices. It is in this sense that my GIS art project can be understood as part of a broader counterhegemonic struggle over GT, as a form of questioning and a form of protest and resistance.

These three experimentations (or moments) of recorporealizing geospatial technologies entail several critical elements. They seek to use these technologies for expressive rather than analytical purposes. They counter the omniscient vision and objectifying gaze in conventional uses of GT through refiguring their dominant visual practices. They put subjectivities and bodies back to the center of geospatial discourse through displacing the notions of scientific objectivity and disembodied researchers and users. They reveal the contestability of the meanings and uses of GT, and they suggest some of the ways in which the politics of resistance may be realized with regard to GT.

Toward Passionate Politics

Without bodies, there is no knowledge, no violence, and no fear. Without bodies, there is no passion, no feeling, and no emotion. The wars that followed 9/11 have taken an enormous human toll, sometimes with the assistance of GT, such as GPS and remote sensing (Gregory, 2004; Hannah, 2005; Hyndman, 2005). The failures that Hurricane Katrina reveals, which many had hoped to be able to avoid with the help of GT, are also extremely disconcerting. Feminist geographers with an interest in GT need to reflect on the kind of geospatial practices that are truly helpful to the contemporary world. Critical engagement that would facilitate a less violent and more just world should be their primary concern. In this chapter I have argued that embodied practices and passionate politics of GT that is attentive to bodies, subjectivities, and emotions will help us move beyond software and data to focus on real people, real bodies, and real experiences (Moss & Kwan, 2004).

As Elaine Hallisey (2005) rightly argues, cartographic visualization can be based on various epistemologies and politics. I have also suggested that being a GIS practitioner does not necessarily mean having a lack of critical sensibilities or intellectual rigor (Kwan, 2002a, 2004). Feminist epistemologies and politics can surely afford “a distinct critical edge” to practices of GT (Jenkins et al., 2003, p. 59), as they provide a rare discursive space for us to make emotions, feelings, values, and ethics a central part of our work (Ekinsmyth, Elmhirst, Holloway, & Jarvis, 2004; Kobayashi, 2005; Sharp et al., 2004; Trauger, 2004). Mobilizing emotions and values in our work not only represents an important element of the feminist project that seeks to recenter bodies in geospatial practices but also entails experimentations with more expressive or sensual forms of visual practices for conveying strong feminist messages. As video artist Pipilotti Rist suggests, “Messages that are conveyed emotionally and sensually can break up more prejudices and habitual behavior patterns than . . . intellectual treatise” (cited in Riemschneider & Grosenick, 2001, p. 142).

Feminist practitioners of GT need to see the connections between the imminent and obvious issues at hand with their larger contexts—for example, neoliberalism, globalization, international politics, or commodification of knowledge (Mitchell, 2004; Sheppard, 2004; Sparke, 2005)—and thereby need to judge whether GT will be effective (or even suitable) for dealing with specific issues. It is important to scale our care or concern from the personal/local level up to their larger contexts and to scale our geospatial practices up to the power relations and political processes that can truly address the problem at hand.

Feminist geographers should develop innovative means to protest against the use of GT for violence and to engage in political activism that turn violence and fear into hope. Only when emotions, feelings, values, and ethics, as well as a commitment to social justice, become integral elements of our geospatial practices will moral geospatial practices become possible. Only then can GT help create a less violent and more just world.

References

Banks, M. (2001). *Visual methods in social research*. London: Sage.

Chomsky, N. (1988). *The culture of terrorism*. Boston: South End Press.

Chomsky, N. (2003). *Power and terror: Post 9–11 talks and interviews*. New York: Seven Stories Press.

Cieri, M. (2003). Between being and looking: Queer tourism promotion and lesbian social space in Greater Philadelphia. *ACME, 2*, 147–166.

Cope, M. (2002). Feminist epistemology in geography. In P. Moss (Ed.), *Feminist geography in practice: Research and methods* (pp. 43–56). Oxford, UK: Blackwell.

Curry, M. (1994). Image, practice, and the unintended impact of geographical information systems. *Progress in Human Geography, 18*, 441–459.

Deleuze, G. (1986). *Cinema 1: The movement-image* (H. Tomlinson, Trans.). Minneapolis: University of Minnesota Press.

Domosh, M., & Seager, J. (2001). *Putting women in place: Feminist geographers make sense of the world*. New York: Guilford Press.

Ekinsmyth, C., Elmhirst, R., Holloway, S., & Jarvis, H. (2004). Love changes all: Making some noise by "coming out" as mothers. In J. Sharp, K. Browne, & D. Thien (Eds.), *Geography and gender reconsidered* (pp. 95–107). London: Women and Geography Study Group of the Royal Geographical Society.

England, K. V. L. (1994). Getting personal: Reflexivity, positionality, and feminist research. *Professional Geographer, 46*, 80–89.

Enloe, C. (1989). *Bananas, beaches and bases: Making feminist sense of international politics*. Berkeley: University of California Press.

Foucault, M. (1977). *Power/knowledge: Selected interviews and other writings, 1972–1977*. New York: Pantheon Books.

Gibson-Graham, J.-K. (1994). "Stuffed if I know!": Reflections on post-modern feminist social research. *Gender, Place and Culture, 1*, 205–224.

Gregory, D. (2004). *The colonial present: Afghanistan, Palestine, Iraq*. Oxford, UK: Blackwell

Hallisey, E. J. (2005). Cartographic visualization: An assessment and epistemological review. *Professional Geographer, 57*(3), 350–364.

Hannah, M. (2005). Virility and violation in the US "war on terrorism." In L. Nelson & J. Seager (Eds.), *A companion to feminist geography* (pp. 550–564). Oxford, UK: Blackwell.

Haraway, D. (1991). *Simians, cyborgs, and women: The reinvention of nature*. New York: Routledge.

Harding, S. (1991). *Whose science? Whose knowledge? Thinking from women's lives*. Ithaca, NY: Cornell University Press.

hooks, b. (2000). *Feminism is for everybody: Passionate politics*. Cambridge, MA: South End Press.

Hyndman, J. (2005). Feminist geopolitics and September 11. In L. Nelson & J. Seager (Eds.), *A companion to feminist geography* (pp. 565–577). Oxford, UK: Blackwell.

Jenkins, S., Jones, V., & Dixon, D. (2003). Thinking/doing the "F" word: On power in feminist methodologies. *ACME, 2*(1), 57–63.

Jiang, H. (2003). Stories remote sensing images can tell: Integrating remote sensing analysis with ethnographic research in the study of cultural landscapes. *Human Ecology, 31*(2), 215–232.

Johnson, L. (1990). New courses for a gendered geography: Teaching feminist at the University of Waikato. *Australian Geographical Studies, 28*(1), 16–27.

Kobayashi, A. (2005). Anti-racist feminism in geography: An agenda for social action. In L. Nelson & J. Seager (Eds.), *A companion to feminist geography* (pp. 32–40). Oxford, UK: Blackwell.

Kwan, M.-P. (2002a). Feminist visualization: Re-envisioning GIS as a method in feminist geographic research. *Annals of the Association of American Geographers, 92*(4), 645–661.

Kwan, M.-P. (2002b). Is GIS for women? Reflections on the critical discourse in the 1990s. *Gender, Place and Culture, 9*(3), 271–279.

Kwan, M.-P. (2004). Beyond difference: From canonical geography to hybrid geographies. *Annals of the Association of American Geographers, 94*(4), 756–763.

Kwan, M.-P. (2007). Affecting geospatial technologies: Toward a feminist politics of emotion. *Professional Geographer, 59*(1), 22–34.

Laws, G. (1997). Women's life courses, spatial mobility, and state policies. In J. P. Jones, III, H. J. Nast, & S. M. Roberts (Eds.), *Thresholds in feminist geography: Difference, methodology, representation* (pp. 47–64). New York: Rowman & Littlefield.

Lawson, V. (1995). The politics of difference: Examining the quantitative/qualitative dualism in post-structuralist feminist research. *Professional Geographer, 47*(4), 449–457.

Longhurst, R. (2001). *Bodies: Exploring fluid boundaries*. London: Routledge.

McLafferty, S. (1995). Counting for women. *Professional Geographer, 47*(4), 436–442.

McLafferty, S. (2005). Geographic information and women's empowerment: A breast cancer example. In L. Nelson & J. Seager (Eds.), *A companion to feminist geography* (pp. 486–495). Oxford, UK: Blackwell.

Mitchell, D. (2000). *Cultural geography: A critical introduction*. Oxford, UK: Blackwell.

Mitchell, D. (2004). Geography in an age of extremes: A blueprint for a geography of justice. *Annals of the Association of American Geographers, 94*(4), 764–770.

Moss, P. (1995). Embeddedness in practice, numbers in context: The politics of knowing and doing. *Professional Geographer, 47*, 442–449.

Moss, P. (Ed.). (2002). *Feminist geography in practice: Research and methods*. Oxford, UK: Blackwell.

Moss, P., & Kwan, M.-P. (2004). "Real" bodies, "real" technologies. In S. D. Brunn, S. Cutter, & J. W. Harrington, Jr. (Eds.), *Geography and technology* (pp. 383–400). New York: Kluwer.

Nash, C. (1994). Remapping the body/land: New cartographies of identity, gender, and landscape in Ireland. In A. Blunt & G. Rose (Eds.), *Writing women and space: Colonial and postcolonial geographies* (pp. 227–250). New York: Guilford Press.

Nelson, L., & Seager, J. (2005). Introduction. In L. Nelson & J. Seager (Eds.), *A companion to feminist geography* (pp. 1–11). Oxford, UK: Blackwell.

Nightingale, A. (2003). A feminist in the forest: Situated knowledges and mixing methods in natural resource management. *ACME, 2*(1), 77–90.

Parks, L. (2001). Plotting the personal: Global positioning satellites and interactive media. *Ecumene, 8*(2), 209–222.

Pavlovskaya, M. E. (2002). Mapping urban change and changing GIS: Other views of economic restructuring. *Gender, Place and Culture, 9*(3), 281–289.

Pavlovskaya, M. E. (2004). Other transitions: Multiple economies of Moscow households in the 1990s. *Annals of the Association of American Geographers, 94*(2), 329–351.

Pickles, J. (Ed.). (1995). *Ground truth: The social implications of geographic information systems*. New York: Guilford Press.

Pile, S. (1997). Introduction: Opposition, political identities and spaces of resistance. In S. Pile & M. Keith (Eds.), *Geographies of resistance* (pp. 1–32). New York: Routledge.

Pink, S. (2001). *Doing visual ethnography: Images, media and representation in research*. London: Sage.

Pratt, G. (2000). Feminist geographies. In R. J. Johnston, D. Gregory, G. Pratt, & M. Watts (Eds.), *The dictionary of human geography* (pp. 259–262). Oxford, UK: Blackwell.

Riemschneider, B., & Grosenick, U. (2001). *Art now*. London: Taschen.

Rocheleau, D. (1995). Maps, numbers, text, and context: Mixing methods in feminist political ecology. *Professional Geographer, 47*(4), 458–466.

Rose, D. (1993). On feminism, method and methods in human geography: An idiosyncratic overview. *Canadian Geographer, 37*(1), 57–61.

Rose, G. (1993). *Feminism and geography: The limits of geographical knowledge*. Minneapolis: University of Minnesota Press.

Rose, G. (1997). Performing inoperative community: The space and the resistance of some community arts projects. In S. Pile & M. Keith (Eds.), *Geographies of resistance* (pp. 184–202). New York: Routledge.

Rose, G. (2001). *Visual methodologies: An introduction to the interpretation of visual materials*. London: Sage.

Sharp, J. (2005). Geography and gender: Feminist methodologies in collaboration and in the field. *Progress in Human Geography, 29*(3), 304–309.

Sharp, J., Browne, K., & Thien, D. (2004). Introduction: Why study feminist geography? Do we still need to bother? In J. Sharp, K. Browne, & D. Thien (Eds.), *Geography and gender reconsidered* (pp. 1–4). London: Women and Geography Study Group of the Royal Geographical Society.

Sheppard, E. (1993). Automated geography: What kind of geography for what kind of society? *Professional Geographer, 45*, 457–460.

Sheppard, E. (2004). Practicing geography. *Annals of the Association of American Geographers, 94*(4), 744–747.

Sparke, M. (1998). Mapped bodies and disembodied maps: (Dis)placing cartographic struggle in colonial Canada. In H. J. Nast & S. Pile (Eds.), *Places through the body* (pp. 305–337). New York: Routledge.

Sparke, M. (2005). *In the space of theory: Postfoundational geographies of the nation-state*. Minneapolis: University of Minnesota Press.

Taylor, M. (n.d.) *Time pieces*. Retrieved October 28, 2005, from *www.users.ties.k12.mn.us/~taylor/timepieces/time.htm*

Trauger, A. (2004). Beyond the nature/culture divide: Corporeality, hybridity and feminist geographies of the environment. In J. Sharp, K. Browne, & D. Thien (Eds.), *Geography and Gender Reconsidered* (pp. 21–34). London: Women and Geography Study Group of the Royal Geographical Society.

Virilio, P. (1997). *Open sky* (J. Rose, Trans.). London: Verso.

CHAPTER 30

Neural Networks as an Emergent Method in Quantitative Research

An Example of Self-Organizing Maps

Natalia Sarkisian

It's easy to believe that the 10-million-fold increase in computational power we've seen will make statistics deeper as well as bigger.

—EFRON (as cited in Holmes, Morris, & Tibshirani, 2003, p. 281)

Many statistical models have existed in their theoretical forms for decades, but their implementation was hindered by the complexity of calculations involved. For instance, the maximum likelihood (ML) estimation that is now the basis of many advanced statistical analyses was developed by Fisher in the 1920s, but it was technically difficult, if not impossible, to apply this knowledge in practice before the advent of fast computers (Rindskopf, 2004).

That situation changed in recent decades with the rapid advances in computing speed and power and the related developments in statistical software. Fast computers made it possible to solve many linear equations at the same time, enabling researchers to use complex multivariate regression models, while convenient, low-cost computer programs popularized such models. The development of techniques for finding eigenvectors and eigenvalues further extended the range of available multivariate techniques, including factor analysis, cluster analysis, and discriminant analysis, among others. Furthermore, the advances in numerical methods and computing hardware made ML estimation routine (Long & Cheng, 2004), as well as enabled utilization of other iterative algorithms. This broadened immensely the range of analytical possibilities.

Importantly, the increasing computing power and the expanding supply of computer applications brought about a change toward greater realism and complexity of statistical models and made such complexity increasingly more accessible for an average researcher (Rindskopf, 2004). One important shift toward more realistic analysis involves the development of multilevel models for nested data, such as, for example, data collected from students clustered in schools or from individuals nested in neighborhoods, or even data that contain repeated measures from the same individuals (Luke, 2004; Raudenbush & Bryk, 2002; Snijders & Bosker, 1999).

Furthermore, contemporary data analysis methodologies, such as structural equation modeling (SEM), eschew the notion that measurement can be made without error and allow estimating latent variables on the basis of the measured variables while explicitly taking the measurement error into account (Kline, 2005; Kaplan, 2000). SEM also allows estimating models in which the same variables serve as both dependent and independent variables, including models with reciprocal relationships (Kline, 2005).

Furthermore, the range of methods available to deal with the missing data has been expanding (Allison, 2001; Little & Rubin, 2002). Unlike deterministic imputation techniques of the past, contemporary methods for dealing with missing data take into account the uncertainty of imputation. Some of them generate and analyze multiple imputed datasets and rely on the variation in estimates to assess the uncertainty. Other methods utilize full information maximum likelihood (FIML) to estimate models on the basis of all available data points.

Contemporary techniques of statistical analysis also take into account complex sampling designs, enabling accurate inference when the data were obtained from clustered and stratified samples (Lee & Forthofer, 2006). Furthermore, the development of resampling techniques such as bootstrapping harnessed the power of high-speed computers to obtain reliable standard errors and confidence intervals without relying on particular parametric model assumptions (Davidson & Hinkley, 1997).

Thus the developments in computer technology not only made it possible to apply in practice those methods that already existed as theoretical constructions but also gave birth to many new methods and techniques. Furthermore, these developments have opened up the possibilities for entirely new approaches to statistical analysis to emerge. One of these emergent approaches, neural networks, is the focus of this chapter.

Neural Networks: An Emergent Field

> Neural networks represent a new way of thinking: a wildly polygamous conjunction of computer science, biology, linguistics, engineering, psychology, and statistics that [has] the thrill of 1960s rock and the roar of a thousand central processors hooked up in parallel.
>
> —JENKINS (1991, as cited in Garson, 1998, p. 8)

Neural networks is an emergent field that in recent years has been receiving a lot of attention. It originated in neurobiology and was further developed by engineers and computer scientists, who aimed to design electronic networks of highly interconnected computing elements with attributes that closely resemble those of biological neural networks. These electronic circuits, termed artificial neural networks (ANNs), have been inspired by the capabilities of the human central nervous system.

The neural networks in the brain consist of neurons, complex nerve cells that respond to electrochemical stimuli and operate as signal processing units (Patterson, 1996). An individual neuron in the brain receives input signals from many other neurons via its filamentary input paths, the dendrites. It then processes and combines the multiple signals and sends output signals to other neurons via the axon, which is the neuron's transmission line (Rojas, 1996). A single neuron can be connected to hundreds or even tens of thousands of other neurons, although typically, only a small percentage of these connections are active at a given time. Human cerebral cortex contains 100 billion neurons (Kartalopoulos, 1996), and, combined, they are capable of processing millions of input stimuli in milliseconds (Patterson, 1996). Of course, human brains are orders of magnitude more complex than any artificial neural network existing so far. Nevertheless, ANNs operate on the same principle, as they pass input data through multiple processing units operating in parallel (Garson, 1998). Instead of following a rigid set of preprogrammed instructions as do other statistical techniques, ANNs have the ability to dynamically adapt to the data. Specifically, in the process of training, a neural network model develops a set of parameters (weights) that allow mapping from a set of given data values known as inputs to a desired set of outputs (Swingler, 1996).

The wide variety of different ANNs currently available permits their utilization for a variety of quantitative data analysis tasks. ANNs can be classified in many different ways, but the two key taxonomies emphasize the type of network architecture and the learning method. The network architecture has to do with the way that neurons are organized into a network, as well as with the direction of the signal movement through the network. Neurons in a network are arranged in layers, and the signal typically travels across these layers. Patterson (1996) identifies three main architecture types: single-layer feedforward networks, multilayer feedforward networks, and recurrent networks. In a single-layer network, the signal from the inputs arrives to the single layer of neurons, which then directly produce the output. For instance, in a multivariate regression application of a single-layer feedforward network, the values of independent variables are the inputs, and the outputs are the predicted values of the dependent variable. In contrast, in a multilayered network, the input signal first arrives to a so-called hidden layer, which then transfers it to the output layer. Such a multilayered structure allows for more complex, nonlinear models, as multiple sets of weights are used to transform the input data into the output values.

The other distinction that is made with regard to the network architecture is that between feedforward and recurrent (feedback) networks. In feedforward networks, the signal travels in a single direction from the inputs to the outputs. In contrast, in recurrent networks, feedback loops are allowed, and the signal can be repeatedly processed by the same neurons. Thus, after getting an input signal, recurrent networks may have to iterate for a long time before producing an output (Garson, 1998).

The second important classification focuses on learning algorithms. In general, a network learns by modifying a set of weight values that determine how the signal is modified by each of the neurons in the network (Skapura, 1996). Three main types of learning algorithms can be distinguished: supervised learning, unsupervised learning, and reinforcement learning (Patterson, 1996). In supervised learning, neural networks are given both the inputs and the correct outputs, and they need to learn how to produce outputs closely approximating the correct ones. A classic example of this strategy is neural network implementation of multivariate regression, mentioned earlier. In unsupervised learning, no correct outputs are available, and the network is trained to summarize the patterns contained in the inputs, performing some type of data compression. Finally, reinforcement learning does not disclose the correct outputs but instead provides rewards and penalties at each step of the training process (Garson, 1998). This type of learning algorithm is rarely used for data analysis, however.

In recent years, neural networks have enjoyed many practical applications. For example, they have been used to control and opstimize industrial processes, to monitor aircraft or train engines, to diagnose patients, to perform signal processing tasks such as speech or handwriting recognition, to manage college enrollment, and to make marketing predictions (Garson, 1998; Patterson, 1996).

Although widely utilized for data analysis in many fields, neural networks can be considered an emergent methodology in the social sciences. The field of economics accounts for the majority of neural network applications in social sciences, as neural networks are widely used in financial analysis, risk assessment, managerial decision making, and forecasting of economic time series (Garson, 1998). Psychology, especially cognitive psychology, has also generated a range of applications, as scholars have used neural networks to explore memory, language acquisition, spatial learning, and other cognitive processes (Martindale, 1991). Outside of economics and cognitive psychology, ANNs have been used to predict crime, drug use, and child abuse (Buscema, 1995; Collins & Clark, 1993; Kelly, Goodman, Kaburlasos, Egbert, & Hardin, 1992), to model the diffusion of innovations (Ilonen, Kamarainen, Puumalainen, Sundqvist, & Kälviäinen, 2006), to classify "undecided" respondents in opinion polls (Monterola, Lim, Garcia, & Saloma, 2002), to predict election results (Kruglov & Dli, 2001), to assess the relationship between social and political views and race and class background (Sares, 1998), to study dating preferences (Suna et al., 2006), to examine the predictors and consequences of TV watching habits (Paik, 2000b; Paik & Marzban, 1995), to analyze international relations events (Garson, 1991; Schrodt, 1991) or predict levels of democracy (Kimber, 1991), and to examine social mobility and inequality (Meraviglia, 1996), among other applications. A few applications also used ANNs for simulation of human behavior rather than for data analysis (Acerbi & Parisi, 2006; Bainbridge, 1995; Duong & Reilly, 1995; Hutchins & Hazlehurst, 1995; Macy, 1996; Parisi, Cecconi, & Cerini, 1995).

It is likely that we will see more social science research utilizing ANNs in the years to come, as neural networks offer a range of new possibilities to social scientists. As Garson (1998, pp. 14–15) writes, "Neural networks present the social scientist with a tool which has been shown to be powerful across a broad range of problems, frequently to outperform many standard procedures, and to be appropriate even for fuzzy data environments common in social sciences."

Although neural networks are sometimes used as substitutes for traditional statistical techniques, they can serve functions beyond that. Neural network models allow the simultaneous analysis of data with hundreds of variables. They can work with highly unstructured, noncontinuous, and noisy data and with very large, as well as very small, samples, and they model a wide range of nonlinear relationships, providing robust results. According to Garson (1998, p. 1), "neural networks may outperform traditional statistical procedures where problems lack discernible structure, data are incomplete, and many competing inputs and constraints related in complex, nonlinear ways prevent formulation of structural equations." They also allow a simultaneous analysis of quantitative and qualitative data and can blur the boundaries between these two types of analysis (Castellani, Castellani, & Spray, 2003).

This chapter further explores some of the advantages and disadvantages of neural network models by focusing on self-organizing networks and, more specifically, self-organizing maps (SOMs) developed by Kohonen (1984, 2001), also known as self-organizing systems or Kohonen networks.

SOMs: An Introduction

> SOMs are the beginning of requiring our systems to not only handle our data, but to think about it.
>
> —Douglass (2001)

The SOM is one of the newer neural networking techniques that arises from the field of complexity theory (Garson, 1998) and is based on one of the most important concepts for understanding complex systems, the concept of self-organization (Castellani et al., 2003).

Neural networks' ability to self-organize is one of the most captivating topics in the neural networks field. Self-organizing networks are unsupervised neural networks that find patterns and correlations in the input data and adapt to these patterns. The neurons of self-organizing networks learn to recognize groups of similar data points and move toward them (by adjusting the corresponding weights) in such a way that those neurons that are physically located near each other move toward similar sets of data points. In the case of self-organizing maps, the map units adjust to the probability density of the input data. The result is a topological "map" of the input data, dense where many data points are located and more dispersed where the data density is low.

Like many other neural network applications, the SOM was inspired by the connectionist architecture and self-organizing processes in the human brain (Garson, 1998) and, more specifically, by the way the brain organizes sensory perceptions. In the brain, sensory input is neurologically mapped via the creation of spatial relationships among the neurons that correspond to the spatial relations among the input stimuli (Kohonen, 2001; Rojas, 1996).

In the case of self-organizing maps, such a process relies on a single-layer feedforward network operating under the *unsupervised competitive and cooperative learning* paradigm (Kohonen, 2001), also known as soft competition (Principe, Euliano, & Lefebvre, 2000). The idea behind competitive learning is that of a competition among map units, making them gradually move toward the more densely populated parts of the observation space. In each round of the competition, the map unit most similar to a specific data point becomes the winner; it then moves even closer to the data point (Sarle, 2002). The learning process in SOM is not only competitive but also cooperative, meaning that the winner selects several of the nearest units to form a cooperative team that will move together in order to adapt to the input data. The specific details of this process are addressed later.

Unlike many other neural network techniques, self-organizing maps do not have an easily identified counterpart in traditional statistical methodology, although some compare them to factor analysis and cluster analysis (Garson, 1998), to multidimensional scaling (Ripley, 1996), or to principal curves (nonlinear counterparts of principal components) (Cherkassky & Mulier, 1994; Sarle, 2002). SOM is also a nonlinear technique that can be used for data visualization, classification, segmentation, novelty detection, and many other purposes. Most important, it can analyze large quantitative databases and find the patterns and relationships among the variables that were not initially apparent. As Kohonen (2001) puts it:

> The Self-Organizing Map (SOM) is a new, effective software tool for the visualization of high-dimensional data. In its basic form it produces a *similarity graph of input data*. It converts the nonlinear statistical relationships between high-dimensional data into simple geometric relationships of their image points on a low-dimensional display, usually a regular two-dimensional grid of nodes. (p. 106)

The SOM is probably the most widely used unsupervised neural network model. It has been applied to a variety of tasks, especially those requiring pattern recognition—such as face recognition (Lawrence, Giles, Tsoi, & Back, 1997) and handwriting recognition (Cho, 1997); medical diagnostics, such as tumor detection, depression assessment, or match of organ donors and recipients (e.g., Haydon et al., 2005); epidemiological research seeking to identify disease trends (Kohonen, 2001); and other intelligent data mining. Recently, some social science applications of SOM have started to appear as well. For example, a study of housing market segmentation (Kauko, 2004) used SOMs to identify market segments in Amsterdam and to compare segmentation in Amsterdam with segmentation in Helsinki. The study found that Amsterdam is more fragmented than Helsinki and that price alone is an insufficient criterion for fully understanding segmentation in either of the two markets. In another application of SOMs, Ilonen and colleagues (2006) created a map of the economic, technological, and social characteristics of specific markets and then examined how these characteristics affected the diffusion of innovation, using the example of cell phone and Internet use across countries. Another study by Suna and colleagues (2006) analyzed data on individuals' preferences and opinions collected by an Internet dating service (approximately 300 variables and 5,000 observations). Based on their findings, Suna and colleagues developed the concept of "cultural age," defining it as a body project, a social representation of one's biological age that manifests itself in opinions and relationship preferences expressed by individuals. They concluded that "the SOM approach offers a well established methodology that can be easily applied to complex sociological data sets" (p. 1).

Basic Concepts, Elements, and Processes of SOM Analysis

A wide range of software provides implementations of the SOM algorithm. These include specialized public domain software packages developed for self-organized maps, such as SOM_PAK, operating in Unix or MS-DOS, a more user-friendly Nenet (Neural Networks Tool), and a free software addition to Matlab, SOM Toolbox. Many commercial software packages have SOM capability as well; this includes, for example, SAS Neural Network Application, MATLAB Neural Network Toolbox (which is different from SOM Toolbox), SPSS Clementine, STATISTICA Neural Networks, NeuroShell 2, Viscovery SOMine, Trajan 6.0 Professional, NeuralWorks, havFmNet++ and havFMNet Java, and NeuroSolutions 5.0 (see Kohonen, 2001, and Deboeck, 1998, for more detail on SOM capabilities of many of these packages).

To demonstrate SOM methodology in this chapter, I use SOM Toolbox, the free Matlab function package implementing the SOM algorithm, that is available at *www.cis.hut.fi/projects/somtoolbox/*. I use this package in the Matlab 7.2 environment, but it was originally developed under Matlab 5; thus it works pretty well with that version and all other subsequent versions.

For these examples, I use a set of variables on time use from the Family Interaction, Social Capital, and Trends in Time Use (FISCT) dataset, collected in 1998–1999 (Robinson, Bianchi, & Presser, 1999). The data were obtained from a representative sample of 1,151 respondents age 18 and older via a telephone interview. For my examples, I use 12 variables containing the data on weekly recall estimates of time spent on paid employment, housework, religious activities, and television viewing (see the list of questions in Appendix 30.1), as well as the information on respondents' gender, age, marital status, and parental status. These data were collected from one-half of the sample, randomly selected ($N = 567$). There were a small number of missing data points on the 12 time-use variables. Fortunately, SOM Toolbox has the ability to deal with the missing data. The missing data points should be coded "NaN" in order for the SOM Toolbox to recognize them as such. If an observation is missing a value on a specific variable, that variable is omitted from the distance calculations for that observation. For the four demographic variables used to explore the results (sex, age, marital status, and parental status), I used the imputed variables generated by the FISCT staff. For simplicity, I also imputed 30 missing data points on the age variable using single regression imputation.

It is typically recommended that researchers rescale (normalize) their data before applying the SOM algorithm due to the fact that it is based on Euclidian distance measures that are sensitive to variables' measurement units (Vesanto, Himberg, Alhoniemi, & Parhangankas, 2000). The variables with different measurement units can have differential impacts on the results; it can be especially problematic if one of the variables has a much larger range of values than the other variables, as this variable can end up dominating the entire map organization (Swingler, 1996). The most common way to normalize the variables in SOM Toolbox is to standardize them so that all of the variables have the variance of one. Note that for the purposes of visualizing the results, the data are typically transformed back, or denormalized, to ensure interpretability. The choice of scaling can substantially affect the results. Therefore, it is important to carefully consider this choice, possibly comparing maps based on multiple scaling options (Kohonen, 2001). For the examples used in this chapter, I do not normalize the data because all of the variables used have the same measurement units (hours).

Creating the Map

For the first example, I use a subset of the larger time-use dataset; this subset contains only two variables, time worked for pay and time spent on preparing meals. The analysis starts by creating a neuron grid of specified shape and size. This grid is typically two-dimensional, but if desired, grids with one dimension or with three or more dimensions can be used, although when dimensionality is higher than two, the visualization of the resulting map will be difficult.

The lattice of the grid can be either hexagonal or rectangular (see Figure 30.1); hexagonal lattice is typically preferred, because in a rectangular lattice, the distance to the four diagonal neighbors of a neuron is larger than the distance to the adjoining four, whereas in a hexagonal lattice, all six neighbors are equidistant, which results in smoother maps (Kohonen, 2001; Vesanto et al., 2000). Figure 30.1 also shows the three possible shapes of the map: a sheet, a cylinder, and a toroid. Sheet maps are most commonly used; toroid and cylinder maps are recommended only if the data are known to be circular (Vesanto et al., 2000).

The map size can be defined by the researcher, or it can be determined automatically based on the formula: The number of units = $5*\sqrt{N}$, where N is the number of observations. If the researcher selects the number of units manually, it is recommended that the selected number be fairly large—typically between 100 and 500, even for small datasets; the larger the map, the more flexible it can be in the training process (Vesanto et al., 2000). Nevertheless, the number of neurons should not be too large, because computation will become too time-consuming.

Once the number of map units is identified, the map size should be determined. In SOM Toolbox, the map size is defined as follows: The ratio of the two largest eigenvalues of the data becomes the ratio of the length of the map to its width. Even if one chooses not to rely on eigenvalues, it is nevertheless recommended that the length of the map be selected to be larger than its width. In our example, we allow the program to determine map size automatically, which then calculates that the map should have $5*\sqrt{567}$ elements—120 map units—and then creates a 24×5 map. The results of SOM analysis can be sensitive to the map size and dimensionality, but it is difficult to guess the best set of these parameters before analyzing the data. Some researchers are attempting to develop growing SOMs, in which these parameters are modified in the process of training (e.g., Fritzke, 1994).

SOM Training Process

Each map unit has two sets of coordinates: (1) those in the output space, representing a unit's position on the map, and (2) those in the input space, defined by the values of all the input variables. Because of the double

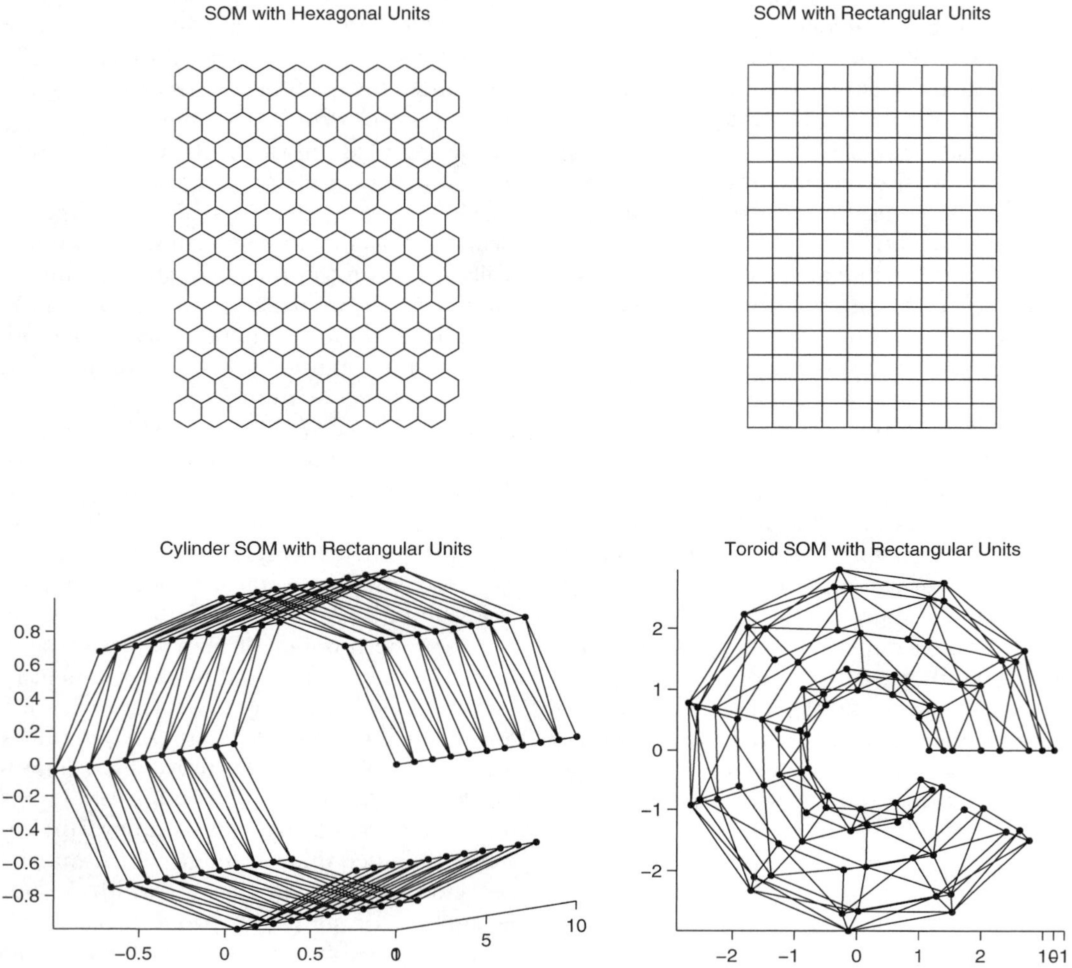

FIGURE 30.1. Types of self-organizing map grids.

sets of coordinates for each unit, we can view SOM as a nonlinear projection from the multidimensional input space to a two-dimensional output space (Vesanto et al., 2000). The coordinates in the output space are allotted once the map is created, assigning each unit a specific position on the grid, whereas the coordinates in the input space change over the course of map training.

Once the map is created, it must be initialized. This process generates the initial coordinates in the input space for each map unit. That is, each map unit is assigned a set of values on each of the input variables. The final result is not influenced much by the choice of the values used at this point; only the speed of convergence is affected. In SOM Toolbox, two types of initialization are available: random initialization and linear initialization. Linear initialization is usually preferred because it starts with the values based on the two principal eigenvectors, whereas random initialization utilizes randomly selected values (Kohonen, 2001). Linear initialization is usually used as default, unless it is not possible to calculate the eigenvectors, in which case random initialization is used (Vesanto et al., 2000).

For this first example, we start with a randomly initialized two-dimensional map. The first and the second panels of Figure 30.2 demonstrate how a randomly initialized map looks in both the output and the input space. In the first panel, we can see the map in the output space represented as the grid structure, where the dots show positions of map units and the gray lines connect neighboring units. In the second panel, we can see the map in the input space. When the map is randomly initialized, as is the case in this example, the coordinates in the input space are randomly assigned, resulting in large distances between units that are neighbors in the output space. The crosses in the second panel of this figure represent the original data points.

During the training process, the map learns the positions of data points, and the map units are moved toward them as a part of the competitive and cooperative learning process. An SOM algorithm tries to arrange the map in such a fashion that any two map units that are close to each other in the grid space also become close in the input space (i.e., have similar values of input variables). Two different algorithms can be used for training a self-organizing map: the sequential training algorithm, also known as pattern algorithm, and the batch training algorithm (Swingler, 1996; Vesanto et al., 2000). The sequential training algorithm operates as follows. In each training step, it randomly selects one observation from the dataset and calculates the distance between this observa-

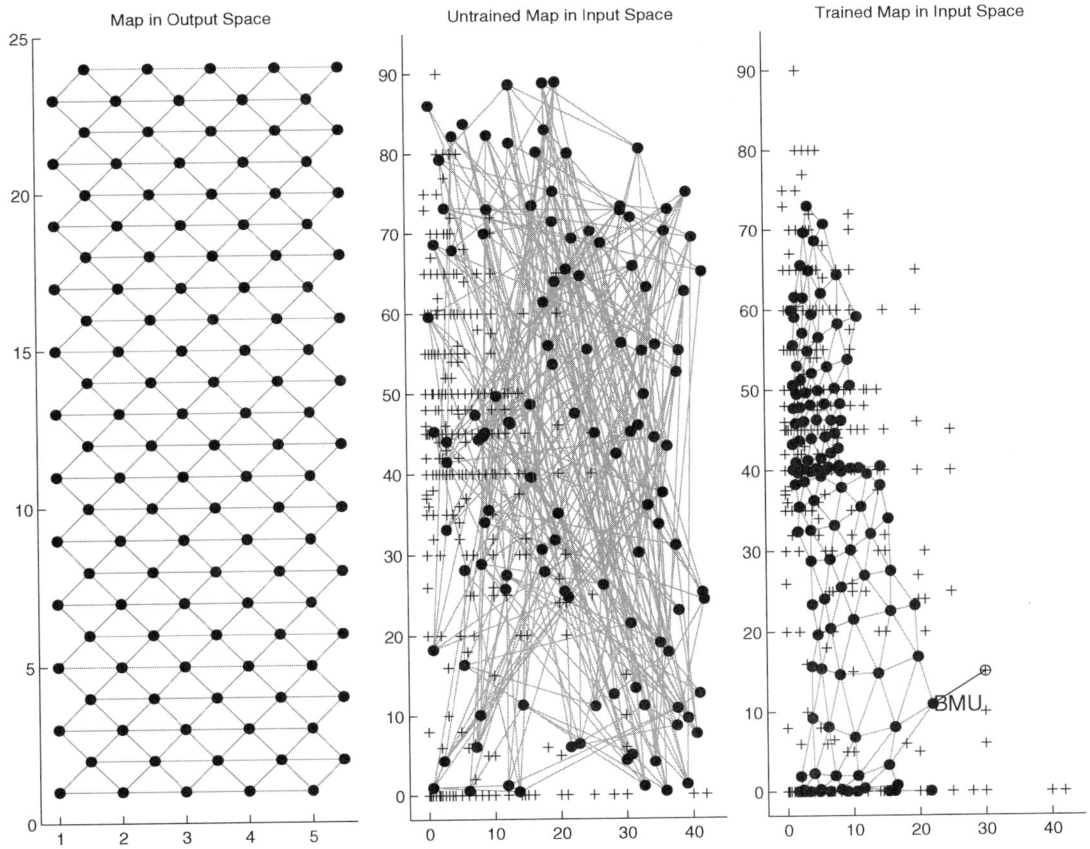

FIGURE 30.2. Creating an SOM for a dataset with two variables.

tion and each of the map units. The map unit that is the closest one to the selected observation is the best-matching unit (BMU) for this observation, that is, the unit that best resembles that observation. This unit becomes the "winner neuron" in this training step. Once the winner is located, that winning unit itself and its topological neighbors are moved closer to the selected observation; that is, their input space coordinates are adjusted. The amount of adjustment for the winner depends on the so-called learning rate, which typically decreases over the course of training at a rate inversely proportional to training time, which ensures that all data points have similar influence on the final result (Vesanto et al., 2000). The adjustments for the topological neighbors depend not only on the learning rate but also on the neighborhood parameters that are discussed later. Once the adjustments are applied, the next training step starts.

The batch training algorithm involves similar calculations; the main difference is that no map units are moved until all of the observations are evaluated. The map is then updated with the net effects of all observations, and the algorithm moves to the next step (Ripley, 1996; Swingler, 1996). The batch training algorithm is used by default in SOM Toolbox because it is much faster; moreover, unlike the sequential algorithm in which further moves are always possible, the batch algorithm frequently converges (Vesanto et al., 2000).

Neighborhood Parameters

As it is the spatial neighborhood that makes SOMs so different from other competitive neural networks (Principe et al., 2000), in both algorithms, neighborhood parameters deserve a special consideration. Specifically, we have to consider two issues: (1) which units are viewed as the winning unit's topological neighbors and (2) to what degree the neighbors' positions in the input space are adjusted along with the winner's position. Although the direct neighbors of each unit are easily identified, these constitute only the smallest possible neighborhood in SOM—the one with the radius of 1. Larger neighborhoods can be constructed that include neighbors of the neighbors as well.

Typically, early in the training process, large neighborhoods are used. Specifically, SOM training has two phases (Vesanto et al., 2000). The first phase is the rough training phase; it utilizes a large neighborhood radius and brings the SOM to approximately the same space as the input data. However, if the map is initialized using linear initialization procedure, the rough training phase can be omitted, because the map is already located in the same area of space as the data. The second phase is the fine-tuning phase that uses a small neighborhood radius for more precise adjustment of the map to the data. In both of those phases, the neighborhood radius decreases as the training progresses, typically going down to 1, and the learning rate decreases as well (Principe et al., 2000). The neighborhood size is not allowed to shrink all the way to 0; in that case, the SOM algorithm degenerates into another type of algorithm, Kohonen vector quantization algorithm (Kohonen, 2001), that produces results similar to the *k*-means clustering technique (Balakrishnan, Cooper, Jacob, & Lewis, 1994; Ripley, 1996).

The final neighborhood size is an important parameter of an SOM, for it can substantially affect the results. In this sense, SOM can be compared to nonparametric regression models, in which the degree of smoothing can also dramatically affect the results. Unfortunately, there have not been any systematic studies to determine how to best choose the final neighborhood size for a particular research project (Vesanto et al., 2000). A researcher might want to vary the final neighborhood size and assess the variation in the resulting maps.

The degree of position adjustment applied to the more distant neighbors relative to the more proximate neighbors is another issue to consider. This position adjustment is regulated by the neighborhood function.

This function specifies how big a pull factor the winner can exert on other neurons, both those close by and those far away. The simplest neighborhood function is called the bubble. This function is constant over the whole neighborhood of the winning neuron. That is, the whole neighborhood is moved in a similar way, and the elements outside of the neighborhood remain in place. More complex neighborhood functions are typically used; these functions specify the largest adjustments for the closest units and reduced adjustments for the units that are farther away from the winner. In a way, SOMs work by smoothing map units in a manner similar to kernel estimation used in nonparametric regression models (Mulier & Cherkassky, 1995), although this smoothing takes place in the neighborhoods in the output space instead of in the input space (Sarle, 2002). Still, similar kernel functions are used, such as Gaussian or Epanechnikov. Unlike the neighborhood size, the exact shape of the neighborhood function itself (e.g., bubble vs. Gaussian vs. Epanechnikov) does not appear to have a substantial effect on the results (Vesanto et al., 2000).

Examining the Trained Map

Once the map is trained, each unit on it is a prototype, a model unit that should be viewed as an ideal type or a model individual representing a number of original observations. To better understand what a map unit represents, we can examine its coordinates in the input space. We can also examine the set of observations represented by it, that is, those observations for which the selected map unit represents the BMU. As mentioned earlier, BMUs are identified using distance measures; we can calculate the distance between each observation and each map unit and identify one unit that has the minimum distance to a given observation. That map unit will be the BMU of this observation. For example, in the third panel of Figure 30.2, we can see the BMU for an individual who works for pay 15 hours a week and spends 30 hours per week on meal preparation. The BMU has coordinates of [22.1;10.9], which means that the prototype individual representing the selected person spends 10.9 hours a week in paid work and 22.1 hours in meal preparation. In SOM Toolbox, such coordinates for prototypes are stored in the codebook matrix as the prototype vectors (i.e., the rows of the matrix are the map units and the columns are the variables); later I utilize this matrix to calculate correlation coefficients based on prototypes.

In the example I have considered so far, the map has the same dimensionality as the input space. Both are two-dimensional because the data used contained only two variables. In SOM, any number of input variables can be used; the only restriction is that the number of variables should not be smaller than the dimensionality of the map (i.e., for a typical two-dimensional map, we should have at least two variables). Typically, input data contain more than two variables, and therefore the input space dimensionality is much higher than the two dimensions of the map. In such circumstances, the two-dimensional map folds itself into the higher dimensional space of the dataset in order to capture the patterns in the data. In this process, the map is embedded into the input data space so that every observation is close to one of the map units but the degree of bending or stretching of the grid is minimal (Sarle, 2002).

Figure 30.3 demonstrates this process using a dataset with three variables: time spent preparing meals, time spent watching TV, and time spent working for pay. The first panel presents a three-dimensional scatterplot of the data. The second panel shows the map after the linear initialization. Finally, the third panel shows the trained map that has folded to follow the data patterns.

To better understand the resulting map, it is useful to examine its relationship to the three original variables (components). Figure 30.4 presents the three component

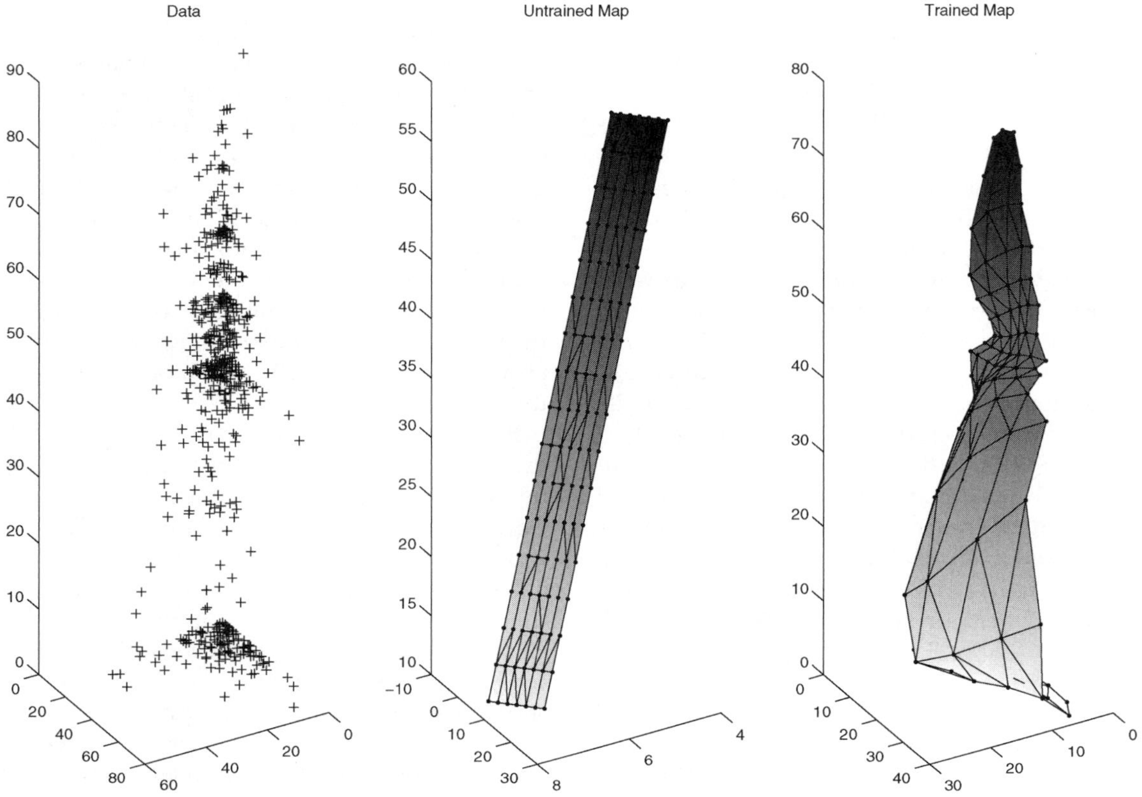

FIGURE 30.3. Creating an SOM for a dataset with three variables.

planes, as well as the "U-matrix" for this map. The U-matrix is the matrix that shows the distances between neighboring map units. The U-matrix has many more hexagons than the actual map contains (compare the U-matrix with the component plane plots). The reason is that it includes the actual distances as additional hexagons between each pair of map units. Thus the shade intensity of the map unit itself shows the average distance of that map unit to its neighbors; the shade level of the hexagon between two specific map units indicates the distance between those map units. Here, high values on the U-matrix are represented by darker shades, meaning larger distances between neighboring map units. The U-matrix helps visualize the cluster structure of the map. Clusters are typically uniform areas of low distance values, and the U-matrix clearly shows the cluster borders as those places at which the units are separated by large distances. Here, we can see one clearly pronounced cluster border between those who work full time or overtime and those who work fewer hours for pay or not at all; some of these individuals also spend substantial amounts of time on meal preparation.

The three component plots included in Figure 30.4 are different visualizations of the same SOM analysis; these plots help us understand the relationships between the map and individual input variables. The component plane plot for a specified input variable shows each variable value for every given map unit; in other words, for each map unit, it shows the input space coordinates with regard to the selected variable. The map units in these plots are arranged in the order of the output space grid; thus the plots are linked in the sense that a given map unit has the same position on all three subplots. The input space coordinates of each unit are reflected by their grayscale shades rather than their positions. The bar on the right shows what specific shades mean for each variable. For example, the darkest areas in the "Meal Preparation" component mean that the individuals represented by these map units spend more than 20 hours per week on meal preparation.

Note that in SOM Toolbox, these plots are typically viewed in full color, which greatly enhances the visualization. (To see some of the graphs used in this chapter in color, go to *www.sarkisian.net/som.html.*) Sometimes, it can be easier to see the patterns with fewer color gradations. Figure 30.5 presents the U-matrix and the three component planes in

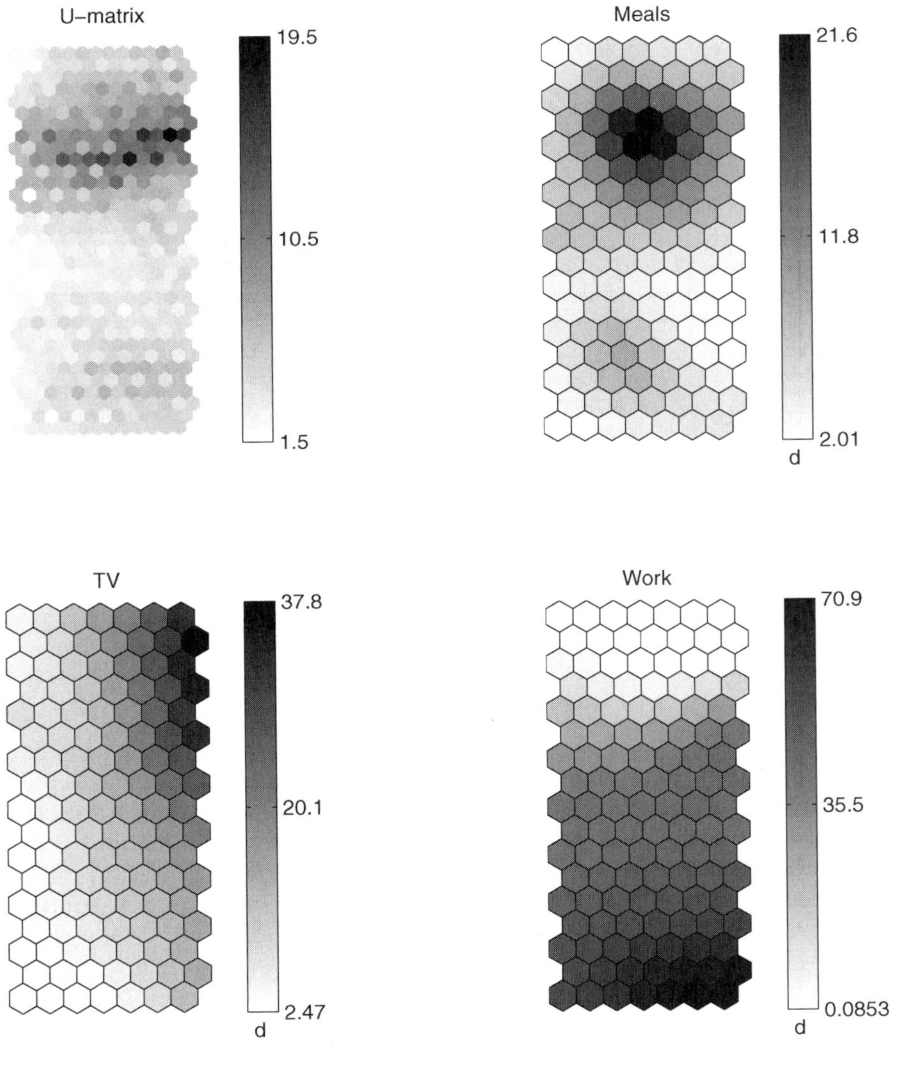

FIGURE 30.4. U-matrix and SOM component planes for a dataset with three variables.

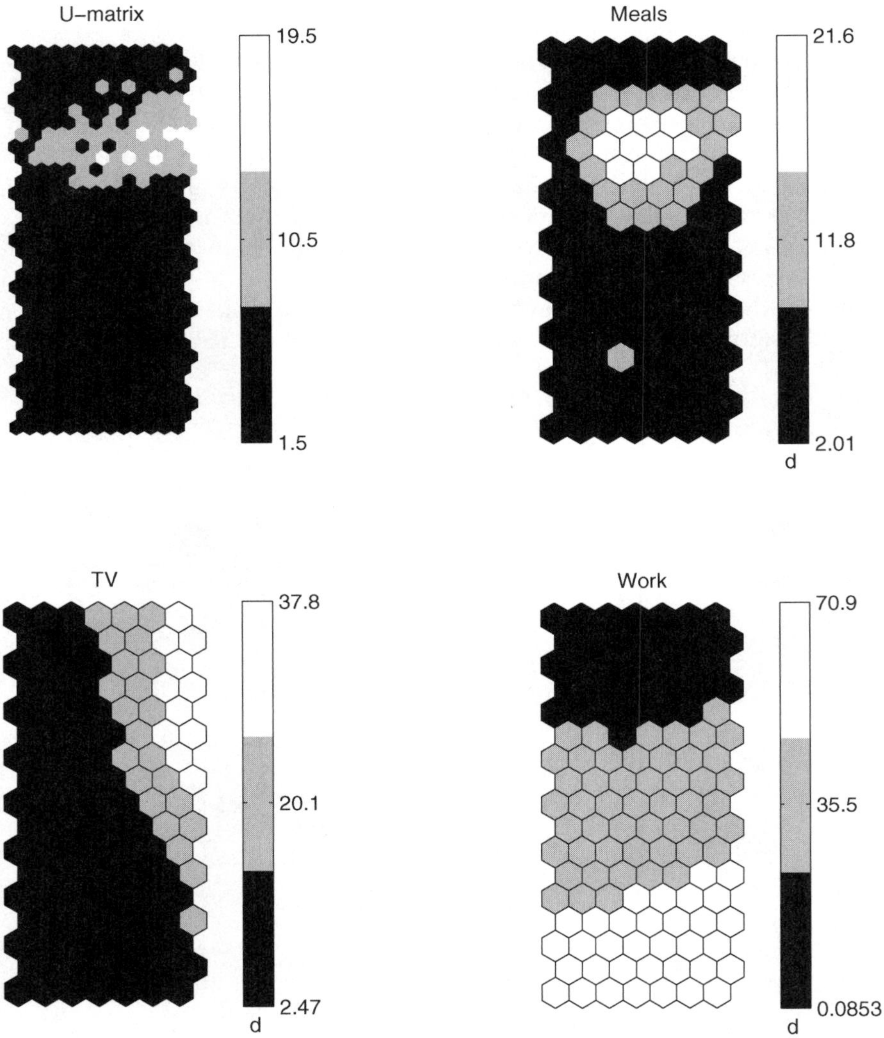

FIGURE 30.5. U-matrix and SOM component planes: Reduced color gradation.

three colors: white, gray, and black. This allows us to clearly see the role each variable plays in determining the unique characteristics of map units.

The SOM training process involves a compromise between the smoothness of the topological mapping and the accuracy of (1) data point representation and (2) dataset topology representation. Therefore, to measure the quality of fit for a self-organizing map, it is useful to examine measures of both data representation and topology representation (Kohonen, 2001). Data representation accuracy is typically measured using average quantization error computed as the average distance between each data point and its BMU. To assess the accuracy of the topology representation, SOM Toolbox utilizes the topographic error measure, which is calculated as the proportion of all data points for which their first and second BMUs are not neighbor units (Vesanto et al., 2000).

In our example, the quality measures for the untrained map with random initialization are: quantization error $q = 8.35$ and topographic error $t = 0.93$. If we use linear initialization and again examine the untrained map (which is approximately equivalent to completing the rough training phase), we get the quantization error $q = 7.98$ and the topographic error $t = 0.0$. Finally, for the trained map, the quantization error is greatly reduced, with $q = 3.98$, but the topographic error increases slightly in comparison with the linearly initialized map, to $t = 0.03$. This illustrates the fact that usually, during the training, the SOM reduces the quantization error, but the topology representation capability suffers. If we were to use a larger final neighborhood radius in the training, the map would be less "smooth" and have larger quantization error, but it could better reflect the topology of the dataset (Vesanto et al., 2000).

Applying SOM Methodology to Time-Use Data

Now that we addressed the basic elements and processes of SOM analysis, let us examine a more complex example and demonstrate some additional visualization tools and interpretation strategies. Here the full dataset with the 12 input variables from our example is used.

Combined-Sample SOM Analysis

First, using the whole dataset, we train the map and separately examine its 12 components (see Figure 30.6). Note that, if desired, it is possible to examine more than one input variable at a time by using these variables as axes and plotting the input space coordinates of the map units. For that kind of plot, however, we would have to select the three variables to serve as axes, as we cannot visualize more than three dimensions. It is possible, however, to add the sense of the fourth dimension by using color or by scaling the size of each element according to its position in that dimension.

In Figure 30.6, like in the simpler example in Figure 30.4, work for pay is clearly an important organizing dimension that is very distinct, although it is linked to other components in revealing ways. However, unlike the previous example, in which each of the three variables appeared to create its own separate dimension in terms of classifying the map units, this example demonstrates a number of variables that have strong relationships to each other, therefore exhibiting similar patterns in component plane plots. More specifically, when the high-value areas coincide on two component planes, this suggests a positive correlation between the two variables; when the high-value areas of one variable coincide with the low-value areas of another variable, this suggests a negative correlation between these variables.

We can clearly see similar patterns for variables representing stereotypically "female" household tasks: cooking, doing dishes, cleaning, shopping, doing laundry, and chauffeuring others. Furthermore, interesting patterns are observed for paying bills. It appears that some of those spending a lot of time on bills are also those spending much time on "female" household tasks, but there is also another group located among those who work long hours for pay.

The two stereotypically "male" tasks—outdoor work (including repairs to the house) and auto repairs—also seem to be linked. The map units with high values of those variables seem to appear in the same region, although an additional set of units also appears in the area where little other housework is located; it is possible that these are individuals who use outdoor work, such as gardening, for recreation.

The pattern observed for the time spent attending religious services is pretty interesting. There appears to be a strong relationship between spending time on "female" household tasks and spending time in reli-

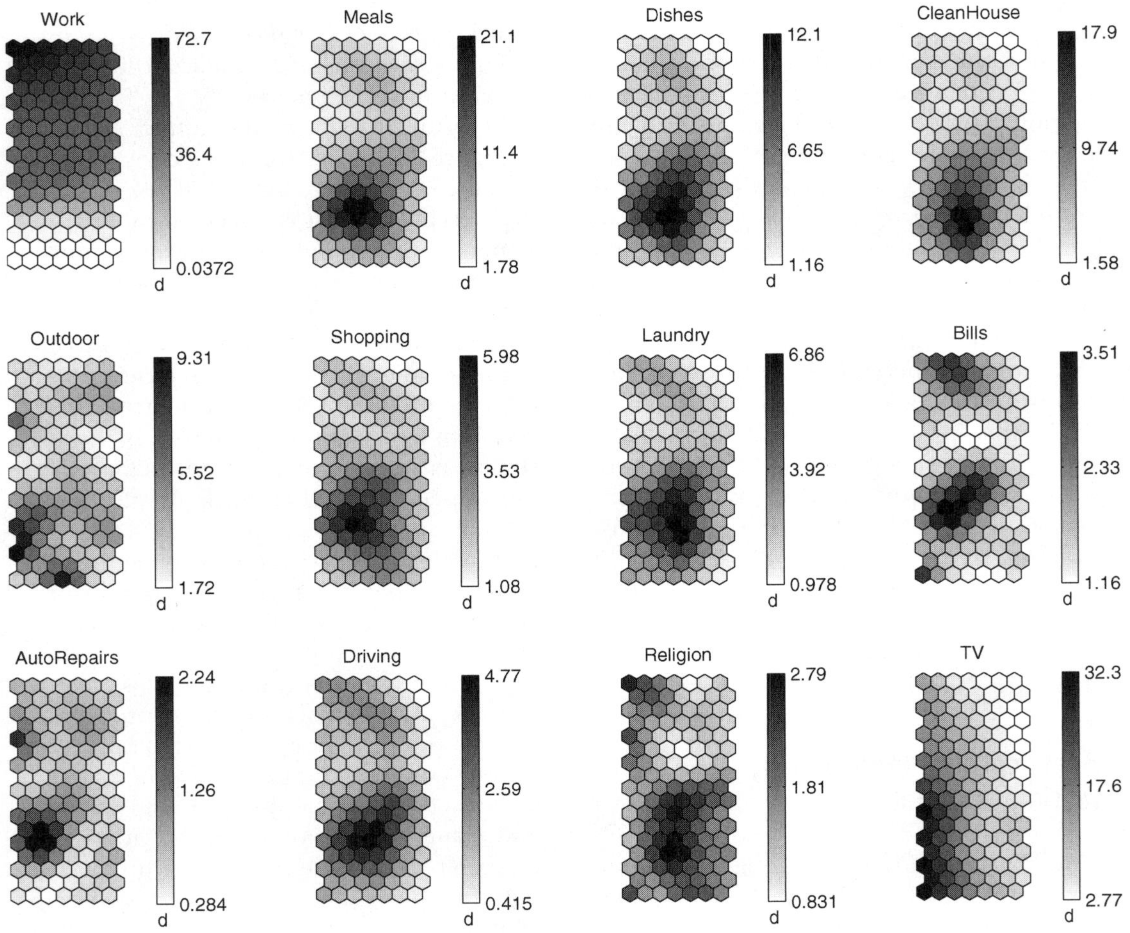

FIGURE 30.6. SOM analysis of time-use data: 12 components.

gious services, although they do not overlap entirely. It is especially interesting to observe a cluster of higher levels of religious service attendance among those who work long hours in their jobs. Finally, watching TV appears to be its own dimension, although not entirely independent of working for pay, doing household tasks, or spending time on religion. The "heaviest" TV watchers are concentrated among those who spend few hours in paid jobs and household labor, although there are also some moderate to heavy TV watcher groups among those working a substantial number of hours for pay.

To further understand how SOM analysis fleshes out the relationships among variables in the dataset, it is helpful to examine the correlation matrix for these variables in the original dataset and then compare it with the correlation matrix based on map unit values of those variables. Table 30.1 presents the original correlation matrix, utilizing 567 observations in the input dataset. Table 30.2 presents a correlation matrix calculated using the prototype coordinates for 119 map units. Comparing those tables, we find that the correlations in the prototype matrix reflect those in the original matrix in terms of their direction, but they are greatly

TABLE 30.1. Original Correlation Matrix

	1	2	3	4	5	6	7	8	9	10	11	12
1 Work for pay	1.00											
2 Meals	−0.23	1.00										
3 Dishes	−0.22	0.62	1.00									
4 Cleaning	−0.24	0.44	0.52	1.00								
5 Outdoor tasks	−0.09	0.03	0.06	0.09	1.00							
6 Shopping	−0.12	0.41	0.33	0.26	0.12	1.00						
7 Washing	−0.11	0.43	0.39	0.47	0.00	0.38	1.00					
8 Bills	0.03	0.07	0.13	0.18	0.05	0.25	0.41	1.00				
9 Auto repairs	0.04	0.08	0.04	0.03	0.30	0.09	0.00	0.13	1.00			
10 Drive others	−0.01	0.18	0.24	0.24	0.02	0.26	0.24	0.15	0.15	1.00		
11 Religion	−0.07	0.21	0.09	0.12	0.01	0.26	0.11	0.07	0.01	0.09	1.00	
12 Watch TV	−0.29	0.07	0.07	0.11	0.07	0.03	0.08	0.04	0.06	0.01	0.04	1.00

Note. $N = 567$.

magnified in terms of their size. This is a typical outcome of SOM analysis, as this technique seeks out the relationships among input variables and then emphasizes these relationships, making them more prominent. Note that many of these relationships could be invisible to standard data reduction techniques such as factor analysis because of the weak correlations. This is a good demonstration of the usefulness of SOM in terms of reducing the effects of noise and outliers and its ability to reveal dependencies among variables that might otherwise remain hidden (Suna et al., 2006).

Figure 30.7 allows us to examine the U-matrix for this analysis. Note that the cluster border separating those working part-time or less from others that we saw in a simpler analysis earlier is still pronounced in this matrix. The second panel of this figure allows us to clearly separate the actual map units and the distances between them. Here, each map unit is presented as a hexagon proportional to the number of cases that this map

TABLE 30.2. Prototype Correlation Matrix

	1	2	3	4	5	6	7	8	9	10	11	12
1 Work for pay	1.00											
2 Meals	−0.48	1.00										
3 Dishes	−0.54	0.97	1.00									
4 Cleaning	−0.59	0.91	0.95	1.00								
5 Outdoor tasks	−0.43	0.46	0.48	0.45	1.00							
6 Shopping	−0.43	0.92	0.92	0.85	0.43	1.00						
7 Washing	−0.39	0.92	0.94	0.90	0.40	0.94	1.00					
8 Bills	0.14	0.50	0.48	0.37	0.25	0.60	0.62	1.00				
9 Auto repairs	0.12	0.44	0.35	0.24	0.46	0.52	0.38	0.62	1.00			
10 Drive others	−0.22	0.90	0.90	0.79	0.36	0.87	0.92	0.70	0.48	1.00		
11 Religion	−0.37	0.66	0.72	0.73	0.25	0.74	0.74	0.54	0.26	0.72	1.00	
12 Watch TV	−0.37	0.28	0.28	0.30	0.55	0.32	0.30	0.26	0.40	0.19	0.20	1.00

Note. $N = 119$.

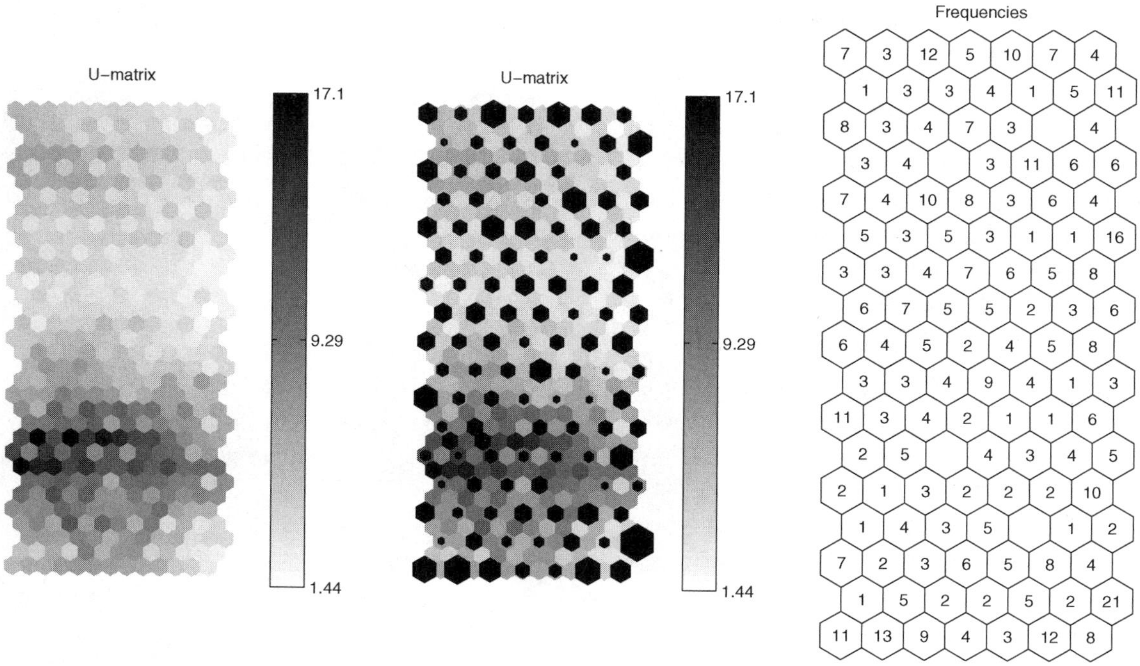

FIGURE 30.7. The U-matrix and the frequency distribution for map units.

unit represents (i.e., serves as their BMU). Similarly, the third panel of Figure 30.7 shows specific numbers of observations corresponding to each map unit. In this panel, we also see that there are four map units that do not correspond to any observations; such map units are called "interpolative" or "dead." That is, in theory they could be populated, but in our dataset, there are no observations that match them.

Figure 30.8 demonstrates another tool for examining the multivariate distances between map units: the distance matrix, also known as D-matrix. The first panel of this figure presents the already familiar U-matrix. The second panel shows the D-matrix, which is similar to the U-matrix in that it color-codes the distances so that the darker shades correspond to larger distances. But the D-matrix shows only the average distances for each map unit; it does not include distances between individual units. Thus the picture it presents is somewhat simplified as compared with the more complex U-matrix and therefore can more clearly indicate the patterns of difference and similarity. The third panel of Figure 30.8 presents an alternative rendition of the D-matrix, in which the distances are indicated by the size of hexagons rather than their color. Large hexagons correspond to those units that are close to their neighbors, whereas the smaller hexagons are those units that are located at larger distances from their neighbors. Once again, if we are interested in clustering, the sets of small hexagons can indicate where the borders between clusters are.

Figure 30.9 demonstrates another way to visualize the distance matrix. Here, it is presented as a three-dimensional surface plot in which the additional dimension represents distance. In fact, both the intensity of shading and the *z*-axis coordinate for a specific point on the map indicate its average distance to neighboring map units. When using SOM Toolbox, we can easily rotate this sur-

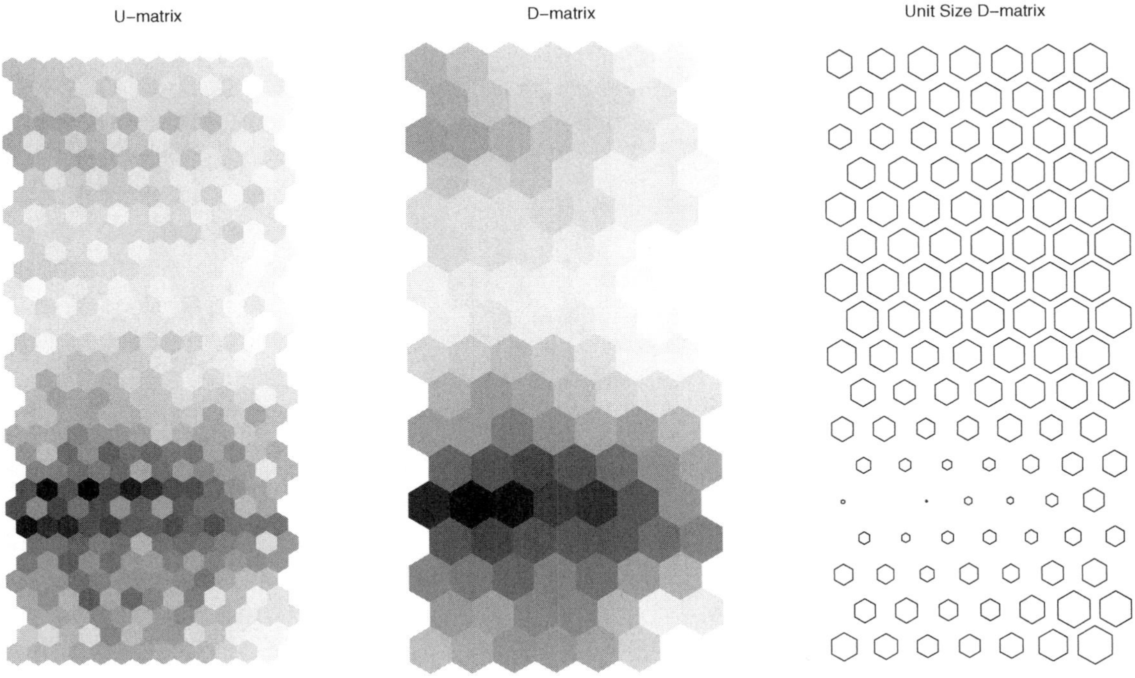

FIGURE 30.8. U-matrix and distance (D-)matrix.

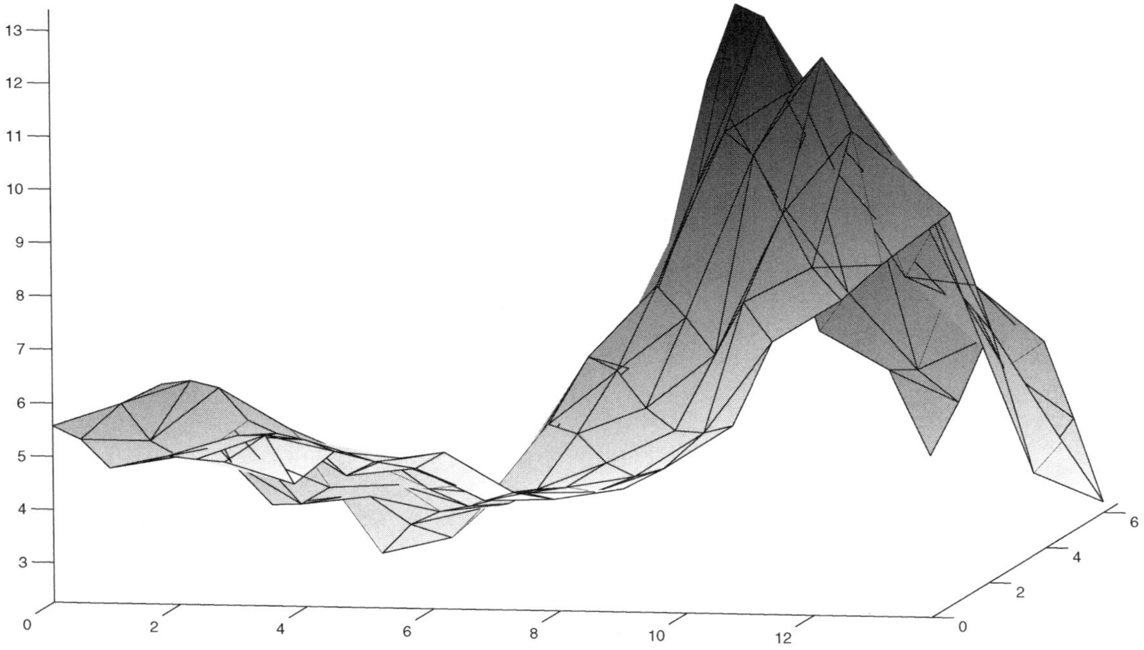

FIGURE 30.9. Distance matrix: A three-dimensional view.

face plot to see it from different directions, which helps us better visualize the distances among the map units.

Introducing Age and Gender

Next, we examine how this map is related to some demographic characteristics of our sample, specifically, age and gender. These demographic characteristics were not a part of the analysis. They were not included when SOM was trained; instead, they are added to the data as string variables serving as labels attached to each case.

In Figure 30.10, I use age labels to indicate the modal age category for each map unit. These labels are shown on the empty SOM grid. Here we can see that although most age categories appear to be mixed on the map, the map units located on the lower rows of the map are much more likely to include individuals age 66 and above. The reason is clearly that many of these individuals are fully retired and do not work for pay or work very few hours.

This pattern is further verified by the hit histograms presented in Figure 30.11. These hit histograms indicate the size of the groups of cases represented by each specific unit. Here, the hit histograms are presented separately for each of the four age groups. Again, we see a distinct pattern for those ages 66 and above in that they are concentrated in the lower portion of the map. In terms of the other three groups, they are much less differentiated on the map, although those 36–45 years old are especially likely to work long hours.

Figure 30.12 presents similar analyses for gender. The first panel of this graph is similar to Figure 30.10 in that it uses gender labels to indicate the modal gender category for each map unit. The second panel combines hit histograms for women and for men: the frequencies for men are presented in gray, and the frequencies for women are presented in black. These frequencies are also presented separately in the third and fourth panels of Figure 30.12. Here, we can

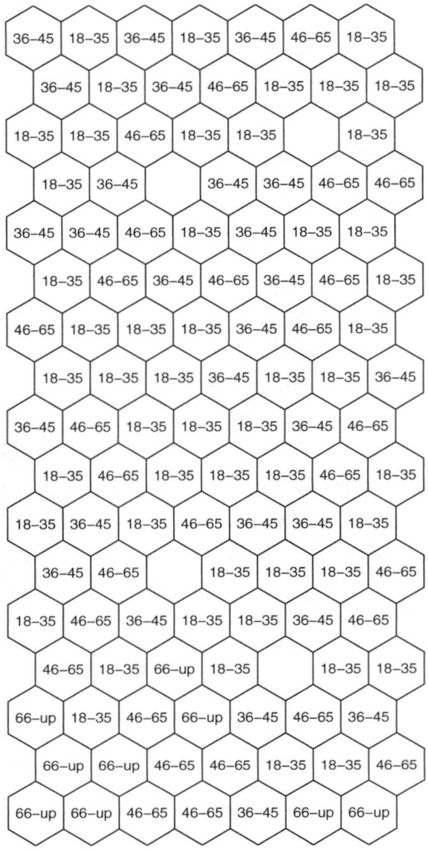

FIGURE 30.10. Modal age distribution for prototypes.

see a clear gendered pattern in frequencies, suggesting that gender is important in defining individuals' time use. Specifically, more men are located either at the top portion of the map, where employment hours are high, or at the very bottom, where many retirees are located. The middle area of the map with lower employment hours and higher household labor hours is dominated by women. I would like to stress once again that neither age nor gender were taken into account when creating and training the SOM for this analysis; they are introduced only in the interpretation stage. That is, without any information about the gender of individuals, the SOM algorithm produced a map that indicates distinct gender differences.

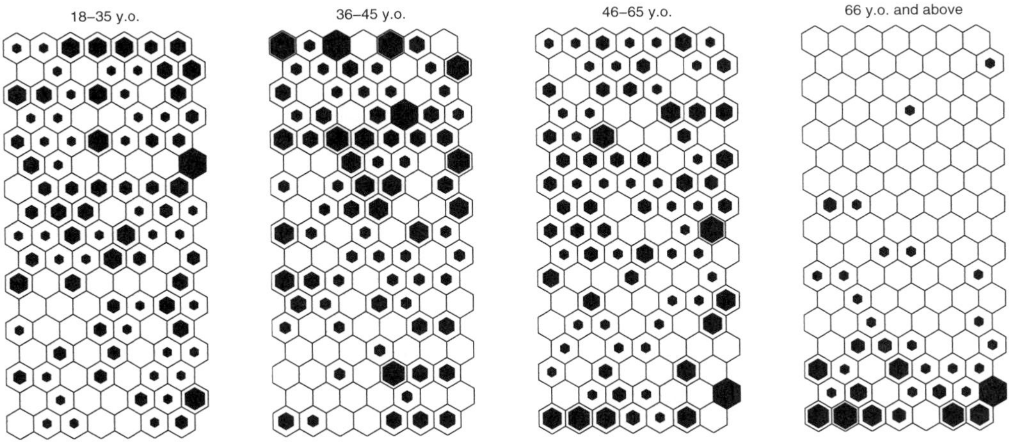

FIGURE 30.11. Age category frequencies for map units.

Separate Analysis by Gender

Given these pronounced gendered patterns, the next logical step would be to create a separate SOM for both women and men to facilitate comparisons. Figure 30.13 presents the 12 component planes for the separate SOM for women, and Figure 30.14 presents the 12 component planes for the SOM for men. Note that because these analyses were conducted separately, the units of these two maps are not linked in any way—that is, the same position on the map grid in Figure 30.13 and in Figure 30.14 does not represent the same map unit. In fact, even the map dimensions are different for the two gender groups—the men's SOM has a larger vertical dimension than the women's SOM. Given that the vertical dimension is clearly linked to employment hours, this demonstrates the more dominant function of paid employment in organizing men's time in comparison with women's time. Nevertheless, in both groups, paid employment plays an important role in shaping people's time use.

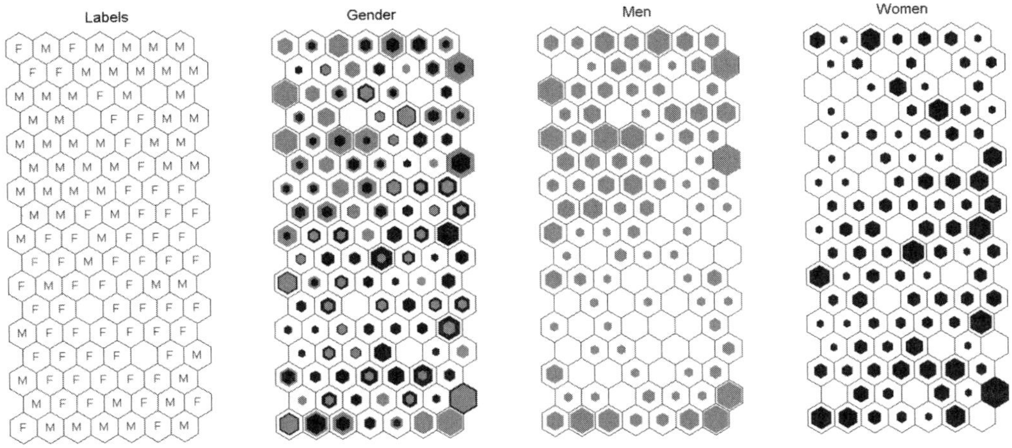

FIGURE 30.12. Gender distribution for prototypes.

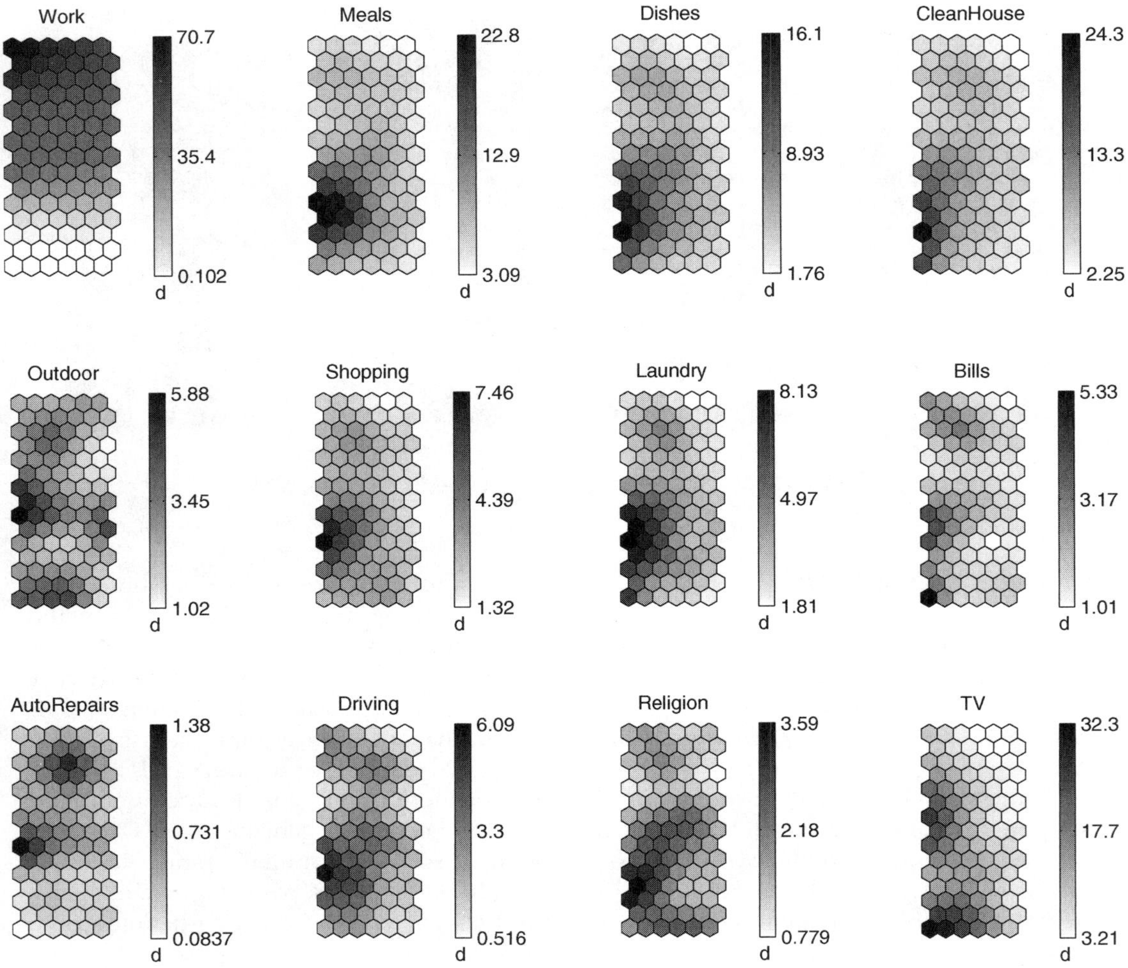

FIGURE 30.13. Separate analysis for women: 12 components.

Next, the comparison of the two figures also makes it clear that the time spent on stereotypically female household tasks (meals, dishes, cleaning, shopping, and laundry) makes a more pronounced contribution to organizing the women's map as compared with the men's map. It is clear that the correlations among these variables are stronger in the women's sample than in the men's sample. Furthermore, the women who spend the most hours on the stereotypically female household tasks are usually those women who are employed part time. In contrast, among men, it seems that there are separate clusters of higher housework involvement in all levels of paid employment, including among those who work very long hours. Note, however, the different ranges in the scales for women and men—among women, those who spend a lot of time on household tasks spend many more hours doing so than those men who spend a lot of time on housework. Thus what we are observing are the relative levels of housework involvement within one's own gender group rather than the absolute levels.

Moving on to traditionally male types of household labor, we note that the high

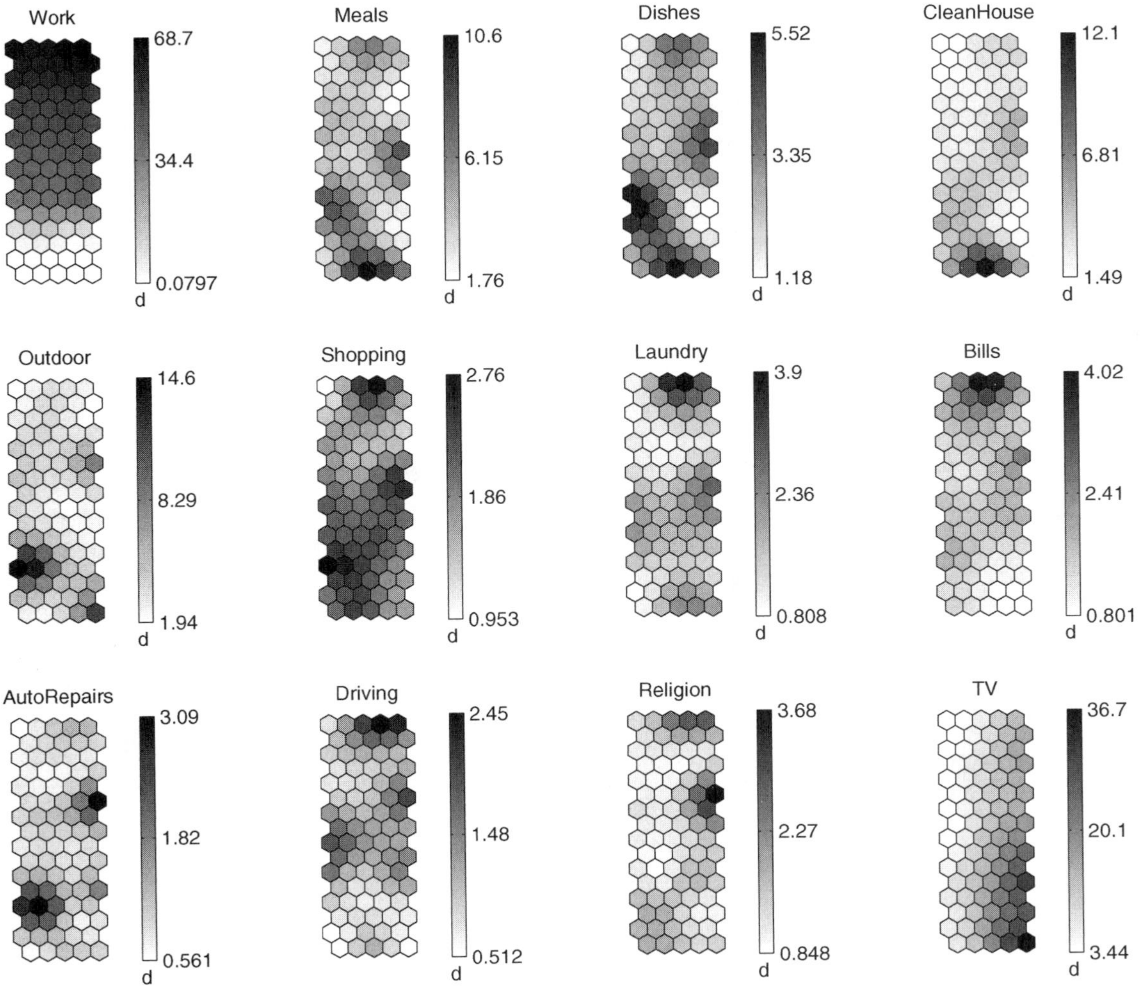

FIGURE 30.14. Separate analysis for men: 12 components.

amounts of time spent on outdoor labor seem to be more clustered for men but dispersed across the map for women. For men, the patterns for outdoor work also seem to be highly related to the automobile repair patterns, but for women that is not the case. An interesting finding is that among women, those who spend time on car repairs are usually those who work part time or overtime.

Another interesting finding is that the group of map units with high values on time spent on bills that we observed in the upper portion of the combined map in Figure 30.6 can be attributed almost entirely to a pattern among men wherein a group of men with high employment hours also spend a lot of time on bills. The same men, however, also seem to spend substantial amounts of time on meals, dishes, shopping, laundry, and driving others, which suggests these could be men with low socioeconomic standing who cannot afford to pay for such services.

The pattern of religiosity also appears to be different for women and for men. For women, religious service attendance is the highest among those not employed or working only part time, whereas among men, it is those employed full time or working very long hours who spend the most time in religious services. The patterns of watching TV also differ by gender: In the women's map, two clusters of heavy TV watching seem to exist, one among those who work few hours for pay and the other one among those who work 30 hours or more. Among men, however, it seems that long hours of watching TV are more concentrated among those who work under 20 hours per week.

Finally, it might be interesting to examine how these maps for women and men are related to the marital status and parental status of individuals. Figure 30.15 presents modal categories and frequency distributions for the four combinations of marital and parental status: single with no children, married

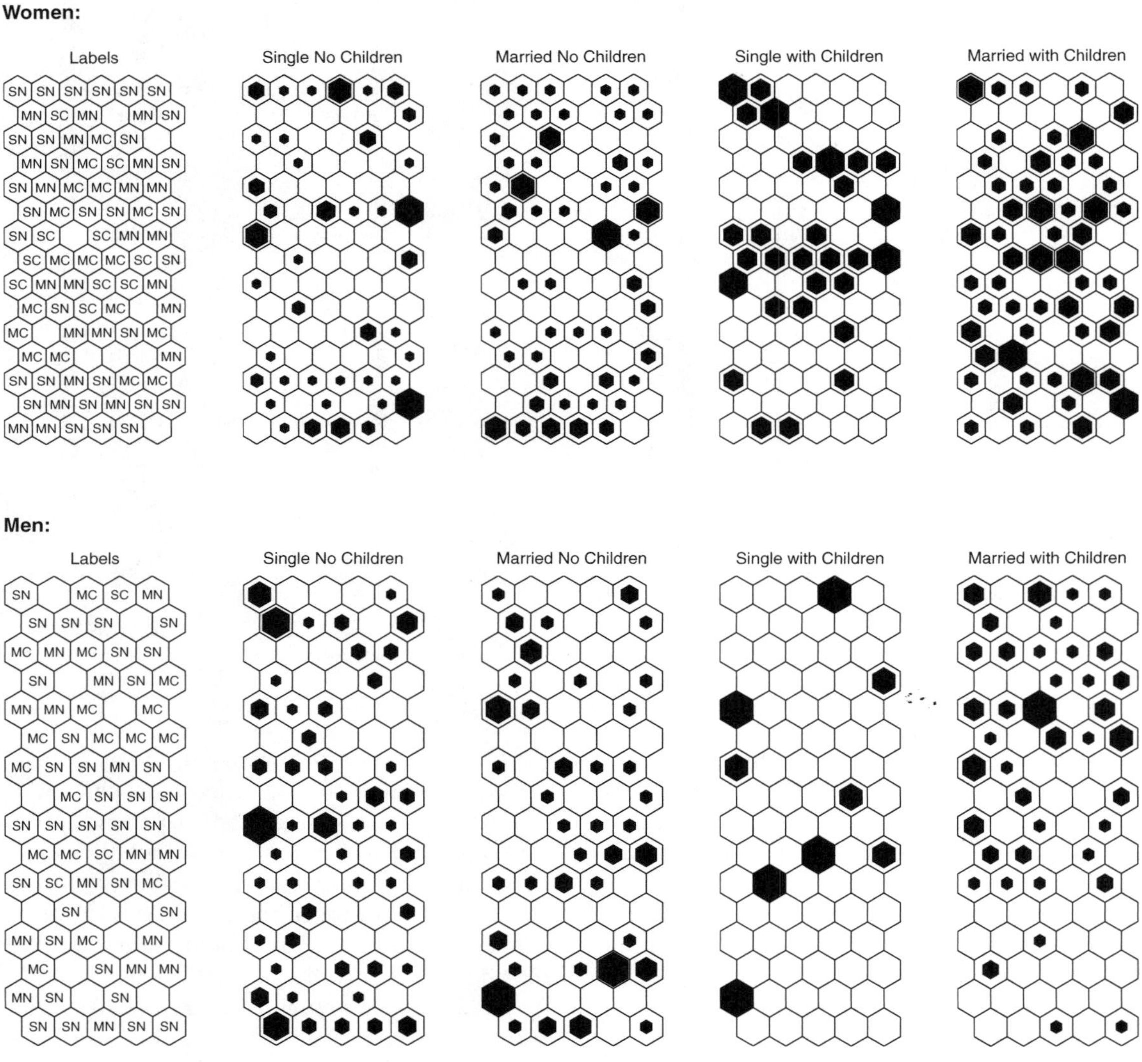

FIGURE 30.15. Marital/parental status distributions among women and men.

with no children, single parents, and married parents. For both women and men, the patterns of marital and parental status are not very clearly pronounced, suggesting that other factors, such as age, education, income, or gender ideology, might be more important in defining how women and men structure their time. We do, however, observe a pattern among men, wherein fathers—whether single or married—appear to be more concentrated in those map units associated with higher employment hours compared with those men who do not have minor children. For women, the most pronounced pattern is the greater concentration of married women with children in the area of high housework hours, although a substantial number of married mothers are also located outside of that area. In general, if we focus on married parents, we find that there is more variation in terms of their location on the map among women than among men. Future research could examine this variation by linking it to characteristics such as age, education, or income.

Note that this demonstration includes only some of the visualization tools available in SOM Toolbox; there are many more. For instance, those tools that primarily rely on color to link observations were not used, as these are difficult to view in grayscale mode. Furthermore, I should emphasize that there are many variants to the basic SOM described here. Some variants try to enable an SOM to better follow the topology of the data and to achieve lower quantization error by using different neighborhood sizes for different units or by allowing adaptive or flexible neighborhood definitions (Vesanto et al., 2000). Another version of SOM allows growing map structures (Fritzke, 1994). Such methods, however, require much more computational resources, and they often make visualization more difficult (Sarle, 2002). Furthermore, some versions of SOM are supervised (Kohonen, 1995); that is, not only the input data but also an outcome variable are provided to the algorithm, and the goal of the map is the classification of outcomes based on the input data. SOM Toolbox includes some of these variations, such as the modules for neural gas (neural_gas.m) and supervised SOM (som_supervised.m) estimation (Vesanto et al., 2000).

Advantages and Limitations of Neural Network Models

Neural networks in general, and self-organizing maps in particular, offer a range of new possibilities to social scientists. Although some scholars view neural networks as mere substitutes for traditional statistical techniques, they are clearly much more than that. First, neural network models allow the simultaneous analysis of data from lengthy questionnaires consisting of hundreds of items; they also allow a simultaneous analysis of quantitative and qualitative data. The SOM is especially useful for identifying patterns in complex data sets, because this technique is capable of extracting useful and interpretable results from the large quantities of diverse data or from data that contain a lot of noise. SOM enables researchers to cluster the data into meaningful sets, to visualize the patterns in the data, as well as to examine group differences and similarities in these patterns, and to preprocess the data for subsequent analyses (Suna et al., 2006).

Second, social relationships are typically nonlinear and quite complex; it is rare that we actually know the functional form of the relationships that interest us. But the types of models typically used in social sciences assume linear functional forms and utilize some simple transformations in an attempt to achieve linearity. In contrast, neural network techniques can easily model a wide range of nonlinear relationships; they have a clear advantage when the data of interest involve complicated, nonlinear associations and processes (Suna et al., 2006; Zeng, 1999). Indeed, simulation studies demonstrate that, with complex data, neural network models perform significantly better than the generalized linear models, as neural network results closely approximate the "true" models underlying the data (Zeng, 1999).

Third, unlike the traditional statistical methods that focus on means and average-case relationships, SOM pays much more attention to the patterns of variation in the data. As we saw earlier, although examining SOM component planes allows us to identify patterns of correlations among variables, we can also examine relationships among variables for specific subgroups of individuals by assessing different portions of the map.

Fourth, SOM analysis strategy itself is much less linear than the strategies of standard statistical analyses. The data mining philosophy of neural networking in general, and SOM in particular, implies that the analysis usually involves multiple iterations (Castellani et al., 2003; Han & Kamber, 2001). The researcher trains a self-organizing map, examines the results, and then decides whether some additional information is needed or whether something should be discarded from the model. The process is then repeated. Thus, although the formal terminology calls SOM an unsupervised learning algorithm, the researcher is closely involved in the process. As Castellani and colleagues (2003) put it, this is "a process of discovery, assessment, elaboration, and refinement" (p. 584).

Fifth, some argue that neural networks in general, and self-organizing maps in particular, blur the boundaries between quantitative and qualitative data analysis and allow a postpositivist, neopragmatic approach to quantitative data analysis (Castellani et al., 2003). Specifically, Castellani and colleagues (2003) argue that SOM enables the application of the grounded theory approach (Glaser & Strauss, 1967) to quantitative data. The grounded theory approach emphasizes data-driven theorizing, wherein the researchers closely and systematically examine the data at hand and uncover "the 'hidden' and 'underlying' theoretical framework holding the data together" (Castellani et al., 2003, p. 579). The grounded theory approach is applicable to both the qualitative and quantitative data, but in practice, this approach has been usually applied to qualitative data. One of the main reasons can be located in the nature of traditional statistical techniques: They do not allow the kind of analysis that would be useful for the grounded theory approach, as they emphasize the so-called "verification paradigm"—hypothesis testing, parameter estimation, linear models, and significance tests. In contrast, SOM is neither driven by specific hypotheses nor constrained by the assumption of linearity. For that reason, Castellani and colleagues consider SOM to be the most useful technique for analyzing quantitative data from the perspective of the grounded theory approach. Indeed, as demonstrated earlier, the output of the SOM procedure does not provide any regression coefficients or significance tests—it is primarily visual and requires open-ended interpretation. Consequently, Castellani and colleagues argue that, "to make sense of the nonobvious patterns and trends found, the researcher must apply traditional grounded theory techniques, including coding, memo writing, and theoretical sampling" (p. 578). They call this strategy "grounded neural networking."

To be sure, the researchers have to exercise caution when choosing to use neural networks for their analyses. One possible problem with neural networks lies in model complexity. Whereas the complexity of output might be seen as an advantage by those emphasizing grounded theory, others may be less likely to appreciate it. For instance, when neural networks are used for prediction, they essentially operate as "black boxes" (Mola, Davino, Siciliano, & Vistocco, 1997). Their predictive capabilities might be superior to linear regression models, but it is usually impossible to describe the functions used to calculate predicted values (Paik, 2000a). This problem stems from their nonlinear nature, and, in fact, other nonlinear models have similar problems. Thus, for some purposes, this problem might translate into a disincentive to use neural network methodologies. For instance, it may often be of interest to social scientists to be able to determine the predictive strengths of specific variables, but neural network models usually do not allow such an assessment (Mola et al., 1997).

Second, neural network models are not automatically superior to standard statistical models (Mola et al., 1997; Paik, 2000b). If the true relationships are indeed linear or can be rendered linear, and if relationships are well defined and there is little noise in the data, standard techniques typically perform quite well (Mola et al., 1997). Thus in such situations neural network methodologies have little to offer above and beyond traditional methods of data analysis. The simplicity of standard statistical techniques may be preferred in such cases.

Third, the "artificial intelligence" of neural networks often creates a temptation to avoid any preprocessing of the data. Neural networks are often presented as an assumption-free method of data analysis, in that it is expected that neural networks will be able to provide good output results free of error and bias no matter what (Mola et al., 1997; Paik, 2000a). Thus the good old rule of "garbage in, garbage out" is often neglected when using neural network methodologies. But, although neural network models are more robust, they are not assumption-free (Bishop, 1995); their assumptions are just milder and less explicit and, unfortunately, more frequently ignored (Paik, 2000a). Furthermore, as for standard statistical methods, data screening and preliminary descriptive analysis are essential for neural network models; the data might need to be transformed before being used as the input. For instance, as mentioned earlier, in SOM it is important to consider the issue of normalization.

Finally, an additional possible difficulty in using SOM is that it requires a fair amount of creativity and analytical insight in interpretation. The researcher must be able to figure out how to interpret the map, to identify the important conceptual domains, to explain what they mean, and to examine how they are related to each other (Castellani et al., 2003).

Overall, we do not yet understand the full range of advantages and disadvantages of applying neural network methodologies rather than the standard statistical techniques. The future will reveal how the neural network techniques will be integrated into the standard body of statistical theory. Nevertheless, one thing is clear: As larger amounts of social science data become available, and as we are interested in more complex questions, nonlinear models such as the ones generated by neural networks methodologies will likely become increasingly popular. In addition, further developments in the software available to estimate such models is also likely to encourage social scientists to use neural network models to answer their research questions.

References

Acerbi, A., & Parisi, D. (2006). Cultural transmission between and within generations. *Journal of Artificial Societies and Social Simulation, 9*(1). Retrieved June 15, 2006, from *jasss.soc.surrey.ac.uk/9/1/g.html*

Allison, P. D. (2001). *Missing data.* Thousand Oaks, CA: Sage.

Bainbridge, W. S. (1995). Neural network models of religious belief. *Sociological Perspectives, 38,* 483–495.

Balakrishnan, P. V., Cooper, M. C., Jacob, V. S., & Lewis, A. (1994). A study of the classification capabilities of neural networks using unsupervised learning: A comparison with *k*-means clustering. *Psychometrika, 59,* 509–525.

Bishop, C. M. (1995). *Neural networks for pattern recognition.* Oxford, UK: Oxford University Press.

Buscema, M. (1995). Squashing theory: A prediction approach for drug behavior. *Drugs and Society, 8*(3–4), 103–110.

Castellani, B., Castellani, J., & Spray, S. L. (2003). Grounded neural networking: Modeling complex quantitative data. *Symbolic Interaction, 26,* 577–589.

Cherkassky, V., & Mulier, F. (1994). Self-organizing networks for nonparametric regression. In V. Cherkassky, J. H. Friedman, & H. Wechsler (Eds.), *From statistics to neural networks: Theory and pattern recognition applications* (pp. 188–212). Berlin: Springer.

Cho, S. B. (1997). Self-organizing map with dynamical node-splitting: Application to handwritten digit recognition. *Neural Computation, 9,* 1345–1355.

Collins, J. M., & Clark, M. R. (1993). An application of the theory of neural computation to the prediction of workplace behavior: An illustration and assessment of network analysis. *Personnel Psychology, 46,* 503–524.

Davidson, A. C., & Hinkley, D. V. (1997). *Bootstrap methods and their application.* Cambridge, UK: Cambridge University Press.

Deboeck, G. (1998). Software tools for self-organizing maps. In G. Deboeck & T. Kohonen (Eds.), *Visual explorations in finance: With self-organizing maps* (pp. 179–194). London: Springer-Verlag.

Douglass, J. (2001). *Self-organizing maps: A tourist's guide to neural network (re)presentation(s).* Retrieved March 2, 2007, from *www.english.ucsb.edu/grad/student-pages/jdouglass/coursework/hyperliterature/soms/*

Duong, D., & Reilly, K. (1995). A system of IAC neural networks as the basis for self-organization in a sociological dynamical system simulation. *Behavioral Science, 40*(4), 275–303.

Fritzke, B. (1994). Growing cell structures: A self-organizing network for unsupervised and supervised learning. *Neural Networks, 7*(9), 1441–1460.

Garson, G. D. (1991). A comparison of neural network and expert systems algorithms with common multivariate procedures for analysis of social science data. *Social Science Computer Review, 9*(3), 399–434.

Garson, G. D. (1998). *Neural networks: An introductory guide for social scientists.* Thousand Oaks, CA: Sage.

Glaser, B., & Strauss, A. L. (1967). *The discovery of grounded theory: Strategies for qualitative research.* Chicago: Aldine.

Han, J., & Kamber, M. (2001). *Data mining: Concepts and techniques.* San Francisco: Morgan Kaufmann.

Haydon, G. H., Hiltunen, Y., Lucey, M. R., Collett, D., Gunson, B., Murphy, N., et al. (2005). Self-organizing maps can determine outcome and match recipients and donors at orthotopic liver transplantation. *Transplantation, 79,* 213–218.

Holmes, S., Morris, C., & Tibshirani, R. (2003). Bradley Efron: A conversation with good friends. *Statistical Science, 18*(2), 268–281.

Hutchins, E., & Hazlehurst, B. (1995). How to invent a lexicon: The development of shared symbols in interaction. In N. Gilbert & R. Conte (Eds.), *Artificial societies: The computer simulation of social life* (pp. 157–189). London: UCL Press.

Ilonen, J., Kamarainen, J., Puumalainen, K., Sundqvist, S., & Kälviäinen, H. (2006). Toward automatic forecasts for diffusion of innovations. *Technological Forecasting and Social Change, 73,* 182–198.

Kaplan, D. (2000). *Structural equation modeling: Foundations and extensions.* Thousand Oaks, CA: Sage.

Kartalopoulos, S. V. (1996). *Understanding neural networks and fuzzy logic: Basic concepts and applications.* New York: IEEE Press.

Kauko, T. J. (2004). A comparative perspective on urban spatial housing market structure: Some more evidence of local submarkets based on a neural network classification of Amsterdam. *Urban Studies, 41*(13), 2555–2579.

Kelly, A. J., Goodman, P. H., Kaburlasos, V. G., Egbert, D. D., & Hardin, M. E. (1992). Neural network prediction of child sexual abuse. *Clinical Research, 40*(1), A99.

Kimber, R. (1991). Artificial intelligence and the study of democracy. *Social Science Computer Review, 9*(3), 381–398.

Kline, R. B. (2005). *Principles and practice of structural equation modeling* (2nd ed.). New York: Guilford Press.

Kohonen, T. (1984). *Self-organization and associative memory.* Berlin: Springer-Verlag.

Kohonen, T. (2001). *Self-organizing maps* (3rd ed.). Berlin: Springer-Verlag.

Kruglov, V. V., & Dli, M. I. (2001). Application of neural networks notion to analysis of sociological data. *Sotsiologicheskie Issledovaniya, 27*(9), 112–114.

Lawrence, S., Giles, C. L., Tsoi, A. C., & Back, A. D. (1997). Face recognition: A convolutional neural network approach. *IEEE Transactions on Neural Networks, 8*(1), 98–113.

Lee, E. S., & Forthofer, R.N. (2006). *Analyzing complex survey data* (2nd ed.). Thousand Oaks, CA: Sage.

Little, R. J. A., & Rubin, D. B. (2002). *Statistical analyses with missing data* (2nd ed.). Hoboken, NJ: Wiley.

Long, J. S., & Cheng, S. (2004). Regression models for categorical outcomes. In M. Hardy & A. Bryman (Eds.), *Handbook of data analysis* (pp. 259–284). Thousand Oaks, CA: Sage.

Luke, D. A. (2004). *Multilevel modeling.* Thousand Oaks, CA: Sage.

Macy, M. (1996). Natural selection and social learning in prisoner's dilemma: Coadaptation with genetic algorithms and artificial neural networks. *Sociological Methods and Research, 25*(1), 103–137.

Martindale, C. (1991). *Cognitive psychology: A neural-network approach.* Pacific Grove, CA: Brooks/Cole.

Meraviglia, C. (1996). Models of representation of social mobility and inequality systems: A neural network approach. *Quality and Quantity, 30,* 231–252.

Mola, F., Davino, C., Siciliano, R., & Vistocco, D. (1997). Use and overuse of neural networks in statistics. In *Proceedings of the Fourth International Meeting of Multidimensional Data Analysis* (pp. 57–68). Bilbao, Spain: CISIA.

Monterola, C., Lim, M., Garcia, J., & Saloma, C. (2002). Feasibility of a neural network as classifier of undecided respondents in a public opinion survey. *International Journal of Public Opinion Research, 14*(2), 222–229.

Mulier, F., & Cherkassky, V. (1995). Self-organization as an iterative kernel smoothing process. *Neural Computation, 7,* 1165–1177.

Paik, H. (2000a). Comments on neural networks. *Sociological Methods and Research, 28*(4), 425–453.

Paik, H. (2000b). Television viewing and high school mathematics achievement: A neural network analysis. *Quality and Quantity, 34*(1), 1–15.

Paik, H., & Marzban, C. (1995). Predicting television extreme viewers and nonviewers: A neural network analysis. *Human Communication Research, 22*(2), 284–306.

Parisi, D., Cecconi, F., & Cerini, A. (1995). Kin-directed altruism and attachment behavior in an evolving population of neural networks. In N. Gilbert & R. Conte (Eds.), *Artificial societies: The computer simulation of social life* (pp. 281–251). London: UCL Press.

Patterson, D. W. (1996). *Artificial neural networks: Theory and applications.* Singapore: Prentice Hall.

Principe, J., Euliano, N. R., & Lefebvre, W. C. (2000). *Neural adaptive systems: Fundamentals through simulations.* New York: Wiley.

Raudenbush, S., & Bryk, A. (2002). *Hierarchical linear models: Applications and data analysis methods* (2nd ed.). Thousand Oaks, CA: Sage.

Rindskopf, D. (2004). Trends in categorical data analysis: New, semi-new, and recycled ideas. In D. W. Kaplan (Ed.), *The Sage handbook of quantitative methodology for social sciences* (pp. 137–149). Thousand Oaks, CA: Sage.

Ripley, B. D. (1996). *Pattern recognition and neural networks.* Cambridge, UK: Cambridge University Press.

Robinson, J. P., Bianchi, S. M., & Presser, S. (1999). *Family interaction, social capital, and trends in time use (FISCT), 1998–1999* [Computer file, ICPSR version]. College Park: University of Maryland Survey Research Center.

Rojas, R. (1996). *Neural networks: A systematic introduction.* Berlin: Springer-Verlag.

Sares, T. A. (1998). Sociopolitical viewpoints as narrated by family and educational background. *Journal of Social Psychology, 138*(5), 637–644.

Sarle, W. S. (2002). *How many kinds of Kohonen networks exist?* Retrieved January 10, 2007, from *ftp://ftp.sas.com/pub/neural/FAQ.html#A_Kohonen*

Schrodt, P. A. (1991). Prediction of interstate conflict outcomes using a neural network. *Social Science Computer Review, 9*(3), 359–380.

Skapura, D. M. (1996). *Building neural networks.* Reading, MA: Addison-Wesley.

Snijders, T. A. B., & Bosker, R. J. (1999). *Multilevel analysis: An introduction to basic and advanced multilevel modeling.* Thousand Oaks, CA: Sage.

Suna, T., Hardey, M., Huhtinen, J., Hiltunen, Y., Kaski, K., Heikkonen, J., et al. (2006). Self-organising map approach to individual profiles: Age, sex and culture in internet dating. *Sociological Research Online, 11*(1). Retrieved April 24, 2006, from *www.socresonline.org.uk/11/1/suna.html*

Swingler, K. (1996). *Applying neural networks: A practical guide.* San Diego, CA: Academic Press.

Vesanto, J., Himberg, J., Alhoniemi, E., & Parhankangas, J. (2000). *SOM Toolbox for Matlab 5.* Retrieved December 19, 2006, from *www.cis.hut.fi/projects/somtoolbox/package/papers/techrep.pdf*

Zeng, L. (1999). Prediction and classification with neural network models. *Sociological Methods and Research, 27,* 499–524.

APPENDIX 30.1. Time-Use Questions from FISCT Survey

1. What is the approximate number of hours per week that you spend working for pay?

2. What is the approximate number of hours per week that you spend preparing meals?

3. What is the approximate number of hours per week that you spend washing dishes and cleaning up after meals?

4. What is the approximate number of hours per week that you spend cleaning house?

5. What is the approximate number of hours per week that you spend doing outdoor and other household maintenance tasks (lawn and yard work, household repair, painting, etc.)?

6. What is the approximate number of hours per week that you spend shopping for groceries and other household goods?

7. What is the approximate number of hours per week that you spend washing, ironing, and mending?

8. What is the approximate number of hours per week that you spend paying bills and keeping financial records?

9. What is the approximate number of hours per week that you spend on automobile maintenance and repair?

10. What is the approximate number of hours per week that you spend driving other household members to work, school, or other activities?

11. What is the approximate number of hours per week that you spend attending religious services?

12. What is the approximate number of hours per week that you spend watching TV?

CHAPTER 31

User-Centered Perspectives on Qualitative Data Analysis Software

Emergent Technologies and Future Trends

Sharlene Nagy Hesse-Biber
Christine Crofts

A Data Analysis Tale

Dissertation data had been occupying one room of my apartment, often spread out over the floor organized into neat and sometimes not so neat piles. Many months had been spent in this room devoted to managing and analyzing a set of almost 80 in-depth intensive interviews. With scissors in hand, I would read over a set of new interviews and proceed to "cut up" all relevant chunks of textual data from each interview and paste similarly coded data bites into a separate file folder. However, each time my analytical/conceptual scheme changed, categories would have to be completely altered. If I wanted to apply a different code to the same chunk of text, I needed to recopy the segment. As my data analysis proceeded, I found myself revising and deleting some previously coded category. This also required me to photocopy interviews again and repeat part of the coding process. My ability to assign multiple codes to text and to recode different segments was often thwarted by the "cut and paste" procedure. Although I liked the idea of seeing and handling all of my data in their entirety, as the interviews increased, it became more and more difficult to see the "big picture." Creating memos on different aspects of my analysis and coding procedure was a critical step in assisting with the discovery of some major code categories and themes in my data, as well as relationships between code categories. It was during this time that I discovered a set of "key sort" data cards, or "edge-punched cards." These cards were the new technological rage at the time, especially among anthropologists working in the late 1970s and early 1980s. They were 8″ × 3″ cards ringed with holes that were numbered across the edge of the card. I placed all my interview material on these cards and proceeded to code the data on each card by punching open the numbered ring corresponding to that code. You could conceivably have up to 100 codes for any given card, but usually I had between 5 and 20 codes per card, given the information contained on any given hole card.

Periodically, I would assemble or "stack up" all the cards and begin to retrieve my code categories from the deck of cards using a rod, or what I called my "knitting needle," which was inserted through the circular holes in my stack of cards. If I was interested in retrieving a particular code or set of codes for my study, I would put my knitting needle through those relevant code-numbered holes, shake the pile, and out would drop all the data chunks for that code. In fact, I would sometimes have a great time shaking the deck, and I can remember curious onlookers asking me if I was "OK" as all my coded cards came tumbling out of the pile so I could retrieve my data bounty to analyze. I would repeat this process of coding and retrieving as my analysis process proceeded by hand until I felt I had sufficiently captured the meaning of a specific code by comparing and contrasting different chunks of similarly coded data or latched onto a significant pattern in my data. —SHARLENE NAGY HESSE-BIBER

The preceding narrative-analysis tale is by no means unique for this time before the advent of computerized software for qualitative analysis. Until several decades ago, most qualitative research consisted of amassing and manipulating data by hand, using these types of manual procedures. Ethnographers, sociologists, educators, and other social and behavioral scientists were analyzing their pages of textual data (such as interview transcripts or field notes) by copying and recopying them, and segments of text were literally cut out of pages and pasted onto other sheets or note cards. Various complex categorization systems, often involving color-coding or the punching of hole cards and insertion of rods or "knitting needles" were used to assist researchers with sorting and sifting through their data. Oftentimes the mechanical aspects of keeping data organized and conducting analyses became tedious and overwhelming, to the detriment of the real work of engaging with the data. However, some researchers still prefer to analyze their qualitative data using these procedures or variants of these techniques, viewing their work as craft that should not be subjected to computerized methods. They often point to the positive aspects of having tactile contact with their data and fear that they will lose control and creativity by computerizing some of these analysis functions.

In the late 1970s and early 1980s, some researchers decided that the existing approaches to data analysis did not allow them to engage most effectively with the data they had worked so hard to collect (especially when they were analyzing large amounts of data). The increasing availability of microcomputers also made it feasible to create software that could assist them in their research and analysis efforts. The endeavors of several key social scientists led to the creation of a field of products that would significantly change the way in which qualitative analysis was carried out, namely qualitative data analysis software. This chapter takes a brief look at the history of this family of software, from its beginnings in the minds of a few qualitative researchers to its contemporary state of broad use and diverse application of software programs for microcomputers. We also speculate on the directions these programs will take in the near future.

Qualitative Research and Analysis: The Foundation of Qualitative Data Analysis Software

To understand the origins of qualitative data analysis software, it is first necessary to consider some of the basic features of qualitative research and data analysis, because these programs were specifically created to assist this type of work. Unlike quantitative research, in which data is expressed in *numerical* form, qualitative data can be expressed in visual, auditory, and textual forms. Qualitative researchers utilize interviews, focus groups, participant observations, and oral histories, as well as unobtrusive methods such as historical archival documents, letters, artifacts, diaries, and other forms of "nonliving" data to get at "meaning" and "understanding" from the perspective of the researched. The work of qualitative researchers operates under the assumption that gaining understanding of people and their lives requires a deep and multifaceted engagement with the expressions and representations of those people's experiences in the context of their lives and positions in the world, rather than a detached measurement of particular details. In other words, the qualitative approach to research is one of *holistic engagement* with the researched and their contexts (both living and nonliving). In addition to working with nonnumerical data and taking a holistic approach to gathering and understanding that data, another basic feature of qualitative research is that it is not only a method but a *craft*. Rather than being a strict set of methodological procedures, qualitative methods allow researchers to creatively develop their own approaches to engaging with and learning from their participants' experiences and narratives (Taylor & Bogdan, 1998). Considering some of these fundamental features of qualitative research, it becomes clear that the actual practice of these methods involves an intense "living" relationship with data and requires a great deal of time and effort.

Despite the innovation and individuality of approaches that can be taken by researchers in their practice of the craft, most qualitative *data analyses* also have several basic features in common. Pfaffenberger (1988) notes that qualitative data analysis consists of breaking down material into its "constituent elements that need to be compared, named, and classified so that their nature and interaction becomes clear" (p. 26). *Comparison* in qualitative data analysis is a twofold process of *decontextualization* and *recontextualization* (Tesch, 1990). In decontextualization, portions or segments of the data are examined in isolation from their particular contexts. These segments are then related to other decontextualized segments that seem to have similar meanings or express similar ideas. The process of assembling related segments into groupings or categories allows the researcher to discover themes and patterns that elucidate connections in and make sense of the data they have gathered, thereby recontextualizing the data into new conceptual "contexts." Another feature that typically characterizes qualitative data analysis is *reconsidering* the data that have been decontextualized and recontextualized. Researchers repeatedly reconsider data segments in light of their original contexts, testing and challenging the concepts and themes they have discovered, looking for "negative cases" in which to challenge their findings in an effort to conduct the most authentic analysis possible. Instead of being one distinct step or set of steps that occurs at one point during the research process, analysis is being performed by qualitative researchers throughout their research journey. For example, early field notes or interview data may help to clarify whom you may need to sample next in your research project (theoretical sampling) or what new patterns appear to be emerging in your data. Early attention to data can also assist with identifying an emerging code category or theme in your study and perhaps even allow you to "test out" some initial "hunches" or ideas on your data as you proceed. A computer program would be useful in assisting with the process of attaching a category name to a basic unit of data (chunk of text) and allowing the ability to easily retrieve similarly coded chunks of text for comparison.

It is in this sense that the data are analyzed while they are being collected, and such analysis can lead researchers to change or refine their research questions or approaches to data collection. Contained in these processes are memo writing and rewriting as well as coding and recoding of data, looking for patterns and relationships between categories or themes and querying and retrieving of code categories. Qualitative analysis also includes a variety of ways to display data, especially displays of conceptual thinking in terms of a matrix, network diagram, or outline. Computers would be useful in assisting with many of these analysis and interpretative functions.

It is crucial to remember, however, that not all qualitative research approaches and traditions use inductive analytical methods (such as a "grounded theory approach" to analysis). Narrative analysts are interested in stories and want to code and retrieve narratives looking at their inherent structure, such things as the chronological sequence of events in a narrative. Other researchers prefer to analyze their data utilizing theories prior to their collection of data. Burawoy (1991) suggests an "*extended case method*" of data analysis that begins with explicit theorizing about what the researcher hopes to find in conducting a given research project. This method then uses the specific research study to test out critical components of the researcher's theoretical framework with the idea that data are collected in order to reconfigure existing theory by subjecting them to empirical verification. The researcher's theory drives all aspects of the data project. Burawoy notes the following concerning this method of analysis utilized during an ethnographic project: "We begin by trying to lay out as coherently as possible what we expect to find in our site *before* entry. When our expectations are violated–when we discover what we didn't anticipate–we then turn to existing bodies of academic theory that might cast light on our anomaly."

Each of these qualitative research traditions, then, will require a different configuration of software functions.

Prequalitative Data Analysis Software (First-Generation) Uses of Computers

Hoping to address the issues of data disorganization and the tedium of manual analysis, qualitative researchers began to use computers to deal with their data by the early 1980s. The first programs for analyzing textual data utilized mainframe computers and were geared toward quantitative content analysis that was primarily utilized by researchers in the humanities (Kelle, 1995). The best known of this group of IBM mainframe programs was the General Inquirer, a dictionary-based program developed in the early 1960s (Stone, Dunphy, Smith, & Ogilvie, 1966) that allows the researcher to code words in any given text to specific categories that appear in an existing dictionary (such as the *Lasswell Value Dictionary* or the *Harvard IV Psychosocial Dictionary*) or one created by the user. The program provides a frequency count of the number of occurrences and co-occurrences of specific words in each category of interest to the researcher and allows the researcher to easily group words that share a similar meaning (Kelle, 1995, pp. 1–2).

Yet it was not until the onset of the development of the microcomputer that qualitative researchers began to utilize computers (Figure 31.1) to assist them in qualitative data analysis (Fielding & Lee, 1998; Mangabeira, 1995b). Before personal computers, many qualitative researchers could not reconcile their perceptions of computers–they saw them "as calculating machines; useful in the social sciences only for statistical analysis" (Kelle, 1996a, p. 35)–with their own nonnumeric, interpretative philosophies of data analysis. As they became increasingly proficient in and comfortable with the use of computers, many qualitative researchers began to change their attitudes about the technology and its range of capabilities, and they discovered many possible opportunities to use computers to improve on their manual systems of analyzing data.

Because no software specifically geared toward such use had yet been developed, researchers adapted already existing programs in many different ways to meet their analysis needs, creating what has been called the *first generation* of computer use for qualitative

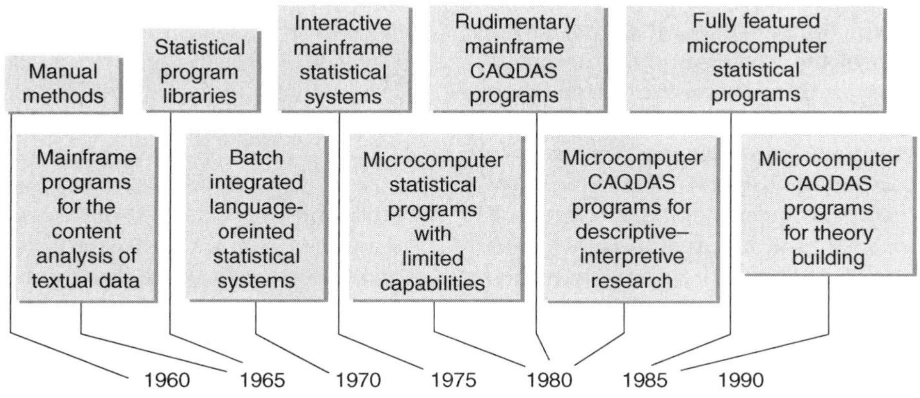

FIGURE 31.1. Historical development of data analysis software. From Fielding and Lee (1995). Copyright 1995 by Sage Publications, Inc. Reprinted by permission.

analysis (Fielding & Lee, 2002; Kelle, 1996a; Mangabeira, 1995a). One of the most commonly utilized types of first-generation programs was the *word processor*, which provided an immediate advantage in terms of reducing the need for paper printouts. Word processors were also used in conjunction with the "embed-and-retrieve" technique, which involved "embedding" alphanumeric codes into the data to mark instances of a certain condition or to assign a text segment to a category. These codes could later be searched for and used to "retrieve" information pertaining to whatever the code was meant to represent (Fielding & Lee, 1998; Tesch, 1990). Another nonspecific type of software used was the *text retriever*, which allowed the user to search for strings of characters within text, often by way of Boolean searches, proximity searches (which search for occurrences of one string of characters within a certain distance from another string), and pattern searches (which search for patterns of characters within the text) (Fielding & Lee, 1998). Examples of these programs are ZyINDEX and WordCruncher. *Textbase managers*, which allowed the researcher to further organize textual information, often by entering it into structured "fields" (columns in a data matrix) or "records" (rows in a matrix), were also used (Fielding & Lee, 1998; Miles & Weitzman, 1996). FileMaker Pro and Textbase Alpha are examples of this type of program.

Development of Early Qualitative Data Analysis Software (Second-Generation) Programs

By the 1980s, social scientists were beginning to develop software that not only fulfilled the type of organizational and searching functions performed by nonspecific programs but that also addressed their particular needs as qualitative researchers. These dedicated qualitative analysis programs were created directly out of the experiences of the researcher/developers themselves, and were, as one of these individuals writes, efforts to "reproduce the mechanical aspects of qualitative data analysis in the formulas of a set of computer programs" (Seidel & Clark, 1984, p. 112). Several groups of researchers in a number of countries (e.g., Australia: NUD*IST and N.Vivo; Germany: ATLAS/ti, WinMax, AQUAD; United States: Ethnograph, HyperRESEACH) began developing qualitative data analysis software independent of each other, tailoring their programs to their particular analysis needs. This growing "parallel development" in software for qualitative analysis strove to fill a basic need for researchers to come to grips with the growing complexity of their analysis of textual materials. Although these researcher/developers each employed somewhat different data analysis techniques in their research practice and consequently fashioned their programs to address their specific technical needs, a common analytical approach with which many of these software programs identified was that of grounded theory, which was very popular in the field of qualitative research in general at that point in its history.

First developed by Glaser and Strauss (1967), grounded theory is a method in which the researcher develops theory based on concepts and ideas discovered in the data analysis process; put another way, the grounded theory researcher "has to set aside theoretical ideas to allow a 'substantive' theory to emerge" (Dey, 1999). From a grounded theory perspective, conducting analysis takes place in a "constant comparative" fashion. Conceptual categories are derived from the data and applied to relevant data segments through the process of coding, and categories are refined by comparisons between cases. Examining the connections between categories allows the researcher to generate theoretical hypotheses about the data. All of this continues in an iterative manner as new data are collected and analyzed (Coffey & Atkinson, 1996; Dey, 1999; Glaser & Strauss, 1967; Strauss & Corbin, 1994).

Some of the earliest developers of qualitative data analysis software programs explicitly noted their use of grounded theory and its connection to the software they created (Muhr, 1991; Richards & Richards, 1991; Seidel & Clark, 1984). Thomas Muhr, developer of ATLAS/ti, notes:

> During the development of the program we were stimulated by the ideas, terminology, and methodological processes associated with "grounded theory." . . . This influence is partly discernible in terms used in the system's user interface (menus, windows, etc). This does not mean, however, that the tool is restricted to a certain methodology. The functions offered by ATLAS/ti are "generic" in the sense that they may be the building blocks that serve other approaches as well. (1991, pp. 351–352)

Because these developers were social scientists and not, for the most part, computer programmers or software development professionals, they were uniquely able to tailor their products to address the particular analytical needs they experienced in their own research. Thus their programs were fashioned to handle the coding and theory-generation tasks that were essential to the grounded theory methodological approach. Their packages contained features that facilitated the creation, application, and retrieval of codes and that aligned segments of coded textual data with conceptual categories. This type of software, specifically geared toward coding and the search for and retrieval of coded segments, made up the second generation of qualitative analysis computer use (Fielding & Lee, 2002; Kelle, 1996a; Mangabeira, 1995a). The features included in these programs responded to qualitative researchers' interest in allowing patterns and themes to "emerge" from the data, a process that both shaped and supported their theories and hypotheses. By aiding the researcher in delimiting and locating sections of the text according to their relevance to broader concepts, second-generation qualitative data analysis software programs "allowed the researcher to analyse more data more systematically and carefully and thus increased the possibility to find evidence or counter-evidence for their hypotheses" (Kelle, 1996a, p. 43). Lonkila (1995) further clarifies the connection between grounded theory and these second-generation programs by discussing the analytical procedures that the two have in common, including coding, making constant comparisons, creating linkages, memoing (or the process of taking theoretical notes during the analysis process), and theory building. At the same time, *not* all second-generation qualitative data analysis software programs were entirely focused on a coding-based grounded theory approach (as some gave equal or greater emphasis to other analysis techniques, such as memo writing). In general, although the first researcher/developers often found the principles of grounded theory useful and applied them to their own research interests, they did not intend for their software to *embody* grounded theory methodology (or any particular methodological approach). Rather, they developed programs to mechanize some of their more tedious or cumbersome analysis techniques, techniques that many other qualitative researchers–both those dedicated to grounded theory and those with other methodological preferences–also happened to employ.

There is no doubt that grounded theory had some influence on the developers of early qualitative data analysis software programs. However, recent debate has focused on whether these and other qualitative analysis programs, because of their link to grounded theory, force the user to employ certain methods techniques or exclude those with certain methodological approaches. Coffey, Holbrook, and Atkinson (1996) suggest that the strong connections between grounded theory and qualitative data analysis software direct software users to approach, handle, and analyze their data in a particular "taken-for-granted" way. They caution that the emphasis on coding found in most analysis programs inappropriately attempts to liken qualitative research to quantitative research by giving it a "scientific gloss." They also warn that users run the risk of thinking that simply assigning codes to their data in their computer program of choice is all they need to do in terms of analysis (1996, Section 7.6). In response to these authors' contentions, Lee and Fielding (1996) argue that qualitative data analysis software does not compel users to conduct their analyses in particular ways (an assertion that they base on their own research on user experiences, which is discussed in Fielding & Lee, 2002). They also cite the wide variety of advanced features that current qualitative analysis programs include and "the general willingness of developers to incorporate features desired by users even if these do not always accord with the epistemological preferences of the developer," arguing that the orientations of developers do not determine how their programs can be and are being used (Lee & Fielding, 1996). A similar position was also articulated by Kelle, who argued that "in practice, researchers tend to cease using a certain package rather than submit themselves to the logic of a software program totally different from the logic of inquiry they wish to employ" (1996b, p. 239). Furthermore, Kelle has pointed out that, despite the links and references to grounded theory that can be found in documentation of and literature about many qualitative data analysis software programs, their developers actually had quite "differing conceptions of how knowledge of social reality is produced," and he suggests that the similarity between their development approaches lies in the "code-and-retrieve" technique, which, rather than being specifically aligned with grounded theory, is "an 'open technology' applicable in various theoretical and methodological contexts" (Kelle, 1997, p. 6).

Although this recent debate is useful in highlighting some important issues regarding the use and potential misuse of qualitative data analysis software programs, it does not indicate that the development history of these programs restricts or limits their use to those with a particular theoretical or methodological preference. Coffey and colleagues (1996) are justified in warning of the dangers of relying too heavily on software for analysis, but it seems that this relates more to individual users' application of data analysis software than to any qualities of the software itself (and even less so to the methodological orientations of early developers).

So, too, can the coding process lend itself to a "quantification" of qualitative data if the researcher chooses to count codes rather than to use them to clarify broader concepts and themes in the data, which is again a decision of the user, not a demand of the software. Indeed, as is discussed later in this chapter, researchers from many disciplines and with many different methodological preferences currently use qualitative data analysis software, suggesting that not only those partial to grounded theory can benefit from incorporating software into their analysis repertoire.

Development of Advanced (Third-Generation) Programs and Features

As the field matured, existing and new qualitative data analysis software programs began to respond to increasingly sophisticated analysis needs. Whereas the two previous generations of computers in qualitative analysis essentially served to automate techniques that were already being done manually, this *third generation* introduced features that "widely exceeded the analytic possibilities offered by manual methods" (Kelle, 1996a, p. 43). In other words, new programs introduced analytical techniques that may not have been feasible without the use of a computer. Such innovations included the capability to do more advanced code searching and to create linkages and networks between conceptual categories. Programs could use elaborate search methods to "discover" patterns and themes on their own (which, although they would of course have to be examined and verified by the researcher, could uncover linkages within or between cases that might have escaped the researcher's notice). The purpose of including such features was to enable the software to support inductive theory building and hypothesis testing (Fielding & Lee, 2002; Kelle, 1996a; Mangabeira, 1995a).

Categorizations of Qualitative Data Analysis Software Programs

Many qualitative data analysis software programs have been developed since the 1980s, each with somewhat different interfaces, features, and analysis goals. A number of efforts to categorize the variety of programs available have been made over the years to assist current and potential users in understanding how various programs might fit their needs. Such categorization has primarily focused on the main *analysis functions* that each program is able to perform and the types of analysis goals that it can successfully assist the researcher in achieving.

The *first-*, *second-*, and *third-generation* way of thinking about qualitative data analysis software programs discussed here (and further addressed in Kelle, 1996a, and Mangabeira, 1995a) presents one categorization method. This method takes a historical approach to creating categories and truly addresses the overall development of computer usage in qualitative analysis (not just data analysis software), as its first generation pertains to software not exclusively geared toward qualitative analysis. The second and third generations refer specifically to dedicated qualitative data analysis programs, distinguishing them by the level of analysis they support; those that simply code and retrieve are second generation, whereas those that allow for theory building and/or hypothesis testing belong in the third.

One of the earliest methods of categorizing qualitative data analysis software programs was developed by Renata Tesch (1990) and focused on the *analysis goals* that programs were able to support. In her estimation, most programs available at that time shared similar main functions and differed in terms of the more advanced features they offered. Because of the variety of dimensions along which the specific features of the programs differed, Tesch opted to categorize them based on what purpose each program was ultimately designed to achieve for the user, rather than the particular features it contained. The two categories Tesch established were "programs for descriptive/ interpretive analysis" and "programs for theory-building." Although she admitted that it could be difficult to determine to which of these categories some programs should belong (noting that the difference between programs' purposes "is one of degree; it is not absolute"; Tesch, 1990, p. 147), Tesch's categorizations emphasized the type or level of analysis that each program could support. In terms of their actual classification of programs, these categories quite closely parallel those of the second and third generations discussed earlier. However, Tesch contributed a crucial dimension to our thinking about qualitative data analysis software programs—namely, the importance of considering how the *user* relates to and utilizes a software program (in terms of discovering "which program best suits the research projects you usually conduct, or are currently engaged in" and learning "which program is most congruent with your work style"; Tesch, 1990, p. 177). Tesch wanted researchers to carefully consider in a step-by-step fashion what program met their own needs. Some of her advice: "If a program does not have the capabilities you'd like to use for your research, pay no further attention to it" (p. 178). Style of thinking was also something Tesch pointed out as a consideration in purchasing software, and she noted that "some programs might fit your style of thinking and working more closely than others" (p. 178). The degree of a user's "comfort" was also of great importance to Tesch. In order to attain a level of comfort, she advised the researcher to "visualize your own data there and imagine which one would be most helpful for your interpretation" (p. 178). Lastly, Tesch asks users to be open to serendipity by suggesting they browse through program descriptions, even among those "you don't expect to serve your research purpose. You might discover that some program will let you perform operations quite likely to enrich your analysis, in ways you would never have thought of" (p. 178).

Another important system of program categorization was put forward by Weitzman and Miles (Miles & Weitzman, 1996; Weitzman & Miles, 1995) and focuses on the primary and/or highest level features of programs used for qualitative data analysis. This "features-based" categorization, like the "generations method of categorization," provides a range of groupings—word processors, text retrievers, and textbase managers (nonqualitative data analysis software programs) and code-and-retrieve programs, code-based theory builders, and conceptual network builders (dedicated qualitative data analysis software programs) that emphasize the "functional" characteristics of each software package (Miles & Weitzman, 1996). Programs are assigned to categories based on what types of analytical tasks they are capable of performing. Implicit to this categorization system is a hierarchy of program complexity; each level represents a more advanced, feature-enriched group of programs than the one preceding it. According to Weitzman and Miles (1995), each program was assigned to a category based on which functional level was at its "heart and soul" (p. 16). Thus, although a program might (and often did, as Weitzman and Miles conceded) have features that would seem to place it in more than one category, a decision was made by the categorizers to isolate its "truest" function. Weitzman and Miles start their review of software by taking a *user* perspective. They emphasize the importance of each user's paying attention to several key questions: What type of computer experience have you had? What type of project do you plan to use this software for? What kind of database and analysis? (p. 7). Yet in the end, their emphasis shifts from user to expert, as is evidenced in their display of program function tables, which present a "hierarchy" approach to categorizing programs emphasizing an *"expert" rather than a user perspective*. The "expert" approach to categorizing programs gained wide acceptance in the field and is borrowed by many others who have written about this family of software in recent years (e.g., Fielding & Lee, 1998; van Hoven & Poelman, 2003; Lee & Esterhuizen, 2000; Mizrach, 1999; Morison & Moir, 1998).

Since the time these systems of categorization were developed, qualitative data analysis software programs have continued to expand and refine the types of features they offer and the analysis goals they support, making them increasingly difficult to assign to one particular category. Similarly, as the community of users and the types of analysis goals they are trying to achieve become ever more diverse, groupings that focus on one particular functional quality or analysis purpose begin to lose relevance.

An alternative approach to thinking about qualitative data analysis software programs is to analyze their strengths and weaknesses in various "areas of performance." Such an approach is taken by Creswell and Maietta (2003), who have developed eight criteria (in areas such as *ease of integration*, *memo writing*, and *categorization*) by which qualitative data analysis software programs can be evaluated. This type of system does not provide an opportunity "to declare a 'best' program that covers the universe of qualitative data analysis software" (Creswell & Maietta, 2003, p. 165) because it is based on the presumption that the criteria are of *varying* importance to each user. Furthermore, such a system does not claim that each program fits into only one functional or purposive category. Rather, Creswell and Maietta create a method by which each researcher can determine which program best suits his or her "category" of need. Although definitely more responsive to the user perspective than Miles and Weitzman's approach, this type of loose categorization still assumes an "expert" position. By rating each program based on how well it supports the eight criteria, Creswell and Maietta suggest that programs have an inherent value in each criterion area that can be discerned by experts, rather than by individual users. Though not the intention of its authors, such a listing of criterion areas may encourage an *additive approach* to thinking about what is the "best" qualitative data analysis software program, with the user simply "adding" the ratings for each criterion for specific programs and selecting the program that "scores" the highest.

Although each of these categorization systems uses a different language to describe what they seek to portray, all of these systems (with the possible exception of Tesch's) seem to share several underlying assumptions. First, they all seem to agree that the particular features or specialty areas of each program should determine the researcher's selection of which program to use. In other words, they suggest that if the prospective user chooses a program from the appropriate functional category or with strengths in the proper feature areas, he or she will have found the "right" technology for job.

Although it is likely not the intention of those who developed systems of categorization, this seems, to some extent, to remove a sense of user empowerment and accountability from the computer-assisted-analysis process. In one sense, the user feels no authority in deciding which program he or she should use, needing to defer to expert opinion about which software will best meet his or her needs. In another sense, the process of selecting a program based on "what it can do" may cause the user to expect that program to "perform" the analysis on its own; when a program is invested with the ability to carry out certain functions, there is a danger that the user will forget that he or she is actually doing the analysis and that the software is only supporting that process.

For these reasons and because of the increasing diversity of programs and features, attempts at categorizing or grouping qualitative data analysis software programs seem somewhat limiting. Retaining Tesch's imperative to acknowledge the user's role in determining how qualitative data analysis software can be used appears to be the crucial element in any evaluation of software. This evaluation approach can be thought of as reflective, user based, and nonhierarchical. From this perspective, the user takes on the role of "expert" in the decision-making process. Tesch's two user considerations evolve around the type of research project the user is engaged in or usually engages in and the user's work style (Tesch, 1990, p. 177). Before simply selecting a program based on its performance of a particular function or its "rank" along the hierarchical continuum, the user is urged to consider a number of questions that will encourage reflection about how the software will fit into the larger scheme of the user's own research agenda. The following set of reflective questions are derived from Tesch (1990), from Weitzman and Miles (1995), and from Creswell and Maietta's (2003) analysis of the user's perspective, as well as from our own suggestions about what questions users might consider when selecting a software program. It would be important for the user to prioritize which questions are most relevant for his or her research agenda.

1. What is your level of computer literacy? Here the emphasis would be on discerning how comfortable you are with working with computers in general. Do you consider yourself a novice user or, going to the opposite extreme, do you write your own computer programs?
2. What type of computer system do you prefer to work on or feel most comfortable working on? Does the program support your operating system? Do you need to upgrade your system or perhaps to purchase a new computer to meet the requirements of a specific program? Do you like the look and feel of a program's interface? What excites you about this program at a visceral level?
3. Does the look and feel of the program fit well with your own research style? What is your analysis style? How do you plan to conduct your analysis, and how might computers fit into that style? How might each program enhance (or detract from) your analysis? In what sense? For example, do you plan on coding most of your data? What type of coding do you want to do? How do you prefer your data be retrieved and how important is it to you to be able to look at the full context from which the data were taken? Are you a visual person? Do you like to see relationships and concepts selected in some type of diagram or network? Do you anticipate quantifying any of your data?
4. For what research project or set of projects do you anticipate using a computer software program? What type of data does your project consist of—textual or multimedia?
5. How do you want a computer program to assist you? What tasks do you want to mechanize? What specific tasks do you want computerized? You may not want all the features espoused by these programs. What are your expectations of what the program will be able to assist you in doing? Are your expectations realistic?
6. What resources are available to you? Which programs can your computer support? Which programs can you afford? What necessary resources (time, personnel, material) for learning how to use this program are available to you?
7. What are your preconceptions about these programs? How have other users' opinions, product marketing, or other sources of information about qualitative data analysis software programs influenced your preferences? Are your assumptions about programs accurate? What more would you like to learn about particular programs?
8. Which of these questions and concerns are most important to you? How would you rank order your most important factors in considering a software purchase? What questions have been left out?

Reflecting on these types of user concerns *before* attempting to select a qualitative data analysis program puts users in the position to critically evaluate for themselves how each program might be integrated into their unique research programs. By examining detailed descriptions of program features and examples of how others have used the software, users can develop their own sense of how various programs can be of service to them. In addition to assisting them in the selection process, this reflective approach also reminds users that they are in control of the analysis process and that no technological tool, regardless of its features, can independently "perform" analysis. Through this type of program evaluation, both user empowerment and accountability are strengthened.

Trends in Qualitative Data Analysis Software Usage and Application

The emphasis on the unique perspective of each user seems especially relevant in light of recent trends in qualitative data analysis software usage. Just as the features and foci of these programs have changed and expanded over the years, so has the community of researchers that utilize them. In the field's early days, most users were, as Fielding and Lee write, "better-than-average technically oriented and were also likely to be sophisticated in their grasp of qualitative method" (2002, p. 198). They were mostly academics, functioning within the same professional circles as the researchers who developed the early qualitative data analysis software programs. Today, as communications via the CAQDAS (Computer-Assisted Qualitative Data Analysis Software) Networking Project (2003) and Fielding and Lee's considerable research on patterns of qualitative data analysis software adoption and usage demonstrate, the range of fields in which these programs are being used and the types of researchers who use them have broadened tremendously. In addition to the traditional social sciences, qualitative data analysis software programs are now widely used by medical professionals (such as clinicians, nurses, and health researchers), marketing and consumer researchers, and many applied researchers with no particular discipline affiliation who simply want to manage or analyze a lot of textual data (Fielding & Lee, 2002). Many of the articles about qualitative data analysis software that have been published in the past decade have been written by members of these more recent groups of software users. (e.g., Dembrowski & Hanmer-Lloyd, 1995; Hinchliffe, Crang, Reiner, & Hudson, 1997; van Hoven & Poelman, 2003; Tak, Neid, & Becker, 1999).

Another way to think about trends in qualitative data analysis software usage is to note the change in attitudes toward software for qualitative analysis. Duchastel and Armony (1996, p. 274) have characterized four types of responses to the idea of using this software that have typically existed: *hostility* or *indifference*, which was expressed by those who either preferred their manual methods and/or thought computers were not appropriate for interpretive analyses; *naive enthusiasm*, or an uninformed acceptance of any program that does qualitative data analysis; a *utopian attitude*, which includes the idea that any analysis task can and likely will one day be performed by computers; and *pragmatism*, or a balanced and informed perception of how computers can aid analysis. Fielding and Lee (2002) are key promoters of this pragmatic attitude, and they suggest that formal instruction in qualitative software would significantly promote its spread: "the increasing acceptance of CAQDAS into the methodology curriculum will produce a new generation of academics with a clearer understanding of what CAQDAS is and is not" (p. 202). The growing presence of qualitative data analysis software in academic settings, as well as the spreading of its use to nonacademic fields, suggests that what used to be a climate with a good share of hostility and indifference toward the software has given way to a new, more accepting attitude about these programs. However, this growing acceptance of the capabilities of qualitative data analysis software is also occurring in a climate in which many users lack sufficient grounding in qualitative methods per se, and the heavy marketing of certain programs may mean that much of this earlier hostility and indifference to qualitative software has been replaced with inexperienced enthusiasm or utopianism, rather than the user self-reflection we noted earlier that would be more appropriate in approaching the use of such programs.

Perceptions of the Limitations and Benefits of Qualitative Data Analysis Software

Although the user base of qualitative data analysis programs has expanded significantly over the years, concerns over possible limitations of the software and its applications have been voiced often since its inception, and they continue to endure in the minds of many users and nonusers alike. Hesse-Biber (1995) summarizes many of these apprehensions with the metaphor of "Frankenstein's monster" (see also Lee & Fielding, 1991); many researchers have expressed fears that "while computers have the potential to revolutionize the field, there is also a possibility for things to run out of control" (p. 26). One concern is that using computerized analysis techniques removes the element of "craft" from the qualitative method, that the connection to the participants and their experiences or the creative aspect of the process is disrupted by the interference of computers (Hesse-Biber, 1995; Hinchliffe et al., 1997). Similarly, there is a concern that users of qualitative data analysis software become "distanced" from their data and that coded and retrieved segments of text can (especially in the use of some programs) easily be disconnected from their context (Hesse-Biber, 1995; Hinchliffe et al., 1997; Lee & Esterhuizen, 2000). Others feel that computers impose an inherently quantitative logic onto qualitative data, causing it at times to resemble survey research more than qualitative inquiry (Coffey et al., 1996; Hesse-Biber, 1995; Lee & Esterhuizen, 2000). The cataloguing of textual, audio, or visual information in computerized systems also brings up new issues of data protection and confidentiality, as different protocols need to be established to account for the changed avenues of accessibility to this personal information (Akeroyd, 1991; Hesse-Biber, 1995). Additionally, the issues of inadequate user training and accountability discussed earlier limit the potential for qualitative data analysis software to be used effectively and appropriately (Fielding & Lee, 2002; Miles & Weitzman, 1996). As discussed earlier in the chapter, the fear that using the software restricts the user to conducting research in certain ways is often expressed; as Hinchliffe and colleagues write:

> one worry is that as we continue to use the procedures contained in computer packages they will "police" our habits and the tendency will be to conform to certain patterns of ordering our research. The danger is that, as more and more of our research time is spent at the screen, the active forgetting of the processes with which we are engaging means that we might start to act as if we were "information processors," locked into essentialist versions of the world. (1997, p. 1117)

Some have also noted that those researchers who are particularly fond of using qualitative data analysis software can sometimes seem to present computer-assisted analysis as the only way of analyzing data. Their excitement over the benefits and possibilities that qualitative data analysis software provides can be perceived as a condemnation of other approaches. As one admitted "pusher" of the use of computers for data analysis suggests, "A mentor's enthusiasm and preference for microcomputer-assisted qualitative research [could] be misinterpreted as an attempt at religious conversion or a discommendation of more conventional, low technology/manual methods of data management" (Tallerico, 1991, p. 282). Adding to these concerns about unquestioning acceptance of computer-assisted analysis as the gold standard of analysis approaches, Froggatt (2001) emphasizes that time constraints may make using software impractical for some researchers, asserting that time needed to learn how to use a package must be weighed against the time saved by using it.

Although these and other misgivings about the possible limitations or harmful effects of qualitative data analysis software persist for some, just as many perceived benefits seem to balance the scale of attitudes about the software. All of the functions and features discussed earlier have been cited by some as benefits to using software instead of manual methods. To some, the use of a computer program to manage and organize data can actually prevent rather than cause distancing from the data. Being able to move more freely and efficiently through the data may allow the researcher to stay connected to portions of the data that otherwise may have been overlooked. As one user told Smith and Hesse-Biber (1996), "One of the nice things I like about more qualitative techniques, and HyperRESEARCH certainly fits into this category, is that it almost forces you to look at your data, to become really immersed in your data, to really get to know your data and have stuff come out of your data. . . . And that's valuable" (p. 427).

The ability to deal with large volumes of data is one of the most basic perceived benefits of qualitative data analysis software (although this can also be seen as a disadvantage, if it encourages researchers to amass more data than they are capable of analyzing) (Fielding & Lee, 1998). To the extent that it allows researchers to automate the more mechanical, less analytical tasks of the analysis process, qualitative data analysis software is seen by many as a way of dealing with the enormity of textual data that qualitative research generates. Tallerico (1991) suggests that this software can sometimes be a motivator to those researchers who feel intimidated by the complexity of the analysis process and that using it may "generate some degree of momentum (some sense of 'getting over the hump,' of launching oneself toward meaningful engagement with the data)" (p. 281). This would seem to be reflected in users' experience. As one user stated, "Because the coding is um so difficult and so time-consuming . . . to get the correct codes . . . I mean for me it was–it became a drudgery. And uh but once we got past that, entered it in, then we could, y'know, manipulate it . . . see what was going on, and then go back out into the field and, and it was fun . . . at that point (Smith & Hesse-Biber, 1996, p. 426).

Another possible strength of qualitative data analysis software is the level of transparency it provides; unlike many manual methods, computer-assisted data analysis offers an opportunity for the researcher's analysis process to be examined and checked for inconsistencies (Fielding & Lee, 1998; Kelle & Laurie, 1995). Put another way, the researcher leaves "a so-called audit trail that helps [one] to be aware of and reflexive about validity and reliability in [one's] analysis" (van Hoven & Poelman, 2003, pp. 117–118; see also Hesse-Biber, 1995). Another position in support of the software (and responsive to many of the limitations discussed earlier) relates to the importance of user responsibility and accountability. Although many programs do have the potential to be misused, this is not necessarily a limitation of the programs themselves. Morison and Moir (1998) effectively summarize this approach to thinking about the relative limitations and benefits of qualitative data analysis software:

> The fault lies not so much with the computer software as with the researcher who uses it inappropriately. The use of computer software to facilitate theory generation and testing does not replace the right brain's ability to make conceptual connections from data from social situations that appear at first to be quite different. Instead, by facilitating and greatly speeding up the clerical tasks associated with data handling, it can free up the researcher's time (Tesch 1990, 1991) to discover theory creatively and intuitively. (p. 109)

Future Directions for Qualitative Data Analysis Software: The Movement toward a Fourth Generation of Software?

Although is difficult to predict where qualitative data analysis software may be headed in the future, several issues that have received consistent attention in recent years will likely be addressed (and are already in the process of being addressed) in the development of new software and updated versions of existing programs. Many hope for some type of *standardization* of program commands, function names, and procedural protocols or for some move toward interprogram compatibility. This would not only assist users in understanding how software works (by reducing confusion associated with the tendency of each program to have a different name for the same technique) but could also allow users to optimize their analyses by using features from a number of programs simultaneously (Alexa & Zuell, 2000; Mangabeira, 1996). Several promising steps have already occurred in this regard. A computer program that allows for multimedia file formats such as HTML (hypertext markup language) or XML (extensible markup language) formats is desirable. Brown (2002) notes that these formatted languages

> have the advantage of agreed standards. . . . HTML text is currently the most practical way of representing qualitative data because the researcher can immediately convert an MS Word document into HTML. . . . XML editors will soon replace these with far more powerful options, but HTML documents should be quickly convertible, and therefore not become obsolete for some time to come. (paragraph 25)

XML (eXtensible Markup Language) holds the promise of providing a standard data format for qualitative data analysis. Carmichael (2002) notes that this format allows a universal template to mark up text through its external referencing of other multimedia data. XML language allows for the identification of content but does not determine how the data should be specifically organized. Carmichael notes:

> XML's "unencumbered" nature—with no superfluous application-specific formatting information—makes it ideal as a data exchange format. . . . The promise of XML for those involved in Qualitative Data Analysis is that, as in other areas of networked collaboration across the Internet, "raw" datasets, proprietary software . . . and other project-specific applications can coexist, linked by an underlying common data format. An extension of this functionality, aided by the publication of the "schemata" used to structure documents, would be the physical separation of the original datasets from analytical tools and analyses, as long as the underlying data formats are consistently applied, an XML-based CAQDAS application would, like applications in other fields, be able to run transparently across a network. (paragraph 13)

The movement toward digitized multimedia data may even foster the movement in this direction as digitized formats drive the demand among users for a standard data format whereby the researcher can transfer his or her files from one software program to another (Gibbs, Friese, & Mangabeira, 2002). Whether this will occur is uncertain, as the differing philosophies and individual commercial interests underlying many programs may limit collaborative efforts.

The rapid dissemination of digital technology—especially digitized video and audio—allows more ways in which data can be analyzed, expanding the variety of data collected and creating new ways to enhance our understanding of meaning through multimedia analysis. Some CAQDAS programs allow researchers to code images, digitized speech, and video. New data can be collected as well in terms of text Web pages, discussion lists, and so on. Using HTML and PDF formats facilitates this process by enabling the researcher to connect a wide array of multimedia research data (Gibbs et al., 2002). Brown (2002) suggests that a "digital convergence" will enhance the ability of researchers to work with a range of qualitative multimedia data–text, audio, video, and graphic files. Digitizing video, audio, and graphic files is now technologically feasible, and digitizing analog video is now within reach of many researchers, as the cost of this interchange equipment has drastically decreased. The new digital technology makes high-quality audio, video, and still images available for computerized analysis. This new technology is more portable, and the price of digital equipment is substantially decreasing. For example, digital camcorders are small enough to easily fit in the palm of the hand and make for a less obtrusive technology for qualitative research.

Some contend that the analysis of multimedia data is a particularly important future direction for qualitative data analysis software development (Gibbs, 2002; Hesse-Biber, 1995; Koch & Zumbach, 2002; Smith & Short, 2001). Not only does this free up time that the researcher might normally spend on the intermediate step of transcription (which is often overwhelmingly time-consuming), but it also may allow the researcher to code nonverbal behaviors and to engage more directly with images and sounds from the research site and/or participants' accounts of their experiences. The benefits of being able to conduct analyses of original audio or video data could be especially important when research participants are members of oppressed groups for whom language is a location of disempowerment (Charmaz, 1995). Multimedia allow a range of interpretations of the data, not just a linear interpretation.

Expanding the features of software programs that permit teams of researchers, both on site and off site, to work collectively on a given research project is also in need of further development. Miles and Weitzman (1996) note the paucity of programs that are configured for network usage, which precludes the possibility of more than one researcher working on a common database (p. 223). Few programs allow for the identification of which research team member coded what file and transferring work completed (coding schemes, coded text, and memos) on a given project from one team member to another (p. 223).

Software that effectively supports a mixed methods (both quantitative and qualitative) approach to research is also desired by many users (Miles & Weitzman, 1996). Programs may not only move toward allowing the analysis of both numeric and textual data of the same program, but they may also integrate features that facilitate translation of data from qualitative to quantitative form. Furthermore, this "quantified" data may be formatted in such a way as to be compatible with popular statistical analysis software. Such features and modifications could potentially further increase the disciplinary and paradigmatic diversity of qualitative data analysis software usership.

Additionally, many researchers feel that further integration of hypertext into qualitative analysis programs would greatly enhance a range of analysis techniques. The ability of hypertext to easily navigate through different types of data within an analysis project–from transcripts to specific codes to visual images–will serve to defy traditional linear ways of interacting with data and is suggested to be especially beneficial for those researchers with a postmodern or poststructural orientation (Coffey et al., 1996; Colon, Taylor, & Willis, 2000; Fielding & Lee, 1995; Lee & Esterhuizen, 2000; Weitzman & Miles, 1995). By taking advantage of a more multidimensional and complex linking of data and concepts, many researchers believe that their analyses may more closely mirror the intricate meanings embodied in the data they gather. As Coffey and colleagues (1996) note:

> Many people working with qualitative data, whether they use fieldnotes, interviews, oral history or documentary sources, feel frus-

trated by the necessity of imposing a single linear order on those materials. It is, after all, part of the rationale of ethnographic and similar approaches that the anthropologist, sociologist, historian, psychologist or whoever, recognizes the complexity of social inter-relatedness. We recognize the over-determination of culture, in that there are multiple, densely coded influences among and between different domains and institutions. It is, therefore, part of the attraction of hypertext solutions that a sense of dense interconnectedness is preserved, enhanced even, while linearity is discarded. (paragraph 8.5)

As qualitative data analysis programs continue to evolve, there is an increasing movement of programs toward theory construction and model building. These programs utilize *artificial intelligence*–knowledge-based expert systems. There is a great potential for programs to enhance the creativity of the research process. HyperRESEARCH's hypothesis tester allows for the development of "if . . . then" propositions or hypotheses. HyperRESEARCH supports the use of production rules similar to those typical of expert system software to help researchers discover and create relationships between coded text segments and to formulate and test hypotheses about these relationships. AQUAD (analysis of qualitative data) also has the capacity to formulate and test relationships in textual data (see Heise, 1991; Heise & Lewis, 1988; Hesse-Biber & DuPuis, 1995) is a software program that allows for "event structure analysis" that looks at the temporal ordering of recorded events and examines the logical temporal sequence of relationships between events based on causal accounts within data. Heise (1991) notes:

> Event structure analysis . . . materializes expert understandings about processes that might be impenetrable to the uninformed. Dealing with recorded incidents, an analyst defines events, defines logical relations among the events, and defines how each event enables and expands other events. The result is a grammar of action accounting for recorded incidents, and this model can be displayed graphically, employed for simulations, and compared with related grammars, for purposes of contrast of generalization. (p. 136)

Other expert systems have evolved to assist in the coding process. Some programs (such as the software program QUALRUS) already have functions such as "autocoding" of text documents, which includes ways to track, via artificial intelligence, the types of codes users have utilized and suggestions for coding of text based on prior coding schemas (Gibbs et al., 2002).

Some researchers look to artificial intelligence to truly move the field toward a "fourth generation" of computer development and envision the incorporation of expert systems to enable the researcher to perform the "human" tasks involved in the coding, especially that coding involved in conducting a content analysis (Gibbs et al., 2002). As Evans (2002) notes:

> Ultimately, we can expect a system that will monitor, process, and code texts and images with little human intervention. This system may be able to retrieve and manage great quantities of material and may actively identify opportunities for content analysis, devise and test content analytic hypotheses, and even learn as it does so. In other words, it is not feasible to begin working toward a kind of magic in content analysis. Furthermore, this magic is appropriate and even necessary if content analysts are to take full advantage of opportunities afforded by the emerging era of electronic databases and interactive media. (p. 78)

Whatever changes do occur in qualitative data analysis software in the coming years, it is likely that they will be greatly influenced by user feedback, just as has been the case since the field's inception. It is therefore important that the lines of communication between users and developers be strengthened in the future. The growing number of online user support groups and the development of online support by developers and electronic mailing lists for users of specific computer software programs is a ripe venue for the exchange of ideas between users and developers. Trends in the prevalence of qualitative data analysis software use in various disciplines and fields are also likely have a particularly strong impact on the directions in which program developers choose to take their work.

References

Akeroyd, A. V. (1991). Personal information and qualitative research data: Some practical and ethical problems arising from data protection legislation. In N. G. Fielding & R. M. Lee (Eds.), *Using computers in qualitative research*. London: Sage.

Alexa, M., & Zuell, C. (2000). Text analysis software: Commonalities, differences and limitations: The results of a review. *Quality and Quantity*, *34*, 295–391.

Brown, D. (2002, May). Going digital and staying qualitative: Some alternative strategies for digitizing the qualitative research process. *Forum Qualitative Sozialforschung/Forum: Qualitative Social Research*, *3*(2). Retrieved September 12, 2007, from *www.qualitative-research.net/fqs-texte/2-02/2-02brown-e.htm*

Burawoy, M. (1991). *Ethnography unbound: Power and resistance in the modern metropolis*. Berkeley: University of California Press.

CAQDAS Networking Project. (2003). *Computer Assisted Qualitative Data Analysis*. Retrieved September 12, 2007, from *caqdas.soc.surrey.ac.uk*

Carmichael, P. (2002, May). Extensible markup language and qualitative data analysis. *Forum: Qualitative Social Research*, *3*(2). Retrieved September 12, 2007, from *www.qualitative-research.net/fqs-texte/2-02/2-02carmichael-e.htm*

Charmaz, K. (1995). Grounded theory. In J. A. Smith, R. Harre, & L. V. Langenhove (Eds.), *Rethinking methods in psychology*. London: Sage.

Coffey, A., & Atkinson, P. (1996). *Making sense of qualitative data: Complementary research strategies*. Thousand Oaks, CA: Sage.

Coffey, A., Holbrook, B., & Atkinson, P. (1996). Qualitative data analysis: Technologies and representations. *Sociological Research Online*, *1*(1). Retrieved September 12, 2007, from *www.socresonline.org. uk/1/1/4.html*

Colon, B., Taylor, K. A., & Willis, J. (2000). Constructivist instructional design: Creating a multimedia package for teaching critical qualitative research. *Forum: Qualitative Social Research*, *5*(1/2). Retrieved September 12, 2007, from *www.nova.edu/ssss/QR/QR5-1/colon.html*

Creswell, J. W., & Maietta, R. C. (2003). Qualitative research. In D. C. Miller & N. J. Salkind (Eds.), *Handbook of research design and social measurement*. Thousand Oaks, CA: Sage.

Dembrowski, S., & Hanmer-Lloyd, S. (1995). Computer applications: A new road to qualitative data analysis? *European Journal of Marketing*, *29*(11), 50–62.

Dey, I. (1999). *Grounding grounded theory: Guidelines for qualitative inquiry*. San Diego, CA: Academic Press.

Duchastel, J., & Armony, V. (1996). Textual analysis in Canada: An interdisciplinary approach to qualitative data. *Current Sociology*, *44*(3), 259–278.

Evans, W. (2002). Computer environments for content analysis: Reconceptualizing the roles of humans and computers. In O. V. Burton (Ed.), *Computing in the social sciences and humanities* (pp. 67–83). Urbana: University of Illinois Press.

Fielding, N. G., & Lee, R. M. (1995, May). The hypertext facility in qualitative analysis software. *ESRC Data Archive Bulletin*, *59*.

Fielding, N. G., & Lee, R. M. (1996). Diffusion of a methodological innovation: CAQDAS in the UK. *Current Sociology*, *44*(3), 242–258.

Fielding, N. G., & Lee, R. M. (1998). *Computer analysis and qualitative research*. Thousand Oaks, CA: Sage.

Fielding, N. G., & Lee, R. M. (2002). New patterns in the adoption and use of qualitative software. *Field Methods*, *14*(2), 197–216.

Froggatt, K. A. (2001). Using computers in the analysis of qualitative data. *Palliative Medicine*, *15*, 517–520.

Gibbs, G. (2002). *Qualitative data analysis: Explorations with Nvivo*. Milton Keynes, UK: Open University Press.

Gibbs, G., Friese, S., & Mangabeira, W. C. (2002). The use of new technology in qualitative research. *Forum: Qualitative Social Research*, *3*(2). Retrieved September 12, 2007, from *www.qualitative-research.net/fqs/fqs-e/inhalt2-02-e.htm*

Glaser, B. G., & Strauss, A. (1967). *The discovery of grounded theory: Strategies for qualitative research*. Chicago: Aldine.

Heise, D. (1991). Event structure analysis: A qualitative model of quantitative research. In N. Fielding & R. Lee (Eds.), *Using computers in qualitative research* (pp. 136–163). London: Sage.

Heise, D., & Lewis, E. (1988). *Introduction to ETHNO*. Raleigh, NC: National Collegiate Software Clearinghouse.

Hesse-Biber, S. (1995). Unleashing Frankenstein's monster? The use of computers in qualitative research. *Studies in Quantitative Methodology*, *5*, 25–41.

Hesse-Biber, S., & Dupuis, P. (1995). Hypothesis testing in computer-aided qualitative data analysis. In U. Kelle (Ed.), *Computer-aided qualitative data analysis*. Newbury Park, CA: Sage.

Hinchliffe, S. J., Crang, M. A., Reiner, S. M., & Hudson, A. C. (1997). Software for qualitative research: 2. Some thoughts on "aiding" analysis." *Environment and Planning*, *29*, 1109–1124.

Kelle, U. (Ed.). (1995). *Computer-aided qualitative analysis*. London: Sage.

Kelle, U. (1996a). Computer-aided qualitative data analysis: An overview. In C. Zuell, J. Harkness, & J. H. P. Hoffmeyer-Zlotnik (Eds.), *Text analysis and computers*. Mannheim, Germany: ZUMA.

Kelle, U. (1996b). Computer-assisted qualitative data analysis in Germany. *Current Sociology, 44*(3), 225–241.

Kelle, U. (1997). Theory building in qualitative research and computer programs for the management of textual data. *Sociological Research Online, 2*(2). Retrieved September 12, 2007, from *www.socresonline.org. uk/socresonline/2/2/1.html*

Kelle, U., & Laurie, H. (1995). Computer use in qualitative research and issues of validity. In U. Kelle (Ed.), *Computer-aided qualitative analysis*. London: Sage.

Koch, S., & Zumbach, J. (2002). The use of video analysis software in behavior observation research: Interaction patterns in task-oriented small groups. *Forum: Qualitative Social Research, 3*(2). Retrieved September 12, 2007, from *www.qualitative-research.net/fqs/fqs-e/inhalt2-02-e.htm*

Lee, R. M., & Esterhuizen, L. (2000). Computer software and qualitative analysis: Trends, issues and resources. *International Journal of Social Research Methodology, 3*(3), 231–243.

Lee, R. M., & Fielding, N. G. (1991). Computing for qualitative research: Options, problems and potential. In N. G. Fielding & R. M. Lee (Eds.), *Using computers in qualitative research* (pp. 1–13). Newbury Park, CA: Sage.

Lee, R. M., & Fielding, N. G. (1996). A comment on Coffey, Holbrook and Atkinson. *Sociological Research Online, 1*(4). Retrieved September 12, 2007, from *www.socresonline.org.uk/1/4/lf.html*

Lonkila, M. (1995). Grounded theory as an emerging paradigm for computer-assisted qualitative data analysis. In U. Kelle (Ed.), *Computer-aided qualitative data analysis: Theory, method and practice*. London: Sage.

Mangabeira, W. (1995a). Computer assistance, qualitative analysis and model building. In R. M. Lee (Ed.), *Information technology for the social scientist*. London: UCL Press.

Mangabeira, W. (1995b). Qualitative analysis and microcomputer software: Some reflections on a new trend in sociological research. In R. G. Burgess (Ed.), *Studies in qualitative methodology: Volume 5. Computing and qualitative research*. Greenwich, CT: JAI Press.

Mangabeira, W. (1996). CAQDAS and its diffusion across four countries: National specificities and common themes. *Current Sociology, 44*(3), 191–205.

Miles, M. B., & Weitzman, E. A. (1996). The state of qualitative Data analysis software: What do we need? *Current Sociology, 44*(3), 206–224.

Mizrach, S. (1999). *Using computers in qualitative research*. Retrieved September 12, 2007, from *www.fiu.edu/~mizrachs/comp-in-qual-research.html*

Morison, M., & Moir, J. (1998). The role of computer software in the analysis of qualitative data: Efficient clerk, research assistant or Trojan horse? *Journal of Advanced Nursing, 28*(1), 106–116.

Muhr, T. (1991). ATLAS/ti: A prototype for the support of text interpretation. *Qualitative Sociology, 14*(4), 349–371.

Pfaffenberger, B. (1988). *Microcomputer applications in qualitative research*. Newbury Park, CA: Sage.

Richards, T. J., & Richards, L. (1991). The NUD.IST qualitative data analysis system. *Qualitative Sociology, 14*(4), 307–324.

Seidel, J. V., & Clark, J. A. (1984). The ethnograph: A computer program for the analysis of qualitative data. *Qualitative Sociology, 7*(1–2), 110–125.

Smith, B. A., & Hesse-Biber, S. (1996). Users' experiences with qualitative data analysis software. *Social Science Computer Review, 14*(4), 423–432.

Smith, C., & Short, P. (2001). Integrating technology to improve the efficiency of qualitative data analysis: A note on methods. *Qualitative Sociology, 24*(3), 401–407.

Stone, P. J., Dunphy, D. C., Smith, M. S., & Ogilvie, D. M. (1966). *The general inquirer: A computer approach to content analysis*. Cambridge, MA: MIT Press.

Strauss, A., & Corbin, J. (1994). Grounded theory methodology: An overview. In N. K. Denzin & Y. S. Lincoln (Eds.), *Handbook of qualitative research*. Thousand Oaks, CA: Sage.

Tak, S. H., Neid, M., & Becker, H. (1999). Use of a computer software program for qualitative analysis: Part I. Introduction to NUD.IST. *Western Journal of Nursing Research, 21*(1), 111–117.

Tallerico, M. (1991). Applications of qualitative analysis software: A view from the field. *Qualitative Sociology, 14*(3), 275–285.

Taylor, S. J., & Bogdan, R. (1998). *Introduction to qualitative methods: A guidebook and resource* (3rd ed.). New York: Wiley.

Tesch, R. (1990). *Qualitative research: Analysis types and software tools*. New York: Falmer.

van Hoven, B., & Poelman, A. (2003). Using computers for qualitative data analysis: An example using NUD.IST. *Journal of Geography in Higher Education, 27*(1), 113–120.

Weitzman, E. A., & Miles, M. B. (1995). *Computer programs for qualitative data analysis*. Thousand Oaks, CA: Sage.

CHAPTER 32

The Role of Computer-Assisted Qualitative Data Analysis

Impact on Emergent Methods in Qualitative Research

Nigel Fielding

It can be somewhat of a shock for those who have been involved with an innovation when the innovation does not just become mainstream but begins to evolve. We might think with some sympathy about the feelings of the developers of the biplane when the monoplane came along, or those of the engineers busily refining the propellor engine when jets suddenly appeared over European skies in the late stages of World War II. For many researchers and methodologists, computer-assisted qualitative data analysis (CAQDAS) is not yet even mainstream, but those involved in its development can now look back on 20 or so years' experience, and change is fast in the computing world. Standard typologies already list several distinct generations of qualitative software, and new possibilities are arising from the capacities of what is now a mature field of social science computing, whereas others are arising from new computational resources that are just beginning to be applied to qualitative research.

To see where we are going, we have to know where we have been. The task of this chapter is therefore to provide an account of qualitative software and what it can currently do as a basis from which to then profile the new, incoming, and over-the-horizon possibilities being opened up. I begin with a discussion of the emergence of qualitative software and then review the different types of qualitative software and the kinds of work that researchers can do with them. I then look at an emergent technique that has lately arisen from capacities that have been associated with CAQDAS for some time but have been underexploited–namely, methodological integration, the interrelation of qualitative and quantitative dimensions of social phenomena in the pursuit of fuller and more valid analyses. Finally, I profile some new emergent techniques that can be glimpsed at their formative stage. These techniques relate to new developments in grid computing and high-performance computing (HPC).

Qualitative Software Emerges

The social sciences have long had an engagement with computing. One of the very first computer applications was the formal analysis of textual databases in the fields of political science, linguistics, and sociolinguistics. However, the mode of analysis was quantitative, as delineated by one of the field's principal authorities, who wrote that such work pursues "objective, systematic and quantitative description of the manifest content of communication" (Berelson, 1952, p. 489). Computer power made much less laborious the management of the large bodies of text associated with such work, and early computer programs were suited to performing the relatively small repertoire of rule-based analytical routines that were involved. Text units were treated as variables, and the principal objective was the production of organized lists of words and phrases ("concordances") showing, for example, how frequently particular pairs of words (e.g., *emergent* and *methods*) co-occurred. Content analysts also required tools with which to rapidly access the context around given words or text segments, termed *KWIC* searches, for *key words in context*. The treatment of terms as variables, and the other routines noted, made for a form of analysis that was statistical and that struck a certain posture on the nature of social science data, a point signaled by Berelson's mention of "manifest content" (not latent or hidden content but surface content) in the preceding quote. Thus, although one mark of qualitative data analysis is that it has customarily focused on text, traditional content analysis had little else in common with qualitative data analysis. The computer programs written to support it did not support qualitative data analysis, although when CAQDAS packages emerged, many contained the simpler kinds of content analysis tools, used primarily to get a first sense of the data.

Before 1960	Manual methods
1961–1965	Mainframe programs for the content analysis of textual data
1966–1970	Statistical program libraries Batch, integrated language-oriented statistical systems
1971–1975	Interactive mainframe statistical systems
1976–1980	Microcomputer statistical programs with limited capabilities
1981–1985	Rudimentary mainframe CAQDAS programs Microcomputer CAQDAS programs for descriptive–interpretive research Fully featured microcomputer statistical programs
1986–1990	Microcomputer CAQDAS programs for theory building
1991–1995	Microcomputer CAQDAS programs with support for direct coding and manipulation of audio and audiovisual files
1996–2000	Microcomputer CAQDAS programs with support for operating other programs within the CAQDAS program
2001–2005	XML/HTML applications for qualitative analysis over networks

FIGURE 32.1. Historical development of social science data analysis software. Data for pre-1990 material from Brent and Anderson (1990) and Tesch (1990).

During the 1980s computer programmers and social scientists in several countries, chiefly Australia, Germany, and the United States, began independently to work on developing software tailored to support qualitative data analysis, particularly the approach to it associated with grounded theory (Glaser & Strauss, 1967). A timeline of social science computing developments in this field is given in Figure 32.1.

In the years between the early development of content analysis programs such as the General Inquirer and the emergence of CAQDAS, important changes had happened both in technology and social science. In technology, the audiocassette recorder had emerged, enabling researchers to cheaply and unobtrusively capture the exact words of respondents, a substantial boost to interview-based research (Lee, 2004) and one that played to the increasing familiarity of interview methods to the populations of advanced industrial democracies in what some commentators called the "interview society" (Gubrium & Holstein, 2001). While a boon to data collection, this development was a challenge for data management and data analysis, as there was no longer any technological restriction on the number or length of interviews that could be conducted. An even more important technological development was the emergence of desktop computers and accessible operating systems to run them, making everyday computing available to a far wider range of users than were involved with mainframe computers.

In social science, a key development was the revival and gradual restoration to legitimacy of qualitative research methods, beginning in the late 1960s. Glaser and Strauss (1967) actually wrote their seminal text in the conviction, plausible at the time, that if something were not done, qualitative methods would literally disappear from the curriculum and the social science tool kit under the weight of assault on such methods from a social science establishment that firmly believed that its claim to scientific status could be secured only on the basis that it used quantitative data and statistical analysis to create testable hypotheses with which to model social behavior. Institutional changes, such as the founding of new social science departments during a period of expansion in higher education, and external changes, such as the rise of a counterculture from opposition to segregation, apartheid, and the Vietnam War, influenced the discipline, too, bringing new critical perspectives that associated quantitative methods and positivist heuristics with the "machine science" that fed an increasingly unpopular political establishment (Fielding, 2004).

A space was thus reopened for qualitative methodology that had nearly been lost, and during the 1970s and 1980s new intellectual currents from feminism, libertarian Marxism, and postmodernism helped extend the toehold that qualitative methodology had gained. To more than one generation of students, qualitative methods, with their accessibility and flexibility, seemed somehow more "democratic" and naturally allied with the underdog and the unrepresented than did quantitative methods.

In short, the period was one of change and new thinking in both the computing world and the social sciences. The productive coincidence of new computing resources and a critical mass of qualitative researchers keen to secure the position of qualitative research in social science (Agar, 1991) provided the context in which the earliest CAQDAS programs, such as The Ethnograph and NUD*IST, came into being. A mark of this field has always been the close involvement of social scientists as developers, either working in tandem with programmers in long-standing collaborations or writing the software themselves. Nearly all early CAQDAS emerged in noncommercial environments, and although commercial considerations do now apply, this is a field of computing in which developers are especially close to users, and one in which developers also interact closely with other developers. It is also a field in which there is long established and useful freeware available, and increasingly one in which there are open-source applications.

Thus, computers came to have a significant part to play in qualitative research. A key publication by Weitzman and Miles (1995), the sourcebook for many in their first encounters with evaluating, choosing, and using qualitative software (but unfortunately now obsolete in its reviews of specific programs), demonstrated how computers were routinely used in each stage of qualitative research projects, from research design through data collection and data analysis to presentation of findings. Although much early effort was devoted to the refinement of the basic procedures of data management, code assignment, annotation of extracts or codes, and the search-and-retrieval process of data analysis, another contribution of CAQDAS is less obvious. It is not simply that qualitative software supports the key stages of qualitative projects but that it does so in ways that are transparent and self-documenting, creating an "audit trail" that allows researchers and their audiences to trace how given findings have been derived and conclusions have been drawn. This speaks to one of the principal criticisms raised against qualitative methods—that the analytical process takes place "in the researcher's head" and is thus nonreviewable, intuitive, and unsystematic. Whatever the truth of that criticism, the audit trail features of qualitative software help researchers rebut it in respect to their particular projects.

Many data management tasks are repetitive and tedious, and these conditions make for error. The support that CAQDAS provides for formatting, segmenting, and marshaling data into meaningful units ready for analysis helps here. Computers do the same thing the same way every time, and, once the data are in, they do not let the user forget that they are there, a stimulus to more thorough analysis and an antidote to the temptation to focus on the most vivid data. CAQDAS also addresses other major bottlenecks, such as transcription. For example, the HyperTRANSCRIBE tool produced by the developers of the HyperRESEARCH qualitative software package transcribes both digital audio and video and podcasts (HyperTRANSCRIBE is a "stand-alone" product and can be used independently of qualitative software). A number of CAQDAS packages can handle video data, in some cases offering the full suite of tools developed to manage and analyze conventional text. Such multimedia capacities reflect the increasing orientation of social science to nontextual data and multiple forms of representation. For many, qualitative software's data management capacities are the principal attraction, and there is evidence that some of the more sophisticated analytical features are underused (Fielding & Lee, 1998), although research on user experiences is limited and the pattern may be changing. Moreover, most users will make use of the essentials of the code-and-retrieve data analysis routines, Boolean retrievals (discussed later) are offered by all current qualitative software, and there is now robust support for more sophisticated analytical operations, including graphical tools for idea mapping, procedures and tools to handle quantitative data and even to operate other software directly within the qualitative program, and features to handle nontextual data, such as still or moving images and/or sound. Not every feature is available in every package, and not every user or project will require the same features and tools, so informed choice is crucial. To some of these variations we now turn.

Types of Qualitative Software

Classification into types is an essential element of qualitative research, so it is unsurprising that, when CAQDAS first emerged, typologies soon followed. In the first such typology, Tesch (1990) established the important principle that, in answering the question What is the best package?, the prospective user needed to be clear about what kind of analytical work he or she wanted to do, both in his or her current project and in the future. Consequently, Tesch organized her typology on the basis of different kinds of analytical work. It is here that we can apply the English saying that one "chooses horses for courses." As well as one's own patterns of use, the competencies and degree of engagement with information technology that one has are factors. We would not expect a sensible answer to the question What is the best car? without qualification: Is the car needed for off-road use? Commuting? As a status symbol? So it is with qualitative software.

The process of choice begins by learning what is available. The best-known typology is Weitzman and Miles's (1995) straightforward three basic types, named for the analytical work that characterizes them: text retrievers, code-and-retrieve packages, and theory-building software. The distinctions are elaborated in what follows, after noting that Kelle (1997) argues that the typology represents successive generations and that Mangabeira (1995) makes an important qualification by arguing that the distinctive feature of third-generation software is that it supports the building of models. Although the Weitzman and Miles typology remains broadly valid, with most of the more popular packages reviewed there still available (in updated versions), it is important to note that recently there has been a considerable convergence of features. Developers have learned better what users want and have also learned what other developers are providing. There are several instances of features that were formerly distinctive of a particular package later turning up in others.

I now look at Weitzman and Miles's (1995) typology in more detail. "Text retrievers" are most similar to the content analysis programs mentioned earlier. They chiefly support the recovery of data using keywords in the data that the user selects. Thus a search for the word *emergence* will retrieve every instance in which it appears in the chosen text. Users can also retrieve strings of characters that are not words, search only in a subset or across all files, or search for things that sound alike or have equivalent meanings. The ability to search for strings that mix characters and numbers can be useful for searching within bureaucratic documents such as social security card unique identifiers. Users can also link analytical memos to the segmented data, to the code terms, or to the beginning of each case (e.g., to the header of an interview transcript). Like content analysis software, text retrievers retrieve basic data very quickly and can handle very large documents, but their functionality is somewhat limited.

With "code-and-retrieve" packages, one gets into the core ground of qualitative software. Recall that CAQDAS developers aimed particularly to support the grounded theory approach to qualitative data analysis, the essence of which is the generation of a thematic analysis based on assigning codes that express aspects of the themes to data derived from field notes, interviews, documents, and, indeed, any other source of information. Code-and-retrieve packages thus provide particular support for dividing texts into segments, attaching code terms to the segments and then retrieving segments by code. Retrievals can also employ combinations of more than one code. Users can perform retrievals based on particular respondents, and they can construct searches based on how codes relate to each other, for example, where data assigned the code "emergent methods" coincides with data assigned the code "resistance to change." Users can include, in their code set, classifications relating to universally applicable information that has been collected for all respondents, such as sociodemographic variables such as age, sex, and marital status or organizational information such as number of days' stay in the hospital in a sample of surgical patients. Retrievals can then be made on combinations of conceptually based codes and sociodemographic or organizational features, such as length of stay by all patients under age 40 who had expressed the attitude "fatalistic resignation" in their interview compared with lengths of stay by patients under age 40 who had expressed the attitude "cheerful confidence." Complex searches using the basic Boolean operators AND, OR, NOT, and XOR can be performed, such as a search to recover only data in which two characteristics apply but not a third, for example, data from MALE respondents who were RELEASED ON THE DAY OF SURGERY who are NOT married. Proximity operators such as NEAR and CO-OCCUR are also usually provided.

As software has become more sophisticated, the differences between code-and-retrieve software and theory-building software have become less distinct. While providing good code-and-retrieve capacities, theory-building software also provides support for users to create higher order, more abstract classification schemes, semantically oriented typologies, and ways of representing data other than those derived in the coding process, such as tools with which users can formulate a proposition and test its application to the data using hypothesis-testing features. Theory-building software also offers graphical features that enable users to visually represent the relationships between different codes. The code names or any other object within the worked project, such as analytical memos or header file information, is displayed as a node, and users can then link them to other nodes and assign values (numerical scales indicating strength of association), or relationship types, to the links (such as "leads to," "is a kind of," "causes," and so on). In the case of some packages, such as MAXqda, the link is simply a visual representation, their function being confined to symbolizing relationships in the map in which they are displayed. In packages such as Qualrus, N.Vivo7, and ATLAS.ti, the links are functional. Coded data can be retrieved based on the links between them. In ATLAS.ti, the data associated with an expressed relationship can instantly be inspected to check the applicability of the relationship the user is considering (see Figure 32.2). In N.Vivo7, relationship nodes give an alternative way to link categories. Here the linking is based on coding, and the relationship itself acts as a code. Again, there is a benefit to users in being able to keep track of the evidence for the relationships (see Figure 32.3).

Some theory builders go further by employing artificial intelligence system features. For instance, the user of Qualrus can design a set of criteria that must be satisfied for a code to apply to a given extract, and if the criteria are not satisfied the program will prompt the user that he or she has violated the rule he or she has set. The software will suggest codes to the researcher based on a number of computational strategies, one of which reflects the theory of constant comparison. On selecting a text segment for coding, the researcher is reminded of the codes applied to the previous coded segment to assess whether the segment is also relevant to those codes (see Figure 32.4). The researcher remains in control of which codes are applied. Other software offers "system closure," whereby the results of every analytical query are "banked" and added to the dataset or the composition of a complex retrieval is retained so it can be repeated as new data are added. Automated coding based on the previous retrieval can then be performed each time the dataset is changed.

One of the few CAQDAS packages developed for Apple Macs as well as PCs, HyperResearch, provides a hypothesis test feature that enables users to test a hypothetical relationship between the occurrence of one entity in the data and the occurrence of another, formally IF "this," THEN "that," the basic form of inference and integral to causal modeling. The function is iterative: When co-occurrence is found, this can be used as an element of another hypothetical relationship. The IF/THEN rules are constituted from the codes assigned to the data. A rule can take the form "For a given case, IF code A is present AND code B is present AND code C is present THEN ADD code

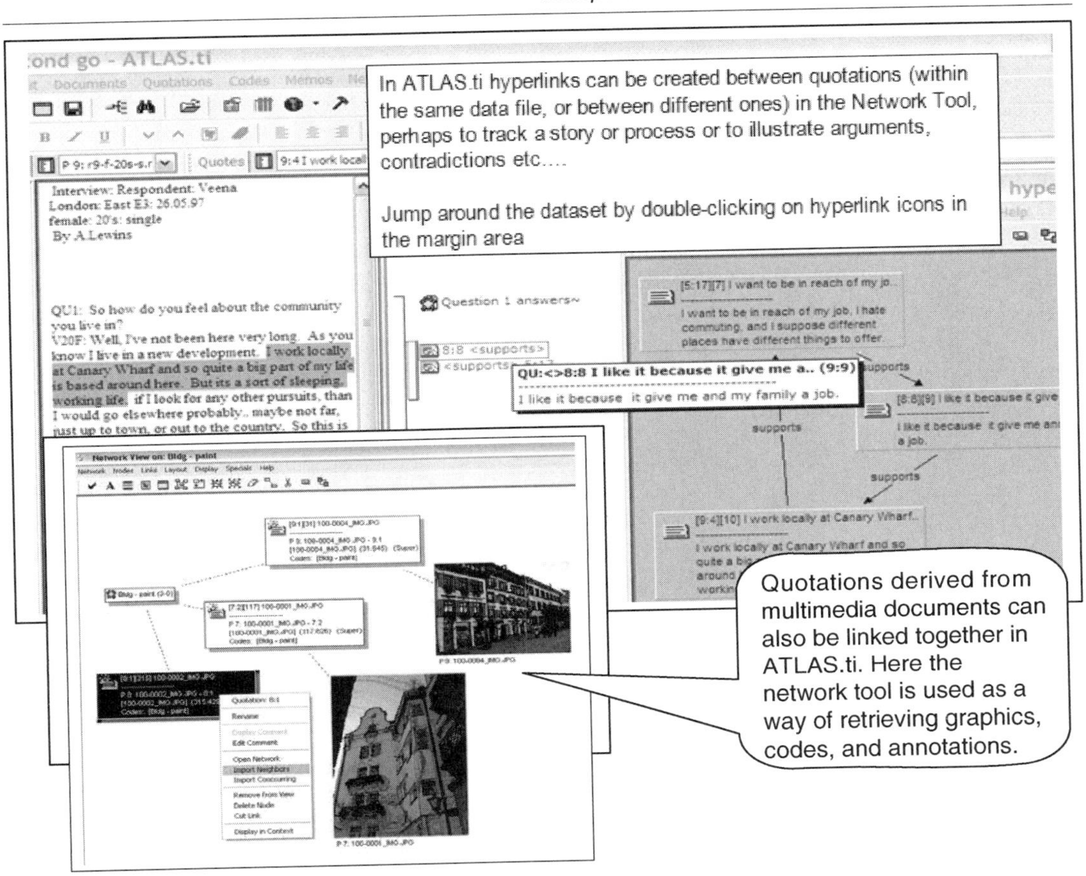

FIGURE 32.2. Hyperlinking in ATLAS.ti version 5. From Lewins and Silver (2006). Copyright 2006 by Sage Publications. Reprinted by permission.

D." To construct a testable hypothesis, the user may need several IF/THEN rules. The tool searches for instances in the data in which the code words appear in the combinations required by the proposition. When they do, the case supports that proposition. As with other theory-building features, the user's attention is primarily on work with the coding scheme rather than work with the data. One response to this is to perform what Hesse-Biber, Dupuis, and Kinder (1991) call "directional" coding rather than "coding for content." To simply use a term such as *self-image* as code does not help when it comes to hypothesis testing. To signal direction, one needs two codes, *positive self-image* and *negative self-image*.

Thus, the user has to have the hypothesis-testing objective in mind during coding and, indeed, has to look ahead, perhaps more than is usual, to the likely analysis. Moreover, a decision needs to be made on how many cases in accord with a hypothesis are needed to be certain of an inference, implicitly moving the qualitative analysis in the direction of a quantitative analysis. Such features therefore tend toward a hybrid methodology. This approach is clearly attractive when causal explanation, modeling, and prediction are the objectives, but it just as clearly relies on particular practical and epistemological assumptions. As well as being satisfied that the data have been coded in a consistent way throughout the coding pro-

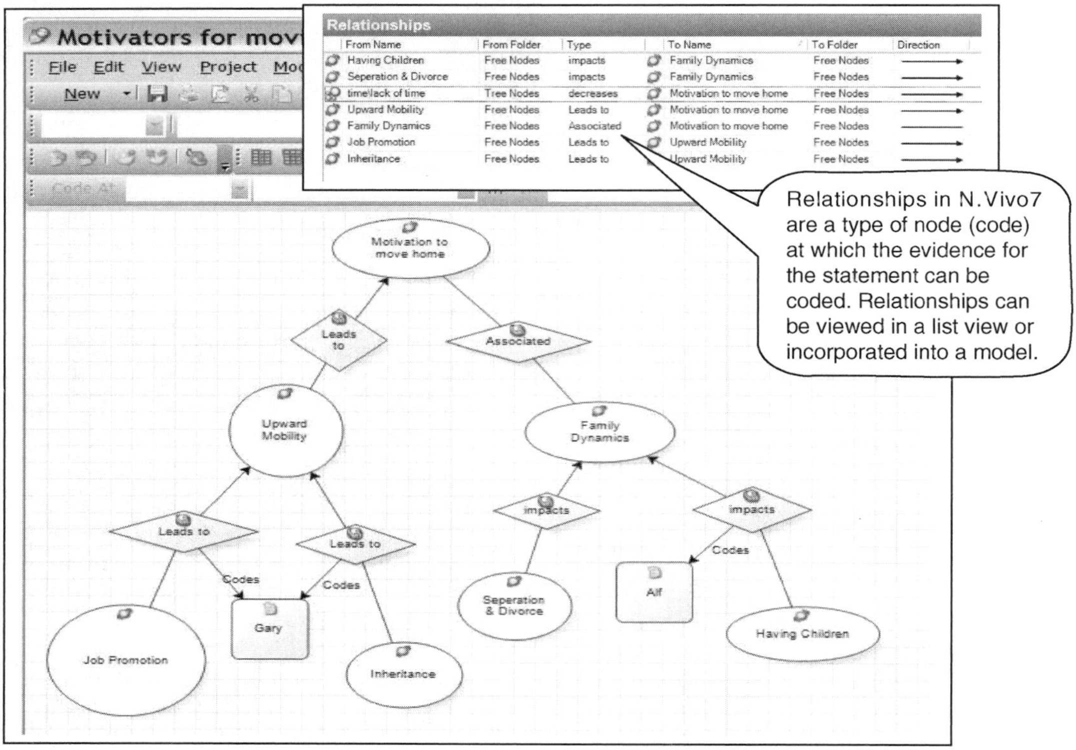

FIGURE 32.3. Code relationships in a N.Vivo7 model. From Lewins and Silver (2006). Copyright 2006 by Sage Publications. Reprinted by permission.

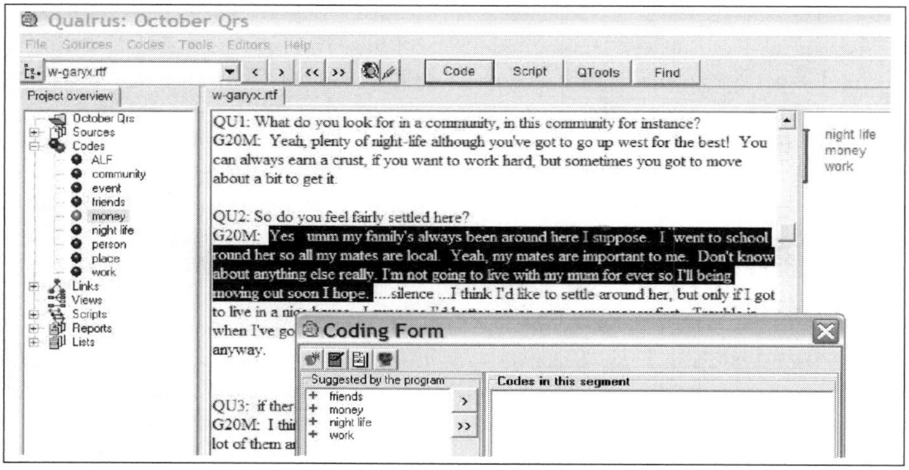

FIGURE 32.4. Code prompting in Qualrus. From Lewins and Silver (2006). Copyright 2006 by Sage Publications. Reprinted by permission.

cess, with the same code being applied to equivalent data on each occasion of coding so the data in different parts of the data set are genuinely comparable, users must also hold an epistemological perspective that regards qualitative data as reliable, valid, and a secure base for generalization. The grounded theory practice of writing detailed "code definitions" as analytical memos can be an effective way to ensure consistency of coding, and, as mentioned, some packages have features to check adherence to the definition whereas all packages provide the next best thing, annotation tools that can offer the definition for inspection by the researcher during code assignment or when codes are revisited. As noted earlier, a way of thinking about the difference between code-and-retrieve software and theory-building software is that the former concentrates analytically on the relationships between codes and data and the latter on the relationships between codes.

Summing up, CAQDAS packages provide tools to organize, manage, explore, interrelate, and interpret qualitative data. In light of recurrent misperceptions that qualitative software can "do the analysis for you" or even "take over your project," it is worth emphasizing that the user decides what tools to use out of those the package provides and the order in which to use them. The user decides what constitutes a segment (and, indeed, whether to analyze at case level or use codes), the user decides on and defines the codes to apply, the user has to think of what retrievals to perform, and the user has to decide whether the results are analytically significant. Qualitative software can do a great deal, as Figure 32.5 indicates, but the figure also shows that users have many choices to make. Sources that provide a detailed account of the features of a wide range of CAQDAS packages (e.g., Lewins & Silver, 2006), rather than confining them to a single package, give particularly valuable assistance in making these choices.

The word *analysis* in the term *computer-assisted qualitative data analysis software* could be regarded as somewhat of a misnomer in that these software packages function, and are primarily used, as project management tools. They provide an electronic filing cabinet and offer users flexibility in handling their data and ways of integrating the different kinds of data available in projects. The "audit trails" mentioned earlier make the user's work more accountable because they can be used to show how a given finding or interpretation was produced. Moreover, this facility helps users to monitor their own work, giving insight, for example, into how a puzzling or suspect interpretation was arrived at.

Many features of qualitative software provide generic support that is functional regardless of the researcher's analytical approach. This is important to note because it is sometimes suggested that CAQDAS is primarily aimed at "code-based" analysis, a perception engendered by developers' early emphasis on how their software supported grounded theory research. Although grounded theory and other code-based techniques probably account for the largest proportion of contemporary qualitative analyses, they are certainly neither the only approach to qualitative work nor the only approach that can be supported by software, as I discuss next.

Case-Based Qualitative Research

Although code-based analysis predominates in contemporary qualitative research and is the basis of most of the analytical approaches discussed previously, it is entirely possible to use qualitative software to support case study research and case-based reasoning. Indeed, the moves toward methodological convergence based on qualitative software, discussed in the next section, involve case-based reasoning. Before moving to this point I should note that there is specialist software to support one principal form of case-based analysis, Ragin's (1987) Qualitative Comparative Analysis (QCA).

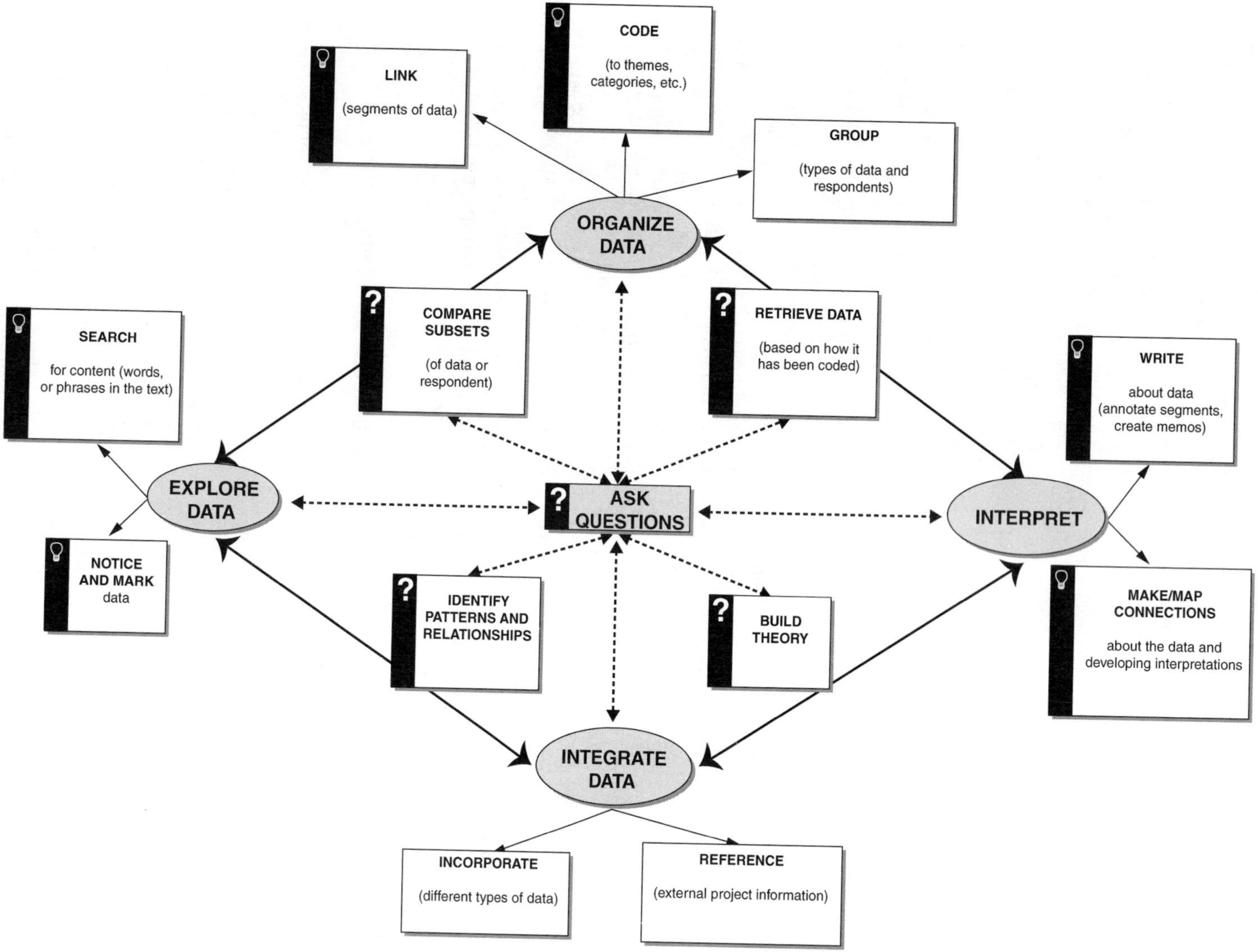

FIGURE 32.5. The affordances of qualitative software. From Lewins and Silver (2006). Copyright 2006 by Sage Publications. Reprinted by permission.

QCA is based on the Boolean algebra mentioned earlier, the algebra of sets and logic. QCA pursues patterns of causation in small to moderate numbers of cases. The technique involves analysis of the configuration of possible causal elements associated with the presence or absence of the outcome whose causes one wishes to determine. Focusing on configurations allows for the possibility that different combinations of conditions can produce the same outcome and accommodates contradictory patterns of causation, in which a given condition combined with certain variables may produce a positive outcome but produce a negative one when combined with others. The technique also allows one to eliminate irrelevant causes.

The process is one of Boolean minimization. The researcher produces a "truth table" that lists the various combinations of variables that appear in a dataset. Each case, listed as the rows of a truth table, might be an interviewee. Each variable might be an attribute or an attitude that was or was not associated with the interviewee. Computer programs such as Ragin's own QCA and fsQCA (fuzzy set) programs or the CAQDAS package AQUAD systematically compare each configuration in the truth table with all the others in order to remove ineffective configurations. When two rows differ on only one causal condition but eventuate in the same outcome, the condition that differs between the rows can be considered ineffective and can be removed, creating a simpler combination of causal conditions (see Table 32.1).

In considering configurations in Table 32.1, imagine that you had two cases. Uppercase letters in the following show the presence of a condition, lower case its absence. The dot between the terms signifies an AND relation.

Case 1: DEBT • DIVORCE• CHILDREN LEAVE HOME • job relocation = MOVE

Case 2: DEBT • divorce • CHILDREN LEAVE HOME • job relocation = MOVE

In case 1, a house move occurs when debt is present, a divorce has occurred, and the children leave home but employment continues as before. In case 2, a house move occurs with debt present and when children leave home, but no divorce and no job change have occurred. The house move happens in one case in which there has been divorce but not in the other. One can thus infer that divorce is not necessary for a house move to occur. The two configurations can thus be combined by excluding divorce, yielding

DEBT • CHILDREN LEAVE HOME • job relocation = MOVE

House moves, in these two cases, occur in the presence of debt and children leaving home and the absence of a job change. The result of the simplifications of conditions is a Boolean expression that contains only the logically essential "prime implicants." As a systematic approach to the formal analysis of case study data, QCA has much to recommend it. QCA can be used with smaller data sets than are needed for multivariate statisti-

TABLE 32.1. A QCA Truth Table

Case	Debt	Divorce	Children leave home	Job relocation	House move
A	0	0	1	1	1
B	1	0	1	0	0
C	0	1	1	1	0
. . .					
n	1	0	0	1	1

cal analysis, and it makes no assumptions about the nature of the variables and views causation as conjunctural rather than additive (Fielding & Lee, 1998).

All data analysis is a process of data reduction. In the case of QCA the reduction is quite radical. In contrast to much qualitative analysis, QCA forces researchers to select cases and variables systematically, which reduces the danger of ignoring "inconvenient" cases. It also recognizes the context-specific character of causation. Although the broad concept is straightforward and attractive for the particular purpose of causal modeling using case studies rather than multivariate methods with findings based on statistical variance, the method's elegant simplicity is more challenging on close consideration. One issue is the determination of what should be the input conditions (Amenta & Poulsen, 1994). The combinations of dichotomous variables grow exponentially from a base of 2, and if there are many independent conditions, QCA becomes unwieldy, and size also decreases the chance that any given combination will have an empirical referent. That is, a combination may be logically possible but highly unlikely to occur empirically or to be feasible to detect or measure empirically. Moreover, if we try to derive conditions directly from empirical data rather than logical possibilities, it is hard to know what to select. We might try to do so based on a theory, but this risks the replication of orthodoxy and could miss conditions that are important variables. Neither approach guides us as to what conditions might fruitfully be combined, either. Another issue is how the input conditions are to be defined and measured. QCA needs dichotomous variables and, if we are working from qualitative case data, some prior means of data reduction is needed. Thus, although the software helps manipulate the key elements of the data, it is a relatively limited part of QCA work, with the bulk of key decisions occurring offline before running the software. I return to QCA in discussing on-the-horizon emergent methods.

Contemporary Emergent Methods: Methodological Integration via CAQDAS

Having surveyed the broad capacities of CAQDAS and the kinds of analytical work that may be done, we can consider an application of CAQDAS that has lately engaged substantial numbers of researchers, involving a number of new approaches to methodological convergence. Interest in systematically interrelating qualitative and quantitative methods originated some years ago in psychology (Campbell & Fiske, 1959). An established reason for interrelating quantitative and qualitative methods is that the qualitative element can suggest types of adaptation or experience for which the quantitative element can then test, permitting conclusions concerning the statistical frequency of the types. Qualitative research is good at identifying the characteristics of types but can seldom indicate precisely what proportion of a population falls within each type. Used together, qualitative and quantitative elements can reveal more about the dimensions of the types and the extent of regularities. However, as originally practiced, methodological interrelation usually involved one method taking precedence over the other (Creswell, 1994). Qualitative components were seldom the basis of the main analysis but were used for pilot work or follow-up with a subsample. Closer and more even-handed combinations subsequently emerged. For example, Caracelli and Green (1997) classify mixed method designs into component designs (such as "complementary" or "comparative" designs) and integrated designs (including "iterative," "nested," and "holistic" designs). From the earliest stage of their development, CAQDAS packages have included quantification features, and it is increasingly being realized that these features can be exploited in research designs that embrace Caracelli and Green's integrated approach. At minimum, most qualitative software counts "hits" from specified retrievals and offers a port to export data to SPSS and import quantitative data tables.

In the view of some, the features I discuss next are bringing about a hybrid methodology that transcends the quantitative–qualitative distinction. Bazeley (1999) suggests a "fusion" of quantitative and qualitative data, Bourdon (2000) refers to a new, "quantilative," form of method, and Richards (2000) refers to a "dialectic" of qualitative and quantitative approaches. Richards elaborates an approach termed "pattern analysis." It involves seeking patterns in qualitative data by importing demographic or other descriptive data as a means to sort the qualitative data, a quasi-variable form of analysis that often involves the incorporation of each round of comparative work into the overall dataset in a series of steps forming an iterative process. This approach requires software that enables statistical information to be imported into qualitative databases and used to inform coding of text, with coded information then being exported to statistical software for further quantitative analysis. An instance is NUD*IST, whose table import and export functions can be used to manipulate exported data either as information about codes that have been applied to the text or as a matrix built from cross-tabulated coded data. In the other direction, quantitative data can be imported to inform interpretative work before detailed coding, such as segmenting an interview subsample on the basis of divisions that were apparent from the responses of the full sample completing a survey questionnaire.

Qualitative software opens up a range of ways to interrelate data, from sorting qualitative comments by categorical or scaled criteria to incorporating the results of qualitative coding in correspondence analysis, logistic regression, or other multivariate techniques. Connections with the original context of the data are preserved, because categorized response sets exported to a statistics package are still linked to the qualitative data from which they were developed. For example, when working with data matrix tables in N.Vivo, one can access qualitative data from each cell of the matrix produced when a cross-tabulation-type search is performed across data files. Users can examine any number of sociodemographic characteristics against any number of selected codes. Color graduation of table cells flags the density of coding in each cell so users can judge how well supported empirically a given code or theme is. Combinations of interpretive coding and coding representing sociodemographic details can be used to constitute retrievals.

Thus CAQDAS has helped to bring about a greater degree of integration between methods. Previously, methodological integration was chiefly done at the stage of the final interpretation of findings. Bryman (2006) reports that most social science studies employing multiple methods combined a survey instrument and qualitative interviews (57%); and, for a further 27%, coanalyzing results from closed- and open-response questionnaire items sufficed to support claimed methodological integration. The strategies we are considering go well beyond this. Importantly, the move to more integrative strategies was under way before this aspect of qualitative software was much developed or used. Thus Caracelli and Greene (1993) offered four integration strategies without reference to qualitative software. One involved data transformation, in which one form of data was transformed into another for further analysis; the second, typology development, involved the application of concepts or categories developed from one set of data to data of another type; the third, extreme case analysis, explored outliers or residual data from one form of analysis using alternative data or methods; and the fourth, data consolidation, combined datasets to create new variables for further analysis in its merged form. It is not, therefore, a matter of qualitative software imposing a new approach but of its enabling an approach to which developments in methodology had independently found their way.

Bazeley (2006) suggests two main "routes to integration" that underlie software-based integration. These are the combination of data types within an analysis—for example, the use of categorical or continuous variables both for statistical analysis and to compare coded qualitative data—and conversion of data from one type to another, such as qualitative codes to codes used in a statistical analysis, or where quantitative data contribute to a qualitative analysis, such as by providing a means to subdivide cases for comparative analysis. The kinds of strategies that Caracelli and Greene (1993) suggest are likely to involve both conversion and combination.

Spreadsheet and database software can be used to construct data matrices (Miles & Huberman, 1994), holding, for example, summaries of interviewees' comments on each analytical theme, with themes making up the columns and interviewees making up the rows, and additional columns showing quantitative data that categorizes respondents, which can be used to sort textual comments in pursuing patterns of response. But qualitative software can take things much further toward integration than spreadsheets and databases can. A number of CAQDAS packages support autocoding text for the question to which the text was a response and can import matching statistical data for each respondent, such as sociodemographic information. Although any database can sort text responses by precategorized response variables, CAQDAS offers more flexible coding systems so that the text material can be easily "coded on" into emergent categories or themes. Text then assigned to the new categories can be compared by demographics or to responses relating to other themes. In an example detailed by Bazeley (2006), this technique was used to combine analysis of responses to both closed and open questions on attitudes toward organ donation in a sample of those who had been faced with the issue (Pearson, Bazeley, Plane, Chapman, & Robertson, 1995). Responses given for choosing to donate were coded on into categories representing altruism, pragmatism, and anxiety about bodily integrity. The differently categorized responses could then be related to "grief resolution" and other variables.

Bazeley (2006) notes that being able to combine qualitative data with demographic, categorical, or scaled information increases the number of analytical strategies available. Variables based on whole cases, such as an individual respondent or field site, can be combined with coded qualitative data by using the values of the variables to sort the text for a particular coding category. As well as enabling researchers to compare how different subgroups respond to an issue of interest, Bazeley demonstrates that the procedure can be used as an anchor point for scaled responses. She illustrates this with the example of Coll (n.d.). Following outpatient surgery, patients completed a "visual analogue scale" to record how much pain they were feeling and were interviewed. Descriptions of pain from the interviews could then be sorted by the rating they had given for pain levels. It was thus possible to determine what each point on the pain scale meant for patients expressing it.

One might reasonably argue that social science fundamentally proceeds by comparison. Indeed, one major analytical approach, grounded theory, is explicitly organized around the "constant comparative method" (Glaser & Strauss, 1967). The use of qualitative software enhances researchers' ability to perform this fundamental activity by enabling respondents' stated views, reports of experience, and their behavior, captured by observation, to be systematically matched to their sociodemographics or information from rating scales or survey responses. As Bazeley (2006) observes, grouping types of response to open-ended survey items and progressively reducing the groupings to form a small number of analytically related categories is a long-standing means of dealing with open-ended questionnaire responses. Statistical programs such as Wordstat and SPSS can automate this process by automatically categorizing responses based on co-occurrences of words. Responses can be related to other statistical data. The problem is that if one does this manually, it is time-consuming, and if one automates it, one loses any sense of the context of responses. CAQDAS addresses these problems more satisfactorily. Virtually any CAQDAS package will report the frequency of occurrence of categories, themes, and other traits of response and will export individual coding information to a statistics package, which can then treat the information as a case-by-variable matrix. Some programs enable the export of more complex associations between variables as a quantified matrix, such as a similarity matrix. In contrast with approaches that use statistics software, the CAQDAS-based "quantitizing" of qualitative data (Tashakkori & Teddlie, 1998) still permits ready access to the original data and its context.

Integrative operations need not be complex to be analytically useful. Although it is a very simple transformation of data, counting occurrences of a theme or category can be highly informative, and qualitative software readily provides various kinds of counts, such as the number of data segments or cases with a given code, how many segments have been coded and how many are "noise," and so on. Some quite sophisticated inferences can be supported using simple counts. Anderson and colleagues (2001) monitored the number of lines of text between the appearances of codes representing children's reasoning; the decreasing number of lines verified an increasing convergence of argumentation strategies between the children as they worked in problem-solving groups.

More sophisticated software-based methodological integration chiefly requires the transformation of some aspect of qualitative data into variables. When codes derived from qualitative data are recorded separately for each case (as the presence or absence of the code in each particular case or as a frequency of the code's occurrence), a case-by-variable matrix can be derived. Statistical techniques such as cluster analysis, correspondence analysis, and multidimensional scaling can be applied to such "quantitized" qualitative data. There are a number of hybrid techniques that interrelate quantitative and qualitative methods. For example, types of adaptation to labor force position that have been documented in nonstandardized interviews can be made the basis of a probabilistic cluster analysis in order to relate perceived social class to income measures. The proximity and probability of classification of each respondent toward the center of the relevant cluster (i.e., type) can thus be visualized and categories reduced to a smaller number of dimensions by multiple correspondence analysis. Kuiken and Miall (2001) used this technique to specify experiential categories they had identified from interview responses in social psychological research comparing different readers' impressions of the same short story. After identifying attributes qualitatively, categories were specified by a quantitative cluster analysis that systematically varied the presence of individual attributes. Then a further qualitative inspection of the clusters was done in order to further differentiate the types.

In methodological research on the research design of mixed methods projects, Niglas (2004) used scales to measure variation among projects on various research design characteristics. Cluster analysis produced eight distinctive groups and indicated the characteristics that best differentiated them. She then compared the characteristics to commentaries she wrote during her initial reading of each project to produce summary descriptions of the eight groups. The descriptions were used as elaborated definitions to assign studies into categories representing variables for further statistical analysis. These alternating quantitative and qualitative procedures do not challenge the essential integrity of the quantitative and qualitative methods being interrelated in multimethod projects. They represent genuine interrelation rather than using one method in a subordinate role simply to illustrate findings from the main method in use.

To use such procedures, several conditions need to be satisfied. There have to be enough cases to give a sample of the size required by the chosen statistical method. Second, the researcher must decide whether to use simple absence or presence of the code or to capture in a measure the amount of data in each case assigned given codes. Third, further coding may be needed to accommodate nondirectional codes that do not include an outcome. Bazeley (2006) uses the example that a code may simply raise the issue of the character of a witness without identifying the conclusion that was reached following legal argument over his or her character. A more specific code indicating whether there was a positive or negative assessment of witness character would be needed. Researchers must also ascertain that the underlying data are robust and commensurate. For example, the absence of a code in particular cases may not signal a genuine lack of applicability but reticence, withholding, or inattention.

Integration of analyses from different methods using qualitative software is helpful for several purposes. Bazeley (2006) notes that it can stimulate new perspectives in an exploratory study, create and/or validate scaled measures, help in the development of typologies, and be used to suggest factors predictive of an outcome. Integrative strategies enable more iterative approaches to analysis, with results from merging data sources being used to create new composite variables that are then added to the analysis (a procedure that is helped by the "system closure" feature mentioned earlier).

Emergent CAQDAS-Based Methods Just Over the Horizon

New computational tools have become available to social scientists since the emergence of grid and high-performance computing in the late 1990s (see Fielding, 2003). Gains in computing resource offer new data-handling capacities and analytical procedures. These extend to a range of fields in social science, both those that are already computationally based in large measure and those that have not yet seen significant impact from computing applications. Here I survey only those relating to qualitative software.

New Computational Technologies for Qualitative Secondary Analysis

Grid and HPC technologies have a prime role in managing databases of archived qualitative data. Secondary analysis of qualitative data remains limited relative to quantitative secondary analysis, but recently interest has grown in collaborative archival research and distributed analysis. Linking qualitative and quantitative data and linking material such as personal biographies to census data, maps, and so on is a large incentive to work with archival data. Data grids enable researchers to share annotations of data and to access multimodal, distributed archival material. Empirical phenomena can be represented in many ways, and being able to use multiple modes of representation makes for a richer analysis but requires multiple tools (for sound, image, transcripts, statistics). "Asset management" software, such as Extensis Portfolio and iVIEWMEDIA Pro, enable a range of data types to be held in an integrated environment. Such an approach was used in a multimedia ethnographic study of a heritage center (discussed in Fielding, 2003). Grid computing resources were used to distribute large audio and video datasets for collaborative analysis. Hypercam software was used to record "physical" interaction within a three-dimensional graphical environment in order to model different visitor behaviors in heritage centers. The 3-D files could be streamed over networks via the Internet, enabling researchers at several centers to work on the models in real time. Data grids enable researchers to access image, statistical, or audio files stored at remote archives and work on them over networks (e.g., collaboratively, or using specialist software not available locally) or download them.

Data grids can enable research teams to create and share annotations among themselves and external participants. To handle sound, image, and text, such applications require multiple tools; for text alone these range from simple text editors to automatic speech transcription and CAQDAS. Qualitative software thus becomes but a part of a fully specified analytical system. The decision is whether to maintain the CAQDAS component as a proprietary program or to develop XML to offer similar functionality, the advantage of the latter being the capacity of XML to operate over networks. In the context of work with remote archives and in team research in which team members are at dispersed locations, this advantage may prove telling. But these developments raise a core epistemological issue: whether qualitative researchers who did not collect a given body of data can fully understand it or whether context effects obstruct productive comparison (Bishop, 2005). A number of technological means can be used to address this concern. Among these are annotation tools, tools to overcome data source format differences ("extensibility" protocols, standard format conversion), the incorporation of CAQDAS-type links back to the original data to check context, and support for multimodal representation. The effectiveness of these measures awaits full-scale trials on real datasets, but, as we see in the next section, the basis for such trials is in place.

"Scaling Up" and Methodological Interrelation

In fields such as health, social welfare, household economy, and family studies, there is a lot to gain from better integrating findings from qualitative research with those from other research modes. However, integrating qualitative findings alongside those from epidemiological and statistical research faces serious obstacles. Sample size, nonstandardized definitions, and noncumulative patterns of inquiry inhibit the integration of qualitative with quantitative research (Fielding & Schreier, 2001). Studies of family formation, the household economy, and health-related behavior are among areas in which a number of qualitative studies, rich in themselves, have proved unable to talk to each other due to varying conceptualizations addressing fundamentally rather similar characteristics. Grid resources can enable the scaling up and meta-analysis of findings from small-scale studies. One approach uses XML to create a metadata model to collate contextual features mutually relating to the phenomenon of interest in different studies or fieldwork sites. It builds the links between researcher, data, context, and interpretation that make for context specificity into a protocol by using an XML data model and wrappers around each individual study, so that the metadata model can access and query individual datasets. An ontology is used to specify a common vocabulary for the methodological and substantive facets of the studies.

The ontology is a practical mechanism for reconciling quantitative and qualitative epistemology. In the process of defining it, different constructions of the features of the same phenomenon are drawn out, and conventions can be agreed on to handle them. The procedure of matching up the disparate terminologies employed by different researchers in independent studies enables a scaling up of findings. The ontology "translates" between projects (so that what study A calls "trouble with neighbors" is matched to "boundary dispute" in study B, etc.), enabling the generalizations and heuristics derived from the different studies to be combined in a reliable and comparable way while revealing genuine differences and preserving them.

As we have seen, current-generation CAQDAS offers considerable support for methodological integration, but the size of datasets it can handle remains limited. We noted that command languages to automate large-scale or repetitive routines can enable autocoding of participants' responses or field site information, but the benefits of this are vitiated if resulting datasets exceed the computing capacity of the program running on a desktop computer. The integrative analytical strategies profiled earlier–including the ability to operate software output such as spreadsheets and other non-CAQDAS programs and to manipulate it within the coded text of a CAQDAS project so users can "eyeball" output and relate it to textual data and "merge" functions that allow separately created analyses to be combined and enable researchers to explore differences between them–offer much scope for methodological interrelation, but response times can be unacceptably slow, and extensive queries can crash the program. CAQDAS programs with grid resources could enable the use of these features with larger datasets and provide finer grained analyses of very large data sets than is possible with content analysis software.

The Role of XML and HTML Applications in Opening Up Qualitative Research

For all the cooperativeness and productive exchange that has marked the CAQDAS field, proprietary software dominates current approaches to computer-supported qualitative data analysis, but XML and HTML applications are increasingly able to offer similar functionality and to do so over networks, either within institutions or over the Internet. Researching accounts posted online by cancer sufferers, Seale (2002) preprocessed the data with a customized Visual Basic program, coded the data using N.Vivo, and used a concordance generator to provide a content analysis of response patterns that informed the overall analysis. Such integrated software use depends on the ability to easily import and export data. Digital convergence reinforces the demand for universal, standard data formats so that files can be easily transferred. Some CAQDAS packages (e.g., Tatoe and Atlas.ti) already use XML/HTML to export data files. But nearly all CAQDAS applications are customized database solutions and, because they focus on facilitating semiautomated analyses, are less concerned with supporting the range of file formats and platforms that mainstream database products can support. CAQDAS also generally lacks the client server or three-tier networked architecture that is necessary for secure multiuser access to networked data repositories. A trait of XML is that raw data are separated from subsequent layers of mark-up, so source data are protected (advantageous in making analytical decisions transparent and a constraint with some CAQDAS packages).

The use of XML and software to read and edit XML documents allows qualitative data analysis facilities to be incorporated into groupware applications such as document bases and collaborative workspaces and used across networks (Carmichael, 2002). Current collaborative systems have largely focused on work with whole documents, and the "pencil-level richness" of CAQDAS applications has been lacking. But combining XML with a scripting language such as Perl makes it possible to approach CAQDAS-type functionality (retrieval by text and codes, attachment of memos to text segments, generation of tables, matrices, and other means of summarizing the data) via a standard Web browser. An attraction is that being able to provide an ongoing project over the Web can deepen research participants' engagement in research, extending their role from providing data to participating in its interpretation. This can enable an "expert system" approach to qualitative data analysis, applying progressively elaborated interpretive schemes informed by research users and respondents' views to the analysis. These data exchange and expert system capacities make XML the putative standard tool for CAQDAS-type qualitative data analysis by distributed research teams, and grid resources can facilitate the coexistence of raw datasets, proprietary CAQDAS software with XML integration, and other project-specific applications. With open publication of schemata used to structure documents, XML-based CAQDAS applications would be able to run transparently across a network. A number of challenges remain, including access/licensing, the need to assess which languages best support XML processing, the need to establish new methods to code and perform other analytical operations interactively, and to agree on ways to preserve data integrity in a context of co-analysis.

Case-Based Analysis in a Grid Environment

As to case-based analysis, we earlier discussed the QCA approach to systematic case-based analysis, a procedure based on mathematical truth tables and fuzzy-set theory. Modeling social phenomena with a view to identifying causes and making predictions is an increasingly important application of social research, and QCA procedures systematically elaborate outcomes against conditions, enabling the causally significant conditions to be identified. However, we earlier noted difficulties in defining input conditions and in handling the exponential growth in combinations of conditions from a base of 2. QCA remains at core a qualitative method, as field data are used to document the conditions in each case studied, but its effectiveness is restricted by the richness of field data, which make for a multitude of choices when it comes to defining input conditions. It is just this kind of problem that HPC resources can help with. Grid computing could enable the QCA and fsQCA software to analyze definitive volumes of cases and conditions and support the large number of combinations generated by the exponential proliferation of logically possible input conditions.

Conclusion

I began with the observation that change is fast in the computing world. Hopefully, this chapter has also demonstrated that social scientists are adaptable and quick to respond to new resources in innovative ways. In that sense, methodological emergence is not a once-and-for-all phenomenon but an ongoing process. Moreover, the story of qualitative software is not purely a story of innovation but has the important effect of helping us to better understand the essentials of qualitative methodology that have long been taken for granted and have often been insufficiently elaborated. Much as the attempt to model language in order to create better computational tools for Natural Language Processing has forced sociolinguists to identify gaps in accepted understandings, the writing of programs to support qualitative data analysis has forced the field to better articulate cherished assumptions and accustomed procedures. Qualitative software has encouraged a more systematic approach to data management and stimulated fresh interest in more formal approaches to data analysis. Moves to widen the evidence base via computing support for visual and multimedia data, moves toward formal techniques such as hypothesis testing and case study modeling, and the ability to engage new audiences and deepen research participants' involvement, are developments that have helped qualitative research to be not only more precise but also more expansive. We can confidently expect the qualitative software field to remain a site from which productive new methods will continue to emerge.

This said, qualitative research gains its strength from grounding its analyses in closeness to context, receptiveness to the voices of those it studies, and respect for the complex multidimensionality of social phenomena. It will always remain necessary for qualitative researchers to evaluate qualitative software against these fundamental standards. Indeed, it is noticeable that, as each generation of researchers confronts qualitative software, it asks similar questions and expresses similar concerns as those raised in the field's first encounters with software support for qualitative data analysis. Worries about the computer "taking over," which Ray Lee and I (Fielding & Lee, 1991) likened to the fear of Frankenstein's monster, are more resilient than we supposed, but, provided that the fear engenders a genuine engagement with what the software does and does not do, it may also be more functional than we thought. As CAQDAS increasingly acquires artificial intelligence features, exploits new computational techniques enabling semiautomation based on Natural Language Processing, and involves the transformation of qualitative data into quantitative forms that can be manipulated statistically and by formal (mathematical) methods, qualitative researchers will no doubt continue to assess CAQDAS against the fundamental standards that give qualitative research its distinctive character.

References

Agar, M. (1991). The right brain strikes back. In N. Fielding & R. M. Lee (Eds.), *Using computers in qualitative research* (pp. 181–194). London: Sage.

Amenta, E., & Poulsen, J. (1994). Where to begin: A survey of five approaches to selecting independent variables for QCA. *Sociological Methods and Research, 23,* 22–53.

Anderson, R., Nguyen-Jahiel, K., McNurlen, B., Archodidou, A., Kim, S., Reznitskaya, A., et al. (2001). The snowball phenomenon: Spread of ways of talking and ways of thinking across groups of children. *Cognition and Instruction, 19*(1), 1–46.

Bazeley, P. (1999). The bricoleur with a computer: Piecing together qualitative and quantitative data. *Qualitative Health Research, 9*(2), 279–287.

Bazeley, P. (2006). The contribution of computer software to integrating qualitative and quantitative data and analysis. *Research in the Schools, 13*(1), 63–73.

Berelson, B. R. (1952). *Content analysis in communication research.* Glencoe, IL: Free Press.

Bishop, L. (2005). Protecting respondents and enabling data sharing. *Sociology, 39,* 333–336.

Bourdon, S. (2000). QDA software: Enslavement or liberation? In *Social science methodology in the new millenium: Proceedings of the Fifth International Conference on Logic and Methodology*. Koln, Germany: Zentralarchiv fur Empirische Sozialforschung.

Brent, E., & Anderson, R. (1990). *Computer applications in the social sciences*. Philadelphia: Temple University Press.

Bryman, A. (2006). Integrating quantitative and qualitative research. *Qualitative Research, 6*(1), 97–113.

Campbell, D., & Fiske, D. (1959). Convergent and discriminant validity by the multi-trait, multi-method matrix. *Psychological Bulletin, 56,* 81–105.

Caracelli, V., & Green, J. (1993). Data analysis strategies for mixed method evaluation designs. *Educational Evaluation and Policy Analysis, 15*(2), 195–207.

Caracelli, V., & Green, J. (1997). Crafting mixed method evaluation designs. In J. Green & V. Caracelli (Eds.), *Advances in mixed method evaluation* (pp. 255–274). San Francisco: Jossey Bass.

Carmichael, P. (2002). Extensible markup language and qualitative data analysis. *Forum Qualitative Sozialforschung/Forum: Qualitative Social Research, 3*(2).

Coll, A. M. (n.d.). [Experience of pain after day surgery]. Unpublished raw data, School of Care Sciences, University of Glamorgan, Wales.

Creswell, J. (1994). *Research design: Qualitative and quantitative approaches.* Thousand Oaks, CA: Sage.

Fielding, N. (2003). *Qualitative research and e-social science: Appraising the potential.* Swindon, UK: Economic and Social Research Council.

Fielding, N. (2004). The resurgence, legitimation and institutionalisation of qualitative method. In M. Bergman & T. Eberle (Eds.), *Qualitative inquiry: Research, archiving and re-use* (pp. 27–37). Bern, Switzerland: Swiss Academy of Humanities and Social Sciences.

Fielding, N., & Lee, R. M. (1991). Computing for qualitative research. In N. Fielding & R. M. Lee (Eds.), *Using computers in qualitative research* (pp. 1–13). London: Sage.

Fielding, N., & Lee, R. M. (1998). *Computer analysis and qualitative research,* London: Sage.

Fielding, N., & Schreier, M. (2001). On the compatibility between qualitative and quantitative research methods. *Forum Qualitative Sozialforschung/Forum: Qualitative Social Research, 2*(1).

Glaser, B., & Strauss, A. (1967). *The discovery of grounded theory,* Chicago: Aldine.

Gubrium, J., & Holstein, J. (2001). From the individual interview to the interview society. In J. Gubrium & J. Holstein (Eds.), *Handbook of interview research* (pp. 1–19). London: Sage.

Hesse-Biber, S., Dupuis, P., & Kinder, T. S. (1991). HyperResearch: A computer program for the analysis of qualitative data with an emphasis on hypothesis testing and multimedia analysis. *Qualitative Sociology, 14,* 289–306.

Kelle, U. (1997). Theory building in qualitative research

and computer programs for the management of textual data. *Sociological Research Online, 2*(2).

Kuiken, D., & Miall, D. (2001). Numerically-aided phenomenology: Procedures for investigating categories of experience. *Forum Qualitative Sozialforschung/ Forum: Qualitative Social Research, 2*(1).

Lee, R. (2004). Recording technology and the interview in sociology, 1920–2000. *Sociology, 38*(5), 881–901.

Lewins, A., & Silver, C. (2006). *Using qualitative software: A step-by-step guide*. London: Sage.

Mangabeira, W. (1995). Computer assistance, qualitative analysis and model building. In R. M. Lee (Ed.), *Information technology for the social scientist* (pp. 25–40). London: UCL Press.

Miles, M., & Huberman, A. M. (1994). *Qualitative data analysis: An expanded sourcebook*. Thousand Oaks, CA: Sage.

Niglas, K. (2004). *The combined use of qualitative and quantitative methods in educational research*. Tallinn, Estonia: Tallinn Pedagogical University.

Pearson, I. Y., Bazeley, P., Plane, T., Chapman, J. R., & Robertson, P. (1995). A survey of families of brain dead patients. *Journal of Anaesthesia and Intensive Care, 23*, 88–95.

Ragin, C. (1987). *The comparative method: Moving beyond qualitative and quantitative strategies*. Thousand Oaks, CA: Sage.

Richards, L. (2000). Integrating data: Can qualitative software do it?. In *Social science methodology in the new millenium: Proceedings of the Fifth International Conference on Logic and Methodology*. Koln, Germany: Zentralarchiv fur Empirische Sozialforschung.

Seale, C. (2002). Cancer heroics: A study of news reports. *Sociology, 36*(1), 107–126.

Tashakkori, A., & Teddlie, C. (1998). *Mixed methodology*. Thousand Oaks, CA: Sage.

Tesch, R. (1990). *Qualitative research: Analysis types and software tools*. New York: Falmer Press.

Weitzman, E., & Miles, M. (1995). *Computer programs for qualitative data analysis*, Beverly Hills, CA: Sage.

Author Index

B

C

D

E

F

G

H

I

J

K

L

M

R

S

T

U

V

W

Y

Z

Subject Index

Page numbers followed by *f* indicate figure; *n*, note; and *t*, table

D

E

F

N

Q

R

S

T

U

V

About the Editors

Sharlene Nagy Hesse-Biber, PhD, is Professor of Sociology and director of Women's Studies at Boston College in Chestnut Hill, Massachusetts. She has published widely on the impact of sociocultural factors on women's body image, including the book *Am I Thin Enough Yet?: The Cult of Thinness and the Commercialization of Identity* (1996), which was selected as one of *Choice* magazine's best academic books for 1996, and *The Cult of Thinness* (2007). Dr. Hesse-Biber is coauthor of *Working Women in America: Split Dreams* (2005) and *The Practice of Qualitative Research* (2006); coeditor of *Feminist Approaches to Theory and Methodology: An Interdisciplinary Reader* (1999), *Approaches to Qualitative Research: A Reader on Theory and Practice* (2004), and *Emergent Methods in Social Research* (2006); and editor of the *Handbook of Feminist Research: Theory and Praxis* (2007), which was selected as one of the Critics Choice Award winners by the American Educational Studies Association and one of *Choice* magazine's outstanding academic titles for 2007. She is also a contributor to the *Handbook of Grounded Theory* (2008) and author of the upcoming *Mixed Methods for Social Researchers*. Dr. Hesse-Biber is codeveloper of the software program HyperRESEARCH, a computer-assisted program for analyzing qualitative data, and the new transcription tool HyperTRANSCRIBE.

Patricia Leavy, PhD, is Associate Professor of Sociology at Stonehill College in Easton, Massachusetts, where she is also the founder and director of the Gender Studies Program and currently serves as chair of the Sociology and Criminology Department. She is the author of *Iconic Events: Media, Politics, and Power in Retelling History* (2007) and the forthcoming *Method Meets Art: Social Research and the Creative Arts*; coauthor of *The Practice of Qualitative Research* (2006) and *Feminist Research Practice: A Primer* (2007); and coeditor of *Approaches to Qualitative Research: A Reader on Theory and Practice* (2004) and *Emergent Methods in Social Research* (2006). Dr. Leavy has published articles in the areas of collective memory, mass media, popular culture, body image, feminism, and qualitative research methods, and she is regularly quoted in newspapers for her expertise on popular culture, current events, and gender.

Contributors

David Altheide, PhD, is Regents' Professor in the School of Justice and Social Inquiry at Arizona State University, where he has taught for 34 years. His work has focused on the role of mass media and information technology in social control. Dr. Altheide received the Cooley Award three times, given to the outstanding book in symbolic interaction by the Society for the Study of Symbolic Interaction: in 2007 for *Terrorism and the Politics of Fear* (2006), in 2004 for *Creating Fear: News and the Construction of Crisis* (2002), and in 1986 for *Media Power* (1985). He received the 2005 George Herbert Mead Award for lifetime contributions from the Society for the Study of Symbolic Interaction, and the society's Mentor Achievement Award in 2007.

Carol A. Bailey, PhD, is Associate Professor of Sociology at Virginia Tech. She specializes in evaluation research. Dr. Bailey's list of evaluations includes drug and alcohol treatment programs, a mobile chemistry lab, a therapeutic day treatment program, a science camp for girls, a driver's education program developed by teenagers, and a workshop on nanotechnology for high school teachers. Her recent focus is on evaluating programs that serve children with severe mental illnesses and their families. The second edition of her book, *A Guide to Qualitative Field Research*, has been recently published. Dr. Bailey has won numerous teaching awards, including the university-wide Alumni Award for Teaching Excellence, and was once the director of the University Writing Program.

Himika Bhattacharya, PhD, is the managing editor of the journal *International Review of Qualitative Research* and Associate Director for the Annual International Congress of Qualitative Inquiry. She has contributed entries to the *Sage Encyclopedia of Qualitative Research* and is the guest editor for a special issue of *Qualitative Inquiry*. Dr. Bhattacharya's main research interests lie in the broad areas of interpretive research practices, culture and communication, gender and women's studies, and critical development studies. She has conducted action-based research on projects dealing with domestic and sexual violence against women in Lahaul, India; Champaign, Illinois; and New York City.

Ellen Block, MA, is a doctoral student in the Joint Doctoral Program in Social Work and Anthropology at the University of Michigan. She does ethnographic fieldwork on care practices for AIDS orphans in rural Lesotho. Her research addresses issues of kinship, gender, and the intersection of illness and culture.

Kathy Charmaz, PhD, is Professor of Sociology and coordinator of the Faculty Writing Program at Sonoma State University. She has written or coedited seven books, including *Good Days, Bad Days: The Self in Chronic Illness and Time*, which won awards from the Pacific

Sociological Association and the Society for the Study of Symbolic Interaction; *Constructing Grounded Theory: A Practical Guide through Qualitative Analysis*; and, coedited with Antony Bryant, *The Sage Handbook of Grounded Theory*. Dr. Charmaz has served as president of the Pacific Sociological Association; vice president of the Society for the Study of Symbolic Interaction; vice president of Alpha Kappa Delta, the International Sociology Honor Society; editor of *Symbolic Interaction*; and chair of the Medical Sociology Section of the American Sociological Association. She received the 2001 Feminist Mentors Award and the 2006 George Herbert Mead Award for lifetime achievement from the Society for the Study of Symbolic Interaction.

Frederick G. Conrad, PhD, is Research Associate Professor at the University of Michigan, Institute for Social Research, and University of Maryland, Joint Program in Survey Methodology. His research interests include survey measurement error and techniques for reducing it. Currently, much of his work is focused on web surveys and the consequences of building some features of human interviewers into the user interface, for example, virtual, animated interviewers that can detect respondent confusion and try to help.

Lisa Cosgrove, PhD, is a clinical and research psychologist and Assistant Professor in the Department of Counseling and School Psychology at the University of Massachusetts at Boston. She is coeditor, with Paula Caplan, of *Bias in Psychiatric Diagnosis* (2004) and author of several of its chapters. Dr. Cosgrove has published articles and book chapters on theoretical and philosophical issues related to clinical practice and research methods and on social policy issues such as conflict of interest in the psychopharmaceutical industry. Her research has been supported through grants from the National Institute of Mental Health (to the Murray Center, Harvard University) and from the University of Massachusetts. She was a fellow in the William Joiner Center for the Study of War and Social Consequences (2002–2003) and has conducted research on the intergenerational impact of war-related posttraumatic stress disorder.

Michael Coyle, PhD, is Assistant Professor in the Criminal Justice Program, Department of Political Science at California State University, Chico. His scholarly focus is on language of justice research: language studies that ask critical questions about everyday social and criminal justice discourse as a whole and its relationship to social control and moral entrepreneurship. Dr. Coyle's research interests include social and criminal justice theory and practices, restorative justice, and qualitative research methods. He also writes public policy analysis for think tanks and national and local media focusing on the social cost of America's imprisonment binge, the death penalty, and more. Dr. Coyle's work focuses on the least powerful who disproportionately bear the costs of our social and criminal justice system.

John W. Creswell, PhD, is Professor of Educational Psychology at the University of Nebraska–Lincoln, where he teaches courses and writes about qualitative methodology, research design, and mixed methods research. Dr. Creswell has authored 10 books, many of which focus on research design, qualitative research, and mixed methods research. He also codirects the Office of Qualitative and Mixed Methods Research, which supports scholars incorporating qualitative and mixed methods research into projects for extramural funding. He is coeditor of the *Journal of Mixed Methods Research*. Dr. Creswell is currently a Senior Fulbright Scholar and makes international presentations on mixed methods research.

Christine Crofts, BA, is a doctoral candidate in the Department of Sociology at Boston College. She has published in the area of the sociology of science and technology, and her current research centers on the social implications of various scientific and medical technologies, including innovations in genetics and tuberculosis diagnostic tests.

Christine S. Davis, PhD, is Assistant Professor in the Communication Studies Department at the University of North Carolina at Charlotte. Her research interests are in the intersection of family, health, and disability and in the ways in which liminality in health status affects identity. At the University of North Carolina at Charlotte, Dr. Davis is currently involved in several participatory community action projects, studying the role of communication in the lives of patients with traumatic brain injury and their families, health literacy among caregivers of children with severe emotional disturbances (SED), and social support among caregivers of children with SED. She is also conducting autoethnographic research on body image and aging.

Katie DeVriese, MA, is a doctoral student in the School of Justice and Social Inquiry at Arizona State University.

Bella Dicks, PhD, is Reader in Sociology at Cardiff University, Wales, United Kingdom. Her research interests and publications include digital methodologies, heritage and cultural display, regeneration, and qualitative studies of place and locality. Her coauthored monograph, *Qualitative Research and Hypermedia* (2005), represents groundbreaking new work on ethnography in the digital age.

Carolyn Ellis, PhD, is Professor of Communication and Sociology at the University of South Florida. She is interested in interpretive and artistic representations of qualitative research, in particular, autoethnographic narratives. Her books include *Fisher Folk: Two Communities on Chesapeake Bay* (1986), *Final Negotiations: A Story of Love, Loss, and Chronic Illness* (1995), and *The Ethnographic I: A Methodological Novel about Autoethnography* (2004).

Collin Fellows, MA, is a graduate student in the Department of Sociology at Portland State University and program manager of Students First Mentoring Program. His research interests focus on making higher education accessible to those who are first-generation college students. He is also working on developing a practical measure of expertise and advancements in qualitative research methodology.

Nigel Fielding, PhD, is Professor of Sociology at the University of Surrey, United Kingdom, codirector of the Institute of Social Research, and codirector of the Economic and Social Research Council–supported CAQDAS Networking Project, which provides training and support in the use of computers in qualitative data analysis. His research interests are in qualitative research methods, new technologies for social research, and criminal justice. Dr. Fielding has authored or edited 20 books, more than 50 journal articles, and more than 200 other publications. His authored books include *Linking Data* (1986), with Jane Fielding, and *Computer Analysis and Qualitative Research* (1998), with Ray Lee. Edited and coedited books include *Using Computers in Qualitative Research* (1991), with Ray Lee, and a four-volume set, *Interviewing* (2002). Dr. Fielding is presently researching high-performance computing applications to qualitative methods.

Michael Frisch, PhD, is Professor of History and American Studies and Senior Research Scholar at the University at Buffalo, State University of New York. He has been involved for many years in oral and public history projects, often in collaboration with community history organizations, museums, and documentary filmmakers. Dr. Frisch is the author of *Portraits in Steel* (1993), a book and associated traveling exhibit created in collaboration with the noted documentary photographer Milton Rogovin. The book received the Oral History Association's Best Book prize for 1993–1995. Dr. Frisch is also the author of *A Shared Authority: Essays on the Craft and Meaning of Oral and Public History* (1990), among other works. He has served as editor of the Oral History Review (1986–1996), as President of the American Studies Association (2000–2001), and as a board member of the New York

Council for the Humanities and the Federation of State Humanities Councils. His recent work is in oral history applications of new audio–video indexing technology.

Denise O'Neil Green, PhD, is Associate Vice President for International Diversity at Central Michigan University. Her research focuses on the development and implementation of qualitative research designs that aid social science and education researchers, policymakers, and administrators in understanding diversity issues and diverse populations in public policy, higher education, and K–12 education. In particular, her research examines methods, practices, and strategies employed in qualitative studies that explore phenomena associated with racially and ethnically diverse populations.

Jaber F. Gubrium, PhD, is Professor and Chair of Sociology at the University of Missouri–Columbia. He has a long-standing program of research on the social organization of care in human services institutions and has pioneered in the reconceptualization of qualitative methods and the development of narrative analysis. His publications include *Living and Dying at Murray Manor* (1975); *Old-Timers and Alzheimer's: The Descriptive Organization of Senility* (1986); and, with James A. Holstein, *The New Language of Qualitative Method* (1997) and *The Self We Live By: Narrative Identity in a Postmodern World* (2000), as well as numerous articles on aging, the life course, medicalization, and representational practice in therapeutic context.

Heather Guevara, MA, is Adjunct Instructor in Sociology at Portland State University, where she used focus groups to examine the transition experiences of new graduate students. Her current research interests include examining the successful adjustment of students new to the college environment, as well as improving the scholarship of teaching and learning in the classroom.

Simon J. Harrison, MSc, is currently pursuing a PhD at the University of Leeds in the use of metaphorical inference to communicate risk. In this project he is attempting to develop a method of metaphorical analysis that allows the insights of Lakoff and Johnson to be combined with a discursive psychological approach.

Monique M. Hennink, PhD, is Associate Professor in the Hubert Department of Global Health in the Rollins School of Public Health at Emory University. She has extensive experience in designing, conducting, and evaluating qualitative research, particularly in developing country settings. Dr. Hennink has conducted intensive training workshops for researchers, professionals, and students in China, India, Pakistan, Uganda, Malawi, South Africa, the Netherlands, and the United Kingdom. She is author of *International Focus Group Research* (2007), and is currently writing several other textbooks on qualitative research.

Sharlene Nagy Hesse-Biber (see "About the Editors").

Claire Hewson, PhD, is Lecturer in Psychology at the Open University, Milton Keynes, United Kingdom. She has also been Research Associate in the Human Communication Research Centre, University of Edinburgh, and Lecturer in Psychology at the University of Bolton (formerly Bolton Institute). Dr. Hewson's research interests include folk psychology, lay theories and beliefs, use of the Internet as a data-gathering tool in social and behavioral research, and the use of information technology in teaching and learning. She has coauthored the book *Internet Research Methods* (2003) and has published various articles on this topic.

Christine Hine, DPhil, is Senior Lecturer in Sociology at the University of Surrey, United Kingdom. Her main research centers on the sociology of science and technology. She has conducted ethnographic research into the deployment of information and communications technologies in scientific research, focusing on development of mobile and connective approaches to ethnography that combine online and offline social contexts. She has a major interest in the development of ethnography in technical settings and in "virtual methods" (the use of the Internet for social research). She is author of *Virtual Ethnography* (2000) and *Systematics as Cyberscience: Computers, Change, and Continuity in Science* (2008), and editor of *Virtual Methods: Issues in Social Research on the Internet* (2005) and *New Infrastructures for Knowledge Production: Understanding E-Science* (2006).

Gunilla Holm, PhD, is Professor of Education in the Department of Education at the University of Helsinki, Finland. Her research interests are focused on qualitative research methods, as well as issues in education related to race, ethnicity, class, and gender. She has also published widely on multicultural education, adolescent cultures, and schooling in popular culture. Dr. Holm has coedited several books, including *Schooling in the Light of Popular Culture* (1994) and *Contemporary Youth Research: Local Expressions and Global Connections* (2005).

James A. Holstein, PhD, is Professor of Sociology in the Department of Social and Cultural Sciences at Marquette University. His research and writing projects have been concerned with social problems, deviance and social control, and family and the self, all approached from an ethnomethodologically informed constructionist perspective. His books include *What Is Family?* (1990), *Court-Ordered Insanity* (1993), *The Active Interview* (1995), *The Self We Live By* (2000), and *Handbook of Constructionist Research* (2008), all with Jaber F. Gubrium; and *Reconsidering Social Constructionism* (1993) and *Challenges and Choices* (2003), with Gale Miller.

Pilar S. Horner, MSW, is a doctoral candidate in the Joint Program in Social Work and Sociology at the University of Michigan. Her research interests include methodology, epistemology, and the regulation of female sexuality. Her current work looks at issues of sexuality, work, and professionalization in the home sex toy industry.

Sarah Irwin, PhD, is Reader in Sociology at the University of Leeds, United Kingdom. She is Deputy Director of Real Life Methods, part of the Economic and Social Research Council National Centre for Research Methods. Real Life Methods is exploring the use of diverse methods in researching social relationships and contexts in the areas of family, youth, and community. Dr. Irwin has also conducted research and published extensively on youth transitions, family, gender, employment, care, inequalities, and social change. She is the author of *Reshaping Social Life* (2005), among other books. She is a codirector of the Centre for Research on Families, Life Course and Generations (FlaG) at the University of Leeds.

Burke Johnson, PhD, is Professor in the Department of Professional Studies at the University of South Alabama. He is coauthor of *Educational Research: Quantitative, Qualitative, and Mixed Approaches*, now in its third edition (2008). He is author or coauthor of numerous articles and chapters and has published in *Educational Researcher*, *Journal of Educational Psychology*, *Evaluation Review*, *Journal of Mixed Methods Research*, and *Evaluation and Program Planning*. Dr. Johnson was the guest editor of a special issue on mixed methods research in the journal *Research in the Schools*. His current interests are in research methodology (especially mixed), the philosophy of social science, and social theory.

Joke Kort, MSc, worked at the Institute for Perception Research at the Technical University of Eindhoven, the Netherlands, in User System Interaction from 1998 to 2000. Since 2000 she has been a researcher and consultant at TNO, an independent research and consultancy organization in information and communication technology. Ms. Kort's work focuses on researching and applying user-centered design and user experience methods. Most of her current work is done in (inter)national research programs and commercial projects for (mobile) telecommunications providers. Ms. Kort was co-organizer of a workshop on usage analysis held in conjunction with the Association for Computing Machinery conference on Computer–Human Interaction in 2005.

Mei-Po Kwan, PhD, is Distinguished Professor of Social and Behavioral Sciences at Ohio State University, where she is the chair of graduate studies in the Department of Geography. Her research interests include geographies of gender, race, and religion; information and communications technology; geographic information systems (GIS); and feminist perspectives on geospatial technologies. Dr. Kwan is editor of the *Annals of the Association of American Geographers* (Methods, Models and GIS Section), an associate editor of *Geographical Analysis*, and a member of the editorial board of *The Professional Geographer*. She received the 2005 Research Award for outstanding contributions to GIScience from the University Consortium for Geographic Information Science and the Edward L. Ullman Award for outstanding contributions to transportation geography from the Association of American Geographers. She has been recognized as a Joan N. Huber Faculty Fellow for outstanding scholarship at Ohio State University in 2005 and as an Ameritech Fellow.

Patricia Leavy (see "About the Editors").

Melvin M. Mark, PhD, is Professor of Psychology at Penn State University. He is a past president of the American Evaluation Association and has served as editor of the *American Journal of Evaluation*, where he is now editor emeritus. Dr. Mark's interests include the theory, methodology, practice, and profession of program and policy evaluation. He has been involved in evaluations in a number of areas, including prevention programs, federal personnel policies, and various educational interventions. Among his books are *Evaluation: An Integrated Framework for Understanding, Guiding, and Improving Policies and Programs* (2000), with Gary Henry and George Julnes; *The SAGE Handbook of Evaluation* (2006), edited with Ian Shaw and Jennifer Greene; and the forthcoming books *Exemplars of Evaluation* (with Jody Fitzpatrick and Tina Christie) and *Social Psychology and Evaluation* (with Stewart Donaldson and Bernadette Campbell).

Bruce Mason, PhD, is a postdoctoral research fellow at De Montfort University, Leicester, United Kingdom, where he has worked on projects using ethnographic methods to help explore Web 2.0 phenomena such as folksonomy and wiki-based collaboration. He expanded his interest in new forms of ethnography through a trio of research projects with a team at Cardiff University focusing on the use of hypermedia in conducting, presenting, and sharing ethnographic work. He collaborated in the authoring of many articles and the book *Qualitative Research and Hypermedia*.

Joseph A. Maxwell, PhD, is Professor in the College of Education and Human Development at George Mason University. He is the author of *Qualitative Research Design: An Interactive Approach* (2nd edition, 2005) and, with Diane Loomis, of a chapter on designing mixed methods studies in the *Handbook of Mixed Methods in Social and Behavioral Research* (2003), as well as articles on qualitative methodology, sociocultural theory, Native American societies, and medical education. His current research focuses on using qualitative research for causal explanation, the value of philosophic realism for qualitative and mixed methods research, and the importance of diversity and dialogue among research paradigms and methods.

Maureen McHugh, PhD, is Professor of Psychology at Indiana University of Pennsylvania. Her work focuses on gender differences, feminist methods, and violence against women. She has coauthored a key article on nonsexist research in psychology in *American Psychologist*, and has published with Lisa Cosgrove on feminist approaches to research on gender. Dr. McHugh and Irene Frieze received the Distinguished Publication Award from the

Association for Women in Psychology (AWP) for their coedited special issue of *Psychology of Women Quarterly* on measures of gender role attitudes. Also with Irene Frieze, she coedited two additional special issues of *Psychology of Women Quarterly* and *Sex Roles* (both in 2005). She has received the Christine Ladd Franklin Award for service to AWP and to feminist psychology.

Barbara A. Miller, EdD, is codirector of the Center for Leadership and Learning Communities at the Education Development Center, Inc., in Newton, Massachusetts. She is currently the co-principal investigator for the National Science Foundation–funded Mathematics and Science Partnership Knowledge Management and Dissemination project; lead evaluator for the University of Pittsburgh's NSF-funded K–12 project; director of a turnaround partner effort with an underperforming Massachusetts school district, under contract with the Massachusetts Department of Education; and consultant to various districts on the development and implementation of teacher and administrator leadership programs. Dr. Miller has coauthored a handbook on strategic leadership for large-scale reform and authored casebooks on teacher leadership and school reform issues. Her major interests are development of leadership in teachers and school reform.

David Morgan, PhD, is University Professor at Portland State University, where he also holds an adjunct appointment in sociology. He is the author of three books and numerous articles on focus group research. In addition to his work on focus groups, Dr. Morgan's current interests center on issues in research design, with an emphasis on topics related to combining qualitative and quantitative methods.

Ingrid Mulder, PhD, is Professor of Human-Centered ICT at the Institute for Communication, Media, and Information Technology at Rotterdam University in the Netherlands. She is also a scientific researcher at Telematica Institute in Enschede, the Netherlands. Her research activities mainly focus on the development of methods and techniques for capturing innovation, experiences, and latent user needs, as well as methods for the design and evaluation of innovative technologies from a human-centered perspective. Dr. Mulder has authored more than 80 articles for international conferences and journals, is a member of the consulting board of *Computers in Human Behavior*, an international reviewer for the Association for Computing Machinery (Computer-Supported Cooperative Work and Computer–Human Interaction) and the *Journal of Educational Technology and Society*, and an international evaluator of national research programs. In September 2008 Dr. Mulder will serve as conference co-chair of the ACM Mobile Human–Computer Interaction Conference.

Vicki L. Plano Clark, PhD, is codirector of the Office of Qualitative and Mixed Methods Research and Research Assistant Professor in the Qualitative, Quantitative, and Psychometric Methods Program housed in the University of Nebraska–Lincoln's Department of Educational Psychology. She teaches research methods courses, including foundations of educational research and mixed methods research, and serves as managing editor of the *Journal of Mixed Methods Research*. She specializes in mixed methods research designs and qualitative research, and her research interests include the procedural issues that arise when implementing different designs, as well as disciplinary contexts for conducting research. Dr. Plano Clark has authored and coauthored over 25 articles, chapters, and student manuals, including the book *Designing and Conducting Mixed Methods Research* (2007). Her writings include methodological discussions about, as well as empirical studies using, qualitative and mixed methods approaches in the areas of education, family research, counseling psychology, and family medicine.

Lindsay Prior, PhD, is a medical sociologist and Professor of Sociology at Queen's University, Belfast. His recent work has focused on public and professional understandings

of a variety of health risks, including specific forms of genetic and public health risks. Dr. Prior has been Director of the Health and Risk Research Program at the University of Wales College of Medicine and Cardiff University and has worked in U.K. university departments of general practice, as well as in departments of sociology and social science. His most recent book is *Using Documents in Social Research* (2003).

Sue V. Rosser, PhD, has served as dean of the Ivan Allen College of Liberal Arts at Georgia Tech since 1999, where she is also Professor of Public Policy and Professor of History, Technology, and Society. She is the author of more than 120 refereed journal articles and 10 books in the theoretical and applied issues of women and feminism in science, technology, and health. Her two most recent books are *The Science Glass Ceiling* (2004) and the coedited volume *Women, Gender, and Technology* (2006).

Elisabetta Ruspini, PhD, is Associate Professor of Sociology at the University of Milano–Bicocca, in Italy. Her research interests include the social construction of gender identities, changing femininities and masculinities, new forms of parenthood, social policy and heteronormativity, and the gender dimension of poverty and social exclusion, as well as gender issues in social research, the analysis of social change, longitudinal research and the issue of comparability, and design and collection of longitudinal datasets. Dr. Ruspini is the author of *Introduction to Longitudinal Research* (2002) and has coedited *The Gender Dimension of Social Change: The Contribution of Dynamic Research to the Study of Women's Life Courses* (with Angela Dale, 2002) and *A New Youth?: Young People, Generations and Family Life* (with Carmen Liccardi, 2005).

Natalia Sarkisian, PhD, is Assistant Professor of Sociology at Boston College. Her research examines the differences and similarities in family experiences by race/ethnicity, gender, and marital status and explores the structural circumstances and cultural values that may account for these differences and similarities. Dr. Sarkisian has published articles in *American Sociological Review, Social Forces, Journal of Marriage and Family, Contexts,* and *Family Relations.* She received the 2005 Rosabeth Moss Kanter International Award for Research Excellence in Families and Work.

Christopher Schneider, MA, is a doctoral student in the School of Justice and Social Inquiry at Arizona State University. His current research concerns music, media, and everyday life, specifically focusing on rap music and how this music is discussed and treated in the mass media in an effort to better comprehend how and in what ways this process contributes to issues of social justice.

Michael F. Schober, PhD, is Dean and Professor of Psychology at The New School in New York City. His research examines coordination in pairs and groups in various face-to-face and mediated settings. Dr. Schober also studies social presence effects in human–computer interfaces with various degrees of anthropomorphism. He is coeditor, with Frederick G. Conrad, of *Envisioning the Survey Interview of the Future* (2007) and editor-in-chief of the journal *Discourse Processes*.

Ronald J. Shope, PhD, is Research Associate Professor at the University of Nebraska–Lincoln; research associate in the Office of Qualitative and Mixed Methods Research and the qualitative consultant in the Nebraska Evaluation and Research Center; and Professor of Communication and Research and director of assessment and institutional research at Grace University in Omaha, Nebraska. He specializes in grounded theory and case study designs, has worked on mixed methods research projects, and has coauthored conference papers dealing with technology in teacher education and mixed methods research in mass communication, as well as instructor materials for several textbooks.

Lynn Sorsoli, EdD, is a research scientist at the Center for Research on Gender and Sexuality, where she directs the Adolescent Sexuality Project. Dr. Sorsoli focuses on developmental and relational processes, including the disclosure of sexual abuse and sexual orientation, and on research design and methodological issues, both quantitative and qualitative. She has published her research in the *Journal of Emotional Abuse*, the *Journal of Aggression, Maltreatment, and Trauma*, *Psychology of Men and Masculinity*, and the book series *The Narrative Study of Lives*.

Karen M. Staller, PhD, JD, is Assistant Professor at the University of Michigan School of Social Work. Her recently published book, *Runaways: How the Sixties Counterculture Shaped Today's Practices and Policies* (2006), reflects her long-standing practice and scholarly interest in runaway and homeless youth as well as in qualitative and historical research methods.

Abbas Tashakkori, PhD, is Distinguished Frost Professor of Research and Evaluation Methodology at Florida International University. He is the founding coeditor (with John Creswell) of the *Journal of Mixed Methods Research*. Dr. Tashakkori has published numerous articles and book chapters and coauthored or coedited three books. His research interests include the planning and evaluation of school improvement programs, minority and gender issues, integrated research methodology, teacher efficacy and job satisfaction, and bilingual education. He is the coeditor, with Charles Teddlie, of the books *Foundations of Mixed Methods Research* and *Research Methods for the Social and Behavioral Sciences: An Integrated Approach* (both 2008).

Charles Teddlie, PhD, is Jo Ellen Levy Yates Distinguished Professor in the College of Education at Louisiana State University. He has been a co-principal investigator on several major research studies, including the Louisiana School Effectiveness Study, the International School Effectiveness Research Project, and the ongoing International System for Teacher Observation and Feedback project. Dr. Teddlie's more than 140 publications include *The International Handbook of School Effectiveness Research* (coedited with David Reynolds) and the *Handbook of Mixed Methods in Social and Behavioral Research* (coedited with Abbas Tashakkori). His latest coedited book (with Abbas Tashakkori) is *Foundations of Mixed Methods Research* (2008).

Zazie Todd, PhD, is Lecturer in Social Psychology at the University of Leeds, United Kingdom. She is an applied social psychologist with an interdisciplinary background, focusing on research of the social psychology of language and communication. Dr. Todd is currently using metaphor analysis to investigate the perception and communication of the risks of terrorism. She coedited *Mixing Methods in Psychology* (2004). Dr. Todd co-proposed the Qualitative Methods in Psychology Section of the British Psychological Society, which was established in 2005. As chair of the Section, she has worked to promote the use of qualitative and mixed methods in psychology. During 2006, Dr. Todd was a visiting scholar at Chulalongkorn University in Bangkok, Thailand.

Deborah L. Tolman, EdD, is the director of the Center for Research on Gender and Sexuality and Professor of Human Sexuality Studies at San Francisco State University. Her research focuses on adolescent sexuality, gender development, gender equity, and research methods. Dr. Tolman's book on adolescent girls' sexuality, *Dilemmas of Desire: Teenage Girls Talk about Sexuality* (2002), was awarded the 2003 Distinguished Book Award from the Association for Women in Psychology. Her current research includes longitudinal studies of the role of sexual content on television and adolescent sexuality and a developmental study of gender, relationships, and sexuality that focuses on how messages about masculinity and femininity affect boys' and girls' abilities to pursue healthy relationships.